OPERATION GEORGE

A Gripping True Crime Story of an Audacious Undercover Sting

Mark Dickens with Stephen Bentley

Hendry Publishing Ltd

LONDON, ENGLAND

Hendry Publishing Ltd
20-22 Wenlock Road
London, N1 7GU, United Kingdom
www.hendrypublishing.com

Publisher's Note: This is a work of nonfiction. Some names have been changed, no characters invented, no events fabricated.

Book Cover Design: 100 Covers

Operation George/ Mark Dickens and Stephen Bentley
 -- 1st ed.

eBook ISBN 9781739813604
Paperback ISBN 9781739813611
Hardback ISBN 9781739813628

'Operation George is brilliant! It's a unique insight into the undercover world, the ingenious tactics, the outwardly serene UCOs and the fastidious adherence to rules and training are nothing like I've ever read before.

Devoting the majority of the second half of the book to the trial was inspired. It's all very well for readers to have that amazing peek into the undercover world (and the way the team created a totally illusionary one for Fulton at huge potential risk to themselves given his background and connections) but to show how the evidence obtained stands or falls in court does the whole tactic justice.'

- Graham Bartlett, former UK senior police officer and co-author with international best seller, Peter James, of a *Sunday Times* Top Ten bestselling non-fiction book, *Death Comes Knocking – Policing Roy Grace's Brighton*

Dedicated to all the peacemakers in the world and to all undercover police officers plying their tradecraft in the war against serious crime and terrorism in a world with insufficient peace.

Chaque légionnaire est ton frère d'armes, quelle que soit sa nationalité, sa race ou sa religion. Tu lui manifestes toujours la solidarité étroite qui doit unir les membres d'une même famille. – Article 2 Code of Honour, French Foreign Legion

"I just wish people would speak to each other and recognise that most solutions can be achieved by simple dialogue and negotiation.".

— Rosemary Nelson, Lurgan Mail, 11 February 1999

GLOSSARY

The following may be useful to understand the acronyms and vernacular used in this book. You may wish to bookmark this page for ease of reference.

40/20-Footer: Forty- or Twenty-foot cargo container or trailer.

At the race(s): The time of a planned event.

Backup: Physical support on the plot provided by the Operational Team or Cover Officer.

Bandit Territory: The opposition's geographical area which could refer to their housing, business locations, social venues or areas in which they conduct their criminality.

Bit of Work: The term used when you are first contacted by the Undercover Office enquiring if you are available or interested in a deployment. This could be within a new operation or an ongoing operation.

Can you Talk: When a UCO is deployed, and his/her Cover Officer needs to speak with them over the phone the Cover Officers start the conversation with, 'Can you talk?' This means can you speak freely.

Clean Myself: Counter and anti-surveillance conducted by the UCO before and after a meeting with the opposition.

Cover Officer: A trained UCO who acts as the handler of another UCO in the field. Looks after the safety and welfare of the UCO on the plot and acts as liaison between the UCO and the 'boss.'

Factory/Nick: Police Station.

Firm: Detective speak for an OCG.

Flop: Accommodation used by a UCO on an ad hoc basis to rest and sleep.

Job: Operation.

Legend: UCOs will spend time in certain locations establishing their faces by socialising and getting to be known in the area as Mr X or Mrs Y.

Lumped Up: Premises or vehicle has been fitted with a technical equipment such as a 'brick' (tracking system) or an audio recorder deployed to monitor, track and secure evidence. In some cases, provide additional safety for the deployed UCO i.e., a UCO deployed either within or outside a plot area may have a 'lump' fitted to his vehicle so that the Cover Officer and/or surveillance team can monitor their position and react accordingly if the UCO's safety becomes an issue.

MIT: Major (or Murder) Investigation Team.

Moody: A plan, situation or a person that just does not seem or sound right.

MPS or Met: Metropolitan Police Service.

OCG: Organised Crime Group (criminal gang).

Old Bill: Police.

On the Pavement: A term used by UCOs confirming they are deployed.

Opposition: A term used when referring to the criminal subjects in operational briefings.

Parcel: The stolen goods, drugs etc.

Plot: Area of undercover deployment where the action takes place.

Plotting Up: The meeting between the UCO and the criminal will be covered by the operational team either technically or with surveillance officers.

PSNI: Police Service of Northern Ireland.

Real Police: When a UCO is deployed, they may have experienced a situation where uniformed or plain clothes police officers have entered their plot. The UCO would refer to these as 'Real Police' as they do not form part of the operational team.

RUC: Royal Ulster Constabulary.

Safe Location: A secure safe location where the boss and selected members of his team can meet, brief, debrief and task the UCO. The Cover Officer will always be present at these meetings.

SB: Special Branch.

SIO: Senior Investigating Officer or 'boss' used instead of SIO by UCOs.

Slaughter: Slang for a warehouse to keep stolen goods/drugs or to distribute criminal proceeds.

Snide: Counterfeit goods or money.

Snout/Grass/Tout: Police Informant or Covert Human Intelligence Source (CHIS).

Strike: The arrest stage of the operation.

Time: Length of Prison Sentence.

Throw Away/Burner Phone: 'Pay as you Go' mobile phone.

UC or UCOs: Undercover officer(s).

Wheels: Car.

CONTENTS

CHAPTER 1

The Targets

The following true story is not about Rosemary Nelson, the Troubles *per se* nor Northern Ireland, although they feature out of necessity.

We feel that from the outset it is worthwhile to set out a background to the events and locations of this book and a brief history of the Troubles in that part of Northern Ireland. Whilst this book tells the amazing story of possibly the most audacious undercover sting in the world, we also acknowledge the grief suffered by so many on both sides of the sectarian divide in that part of the United Kingdom. In writing this book, we can assure you we also felt the pain endured by so many innocent people.

William James Fulton and Muriel Gibson were from Portadown, a small town in County Armagh, Northern Ireland. Sadly, it is better known as the scene of the Drumcree conflict rather than the birthplace of notable people like Lady Mary Peters (Olympic athlete), Gloria Hunniford (TV personality) and Martin O' Neill (football manager). It is located about twenty-five miles southwest of Belfast. In the 1980s and 1990s its population was made up of about seventy percent Protestants and almost thirty percent Catholics. Garvaghy Road is in the middle of an area of housing that is largely populated by Catholics. Lurgan is a short drive away; about six miles separates it from Portadown. Lurgan was the location of Rosemary Nelson's law practice.

The Drumcree conflict is a dispute over the right of Protestants and loyalists to hold parades mainly to commemorate the so-called Glorious Revolution of 1688. The occasion is known by many as 'The Twelfth.' It was first held in the late 18th century in Ulster and it celebrates the victory of Protestant King William of Orange over Catholic King James II at the Battle of the Boyne in 1690, which began the Protestant Ascendancy in Ireland. Residents of Garvaghy Road and the surrounding Catholic district object to what they view as "triumphalist" Orange marches through their area. Rosemary Nelson, a Catholic solicitor, was the figurehead and spokesperson for the Garvaghy Road Residents' Coalition as well as representing the coalition in legal matters until she was assassinated on 15 March 1999. Sam Kinkaid, the RUC officer who played a leading role in the investigation of Rosemary Nelson's murder, described the area (Portadown) as "second only to North Belfast in terms of sectarianism.[1]"

The sophisticated bomb device that blew up Rosemary Nelson's car and killed her is where our story begins. A loyalist paramilitary splinter group naming themselves the Red Hand Defenders claimed responsibility for the killing. At that time, William James Fulton and Muriel Landry née Gibson (referred to as Gibson throughout the remainder of this book) were members of the Loyalist Volunteer Force – the LVF. Soon after the bombing, Fulton fled to the United States and Gibson relocated to England.

In this story of Operation George, all the names of the undercover police officers (UCOs) used are pseudonyms. Some are the same aliases as used in evidential transcripts and sanctioned by the judge to preserve their anonymity whilst giving evidence at the trials of William James Fulton and Muriel Gibson at Belfast Crown Court. The names or nicknames of other UCOs and Cover Officers are fabricated aliases to protect their anonymity and thus prevent any kind of criminal

---

[1] Para 6.7 Nelson Inquiry. Full report can be accessed at https://www.gov.uk/government/publications/the-rosemary-nelson-inquiry-report

retribution against them or their families. In the same vein, the authors are sparing in using details of any undercover officer such as physical descriptions, accents, backgrounds, and the like to preserve anonymity.

When Julie Met George

Operation Julie and Operation George are light years away from each other in more ways than one. Undercover policing has drastically changed owing to modern 'UK Police PLC' attitudes and policies. The contrasts between 1970s Operation Julie and 21st Century Operation George undercover policing are like night and day.

Perhaps now is an opportune moment to explain what is entailed to become a Level 1 UCO then to be entered into the national register. It's a world apart from the Operation Julie days when straight from being a member of a surveillance team, a detective would be asked by a boss if they wanted to go undercover. No training in those days. They made up a back story on the fly and then they were straight into the deep end. Sink or swim!

For some time now, undercover officers are recruited and must attend a national training course. They are evaluated to see if they are suitable and are eventually set free to establish a legend and back story. Those are the two things they will fall back on and carry with them for the remainder of their undercover careers. Essentially, it's a case of who they say they are and not who they really are. They will spend time in certain locations, establishing their faces by socialising and getting to be known in the area as Mr X or Mrs Y. That strengthens their credentials if someone checks them out. Occasionally, they may have to repeat that exercise if there is a good reason to change location. If an UCO has special skills, so much the better. For example, Robbie, one of the Operation George UCOs, appeared to have a licence to drive trucks, as it's known from the transcripts that he held himself out as a lorry driver in his dealings with Jim Fulton.

Unlike Bentley's pioneering undercover days, as described in his memoir Operation Julie[2], these Operation George officers belong to a modern era of covert policing. The story of Operation George highlights the sophisticated methods deployed by modern law enforcement. Those methods and techniques are all Bentley hoped and wished for when he wrote the chapter 'The Future of Undercover Policing' in his memoir. Indeed, they go beyond that and demonstrate the changes in policing attitudes and a resolute commitment to engage in proactive intelligence-led policing to combat organised crime and terrorism.

We need to add that even in Seventies undercover work, the targets of investigations were aware of undercover methods. As time passes, covert operations step up, invent new tactics, use the latest technology, all to keep one step ahead of the smartest criminal enterprise. The future may involve the use of drones, negating the need for human covert policing. It is not far-fetched to suggest that criminal activities, including meetings when crimes are planned, may soon be recorded both in audio and video. It is not hard to imagine with the arrival of 'smart cities', as referenced by the head of the UK intelligence agency, GCHQ[3]. No wonder many criminals are paranoid. Even now, they will challenge innocents in a belief they may be undercover officers (UCOs). In fact, Jim Fulton did just that when telling the Operation George detectives he thought some of his neighbours in Cornwall were MI5 undercover people.

He was wrong. The "undercover people" were surrounding him, socialising with him, working with him, paying him as an employee, talking to him daily for the best part of two years. During that time, he was recorded on audio tapes, the 'product' of which eventually became the damning evidence sending him to jail with no prospect of release for twenty-five years.

---

[2] Stephen Bentley, *Undercover: Operation Julie – The Inside Story,* Hendry Publishing, 2017 and *Operation Julie: The gripping inside story of Britain's biggest drug bust,* Ebury Spotlight, 2022
[3] https://www.bbc.com/news/technology-56851558

CHAPTER 2

Genocide

Over fifty thousand hours of conversations between William James Fulton and undercover officers engaged on Operation George were secretly recorded. In one of those recordings, Fulton said, "... They've got to shoot a Catholic once a week ... about once a week and that's why they broke away. That's why the LVF broke away from the UVF was because they weren't killing enough Catholics. And the LVF wanted a Catholic per week killing."

Put yourself in the shoes of that undercover officer – how would you react to such disturbing words? These undercover officers are to be admired as the consummate professionals they truly are. They don't flinch, berate, judge or ask questions. Instead, they associate, infiltrate, befriend their target, and covertly gather the evidence for a future day of reckoning.

On the 11th of March 2021, a BBC World News article[4] reported that, "The term genocide was coined in 1943 by the Jewish-Polish lawyer Raphael Lemkin, who combined the Greek word 'genos' (race or tribe) with the Latin word 'cide' (to kill). After witnessing the horrors of the Holocaust, in which every member of his family except his brother was killed, Dr Lemkin campaigned to have genocide recognised as a crime under international law.

---

[4] https://www.bbc.com/news/world-11108059

His efforts gave way to the adoption of the United Nations Genocide Convention in December 1948, which came into effect in January 1951. Article Two of the convention defines genocide as 'any of the following acts committed with the intent to destroy, in whole or in part, a national, ethnic, racial or *religious* [our emphasis] group …'"

This Operation George story has genocide at its centre. It's also the remarkable story of a brave, experienced, elite group of undercover officers and their forward-thinking boss, who conceptualised then executed a most brilliant plan to bring a terrorist to justice.

CHAPTER 3

Interview Room, Belfast

On 12 June 2001, Constable Pierce of the Devon and Cornwall Constabulary, together with a specialist armed arrest team, arrested Jim Fulton at his Plymouth home under the Prevention of Terrorism Act. To Fulton's surprise, he was flown to Belfast under armed guard in a military helicopter. His surprise turned to fear as he started to cry like a baby, dreading that he was about to be assassinated and thrown into the dark waters of the Irish Sea.

By the time he had been processed at a Belfast holding centre, Fulton had reverted to type: a cocksure individual who thought he had nothing to worry about. That overconfidence was on display at the earliest stages of the disclosure interviews. Those interviews are mandatory under the umbrella of the Police and Criminal Evidence Act (PACE) and were conducted in the presence of a well-known Belfast solicitor.

Fulton was settling into a chair in the stark interview room, listening closely to the introductory disclosure material articulated by an interviewing officer, undoubtedly thinking, *I'll be out of here soon.*

Then his world shattered. He rocked back on the chair, almost losing balance, whilst he took in what he had just heard: "Those people back in Plymouth. You know Neil, Robbie and the others in that firm you were working for. I must inform you they were all undercover police officers. Furthermore, they recorded your many conversations with them."

Fulton rocked forward, regaining his balance, then held his head in his hands. Once more, he started to blubber, but only for a moment. He quickly gathered himself and started to put his defence on tape – for the sake of the record.

"I mean, I thought I'd got in with a big firm in England and I just wanted to make myself more important, make myself seen that I was a big man," Jim Fulton said.

"A firm as in gangsters?" asked a detective.

"Right. So, I wanted to make myself out to be a big man."

"Right and so you decided what?"

"Just waffle."

A firm as in gangsters? the interviewer asked. I ask you to remember that word – 'firm' – because this is a true story about the firm that wasn't a firm at all.

Just like Jim Carrey's character in *The Truman Show,* Fulton's environment had been controlled and his life manipulated. He believed he'd been living cheek by jowl in the company of gangsters in Plymouth, England from 1999 to 2001. In fact, he'd been living in a bubble not of his own creation.

The rest of the cast in the 'firm' playing the parts of members of an organised crime group (OCG) are real enough but not genuine. They are all skilled undercover detectives and part of Operation George. This extraordinarily successful police operation was set up in the wake of the murder of the prominent human rights solicitor Rosemary Nelson in Lurgan, Northern Ireland in 1999, and therein lies the catalyst for what came later.

CHAPTER 4

The Nelson Family Home

Monday 15 March 1999 was like any other day. The only anomaly was that Rosemary Nelson slept a little later than usual as she was feeling under the weather, partly because of how she was feeling and also because two of her children were away on a school holiday in France.

It was late morning when her friend, confidante and secretary Nuala McCann called by to find her friend still getting ready for work. They planned to have a coffee before travelling in separate cars to the law firm's office a short distance away in Lurgan town centre.

Based on the known facts, it's easy to imagine this is what happened that morning. Letting herself in with a key entrusted to her, Nuala called upstairs, "I'm here, are you ready?"

"I'll be down soon but can you do me a favour?"

"No problem. What is it?"

"Get the *Irish Times*, please. I want to read the Drumcree article and see if they published my picture."

Exchange over, Nuala went to a local newsagent to buy the paper. On her return, both women sat in the kitchen and over coffee briefly chatted about the article and their amusement at Rosemary's picture. "They never use a flattering photo, have you noticed?" Rosemary said and both women laughed.

Nuala drove to the end of a nearby road, expecting to see Rosemary driving her silver BMW past on Lake Street. Confused as to why

Rosemary hadn't passed her, Nuala drove around looking for her friend, until she came around a corner to a scene of devastation. Rosemary's BMW was a mass of twisted metal, the work of a terrorist bomb. Nuala rushed to the driver's seat. Her friend was covered in black dust and seemed gravely injured.

Nuala ran to a neighbour's house and asked her to call 999. On returning to her friend, Nuala found another neighbour, a qualified nurse, had arrived. The nurse had heard the explosion and ran to the scene. A short time later a local doctor arrived, followed by an ambulance, paramedics, the fire service, and the police. It should come as no surprise, owing to both her legs having been blown off by the blast, that medics struggled to stabilise Rosemary Nelson or relieve her pain. By the time she was cut her free from the car and taken to Craigavon Hospital there was no more to be done to save her life. Rosemary Nelson died shortly after three o'clock that afternoon.

Later that same day, the Red Hand Defenders, a splinter Loyalist paramilitary group who some claimed was a front for the LVF, claimed responsibility for the bomb in a telephone call to the BBC Newsroom in Belfast.

This gruesome murder was a catalyst in bringing Fulton to justice for other crimes. Though there is no evidence Jim Fulton was implicated in the murder of Rosemary Nelson, he was one of many suspected who had connections to Loyalist paramilitary groups. It was her murder that acted as a mechanism for bringing him and Muriel Gibson to justice for other terrorist crimes including the murders of innocent Catholics and RUC police officers. Fulton was a Nelson murder suspect, but there is no evidence implicating him at all, even to this day.

Soon after Rosemary Nelson's death, both Fulton and Gibson fled Northern Ireland; Fulton flying to California and Gibson relocating to the West Country in England. Fulton thought he was safe. What he didn't know was that he would soon come to the notice of American law enforcement, including the FBI.

CHAPTER 5

California Dreaming

Murrieta is a township in Riverside County, about eighty miles south of downtown Los Angeles. Nearby Temecula is known for its wine trail and is one of the many attractions in this region of Southern California.

Muriel Gibson had connections to Murrieta. Her former husband, William Landry, and their children lived there in a battered looking yellow house. In September 1999, Jim Fulton flew to the United States then took refuge in that house together with his wife, Tanya, no doubt waiting for the hullaballoo to die down back in Belfast. But Fulton's attempts to lie low were undermined when Tanya discharged a loaded weapon in the grounds of the house. The shots rang out and were heard by some nearby brickyard workers who instinctively ducked for cover. The two workers, Johnny Buckles and Nathan Rouse, were stacking bricks with a forklift truck. Buckles later said, "Two or three shots went off. Then the fourth or fifth went zipping by us a little closer." Rouse claimed they had heard at least a dozen shots. The workers reported the shots to Murrieta police.

Local law enforcement officers arrived to find the Fultons and three other adults at the home. Inside, they found two rifles, expended cartridges, ammunition, and a gun on a shelf. They also seized a .32-caliber handgun and a black T-shirt emblazoned with the slogan "Loyalist Volunteers lead the way."

A news article[5] said, "Police reported finding a number of .22 calibre rifles, an M-72 "spent" anti-tank rocket launcher, a six-inch cannon, mounted on a wooden base, two inert pipe bombs, hollowed out hand grenades with some gun powder residue, as well as 5.5 ounces of hashish and a small amount of methamphetamine."

It continued: "Police said a 33-year-old Las Vegas woman and 29-year-old Tanya Fulton admitted to having fired a handgun out a rear window of the home. Tanya Fulton's lawyer said the shooting erupted after the Las Vegas woman told his client it is legal to own firearms in the United States. The lawyer added, 'Tanya had never fired a gun, and she was told there was a big open field there and apparently a couple of shots were fired out of the window.'"

The Murrieta Sheriff's Department arrested the Las Vegas woman, William James (Jim) and Tanya Fulton, as well as residents Odysseus Landry, 29, and Mahatma Landry, 28, on child-endangerment, drug, and weapon charges. The child endangerment charges were levelled at Jim and Tanya Fulton owing to the presence of their two young children at the house in Murrieta. The children were taken into protective care and were returned to Northern Ireland after their parents were arrested.

The arrests took place on the 16th of December 1999, just nine months after the bomb explosion that killed Rosemary Nelson. Local law enforcement authorities in the town were notified by the FBI to put major security around Fulton almost immediately after they arrested him but were not told the reason. Many questions then started to flow about Fulton and his presence in the United States.

The US press, alerted by reports in Ireland, became aware of the implications of the case. A nationwide TV network[6] referred to Fulton and those arrested with him as a "cell of a dangerous, international Irish terrorist organization." Following that, the Californian arresting officer told the media he had not been approached by the RUC but confirmed police reports from Belfast giving details of prior convictions and other

---

[5] http://www.nuzhound.com/articles/tlac1-23.htm
[6] Ibid at 5.

background material on the five people arrested had finally been sent to the US.

On Fulton's appearance at a court remand hearing, the District Attorney told the court the $100,000 bail being asked for each defendant was higher than the normal $5,000 per defendant in such a drug case, but he declined to say why. Jail officials later said, "Regardless of whether Fulton can make bail, the immigration hold will bar his release."

Fulton's California arrest caused quite a commotion at that week's official State Department briefing for journalists at the White House in Washington, with one journalist asking,[7] "What do you know about the arrest last month of a man in Southern California who is suspected of having planted a car bomb that killed Rosemary Nelson in Northern Ireland?"

The terse answer from spokesman James Rubin was, "Yeah, that sounds to me like a domestic law enforcement matter, and I would refer you to the law enforcement agencies."

The same article also reported that "the Assistant Chief Constable of Norfolk Constabulary, Colin Port, who's heading the investigation into Nelson's murder in last year's March 15th car bombing, however, told [us] on Sunday last week that he was aware of the arrest, but had no plans to interview Fulton."

Richard Harvey, a New York-based lawyer, of the Rosemary Nelson Campaign also started asking how Fulton came to be in possession of an arsenal of weapons, including explosives, and why all charges, except possession of drugs, were dramatically dropped that week. He also asked how Fulton got entry into the US and why he could remain on in contravention of immigration law. All this was going on in the background as United States Congress was holding hearings to bring pressure on the British government to hold an independent inquiry into Nelson's murder.

---

[7] Ibid at 4 and 5.

The explosives and weapons charges were eventually dropped, against the wishes of the local district attorney, who was controversially overruled. The district attorney and arresting officer were only informed about Fulton's loyalist connections when phoned by the *Ireland on Sunday* newspaper almost two weeks following the Murrieta arrests.

Colin Port was undoubtedly truthful but possibly disingenuous when telling the press there were no plans to interview Jim Fulton. That point was a long way off. What few people knew was that Colin Port, as head of the investigation into the Rosemary Nelson murder, had already put a covert operation in place once Muriel Gibson had been located in Plymouth, Devon, England, and after the arrest of the Fultons in California, the first phase of Operation George had commenced with the assistance of the FBI who were undoubtedly instrumental in dropping the charges against Fulton. Jim Fulton's California dreaming would soon become his nightmare

CHAPTER 6

Colin Port

International pressure was building for a thorough and independent inquiry into the horrific murder of Rosemary Nelson.

As early as 17 March 1999, two days after Nelson's car was blown up, a resolution condemned the murder of Rosemary Nelson,[8] which was referred to the US House of Representatives Committee on International Relations. Amongst other things, it referred to "public knowledge that Rosemary Nelson's life was threatened on a number of occasions by the RUC Special Branch... the North's human rights group, the Committee on the Administration of Justice, has called for an independent investigation into Rosemary Nelson's murder and said it would be 'untenable' for the RUC to head the inquiry... the United States should fully support the implementation of the United Nations Special Rapporteur's recommendation for an independent inquiry into the killing of Belfast lawyer Pat Finucane... calls on the United Nations to condemn these bombings and seek an independent investigation apart from the RUC; calls on the United Nations to form an independent inquiry into the harassment by the RUC of human rights lawyers and the killings of Rosemary Nelson and others."

The Good Friday Agreement (GFA), or Belfast Agreement, are two agreements, not one, but almost always referred to in the singular. They

---

[8] https://www.govinfo.gov/content/pkg/BILLS-106hconres59ih/html/BILLS-106hconres59ih.htm

were signed on 10 April 1998, designed to end the violence of the Troubles, which had ensued since the late 1960s. It was a major development in the Northern Ireland peace process of the 1990s. Northern Ireland's present devolved system of government is based on the agreement. The agreement also created several institutions between Northern Ireland and the Republic of Ireland, and between the Republic of Ireland and the United Kingdom.

With that in mind, on the day of Rosemary Nelson's murder and recognising the need for an independent element in the murder investigation, Sir Ronnie Flanagan, then RUC Chief Constable, sought assistance from HM Inspectorate of Constabulary and the Director of the Federal Bureau of Investigation. The result was that Colin Port, the Deputy Chief Constable of Norfolk, was appointed to act as Officer in Overall Command (OIOC) of a murder investigation team (MIT) which became the most extensive murder investigation in the history of Northern Ireland.

Colin Port had spent most of his police career investigating crime, initially with the Greater Manchester Police, rising through the ranks from Detective Constable to Detective Superintendent in charge of Crime Operations and later as a Detective Chief Superintendent. He became the Head of the Criminal Investigation Department (CID) with the Warwickshire Constabulary. In 1994 he had been appointed Investigations Coordinator to the UN International Criminal Tribunal for the former Yugoslavia and in the following year Director of Investigations to the UN International Criminal Tribunal in Rwanda. In 1996 he became Head of the Southeast Regional Crime Squad. He then became Deputy Chief Constable of Norfolk. He went to Northern Ireland with a great deal of experience, particularly the targeting of serious and organised crime groups, using informants, surveillance, undercover officers and intrusive techniques.

Port was not the first to suggest that the best hope of developing a case against those suspects named in the early intelligence lay in pursuing a proactive investigation which could include both human and technical surveillance. Port had referred to it as a possibility at a meeting on 26 March 1999, when Kent police officers from England, FBI Special Agent John Guido, and senior RUC Special Branch (SB) officers, discussed 'technical issues and possible opportunities' and held a 'general discussion about intelligence versus evidence difficulties and the need to protect intelligence gathering tactics whilst exploring every opportunity to secure evidence in this very important case'. Owing to internal RUC politics, it was clear the SB had some reservations about such a course.

However, in the latter half of 1999, significant opportunities arose which enabled the MIT to initiate surveillance without the assistance of SB, using techniques that were less familiar to those targeted and at times and in places when they were almost certainly less watchful. These opportunities arose when two of the murder suspects left Northern Ireland. In September 1999 one of them, William James ('Jim') Fulton, travelled to the USA; another, Muriel Gibson, moved from Portadown, initially to Plymouth and later Cornwall in England. When Jim Fulton returned from the USA to Northern Ireland, he was warned that a threat had been made against his life and so he also moved to Cornwall, where he resided temporarily with Muriel Gibson before finding accommodation of his own. From time to time during the following months both Jim Fulton and Muriel Gibson were visited by others whom the Port MIT regarded as suspects involved in Rosemary Nelson's murder.

Port was also familiar with the CHIS – covert human intelligence source – database back in England. It was originally planned to establish a single database containing details of undercover police officers and confidential informants ('snouts', as they were informally known). That idea was scrapped, resulting in a separate database of nationally accredited undercover officers (UCOs). With Gibson's new location in Plymouth and Fulton's return in mind, Port and others started collating a list of experienced Level 1 undercover officers, those with deep infiltration experience. This list contained the details of the undercover officers who would soon form two teams on the covert intelligence operation, code named George.

CHAPTER 7

Down the Rabbit Hole

Unlike in the pioneering undercover cop days of Operation Julie, covert policing is now highly regulated, whether using human or technical resources. If the rules and regulations are broken, even bent or twisted a little, any evidence gleaned is certain to be ruled inadmissible in court hearings. The modern undercover officer is trained to 'open doors', in that a target or suspect is unwittingly put in a situation where they have a genuine choice to talk about past or future crimes or voluntarily offer up vital intelligence which may or may not be potential evidence.

The target cannot be subjected to questioning, otherwise the provisions of Code C of the Police and Criminal Evidence Act 1984 (PACE) come into play. The real issue is whether the undercover officers conducted an interview; in English law that means a conversation including questioning regarding an offence. Answers received by UCs not having cautioned a target who is now a suspect may, depending on the judge, not be used in court as evidence.

The preparation for any operation involves the UCO meeting with his boss to work out the parameters. All sanctioned actions on the part of any UCO are signed off in advance. In that way, the UCOs know exactly how far they are lawfully allowed to go within each step of the operation.

Elite Level 1 officers know and live by a rule of not disturbing a pre-existing environment. They do not act like a bull in a china shop because if they do targets are more likely to suspect them and no one will trust them. It becomes a long-term process when infiltrating an organised crime group (OCG). In that way, it increases the chances of obtaining the information necessary to prosecute the gang members.

Now that Colin Port had a list of elite UCOs, how best to deploy them against the targets of Jim Fulton and Muriel Gibson?

Through close liaison with the FBI, Port and the embryo Operation George team (which by now was a spin-off from the Rosemary Nelson murder investigation) learnt Fulton was to be deported from the United States back to the United Kingdom. The team realised its best chances of infiltrating the Fulton/Gibson axis – a cabal of two – was to ensure Fulton did not reside in Northern Ireland where the recognised surveillance problems could prevent the effectiveness of any attempted infiltration. Besides, Port's list of UCOs was full of cops from England, though not necessarily English. Embedding them in Ulster would have been both futile and presented a grave risk to their personal security.

What happened next was a master stroke by any standards. One undercover team consisting of a man and a woman was deployed in Cornwall with the brief to establish themselves in the local community. They were known as Dave S and Sam, and they set about starting up a small business as market traders in Camborne.

Liz, another UCO, was deployed to Plymouth where Gibson had been located. Liz was tasked with making the first approach to Gibson in a natural way. As you will see, she succeeded. Eventually, Liz paved the way for Muriel Gibson to tell Jim Fulton that Liz's fella, who was another UCO called Neil, was looking for a driver.

Simultaneously, someone or possibly more than one person whispered into Jim Fulton's ear whilst he was still in California, "You want to think twice about where to go when you get back to the UK."

"Why?" Fulton asked.

"There's a story doing the rounds, you're on a hit list back in Belfast."

Was one of the whisperers someone from the FBI? Your guess is as good as ours, but we know they were actors on the stage at this time and close to Port's MIT. It's also known that Fulton was covertly recorded whilst in custody in the United States when he denied killing Rosemary Nelson to a fellow prisoner. That sounds like the FBI.

That same 'story' may have also been fed to Muriel Gibson, who would undoubtedly pass it on to Fulton, probably through his lawyer in the States or her kids in Murrieta. It's an educated guess the 'rumour' was deliberately started at the instigation of Port, who utilised the array of law enforcement and security services in Belfast and elsewhere to propagate the rumour throughout all the loyalist haunts. The Metropolitan Police Service (MPS or Met) Special Branch also played its part. Dame Stella Rimington, former Director General of the Security Service, explained in a lecture[9] how "Special Branches [act] as the main interface between the Security Service and the Police Service as a whole." The Met's SB has responsibility for policing Heathrow and other major ports. Have you ever noticed the man in plain clothes standing close to the passport control booths at the airport? You know, the guy with the frown. The chances are he's Special Branch and keeping a close eye on arrivals. One did when Fulton arrived at Heathrow and took him to a nearby interview room where Fulton once more was told about a death threat. Despite the reinforcement of the message, Fulton carried on and returned to Belfast, undoubtedly because he wished to be reunited with his wife and children who had all returned from California at an earlier time.

Nonetheless, Fulton and his family did return to England after he had spent one month in his County Armagh hangouts, owing to a combination of unease on his part and Gibson telling him about a golden opportunity. All these initial steps were part of creating an 'open door', inviting Fulton to walk in and join his friend Muriel Gibson to

---

[9] https://www.mi5.gov.uk/cy/node/412

'disappear down the rabbit hole'. In the controlled vacuum created by Operation George, the task would be to create an environment in which Fulton and Gibson would talk freely about events in Northern Ireland.

Some of the players in the Operation George sting would soon be in place, but it would be a long way from the denouement, one which draws comparisons with the movie *The Sting*. The title refers to the moment when a con artist finishes the "play" and takes the mark's money. If a con is successful, the mark does not realize he has been cheated until the con men are long gone, if at all.

The Sting? *The Truman Show*? *Alice in Wonderland*? Get the picture? Pun intended.

CHAPTER 8

Liz

The first thing Liz knew about Operation George was late September 1999, when Trevor in the Undercover Office called her asking if she, "Fancied a bit of work?" That was a question she had been asked many times before, owing to her lengthy experiences of undercover roles infiltrating criminal gangs.

"Oh yeah, what is it this time, a handbag on the arm of … let me guess…"

Trev cut across her. "No Liz, this is a proper bit of work. It does not come without a slice of risk, and you'll be working alone initially. I can't say anything more now over the phone – the boss wants you to come into the office for a sit-down chat tomorrow at two. Can you make it?"

"Bloody hell, Trev, you know how to get a girl excited. Two it is!" Liz killed the call and carried on completing the report she was crafting about her latest deployment. Liz was a seasoned UCO who had worked on infiltrations for many years across the UK. This next role was different: rather than a gang, there was just one person's world she was to infiltrate.

At five to two the next day she walked into the Cover Office and acknowledged Trev with a nod and a swift hello. Trev, just finishing off the final touches to three coffees, asked, "No sugar, right?"

"Right, no sugar, what's the job about, mate?"

"I honestly can't say a word. I've been sworn to secrecy, as will you in a minute. The boss is on the phone as we speak. When he's finished, we're in and everything will be made clear. But I can tell you this: it's fucking big and you have been handpicked."

Liz grabbed her brew and sat at the nearest empty desk. She knew she wouldn't be disturbed by its regular occupant, Sam, as she was out on the plot in another part of the UK working a market stall with Dave, usually known as Dave S, owing to Dave being a common name for UCOs.

After a few minutes, the boss's door opened and Len, the gaffer, crossed the office to Liz and greeted her with a handshake and invited her and Trev into his office. Making his way to his desk, he said, "Right, Liz, what's Trev told you about this bit of work?"

Settling into a chair, Liz avoided eye contact with the boss until the last few syllables of his question. "Zero, nothing, nada, jack shit, boss, other than there is a bit of risk wrapped round it and I'm on my own. So apart from that, nothing, boss."

Satisfied, the boss took his seat behind his sparsely furnished desktop decorated with only a landline telephone, a mobile phone, and a twenty-pack of Silk Cut cigarettes besides a lighter inscribed: 'To Len, best of luck on your promotion.' From a drawer, he pulled out a chunky blue folder marked 'Operation George.'

On setting down the folder, his piercing eyes locked on to Liz's. "Good, and that's how we're going to play this one, Liz. Before I go any further, what have you got in your diary for the next three to six months?"

Liz knew this wasn't an unusual question for a UCO to be asked when there is the possibility of a bit of work on the table. Undercover officers are like every other grown-up on the planet; they have stuff they have to deal with in their private, home and working life. Liz was no exception to this rule. She had a fella, Tommy, who wasn't a cop but was supportive in her chosen role. He knew there were times that she would be away on a job for prolonged periods of time. Contact wasn't easy. He couldn't just pick up his phone and call her throw-away phone from his mobile or house phone. That would leave a footprint on Liz's phone record which in time could be pored over by a defence team of barristers. Her job phone or personal mobile would be switched off and held by her Cover Officer when she was on the plot. To keep a line of communication open for emergency, Liz always ensured that Tommy had a list of the first names of the Cover Officers and their job mobile numbers, just in case. Tommy knew the Cover team from downtown piss-ups and barbeques in the back gardens of their homes. He was trusted and part of the undercover family and therefore looked after by all the team members.

So, family life and potential issues. No issues. Tick that box.

The job Liz had just finished would take more than six months to get anywhere near the Crown Court and if she, the Operational Team and the Crown Prosecution Services (CPS) had done their jobs correctly, her role should have been protected under Public Interest Immunity (PII[10]). However, there was always the chance that she could be called for a closed-door hearing with the trial judge over a part of her submitted evidence and or role. You can't call the odds on that, and you just have to roll with it.

So, work issues. None. Tick.

Privately, Liz was thinking of settling down to a more stable lifestyle and maybe sitting the promotion exam to boost her pension and to share her knowledge and experience with the new breed of police officers who were prepared to enter this challenging and exciting world of undercover policing. *Well*, Liz thought, *another six months isn't going to make that much of a difference.*

So, private issues. None. Tick.

---

[10] Public Interest Immunity or PII as it is often called; previously known as Crown privilege, is a principle of English common law under which the English courts can grant a court order allowing one litigant to refrain from disclosing evidence to the other litigants where disclosure would be damaging to the public interest.

Breaking free from her thoughts, Liz said, "Just finishing off my report and exxies [expense claims] from the last op, boss. A week away with Tommy, it was going to be two weeks, but he's arranged and paid for a trip to Spain golfing with his mates because he didn't expect me home for another couple of weeks. Typical. So, I'm all yours. What you got, boss?"

"What I've got in this folder is 'Operation George'. This is going to be a trail blazer. Never have UK Police Plc done anything like this, it's unique. What you are about to hear doesn't leave this office. I'll give you an outline without going into detail because if you don't fancy it, no worries, walk away and no one will think less of you. But before going into the finer detail, I have to know that you want this job."

Liz looked at Trev and then at Len with a frown. "Bloody hell, you're asking me to sign up for a job you've told me nothing about. I can walk away, no bother. I'll be working alone and there is, in your words, a slice of risk. Where is it and what is it, can you tell me that?"

"Okay," said Len and then, after a slight pause, "there is a female in the West Country that we want you to befriend. She is of great interest to several UK law enforcement agencies. She is the key to an international operation, and we need someone to turn that key. That someone could just be you, Liz. In or out?"

Not one for using bad language in front of the boss but having a full vocabulary when needed and appropriate, Liz responded, "For fuck's sake, I'm none the wiser but you have got my complete and undivided attention. Count me in on this once in a lifetime opportunity. I'm intrigued and a hundred percent in. Now for god's sake, tell me what the fuck it's all about."

The atmosphere in the boss's office lightened and Len opened the file. He began, "Operation George is a deep undercover operation. It is a post-murder enquiry into the killing of a prominent Catholic solicitor, Ms Rosemary Nelson. The murder took place in Northern Ireland on 15 March 1999. We suspect the LVF. One of their members, Muriel

Gibson, has left Northern Ireland and taken up residence in a bed and breakfast in Plymouth."

There was enough in this short summary to get Liz's mind working. She snapped off three questions: "Do we have a plan? Who am I working for? Who's my cover?"

Trev replied without hesitation, "I'm going to cover, and I've got an idea of a plan about why you have just suddenly dropped out of the sky. I have read the file inside out, backwards forwards and upside down and there is stuff in there that you don't need to know. Trust me."

"Always," Liz replied.

Trev continued, "You know your safety is paramount at all times and I won't hold back on any info that compromises that. But there is stuff we'd rather you found out for yourself by getting close to Gibson and winning over her confidence."

"Yeah, I get that, and I much prefer it coming from the target, then my reaction to it is very natural. Who am I working for?"

Len took over. "This is a Royal Ulster Constabulary job being run out of Northern Ireland. the OIOC [Officer in Overall Command] is Deputy Chief Constable Colin Port from Norfolk Old Bill. Port is a top, top, cop, career detective with some big jobs under his belt; he's been appointed head of the investigation."

Liz looked somewhat puzzled. "Excuse me for asking, but why is the DCC of Norfolk heading up a job for the RUC?"

Len looked across at Liz with an eyebrow raised. "That's a good question, Liz. Let's just put that down to politics and park that there for the mo, mate."

"Okay. What's my way into this Muriel Gibson of Plymouth, pray tell?" asked Liz.

"How do you feel about escaping a domestic situation, Liz, as a cover story? That could explain why you have moved into B&B accommodation," Trev said.

"Yeah, I can work something around that, let's build on it a bit more. I don't want to appear vulnerable or a pushover to this target. Been there, done that, too many pitfalls. We need to be thinking two steps ahead so let's not open doors for her. I'll take the domestic angle but not violence; I don't really want to appear a victim. How about the domestic thing is I'm married and having a relationship with a guy, long term relationship, and we're looking at taking it to the next level and leaving my other half is the next step. That's why I'm in Plymouth, and it will give me an excuse for going on the missing list now and then. Dirty weekend away with my fella! I'm liking the sound of this bit of work now."

Trev chipped in with a touch of caution in his voice. "Easy, Liz, it's only make believe and Tommy's a mate. I get your point about appearing vulnerable and a victim. So shagging, notionally of course, mate, some fella from Plymouth might be a good line to run out. Yeah, I like that, and it gives us some flexibility on the plot."

"Listen, Liz,' Len said, 'this job, this bit of work, *it will be,* and *you will be* tightly controlled and directed. Every idea you come up with or we come up with, every next move you want to make, has got to be given the green light by the Op Team. There is no fucking about with that. You are going to be a cog in a machine. There is stuff going on here, over in Ireland and in other places, a lot of moving parts. It's a bit like three-dimensional chess, and Colin Port and his team can see the whole of the board and they decide what piece moves next and where it moves to. I can't stress that enough, Liz."

Liz sucked up a lung full of air then exhaled. "Wow! What about going to the loo? Do I need permission, or can we assume that's a given?" Both men smiled as she continued, "No, seriously boss if you say jump, I'll ask how high before I take off. I trust you guys to look after me and to watch my back, if you're happy with what's going on I'm totally relaxed about it."

The next steps were put in motion over the next few days, the three of them having further meetings to plan it all.

Liz was going to use one of her covert identities that was locked away in a secure steel cabinet bolted to the floor and wall inside the office. She picked out a sealed brown envelope with the name Liz Taylor written across the front. Tipping the contents out, she checked the driving licence and refreshed her memory with the address and postcode. There were also a Lloyds Bank debit and credit card in the same name registered to the same address as the driving licence. A Tesco club card, B&Q loyalty card in the name of Taylor, half a book of postage stamps and a Costa Coffee loyalty card made up the remainder of the contents of the Liz Taylor alias. She gathered them up and placed them into the various pockets and compartments of an empty designer purse she had picked up at a car boot sale a few weeks earlier for a couple of quid. *I knew this was a good buy*, she thought. Trev gave her £180 in various notes from the cash box which Liz stuffed into the YSL purse together with some coins from her own purse. Trevor then picked up a couple of Undercover Officers' Notebooks and secured them in his own rucksack.

"We haven't mentioned a car. What am I going to use as transport, Trev?" Liz enquired of her Cover Officer.

"Your car is being fitted out as we speak. They had a bit of a technical issue with a piece of kit and the hard wiring or something. The guy did explain it to me, but it was all rocket science to me and went straight over my nut. It's coming, don't worry, might not be here till next week. I'll drop you by the train station and you can get a cab from there."

"Why can't we just wait a week, Trev?"

"They want you on the ground this week, Liz. Remember what the boss said: three-dimensional chess. On another point, this fella you've left home for, has he got a name?"

"A name? 'Course he's got a name!"

"What is it?" Trev said.

Liz thought, *Keep the lie as close to the truth as possible, easy to remember that way.*

"Before me and Tommy got together, I had a fling with a guy who would have given his world for me, but the timing wasn't right. He was called Neil. So, let's call my fella Neil," she said.

"Okay. They want you to give Neil the profile of a wealthy businessman who has his fingers into several pies. The sort of guy that on the face of it looks hundred percent legit. Neil plays his cards close to his chest, but he's got properties and business interests in the UK and Europe. Don't go into detail about Neil's business, but make sure you let Muriel think he's not a straight runner, that he has an edge to him."

"Is this the new man in my life then? He'd better not be a minger or a fat bastard. I've got standards, Trev, and I'm not dropping them for Colin Port," Liz said.

Both officers laughed and finished off their preparations. Trev tossed a box towards Liz that contained her new throw-away phone. Trev had paid cash for the phone from a phone shop out of the area and paid for the call credit in the same way. It wasn't traceable to any individual. "Here you are, Liz. I've plumped my new number in under Trev, the rest is up to you to download apps and numbers. You don't want to look like billy-no-mates on the plot, do you?"

Liz took the phone out of the box and discarded everything other than the charger and the USB connector. "Where did you get this, Trev? Toys 'R' Us? It's a piece of crap, mate, and the colour is awful. Why couldn't you let me get my own phone?"

"The op team needed your number on the hurry up. Sorry about the colour, Liz, but it suits your eyes," Trev said.

"It's bright red, Trev."

"As I said, it suits your eyes."

Liz shook her head and said in her best West Country accent, "Wanker!"

Trev, laughing, said, "It's the West Country you're heading for. So why the fuck are you speaking Welsh?"

"Wanker!" Liz repeated in what she believed was a West Country accent, but there was no discernible difference between both attempts.

CHAPTER 9

Exeter

The next morning Trev and Liz travelled to a hotel just outside of Exeter and went straight to room 26. On arrival at the room, Trev gave a soft tap. The door opened for Liz to see a man who was a stranger to her. She later found out his name was Barry. It was clear from the greeting that Trev and Barry had met before, and Liz speculated they had met and had numerous phone calls leading up to this meeting. On entering the room, Liz saw another woman who stood to approach Liz and introduced herself as Kate, and then busied herself with arranging hot drinks. Liz was under the impression that Barry outranked Kate and herself. Not that it was any big deal, for Liz knew, as did all experienced UCOs, it's your role not your rank that dictates your status in the group. Barry informed the small group they were just waiting for the Detective Inspector (DI) to arrive.

It was the DI's job to brief Liz and issue her with a Pocket Notebook (PNB): a process that all in the room had taken part in before. There was a lot of small talk going on about this and that but nothing about Liz's deployment. This weighed on Liz's mind a bit, but not to the point of 'what the fuck, can we talk about the elephant in the room'. She knew this was different to anything else she had been involved with before and started to realise that she was the key, the starter cog of what was clearly going to be a long job. Liz had been deployed on infiltrations before, but always with a partner. This was different. She was going to be gathering evidence and not intelligence. That evidence would have to be eventually transformed into reams of typed transcripts of covert recordings suitable to put in front of a judge. She was to work alone and knew that first in was the most difficult part of any undercover operation. You fail then the job fails.

After another soft tap at the door a young guy who introduced himself as Andy Stevens entered. Liz correctly guessed that he was the DI. A mug of coffee was pushed his way and there were smiles all round. Liz was expecting an Irish accent, but this guy was a cockney. He gave the room an up-to-date briefing on the operation so far. Muriel Gibson was living in the B&B; she used the phone box at the end of the street once a week on a Wednesday at around six pm. She enjoyed a game of bingo on a Thursday night. Her favoured café was 'Beach Cafe' where she would go to for a sandwich with coffee during the day and read trash mags. Muriel had found herself a local drug dealer who was known to police for supplying class 'B' Cannabis and Class 'A' Cocaine and Ecstasy. She was also obtaining drugs on prescription from her doctor.

Liz thought, *This is going to be challenging – a pot smoking, pill popping, bingo nut who reads fucking trash mags.*

Many outside of the police force, and even some inside it, think that undercover work is sexy and high adrenaline stuff. Liz, on hearing about her target, would have begged to differ.

Andy continued his briefing, treading carefully so as not to give Liz information that she would not need. "Your job is to befriend Gibson and let her talk. See what she says. Record it and bring it back to me. Remember, this is a post murder inquiry. Be careful when you engage her in conversation that you don't interview her. Let her talk. It's not your job to question her about any criminal offences. Code C and PACE always apply. I repeat, always. Clear, Liz?"

"Clear, boss," Liz said.

Andy continued, "The guy Neil, your fella. Just gently introduce him by name and that you and he are close. Leave Gibson with the impression he's a bit of a gangster type of guy. Don't go too deep into it. We just want him painted into the background at this time in case we can work something in later. Okay?"

"Got it boss, no problem," Liz said.

Trev crossed the room and handed Liz her recording device and a supply of tapes. "That will keep you going for a while, Liz," he said as she took the equipment from him.

The boss produced photographs of Gibson. They were a mixture of surveillance and mug shots. Liz made a mental image in her head of Gibson's face. *Never to be forgotten.* The DI concluded by informing Liz that there was a 'Vacancy' sign in the window of the B & B right now. Liz thought, *Bite the bullet, girl, and go get yourself a bed for the night.* Then she said, "Right then, let's get this show on the road." Liz looked towards Andy and asked if he had a phone number of the B&B. "I'll try booking a room over the phone," she said to no one in particular.

Liz took herself off and, sitting in Trevor's car on the car park outside, she made the call. The phone in the B&B was answered by a female who introduced herself as Marie. Liz enquired about any vacancies and the cost and was booked into room 3 within minutes. "Yeah, Liz Taylor, thanks. I'll see you soon, thank you so much, you're a godsend, Marie." Liz finished her call and returned to the hotel room. She updated the group and started to write her notes in a PNB given to her by Trev. She recorded that she had been briefed by DI Stevens; she had seen photographs identified by their exhibit marks and made a phone call to the B&B; she had then spoken with Marie and booked into room 3. The boss signed off the notes, as did Liz, and handed the book back to Trev for safe keeping.

When the meeting broke up, Liz and Trev got into Trev's car. Liz handed over her job and personal mobile phones, and handbag containing her real life. Trevor placed the items into his rucksack and checked that Tommy had his number if needed. "Yeah, he's got it, do me a favour will you? Just drop him a text every day or so and let him know I'm alive and kicking mate, ta," Liz said.

"As always, mate," he replied. Trev dropped Liz off outside the train station. Just before she got out of the car they agreed on a safe word or phrase: something the UCO could use in a telephone conversation without attracting attention from others. It would alert the Cover Officer that the UCO was in danger of some kind and needed extracting immediately. It was essential the word or phrase had to fit into a normal conversation. They decided on, 'What fucking sunshine?'

Liz stood outside the train station with her suitcase. Just in case someone had noticed her getting out of the car, she made her way into the ticket hall and bought a newspaper, then made her way into the buffet bar for a coffee. She was now alone and about to enter the world of a terrorist, Muriel Gibson. She thought for a moment about the people sat around her. What would they think if they knew she was an undercover police officer, deployed against a Northern Irish Terrorist? These people were just going about their daily routine, but there she was amongst them, a lone female on a dangerous deployment. None of them knew the real Liz, who had a four-bedroom detached house in Middle England, took expensive holidays with the love of her life, organised barbeques in her back garden and got pissed with girlfriends on a Saturday night. Like all experienced UCOs, Liz was now in role, dismissing all thoughts of her personal life, and started to look forward to a cheap B&B in Plymouth.

It was a short journey on the train from Exeter to Plymouth. On arriving at Plymouth, she walked out of the station towards the taxi rank. From there, she took a cab to her new home. She paid the driver while still seated in the back seat. Once out of the cab, she put her throw-away burner phone to her ear with one hand and activated her recording device with the other. Liz didn't know who she would run into when she entered the B&B. It could possibly be Muriel Gibson. So, on went the device. The first of many recordings that Operation George would generate.

Tape one. Day one.

Liz was greeted by the lady she had spoken to on the phone. "Is it Liz?" she asked.

"Yeah, that's me, and you must be Marie, pleased to meet you and thanks for doing this at short notice."

Marie gave Liz the keys to room 3 and directed her towards the first floor. Once in the room Liz gave it the quick once over. It was clean, spacious and had a window that looked out over the street. *First things first, let's find a hide for the tricky stuff,* she thought. The room had an ensuite. Liz managed to pull the plastic trim away from under the shower tray which provided an ideal place to stash her recorder and tapes.

The first week Liz made sure she visited the 'Beach Café' every day to build up a relationship and legend with the café staff. She addressed Pauline behind the counter as if she had gone to school with her. "Morning Liz, coffee no sugar?" Pauline would call out as Liz walked in.

Job done, I'm a local, well as far as Pauline is concerned. Liz hinted about her complicated love life when chatting with Pauline, knowing that the gossip would spread Liz's story around the café and local community. Liz knew that was good trade craft. She also fostered the habit of taking a jog along the sea front at around six most evenings. Her route took her along the coastline, passing a public phone box at the end of the street near to the B&B.

In a constant state of readiness, Liz always carried her recording device ready to activate if she saw Gibson, just in case there was a chance of a verbal exchange. On two occasions in the first week she acknowledged a female who was waiting outside the phone box, who had commented on her running. The woman spoke with an Irish accent. As Liz got closer and recognised Gibson, she switched on the device, believing a wasted tape is better than a missed opportunity, but that opportunity had not yet presented itself. One week went by and Liz and Gibson never crossed paths in the B&B. Liz was taking the opportunity to download her daily events to Trev via the burner phone on her early evening runs. She thought, *A slow start, but that's the best way. Only fools rush in.*

But then on a Thursday morning Liz popped down for a light breakfast of tea and toast in the breakfast room of the B&B. She was a little later than usual and found the room busy. Gibson was sitting at a table in the bay window with a free seat to her left. *Device on and into the room.* "Hi, do you mind if I join you?" Liz said.

"No, for sure I'd enjoy the company, come on sit yourself down," Gibson replied. *First contact.*

"I'm Liz, how are you doing?"

"Oh, you know, good days and bad days. Today looks like it might be a good day," Muriel said in that strong, unmistakeable Northern Irish accent.

Liz thought, *Yeah, good day for me, but a shit day for you, love.*

Muriel mentioned that she had seen Liz around the place and didn't want to intrude because she seemed preoccupied. Liz didn't push the relationship and reacted to Gibson's comments with, "Well, you know what they say, men…you can't live with them, and you can't live without them."

Muriel laughed. "I could give you lessons in men, love."

The new friends continued with social chit chat. After breakfast, the two women went their own way. Liz had signed up at the local leisure centre that was equipped with a pool and gym. *The job was paying so let's enjoy it* was her motto. The rest of her days were filled by walking around the city centre, window shopping, or reading a good book on Plymouth Hoe, the large south-facing open public space. It was impossible not to think of her real life during the 'idle hours.'

The arrangements around this deployment effectively meant Liz had no real life for the first two weeks. But Tommy would be home soon from his trip abroad. She contacted Trev and asked if she could clear the plot early on Thursday. Trevor suggested he pick her up at the drop off point on Wednesday after breakfast, and they could make their way to the hotel in Exeter for a bottle of vino and a meal, followed by a debrief on Thursday, and then Liz was free for a long weekend.

When an undercover officer says he or she worked undercover for five or ten years or more, it does not mean they worked undercover for three hundred and sixty-five days every year of their undercover career. All UCOs all have a life outside the job. Liz was no different. So, with the offer of a long weekend on the table there was no contest. "Yeah, that sounds like a plan, Trev, let's do it. Dinner's on you. Cheers, mate."

CHAPTER 10

Cornwall

The following day, Liz was sitting on Plymouth Hoe reading a romantic paperback she had picked up in one of the charity shops. Always aware of her surroundings, she noticed Gibson heading her way. *Bang. On went the recorder.* Liz knew that Gibson would stop and chat.

"How's it going, Liz?"

"Oh, hi, Muriel," Liz said with nonchalance before adding, "Yeah, it's going as good as it can be. What about you?"

Muriel sat down on the bench next to Liz, looking out to sea. "I've been down the council banging the desk about getting a house. That B&B is driving me fucking nuts. Apparently, the council here have an agreement with other councils, and I could end up in a place in Devon, Dorset, Somerset or Cornwall, which ever one comes up first. What about yourself, love?"

"I'm in a different situation to you, Muriel. I've got a house, but I can't live in it any more with him. It's a long story for another time maybe."

"Don't worry love, Pauline in the café mentioned you had men problems. We've all been there. If you ever need a friend to just talk to, I'm here for you, love."

"That's kind of you, Muriel, thanks. My sister has invited me down for a few days. I might take her up on it. Her husband is away working, and we can have some girlie time."

"That's the spirit, love, get yourself off and have a change of scenery for a few days, it will do you the world of good. I'm off to the Beach Café for a late dinner or an early tea. I'll see you later, love." With that, Muriel stood up and walked off in the direction of the café.

That is one of the fundamental bits of trade craft a UCO must develop. It's okay having a story about what you're doing in a place and where you came from. What you must have, is a believable and sustainable reason on why you disappear every now and then. "Where do you go to?" is a common question. So, you've got to have a reason why you disappear. UCOs all have a normal life with the same demands as everyone else. So, Liz dropped her sister into the mix.

Liz switched off the device, smiling inwardly, and continued reading her book. She thought, *I've got something for the op team. Contact made, looking at moving, could be Devon, Cornwall Somerset or even Dorset.* Liz picked a bottle of half decent red and dinner from the Co-op on the way back to her room. She planned an early night curled up watching TV in her room and finishing her book. What Liz was not aware of, owing to the sterile corridors[11] of undercover work, was that the operational team was already lining up accommodation for Gibson in Cornwall where she would become a neighbour to Dave S and Sam.

The following morning, Liz missed her tea and toast and waited to see Muriel leave the B&B, heading off in the direction of town. Liz had her bag ready to go and called a cab. She had some time to kill so grabbed a coffee and a *Sun* newspaper – not her preference but she was in character and the *Sun* seemed like the right paper. Within half an hour she would be back in her normal world with normal people enjoying normal things. She stepped out of the cab and walked into the station. Arriving in Exeter, she knew Trev would call so she could sit and relax.

Five minutes later her phone rang. "I'm outside, Liz," the familiar voice said.

"On my way," Liz said.

---

[11] Sterile corridors in covert policing means forms of cut-offs based on a 'need to know' policy.

Trev's BMW was waiting in the pick-up bay. She threw her bag on the back seat and jumped into the front passenger seat and greeted Trev with, "All right mate, get me the fuck out of here."

Trev had booked two double rooms across the corridor from each other. He'd use his room for the debrief the following day. He handed Liz her PNB so she could record her activities over the week without going into too much detail. The tape was the contemporaneous record of all meetings with Gibson. All Liz had to do was record each of the tapes as exhibits and the onward continuity to preserve the integrity of the exhibits. The last thing to do was her exxies. Once completed, a shower, change of gear, and an early bottle of vino in some wine bar rubbing shoulders with city slickers. The type who told everyone that they had the best job in the world. Little did they know that the unassuming couple stood next to them, Liz and Trev, led a far more exciting life than they could even dream of.

Both officers retired for the night at around ten o'clock and were dressed, fed and watered for the eleven o'clock debriefing the following morning. Liz and Trev were waiting in the hotel room for the Op team and DI to arrive. Bang on time there was a gentle tapping on the door. The team of three walked in, headed by Andy Stevens with Barry taking up the rear. Liz verbally debriefed the team on the events of the week. She handed the recordings (Product) to Kate and recorded the fact in her PNB and then handed the book to Andy to sign off.

"Any mention of Neil yet?" Andy asked.

"No not yet, boss, but I've dropped the hint my reason for being here is man trouble. She has offered to lend a sympathetic ear if I need one. I didn't want to push it too hard in the first week or so."

"No complaint here Liz," said Andy, "you've done great. The relationship between you and Gibson will grow. I'm sure of that.'

CHAPTER 11

Lizzie

The next few weeks saw Liz spending more and more time with Muriel, who began to talk about her life in Northern Ireland and the USA. Muriel would often smoke cannabis in Liz's company. On one of the first occasions Muriel offered Liz a draw. Knowing it was bound to happen, Liz was geared up with her excuse.

"Fancy a wee bit yourself, Lizzie?" asked Muriel.

"Not for me darling. I had a bad turn with it once. When I was young, I suffered from asthma. I had all kinds of medications, hormone treatments and inhalers, you name it. It was really bad. And you know how it goes when you try things when you're young. Well, I nearly died. Honest, I had to go to hospital and get put on a breathing machine. I nearly bloody died. So that was it for me, never again. So, thanks but no thanks, you crack on, love."

That was it. Muriel never offered Lizzie, as Muriel now called her, a draw again.

As the relationship developed, Liz spoke more and more about her fella, Neil. She told Muriel how she would go off for weekends or a few days in the week with him, telling her tales of trips up to London enjoying the shops and the night life, and how Neil was very good to her, spending a lot of money on her. These notional trips with Neil gave Liz a believable and sustainable reason for her not being on the plot. In truth, they gave Liz down time to be with Tommy. Over the Christmas and New Year period the story went that Neil took Liz off to a castle in Scotland. To bolster this story, Liz purportedly sent Muriel a postcard of Loch Ness wishing her a Merry Christmas and Happy New Year. A Scottish UCO, belonging to the now defunct Scottish Crime and Drug Enforcement Agency, and Trev's friend, had bought the card and posted it from Scotland at Trev's request, but not before Liz had written the message and signed it. It was then handed over to Trev who posted it to his Scottish UCO friend who then did his bit in the subterfuge.

When in Liz's company, Muriel began to open up about her involvement with a paramilitary organisation. She spoke about her many associates within this group, one of whom was a guy called Jimmy. Owing to a 'need to know' protocol, only the most senior officers would realise the significance of Gibson's revelations. At that time, Liz was unaware Jimmy was William James Fulton, leader of the LVF in Portadown. On the first debrief when Liz attended and mentioned the guy 'Jimmy' there was no reaction from the Op Team or Cover Officer. It was recorded in the debrief note in the usual manner and even regarded by Kate as an insignificant bit of info. At the end of the debriefing, Andy again thanked Liz for her work and instructed her to continue in the same vein using the same tactics. However, Liz couldn't continue to live in the B&B forever. It didn't look right, plus Gibson was about all day and every day. It didn't fit the picture Liz painted of her boyfriend, Neil. So, after about six weeks Liz moved out of the B&B and into one of Neil's flats that had supposedly recently become available and freshly decorated.

Of course, Liz told Muriel she was free to call in for a catch up and a coffee anytime. After all, Liz and Muriel were now good friends. Their relationship was on solid ground and Muriel trusted Liz with some stories about her activities across the water and her friend, Jimmy. Liz continued to debrief on Jimmy's involvement in terrorism in Northern Ireland and the team continued to record her information without a flicker of interest. Later, after learning the truth, Liz told Kate that she would never play poker with her.

Dave S and Sam

About this time, Muriel had been offered a house in Camborne, Cornwall. The local authority told her that if she refused the move, she would be placed at the bottom of the list and it might be a further six months before she received another offer. Muriel agreed to view the property and was driven down to Camborne by a member of the relevant department. The house was in a nice location and freshly decorated. The couple living next door were out doing some gardening when Muriel turned up. Not shy at coming forward, Muriel called out towards the couple in her Northern Irish brogue. "How you doing? Looks like we might be neighbours."

Both stopped what they were doing and walked towards the fence between the two houses. "Pleased to meet you, I'm Dave and this is Sam."

"Good to meet you," Sam said shaking Muriel's hand.

"I'm Muriel, it seems nice and quiet around here, no noisy kids and barking dogs."

Dave went on to say there were some young kids, but they were well behaved and the guy across the way had a Lab that was as soft as shit. Muriel was satisfied and agreed to take the place, then made the arrangements to move from Plymouth to Camborne in Cornwall, which are about sixty miles apart. Whilst she was making those arrangements pending her relocation, the Op Team got busy, applying for authorities to deploy probes, and then fitting without attracting the attention of the neighbours. Well, not all the neighbours. Dave and Sam knew what was going on. They had been patiently waiting for this day since they were first deployed to Camborne.

At a briefing soon after Muriel's trip to Camborne, Liz was instructed to mention to Muriel that Neil had recently lost one of his trusted drivers. The driver had suffered a heart attack and wouldn't be fit for work for some time or maybe never again. The story, according to Liz, was this situation was giving Neil some stress because this guy was trusted and a loyal member of his firm. There was a strong hint that 'firm' meant a criminal firm. Unbeknown to Liz, the plan was to entice Jimmy Fulton to the mainland with some things he would likely want: a driving job with a dodgy outfit; a chance to make money; to distance himself from possible execution which was likely if he stayed in Belfast; to become closer to Muriel Gibson, a trusted LVF member. The RUC's Special Branch (SB) gave Fulton a full Osman warning[12] to reinforce the same message issued to him on his arrival at Heathrow following his deportation from the United States.

After a couple of weeks, Muriel picked up the keys to her lovely new house in Camborne and began turning it into a home. She loved her neighbours – Dave and his lady, Sam. They were so helpful and friendly. So, a friendship began to develop. Dave and Sam had a market stall selling baby stuff: second-hand push chairs, baby clothes, highchairs, baby baths and the like. On one occasion, Sam took ill, leaving Dave needing a hand on the stall, so he asked Muriel if she could help for a few bob to be paid cash in hand. Muriel jumped at the chance and seemed grateful for the opportunity.

Dave used a long wheel Transit van for the market business. It also came in handy when Muriel needed any large items moving that she'd bought locally from charity shops to furnish her new house. Dave and Sam also had a small lock-up garage that Muriel visited when she helped on the market stall. She would go there with Sam or Dave to help load and unload the Transit. It was no accident that she noticed cases of booze, wine, spirits and fags stashed in the back. Dave and Sam obviously had a side-line in cheap fags and booze, Muriel must have thought, and that was the object of the deception. Muriel's contact with Jimmy was now daily and it was clear from the probe and phone taps that he was seriously looking at coming across to spend some time with

---

[12] It is a warning of a death threat or risk of murder, issued by the British police or authorities to the prospective victim. It comes from the 1998 legal case of Osman vs United Kingdom which was heard by the European Court of Human Rights.

her. Time for the Op Team to turn the screw on Muriel and Jimmy via Liz.

So, the stage was now set for Jimmy. Muriel was settled into her house in Camborne. Dave and Sam had befriended her and won over her trust. Jimmy had been kicked out of the USA. Neil was set up back in Plymouth needing and looking for a good, trusted, loyal driver to join his team. Muriel had been picked up on the probe and phone taps talking to Jimmy who was now back in Portadown but believed he was not safe in Northern Ireland.

"Get yourself over here, Jim. There's a job here and you can get your head down with me until you and Tanya get sorted out. I've been telling my mate Liz that you're a top fella and she's mentioned it to her man, Neil. The word is that it is not safe for you back home," was the gist of Muriel's communications with her long-time friend Jim Fulton.

In March 2000, Fulton arrived in Camborne. The final piece of the jigsaw had just walked into place under his own free will. It was an amazing bit of police work, but now even more extraordinary police action was to follow. It was as if Jimmy Fulton had walked onto the set of *The Truman Show*. Welcome, Jimmy! Welcome to a world created and populated by Colin Port and his team of dedicated covert officers.

Muriel called Liz in a state of excitement. "Hi, Liz, yer man's here. He arrived last night. Is Neil still looking for a driver?"

The day after the call to Liz, the UCO known as Neil drove his car down to Camborne with Liz as his passenger to meet Jimmy. He dropped Liz off at Muriel's house and he and Jimmy went out for a drive and a chat. After about five minutes, Neil pulled over and said, "Right, let's see how you drive, son. Swap places." Jimmy took control of the black Lexus with tinted windows and drove round for half an hour with Neil giving him directions. Jimmy seemed a little nervous – not surprising as he thought this was a driving test. If he failed, no job. *Nothing to get nervous about, Jimmy, son*, thought Neil, the *fucking job's yours. It's a done deal, you're on the books.*

William James Fulton was now the property of Operation George. The first stages of the plan had succeeded; a plan first devised whilst Fulton was in custody in the USA for firearms and drugs offences. It was a cunning, audacious and exceptional plan, expertly executed under the supervision of Colin Port together with assistance from the FBI and the British government, to ensure that Jimmy was extradited from the USA and returned to the United Kingdom. Colin Port needed Jimmy on the mainland. Now he was.

CHAPTER 12

Neil

After the Cornwall undercover team had whispered words in Muriel Gibson's ear, Neil was one of the first Plymouth-based UCOs to engage with Jim Fulton. Neil had an air of authority and a panache which easily lent themselves to his role as the crime lord of the Plymouth organised crime group – the firm. It was a role he carried off to perfection and it wasn't long before Jimmy Fulton was shooting off his mouth to ingratiate himself with Neil, the boss, following his recruitment into the Plymouth firm. Initially, Neil engaged Fulton in conversation over breakfast in Plymouth's Port O' Call café, talking to him about family matters once Fulton had mentioned names. Neil was then able to ask about Jim's wife, Tanya, his brother Mark's release from prison on parole, and could query the possibility of Jim recruiting a friend, Phillip McLean, into the firm. They were normal friendly conversations and extended to Neil inquiring about Mark's children and Muriel Gibson's family in California. These conversations were all based on facts freely offered by both Gibson and Fulton so Neil was safe in discussing these matters.

After breakfast, Jim drove Neil to London after Neil had told him he needed to collect some money. That gave Neil most of the rest of the day to hear what Fulton had to say on the journey out and back. Jim carried on talking about family, including Gary Fulton's sister who was married to an RUC police officer. But later, and possibly prompted by the mention of the RUC, Jim started talking about Drumcree when Swinger (Mark Fulton), his brother, was in jail. He explained about the huge security presence because of the events of the previous year and his assurance to the 'Orangemen' he wouldn't bring any weapons to the protests.

Jim said, "They got their faces reddened the year before when we got the machine guns and all out like."

Then there was more chat about Drumcree, Northern Ireland and about Billy Wright and his finances. Wright was the former leader of the LVF but now deceased. After a long period of quiet Fulton said, "One time, Swinger, Billy and Tony and Jamesy went out and stiffed the Boyle brothers, two of them, both Provies... fucking just out the other side of Lurgan. And they stiffed them that quick... got back in the car. The weapons were taken away, but they were still covered for you know forensics. They drove into Lurgan … but into a check point. And Billy says 'right everybody act drunk.' And you know they hadn't even, they hadn't got word about the shooting. They'd had no reports come in."

"Oh, right," Neil said. It was important for him to seem only half interested, when in reality he knew he was potentially recording crucial detail about a murder.

Neil's frequent trips to the bank with Jimmy driving would involve the round trip from Plymouth to London. Owing to previous visits, Jimmy knew it was a private bank in Mayfair. Neil told him he had a safety deposit box there and he often mentioned Stuart, the first name of his personal banking manager. It was often the case, after the visit to the bank, that Neil told Jimmy the next stop was a business meeting in the Ritz Hotel with an associate and friend who was stopping off in London for a few days before flying back to his mountain villa high in the Canadian Rockies.

Neil was a master at creating these intriguing scenes for Jimmy to imagine, using simple suggestions and veiled speech. Jimmy revelled in the kudos that came with having a boss who moved in such exciting circles, visiting high-flying associates in world-famous venues like the Ritz in Mayfair. Neil would sometimes carry a package or briefcase into the bank, making sure to mix it up. Jimmy would always drop his 'boss' directly outside the bank and drive off and wait in a residential street just off the main road. To keep things looking real, Neil did have a deposit box inside the bank so he could go into the building and gain access to the box. He'd place the package or the contents of the briefcase into his box or depart with a package that he had placed there a few days before without Jimmy's involvement or knowledge. Neil would wrap the package to suggest it was a bundle of bank notes by its size and shape. He would take advantage of this time alone to put a fresh tape into his recording device ready for the next two-hour session with Jimmy.

On leaving the Mayfair bank, Jimmy would drive to Neil's lunch appointment at the Ritz Hotel. Jimmy would drop Neil outside the hotel and drive off. Walking into the hotel reception area, Neil would wait for a call to say Jimmy had cleared the plot. Neil now knew it was safe to leave the hotel without being spotted by Jimmy. Forever the professional, Neil had a cover story ready for any staff member who might ask if they could help. "No thanks, it's okay. I'm just waiting for my colleague to join me; he'll be here in a minute. Thanks."

Within seconds, Neil's phone would ring and he would get a cryptic message from his Cover Officer that Jimmy was away. Neil would reply in an equally enigmatic message that suggested to anyone who may overhear him that he understood and would meet him there [a pre-arranged location] in a minute or two. Neil would leave the hotel without disturbing the environment or attracting suspicion and make his way the short distance to the agreed meeting location with his Cover Officer. On arrival, Neil would go to the toilet to deactivate his recording device before talking to the Cover Officer. These locations weren't the Ritz, but the coffee and pizza were delicious and courtesy of Colin Port. When deemed appropriate, Neil would reactivate his device and put a call into Jimmy and ask him to pick him up. "Okay, Jimmy, fed and watered. Come and pick me up please. I'll be on the pavement on the opposite side of the road across from the hotel."

"No problem boss, I'll be there in two," Jimmy would reply.

Jimmy was in his element. He would often tell the other UCOs over a few beers how he enjoyed playing cat and mouse with who he called the "Stasi" (London traffic wardens). He told them how he would sit on a parking meter without paying with a view of the street and pavements looking out for the Stasi. He said it reminded him of 'operations' in Ireland and if he could operate on the streets of Northern Ireland and not get nicked, an over enthusiastic traffic warden pounding the streets of London wasn't going to worry him. As soon as Jimmy saw the warden approaching, he'd drive off round the block to where he thought the warden had come from, then park again. Jimmy's rationale was that the guy had a route; a set pattern of patrolling his patch like a soldier and therefore would not be back in Jimmy's new location for some time.

Jimmy would delight in saying, "You boys want to take a few lessons from the master of trickery." The UCOs present would smile inwardly at Jimmy's words, safe in the knowledge that only they understood the irony.

To foster his grand deception, Neil told Fulton he had a flat in London, as well as his place in Plymouth. He also mentioned stocks and shares to Fulton, letting the target think he was a wealthy and successful crime boss. This was reinforced by hints of other dubious activities. He also hinted he was a millionaire, throwing in mention of a portfolio of properties in Spain and Portugal, but in a quite a casual way. The understatement was deliberate. Neil wished to give the impression that he was successful because he and his firm stayed off the law enforcement radar. He said nothing to dissuade Fulton that it was he who had financed the purchase of a Renault Laguna for Jim's sole use. The arrangements were made for Fulton to be paid for his new driving job for the 'firm.'

Later, Fulton called his mum in Northern Island and the conversation was recorded as he talked proudly about his new job, leaving out all the dodgy bits. He also told his mother he was being paid £2,500 every fortnight.

Neil later commented, "He probably wanted his mum to think that he had a proper job, and he wasn't involved in anything else." The rest of the UCOs thought the same.

Fulton was paid by the firm for his work as a driver over a period of sixty-four weeks. He received an average weekly wage of £455.27, or £1,821.06 a month. The payments varied in date and amount depending on the work Fulton had done. For example, in one five-week period no payments at all were made to Fulton for wages, but on some occasions large amounts were paid: in July 2000 and April 2001 he received £1,000; in March 2001, £900, and another £570 in April 2001, plus £500 in December 2000. On top of his wages, Fulton also benefited from the generosity of the undercover officers, who paid for meals and refreshments. Once more, human nature plays its part in Fulton trying to advance himself in the hierarchy of the firm. He thought he was on to a good thing.

CHAPTER 13

First Meeting

Just like actors on stage and screen, UCOs need a rest occasionally. But a key difference is that UCOs are paid as usual even when not 'working', as opposed to actors using the euphemism of 'resting' to disguise the fact they are temporarily unemployed.

A UCO with the alias Robbie was sitting at his desk when his legend mobile phone rang.

"Do you fancy a bit of work?"

It was the boss in London. The boss, a senior investigating officer (SIO) met Robbie in London and briefed him to deliver a car to Plymouth where he would meet another UCO and the target of the operation – Jim Fulton. At that stage it was supposed to be a quick in and out job. Deliver the car and that's it. When Robbie got to Plymouth, driving there in his own car,[13] he had another briefing where he was told the operation was top secret and nothing about it could be disclosed. He was also told never to mention a thing about his military background. Before the briefing was over, the briefing officer, glancing at some notes, said, "And not a thing about being a Catholic." Robbie, feeling a little perplexed initially, soon came to realise the vital importance of those instructions.

---

[13] Notionally 'his car' but owned by the police authority and used by Robbie as 'his car.'

Robbie then returned to London to collect the car that was to be delivered to Fulton – a Renault Laguna – and drove it to Plymouth. As per his instructions, he headed to a pub where he was to meet another UCO – Neil – and Fulton. Robbie already knew Neil from other operations and, as part of the usual steps, had called him while on his way to Plymouth to firm up arrangements for the meet. Robbie met up with Neil and Fulton inside the pub. Neil, making out he was someone 'big' in the firm, told Robbie to hand over the car keys to Fulton.

All went well until Neil pulled Robbie over, out of Fulton's sight and hearing, and told him he was feeling ill. "I mean ill… really ill… genuinely ill. I'm going to have to go back to the flat. Will you be okay?"

"I'll be fine," Robbie said. "No problem."

Robbie and Jim whiled away the hours, chatting away like 'new best friends,' and that was the start of almost two years Robbie spent in the company of Jim Fulton, a relationship Fulton never realised was a fabrication. After Robbie slept overnight in the Plymouth flat, a safe house, he met up with Jim again the following morning by mutual arrangement and sanctioned by a Plymouth Cover Officer.

They strolled through a trailer park near the docks close to a freight terminal when Jim started to talk, entirely unprompted, about his days in Belfast. He told Robbie about his bomb maker. Jim said, "He's good. He can make a bomb so wee it fits inside a cigarette packet." After that, Fulton went his separate way, using the car Robbie had delivered as his wheels. Fulton was unaware that car had been doctored, lumped up – kitted out with listening devices and an immobiliser.

Following the usual routine, Robbie went to meet a Cover Officer for a debrief. It was at that Plymouth debriefing where he again met Neil, a UCO who played a major role in the operation. Neil played the part of the boss of the crime gang and explained to Robbie that the objective was to gain Fulton's confidence by recruiting him into the Plymouth-based organised crime group, initially as a driver. Hence the reason for the Renault Laguna that Robbie had driven down from London.

During the debrief, Robbie relayed what had happened with Fulton, which was all recorded, and whilst Robbie was making his own notes in his pocket notebook, one of the team said, "Do you think you can hang around for a few days?"

"Yeah, I'm sure I can," Robbie said. That was the start of Robbie's long so-called friendship with Jimmy Fulton. Neil, Robbie and the rest of the UCOs came to address Fulton as 'Jimmy' rather than a more formal 'Jim' as they got on friendly terms.

CHAPTER 14

Robbie a Fixture

Now Robbie was a fixture on the team, plans were laid as to how best to control Jimmy Fulton in the hope he might say something about the Rosemary Nelson murder. That was the prime objective. From Colin Port downwards, the whole Operation George team was conscious Fulton was a ruthless terrorist, and accordingly it was vital he did not engage in any terrorist activities on the English mainland, or elsewhere for that matter. It is somewhat otiose to consider the implications if he were to explode a bomb in England whilst part of the Plymouth 'firm.'

Neil, Dave, Robbie and one other were to become the nucleus of the UCOs 'palling up' to Fulton. It was they, together with the Cover Officers, who discussed the various scams or subterfuges designed to bring Fulton closer to the 'firm' and thus increasing the opportunities for the target to talk freely. All these conversations were to be recorded using gadgets hidden on the UCOs, secreted in vehicles, and later using probes hidden in the homes of both Fulton and Muriel Gibson in Cornwall.

The Cover Officers would rotate from time to time, but one of them would always be close by and staying in a hotel. The deceptions were freely discussed between all present; sometimes a Cover Officer would float an idea or more often the scams were thought up by one of the UCOs. Robbie's legend was partly built on a background of the haulage industry and Robbie had a valid HGV 1 licence. To be precise, there were two. One in his real name and one in an alias for undercover work. This was ripe for introducing Fulton to a world of high value thefts of lorry trailers and their cargo. Trailers loaded with booze, cigarettes, or computer parts were the favourites, but one or another of the team would throw in an idea based on real jobs they had worked on in the past.

Once an idea had been adopted, the UCOs and Cover Officers would approach the Operational Team to discuss the logistics: the 'what, where and how' of the scam. The Operational Team would then locate and obtain the resources, whether they be radios, lorry loads of booze or fags, and on other future scams an armoured car and a priceless work of art. These deceptions were vital if they were to control Jimmy Fulton. That control was a given. They needed him in their company as much as possible to allow him to talk, which was all recorded.

It wasn't always a planned staged theft. Sometimes he would be invited to drive them to different places all over England. In a typical job, he would drive one or more of the UCOs to London. He'd drop them off and the UCO or UCOs would disappear, telling him they were going to an important meeting. The way it was said was designed to let him believe it was something dodgy. He would wait in the car thinking, *I've landed on my feet here with this gang.* On occasions he would drop one of the UCOs off at a bank, usually Neil because he had a safety deposit box there. That was designed to make him think they were real big-time players in the criminal underworld.

These subterfuges were gradually ratcheted up so sometimes Jimmy would be told to come inside to the meeting but to stay in the corner to keep an eye on the parked car or 'Old Bill.' The meeting was all pre-arranged so one of the UCOs would be meeting up with another UCO, not part of the operation but playing a minor but important role in the grand deception. The two UCOs would sit and talk about anything, but out of earshot of Jimmy. Once the meeting was over, Jimmy would drive back to Plymouth with the UCO and talk all the way. These subterfuges were all sanctioned, recorded in writing and authorised by the boss. It was then the logistical support kicked in, supplying whatever was required for any one scam. Although the UCOs knew this operation was deadly serious, they did have fun coming up with the ideas for the scams. Some were actioned and others put on the back burner. But all had the same intention: to keep Jimmy Fulton thinking he was running with a firm of serious proportions.

CHAPTER 15

Slough

"I need you to do a bit of work with Robbie for a few days. You okay with that, Jimmy?' Neil asked.

"I'm yer man," Jimmy replied, all too keen to impress Neil, and he was now on the payroll of the Plymouth gang.

"Okay then. Meet him at the Port O' Call at eight tomorrow morning," Neil instructed.

Plymouth's Port O' Call café was near to the Hoe and a regular meeting spot for Jimmy and the UCOs. It served what some call a 'big boys' or 'fat boys' breakfast. Others call that huge cholesterol laden English breakfast by other names, one of which is amusing and often used in Sheffield – 'the full train smash.' Over breakfast, Robbie said, "Right, we're going to have a drive up to Slough. There're loads of industrial estates there and we need to have a mooch around and check out a trailer worth nicking. I'm told there is, but I need to see with my own eyes."

"Right yer are, Robbie," Jimmy said, delighted to be placed in a position of trust within the firm.

It was mission accomplished in that Robbie and Jimmy would be spending five hours or more together in the confines of a car wired for sound, as was Robbie. The people who'd listen to those tapes were located many miles from Plymouth and buried away in a police headquarters back office. They would listen after the event and make notes before passing the tapes on to the transcribers. Those transcripts were typed documents and, in the future, would be used as evidential material in the case against Fulton and Gibson.

In one revealing moment during that recording, Jimmy laughed about when he'd invite people round to tea. He went on to explain that in his world back in Northern Ireland getting invited around for your tea means you're going to get punished – a shooting or kneecapping. He did so with a laugh and a smile in his eyes. Robbie stayed calm… and silent. Fulton went on to demonstrate to Robbie how he'd kneecap somebody. If it were somebody he liked, he'd put it through the fleshy bit of the thigh, close to the knee. If it were somebody that he didn't like and deserved the worst he could possibly get, he'd put the bullet through his kneecap and cripple them for life. All through this, Fulton laughed and joked and suddenly switched to how he had grown up in Belfast. Robbie gained the impression Fulton wasn't a soldier. He wouldn't have gone gun to gun – mano a mano. But Robbie remained silent, keeping his innermost thoughts private.

With every recording it felt like they were getting closer to snaring Jimmy Fulton, but he still hadn't mentioned the Rosemary Nelson murder. After some consultation the team decided to up the stakes. In three weeks they would stage a lorry theft. By upping the stakes like that, they could convince Jimmy how serious they were. The question remained: would he finally give them what they needed, or would everything unravel before they got their man?

CHAPTER 16

Cash in Transit

The team more and more enjoyed the surreal nature of the deceptions and delighted in the private references to the *Truman Show*. They decided to give Jim bigger parts to play to make him feel even more part of the 'gang.' Someone came up with the idea of staging a cash in transit robbery. It was a risk, bearing in mind it would possibly involve violence which was Jim's bread and butter.

The plan went ahead with Robbie and Jimmy driving to a hotel in the home counties. The idea was for them to meet up with Neil and other members of a crime gang that Robbie and Neil had previously worked with. The other players were, of course, UCOs who all knew each other well. The main player on their side was a guy called Bobby. At the meeting in a hotel bedroom with Jimmy present, Bobby started telling Robbie and Neil about a job he was planning, but he needed some extra bodies with certain talents to pull it off. There were about five men in the room when Bobby unveiled the plan for this job.

Completely off the cuff, Robbie started digging and asking questions about details. Bobby and Neil knew to play along even when things got a bit heated.

"I hear you but I gotta know, whose bit of work is this?" asked Robbie.

"Can't tell you that," Bobby said.

"Well, okay, who will be on the pavement at the time of the race [the planned event]? You're talking millions in cash so there's a good chance armed cops would be close. I need to know the head honcho will be there with me, so I know it won't turn to shit," Robbie said, almost shouting. It was getting heated and turned up a few notches by Bobby and Robbie yelling and stabbing the air every time they were making a point. Neil gave Robbie a certain look which was code for enough. The scene was now set.

The meeting broke up and Robbie and Jimmy went for a pint in the hotel lounge. Bugsy, one of Bobby's gang (in reality another UCO), joined them.

"What the fuck's up with your boss?" Robbie said.

"Ah, don't worry about it. He's okay. No problem," Bugsy said.

After finishing their drinks, Jimmy and Robbie drove back to Plymouth, some four hours away. Fulton talked about this job incessantly and said, "Right up my street. Guns, violence and money." He seemed upset about the argument back in the hotel room.

"Forget it," Robbie said.

"Don't you worry, Robbie. I'll dig two holes, one for the money and one for that cunt Bobby. No one talks to you like that in front of me and gets away with it," Fulton said.

Later that night at a debriefing session, Robbie was finally able to laugh at what had happened, especially Jim Fulton's 'two holes' comment. Unable to resist a bit of leg-pulling, Robbie saw his old mate Bobby and said, "You're a dead man walking."

It was then back to serious work. The team needed to plan the staged cash in transit job. As always it was a case of keeping Jimmy occupied and under control so they would go and recon the plot. This gave them ample time with Jimmy travelling to London and capturing his admissions on tape. The first stage of planning involved the Operational Team and Cover Officers obtaining an armoured car and access to a disused secure bonded warehouse somewhere in East London. A UCO from outside the team was briefed to drive the armoured car.

The Plymouth team had arranged for the Cover Officer to get hold of some walkie-talkies for the scam. True to form, the Metropolitan Police Service (MPS) Cover Officer went out and purchased the best, all singing and dancing two-way handheld walkie-talkies. They were complicated to the uninitiated, with a complex array of switches, buttons and dials.

As one forthright UCO exclaimed on first testing one of the radios, "For fuck's sake mate, is this kit supplied by NASA? You could hold a conversation with someone stood on Mars with these things. They must have cost thousands. The only problem is you need a PhD in electronics to switch the fucking thing on."

Following the plan, Robbie and Jim set off from Plymouth to London on another exciting day of murderous conversation between them. Robbie's ploy to make sure the recordings were clear was turning off the in-car radio when he got in. Covering his real motive, he said, "I don't like that shit that comes across the airways." It was reputed Robbie loved his music and prided himself as a pop aficionado, sometimes telling anyone who would care to listen that popular music was his thing in any pub quiz round. So now pop music was added to the list he couldn't disclose in his legend, along with the truths he was once a soldier and is a Roman Catholic, albeit of the lapsed kind.

At some point on the journey, Robbie, who was in the passenger seat, retrieved the walkie-talkies from a bag on the back seat. He examined the mass of dials and switches, trying to figure out how to turn them on. Pressing some buttons, Robbie was horrified to hear the car radio clicking as if in weird electronic duet with the walkie-talkie. Panic set in. Robbie's thoughts were filled with expletives, and he could sense a cold sweat running down his back. He suddenly realised the car radio and the walkie-talkie were on the same wavelength. Worried that Jimmy would become suspicious, and desperately concerned that the whole operation was about to go tits-up, he managed to shrug the whole thing off in front of Jimmy.

Sometime later, they arrive at the disused bonded warehouse in East London and met up with another UCO called Hands (on account of having hands the size of large shovels). Robbie gave Hands one of the walkie-talkies and a quick lesson on how it worked, though Hands seemed a little distracted. Robbie conducted a test call, deliberately avoiding using any recognised voice procedure or knowledge of how you should talk over a radio with words like 'over' or 'out.' He spoke as if he was talking to him face to face. Jimmy interrupted and started to say things like, "Press the PTT button, Robbie." He was eager to help in any way he could, undoubtedly thinking of all those millions.

Robbie knew from his former military life that PTT was short for 'Press to Talk' or 'Press to Transmit.' It was clear to Robbie his feigned ineptness in radio management, voice procedures and protocols were both amusing to Jimmy and frustrated him, to the point where Jimmy said, "Robbie, you drive, and I'll do the fucking radio." Robbie did just that, jumping into the driving seat and letting Jimmy take over the radio. Robbie was impressed with Jimmy's expertise as he listened to him using phrases like "Hello one. This is zero, over," and "Standby, standby one. There is movement at the premises."

A friendly insider at the warehouse had told the team what time to expect the armoured car to exit. At the precise time, out came the money truck. Robbie and Jimmy noted the time and the direction of travel, knowing Hands was in position a bit further away as a second pair of eyes as part of the staged recon for the job itself. Once they had seen what they needed, Robbie and Jimmy called up Hands so he could make his way over to them. They had a brief conversation where there was a load of piss taking at Robbie's expense about his radio techniques. Then Hands walked away, with Robbie still in the driving seat. Robbie soon realised Hands' walkie-talkie was on open mic, but still in his pocket. If Hands was to call his Cover Officer to update them on what had just happened, the conversation would come through the walkie-talkie, and the entire operation would be blown. Jimmy still had the walkie-talkie so Robbie couldn't turn it off. Trying not to panic, Robbie's brain went into warp speed to come up with a plan.

Robbie could see Hands and was dreading him taking his phone out. Robbie's first thought was to drive at him and knock him over if he reached for his phone. He would try to avoid causing him serious injury, just wing him a bit, anything to stop him reaching for and using his phone. Lucky for Hands, Robbie had a second thought.... he rang him. Robbie managed to indicate cryptically what the problem was. After some initial confusion on the part of Hands, he twigged what Robbie was saying, reached into his pocket and turned the walkie-talkie off. Though they were able to laugh about it in the debrief that followed, Robbie had been so close to the operation collapsing that he must have had nightmares about it. Jimmy had talked about his previous violence. Who knows what he might have done in that van when he realised how he'd been hoodwinked.

CHAPTER 17

The Reversing Lorry

The cash-in-transit job was eventually abandoned, but not until several dry runs following the armoured car with Jimmy for company in the wired-for-sound car. That provided many hours for Jimmy to talk, and he did talk. In addition to following the armoured car, UCOs and Jimmy scoped various likely places to ambush the truck. Most of them were in the New Forest, a popular tourist area, which was a factor in calling off the plan – along with complications around having to use real weapons to make it all look genuine. Every one of the team, never mind the bosses in Belfast and London, knew this was a big no-no as far as Jim Fulton's involvement was concerned. The team deflected Jimmy's interest into helping steal a high-value load of cigarettes instead. Over one million quid's worth to be exact. The load 'belonged' to a government agency and for them to play ball, Colin Port had to hastily arrange for the entire load to be underwritten to the tune of £1.2 million, now just over £2 million in today's money, which included the vast amount of taxation due on the cigarettes. Daniel Defoe was correct when he wrote in *The Political History of the Devil*, in 1726: "Things as certain as death and taxes, can be more firmly believ'd." H.M. Government was prepared to 'lose' the goods but not the taxes.

Robbie was the UCO with a licence to drive big lorries and he set off to a bonded warehouse near to the docks in Dover, Kent, to collect the load in a forty-foot long, nondescript curtain-side trailer. Spare a thought for Robbie right now. Can you imagine a non-ranking detective signing for and being responsible for £1.2 million worth of product? If this had been a drug deal or some other sort of undercover operation with a parcel of that value on the pavement the boss would have had a fully armed surveillance team with eyes on that the parcel 24/7. Some UCOs have done jobs with much less money on the plot and there were more guns deployed than they had at the Alamo.

In the real world, loads of this value would have tracker devices buried in the trailer or load. Robbie's experience was invaluable. Some of that was from other undercover work and some gleaned from real haulage industry experience. He knew how to combat any challenge Jimmy might come up with because he would say they had a man on the inside of the knock-off. He would explain the guy had reassured him that any tracker had been sabotaged. Jimmy never asked. The easiest question to answer is the question that is never asked, but he was ready if asked.

Setting up all these staged jobs would involve casing the locations, planning routes, working out time and distance, arranging access to a 'slaughter' (criminal slang for warehouse) where the parcel would be broken up ready for distribution to trusted buyers. All this gave the time for the UCOs to be with Jimmy for hours on end or a one to one where all sorts of conversations took place.

Robbie did a few recons with Jimmy on the cigarettes theft just to spend time with him and generate conversation. Eventually, Robbie did the job of hitching up the tractor unit to the trailer with Jimmy acting as his third eye. Robbie smoothly had the trailer away and set off for the slaughter. Jimmy was following in the Laguna with both men in contact using mobile phones. Robbie instructed Jimmy to drive ahead to a choke point to check if anything was following the lorry. Once Jimmy gave Robbie an all clear, Robbie told Jimmy to follow at a distance to monitor any vehicles that were in convoy with the lorry. He got Jimmy to carry out anti and counter surveillance.

"This is the dog's bollocks," Jimmy said over the phone. He was loving it, thinking he was back operating in Northern Ireland. Robbie, sat in the cab of the truck, couldn't resist a wry smile. He knew these antics gave the Plymouth firm a professional aura and credibility. *But there's still a lot that could go* wrong, he reminded himself.

Robbie and Jimmy arrived at the warehouse, which had all been arranged by the Plymouth cover team beforehand. The team had always wanted Jimmy to feel he was working his way up the ranks of the firm and gaining their respect and trust. This was paying dividends. Unbeknownst to Jimmy, prior to arriving at the warehouse the technical team had worked their magic for sound, after which they had handed over the warehouse keys to the UCOs. A Cover Officer would give a crash course, showing how to activate the sound and the best locations for best quality recordings. What nobody could change was the physical layout of the industrial estate where the warehouse was located. It was best suited to large Ford Transit vans and not forty-foot trailers. The access roads were cramped and ram full of delivery vans during daylight hours. Not the best scenario for backing in a forty-foot trailer into a warehouse never designed to accommodate large trucks. Together, Robbie and Jimmy had visited the 'slaughter' a few times before the day of the race [the event] to familiarise themselves with the location, locks, light switches, door operation and stuff like that. These trips again generated opportunities to spend time with and occupying Jimmy. That was the name of the game in their world.

Robbie soon realised a forklift truck and a pallet truck were needed. The pallet truck proved easy for the cover team and was sourced locally. Robbie had no idea where it had come from. Cover Officers from the cover team put it inside the warehouse until needed.

That part is now sorted, but what about the forklift truck? Robbie thought. After all, there was no way they could handball forty feet of fags off a trailer. One of the team found a plant hire place on the estate that rented out forklift trucks and other plant out by the day. Robbie was the only UCO on the team who had a licence to drive a forklift truck, so it fell on him to arrange the hire. No problem, as he had all the necessary covert documentation to produce to the guy in the hire centre: a driving licence, a separate forklift licence, proof of address and most importantly to the hire guy, bank details for the hire payment.

Robbie arranged to collect the truck the following day without Jimmy being there, as the plan was to meet Hands to run the plans by him to ensure all went like clockwork. On arriving at the warehouse, Robbie spotted Hands' car parked up but no sign of his colleague anywhere. Robbie later told the team, "I'm the only person with keys to the warehouse so I know he's not playing one of his stupid games of hiding inside from me ready to jump out to scare the shit out of me. I know the tea van round the corner does a nice brew and bacon butty, so I head off round there thinking that's where he'll be. As I'm making my way round to the van what do I see?"

Robbie continued to describe Hands driving towards him in the forklift truck, right down the middle of the road. He was holding up a line of traffic that couldn't pass because of his road position. Robbie added, "He was smiling from ear to ear and shouted out to me, 'A piece of piss this mate, don't know what all the drama is about who can drive what.'" Hands had told Robbie as he was on the plot early, he'd go and pick up the forklift. He informed the hire guy that he worked for Robbie and he'd sent him to pick up the truck.

"Convincing people to believe us is part of being a UCO, I guess," added Robbie at the end of telling the tale to the assembled team.

And so the scene was set. The team had the warehouse, the listening device, a forklift, the lorry, the trailer and the cherry on the cake: a load of fags to the value of £1.2 million.

At around 2:00 am Robbie called Hands on the mobile and told him he was five minutes out and to get ready. Five minutes later, Robbie pulled into the industrial estate and positioned the lorry so he could reverse around the corner of the building line and come to a halt alongside the warehouse shutter door. As he braked to a halt with that unmistakeable hiss of air brakes, Jimmy, with the keys in hand, was off like a dog with a bone to open the door and switch on the lights and, unbeknownst to him, the listening devices planted in the warehouse.

Robbie started the tricky manoeuvre of reversing and turning the trailer at the same time. It was a tight fit but doable. Hands was on foot, keeping pace with the trailer from behind, helping to guide Robbie round the corner and into the best position by the shutter door. The trailer started coming round like a dream. Hands was doing a great job, shouting out, "Keep coming, keep coming, a bit of left hand down." Then, as Robbie later put it, "My eyeline clears the side of the building line and my retinas are destroyed by a brilliant white light. I can't see a fucking thing."

Hands continued to shout, "Keep coming mate, keep it on that, keep coming."

Luckily, Robbie sussed out what was going on. He looked up at the source of the bright lights, shielding his eyes, and could just make out that Hands had parked his car at the top of the yard with the headlights on main beam, no doubt trying to help.

Later, Robbie continued his story, "All he's done is blind me... bloody hell, Hands! I try to get his attention by shouting, 'Hands, mate, I can't see fuck all, switch the fucking lights off.'

"Hands continues to shout out, 'Come on, keep coming, keep coming.'

"I'm shouting 'Hands, Hands, switch the fucking lights off, I can't see.'

"All I heard was Hands, 'Keep coming, keep coming.'

"Over the noise of the truck and Hands calling out I can't hear a word. Out of frustration I shout out Hands' real nickname, 'Lucky, shut the fuck up and switch those fucking lights off.' That did the trick, as Hands stopped shouting. I could see his silhouette in the wing mirror walking towards me along the side of the trailer.

"He stopped by the driver's door and looked up at me with wide eyes and said, 'You've just called me by my nickname.'

"'Yeah, I know mate, but you weren't responding to Hands.'

"'You've just called me Lucky on the tape,' he said.

"'Yeah mate, and you've just done it now,' I said.

"'Fucking hell that's shit,' he said.

"So, I said, 'Yeah, I'm sorry mate, but do me a favour, switch the fucking headlights off. You're blinding me. I can't see shit.'"

At the official debriefing the team heard how Hands complied with Robbie's request and deftly manoeuvred the trailer into A1 position. It was confirmed that Jimmy had been in the warehouse and heard and saw nothing. Robbie had jumped down from the cab to where Hands was standing as Jimmy opened the barn doors at the rear of the trailer. Robbie then went into the warehouse and within seconds reappeared driving the forklift. Jimmy stayed in the warehouse, directing where to drop each pallet according to brand. He oversaw handing over the booty to the buyers throughout the next twenty-four hours. Robbie lifted the first two pallets off and into the warehouse and then started moving pallets to the rear of the trailer, using the hand-operated pallet where his now ex mate Hands was waiting to use the big forklift truck. The job went like clockwork, and they unloaded the fags in record time. Jimmy's job now was to stay there and slaughter the load to numerous vans and small lorries that would be arriving over the next hours. Every van and lorry were driven by a motley crew of UCOs all drafted in solely for this scam. Hands and Robbie left Jimmy in charge. Hands set off in his car with Robbie leaving in the lorry to dump the empty trailer. But not before Robbie dissuaded Jimmy from his plan to torch the trailer.

Jimmy was relieved sometime later by Hands so Jimmy could go home and get some sleep. Once Jimmy was indoors and a suitable time allowed for him to drop off, the operation in reverse had to take place. The load had to go back. Jimmy was monitored by the technical people using the probes and once he seemed to be in dreamland after a successful job, the same fleet of vans and lorries returned all the fags to the warehouse. The building and its valuable contents were secured, and someone stayed there until the area around the warehouse had fallen silent again. That was Robbie's cue to return with the tractor unit and trailer to reload and return the goods to the rightful owner.

During the operation debriefing, Hands was heard to demand, "That part of the tape needs PII cos dickhead Robbie called me by my nickname."

Robbie said immediately, "Sorry, Lucky, no harm done mate."

One further point was up for discussion at the debriefing when someone asked, "Did anyone else see the real police in that marked police car?"

"No, we were too busy unloading over a million quid's worth of fags," said a voice at the back of the room.

"Lazy bastards, three in the morning and they can't be arsed to ask us what we're doing," said another.

CHAPTER 18

Work of Art

As always, a new scam was conceived at a joint meeting of the UCOs, with the cover team sitting down and dreaming up a 'bit of work' that they could run out over a prolonged period. They also kept the prime objective in mind: to spend time with Jimmy to occupy him and let him talk about his life in Northern Ireland 'fighting the fight.' They had to create scenarios that would genuinely play out over several deployments and structure them in a criminal way. They knew each bit of work had to be milked for everything they could get out of it. This was how the 'stolen and priceless work of art' scam was invented.

The possibility of a 'big earner' was casually floated around by the UCOs in Jimmy's company, so he had some idea that a big job was in the making and come the time the firm would sit down and discuss it. Those talks would involve Jimmy too. The germ of an idea had taken hold in Jimmy's mind, so much so, on a full day road trip with Robbie, he said, "Has Neil mentioned anything to you about a big job coming off?"

Robbie played dumb. Jimmy, hardly able to conceal his excitement, continued, "For fuck's sake, Robbie, don't let on I've mentioned it but it's to do with a fucking expensive painting."

The scam was in play. They had created a scenario for Jimmy, and he was walking wide eyed into it. Sometime later, Neil called the meeting. Neil, Dave, Robbie and Jimmy attended when Neil laid out the plan. Robbie at that point looked across at Jimmy who wore a 'told you so' smile. Neil made it clear they were going to have a fat pay day for doing next to nothing but with a bit of risk around it. He explained that he was middling the sale of a stolen, priceless work of art, and had an overseas buyer for the painting.

"Our buyer is the front. I happen to know he's working for a Belgian firm but as far as anyone is concerned, I'm doing business with only the buyer, the front man. Likewise, the real seller is known to no one," Neil said, deliberately sounding mysterious as to who had possession and control of the painting at this time. He added that "the market for works of art is a mystery to me but none of us need know anything about it or who the real buyer and seller is. That's where we come in with the Belgian outfit, to keep the real identities of the parties a closely guarded secret. That's how it works."

Neil carried on laying out the next steps which were to meet up and have preliminary talks with the Belgian firm and agree an acceptable method of how the trade would go down. The selling price was disclosed to the Belgian firm who would seek agreement from the buyer. In that way the trade would go down between them and the Belgian guys.

The first meeting was in a motorway hotel. The Belgians had made their way there from the airport and booked a couple of rooms for the night. The UCO team had done the same but with no intention of staying the night as this was business, not a social meeting. They also knew there would be time for a few beers with their European cousins later. The Plymouth team had no idea how many Belgians would arrive so they decided all four of them would travel to the motorway hotel. That was Neil, Dave, Robbie and Jimmy. Neil made a point of matching each one of them one for one at the meeting table, stipulating that any Belgian extra bodies would have to sit off to the side. That was designed to prevent the meeting being overcrowded and possibly to ruffle a few feathers.

Before the meeting, Neil said, "There's no reason to mistrust these guys, but Europeans tend to work a bit different to us and there is always a good chance they might bring guns to the meeting."

"That's most unlikely on this first meet as there is no valuable commodity at the venue," Dave interjected.

"Correct," Neil said, and set out a sort of batting order for the meeting. It was agreed that Dave and Neil would be one and two on the team with Jimmy in three and Robbie in four. Jimmy smiled at Robbie again. His face gave away his meaning as if he had said, "Me three, you four." Robbie, as imperturbable as ever, thought, *That's okay, Jimmy. I bet there are only two Belgian guys at the meeting so me and you will both sit it out.*

It was clear Jimmy was disappearing further down the rabbit hole as he was getting more involved, and the team were stroking his ego, not to mention stoking his sense of growing importance in the Plymouth firm.

As the four walked into the meeting venue, they saw two guys seated at a table close to the window overlooking the car park. They all guessed correctly. These were the men from Brussels. One guy was mister average, nothing to write home about, but on the other hand, his mate was a contender for the stereotype of the 'muscles from Brussels.' He was huge, and as Jimmy later remarked, "A fucking big guy." Both appeared to be in their mid-forties and dressed like businessmen in smart trousers, jackets and open-neck shirts.

Neil and Dave followed the plan and sat *tête-à-tête* at a table with the two Belgians. Robbie and Jimmy sat at a separate table watching on. Once Robbie and Jimmy were seated at a separate table, and out of earshot of the four main players, Robbie whispered, "If things kick off, I'm fighting the little fucker, the hulk is yours."

Jimmy replied, "No worries, Robbie, the bigger they are the harder they fall. He won't know what's hit him." At that, they lapsed into a quiet fit of the giggles with them agreeing these two Belgians were now to be known as 'Tom' and 'Jerry', Tom being the bigger of the two. The Plymouth firm referred to them as that from then on.

The meeting went on for almost two hours over coffee and sandwiches with Robbie and Jimmy sat to one side. Jimmy insisted on keeping a close eye on Neil and Dave and positioned himself at his table with the best possible vantage point. Robbie thought, *Ten out of ten on the basic surveillance course, Jimmy. That's the position I would have taken up.*

As the meeting ended, all four at the main table stood up and shook hands with each other. Tom and Jerry walked away in one direction. Neil and Dave walked towards Robbie and Jimmy. It was time for the long drive back to Plymouth with Jimmy at the wheel. On the journey back Neil went over the details of the meeting for the benefit of Robbie and Jimmy. Jimmy soaked it all in and occasionally asked a question or made a comment. Neil made a point of mentioning how professional the guys were and on the day of the race they would match them. He said he wanted them all suited and booted. This was a problem for Jimmy who didn't possess a suit.

On arriving back in Plymouth, Neil produced some folding from his pocket and handed some cash to Jimmy. "There you go, Jimmy, problem solved. Buy yourself a decent whistle but do me a favour and make sure it's black," Neil said.

The team purposefully allowed a few weeks to pass, during which time Jimmy would be engaged on his usual driving jobs, ferrying one or the other of Neil, Robbie or Dave around. When driving Neil, he would feed Jimmy updates and bits and pieces on the development of the art job. Jimmy would tell the others in passing conversations. Neil had instructed Jimmy that on the day of the trade he was going to be with him and Robbie, together with Tom and Jerry and the art expert who was to validate the provenance of the painting. He told Jimmy he was to search all three for guns before they got into the hotel room with them and the painting. Jimmy's face was a picture. This role was icing on the cake. Later, Jimmy said to Dave, "Search them for guns? Now you're working in my sort of world."

Unlike the 'stolen' cigarettes, the painting was a fake. It was depicted as a genuine but stolen Lowry known as the *Factory Gates*. It had a cheap two-bob frame and even a casual scrutiny could have given the game away. There were some misgivings within the UCOs and the cover team over this scam, so they decided to limit exposure to the 'stolen work of art', especially where Jimmy was concerned. In some ways, this exposure limitation was realistic because if it were the real thing, any professional gang would keep it under wraps as much as possible. Therefore, it was necessary for Neil to attend further notional meetings with Jimmy as the driver. Neil, in Jimmy's presence, had several cryptic phone calls about the trade to help reinforce the illusion. Those phone calls referred to a motorbike. Jimmy knew that was code for the painting, and he probably also knew this was common practice in the criminal fraternity to mask the nature of the real parcel.

The deal was structured like this. Two hotels were picked on opposite sides of Exeter. One hotel for the Belgian money men and Dave plus another UCO called Dave who was drafted in for this play. A second hotel was for Neil, Robbie, Jimmy, Tom, Jerry, and their Belgium art expert plus the 'motorbike'.

The regular duo of Dave and Robbie stayed in a small bed and breakfast the day before the trade. The others were coming across with Jimmy the next day. Dave and Robbie enjoyed a couple of beers the night before and were up nice and early for the typical large English breakfast that put the 'breakfast' into the B&B abbreviation. Both had arranged to meet on the landing outside their rooms before going down for breakfast. They could not believe what they saw when they came onto the landing. Hanging there were three miniature prints. All three were Lowry's work and the middle one was the *Factory Gates*. On seeing them, Robbie said, "This bit of work is jinxed and has been since the Cover Officer walked in with the 'Lowry' weeks before."

By mid-afternoon on the day of the trade, all the Plymouth Operation George UCOs were in their respective locations. Jimmy and Neil were the last to arrive. Jimmy believed Dave was in his notional hotel awaiting the Belgian money men. He was, in fact, in a hotel room with the Cover Officer. Robbie and the other Dave were in the hotel room that was going to be used for the trade. Neil rang to inform them he was about five minutes away. That was a heads-up call to be ready with recording equipment on and running.

Following a light tap on the door, Jimmy and Neil entered Robbie and Dave's room. Jimmy walked in front of Neil who was smiling. Once Robbie took in Jimmy's appearance, he knew why there was a smirk on Neil's face. Jimmy's new set of clothes were black shirt, black trousers. black shoes and a three-quarter length black box jacket. It looked like one of those jackets you would see on the front of a 1960s pop album. Robbie said to Jimmy, "What the fuck is *that,* Jimmy? You look like one of the Beatles back in the sixties."

Jimmy was quick to defend himself and there followed some intermittent piss-taking between the four. Dave started to hum and sing every Beatle song he could recall. Jimmy carried on oblivious, justifying his choice and style. The next time Robbie saw this jacket was when he walked into the Crown Court in Belfast some six years later to give his evidence at Fulton's trial.

Once the banter had died down, Neil placed a box in the wardrobe. He had carried the painting into the room wrapped in cloth and protected in an open box. A hush fell upon the room as Neil set about telling each of them what to expect and what he wanted them to do. He started by saying that Tom and Jerry, together with the expert, were to call Neil when they were in the reception. They had not been given the room number for security reasons. Once that call was made, Robbie and Jimmy were to go down to the reception and bring them up to the room using the lift. Once in the lift, Jimmy was to pat down all three for guns. Robbie was there to make up the numbers and if a gun was found he was to tell them that the deal was off and take the lift back down to the ground floor and then bid goodnight to their guests.

Neil's phone rang on cue and he had the conversation with Tom or Jerry. Robbie and Jimmy now made their way down from the third floor. On the way down in the lift, Jimmy looked at Robbie. He nodded and with a wink of the eye said, "Game on, Robbie, now you'll see how an operative works."

Robbie looked at Jimmy in his three-quarter length jacket and said, "Fuck off, Ringo." Both men burst out in laughter, struggling to regain their composure before the doors opened on the ground floor. Now straight-faced as the lift doors opened, they saw Tom and Jerry together with a third man who would act as their art expert. After the deed, and still in jocular mood, Robbie and Jimmy gave him the soubriquet of Lester – as in Lester the Tester.

Lester had a briefcase in his left hand and offered his other hand towards Jimmy, looking for a handshake. Jimmy declined the invitation and instructed the three to follow into the lift. The doors closed and Robbie pressed the button for the top floor. As he was doing so, Jimmy directed the three men to stand to one side of the lift. He then asked the expert to open the case, which he did. There was nothing sinister in it. It contained some bottles containing clear liquids, brushes, a pallet knife, UV light, cloth, and some other small bits and pieces. Jimmy then patted him down face to face and once done got him to turn and face the wall of the lift and repeated the same routine down his back, sides, legs and arms. The same routine was carried out on Tom and Jerry. Jimmy looked like a dwarf next to Tom. The searching was complete by the time they reached the top floor. As the lift door opened, Lester made to step out. Jimmy gently tapped his arm and said, "No, no, my friend. We're not there yet." Robbie pressed the button for the third floor and off they went again.

The lift stopped on the third floor and Robbie led the way from the lift to room 302. A tap on the door and it was opened by Dave. Dave shared a greeting with Tom and Jerry and they in turn greeted Neil with a friendly handshake. Lester was introduced to Neil and explained he had some test kit with him. All this had been agreed at a previous meeting and phone calls between Tom and Neil. Lester asked if he may see the 'motorbike.' Neil took the box from the wardrobe and placed it on the bed and pulled back the cloth. Lester reacted as if he'd just clapped eyes on the Holy Grail. He asked Neil if he could take the painting into the bathroom to carry out a few tests to authenticate its provenance. Tom invited one of the English firm to accompany Lester, but Neil thanked him for the offer and declined as a show of trust and mutual respect.

About ten minutes later, Lester reappeared with the masterpiece wrapped in the cloth and placed it back in the open box. He turned to Tom and Jerry and gave his expert opinion that it was the genuine painting and worth every Euro. Tom called his man as Neil rang Dave in the other hotel. Tom spoke in Flemish to the mystery buyer. Jerry translated, telling them he was authorising the release of the money. Neil then told Dave to count the money and call back when happy. Twenty minutes later Dave rang to confirm that all the 'paperwork' was there, and all was good to make the exchange. Everyone beamed in that hotel room. There were handshakes all round, then the Belgians headed off into the sunset with their 'priceless Lowry.'

Jimmy beamed once more shortly afterwards as the Plymouth crime gang prepared to drive away. Neil called him over and handed him £500 in a bundle of banknotes saying, "Nice one, Jimmy. Not bad for very little work, eh."

CHAPTER 19

A Thousand Fags and Friction

Om Malik is quoted[14] as saying, "As someone who has been wrong often, I can tell you one thing for sure: hindsight reminds you of your follies every day." So, at the risk of sounding foolish (not for the first time) perhaps hindsight tells us something about the subterfuge surrounding the 'stolen' work of art. It was risky. Clearly, there were no culture vultures as part of the operational team as it could be argued the choice of Lowry's Factory Gates was flawed in more ways than one. It had not been the subject of news reports telling all who cared that it had been stolen, nor was it an enticing work, especially to involve overseas buyers. It was no fake Rembrandt or Holbein. It was also a cheap print in an even cheaper gilt frame. Hats off to these UCOs who pulled the wool over Jimmy's eyes, and who was obviously not much into culture himself. They got away with it. Sometimes one does… if the plan is audacious, and it was delightfully daring.

The Lowry plan, originally initiated by Mary, a Cover Officer, was a source of friction within the Plymouth UCOs. Naturally, Mary was keen on the plan and supplied the 'work of art', but others weren't convinced. As Mary produced the painting, some would have been thinking, *Okay, a painting. It's only a fucking Lowry, not any old Lowry but probably the most famous Lowry painting ever. She's turned up with*

---

[14] https://5quotes.info/quote/218656

the Factory Gates *and it's in a ten pence frame that you'd pick up at a car boot sale. What is she thinking of? If this painting had been nicked it would be all over the six o'clock news and every newspaper in the fucking world.*

Neil piped up in a jovial tone, "Mary, are you pissed? A fucking Lowry! I know the square root of fuck all about paintings, but I know what that is before you tell me. It's like one of the most talked about paintings in modern time."

The team of UCOs all chipped in with a mixture of serious and piss taking comments and the tension coupled with the disbelief in Mary's choice of material lightened. Dave added, "Didn't they have a painting of a fucking horse eating grass in a field by John Stubbs?"

Robbie said, "George."

Dave again. "George? What do you mean 'George'? What the fuck are you on about, George?"

"George, his name is George Stubbs,' Robbie replied. "The guy that paints horses eating grass in fields, his name is George Stubbs, you fucking philistine."

The tension evaporated as the room burst into laughter, but it allowed Dave to think of a retort. "Fuck off, Robbie, you cock. You know who I meant, George fucking Stubbs. Una's dad, painter and decorator out of Watford."

The score was now two-one to Dave as all except Mary laughed at this side show. Mary frowned and tried to ignore the ribaldry. But Dave, sensing he was ahead, carried on. "What about a painting of a Cavalier wearing a big fuck off hat, drinking a pint at the bar?"

Cue more laughter, coupled with coughing, and choking noises from those sipping coffee or puffing on a cigarette. Everyone in the room could see that Mary wasn't joining in or enjoying being the butt of every joke. Neil brought the stand-up comedy show to a gentle end by saying, "We can work with this. We'll just be smart about what Jimmy sees and when he sees it. Thanks, Mary."

Dave thought, *Yeah, thanks, Mary you've just made my job ten times harder. A fucking Lowry, for fuck's sake and Robbie, what's a fucking philistine?*

This was a tight knit group of forceful characters who were all seasoned, nationally accredited undercover officers. They were living and working in a stress-filled atmosphere laden with potential danger to themselves, and possibly subconscious fears about the catastrophic consequences of operational failure. That last lengthy sentence and its precursor amounts to tinder awaiting the carelessly discarded match.

One of the UCOs knew trouble was brewing and the Lowry incident only served to reinforce his instincts. He didn't hit it off with Mary and often felt like he was skating on thin ice where she was concerned. As usual, the team got busy dreaming up a short 'bit of work.' That was their brief until such time they were told differently. The scam involved Neil who had a mate in Exeter who had asked him for a parcel of ten thousand fags as a favour and on the hurry up. Neil embellished the story by telling Robbie and Jimmy to jump in the car and make the delivery pronto as his mate was in a jam. Robbie was of course ready to react but Jimmy wasn't going to have much notice so he may have had to change his plans to accommodate Neil's request. The team saw that as a test of Jimmy's commitment to the firm and an effort to build up his role and status within it. The ops team and the Cover Officer directed that Robbie and Jimmy were to walk into a pub carrying two black bin liners stuffed with the fags. The plan then was for Robbie to recognise Neil's 'mate' and walk up to him. After a short conversation, the handover would happen. The parcel of fags in exchange for the agreed price, then Robbie and Jimmy were to exit the pub. That was the plan thought up and designed by the cover and ops team without any input from Robbie, the man on the ground.

Robbie in due course attended a briefing just before deployment. Mary, two members of the ops team and Robbie met in a hotel room. These officers represented the ops and cover teams plus the man on the ground. The plan was laid out and Robbie's role was explained as above. As the bit of theatre was being delivered to Robbie, it must have been clear to the others he was not happy as it was written all over his face. He looked at Mary and she seemed to have sensed Robbie's discomfort. At the end of the briefing the ops team asked if Robbie had any questions. He did.

"So, let me get this right. You want me and an Irishman to walk into a pub we don't know, and no one knows us. Carrying ten thousand fags in black bin bags. Sit at a table with another guy that no one knows in this pub. Conduct what can only look like a dodgy deal for cash in exchange for the fags. In front of everyone, including the landlord, and walk out. That's the plan?" Robbie's scathing contemptuous interpretation was the flame in the room full of petrol fumes. Nevertheless, he continued, "Okay, I'll do it. I think your plan is wonky, but if that's how you want it done, I'll do it just like that."

The proverbial pin dropped in the room. One of the ops team was first to respond and he invited Robbie to say what needed changing. Robbie took up the cudgel and stressed the optics of their plan of walking into a strange pub with a parcel of fags, and maybe the landlord's reaction to a criminal act on his premises. He added, "We're selling fags under his nose, and he might well be selling fags via a vending machine or from behind the bar at the real price. It's wonky." Instead, he suggested that Jimmy and he walk into the pub empty handed having left the fags in the boot of the car, meet with the buyer and have a drink together, making sure Jimmy was on soft drinks, then off to the car park and do the business out there; job done without disturbing the environment.

All agreed. Robbie stood and walked out of the briefing and crossed the road to a café. His phone rang within a few minutes. It was Mary. She asked where he was and then asked him to wait there. A short time after Mary walked into the cafe and sat down. She said, "You have to stop arguing with the operational team, Robbie."

He said, "Yeah, you're right, Mary. You should be doing it on my behalf."

The scam went ahead with no problems. Jimmy enjoyed being called on at short notice and given additional responsibility. During the journey he spoke about kneecapping people, again using the phrase, "Invite them round for tea." Robbie asked Jimmy to remind him never to come round his house for his tea

CHAPTER 20

Torch the Trailer

Despite the friction, the scams continued. This time all concerned agreed on the latest bit of work. It was arranged that Robbie was going to do another lorry load. This time the parcel was going to be forty foot of booze. The deception was built around Robbie knowing a haulier who was struggling financially and needed a lump of cash on the hurry up. Robbie gave the non-existent haulier the name of Johnny who had a contract with a brewery company in Reading. The contract was pulling forty foot of booze from the brewery to the Tesco supermarket distribution warehouse in Southampton. Again, this was all designed so they could spend time with Jimmy, keeping him busy and under control and letting him disclose his evil deeds. At the same time, it reinforced the notion he was in with a proper firm of villains. It was a precondition of this scam that the lorry driver would have to be in the know on this, unsurprisingly, as they planned to heist not only the load but also steal the tractor unit and trailer. Furthermore, with Jimmy's presence they didn't want to use or threaten to use violence.

Neil set up a meeting with Robbie and Jimmy in the warehouse, the same one used for the cigarettes scam. Now acting out their respective roles, Robbie told Neil that he was going to have a further meeting or two with Johnny if needed and walk him through the way the job would go down. Robbie also told Neil that Johnny was looking for £10,000 for his part in the theft. Neil said, "I'll start getting the booze placed with buyers. I know a good few who would be interested in cheap booze."

Robbie turned to Jimmy, saying, "I'll take you along with me on the day of the race to ride shotgun."

"Riding shotgun with you Robbie, I like the sound of that. Do I get a real shotgun?" Jimmy said.

Robbie smiling, looked at Jimmy and replied, "I wouldn't trust you with a super soaker sat next to me, you crazy fucking Irishman."

Neil, who was smoking a cigarette, burst into a fit of coughing and laughter. Now the scene was set, and Jimmy was walking into it with both eyes wide open.

Robbie reported back that he'd had his notional meetings with Johnny and his driver. He kept Jimmy informed on the progress of the job, drip feeding him bit by bit. He told Jimmy that it would be a plain tractor and trailer. There were no markings or indication of what the load was. It was also a Scania tractor unit which made Robbie happy because he enjoyed driving that make and model.

Back at the office, the planning continued. A couple of scenarios were suggested by Neil, Robbie and Dave, another of the Plymouth UCOs. They included faking a Ministry of Transport routine check at one of the service stations. That was discarded. "Too many moving parts," commented Robbie. "Keep it simple, lads. He's giving it away, no need for a complicated high manpower plan. The driver has a time slot he must arrive at the warehouse. If, as on previous occasions, he is ahead of time he parks up short in a layby just off the M27 motorway. Jimmy and I have been up and had a look at the layby and it will be ideal. We will just take the keys off him. Jimmy and I will drive the load off to here and unload it. I'll need Hands for that and to drop me and Jimmy off around Southampton."

"Yeah, he knows a bit of work is in the offing," Neil replied.

"I've told the driver he'll be left tied up with a sack over his head nearby where he'll be found at least one hour after giving us a bit of a head start. I've told him exactly what to say to the old bill when they interview him. And it won't be the locals that deal with this, it will be those Regional Crime Squad boys," Robbie said. He continued, "I'll have a moody set of plates to stick on the tractor and trailer giving us that extra bit of comfort. We'll need a nicked motor to take the driver off in. Can I leave that with you, Dave?"

A nod of the head from Dave. "No worries, mate."

Robbie finished running out the plan. "Jimmy will have left his car here in the warehouse, so once we've tipped the load Jimmy can drive home. I'll take the empty trailer on a nice long drive up the motorway and ditch it. Dave can collect me and the job, as they say, is a good one."

Once all had been agreed, it was time to bring Jimmy into the further chit chats with each member of the firm, going over the finer details of their roles. Jimmy threw a suggestion in from left field. "Are you going just to ditch the lorry, Robbie? Why don't we burn the fucking thing?"

Robbie thought, *Because, Jimmy my good man, that tractor and trailer belong to the Chief Constable and he wouldn't be too pleased with Mr Colin Port if we were to do that.*

Neil came to the rescue. "Nothing like having a fucking bonfire to let the old bill know where you are. You fucking idiot!"

The usual laughter and piss taking followed, with each giving and taking the banter. The meeting broke up with Jimmy driving Neil back to Plymouth. This bit of theatre was kept flexible as to timing, so keeping Jimmy on the hook.

With Jimmy and Neil gone, Robbie got in the 24-valve Mondeo with Dave driving. Robbie knew this was likely to be another terror drive with Dave at the wheel of the Mondeo. Rumour had it that Dave and the Mondeo were on the local police traffic department's 'most wanted list.' Dave was an excellent driver and safe at speed. He had no time for lesser mortals so he would often inform and instruct other road users where they were lacking in his absolute best Anglo-Saxon English. "Fucking tosser, get out of the fucking way."

Eventually, the day for the bit of work was agreed. Jimmy drove Robbie to the warehouse where they met with Hands. A forklift truck and pallet truck had been picked up and were in the warehouse ready to go. Jimmy locked his car inside and all three set off for Southampton. Robbie carried two number plates which he tucked under the front passenger seat. The numbers were ghost plates which would match the tractor and trailer they were going to 'nick.' One set was fitted with thick rubber bungees that would go round and secure the plates over the original ones. That was intended to go on the back of the trailer. The front number plate was different as there was nowhere on the front of a tractor unit to affix the hooks at the end of a bungee cord. That plate had industrial strength double-sided tape running all the way along the perimeter of the inside of the plate.

The driver had been told to be in the layby at 8:00 pm, then switch off the engine and leave the keys in the ignition. He was also told to extinguish all the lights. The layby was just big enough to fit a lorry and trailer and at best two cars, eliminating the risk of another lorry's unwanted presence. Dave had got there early. Robbie, Hands and Jimmy arrived at around 7:45 pm. Parking their cars in the layby, they heard the lorry approach so both cars moved forward, allowing the wagon to pull up behind them. Jimmy and Robbie jumped out of the cars with Jimmy racing to the rear of the trailer to fit the new registration plate. Likewise, Robbie went to the front to fix the front plate. Johnny's haulage driver, following his instructions, got out of the cab passenger door and jumped into the back of Dave's car. By the time Jimmy had fitted the plate, the compliant driver was seen sitting in the back of Dave's car with a hessian bag pulled over his head. On seeing this, Jimmy jokingly said, "It reminds me of home."

Robbie replied, "You're that ugly you'd need two sacks over your head." With that, Robbie climbed into the cab of the Scania to head for the warehouse where Hands would be waiting, ready to unload the twenty pallets at warp speed. Jimmy 'rode shotgun' at Robbie's side, filling the time on the journey with the telling of more stories of the life of an operator in Northern Ireland. It was all recorded on Robbie's hidden device.

On arrival at the warehouse Hands was ready to go. Robbie reversed the trailer into A1 position, without the assistance of Hands and his headlights this time. Jimmy was taking the cord out of the curtain side and pulling the curtain back. Hands was on the other side doing the same. Robbie went into the warehouse and came back out in seconds, driving the forklift. It was such a slick operation they didn't even have to talk to each other. They worked together like clockwork. Jimmy got in the warehouse and was guiding Robbie as to where the pallets should go. Jimmy used the hand-operated pallet truck to position the odd one that was slightly out of line, telling him that his boy could do a better job. The trailer was unloaded in record time. The warehouse was now locked and secure.

The trailer curtains were fastened, then Jimmy jumped into his car and shouted at Hands and Robbie as he drove away, "Happy days, boys."

Hands got into his car and followed Jimmy. As they approached a junction Jimmy indicated left and Hands right. Jimmy's car was being tracked in real time by the backroom staff, and once he was safely away they informed the Cover Officer, Gucci Gary, who in turn told the UCOs.

Like all the other deployments, the Cover Officers dictated the play or called the shots as to exactly how the job was to be executed. The Cover Officers instructed the UCOs to reload the trailer ready to be later driven away by another driver (UCO). Robbie and Hands began the reload. After loading about fourteen of the pallets Hands did one of his famous shutdowns. Anyone who had worked with Hands will know exactly what that means. He just stares at you like one of those soldiers you see in those Vietnam war movies when they have been under fire for days on end – the thousand-yard stare. Hands was giving Robbie the stare.

He told Robbie, "Mate, I'm fucked, we'll finish this off in the morning." Hands was a supporting actor on this production and had there been Oscars for this operation he may have been a contender for best supporting actor. Robbie reminded him they were instructed to load the trailer and that is what they should do. Hands wasn't having any of it. With that thousand-yard stare he said, "I'll tell him [the Cover Officer], don't worry about it."

Robbie decided to play along with Hands as his colleague now looked like an anti-social psychopath from the film *One Flew Over the Cuckoo's Nest*. They locked down the trailer and made their way to Gucci's hotel room. It was getting late in the day. Gary was sitting in an armchair, smoking a posh fag, and had a pricey bottle of red on the go. Robbie had the impression Gary had been wearing a three-quarter length smoking jacket but had taken it off when he knew the UCOs were on their way. Gary asked how it went.

Robbie piped up, "Go on, tell him then. Mister fucking Sinatra."

Hands, still with that vacant stare, said, "I did it my way."

Gary said, "What do you mean you did it your way and why are you looking at me like that?"

Robbie chipped in, "We've got about another five or six pallets to load but he just zoned out on me and said he'd had enough for today. What can I do?"

Gary, a cheeky smile on his face, said, "You can get that fucking vacant look off your face and the pair of you get back down there and finish the job. I got a driver coming down in a few hours to pick it up and take everything back."

Hands had a quick coffee and after splashing cold water on his face he seemed to return to normal, or the nearest to normal in his case. Robbie could never work out what the issue was with Hands and the warehouse. Every time there was the combination of Hands and the warehouse something went wrong. He'd burnt out Robbie's retina with the car headlights. He zoned in and out of the job doing it like Sinatra in *My Way* and held up a ton of traffic driving the forklift, bringing unnecessary attention to himself.

CHAPTER 21

On the Piss in Plymouth

There were occasions during the operation when Jimmy would stay over at the flat. It would usually follow a night out on the piss. The amount of alcohol consumed or tipped down Jimmy's neck was an area that his defence counsel would come to question and challenge during the trial. One of the team's major challenges was keeping Jimmy under control and keeping him occupied, to prevent him going rogue on the mainland. Imagine the consequences for Colin Port if Fulton committed a major crime, possibly a murder on the mainland whilst was being funded by 'UK Police PLC.'

That was not farfetched, just think back to his recent sojourn in the USA when he managed to get his hands on guns and explosives. Finding contacts on the British mainland to access guns and explosives would have been a walk in the park for this guy. So, keeping him busy was essential. In general, when a gang of criminals go out for the evening, they don't drink orange juice and talk about their holidays and families. There is no political correctness in their dialogue or lack of racist comments. They are people who live outside the law and acceptable societal standards.

The UCOs in the Plymouth 'firm' knew all conversations were recorded and many would be likely played in court at some future date. So, any one of them might laugh at a racist comment without endorsing it in the real world. It can be a difficult moment. When UCOs are on the plot, their thoughts are often working at warp speed. They are listening and responding in a natural way without facial expressions giving anything away and no unnatural delays in verbal responses.

Some experienced UCOs use the 'Two Ronnie's' technique to overcome these awkward moments. At the end of that TV show, little Ronny would sit in a chair to tell a story during which he would hop from topic to topic, telling a different story than expected. That's how some avoid answering a question or the need to comment on any given issue. As all humans are different, some naturally gravitate to this type of diversion and others initiate their own ruses to complement their character. Thinking quickly is the common denominator no matter the technique. It becomes second nature to a long-in the-tooth professional UCO.

Another factor to be borne in mind, knowing all conversations are recorded, is the necessity to avoid direct questions. There must be no hint or semblance of any questioning or conversation that could be deemed as originating from an *agent provocateur*. This is not only for legal reasons, but a UCO does not wish to say something that makes the target think, *What the fuck did he just say?*

The plan with Jimmy was to manage his and the team's alcohol consumption. The UCOs would dump their drinks around the pub. For example, they would go over to the fruit machine and play a few bob and come back with no drink. On other occasions when Jimmy went to the loo, the drinks would be quietly disposed of. When Jimmy had finished his drink, they would move on to another pub leaving their unfinished drinks. The problem was Jimmy was not playing the game by following the same rules. Later at trial, the defence made a big thing about filling him up with alcohol in a futile effort to taint the admissibility of his admissions on the covert recordings. The team knew this was a soft underbelly for attack at any future trial by his defence team. Alcohol and evidence of admissions are bit like drinking and driving, not a good mix.

The listening post had picked up from the probe in Jimmy's Renault Laguna that he was possibly drink driving while not with any of the

UCOs. Once again, this was a potential banana skin for Colin Port. Just imagine if he had killed someone whilst drink driving. The team were constantly reminded at briefings, and in particular Neil, to tell Jimmy not to drink and drive and attract attention to himself from the real police and thereby attract attention to the Plymouth firm. This missive came down from on high. Colin Port... balls of steel.

Notwithstanding the protocols and operating procedures, the team still had a job to do, and they were going to do it to the best of their abilities. So, it was natural for the team and Jimmy to go out on the piss; a gang of fellas enjoying spending their ill-gotten gains from their latest heist. They were celebrating. The beer, wine and good meals ordered and consumed was followed by more beer and a whiskey nightcap. Often at the end of the night take-away meals would be taken back to the flat. The UCOs would all be carrying recording devices that remained in place until one by one they made their excuses and left the company to retire to bed. On nights such as these, Jimmy would sleep on the sofa whilst the rest of them slept in a bedroom. Neil had the master bedroom because he was the boss. Robbie had a single bed in a small room. It was a flop, really. Just a place where the team got their heads down while in Plymouth. Sometimes, one of the UCOs would slink off and stay in a nearby hotel.

The Cover Officer at first insisted they hand over their recording devices and tapes before going to bed. The Cover Officer wanted them to leave the flat once they had pretended to go to bed and then hand over the stuff to prevent Jimmy having a sniff around and discovering the recording kit. No way was that going to work. With some low cunning and imagination, the UCOs found their own methods to do it their way.

One removed all his recording kit, including tapes, and placed it between the mattress and base of the bed. He figured that if Jimmy were to go looking for it, a fight would have broken out and he could bluff his way out without Jimmy finding the stuff. They also felt safe in the knowledge the flat was wired for live recording which meant someone in the listening post faraway would be monitoring Jimmy all night.

The morning after these nights out would typically involve Neil taking all the 'firm' including Jimmy to the Port O'Call café for the big boy's breakfast. Before leaving the flat, the UCOs secreted their recording devices and privately carried out the protocols ready to record the day's conversations with the target. Breakfast over, another day, another scam with Jimmy at the centre. That day's scam would have been scripted and agreed at a previous team meeting designed to give Jimmy the opportunity to talk over many hours. A case of 'here we go again.' Yet another trip down the rabbit hole and some scene changing in *The Truman Show*

CHAPTER 22

Play Fighting

It became clear that Tanya and the kids were going to move to Plymouth after Jimmy found a home to rent. This big and new development brought its own challenges.

Once Jimmy had moved into his own Plymouth house together with his wife and the kids, extra problems arose. Play fighting with Jimmy Fulton's young son caused an issue on those occasions one of the UCOs visited Jimmy at his home. He was a lively little thing and always started to play fight, well they thought it was play fighting, but who knows? Robbie was the first to encounter the problem. He had a recording device strapped to him. Imagine it: the little tyke grabbing and pulling at him with his little arms around Robbie's legs, calling out, "Come on Robbie, let's fight." He felt like a postman trying to shake a yapping dog off his leg. It was worrying, so naturally it was up for discussion at a debrief, resulting in an SIO's policy decision that there would be no carrying of recording equipment when entering Jimmy's house. Ultimately, Colin Port would have signed it off as standard operating procedure (SOP).

The UCOs on the team would also get to meet other members of Jimmy's family including his mother. The team perceived her to come from good stock. She carried herself well and dressed stylishly. She would often be seen sitting in an armchair, her back upright and not slouching. Sometimes, she would have the King James Bible on the armrest of her favourite chair. At least one of the UCOs found this hypocritical as he felt sure she knew what her sons were and what they had done under the banner of 'The Cause.'

Most of the team also met Tanya, Jimmy's wife. They figured Tanya and Jimmy had a volatile relationship, but she could hold her own with Jimmy. She benefited in many ways being married to him. Holidays were paid for from money which was either stolen, extorted, or donated to the LVF. There were kudos in being Mrs Fulton and the privileges that came with that title within their community. Tanya stayed in the UCO's Plymouth flat for a week's holiday before they found the house where Jimmy was later arrested. Tanya befriended a female who lived round the back of the flat during her holiday. This was important to the Plymouth team, knowing that she now had a new best friend living next door to them. They sharpened up on their tradecraft and behaviour while coming and going. They knew they had to be at the top of their game because it was impossible to know who might be connected to Jimmy and his wife via this new friend. Tanya was treated as an extension of her husband, and some viewed her an active member of the LVF after Jimmy told Robbie how he used her and their child in a pram to smuggle a firearm into the church at Drumcree. Jimmy also claimed the RUC wouldn't search her because of who she was. Whatever the truth of that claim, Tanya appears to have cashed in on her husband's name and reputation.

It was better all round for the Plymouth team after Jimmy, Tanya and their kids moved into the house on one of Plymouth's largest housing estates and mostly built in the post-WW2 era to accommodate many Janners, the regional nickname for Plymothians. Far removed from being a Janner, the relocation removed Tanya from proximity to the UCO's flat and gave the team, with the invaluable expertise of the technical team, opportunities to record conversations whether the UCOs were present or not. Just when things were looking up, the technical listening devices fitted in the house failed. The team was tasked with coming up with a ploy to get the family to vacate for a day while the tech people went into the place to fix it. More by accident rather than design Robbie had already got the solution: fitting coving to the ceiling.

The previous occupant of Jimmy and Tanya's house had coving fitted to the lounge ceiling and walls. Sometime later, an occupant had removed the coving and it looked a mess with the painted walls stopping short of the ceiling. Robbie had mentioned to Jimmy a few times that Jimmy should replace the coving or redecorate the room. Tanya also got on Jimmy's case about it. Robbie didn't waste time in telling the Plymouth team that he was a dab hand at DIY. In a former life, he had gained qualifications for painting and decorating. Who would have thought when he completed his City and Guilds it would become a tool in the toolbox of his undercover career?

The fledgling plan was developed. Fledgling… and cunning, like Baldrick – he of "I have a cunning plan" in the *Blackadder* comedy show. Jimmy was to drive Neil to Exeter for a business meeting. As a treat, Neil invited Tanya along for lunch, promising he would pay. Possibly the real cunning part, Jimmy was to be brought in on the plan under the guise of surprising Tanya when they got back from Exeter and finding the coving done. He was told to leave a key under the door mat so Robbie could let himself in. What neither Jimmy nor Tanya knew was Robbie would bring the tech team along with him. Once the job was done, Robbie was to replace the key under the mat and leave the house: coved, clean, tidy and fully wired for clear audio product.

At one stage Dave was going to do the coving with Robbie, and Robbie was happy about that. However, Dave – with his great command of the English language, used his stock phrase, "Fuck off," before adding, "I'm an undercover police officer, not a lackey to some Irish terrorist. I'm not doing it."

A hush filled the room. You could cut the atmosphere with a blunt knife. Robbie piped up and broke the deadly silence with, "No worries, I can do it alone." Everyone in the room began to breathe again.

As for Dave, it was water off a duck's back. He was quite within his rights to turn down the proposal. The meeting broke up and the plan was actioned for the following day. In preparation, Robbie headed off to B&Q for the tools, fixings and lengths of plaster coving. Neil called Jimmy and arranged the trip to Exeter with Tanya after they had dropped their lad off at school. The technical boys were put on standby. Dave arranged to take the day off.

The following day the plan sprang into action. Jimmy, accompanied by his wife, set off in the car from his house to pick up Neil from the city-centre flat. At the same time Robbie set off for Jimmy's house. It is feasible Jimmy and Robbie must have passed each other at some point. Robbie arrived at Jimmy's and found the key as arranged. Letting himself in, he left the door on the latch as he went to and from his car to collect the tools and materials. The technical team also entered to do their stuff at this time.

Robbie cracked on with fixing the coving. He tackled the most difficult first: the awkward cuts and angles like around the chimney breast and around a few pipes running from the ceiling to the floor and onto the radiators. He left the easier long straight runs of coving until the end. He knew they could be done with speed and fewer cuts. They had an idea of the time Jimmy and Tanya were to return home and the technical team had finished with about an hour to spare. Not that they were too worried as Neil had them both under control and they were confident that Neil would have warned Robbie if there were any unforeseen hiccups.

That was viewed as luxury by the tech team as it wasn't often they were afforded that type of protection. Showing their gratitude, they gave Robbie a hand finishing the long straight runs of coving and cleaning up. Both of those tasks are best carried out by more than one pair of hands. It was excellent teamwork. No one disturbed the environment or attracted attention to themselves.

Later that day and after Jimmy and Tanya had returned home, Robbie received a phone call from Tanya in which she thanked him for the surprise. She was also complimentary about the standard of workmanship and pleased there was no mess.

Robbie made light of it by saying, "No problem. I was in the area, my pleasure." Neil, Robbie and Dave went out for a beer that night and perhaps unsurprisingly considering Dave's earlier outburst, the day's activities were never mentioned. The revamped audio was working again. Now, to catch Jimmy in the act.

CHAPTER 23

Swinger

Mark 'Swinger' Fulton was the leader of the Loyalist Volunteer Force (LVF), having taken over its command following the assassination of Billy Wright in the Maze Prison in 1997 by members of the Irish National Liberation Army (INLA).

Journalist Susan McKay alleged Fulton carried out a dozen sectarian killings in the 1990s.[15]

During the operation, Jimmy's family from Northern Ireland would come and visit him. As well as Tanya's visits, Jimmy's mother would make trips over. She was a well-presented woman. She came from good stock and her style and manner of speaking underlined this. Her manner of dressing, her deportment and her command of the English language all bore testament to her good upbringing.

But the visitor from Northern Ireland who was a real person of interest was Jimmy's brother, Mark Fulton, known by many as Swinger. He had recently been released from jail after serving a term for a terrorist offence along with Billy Wright. Jimmy had invited Swinger to see him in Plymouth saying, "Come and meet my new mates, the Plymouth firm. They are good boys and bang at it. What's more, they pay well." Swinger accepted, but this caused a kerfuffle in Colin Port's MIT back in Belfast, not to mention in London. Not only did they now have one

---

[15] https://belfastchildis.com/tag/mark-fulton/

paramilitary terrorist on the mainland, but the prospect of two of the deadliest running around the mainland hand in hand, maybe itching to pick up from where they had left off. Worse, if things did start to go *boom* on the mainland, many would have rightly observed it was all sponsored by 'UK Police PLC.'

After returning to Belfast and following the arrest of his brother, Jimmy Fulton, he committed suicide while in custody awaiting trial. He was found dead in his prison cell at Maghaberry Prison and possibly could not face the rest of his adult life in prison. Either that, or he was embarrassed the leader of the LVF had been duped by a handful of undercover cops. It's strange being ensnared by undercover officers is not something prisoners brag about on the streets of Northern Ireland nor on a wing inside a high security prison.

By the time of Swinger's visit, Jimmy was living in the house in Plymouth. Before he moved in the technical team had wired it from top to bottom with listening and recording devices. The two brothers also visited Muriel in Cornwall where the electronic eavesdropping continued. Neil, as boss of the firm, made it clear to Jimmy he must take some time off whilst his brother was visiting. He said, "Jimmy, son, when your brother comes across, I want you to enjoy yourself. Take some time off and catch up on things. We'll be okay for a few days or a week or so without you. I got some family stuff to take care of so no worries."

Jimmy was grateful for this act of friendly kindness and was quick to say so. "That's good of you, boss. But you'll have to meet up with him while he's here. He's a good man and good operator [the word he used to describe a paramilitary member] and you never know, he might be looking for a job now that's he's out and on the straight and narrow."

Robbie chipped in. "Yeah, that's a fucking good idea. Jimmy, my man, you can take us out for a Chinese and you can pay."

Jimmy said, "For fuck's sake, Robbie, I paid for the tea in the caff this morning. It's fucking your turn to pay."

This banter produced much laughter and a degree of piss taking. But Neil and Robbie had that feeling of internal satisfaction and professional pride that they had just laid out the blueprint to the next chapter in *The Truman Show* starring Swinger Fulton. *Poor Jimmy, you just don't get it*, they thought. *We want you and Swinger together enjoying yourself, relaxing and talking over old times.... that's not kindness, Jimmy, it's just good old bill*. Human nature is human nature. We all do similar things and have similar character traits when it comes to meeting up with family and friends we haven't seen for some time. We bring them up to date on what we've been up to and talk about old times, and that was exactly what they did.

Owing to the sterile corridors of covert policing, the team imagined Swinger left Belfast in the company of a surveillance team and was picked up on the mainland by the same Belfast-based team but with different faces. Most working undercover cops love surveillance. Many get a kick out of following someone for days on end, gathering evidence.

Operation George was different. They were not following anyone. They had invited Jimmy into a parallel world that they controlled and sealed it off as if it were a vacuum. He was like a goldfish in a bowl they had made.

Jimmy collected Swinger from Bristol airport in the all singing, all dancing wired-for-sound Laguna. The flight was direct from Belfast to Bristol with EasyJet. This visit also gave the team a little respite as they had little to do with them over the period he was there. But the main operational team did not sleep. There was around the clock monitoring by fixed probes and mobile probes together with Swinger's Belfast watchers. Yet, there was one memorable evening, prompted by the earlier banter about the Chinese meal.

There was a Chinese restaurant in the square close to the flat used by the UCOs. Like all good UCOs, the Plymouth team built a rapport with the management and staff by being frequent big spending customers. This was designed to give the impression to other diners that they were local, and this was their 'go to' restaurant. Over time, they built the restaurant into their deep cover so that by the time Swinger walked in there with them it was clear the team were 'real people' who belonged and were popular and respected within the local community. They didn't portray themselves as loud and cocky, the sort of guys that would annoy and or disturb other diners. They were friendly, polite and likeable guys. They didn't disturb the environment.

Swinger bought straight into this illusion. He applied the trick to himself. The friendly restaurant owner had arranged a table in a corner, off to one side; it was perfect. The position of the table meant that all could talk freely and openly about their 'business' and the Fultons could do the same without others hearing a thing. Swinger came down the rabbit hole.

The UCOs took a listening device into the restaurant and in addition the UCOs were recording all conversations with separate hidden recording equipment. The listening device was for officer safety. It allowed a monitoring team to listen in to the conversation and react if it all went tits up at the table and Swinger were to go into one and kick off violently. They knew Swinger was more volatile than Jimmy, so the cover and the operation teams insisted on this listening device being deployed.

They all met up in a local pub close to the restaurant and introduced themselves to Swinger. He looked like the typical LVF member. Pictures of Billy Wright, James Fulton and Swinger Fulton made them look like brothers. They all had the same hair style, same build, same style of dress, same tattoos and the same strong Northern Irish accent. They were like clones of each other. Swinger came across as a bit of a thinker.

Both Fultons extolled Billy Wright's virtues and what a great orator he was and how the British government had him killed (the murder was attributed to the Irish National Liberation Army – INLA) because he was unafraid of the government or anyone else in that case. Swinger was in jail at the time of Billy Wright's murder and Jimmy had to arrange the illegal and unauthorised paramilitary funeral – a bunch of men and youths would congregate, dressed in a mish mash of military type uniforms, wearing balaclavas and sunglasses to hide their identities and marching like youngsters in the Boys Brigade. At the graveside a mixture of firearms would be produced, rifles and pistols, then a volley of shots fired over the coffin of the poor unfortunate lately departed terrorist. Amen.

The team sat straight faced as Jimmy spoke about how he organised this 'military operation' and mentioned the names of the pall bearers. One was Philly who lived near Bristol at this time. The team later tried to pull Philly down the rabbit hole, but he never accepted the invitation which came straight from Jimmy's lips. On one visit to Jimmy's house, he produced a photograph of the cortege in the sunglasses and balaclavas, standing by the coffin. He very kindly pointed at each of them and named them for the record.

Back at the restaurant, the UCOs sat at their 'special table.' There was Neil, Dave, Robbie, Jimmy and the new cast member, Swinger. The listening device was placed naturally and deftly in the middle of the table, together with phones and sundry bits and pieces, including the usual crockery and cutlery. The sundries also included things like spectacles cases, fag packets, lighters, car keys cluttering the table. Free space was now at a premium.

Swinger, without notice or warning, decided the table needed sorting out. He picked up the item containing the listening device to move it. The three UCOs breathed a collective deep breath and thought in unison, *Fuck! What's he picked that up for?* Robbie said later, "I thought, has it got a little red light flashing showing it's on a call? Bollocks, stand by for action. It's all going to go off at Haydock any second now."

No doubt all three wondered what the listeners were thinking as they tried to interpret what the change in sound was all about. Their thoughts were rushing at something approaching Mach One speed. Within seconds panic subsided. Swinger had placed the device on a small shelf next to his head. The UCOs couldn't have re-located it to a better position. *There is a god*, Robbie thought as he downed a large mouthful of fine wine. In addition to them talking about Billy Wright and the LVF, the UCOs gently steered the conversation to finding some work for Swinger within their gang. He didn't dismiss the proposition but wanted to consider his options after he returned to Northern Ireland. They didn't push the subject any more than that. A great night was had by all, the meal finished, and they all went their separate ways.

The team wasn't to see Swinger again. He finished his visit and returned home to Portadown where he remained until his arrest in June 2001. He was found dead in his prison cell at HMP Maghaberry, Northern Ireland on June 10, 2002.

CHAPTER 24

Barbara Windsor

Neil and Jimmy set off on the long journey back to Plymouth from one of their trips to London. Starting out on the A4, which is always slow with heavy traffic, they then headed on to the M4 towards Bristol. Neil had worked out that his tape would need changing around Chieveley Services, situated on the M4 close to the A34 junction.

He figured this could take between an hour and a half to two hours depending on traffic. Once they clear the A4 and hit the M4 motorway, Jimmy hit a cruising speed of between seventy and seventy-five miles per hour. Neil always insisted on this maximum speed to avoid traffic stops and attention from the 'real police.' Jimmy knew which side his bread was buttered so complied. On one of the first such journeys along this route, Neil had pointed out to Jimmy two mobile masts in the middle of woodland adjacent to the motorway on the eastbound Carriageway near Chieveley Services. These masts were disguised to look like trees so that they didn't stick out and spoil the natural environment. Jimmy must have been impressed, for he never tired of repeating the story and pointing at the disguised masts to whomsoever happened to be in the car with him. He was fond of saying, "How clever is that? Imagine disguising them as trees." *Masts? Trees? Undercover officers?* Another piece of irony. Back to their journey, where Neil was aware that his two hours were almost up. He asked Jimmy to pull in at the next Services so he could have a coffee and a leak. Jimmy, as always, agreed.

On arriving at Chieveley and after Jimmy made refence to the disguised masts for what felt like the millionth time, Jimmy parked up in the furthest space away from the entrance. Neil gave Jimmy a sideways look and asked Jimmy to call a taxi for him.

"A taxi? What do you want a taxi for, boss?" Jimmy asked.

"To get me to the fucking door. Go and park up by the building, you wanker," came the reply.

Jimmy knew that was just Neil's sense of humour, so no offence was taken. He drove over to the disabled parking bays right by the entrance to the building. As both men alighted and were walking to the Services entrance doors, Neil spotted Barbara Windsor coming down the steps towards the car park. He nudged Jimmy and pointed in her direction. "Look who that is coming this way."

Jimmy said, "Where? Who?"

"The two women walking towards us; the one in the purple leather jacket and trousers. It's Barbara Windsor."

"Oh! fuck me, so it is. I'm going to ask her for an autograph."

On approaching the two women, Jimmy shouted out in that heavy and distinct Northern Irish accent, "Hey! Babs, what about a wee autograph?"

This request was so loud it attracted the attention of other members of the public in the area and everyone turned to look towards Jimmy and Neil.

Don't attract attention, thought Neil, *Fucking good job, Jimmy. We've got the whole population of Berkshire looking at us.*

The lady accompanying the celebrity, possibly Ms Windsor's agent or a management team member, looked directly at Jimmy. Shock and surprise were etched over her face. She took Barbara's elbow and guided her away with an understandable excuse that they were running late and had to dash. Unabashed, Jimmy added a few more requests for an autograph while the agent steered Barbara away from this loud in-sistent Irishman.

Both men entered the Services building. Neil handed Jimmy a tenner and asked him to get the coffees. Taking the cash, Jimmy made his way to the self-service counter as Neil headed off to the toilet to do what the stop was really all about. Leaving the toilets, Neil could see Jimmy just paying for the drinks. Neil, now holding his mobile phone to his ear spoke in hushed tones. "Today's date is Friday the 12th of May 2000 and the time is 4:20 pm. I'm at Chieveley Services on the M4 motorway and I am just going to re-join Jim at the table." Both men arrived at a table at the same time as Neil finished his phone conversation with, "Yeah, we've just pulled in for leak and a coffee. We should be back down there in a few hours, Robbie. I'll call you then, mate. Okay?"

Phone off. Tape changed, coffees on the table. It's showtime again. *Quiet please, places everyone, lights, camera and action.*

Coffee done, and back into the car, they continued their journey to Plymouth. The M4 turned into the M5. The Highways Agency were carrying out major repair works on the motorway bridge that spans the River Avon. It was guaranteed to slow down the journey time, but once across the bridge it almost feels like you are nearly home. They stayed on the M5 until it finished at Exeter where it runs into the A38 down to Plymouth, taking them by the Little Chef where Dave and Robbie shook off surveillance. Neil was aware another tape change was needed before Plymouth. The area surrounding Cullompton in Devon was a favoured location by all the UCOs for such changes. It is about two hours driving from Chieveley, traffic permitting. There were a few suitable places around there so the UCOs would chop and change the locations, so Jimmy didn't start forming a pattern in his head. At debriefs, the UCOs would always mention where they had stopped and changed tapes, so everyone knew to mix it up. Good tradecraft.

On arrival in Plymouth, Neil would follow his usual routine of pay-ing Jimmy for his day's work, then Jimmy would drive home under control of the tracker and listening device fitted to his car. That was the end of a typical day's deployment but not the end of the working day for the UCOs. The paperwork needed doing. Notes to be made. Tapes to be marked up with exhibit identification marks and either a hot debrief to the Cover Officer or a full debrief with the operational team depending on the time, location, and operational necessity.

As an aside, notes in an undercover officers' pocket notebooks in a situation like Operation George are intended as an *aide memoire.* They are not for filling with copious notes, and it isn't a good practice. The contemporaneous record of the deployment is the tape.

Once all the 'admin' had been taken care of it was time to relax and unwind after a day of listening to Jimmy talk about his activities and horrendous crimes whilst in Northern Ireland. It had been another day of thinking, *How do I get him to disclose more without asking him a direct question? How do I get him back on to that subject?* In Jimmy's company it felt like the brain was processing information at high speed, listening, reacting, thinking of tradecraft, and countless other thoughts: *How much recording time have I got left? What's the rules of evidence around my questions? Can I say this?* The list was endless, and each deployment with Jimmy had to be managed on its own merits.

CHAPTER 25

Paranoia

Working undercover for any length of time can make the most stable people become paranoid.

Over time and since the Operation Julie days of the Seventies, the police service has recognised the need for psychological support for UCOs owing to the often dangerous, difficult and stressful roles they undertake. They must attend appointments with a psychologist at regular intervals. Indeed, the Operation George UCOs were offered professional help on tap if they felt they required support. In modern times, a new UCO would pay a first visit to see the professional, usually a psychologist, soon after s/he has completed and passed the National Undercover Course.

In the words of one undercover officer, "I attended an office block in London and checked in with the receptionist using a moody name and informed her I had an appointment with Mr Smith (not his real name). After a few minutes, a small wiry guy came down and spoke to me using the moody name then led me to his office. Mr Smith sat down with a pen in his hand with a writing pad on a coffee table in front of him. Unsure how to kick off the session, I said, 'What do you want to know?'

"He said, 'Anything you want.'

"'Well, what do you know about me?'

"'I know your National Number and that's all. I don't even know your name, just a number.'"

That was the start of a long relationship between that UCO and the psychologist. By the end, the psychologist knew more about that UCO than any other person on the planet. He kept a file full of notes completed with fresh material after each visit. The officer shared information about his family, his jobs, police life, and private life except for his extra marital affairs. "Some things are too private to share," he added. Such appointments were scheduled every six months. Everything shared is strictly confidential, not even shared with police management unless it was thought you were unstable, or a threat to yourself or others; then he was duty bound to tell your line manager.

Back to the anonymous undercover officer who told this story. "The only time I showed any emotion with him was when I recounted an incident that took place whilst I was on holiday. I saw a child aged about five or six lying on the bottom of the swimming pool. It turned out the pool attendant, who wasn't a lifeguard, went to rat's shit and did fuck all other than panic. He was screaming and running around like a headless chicken. My training kicked in and with another Brit I got the lifeless body out of the pool and started working on him. You know, mouth to mouth and CPR on this kid. He started to breathe then vomit all over the place. I turned the kid into the recovery position and forced his mouth open to clear his airway. I'd never done that before on a real person and I was surprised how difficult it was to open the casualty's mouth.

"A crowd of Spanish and Brit onlookers surrounded us and started giving me shit for forcing his mouth open and sticking my fingers into his mouth to clear his airway. The ambulance came and took over. The kid was in hospital overnight and after that he was back on site and in the pool. It was some time after I got a bit of PTSD. I kept thinking what would have happened if my efforts to revive him had failed. I was recounting this story to the shrink through floods of tears. It was the only occasion I showed or even felt any emotion in front of him."

Police National Computer (PNC)

As far back in the early days of undercover policing, UCOs sometimes got paranoid. It may be the case that it comes with the territory because of deception and duplicity becoming the norms. Take Bentley in his pioneering Operation Julie days, for example. For a long time, he harboured a serious belief that the two characters he met on the cocaine importation plot in Liverpool were themselves undercover agents for a rival law enforcement agency, either in the UK or the States.

On Operation George, Robbie and Jim Fulton were the only ones who knew of the registration number of the tractor unit. But it was checked by way of the RUC and the Garda as part of a batch of ten vehicle registration numbers. This lorry on that number had only been out once before, and that was a week before when Robbie and Jim took it out for a dry run of the job they were planning. Before Robbie had driven it or Jim had ridden in the cab, a guy delivered it and told Robbie the number had been PNC checked. The guy knew nothing and had no idea of what Robbie was engaged in. All he was doing was delivering a lorry to him at a service station on the M25. Robbie, thinking it was strange, started to drive to Weston-Super-Mare, planning to park the tractor unit on an overnight lorry park. Thinking more about the brief conversation about the PNC check, Robbie called the ops team. He told them the story and they assured him they would investigate it.

Still bothered, Robbie then called Dave. "Mate, come to Gordano Services on the M5. Don't approach me though, we'll chat on the phone once you get there but make sure you eyeball me because I need you as a third eye." On arriving at the services area, Robbie called again. Dave now had Robbie and the tractor unit in sight. Between them they hatched a counter-surveillance plan for Robbie to drive out, followed by Dave as the third eye.

After a while and still in contact over the phone, Dave said, "There's nothing. Can't see anything. Nothing at all."

It is difficult to conduct counter or anti-surveillance in a tractor unit or a lorry with trailer behind because the lorry isn't fast enough to get away. So Robbie instructed Dave to get off the motorway and make his way to a choke point to see if anyone was following the lorry. Once more, Dave reported he had seen nothing.

Robbie now drove into the lorry park in Western-Super-Mare, but not before he had driven through a normal car park designed for only cars. At the far side of the regular car park is where all the heavy lorries and coaches park up overnight. Dave still followed. Robbie looked everywhere, as he was still in anti-surveillance mode. He looked right, left, straight ahead, checked his mirrors and looked overhead. Then, he saw an overpass: a service road straddling the car park. More importantly, he then saw a man and woman sitting in what appeared to be a four-door, two-litre car. She had a handbag over her shoulder and it seemed to Robbie she was looking for something inside the bag. *Typical female surveillance ruse*, thought Robbie, *she's got a covert radio stashed in the bag.*

Robbie glanced up again at the flyover and spotted a bloke eating from what looked like a bag of fish and chips. With that, he spoke to Dave over the mobile phone. "Looks like we have just driven into a choke point."

Dave said, "Yeah, I see him and the car."

Robbie said, "Let me park up then I'll get my overnight bag. Then I'm going to walk up to your car." Robbie did that and on getting into Dave's car, he said with a smile, "Come on, we'll have a bit of a laugh on this." Robbie opened his bag. Dave, acting out the role, peered into it, poked inside and started grinning, giving lots of thumbs up signals as if it were a parcel, before placing the bag in the boot. The bait in place, Dave drove off in the 24-valve Ford Mondeo. The fish was hooked. The Mondeo was followed out of the car park.

What the followers did not know was that Dave was one of the most wanted drivers in his force area. Wanted because he was fast but safe.

Robbie, if asked, would have put it a different way: "He drives like a nutcase!"

Dave gunned that car all the way from Weston-Super-Mare south-west down the M5 until he reached the Little Chef next to Exeter Race-course, covering the sixty miles or so in much less than an hour. There was still a Golf GTI on his trail, so Dave pulled into the car park of the Little Chef. The GTI driver was now on his own and utterly compro-mised, so he turned around and left the car park. He didn't go in the restaurant nor the petrol station next door. He simply disappeared. It was time for a debrief.

At the debrief, the operational team downplayed the possibility of a team on them. In fact, they dismissed the idea completely out of hand. For weeks after the car chase, Robbie kept asking for any updates on the surveillance. No, was the stock answer and Robbie was urged to 'move on.' It seemed they just wanted it to treat it as a 'sleeping dog.' But when one adds up all the unusual spooky events, Robbie felt it was more than a possibility. He knew what surveillance looked like, so he was convinced some other team or outfit was watching him and the Op-eration George team. As soon as he drove into that lorry park, he saw them.

The morning after the race to Exeter, Dave and Robbie drove to the flat in Plymouth. As they came off the main dual carriageway they got picked up by a surveillance team again. In haste, they made towards the flat. Robbie and Dave clocked the same car that had taken up position behind them coming off the dual carriageway. Dave made a quick left into a square and they watched the car drive on by. They both suspected some foot men may have lain in wait near the flat, so they carried on driving out of the square to head for the Port O'Call café. Dave parked up outside before they went in and ordered two big boy breakfasts.

The UCOs were not at all surprised to see a stranger enter the café on his own. He took a seat and was joined by a female some three or four minutes later. They too ordered the big boy breakfasts. Robbie and Dave waited for them to be served with their breakfasts. As soon as they were placed on the table, Dave and Robbie got up and walked out the café. They had burned them. All activities were cancelled that day because Dave and Robbie maintained they were under surveillance, despite the ops team denying it.

Besides Robbie, the only person who had prior knowledge of that lorry registration number was Jimmy. That provoked some theories: one, Jimmy might've served it up for some reason no one could explain. Two, some other law enforcement organisation had taken interest in the paramilitary terrorist. Three, perhaps MI5 had set a team of watchers on to them. Robbie felt somehow these clandestine activities had contaminated him via the lorry. He wondered if that was how the lorry registration got fed into the PNC. Or maybe it was just a coincidence or a typo along the line somewhere. But, deep down, he knew something was wrong.

The team cancelled what it planned that weekend and they decided to move the job to a later date. When the plan was reactivated, a fixed-wing aircraft followed the lorry at a discreet distance. During the journey with Jimmy in the cab of the lorry, Jimmy got talking to Robbie about police surveillance back in Northern Ireland. At one point, he said, "Don't you worry, Robbie, I can smell the police."

Little did Jimmy know he was sitting next to one and with another one flying above his head.

Some on the Operation George team reflected on this strange episode years later. One was convinced there was bound to have been twenty-four-hour surveillance on Swinger, Jimmy's brother, if not in the form of the many listening devices deployed, as a surveillance team to cover him moving under his own steam from A to B. Some were also convinced looking back that some parts of the jigsaw didn't quite fit. And possible explanations for things that seemed like minor miracles at the time. It was Robbie's guess this surveillance team may have been used on other aspects and events on the job. For example, the ghost team that Robbie and Dave experienced in the chase to Exeter and the café the next day, the god sent car that made space outside Jimmy's house the night before his arrest. And, later, you will read about the big fella Robbie met in a Belfast hotel. If you work undercover for a long time, you get those intuitions. You know when something doesn't smell right. As they say, if it looks like a duck and quacks like a duck, it's a fucking duck.

Jimmy and the RUC Officer

Throughout the UCOs' operational deployments and the hundreds of hours of recordings captured from house and car probes, Jimmy never admitted to the murder of Rosemary Nelson. It was a common feature at most debriefs for the UCOs to report Fulton claimed that she was killed by the British Government. He never once indicated or claimed that he did it or ordered the murder. He repeatedly pointed towards the British Government in collusion with the military, police and security services. Jimmy didn't hesitate to talk about all the offences he was eventually indicted for. Most of the team believed if he were culpable in any way for Rosemary Nelson's murder, he would have disclosed it to the team in one of the many captured conversations. In Fulton's bloated self-esteem, it would have been a massive feather in his cap and great kudos. So the Plymouth Operation George team believed Jimmy didn't do it nor have any knowledge of who did.

Coupled with the collusion statements about the British authorities being instrumental in Nelson's murder, Jimmy also spoke often about an RUC officer. He did name him, but the authors choose not to reveal his name or rank. Jimmy always spoke in high regard of this officer and talked about meeting him in Northern Ireland on several occasions. The meetings didn't take place in police stations, but they were the sort of venues and environments that a seasoned informant handler would choose for a meeting. The team gained the impression that their relationship was that of informant and handler.

This situation on the mainland would have warranted someone like Jimmy to be registered as a 'Dangerous Informant.' He would be seen as high-risk by any informant handling controller owing to him being a known terrorist. It is likely the rules about handling informants in Northern Ireland may have been different. On the mainland, it would not have been good practice or policy to meet someone of Jimmy's character alone. Meetings with 'Dangerous Informants' are always two handed. Accurate contact reports would be completed immediately after the contact and both officers would sign the report and it would be submitted to the controller. Despite those policy and practice differences, in the opinion of some of the team, this RUC officer's relationship with Jimmy was totally professional and many believed that Jimmy was possibly a snout – an informant.

One of the disclosures Jimmy made to the UCOs about the RUC officer was that he (Jimmy) handed over four ounces of explosives to the officer at a clandestine meeting. Jimmy told them it was the same amount of explosives that was used to killed Rosemary Nelson. Jimmy went on to claim that the explosives were taken from a secure police storage facility and used in the bomb. All of this was dismissed as a figment of Jimmy's imagination and another attempt to bolster the conspiracy theories surrounding the death of Rosemary Nelson. It was, however, recorded in the debriefing notes.

Of course, any mention of Rosemary Nelson by our target would reach the eyes and ears of Colin Port. He was in the habit of visiting the Plymouth officers about once a month to inform the group how things were progressing. The team valued these visits which were another component of Colin Port's excellent leadership skills. He didn't have to attend; he could have sent one of his Senior Management Team (SMT). But he took the trouble to sit down with the detectives who were walking a dangerous line day in and day out. At the end of each meeting Colin Port would ask if anyone had any questions. There were the normal serious questions and a few funnies. The meetings were always relaxed and if a stranger had walked in, God forbid, they wouldn't know Colin Port was a Deputy Chief Constable (DCC). During one of the question-and-answer sessions, Colin Port was asked by one of the

UCOs about the RUC officer. The UCO asked if much was known about the officer and what, if any, was the relationship between him and Jimmy. Without any hesitation, Colin Port replied with words to the effect of: "If I had any concerns about the officer, he would not be involved in this enquiry. He has my full confidence."

His reply was like an explosion in the room. Heads dropped amongst the Cover Officers and operational team. They avoided any eye contact with the UCOs. For their part, the UCOs all looked at each other open mouthed. Colin Port continued with words of confidence in the character of the officer.

Then one of the UCOs asked if the RUC officer knew about them and their role with Jimmy. Port told the assembled team that he knew they were undercover officers. He knew their pseudonyms but had no idea of their real names or where they were from.

This development was surprising and unusual, but the collective wisdom and reasoning of all in the room was if Colin Port was good with the situation so were they. They knew Colin Port as an outstanding leader, and he had the full confidence of every team member no matter their role. It was obvious that they (the Belfast MIT) had been in possession of this information every time the UCOs debriefed and mentioned this officer by name. The team, for its part, had no issue with that. Information gets held back for all sorts of valid reasons. It goes with the territory of covert policing. It is better to withhold certain information if it could affect your reaction and conduct on the plot in an adverse way. So the decision to withhold this officer's role from the UCOs was the right thing to do, but someone should have copied Colin Port into the script.

CHAPTER 26

The Cutting Room Floor

"The best laid schemes of mice and men

Go often askew," ¬ Robert Burns

Continuing in the vein of using the *Truman Show* analogy, we bring you some of the scenes left on the cutting room floor. The Operation George undercover officers, though professionals, were human and sometimes made mistakes. Some of them were potentially serious. Some also demonstrate the stresses of undercover work and others the behind-the-scenes humour, or a mix of the two.

The Sherpa Hat

Neil, Robbie and Dave comprised the crew charged with most of the heavy lifting in the scams involving Jimmy. They knew their roles backwards when in Jimmy's company. The professional bond between those UCOs was as strong as any they had known, and they had worked undercover on many serious cases. They depended on each other, had each other's backs, trusted each other. They were tight. Off stage, in the privacy of the safe house, they were friends and those were the moments they could relax. They even felt at ease disagreeing with each other and leg-pulling was an art between them. The regular piss-takes were part of the glue holding them together as a unit. They never fell out and if there were any serious disagreements, they would hammer it out and then move on as one.

As a crew they switched that mental trigger as soon as they were about to go into action. They also hit the physical switches on their recording devices hidden somewhere on their bodies or in an item of clothing. *Game on.* The UCOs were now mindful of their casual conversations. Anything they said now could end up being disclosed to Jimmy and his defence team at some future point. All conversations from now would be in role and a minimum of chit chat took place.

A typical day began with a briefing in the holiday let used as a safe house. The cover team had rented for it for a couple of months in a small Devonshire village. Dave had turned up at the briefing in a jovial mood wearing what looked like a Sherpa hat. It was multi coloured with ear flaps and long tassels hanging off the flaps and a colour matched bobble on top. It's the sort of hat you might have seen Sherpa Tensing wearing, standing at the top of Everest posing for a photo with Edmund Hillary. There is a time and a place for everything, and Dave's choice of head gear was out of sync with the environment, climate and temperature. This was the sort of location that your elderly relatives went to for a couple of weeks in the summer, not where you would find a Sherpa in the local shop. The safe house was near to a small village shop full to the gunnels with everything you could imagine. The UCOs would often try to outdo each by mentioning something obscure that they were going to buy at this shop.

Back to the briefing, on entering the room the operational team briefing officers and the Cover Officer first looked at Dave and then at Neil and Robbie with an inquisitive glance and what seemed to be a disapproving tilt of the head. Robbie shook his head sideways as a signal before saying, "Okay, Dave. You can take the hat off now, mate. We've all seen it; you've made your statement."

Without a glance at Robbie, Dave just said, "What?"

Neil said, "The fucking stupid hat, we've all seen it. Now you can take it off."

Unfazed, Dave replied, "I'm going to the shop to get some milk and a MIG welder. Anyone want anything?" Everyone present laughed, used to Dave's idiosyncrasies. Dave made to walk out on his way to the shop.

Robbie called out after him, "Mate! Can you get me a Daily Mirror? If they haven't got the Mirror, get me anything." The team settled down. The kettle was on and Dave was fetching the milk. The room filled with idle chatter until Dave's return.

Dave said loudly, "Robbie, they didn't have the Daily Mirror, so I got you this." He tossed a cold meat and potato pie towards Robbie.

Robbie smiled, saying, "Very funny, Dave. You're wasting your time on this job, you funny git."

"Well, you did say if they didn't have the Daily Mirror, get you anything. So, I had a look around the shop and got you a pie. What's the problem with that?" Dave said with a straight face.

More sarcastic comments and laughter at Robbie's expense. Dave felt chuffed with himself, and the stunt gave Robbie a cheesy grin every time their eyes met. Robbie just mouthed the word 'twat' back at him.

Neil and Robbie had agreed behind Dave's back not to make mention of his hat. They had decided he was wearing it to cause a stir and attract comment. Neither man was going to play into Dave's hands.

PAG-IN-TON

After the briefing, the three men left in Robbie's car and made their way to Plymouth. Neil put a call to Jimmy and told him to be ready for a pickup at seven. On the way, Robbie stopped for fuel at a petrol station in the middle of nowhere. Neither Neil nor Dave made a move to assist in putting the fuel in or suggesting they would be going into pay. Robbie said in his best sarcastic tone, "I'll do it, lads, you just take it easy."

"Okay," said Dave.

As Robbie was just about to finish filling up Dave got out of the car with the map book in his hand and said to Robbie, "Get ready for this, mate." Robbie followed into the shop a few seconds behind Dave who was now talking to the attendant in an American accent.

Robbie heard Dave say, "Is this the road to Pag-in-ton? We're trying to get to Pag-in-ton."

The attendant pushed his bottom lip over his top lip and moved his head left to right and in a strong Devon accent said, "I've never heard of it round here."

Dave, now getting louder and more animated, pointed left and right out the window and exaggerated his pronunciation. "Pag-in-ton, man." He then opened the map book and pointed at the town of Paignton. He continued, "Pag-in-ton."

The attendant chuckled at Dave's interpretation of the word Paignton and pointed out to the 'American' the English way of saying it, "It's pronounced Paynton."

Robbie was working hard to contain himself with Dave's performance. Dave was on top form with his wacky sense of humour starting with his Sherpa hat, Robbie's pie and his role as an American lost in the Dartmoor National Park.

Lucky Robbie

Close to Jimmy's place, Dave put a call in to Jimmy telling him to be outside in five minutes. The three UCOs all reached for their recording devices and hit the on button. *Game on.* They had arranged to meet up with Jimmy and have a couple of drinks in Plymouth in and around the area of the flat (safe house). These social gatherings were always difficult to manage for the Plymouth team of UCOs. They knew they were exposing themselves to a defence team pulling any evidence apart because of the introduction of alcohol. Another concern was Jimmy driving home at the end of the evening. This concern was dealt with by one of the team, who on their way back into Plymouth would volunteer to pick Jimmy up at his house, thereby leaving his car at home, and a taxi was arranged to take him home. Job done, no chance of Jimmy drink driving.

As Robbie drove along, he saw Jimmy on the opposite side of the street from his house. The car pulled up and Jimmy jumped in the back next to Dave who greeted him with a string of insults and put downs about Jimmy's dress sense. Jimmy had the collar of his purple shirt over the collar of his black jacket. Robbie looked at Jimmy in the rear-view mirror. "You look like an Irish John Travolta." The usual volley of follow-ups filled the next five minutes. Robbie pulled up outside the pub and the other men got out and made their way into the pub. Robbie switched off his recording device, then drove the short distance to the flat to drop the car off. He put a short call into the Cover Officer to give him an update and told him they were looking at getting back to the flat around eleven.

Just before leaving the flat Robbie was aware that the micropore tape holding his device in place needed adjusting. After he had removed the device, he discovered that he didn't have any tape. He was frustrated by his oversight and took the chance of slipping it inside his sock. He tested it by walking up and down the stairs a few times. It seemed to be secure, so he activated the device then stuck it down his sock. Pulling up the sock, he set off for the pub.

As Robbie arrived, Jimmy stood up and headed for the bar to buy Robbie a pint. "Usual for you, Robbie, my man?"

"Yeah, cheers mate," Robbie said.

By the time Jimmy and Robbie had joined Neil and Dave at the table, those two were sitting with empty glasses. Robbie knew exactly what had occurred while Jimmy's back was turned. The two experienced UCOs had lost their drinks. The two partly drunk pints would now be on an empty table with an explanation ready if Jimmy asked any questions. Losing drinks was a tactic for avoiding going pint for pint. The group visited two or three of their favourite haunts, after which Neil invited the men to a curry at his expense. Everyone agreed, grateful for the offer, then followed Neil to the door with the UCOs leaving various amounts of beer in their glasses.

As they left, Dave put his arm around Jimmy's shoulder and playfully pulled him in towards him, still piss taking about his shirt and jacket. Stepping down from the pub doorway on to the pavement, a loud sound of metal landing on paving stone rang out. To Robbie, this sounded like Big Ben striking. He knew what it was. The device had worked its way out of the sock and had hit the pavement. The wire was still plugged in, and the bloody thing was being dragged along behind him.

Dave, still with an arm around Jimmy, continued without breaking step. Robbie, with lightning speed, dropped to one knee and within a split second the device was back in place. No harm done. Robbie knew how lucky he was. A schoolboy error: one that he would never repeat in his undercover career. The men had their curry at Neil's expense. Jimmy was put into a taxi and the three UCOs headed back to the flat. Dave had not finished his comedy show quite yet. He'd been on a roll all day, and this was his finale. The UCOs got back into the flat and deactivated their devices. A phone call was made to the Cover Officer to let him know the men were back in the flat safe and sound. He was able to tell the UCOs that Jimmy was back home and on the probe. Following routine, the tapes were marked as exhibits and together with the device secured in the flat until morning and debrief.

Once that routine was completed, the men sat around with a tin of beer and relaxed. Dave asked the group of UCOs, "Did anyone hear that fucking clunk as we left the last pub? It sounded like some wanker had dropped his recording device on the pavement in the company of the target. Then, I thought no one would be that stupid. Would they, Robbie? You cock."

Robbie, taking up the cudgel, said, "Mate, it couldn't have happened at a better time. As soon as it hit the pavement, I looked towards Jimmy and saw you had him in a hug and joking with him. It was like slow motion. I was down, grabbed the thing and shoved back in down my sock and back up again. That could have ended badly, to say the least. Doesn't bear thinking about, mate. I owe you one. Sorry lads. Fucking schoolboy error."

Neil, nonplussed by the event said, "No harm done, mate. You can buy the pies tomorrow. Good night, lads."

The Kebab Shop

Working undercover on the plot for a long time brings its own burdens and stresses. On occasions when Jimmy wasn't with them, some of the UCOs let off steam. One such time involved Robbie and Dave who were close friends as well as colleagues.

One night they went out drinking together free from the presence of Jimmy Fulton. They relaxed and let their hair down because they are human. That's what people do. At the end of a heavy session, the pair ended up in a kebab shop. It's fair to say by the time they arrived there, slurred speech was the norm. They managed to place their orders but when Robbie got his, he told the man behind the counter it wasn't what he had ordered. An argument then broke out between Robbie and the Turkish guy who suddenly produced a huge, evil looking knife and started swinging it around in front of Robbie's face. Robbie, no doubt fearless in drink, got ready to fight but Dave stepped in to try to defuse the situation. Lucky for Robbie, Dave could handle himself having served in war zones in the employ of a foreign country. Robbie knew Dave was a real warrior who didn't talk or brag about his experiences.

Dave, using his wits and common sense, decided the best course of action was to drag Robbie outside. Dave pulled him away from the blade and towards the shop door. Befuddled Robbie took objection and a push and pull session started between the two pals. The other Turks in the shop helped by calming down their knife-wielding compatriot so Dave and Robbie could get outside and on to the pavement. The trouble was Robbie still wanted a scrap. He offered Dave out, "Right fucking here and right fucking now!" You can imagine Robbie doing a passing imitation of a Hollywood drunk. He swayed from one foot to another which he probably thought was a fighting stance and continued baiting Dave. Dave's reaction was classic. He simply burst into fits of laughter on seeing his mate's antics. Robbie later realised Dave could have knocked seven bells out of him.

The last Robbie saw of Dave that night was his mate walking towards the flat (safe house) shouting his favourite phrase, "Fuck off! Wanker!" Robbie eventually crashed out in his own bed in the flat.

The next day in the Port O'Call café, tucking into a big boy's breakfast, they laughed and counted their blessings the local old bill hadn't been called. Had they got nicked they would have stayed in role in the police station and awaited the arrival of their brief or role-playing Cover Officer. Taking a nicking and bringing attention to themselves would have resulted in an immediate withdrawal from the plot.

Roof Lining

Robbie drove a Range Rover Vogue, a decent car, to go with his image and legend of having a successful haulage company. He left the plot on one occasion to drive to his home. It was daylight when he set off, however it got dark later. Once it was past dusk and with his lights switched on, Robbie first noticed the interior light was flashing on and off at irregular intervals. His first thought was someone's lumped up his car (fitted a device to it). *Why would they do that?* he thought. Then he swore silently, *Twats*.

Pulling off the motorway at the first opportunity, he inspected the light fitting whilst giving a running commentary of what he was doing. He was convinced that someone was listening to him. "Right, you fuckers, wherever you are, I'm going to pull this car apart till I find your bug." This was followed by "wankers," "twats" and "you piece of shit." He started trying to remove the plastic that covered the bulb. That didn't work. Then he forced the whole light fitting out of its housing in the roof lining. That didn't really help. So, he pulled down the roof lining.

That did the trick and using the flame from a cigarette lighter, he saw into the space between the lining and the steel of the roof.

Robbie knew this car had been deployed on numerous jobs before Operation George and most likely had technical fits (listening/tracking/video) installed in it. That seems to be confirmed as he looked at a confusing mass of internal wiring stuck together with insulating tape. It was impossible for the untrained eye to tell if there was a current live technical fit. At that point, Robbie continued his monologue with the 'listening team' and called them all the names under the sun and decided to continue his journey home. Problem. He was unable to get the roof lining back into position. Only one thing for it. He drove home with the roof lining resting on his head. Every little bump in the road reminded him by the lining giving a gentle tap to his head.

On arriving home, Robbie went to remove his stuff from the boot. A Range Rover is a large hatchback and built in such a way that the rear window can also give access to the boot space. This was the moment he discovered that the rear window wasn't shut properly and had been tapping on the contact that switched the interior light on and off. The following day was spent putting the roof lining back in place and chuckling to himself, thinking about the soliloquy he'd delivered the previous night.

Then there was the incident of the missing pocket notebook which was as far removed from humour as anyone can imagine.

CHAPTER 27

Missing Notebook

Back to the heading of 'paranoia', another RUC officer loomed large in the Operation George saga. In what is believed to be the first and only time an RUC officer was despatched to the mainland to fire a police officer serving in one of the forty-three police forces in England and Wales, he arrived to officially inform one of the Plymouths UCOs his 'services were no longer required.' He was off Operation George for good. His 'crime' wasn't as nefarious as you might think.

The Plymouth team of UCOs had a safe house in Brixham. It was somewhere they could chill out without bumping into Tanya and Jimmy or any of their new friends and associates in Plymouth. They soon discovered there are four things to know about Brixham. It gets full of pensioners who arrive on coaches every day. That's a little surprising owing to the steep hills. The town sits across the bay from Torquay, which is livelier and in the UCOs' opinion, infinitely more desirable. But the Cover Officers were in control and sorted it out for them. The last thing to know is how the locals refer to Brixham. Depending on your employment seems to dictate how you refer to it. It's either Cow Town or Fish Town, and the two tribes of farmers and fishermen do not get on or indeed live in complete harmony together. Their relationship is like City and United or Celtic and Rangers. There is a fierce rivalry that spills over into punch-ups on a Friday and Saturday night after the old dears and their husbands have long gone. The farmers have their pubs and the fishermen have theirs.

There was one pub on the quayside that both sets would be attracted to because it was where the girls hung out. A fight broke out on one occasion in this pub where a massive bloke – he must have been a farmer because he would not have fitted into a fishing boat – threw a punch, sending his opponent flying horizontally and resulting in the poor guy landing on the far side of the room. The UCOs were unanimous in deciding this was a venue to be avoided at all costs. Instead, they chose to drink in a small local which just happened to be the first pub on leaving the safe house.

The UCOs invented a cover story as to why they were in Brixham. They put it about they were IT engineers employed by a London based company, working in and around Devon and parts of Cornwall. Robbie wasn't the savviest around IT so Dave told him to say that he did the 'ergonomics.' Robbie could hardly pronounce the word let alone spell it or know its meaning. Dave went on to explain, "Right, I'll say we do IT installations for a company based in London and we all have different parts of the business, and you do the ergonomics."

"Dave, mate, excuse my lack of knowledge but what the fuck does that word mean? It's best to stick to something I know and can talk about," Robbie said with genuine concern.

"Listen, all you have to say is you plan where the workstations, desks and cable runs go and that's it. Leave the rest to us," Dave assured him.

The safe house was about a five-minute walk up the hill from the quayside. It was someone's second home that was rented out as a holiday let to bring in an extra income stream out of season for the owner. The lads all had a room each which were off a first-floor landing. In the roof section above the landing was a Perspex domed skylight which gave an open, bright feeling to the landing. Sadly, it was also a resting place for huge seagulls to tap on at first light. The birds constant tap-tap-tap woke the team at dawn every morning, much to their annoyance.

The landing window gave a great view across the bay to Torquay and the beautiful Victoria Hotel looking splendid in white. At this sight, they understood why Torquay is known as the English Riviera. The team sarcastically referred to their safehouse as the 'des-res' but were comforted when the Cover Officers often arranged briefings and de-briefing at the Victoria Hotel. The UCOs ensured the complimentary bar was left empty on those occasions.

On one occasion, one undercover officer we shall call Mike was away for the day with Jimmy. The other team members were mooching around the town, which didn't take too long. It was a regular tactic for a Cover Officer to tag along out of sight of any UCO and Jimmy. Jimmy had dropped Mike off at the flat in Plymouth and he waited for Jimmy to clear the plot before setting off down to Brixham to join the other lads. The Cover Officer on this occasion, we will call him John, did the same, setting off about ten minutes before Mike. As John was nearing Brixham he called Neil to see where the team was as he fancied a quick half before retiring to his accommodation. Neil told him they were in their local and John agreed to meet them there. After about ten minutes, John walked into the bar and joined the team of IT Engineers. Dave soon got the conversation round to ergonomics and taking the piss out of Robbie and how he'd made a gigantic cockup on the job that day. It was all cock and bull, but it served a purpose if anyone was earwigging the conversation. Within ten minutes of John arriving, Neil got a call from Mike asking where they were. Neil told him they were in the pub and Mike agreed to join them there. At that point, the UCOs present in the pub had no inkling of any untoward issues. But alarm bells started to ring in John's head.

Mike walked into the pub and joined the team. John quietly asked Mike if he had completed his work, gesturing writing on his hand with a pen: code for have you done your notes? Mike answered in the affirm-ative, but John was unconvinced, though he held off, probably believing this wasn't the time or place to hold an inquisition. John left the com-pany, and the remainder of the evening followed the usual pattern – beer quaffed followed by either a sit-down meal or fish and chips from the local chippy. Robbie had to be up early the next day to meet up with John at the Gordano Service Station on the M5 motorway. They planned to go into Bristol to look for a lock up. Just as Robbie was turning in for the night, Mike asked if he could come along in the morning just for something to do.

"If it's okay with John, it's okay with me. I'm off at 7:30ish," Robbie said.

"Fine, I'll speak to John and see you in the morning," Mike said.

The following morning arrived with Robbie up and ready to go, looking forward to a full English at the motorway services or a nice greasy spoon cafe in Bristol. He knocked on Mike's door and discovered Mike fast asleep. Robbie shouted out that he was going now. Mike mumbled, "Okay, I'll come up in my car and meet you at the services."

Robbie drove the hundred-mile journey to the service station, a journey of about two hours for him but just over the hour for Dave, Devon and Cornwall's most wanted road hog. Robbie and John met up and made their way to the self-service café. They decided to give the rubber-like egg and cold sausage a miss and elected for the Bristol greasy spoon option. Robbie told John Mike was about ten minutes away so they should wait there for him. John looked surprised and said he didn't know Mike was coming. That was when Robbie informed John about the earlier conversations he'd had with Mike. Robbie had no idea anything was out of place, but he sensed John was wondering what the hell was going on.

Robbie called Mike to find out where he was and to tell him two guys were waiting on him at Gordano, and they were starving. Mike told him he was stuck in traffic on the motorway, but he could see the motorway one-mile advance sign for the services. Robbie and John were able to see the motorway traffic and noted there weren't any delays or hold ups. At that, John phoned Mike and told him to meet them in the first layby as he exited the M5 at Junction 19. The plan was to leave two cars there and all three of them would continue into Bristol in one motor.

John and Robbie made their way to the large layby and waited for Mike. After some delay, Mike called John to say he'd missed the exit and would have to continue to the next one at Junction 18 which was on the other side of the major road works to the bridge over the River Avon. These road works always caused delays, but this was a Saturday morning, and the traffic was light. The UCO and the Cover Officer waited in silence for the most part. John was obviously working through things surrounding Mike's recent performance.

Robbie was just plain hungry and regretted agreeing to have Mike come along. Then like something out of a Disney cartoon a Black BMW approached, steam coming from the bonnet; it was travelling at best ten miles per hour. The front wheels were splayed and out of line with the front wings. Every panel was damaged including the roof, and there was no windscreen. Had it not been for recognising Mike behind the wheel aiming the wreck towards them, neither of the guys would have thought it was the nice shiny black beamer that was once in apple pie condition.

Shrugging, Mike got out of the wreck and looked and acted totally nonchalant. He offered an opinion it wasn't as bad as it looked. He was utterly unfazed, unlike John who fired off a barrage of questions, "Mate what in fuck's name? Have you driven that down the motorway like that? What's happened?"

Mike began to tell his tale of woe. He'd come off at Junction 18 and exited the roundabout to head back towards Junction 19. As he was about to head west on the main carriage way, a fox ran across the slip road. He hit the brakes and turned the steering wheel to avoid the quick brown fox and went down the embankment, rolling over and ending up back on the wheels. A lorry driver stopped and pulled him out with a tow rope that he just happened to have. Once on the slip road, he started the engine and drove along the hard shoulder to meet up at the layby. Robbie, listening with incredulity, thought, *What a load of shite! This is for John to sort out, it doesn't involve me and a lock-up is still to be found.* This was the last time Robbie saw Mike.

Robbie continued into Bristol and stopped at the first place that sold hot food, after which he went into Bristol and secured a lock-up in the form of a 'To Rent' private domestic garage advertised in a newsagent's window. It was in a block of garages behind a high-rise tower block in a working-class area of Bristol. The lock-up was ideal for a future plan involving Jimmy and a dodgy motor.

Meanwhile, John and Mike had to arrange for a local recovery company that would be prepared to recover the beat-up BMW back to a secure police workshop in London. Once the BMW was being piggy backed to London, Mike and John headed back to Plymouth to meet up with the operational team members and give them a full debrief on the events. It was during this question-and-answer session that the subject of Mike's pocket notebook (PNB) arose. The PNBs were always left with the Cover Officer or ops team or secure in the safe house. It never went onto the plot. Mike claimed his book was safe and secure in his hiding place in the safe house in Brixham. The team in Brixham were called and directed to the hiding place and asked to retrieve Mike's PNB. The safe house was searched top to bottom with a negative result, as was the Plymouth flat which was searched by Mike and John.

Mike then said it may have been in the crashed BMW which by now was in a secure police garage in London. A member from the London Undercover Office was called out to gain access to the garage and search the BMW inside out. Once more, no PNB. Mike then admitted he had it in his holdall when he went to a public gym in Plymouth a day or so ago. Things now were serious. The UCOs, including Robbie, were all together in the safe house in Brixham. John called them to offer a quick explanation of the day's events. He also instructed them not to return to Plymouth under any circumstance and not to take any calls from Jimmy. What is more, he instructed them to return to their home addresses and stay there until contacted.

A sombre atmosphere fell over the team of UCOs. *What if someone found it?* They knew the whole job could now be destroyed by one of their own. Anyone could be in possession of that PNB. *What if it found its way into the hands of a local hack reporter? What if it was in the hands of a real Plymouth criminal? What if Jimmy had it?* That's a lot of 'what ifs,' but any of those could have proved fatal in more ways than one.

Just like a starburst, the UCOs from Brixham headed off in the directions of their homes in this cloud of uncertainty. They had all agreed to keep in contact with each other using their personal mobiles so that they could report on any contact made by Jimmy. They could also keep in the loop about any updates from the cover and operational teams or discuss between themselves any suggested course of action for the teams. Independently from each other, the undercover officers started to mull things over as they drove in different directions. These were ultra-smart guys that could nit-pick the bones out of a series of events and dialogue. They had been told that the PNB may have been lost for a few days when Mike said he had it in his hold all in Plymouth gym. They knew that alone was a cardinal sin, punishable with the sack. *What was he thinking, taking it there? It was placing his colleagues in danger. There wasn't sufficient time so how could Mike have completed his notes before joining the team in the pub on the previous night. Lying to the Cover and his colleagues to cover up his fuck-up; how could these men trust him again? Simple and short answer to that question was, never.*

In this line of work, when you are in a team behind the lines you depend and trust on the guy or gal next to you to do their part. Mike, at worst, had knowingly put these guys in real danger. At best, he had done it unwittingly. His colleagues had families, children, wives, brothers, sisters, loved ones. *Unforgivable.* A thousand questions and scenarios ran across the minds of the undercover team as they drove in different directions to the safety of their homes and families. The one comforting thought was there was no connection between Plymouth, Jimmy or

Mike that would lead anyone to their front door. This responsibility ultimately was in the hands of the individual officers. Each knew a sterile corridor was in place that stopped any contamination from their murky undercover lives spilling over into their peaceful home and family lives.

Once home, the team called John to let him know they had arrived safe and sound. Neil, Dave and Robbie all rang each other and slagged Mike off. They agreed never to work with him again. As far as they were concerned, Mike was now *persona non grata.* What is more, all agreed that status should be recorded in the Undercover Officers National Index. They strongly felt Mike was finished as a UCO. *Good riddance to bad rubbish*, they thought.

Another point that the three undercover officers raised with each other was the amount of detail Mike wrote in his notes. We have briefly mentioned previously the danger of writing too much detail and copious notes. It's a car crash waiting to happen. Not normally because some wanker has lost his PNB, but it gives the defence team at any future trial a massive area to attack an officer's evidence. The contemporaneous record of any conversation is the recording: the tape. Officers who write too much detail into their notes can often contradict the tape recording, perhaps unwittingly. This potentially leads to an uncomfortable cross examination, an experience to be avoided at all costs. The undercovers, the operational and cover team had all sat in debriefings when the UCOs read notes from their PNBs. The PNB is an 'Aide Memoire' and should be written up in that style. If, during a debrief, the topic is about a direct conversation, an address or a phone number and it cannot be recalled, it's best practice to inform the debriefing officer it's on the tape and they can retrieve the exact detail there. However, Mike wrote buckets full of information in his notes. Names, addresses, phone numbers, vehicle registrations, everything went in there. Poor tradecraft and bad practice and unnecessary. That was why the loss of his PNB was such a disaster and caused such an alarm.

The next day was a busy time for everyone involved in Operation George – the listeners, enquiry teams, and those monitoring trackers. Both the ops team and Cover Officers were still on the plot. Jimmy was alone in Plymouth without the undercover team available to step in should he decide to go independent on some scheme. Speed was required to resolve the situation.

The cover team contacted each individual UCO at their homes and told them that the situation had been risk assessed. Mike had informed them that the book did not contain any information that could lead a third party to the Plymouth operation. He added there was nothing in his notes that could compromise the op. Neil, Dave and Robbie knew that was bollocks and told them it was more of Mike's lies and bullshit. They wanted a full risk assessment carried out by Colin Port or his nominated officer before going back on the plot. They strongly felt this was not an event that could be swept under the carpet to avoid embarrassing someone. All three UCOs refused to redeploy until their condition was met. As a result, a senior RUC officer arrived from Belfast to conduct an internal investigation into the loss of the PNB and a further risk assessment. He was satisfied from probe product that Jimmy had no knowledge and his movements and behaviour had not changed. The decision to redeploy was conveyed to the three undercover officers. All three men were asked if they were happy to return to Plymouth. All three said yes. The operation was back on. Mike was never seen or heard of again.

CHAPTER 28

The Voice

The Plymouth team had been operating for a long time by the time of Fulton's arrest, and prior to that day it was business as usual, trying to dream up more schemes and scams to enable them to be close to their target; close enough for several hours a day to let him talk and record those conversations. Dave professed to know more about IT than any of the other UCOs, so it fell to him to propose a scam involving the theft of high-value computer microchips. Luckily for him, one of the Cover Officers knew his computer onions and backed him.

"Didn't know they were made in the UK," Robbie said sceptically.

The Cover Officer wised him up. "Most aren't. They are imported from Asia and the States."

"What about the buyers? Who would buy this stuff? More to the point, what do we tell Jimmy?" Robbie queried.

"There's lots of smaller outfits busy making high end gaming computers. They are the customers as the chips are the most expensive components," Dave added.

"That might work, as I don't think Jimmy knows the difference between a microchip and a potato chip unless it's got McCains on the packet," Robbie said.

"We could say the same about you, Robbie," someone at the back of the room said.

With the plan now sanctioned, Neil arranged for a meeting of the Plymouth firm at the Weston-Super-Mare lockup, which was still wired for sound. Naturally, Jimmy was present as a valued and trusted member of the criminal gang. During this two-hour long planning meeting, all present were unaware persons other than the regular listeners were eavesdropping. They included teams of detectives gathered in preparation for interviewing Fulton and others following their arrests.

Preparing for the end of the operation, Colin Port's team trawled the UK mainland for a team of top detectives to conduct the interviews of Jimmy and his crew. This expedition was conducted by the Special Branch departments of the forty-three geographical police areas in England and Wales. What were the chances of members of the interview teams knowing any of the Operation George UCOs?

Once the interviewing team had been identified it was called to a secret briefing at Colin Port's clandestine operation base on the UK mainland. That briefing was to last over several days. Starting with an overall picture of what Operational George entailed, the assembled detectives were broken down into individual interviewing teams of two. Each team was then given many hours of covert recorded conversations between the UCOs and a target. These conversations, known as product, were all the conversations captured on listening probes in the homes of Fulton and Gibson and Fulton's Renault Laguna. Additionally, there were many hours of covertly recorded conversations captured by the UCOs using hidden recording devices. Within them were the admissions used as evidence to convict Jimmy and his crew in court.

As any seasoned detectives of certain eras know, at any gathering of the 'old school detectives' a natural bonding process begins or is fostered, usually by way of late nights in the bar or sometimes early evenings in the bar followed by curry and then a late night in the bar. This is when the 'war stories' get trotted out: "Do you know such and such? He/she was on my CID course," or "I was giving evidence in number one court at the Bailey," or "When I was on the RCS." The latter is the 'When-I's' favourite. They are known for prefacing every war story with, "When I…"

Two of the detectives selected for this job were two top Johnnys from one of the UK's finest, Clive and Pete, we will call them. Both were highly respected by colleagues no matter what rank. At the risk of sounding controversial in an age of political correctness within the modern police service, they were two modern day detectives who were versed in the more acceptable old school methods and tactics but allied to a complete knowledge of PACE to enable successful interviews resulting in convictions. These guys were comfortable with the task they had been handed and tackled it with the same professional attitude and approach as every other job, big or small. Clive and Pete mixed in well with the other team members and threw themselves into the social gatherings with gusto.

On the second day of the briefing, the teams were gathered, poring over transcripts, making notes, exchanging ideas and strategies, and asking searching questions of the full-time members of the operation team. During one of these sessions one of the listeners came in and announced, "If you guys are interested there is a meeting involving the UCOs and Jimmy taking place in a warehouse in the West Country right now. The boss said you guys can give your ears a treat if you fancy it."

Clive and Pete were on the move before the fella had finished his invitation. Like two thoroughbred racehorses at the start of the big race, they were at the head of the field making the early running with the listening room as their winning post. The new arrivals settled down where they were able. Standing in complete silence, they tuned their ears into the voices emanating from a set of small speakers on a desk. The UCOs and Jimmy were in the warehouse discussing a bit of work that was coming up. Neil was delegating who was going to do what. There was the usual banter between the group, which the interviewing teams interpreted as a relaxed atmosphere and not at all what they expected. But those present who had experienced undercover operations before or had past dealings with similar product knew, contrary to common belief, that all UCOs didn't talk out of the corners of their months, effing and blinding like some Cockney flash Harry.

Clive and Pete listened carefully, staring at the two speakers on the desk as an aid to concentration, when simultaneously they looked into each other's eyes. Not uttering a word, they thought the same thing at the same time, *Fuck me!* Both had recognised one of the voices as one of their own. Clive, Pete and the UCO had all been part of the same shift back on division, in uniform and on CID. As always, both maintained their professionalism, said nothing and maintained their composure. Both made a mental note to speak with each other later away from anyone else.

Before dinner that day while taking a stroll around the sports field, Clive and Pete discussed the situation. They agreed not mentioning it in the listening room was the right thing to do. Their silence effectively protected the UCO being identified. They also agreed to keep the facts to themselves and not share this with anyone at the briefing location. They believed the right thing to do was contact the Special Branch (SB) Detective Inspector (DI) in their own force who had nominated them for Colin Port's interviewing teams. He listened to what they had to say, expressing he had no clue of any of the identities of the UCOs deployed on Operation George. Unfazed by this account, he reassured Clive and Pete he would call the operational team to appraise them of this development. Content they had contacted the SB DI, Clive and Pete went for dinner. After dinner, the two guys sat in Clive's room enjoying a glass of red wine that Clive always seem to have available. They recounted the very second each of them recognised the voice of their old mate and described each other's facial expressions. Naturally, they could not reach agreement as to which of the two was more composed on hearing the UCO in the listening room. They did agree their old mate was buying the first round when this thing was all over. Clive had the last word. "The fucking exxies [expenses] he's on, that's a given, Pete."

After the glass of wine, they sauntered into the bar to have a few pints with the rest of the interviewing teams and contact home using their mobile phones. After a quick chat with their respective wives, Clive's phone pinged. It was a text from the SB DI asking them to attend the ops team's office at 08:15 the next morning to see the boss. He clarified he had not disclosed their friend's alias nor anything else about him. He signed off the text with: *Please acknowledge by text. Regards. Denis.*

Clive read the text and replied with: *'ok ta guv'* and put the phone back in his pocket. Exercising oodles of discretion owing to the presence of too many others, Clive decided to wait to inform Pete of the text. Both were aware the normal working day started at nine in the morning so later that night and showing the text to Pete, he said, "Okay, we had better make up a cover story just in case these nosey bastards see us going across early."

Pete said, "We'll tell them we wanted to get away a bit sharpish tomorrow for a commitment back on Division."

They agreed that they would only refer to the UCO as 'the voice' and not even identify him by his alias. Come the following morning, the two men walked the short distance from the accommodation block across to the office. They found the boss's door open, and he beckoned the two men to enter with a wave of the hand. The boss asked Pete to close the door. The entire story was pored over with the boss agreeing completely with their decision making and the steps they had taken. He fully understood. The boss asked the two officers if they were still happy to be part of the team and no inference would be drawn by him if they felt too close and would rather step down. Both detectives glanced towards each other and without hesitation turned back to the boss and said in unison, "I'm in."

The boss smiled at their double act and said, "Thank you. I think you two will be valuable members of this team. I can only hope the other guys are as switched on and as savvy as you two guys." Some lighthearted chatter followed, mainly about their reaction to recognising the voice and referring to their friend only as 'the voice'.

As Clive and Pete were leaving the office, Clive mentioned their cover story concocted to mask this visit. The boss, without looking up from his desk, shook his head from side to side before saying, "You guys think of everything, get out of here."

Clive and Pete returned to their force the next day and waited for the call to return for a final briefing and allocation of interviews. The UCO got the heads up on the voice recognition episode and parked it in the 'no worries tray.' He knew the two detectives well and had no concerns whatsoever about their integrity nor his identity and safety being compromised.

Months later, following the completion of all the interviews and after Fulton and Gibson had been charged, Clive and Pete returned to their usual daily routine back on Division. Clive was walking through the rear yard of a nick heading for the car park when he saw the UCO, 'the voice', walking towards him. They nodded to each other, but the UCO was sporting a cheeky little smile. Clive, however, after the nod of the head sheepishly dropped his eyes and did not see the smile. Still approaching, the UCO spoke, "It's okay, mate. I heard what happened and how you dealt with it."

"Thanks," Clive replied still a tad bashful. But then recovered his composure, saying, "My pleasure, you owe me wine, lots of wine. You almost stopped my heart when I heard your voice. Good job, by the way."

They both continued walking in opposite directions, the UCO heading for the police station building. He found Pete sitting in the canteen drinking tea and reading a report. The UCO approached him from behind to surprise him. Just as Pete raised the mug of tea to his lips the UCO said, " Have you been listening in to my fucking conversation?"

Once more recognising 'the voice', Pete remained statue-like and without turning around, he said, "Half of the UK police have been listening in to your fucking conversation." Then turning towards the UCO, he stood slowly, turning his face towards his mate, beaming a huge smile and offering a man hug.

"What the fuck! Get your paws off me," the UCO exclaimed.

"Mate, you owe me and Clive dinner and beers but vino in Clive's case. Are you okay? That was some bit of work you were on."

The UCO strolled off to get two more cups of tea and they continued talking about their different experiences on Operation George. Pete was amazed how they, the UCOs, had managed to keep the illusion going for so long. Following this encounter, there were always conspiratorial nods and winks passed between them with Pete or Clive often asking, "Where's my fucking dinner?" On occasions it would be a jovial inquiry asking the UCO if he had been down to the warehouse lately. The UCOs deployed on George came from all over the UK, as did the interview teams. What are the odds of the interviewing teams knowing the UCOs? Perhaps as high as a million to one.

CHAPTER 29

The Strike

Despite the stumbles and some disharmony in the Plymouth undercover team, activities continued on a professional level. However, there could be no doubt some pressure was being put on Colin Port to bring down the final curtain on the *Truman Show*. It was obviously costing bundles to finance and Port possibly had eyes on legal issues such as an allegation of abuse of process. He would have also assessed what new stuff was coming out of Jimmy and the stresses, strains and mental conditions of the gang of three in Plymouth – Neil, Dave and Robbie. Those three did all the heavy lifting when it came to occupying and controlling Jimmy.

Some friction had started to develop between those three and some of the Cover Officers. This had also been noticed by the operational team, that's to say the team based away from Plymouth who oversaw the operations in Plymouth and Cornwall, reporting directly to Colin Port in Belfast. That team was responsible for briefing and debriefing both Operation George teams, including the UCOs and the Cover Officers. To the credit of the operational team, its practice was not to become involved in the disagreements but to leave the UCOs and Cover Officers to sort it out between themselves. The imminent arrest of Jimmy Fulton was perhaps timely.

On Monday, 11 June 2001, the evening before his arrest, Neil, Dave and Robbie, together with Jimmy, were having a quick drink in a pub just up from Jimmy's Plymouth house. The house was part of a large estate to the north of the city centre. By now, Jimmy's wife and kids were also living with him. There was no off-road parking on the estate and trying to find a parking spot was always a hassle as they were at a premium. However, Jimmy had managed to find a spot directly opposite his lounge window but on the opposite side of the road from his house.

Earlier, Robbie had travelled with Jimmy, and they met with Neil and Dave in the pub on the estate. Robbie planned to get a lift back with the other two UCOs. All four had been in the pub for five minutes or so when Robbie's mobile phone rang. It was the Cover Officer using the cryptic coded question, "Are you all right to talk?"

Robbie, following protocols and his training, said, "Yeah mate, everything go all right with that load?" He often used words and phrases that a third party would associate with haulage. That was his back story with Jimmy, that he had a haulage company that was a part front to launder his criminal proceeds. Jimmy was by now used to Robbie receiving such calls and walking away from the group. Once alone out on the pub car park, Robbie was able to continue the conversation, ensuring Jimmy remained in view to prevent the target catching him unawares and possibly hearing something he should not.

Confident he was alone, Robbie told the Cover Officer to go ahead.

"I've had a request from the operational team, so don't shoot the messenger."

"What the fuck is it now?" Robbie said.

"The firearms team have asked that the car is parked the other way round so that the driver's door opens into the road. As it is, the driver's door is kerbside, they want him to turn it around."

Words dripping with more than a little irony, Robbie said, "No worries. I'll explain it to Jimmy, I'm sure he'll understand. Do they want Jimmy to wear a Hi-Vis vest in the morning so they know it's him, mate?"

Following a little more banter, Robbie agreed to sort it out, but he wasn't yet sure how. He walked back into the pub and joined the group. Neil played his part by saying, "Everything okay with that load, Robbie?"

Quick thinking as ever, Robbie said, "Yeah, no worries mate. I need to make a phone call from a box. Jimmy, can I borrow your car?"

In private thoughts, Robbie guessed the armed arrest team boss had taken a drive past to get an accurate mental picture of the scene, so he was able put his arrest plan together.

Unhesitating, Jimmy replied, "No worries, my man, here you go," as he tossed over the Laguna keys.

Robbie walked the short distance to Jimmy's house and was engrossed by some troubling thoughts. *Parking spots are like rocking horse shit in this street so the chances of me getting the same spot is a million to one shot. The new parking spot might not suit the firearms boys and we could be playing this musical car game all fucking night.*

On reaching the car, he had another thought – *Tanya's indoors, so I'd better make this look real. No use just moving it in case Tanya spots me. I'd better make this good as it's the finale and I don't want to fuck it all up.*

With these thoughts battering his brain cells, Robbie drove off in the direction of the phone box he knew on the estate. He went as far as going into the phone box and making an imaginary call just in case one of Jimmy's neighbours saw his car with a stranger sitting in it outside a phone box. After five minutes, Robbie got back in the car and drove back to find a parking place near Jimmy's house. Not for the first time, Robbie thought, *Well, the gods are smiling on me.* As he approached the spot where Jimmy's car had been parked, he saw it was already taken. But then the car directly in front pulled out, leaving the perfect spot for him to park Jimmy's car afresh. *Job done*, he thought.

As he was locking the car door, Robbie was startled to hear that that distinctive Northern Ireland accent call out, "Tell that man of mine to get home. His tea's on the table." It was Tanya. Robbie gave a cheery wave in acknowledgement that he would pass on the message to Jimmy. With that, he walked back to the pub and re-joined his mates.

Handing Jimmy his keys, Robbie reassured Neil with, "All sorted, Neil, no worries. Jimmy, I saw Tanya and she says your tea's on the table." Robbie and Neil could not help thinking, *I'm glad it wasn't one of Jimmy's 'invitations to tea.'*

The get together in the pub ended with all three UCOs leaving and Jimmy walking home for his tea – the last time he'd be eating tea with his family for a long time. Before the parting of the ways, arrangements were made for Jimmy to pick Robbie up from the flat at 6:30 the following morning, Tuesday 12 June 2001. Neil and Robbie knew it was a fifteen-minute drive from Jimmy's house to the flat so he would be leaving his place at around 6:15 am. That would be the time his whole world would fall around his ears, and he would start to pay for his crimes. The vehicle had a remote-controlled immobiliser fitted so the firearms boys could allow him to get inside the car and then hit the immobiliser. Jimmy would be trapped and under control in a car that wasn't going anywhere. Checkmate Jimmy Fulton!

The UCOs went back to the flat, packed up their personal kit, loaded their cars and drove out of the square for the last time and into the sunset. It made absolute common sense for them to get out of town just in case something went wrong. In the event something did, there were always the phones to contact Jimmy if they needed to call him or if he decided to go out that night with or without the car. There were a few possible permutations: likely or unlikely events. Nothing ever goes to plan. They say in battle the game play goes out the window as soon as the first round is fired. Fortunately, everything went to plan. The long-time target, Jimmy Fulton, was arrested in a dawn swoop by armed officers of the Devon and Cornwall Constabulary. He was driven a few miles to a nearby airfield where a military helicopter awaited. Soon after take-off, he was locked up in a Northern Ireland holding centre to await questioning.

Safe in that knowledge, the UCOs and the Cover Officers drove to Exeter on the evening of the day of Jimmy Fulton's arrest. Hotel rooms were booked, and they went out for a meal together. They don't recall giving Jimmy much thought and the mood was more a relief it was over than of celebration. They knew as seasoned professionals it was the end of an amazing 'bit of work.'

CHAPTER 30

Interviews

The RUC interview team dedicated to William Fulton, known as Jimmy, had prepared their strategy, structure and staged disclosure for months. No stone would remain unturned. These diligent detectives would do their best to ensure as many victims and the families of those victims as possible would have their day in court. Jimmy had killed, maimed, terrorised and ruled his corner of Northern Ireland with fear and savage violence. Not any more, Jimmy, son. Your time is over. Make way for the rule of law.

This was the mantra of two experienced detectives we will call Detective Inspector Eddie Roche and Detective Sergeant Dennis O'Brien. They were close friends as well as colleagues. The two men worked from an office within shouting distance of the Stormont Parliament Buildings in Belfast. On their desks lay files of unsolved open cases ranging from murder, kidnapping, bombings, robbery, drug dealing and punishment shootings. Jimmy Fulton's blood-stained dabs were now all over them. Not as a result of a tout, victim or an eyewitness but by Jimmy himself. Self-confessed involvement. Eddie and Dennis already had Jimmy's confessions; the interviews were almost a formality.

The day of reckoning had finally arrived. Eddie and Dennis watched from the window of the Special Branch (SB) Office at Belfast Airport as the military helicopter touched down a short distance away from them. The chopper's rotors stopped, and the engine fell silent. From the opened door stepped a guy in military dress wearing an aircrew helmet, followed by an RUC policer officer colleague dressed in a suit. Then came Jimmy dressed in jeans and a polo shirt, instantly recognised by the two detectives from interviews, posters and mug shots around the SB Offices in the province. Eddie and Dennis knew that Fulton wasn't getting off the hook this time. He was oven ready, and the oven was at the right temperature to slide him in and watch him cook in his own juices. "Mr William James Fulton you are well and truly fucked this time," whispered Eddie.

There was the normal custody procedure to follow so the two detectives waited to get the ball rolling with their interview strategy. It was agreed at SIO level that the disclosure would be staged. Interview one would be focused on dates and events. Two would be further detail around those dates and events. Three would be associations. Four would be when Eddie and Dennis pulled the pin out of the hand grenade and monitored Fulton's reaction. Stage four was the disclosure that his best friends on the mainland were undercover cops and they had covertly recorded every conversation he had with them.

The moment finally arrived when Eddie and Dennis signed the custody record, taking charge of Fulton in the presence of his solicitor, and walked him to the interview room. The four men sat around a table and Dennis pushed the record button on the wall mounted recording machine. After the prolonged buzzing sound Eddie made the customary introductions which included asking Fulton to state his name.

Looking at Fulton, Eddie invited him to introduce himself. "Would you please state your name for the tape, please."

Fulton remained silent with his eyes fixed on a stain in the paintwork above the heads of Eddie and Dennis. Fulton was exercising his anti-interrogation techniques. He was taking himself mentally out of the room and focusing on anything and everything other than the two officers and their questions. This silence and anti-interrogation methods continued through the next two interviews, but the officers stuck to their planned structure and questions. The staged interviews and questioning zeroed in towards the moment the detectives were to deliver the knock-out punch.

Interview four followed along the lines of the previous three. On this occasion, Fulton was attempting to balance his chair on two legs. He had his fingertips on the end of the table, his feet raised off the floor and trying to find the point of balance where he could remove his fingertips and hold his position in the chair without support. In no rush to spoil Fulton's day and piss all over his fireworks, the two officers stuck to the plan. Eddie took the pin out and threw the grenade onto the table right under Fulton's nose.

Eddie fixed his eyes on Fulton and expressing no emotion said, "Your associates on the mainland. Your friends, Neil, Dave, Robbie, Gary, Hands, they are all undercover police officers and have been covertly recording all your conversations with them." That got his attention. Fulton's face expressed his thoughts – *What did he just fucking say?*

Fulton's face wore a glum expression as he set the chair down on all four legs and looked directly into Eddie's eyes. "That's right, all cops like me and Dennis. Cops that had you talking for hours and hours and hours about your involvement in countless crimes from murder to drug dealing," Eddie said, and then in a subdued tone of triumph, added, "I imagine you would like to have a consultation in private with your solicitor now. Interview concluded."

Dennis reached across and pressed the stop button on the recording device. The tape labels were completed in deadly silence. You could have heard a pin drop in the room. Fulton was first to his feet and keen to get out of the room. His world had just collapsed. He must have thought, *What the fuck have I said? What do they know?* The answer was simple, one word. Everything.

Eddie and Dennis escorted Fulton and his solicitor back to the custody staff. They guessed it would be some time before Fulton and his solicitor would be ready for the next interview. The two friends put an arm around each other's shoulder. Eddie pulled Dennis into him as if they had just won the Champions League Final with a late goal and said, "Take that, you fucker."

The two detectives walked into the SB office and were surprised to find so many of their colleagues still sitting at their desks. Tim, a short bald detective, couldn't contain himself. He shouted across at the interviewing officers. "How did it go, boss? What did he do when you told him about the boys on the mainland?"

Dennis got in first. "He shite his pants right there in front of us. I kid you not. Shite himself."

"You're joking me, come on. Did he really?" asked Tim.

The office broke out in hand clapping, cheers, back slapping and laughter. They had Fulton on the hook and he was going nowhere... except prison for a long time.

Much later and after her son's arrest whilst Fulton was on remand, his mum was picked up on a mic while visiting Jimmy in jail. She was heard asking Jimmy, "Is that nice man Robbie a policeman?"

Jimmy replied, "Yes, Mother, even that nice man Robbie. And stop calling him Robbie, it's not his real name. He and the others all used false names and were undercover policemen."

But it wasn't quite over yet – there were legal battles ahead.

CHAPTER 31

Bail

Before the legal battles proper were enjoined, Fulton's defence team won an early skirmish in that they successfully applied for bail in the wake of his brother, Mark 'Swinger' Fulton committing suicide in his Northern Ireland prison cell. He was granted bail so he could attend his brother's funeral. Such a bail hearing would have taken place in front of a single judge in private with both defence and prosecution arguing their respective cases. It is highly likely the defence argued that the whole case against Jim Fulton would collapse if the covertly recorded admissions were to be ruled inadmissible. The prosecution probably agreed because that scenario was true. So, with conditions, Fulton was bailed.

Later, Robbie was on holiday in the South of France. It was his habit to always take the whole month of August off. He had set off with his children with a caravan in tow. The idea was to spend about two weeks travelling to the *Cote d'Azur* and back again. Avoiding motorways, he would take the scenic route through northern France, across into Germany, Austria, Switzerland, Italy, Monaco and back into France, meeting his wife at Nice Airport for a two week stay at a camp site.

Relaxing at the camp site, Robbie received a call on his job mobile. At any one time, he may have had several mobile phones with him: personal, his job mobile, his legend mobile and a phone for any UC job he may be involved with. It was one of the Plymouth Cover Officers, the one who had planned the Lowry painting scam.

"Can you talk?" she asked, using the usual code phrase.

Robbie thought, *Fuck, what's happened? She knows I'm on holiday and out of the country because of the ring tone. Do I need to get back to the UK for a court case? Has a job gone tits up and I need to get back in there to protect an informant? What is it?!*

"Yeah, I'm okay to talk."

"I have some bad news for you," she said, adding swiftly, "Jimmy's has been released on bail."

All Robbie could say was, "What the fuck are you doing phoning me up to tell me that?"

It was a brief call. Robbie undertook a brief self-risk assessment (and risk to his family) and concluded there was nothing he could do about it and the chances of Fulton coming on his holidays to the same site was a one in a billion chance. He told no one and got on with the rest of his holiday.

But a scare was to come just a few days after this call. The family visited a different camp site to use their facilities on a day basis. The sunbeds were set up by the pool when the blood in Robbie's veins ran ice cold. He was relaxing, eyes half shut, when he heard people arriving behind them to set themselves up. Startled, he heard the adult voice of a male speaking in that unmistakable Northern Irish accent. *Fucking no way!* he thought. Positioning his head to get a look at the fella, he saw he was tattooed, had cropped hair and aged about the same as Jimmy Fulton. His heart skipped a beat at the sight before he convinced himself it wasn't him despite an uncanny likeness. *How spooky is that?* he thought. Robbie could see this guy had all the trademarks of a paramilitary and he was sure if he'd asked him if he knew Jimmy Fulton he would have said, 'Yes.' Robbie had met both Fulton brothers and had been shown photographs of Billy Wright – the top echelon of the LVF and knew how similar they looked. Considering his family's welfare and that of his own, they left for the safety of their own camp site and never returned to the scene of the scare.

CHAPTER 32

Belfast

Finally, the trial of The Queen v William James Fulton was scheduled to take place at Belfast Crown Court. It was held with no jury present under the Diplock courts arrangements for Northern Ireland. Diplock courts were criminal courts in Northern Ireland for non-jury trial of specified serious crimes used for political and terrorism-related cases during and after the Troubles. They were abolished by legislation introduced in 2007. However, non-jury trial remains possible in Northern Ireland on a case-by-case certification basis rather than automatically applying to scheduled offences.

Robbie was warned to give his evidence at court on many occasions. Most times, it was cancelled at the last moment, usually owing to legal arguments forcing the hasty revision of calling witnesses to give live evidence. Sometimes, he would receive notice of cancellation before leaving home but sometimes, he would be sitting in an airport waiting to board his Belfast flight. Eventually, he boarded to land at Belfast airport in the knowledge there was a full security plan in place to afford him protection. He travelled on another alias using a new covert identity and passport. On the aircraft touching down, he made sure he was the last passenger to deplane and that was the cue for two armed PSNI officers to escort him into a back room in their Special Branch office.

Next, a people carrier type vehicle with blacked out windows was used to drive him to a police station that looked more a prison than cop shop. There were high barbed wire fences, concrete chicanes and blast walls. Though Robbie had served in the military, he had never set foot on Northern Irish soil, so he considered the sights of fortified police buildings as a novel experience. Inside the safety of the police yard, he would change vehicles again – more blacked out windows – to set off for the hotel. At the hotel, he was handed over to one of the regular Cover Officers from the London office who told him the arrangements for his attendance at court. Robbie would be met by an armed PNSI officer who would escort him to Belfast Crown Court and sit beside him in the court room as his protector and bodyguard.

A few things struck Robbie about his protector. The PSNI officer was quick to tell him how much he detested the changes to the uniforms since the RUC changed to the PSNI in 2001. He hated the removal of the old Royal Crown. The new PSNI badge still had a crown but not that associated with the British monarchy. Instead, it featured the St. Patrick's saltire, and six symbols representing different and shared traditions: the scales of justice (representing equality and justice), a crown (a traditional symbol of royalty but not the St Edward's Crown worn by or representing the British Sovereign), the harp (a traditional Irish symbol but not the Brian Boru harp used as an official emblem in the Republic), a torch (representing enlightenment and a new beginning), an olive branch (a peace symbol from Ancient Greece), and a shamrock (a traditional Irish symbol, used by St Patrick, patron saint of all Ireland, to explain the Christian Trinity). Robbie found this baffling but many steeped in the history of the province may conclude it is but one small piece of evidence illustrating the deeply ingrained sectarianism rooted within the minds of many people in Northern Ireland.

The bodyguard must have known that the man in the dock, though not yet convicted, was a Loyalist paramilitary terrorist who had been suspected at one time of murdering Rosemary Nelson and wanted to kill a Catholic a week. Yet, Robbie felt more in danger from him than Jimmy. In Robbie's mind's eye, it wasn't hard to imagine his bodyguard sitting in court beside him twiddling his gun round his finger like a cowboy in a western movie, pointing it at him and mouthing the word 'BANG! They did not exchange phone numbers on his departure from the province, especially in light of other incidents.

This PSNI officer was Robbie's regular escort and bodyguard. He took him to and from court every day during Robbie's stay in Belfast. On one of the trips, Robbie asked him to stop at a local Co-op store as they were passing by so Robbie could buy a bottle of wine to drink later that day. He kindly agreed and he pulled up outside the shop. This was outside of the security procedures agreed between London and the PSNI but Robbie had no intention of telling anyone about it. In vain, Robbie checked all the aisles and shelves for a decent bottle of vino. Frustrated, he asked the guy behind the till where it was kept, only to be informed that they didn't sell alcohol. On returning to the parked car, Robbie told him that they don't sell alcohol.

The PSNI man said, "Yeah, I know that. None of the wee shops do. It's not like on the mainland."

Robbie was speechless but thought, *Twat!* Undeterred, Robbie asked him to stop at a big Sainsburys store further up the road. You could cut the atmosphere. Once more, the officer parked with Robbie off on his quest again. Success this time, as he triumphantly carried two bottles of plonk in a bright orange Sainsburys carrier bag back to his waiting escort. The drive to the hotel was accompanied by a deafening silence. Without a word, Robbie got out of the car to walk into the hotel reception area where he was met by the London Cover Officer who, on spotting the bag, said, "Where did you get that from?"

Robbie, still peeved by the PSNI officer's antics said, "Fuck me, Sherlock, you're meant to be a detective, the country's finest, the clue is on the bag." Not wishing to offend, Robbie added it was from Sainsbury's, just in case he was still struggling with the big clue. He told him his bodyguard had stopped on the way back. He also informed the Cover Officer all about the Co-op fiasco.

By the time of the Belfast trial, about six years had passed since Robbie last saw Jim Fulton in the Plymouth pub the night before his arrest by the armed Devon and Cornwall police team. By prior arrangement and in the company of his new best friend the bodyguard, Robbie entered the Diplock court by way of the judge's chambers. Although Muriel Gibson was tried on the same indictment, only Fulton occupied the dock. There were two sets of counsel, one for the prosecution and the other representing Fulton. Mr Justice Hart was sitting in a chair high above all else. As soon as Robbie entered the courtroom Fulton had him in his direct line of sight. They locked eyes as Robbie walked towards the witness box. Jimmy had a half smile on his face. Fulton nodded slightly, his chin almost imperceptibly rocking towards his chest then back once more. Most people would not have noticed. Robbie looked back and raised his eyebrows once in a gesture of recognition. It was only then Robbie noticed what Jimmy was wearing. It was the black suit he had bought with the money given by Neil for Jimmy to wear for the fake Lowry scam. Robbie thought he looked like one of the Beatles dressed in a three-quarter length box jacket depicted on a Sixties album cover. With supreme self-control, Robbie kept his face straight.

Later, Robbie often wondered how Fulton felt at that moment when Robbie changed from just a name in the court papers to a living, breathing undercover cop whom Fulton had considered a mate. Mates who for such a long time drank, ate, laughed and schemed criminal plots together, only for him to discover Robbie had tricked him. Robbie was the last man standing after the con had been executed.

Another incident of note happened in Robbie's hotel in Belfast. The hotel was situated directly opposite the cemetery where George Best is buried, so on most days people would visit his grave to pay respects to a gifted footballer. One early evening Robbie was sitting in the hotel and became aware of a big fella sitting on the stool next to him. They struck up some small talk conversation with Robbie primed to trot out a creative cover story if needed.

Robbie, acting naturally, said, "What is it you do for a living, big fella?"

Big Fella said, "I'm a police officer."

"Fuck me, mate, that must be a bit hairy over here, a police officer. How dangerous is that... respect to you, big man."

Big Fella said, "It is, and it's more dangerous for me because I'm an undercover police officer. A UCO."

Robbie, keeping a poker face and not knowing if this man was crazy, said, "Wow! You must be so tough and brave to work undercover. I don't think I could do anything like that. One hundred and one percent total respect to you, big man. What sort of stuff do you do, can you talk about it?"

Big fella replied, "I drive HGVs. That's about all I'll say..." He left it there with those words hanging in the air.

Robbie wanted to say, but dare not, "You're joking me, who would have thought two undercover police officers who drive trucks, coming from different countries, would bump into each other at a hotel bar in Belfast."

Robbie later told a UCO colleague that what happened was something he might do in the right circumstances. He would do it for the devilment and respect for a brother UCO. Robbie did add, "The big fella could have been an extra layer of officer safety, a covert protection team detailed to cover us while in the hotel. That would be standard operating procedure (SOP) on such a high-profile case. Maybe the guy was giving me the nod, you know, like drop it into the conversation that he's got my back. But the mention of HGVs made me think of the surveillance team when we were in Weston-Super-Mare, the chase to Exeter and the following day when Dave and I cleaned ourselves after we were followed into the caff. If we had a ghost team looking out for us during the operation, it would make sense not to tell us in case we started to act differently in front of Jimmy." Nevertheless, he always thought that was spooky coincidence on what was to be his last day using the alias of Robbie.

CHAPTER 33

The Admissions

The full transcript of the handed down judgement of Mr Justice Hart may be found under the reference of R v Fulton and Another, Neutral Citation No. [2006] NICC 35, Delivered 7 December 2006, Hart J.[16]

In this and following chapters, we include abridged or reduced versions of that full judgement. Just like a chef in the kitchen, the term "reduction" refers to a technique that delivers an intense flavour. The excerpts are intended to give you a taste of the essence of the gravity of the crimes in the case of *R v Fulton and Gibson.*

We have also used two different formats for those excerpts to differentiate those parts where the judge is 'speaking' and the transcripts of the covert recordings *per se.* Those transcripts are unredacted and appear in the same form as they did at the trial.

It doesn't take a great legal mind to know the admissions secretly recorded by the Operation George undercover officers and the probes were the key to securing convictions in the cases of William James Fulton and Muriel Gibson. Without the admissions, there was nothing left of the Crown's case. Mr Justice Hart, the trial judge, put that in legalistic terms:

> *The prosecution case depends entirely upon the alleged admissions by the defendants whilst they were under police*

---

[16] https://www.judiciaryni.uk/judicial-decisions/2006-nicc-35

surveillance, and the inferences to be drawn from those admissions. So far as Fulton is concerned, during the second interview the relevant tapes were played to him. He did not respond, and the third interview was cut short to allow him to consult with Mr Ingram [a solicitor]. In the fourth and subsequent interviews, Fulton accepted that it was him talking. This has not been challenged, and so I am satisfied that he uttered the words attributed to him in the transcripts. It is noteworthy that, unlike Gibson, no suggestion was made to any of the undercover officers or transcribers that the transcripts were an inaccurate record of what Fulton said, although, as we shall see, there were issues about whether everything relevant to the issues in the case had been recorded. As I am satisfied that Fulton uttered the words said to him, for the sake of brevity I will henceforth simply refer to them as the "admissions."

Undercover police officers are exactly that. They are still police officers masquerading as someone and something else. When deployed they are still police officers and all the rules that apply to everyday officers still apply. So, in simple terms, if they were to ask a question of someone stopped in the street that goes to the heart of the investigation: a direct question (*R v Bryce*), they must under Code 'C' of PACE caution that person. A short and unsuccessful career as a UCO would follow in that scenario so they must avoid the direct question and instead ask an indirect question (*R v Christou and Wright 1992*).

The case law of *Bryce, and Christou and Wright* was always at the forefront of the UCOs' minds when with Jimmy. He would start to talk about an event in detail. In simple terms he was giving the UCOs the evidence from his own utterance to convict himself. The UCOs' questions would have to be indirect questions so as not to make the 'conversation' inadmissible and rule out at any future trial. Otherwise, his self-admissions would have been deemed as inadmissible under Code C of PACE and never would have seen the light of a courtroom. To avoid the trap of 'direct questions' but to keep the conversation going in a natural way the Plymouth team of UCOs would say things such as, "Fuck me, Jimmy," or make an acknowledging grunt or similar noise, and Jimmy would continue with his talking about his involvement in the murders, robberies, pipe bomb and gun attacks, and other offences.

Before we turn to the details of the case against Fulton, here are some procedural points involved when undercover officers must give evidence at trial. In general, in the courts of England and Wales, when an undercover officer enters the witness box and has sworn the oath or affirmed, they will address the judge to inform the court that they are a serving police officer in the United Kingdom and for the purpose of this operation they were known as John or Jane. They then ask for the leave of the court to give evidence in that name. They often inform the court that they are in possession of a police warrant card if the judge wishes to see it. The UCO will have that warrant card ready to produce in case it is asked for. It will be tucked away inside an envelope safe in John's pocket or Jane's handbag.

At Belfast Crown Court in front of Mr Justice Hart, the procedure was different in that the UCO would write his real name and home police force on a slip of paper then placed inside a small envelope. That note was passed to the court usher who in turn handed it to the judge. He would open the envelope, read the information, and peer over his spectacles at the officer standing in the witness box a few feet away. The slip was then replaced into the envelope, sealed and placed with the judge's papers on the bench.

The preliminaries now completed, it's time for the fun and games to commence. It has been said criminal trials are not a search for the truth. Instead, trials are about what can be proved through evidence, using the rules of evidence. One of the aspects of the trials of Fulton and Gibson is in some ways it ran counter to the perceived wisdom of the penultimate sentence. The admissions were either true or not.

So many parts of a criminal trial can be fairly described as the play within the play. The examination and cross examination of any single witness can be as dramatic as any chapter in a book or film scene. It sticks in the memory like this exchange between Fulton's counsel and

Robbie at trial because in our view it can also be seen as the play within the play.

Fulton's counsel posed this question to Robbie. "Did you ever ask a direct question about any offences when in the company of Mr Fulton?"

Immediately with Code C in mind, Robbie said confidently, "No, my Lord," as he addressed the judge.

Inevitably, the barrister challenged Robbie's strong denial, affecting an air of incredulity, "No, officer?"

Robbie, knowing he was on solid ground replied, "No. Not once, my Lord."

The barrister shuffled through the bundle of papers in front of him and directed Robbie to a particular bundle and page number. Robbie was now looking at a bundle of exhibits including transcripts of the tape summaries. These were transcripts he had helped to prepare some six years previously. He quickly took in what was typed and recalled the gist of the actual conversation. It was about an episode Fulton had recounted when he and others had driven out to the countryside in his wife's car, intending to murder a Catholic.

With no sense of haste, counsel permitted Robbie to settle before saying, "You are now on that page, yes?" Robbie confirmed he was. "Very well. This conversation took place between you and Mr Fulton on 18th September 2000 during a journey where my client was driving, and you were the only other person in the vehicle. Is that correct?"

"It is, my Lord," Robbie said.

"I will read the part of Mr Fulton and you will read your part, your words. Is that clear?" Counsel said.

Robbie had played this 'he said, she said' scene on many occasions in Crown Courts up and down the mainland. Robbie cleared his throat with a couple of light coughs and replied, "Understood, sir."

"Very good. Please start with your words at the middle of the page."

"What's been the biggest fuck up you've had though?" Robbie said.

Fulton's counsel began to read Jimmy's words, "Oh for fuck's sake, Robbie. I'll tell you..." He continued until the end of Fulton's comments before looking at Robbie, saying, "Please look at those words of yours once more, officer. Those that prompted what Mr Fulton had to say."

Robbie knew what counsel was referring to but said, "You mean, 'What's been the biggest fuck up you've had though?'"

"Yes. That was a direct question, officer. Wouldn't you agree with that proposition?"

Robbie replied without pause, "No, sir. That was not a direct question. I asked your client, 'What's been the biggest fuck up you've had though.' He could have told me he'd once fallen off a ladder or something of that nature. He didn't. He chose to tell me about his attempt to murder a Catholic."

A silence fell on the courtroom. In this vacuum, Robbie sensed the defence barrister's eyes burning into the skin of his forehead like two laser beams. He also thought, *Yes, you can see the words 'I'm not a twat' etched into my skin.* The barrister moved on to a few more secondary questions that were answered with yes or no replies. Then suddenly with no warning or indication he said, "No further questions, my Lord," and sat down. The Judge confirmed that he had no further questions and turned to the Prosecuting Counsel who also confirmed he had no more questions.

Robbie then heard the words that every police officer longs to hear, "You are released, officer, thank you."

Robbie returned the respectful dismissal with four simple words, "Thank you, my Lord."

Robbie glanced across the court room at Fulton, taking him in for the last time. There was no more raised half-smile on his face. No more nodding of the head. No more friendship. Just a look of betrayal. Robbie had knocked the last few nails into the lid of Jimmy's coffin. Jimmy was alone down the rabbit hole, in the dark with no friends around him anymore. Robbie turned his back on him and walked out of the courtroom, followed by his assigned bodyguard. Operation George had finally come to an end for Robbie. The longest trial in Northern Ireland's legal history.

Alcohol and Drugs

Mr Justice Hart also had to apply his mind to a question he often posed to himself in the judgement handed down on 7 December 2006. At one point in that document running to over ninety thousand words, the judge stated:

> *I have considered, amongst other things, whether there is any reason to believe that this is, or may be the case, in each evidential tape, and I excluded a number of tapes because the prosecution were unable to show that Fulton was not, or may not have been, affected by alcohol and/or drugs. So far as the remaining tapes that were admitted are concerned there is no evidence to suggest that Fulton was affected by drink or drugs in any of them, and therefore no reason to doubt their reliability on that score. Had there been such evidence no doubt defence counsel would have asked me to listen to the tapes, as was done in relation to several of the tapes relating to Gibson.*

The undercover officers Neil, Robbie, Dave, Max and Gary were cross-examined on this topic and gave the following evidence:

> *On 16 March 2006 at pages 9 and 10 of his cross-examination Max described how Fulton smoked some cannabis when they were on the move together in a car, although Max could not say whether Fulton or himself was driving at the time. Max was not surprised by this, and did not remonstrate with him, saying that it was not take [sic] significant because "the vast majority of the public smoke cannabis nowadays". Robbie took the same view when Fulton told him that he had smoked cannabis whilst having a drink at Gibson's house.*

> *That on one occasion Fulton smoked cannabis whilst he and Max were traveling together lends support to the suggestion that Fulton may have used cannabis on occasions when he was traveling in a car, although I consider it most unlikely that on*

the occasion Max described Fulton smoking cannabis in the car Fulton was driving at the time because of the obvious risk to Max from such conduct. Whatever risks Fulton may have been willing to run, I do not believe that Max would have allowed himself, and other road users, to be endangered. It would also go against the strict policy laid down by Neil to which Gary referred. I remain of the view that I expressed at page 9 of my ruling of 8 May 2006, namely "that Fulton was anxious to show that he was reliable and conscientious individual in order to retain the favour of the undercover officers who he believed were employing in their criminal enterprise." That is a factor which would have influenced Fulton against driving under the influence of drink or drugs whilst he was with a member of the firm.

Whether Fulton was affected by cannabis on any other occasion when he made admissions is a separate issue. If he was smoking cannabis when undercover officers were present, or had been smoking beforehand, I am satisfied that would have been obvious to them because their previous experience as uniformed officers would have enabled them to recognize the signs of someone having taken drugs or alcohol. For an example see Dave's evidence on 28 March 2006 at pages 86 to 89 where he described various symptoms of drug or alcohol use. On those occasions where they were not present, the only people who can say whether Fulton was affected by drugs or alcohol are Fulton and those who are present. Only if something is said, or there is something about the way people spoke, or there is some other evidence which would alert listeners to the conversation to this possibility, could the recording throw light on whether he was affected by drugs or alcohol. Any listener is dependent upon the recording in order to determine whether or not Fulton was affected by alcohol or drugs at the time.

Mr Berry cross-examined Gary, seemingly on the instructions of his client, Fulton, putting to him that on three occasions he had given cocaine to Fulton. Firstly, in a pouch after Gary had visited the toilet in a wine bar, secondly, in Neil's flat after Neil had gone to bed, and on the third occasion a few weeks later when he allegedly gave Fulton a small toiletry bag to keep for a few days, accompanied by an invitation to sample the cocaine it impliedly contained. We say "seemingly" as it appears these allegations were a smear tactic dreamed up by Fulton in a desperate attempt to discredit the UCOs and the admissibility of the secret recordings.

Gibson Legal Issues

Just as in Fulton's case, the Crown's case against Muriel Gibson depended entirely on the admissions she made both to undercover officers and recorded on the hidden probe that recorded her conversations at her home. However, it seems as if her legal team explored more avenues than Fulton's team did in trying to have the admissions ruled inadmissible. At an early stage of police interviews, she claimed not to recognise her own voice on a tape that was played to her. Indeed, apart from one brief passage, it was never admitted by Gibson nor her legal team that she was present on any occasion [of the recordings], or that it was she who said the words attributed to her by the transcribers [of the recordings]. However, Mr Justice Hart in a ruling on the issue said:

> *... I was entirely satisfied that, with the exception of one brief passage, Gibson had been correctly identified as the speaker in the passages attributed to her.*

He gave his reasons for reaching that conclusion and also added:

> *For the avoidance of doubt I repeat that I am satisfied that she was the speaker on all the occasions attributed to her unless I say otherwise.*

Again, like in the case of Fulton the issues of alcohol, drugs and direct questions put by undercover officers were all matters her defence team used to persuade the trial judge some or all her admissions were inadmissible. Part of the defence case was she was a heavy consumer of illicit and prescription drugs on occasion and material was placed before the court to persuade the judge of the validity of the defence submissions. Medical evidence was also before the court which the defence submitted went to the issue of an "abnormality of mind." In layman's terms there was some medical evidence that could mean any admissions were unreliable and therefore ought to be excluded from evidence.

The defence also suggested that the officers transcribing the transcripts "have sought to deliberately remove references to alcohol." But the judge made it clear that:

> ... each of these evidential tapes has been excluded from evidence and were there a jury hearing the case the jury would not be permitted to consider the contents of the excluded tapes, and, unless the tapes were excluded after the voir dire, would not be aware of the contents. I agree that is a correct statement of the law and I must therefore ignore the contents of the excluded tapes.

The judge also considered that "a number of general submissions were advanced in the closing submissions on behalf of Gibson... that as the admissions were not made under caution, and in an informal setting... [so] she had no reason to appreciate the importance of the occasion and the imperative to be measured and accurate in responses to specific police questions."

The judge continued:

> It is difficult to overstate the importance of the obvious fact that none of the alleged admissions was made under caution. This is not a mere technical requirement in the system under PACE... At no stage during any of the recordings relied upon against Mrs Gibson did she have any reason to take care to avoid inaccuracy or exaggeration or to expect that anyone would place any reliance on anything she said. It is a common human characteristic, more marked in some than others, to embroider or even invent stories or inflate the importance of one's own role in a given situation. Casual dishonesty of this nature is inevitably more likely to occur in the kind of informal settings in which

all the assertions relied on by the Prosecution were made by Mrs Gibson.

The judge then went into further detail about:

... the dangers associated with placing reliance on assertions made privately in relaxed circumstances are compounded where the individual in question...

He then listed those dangers and concluded:

All of these factors are present to a greater or lesser degree in Mrs Gibson's case. [the judge then turned to further defence submissions] There are a number of comments I make about these points. The first is that there was nothing improper in the undercover officers demonstrating enthusiasm or interest in the topic of Loyalist terrorism, provided that they did not circumvent the protections for suspects contained in PACE. Indeed, their usefulness would be severely limited if they did not display such enthusiasm and interest. The second is that, as will appear, many of the admissions were made when no undercover officers were present. Gibson's willingness to discuss terrorist crimes at length with her family, and friends such as Fulton, shows that she needed no encouragement to discuss such matters. Admissions made in those circumstances cannot be said to have been made because of her contact with undercover police officers. The third is that to characterise the contacts between her and the undercover police officers as amounting to offers to her "of a range of inducements" to make incriminating statements is unjustified. The use of the term "inducement" implies that an improper incentive has been offered to the accused, as a result of which she has made an unreliable confession.

Looking at the evidence as a whole I am satisfied beyond reasonable doubt that Gibson did not suffer from an abnormality of mind at the time covered by these tapes... That is not to say there may not have been occasions when she was affected by alcohol or a combination of alcohol and prescription drugs, and occasionally cannabis, which may on occasion render her admissions unreliable and where there is evidence suggesting that was or could have been the case, I will exclude the relevant

tape... I do not accept that, as her instructions suggested, she
was drinking heavily or misusing prescription drugs, or taking
illicit drugs on a virtually daily basis throughout this period.

The issue of direct questioning was the subject of written submissions by the defence who submitted "all of the taped conversations between the defendant and Sam and or Dave S amounted in effect to the functional equivalent of an interrogation and should be disregarded."

The judge responded:

To a considerable extent these submissions repeat points which
I have already considered when ruling on the admissibility of
the evidential tapes and I do not propose to rehearse again my
reasons for holding that the evidential tapes which have not
been excluded were not the functional equivalent of an interro-
gation... A point upon which considerable reliance is placed is
that Gibson was no longer free to resile from admissions she
had made in conversations that have been excluded, and indeed
was liable to expand upon them. Even though the admissions
may be separated by significant periods of time, it is impossible
to say that the later (admissible) admissions would have been
made even if the earlier (inadmissible) admissions had not. This
is a factor that ought to weigh heavily with the Court in respect
especially of admissions made to Dave S and Sam, who repeat-
edly breached the rule that direct questions were not permitted
to such an extent that they were removed from the covert sur-
veillance operation.

Mr Justice Hart continued:

As the defence concede the court is bound to exclude from its
consideration the contents of other tapes that have already been
ruled inadmissible. Where the admission was not prompted,
then there is nothing to cause the defendant to choose to speak,
even if she repeated or expanded upon admissions she had
made on other occasions, usually weeks, if not months, before.
In those circumstances I do not consider that what Gibson may
have said in an excluded conversation can be said to "taint" a

later admission. On the later occasion she was completely free to decide whether to talk or not, and the admissions appear to be entirely voluntary and spontaneous. To suggest that her decision to talk about criminal offences she had apparently committed could be regarded as "tainted" by what happened long before is, in my opinion, unsustainable. She, like Fulton, was quite prepared to boast about her terrorist activities to those she thought she could trust, such as her family and/or Fulton. Unfortunately for her, her loquaciousness betrayed her when she was speaking to people who were, unbeknown to her, undercover officers. I consider that there is no basis for regarding her admissions as unreliable on that ground.

In his final written judgement, Mr Justice Hart returns to the question of alcohol and drugs in relation to every single admission or admissions that the Crown say is sufficient to convict Fulton and Gibson. We now turn to some of the grave crimes they were accused of and they are an essential part of the whole story of Operation George because the result justified the resources and cost of such a long-running covert operation.

CHAPTER 34

The Crimes with the Evidence

William James Fulton

The Events of 4 and 5 June 1999

Counts 1 – 13 of the indictment cover three incidents that occurred on the night of 4 and early hours of 5 June 1999. They occurred shortly before Fulton went to America. By then it is apparent that he had long since transferred his allegiance to the LVF, and to judge from the admissions relating to the events of that night, was the leader of the LVF in Portadown at that time.

The Attack on Mr Murnin's House

The Narrative

Mr Murnin lived in a bungalow in Hilltown which is about midway between Newry and Newcastle. It is about twenty-four miles south east of Portadown and normally about a forty-minute drive. On 4 June 1999, Mr Murnin was in the house with his four children aged between seven years and six months. His wife was out at a church function and the children had just gone to bed. His nephew Mark Murphy was also there as he was staying the night. Mr Murnin was sitting watching TV in the chair in the corner of the room, close to the large window that faces out to front of the bungalow. As was his usual practice when watching TV, he had switched on two wall lights either side of the fireplace.

At about 11:30 pm he heard something rattle on the roof but thought nothing of it. Moments later, he heard an object hitting the window then heard a loud explosion. The glass from the window rained in all around him but he was uninjured. He then heard squealing tyres outside at which he checked to see if his children were unharmed. Thankfully, he found they were fine and moved them to a backroom, asking his nephew to watch over them whilst he went outside. Mark Murphy had been in bed at the time, but he told his uncle he also had heard glass smashing and a car screeching away.

Venturing outside his home, Mr Murnin, as a matter of caution, did not go round the front of the house but checked from the side of the bungalow. He saw there was damage to the front window and to the kerb outside. He also noticed white fragments on the roof that hadn't been there before the incident. He also saw that some of the glass was damaged in his work van parked at the front of the house. Police later arrived confirming the damage to the window, the kerb and the rear doors of the van. A detective found a ring pull and the flyoff lever for a hand grenade, both on a grass bank quite close to the road surface. That area is outside the boundary fence at the front of Mr Murnin's house and beside the road. Prosecution experts later concluded the parts were from a Soviet RGD 5 type grenade thrown at the house. They were described as a factory produced, anti-personnel device and in the experts' opinion had it gone through the living room window and there was a person inside there was the potential for serious injury, if not death. They also observed that it had little use as an anti-property device, and that it was primarily used by loyalist terrorists.

As for the "screeching of tyres," the prosecution case was that Fulton drove from Portadown with the others to the scene of this attack in a Renault 5 belonging to his wife Tanya. After the attack he drove them back to Portadown because it was part of his plan that he intended to get back to his house before the other two attacks were carried out, in order that he would appear to have an alibi when the police came to see if he were at home, because suspicion would inevitably fall on him.

About 12:45 am on 5 June, the second and third incidents occurred virtually simultaneously in Portadown. Sergeant Bingham of the RUC heard two simultaneous explosions when he was carrying out a visual check point (VCP). Jayne Humphreys, a neighbour of Janelle Woods, heard a large bang at about a quarter to one in the morning of 5 June. Sergeant Brown, another RUC officer, went to the scene of what transpired to be the graver of the two incidents at the home of Mrs O'Neill because of a call timed at 0048, so these attacks were both carried out at about a quarter to one that morning. As we shall see, a blast bomb had been thrown into Mrs O'Neill's living room through a hole broken in the window with a brick.

The Murder of Mrs O'Neill

The Narrative

By 4 June 1999, Mrs Elizabeth Mary O'Neill and her husband had lived at their Portadown home for some thirty-six years. About 12.30 am on 5 June 1999, Mr O'Neill went upstairs to bed leaving his wife watching television. Before he could fall asleep, he heard a bang at the front of the house, followed by his wife shouting. Mr O'Neill had no idea what she was shouting, so he got up and started to make his way downstairs. Almost at the foot of the stairs, he saw his wife in the doorway leading from the front hall into the living room. Then an explosion that proved fatal for the fifty-nine-year-old grandmother. The pathologist described the injuries to her chest and heart as "a massive haemorrhage both externally and into the left chest cavity." There was also "sustained extensive mangling of her left hand consistent with her having been holding the device close to her body when it exploded."

From subsequent police investigations and forensic examinations, it was clear that the window at the front of the house was broken with a concrete brick and the explosive device was then thrown through one of the holes into the living rooms. Mrs O'Neill picked it up, no doubt in a vain attempt to throw it back into the street, but tragically the device exploded in her hand before she was able to do this, inflicting massive injury which caused her death.

Dr Murray of the Forensic Science Agency of Northern Ireland examined fragments of the explosive device and found several grooves on one of the fragments, and explained that, "The purpose of putting the grooves into the metal is to create lines of weakness – so that you have reduced the thickness of the metal to make it easier for the pipe to break up." Clearly, that was done to cause maximum injury to anyone close to the explosion.

The Attempted Murder of Janelle Woods

The Narrative

The third incident occurred at the home of Janelle Woods. Again, a blast bomb was thrown at the window, which it appears to have broken before it fell to the ground and exploded. The blast bombs used in both incidents in Portadown were described by Dr Murray as being devices of a type intended primarily as anti-personnel weapons.

Janelle Woods was 20 years old and lived close to the O'Neills in Portadown in 1999. On the night of 4 and 5 June Ms Woods, her eight-month-old child, her seventeen-year-old sister, and her boyfriend Steven Black were at home. Steven Black had fallen asleep whilst watching TV on a couch. He was awakened by a bang which was one of the two explosions heard by Sergeant Bingham. On opening the curtains, Mr Black found that the left-hand panel of the front bay window had been broken. Later, a pipe bomb in the form of a piece of metal plate approximately 80 millimetres square with a centrally drilled hole in it was discovered. It was lying amongst broken glass and wood outside and below the broken window. Dr Murray described these items as the remains of a pipe bomb: an improved explosive device which he described as a small hand-thrown device intended primarily as an anti-personnel weapon. A former boyfriend of Ms Woods stated how on an occasion when she was pregnant some drunken young men came to the house and said that her father was a Catholic, and that when the child was born, they would have to leave the estate.

The Admissions

Mr Justice Hart said:

> *When considering the charges in relation to Mrs O'Neill's death I have set out those passages in which Fulton admitted that he had ordered and planned the two attacks on Catholic houses that night and I do not propose to repeat them. I have already concluded that his admissions were true, and I am satisfied that the attack on Ms Woods was the second of the two attacks to which he referred. It is unnecessary to repeat the considerations that led me to conclude that Fulton's intention was to kill Mrs O'Neill. The same considerations satisfy me that his intention was to kill Ms Woods. The method and device used were the same, and it was the third attack of the three he directed and planned were to be carried out that night.*

> *Fulton referred to the murder of Mrs O'Neill, and to the part he played in it, on several occasions over a period of eight months between 22 March 2000 and 16 November 2000. The first occasion was on 22 March 2000, when Fulton, Gibson and her daughter were present in Gibson's house in Cambourne. No undercover officers were present and the recording, which covers the period from 17.09 to 21.24, came from a probe. This conversation took place shortly after Fulton had returned from the United States and moved to Plymouth. Fulton and Gibson were discussing the time they have spent in Gough Barracks and Fulton refers to Mrs O'Neill's murder. This was one of the occasions he got her Christian names wrong, saying she was Rosemary O'Neill, whereupon Gibson emphatically corrected him, saying she was Elizabeth Mary O'Neill. There then occurs a lengthy discussion in which he and Gibson refer to themselves and others being arrested and questioned following the murder, in the course of which differing recollections are expressed as to who was actually arrested. I have earlier referred to Fulton's alibi that he had given Dale and Rory a lift to the Coach, and he*

explains how he told the police that he wouldn't say who the people were that he had given a lift to, a position he maintained throughout the period he was questioned. He also referred to Dale in a fashion that shows he knew him well, even though, as we have seen, he told the police at one stage during his interviews that he did not know Dale's surname. This account of their common experiences leaves me in no doubt that Fulton deliberately lied to the police about his knowledge of Weatherhead when he was questioned after this arrest in 2001.

The second reference to the murder of Mrs O'Neill came two days later, on 24 March 2000. Again, this recording, which was between 13.00 and 16.56, came from a probe, and those present where the same as on 22 March 2000. He makes a passing reference to the murder of Mrs O'Neill, and then there is a discussion about why "Bug" (Philip Blaney) had admitted to involvement in Mrs O'Neill's murder, and to his apparently having implicated Fulton in one of the attacks that had taken place that night. Fulton then says, "It couldn't possibly have happened", and the exchange to which I've earlier referred takes place between himself and Gibson in connection with the Murnin incident.

The third reference to Mrs O'Neill's murder comes on 18 May 2000. Fulton drove Neill from Plymouth to Exeter and back in the morning. In the course of his description of the attack on Mr Murnin's house Fulton says:

"We went out and fucking, (inaudible) I gave the boys pipe bombs like", and later "I'd ordered the fucking two houses hit, with Catholics in them in our area"… "But they were only about fucking about a two minute walk from my front door, you know. So, fucking, I couldn't be in the area…"

The fourth reference to Mrs O'Neill's murder occurred on 13 July 2000. This is the result of a probe tape when Fulton, his wife Tanya and their children visit Gibson. No undercover officers are present. There is another discussion about Bug being charged, and Fulton is unsure about Mrs O'Neill's name, asking was she McNeill or O'Neill, and again Gibson puts him right, saying she was Elizabeth O'Neill. It seems that this remark was probably made shortly after a phone call at 19.30.

*A more significant reference is the fifth, which occurs when
Fulton and Dave are on a journey from Plymouth to London on
the morning of 16 August 2000. In the course of this conversation in the following passage Fulton says that he planned all
three attacks. He also explained the sectarian motive behind the
attack on Mrs O'Neill's house, the way the attack was carried
out and why he had taken a grenade and not a blast bomb.*

...and the one we all got arrested for fucking O'Neill Rosie
O'Neill...that silly old bat fucking it was the night I fucking
planned 3 of them what do you call it er I wouldn't throw them
no more after the last one I threw fucking wick bent on it
cracked when I lit it went to throw it, it bounced jumped on the
top of the wick right into the fucking neck of the fucking blast
bomb it got about 4 fucking foot from my hand and went off.

Dave: Fucking hell.

Jim: So the night I planned the three of them three different
units going out three different places I went out with a grenade
but I went into provie country right into where the provies live.

Dave: Yeah.

Jim: But er 3 of the other guys they went ...cracker like I must
admit it was a fucking real real strong fucking type, different
from the design we were using but it was out the same batches,
anyway so they put the window through first with a brick and
then tossed that in and she's so fucking house proud what's she
do she's sitting in the living room instead of fucking running
out that's sitting going psst on the floor instead of fucking running out frightened she picks it up and goes to throw it back out
of window she picks it up lifts it up to here and it goes off here
just completely blew her torso off from there...

Dave: Shit.

Jim: Just dismantled her.

Dave: What was she then.

Jim: She was a prod (laughs) well she er it was a mixed family.

The sixth reference to Mrs O'Neill's murder occurs on 30 August 2000 during a meeting with Gary where Fulton refers to being arrested and questioned about the murder, but he makes no admissions in relation to it. The seventh reference occurs on 19 September 2000 when he again referred to her murder in a passage in the course of a conversation with Robbie. His admissions relate not to his participation in the murder of Mrs O'Neill, but to the attack on Mr Murnin.

The eighth reference occurred on 25 September 2000 during a journey with Neil when he drove Neil to Great Portland Street in London. This the recording is from 0902 until 1110. The conversation turns to Bug who Fulton says had phoned him. He then goes on to describe how Bug has told them that he had implicated Fulton and Mahatma in Mrs O'Neill's murder. Fulton continued at page 151:

Well that's an impossibility for the simple reason is Bug was nowhere near me that night. He didn't even see me that night. I know he was on one of the moves but he what do you call er he didn't see me.

Whilst what Blaney might have said about Fulton is not evidence against Fulton, what is significant is Fulton's knowledge that he knew Blaney "was on one of the moves", in other words that he knew Blaney was involved in one of the episodes on the same night. He continued to discuss Blaney's activities, and refers to his actions that night, and to his being questioned by the police after the murder, saying "they [the police] already know I never done it". That is a clear denial of taking part in the attack on Mrs O'Neill. But he goes on to refer to his getting back to his house before the murder.

Jim: They already know they already know I never done it, but all they're trying to do was eh get me for ordering it cause actually when hers went off low and behold. Me and the wife were, I got back to the house before there's I had time it, what do you call it we had done ours I had time to get back to Portadown in County Armagh get into the house.

Neil: Ah.

Jim: Before that one went off and what do you call it I was in the house and the wife er, I wanted to stay downstairs the whole night just in case any fucking body come near the door what not. So we pulled a two seater sofa bed out, me and the wife. Got the big er sleeping bag down, lying there, we heard it going off.

The ninth reference by Fulton to Mrs O'Neill's murder occurs on 16 November 2000 during a conversation between himself, Gibson and one of her daughters. This conversation was recorded by a probe during the mid-afternoon between 1547 and 1656. Fulton refers at some length to allegations that appear to have been made in the United States about his involvement in the murder of Rosemary Nelson and other crimes, and in the course of his denials he referred to Mrs O'Neill's death.

No no no I actually thought that would have been you know what I mean but (inaudible) and this one cunt that's leading the congressional enquiry. The senate. I can't remember his fucking name. Fuck he has it fucking in for me. He's me a convicted LVF terrorist and everything like, (inaudible) leading fucking protestant fucking murder squads fucking responsible for over fourteen fucking murders and all.

Muriel: Mary Elizabeth O'Neill for instance.

Jim: Aye that's another reason why what the disagreement was ordering, me ordering me the death of Mary O'NEIL and throwing blast bombs.

Muriel: Mary Elizabeth O'Neil, 59 year old grandmother.

Jim: Went strictly against Billy WRIGHT's wishes that she was not to be touched. An order was given that she was not to be touched.

Muriel: Billy was already dead. (laughing).

Jim: That she had not to be touched, only I made sure she was, and then there was a policeman with a blast bomb (inaudible). We, I ordered everybody all our men to stay away from all that. None of our men were ever near there when that cop got blew up. They just thought those old (inaudible) with Mary.

I am satisfied that in the sentence beginning "He's me a convicted LVF terrorist" Fulton was recounting the way he was being portrayed in the congressional enquiry, and not admitting to his supposed activities. However, when he responds to Gibson's interjection about Mrs O'Neill what he says is quite different. He is plainly saying that he ordered her death and the throwing of the blast bombs, and that despite an order from Billy Wright that Mrs O'Neill was not to be touched, in his words "Only I made sure she was".

The tenth and final reference to his part in Mrs O'Neill's death occurred on 12 January 2001. This conversation occurred in a recording between 0950 and 1148 that morning. Dave's evidence was that after breakfasting together at the Port O' Call Café in Plymouth Fulton drove him to Reading Services. Fulton referred to the preparation for the various attacks, saying "I'd to give the order that all the rest of the boys were going out and everybody had their check times", and that he and his companions were going to go first to give them time to get back into town "before they went, they went, so think it was four attacks all together but they all had blast bombs".

The prosecution case is that Fulton planned all three attacks, and himself took part in the attack on Mr Murnin's house, as can be seen from the accounts he gave to two of the undercover officers. Speaking to Neil on 18 May 2000, he said:

I'd ordered the fucking two houses hit, with Catholics in them in our area, and

But they were only about, fucking about a two minute walk from my front door, you know. So, fucking, I couldn't be in the area but I, so I took two guys with me and we drove away up to fucking near Newcastle. Up to a Provie contractors house and I was using the wife's wee Renault 5 and it wouldn't go over 60 mph see.

He made the same assertion on 16 August 2000 when he was speaking to Dave, saying:

...the one we all got arrested for fucking O'Neill Rose O'Neill...that silly old bat fucking it was the night I fucking planned three of them.

Then on the same page he repeats that he had planned all three, saying:

So the night I planned the three of them three different units going out three different places I went out with a grenade but I went into Provie country right into where the Provies live.

In his submissions at the direction stage Mr Kerr pointed to further remarks by Fulton on 12 January 2001 where he again described to Dave how the attacks were part of a coordinated plan, part of which was that the attack on Mr Murnin's house was to be the first, and the others were to be carried out after sufficient time had elapsed to allow Fulton and his companions to return to Portadown. In B12 at page 193 occurs the following, which arose in the context of a discussion about Fulton's use of hand grenades which precedes it, and the description of the incident which follows unmistakeably refers to the attack on Mr Murnin's house.

I'd give all the order that all the rest of the boys were going out and everybody had their check times. We were, we were away outside country like so we were, we're going to go first, that would have give us time to get back into town before they went, they went, so, I think it was 4 attacks altogether but they had all blast bombs.

The prosecution rely on the inferences to be drawn from the use of anti-personnel devices in all three attacks and on Fulton's planning all three. If these accounts are true, then not only did Fulton decide that all of these attacks were to be carried out, and plan how they were to be carried out, but he was aware that anti-personnel devices were going to be used in each attack. These matters are relevant to the charges he faces in respect of Mrs O'Neill and Janelle Woods because they have a bearing on the intent that has to be established in respect of the first eight counts on the indictment.

In relation to counts 8, 9, 10 and 11 the prosecution case is that he planned and directed the attack, telling the others what to do, but the grenade was thrown by someone else, although Fulton was present. However, on his account, he also armed the hand grenade in his house before the attack, see B12 at page 193, and took it from one of the other attackers and straightened the pin before handing the grenade back to his companion and telling him to throw it. At B12 pages 193 and 194 he said:

…I had to grab a fuck sake give me the fucking thing. Pulled it off him and I straightened the pin out but eh then pulled it out there was only a fucking millimetre left, hear [sic] me there now pull it out and throw the cunting thing.

Therefore, although he is indicted on counts 8, 9, 10 and 11 as a principal offender, he did not throw the grenade. However, his presence, his actions in planning and preparing for the attack, taking part in it, and adjusting the pin to enable the grenade to explode when thrown, show that on his account he was taking part in a joint enterprise as an aider and abettor of the person who threw the hand grenade. It is from his avowed actions, as well as his declarations as to the purpose of the attack, that his intent is to be inferred. So far as count 12 is concerned, he was also taking part in a joint enterprise which, on the basis of his account, resulted in an explosion being caused, and he aided and abetted that by his actions, both before and during the attack. In respect of count 13, on his account he had actual possession of the grenade with knowledge of its properties when he armed it in Portadown and adjusted the pin at the scene of the attack, and therefore had possession as a principal offender, and not just as an aider and abettor.

…that wee car wouldn't do more than fucking 60 round the country roads. I was ripping, but I got away like back to Portadown.

The reference to "round the country roads" suggests that minor roads were used.

Fulton described this episode in four conversations with undercover officers, first to Neil on 18 May 2000, then to Dave on 16 August 2000, then to Robbie on 18 September 2000, and again to Dave on 12 January 2001. The first conversation with Neil on 18 May 2000 is contained in B3. The recording started at 0750, although there is no evidence when it finished. They are described as leaving the flat together and they drove to a café for breakfast, after which they continued their day's work with

Fulton driving, and Neil's evidence was Fulton drove him from Plymouth to Exeter and back. During that recording Fulton talked about hand grenades. At pages 30 to 31 he referred to his having thrown a Russian hand grenade and borrowing his wife's car because his was not working, and her car would not go over 60 mph. He described how he took two men with him "...and we drove away up to fucking near Newcastle. Up to a Provie contractors house..." He described how he had to reverse down the driveway, and then instructed Rory to use a breeze block to break the window, saying that "Dale put the grenade through the fucking window after the breeze block went through".

He then described how the person who had the grenade panicked and was unable to pull the pin out to activate the grenade.

Jim: A straight pull. He said Jim I can't get the pin out. Rory had already fucking broke the window, says Jim I can't get the pin out of the grenade, here's me fuck sake, give me the fucking thing, ripped it out like that there, hear me, now just fucking hold it, when you let go, throw it just spring it off and throw it, don't try and throw at the same time or it will spring it off some other direction, then, bang, fuck me, (inaudible) threw it it bounced off the fucking sill of the window landed on the driveway.

Neil: Oh no.

Jim: And I fucking don't, two doors were open, fuck want to feel the fucking stones. They near broke my fucking head, smoke just come flying into the car, them two jumped in the car. (Inaudible) and then they scooped everybody, and a week later they fucking scooped me.

Fulton's next reference to these events was on 16 August 2000 and is to be found at B5. As on 18 May the conversation takes place in the morning, the recording starting at 0947, and took place when Fulton and Dave were in a car together. Dave's evidence was that they met at 1047 in Plymouth, and he told Fulton to drive him to London, and on the way they stopped for breakfast at a Little Chef at Ilminster. Fulton referred to the murder of Mrs O'Neill and the use of blast bombs, saying at page 46:

So the night I planned the three of them three different units going out three different places I went out with a grenade but I went into Provie country right into where the Provies live.

At page 48 he said that he drove to the attack, saying that because of the area it was in "It was a real dodgy move like but I wanted this bastard he was er a construction worker."

Fulton then described the attack on the bungalow in this passage at page 49:

Jim: And he had fucking a van and all outside you could hear him sitting in the living room he had one of the wee windows open but just open about that and what do you call it er laughing and getting on with a couple of his workmates so I sent the boys down I says to em make sure you break the fucking window first cos it was a big double glazing window I says now fucking hit, you have to hit...to break a double glazing window that size you throw it at the middle it'll bounce off anything at all even a brick you have to hit it at the bottom quarter panels that's when it'll shatter the whole window I says now lift a good size fucking brick, break the corner of the fucking window and toss the fucking grenade in he says no problem so the 2 guys go out wee man he runs up game as a badger big fucking house brick whack...fucking the corner of the window goes through that was alright so they started jumping about in the house so we had to put it through there and then the fucking other wee guy runs over to me and goes like that Jim I can't get the fucking pin out. Here's me you what , give me the fucking thing, now I'm sitting on your man's driveway in a clean car and the window not even broke and lights were going on just all over the place and I fucking just grips pulls the pin out I says now hold that once you get out of the car let it fucking go and toss it through the window the boy who was letting it go he panicked and fucking threw it at the window all it did it exploded outside the fucking outside the window shattered the rest of the window and fucking threw up shit everywhere.

Fulton's next reference to this episode was to Robbie on 19 September 2000 and is to be found in B8 at page 127. He was discussing how he had been arrested and questioned about the O'Neill murder, and in the course of the discussion said that he had used his wife's Renault 5 for the grenade attack, which is plainly a reference to the attack on Mr Murnin's house:

Because the night O'Neill was killed my car stayed at the house but nobody had knew I'd took the wife's car a wee Renault 5, it was a shit car. It wouldn't go over sixty miles an hour, but it was a clean as a whistle and nobody on this earth I don't care who you are would have contemplated that I'd have used that on a move. But (mumbled word) Robbie I had went near eighty-miles away in to a Provie area with two, two boys with me for the grenade attack in that car, there's nobody Robbie, even if you drove up to the checkpoint and all, being out of the area you got the chance of nobody recognising you, you know at night time and that wee car there you were getting waved on, nobody in their right mind is going out in that car to do something...

Two points arise from this. The first is that Fulton describes how he took a calculated risk in using a small car in poor condition for this attack because it would not go over 60 miles an hour, but he did so because nobody would think he would use it, it was an improbable car to be used by terrorists and so it was unlikely he would be recognised, and for these reasons it was unlikely they would be stopped at checkpoints. The second is that he went into what he described as "Provie area" obviously an area where he would not be welcomed. This description certainly suggests that he was prepared to take risks but the risks were calculated ones. His statement that "I had went near 80 miles away into a Provie area" was emphasised by the defence as not just being inconsistent with the facts, but so exaggerated that it indicates that Fulton's account could not be true. If that is read as meaning that the journey was 80 miles each way, and that is the obvious meaning, then it is grossly inaccurate. It could, however, imply that the journey was 80 miles in all, including both legs of the journey. If that were the case, then the inconsistency with the known facts is much less. That that was the intended meaning is, however, less likely from the words used.

The final references to this incident occurred on 12 January 2001 and are to be found in B12. Like each of the three previous descriptions, this also occurred during a journey when Fulton drove Dave to Reading Services. Robbie was with them earlier in the morning but left them after they had breakfast together, the recording commencing at 0950 when Dave and Robbie met. They meet Fulton and had breakfast, and the recording stopped at 1148. Therefore the conversation between Dave and Fulton took place on a journey before noon. In that conversation there are references by Fulton to the manufacture and use of bombs involving what Fulton refers to as "carbine" (presumably a mistake for "carbide"). Fulton then turns to the subject of hand grenades, again telling Dave about the attack on Mr Murnin's house, going into considerable detail about his role in the preparation of the attack, as well as in the attack itself.

Although Fulton's earlier account of this episode had been quite a detailed one, on this occasion he gave an even fuller account, as can be seen from the following passages at pages 193, 194 and 195.

I have seen them there I've never used one of them but the last one I used. Proper shrapnel grenade was just like a wee round apple just with a wee neck on. Just pull the pin, just let her go. But you want to actually hear the percussion cap going off first before it ignites the explosives.

Dave: Right.

Jim: It's a fuck quare bang off it alone. Know what I mean aye. [redacted]. I'd give all the order that all the rest of the boys were going out and everybody had their check times. We were, we were away outside country like so we were, we're going to go first, that would have give us time to get back into town before they went, they went, so, I think it was 4 attacks altogether but they had all blast bombs. I had the little grenade, so I took the boys way out country, me and Mahatma were in the house first arming it, I had a, I had a bullet-proof jacket on backwards. You know right down here what do you call it I'm sitting like that as if it's really going to fuck'n know save me like sitting with a grenade in my hand just screw it right in once you screw it past a certain point that's it armed. Know what I mean so you can't fuck about with them, so we drive down to this house, Republican build, he was a building contractor, but he's a Republican, way in the middle of a republican area, like 30 miles in any direction like, if you'd have been fucking caught anywhere, know they'd have butchered you, butchered you. But as usual what do you call it eh, short notice I had to grab a fucking a clean car. Fuck'n the wife was driving this stupid wee Renault 5 GTL or something and it was a heap of fucking shit, the cunting thing wouldn't go. It took a big hill to get it up to fuck'n 80 mile an hour. Know what I mean but it was totally clean know what I mean so there was no fucking books on it whatsoever. So there was fuckin 3 of us jumped into it me and the (inaudible). Took us about an hour to get there, we were running against the clock, like. I says right boys, I says you get out I says Robo you grab a brick. Up, break the fuckin now. It's a big double glazed front fuckin window, in this big bungalow, make sure you hit it down about down one of the corners don't throw it in the middle cos it'll bounce back, big brick hit the corner of it, fuckin er that'll break it and then lob the fuckin grenade in or the fucking grenade will just bounce off the window. Ah there's no problem. The two of them gets out, fucking the first one fair enough they'd never used a grenade before know what I mean, and in the heat of the moment, know what I mean I didn't think know what I mean common sense would have know to fuckin its just like you know one of them pins, just flatten the edges out till there (sic) straight and then just pull it like any jubilee clip, so fuckin eh.

(Dave coughs).

Jim: All I hears this crack the window going in then all the fuckin lights in the house going on, er yer wee man comes back to the car and he say I can't get the pin out. Fuckin hell I'm sitting in yer man's driveway in this wee fucking stupid, wee fucking Renault 5. I says for fuck sake give me the fuckin thing. Pulled it off him and I straightened the pin out but eh then pulled it out there was only a wee fuckin millimetre left, hear me there now just pull it out and fuckin throw the cunting thing. But, there was that much activity round the house the wee fella just run to the top of the driveway, just fuckin lobbed it, fuckin thing just bounced off the sill of the window and exploded, fuck me I'm not joking yer wanta see the shit hitting my fuckin car or the wife's car, I had all the windows open just in know what I mean cos the percussion from an explosion it would have put your windows in.

Dave: Oh right.

Jim: You know so I had all the windows down on the side of the car, the fuckin stones, shit hitting my fuckin face. Here's me ya wee bastard will yet get into the fuckin car. You want to see us trying to get away that wee car wouldn't do more than fuckin 60 round the country roads. I was ripping, but I got away like, got back to Portadown. As soon as I got into the house the wife was up staying in my house with the kids, I says right I had a sofa bed downstairs as well. Pull that sofa bed out, were watching T.V. downstairs. Eleven o'clock on the, or five past twelve on the button boom!

From these accounts it can be seen that Fulton described the events in considerable detail on four occasions over a period of twelve and a half months…

I have already referred to Fulton's defence that he was repeating what he had heard from others, that he inserted himself and friends and family into his account to make it seem more authentic, and that he was bragging to make himself appear a big man in the eyes of the firm, and I do not propose to repeat it. He was questioned about the Murnin incident at considerable length during his first interview. He made no reply, even though one of the matters put to him was the possibility that he might want to say that he had read about it in the papers. In the second interview he was played the tape relating to the 18 May 2000 and then questioned about it. It was in the fourth and succeeding interviews that he made the defence that he was repeating a story he had picked up, although he could not be precise where he heard it. At page 44 when saying that he was not involved in the murder of Mrs O'Neill he said that earlier that night he had given Dale and Rory a lift to the Coach, when asked who they were he said he did not know their second names even when asked was he referring to Dale Weatherhead and Rory Robinson. Robinson has an obvious connection with the name "Robo" he used in the passage from page 194 set out earlier. The police returned to this in interview C12(b) at page 148 and Fulton then admitted that he had known Dale for four or five years. It is clear that he was caught out in an attempt to distance himself from Weatherhead by claiming him as an alibi, but then saying that he did not know him that well, when, as he was driven to say at page 151, "Yous are well aware I know

Dale". There is nothing to support this alibi and I am satisfied that it was false for the reasons I give later.

I am satisfied that on each of the four occasions he recounted the part he actually played in the attack on Mr Murnin's house. Fulton was not affected by alcohol or drugs because he was driving for long periods each time, and it is wholly implausible to suggest that he may have been affected in this way. I accept the evidence of the undercover officers on this. As earlier stated there can be no doubt that Fulton was bragging when he discussed these matters, the question is was he bragging about matters he had been involved in, or was he, or might he have been, describing events he had heard about and in which he was falsely claiming a role for himself to improve his standing in the eyes of the undercover officers whom he wrongly believed to be members of the criminal gang? Was what he said about his role in this attack true?

In addition, Fulton did not confine his discussion of his role in the attack on Mr Murnin to conversations with the undercover officers, because he discussed it with Gibson and Ayesha Landry on 24 March 2000 in B2, a recording from a probe when there were no undercover officers present. At page 16 there was a discussion about why "Bug" (Blaney) had admitted involvement in Mrs O'Neill's murder, and there then occurred the following exchange between Gibson and himself which plainly refers to the aftermath of the attack on Mr Murnin's house when he was safely in bed at home before the police came to his house to check his whereabouts. Gibson refers to his being "away doing the other one", and Fulton says "But I was already back home".

Muriel: Because you had went on home as I remember.

Jim: No I was, I wasn't even in County Armagh.

Muriel: Aye, you were away doing t'other one whenever eh Philly went down to do that there.

Jim: But I was already back home, in the house with Tanya.

Muriel: Aye, in bed.

Jim: In, no we were actually put the, we put the, you know the couch bed, we had actually rolled it out to watch TV. We heard it going off and when it went off, me and her were looking through the fuckin blinds and a Landrover come up, parked in front of the house and shone the lights, flood, flash the lights at me and Tanya in the window, you know what I mean, so that was 2 seconds after it happened me and her were sitting, I had nothing on, she was sitting in her pyjamas wave, waving at the police so they knew it had nothing to do with me. You know, all they had me in for was directing it, directing you know all the attacks, that's all.

Muriel: That's what I said to Gabriel I said they are going to try and get Jim on a Directing Charge here.

The significance of this passage is that the account tallies with the account he gave to the undercover officers, eg to Neil on 18 May 2000, B3 at pages 32 and 33, and to Dave on 16 August 2000, B5 at page 51. Not only has he been consistent in his account, but he has given some of the details to Gibson and her daughter, and Gibson's intervention shows that she was aware of his having taken part. This conversation cannot be explained as having been an attempt to impress the undercover officers.

Verdicts

Count 8, the attempted murder of Mr Murnin. Fulton has described how they took a Russian grenade, which was armed by him, and how he pulled out the pin at the scene to enable it to be thrown by one of his companions, who he then told to throw it through the hole in the window to be broken for that purpose. The use of an anti-personnel weapon, and the determination Fulton displayed to ensure that the hand grenade was thrown into the room, leads me to the inescapable conclusion that the occupant of that room, whom he believed was Mr Murnin, would be killed, and that is what he meant when he said at page 89 "I wanted this bastard". Fulton would not have set up such an elaborate attack, involving as it did his taking a calculated and considerable risk that he would be caught, and driving so far, merely to intimidate Mr Murnin out of his house, or to frighten him. I am satisfied that his intent was to kill Mr Murnin, but fortunately the plan miscarried because one of his fellow attackers blundered in his role, and Mr Murnin escaped injury. I am satisfied that count 8 has been proved and I find him guilty on that count.

Count 9 is a count of attempted murder of Mark Murphy, Mr Murnin's nephew. There is no evidence where he was in the house at the time, anymore than there is evidence where Mr Murnin's children were either. When I asked Mr Kerr at the direction stage why there were no counts in respect of Mr Murnin's children, he very reasonably replied that one would not tend to bring a charge in respect of every person who happened to be in the house. Whilst Fulton intended that whoever was in the room into which the grenade was thrown would be killed, that does not necessarily mean that he intended to kill all the occupants of the house, although there is a strong inference that he was indifferent as to who was killed, provided that Mr Murnin was. However, there is no evidence that he knew that there were any other occupants of the house as he makes no reference to them, although he possibly was aware that there were others living in the house. Another factor is that Dr Murray described this type of grenade at page 91 as one where it became less lethal the further people are away from the explosion.

This type of grenade is an anti-personnel weapon designed for use in an offensive role. The fragmentation produced upon initiation of the explosive filling, approximately 110 grammes of TNT, is most effective at close range but the potential for lethality falls off very rapidly with increasing distance from the explosion. Grenades have been accounted [presumably this should be "encountered"] on numerous occasions in Northern Ireland particularly attributable to Loyalist extremists.

There is no evidence where the others where in the bungalow, or to say what the risk was to them had the grenade exploded in the room where Mr Murnin was. These facts might suggest that the prosecution have failed to prove that Fulton had the necessary intention to kill Mark Murphy. That would be to take an unrealistic view of the entirety of the circumstances involved in this attack. Mr Murnin's children had been in the room until not long before the attack. If they, or Mark Murphy, had been in the room with him, would they not have been encompassed by his intention to kill? Terrorists who carry out sectarian murder attempts of this type are completely indifferent to who may be killed provided that their intended victim is killed. I am satisfied that Fulton shared this indifference to the full and I find him guilty on this count.

Count 10 is an alternative to the count of attempted murder of Mr Murnin and I find the accused guilty on this count. Count 11 is a similar charge of attempted grievous bodily harm in relation to Mark Murphy and for the reasons already given in relation to the attempted murder charge relating to him I find him guilty on this count. Given my findings as to Fulton's intention, and as he armed the grenade at his home before setting out, prepared it for use at the scene by partially extracting the pin, and instructed his companion to throw it into the room once the window was broken, Fulton clearly had the necessary intent to endanger life, or to enable others to do so, and had possession of the grenade. I find him guilty on counts 12 and 13

Attempted Murder of RUC Officers at Drumcree on 9 July 1998

The Narrative

The Twelfth[17] approaches and about a quarter to midnight on the night of the 9 July 1998, a bomb explodes, gravely wounding RUC officers deployed as part of a police and army human shield to prevent an Orange parade from passing down the Garvaghy Road after attending a church service at the nearby Drumcree Church. Besides that human shield, the protestors were separated from the police by several physical obstacles. There was a water-filled ditch some several feet wide. It had been built either by digging a new ditch or widening an existing ditch. In addition, lines of barbed wire were in place with a final line of rows of barbed and razor wire several feet thick and some feet high. It took on the appearance of a war zone.

On the other side of the ditch a large crowd were gathered. It was some thousands strong according to one who was present. The crowd had made violent and prolonged attempts to breach the police lines that

---

[17] The Twelfth of July: the height of the Orange marching season.

night. Chief Inspector Barr described a constant hail of missiles consisting of bottles, stones, heavy duty fireworks, and ball bearings thrown at the police. To blind the police, heavy duty lights and laser pens were also directed at them from the crowd. Occasionally, the police moved forward to prevent the demonstrators dismantling the wire using poles and grappling hooks. This precipitated some of the officers coming closer to the crowd. As one group from a RUC Mobile Support Unit was retreating, the pipe bomb was thrown and exploded, injuring the officers named in the four counts.

Chief Inspector Barr suffered severe injuries to his lower left leg with damage to the muscles and tendons, as well as some damage to his right leg above his ankle. In the immediate aftermath, he believed he would lose his left leg. It was two and a half years before he could resume any duty. Reserve Constable Irvine also received serious leg injuries, and whilst being treated for his injuries at Craigavon Hospital his lung collapsed. The severity of his injuries meant that he was unable to resume his duties as a full-time reserve constable. Constable Harkness also received serious injuries to his lower left leg. He was in hospital for several weeks and was unable to resume his duties as a serving officer. The fourth officer to be injured was Constable McBrien. He was operated upon at the Ulster Hospital, and a piece of metal was subsequently removed from his left thigh.

The Admissions

The admissions upon which the prosecution rely to bring home these charges against Fulton are contained in relates to a conversation between Robbie and Fulton on 11 January 2001 between 08.46 and 21.51. Robbie's unchallenged evidence was that during this time they travelled by car to Exeter and back. Although it was not expressly stated, I am satisfied that the journey started and finished in Plymouth as that was where Fulton lived. Robbie's evidence was that they travelled in Fulton's car, and as he was employed by the firm as a driver, I infer that Fulton was driving. Pages 270 to 275 record Fulton describing at some length his presence at various meetings with

*leading Loyalist terrorists, as well as some of his own actions,
and the use of kneecapping and murder to ensure that commands of terrorists such as Billy Wright and Swinger were
obeyed. At page 275 he started to describe the confrontation at
Drumcree between the demonstrators on one side and police or
soldiers on the other. He described how the moat (as he accurately described it) was built, and the rows of barbed wire
created a sense which he said, "was like the Somme", a meta-
phor which accurately conveys the scene portrayed in the
photographs in Exhibit A21. At page 277 he described how the
crowd was used for cover and he threw a blast bomb which exploded amongst the police, several of whom fell to the ground.*

Jim: But you want to see all the people there are thousands of
people just standing upon the bank, what do you call it, just facing over all the police lines and all and we got the fucking and
we got down there, we've come across fucking ambush style
like that there right up in between them and then we turns round
and says right everybody when we say go just part for us and
they just fucking parted throw in one of the grenades (Jim
makes a noise like explosions).

Robbie: Did you get them?

Jim: Oh fuck aye, see my first blast bomb I threw landed right
in the middle of thirty, a group of thirty fucking policemen all
standing with fucking masks on hoods on like that with their rifles and all (inaudible), just parted slightly and I had lit it it's a
fucking about a three second fuse, fucking such a throw like I
have a (inaudible) from throwing it straight in you (inaudible),
just seen it exploding and what do you call it just see peelers
fucking falling to the ground and all like then, up and our fella
came up machine gun then the thirty eight.

*Although he does not give a year for this episode, at page 278
he says, "but then the third year, that's when it came to a fucking head like", which suggests that it was during the third year
of protest at Drumcree that the throwing of the blast bomb he
had earlier described took place.*

*The next reference occurred on 16 May 2001 and is to be found
in B18. This covers the period between 00.52 and 06.00, and
records a conversation between Fulton, his brother Swinger,*

and Swinger's wife Louise. The conversation contains many references to individuals including Fulton's cousin Gary, Mutley (Ian Stewart) and others. The conversation is critical of many of those to whom they refer, particularly Mutley. I have already described the reference by Fulton at page 300 to being ordered by "Brigade Staff" to collect money "for the organisation", and in part there is an element of regret that things in Portadown were not what they were. Given that the conversation is taking place a few weeks before the 2001 Drumcree parade it is not surprising that in the following passage at page 302 they speculate about what might happen at Drumcree that year.

Swinger: Watch Drumcree this year, nobody will be at it.

Jim: What did ... tell Louise.

Swinger: See last year they were firing shots.

Jim: Tell Louise what I said.

Swinger: The year before it up firing shots, I was missing for two years.

Jim: The day of Drumcree last year where wa... where was I. I was in the States, I walked away.

Swinger: See the year before when I was (inaudible) jail Jim.

Jim: I told you before (inaudible) visit, what did I tell you when I was the visit, its finished.

Swinger: Who's the only ones opened up on the police 1998.

Jim: We were.

Swinger: Aye and who's the orangemen give off about them.

Jim: They were.

Swinger: Right, that's it over, its finished, its done, its dusted, its over. They'll stand there for the next twenty years and I will laugh at them. God forbid me but I will laugh at them. No matter who comes to my door.

The final reference is to be found in B112, which contains the discussion between Fulton and Gabriel Yellow between 00.52 and 04.43 on 7 June 2001 to which reference has already been made. As in the case of B18 this is the result of a probe. Fulton describes in considerable detail how to make various types of explosive device, including one he said he made with Mahatma using a spark plug that could be detonated when the engine of the car is turned on. During this conversation Fulton refers to blast bombs in the following passages...

Fulton was questioned in interview about what he had said about throwing the blast bomb at Drumcree. He accepted that he had been at Drumcree on several occasions, saying that he simply stood "with another hundred thousand people" and walked about. At pages 156 and 157 he maintained that he had never thrown a blast bomb, saying that he had gained his knowledge from what he had seen on TV, and when he described how to make blast bombs he was simply saying what was common knowledge.

Fulton: I never threw no blast bomb. It was me just being bravado. Know what I mean I'd seen it on TV, it was know what I mean so it was legitimate, I could know what I mean there was no problem I could get a video and show know what I mean so I could make it beli, so believable...

... It showed you, I don't know whether it was Spotlight or whatever, wee circles round people coming down and getting up, some guy getting up and throwing something. Another guy getting up and letting a shot off. I mean anybody could have know that I mean it was all on TV. They actually put a wee light spot around the heads of the people running down. I mean anybody could have fucking said that.

Q: Well tell us how you do it.

Fulton: I don't know how you do it. I'm only surmising by looking at them. I have never seen, I have never been up close to one so I couldn't tell you.

Q: Well you've told this undercover policeman how to make one.

Fulton: Aye that's me just letting on I know how to make them.
I've never been close to one to tell you exactly how to make
them.

*During interview Fulton said that he had made up this account
of his involvement from what he had seen on TV, and that it was
common knowledge round town how to make blast bombs, and
that he made this up to make him "look real good with the
firm". Although it is conceivable that a person could invent
such a simple account of the type that Fulton gave, his reason
for doing so does not bear examination. Whilst the description... was given to Robbie, and therefore is consistent with
Fulton's explanation, the references in... were not made when
there were undercover officers present, and hence Fulton had
no reason to invent stories in order to impress members of the
firm. On the contrary, his discussion with his brother shows
that they were deeply involved in terrorist activity.*

*Have these admissions been brought about by the effect of
drugs and or alcohol? The conversation in B16 occurred during a car journey when I am satisfied Fulton was driving, and
for the reasons I have given I am satisfied that he was not affected by alcohol and or drugs on that occasion. The
conversations in B18 and B112 both took place after midnight,
and the possibility that he may have consumed alcohol or drugs
to a material extent is one that has to be considered, given Fulton's propensity to drink heavily on occasions, and to consume
cannabis, during this period. However, there is no evidence to
suggest that on either of these occasions he was materially affected by drugs or alcohol, and I therefore discount the
possibility that the reliability of either of these admissions is undermined by these factors.*

Verdicts

*Fulton faces ten charges relating to a serious incident at
Drumcree on the night of 9 July 1998 when an improvised explosive device in the form of a pipe bomb was thrown from the
crowd at the police lines. The pipe bomb exploded near the police, and such was the effect of the explosion that four officers
were gravely injured. Four of the counts are of attempted murder of each of the injured officers, four of wounding with intent*

*of the same officers, and the two remaining counts are of caus-
ing an explosion of a nature likely to endanger life or cause
serious injury to property, and possession of a pipe bomb with
intent to endanger life or cause serious injury to property.*

*Having considered all of the evidence I am satisfied that these
admissions are reliable and true. I am satisfied that Fulton
threw a blast bomb at the police lines, and from the nature of
the weapon and the circumstances in which it was thrown I am
also satisfied that his intention was to kill, or if unsuccessful, to
wound the officers, and that he was fully aware of the nature of
the device he threw. He therefore had the intent necessary to
constitute the offences of attempted murder and attempted
wounding with intent, as well as the offences under the Explosive Substances Act. Accordingly, I find him guilty on counts 14
to 23.*

Attempted Robbery of Conor McAleavy 25 October 1996

The Narrative

Mr Conor McAleavy was the manager of the Ulster Bank in Newcastle,
County Down, and lived with his wife and daughter in that same town.
Just after midnight on 25 October 1996, he was sitting alone downstairs
watching TV, his wife having earlier gone to bed, when he heard someone at the front door. He was unable to see who it was and opened the
door to see a man dressed in a police uniform who said, "Are you Mr
McAleavy?" He replied, "Yes."

The man then said, "The alarm's gone off at the bank."

McAleavy replied, "Not again". He was accustomed to false alarms
on a windy night. But the man in police uniform walked past him into
the house. Before he could protest, he felt an object pushed into his neck
as the first man was followed into the house by three or four other men.
Mr McAleavy was then told to lie down in the inner hall.

One of the men stood over him and said something like, "I'm going to" or "We're going to stiff you."

Mr McAleavy wasn't prepared to just lie there so raising himself to
his full six foot three inches he exchanged blows with the intruders

during which he received a heavy blow to the top of his head. Despite that, he was able to escape upstairs, trying to alert his wife to what was happening. As he was halfway up the stairs, he heard the man following him on the stairs call out, "Give me the gun."

Mr McAleavy got into a bedroom, lay down on the ground and jammed his feet against the door. The robbers decided to flee throwing a dining room chair through a window to affect their escape.

The robbers fled on foot leaving their car behind. The man who was wearing the police uniform made his way through to the banks of the Burren River, abandoning his police tunic and tie as he did so. It is likely that at least one, probably two, of the others accompanied him on this route, because two balaclavas were found in the same area during the subsequent search.

Admissions

The judgement of Mr Justice Hart said:

> *This was plainly a carefully prepared attempt to seize Mr McAleavy and force him to open the bank. A complete police uniform had been acquired so that he could be tricked into thinking that the person at the door was a police officer. The reference to the alarm going off in the bank suggests that their intention was to persuade him to go to the bank, and that they knew that Mr McAleavy would not be surprised at this request. That suggests that they had information about the bank alarm going off from time to time. That there were at least four men involved indicates that they probably intended to hold his family until the robbery was over, an extremely common practice in this jurisdiction when banks, post offices, or businesses where large sums of money are kept, are the subject of planned robberies when the robbers go first to the home of a member of staff. The reference to a gun by the man who pursued Mr McAleavy upstairs; the hard object he felt pressed against his neck, and the references to being "stiffed", strongly suggest that the robbers had either a real or an imitation firearm with them in the house, although Mr McAleavy did not say that he*

saw one. That Moore was soaked when arrested is consistent with his having gone into the Burren River, and Fulton's admissions link him to the crime. That the three men asked to be driven to Portadown is highly suspicious, but no more than that without evidence linking them to the attack, although the time at which they came to the taxi depot is consistent with them being part of the gang who had been stranded in Newcastle because they had abandoned their car.

The admissions relied upon relates to a conversation between Neil and Fulton between 1340 and 1535 on 30 March 2000. Their first meeting had been on 24 March 2000 and this is therefore very early in Fulton's relationship with Neil and the other members of the firm. It refers to Neil giving directions) and asking to be dropped off, so it is clear that Fulton is driving. Neil is recorded as telling Fulton to keep the car clean, no tickets. During the journey the conversation between Fulton and Neil can best be described as a virtual monologue by Fulton, who talks at length about robberies at banks, ATMs, and post offices, as well as the plan to rob Martin Phillips (which is the subject of count 56 – incident 17), and the emergence of the LVF when the followers of Billy Wright left the UVF to form their own organisation, interspersed by occasional remarks by Neil.

Fulton refers to robbing banks by taking over the bank manager's house, and then making the manager open the ATM from inside for example. Having talked about these robberies, and their frequency, in a general way, he then describes how he was responsible for planning the attack on Mr McAleavy.

The next reference is a conversation between Fulton and Dave on 23 August 2000 between 0847 and 1542 in Fulton's council house in Plymouth. Fulton talked at length about the attack on the home of a prison officer (Mr Terry, incident 10 – count 37) and his prominent role in the LVF. They discussed the need to have good intelligence when planning a crime, and how long it can take to prepare some crimes. Fulton then proceeds to describe the attack on Mr McAleavy's home in detail, in very much the same terms as in the first description to Neil but referring expressly to some matters that were implicit in the account he gave to Neil.

The third reference is found in a recording on 30 November
2000 starting at 1218 although the finishing time is not known.
The conversation on this occasion is with Robbie and occurred
on a journey to Bristol with Fulton driving. Robbie's estimate
was that the journey from Plymouth to Bristol could take one
and a half to two hours. It appears that the journey had some-
thing to do with a Belgian buying a picture. During their
conversation there were comments by Fulton about how some
individuals could shoot people but not rob banks, and vice
versa. There was then the following exchange.

Jim: Where as you know what I mean I'm a sort of all round
guy.

Robbie: If he is a sort of Jack of All Trades and Master of
None.

Jim: Yeah exactly. Oh no not really. (Both are laughing).

Robbie: Walked into that.

Jim: I am a master of very few now. Well put it this way I've
made the mistakes in every trade there is to know, what's the
right way and what's the wrong way.

Robbie: What's been the biggest fuck up you've had though.

Jim: Eh one of my jobs but I wasn't on, know what I mean, I
wasn't allowed to go on it because I was running things but I
set the whole thing up and then they used other men through request I used different people and the whole thing fucked up.
Five guys fucking went to a house. Got the house open no problem what do you call eh paid expensive for the clean car and all
because you know what I mean it was hundred per cent certain.
The guys go into the house exactly the way I told them, I had
your man in the policeman's uniform, everything, clipboard and
all bank managers house. Got through the door no problem. He
took the security off the door, let them in, once they got in your
man 45 under the clipboard straight to his head put him on the
ground. The man got down no problem, but then I don't know
what all went wrong I've heard so many different stories about
it. There was four of them on the move, five of them altogether
counting the driver, the other three guys run into the house all

wearing combats and hoods but once he seen them coming your man freaked and it is true when your frightened you do your strength, you know what I mean you do get bursts of strength.

From the end of this passage went on to describe at some length what had happened and how the operation had gone wrong. He repeated that it was his responsibility, saying "... but at the end of the day the buck stops with me, it was my move". He described how he had agreed to use two men at the request, and on the recommendation, of his brother Swinger and Billy Wright as a favour, implying that it was because of these two men that the plan miscarried.

The fourth reference to this episode is to be found later in the same conversation when Robbie said to Fulton that he had not finished the story of the attack on the bank manager. Fulton then explains in some detail what happened after the robbers fled from the scene, and what he did...

When the garage owner who had sold the car to Fulton panicked, anticipating that he would be questioned, Fulton instructed him to leave the car keys under the mat in each car, the inference being that the garage owner could then pretend the car had been stolen and thereby successfully distance himself from any knowledge of what had occurred.

The final reference is to be found in a probe recording of a conversation between Fulton and Yellow in a car driven by Fulton on 7 June 2001 between 2021 and 2224. In the course of the conversation Fulton describes his role in the Newcastle episode in this passage from page 21 onwards.

There's no police on the ground at 12 o'clock in Newcastle and I knew that the alarm at the front of the house was faulty and I knew that the bank had a faulty alarm system, and I'll tell you better (inaudible) to set the alarm off, so the police were regularly, every, you know every couple of months every once a week, you know down at this door knock, knock, knock the alarm's off at the bank. So I sent a wee guy to his door all in the RUC uniform, clipboard, 38 under the clipboard, knocked the door (over talking inaudible). No, Mr McAnally, em, it's the alarm at the bank. His exact words were "Ah for fuck sake, not again, come on in officer". Door open like that, 12 o'clock at night, walked straight in, gun to the head, put him on the ground, no problem. They'd all charged in, no, another three of them charged in after him and when your man, your man he was a tall guy like but as I already said say, he was already on the ground but all he though of straight away when he seen the masks and the combats coming in (audible words) (sic), he, know what I mean he just freaked and the four of them couldn't even hold him down, they pistol whipped him and everything and he headed upstairs to the bedroom, locked the door in the bedroom and called the police.

Gabriel: Aye.

Jim: They even locked themselves in the house and they had to break a big fuckin plate glass window with a big ornate chair to get out the house.

Gabriel: Laughs.

Jim: Cause there was a combination fucking know lock on the front door.

Gabriel: Ah, fuck me Jim.

Jim: Lost the keys to the car too, it was left in the driveway 900 quid fuckin car. Wasn't a cheap car we had paid extra for it because it was fuckin.

Gabriel: Eh.

Jim: Cause the crime was so perfect. I mean I had everything done.

Gabriel: Cost them fuckin money.

Jim: Aye it cost me.

Gabriel: (Inaudible) all the fuckin education behind it, boy and you think (inaudible).

Jim: I had (inaudible) the team to do it only Swinger come, Swinger Swinger and Billy both come to me and said look Jim, one last favour, please let Tony come on this with you. (Audio distorts), I'll bring him round with me I says I'll go over ...

This is therefore a succinct, but comprehensive, summary of the accounts Fulton gave on other occasions, incorporating the essential features of his involvement. In it he again says that the car cost £900. He also says that it was left in the driveway, whereas it was found on the roadside in front of the house.

In these accounts Fulton described how he had planned every aspect of this attack on Mr McAleavy's home, and the objective was to gain access to the bank and steal a very large amount of money. It was an essential element of the plan that an imitation gun was to be used, and so it involved at least the threat of force, and, as the actions of the robbers in trying to subdue Mr McAleavy show, they were prepared to use force if necessary. Mr McAleavy was plainly to be held captive, and was restrained briefly before he escaped, so if these accounts are true then Fulton is guilty of the charges of robbery and false imprisonment. When questioned, Fulton confined himself to saying that it had absolutely nothing to do with him (page 243); that he was not guilty (page 323), although in the next interview he said that he was bored (page 339). Apart from these responses, he made no reply when questioned.

Fulton's defence is that he picked up information from others, and the reference in the passage cited above to having heard "so many different stories about it" at first blush lends some support to it. However, I believe that to place such a construction on these words would be to misinterpret them. I am satisfied that when that remark is viewed in the context of the passage Fulton was saying that he had heard different stories about that part of the episode and given that up to five intruders entered the house, and the struggle between Mr McAleavy and his attackers took place in the hall, it is not surprising that there may have been different accounts given by the intruders themselves of a confused situation because of the subsequent panic.

Did drink or drunks play any part in Fulton's admissions? B19 and B24 relate to occasions when he was driving, and for the reasons already given I am satisfied that he would not have been affected by either drink or drugs when driving on long journeys. B22 relates to a period on 23 August 2000 starting at 0847 and ending at 1542, B113 a period on 7 June 2001 between 2021 and 2224. There is nothing to suggest that Fulton was materially affected by alcohol or drugs on either occasion.

Fulton's defence that he was trying to impress the members of the firm is contradicted by the admissions in B113. These were recorded by a probe when no undercover officers were present. Fulton was talking to Yellow who he knew well. He had no motive to impress Yellow, as opposed to the undercover officers, nor does it seem that Yellow needed to be impressed, because he is talking to Fulton about his desire to obtain a revolver, and not an automatic, for what he describes as "the right price". It is very hard to envisage why Yellow should talk about this to Fulton, or did not contradict, or at least express some scepticism about Fulton's account of the Newcastle robbery, if he thought Fulton was a barfly and a fantasist.

Are Fulton's admissions that he planned this episode true? The admissions themselves are very detailed and have the ring of truth about them. For example, his references to details such as the combination lock, the routes taken by the intruders in the immediate aftermath of the robbery; the imitation 38 being held under the clipboard, all convey a sense of authenticity and personal knowledge, both in planning the attack, and then of debriefing the actual intruders afterwards. His defence that he was trying to impress the undercover officers does not stand examination when his admissions to Yellow are borne in mind. Whilst there are some contradictions between his accounts, they are insufficient to raise a reasonable doubt as to the veracity of his otherwise consistent accounts. I am satisfied that these admissions are true, and I find him guilty on counts 24 and 25.

Conspiracy to Murder Derek Wray and Attempted Murder of William Fletcher – 6 January 1997

The Narrative

Mr William Fletcher was at home in Portadown when he heard a banging noise that made him jump to his feet. At almost the same time, a masked man holding a handgun, entered the living room and said, "Where's Derek Wray?"

"He's not here," was the reply. Then the masked gunman fired several shots at Mr Fletcher.

A total of six spent bullet cases, several distorted bullet heads, and the location of a few strike marks in the living room were found at the scene. An expert concluded that at least six rounds had been fired from a single 9-millimetre calibre self-loading pistol. He also later compared the spent cartridges with cartridges recovered from the shootings at Edenderry Primary School on 3 January 1997 (the shooting of Buchanan, Birney and Doran – incident 7, counts 30 to 33), that is three days before this incident, and concluded that the same pistol had been used in both incidents.

Admissions

The trial judge said:

> The prosecution case is Fulton was the gunman, that he went there expecting to find and to kill Derek Wray, and when he discovered that he was not there fired the shots. Fulton is charged in count 26 with conspiracy to murder Wray; in count 27 with the attempted murder of Mr Fletcher; in count 28 with wounding Mr Fletcher with intent to do him grievous bodily harm, and in count 29 of possession of a loaded handgun with intent to endanger life.

> ... One probe recording relates to a conversation between Fulton and Gibson at Gibson's home at Cambourne, between 0857 and 1310 on 16 March 2000, that is soon after Fulton has come to the West Country. During the morning Fulton described the attack on Fletcher. He described how it seems that it had been originally intended to carry out this attack the night before, but it had been called off because there were three police cars in the vicinity. On the night of the attack, he had smoked a couple of joints and was at his mother's, intending to smoke another joint, when he received a phone call from somebody he only to as "Bugs". This reminds him what he is to do, so he goes to the rear of [name redacted] home, where he is given a gun by a man called [name redacted]. Fulton describes how he checks

the gun and finds that it is "filled", i.e. loaded. He tells
"Philly" (Philip McLean) to come with him and close the door
after them once Fulton has put the door in. He then described
what happened next.

Jim: Soon as I got round to the door so I just fucking how am I
getting in even the day the next day what do you call it you
could see the fucking dust prints know, actually round the Yale
Lock like my short leg fitted right up the top reached, right up
to the Yale Lock. Like the door went to the wall, fair play to
Philly he was straight in I didn't see Philly doing it but he was
straight in and he fucking put his boot to the door and pulls the
phone out and what you call it then, I had (inaudible) take that
door there. The kitchen door was to the left. Him and the
woman were lying on the couch and he jumped off the couch
but to me, to me, I thought he was jumping at me and he was
jumping, but he was jumping at the kitchen door but it was
locked. As soon as he jumped at me I was straight to his forehead, boom like that there and how I missed his head it baffled
me like. See the next thing he jumped the other way and he was
standing right in front of me like that there. By this time Philly.

Muriel: (Interrupting). He went fucking everywhere didn't he
(inaudible).

Jim: Aye by this time he was, see actually. I actually all I
wanted to do was hit him in the limbs cause it wasn't Derek
Wray, I was looking for Derek Wray.

Continuing the description of the shooting Fulton describes how he
fired several shots intending to hit the man in the limbs.

Jim: So I said, Philly, Philly said, Jim he says, I swear on my
life, I swear to God I says, I mean after that I said to Gary like,
he says, I'll do anything you like boys but I'll not, not, I'm not
a shooter. I'm not going to know lie, I'm not a shooter like that
tell Gary, that after it like. I swear to you he's like a break
dancer. I wanted to just hit all the limbs and he's standing right
in front of you I goes boom, boom, boom, boom, boom, boom
(laughs). And you could see the fucking legs going and the
arms going. He was all over the fucking place, but see when I
got out Philly was already up Alexander Avenue.

Muriel: Philly was just away like a fucking rocket.

Jim: Billy had blocked one road off. Swinger had blocked the other road off, somebody blocked the other road off. Philly got everywhere. Philly was right out your back and everything.

Fulton then describes how he made his way to Gibson's house where he waited to hear news of the attack on the radio.

Jim: I dandered across and I dandered across, there was Swinger. He'd left the car on up the walk a wee bit to block the road. Says he where to fuck will ye hurry up. Here's me, right, right, right. I was that shattered and that stoned I could hardly get over your fence. 'Sargy' he was shaking like that (inaudible) you know waiting to take the gun and all. Time I got over the back I was fucked, I mean, I was destroyed, I swear to fuck, that's me, smoking that fucking blow.

Muriel: And then the sitting up the stairs waiting on the fucking radio.

Jim: On the hour every hour then at 12 o'clock a report came in man shot dead. Ah, here was Philly, oh, oh. Oh I'm going to crack up.

Muriel: (Inaudible) dead (laughs).

Jim: Here's me let me tell you something. The rule, the golden rule is the next time somebody tries to attack you (inaudible). It's up to your own decision. (Mimicks Philly). I'm not going to go mad. So they did like started to go mad. Then they started arguing with each other. Swinger and Billy.

Muriel: Then it turned out alright.

Jim: Aye, arms and legs and all (laughs).

Muriel: Those legs and hands fucking shot right through (laughs).

Jim: Through his ankles and all aye. He got hit seven. Seven times he was hit or something.

Muriel: I don't know.

Jim: Seven times cause I always maintain that he run.

Muriel: Philly sitting with a big cigar you know and the bottle of fucking champagne and all the rest of it. He soon walked out with it didn't he.

Although Fulton does not mention Mr Fletcher by name, he says that he was looking for Derek Wray, and it is unmistakeably the shooting of Mr Fletcher to which he is referring. The next reference occurs in a recording made on 1 October 2000 between 0944 and 1406.

And eh, cos I tried to murder one of their men, only he wasn't in the house, but the guy that was in the house I shot him 6 times, didn't try to kill him like. Just shot him in the elbows, the knees and the ankles, you know, what do you call it, left him a message. We want fucking, whoever fucking done that we want him punished. Billy was blamed for it.

Gary: So they were saying whoever did it wanted it.

Jim: They wanted us to punish whoever shot him. And I Billy had a word with me he said now I'm telling you don't you open your mouth in here you check your temper you let me do the talking like. But the wanker that was doing all the fucking talking, one of the old guys you know in his fucking coming into his 50's he was one of the old commanders, never pulled a trigger in his fuck'n life but he's trying to sit on the same plane as us, fuck'n fair enough, a commander all his life you know what I mean he was on the brigade staff, and I just lost it altogether and here's me what do you want to know and you want to fuck, you will, what do you want to punish him well I'll tell you what, I shot the fucker, alright I shot him, now do you want to punish me, his face just dropped like that there.I said, well come on, you fucking sort it out Will, cos I tell you what see if that other maggot had of been in the house I'd have put one in his fucking head. And I said, see when I do find him I will be putting fucking one in his head. So you see long after all the negotiations, this that and the other, the guy that I was looking to shoot, what you call it, they sent a whole fucking er Provost Marshall Team down to a housing estate in my area and I got them the lend of the Community Centre and ordered him up with his men and I made his men stand round in a circle, and the boys came out of the kitchen, had baseball bats and fucking broke every bone in his body.

Gary: Did they, what his own people did it.

Jim: His own people, seeing how serious it was, once I lost it in the meeting, I turns round and says you want the guy punished I said well that's alright you want to do it, and I said cos I'm the one who shot him, here's me you going to punish me boy, I said fuck all, I said you've done fuck all in your fucking life, how dare you try to fucking dictate to me.

The next reference to this episode is to be found in, a conversation between Fulton and Dave on 7 January 2001. The recording was made between 1037 and 1221, although it would seem that Fulton did not arrive until after 1045, when he was expected within 15 minutes, so it covers up to one and a half hours or thereabout. Dave's un-contradicted evidence was that Fulton drove Dave in a Peugeot to Michael Woods Services, which he said was perhaps north of Bristol. During this lengthy conversation he again referred to the Fletcher shooting saying, "er, I was looking for Derek Wray but he wasn't in house so I shot the other wee lad in the arms and legs and all…".

Then there is the following:

Jim: (Laughing). I only tried to kill him the once. Cause he wasn't the one I was going for you know so I'd no intention of killing him but when I come through the door you come through the house front door like that then the door to the living room was right there so when I kicked it open the door to the kitchen was to the left.

Dave: Yeah.

Jim: And he was sitting lying on a couch with his girlfriend that way along that wall.

Dave: What the right hand side.

Jim: On the left hand side as I come through the door.

Dave: Right.

Jim: He was lying on the left hand side of the couch long ways. The TV was the bottom of it but the door to the kitchen was behind that to my left.

Dave: Yeah.

Jim: Well through just you know what I mean, through own self preservation when I burst through the door he was a big tall cunt he jumped up and jumped over the fucking front of the couch towards me which I thought he was making a go for me. He wasn't he was going for the kitchen door.

Dave: Right.

Jim: But I didn't know that there.   So my first shot just went straight for his fucking head like. I mean cause I though he was coming for me. So I just put straight up boom and must have just fucking whistled passed his ear cause he just lit in mid-air he just changed direction went in front of me there then that's when he start Break Dancing. (Jim making the sound of a gun five times laughing).

Dave: Break Dancing (short pause).

Jim: And the rush of the adrenaline and all, I didn't even know, I knew I had to, I knew I had to send to leave a message about Derek WRAY but I didn't through all the adrenaline rush and buzz and all I still to this day can't remember saying it know what I mean cause I had to ask wee Philly after it. I said to Philly did I give the warning. Philly said, aye you fucking right you give the warning alright.

Dave: Who was this Derek WRAY geezer then.

Jim: He was in the UDA I mean all he was is a big bully.

Dave: Right.

Jim: Just fucking beat up. All he done was beat up wee Prods all the time. Fucking he was a big gruff big bastard and a nasty big cunt. And he just kept beating people up and everytime he was warned it was just going through, making us look bad you know what I mean as if we were afraid of going to fucking to sort it out. So we asked the UDA to sort it out and they just kept on saying he's a wanker, he's a wanker. So Billy turned round and says that's alright we'll sort it out.

The defence that these accounts were given to impress the undercover officers is again inconsistent with, and contradicted by, his first description being given not to them, but to Gibson on 16 March 2000 in her home. That account was given in the morning between 0857 and 1310, and whilst Fulton and Gibson resorted to drink and/or drugs on occasion, it is less likely that they would have done so at that time of day, and there is nothing to suggest that Fulton was in anyway affected by drink or drugs on that occasion. For the reasons I have given earlier I accept that he was not so affected when driving on either of the other two occasions.

Having considered all of the evidence I am satisfied that Fulton's admissions are true…

… If he fired the first shot at Mr Fletcher's forehead there could be no doubt that his intention at that moment was to kill him, even though that was not his intention when Fulton entered the house, or even when he turned round after hearing Wray was not in the house. Whilst Fulton's assertions are predominately that he did fire at Mr Fletcher's forehead, they are not all to that effect, and Mrs Fletcher's evidence that the first shot was fired at her husband's lower limbs raises a reasonable doubt as to whether the first shot was fired at his forehead. I find him not guilty on count 27, the attempted murder of Mr Fletcher. However, the subsequent shots were clearly intended to wound him, and I find Fulton guilty on count 28

Punishment shootings of Buchanan, Birney and Doran at Edenderry Primary School on 3 January 1997

Admissions

Fulton is charged with three counts of wounding each man with intent to do him grievous bodily harm, contrary to Section 18 of the Offences Against the Person Act, 1861 (counts 30, 31 and 32); and with possession of a loaded Browning 9-millimetre pistol with intent to endanger life, contrary to Article 17 of the

Firearms (NI) Order 1981 (count 33). The prosecution case is that Fulton ordered each of the three men to come to this spot to be subjected to a punishment shooting, and then shot each man in each thigh.

Fulton referred to this incident on nine occasions between 16 March 2000 and 7 June 2001, sometimes when more than one undercover officer was present. He spoke about this once to Liz, three times to Neil, three times to Robbie, twice to Dave and once to David and Max. The most significant of these conversations were the first two, that is the conversation recorded on 16 March 2000 when Liz was present, and then on 30 March 2000 with Neil, and I shall examine the relevant conversations in chronological sequence.

The first in time relates to a conversation which took in Gibson's house in Cambourne between 1310 and 1633 on 16 March 2000. Fulton, Gibson and [name redacted] *were in the house when Liz called. The importance of what then occurred is two-fold. First of all, Fulton had not met Liz before, and she had no known connection to the firm and was simply there because she was friendly with Gibson. There was therefore no reason why Fulton should wish to impress her so far as improving his standing with the firm was concerned. Secondly, he was quite willing to talk at length about himself and his criminal activities to show that he was well-known, even notorious, not just in Northern Ireland but in the USA, because at an early stage of the conversation he claimed that he had been the most wanted man in the US for a while. Later he said that he had been put on the front page of An Phoblact. It is not without significance that Gibson supported him by saying that he was shown in the Irish press in prisoner shackles and was on the RTE news. He referred in some detail to his criminal activities, including having a bath at Gibson's house and how Gibson would burn his clothes, something which Gibson appeared to confirm when she said, "Naked men and all running around the living room trying to get into the bath". He also described how he narrowly escaped detection when carrying £25,000 in cash on one occasion and an AK47 on another.*

He described how men would be shot through the fat of the leg so that it would be reported that they had been kneecapped. The reason for this was that the victims were at risk of being shot

*dead by various organisations because of their suspected drug
dealing, and this would be regarded by such organisations as a
satisfactory method of dealing with the matter, thereby enabling
them to escape death and so saving their lives. He said how the
last three kneecappings were at his child's school, and because
this caused such a fuss amongst the parents his wife told him
not to shoot anyone in that school again, to which he replied,
"It'll be alright love no more of it so we'll go back to Brownstown Park then."*

*Whilst the reference to three people being shot in this way sug-
gests that Fulton was referring to the episode when Buchanan,
Birney and Doran were shot, taking this conversation in isolation there is insufficient detail to be certain that was the episode
to which he was referring. In addition, his response to his
wife's allegation might be argued to be consistent with him not
being involved in that episode, but saying that, for example, he
would see it did not happen again. Be that as it may, Fulton's
willingness to refer to his criminal activities in such detail to
someone who, so far as he knew, was just a friend of Gibson, is
inconsistent with his defence that he claimed involvement in
crimes because he wished to impress the firm. He was clearly
willing to impress others also.*

*Just two weeks later 30 March 2000 occurred the next refer-
ence which records a conversation on a car journey (see
Fulton's query "is this Plymouth?"). Fulton and Neil first met
on 24 March 2000 and Fulton believed that he was now working for Neil which covered the period between 1340 and 1535
that day. Neil had told Fulton that he was to behave himself
and that he could not be drink driving, and told him to keep the
car clean, no tickets. Given Fulton's need to keep in with Neil
at the beginning of Fulton's involvement with the firm, and that
he was driving during this conversation, it is in the highest degree implausible to suggest that Fulton may have been affected
by drink or drugs and I am satisfied he was not.*

*Fulton gives the fullest of the nine descriptions of his involve-
ment in this episode when he described it in the following
terms:*

Jim: I've deliberately ostracised people even though they were friends of mine in the drug trade. I mean their friends of mine who fucking..

Neil: Or ain't gonna go near somebody, I mean if he's, if he's been looked at then soon as you meet or they see you, your being looked at aren't you.

Jim: Exactly know what I mean, its only a matter of going up and explaining to them. Listen I'll not be calling at the house no more. I've done it on 4 occasions. I've shot 3 of my friends over drugs. Billy told me to do it. Billy's right hand man. I shot both of them, him in both his legs, guys. Big Ron I shot him and Billy, Billy says because fucking they were going fucking after Billy for drugs. So Billy had to show some of them and then we shot one of the UFF boys and er they said they sent word out, over drugs that you know were going to stiff the first drug dealer in Portadown we get our hands on. So that meant Ron. Fat Ron was dealing for Billy.

Neil: Oh right.

Jim: So to fucking save Ron's fucking neck and see give Billy good pub.. publicity. Says right Jim he says er Ron wee guy TYLER he says and wee Danny from Lisburn. He says but wee Danny doesn't want to do it and he said wee Danny doesn't want to turn up. I said do you fucking blame him Billy. This is another wee guy I was friendly with. So I had to go and me down it took me an hour and half to fucking talk this wee lad into coming up to Portadown and let me shoot him. I had to talk him into letting, me shoot him like (laughs). Some of them things are so comical like. I felt sorry though for Ron that night but fucking er.

Neil: Did he come.

Jim: Oh fuck aye. (Inaudible) aye. He'd nothing to lose (inaudible) (laughs). (Inaudible) fucking it was to save Billy's face but also to save Ron's life cos the UFF would have shot him dead like to prove a point. Cos we shot one of their men. So, I brings I sends for them I says aye be in my kids school their primary school. I says to be in the back of the primary school because if there's a shooting in a school ground or anywhere like that at all the Police will not come into it instantly in case its a set up. Cos they don't know what's waiting for them. So you always use a school. So I had the 3 of them. So I comes dandering across from the park with a nine mil and what do you call it er I says right boys lay down. Big Ron says Jim do me first, big Ron's a fucking good bit of fat on him like and because they're mates all I done was squeeze the fat of the leg out.

Neil: Yeah.

Jim: And I fucking I was putting the its like ramming a nail through your fucking leg through the skin of your leg. No big deal. But it comes out in the papers kneecapping, you know and it does the public know what I mean gives the public what they want and all that. So I goes to Ron first, bang. I shot Ron in the fucking this leg right but when I shot him fucking the gun re-coiled and hit either my hand or else my hand moved down and the foot clip came out about a fucking couple of mil.

Neil: (Overtalking) Right.

Jim: Just caught the clip slip. See when I went on to the next leg. Click. Pulled the fuck cocked it again. Click. Cocked it about 3 times. Here's Ron for fucks sake. Jim hurry up (laughs) pitch black like, so I had to feel over the gun and I felt the clip and banged it again and cocked it, boom. The next fucking two, they're sitting beside him. Ron says ye bastard ye. I went up to see him in hospital aft.. about an hour later after I got washed up and cleaned.

Jim: I walks to the hospital first of all there's a peeler standing at the door, me and Philly (inaudible) Fulton your nothing but a sick bastard, he said shooting em an hour ago and up visiting them an hour later (laughter) . You're nothing but a sick cunt here's me now come on boys you know they're my mates (in-audible) all their families know and knew as well.

Neil: Yeah.

Jim: But they had told their families that, listen if that didn't happen the UFF were going to shoot us dead.

One element of the account which is of particular importance is Fulton's description of the interruption of the shooting and the trigger clicking but the gun not firing. This very closely corresponds with descriptions of Buchanan and Doran, and it very strongly conveys the impression that Fulton was describing events in which he had participated.

... It is also significant that, with one exception, each reference was made by Fulton when he was driving a car on a long journey. I have already stated why I do not consider he was affected by drink or drugs on such occasions.

The exception is on 28 June 2000 when Fulton was with Neil and Dave in a pub watching a football match on TV. This was the second occasion on which Fulton spoke to Neil about this episode. The recording commenced at 1615. It was not the subject of attention by counsel when Neil and Dave gave evidence and I admitted it on the voir dire. However, at that stage I did not appreciate that the entry for that day on the transaction master sheet suggests that Fulton had at least five, and possibly six, drinks whilst they were in this pub. In those circumstances I cannot be satisfied that Fulton was not adversely affected by drink and I propose to disregard that tape completely because it cannot be considered reliable.

The remaining references are the following...

Verdicts

I am satisfied that the admissions... are reliable. They gain support from those contained in... which cannot be said to have been made because Fulton wanted to impress any member of the firm. They are confirmed by the other admissions to which I have referred, and I am satisfied that they are true, and I find Fulton guilty on counts 30, 31 and 32. By using the 9mm gun to carry out these attacks Fulton clearly intended to endanger life because such attacks always endanger life, even if, fortunately, death does not usually result. I find him guilty on count 33 also

Hijacking of a Post Office Van on 10 July 1996 to be used for a hoax bomb

The Narrative

At 5:15 PM on Wednesday 10 July 1996, Calvin Rowe was making his rounds collecting mail in Portadown. As he drove towards the collection box beside the bridge over Northway in Edgarstown, he found it impossible to park close as there were burnt out vehicles across the road owing to widespread disorder in the area at the time. Mindful of his duties, he was in the process of removing letters from the box when he was approached by a man wearing a balaclava who produced a pistol. The gunman forced him to surrender the keys to the vehicle and at gunpoint then made him drive the van to an area close to the Golden Hind pub. The gunman placed a yellow cylindrical Calor gas bottle in the back of the van. The gunman then ordered Mr Rowe to drive the van to the police lines, which he did. The gas cylinder was later found to be a hoax bomb.

Admissions

There can be no doubt that the masked gunman hijacked the Post Office van by threatening the driver, and that, provided it can be proved that the gun was a real gun, he had the gun with him to hijack the van. The prosecution case is that Fulton was the masked man and was carrying a 9-millimetre pistol. If that is proved, then he is clearly guilty of both charges.

The prosecution case rests on admissions made by Fulton on 28 March 2001 during a journey with Dave, which was recorded. This covers the period from 08.48 to 17.53 and commenced when they met at Exeter Services on the M5. Fulton was driving. During the journey Fulton referred to an episode which he said involved a postman who he described as the stupidest person he had ever seen, apparently because the postman was undeterred by the disorder around him and continued to do his duty by collecting mail. He did this from a letterbox which appears from the evidence to have been in a no man's land between the demonstrators and burnt vehicles on one side, and the police lines some distance away on the other. Fulton's description of events is to be found between pages 698 and 702. I do not propose to set it out, but it corresponds with Mr Rowe's account.

Some support for the reliability of Fulton's account is to be found in the evidence of Major Seddon and WOII Lamb, who were involved in dealing with the device. Major Seddon's statement says that he saw Billy Wright and one of the Fulton brothers, he could not say if it was Mark or Jim, watching from some distance away. Fulton says Billy Wright was at the scene and had given the order to carry out this opportunistic hijacking when he saw the Post Office van approaching.

Verdicts

When interviewed, Fulton denied involvement and said that he was not guilty. No defence submissions were made specifically in respect of this incident. Are Fulton's submissions reliable? He was driving the vehicle for a long period and I am satisfied he was not affected by drink or drugs. His account of events corresponds very closely with Mr Rowe's account. In particular Fulton's reference to Mr Rowe being in the process of removing the letters from the collection box when Fulton approached him with a 9-millimetre pistol has the ring of truth. I am satisfied that Fulton was recounting events he had been personally involved in and that these admissions are reliable. I find him guilty on both counts

Possession of a .22 pistol with intent to endanger life at the time of the murder of Michael McGoldrick

The Narrative

Michael McGoldrick was a Roman Catholic taxi driver who was murdered some time on the night of 7 July or in the early hours of 8 July 1996. His body was found in his taxi at a remote spot on the Montiaghs Road, Aghagallon, at 6.30am on 8 July. Dr Carson performed the post-mortem examination and concluded that the cause of death was five bullet wounds to the head. Mr Rossi's examination of the bullets established that they had been fired from a single .22 weapon. On 20 July 1996 a .22 pistol and 30 rounds of .22 ammunition were found during a planned search of a potato field off the Soldierstown Road, Aghalee.

This weapon was also examined by Mr Rossi, and he established that it had been used to murder Mr McGoldrick, as well as being used in another fatal shooting, the only information about that death contained in his report being that the victim was Bertie Martin who was killed on 15 July 1997.

Admissions

Fulton is charged in count 36 with possession of a Star .22 pistol with intent to endanger life, or to enable some other person by means thereof to endanger life, on a date unknown between 1 July 1995 and 8 day of July 1996. This is based upon his admission that he had brought the weapon from Belfast and test fired it in the country, and that he had the gun brought to him during the Drumcree protests of 1996. It is a significant part of the case against him that in his admissions he implicated his wife in the possession of the gun: saying (a) that she was with him when he took it out to the country and test fired it; and (b) that at his direction she brought the gun up to him at Drumcree.

It is also a significant element of the case against him that he is alleged to have instructed his wife to put forward a false explanation of how she brought the gun to Drumcree if she were to be questioned about it by the police. This allegation relates to the contents of the letter exhibit DE1A which is shown in exhibit A67, and to which I have already referred, see [81] to [83]. As Fulton is charged in count 43 with doing an act tending and intended to pervert the course of public justice by composing this false account, it is convenient to deal with the evidence relating to the discovery and authorship of the letter at this stage.

The unchallenged evidence was that his wife Tania Fulton was searched by [name redacted] during a visit to Maghaberry Prison on 26 July 2001, by which time Fulton was in custody on remand, having been arrested the previous month. During the search, the message which is now exhibit DE1A was found by [name redacted] in the left breast pocket of Tania Fulton's jacket. Another searcher, [name redacted], described how Tania Fulton then tried to lift the paper and rip it up but was prevented from doing so. Tania Fulton was known to [one of the prison officers] from previous prison visits and did not deny that the paper was hers when informed by Principal Officer Alexander that the document would be confiscated. The document was later examined by Mr Craythorne, a questioned document examiner and a senior scientific officer at Forensic Science NI and compared with other documents ostensibly written by Fulton. He concluded that the document seized from Fulton's wife had been written by Fulton.

The document starts with the following passage.

Tania. Neil once asked me was I never afraid of you ever squeeling (sic) of me to the police, so I said that you couldn't because you had brought the gun that killed the taxis (sic) driver at the first Drumcree up to me. So if you are ever asked about it this is what you say.

The letter then sets out a detailed story that his wife was to tell. In essence this was that whilst he was at Drumcree he asked her to go out to their home to get him a change of clothes, which she did. Some months later he said that she could not get back at him because she had brought a gun up to him at the barricades. She got angry, he said he was only joking, but from time to time over the years he would repeat this allegation, which she thought he only did to wind her up, she knew he was lying.

I am satisfied that Fulton wrote this letter to his wife and I shall return to this part of its contents and its possible significance later.

There are four evidential transcripts that contain relevant admissions… The first in chronological sequence which relates to 16 May 2000 when Fulton and Dave were on a journey from Bristol Airport to Plymouth, covering the period from 1400 to 1922. At page 722 they were talking about Tania when the following exchange occurred.

Jim: Ah well a wife's good you see and I have my wife in a perfect position. She could never say anything about me. She could never do anything about me because, one of the most famous murders was the first the first Drumcree, first Drumcree, when Michael McGoldrick a catholic taxi driver was shot dead with a star 22 with a star 22 pistol…

Dave: Right.

Jim: Er an automatic. Ah well I had, I had to go down to Belfast on a motorbike to lift that. That was actually brought up for for a knee capping, so the fella he left the country so I went and put it away. So I got the wife to come on the back of the bike with me. First of all to test fire it. I had an old chopper, a hard tail chopper with a straight cut off pipe.

Dave: Yeah.

Jim: Real loud so out in the country. Just got her to sit on the bike. Rev her flat out and I just let three or four rounds off her. Working perfectly. Went out the road with the wife, says right into the, stick that into the hedge there, I says, beside the back of that give way sign and (Inaudible) , all wrapped in a grease er in a cloth in a plastic bag and stuck down. So that was al-right. It was left there for months. Then Drumcree happened. Nobody was expecting Drumcree to be banned.

Dave: Yeah.

Jim: Bang all of a sudden bang we were still in the UVF at the time. So we decided what to do Billy come to me he says right, it was the second day, the third, second, no the third day, Billy says to me right he says get that wee star in, there was only one way of getting it in cos everyone of us everytime, no matter, if we passed 40 times a day going up and down in our cars we were stripped I mean even coming out of it.

Dave: Right.

Jim: They had to do it by, know what I mean so there was only one way of doing it I says right, I says to the wife, away an get that package, that wee package an she fucking she was really fascinated with it cos it was a beautiful wee weapon, Dave it was only about you could hold it in your whole hand.

Dave: Yeah.

Jim: And it was pure fucking nickel plated.

Dave: Oh right.

Jim: With a bone handle with a fucking silver star on the handle, it was a star 22 a beautiful wee weapon boy it was lovely an I says away an get that wee fucking package, I says I'll get you a taxi to bring you in, I says get dropped off before the barricades and before the police lines and walk up with it. So she arrives in the taxi and the taxi pulled up. Billy says don't bring it in he says just get it left on round the fucking such an such, so I went over to the wife I says right just walk, on round to such an such house I says and hand that over.

Dave: Yeah.

Jim: Hah that's what shot Michael McGoldrick.

Whilst Fulton correctly links the gun to McGoldrick's murder, and describes it as a .22, he was wrong to describe it as having a bone handle with a silver star on the handle, errors which he was also to make in later references to this incident.

Fulton again referred to this in B44 on 9 July 2000 which relates to the period between 1947 and 2114 when he was in a car with Neil while they were returning from Penzance. A general conversation takes place re domestic matters. Jim then speaks about his wife Tanya and what she has done for him and the LVF.

Jim: She must have been thinking about, she must have been thinking about Drumcree (inaudible) you know something love it wasn't last year I brought you the guns up to Drumcree. What, she says no it wasn't she says last year you wouldn't let anybody cause any trouble shes right it wasn't last year I (unfinished word) I wouldn't let any LVF members (inaudible) or up to it. It was the year before she brought the weapons up. I know what it was she was listening, she was on about McGoldrick the taxi driver (inaudible). She never ever ever mention it.

Neil: She never mentions it why not.

Jim: She mention about bringing the guns an all up, she will never ever mention about bringing that fucking one gun cause she knows it implicates her into a murder. She'll mention about all the other guns she hides and moves about never ever ever mention that Star 25 shes got a complex about it.

Neil: Not only got a complex, probably a bag of nerves about it.

Jim: The only person can do her any harm is me.

Neil: Is it.

Jim: Aye, I'm the only one knows she brought it in.

Neil leaves the vehicle and Jim travels home and makes two phone calls which appear to be of a social nature. As can be seen from this passage Fulton reiterates how he holds over his wife her involvement in moving the gun, but wrongly describes the calibre, though not the make, of the gun.

The next reference to this matter is to be found in B29, which relates to 1 October 2000 between 0944 and 1406 when Fulton and Gary were travelling from Cornwall to London in Fulton's car. I do not propose to set out the entire passage between pages 540 and 542, but the following points are relevant.

The judge continues to list four points before adding:

When questioned in interviews... he denied involvement, saying... that it was totally fictitious. He made no reply when asked about the letter... or whether he wrote it.

Verdict

However, these are not the only matters to be considered. There is also the letter written by Fulton and seized from his wife. In it he confirms what he had said to Neil. Nowhere does he say that was untrue. Instead, he goes to considerable lengths to construct a story which his wife is to tell if questioned about this gun (and another episode), a story which from its very nature and content is plainly false. The natural inference is that in doing so he was seeking to ensure that his wife would not tell the truth if questioned, the truth being that she did bring the gun to him at Drumcree as he had admitted. I remind myself of the warning in R v Lucas about a defendant's possible motives for lying, but I am satisfied that Fulton's reason for constructing this elaborate story was to cover up the truth. Notwithstanding the repeated errors he made in the calibre and

appearance of the gun, having considered the letter to his wife
in particular I am satisfied that the admissions that he had the
gun in his possession are reliable and are true. I find him guilty
on count 36.

Attack on a military patrol near Union Street, Portadown, on 9 July 1998

These counts on the indictment were in part supported by the following covert recordings:

> Jim: I nearly broke my leg that night. Me, Philly and Gary standing at the back of the (inaudible) behind Billy's house, near (inaudible) place and all the Land Rovers were parked right down that bit of slip road, you know as you go onto Northway and we could hear them all talking. They were all talking and joking and all the wee (inaudible) all standing on the Landrovers. Two lines of Land Rovers blocked the whole road (inaudible). We're only holding (inaudible) and a blast bomb. What do you call it. Decided it was definitely me who could throw it the furthest like and I says right, cos nobody noticed we had to walk around two wheelie bins you know to get up the back garden. Nobody thought about moving them out of the way. You know for us, so that's alright. That cunt Gary, what does he fucking do? I said right light it and what do you call it, once it's lit you know what I mean there's only a wee tiny fuse like. (Overtalking) here's me wallop. Straight up in the air and we sat and our Gary (inaudible) fucking mine must have landed on the fuse went right up and came straight down on top of the Land Rover. Right down on top of it. And you could just hear it hitting it and clinking off it you know ran like fuck. That bastard Gary run past laughing and pulled the fucking front bin down. Philly hit it first and went head over heels. I fucking hit it and nearly broke my leg. I swear to God, you know what I mean.

The second passage relied upon by the prosecution is to be
found in B12, which relates to a period between 0950 and 1148
on 12 January 2001 when Fulton drove Dave and Robbie from
Plymouth to Finchley in London. Fulton, who had been talking

at length about blast bombs, pipe bombs and grenades and their characteristics, then said at page 199 that pipe bombs were unpredictable, and that he nearly got his arm and his head blown off by one. He continues at page 200.

Jim: Know what I mean. Just soon as it lit, I fucking, I just straight up over the wall straight at the fucking Brits and it got about 10 foot from my hand and went off know what I mean, fuck'n just as well as I threw it. I went straight down behind the wall again. Because it just you want to hear them chip lumps of bricks coming off the wall fucking on top of me.

When questioned in interview... he said that he heard others who had been involved talking about the incident in the Buffs' Club.

Verdicts

Whatever Fulton is describing, and whether or not his description of his involvement is true, the incident(s) he is describing bear no relationship to the incident described by the soldiers, and so the evidence falls very far short of linking him with this episode. I find him not guilty on counts 38, 39 and 40

Intending to pervert the course of justice and possession of a handgun with intent

Admissions

As count 43 (doing an act tending and intending to pervert the course of justice) and count 44 (possession of a handgun with intent contrary to Article 17 of the Firearms (Northern Ireland) Order 1981) are linked by the letter Exhibit DE1A to the matters just considered it is appropriate to deal with them together at this stage. At [281]–[283] I have already referred to the evidence that has satisfied me that Fulton wrote this letter, and I do not propose to repeat it. As I said, I am satisfied that Fulton's reason for constructing the elaborate story relating to the gun that killed McGoldrick was to cover up the truth.

The second part of the letter relates to a different episode, again involving his wife, when she brought a loaded .45 Webley through the police lines to him at Drumcree, successfully calcu-lating that she would not be searched because the police had been led to believe, wrongly, that he and his wife despised each other. The relevant admissions are to be found in B67, which relates to 26 October 2000 between 1027 and 1430 when he was travelling with Robbie on a journey from Plymouth to Avonmouth, Weston- Super-Mare and back to Plymouth. There had been a discussion about wives and Fulton then referred to this incident at page 932.

Jim: No my wife's done, my wife's done a lot Robbie (inaudi-ble) she's walked through fuck'n checkpoints and all with she came actually through one checkpoint up at Drumcree with a loaded .45. A big 45 Webley with a child's buggy and all the cops knew, knew, but then me and her had the perfect situation for all the cops.

Robbie: What do you mean all the cops knew?

Jim: All the cop, everybody knows who, know what I mean, my wife and all is.

Robbie: Oh right.

Jim: But what do you call it, the perfect situation was that (mumbled speech) cops thought that me and her despised each other we were always fucking fighting and all.

Robbie: (Inaudible) (overtalking).

Jim: And that's the way we always kept it. The cops would never go near her house, wouldn't search her house or nothing, cos I could actually plank stuff in her house (inaudible).

Very soon afterwards Fulton repeated this statement, adding that the gun was brought to him at his request.

So at Drumcree the fuck'n year that we all opened up on the fuck'n Army and the Police. She, what do you call it, we were short of one weapon. The only one we couldn't get in. I fuck'n sent a girl to tell her I says, you tell the wife I says, that er, I sent such and such out to the house for her to bring up it to me, and she walked right up through all the fuck'n ranks, through the checkpoints, through everything with a Webley 45, loaded and all.

The obvious inference is that Fulton received the gun at Drumcree, but in any event as she was bringing the loaded gun to him at his direction they were involved in a joint enterprise. Although he did not have physical control of the gun when his wife was bringing it to him, she was acting at his direction, and as such he had possession of the gun... In either event I am satisfied that if his account is true he was in possession of the Webley revolver. The purpose of bringing a loaded revolver to Drumcree was to enable shots to be fired, thereby endangering life, whether they were to be fired by Fulton or one of his companions.

When questioned in interview at C32(b) at page 381 about this and other allegations Fulton replied that it was fictitious... That the account was true gains significant support from the content of the story he instructed his wife to tell in exhibit DE1A. This was carefully constructed to provide her with a story which would exculpate her if questioned. Why would Fulton go to such lengths unless he believed that his wife might say something else if questioned, questioned in this context unmistakeably meaning questioned by the police, unless there was a risk that she might tell the truth, and thus be at risk of prosecution? It is the case that he says it was Neil he had told, but the circumstances of the account to Robbie correspond with what he wrote to his wife.

Verdicts

I am satisfied that Fulton's account of this incident is true, and I find him guilty on count 44, possession of the firearm with intent.

The references in the letter to "this is what you say", together with the words "so if you are ever asked about it", "it" being Fulton's statement to Neil that she brought him the gun that killed Mr McGoldrick, incontrovertibly refer to being questioned by the police. I can conceive of no other meaning, nor has one been suggested. To instruct someone to tell a false story

if questioned by the police about a suspected offence is an act
tending and intended to pervert the course of public justice of
the clearest kind. I am satisfied that Fulton composed this letter
with that intention, and I find him guilty on count 43.

Attempted wounding with intent to do grievous bodily harm to William Terry

The Narrative

William Terry lived in Portadown and retired as a senior officer at the Maze Prison early in 1997. He and his wife and other members of the family returned to their home at about 10:30 PM on 13 August 1997. Shortly after, shots were fired at his home.

Police investigations established that the shots had been fired from a 7.62-millimetre calibre weapon of an unspecified type which Mr Thompson of the Forensic Science Agency described as being of a type usually associated with Loyalist terrorists.

The strike marks which can be seen clearly are grouped on the upper part of the wall, indicating that the gunman fired upwards at the side of the house, apparently aiming at the area between the upstairs windows, with most of the strike marks being in the region of the floor level of the first floor. Fortunately, the only bullet which penetrated the house was that which went through the upstairs window, and no one was physically injured.

Admissions

In count 37 Fulton is charged with aiding, abetting, counselling
and procuring others with attempting to wound Mr Terry with
intent to do him grievous bodily harm. This charge is based
upon Fulton's admissions in B22, a conversation with Dave on
23 August 2000. After discussion of contract killings, the con-
versation turns to the effect of 7.62mm rounds when fired from
an AK, clearly referring to a gun of the AK47 type. Fulton then
referred to a warning given to the security forces, including

prison officers, that they should lay off Loyalist prisoners; the implication being the officers should not enforce prison discipline strictly; or else there would be reprisals. He then described how his cousin Gary came to him at his holiday caravan and told Fulton that Swinger (ie his brother Mark) had left them "a job", the "job" being described by Gary to Fulton as "we'll be hitting fucking screws". Fulton then gave Gary directions to the only prison officer's house he could think of at the time, a house which was two doors from Fulton's mother's house. He then described in considerable detail what was plainly the gun attack on Mr Terry's house.

If Fulton's admissions are correct, he set up the attack on Mr Terry's house by nominating him as a target. During interview Fulton denied being involved, saying he had heard about the attack when he went to his mother's house the next day. However, it is unnecessary to dwell on the plausibility or otherwise of this explanation because Mr Treacy's submission was that at best whilst the evidence reveals offences of criminal damage and attempted intimidation, it falls short of proving that the gunman had the necessary intent to wound Mr Terry with intent to do him grievous bodily harm because what the gunman did was to spray the back of the house with gunfire.

Verdict

Fulton's reference to "hitting screws" is certainly consistent with knowing that the attack was intended to injure Mr Terry, an inference strengthened by the number of shots fired at the house. However, it is somewhat ambiguous, and it is by no means impossible that it meant an attack on the house designed to frighten and intimidate prison officers in general. This possibility is supported by the gunman firing upwards at the house at a point where all the strike marks but one was on a part of the building away from windows. I am not satisfied beyond reasonable doubt that the object of this attack was to wound Mr Terry, as opposed to causing fear and intimidation of prison officers, and I therefore find him not guilty on count 37.

Attempted armed robbery and false imprisonment of the McCrea family in December 1991

Admissions

*Fulton is charged with five counts relating to the holding hos-
tage of Mr McCrea and his wife by two armed men. Mr
McCrea, who held a senior position in the headquarters of the
Northern Bank in Belfast, had formerly been the manager of the
Crossgar branch of the bank, and he and his wife lived in
Crossgar with their children at the time of these events in mid-
December 1991. What was undoubtedly a prolonged and extremely frightening, indeed in all probability a terrifying
experience for the McCrea family, was perpetrated by two
armed men who were undoubtedly part of a carefully prepared
plan which involved Mr McCrea being led to believe that the
safety of his family was at stake, thereby forcing him to cooper-
ate with their kidnappers to rob the Northern Bank in Crossgar
of a large amount of money. However, it seems that the robbers' information was out of date, and they were unaware that
he had been transferred from the Crossgar branch.*

*The only evidence against Fulton on this matter is to be found
in the following passage at pages 312-314. As is apparent from
this passage there is no reference whatever in it to the incident
involving the McCreas. It is correct that Mr McCrea said that
he found a bank security leaflet when he came home later, but
this does not advance the prosecution case to any material extent because he said that he had such leaflets in his briefcase,
and they went through the briefcase. This does not correspond
to the reference by Fulton to leaving glossy magazines open at
the home security section.*

Jim: Oh aye that there and robbing post offices they don't mind
banks as much either. But see post offices. See anything to do
with the Royal with the fucking Queens head or anything boy,
do they take that thick. Used to leave calling cards in all for
them.

Neil: Calling cards.

Jim: Aye they weren't actually calling cards. We used to do a
bank managers house. Take over the bank managers house. At
one stage like there was us, a unit of us who was doing that
fucking 7 days a week. So we were taking about 3 different
bank mangers a week. You know what I mean out of fucking 10

banks we got one you know what I mean you're fucking you're set like for a few quid so they started publishing these anti terrorist magazines for all the businessmen and fucking banks, bank holders and all, they're all a big glossy magazines come in a group of 12 and you're meant to buy one every week. So every bank fucking manager we hit fucking he'd always the whole fucking 12 in fucking a nice mahogany case so we started opening them at fucking home security (laughs) (inaudible) of the cabinets and all and setting them all up round the fucking living room leaving them for the peelers to come in. (Inaudible) these bad tempered sarcastic fuckers everytime they questioned me like.

Neil: You wouldn't want to be a bank manager over there then would ye.

Jim: Wait till I tell you something they're as crooked as fuck. I have seen, I have seen dozens of them asking for money out of the …

Neil: Have you.

Jim: Oh fuck aye. You get them to drive ye and all know what I mean in their car fucking pick money up and all thems going like what about me now I'm going to be all, throw us a couple of grand. I says no. See that wee cunt Tony I see him pistol whip one cos yer man actually started arguing with him in the car trying to get money of him. Him being fucking held by a gun. Tony fucking whacking him on the back of the fucking head when he's driving.

Verdicts

The defendant denied involvement in this episode in interview. Mr Treacy submitted that the passage relied upon by the prosecution "is too general, vague and non-specific to ground a conviction". In essence the prosecution have to rely on a general admission that Fulton committed many bank robberies which involved breaking into the homes of managers as proof of a specific episode to which he has made no specific admissions. I consider that the defence submissions are well-founded, and I find the defendant not guilty on counts 45, 46, 47, 48 and 49.

Hijacking and false imprisonment of Mr McCallum in March 1992

Admissions

Fulton is charged with three counts relating to the hijacking of a car and the false imprisonment of the driver on 6 March 1992. Count 50 alleges that he hijacked a Vauxhall Vectra driven by Mr McCallum; count 51 that he falsely imprisoned Mr McCallum and count 52 that he had a firearm with him with intent to commit an indictable offence, namely hijacking.

The admissions are to be found in a conversation between Fulton and Dave on 7 January 2001 between 1045 and 1221 when he drove Dave from Plymouth to Michael Woods Services which he thought was north of Bristol, again a lengthy car journey. Fulton spoke at length, and the conversation turned to bank robberies, and he referred to the events which the prosecution allege include the events which give rise to counts 50-52. He first described how he and another man went early one morning to a banker's house somewhere out in the countryside which they had kept under surveillance for some weeks. They went to the door expecting his wife to be in and to answer. The unmistakable inference is that she, or her husband, was to be held hostage as part of a bank robbery. However, there was no answer when they knocked at the door, so they decided to wait in a nearby driveway in their two-litre Cortina. As they did so a car which they recognised as a police car appeared, whereupon Fulton, believing that the police were suspicious, drove off at high speed. He then described a car chase with both vehicles travelling at extremely high speed. So far, the events occurred in an unidentified country area, but at this point in the pursuit the cars were approaching an urban area. A petrol tanker jack-knifed, and Fulton was able to escape, but he then lost control of the car as he took evasive action to avoid a pedestrian crossing the road and crashed through a stone wall into a garden.

The narrative continues when he describes how he and his companion abandoned their car and fled on foot, pursued by the occupier of the house into which they had crashed in a car he described as a Cavalier RSI. He described how one of them produced a snub nosed .38. They intended to hijack that car, but it drove off at speed, so they took a white Astra which Fulton saw sitting at a nearby bus stop with several children in it. Both men got in, and the driver, a fireman bringing his children to school, was made to hand over his driving licence and then told to drive them to East Belfast. Fulton then told the driver:

Now I tell you, we're not the fucking IRA, we're the Mid Ulster UVF, now I says if you identify us, or anything like this, well come back on you, now I'm telling you drive us into East Belfast.

Fulton was questioned about this, and he said that he had heard about this episode and had superimposed himself on the account he had heard. He said that he was never involved. No specific defence submissions were made in relation to this incident.

This conversation occurred whilst Fulton was driving and I am satisfied that he was not affected by drink or drugs. The description of events he gives corresponds closely with the accounts of Mr Adams and Mr McCallum in the following respects...

Verdicts

The only improbable feature of Fulton's account is his description of Carryduff as "a big Provie area". As against this, whilst the description of the events is given in dramatic terms, for example the description of the car chase, it is detailed and includes small details which strongly suggest that he was recounting events he had taken part in, such as the reference to crossing the cattle; removing the gear knob; losing the keys of their own car that they had left in a carpark, impliedly in Carryduff. In addition, Fulton was describing something that had occurred almost nine years before. I do not believe that he was adding himself to something he had been told about that happened the best part of a decade before. The entire tenor of the account, and the detail, render that wholly implausible. Having considered all of the evidence I am satisfied that this account is reliable, and that Fulton was describing events in which he took part. His actions establish all the necessary ingredients of each of these accounts, and I find him guilty on counts 50, 51 and 52

Conspiracy to murder by bombing the Sinn Fein offices in Newry in May 1994

Admissions

Fulton is charged with three counts based upon his admissions. Conspiracy to murder people in, or in the vicinity of, the Sinn Fein centre, count 53; doing an act with intent to cause an explosion in that he tried to repair a broken timing mechanism on this device, count 54; and possession of the device with intent to endanger life or cause serious injury to property, count 54.

The admissions are to be found in a discussion with Dave on 12 July 2000 between 1818 and 1949, during a journey when Fulton drove Dave to Bristol city centre. During the conversation, Fulton describes how he was unwittingly recruited by his brother to take part in what turned out to be an unsuccessful attack on the Sinn Fein offices in Newry. He was unwittingly recruited because Swinger did not tell him that there was a bomb involved, and Fulton had always sworn that he would have nothing to do with, or go near, explosives. He described how he agreed to drive Swinger, and another man only referred to as "Turkey", towards Newry in Fulton's wife's newly acquired 1300 Fiesta. During the journey Swinger asked if could drive. While Swinger was driving, he pulled into the side of the road, another Fiesta pulled up beside them and a tea flask was passed over from the other vehicle. It emerges when they park in a street away from the Sinn Fein offices that Turkey is to plant the bomb. They watch Turkey scale a wall with an iron door in it and then disappear. A few minutes later Turkey is seen running back towards the car, and en route he throws the flask into a bin. It transpired that Turkey could not get to the back of the Sinn Fein centre, so Fulton agreed to Swinger's request that he go with Turkey and help him to set the bomb by showing him how to get to the centre, Swinger knowing that his brother had gone over the wall when he and Billy Wright intended to carry out a machine gun attack on the Sinn Fein offices on an earlier occasion. Fulton agreed to do so, and went through the iron door, having allowed Turkey to struggle over the wall for a second time.

Fulton's narrative continues.

> I got up another wall and put a plank across onto the side roof of the fucking, walked across the plank, got down into the back of the Sinn Fein Centre. He came over and handed me the bomb down I says, right set the fucking thing, so I get's up and goes to the other side of that wall. I'm sitting, I said have you set it yet, I cant get the watch to work, I says what, I cant get the watch to work. By this time my blood was boiling it was just an active service move. So I climb back over the wall and I swear to god this is me now, with the way the fucking it was a stop watch on a bar wee a real fine screw or drill bit wee tiny drill bit, a watch drill bit drill through it put a pin through it, so when the hand comes round once the hand touches it, its wired to the battery and basically for the connection. So I said, he said, it won't wind up, the fucker I didn't know, at the time he had broke it see when he came over and threw it in the bin. He had fucking broke it, so I'm sitting like that I said give me the fuck- ing thing, well I took the lid off, opened it, fucking stop watch sitting there, here's me I'm sitting like that, turned my head away like as it was going to know what I mean, if the bomb goes off you're obliterated. I was sitting like that, screwing the fucking stop watch and then listening to it, the fucking bastard thing watch broke, so we had to take it away with us again.

If Fulton's admissions are true, then he is plainly guilty on each count.

Verdicts

Are these accounts true? Dave's un-contradicted evidence was Fulton was driving, and I am satisfied that he was not affected by drugs or alcohol. As in incident 15, Fulton purported to de- scribe events that occurred many years before, in this case seven years before. I do not believe that he could recount in such detail events he had only heard about, but not taken part in, so long before. On the contrary, his description of details such as opening the metal door, but letting Turkey climb the wall the second time, and the other Fiesta being red give an air of authenticity to his account. I am satisfied that these admis- sions are true and I find him guilty on counts 53, 54 and 55.

Conspiracy to rob Martin Phillips in December 1996

Admissions

There can be no doubt that this was an attempt to rob Mr Phillips when he returned home because he was expected to be carrying money, hence the initial demand for money. The prosecution case is that Fulton organised and planned the operation but did not take part in it. The admissions upon which reliance is placed to prove count 56, conspiracy to commit an armed robbery of Mr Phillips, commenced with a conversation between Fulton and Neil on 30 March 2000 between 13.40 and 15.35, during which Neil tells him to keep the car clean and not to get any tickets. This is after they meet at Plymouth station, and Fulton is driving. Neil tells him to slow down. This is a few days after their first meeting, and I am satisfied Fulton was unaffected by drink or drugs because he was driving and anxious to make a good impression on Neil.

During the references to this incident Fulton tells Neil that Phillips was believed to have large amounts in cash in the house, and that he met his managers every Thursday in a pub where they gave him the takings. Although he set it up, he was unable to take part himself because, as he put it, "the wife never came home in time for me to go". He sent three men to commit the crime who did exactly what he told them. He described how Mrs Phillips' daughter opened the patio door and let the men and her mother in. He also described how the two women and three children were put in the bathroom and tied up. Then one of the men departed from the plan by waiting outside with one of the others. When Mr Phillips returned, he pulled the mask off this man, whom Fulton named as Tony. It was expected that Mr Phillips would have anything between £5,000 and £30,000 on him. The informant about the money was said to be Mr Phillips' brother-in-law.

On 30 November 2000, in a conversation starting at 12.18 with Robbie during a journey to Bristol, Fulton again referred to this incident. This time he said that he could not take part in the robbery because he and his wife had had a row and she left him sitting in the house, the implication being that he could not leave as there were children to be minded or something of that sort. He therefore had to send someone else in his place, someone who had been recommended by Billy Wright and Swinger. Fulton had trained the other men himself, and he expected that the proceeds of the robbery would be £158,000; £100,000-£120,000 of which would be in the safe, with another £38,000 being on Mr Phillips' person. Again, he referred the family being tied up, and the plan being changed by going outside to wait for Mr Phillips. He said the information came from one of Phillips' own men. The third description is that of 28 March 2001 when Fulton met Dave at Exeter Services on the M5. It covers the period from 0848 to 1735. Fulton returned to this episode, and a summary of the conversation refers to the house of the owner of four carpet warehouses, £120,000 is talked about, and the informant who provided the information about the money was said to be one of the man's managers. I am satisfied this referred to the attempted robbery of Mr Phillips.

Verdict

In his closing submissions, Mr Treacy relied on [inconsistencies]. While some of these inconsistencies are less important than others, and some might have been resolved if Mr and Mrs Phillips had given evidence, the cumulative effect of them is to create a reasonable doubt as to whether Fulton really was describing an episode in which he had been involved and I find him not guilty on count 56.

Importing and supplying Class A and Class B drugs in 1998 and 1999

Admissions

Fulton faces four counts relating to the importation and supply of Class A drugs in the form of Ecstasy, and Class B drugs in the form of Cannabis or Cannabis Resin. Count 57 alleges the supply of Ecstasy; count 58 the possession of Ecstasy with intent to supply; count 59 supply of Cannabis or Cannabis Resin and count 60 possession of Cannabis or Cannabis Resin with intent to supply. In each case the offence is alleged to have occurred between 1 January 1998 and 30 September 1999. It is alleged that Fulton was involved in importing the drugs into Northern Ireland concealed in gym equipment delivered by post to a gym in Portadown and then sold or distributed. Evidence was given by Robert Jameson that in 1999 he owned a unit in the Brownstown Business Centre in Portadown which he rented to various people who used it as a gym during that year. A number of people ran the business at various times until it finally closed down, the last of whom was Gary Fulton who took the equipment away in November 1999. Jameson said that he saw the defendant at the gym on occasions. None of his evidence was challenged, nor was the statement by Detective Constable Butler who confirmed, if confirmation were needed, the meaning of drug slang used by Fulton, as well as giving evidence about the relevant prices for Ecstasy and Cannabis at the time described by Fulton and at the time the statement was made.

These charges are based upon admissions on 30 March 2000 when Fulton and Neil are in a car, and the recording starts at 1615. In a passage which is described in indirect, and not direct, speech Fulton is recorded as saying that he got what he describes as a "9 bar" a week from a friend in London for £380 which he then sold on to Gibson. It is also stated that "he talks of smoking blow and making money through drugs". Whilst there is a strong probability that Fulton is referring to himself in these summarised passages, in the absence of the actual words used in a verbatim transcript I am not satisfied that his guilt can be proved to the requisite standard because a summary may result in a distortion of meaning or place an inaccurate meaning on the actual words uttered. This defect does not affect the 19 September 2000 when Fulton travelled to Reading from Plymouth with Robbie, and the recording starts at 1235. During the conversation Fulton describes how he was involved in bringing what he refers to as "blow" ie Cannabis, at the rate of "40 or 50 kees [kilograms] of stuff every week" by post to a gym in a business complex owned by Bobby Jameson. This is a succinct description of his earlier account.

Finally, Fulton again refers to this topic on the 6 June 2001 when Fulton, David and Max travel to Reading together. After Max leaves, Fulton and David returned to the vehicle and

continued to Bristol, during which journey Fulton again turned
to the importation of drugs into Northern Ireland.

Jim: We used to (inaudible) fucking getting the gear to come in
the storage heaters, you know that auld fucking like glue, like a,
its like a paste that's inside, well that stuff fucking comes off
nothing like (inaudible) in there and 30 ki. We brought them in
in storage heaters. Well done like. Then I got them in the next
time, and er we had our own multi gym, bogus name but it was
the biggest multi gym in Northern Ireland. I'd fucking (inaudible) rowing machines and all, jogging machines all them uns
coming in with all the fucking blow in them. Perfect so it was
cos the units where we had the gym was owned by the JAME-
SON's and they have er police guards with them all the time,
they do security work, so this whole place is just fucking know
what I mean, there's police on the gates, there's police walking
in the grounds. CID with him at all times, for they know we go
in there and train seven days a week. I'm sitting there, what do
you call it. I knew it was coming, nobody else knew it was
coming. I just printed on this wee card TNT leave parcel and
get one of the, one of the guys to sign for it and put the boy
whose name it was in just put his signature at the bottom of it
and pinned it on the noticeboard. I'm sitting on the bike that
morning and wee Philly's sitting beside me just finishing off the
training (inaudible) in comes the TNT boy, he went to walk out
again. I said hey is that not for you there, pointed at the notice.
That'll be me, says will one of you's boys give us a hand in
with these. I say's what is it, rowing machine, jogging machine.
I say's aye I'll give you a hand in (inaudible) lifted it off and all
and brought it in all (inaudible) like that there, sign for that
there. Here's me no problem, wee squiggle (inaudible). Squiggle. Here's him right that one's yours dead on. I'm straight on
the phone, well mate, come down and get this stuff. Straight in
that door, out the back door and away in the car, perfect cover.
Police all around you and CID everywhere.

Verdicts

When interviewed Fulton denied any involvement with drugs in
any way. In his closing submissions Mr Treacy correctly
pointed to the absence of any reference to Fulton himself being
involved in the importation of Class A drugs in the form of

Ecstasy, and I find him not guilty on the Ecstasy charges,
counts 57 and 58. Mr Treacy also submitted that there was in-
sufficient evidence to link the Cannabis charges with the period
covered by the charges, but the evidence of Mr Jameson as to
the use of one of these units for a gym during 1999 provides
that link. I have already explained why I believe Fulton would
not have been affected by drink or drugs while driving, and that
reasoning applies equally to these occasions. Whilst there is no
extraneous evidence, other than that of Mr Jameson, to support
Fulton's account, as the account was clear, consistent and re-
peated on one than one occasion I am satisfied that it was true.
Fulton had the necessary connection with the physical trans-
portation of the Cannabis that was imported through delivery to
the gym, as well as the necessary intent, and I therefore find
him guilty on counts 59 and 60.

Attack on Mark Fulton on 10 February 1998

Admissions

Fulton faces two charges relating to 10 February 1998, count
61 that he had possession of a .38 revolver and ammunition
with intent to endanger life, and count 62 alleges that he had
possession of them in suspicious circumstances. These charges
relate to what is alleged to have been a staged attempt on the
life of Fulton's brother Mark "Swinger" Fulton by the defend-
ant. This was suggested and carried by the defendant with the
connivance of Swinger and their cousin Gary and was intended
to remove threats to them and their associates from the UVF,
threats connected with drug dealing. It was believed that be-
cause the UVF would inevitably be blamed for what would
appear to be an unsuccessful attempt on Swinger's life, to avoid
retaliation leading members of the UVF would ensure that the
threats against the Fultons would be removed.

That there was an incident involving Swinger Fulton in which
shots were fired on 10 February 1998 was not challenged. On
the afternoon of that day Peter Robinson, MP for East Belfast,
received a message that Mark Fulton wished to speak to him,
and a telephone number was given at which he could reach
Mark Fulton. Mr Robinson rang Mark Fulton at about 5:45 PM

and was told by him that meeting of the PUP and UVF had decided that Mark Fulton was to be killed, to which Mr Robinson replied that he would have to inform the police. Later that night Mrs Robinson received a message from a Pastor Kenny McClinton which she passed on to her husband. The message was that an attempt on Mark Fulton's life had been made about 9:15 PM but he had not been injured.

At, or shortly after, 8:30 PM Mrs Mary Gibson and her 12-year-old daughter Louise were in their home at 38 Westland Road, Portadown. Their house is opposite the junction with Hartfield Avenue, and overlooks Flat 2d Hartfield Avenue, the entrance to which is at the junction. Mrs Gibson heard what she described as "two thuds", and Louise saw a man running from a point close to the entrance to 2d. The man ran past the front of their house and passed their car and seemed to put his hand on the front of the car as he passed. This man appeared to be wearing a black woolly hat or a black balaclava; either a dark coloured tracksuit top or lightweight coat, and what looked like black tracksuit bottoms. Mrs Gibson saw Swinger and a man she knew as "Philly" standing in the doorway of the flats, and she thought that Philly had been shot as he had his hand over his mouth and was holding his stomach. She approached them and asked if they were alright, they said they were and asked for the police to be called.

As it happened Constable Reid had driven along Hartfield Avenue at about 8.30pm and seen a green Citroen Xantia normally used by Mark Fulton parked with its lights on near the junction of Hartfield Avenue and Westland Road. Constable Reid drove onto Westland Road and saw a black Honda Civic driven by Gary Fulton pass by. There were no passengers in this car. Gary Fulton lived at 2d Hartfield Avenue. Very soon afterwards Constable Reid heard a radio report that shots had been fired, and he returned to Hartfield Avenue and Westland Road, arriving at 2037. He was then approached by Mark Fulton and Philip McLean and spoke to them. A police search of the area led to the discovery of two bullet heads in the vicinity of the front door of 2d Hartfield Avenue. The first can be seen on the pathway 0.85 metres from the door in Exhibit A73 photograph 4, and the other appears in photograph 5 somewhat further from the door. Mr Rossi examined them and established that they were .38 Smith and Wesson, round nose, lead revolver bullets. They cannot be microscopically matched, but he thought that they had been discharged from the same barrel, which was either homemade or reworked.

These charges relate to admissions made by Fulton on 1 October 2000 when he travelled from Cornwall to London with Gary, and are to be found in the period between 0944 and 1406. During the journey Fulton spoke at length about several matters, and he referred to this incident. I do not propose to set out all, or even part, of his description. It contains the following.

There was a staged attempted on Mark "Swinger" Fulton's life planned and carried out by Fulton. The objective was to convey the impression that the attack had been carried out by the UVF. Because it would be attributed to the UVF, the UVF would be scared that their members would be attacked in retaliation, and as a result the UVF would stop threatening Fulton and his associates, whom they had been accusing of drug dealing.

(ii) Fulton, his brother Mark and their cousin Gary discussed and agreed to the plan, but they deliberately kept their henchman "Philly" (Philip McLean) in ignorance of the plan, with the result that when the attack was staged on Mark Fulton when Mclean was with him McLean believed that his life was in danger as well.

(iii) On the night the plan was carried out Swinger drove down to the spot with Philly in the Citroen Xantia and parked. Gary was to follow a short distance behind.

(iv) Fulton, who was to be the gunman, dressed in a tracksuit and baseball cap.

(v) When Swinger got out of the car Fulton ran over and fired a number of shots, pretending to fire them at Swinger. Four shots in all were fired, and Fulton described how some were damp, saying that he actually saw the bullets come out of the barrel of the gun, one of which hit the wall.

*(vi) Philly, who was not in on the plan, not surprisingly be-
lieved that it was a genuine attack. He crawled under the
dashboard of the Xantia to hide. He had his mobile phone with
him which accidentally recorded what happened.*

*(vii) The police were very quickly on the scene, and Fulton also
arrived in the Honda with Gary very soon afterwards.*

*(viii) Fulton and Gary then went to the house of Jameson, a
member of the UVF, and in a shouted exchange through a
closed door threatened retaliation. Jameson then came to the
scene straight away in an effort to persuade Swinger that he
had not been responsible for what happened.*

*(ix) The implication is that Jameson then drove straight to Bel-
fast where a Brigade staff meeting was summoned in the middle
of the night to find out who was responsible for the attack on
Swinger.*

*(x) The UVF were frightened as they thought that this had
been a genuine attack, as did Philly, until Fulton told him three
months later what had really happened.*

*(xi) As Fulton ran away from the scene he jumped over a car,
and as he did so he rested his hand on the bonnet, although he
was wearing rubber gloves at the time.*

*(xii) Fulton recounted how the description of himself by a num-
ber of witnesses were contradictory, and wrong in some
respects. Whilst they were correct in referring to the tracksuit,
and the baseball cap, the reference to his wearing red and
white trainers was wrong as he was wearing lime green trainers.*

*(xiii) He said that the police found the first round that "fizzled
and popped out" of the .38 he used.*

*(xiv) He explained this phenomenon by saying that the rounds
were damp, but if a few grains of powder were dry they are
"the ones that fizzle it just enough to ignite them and pop it"*

Verdicts

Fulton was not specifically questioned about this. Mr Treacy confined his specific submissions to the point that on Fulton's story there could be no intent on his part to endanger life, or to cause serious injury to property, or to enable others to do so. I agree that there was no intent to endanger life. There is insufficient evidence to say whether any of the bullets hit the building, and nothing to suggest that there was any damage to property that could be described as serious. I therefore find the defendant not guilty on count 61. However, if Fulton's account is reliable and true, it cannot be suggested, nor has it been suggested, that to stage a mock murder attempt, and to fire shots during it, with a view to resolving differences between rival groups of terrorists, can be said to be a lawful object. That being so, if Fulton's account is true then he is guilty of count 62, possession of the gun and ammunition in suspicious circumstances.

Are these admissions reliable and true? For the reasons I have already given I am satisfied that Fulton was not affected by drinks or drugs during this conversation. There is a high degree of conformity with the known facts about the case, such as the type of cars involved, the personnel who were present, and the type of weapon involved. As Fulton describes how the other main actors were his brother and his cousin, it can be argued that he was in a position to learn the details from them, and it would therefore be easier for him to place it in the narrative. As against this, the sheer volume of detail in his account suggests that it is true, in particular his saying that he touched the bonnet of the car. Is it at all likely that he would have been aware of such a detail if he had not taken part? He refers to having not worn red and white trainers but lime green ones. There is no evidence that anyone described the colour of the trainers, but is it really possible that someone who has picked up details from listening to others describing events in which he played no part would have invented such a detail as wearing lime green trainers? As against this, there is his description of the bullets popping out of the gun, which, in the absence of any forensic evidence, seems improbable to say the least. Nevertheless, this was an incident which purported to be an attack on his brother's life, and taking the evidence as a whole, I am satisfied that Fulton's account of what happened is reliable in its essential components and true. I find him guilty on count 62.

Directing the activities of, and membership of, the LVF between 5 June 1997 and 30 September 1999

Admissions

I have left counts 41 and 42 to the end because they involve consideration of the evidence relating to the other counts faced by Fulton, but before turning to the evidence I have to say something about the nature of the charges, and this includes the dates contained within both counts. Count 41 alleges that Fulton directed terrorism...

The judge went on to discuss certain legal issues raised in Fulton's case regarding these counts on the indictment. He concluded:

For these reasons I consider that there are only a limited number of admissions that may prove either the directing or membership counts... I am satisfied that what is required is proof that an accused was in a position in a terrorist organisation that enabled him to give orders to commit terrorist acts in the expectation that other members of the organisation would carry those orders into effect, whether the order was of a specific or a general nature. The inclusion of the words "at any level" make it clear that a subordinate who has such a position over others can commit this offence, and that the offence is not confined to those at the head of such organisations.

Of the individual episodes already considered, the three which comprise counts 1 to 13 relating to the murder of Mrs O'Neill, the attempted murder of Janelle Woods, and the attempted murder of Mr Murnin on the night of 4 and the early morning of 5 June 1999 can be relied on in support of the charge of directing terrorism as they occurred within the relevant period. I have already dealt with the circumstances of these offences, and Fulton's role in them, and it is unnecessary to repeat the evidence and my conclusions. I need only refer to the following remarks which related to the events of that night.

(i)   B5, page 46 "so the night I planned the three of them three different units going out three different places".

(ii)   B12, at page 193 "I'd give all the orders that all the rest of the boys were going out and everybody had their check times".

(iii)   B3, at page 30 "I'd ordered the fucking two houses hit, with Catholics in them in our area".

(iv)   B45, at page 46 "I fucking planned three of them".

These admissions plainly amount to directing acts of terrorism on that night. Two of the attacks were carried out by others at his direction, and the third was also carried out at his direction but he also took part in it. A person who plans such an attack and also takes part in it directs the attack as much as an officer who plans a military operation and then leads his men into action to carry that plan out...

The judge then lists several passages from the admissions.

The remaining admission, which can be identified as relating to the 28 month period covered by the charges, is to be found in B63 at page 909. Fulton and Dave had been talking about the death of a police officer on an occasion when a pipe bomb was thrown from a protestant crowd. The following exchange then took place.

Dave: So I mean how does it work, is it like cause I mean I don't know a lot about it. Is it like you've got like a load of people that are fucking in charge that say right you go out, and you do this you go out and you do that. How's it.

Jim: What do you mean the paramilitaries?

Dave: Yeah. How's it work like.

Jim: Well, I'd ave been in charge. Before I left I was in charge so I'd ave been fucking arranging everything.

Dave: Right.

Jim: I'd be saying right you boys at such and such a time yous be there yous do that there, and then everybody in the whole town knows who you are, so once the crowd builds, you're getting the ordin, the ordinary protestors.

I am satisfied that Fulton was referring to the period when he went to America at the end of 1999 (which provides the closing point of the 28-month period in the charges), and that his statement that he "was in charge" before he left is confirmation that he was the leader of the LVF in this area up until he went to America. That being so, if the admission is reliable it is evidence both of his membership of the LVF and, as he was in charge, that he was directing its activities in this area, a role which amongst other things involved the organisation of demonstrations. B63 relates to a car journey on 24 October 2000 and covers the period between 2356 and 2254. I am satisfied that Fulton is driving on this occasion as Dave's evidence was that Fulton drove him to Reading Services to meet another undercover officer called Ron. They then returned to Plymouth, and it is recorded that Fulton dropped Dave off in Plymouth. For the reasons I have already given I am satisfied that Fulton was not affected by drink or drugs on this occasion. His admission is consistent with his repeated accounts of how he was under the patronage of Billy Wright and rose through the ranks of the terrorist groups that he was in, succeeding to more important positions when the other leaders were in prison, so that in due course he became the leader of the LVF in the Portadown area. I am satisfied that these admissions are reliable.

In support of the inferences that can be drawn from these passages, the prosecution also rely on a number of photographs, and a video of Billy Wright's funeral, items which were seized during the investigations in this case. I shall deal with the latter first. I have watched the video and it shows a group of men dressed in white shirts and other items of matching clothing who form a guard of honour beside the hearse containing Wright's coffin as the cortège forms up and then moves off through the streets. In his witness statement, which was agreed, Detective Sergeant Carson identified Fulton as one of these in the guard of honour. Whilst Fulton's presence as a member of this guard of honour on its own may not prove that he was a member of the LVF at the time of Wright's death, at the very least his presence in such a group gives rise to a strong inference that he was a close associate of Wright, and not just someone who was a barfly who picked up crumbs of information from Wright and other terrorists.

This inference gains additional support from the contents of Exhibit A107, and Fulton's reaction to some of the photographs, particularly numbers 5 and 7. Photograph 7 shows what is plainly a LVF flag being held over the headstone of Billy Wright's grave, the standard bearer is flanked on both sides by men with what appear to be automatic pistols, and all three are wearing balaclavas and military clothing. The same scene can be seen in photographs 1 and 5. From the headstone in photograph 7 it is possible to make out that Wright died on 27 December 1997. This is therefore at the least prima facie evidence of the date of his death. Neil's statement.. he describes Fulton pointing to one of the photographs.

On seeing the photographs he said `Don't I look well'. He pointed at one of the photographs, which depicted three men in camouflage clothing, standing over the grave of Billy WRIGHT. Jim identified to me that the man in the centre was Mark Foulton (sic), with Jim Foulton (sic) on the right and Gary Foulton (sic) on the left of Mark Foulton (sic).

... Fulton's identification of himself as one of the party is extremely strong evidence that he was not only a member of the LVF, but a prominent one, and is a further contradiction of his assertion that he was a wannabe, a barfly and never in the LVF.

Verdicts

Fulton made no admissions during interview and said that his remarks were complete fiction. No specific defence submissions were made on these charges. It can only be the LVF to which Fulton was referring when he said that he was the leader before he went to America, and I am therefore satisfied that the prosecution have proved that he was a member of that organisation within the 28 month period covered by count 42 and I find him guilty on that charge. The events of 4 and 5 June 1999 occurred shortly before Fulton went to America. By then it is apparent that he had long since transferred his allegiance to the LVF, and to judge from the admissions relating to the events of that night, was the leader of the LVF in Portadown at that time, Wright's death having occurred on 27 December 1997. I am satisfied that count 41 has been proved and I find him guilty on that count also.

CHAPTER 35

Muriel Gibson

Withholding information about the shooting of William Fletcher on 6 January 1997

The facts of this count on the indictment may be found previously under the case against Fulton. He was found guilty on count 28 intending to wound Mr Fletcher by shooting but not guilty of his attempted murder. This was the incident where Fulton was looking for Derek Wray.

Gibson faced a count of failing to give information about this shooting of William Fletcher which happened on 6 January 1997. In interview, she was questioned about her knowledge of this episode. She was again questioned about this during further interviews. She replied no comment when the matter was raised, except she said that she would not know if Mark (that is Mark Fulton), and Billy (that is Billy Wright), were seen by the police in Deramore Drive that night.

Admissions

Referring to the recordings, the judge recounts how Fulton describes how he found that Philly (Philip McLean) had already gone up Alexandra Avenue, at which point Gibson interjects *"Philly was just away like a fucking rocket"*. Fulton then described how he made his way back to Gibson's house. There then occurred the following exchange[18] between them. The judge continued:

Gibson's references to Fulton "sitting up the stairs waiting on the fucking radio", and to Philly sitting with a big cigar and champagne very strongly suggest that she is recalling what she observed that night, and that in the immediate aftermath of the shooting she was fully aware of what had occurred, and Fulton's part in it." He added, "... the portion relied on starts at 12.36. Throughout Gibson could be clearly heard, she spoke precisely, and her speech flowed easily. At all times she sounded as if she was speaking perfectly normally and there was nothing to suggest any impairment of thought or speech either by alcohol or drugs. No request was made for any other portion of the tape to be played... As no undercover officer was present there is no basis upon which it can be argued that what transpired was the functional equivalent of an interview. I am satisfied that her account on that occasion is reliable, and that she and Fulton, who had recently come to the West Country following his return from America, were reminiscing about what they had done.

In another tape recorded some fourteen months later, the judge commented:

This conversation occurred in mid-afternoon. Having listened to the tape I was satisfied that she was not affected by alcohol or drugs, and the reliability of her admissions is not therefore called into question by these factors. In her account Gibson describes what Fulton, who is not present during this conversation, has said about the shooting in the past. She then described what happened in her house.

Muriel: I think, I think I've put about, er, five in him, he said. Billy goes 'right' and he had a bottle of champagne and a cigar and then the next thing it come on the news. A man has been shot dead, (inaudible) sitting quiet cos I was burning all the

---

[18] The transcript of this exchange is to be found under the count against Fulton: Conspiracy to Murder Derek Wray and Attempted Murder of William Fletcher – 6 January 1997

clothes, it was summertime and the house was just boiling, you know, and then I was burning all the clothes and they were sitting around in shorts, listening, our man has been shot dead, went "yes", in Belfast, went that's not him and another man has been shot in Portadown, but not killed. (Laughter) (inaudible) (Rain speaks). It came out all perfect about your mans has been fatally wounded, and we're all 'yes' (inaudible). He did take five bullets but he took them everywhere (laughter). (Pause). It was fucking hilarious that night because Thelma kept, she, thought that I was screwing Swinger and she kept phoning up and I couldn't tell her there was an operation going on (inaudible). I know he's there, I heard his voice. I know he's there, and im going he's not fucking here I don't know where he is, and I know theres listening on the phone and Im saying I'll kill her Swinger, I'll kill her and Swingers going you're not going to have to I'll kill her I'll kill her, I can hear his voice an all she's shouting into the phone, I'm going I haven't seen Swinger, I don't know where he is. Sitting with the big cigar (pause).

The judge points out some differences in this account from her earlier account before turning to the verdict.

Verdict

In view of her very clear admissions fourteen months before I do not consider that her mistake about the season is sufficient to raise a reasonable doubt as to the reliability of her admissions, and I am satisfied that on 6 January 1997 she knew that Fulton had committed an arrestable offence because he came back to her house after the shooting and told those present, including her, that he shot Mr Fletcher several times, and it was not until they heard the news on the radio that they realised that Mr Fletcher had not died. Once she had learnt what Fulton had done, she was under a duty to give that information to a constable within a reasonable time. She did not do so, and there is no suggestion that she had a reasonable excuse for not doing so, nor can I conceive of one. I therefore find her guilty on count 65

The murder of Adrian Lamph and possession of a handgun and ammunition with intent to endanger life

Admissions

I am satisfied that the murder of Adrian Lamph was a sectarian murder; that the gunman was the person seen on a mountain bike by Mr McCandless; that the gunman removed his clothing soon afterwards, and that it was burnt in the alleyway in an attempt to destroy all the clothing, and hence destroy evidence linking him to the crime. A local shop keeper sold two tins of Swan lighter fuel over a 10-minute period at about 11.30 on the morning of the shooting. This was unusual as normally she would only sell one tin a week. I am satisfied that the lighter fuel had been purchased from her in preparation for, and was used for, the attempted destruction of the clothes worn by the gunman in the fire.

Although extensive searches of the area were made by the police in the aftermath of the murder, and in succeeding days, the bike has not been recovered. On the morning of Wednesday 22 April Sergeant Beck found a new, black "Townsend Beartooth" make mountain bike in the back yard of a building he ultimately established was 84 West Street, and it was pointed out to Detective Constable Jones. However, there was some difficulty at the time in establishing precisely to which house the yard belonged, and when Detective Constable Jones returned at 09.30 on 23 April this bike had gone. Whether this was the bike used by the gunman cannot therefore be established.

Gibson is charged with the murder of Adrian Lamph – count 66; and with possession of a handgun and ammunition with intent to endanger life. The prosecution case is that she assisted in the preparations for the murder, whether she knew that Adrian Lamph was to be the specific target, or because, as Mr Millar put it in his written closing submissions, "she knew the specific target in advance her experience would have led her to know the nature of that attack and that death or really serious bodily harm was the intended result".

However, he submitted that were Gibson to be found not guilty of murder, it would be open to the court to return a verdict of guilty of the offence of assisting offenders on this count. Gibson is charged with possession of the handgun and ammunition on the basis that she took it from the gunman afterwards and helped to spirit it away.

The prosecution have to rely on four evidential tapes, the first tape relates to a period starting at 2123 on 25 May 2000 and finishing on 26 May at 0007. No undercover officers were present, and the recording commenced when Gibson and her daughters returned to Gibson's house having been at a pub. One of the daughters introduces the topic of someone called "Sargy" telling her about a shooting. It has been established that she started to discuss this at 2324. Gibson then joins in by describing her part in the events relating to the shooting of Adrian Lamph and she says a number of things.

(i)   It was Philly (Philip McLean) who was supposed to burn the clothes afterwards, but he was late.

(ii)   When Gibson arrived Gary (ie Gary Fulton) had already stripped off his clothes and was naked because he had nothing to change into, so she told him to hide behind a gate.

(iii) She said she would take the clothes and the gun because Philly had not turned up.

(iv) She got away with the gun.

However, these admissions came after, and have to be viewed in the context of, her opening remarks on the matter, remarks which are the basis of the prosecution case on the murder charge. At page 950 there occurred the following.

Muriel: I know, I know, tell me about it. After LAMPH was shot.

Female Landry: Aha.

Muriel: And I run away with the gun, Philly was supposed to burn the clothes, I was supposed to take the gun away.

Female Landry: Philly was late and you had to fuck'n.

Muriel: Philly showed up late. Poured lighter fluid all over the clothes (overtalking) put it next to a gas tank, in somebody's back so they called the Fire Brigade, they put it out and got half a Tee-Shirt with Stoned Again.

The reference to lighter fluid being poured over the clothes is consistent with Gibson burning the clothes because Philly was late. However, if he was to do this, how was she equipped to do so? The key phrase is "Philly was supposed to burn the clothes, I was supposed to take the gun away". This, the prosecution submit, shows that Gibson's role was made known to her before the shooting, in which case she must have known that a murder was intended, and so is guilty of murder as a participant in a joint enterprise, or conspiracy, where she knew her part before the murder, and not that she simply helped afterwards without knowing what was intended beforehand. This is a crucial distinction, and the defence addressed it in of their written submissions.

Indeed, later in the same tape, Mrs Gibson is recorded as describing how she was running up Ranfurley Road when she heard a bang which she was clearly not expecting. She is recorded as saying "I said oh fuck that's somebody's killed". The prosecution's reply to this on the application for direction was that Mrs Gibson was not talking about the Lamph shooting but was more likely to be expressing her concern about Gary or Philly. That is an illustration of the problems associated with the interpretation of ambiguous comments made loosely in a casual conversation. As with the earlier comment ("I was supposed to take the gun away"), it is open to more than one interpretation. In other words, the Court cannot exclude the reasonable possibility that Mrs Gibson was either referring to an arrangement made after the event or to an arrangement which did not embrace anyone's murder.

The inescapable conclusion is that all of the comments attributed to Mrs Gibson in this tape are explicable on the basis of involvement in assisting offenders after an event the nature of which was unknown to her.

Before commenting on these submissions, I propose to deal first with the submissions that had been made about the reliability of Gibson's admissions. As already indicated, she and her daughters had just returned from a pub, and the defence submit that the court must have doubts as to the accuracy and reliability of the admissions Gibson made because of the amount of drink she had consumed in the pub and consumed, or may have consumed, after they returned home. Parts of the tape were played on several occasions during the trial, and I have again listened to the material parts of the enhanced tape on the equipment provided by the defence. I have considered all the points made during the trial, and those of the defendant's written submissions. In view of the conclusion, I have come to on the remaining evidence on this charge it is sufficient to say that, whilst there is evidence that Gibson had been drinking, she is speaking clearly, fluently and unambiguously at all relevant times and I see no reason to doubt that the reliability of her admission is impaired.

The next evidential tape relates to 3 July 2000 and covers the period between 0816 and 1226 when Gibson is in the company of Dave S. At their height, these admissions only relate to what happened afterwards and do not support the case that she had prior knowledge of what was intended. I am satisfied Gibson was not affected by drink or drugs when she made these admissions.

I will refer to a conversation at this stage even though that is to take it out of chronological sequence as it relates to a conversation on 15 September 2000 between 1651 and 2057 when Gibson is speaking to her daughters. No undercover officers are present. Gibson says that she was seen by John Smith and someone she refers to as "Wee Michael" when she went out to pick up the gun after the Lamph shooting and found Gary Fulton naked in the alleyway. This does not indicate prior knowledge, although it does provide further confirmation that she moved the gun afterwards. I am satisfied that she was not affected by alcohol or drugs when she said this.

I now turn to a conversation between Gibson and an English friend named Vanessa at Gibson's house between 1306 and 1711 on 25 July 2000. The prosecution now rely on the passage starting with the words "that's a lot of bollocks" and it has been established that this portion starts at 1432. In an extended passage lasting until 1444, some 12 minutes, Gibson describes her role in the events relating to Adrian Lamph's murder in considerable detail. I do not intend to set out the entire conversation, but the following are the relevant admissions.

(i)   The rider was wearing a red, white and blue scarf around his face, a baseball cap and a t-shirt that said `stoned again'.

(ii)   Gibson dressed "them all up for the occasion. I didn't know what I was dressing them up for but I was dressing them up anyway."

(iii) The gunman rode the bike past Lamph, called to him and "shot him right between the eyes, took the whole head off".

(iv) She ran up to "Ronnie and Jill's yard" and found the gunman naked. "And I go, what, what, what do you want me to do what have you done."

(v)   The gunman then told her to take the gun, which she did and arranged for it to be hidden.

(vi) As she was receiving the gun Philly came up, was given the clothes and told to burn them. The implication is that it was the gunman who did this, although Gibson had asked him to give her the clothes.

(vii) Philly then poured lighter fuel over the clothes in the alley.

(viii)Only part of the t-shirt was burnt. It had what she described as "two big round squibley eyes on it".

(ix) She then arranged for some boys to collect the bike. The bike is collected by "Don" and he brings it to her house, so she tells him to put it anywhere, in somebody's alleyway.

(x)   Very soon afterwards her grandson comes and tells her that he is riding about on the bike which has been left in "our", i.e. his alleyway.

(xi) Gibson then phones Don and berates him for leaving the bike in her daughter's alleyway and tells him to move it.

(xii) She tells Don to throw it in the river which he does, and so the bike is never found.

(xiii)She told Swinger that she had lent him, i.e. the gunman, the t-shirt. She described it as unique.

(xiv) When it is realised that because the t-shirt is so distinctive she destroys six photographs of men wearing it.

I am satisfied that the admissions are reliable. They were entirely unprompted by any undercover officer or agent of the State. Gibson chose to describe her exploits to her friend Vanessa. The admissions were made over a 12-minute period in the early afternoon. The tape was played in court and there is nothing to indicate that Gibson was affected in any way by drink or drugs. In this instance it is not just Gibson's voice in the tapes that allows that conclusion to be made, but, as I pointed out at 1424, that is 8 minutes before the start of the passage relied upon, Gibson said "I'm fully recovered I got back on the wagon", and then "I died the death last night about 11:00 last night". I am satisfied that she meant by this that she had recovered from having been drinking two days before and had not been drinking on this day.

That tape contains the fullest account by Gibson of her involvement in the Lamph murder, and the tenor of it is unmistakably that she did not know beforehand what was intended. She said that she did not know what she was dressing them up for, and her statement to the gunman "what do you want me to do, what have you done", if true, suggests that she did not know in advance that her role was to take the gun afterwards. It is thereby at variance in her statement at another time that "I was supposed to take the gun away".

Some interviews were deleted from the papers. In the remaining interviews Gibson made no reply when questioned about the Lamph murder, save that in [in one tape] she said that she was sorry for the Lamph family and their loss.

Verdicts

The judge concluded:

I am not satisfied that the prosecution have proved beyond reasonable doubt that Gibson had prior knowledge of what was intended, nor am I satisfied that she knew that death or really serious bodily harm was the intended result when she dressed "them", whoever "them" may be. I am, however, satisfied that she played a major role in what happened afterwards. She came across Gary and was in no doubt that there had been a shooting. She did everything she could to ensure that all evidence would be destroyed or removed by asking for the clothes, and then taking the gun, which she said was "still hot", away and arrange for it to be hidden. When she learnt that the bike had not been removed, she took steps to see that it was, and arranged for someone to throw it in the river. I am further satisfied that this person, whom she referred to as "Don", was in fact Don Marno to whom she made several telephone calls on Wednesday 22 April (1), and Thursday 23 April (6), accordingly to an analysis of the phone calls. By removing the gun, she was not merely determined to impede the gunman's apprehension or prosecution but intended that it would be preserved for another occasion.

For these reasons I find Gibson not guilty of murder on count 66, but guilty of doing without lawful authority or reasonable excuse an act with intent to impede the apprehension or prosecution of the murderer of Adrian Lamph. I also find her guilty on count 67.

Conspiracy to place a bomb in Dundalk in 1997

Admissions

Gibson faces two counts relating to this bomb both between 1 January and 25 May 1997. The first is count 70, conspiracy to cause an explosion of a nature likely to endanger life or cause serious injury to property in the Republic of Ireland. The second is count 71, possession of the device with intent by means thereof to endanger life or cause serious injury to property in the Republic of Ireland, or to enable some other person to do so. These charges depend upon admissions made by Gibson on two occasions.

The first is the result of a probe where no undercover officers were present and covers the period between 2143 and 2337 on

30 March 2000. Two portions and then a further passage are brief, with the latter portion of the transcript established as starting at 2243 and lasting for 42 seconds. One of the issues raised by the defence at an earlier stage was that [a tape] should be ruled inadmissible because Gibson was affected by drink or drugs. I rejected this contention at my ruling of 23 May 2006. As part of the defence case an enhanced copy has been produced, and it is submitted on behalf of Gibson that it sounds as if she under the influence of alcohol. In view of my conclusion on these counts I do not propose to deal with this issue at this stage, although I will return to it in connection with some of the remaining counts.

The portion of the tape upon which the prosecution rely in support of these charges is to be found is as follows.

Muriel: No you, see whenever he brought me them detonators you know before the bomb in Dundalk, he brought me them detonators and, he was expecting Swinger to be there, eh, it was a total shock to him. think it was his way of putting Swinger in a hole.

Jim: Yeah.

Muriel: And ah, Swinger sent me and I said have you got eh something for Swinger and he says eh aye I have, but em, but I dont think I should be giving it to you and I says, well then you wont be giving it to anybody and then he went out and he put them all in a sock and give them to me. But the powergel that we got from him didn't work.

Jim: I know it didn't work, fuck sake, sure (inaudible) didn't we swap fucking weapons for it.

Muriel: Mmm.

Jim: Fuck sake, twice.

Muriel: It didn't work, I was, I smelt it, it was fucking like rotten eggs and it kept bubbling, then it kept settling down, then it kept bubbling, it wasn't, it isn't right.

Jim: Powergel, that powergel was off fuckin a long time ago for fuck sake.

Muriel: I actually think there was something added to it.

Jim: No, it was just, it was old stuff, fucking sell past date, long sell past, date stuff been lying fucking years and they kept on blaming the detonators. The detonators, the detonators, the detonators weren't powerful enough to set it off.

Muriel: Well the detonators came from Sparky too.

Jim: Aye, but don't forget they weren't fucking eh, military dets, they were only small commercial dets.

Muriel: I know.

Jim: For one wee stick of fuck'n, what do you call it, powergel.

Muriel: Ahem.

Jim: Know what I mean they were sticking fuckin 2 or 3 in them try and set off a fucking a bomb then fucking height. The military det was a big fucking, big fucking.

Muriel: He knew.

Jim: Course he fucking knew, he was in the Army. He was handing over fucking commercial detonators.

Muriel: But that night that I went to pick up them detonators, that really really shocked him, because he, he (pause) and Kathy KERR was in on it.

In this passage Gibson admits that she obtained a quantity of detonators for Swinger from someone she refers to as "Sparky", and then says "But the Powergel that we got from him didn't work", to which Fulton replies "Didn't we swap fucking weapons for it". Gibson put this "before the bomb in Dundalk". However, there is no reference to either the detonators or the explosive being intended for use in the Republic of Ireland. Whilst Gibson is clearly familiar with its properties, she says the Powergel did not work to which Fulton replies that it was swapped for weapons, an exchange which suggests that this consignment of Powergel could not have been used in the Dundalk bomb.

The connection with the Dundalk bomb in particular depends another tape. This relates to a recording of Gibson and Dave S on 3 June 2000 as they work at a market stall from 1230 onwards.

Muriel: The problem with the Prods is they could never make fucking decent bombs (Dave S laughs). Honest to God they couldn't (inaudible) blowing up all kinds of fucking things, trying to make bombs. No good. They're good at shooting.

Dave S: Yeah.

Muriel: Good accurate, accurate marksmen you know. That's why you always here (sic) about Catholics getting shot and Protestants getting blew up (inaudible).

Dave S: Cause they're trying to make their own bombs.

Muriel: (Inaudible) (Dave S laughs) (pause) the last one we sent down to Dublin went off in fucking Dundalk.

Dave S: How far's that from Dublin.

Muriel: About er half way there.

Dave S: (laughs) what like. On a timer or just.

Muriel: Well see, I was running round for days buying these er wind up watches. You couldn't have.

Dave S: What the old style.

Muriel: Do you know how hard they are to find now. They're really hard to find now.

Dave S: I think you'd have to buy like erm you know those railwayman's watches.

Muriel: Yeah.

Dave S: Things where you gotta pull the thing out like that.

Muriel: Yeah.

Dave S: Yeah. That's the only ones I've ever seen like of like.

Muriel: Well you need one of them you need a wind up watch. I had every wind up watch in the town (inaudible) run round in the taxi (inaudible) was hilarious so it was. Then we sent that one down.

Dave S: (Inaudible talk and laughter) was anyone hurt.

Muriel: Yeah, there were a couple of them (inaudible) but none of ours I can tell you. They (inaudible) fucking smelt it burning you know.

Dave S: (Inaudible).

Muriel: (Inaudible).

Dave S: Does it.

Muriel: Yeah. It starts to bubble and then it starts to stink.

Dave S: And you can hear it.

Muriel: Ah ha. You can see it (laughs) you can see it bubbling (inaudible) fuck. Get out of here (laughs).

Dave S: Jesus Christ. Get out of that fucking things as quick as you can say jack shit.

Muriel: You're supposed to keep it er at the same temperature all the time.

Dave S: What is it.

Muriel: Its em power gel.

Dave S: Its what.

Muriel: Power gel.

Dave S: Whats that.

Muriel: I don't know, I just know it, eh, to see it (inaudible) the smell of it. I could pick the smell of it out a mile away. It smells like fucking rotten eggs (inaudible).

Dave S: (Laughs) but what causes it to heat up.

Muriel: Just on its own, it fucking, it sweats, it sweats (inaudible sentence)

They then deal with customers at the stall for several minutes and Muriel talks to a customer about Ireland. She then continues talking to Dave S.

Muriel: Yes its starts to bubble then and then it starts to seep, fuck and you can't get it offa yer.

Dave S: (Inaudible) a liquid or.

Muriel: Yeah (pause) its gel (inaudible) starts bubbling you can't stop it, you know.

Dave S: (Inaudible) (laughs).

Muriel: No you can't stop it unless you've got a freezer, something sitting there you can stick it in, you know and stop it.

Dave S: (Inaudible).

Muriel: Ah ha that's it (inaudible).

Dave S: (Dave and Muriel overtalking).

Muriel: No (inaudible) Dundalk the next day (serious interference) blew up in the (inaudible) and caught a couple of boys that were coming out (both laugh) it was (inaudible) after that.

Dave S: Oh well.

Gibson discusses the properties of the bomb in detail, showing considerable familiarity with the properties of Powergel. Twice she refers to "we" sending the bomb down, and she refers to her obtaining the timing devices. The use of the term "we" in conjunction with her description of herself obtaining devices to be used as timers, together with what she said in B48, raises a strong inference that she was an active participant in the preparation of a bomb that was to be exploded in Dublin.

Nevertheless, there are three respects in which her admissions are inconsistent with her involvement in the preparation of the device found in Dundalk on 25 May 1997.

(i)   She twice refers to obtaining watches for use as a timer but the evidence is that a clock, not a watch, was used in the Dundalk bomb.

(ii)   The reference to the device having "blew up" is consistent with its partial explosion, but she goes on to infer that two people were injured in the explosion when she says it "blew up in the (inaudible) and caught a couple of boys that were coming out". There is, however, no evidence of anyone being injured.

(iii)   The reference to the Powergel not working.

Verdicts

These are significant inconsistencies and weaken the otherwise strong inference to which I have referred. In interview she was questioned about this allegation and she denied involvement. At one point she said that she had heard about it in a bar, and at another she said that she was not involved in making this bomb. And another, she said that she had "heard it in the pub anyway". Whilst it may well be the case that Gibson had possession of detonators and other materials used in the construction of explosive devices at some time prior to 25 May 1997, these inconsistencies give rise to a reasonable doubt as to whether she was implicated in the preparation of the bomb that was found in Dundalk on that day, and I find her not guilty on counts 70 and 71.

Possession of detonators

Admissions

Count 72 charges Gibson with possession of detonators with intent "by means thereof to endanger life or cause serious injury to property in the United Kingdom or in the Republic of Ireland, or to enable some other person so to do" between 1 January 1995 and 30 September 1999. This charge depends upon the references to Gibson being given detonators in the passage already quoted. In this passage the time to which Gibson is referring is only identified as being "before the bomb in Dundalk", which infers that it was before 25 May 1997, but is not otherwise precise. She describes how Swinger sent her to someone she refers to as "Sparky", who put detonators in a sock and gave them to her. In the closing submissions it was argued that it was not clear whether Gibson was aware that she was in possession of detonators, but her references to detonators are clear evidence that she was fully aware of what they were after she had received them from Sparky, and I am satisfied that if the admissions are reliable there is ample evidence to establish that Gibson had physical possession of the detonators, that she knew what they were, and that she intended that they would used to initiate a bomb on some occasion.

Also, in the closing defence submissions it is argued that there is no evidence that they were used either in the Dundalk bomb or any other explosion where life or property was endangered. That is correct. But the count alleges that the intent was to endanger life or cause serious injury to property, not that life was endangered, or that serious to property was caused. It also alleges that this was to be in either the United Kingdom or the Republic of Ireland, and any Loyalist explosion would be bound to be in either jurisdiction. Finally, the intent is alleged "to enable some other persons so to do". The admissions on their face clearly establish the necessary elements of the offence alleged.

During interview Gibson denied involvement in making the Dundalk bomb, and although she was not asked about possession of the detonators separately, her general denial of involvement in the Dundalk bomb should be treated as a denial of this charge.

Verdict

The tape is the sole basis for this charge, and when referring to it, I said that I would return to the issue whether Gibson was affected by drink or drugs during that conversation, and I now do so. The tape covers the period between 2143 and 2337, and the admissions are contained in a passage that comprises most of the 42 second period from the foot of that page to the end of direct speech at the bottom of a following page. It is asserted by the defence that the enhanced tape, presumably the other tape prepared by Mr Kielty, shows that "the defendant sounds as if she is under the influence of alcohol. Her speech is slow and

halting". Whilst preparing this judgment I have listened care-
fully to this passage on the enhanced tape several times, and I
remain of the view I expressed in my ruling of 23 May 2006.
Gibson can be heard speaking clearly, distinctly, coherently,
with no sign of confused thought or expression, nor is there any
apparent slurring of speech. Although this conversation takes
place late at night at 2243, I am satisfied that there is nothing
to suggest that Gibson is affected by drink or drugs. I am satis-
fied that the admissions are reliable, and I find her guilty on
count 72.

Possession of pipe bombs

Admissions

Count 73 alleges that she had possession of a quantity of pipe
bombs with intent to endanger life etc. This charge appears to
be based solely on the following brief extract from B85, a re-
cording covering the period between 0900 and 0930 on 9 July
2000. This part of the conversation comes after a discussion be-
tween Gibson and Sam, one of the undercover officers, a
conversation brought about by the news coverage about
Drumcree. During that conversation Gibson is recorded as
having spoken about plastic bullets and injuries which individu-
als have received from them in previous years.

Muriel: I got hit on a rebound, so I did, fucking, my leg was
black, you know crawling across that no mans land, you know
the field. There were they dig it all up and they'd put a moat
around it you know and filled it up full of old muddy water you
know and we got this corrugated tin and threw it down over it,
you know, so that we could crawl across it and get into the
field, you know to get closer to the Police, you know so we
could you know distract them while the other ones threw the
blast bombs at them. And we were, we were lying in that field
and all of a sudden, they done a big switch around (inaudible)
before us going what the fuck are they doing you know and I
said hit the ground, everybody, everybody hit the ground. And
the bullets just came fucking flying, you could hear them going
right past your ears and I got a rebound one. Rebounded off the
ground, hit me on the leg and that was, I mean I was limping. It
was fucking black, it was really, really black, and that was just

a rebound, you know if would have hit my leg it would have broken it.

Sam: Is a blast bomb over there, what we call a petrol bomb here.

Muriel: No, a petrol bomb is made in a milk bottle, with sugar and petrol and a rag, a blast bomb, its made of a piece of steel pipe and er, you fill it full of black powder and then you fill it up, or part of it full of, you know the pebbles out of a cartridge.

In order to secure a conviction on this count the prosecution have to show that Gibson was party to a joint enterprise whereby she would assist others who had physical possession of blast bombs by creating a diversion to enable the blast bombers to get closer to the security forces so that they could throw their blast bombs at the security forces.

Although Gibson does not refer directly to Drumcree, it is clear from the context of her earlier comments about Drumcree, and from those comments being made on 9 July 2000, a time when the tension over Drumcree would be high, that her description does relate to Drumcree. Her description of the ditch also makes it clear that she is referring to the confrontations between the demonstrators and the police that were a feature of Drumcree, and which, for example, gave rise to the charges relating to Fulton considered earlier in this judgment.

Gibson was questioned about these remarks in interview when the relevant parts of the tape were played to her. She either said "no comment", or she denied strapping the blast bombs around herself. This conversation occurred between 0900 and 0930 and there is no suggestion that she was affected by drink or drugs at that time of day. The defence submission was put as follows.

She was claiming that she was trying to get closer to the police so that 'we could you know distract them while the other ones threw the blast bombs at them.' She does not claim to have been party to a joint enterprise to throw blast bombs at the police. Nowhere in the conversation does she claim to have been in possession or control of pipe bombs. The fact that she was able to describe how they are made does not constitute evidence of possession. Nor is her suggestion that 'you could strap them all the way round you and walk them through the fields '.

Verdict

Her statement that she was doing this "... to get closer to the Police, you know so we could you know distract them while the other ones threw the blast bombs at them" is an unequivocal admission that she was acting as a decoy with full knowledge that others had blast bombs which they intended to throw at the police, and that her intention was to help the bombers by distracting the police. By doing so she was aiding and abetting the bombers and was part of a joint enterprise to attack the police with blast bombs. I am satisfied that her statement is reliable, and I find her guilty on count 73.

Possession of firearms

Admissions

Count 74 alleges that that Gibson had possession of a quantity of assault rifles with intent to endanger life or cause serious injury to property, or to enable some other person by means thereof to endanger life or cause serious injury to property. The offence is alleged to have occurred between 1 January 1995 and 30 September 1999. This charge depends upon a brief extract from a conversation between Gibson and Liz, one of the undercover officers, whilst they are in a car together on 24 February 2000 between 1343 and 1738. When Liz was cross-examined on 13 March 2006 it was established that they drove to Plymouth that afternoon, although they were in each other's company for the rest of that day as well, and into the early hours of the next day.

Parts of the recording are of poor quality, but the relevant passages are to be found here.

Muriel: You know I don't know how many of them there was but apparently there was quite a few (inaudible) but they must have all, eh prepared their weapons and everything in (inaudible) house because eh, there must have been residue on everything, must have been real sloppy about it, like I mean I've had A, AK's lying on the floor, everything, and they've never found no, eh residue, you can always put down a black plastic bag and newspaper and eh, you know put something like that on the carpet.

When Liz was cross-examined about this episode it was suggested to her that she had newspaper cuttings in the car which she handed to Gibson, and the cuttings had at least one photograph of rifles on the floor of a house that had been raided in Northern Ireland. It was suggested to Liz that it was the production of the newspaper clipping that led to the remark about guns, and that Gibson was talking about somebody else, something she does not really know much about. Liz responded that she could only go by what is on the transcript of the conversation.

No suggestion was made to her that Gibson was, or could have been, affected by drink or drugs on that occasion, nor was I asked to listen to the tape. I see no reason to assume that she was so affected on this occasion. As Gibson has not given evidence there is nothing to support this suggestion that, as I understand the cross-examination, she was simply commenting on pictures that she was being shown. Whilst her initial words infer that she was commenting on something that had happened earlier, her statement "like I mean I've had A, AK's lying on the floor and they've never found no, eh residue" is a definite statement that she had AK's in her presence on the floor on some occasion, and that residue from the weapons had not been found when her house has been searched. When questioned Gibson denied having possession of any of the guns she was asked about. The defence submissions there is a reference to part of a tape that was transcribed by the defence, but this excerpt from the tape does not appear to have any bearing on the passage relating to AK's quoted above.

I am satisfied that the reference to "AK's" is to assault rifles of the AK 47 type, and that Gibson was saying that she, not others, had such weapons lying on the floor in the past. In the absence of any other explanation, that is sufficient to establish that she had the necessary physical possession of these weapons, and the knowledge that they were firearms, that would render her guilty of possession of assault rifles with the necessary intent to

*endanger life or enable others to endanger life under Article
17. No other explanation has been forthcoming, nor can I conceive of one.*

Verdict

*While count 74 alleges that the offence was committed on "a
date unknown between the 1st day of January 1995 and the
30th day of September 1999", unless the date is an essential
part of the alleged offence it is well settled that the date is not a
material matter. Here there is nothing in Gibson's remarks to
suggest when she had such weapons lying on the floor, and as
the date is not an essential part of this offence it is not necessary for the prosecution to establish that she was referring to a
time within the dates averred in the particulars of offence. I find
her guilty on count 74.*

Membership of the LVF

Admissions

*The last charge Gibson faces is count 75, membership of the
LVF "on consecutive dates unknown between the 5th day of
June 1997 and the 30th day of September 1999." In support of
this charge the prosecution rely on material found in her home;
on various remarks that she made recorded in the evidential
tapes; and, as Mr Kerr put it when opening the case, on her admitted activities on behalf of that organisation.*

*The pictures and other items seized from Gibson's home in
Cornwall demonstrate that Gibson was very interested in the
LVF. On their own they do not establish membership, but they
certainly suggest a keen interest in that organisation, and the
photograph of her holding a placard at a demonstration referring to "LVF prisoners' of conscience" suggests that her
interest was not merely academic, but that she was at least a
supporter of the LVF.*

*The nature and extent of her interest in, and support for, the
LVF was described by Liz during her cross-examination on 13
March 2006.*

A. But the way she has portrayed herself to me from the day I first met her was that she was very proud of her involvement in the LVF. She very proud of the people, they are very close, and she considered herself – this is how it came across to me – she considered herself to be important and played an important role, and she often use to crack jokes about having to get them out of trouble, 'the boys' as she called them, getting them out of trouble when they got in trouble.

Q. She didn't know how they could survive without her?

A. She gave the impression to me that she considered herself to be important to them, yes, and they were all very close.

I accept that this assessment of Gibson's attitude is truthful, not least because it is consistent with the many references by Gibson to the LVF and individuals prominent in it, such as Billy Wright, that appear throughout the evidential transcripts, and her subsequent denials of membership of the LVF when questioned has to be weighed against this interest and support. These documents and her interest in, and support for, the LVF and its leading personalities in the Portadown area do not of themselves establish that she was a member of the LVF at the time alleged in the charge, but they are relevant when considering the remarks made by her and on which the prosecution also rely, and her other admissions about her activities.

The first direct reference by Gibson to the LVF in this context is to be found in her discussion with Vanessa who says:

But it looks like Loyalists and the UFF are joining together.

To which Gibson replies:

The LVF and the UFF, the Loyalist Volunteer Force, that's us.

I have already explained why I am satisfied that the admissions in that tape are reliable, and that there was nothing to indicate that Gibson was affected by drink or drugs. In the defence submissions the following points are made about the inference that might be drawn from these remarks.

As this submission concedes, Gibson is still identifying herself with the LVF when she makes these remarks. But whether this is

*no more than "an expression of identity or support" is some-
thing that cannot be decided in isolation from the entirety of the
evidence relating to this charge, and that applies equally to the
remaining passages upon which the prosecution rely.*

*The next reference on which the prosecution rely is to be found
in a conversation on 19 June 2000 between 2109 and 2218.
Gibson, her daughters and Dave S are present. Gibson telephones a friend called [name redacted] who, to judge by the
content of Gibson's remarks, is in Northern Ireland. A daughter
then speaks to her mother's friend, whereupon Gibson interjects and then resumes her conversation with her friend.*

Muriel: Tell [name redacted] I want her to take my place over
in the LVF. (Laughter).

Muriel then speaks to [name redacted] on the phone again.

Muriel: [Name redacted], you're going to take over my place
over there cause I, I gave the prisoners all your numbers is that
alright? (laughs) they need somebody to help them out over
there and I thought well like you're not doing nothing so I gave
them your ma's number and your mobile number is that alright
so they'll give you a wee ring whenever they need a protest or
anything like that alright (laughs). It'll give your Ma something
to do as well.

Overtalking from the daughter.

Muriel: Alright and we're going to show you where the arms
dumps are alright where all the weapons are you can only give
them out if they're fucking sober right don't give them to anybody drunk okay (laughs) that's the only rules okay oh good
(laughs) thanks Lisa.

*Whilst Dave S was present, there is nothing to suggest that he
instigated, or played any part in, this conversation. It cannot
therefore be impugned as being the functional equivalent of an
interrogation. This tape was played. Gibson can be heard
speaking very clearly and distinctly, and I am satisfied that she
was not affected by alcohol or drugs. As is apparent, these remarks were made in a jocular vein, but that does not
necessarily mean that they do not have an element of truth in*

*them. At paragraph 128 of the defence submissions it is said
that:*

*Dave S, who was present during this conversation, agreed that
Mrs Gibson 'could well have been [joking]'.*

*It is, however, clear from the entirety of the remarks of Dave S
on this issue during his cross-examination on 21 March 2006
that he was not conceding that Gibson was necessarily joking.
As he said on several occasions, when asked if these remarks
were consistent with being said in jest, they could be taken "either way". The full answer in which he said that Gibson could
have been joking also made this point.*

A. Oh, she could well have been. I mean, at the end of the day, I
don't, I don't know who she is speaking to on the other end of
the phone.

*Another tape records remarks made by Gibson to Dave S be-
tween 1345 and 1500 on 5 August 2000 when they were
working on a market stall. There is nothing to suggest that she
was affected by alcohol or drugs, nor was any suggestion that
she was, or may have been, made to Dave S when he was cross-
examined on 22 March 2006. I am satisfied that she was not so
affected.*

*One of the passages relied on in this tape is where Gibson de-
scribes how money was extorted from various sources such as
bars and building sites. As will be seen, at one point she referred to building workers as being beaten up, implying on one
reading that she had done so. Gibson is a small woman, and as
Dave S accepted, it would be nonsensical to think that Gibson
would be able to do this herself. In part of the defence submissions it is suggested that this tape could not seriously be relied
upon to support the contention that "Mrs Gibson went round
building sites intimidating workers and claiming to be in the
LVF". However, Gibson's remarks on this have to been in the
context of the entirety of her admissions on this topic.*

Muriel: But I used to give him an envelope twice a year and I'd
go round all the businesses twice a year and put in an envelope,
Loyalist prisoners of war on it donations please, but it wasn't
donations if you don't put nothing in it you'd fucking get petrol

bombed. Collect (inaudible) every single shop in town had to pay, every pub. A pub couldn't give you under forty quid a taxi service couldn't give you under a hundred.

Dave S: Really.

Muriel: And then if you got a builder, say we had a Catholic builder in a Protestant area building, used to watch out for them. Go up to them and say to them I'm with the LVF its gonna cost you five grand to work here or else your going be run off this site, the contracts going to somebody else.

Dave S: They'd pay up.

Muriel: Yeah.

Dave S: And then you just walked away.

Muriel: No you'll let them do their building they're not gonna build in our areas for nothing, you know, if they didn't then they'd one at the time you'd grab the workers and got them on their own, beat the shit out of them left them out the road you know, then they always paid up.

Dave S: Bad way of doing business.

Muriel: (Laughs) we had what 30 fucking families or something to take care of (inaudible) shit what are we going to do this week you know.

It is apparent from the entirety of this passage that the process Gibson described did not involve her personally attacking building workers. What she described was a process that involved a demand by her for payments from businesses, backed up by the implied threat of violence, in other words that she was demanding money with menaces to use the old expression. There is nothing implausible about her doing that on behalf of the LVF as she could call on Fulton and others to back up her demands. What she went on to say was that if a Catholic builder did not pay up then one of the workers would be beaten up. She said "you'd grab the workers", not that she would do it herself. There have been many prosecutions of Loyalist terrorists for attempts to distort money from builders and other businessmen, and Gibson's description of systematic extortion is all too real. It is suggested that inviting donation for Loyalist prisoners of war "does not amount to evidence of membership of the LVF." However, I consider that this is unrealistic for the following reasons. First of all, Gibson describes how the person who goes up to the building worker says "I'm with the LVF" and, secondly she concludes her remarks by saying "We had what 30 fucking families or something to take care of." These remarks reveal the reality of the situation, namely that she was involved in extorting money to provide financial support for the families of LVF prisoners. Providing financial support for the families of members in this way is a function that is integral to the operation of all terrorist groups in Northern Ireland, and one that is most unlikely to be placed in the hands of a non-member. When considering this passage, I have excluded the passage which follows in which Gibson is said to have referred to telephone conversations because it is not in direct speech for the reasons I have given in relation to other such passages earlier in this judgment.

A central function of any terrorist organisation is the storage and safeguarding of its weapons and ammunitions. Whilst use might be made on occasions of sympathisers to make premises or vehicles available for the storage or transportation of munitions, where an individual is clearly involved in these matters on more than one occasion, I am satisfied that such a level of involvement may, depending on all the circumstances, support an inference that the individual is not merely a supporter of, but is a member of, the organisation concerned. However, while such activity could support such an inference, other evidence of membership would also be necessary before such activity could prove the charge of membership of a proscribed organisation. Were other evidence not required, then merely to supply arms, or to be involved in the transportation of them from a supplier to a terrorist organisation in question, could of itself justify a conviction for membership even if the supplier or transporter was plainly not a member of that organisation. That would clearly be wrong.

One of the occasions when Gibson describes possession of weapons in circumstances that suggest she was responsible for their safe keeping was in the passage which immediately preceded, and lead up to, the money gathering activities considered in the preceding paragraphs. Gibson described how she would never allow individuals such as Philly (Philip McClean) to take weapons from her when they were drunk. It is clear from this that she was entrusted with the guns and had sufficient standing to refuse to hand them over to someone who was drunk. Although there is nothing in the references to the weapons to show that this occurred between the dates alleged in the charge, it is plainly within the overall context of the activities of the LVF she was describing. This can be seen from the references to the LVF and the extortion of money on its behalf that occur in the passage which follows in the transcript and which has already been cited.

Muriel: I would never have let them have weapons whenever they were drinking you know.

Dave S: No.

Muriel: They'd have to come to me to get them, I would never le them have them, I got called some names fucking bastard you give us a gun you know.

Dave S: I bet they thanked you for it after though.

Muriel: No, there was nothing said really after it only thing they'd say afterwards would be don't fucking tell Swinger I was down here drunk looking for a gun, please don't tell him, sure you wont tell him yeah I'm gonna tell him, fucking right I'm telling him. Whenever they were getting all these engraved they wanted to put on mine I'm telling Swinger (laughs).

Dave S: Smart that actually.

Muriel: That (inaudible).

Dave S: What's the actual thing on the front.

Muriel: The LVF.

Dave S: It is.

Muriel: Lead the way.

Dave S: Solid gold, its nice. What that say.

Muriel: No comment (pause) they're all saying what do you want put on yours, what do you want put on yours some were getting on the rat pack and some were getting on this that and the other, I said I want no comment put on mine they said is she fuck you're gonna get I'm telling Swinger (laughter) cos they had to be punished but you know what I mean so that they wouldn't keep doing it again and he was the only one that could scare them, so that way they didn't get in trouble, they didn't they just got a smack in the mouth you know and it made them think again before they'd come back drunk again and ask for a gun.

Dave S: Yeah.

Muriel: You had to do something though.

Dave S: Could be fucking bedlam otherwise.

Muriel: A fuck'n madhouse it would be I had Philly at my door at fucking 3 o'clock in the morning get me a gun get me a gun. How long have you been drinking, two days, what what's it to you. Who are you going to kill. The man that owns the pub. By now he should be like killing you, fuck off you're getting nothing.

(Pause in conversation as they tend to customers).

Muriel: Instead of letting Philly shoot the barman, the bar owners, I barred him from the pub you know he's not allowed in that pub no more.

Dave S: (Muddled speech) barman owed you a proper drink didn't he.

Muriel: He gave me forty ounce of vodka.

Dave S: Yeah.

Another occasion when Gibson admitted possession of weapons in circumstances which strongly suggest that she was a trusted associate of members of the LVF was when she removed the gun used in the shooting of Adrian Lamph, an offence which is also within the period covered by this charge.

Verdict

While some aspects of the evidence relied upon by the prosecution in support of the charge of membership of the LVF may be stronger than others, weighing all of the evidence as a whole: that is the photographs; her portrayal to Liz of being involved in the LVF; her remarks about her place in the LVF; her role in extorting money for the businesses for the LVF, and her actions in connection with firearms, I consider that the cumulative effect is to give rise to an extremely strong inference that Gibson was not merely an active supporter of the LVF, but was a member of it. In the absence of any evidence from her to explain or to contradict that inference, despite her repeated denials in interview that she was a member, I am satisfied that the proper, indeed the inescapable, conclusion from all of this evidence is that the prosecution have proved to the requisite standard of proof beyond reasonable doubt that Gibson was a member of the LVF and I find her guilty on count 75.

CHAPTER 36

Sentencing and Appeal

William James Fulton was sentenced to a total of twenty-eight years' imprisonment. Muriel Gibson received an eight-year custodial sentence.

On 26 January 2007, the BBC reported[19]:

A leading member of the Loyalist Volunteer Force has been sentenced to 28 years for the murder of Portadown grandmother Elizabeth O'Neill.

William James Fulton, 38, of Queen's Walk, Portadown, was jailed for 48 terrorist offences including attempted murder of four police officers.

Mrs O'Neill, 59, died in an explosion at her home in the mainly loyalist Corcrain estate in Portadown in 1999.

Mr Justice Hart ordered Fulton to serve a minimum of 25 years. His lawyers had argued at Belfast Crown Court that he should not serve more than 20 years because that was the longest term other paramilitary prisoners served during the Troubles. He was also sentenced to 28 years for the attempted murder of four police officers during the Drumcree dispute in 1998. His co-accused, Muriel Gibson, 57, with an address at Clos Trevithick in Cornwall, was sentenced to eight years for LVF membership

---

[19] http://news.bbc.co.uk/1/hi/northern_ireland/6302441.stm

and destroying evidence following the murder of Adrian Lamph in 1998.

Passing sentence on Fulton, the judge said: "His culpability for what happened is greater than anyone else involved in this episode and I propose to sentence him accordingly. This was a very grave crime with many aggravating features and I think the minimum period necessary to satisfy the requirements of retribution and deterrence before he can be considered for release is 25 years imprisonment."

After the trial, Mrs O'Neill's son Martin said although he was happy that justice had been done, those who made and threw the pipe bomb were still at large and should give themselves up. Mrs O'Neill died after picking up a bomb which had been thrown at her home where she had been watching television.

The Appeal of William James Fulton

The Belfast Telegraph reported the outcome of Fulton's appeal in the following terms[20]:

A leading loyalist secretly recorded talking about the killing of a Co Armagh grandmother has lost his appeal against being jailed for his part in her murder...

Judges branded Jim Fulton a "ruthless and vicious individual" who talked about genocide as a way of wiping out Catholics.

Mrs O'Neill's killing was said to be fuelled by sectarianism because she was a Protestant in a mixed family.

Rejecting submissions that there was insufficient evidence of an intent to kill, Lord Justice Girvan told the Court of Appeal yesterday that Fulton's statement that he "made sure she was touched" related to the attack on the O'Neill house, his use of terrorist methods and furtherance of loyalist paramilitary activities.

---

[20] https://www.belfasttelegraph.co.uk/news/genocide-loyalist-loses-sectarian-murder-appeal-28482820.html

The judge said: "The clear picture that emerges from the entirety of the recorded conversations, including those recorded by probes, is of a ruthless and vicious individual devoid of human sympathy or empathy and steeped in deeply sectarian attitudes and bitterness who was prepared even to give expression to and countenance the desirability of genocide." Lord Justice Girvan referred to one recording where Fulton declared that Catholics had to be "wiped out".

According to the probe evidence he stated: "That's our belief, if it doesn't work out we're finished. We have to kill every Catholic and believe in it." With Fulton providing nothing to back up claims he was under the influence of drink or drugs at the time, the three-judge appeal panel declared themselves satisfied with the verdict.

Fulton, formerly of Queen's Walk, Portadown, shook his head in the dock as judgment was delivered...

His trial was the longest in Northern Ireland's legal history.

Only Fulton appealed his convictions. On 19 June 2009, the Court of Appeal in Northern Ireland handed down its judgement after considering his appeal. He had been sentenced to a total of twenty-eight years' imprisonment with no prospect of any form of early release. The court made it clear after thanking counsel for their submissions that it was also indebted to the trial judge in saying, "We must also pay tribute to the careful and meticulous judgment of the trial judge which sets out his analysis of the evidence and the law and the findings of fact with commendable lucidity."

The court quashed the convictions on Counts 3, 4, 9 and 11 and allowed the appeal to that limited extent. It affirmed all the other convictions. The sentence of twenty-eight years' imprisonment was unaffected by the appeal court's decision.

We must add at this juncture, the quotation above about the trial judge illustrates one of the major benefits of the Diplock courts. The judge did set out both the facts and the law with superb forensic skills and precision. By doing so, it permits any interested outsider to see and understand the reasoning behind not only the guilty verdicts but also the not guilty. That is something that is impossible with a normal judge and jury trial because there is no way of knowing what influenced a jury in returning the verdicts. Unlike the United States, it is forbidden in law for a juror in the UK legal system to speak to anyone about what goes on inside the jury room. The result is that many practitioners and policemen alike are often baffled at jury verdicts.

CHAPTER 37

Unanswered Questions

Despite the sterling efforts of Colin Port and the entire Operation George team including not only the undercover officers, cover officers, but also the listeners, transcribers and every single person involved at any level whatsoever, some questions remain unanswered to this day.

Who Killed Rosemary Nelson?

The public inquiry[21] concluded at page 465:

> *There is no evidence of any act by or within any of the state agencies we have examined (the Royal Ulster Constabulary (RUC), the Northern Ireland Office (NIO), the Army or the Security Service) which directly facilitated Rosemary Nelson's murder. But we cannot exclude the possibility of a rogue member or members of the RUC or the Army in some way assisting the murderers to target Rosemary Nelson. In addition:*
>
> *• We are sure that some members of the RUC publicly abused and assaulted Rosemary Nelson on the Garvaghy Road in Portadown in 1997, having the effect of legitimising her as a target.*
>
> *• We believe that there was some leakage of intelligence which we believe found its way outside the RUC. Whether the intelligence was correct or not, the leakage increased the danger to Rosemary Nelson's life.*

---

[21] https://www.gov.uk/government/publications/the-rosemary-nelson-inquiry-report

• *We believe that some members of the RUC made abusive and/or threatening remarks about Rosemary Nelson to her clients. This became publicly known and would have had the subsequent effect of legitimising her as a target in the eyes of Loyalist terrorists.*

In a special report[22] in Glasgow's *Sunday Herald* dated 16 June 2002, that newspaper's then-Home Affairs Editor, Neil Mackay wrote:

MARK Fulton, the loyalist godfather who killed himself in his prison cell last week, has been named as the killer of Northern Ireland defence lawyer Rosemary Nelson.

Fulton, known in loyalist circles as "Swinger", was discovered by prison warders in Maghaberry jail in County Antrim on Monday morning. Fulton was found in his bed with his belt knotted around his neck. It's believed he was depressed and suicidal over fears that rival loyalist inmates were targeting him for murder.

Sources close to Colin Port[23] - the deputy chief constable of Norfolk Police who is heading the inquiry into the March 1999 murder of Nelson in a car bomb attack in her hometown of Lurgan - said Fulton, who was once the leader of the Loyalist Volunteer Force, was "without question" the man who masterminded her assassination. ...

To some degree, that article based on anonymous sources and dated some nine years before the public inquiry report was published may have some credence in that the inquiry concluded at pages 341 and 342 that:

We believe that neither the RHSB(S) [Regional Head of Special Branch South Region] nor the Detective Inspector from Lurgan [the local Special Branch DI] would have been willing to characterise what was going on as drug-related had they seen the

---

[22]   https://web.archive.org/web/20150924202247/http://www.high-beam.com/doc/1P2-9989660.
[23] All efforts to contact Colin Port have been unsuccessful.

notes that we have been able to examine. In the context of what was known about the RHD [Red Hand Defenders] and the Orange Volunteers, all the signs pointed to something altogether more sinister and we do not discount the possibility that what was missed was in fact the genesis of the plot to murder Rosemary Nelson.

That excerpt is within the context of the inquiry examining the activities of the LVF and Mark 'Swinger' Fulton in the time immediately preceding the murder of Rosemary Nelson. Intelligence reports concluded Mark Fulton had met a Loyalist bomb-maker in Maghaberry prison on 27 February 1999 where Fulton was being held on remand on a charge of conspiracy to murder.

For those interested in a further account of the Rosemary Nelson murder, we recommend reading the related material on the website of The Pat Finucane Centre.[24]

Who Pulled the Trigger?

Just who was the cowardly gunman who rode up to Adrian Lamph and shot him in the head at point blank range? The family of Mr Lamph still seek justice as can be seen from a recent article[25] in the *Belfast Telegraph*. In 2018, the newspaper reported, "The brother of a young Catholic man gunned down by the Loyalist Volunteer Force in Portadown 20 years ago this week has said his family's grief is still as raw as ever." The article continued, "His brother Niall Lamph said: 'We still have no justice for Adrian's murder. We can't remember the last time anyone from the police has been in touch. It is as if we have been forgotten.'"

You may think that on any analysis of the covert recordings in the Operation George saga Muriel Gibson clearly said it was Gary Fulton

---

[24] https://www.patfinucanecentre.org/
[25] https://www.belfasttelegraph.co.uk/news/northern-ireland/family-of-man-shot-dead-by-lvf-still-hoping-for-justice-20-years-after-brutal-killing-36824615.html

who pulled the trigger that fateful day. Here is a reminder of the relevant parts of the judgement handed down by Mr Justice Hart:

I am satisfied that the murder of Adrian Lamph was a sectarian murder; that the gunman was the person seen on a mountain bike by Mr McCandless; that the gunman removed his clothing soon afterwards, and that it was burnt in the alleyway in an attempt to destroy all the clothing, and hence destroy evidence linking him to the crime.

And later referring to a transcript from a probe at Gibson's Cornwall home, the judge summarised the passage as:

When Gibson arrived **Gary (ie Gary Fulton) had already stripped off his clothes and was naked** *because he had nothing to change into, so she told him to hide behind a gate.*

Other passages from covert recordings in the judgement relating to Adrian Lamph's murder include:

Gibson says that she was seen by John Smith and someone she refers to as "Wee Michael" when she went out to pick up the gun after the Lamph shooting and **found Gary Fulton naked in the alleyway.**

... **The gunman** *rode the bike past Lamph, called to him and "shot him right between the eyes, took the whole head off".*

... She ran up to "Ronnie and Jill's yard" and found **the gunman naked.** *"And I go, what, what, what do you want me to do what have you done."*

... **The gunman** *then told her to take the gun, which she did and arranged for it to be hidden.*

... She told Swinger that she had lent him, i.e. **the gunman,** *the t-shirt. She described it as unique.*

... When it is realised that because the t-shirt is so distinctive she destroys six photographs of men wearing it

... I am satisfied that the admissions are reliable. They were entirely unprompted by any undercover officer or agent of the State. Gibson chose to describe her exploits to her friend Vanessa.

Some interviews were deleted from the papers. In the remaining interviews Gibson made no reply when questioned about the Lamph murder, save that in [in one tape] she said that she was sorry for the Lamph family and their loss.

Those excerpts make out a *prima facie* case it was Gary Fulton who shot and killed Adrian Lamph. That proposition is not evidence in a court of law nor is what Gibson said admissible as it is hearsay. Yet, suspects have been arrested and questioned on lesser information. Was Gary Fulton arrested and questioned in connection with this murder? That is what we asked of the PSNI in a Freedom of Information request. The PSNI replied it "could neither confirm nor deny" Fulton had been arrested and questioned about the Adran Lamph murder. They did confirm the case was still "open."

We do know he was convicted of serious crimes connected to Loyalist paramilitary activities as recently as 2013 when the *Belfast Telegraph* reported under the headline 'Jailed - gang who used Barbie typewriter and bullets to blackmail victims out of £15k.' The article[26] said:

Four men, including a notorious loyalist and a convicted killer, who used a Barbie typewriter in a £15,000 extortion plot have been jailed for a total 17 years.

At Belfast Crown Court Judge David McFarland handed three of the gang, Portadown loyalist Gary Fulton (40), Philip 'Bug' Blaney (48) and associate Mark Briggs five-year jail terms each,

---

[26] https://www.belfasttelegraph.co.uk/news/northern-ireland/jailed-gang-who-used-barbie-typewriter-and-bullets-to-blackmail-victims-out-of-15k-29285194.html

and Daniel Hamilton (31) a term of two years and eight months for the 'Red Hand Defenders' (RHD) [the group who claimed responsibility for the bomb that killed Rosemary Nelson] plot.

Fulton, from Gillespie Court in Comber and Portadown men Briggs and Blaney, neighbours on the Westland Road, had all pleaded guilty to two counts of blackmailing £15,000 from two victims known only as witnesses A and B on dates between 21 February and 24 March 2011 ...

Blaney had served a jail sentence for the manslaughter of grandmother Elizabeth O'Neill, who died in 1999 after picking up a blast bomb thrown into her home and Jim Fulton, a brother to Gary Fulton, is currently serving a life term after he was convicted of her murder.

A prosecuting lawyer told the court how the couple known only as Witness A and B had been targeted by two hand-delivered letters containing bullets at their home and business addresses demanding they pay £15,000 or face "action with extreme prejudice by the Red Hand Defenders".

Witness A agreed to pay up after receiving a number of further demands threatening that his house and business would be attacked, but he had also sought the help of police.

He described how the first set of threats were followed up by a petrol canister being placed in a lorry owned by Witness A and, during a mobile phone call the following day, he was asked how he liked his 'present' and warning him the next one would be 'ignited'.

The court heard that the gang had targeted the witnesses because, aside from their legitimate business interests, they had left themselves vulnerable to blackmail and prosecution owing to their cultivating a substantial cannabis farm, for which they had subsequently been convicted.

Judge David McFarland... said, "the gang had engaged in delivering letters with bullets and other threatening behaviour, describing how Briggs, Blaney and Fulton 'had been behind' the plot with Hamilton the 'conduit.'"

Historical Enquiries Team (HET)

The Historical Enquiries Team was a unit of the Police Service of Northern Ireland set up in September 2005 to investigate the 3,269 unsolved murders committed during the Troubles, specifically between 1968 and 1998. It was wound up in September 2014, when the PSNI restructured following budget cuts. The former PSNI Chief Constable, Sir Hugh Orde, described this as a massive mistake.[27]

The team never got around to investigating the murder of Adrian Lamph but it did in the drive-by shooting of James Patrick, known as 'Seamus,' Dillon. He died in Dungannon at the hands of the LVF on 27 December 1997 the same day Billy Wright was killed by INLA. The LVF stronghold of Portadown and largely nationalist Dungannon are a short driving distance apart especially if using the motorway.

In 2005 Muriel Gibson was charged with possession of the murder weapon used in the drive-by shooting but later acquitted. She was charged based on four tapes covertly recorded by the Operation George team. One tape was excluded by the trial judge owing to its inadmissibility because the judge found she was inebriated at the time of the recording. Three others were excluded as they contained no details to support the case against her on that count. In them, she was heard talking about Dillon's murder. There are no references to these in the official judgement because of their inadmissibility.

Bentley[28] has had access to the HET report into the Dillon murder. It names Gibson as a suspect along with several other prominent LVF members. The prominent members at that time were Jimmy Fulton and his brother Mark 'Swinger' Fulton along with their cousin Gary Fulton.

The LVF hid under the cloak of being called a paramilitary organisation. In fact, it was a firm: an organised crime gang specialising in

---

[27] https://www.belfasttelegraph.co.uk/news/northern-ireland/destruction-of-historical-enquiries-team-was-massive-mistake-says-ex-police-chief-orde-34386735.html

[28] Bentley was the author responsible for all research connected to this book.

murder, genocide, punishment shootings, drug dealing, extortion rackets, kidnapping, and robberies. The Plymouth firm headed by Neil brought two[29] of them to justice

---

[29] Mark Fulton was arrested on 3 December 2001 and on the basis of evidence gathered by Operation George he was charged with the offence of conspiracy to murder. He was remanded in custody and committed suicide in Maghaberry prison on 10 June 2002: Para 31.134 Rosemary Nelson Inquiry Report. Gary Fulton was never arrested in connection with Operation George.

CHAPTER 38

A Conversation Between the Authors

Finally, the authors 'talk' to each other about what drew them together to write this book.

Mark Dickens (MD):
Maybe this might be the time to talk about what was the catalyst that brought you and I together; the two points that caused me to reach out to you and ask those questions about almost tipping off Smiles[30] and the hug in the cells. We know Smiles and Jimmy were two different characters. Smiles, if you like, was a nice crook. Jimmy was everything I stood against. He was a murderer, gangster, drug dealer, extortionist, terrorist, blackmailer, to name but a few.

I didn't find Jimmy hard work; he could be funny and good company and he liked to talk, which as we know was his downfall. But I always knew what he really was. I couldn't have hugged Jimmy at the end let alone tip him off. Smiles was a different sort of crime and fella. Jimmy was a disgusting bit of work. I totally understand your emotions and

---

[30] The reference to Smiles is possibly best illustrated by this quote: Undercover Operation Julie - The Inside Story,' documents everyday life of undercover work as the author, Stephen Bentley, won the confidence of the gang members. Bentley tells in his book how he built a "perfect" relationship with Smiles, an important gang member. But this friendship almost undermined the whole operation.- Dominic Blake, BBC News England, October 2, 2016.

connection with Smiles and to be honest I would have maybe thought the same in your shoes.

Stephen Bentley (SB):
Yes, I understand all that, and they were obviously two very different types of lawbreakers. You forgot to mention you were amazed at what you called as me 'GBHing a guy' just to grab his fingerprints and DNA. I must remind you there was no such thing as DNA in the days of Operation Julie.

MD: Ha! Thanks for reminding me.

SB: No problem. I do understand what you say about Jimmy Fulton. I think one of the things that best illustrates his character is him calling the postman in the hoax bomb incident the most stupid man in the world. He said that because the guy was still trying to do his duty in emptying post boxes with burning vehicles all around him. Duty – that's a word the likes of Fulton do not comprehend.

MD: That's correct, and I always thought of the contrast between him and a soldier in a war zone. He never got face to face with an armed opponent. He'd brag about how he used to like rob drugs and sell them and other gangster activities like the extortion racket collecting money for the 'cause'. But he spent the money going on holiday or lavished it on his family. He was just having these people over – these loyalist supporters. There was extortion with shops and businesses and, you know, he ruled by fear and threatened consequences if they didn't pay up. The most disgusting thing was the LVF policy of they've got to shoot a Catholic once a week. He fully subscribed to that.

SB: He wasn't the only one though, was he?

MD: Right, that's why the LVF broke away from the UVF because they weren't killing enough Catholics. And the LVF wanted a Catholic per week killing. And then that's where the 'Rat' comes in. Billy Wright, known as the 'Rat', the first leader of the LVF. Billy Wright was the top man with Mark 'Swinger' Fulton as number two. Billy Wright gets assassinated in jail, that left yours truly Jimmy in charge of everything when Swinger wasn't around or on remand for some crime or other. He always went on about how Billy Wright could get a crowd going, you know, a great orator. I used to think about him like Hitler at the rallies, pumping his fist in the air and changing the pitch of his voice to stress the importance of what he was saying.

SB: Was Jimmy Fulton involved in the arms decommissioning talks?

MD: Jimmy didn't have the charisma of Wright or the reputation of his brother Swinger. But he now saw himself as the leader. Hence, he was the LVF representative in the Good Friday Agreement signed in April 1998. During the numerous covertly recorded conversations Jimmy would brag about his position in the negotiations with John de Chastelain who was appointed to monitor the various factions in Northern Ireland with compliance in the decommissioning of weapons process. Jimmy said how easy it was to have Chastelain over. He would sit at the table negotiating with him and give him any old rubbish about putting weapons out of reach and then handed over some old rusty firearms and crap ammunition. It was just a con.

SB: Back to contrasting my days undercover and yours, I was heartened to learn about the police catering for the mental health of UCOs in your day. As you say, I think, the psychological counselling was available for all UCOs. I needed that back in my day.

MD: Yes, you did.

SB: Is that it?

MD: Yes, any more questions?

SB: Yes, I note you mention things like tradecraft and describe a 'cleaning' operation to get rid of surveillance. It sounds like something out of a spy fiction book.

MD: Yes, deliberately so. UCOs are in the espionage business so it's natural to borrow terminology from the spying game as described in fiction and non-fiction books.

SB: Okay, and that leads me into another question – do you believe books such as this one assist criminals?

MD: No, I don't for these reasons: spy fiction and non-fiction doesn't help modern day spies. Espionage has just become more sophisticated.

Covert policing has also become more sophisticated. Some of the kit used on Operation George is obsolete, replaced by technological wizardry. Besides, as you said earlier in the book, there are places on the internet that give full details of the structure and functions of undercover policing in the UK. That doesn't prevent successful covert policing by the current crop of specialists. I'm also with you in thinking drones may one day replace humans in the undercover cop world. Criminals will always be paranoid. They tend to believe there's an undercover cop lurking in every corner.

SB: I couldn't have put that any better. Before you go, how would you describe your days as an undercover policeman?

MD: Easy! The best job I ever had.

SB: Final questions – do you have any more undercover tales to tell? If so, are we going to write about them?

MD: Yes, and yes. Lots of stories.

ABOUT THE AUTHORS

Mark Dickens

Mark Dickens is a pseudonym. From humble, and sometimes, difficult beginnings in life, Mark served for many years in a British police force with distinction. He was commended on many occasions for his outstanding detective work including many undercover roles involving the infiltration of organised crime groups throughout the U.K. Mark was registered on the national undercover officer index and also ran training courses for undercover officers. Following his retirement, he remains anonymous to protect the safety of himself and his family.

Stephen Bentley

Stephen Bentley is a former British police Detective Sergeant, pioneering Operation Julie undercover detective, and barrister. He now writes in the true crime and crime fiction genres and contributes occasionally to Huffington Post UK on undercover policing, and mental health issues.

Stephen is a member of the UK's Society of Authors and the Crime Writers' Association. His website may be found at https://www.stephenbentley.info/where you may subscribe to his newsletter and view all his books.

ACKNOWLEDGEMENTS

The authors and publisher wish to thank Richard Roper and Sheryl Lee for their invaluable editing expertise. Richard is a nonfiction editor at Headline, part of the Hachette group, and responsible for the developmental editing of this book. Indie authors and publishers can also hire him through Reedsy.com. Sheryl brought her usual professionalism to bear with a final polish of the manuscript. That is why she is Stephen's go-to editor. If there are any editing errors in this book, then blame Stephen Bentley and the publisher, not the editing team. We also ask you point them out by emailing info@hendrypublishing.com.

We also thank the design team at 100 Covers for the striking design of the book cover.

The excerpts from the court judgement are Crown copyright material and are covered by the Open Government Licence permitting reproduction in this book.

Stephen Bentley also thanks those confidential sources who helped with parts of this book that deal with the LVF in Northern Ireland.

We also acknowledge you, the reader, as the most important link in the chain. Thank you. We ask that you consider leaving an honest re-view wherever you purchased the book.

Milton Keynes UK
Ingram Content Group UK Ltd.
UKHW011448040724
445176UK00019B/105

THAT'S ENTERTAINMENT

THAT'S ENTERTAINMENT

100 Years of Chelsea Lodge No.3098

The Centenary 1905 - 2005

Keith Skues

Lambs' Meadow Publications

ISBN 0 907398 04 9 Casebound

© Keith Skues, 2005

First published 2005

Cover design by Ray Donn

Main text imageset in Times New Roman by John Payne
PC Tech-nique, Hunstanton, Norfolk

Printed in Great Britain by Alden Press, Oxford

Published by Lambs' Meadow Publications,
Horning, Norfolk NR12 8PJ, England

British Library Cataloguing in Publication Data
A catalogue record for this book is available
from the British Library

Contents

The Most Hon. The Marquess of Northampton, DL. Pro Grand Master, United Grand Lodge of England

Spencer Douglas David Compton is the son of 6th Marquess of Northampton, DSO (died 1978), and his second wife, Virginia (died 1997), daughter of Lt-Col. David Rimington Heaton, DSO, of Brookfield, Crownhill, South Devon. Born 2 April 1946. Educated Eton and Royal Agricultural College, Cirencester, Gloucester.

Landowner and proprietor of Castle Ashby and Compton Wynyates, Tysoe, Warwickshire (built 1480-1520). At the age of 21 he inherited his family estates in Northamptonshire, Warwickshire, Surrey, London and over-seas. In Northampton he has been President or Chairman of many charities and was made Deputy Lieutenant in 1979 for his services to the county. Married 1st, 1967, Henrietta Luisa Maria (marriage dissolved 1973), daughter of the late Baron Bentinck; one son, one daughter; 2nd, 1974, Annette Marie (marriage dissolved 1977), daughter of C.A.R. Smallwood; 3rd, 1977, Hon. Mrs. Rosemary Dawson - Damer (marriage dissolved 1983); one daughter; 4th, 1985, Hon. Mrs. Michael Pearson (marriage dissolved 1988); one daughter; 5th, 1990, Pamela Martina Raphaela Kyprios. Masonic career: Craft. Deputy Grand Director of Ceremonies 1983-85; Grand Sword Bearer 1992; Senior Grand Warden 1994-95; Assistant Grand Master 1995-2000 with special responsibility for Freemasonry in London; In March 2001 he was installed as Pro Grand Master. Masonic career: Royal Arch. Deputy Grand Director of Ceremonies 1983-85; President Committee of General Purposes 1992-95; Past Third Grand Principal 1996; Pro First Grand Principal 2001. Hobbies: Freemasonry, planting trees, walking, reading, music and art.

United Grand Lodge of England

Freemasons' Hall, Great Queen Street, London WC2B 5AZ
Telephone: 020 7831 9811
Fax: 020 7831 6021

The Most Hon the Marquess of Northampton

Foreword

In 1905 a group of artistes and musicians founded a Masonic lodge which was destined to become one of the best known and best loved in the world of Freemasonry: Chelsea Lodge No.3098.

Only those involved in show business were able to be members and because of this they did things differently from other Lodges. Such was the popularity of the Lodge that they invariably conducted three ceremonies at each meeting to cater for the demand to join. The Lodge met in the early afternoon to allow members to get to their evening performances and then return again later, often still dressed in their theatre costumes, to entertain their visitors at the festive board. This tradition was unique to Chelsea Lodge.

Members have included Music Hall, Variety and Circus artistes, Actors, Pantomime Dames, Comedians, Magicians, Ventriloquists, Jazz and Dance Band leaders and artistes and producers from the worlds of Silent Films, Cinema, Radio and Television.

Chelsea can boast some of the most famous and colourful performers and in telling their story in this well researched and amazingly detailed book, Keith Skues has chronicled an important historical account of not just show business Freemasons, but also 20th Century show business in general.

It is informative and amusing and whether you are a Freemason or not, I am sure you will find it as absorbing and fascinating as I did.

Fraternally

Northampton

Northampton
Pro Grand Master

Preface and Acknowledgments

Within a few months of my joining Chelsea Lodge in 1999 I was flattered to be asked if I would consider compiling a history of the Lodge to mark its centenary in 2005. Having written a history of my Mother Lodge (Harringay No.2763) I was delighted to agree. Within a very short time I learned this was not going to be an easy project as the first fifty years' paperwork, including Minutes, Accounts and Signature books were all missing. Many of the previous secretaries and treasurers had, sadly, passed on to the Grand Lodge above. However, I enjoy a challenge and this has certainly proved some kind of challenge. Fortunately all was not lost as Harry Stanley compiled the *First 75 Years of Chelsea Lodge* in 1980 which helps fill the gap of the names of founder members of the Lodge and those who went on to become Master.

As Chelsea Lodge has produced so many famous names over the last one hundred years I thought I would major on personalities past and present, rather than follow the usual route in a Masonic Lodge history. I should like to thank those members (and past members) of the Lodge who have given me help and encouragement.

The staff at Grand Lodge Library and Museum, particularly Katrina Jowett and her team, have gone out of their way to try to answer impossible requests I have presented to them in order that we can locate every member since 1905. Sadly, Secretarial Returns from 1928 to the 1950s have been destroyed.

Paul Ganjou has ensured I did not have too much spare time in the last four years. As Director of Ceremonies of Chelsea Lodge he is brilliant in organising the meetings, ensuring that the right officer says the right words at the given time. I have to say he is quite adept in organising authors as well. He has chased members on my behalf to ensure we have all the current biographies. Some members have not responded, others did not wish to become involved, so I can only apologise that it is not the complete picture.

The Secretarial side of Chelsea Lodge, David Calderhead and Charles Firth have been most helpful when I wanted to refer back to old Minutes books and correspondence from 1955 to date. They are as disappointed as myself in not having the complete set of paperwork between 1905 and 1954. Our Treasurer Greg Lunnon has been of great help.

I am most honoured that the Pro Grand Master, The Marquess of Northampton, graciously agreed to write the Foreword.

A book of this nature requires pictures and illustrations. Members of the Lodge have been helpful in this respect, but none more so than Lew Lane who has supplied the majority of photographs from his vast collection of show business personalities which he has been collecting all of his life. Roy Hudd, OBE has also been most generous in allowing some of his show business pictures to be reproduced. I should also like to acknowledge the good offices of the BBC and of show business photographer Doug Mackenzie for allowing me to reproduce some of their respective archive collections.

I am also grateful to the following who have made their reference books and documents available to me: Sandra Dawe at the University of Cambridge Music School at Pembroke College, to the British Library and National Sound Archives at St Pancras, the Newspaper Library in Colindale and the City of Westminster Library, Kelly Wissen at Equity, John Adrian from Grand Order of Water Rats, Don Wickes and John A.B. Wright for their research into dance bands and their singers and David Nathan from the National Jazz Archive in Loughton Public Library. Chelsea Lodge descends from Lion and Lamb No.192. I thank Dr. Simon Marner for allowing me permission to reproduce the family tree he has designed which lists seven generations of lodges, descending from the Lion and Lamb, that was consecrated on Christmas Eve, 1789 under the jurisdiction of the Antient or Atholl Grand Lodge. It still meets regularly in London being one of 125 Atholl Lodges still surviving.

Thanks to Betty G. Crane for proofing the show business stories and offering helpful, factual suggestions and to Wendy Anderson for trawling through hundreds of pages of newspapers and magazines relating to music hall and early dance bands and their musicians and for checking their authenticity.

Betty and Wendy, together with Diana Hallard, cast their professional eyes over the whole of the text once all biographies and history had been put in order.

To all those members of the Lodge who have loaned me photographs, handbills and other artwork and assisted in compiling their biographies, my special thanks, particularly to Ted Callister, Ray Donn, Paul Ganjou, John Logan, Ivan Morgan, David Neale and John Star.

In addition to the names which appear in the Bibliography I should like to thank the following for allowing me to quote from their documents or reproduce photographs and illustrations: Louis Barfe, the former Claire Daniels, Arthur Ferrier, Grand Secretary's office, the late Chris Hayes, Angela Heiss, Peter Jay, Rona Leader, Patrick Newley, David Peabody, Marion Rich, Nita Raymonde, Ron Rigby-Saunders, Julian Spear, Don Stacey, Rita Stanley, Louise Watts and David Warren.

Ray Donn designed the front and back covers of the book to whom I am indebted. John Payne managed to pull together all my design wishes, juggling photographs and text in Microsoft Word 97 to QuarkXPress in order that Alden Press could print the manuscript.

Some references and photographs have been obtained from the internet. In certain cases it has been difficult to trace copyright. Should answers and names come forward I will be pleased to rectify the omission in any future edition of this book.

At the end of the day the person whose name appears as author of a book takes the credit or criticism. I can take no credit, but will be happy to accept any constructive criticism. This has been a team effort and my thanks to everyone who has been a part of that team, however small the part they played.

Chelsea Lodge has always prided itself in bringing together top names in the world of show business. It was the case one hundred years ago and the same applies today. I confirm that comedian Joe Pasquale (recent King of the Jungle in ITV's *I'm a Celebrity Get Me Out of Here*) was initiated into Chelsea Lodge on 18 March 2005, the last ceremony to be held before our Centenary Meeting on 20 May 2005. Musician Rick Wakeman will be joining our ranks as a new member in the near future.

Looking back over one hundred years Chelsea Lodge members must feel satisfied with what they and their predecessors have achieved. If all the founders had lived to see the meetings today of the Lodge they started, they would not have been disappointed, and it will be the present endeavour to ensure that, when future generations look back, they will also think well of those who are now carrying on the work so well begun by the Founders one hundred years ago.

Keith Skues
Horning, Norfolk
April 2005

Abbreviations

ADC Assistant Director Ceremonies
ADC Aide-de-camp
AE Air Efficiency decoration, RAF
AIMC Associate of Inner Magic Circle
ARCA Associate of the Royal College of Art
CBE Commander of the British Empire
DC Director of Ceremonies
ENSA Entertainments National Service Association responsible for bringing drama and variety to the troops on active service during World War II years.
GL Grand Lodge
IG Inner Guard
IPM Immediate Past Master
JD Junior Deacon
JW Junior Warden
LGR London Grand Rank
LOI Lodge of Instruction
MBE Member of the British Empire
MM Master Mason
OBE Order of the British Empire
PAGDC Past Assistant Grand Director of Ceremonies
PGStB Past Grand Standard Bearer
PJGD Past Junior Grand Deacon
SD Senior Deacon
SLGR Senior London Grand Rank
SW Senior Warden
WM Worshipful Master

Bold type in the text signifies a member or past member of Chelsea Lodge

Members of Chelsea Lodge at Installation Meeting, May 2003

List of officers for the year 2005-2006

CHELSEA LODGE No. 3098

W.Bro. David Neale, ProvGStwd	Worshipful Master
W.Bro. Ray Donn	IPM

OFFICERS - 2005/2006

W.Bro. Thomas O'Farrell, LGR	Senior Warden
Bro. David Capri	Junior Warden
W.Bro. David Hillman, LGR	Chaplain
Bro. Greg Lunnon, LR	Treasurer
W.Bro. Peter Elliott	Secretary
W.Bro. Michael Ramsden	DC
W.Bro. John Hollingsworth, PProvAsstGReg	Almoner
W.Bro. Paul Wood	Charity Steward
Bro. John Logan	Senior Deacon
Bro. Michael Jerome	Junior Deacon
W.Bro. Frank Holder, LGR	ADC
W.Bro. Robert Allder, PProvSGD	Organist
W.Bro. Ray Donn	Asst. Secretary
Bro. Paul Mills	Inner Guard
W.Bro. Anthony Chaperlin, SLGR	Steward
W.Bro. Cyril Packer, LGR	Steward
W.Bro. Ivan Morgan	Steward
Bro. Roger Kitter	Steward
Bro. Paul Kaye	Steward
Bro. John McMonagle	Steward
Bro. Roy Graham	Steward
Bro. Dennis Davies	Steward
Bro. Mick McManus	Steward
Bro. Nej Salih	Steward
Bro. David Redfearn	Steward
Bro. Gerry George	Steward
Bro. John Star	Steward
Bro. David Ramsden	Steward
W.Bro. Allan Friedman, PProvGSwdB	Tyler

Above left: W.Bro. Ray Donn, Master 2004-2005. Above right: W.Bro. David Neale, Master 2005-2006. Below members of Chelsea Lodge taken in September 2004

Chapter 1

CHELSEA FAMILY TREE

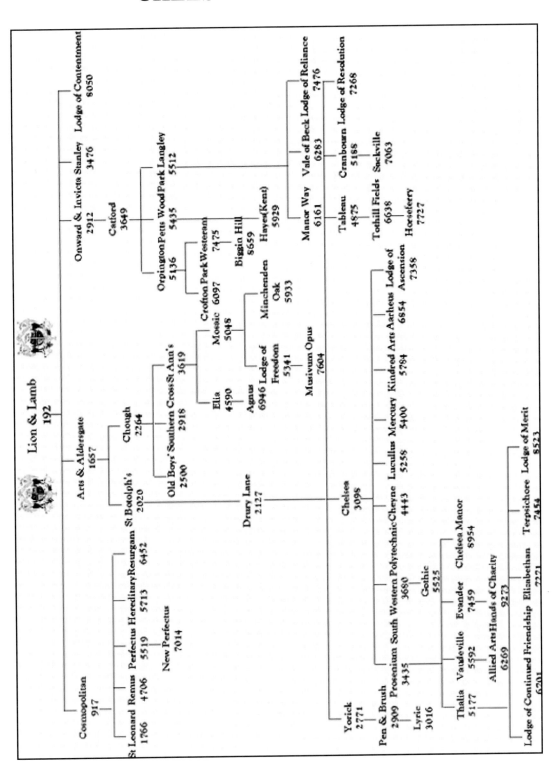

A total of sixty seven Lodges are descended from the Lion and Lamb Lodge spanning seven generations. Below is a list of them all categorised into each generation.

Daughter Lodges (1st generation)	Number	Mother Lodge	Date of Consecration
Cosmopolitan	917	Lion and Lamb Lodge	1862
Arts and Aldersgate	1657	Lion and Lamb Lodge	1876
Onward and Invicta	2912	Lion and Lamb Lodge	1902
Stanley	3476	Lion and Lamb Lodge	1910
Lodge of Contentment	8050	Lion and Lamb Lodge	1965

Grand-daughter Lodges (2nd generation)	Number	Mother Lodge	Date of Consecration
St Leonard	1766	Cosmopolitan	1878
Remus	4760	Cosmopolitan	1925
Perfectus	5519	Cosmopolitan	1934
Hereditary	5731	Cosmopolitan	1938
Resurgam	6452	Cosmopolitan	1947
St Botolf's	2020	Arts and Aldersgate	1883
Chough	2264	Arts and Aldersgate	1888
Catford	3649	Arts and Aldersgate	1913

Great grand-daughter Lodges (3rd generation)	Number	Mother Lodge	Date of Consecration
New Perfectus	7014	Perfectus	1950
Mayfair	8294	Resurgam	1969
Drury Lane	2127	St Botolf's	1885
Old Boys	2500	Chough	1894
Southern Cross	2918	Chough	1902
St Ann's	3691	Chough	1913
Orpington	5136	Catford	1929
Petts Wood	5436	Catford	1933
Park Langley	5512	Catford	1934

4th generation	Number	Mother Lodge	Date of consecration
Yoric	2771	Drury Lane	1899
Chelsea	3098	Drury Lane	1905
Tableau	4875	Drury Lane	1926
Cranbourne	5188	Drury Lane	1930
Lodge of Resolution	7268	Drury Lane	1953
Elia	4590	St Ann's	1923
Mosaic	5048	St Ann's	1928
Crofton Oak	6097	Orpington	1945
Westerham	7475	Orpington	1956
Hayes	5929	Petts Wood	1943
Manor Way	6161	Park Langley	1945
Vale of Beck	6283	Park Langley	1946
Lodge of Reliance	7476	Park Langley	1956

5th generation	Number	Mother Lodge	Date of consecration
Pen and Brush	2909	Yoric	1902
Proscenium	3435	Chelsea	1910
South Western Polytechnic	3680	Chelsea	1913
Cheyne	4443	Chelsea	1922
Lucillus	5258	Chelsea	1931
Mercury	5400	Chelsea	1933
Kindred Arts	5784	Chelsea	1939
Aarheus	6854	Chelsea	1949
Lodge of Ascension	7358	Chelsea	1954
Tothill Fields	6638	Tableau	1948
Sackville	7063	Cranbourne	1951
Agnus	6946	Elia	1949
Lodge of Freedom	5341	Mosaic	1932
Minchenden Oak	5933	Mosaic	1943
Biggin Hill	8659	Westerham	1975

6th generation	Number	Mother Lodge	Date of Consecration
Lyric	3016	Pen and Brush	1904
Thalia	5177	Proscenium	1930
Vauderville	5592	Proscenium	1935
Evander	7459	Proscenium	1956
Chelsea Manor	8954	Proscenium	1980
Gothic	5525	South Western Polytechnic	1935
Mount Carmel	7983	Kindred Arts	1964
Mount Sinai	8993	Kindred Arts	1981
Prospect	7618	Aarheus	1958
Horse Ferry	7727	Tothill Fields	1960
Musivum Opus	7604	Lodge of Freedom	1958

7th generation	Number	Mother Lodge	Date of Consecration
Lodge of Continued Friendship	6701	Thalia	1948
Elizabethan	7271	Thalia	1953
Terpsichore	7454	Thalia	1956
Lodge of Merit	8523	Thalia	1973
Allied Arts	6269	Vauderville	1946
Hands of Charity	9237	Evander	1987

Chapter 2

AIMS AND RELATIONSHIPS OF THE CRAFT

FREEMASONRY TEACHES MORAL lessons and self-knowledge through participation in a progression of allegorical two-part plays, which are learned by heart and performed within each lodge.

Freemasonry offers its members an approach to life which seeks to reinforce thoughtfulness for others, kindness in the community, honesty in business, courtesy in society and fairness in all things. Members are urged to regard the interests of the family as paramount but importantly Freemasonry also teaches and practices concern for people, care for the less fortunate and help for those in need.

Under the United Grand Lodge of England Freemasonry is the UK's largest, secular fraternal organisation. It has over 300,000 members working in some 10,000 lodges throughout England and Wales and 30,000 more members overseas. There are separate Grand Lodges for Ireland (which cover north and south) and Scotland, with a combined membership of 150,000. Worldwide, there are probably five million people who are Freemasons.

Membership is open to men of all faiths who are law-abiding, of good character and who acknowledge a belief in God. Freemasonry is a multi-racial and multi-cultural organisation. It has attracted men of goodwill from all sectors of the community into membership. The early stonemasons were all male and when Freemasonry was being set up, the position of women in society was different from today. There are now two separate Grand Lodges in England restricted to women only.

Each Freemason is required to progress through a series of three degrees (Entered Apprentice, Fellow Craft and Master Mason) where he will gain an insight into increasingly complex moral and philosophical concepts. He will accept a variety of challenges and responsibilities which are both stimulating and rewarding. The structure and working of the lodge and the sequence of ceremonial events, which are usually followed by social gatherings, offer members a framework for companionship, teamwork, character development and enjoyment of shared experiences. He is then entitled to join Chapter and complete the Royal Arch Order.

New members make solemn promises concerning their conduct in the lodge and in society. These promises are similar to those taken in court or upon entering the armed services or many other organisations. Each member also promises to keep confidential the traditional methods of proving he is a Freemason which he would use when visiting a lodge where he is not known.

The much published 'traditional penalties' for failure to observe these undertakings were removed from the promises in 1986. They were always symbolic not literal and refer only to the pain any decent man should feel at the thought of violating his word.

Members also undertake not to make use of their membership for personal gain or advancement; failure to observe this principle or otherwise to fall below the standards expected of a Freemason can lead to expulsion.

Freemasonry is not a religion. It has no theology and does not teach any route to salvation. A belief in God, however, is an essential requirement for membership and Freemasonry encourages its members to be active in their own religions as well as in society at large.

Although every lodge meeting is opened and closed with a prayer and its ceremonies reflect the essential truths and moral teachings common to many of the world's great religions, no discussion of religion is permitted in lodge meetings.

Freemasonry, contrary to what the popular media would have us believe, is not a secret society. However, its lodge meetings are private occasions open only to members.

Members wear regalia, which, like a uniform, serve to indicate to members where they rank in the organisation. They are encouraged to speak openly about being a Freemason, while remembering that they undertake not to use it for their own or anyone else's advancement.

The rules and aims of Freemasonry are available to the public. The Masonic Year Book, also available to the public, contains the names of all national office-holders and lists all the lodges with details of their meeting dates and places.

The meeting places and halls used by Freemasons are readily identifiable, are listed in telephone directories and in many areas are hired out to the local community for activities other than Freemasonry.

Freemasons' Hall in London is open to the public and 'open days' are held in many provincial centres. Many thousands of books have been written on the subject of Freemasonry and are readily available to the general public.

From its earliest days, Freemasonry has been involved in charitable activities, and since its inception it has provided support for many widows and orphans of Freemasons as well as others within the community. All monies raised for charity are drawn from amongst Freemasons, their families and friends, while grants and donations are made to Masonic and non-Masonic charities alike. Since 1995 Freemasonry has raised more than £100m for a wide range of charitable purposes including those involved in medical research, community care, education and work with young people.

Freemasons are proud of their heritage and happy to share it.

W.Bro. Russell Wright was WM in 1970. He issued two cards which he distributed to members of Chelsea Lodge. They are reproduced now.

WHEN IS A MAN A MASON?

"When is a man a Mason?" When he knows how to sympathise with men in their sorrows, yea, even in their sins - knowing that each man fights a hard battle against many odds... When no voice of distress reaches his ears in vain, and no hand seeks his aid without response. When he finds good in every faith that helps any man to lay hold of divine things and sees majestic meanings in life, whatever the faith may be... When he knows that down in his heart every man is as noble, as vile, as divine, as diabolic, and as lonely as himself, and seeks to know, to forgive, and to love his fellow man."

WHAT OF YOUR MASONRY?

What of your Masonry? Is it put by?
Doffed with your apron, forgotten to lie
Dormant and void, inefficient and vain,
Till in the Lodge room you resume again?
Listen, my Brothers, true Masonry dwells
Out in the world, not in dungeons and cells;
It feeds the hungry, defends the oppressed,
Lifts those that languish and soothes the distressed.
Masonry's place is in the shop, street and store,
Fully as much as behind the tiled door.
'Tis not a thing to hide away,
It should be worn, used and lived day by day.
Anon

And we might add:
Take time to enjoy the privileges of the Craft - they are broadening, educational, elevating, recreational and just plain ordinary fun.

Chapter 3

The PETITION

PRELIMINARY MEETINGS OF ORIGINAL PETITIONERS

The first meeting took place on 10 May 1904 in the Chelsea Palace Boardrooms generously loaned for the occasion by the managing director of that Music Hall, Henri Gros, himself an enthusiastic Freemason and Past Master of the Italia Lodge No.2687.

W. Bro. Wolfe S. Lyon, the prime mover among the Founders, and at that time Worshipful Master of the Earl's Court Lodge, No. 2765, presided. Others in attendance at this inaugural session were W. Bros. A. Beales, E. Swanborough, W. H. Hitch, G. H. Cobley, W. K. Walton and E. T. R. Lester and Bros. T. Schreiber, T. S. Burnett, Albert Le Fre, E. A. Bridgen, E. Giles and C. J. Doughty, the last-named Brother acting as organising Secretary.

At this first meeting the name of W. Bro. Edward Swanborough, Manager of the Chelsea Palace, was suggested as the first Master and that the Lodge be called the Chelsea Palace Lodge, to hold regular meetings in the Theatre's Board Rooms on the third Friday, March to October inclusive. On 6 October of the same year it was decided to alter the name to Chelsea Lodge as more acceptable to Grand Lodge.

Following a second meeting of the petitioners it was learned that W.Bro. Swanborough would not be able to accept the office of First Master. Grand Lodge consented to insert the name of W.Bro. J.W. Mathews, PM, of the Asaph Lodge, in his place.

It is worth mentioning that though the Lodge came into being through the efforts of Masons who were allied in some way or another with the Music Hall, its first master was at the time actively identified with the legitimate theatre. W.Bro. Mathews was a New Zealander, born in Dunedin, the son of the famous prima donna, Julie Mathews, the original Grand Duchess of England in Offenbach's comic opera of that name.

The Founders' Petition was forwarded to Grand Lodge on 23 November, 1904. It is given in full, being self-explanatory.

23 November 1904
To the Most Worshipful Grand Master of the United Fraternity of Ancient Free and Accepted Masons of England

We, the undersigned, being regularly registered Master Masons of the Lodges mentioned against our respective names, having the prosperity of the Craft at heart, are anxious to exert our best endeavours to promote and diffuse the genuine principles of the Art; and, for the conveniency of our respective dwellings and other good reasons, we are desirous of forming a new Lodge to be named the Chelsea Lodge.

In consequence of this desire, we pray for a Warrant of Constitution, empowering us to meet as a regular Lodge, at the Board Rooms, Chelsea Palace, King's Road, Chelsea, SW, on the third Friday from March to October and there to discharge the duties of Masonry, in a Constitutional manner, according to the forms of the Order and do recommend Brother James W. Mathews to be the first Master, Brother Albert Le Fre to be the first Senior Warden and Brother Theodore Schreiber to be the first Junior Warden, of the said Lodge.

"The Prayer of this Petition being granted, we promise strict obedience to the commands of the Grand Master and the laws and regulations of the Grand Lodge."

Signed and delivered this 28th day of November 1904
Approved on 4th April 1905
Recommended by the Drury Lane Lodge, 2127
Warrant   £15.15.0d
38 Petitioners at 5/-   £9.10.0d

23 November 1904
To: W.Bro. Sir Edward Letchworth, Grand Secretary

Worshipful Sir and Brother,

In handing you the accompanying Petition for the consideration of the Most Worshipful Grand Master, permit me to point out that the petitioners whose names are inscribed thereto having the prosperity of the craft at heart, and being anxious to exert their best influence to promote the genuine principles of the Art, are prevented from so doing owing to the nature of their calling, viz., the Vaudeville profession and those allied thereto, in consequence of most Lodges being held in the evening at which time they are engaged in their business, and frequently find a great difficulty in regularly attending their respective Lodges. Their object therefore is to obtain a Charter empowering them to hold a Lodge in the interests of the members of their profession in the afternoon of the days and months as stated in the petition, at such hours as will enable them to carry out the duties of Masonry in a Constitutional manner and close the Lodge in time for them to attend to their avocations without detriment thereto.

Thanking you in anticipation for your favourable consideration,
I remain,

Worshipful Sir and Brother,

Yours faithfully and Fraternally,

C.J. DOUGHTY

Names attached to the Petition.
James W. Mathews, Albert Le Fre, Theodore Schreiber, Henri Gros, Wolfe Simon Lyon, Charles John Doughty, Walter H. Hitch, Edward Swanborough, Walter F.K. Walton, Ernest T.R. Lester, Thomas S. Burnett, Alfred W.H. Beales, George H. Cobley, Henry Cumerbrich, Henry H. Griffiths, Angelo Andrew Asher, George H. Dyball, Bert Alexander Bigney, Frederick T. Clay, Albert E. Nicklin, John G. Ellis, Edward H. Bungey, Lauchlan G. Sharpe, Antoine Cloetins, Charles H. Hopwood, William E. Evans, G.E. Wade (George Robey), George H. Hill, Harry T.W. Randall, Charles E. Chapman, William C. Jeapes, J.W. Norton, David George Gillings, (George Mozart) and John W. Woodward.

There were originally 38 names on the Petition. However, four brethren withdrew their names before the Petition was submitted. They were Bros. Ernest A. Brigden, Frederick W. Willatts, George Richter and Harry Long.

A third meeting of the petitioners was convened on 27 January 1905 when the By-Laws were framed, one in particular being worthy of mention, namely article 26, which stated:

There shall be a committee of Installed Masters and PMs formed once in every year at a convenient date previous to the May meeting, whose duty it shall be to examine into the capability of every brother desirous of taking office in the Lodge and to report to the Master upon the qualifications of the brethren so presenting themselves for the efficient discharge of their respective duties.

The final committee meeting was held on 10 March 1905, when its members were told that the Petition for the Charter had been granted by the M.W. Grand Master; also that permission had been given by the Chelsea Borough Council to incorporate the Borough Arms on a banner and as part of the Founders' Jewel.

At all these meetings it was W.Bro. Wolfe S. Lyon who presided. It was he who sowed the seed that has flowered so luxuriously throughout the following 100 years.

Final arrangements for the Consecration were made at a sub-committee meeting held on 13 April 1905, in the offices of the Duke of York's Theatre, St Martin's Lane, London WC2, over which the Master Designate presided. It was here agreed that invitations to the Consecration be sent to the Master and Wardens of the sponsoring Lodge, the Drury Lane Lodge No.2127. Though it seems strange to relate, there is no record of the Drury Lane Lodge playing any part in the Consecration ceremony; neither can it be ascertained why that Lodge is named in the Chelsea Lodge minutes as having been its sponsor. The Chelsea records state that at a meeting of the Drury Lane Lodge at the Drury Lane Theatre on 4 November 1904, it was agreed to sponsor the Chelsea Lodge.

No evidence of this fact can be found in the minutes of the Drury Lane Lodge. In a letter to W.Bro. Fink, dated 17 February 1952, the then Secretary of Drury Lane Lodge wrote:-

Dear Bro. Fink,
In reply to your letter, the Minutes are silent with regard to this Lodge having sponsored the Chelsea Lodge.

Your date, 4 November, does not seem to fit. Regular meetings of the Lodge are held on the second Tuesday in November. The 1904 meeting was held on Tuesday, 8 November. I agree the names of the Master and Wardens.

It seems strange that no mention is made of the signing of the recommendation to accompany the Petition to Grand Lodge, but I do not think we can do anything about it now.

Yours sincerely and fraternally,

LESLIE E. BANKS

Of the original 34 founders, 12 emanated from the Earl's Court Lodge, No.2765; 6 from Asaph Lodge, No.1319; 2 each from Liverpool Dramatic Lodge, No.1609, and St Luke's Lodge, No.144; whilst 1 each came from Lodge Italia, No.2687; Orpheus Lodge, No.1706; Camden Lodge, No.704; Kennington Lodge, No.1381; Brownrigg Lodge, No.1638; Cannon Lodge, No.1539; Emblematic Lodge, No.1321; Blackwater Lodge, No.1977; Becontree Lodge, No.1288; Pimlico Lodge, No.1772; Lodge of Light, No.2721, and Comrades Lodge, No.2740.

WARRANT
of the
CHELSEA LODGE
No.3098

————

To all and every, our Right Worshipful, Worshipful, and Loving Brethren.

WE

ARTHUR WILLIAM PATRICK ALBERT

Duke of Connaught and Strathearn

Knight of the Most Noble Order of the Garter &c &c &c &c

GRAND MASTER

of the Most Ancient and Honourable Fraternity of Free and Accepted Masons of England.

Send Greeting.

Know Ye, that We, by the authority and under the sanction of the United Grand Lodge of England, vested in us for that purpose, and at the humble petition of our Right Trusty and Well Beloved Brethren, James W. Mathews, Albert Le Fre, Theodore Schreiber, Frederick Weir Willets, John Gardener Ellis, Edward Harry Bungey, Lauchlan George Sharpe and thirty-eight others Do hereby constitute the said Brethren into a Lodge of Free and Accepted Masons, under the Title or Denomination of:

THE CHELSEA LODGE, No.3098.

The said Lodge to meet at the Chelsea Palace of Varieties, King's Road, Chelsea, London on the third Friday in March, April, May, June, July, August, September and October empowering them in the said Lodge when duly congregated, to make, pass, and raise Freemasons according to the ancient custom of the Craft, in all ages and nations throughout the known world. And further at their said Petition, and of the great trust and confidence reposed in every of the above named Brethren, We do appoint the said James W. Mathews to be the first Master, the said Albert Le Fre to be the first Senior Warden and the said Thomas Schreiber to be the first Junior Warden for opening and holding the said Lodge, and until such time another Master shall be regularly elected and installed, strictly charging that every member who shall be elected to preside over the said Lodge, and must previously have duly served as Warden in a Warranted Lodge, shall be installed in ancient form, and according to the Laws of Grand Lodge, that he may thereby be fully invested with the dignities and powers of his office. And we do require you, the said James W. Mathews to take special care that all and every the said Brethren are or have been regularly made Masons, and that you and they and all other the members of the said Lodge do observe, perform and keep the Laws, Rules and Orders contained in the Book of Constitutions, and all others which may from time to time be made by our Grand Lodge, or transmitted by us or our successors Grand Masters, or by our Deputy Grand Master for the time being. And We do enjoin you to make such by-laws for the government of your Lodge as shall, to the majority of the members, appear proper and necessary, the same not being contrary to or consistent with the General Laws and Regulations of the Craft, a copy whereof you are to transmit to us. And We do require you to cause all such By-laws and Regulations and also an account of the proceedings in your Lodge to be entered in a Book to be kept for that purpose. And you are in nowise to omit to send to us or our successors Grand Masters, or to our Deputy Grand Master for the time being, at least once in every year a List of Members of your Lodge, and the names and descriptions of all Masons initiated therein, and Brethren who shall have joined the same, with the fees and moneys payable thereon. It being our will and intention that this, our warrant of Constitution, shall continue in force so long only as you shall conform to the Laws and Regulations of our Grand Lodge. And you, the said James W. Mathews, are further required, as soon as conveniently may be, to send us an account, in writing, of what shall be done by virtue of these presents.

Given under our Hands and the Seal of the Grand Lodge, at London, this 1st day March AL5905 AD 1905.

By Command of His Royal Highness the M.W. Grand Master.

(Signed) T.F. Halsey, Deputy Grand Master
E. Letchworth, Grand Secretary

Chapter 4

The CONSECRATION

Friday 19 May 1905

INSTALLATION OF JAMES W. MATHEWS

MANY MEMBERS of the Theatrical profession are enthusiastic Freemasons but their professional duties in many cases prevent them taking that active part in the work which their inclination would desire. Under these circumstances it was a happy thought of Bro. Wolfe S. Lyon, WM 2765 to form a new lodge for their especial benefit, timing it to meet in the afternoon so that the work could be finished before the evening duties of the brethren called them away. The idea having matured, the Directors of Chelsea Palace were approached with a view to their giving the use of their handsome Board Rooms for the purpose of holding the lodge and, permission having been granted, a petition was duly presented to HRH The Duke of Connaught, the Grand Master, signed by thirty-four brethren.

A warrant having been granted, a large assemblage of the brethren met at Frascati's Restaurant on the afternoon of Friday, 19th May 1905, to witness the consecration, which was ably performed by V.W.Bro. Sir Edward Letchworth, FSA, Grand Secretary assisted by V.W.Bro. Henry G. Neville, PAGDC as SW; V.W.Bro. Harry Nicholls, PGStdB as JW; V.W.Bro. Rev. Sir Borrodale Savory, Bart., PGChaplain as Chaplain; V.W.Bro. Frank Richardson, P.Dep.GReg, GD.Cers as DC; and V.W.Bro. J. Percy Fitzgerald, PGStdB as IG.

According to The Freemason dated 3 June 1905 the consecration ceremony was performed in the perfect manner which always characterises the work of the Grand Secretary, and it was listened to with the closest attention by the assembled brethren. Bro. The Rev. Sir Borrowdale Savory, Bart., delivered an oration marked by its eloquence and homely truths.

At the conclusion of the ceremony, Bro. James W. Mathews, PM Asaph 1319, was installed as Master, the following brethren being appointed to assist him during the coming year, namely: Bros. Edward Swanborough, PM 1319; Albert Le Fre, Theodore Schreiber, Wolfe S. Lyon, WM 2765; Charles C. Doughty, G.H. Cobley, 2765; Walter H. Hitch, 2765; A.W.H. Beales, 2765; Angelo A. Asher, 704; and T.S. Burnett. Bros. Walton, Dyball. Bigney and Sharpe were appointed stewards. As Bro. Le Fre was unavoidably absent, his position was temporarily occupied by Bro. Frederick Clay, 1381. Bro. J.F. Norton, PM, was appointed Tyler.

Before the closing of the lodge there were eleven propositions for new members.

The founders were as follows: Lodge No. 144 Bert Alexander Bigney and Charles E. Chapman; Lodge No. 185 Wolfe Simon Lyon; Lodge No.704 Angelo Andrew Asher; Lodge No.1228 William C. Jeapes; Lodge No.1319 James W. Mathews, Albert Le Fre, Edward Swanborough, George H. Dyball, Antoine Cloetins and Harry T.W. Randall; Lodge No.1321 William E. Evans; Lodge No. 1381 Frederick T. Clay; Lodge No.1539 Charles H. Hopwood; Lodge No. 1609 G.E. Wade (George Robey) and David George Gillings (George Mozart); Lodge No. 1638 John G. Ellis; Lodge No.1706 Lauchlan G. Sharpe; Lodge No.1772 J.F. Norton; Lodge No.1977 George H. Hill; Lodge No.2687 Henri Gros; Lodge No.2721 John W. Woodward; Lodge No.2740 Edward H. Bungey; Lodge No.2765 Theodore Schreiber, Charles John Doughty, Walter H. Hitch, Walter F. K. Walton, Ernest T. R. Lester, Thomas S. Burnett, Alfred W. H. Beales, George H. Cobley, Henry Cumberbirch, Henry H. Griffiths and Albert E. Nicklin.

The members of the lodge and their friends, to the number of some fifty, then adjourned to the banqueting suite where an excellent repast was served in the perfect manner for which the Frascati restaurant was noted.

After the toasts of 'The King and Patron of the Craft' and 'HRH the Duke of Connaught' had been duly honoured, the WM proposed the toast of 'The Grand Officers'. He said that he deemed it the most important toast of the evening. but he should not dwell long upon it, because he thought the custom at Masonic functions of making long speeches was to be deprecated, such speeches being too often a repetition of what they had all heard many times before. He desired during his year of office to make his speeches as short as possible. They all knew that Freemasonry was ancient, and he sometimes thought that some of the speeches delivered on occasions like the present were almost as ancient as the craft itself (laughter). But, not withstanding the brevity which he deemed advisable, he was sure that all the brethren present would agree with him that they were very proud indeed to have the opportunity of drinking to the health of the Grand Officers Present and Past.

On behalf of the lodge he tendered to the Grand Officers who had honoured them by accepting their hospitality that night, their grateful thanks for their presence as well as for the admirable manner in which the consecration ceremony had been performed. They were all delighted with what they heard and he hoped that in some future time they might visit them again so as to see the work commenced that day was bearing good fruit.

Bro. Sir Edward Letchworth, on rising, was received with long continuous applause. He said: 'I rise at once to acknowledge the compliments paid to the very distinguished body of which I am a humble representative. The WM would not, I trust measure the sincerity of my thanks by the brevity of my speech. It has given us all the greatest of pleasure to be here to take part in launching this new lodge. I desire to convey our heartiest congratulations to the Chelsea Lodge in having so good a master as the brother I have had the honour of placing in the chair this evening, and I wish him and your lodge every success and happiness.'

Bro. Swanborough next proposed 'the health of the Worshipful Master'. He said that it gave him sincere pleasure to have the honour of proposing this toast. He was present when Bro. Mathews was installed as Master of his beloved lodge, The Asaph. He was glad to see him in his present position, because he felt that it meant complete success to the Chelsea Lodge.

The WM in reply, thanked the IPM for his kind words, and the brethren for the hearty manner in which they had received the toast. He said that when he accepted the responsibility of presiding over the lodge for the coming year, he was quite cognisant of the heavy responsibilities which would be placed upon him as its first Master. Yet, he did not shirk those responsibilities, but hoped he would carry on the work with credit to himself and advantage to the lodge, so that at the end of his year of office, they might say to him that he had acted in all respects as they had expected of him. Before he sat down he had the pleasure of proposing 'the health of the Immediate Past Master'. They all knew that it was the original idea that Bro. Swanborough should occupy the position of first master. It was, however, his (Bro. Swanborough's) good fortune to be a very busy man, and his daily duties prevented him from accepting the office, because he was far too conscientious a man to undertake work that he was not capable of carrying out to the letter. Might he remain for many years closely associated with the Chelsea Lodge! They should make the most of him, because true friends were few and far between. and Bro. Swanborough had shown himself the truest friend, and was beloved by every brother with whom he came in contact.

Bro. Swanborough, in reply, said that his life was made up entirely by the kindness he had received from friends in masonry, first and foremost of whom he must name Bro. Henri Gros. During the many years he had been a Freemason, he had seen no less that four Grand Secretaries occupy that position. It was said that Edwards were always lucky, and he could not help thinking the King and Patron of the Craft was a lucky man. Sir Edward Letchworth was another lucky man, and he might, perhaps, look upon himself also as a lucky man.

The toast of 'The Visitors' was next proposed by Bro. Mathews who said he hoped the Chelsea Lodge would never be behind his sister lodges in the interchange of visits in Freemasonry, which helped very considerably in promoting the universality of the Craft. They had that night the honour of entertaining many distinguished brethren, but in accordance with the desire that speeches should be made as brief as possible, he would call upon only two to respond. W.Bro. Lestocq, an old PM of the Asaph Lodge, he was delighted to see present that evening, and he might look upon him as his father in Freemasonry, and he felt that Bro. Lestocq would view with peculiar interest the position he had been placed in that day. He felt that no-one present was happier in seeing him in that position than Bro. Lestocq. Bro. Charles Cruikshanks had for many years devoted himself to the welfare of his brethren and had rendered assistance on many occasions. There was scarcely a difficulty but what he could suggest a means of overcoming. He hoped the visitors had enjoyed themselves in the company of the members of the lodge as fully as they had in the company of the visitors. If that had been effected then one of the objects of Freemasonry in being happy and communicating happiness had been achieved.

Bro. Lestocq said he had always thought when he was present at a consecration ceremony of a Freemasons' lodge it was one of the most beautiful ceremonies that could be witnessed, and he was certainly of that opinion on that day. He thought he had never enjoyed himself so much. The ceremony had been rendered in a most perfect manner and that starting their lodge, and placing it in the hands of their Worshipful Master, Bro. J.W. Mathews, they might reasonably hope for success for many years. They had been impressed by the high importance and dignity of Freemasonry. He hoped they would carry its beautiful tenets into their daily lives and into their homes with a natural result that they would be better men. He always thought that when a man was known to be a Freemason it should lead the world to think that he was a straight man, for if they, in their everyday life, asked themselves the question is such and such an action Masonic they could not go far wrong. He trusted the lodge founded that day might continue for many generations.

Bro. Cruikshanks said that he was very well satisfied to be a guest of the Chelsea Lodge. He had been for many years connected with the music hall and dramatic professions. He was very glad now that artistes of the variety stage had formed a lodge for their own particular members. Why they had not asked for it years ago he could not conceive. He sincerely wished them every success. He had come particularly to see to Bro. Le Fre placed in the chair of Senior Warden, as that brother might be said to be his child in Freemasonry.

Bro. Wolfe S. Lyon then proposed the toast of 'the Directors of the Chelsea Palace, (Our Home)'. He said that for the sake of the visitors a short explanation was necessary as to why this toast was placed in the programme. The very existence of the Chelsea Lodge was due to the managing directors of Chelsea Palace. The thought originated with himself, that before approaching anyone else he went to Bro. Henri Gros and asked if he would grant the use of his boardroom. This permission was readily granted as he felt sure it would be, having been acquainted with Bros. Payne and Gros for many years. They had included in the toast the words 'Our Home', and those two words were symbolic of all that was lovely, happy and true. The fact that the directors had so kindly given them the use of those rooms meant the saving of considerable fees in the course of every year and this he hoped would enable them to give five guineas a year to each of the charities. (Hear hear!). He asked them to drink heartily to this toast and he called upon Bro. Henri Gros to respond.

Bro. Henri Gros, in reply, said that Bro. Lyon was a very earnest man and one who always spoke the truth and this was probably accounted for by the fact that he had spent some time in the

United States (Laughter). The Chelsea Palace was built two years ago. He did not know whether the architect was a Freemason but he certainly had planned the Palace to include their boardrooms, which fitted admirably for the purpose. He had a little doubt at first as to whether the Chelsea Palace was a proper place to hold a Masonic lodge, but he was reminded of the late George Augustus Sala and his two fellow workers, Bros. Henry G. Neville and H. Nicholls who were there that night. Thinking of them, he had no hesitancy on the subject. He had heard of the hospitality of the Chelsea Lodge, that would warn them that it was by no means to be a fourth degree lodge but essentially a working one. Indeed, they were to have but one banquet a year. He hoped that the lodge would make itself known with the Charities. He thought the principles of masonry higher than the average man could reach but if they took those principles into the streets with them it could but be for their betterment. There was no distinction of creed or nationality. Their Immediate Past Master, Bro. Swanborough, had earned the respect, affection and love of all the directors, none more so than that of himself. He hoped they would go on and prosper, that he might at the end of a year or two find that the Chelsea Lodge had reached a very high point in the reputation and esteem among London lodges.

The WM then proposed the toast of the 'Officers'. He said that the work would be discontinued if any of the officers fell short in the performance of their duties. He had no doubt that the officers who had been appointed that day would do their work perfectly. He asked Bros. Schreiber and Wolfe S. Lyon to say a few words in reply. Bro. Lyon's professional duties threw him among members of two professions and he hoped that the contact between the two would prove that the two professions could work together hand in hand. It behoved them to put their shoulders to the wheel to bring about complete prosperity of the Chelsea Lodge.

Bro. Schreiber returned thanks and assured the Master that he, as well as the other officers, would do their best in the duties that had been assigned to them.

Bro. Lyon said that to him this was a glorious evening. When the idea came to him of a Freemasons' lodge consisting of the dramatic and variety professions, he had remembered that there were among them many ardent Masons eager to take an active part in the work, but he found that in almost all cases they were compelled by the professional duties to leave the lodge early. He saw no reason why a lodge which met in the afternoon might not be formed, having broached the matter to Bro. Gros he received the greatest encouragement, and the result was what they had seen. As regards to his not being the first Master, he would like to say that the position of Treasurer, to which he had been appointed, appealed to him far stronger, perhaps because his father had held a similar position for thirty years.

The Tyler's toast concluded the proceedings.

Among those present as visitors were the following: Bros. B.E. Barnett, 1668; P.H. Basty, 2077; A. Bray, 1348; H, Buckeridge, 1658; J.S.M. Byas, 25; Herbert Chenery, 2978; Tom G. Clare 1319; Clarence T. Coggin, 2127; C.H. Dancocks, 1671; J.C. Davis, 2754; Chas. Cruikshanks, 1319; E. Eddlesten, 1627; D. Frytel, 753; G. Girard, 2765; F.R. Griffiths, 2962; James Hemming, 2398; Hamilton Hill, 1539; J. Hubert, 1604; J. Hunt, 217; Arthur S. Jennings, 73; W.Lestocq, 1319; Harry Lundy, 1733; Wolfe S. Lyon, 1551; W.H. Marler, 452; ProvGDC; H. Massey, 619 and 1928; Henri de Neut, 144; J. B. Nicholls, 84, 168 and 2805, PPSGW, Provincial Grand Secretary; S.J. Price, 3020; Thomas Powell, 2182; T.B. Reid, 15; J.P. Robinson, 2926; T.F. Rowe, 2705; T.W. Rumble, 134; Horace Reynolds, 2182; Henry Saddler, 2076; W.L. Smith, 1638; C.Strong, 2182; E. de Vere, 2712; James Weaver, 862 and 1719; Hubert de Burgh Woolridge, 2741 and Walton Wells, 946; PPGOrg (Middlesex).

The musical arrangements connected with the consecration ceremony were carried out most satisfactorily under the direction of Bro. Angelo Asher, assisted by Bros. Walton Wells, PM, PPGOrg (Middlesex); Thomas Powell, PM; Horace Reynolds, PM; and Charles Strong, Organist.

Consecration of the

Chelsea Lodge

No.3098

at

Frascati's Restaurant, Oxford Street, London W.

On Friday, May 19th 1905

by

V.W. Bro. Sir EDWARD LETCHWORTH, FSA

Grand Secretary

Assisted by

W.Bro. Henry G. Neville, PAGDC....................as SW
W.Bro. Harry Nicholls, PGStB.....……...…….…as JW
V.W.Bro.Rev. Sir BORROWDALE SAVORY, Bart., PGC.....as Chaplain
V.W.Bro. FRANK RICHARDSON, P.DepGReg, GDC...............as DC
V.W.Bro J. PERCY FITZGERALD, PGstB….as Inner Guard

W.Bro. JAMES W. MATHEWS, PM Asaph Lodge, 1319 ... WM Designate
W.Bro. ALBERT LE FRE.......................….SW Designate
Bro. T. SCHREIBER.......................JW Designate

Musical Arrangements under the direction of Bro. Angelo Asher,
assisted by
W.Bros. Wharton Wells, PM, PPGO, Middlesex, Thomas Powell, PM,
Horace Reynolds, PM and Bro. Charles Strong

Organist.....…...........….Bro. ANGELO ASHER

PROGRAMME

1. The Brethren assemble in the Lodge Room
2. The Consecrating Officer accompanied by the Grand Officers, having entered in procession takes the Chair and appoints his Officers pro tem.
3. The Lodge is opened in the Three Degrees.
4.   **OPENING HYMN**
5. The Consecrating Officer addresses the Brethren on the Motive of the Meeting, and calls upon the Chaplain to give the
   OPENING PRAYER
6. Chant (Omnes): "So Mote It be."
7. The Director of Ceremonies addresses the Consecrating Officer
8. The Consecrating Officer replies and gives directions.
9. The Brethren of the New Lodge are then arranged in order.
10. The Director of Ceremonies reads the Petition and Warrant.
11. The Consecrating Officer enquires of the Brethren if they approve of the Officers named in the Warrant.
12. The Brethren signify their approval in Masonic form.
13.   **AN ORATION**
   On the Nature and Principles of the Institution, by the Chaplain.
14.   **ANTHEM**
   Behold how good and joyful a thing it is, for Brethren to dwell together in unity,
   It is like the precious ointment upon the head, that ran down into the beard,
   even unto Aaron's beard, and went down to the skirts of his clothing.
   It is like the dew of Hermon which fell upon the hill of Zion.
   For there the Lord promised His blessing, and life for evermore - SO MOTE IT BE.
15.   **DEDICATION PRAYER** (First Portion)
16. Chant (Omnes): "So mote it be."
17. Sanctus. GLORY BE TO THEE, O GOD
18. The Brethren turn towards the East, and the Consecrating Officer gives
   THE INVOCATION
19. Chant (Omnes): "So mote it be."
20. The Chaplain reads II.Chron., chap.ii., verses OPENING HYMN 1 to 16.
21. The Consecrating Officer directs Lodge Board to be uncovered, and the Consecrating Officer and Wardens carry the Elements of Consecration three times round the Lodge halting in the East at each perambulation (solemn music during the procession.)
22. Before the first circuit the Brethren sing:-
   When once of old, in Israel,
   Our early Brethren wrought with toil
   Jehovah's blessing on them fell
   In showers of Corn, and Wine, and Oil.
23. The Consecrating Officer scatters Corn - the symbol of Plenty
24. Musical Response - GLORY BE TO GOD ON HIGH
25. The Chaplain reads Psalm lxxii., verse 16.

26. Before the second circuit the Brethren sing:-

When there, a shrine to Him alone
They built, with worship sin to foil;
On Threshold and on Corner-stone

27. The Consecrating Officer pours Wine - the symbol of Joy and Cheerfulness
28. Musical Response - GLORY BE TO GOD ON HIGH
29. The Chaplain reads Nehemiah, chap x., verse 39.
30. Before the third circuit the Brethren sing:-

And we have come, fraternal bands,
With joy and pride, and prosperous spoil,
To honour Him by votive hands
With streams of Corn, and Wine, and Oil.

31. The Consecrating Officer pours Oil - the symbol of Peace and Unanimity
32. Musical Response - GLORY BE TO GOD ON HIGH
33. The Chaplain reads Exodus, chap xxx., verses 25 and 26.
34. Before the fourth circuit the Brethren sing:-

Now o'er our work this salt we shower,
Emblem of Thy conservant power;
And may Thy presence, Lord, we pray,
Keep this our temple from decay.

35. The Consecrating Officer sprinkles Salt - the symbol of Fidelity and Friendship.
36. Musical Response - GLORY BE TO GOD ON HIGH
37. The Chaplain reads Leviticus, chap. ii., verse 13.
38. **THE CONSECRATING OFFICER DEDICATES THE LODGE**
39. **ANTHEM**

How amiable are Thy dwellings, Thou Lord of Hosts. My soul hath a desire and longing to enter the courts of the Lord; my heart and my flesh rejoice in the living God. Blessed are they that dwell in Thy house: they shall always be praising Thee. Hallelujah!

40. The Chaplain takes the Censer three times round the Lodge, and halts in the East. (solemn music during his progress.)
41. **DEDICATION PRAYER** (Second Portion).
42. Chant (Omnes): "So mote it be."

43. **THE CONSECRATING OFFICER CONSTITUTES THE LODGE**
44. Chant (Omnes): "So mote it be."
45. **HYMN**
46. **PATRIARCHAL BENEDICTION**
47. Chant (Omnes): "So mote it be.

LODGE BUSINESS

INSTALLATION OF WORSHIPFUL MASTER

ELECTION OF TREASURER AND TYLER

APPOINTMENT AND INVESTITURE OF OFFICERS

PROPOSITIONS FOR INITIATES AND JOINING MEMBERS

CLOSING HYMN

Now the evening shadows closing,
Warn from toil to peaceful rest,
Mystic arts and rites reposing,
Sacred in each faithful breast.

God of light, whose love unceasing,
Doth to all Thy works extend,
Crown our Order with Thy blessing,
Build, sustain us to the end.

Humbly now we bow before thee,
Grateful for Thy aid Divine,
Everlasting power and glory,
Mighty Architect be Thine.

SO MOTE IT BE

H.B. Moody
Printer
345-7 Fulham Road,
South Kensington,
`London SW.

Chapter 5

CONSECRATING OFFICER

Sir Edward Letchworth FSA,

Grand Secretary of England

VERY WORSHIPFUL BROTHER Edward Letchworth, who was Grand Secretary of the United Grand Lodge from 1892 for more than a quarter of a century, was the eldest son of Henry Finch Letchworth of Oak Hill, Surbiton, Surrey, his mother being Maria Elizabeth, daughter of Edward Lane of Reading.

He was born on 13 March 1833, was educated privately, and for a number of years practised as a solicitor. In 1860 he was appointed Chief Steward of Manors to the late Queen Victoria and was sworn in as an officer of the Duchy of Lancaster.

Bro.Edward Letchworth was initiated at Freemasons' Hall, on 23 April 1875, in the Jerusalem Lodge, No. 197, in which he filled the various offices, reaching the chair in 1882, and was Treasurer for some years. In 1881-2 he was President of the Board of Grand Stewards of England. In 1881 he had the honour to propose H.R.H. The Prince Of Wales as M.W.G.M.

He was best known to the Craft as Grand Secretary of England, which office he filled with distinction to himself and great benefit to the Craft from 1892, his previous office being that of Junior Grand Deacon, which he filled in 1884. He was appointed Past Grand Registrar of Middlesex, 1887; a Grand Steward, 1881; Junior Grand Deacon, 1884; Grand Secretary 1892-1917 and Junior Grand Warden (1917). He was Past Master of the Lodge of Antiquity, No.2; Royal Alpha Lodge No.16 (Secretary for 26 years); Jerusalem Lodge, No. 197; Bard of Avon Lodge, No. 778; St James Abercorn Lodge, No. 1579; and Captain Coram Lodge, No. 2737. His services were in constant demand for consecration ceremonies, so much so that he officiated at the inauguration of over 400 Lodges and 150 Chapters from the time he became Grand Secretary, the greater number of which enrolled him as an Honorary Member. For many years he was a member of the Board of General Purposes and of the General Committee of Grand Chapter.

Bro. Edward was exalted in Royal Arch Masonry in the St James Chapter, No. 2, in 1872, became its First Principal in 1882, and subsequently filled the office of Provincial Grand Standard Bearer, 1884. Simultaneously with his appointment as Grand Secretary he became Grand Scribe E (1892-1917). He was twice First Principal of the St James Chapter, No.2; and was a Past First Principal of the Bard of Avon Chapter, No. 778, as also of the Enfield Chapter, No.1237.

He was advanced as a Mark Master Mason in the Carnarvon Lodge, No.7; was a Past Master of the Grand Master's Lodge, and the Ruspini Lodge, No. 363. In 1888 he was elected Grand Treasurer of England, and in 1915 invested Grand Senior Warden.

Other offices held by Sir Edward were those of Inspector-General in the 33rd Degree; Knight Grand Cross of the United Orders of the Temple and Malta; Past Grand Officer of the Royal Order of Scotland; Grand Officer of the Royal and Select Masters, and Honorary Past Grand Master of the Grand Lodge of Quebec.

He was created a Knight Bachelor by HM King Edward VII in 1902. Bro. Sir Edward was a Vice-President of, and served several Stewardships to, the Royal Masonic Benevolent Institution, Vice-Patron and Past Treasurer of the Royal Masonic Institution for Boys, to which he was Steward several times, and for thirty-eight years was a member of the House Committee of the Royal Masonic Institution for Girls of which he was a Patron and to which he had served no less than thirty-six Stewardships. In May 1913, he presided over the 125th Annual Festival of the last-mentioned Institution, when he received such loyal support from the brethren, and especially the members of the London Lodges, that the record sum of £51,071 was contributed, of which London alone provided £34,093.

In 1910, 292 Lodges and Chapters which he had consecrated presented him with a beautifully executed marble bust of himself, the work of Bro. T. Essex, the eminent London sculptor, together with an artistic album containing the names of all the Lodges and Chapters which had taken part in the presentation, and the names of the Committee. Although, at Bro. Sir Edward's request, the ceremony was made a simple one at his London house, the placing in the hands of their consecrating officer of these tokens of appreciation and respect was the occasion of a notable assembly of representative Masons. The bust is about three feet high, is carved out of a block of pure Seravezza marble, and mounted on a black pedestal, the crown of which is a revolving base for the bust and enables the latter to be turned and inspected on all sides.

The esteem in which Sir Edward Letchworth was held by Freemasons was shown in a speech made on his retirement from the position of Grand Secretary by the President of the Board of General Purposes, Sir Alfred Robbins, at the quarterly Communications of Grand Lodge in September 1917: "Sir Edward Letchworth possesses the especially rare and incommunicable gift of growing old gracefully. We, who have watched carefully his work, have marvelled at the fullness of his powers even at an advanced age; we, who have been closest to that labour, have valued it most; but there is not a Mason in the whole Jurisdiction who is not aware of the great influence that has been exercised by that dignified and venerable figure. It is given to few men to win such affection as has been won by Sir Edward Letchworth."

Apart from his long and illustrious record in Masonry, Sir Edward had been identified during his career with patriotic, scientific, philanthropic, and other movements, and retained his connection with institutions related to those interests. When the Volunteer Force (which was superseded by the Territorial Army) was inaugurated he took an active part in this branch of the National Defences, joining the Victoria Rifles in 1859. In the following year he became Captain in the Enfield Rifle Volunteers, and subsequently Captain in the Central Rifle Rangers.

In historic research he took special interest, was a Fellow of the Society of Antiquaries, and his sympathy with social ameliorative work was indicated by his long connection with St Bartholomew's Hospital and the Foundling Hospital, both institutions of which he was a Governor.

Notwithstanding the many interests which have claimed the attention of Bro. Sir Edward Letchworth in the kingdom, he was a great traveller abroad having journeyed extensively in almost all the countries of Europe as well as in Egypt, Morocco, etc. The time he had available for recreation was principally expended in travelling and in outdoor sports, among which riding and rowing formerly took principal places.

Bro. Sir Edward was a renowned bachelor until 1902 when he married Mary Constance, widow of Thomas Blaikie, only son of the late Sir Thomas Blaikie, of Aberdeen. His residences were 14, Cornwall Gardens, SW., and Claygate, Tonbridge, Kent. He was a member of the Junior Carlton and Garrick Clubs.

At the bicentenary celebration of the foundation of Grand Lodge held at the Royal Albert Hall, London in June 1917, Sir Edward received at the hands of the Grand Master, the Duke of Connaught, the jewel of Past Grand Junior Warden and on the following day read the second lesson of the religious service held in the same hall. The following month he was taken ill.

Sir Edward died 8 October 1917, at his London residence, aged 84 years. Such was his fame and the respect and affection of his contemporaries that he was usually referred to in later years as "the Grand Old Man of British Freemasonry".

Chapter 6

FOUNDERS and HONORARY MEMBERS

THE FOLLOWING is a copy of the list of Founders as shown in the records of Grand Lodge, their professions at the time the Lodge was Consecrated, and the Lodges from which they emanated.

Lodge	Name	Occupation
1319	MATHEWS, James W.	Theatrical Manager
1319	LE FRE, Albert	Music Hall Artiste
2765	SCHREIBER, Theodore	Music Hall Artiste
2687	GROS, Henri	Director of Theatres
185	LYON, Wolfe Simon	Theatrical Upholsterer
2765	DOUGHTY, Charles John	Retired
2765	HITCH, Walter H.	Auctioneer
1319	SWANBOROUGH, Edward	Manager, Chelsea Palace
2765	WALTON, Walter F. K.	Comedian
2765	LESTER, Ernest T. R.	Comedian
2765	BURNETT, Thomas S.	Music Hall Artiste
2765	BEALES, Alfred W. H.	Music Hall Manager
2765	COBLEY, George H.	Music Hall Artiste
2765	CUMERBRICH, Henry	Music Hall Artiste
2765	GRIFFITHS, Henry H.	Music Hall Artiste
704	ASHER, Angelo Andrew	Musical Director
1319	DYBALL, George H.	Stage Manager
144	BIGNEY, Bert Alexander	Clerk (Empire)
1318	CLAY, Frederick, T.	Theatre Proprietor
2765	NICKLIN, Albert E.	Manager
1638	ELLIS, John G.	Music Hall Clerk
2740	BUNGEY, Edward H.	Music Hall Clerk
1706	SHARPE, Lauchlan G.	Concert Agent
1319	CLOETINS, Antoine	Musical Director
1539	HOPWOOD, Charles H.	Clerk (Tivoli)
1321	EVANS, William E.	Comedian
1609	WADE, G.E. (George Robey)	Comedian
1977	HILL, George H.	Music Hall Clerk
1319	RANDALL, Harry T. W.	Comedian
144	CHAPMAN, Charles E.	Music Hall Agent
1228	JEAPES, William C.	Cinematographer
1772	NORTON, J. F.	Comedian
1609	GILLINGS, David G. (George Mozart)	Comedian
2721	WOODWARD, John W.	Scenic Artist

Early pictures of Founders Albert le Fre (left) and Serpentello (Theodore Schreiber)
(right), 1906 with Founders Medal 1905 (centre)

Honorary Members, 1905
V.W.Bro. Sir Edward Letchworth, FSA., GS
V.W.Bro. Rev. Sir Boowdaile Savory, Bart., PG Chaplain
V.W.Bro. Albert G. Neville, PAGDC
V.W.Bro. Harry Nicholls, PGStdB
V.W.Bro. Frank Richardson, PDepGR, GDC
W.Bro. J. Percy Fitzgerald, PGStB

Chapter 7

1905 THAT WAS THE YEAR THAT WAS

ONE HUNDRED YEARS have passed since the Chelsea Lodge No.3098 was consecrated in 1905 into a world which, in so many ways, was quite different from our own. Citizens in 1905 sensed they were living in extraordinary times. The country had surgery, sanitation, plumbing and drainage. Optimism was widespread as the country moved into the Edwardian age, following the long reign of Queen Victoria who had died in 1901. King Edward VII was crowned in 1902.

A map of the world showed most of it coloured pink representing the territory of the British Empire and Commonwealth ... Australia, Bechuanaland, British Guiana, British North Borneo, British Somaliland, Burma, Canada, Ceylon, Christmas Island, Cocos, Cyprus, Egypt, Gambia, Gibraltar, Gold Coast, Hadhramaut, Hong Kong, India, Iraq, Kenya, Malaya, Malta, New Guinea, New Zealand, Nigeria, Northern Rhodesia, Sierra Leone, Singapore, Southern Rhodesia, Sudan, Tangyanika, Uganda, Union of South Africa, United Kingdom, Zanzibar, In addition there were dozens of smaller islands and military bases like Amirantes, Andamana, Ascension, Bahamas, Barbados, Bermuda, Caroline. Chagos, Ellice, Falkland Islands, Fiji, Gilbert, Gough, Jamaica, Laccadive, Maiden, Maldive, Mauritius, Nicobar, Pitcairn, Rotuma, Seychelles, St Helena, Starbuck, Tonga, Trinidad, Tristan de Cunha, Tobago. The British Empire was at its height with India 'the jewel in the crown' and Great Britain the most powerful nation in the world. The Prime Minister was Arthur James Balfour.

The radio as we know it today was still a scientific dream, although Marconi had invented wireless telegraphy. Television was light years away.

The petrol driven car had recently been invented and by law its maximum speed was 4 miles per hour with the extra safeguard of a man walking in front holding a red flag. The penny-farthing bicycle and the safety bicycle had recently appeared and were being seen in increasing numbers on the roads. Orville and Wilbur Wright were to make the first controlled flight by a heavier-than-air machine in 1903. Orville Wright flew for just 12 seconds a distance of 120 feet in Kitty Hawk, USA. By 1905 the Wright brothers could fly a full circle of 24 miles in 38 minutes.

St Pancras Railway Station, London in 1905

The most powerful form of transport was rail. London was connected by a vast network of lines connecting most parts of the country with mainline railway stations located at Euston, Kings Cross, Paddington, St Pancras and Waterloo. London's Inner Circle railway lines were electrified. In America it took eighteen hours to travel between New York and Chicago but in 1905 the first train ever equipped with electric lights came into operation.

In world events Port Arthur surrendered to the Japanese in the Russo-Japanese War. Russia suffered other defeats. The Russian revolution of 1905 began on 'Bloody Sunday', 22 January, when troops fired on a defenceless group of protesters in St Petersburg. Strikes, riots and assassinations followed. Sailors on the Russian battleship *Potemkin* mutinied. Reforms, including the first Duma (parliament), were established by Czar Nicholas II's 'October Manifesto.'

In Chicago the organisation 'Industrial Workers of the World' was founded with the hopes of uniting all workers and giving more control to unions. America, whose president was Theodore Roosevelt, had a population of 83,822,000. In England the population was 30,813,043.

Heinz Baked Beans were test marketed in the north of England by Pittsburgh's H.J. Heinz Company. British working class wives were advised that "baked beans make a nourishing meal for men returning home from work."

Ovaltine was introduced by Swiss entrepreneur Albert Wander. Made of malt extract, evaporated milk, powdered eggs, and cocoa powder, the beverage would be prescribed by physicians whose patients were convalescing or suffering from wasting disease.

Isadora Duncan established the first school of modern dance in Berlin. She had developed a spontaneous style that tried to symbolise music, poetry and elements of nature. The first movie theatre opened in Pittsburgh, Pennsylvania. Albert Einstein, the German-Swiss physicist, obtained his doctorate at the University of Zurich and evolved the special theory of Relativity. In Germany Robert Koch won a Nobel Prize for work on tuberculosis, and Polish historian and author Henryk Sienkiewicz won a Nobel Prize for literature.

The world's largest diamond was found in a mine in Pretoria, South Africa on 26 January 1905. Named after Sir Thomas Cullinan, in whose mine it was found, the diamond was a whole 3,106 carats. It was cut into stones for the British Crown jewels and for the collection of the Royal family.

Sherlock Holmes

The Rotary Club in Great Britain is very active but was originally formed in Chicago on 23 February 1905 by lawyer Paul Harris. Today it has grown into an organisation encompassing most countries in the world and does much in the advancement of international understanding, goodwill and peace.

On 31 March 1905, the fictitious hero Sherlock Holmes was resurrected. Sir Arthur Conan Doyle, was initiated into Phoenix Lodge No.257, Southsea on 26 January 1887, at the age of 27 and in the same year created the detective. He then wrote a string of novels which the British snapped up as soon as they were published. For eighteen years Conan Doyle ignored requests for yet another book, but finally relented and wrote *The Return of Sherlock Holmes*.

Other books that were popular in 1905 were: *The House of Mirth* by Edith Wharton, *Where Angels Fear to Tread* by English novelist E.M. Forster, *Kipps* by H.G. Wells, and *The Four Just Men* by Edgar Wallace.

The typewriter made its first appearance in America when L.C. Smith and Brothers sold its first model to the *New York Tribune*. This was followed very quickly by the Royal Typewriter Company, founded in New York in 1905. Their typewriter had innovations that included a friction-free ball-bearing one-track rail to support the weight of the carriage as it moved back and forth, a new paper feed and complete visibility of words as they were typed.

In the world of cricket England won the ashes by beating Australia by two matches to nil, three matches being drawn. Test matches took place at Trent Bridge, Nottingham; Lord's; Headingley, Leeds; Old Trafford, Manchester and Kennington Oval. In the three-day Champion County Match between Yorkshire and the Rest of England played at Kennington Oval, London, Yorkshire won by 65 runs.

A new magazine, *Variety*, covering all aspects of show business, began publication on 18 December 1905.

Music and entertainment played an important part of English life in 1905. Popular tunes of that year included: *Clair de Lune, Daddy's Little Girl, Everybody Works But Father, Forty-Five Minutes From Broadway, I Don't Care, I Want What I Want When I Want It, In My Merry Oldsmobile, In The Shade of the Old Apple Tree, Kiss Me Again, Mary's a Grand Old Name, My Gal Sal, Nobody, Parade of the Wooden Soldiers, Rufus Rastus Johnson Brown, So Long Mary, Wait 'til the Sun Shines, Nellie, Where the River Shannon Flows, The Whistler and His Dog, A Woman Is Only a Woman, But a Good Cigar Is a Smoke* and *Will You Love Me in December*. In London's West End there were musicals galore: *The Cingalee* (Daly's), *Sergeant Brue* (Strand which opened on 22 May 1905), *The Catch of the Season* (Vaudeville), *Lady Madcap* (Prince of Wales), *Peggy Machree* (Wyndham), *The Talk of the Town* (Lyric) and *Miss Wingrove* (Strand).

The theatre world enjoyed *Man and Superman* and *Major Barbara* both by George Bernard Shaw at London's Royal Court Theatre and *Alice-Sit-by-the-Fire* by James M. Barrie at the Duke of York's Theatre.

Amongst those from the entertainment world born in 1905 were Swedish film actress Greta Garbo, trumpeter Charlie Teagarden (brother of bandleader Jack Teagarden), film star Elsa Lanchester, actor Henry Fonda, singer Billy Scott-Comber, orchestra leader Mantovani, trumpeter **Max Goldberg** (he later became a member of Chelsea Lodge), Welsh stage and TV actress Doris Hare and bandleader Ivor Kirchen. The list continues with American film producer Pandro Berman, American trombonist and bandleader Tommy Dorsey, Austrian-born American conductor and opera director Kurt Adler, English film and TV actress Queenie Leonard, American film actress Clara Bow, English stage actress Laura Kendal, American stage and film

director Joseph Cotten, English film actor Robert Newton, American dancer and choreographer Agnes de Mille, Scottish film actor James Robertson Justice, American, stage, film and TV actress Mildred Natwick, Welsh actor, playwright, screenwriter and director Emlyn Williams, American song writers Dorothy Fields, Jule Styne and Harold Arlen, American film actress Myrna Loy, Welsh stage, film and TV actress Rachel Thomas, American jazz musician Earl Hines and English actor Robert Donat. The English playwright, film director and film screenwriter Muriel Box was born in 1905 as was English radio broadcaster and commentator Leslie Mitchell, whose voice opened BBC Television from Alexandra Palace on 1 November 1936 and took part in the launch of ITV's Associated Rediffusion in 1955. During World War II he worked as the announcer for British Movietone News.

Baroness Maria von Trapp, born on 26 January 1905, was the famous nun from Austria who was sent to the von Trapp family as a nurse. There she fell in love with the head of the household, retired navy officer Captain von Trapp, and eventually escaped the persecution of the Nazis by leading her family over the Alps to freedom; her story is recounted in the great musical *The Sound of Music*.

Country singer-songwriter Al Dexter was born on 4 May 1905. He wrote the song *Pistol Packin' Mama* that was a hit record for Gene Vincent in 1960. Another country singer, Tex Ritter, was also born in 1905. He was one of Hollywood's most popular singing cowboy actors.

Other notable personalities born in 1905 include English politician and broadcasting executive Lord Aylestone, French fashion designer Christian Dior, English cleric Cardinal John Heenan the 80th Archbishop of Westminster, English aristocrat Henry Frederick Thynne 6th Mauquis of Bath, Scottish aviator Jim Mollison, English novelist H(erbert) E(rnest) Bates, Swedish diplomat Dag Hammarskjold.

Independence was achieved when Norway broke away from Sweden and dissolved the union which had existed since 18 January 1814, Sweden agreed to the ending of the union.

The Automobile Association (AA) was founded and the first general meeting was held at The Trocodero, London.

Chelsea Football Club was born and they played their first match in September 1905, away, against Stockport. Although it took fifty years to put any silverware in the trophy cabinet Chelsea have, since 1955, been regular cup winners. Their centenary year has been particularly pro-active, winning the Barclays Premiership table.

The Magic Circle was founded at Pinoli's Restaurant, London when some twenty-three amateur and professional magicians got together. Later in the year David Devant was appointed its first President.

Amongst those who died in 1905 were English stage actor Sir Henry Irving, Irish-born social reformer and philanthropist Dr Thomas Barnardo, founder of the homes for destitute children. It was originally known as The National Incorporated Association for the Reclamation of Destitute Waif Children. Today it is simply known as 'Barnardos'. Jules Verne also died in 1905. His writings laid much of the foundation of modern science fiction. He foresaw a number of scientific devices and developments, including the submarine, the aqualung, television and space travel. He is best remembered for *Journey to the Centre of the Earth, Twenty Thousand Leagues Under the Sea* and *Around the World in 80 Days*.

Chapter 8

THERE'S NO BUSINESS LIKE SHOW BUSINESS

FREEMASONRY AND SHOW BUSINESS have run hand in hand for at least two centuries. They are inexorably linked. In whatever branch of the entertainment world one looks one would find many of the major names of the day are Freemasons.

In the world of classical music we have enjoyed the compositions of Beethoven, Handel, Haydn, Listz, Mozart and Sibelius and, more recently, Gilbert and Sullivan. We have been captivated by the memorable tunes written by Jerome Kern, John Philip Sousa, W.C. Handy and Irving Berlin. Many of these tunes were played by the great orchestras of the day - Glenn Miller, Duke Ellington, Count Basie, Lionel Hampton and Paul Whiteman.

On the big wide screen we have come to enjoy the acting talents of Bob Hope, Harold Lloyd, Roy Rogers, Ernest Borgnine, Red Skelton, Clark Gable, W.C. Fields, Al Jolson, Gene Autry, Douglas Fairbanks, Michael Caine and John Wayne, and films directed by such well-respected names as Cecil B. DeMille, Buster Keaton, Louis B. Mayer, Jack Warner, William Wyler and Darryl F. Zanuck.

Singers and musicians are included as well: Roy Acuff, Eddy Arnold, Chet Atkins, Louis Armstrong, Nat 'King' Cole, Burl Ives, Jimmie Rodgers and Mel Tillis. All had one thing in common, they were Freemasons.

Show business was always central to the input of Chelsea Lodge. Over the years its members have come from every facet of the entertainment world - actors, jugglers, magicians, acrobats, impressionists, ventriloquists and musicians, together with those who worked in the circus or the fairground. It has been one great variety show.

From Music Hall to variety, from the silent films to the talkies, from radio to television, members of Chelsea Lodge have played an important part in keeping alive the entertainment business in its wider sense, not just on stage but behind the scenes as well with agents, managers of theatres, producers and directors. The list of Founder members shows that almost everyone was linked with show business in one way or another. There were three theatrical or musical hall managers (including one from Chelsea Palace), seven comedians, three music hall artistes, two musical directors and six theatre or music hall clerks, plus a theatrical upholsterer, a stage manager, a theatre proprietor, a director of variety theatres, two music hall or concert agents, a manager of Chelsea Palace Theatre, a scenic artist and a cinematographer.

MUSIC HALL
The established victuallers who managed the taverns began to see a future in organising the spending of an evening with congenial entertainment. By 1905 Music Hall was in its hey day. Charles Morton, remembered as the father of the British "Music Hall", had begun his working life as a bartender in London, rising to become owner of St George's Tavern. By the time he was twenty-nine he had bought Canterbury Hall in Lambeth and turned it into an elegant and spacious show place, richly decorated with rows of marble-topped tables below the high stage, a wide entrance foyer and graceful stairways curving up to the loggias. The capacity was no less than 1500. It was opened in 1854. Historians have always considered The New Canterbury to be the first true music hall but there are those who would challenge this fact. In their book *British Music Hall*, Raymond Mander and Joe Mitchenson claim that Edward Winder in fact took over and opened the Mogul Saloons on 27 December 1847 and Richard Preece of the Grand Harmonic

Hall at the Grapes, Southwark Bridge Road, had been the first to call his premises the Surrey Music Hall in November 1848, the first use of the name "music hall" in this sense.

Founding member **George Robey** topped the opening bill at the New Canterbury with colleagues Albert Chevalier, George Formby Snr, Gus Elan, Harry Champion and Dan Leno. George was usually billed as "The Prime Minister of Mirth" and was a star of the first magnitude in every branch of the business - Music Hall, revue, musical comedy, legitimate theatre and films. Playing characters both male and female, he became a master of facial expression, with a liking to communicate intimately with his audience. He appeared in the Royal Command Performances at the Palace Theatre on 1 July 1912, and the London Coliseum in 1919. All subsequent performances to date have been shows presented by the Variety Profession which the Royals are invited to attend and members of Chelsea Lodge are still calling the tune both on and off stage.

Three founder members of Chelsea Lodge - Will Evans, George Mozart and a rare picture of George Robey with his first wife Ethel and children Eileen and Edward

Among the Founder members were artistes who became part of Music Hall history. **Harry Randall** was an exponent of the art of burlesque, a great singer of songs and a first-class character actor. **Will Evans**, one of the finest slapstick comedians of the halls, and skits *Harnessing a Horse, Laying a Carpet* and *Whitewashing a Ceiling*, provided a phenomena of pandemonium, much copied but rarely equalled. **George Mozart** specialised in character cameos and was the top of his own particular line; his thumb-nail sketches *An Old Lady Crossing the Street* and *The Family Album* were gems of human observation. Very popular with musical hall audiences were burlesque magicians Walton and Lester (**Walter F.K. Walton** and **Ernest T.R. Lester**). Another Founder member was **Albert Le Fre**. He had made his first stage appearance at the age of six in pantomime at the Criterion, Sheerness, Kent. His London debut was made later at the Old Surrey Theatre in South London. He quickly became a skilful skater, singer, dancer and acrobat, and he appeared in the First Royal Command Performance in London in 1912. Albert was a Founder member of the Variety Artistes Federation.

Music Hall was the first of the mass entertainments. There were over 200 music halls in the 1870s with some 300 in the provinces. Our forbears spoke affectionately of remembering the gold lacquered cupids, feather boas, sweating faces, clinking glasses, waxed moustaches, posters in large black type, musicians tuning-up, bellowing choruses in the gallery. They were indeed "the good old days".

Audiences were given value for money when they could see up to 20 different artistes appearing on a bill. Generally speaking these artistes were a breed of professionals who could face the lights in any town and sing the latest popular song above the noise of the audience. If the song caught on it could sell over a quarter of a million copies in sheet music sales. The audience accepted ballads but the most popular songs tended to be more boisterous and, in some cases, vulgar.

In those days there were no microphones or amplifiers. Singers did not have backing tracks, but they had to have a good pair of lungs to penetrate to the back seats in the theatre.

The audiences wanted to identify with the singers and the sentiments of these songs and join in with the chorus lines. One hundred years later we still remember: *I'm Henery the Eighth I Am, Boiled Beef and Carrots, I Love a Lassie, Roamin' in the Gloamin', After the Ball, I'm a Bit of a Ruin That Cromwell Knocked About a Bit, My Old Dutch, Ta-ra-ra-Boom-De-Ay, Lily of Laguna, If It Wasn't For the 'Ouses in Between* and *The Man Who Broke the Bank at Monte Carlo*.

Music hall singers jealously guarded the sole rights to their songs, but permission to sing the latest successes in various pantomimes around the country over the Christmas holidays were often sold by the owner of the song. *Put Me Amongst the Girls* was one such a success that it was reportedly sung on over 200 pantomimes. The song, written by **Dan Lipton** and C.W. Murphy, was a great success for **Charlie Whittle**. Murphy teamed up with Harry Castling to produce another hit for Charlie in 1909 *Let's All Go Down the Strand* and *Has Anyone Here Seen Kelly* (1911). Although Florrie Ford is associated with 'Kelly', the named singer on Frances Day and Hunter's original published version of the song is Charlie Whittle.

Eating, drinking and entertainment have been close bedfellows as long as one can remember. The large assembly rooms of the Georgian coffee houses and taverns, which catered for both upper and lower classes, were the beds in which the seeds of music hall were sown.

Thomas Edison's invention of the phonograph was being used commercially in 1892 and beginning to attract attention. Performers from the halls were recording on wax cylinders and besides selling for home use, records were to be heard in converted shops, by an intrigued public through stethoscope-like earpieces connected to hand-operated machines. Little did the public imagine that these two novelties would eventually combine and blossom into the talkies and close hundreds of music halls.

The cinematograph was first shown at the Empire in 1896 and soon spread to other halls. The Bioscope with news and events became a recognised "turn" at the end of the evening's entertainment.

By the beginning of the 1900s, social conditions were being created which were provoking a change in popular entertainment and, as in the 1840s, when Morton was the man who emerged and was to co-ordinate all the various activities at the Canterbury, so in December 1902 Oswald Stoll became the man who was to perform a similar feat with the launching of a company, the London Coliseum Limited. He was later knighted.

Music Hall and its close relation, variety, were to remain the dominant forms of entertainment until the 1920s when competition from cheap silent cinema was to mark the decline and eventual demise of the former. Variety soldiered on until the "talkies" took over many of the theatres.

VARIETY and the THEATRE

Variety is a form of theatrical entertainment, similar to broad revue, which emerged as the successor to Music Hall in the twentieth century.

The Victorian public's attitude to entertainment was changing as it passed into the Edwardian era. The middle classes were ready for a family entertainment free from the taint of vulgarity and robust vigour that had kept them away from the music hall.

At the start it was distinguished from its predecessor by the fact it was deliberately less risqué and 'blue' material was precluded in an attempt to make such entertainment more respectable.

The variety programme at the Palace under Alfred Butt had been of a good refined high-class

standard but the old taboos still clung.

It was a new form of variety that Oswald Stoll visualised that would cater for the public he wished to attract. Stoll's dream palace, The London Coliseum, designed by Frank Matcham, was opened on 24 December 1904. The Coliseum was at that time the only theatre in Europe that had lifts. It had a marble staircase and tea room on every tier. Oswald Stoll was a teetotaller who wanted to create entertainment for families. The seats had armrests and for the first time could be booked in advance for performances of which there were four daily. The Royal Variety Performance is staged from time to time at the Coliseum to this day.

Nearly every town in the country had a variety theatre fifty years ago and people flocked to them on a regular basis.

Sir Edward Stoll founder of The London Coliseum

Variety was a mix of musicians, singers, jugglers, dancers, acrobats, actors, poets, dance orchestras, magicians and comedians. It became the creative melting-pot where different acts met and new ones were created. Artistes from different traditions came together, enriching and assisting each other's performances. Acrobats may play musical instruments and musicians might juggle. This form of light entertainment offered a unique mix where all preferences were satisfied in small doses.

The life of the variety artiste could be very solitary. Although they appeared in front of hundreds of people every night they usually had few real friends in the towns they visited. More often than not there was a pub across the road from the theatre to which they retired each evening after the show. They got to know the landlord over the years of visiting the town and it became a second home for them with lock-ins every night after closing time. Unless you were a top line artiste it was not always possible to live in hotels and every town had its theatrical digs where the artistes stayed.

On stage each act was given a number of minutes for their spot, ranging from eight to twenty minutes depending on their importance on the bill. Time was vitally important, especially in twice nightly variety. There was only fifteen minutes between the end of the first house and the second house starting and during that time one audience had to leave the theatre, rubbish picked up and another audience admitted. If

London Coliseum advertising tele-variety in 1935

the first house overran there were problems because the second house would come out after the last public transport had departed. Variety artistes have had the remainder of their dates cancelled because of an overrun.

The Variety Artistes Federation (VAF), based at 13 Charing Cross Road, London WC., was born on 18 February 1906 just nine months after the birth of Chelsea Lodge. Its object was to 'promote the interests of variety artistes and to abolish all abuses detrimental to their welfare.' One of the first moves of the new union was to start a weekly newspaper *The Performer*. The paper ran successfully for 51 years from 1906.

In the 1920s and 1930s **Ernie Mayne** was one of the last of the old-style performers regularly appearing on the halls. The music halls were in decline, a subject on which he aired his views in an interview in *Era*, 3 February 1926:

Variety is by no means dead, and it will never die so long as the right 'stuff' is given to the public. I cannot bring myself to believe that the majority of 'stars' have dwelt too much on their old material. At times the audiences ask for an old number and expect it. The reason why they have not got more variety on the bill is because there are not nowadays sufficient 'stars' to fill the bills as there were in the old days. So many have died, and their places have not been filled, because new talent has not been cultivated. When new talent has presented itself, it has been snapped up by revues, and in these revues it has lost its individuality. Young comedians do not have to fight for their livelihood as we used to do in days gone by. It was that early struggle that produced 'stars' later on. In that struggle individuality generally predominated and won.

Variety reached its peak in popularity in the 1930s before television took a major hold. In the 1930s and 1940s artistes such as Tommy Trinder, Ted Ray, Nellie Wallace, Gracie Fields, Will Hay, George Formby, **Sandy Powell** and Max Miller appeared regularly in variety up and down the country. These were well known names made famous by radio. It was the 'wireless' that was seen as a way to encourage new audiences to come along to see the show. Credits were always given at the end of a radio programme as to where the stars who had appeared on air were currently performing on stage.

The popularity of variety dwindled with the advent of the talking pictures. By the 1930s many theatres had closed or become cinemas. Other forms of entertainment such as revue had become popular and many variety performers made their names through radio, film and later television. In the First World War many former acrobats, aerialists and jugglers were killed in action or injured and could no longer perform, thereby robbing the stage of the variety of acts previously available.

During the Second World War many variety artistes appeared in Combined Services Entertainment, including Norman Wisdom, Harry Secombe and Frankie Howerd. Some toured with ENSA like Tommy Trinder. Theatres in London stayed open during the war and shows played to sell out audiences who remained in their seats even during the heaviest bombing raids. Most theatres had a box each side of the proscenium arch, the one on the left side would light up in red (reading 'air raid' or 'alert') and the one on the right side would be a green light (reading 'raiders passed' or 'all clear').

For many variety performers their first London appearance was at the Windmill Theatre where the famous nude showgirls were the main feature of the show. Almost every comedian appeared there at some point in their careers, but left after a short time because the audiences were only interested in the girls. Most of these acts went on to make their name in television and some in film. Amongst the Chelsea members who worked at the Windmill were **Peter Elliott, Ronnie Bridges, Bob Monkhouse, Dick Emery, Arthur English, Alfred Marks, Charlie Rose, Bernard Spear** and **Peter Sellers**.

Up to the 1960s, performers still learned their skills in the variety theatres. Television stars such as Larry Grayson, Bruce Forsyth, Roy Hudd and Ken Dodd began their careers in variety, playing circuits up and down the country.

The first variety show to become a weekend national viewing habit was *Sunday Night at the London Palladium* (ATV), which was launched on 25 September 1955 by Val Parnell. The show was live for twelve seasons and read like a Who's Who in Show business. Viewing figures reached 23 million in its heyday. The series conferred nationwide fame on a number of comedians and comperes: Tommy Trinder, Dickie Henderson, Hughie Green, **Bob Monkhouse**, Robert Morley, Bruce Forsyth, **Alfred Marks**, Arthur Haynes, Don Arrol, Norman Vaughan, Roger Moore and Jimmy Tarbuck.

The advent of commercial television in the early 1950s saw a quick decline in audiences and theatres began to close. At first it was a small number but by 1956 *The Stage* theatrical newspaper reported that six theatres had closed in the previous week. It was all over in the short period of four years, although from time to time Variety made a brief comeback.

In 1992 impresario Jack Seaton staged a tribute to Ralph Reader and his famous *Gang Shows*, to mark the 60th anniversary of the original *RAF Gang Show*, which starred such people as **Don Smoothey, Rex Roper**, Cardew Robinson, **Reg** 'Confidentially Yours' **Dixon** and **Peter Sellers**. Ralph Reader choreographed and staged many West End shows and on Broadway with Al Jolson. But he will always be best remembered by the arm-waving, woggle-wearing lads singing *I'm Riding Along on the Crest of a Wave*. For the 60th anniversary show Don, Rex and Cardew were joined by Russ Conway and **Jim Davidson**, who began his career in a Gang Show at Golders Green.

Variety acts can still be seen in summer seasons at holiday resorts, on cruise ships, in working men's clubs, and in venues that attract an older audience.

Many members of Chelsea worked in Variety. Forty-five were artistes, fifteen were agents and one was a producer.

The THEATRES, EMPIRES, HIPPODROMES and PALACES

Frank Matcham was by profession a theatre architect. In the final years of the 1800s and first two decades of the 1900s he was responsible for the design of over one hundred theatres in towns and cities throughout the United Kingdom.

These theatres normally had an imposing frontage, illuminated either side by large flame shaped lamps and, high above street level reaching towards the night sky, could be seen two green copper-covered domes separated by an ornate pediment beneath which the word 'Empire', 'Palace' or 'Hippodrome' was portrayed in illuminated letters.

There were many famous places of variety which included Chiswick Empire, Finsbury Park

Empire, Shepherd's Bush Empire, Wood Green Empire, Lewisham Hippodrome, London Hippodrome, Victoria Palace, Chelsea Palace, London Coliseum and London Palladium together

Shepherd's Bush Empire

with numerous provincial theatres. These houses of entertainment are contained in an excellent book *Empires, Hippodromes and Palaces* by Jack Reid (1985). One could eavesdrop in any theatre in the United Kingdom and find Chelsea members making appearances. For example Wood Green Empire hosted **Stanelli**, **Issy Bonn**, **Leon Cortez** and His Coster Pals and the **Joe Loss** Orchestra on different occasions. Suffice here to take one theatre as an example where Chelsea members performed to packed houses. We visit Shepherd's Bush Empire.

This theatre was built for Oswald Stoll and situated at Shepherd's Bush Green in west London. It was designed by Frank Matcham with seating for 1,650. It opened on 17 August 1903. There was hardly a star in the music hall era that didn't play 'The Bush'. **Will Evans** with his *'White-washing the Ceiling'* sketch was reputed to have been the originator of the slapstick kitchen routine which has become a popular feature in practically every pantomime to the present day. Both **George Mozart** and **George Robey** appeared at the Shepherd's Bush Empire.

Between the First and Second World Wars Variety continued at 'The Bush'. **Nervo** and Knox played there in their pre-Crazy Gang days with their hilarious slow motion wrestling act. **Talbot O'Farrell**, singer of *That Old Fashioned Mother of Mine* performed there.

After the Second World War, and until the early 1950s, the theatre continued with weekly Variety and Revues. However, by 1953, in the inevitable sad decline which was to be the fate of so many theatres (like the Chelsea Palace), it succumbed to the tempting offers of television with which it would live on to play a part in the world of entertainment. The last stage performance took place on 26 September 1953 with a variety bill that included Robb Wilton, Hal Monty, Krysta and Krystal, Stan Stennett, Dawn White, The Allen Brothers, The Two Condons, and Tessa Smallpage.

BBC TV took possession of the theatre on 29 September 1953 and almost immediately work commenced to convert the building into a TV studio-theatre. One of the first shows to be televised from Shepherd's Bush in front of a live audience took place in October 1953. *Variety Parade* starred Max Bygraves, Eve Boswell, Gladys Morgan and the Tiller Girls. Other shows which were broadcast included *The Billy Cotton Band Show*, the *Black and White Minstrel Show* and *Jim'll Fix It*. The final programme to be transmitted from the Shepherd's Bush Empire was *Wogan*, in which guests looked back at 38 years of television and also discussed the building's theatrical past. The 'Empire' was the first theatre to become a full time television studio and was also the last to be decommissioned. Known as the Television Theatre it was used by the BBC until the summer of 1991. At a similar time the BBC moved out of the former Gaumont-British studios in Lime Grove.

Once the BBC had vacated the premises, the proprietors of London's Borderline Club moved in and spent much time and money recasting a large area of the plasterwork which had been destroyed by constant use of television equipment. Today the Shepherd's Bush Empire is a thriving music venue.

CIRCUS

The circus can trace its origins back to Greek and Roman times and has stood the test of time. It is not the intention of this book to trace the history of the circus but we must look at its development. Suffice to say that as early as 421BC at a dinner party given in Athens the entertainment for the evening was given by a jester who told jokes, a girl and a boy played music and performed mime and a girl who placed a ring of sharp swords on the ground and did somersaults among them.

These entertainers who attended dinners and banquets were typical of the feats presented by acrobats, jugglers and tumblers who performed for the Greek and Roman empires for centuries.

The 'father of the English Circus' is generally acknowledged to be Philip Astley. He was the son of a cabinetmaker and veneer cutter, born in the Potteries in 1742. Sgt-Major Astley served in Colonel Eliott's 15th Light Dragoon Regiment, where he displayed an

Philip Astley, Esq.

outstanding talent as a horse breaker and trainer. He fought in Germany in the Seven Years War (1756-1763), known as the French and Indian War, and distinguished himself in action by capturing a standard from the French and then rescuing the Duke of Brunswick who had charged through enemy lines and become unhorsed.

Upon his discharge from the Army in 1768 Astley settled in London and opened a riding school where he taught in the morning and performed "feats of horsemanship" in the afternoon. The place featured a circular arena which would later be known as the ring. By the late 1760s Astley's considerable success had outshone his fame as a teacher, and after two seasons in London he decided to bring some novelty to his performances and hired acrobats, tightrope walkers and jugglers, and interspersed their acts between his equestrian displays. He first gave open air displays in a roped off ring at Halfpenny Hatch, Lambeth, London on the south bank of the River Thames located near to what is now Waterloo railway station. Known as Astley's Amphitheatre, the first of these displays took place on 8 April 1768. This roped off area measured 42ft in diameter. This was found ideal for the centrifugal force required to balance a standing rider on top of a horse as it circled at speed. The ring was almost surrounded by pit benches and three huge tiers of boxes or galleries, introduced into the ring of seating and, transforming the shape of the auditorium from a circle to an eclipse, was a large well-equipped stage.

Astley's Amphitheatre retained its name until it closed in 1893. He had also built nineteen amphitheatres in Britain including Leicester, Edinburgh and Birmingham. The name Circus began to creep in towards the end of the 18th century. Charles Hughes was to become a major competitor to Astley. He introduced a conjurer, a tumbler, and a 'learned' horse. Astley responded by extending the range of his shows introducing new kinds of performers to include a 'wise dog', a furniture balancing act, acrobats and a Spanish somersaulter. Hughes came back with the addition of trained birds, a violinist, a tightrope walker and an Italian troupe that did conjuring on horseback. Astley could not rest on his laurels and his new show introduced shadow puppets, a ventriloquist, a zebra, monkeys and a 'learned' pig. The show concluded with fountains and fireworks. Hughes was the first person to use the word Circus (a Latin word for circle) by opening the Royal Circus and Equestrian Philharmonic Academy, London in November 1782.

The first substantial use of a tent or marquee for circuses in England came from America where it had been introduced in the mid-1820s. In 1842 Richard Sands landed in Liverpool with a portable circus which could be erected within a few hours and house several thousand people. In 1843 in Norfolk the first touring circus, owned by William Batty, performed in Norwich under canvas. The tent was 65ft in height and 300ft in circumference and could accommodate 1,400 persons.

The Ringling Brothers Circus was founded in America in 1884. The seven brothers and their father were all members of Baraboo Lodge No.34, Wisconsin. Two members of Chelsea Lodge worked with the Ringling Brothers in America. **Harry Lester** performed an aerial act in 1898 and again in 1913. **Jimmie Dunedin** and his troupe of bicyclists completed a marathon tour of 171 towns over a thirty-weeks season in 1906. Five brothers were involved with the circus: Albert 1852-1916, Otto 1858-1911, Alfred 1861-1919, Charles 1863-1926 and John 1886-1936. The brothers developed their business through shrewd management and by buying up their competition. They purchased the Barnum and Bailey circus, largest of the time, in 1907, merging it with theirs in 1919, making it the world's largest by 1930. The family sold the circus in 1967, but the owners kept the original name.

For their name, most circuses simply adopted the name of their proprietor. The Ginnett family was one of the oldest circus families in Britain. Jean Pierre Ginnett was a French prisoner-of-war, captured at the Battle of Waterloo. On his release he decided to remain in Britain and established a family equestrian act. He went on to own a touring circus and circus buildings. He became the founder of two circus families. Not only was Jean Pierre successful in this country but he also toured America. His son took over the circus and numerous members of the Ginnett family carried on the tradition. **Louis Albert Ginnett** was a circus proprietor in 1926. His son **Frank Jack Ginnett** was a circus artiste. Possibly a relation, Louis Ginnett (1875-1946), was an artist. His work included a design for stained glass windows for the chapel of the Royal Masonic Institute for Girls in 1936.

Although the Ginnett family are still working in English circuses they no longer own any themselves but their name continues. Other members of Chelsea Lodge who were involved with the Circus included **Reco** (Herbert Wroe) as a performer in the 1940s. **William Walker-Dredge** was a circus manager in the 1950s and 1960s.

The only 19th century English circus family still performing today is the Fossetts, recognised everywhere by their red hair and blue eyes. The first of these to have his own circus was Robert, (Sir Robert Fossett's Circus) who started, like Jean Pierre Ginnett, with performing birds in the street. He gradually built up a small family circus, which was on the road by 1866 with five of his children performing. One member of the family was the late **Tommy Fossett**, with his attractive wife Vera, who were not only expert jugglers but, as 'Professor Grimble', Tommy presented a clever red-nosed, baggy-clothed clown act. In addition he was a musician, trapeze artiste and unicyclist. A sister of Robert Fossett was Mary who married Paul Otto (real name Kleinschmidt) from Germany. They had two sons whom they named **Robert Otto Fossett** (Bobby) and Thomas Otto Fossett (Tommy), but they later changed their name to Roberts. Bobby Roberts Snr, himself an 'elder statesman' of the circus world and who was honorary president of the Association of Circus Proprietors, died on 5 April 1999, aged 87 years. The two sons are skilled animal trainers. Bobby's son is also Bobby (**Robert Maurice Paul Roberts**). Bobby junior and Tommy did start a circus with their father after Roberts Brothers Circus (Bobby and Tommy Snrs. parted company). This was called Roberts Brothers Circus Bonanza and Bobby continued as Bobby Roberts' Super Circus, which he still runs to this day. Tommy Junior has horse acts with Zippo's Circus.

Acrobats, jugglers and gymnasts were important ingredients of a circus. Those became members of Chelsea Lodge included **Frank Alber, Coram (Tommy Whitaker), James Harold Fossett** and **Benjamin James Whitely** (acrobats), together with **Jimmie Athlone, Henry Mason, Bob Mezzetti, Joseph Elmer Stanley** and **Edward Robert Stanley** (gymnasts). Jugglers included **Valazzi (Wallace Prouse Hodgson)** and **Will Cromwell. Jimmie Dunedin** managed and trained the Dunedin Troupe of bicyclists.

...It's a Barnum and Bailey world, Just as phoney as it can be, But it wouldn't be make believe, If you'd believe in me...

In America the name Phineas T. Barnum entered circus history in 1871. He was aged 60 and already well known on both sides of the Atlantic. He was persuaded to enter into a business deal, which would form "Barnum's Great Travelling Museum, Menagerie, Caravan, Hippodrome and Circus". Barnum invested money and provided his famous name and promotional genius. The circus toured the whole of the United States of America. It not only featured 55 elephants but also made a star of the worlds smallest man 'General Tom Thumb', even appearing by special request before Her Majesty Queen Victoria. In 1881 Barnum teamed up with another circus man James A. Bailey who would gain control of the company in 1888. They were known as Barnum and Bailey's Circus. Their fame spread to a hit song called *It's Only a Paper Moon*, written in 1933 by E.Y. Harburg, Billy Rose and Harold Arlen:

The biggest circus name in Britain in the later 19th century was 'Lord' George Sanger. With his brother John he launched a circus in London in 1853. They had no circus skills themselves but purchased a 'learned' pony and a ring-trained horse, hired three experienced performers and integrated the younger members of their family as assistants. Within three years they had a stable of 60 horses, plus a group of six lions. Although 'Lord' George Sanger did present his circus before an enthusiastic Queen Victoria, his title was bestowed by himself. Later Robert Fossett added a knighthood to the name of his circus. This was also a masquerade.

In more recent times we have enjoyed the delights of the Bertram Mills circus, which performed at Olympia, London from 1920-1966. Chipperfield's Circus claimed, in the 1950s, to be running the biggest circus in Europe, employing 250 people, and accommodating some 9,000 persons for each performance. Shortly after the Second World War Billy Smart, a fairground operator, began a successful circus but by 1972 it had ceased trading. During its more successful time the circus regularly appeared on television. **Peter Locke**, a cameraman at the time, remembers one occasion he was working on a television programme: "My camera position was 60 feet up in the Big Top. The only way to reach the platform was by Bosun's Chair. Come the performance I had to take my seat in the chair, which was situated in the centre of the circus ring, and be slowly winched up. This, much to the amusement of the audience, to whom I was being the unwilling straight man for the warm up artiste. I didn't let the side down, I gave back as good as I got." The Billy Smart name was revived in 2003 by Circus promoter Tony Hopkins for a nationwide tour in a new show produced by Peter Jay.

The enormous cost of travelling a large circus, of renting grounds and feeding the animals has driven many circuses out of business. The difficulty of finding labour to erect and dismantle the big tents has forced others to close.

Animal Rights protesters have been loud in their condemnation against circuses. In some cases they have stuck stickers 'Circus cancelled' over the original posters to keep people away and in others have persuaded the local council to refuse to let grounds to the circus company.

Brian Austen and Gerry Cottle formed their own circus in the 1970s which had a rather humble beginning in a flower-show marquee, employing just six people: Brian and Gerry, together with their wives and Brian's younger brothers Michael and Patrick. A BBC TV documentary dubbed it *The Smallest Greatest Show on Earth*.

Brian had joined the show when it came to his home city of Cambridge and travelled with it to South Africa picking up the various circus skills along the way. Gerry was the son of a London stockbroker who had a passion for the circus from seeing Bertram Mills Christmas Shows at Olympia. During his school holidays he helped out at the circus at Chessington Zoo and, aged fifteen, he literally ran away from home to join a travelling circus. He later married Betty Fossett of the old circus family having joined her father's show and it was there that Brian and Gerry first met. They were both determined to start their own show *Cottle and Austens Circus*.

The show was small, but it was entertaining, and it could have stayed that way, but Brian and Gerry were ambitious. In 1971 they took the show to the Channel Islands. It was the first circus to go there since the Second World War, and it was a big success. Fifteen people worked for the show and the tent seated 800 people.

Their big break came when they were commissioned by the BBC to provide facilities for a new Saturday night variety series broadcast from a different seaside town every week called *Seaside Special*.

In 1995 Cottle and Austen negotiated to bring the Moscow State Circus to Britain. It has now become an annual event. Gerry Cottle has now left the company and sold his shares in the European Entertainment Corporation (Cottle and Austen Circus, Moscow State Circus, Chinese State Circus) to Brian Austen, who is now owner.

The names of Fossett, Gerry Cottle and the Austen Brothers still fly the circus flag and two towns have permanent circus buildings and mount summer shows. The Great Yarmouth Hippodrome, erected in 1903, still puts on successful summer shows, as does the Blackpool Circus, constructed in 1894 between the legs of Blackpool Tower. It has been described as the most beautiful circus building in the world. Former pop music performer Peter Jay ran the Tower Circus for ten years.

Although there were hundreds of purpose built circus buildings erected over the years only one remains in use for the entertainment for which it was originally intended, and that is the Hippodrome, Great Yarmouth, which celebrated its centenary in July 2003. It was built by Norwich-born George Gilbert, a famous equestrian of the time. Among the artistes who appeared include: **William Permane, Florencio Tomas Jover, Harry Marlow, Charles Grantley, Frank Ginnett, Jack Risket** and **Roberto Germains**. Today. the Hippodrome is one of only three buildings in the world where water spectacles can still be seen, the others being in Moscow and Blackpool. The Yarmouth Hippodrome was sold to **Jack Jay** and his son Peter in 1978. Peter has the distinction of being the longest serving director in the history of the building. His first circus production at the Hippodrome was in 1978. Three years later he revived the water spectacle which remains one of the buildings most talked of features.

The first circus on television was transmitted by the BBC on 4 January 1938 and thereafter for 30 minutes daily for five consecutive days from Bertram Mills Circus at Olympia.

At the end of the World War II, there were 45 circuses in the United Kingdom. There were many special Christmas shows - Bertram Mills at Olympia, Jack Hylton Christmas Circus at Earl's Court and Tom Arnold's Circus at Harringay (over 60,000 seats were sold every Saturday in London alone).

The circus has had to reinvent itself. In the last twenty years circus has changed more than in any other time in its entire 240-year history. Many companies, for political or personal reasons have chosen to leave out performing animals, but others have recently reintroduced horses to their shows.

Today the modern circus presents basic acts of skill and broad comedy, upon which its appeal was originally built. It has incorporated rock and classical music, dance, mime and physical theatre as part of its performance. Hopefully it will survive as long as people want to go to the circus. It is a place where, until recently, animals, men and women almost became one in a joint physical action. The circus is a primeval theatre in the round. Where else can you see music, dance, slapstick, pathos, humour, amazing feats, sleight-of-hand, acrobatic skills, and more, all under one roof from your ringside seat? Quite simply the circus is an international art. As P.T. Barnum said circus is "The greatest show on earth."

TRAVELLING SHOWMEN

This brand of show business is not so much a business as a way of life. People do not choose to be showmen, they are born showmen. One hundred years ago when Chelsea Lodge was formed showmen were travelling the length and breadth of the British Isles first by horse, later by steam and finally by great diesel tractors.

Fairs in this country have a long and ancient history. The Romans used the word 'fair', which is derived from the Latin 'feria' which means a 'holiday'. The tradition is even more deeply rooted. Fairs have their origins in the pagan customs of the people who first settled this land. Two ancient fairs, which survived into the 21st century, are Weyhill Fair in Hampshire and Woodbury Hill Fair in Dorset.

Graham Downie, a former chairman of the Fairground Association of Great Britain in 2000 says: "The Romans did much to make better use of fairs by improving trade and communications. In the centuries following their departure, many fairs and pagan festivals were incorporated into the calendar of the growing Christian Church. Charters granted by the sovereign gave the fairs legal status and increasing importance in the economic life of the nation. Merchants from the continent and beyond were drawn to the great charter fairs of the Middle Ages, bringing with them a wealth of goods - Italian silks, spices from the East, Spanish iron, French wine and furs from the Hanse towns. All these could be found at the principal events like Sturbridge Fair near Cambridge and St Bartholomew Fair held in London's Smithfield. In time these fairs drew not only merchants but itinerant entertainers such as jugglers, musicians, actors and tumblers. These were the ancestors of today's showmen."

By the mid-1800s some fairs consisted almost entirely of amusements. Principal among the competing attractions - acrobats, illusionists, puppet plays, beast shows and freaks - were the booths of the theatrical companies. It was at a similar time that Frederick Savage, an agricultural engineer from King's Lynn, Norfolk, devised a method of driving roundabouts by steam. His invention, a steam engine mounted at the centre of the ride, was to transform the showmen's business. These roundabouts would be made larger, more capacious, faster and most significantly, more heavily ornamented.

The golden age of the fairground had begun. Many of us will remember the carved 'galloping horses' suspended on twisted brass rods and leaping round to the strains of a mechanical organ. There was colour, movement and excitement. Rides were not the only innovations. For many country folk, their first sight of electric lighting was at the local fair. Used to candle, oil lamps or at best gas lamps the rides, a blaze of arc and sodium lamps were indeed a truly wondrous sight. The electrical current was produced by a steam-driven generator mounted on a horse drawn cart.

When cinematography was demonstrated in London in 1896 by the pioneering Lumiere brothers, the fairground world with electricity now available was already well prepared to exploit the novelty of 'moving pictures'. Before television and newsreels the showman produced and developed his own film.

After the First World War a new generation of fairground rides appeared including the 'dodgems' which is, arguably, the most popular attraction to this day.

Graham Downie says: "The story of the fairground is one of continuing evolution. Novelty, the showman's stock-in-trade is the vital element in attracting the public's custom. Fairs may have changed over the years, but their purpose remains the same...to provide the public with a form of entertainment that is unpretentious, exciting and uninhibited."

Michael Thomas was born a showman. He runs Thomas's Leisure Centres in Hunstanton, Norfolk and is a member of the Showmen's Guild of Great Britain, which was founded over a hundred years ago. Its principal object since its inception has remained the same - to protect the interests of its members, travelling showmen who gain their livelihoods by attending funfairs. He says: "One of the founding figures of the Guild was a Suffolk vicar, the Rev. Thomas Horne who was passionately interested in the cause of the showman. He became the Guild's first general Secretary and devoted his life to it. In 1917 the Guild took the most important step forward in its development. It became a Registered Trade Union. The change in status was fundamental; it was no longer just a Trade Association, but a society controlling its own members. There were many famous showmen who were instrumental in its foundations...Lord George Sanger, James Bostock, the Thurstons, the Hollands and the Proctors. But the most remarkable was Patrick Collins. From a humble background he became the most important showman in the land when, at the peak of his career, he was running as many as six fairs each week. His success in business was matched by his achievements in Public Service. Born in Chester in 1859 he went on to become a member of Walsall Borough Council, serving as Alderman and Mayor, and in 1922 was elected as the town's Member of Parliament." Michael Thomas is too modest to mention his own personal achievements, which include four terms as Mayor of Hunstanton, Norfolk. See his biography in Chapter Twelve.

Norman Gray was born into a fairground family. He operates a successful amusements business at Ingoldmells near Skegness. He remembers his grandfather Jim Norman who wore a tuxedo and top hat to work the front of his 'Bioscope Emporium'. This was a travelling cinema before many cinemas were built. They had dancing girls on the front stage to attract customers. The films that were shown were silent and included newsreels of the day.

"I remember my granddad telling me about the time they had a newsreel of the mighty Titanic leaving Southampton. However, before the films were developed and ready to show she had hit an iceberg and sunk. Needless to say everybody wanted to see the film of her departure from Southampton."

Norman goes on: "There are many travelling showmen in Freemasonry. Some of us belong to Chelsea Lodge. Apart from myself and son **Richard Gray**, there are Michael Thomas and his son **Christian Thomas**; Michael's brother **Jimmy Thomas** and his son **Simon Thomas**, also their nephew **John Thomas**. Their mother was a member of a large show land family called The Keeble Family, many of whom still travel today. Also in Chelsea Lodge we have **Harry Hall**, the proprietor of 'Jolsons' at Folkestone, Kent. Harry's family still travel the Nottingham and Derby areas."

The names **Leonard Thomas Best, Herbert John Vockings and William Arthur Williams** are also listed in this profession. Boxer **Freddie Mills** gained experience at the fairground when he joined Sam McKeowen's boxing booth in the 1930s. A challenger was invited to take on a travelling boxer at £5 to win and £100 knockout. Freddie went on to become British and Empire Light Heavyweight champion 1942-1950; European champion 1947-1950 and World champion 1948-1950.

For the showman his business is his life; his job is the fairground and from cradle to grave he will know no other occupation. Most showmen can claim a family history in the business which goes back several generations, some even centuries. Few would exchange their life for another, although it is sometimes far from easy.

Michael Thomas says that despite the vagaries of the weather and the opposition from the ill - informed and prejudiced, the life has its compensations: "There is the security of a family unit, husband and wife work side by side as a team and divorce is virtually unknown. There is the support of the closely knit travelling community and the relative freedom of being one's own boss. He is his own engineer, electrician, carpenter, painter, business manager and accountant. In all of this he is supported by his wife, who shares in what is, after all, a family concern. Showmen are very much like old soldiers, they never die, just simply fade away. There is a well known song *There's No Business Like Show Business*. As far as I am concerned there is no business like it."

PANTOMIME

The Oxford Encyclopedic English Dictionary describes pantomime as follows: "In ancient Rome the Latin pantomimes denoted a player who represented in dumb show (hence the word 'mime') the different characters in a short scene based on classical history or mythology. In England it became the name by which the harlequinade was known. By the 20th century the form of this had changed. The entertainment (still known as pantomime), primarily for children and associated with Christmas, is now based on the dramatisation of a fairy-tale or nursery story, and includes songs and topical jokes, buffoonery and slapstick, and standard characters such as a pantomime "dame" played by a man, a principal boy played by a woman, and a pantomime animal (e.g. horse, cat, goose) played by actors dressed in a comic costume, with some regional variations. Although less popular than formerly, pantomimes remain a feature of the English Christmas season."

The "leading man" or principal boy (when played by a woman) usually wears shorts, fishnet tights and thigh length, high-heeled boots. The character is the hero of the story and wins out in the end. The first female principal boy appeared at Covent Garden in 1815.

The "leading lady" (or Dame) is a man dressed as a woman with bright and elaborate costumes. **Nat Jackley** played the Dame in pantomime as did his father **George Jackley** many years before him. Said Nat: 'You've got to stay the man, really let them know that inside that skirt is a man. You're not a female impersonator. I believe in the part I'm playing, but then I leave that alone and do audience participation - bring the kids up on stage and get them to sing.'

The audience is in no doubt that the Dame is a man dressed as a woman. In 1851 the pantomime *Aladdin* introduced for the first time the famous Widow Twanky at the Strand Theatre. This production confirmed the casting of the male pantomime dame and the female principal boy, which remains to this day. This may seem a little confusing to any of our American visitors to this country. Visitors may have felt more at ease from 1956 had they visited the London Palladium to see the annual pantomime when the company broke with tradition and cast Norman Wisdom in the role of principal boy, launching an era that was to last for fifteen years. The role of 'boy' was filled by stars such as Cliff Richard, Frank Ifield, Frankie Vaughan and Tommy Steele. It was not until Cilla Black played the role of 'Aladdin' in 1970 that the balance was restored, and the Palladium returned to using male performers in the role from 1972 onwards. Sadly the London Palladium ceased staging pantomimes from 1988.

Every memorable pantomime contains an animal. Usually two people play the front legs and the back legs of a horse or cow. One person plays other animals such as the goose and the cat. A number of great characters started their careers by literally playing the back legs of the pantomime horse. The name **Billy Dainty** springs to mind. Charlie Chaplin was different, at the Hippodrome, Stockport, many years ago, he played the front end of the horse.

There is always a "baddie" in a pantomime. These range from a wicked step-mother in *Cinderella* to the wicked Queen in *Snow White*.

One of the essentials in any pantomime is audience participation. They are encouraged to cheer the heroes and boo the baddies.

Another popular part in any pantomime is a scene where someone is hiding behind someone else. This prompts the audience to shout, "It's behind you". It was another Chelsea member **Sandy Powell** who pioneered the techniques of getting the audience to shout out 'Look behind you!' as the villain crept up behind him, or warned him as someone tried to steal the umbrella he had parked on the side of the stage and asked the audience to keep an eye on.

No pantomime would be complete without someone getting covered in something messy. The audience become involved again when two of the characters argue with each other, often the goodie and the baddie, and they normally take the side of the goodie shouting, "Oh no he isn't" and "Oh yes he is".

Drury Lane Theatre became famous for its annual pantomime which included top music hall names

The baddie is often greeted with hisses and boos.

In this country professional theatres always stage pantomimes with famous names in the leading roles. Part of the popularity has to be the fact that actors can deviate from the script and often enjoy the production as much as the audience.

Popular pantomimes include: *Sleeping Beauty, Babes in the Woods, Cinderella, Aladdin, Ali Baba and the Forty Thieves, Snow White, Dick Whittington, Puss in Boots, Mother Goose, Jack and the Beanstalk* and *Goldilocks and the Three Bears*.

During the early part of the 1900s pantomime enjoyed its hey day, but rising costs in the 1960s began to take their toll. Variety was killed by television but it is television that has revived pantomime. The big theatrical promoters know young people will go to see a pantomime if they spot a name they recognize. The stars themselves realize it is a way to reach a broad audience and that it is a form of theatre which people want to go and see. Today there are no West End pantomimes but in the provinces there are some 200 annual professional productions. It is frequently the first live theatre seen by young children who retain affection for it. In later life many bring their own children to enjoy the delights of the pantomime and you can bet the parents will enjoy it just as much as their children.

Just before the finale the technical and construction departments prepare to reset the stage complete with treads (stairs) for the finale walk down. There is a certain amount of noise backstage so a front cloth is normally lowered with a song sheet and the audience is invited to join in. This drowns out any noise on stage for the scene change. When the time is right for the finale a hand normally appears from behind the curtain with a "thumbs up". Today pantomime is much more sophisticated and a cue light informs the musical director to strike up the band.

Many famous names have appeared in pantomime over the years. They include: Moira Anderson, Julie Andrews, Arthur Askey, Max Bygraves, Tommy Cooper, Pamela Cundell, Charlie Drake, Jimmie Edwards, Bruce Forsyth, Edmund Hockridge, Frankie Howerd, Roy Hudd, Engelbert Humperdinck, Joan Regan, Cliff Richard and The Shadows, Helen Shapiro, Tommy Steele, Jimmy Tarbuck, Tommy Trinder, David Whitfield and Norman Wisdom.

Amongst those in Chelsea Lodge who have made appearances up and down the country have been **Ken Barnes, Harry Claff, Jess Conrad, Billy Dainty, Billy Danvers, Jim Davidson, Reg Dixon, Bunny Doyle, Kenneth Earle, Robert Earl, Marriott Edgar, Peter Elliott, Arthur English, Dick Emery, Dai Francis, Bruce Green, Roger Kitter, Lupino Lane, Lee Lawrence, Albert Le Fre, Reg Lever, Ernie Mayne, Alfred Marks, Bob Monkhouse, George Mozart, Sandy Powell, Charlie Rich, George Robey, Peter Sellers** and **Wee Georgie Wood**. **Lewis Leslie** was a pantomime producer and **Peter Elliott** and **Kenneth Earle** later moved into pantomime production. **Tom Arnold** presented major pantomimes throughout the country annually from 1935 onwards.

MAGIC

The story of magic is as old as recorded history. The "Westcar" papyrus, now resting in the Berlin State Museum, written some 4,000 years ago, holds a story of a magician performing centuries earlier in the Pharaoh's court. Magicians performed in the street and marketplaces of ancient Greece and Rome. Almost every society has some form of magic. It has been said that magic is the most universal of the performing arts, because it translates so easily from one culture to another.

Before the year 1750, most magic was performed outdoors in marketplaces, in fairs, and on street corners. Magicians had no stages of their own. Their shows were limited to what they could carry with them - or what audiences were likely to have on hand.

Although a magician or illusionist never topped a Variety bill many appeared as the second turn. A name, which springs to mind, is Harry Houdini, an American who specialised in spectacular escapes. Audiences were amazed at seeing a woman sawn in two. This act was made popular by Selbit in 1921. One of his most sensational escapes was his own creation, the *Chinese Water Torture Cell*, a large tank of water into which he was immersed head downward after his feet were secured in stocks. Houdini also created the illusion of *Walking Through a Brick Wall* and *The Vanishing Elephant*. He was a member of St Cecile Lodge No.568, New York.

Magicians have their own organisation, The Magic Circle, which was founded the same year as Chelsea Lodge, 1905.

In 1906, Nevil Maskelyne edited the first issue of *The Magic Circular*, and on its cover were the signs of the zodiac which, together with the words *Indocilis Privata Loqui,* were destined to

Johnny Hart

become the emblem of the Magic Circle. The words, when translated from the Latin, mean 'Not apt to disclose secrets'. *The Magic Circular* is still published monthly and has a distribution worldwide. The Magic Circle has its headquarters at 12 Stephenson Way, London NW1, just around the corner from Euston Station. Called the Centre for the Magic Arts, the building, which opened in 1998, was refurbished at a cost of £2million and is reputedly the finest magic headquarters in the world. Today there are some 1,500 members worldwide and some of the most famous magicians are members of what has been called 'The most exclusive club in the world'. It is certainly the oldest and most prestigious magical society in the world.

David Devant had personal charm, stage presence and inventiveness. He stands out as the greatest magician Great Britain has ever produced. Television has produced its own magic stars - Paul Daniels, Tommy Cooper, David Copperfield and Lance Burton to name but four.

Magicians who are, or were, members of Chelsea Lodge include **David Berglas, Maurice Fogel, David de Mountfalcon, Johnny Hart, Eugene Matthias, Billy McComb, Ramesis, Dennis Rawlins, David Redfearn, Harry Stanley and John Star. Illusionists include Chris Charlton, Hinsle** and **Morimura**.

David Redfearn says that the difference between magicians and illusionists is that an illusionist will normally work on stage with glitzy boxes, whereas a sleight of hand close-up magician could be two feet away with four silver coins using sleight of hand that has taken many years to perfect: "I am not meaning to decry an illusionist who will have spent a very long time honing in their act. The Pendragons are a good example...pure magic, but if you are attracted to magic you may be tempted to buy some jazzy boxes, stand with a good looking girl on stage, and not have put a great deal of thought into the act. It takes time and a great deal of patience to perfect your act and many hours of practice. In fact it is a 'lifetimes' work."

Magic is a performance, a medium for entertaining an audience. Magicians should not only be skilled in sleight of hand, but also dexterous in showmanship and stage craft. Body language, facial expression and eyes all make a difference to the reaction of an audience.

David Redfearn

VENTRILOQUISM

Ventriloquism is currently enjoyed as an amusing facet of the performing arts. Those researching the cultural history of ventriloquism will relate it was part of a mystic divinatory practice, employed by the ancients to call up the spirits of the dead. There were numerous references to the subject in the Bible and the practice became a debating point among the early Christian fathers who condemned it as a tool of the Devil.

The Oxford Dictionary describes ventriloquism as "the skill of uttering sounds so that they seem to come from the speaker's dummy or a source other than the speaker". The word ventriloquist' is derived from the Latin *ventriloquus* meaning 'belly-speaker' and its exponents were regarded as demonic conjurers possessed by unclean spirits that lurked in their entrails, whence they gave their utterances. The practice of ventriloquism often resulted in imprisonment and death.

During the eighteenth and nineteenth centuries ventriloquism emerged as an entertainment but was still largely misunderstood. Many believed it to be a special talent that enabled certain individuals to throw their voices in any direction. Ventriloquist and author Valentine Vox spent twelve years researching the subject and in his book *I Can See Your Lips Moving* he says Ventriloquism is a vocal illusion which can be acquired by application and practice. "The ventriloquist does not speak from his stomach, except that he employs his stomach muscles in the same manner as an actor or singer does, to assist the diaphragm to give vocal and tonal strength to the voice."

However, references to speaking from the belly are recorded in the annals of history. Thomas Cranmer was a former Archbishop of Canterbury, who declared King Henry VIII's marriage to Catherine of Aragon null and void. He crowned Anne Boleyn queen, thus finalising a split with Rome. In 1523 he made references in his diary to a nun, Elizabeth Barton, who became known as the Holy Maid of Kent. She made ventriloquial utterances in her disapproval of this Royal union. "There was a voice speaking from within her belly, as though it were a tongue, her lips not greatly moving." The maid's prophecies opposing Henry's marriage to Anne Boleyn led to her arrest. She was tried and found guilty of high treason and executed at Tyburn on 20 April 1534.

Three hundred years later ventriloquism played an important part in the world of entertainment. An Englishman, William Edward Love, became a professional ventriloquist in

Coram and "Jerry"

1826 and began touring throughout the major towns in the United Kingdom. He went on to tour Europe and America. Others followed at a similar time. Love, together with Frederic Maccabe and W.S. Woodin, were masters of the ventriloquial art during the nineteenth century. It was about this time that automatons began to appear. Music hall or vaudeville was a new challenge to the entertainer. It was competitive and the limited time on stage allowed each performer to give of his best. The marriage of puppets and ventriloquism proved an attractive form of entertainment. In the early days many of the puppets were crudely made and sometimes grotesque, but the 'speaking doll' or 'dummy' soon became a fixture of variety entertainment.

One person who specialised in perfecting the dummy was **Len Insull**, a master craftsmen who began his career in the theatre as a comedy illusionist appearing under the name **Hinsle**. He spent twenty years performing in theatres around the world assisted by his wife, who appeared as Miss Gertie Ross. Shortly after World War I, Insull began a stage property business in Wolverhampton. It was here that **Coram** challenged him with the words "I bet you couldn't make me a dummy". Insull rose to the challenge and produced a figure called "Jerry". Among his famous creations were Archie Andrews made for Peter Brough and Lord Charles for **Ray Alan**.

Other famous ventriloquists during the last 100 years have included Edgar Bergen, G.W. Jester, E.D. Davies, **Fred Neiman,** Fred Russell, **Tom Edwards,** Valentine Vox, Arthur Worsley,

Dennis Spicer, Shari Lewis, **Sandy Powell, Jim Henson, Terry Hall, Keith Harris** and **Roger De Courcey**.

JAZZ and DANCE BANDS

Many have thought the Victorian era was harsh. The Edwardian years were, arguably, as bad if not worse. If you were living in London there were opportunities to enjoy yourself with concerts and the theatre. For those living in the country, life was more difficult. The highlight was possibly a show or concert at the village hall. Many people entertained themselves in the confines of their own home, sitting around their piano and having a sing-song.

The nearest town possibly had a picture palace (cinema), which screened silent movies. On the other side of the pond - in the USA - life was totally different. A new style of music was rapidly spreading across the whole country. Based on Negro folk traditions of the Deep South, jazz was beginning to take a hold. In time it would spread across the whole world.

We in Britain first caught sight of an American white group called The Original Dixieland Jazz Band who appeared at the London Hippodrome in April 1919. Chelsea Lodge member **George Robey** was the star of the show and he was not best pleased with the arrival of this jazz band, possibly seeing a threat to his position. He presented producer Albert de Courville with an ultimatum: either he or the ODJB would have to go. In the event the ODJB went, but their setback was temporary. After a tour of various variety theatres they secured a booking at the Hammersmith Palais, commencing on 28 November 1919 and running for a total of nine months. In a nutshell they turned the British popular music scene on its head. This syncopated extrovert brand of music attracted young people in their thousands to listen and dance to the music. The musicians were elevated to star status.

By 1920 we were into the Roaring Twenties. It was at a similar time that we experienced national wireless stations playing popular gramophone records. By 1925 record companies were producing electrical recordings with much improved sound. The silent cinema introduced sound with their films - "talkies". We were more mobile as a nation and public transport became more available which meant people could move around more freely to visit the cinema.

A decade later dance bands were playing at all major West End clubs and restaurants. Up market hotels also got in on the act and engaged resident orchestras. Dance band music became really popular throughout the whole of the British Isles from John O'Groats to Land's End. If you couldn't attend a particular club or restaurant the old wind-up gramophone at home would keep you entertained with dance music. Gramophones were a luxury those days. More people had radios. Dance Music was regularly heard on BBC Radio. The first nationally famous band was the Savoy Havana Band who made their initial broadcast for the BBC in April 1923 and became the first dance band to have regular weekly broadcasts relayed from the Savoy Hotel, next door to the BBC Studios in Savoy Hill. Historically the band was important because of its pioneering role in dance band broadcasting. The Roaring Twenties had moved smoothly into the Thriving Thirties.

A large number of the big band leaders who appeared on BBC radio programmes throughout the 1940s were sons of Jewish immigrants who lived in London's East End. Whilst their parents had wanted them to play the piano or violin, the sons realised there was more money to be made by fronting an orchestra or band.

Chelsea Lodge has had amongst its members a number of Dance Band leaders including: **Stanley Black, 'Miff' Ferrie, Roy Fox, Harold Geller, Phil Green, Benny Loban, Joe Loss, Jack Nathan, Woolf Phillips, Ivor Raymonde, Edmundo Ros, Cyril Stapleton, Eric Tann** and **Nat Temple**. Other musicians appeared in orchestras and bands including **Tito Burns, Joe Daniels, Grisha Farfel, Max Goldberg, Alfie Noakes, Tony Thorpe, Tiny Winters** and **Bob Wise**.

*A rare picture from the scrapbook of **Tony Harrison** showing members of the Savoy Havana Band in October 1925. Left to right: Hal Evans, **Tony Thorpe**, Dave Thomas, Laurie Huntingdon, Reg Batten, Harry Howard , **Max Goldberg**, Les Bates and Van Phillips. The Savoy Havana band began making recordings in 1922 for Columbia and later Vocalion, HMV and Broadcast labels. They made over 300 recordings in seven years. The band made its initial broadcast, from a BBC studio, in April 1923, and five months later became the first dance band to have regular weekly broadcasts direct from the Savoy Hotel.*

The dance bands had their singers. **Les Allen** sang with Henry Hall and the BBC Dance Orchestra, **Alan Breeze** was vocalist with the Billy Cotton Band, **Franklyn Boyd** with Teddy Foster and Eric Winstone, **Gerry Brereton** with various bands, **George Elrick** with Ambrose, Henry Hall and BBC Dance Orchestra and **Frank Holder** with Johnnys' Kerrison and Dankworth.

As no Minutes Books of Chelsea Lodge are available for the first 50 years it is not known whether or not the Lodge actively wanted musicians to become members. The most popular profession between 1905 and 1930 was Vaudeville Artistes. However, between 1930 and 1935 of the 61 Initiates, 37 (60%) came from the music industry.

There were many great dance bands in London in the 1930s and they all have their champions as to who was the best. Arguably the number one show band in the country belonged to Jack Hylton. Many would say that none could compete with the Bert Ambrose Orchestra which comprised some top-flight musicians and vocalists. Others would say that Lew Stone ran a tight ship. Those and many more were competing for top honours. They included Sidney Lipton at the Grosvenor House Hotel, Jack Jackson at the Dorchester, and Jack Payne and Henry Hall at the BBC. They and Harry Roy, Billy Ternant, Maurice Winnick, **Roy Fox** and Jack Harris attracted large audiences to their performances.

It would be true to say that a good number of musicians who worked for the top bands of the day were members of Chelsea Lodge. They included **Robert George Somers** (oboe) brother to musical director Debroy Somers, of St Asaph Lodge No.1319. He played with the band from

1927-1945. **Lewis Davis** (trombone) was a member of the Jack Harris and the Ambrose Orchestras, Harry Hudson's Melody Men, Jack Hylton Orchestra, Billy Mason Band, Lew Stone Band and the Ray Noble Orchestra. **Harry Karr** (clarinet, alto saxophone and flute) played with George Glover and His Band, Jack Harris Orchestra, Jack Hylton Orchestra, Brian Lawrence Orchestra, Maurice Winnick Orchestra and the New Mayfair Dance Orchestra. **Wally Morris** (string bass) worked with the **Phil Green** Orchestra, Jack Hylton Orchestra, Ronnie Munro and His Dance Orchestra and Van Phillips and His All Star Orchestra. **Eric Breeze** (trombone) played

with the Ambrose Orchestra, Geraldo and His Orchestra, Jack Harris Orchestra, Jack Hylton Orchestra, Lew Stone Band and the Royal Air Force Dance Orchestra; and **Dick Ball** (sousaphone or tuba, string bass) was a member of the Ambrose Orchestra, The Durium Dance Band, The Ambassador Club Band, Jack Harris Orchestra, Howard Jacobs Orchestra and the Jay Wilbur Band. **Edward Owen 'Poggy' Pogson** (clarinet, alto saxophone, baritone saxophone, flute, oboe) played with Bert and John Firman Orchestras, George Glover Band, Jack Hylton Orchestra, Jack Jackson Orchestra, New Mayfair Dance Orchestra, Jack Payne and BBC Dance Orchestra, Hugo Rignold Orchestra, Victor Silvester and His Ballroom Orchestra, Billy Ternant Orchestra and Jay Wilbur Orchestra. **Jim Easton** was a clarinet and alto saxophone player with the Lew Stone Band. **Laurie Bookin** also worked with Lew Stone and played alto and tenor saxophone.

Dick Ball

When Jack Jackson formed his first dance band in 1933 to play at the Dorchester Hotel, London, three members of Chelsea were selected to join him - **Stan Andrews**, alto saxophone and violin, **Tony Thorpe**, trombone, and **Poggy Pogson**, clarinet and alto saxophone. Within two months **Fred Latham** joined as a vocalist. They made recordings for HMV. **Aubrey Frank** was a brilliant tenor saxophone and clarinet player. He worked with a number of bands including Josephine Bradley, The Skyrockets, Geraldo, Ambrose, Ted Heath, **Frank Weir** and **Jack Nathan**. From the 1950s onward he specialised in studio and session work with BBC Review Orchestra, BBC Concert Orchestra, BBC Big Band and London Symphony Orchestra. **Harry Conn** played alto and tenor saxophone and was a member of the Oscar Rabin Band, Eric Winstone Band, Ambrose, Carroll Gibbons and the Savoy Hotel Orpheans and the Victor Silvester Orchestra. **Judd Solo** was resident at the Hilton Hotel, London for seventeen years.

There was one period in the early 1930s when the New Mayfair Dance Orchestra, directed by Ray Noble, had more than half its musicians as members of Chelsea Lodge.

Trombone player **Lew Davis** remembers, as a musician, there was not much time for relaxation: "There was so much to do, we never stopped. One night sticks in my memory. We'd been to the Decca recording studios in the morning and there was an afternoon rehearsal. The Lew Stone Band were playing one of the London Variety Theatres - I think it was Streatham - so there was all that dashing about as well as our usual dancing and cabaret duties at the Monseigneur. When we finally packed up, it would have been at least 2.00 a.m. and we were all

The **Edmundo Ros** Orchestra appeared in the Royal Variety Performance of 1962 and was featured on BBC's Come Dancing programme. Edmundo also had his own night club in London.

The Ray Noble Orchestra in Holland in 1933 prior to a tour of America. Various members of Chelsea Lodge were musicians in the band. Left to right; **Tiny Winters**, Nat Gonella, Al Bowlly, Mrs Gladys Noble, Ray Noble, Harry Berly, **Lew Davis, Bob Wise**, Mrs Gardner, Freddy Gardner and **Alfie Noakes.**

glad to be done at last. However, without any warning, we were whipped across the road to the Criterion with no idea what was going on and they'd laid on this supper for us. Then we were all crammed into a coach and off we went to Elstree Studios in the middle of the night to record the score for a film Lew was doing. I never knew why they had to have it by dawn or how we saw the notes straight. I certainly don't remember how we got through the next day."

Bass player **Tiny Winters** also worked with the Lew Stone Band and remembers one of the studios, Upper Thames Street, London, where they recorded for Decca: "Studio is a bit of a laugh really because how they thought that place up, I'll never know! It was on the edge of the City near the river and the entrance was through a graveyard. You went into this vast warehouse, up a wooden stairway with only a rope to hold on to. It was a barn of a place with a green haircord carpet stretching into the distance and with just one microphone hanging up on a boom and another on a stand, fold-up music stands, bleak chairs and a little box-place where Arthur Lilley, the engineer, used to operate from. It was remarkable how good the sound was in the 1930s. There was an excitement. The band did its own internal balance and the engineer's job was to get that down on wax. There's something lost now, for all the technical advances."

A change was taking place in Britain in the late 1930s when, in 1939, we were once again at war with Germany and many musicians were called up to serve King and Country. Some worked with ENSA while others appeared with 'Stars in Battledress'. Every branch of the armed forces had its own musical entertainers who were known collectively as the Service Bands.

The Squadronaires (officially called the RAF No.1 Dance Orchestra) was formed in 1940 with

musicians drawn mainly from the orchestras of Lew Stone and Ambrose. Led by Sgt Jimmy Miller, the musicians wore Air Force blue and were given the rank of Aircraftman Second Class, the lowest rank in the RAF. Their pay was 3s 6d (17½p) per day and they were accommodated at the RAF School of Music at Uxbridge, Middlesex. They were required to carry out normal station duties during the day and entertain with concerts and dances in the evening. The musicians included trombone players George Chisholm and **Eric Breeze**, trumpeters Tommy McQuater, **Clinton 'Froggy' French** and Kenny Baker, saxophone players

Lady listening to gramophone record   Andy McDevitt, Cliff Townshend (father of

Peter Townshend of the rock band The Who) and **Jimmy Durrant**, who also played clarinet, drummer Jack Cummings, guitarist Sid Colin and pianist Ronnie Aldrich, who later led the Orchestra.

The Squadronaires played a mixture of contemporary dance music and jazz numbers and were, arguably, the most successful of the Service Bands. Their first recording session took place at the Decca studios on 10 January 1941. One of their first records really to catch the public's ear was an arrangement, by George Chisholm, called *That's a Plenty*, also recorded in 1941, and which used the Chisholm/**Eric Breeze** unison. The Squadronaires made numerous broadcasts on BBC Home Service and BBC General Forces Programme. Chelsea member **Reginald Leopold** appeared in a number of BBC broadcasts with the Squadronaires with his Singing Strings from the Paris Cinema, Lower Regent Street, London in 1944 and 1945. The Squadronaires featured in the 1943 film *The Life and Death of Colonel Blimp*, which starred Roger Livesey. The band played on into the post-war era under pianist and arranger Ronnie Aldrich, disbanding as a civilian group of musicians in 1964. The band was revived in 1987 by Harry Bence, another wartime RAF musician, under the name 'The New Squadronaires', who perform to this day. They have made several recordings including CDs.

The Skyrockets were the main rivals to the Squadronaires. They were formed in 1940 from musicians who were training to become balloon rigger fabric workers. Its first director was George Beaumont, followed by Paul Fenhoulet. When Paul left in November 1947 to conduct the BBC Variety Orchestra his place was taken by **Woolf Phillips**. The band later became resident at the London Palladium and finally disbanded in the mid-Fifties. Violinist **Maurice Sterndale** joined the Skyrockets when they moved to the Palladium. He also conducted the orchestra on occasions.

The Blue Rockets (Royal Army Ordnance Corps) was formed in early 1941 under the leadership of Eric Robinson. The band specialised in swing arrangements of light classics, and backing entertainers at ordnance factories and warehouses all over the United Kingdom. Later, the band made BBC radio broadcasts on both Home and General Forces programmes.

Around September 1941 Eric Robinson was transferred to the Army Radio Unit and the leadership of the Blue Rockets was taken over by trombonist **Eric Tann**. He had worked pre-war for **Roy Fox**, Henry Hall and Lew Stone, and was well respected by all the musicians under his command. Under Tann, the band began to play more varied music and, in 1942, a recording contract was signed with HMV. Around this time it was rumoured in the press that the Blue Rockets were to be featured in a film for the Ministry of Information, entitled *Swinging into the Attack*. For the film, arranger **'Miff' Ferrie** was to re-orchestrate several Spike Hughes compositions. Eric Tann was invalided out of the Army on 2 April 1943 and Benny Daniels took over as director of the band.

Other Service Bands included The Skyliners, The Skyrockets, The Royal Navy's Blue Mariners, and the Regimental Band of the Allied Expeditionary Forces, directed by Regimental Sergeant Major George Melachrino, and which was formed in July 1944. Two of their musicians, who were members of Chelsea Lodge, were **Alec Firman** and Sgt **Laurie** 'Nobbie' **Clarke**.

The Service Bands contributed significantly to the morale of servicemen and women during the Second World War. Once the war was over, many musicians enjoyed successful careers in Civvy Street.

Dance Bands regularly toured the seaside resorts, as well as inland venues, throughout the 1950s and 1960s. Even to this day one or two of the more famous names carry on like Ray McVay, Syd Lawrence, James Last, Bert Kaempfert, BBC Big Band and Ray Conniff although, in some cases, their leaders may have either taken a back seat or died.

SILENT FILMS, TALKIES and the CINEMA

Images recorded on a continuous strip of film on a cellulose acetate base and projected onto a screen sufficiently fast to represent continuous motion, became available to the general public from about 1895. The earliest pictures, shown either as sideshows at fairgrounds or as items in music hall programmes, were all short and silent; they included slapstick comedy, trick pictures, short romances and five-minute dramas.

In 1889 William Friese-Green of Bristol patented the cinematographic technique. The first public screening in Britain was given by Birt Acres at the London headquarters of the Royal Photographic Society, 14 Hanover Square on 14 January 1896. The programme comprised of a series of films by Acres himself and were: *The Opening of the Kiel Canal, The Derby, Boxers, Three Skirt Dancers* and *Rough Seas at Dover*. It was Birt Acres who gave the first commercial show outside London to a paying audience at Cardiff Town Hall on 5 May 1896.

Will Barker was a pioneer of the British film industry. He began by making films as an amateur in 1896, the year that the Lumiere Brothers exhibited their moving pictures in London. He had bought one of their cameras for £40. Barker turned professional in 1901.

Leon Gaumont had produced 'talkies' as early as 1900 when he demonstrated synchronised phonograph cylinders and films at the Paris Exposition. His company continued to refine its sound equipment and, on 21 November 1904, the Gaumont Chronophone was introduced as a regular feature of the variety programme at the London Hippodrome. Chronophone films consisted of scenes with an obvious sound content and included music hall singers who were pre-recorded on disc and then mimed to a playback at the company's open-air studios. Amplification was provided by a compressed air system which gave sufficient volume to fill a large hall. One famous name of the time was **Ernie Mayne** who appeared in two Gaumont Chronophone films *Excelsior (1906)* and *Cupid (1907)*. The films were shown at provincial halls and may have been produced in considerable numbers, but it is unlikely that any of them survive.

The Story of Kelly was the first feature film shown in the United Kingdom which had its premiere at the Assembly Rooms, Bath, in January 1908. The film, made on location in Australia and a biopic of Ned Kelly, the infamous bushranger, was produced by Charles Tait and released by the Colonial Pictures Combine. The film lasted for just over an hour and was made on a budget of £440. No complete print of the film survives to this day although there have been several remakes over the years including a more recent version starring Rolling Stones, Sir Mick Jagger.

The first feature film to be produced in Britain was *Oliver Twist* (four reels), directed by Thomas Bentley starring Ivy Millais, Alma Taylor and John MacMahon and released in August, 1912. The same year Will Barker made the first screen version of *Hamlet* which cost him £180. It was Barker who also made what at the time was described as 'the first really important film' *Henry VIII*. Barker established the first Ealing Film Studios and was proud to show the true British spirit in his productions as was evident in his epic on Queen Victoria *Sixty Years On*.

On a much smaller scale **Will Evans** and F.L. Lyndhurst founded the Sunny South and Sealight Film Company in 1913 utilising part of an old fort at Shoreham, Sussex. It was the only studio in the UK to rely on daylight during and immediately after the First World War. Four years later it was destroyed by fire. The studio had produced two popular films of the day in 1914 *Building a Chicken House* and *The Jockey*.

From 1900 to 1914 the film industry was international, led by France, Italy, Britain and America. The duration of films began to get longer from a few minutes to two hours. During the First World War the demand for films grew at a time when European producers were least able to meet it and America became the foremost film-making country.

It was a French pioneer in the film industry, Charles Pathé, who initiated the system of leasing (rather than selling) copies of films. In the early years of the 20th century he and his brothers built up a company, which dominated the manufacture of stock and equipment and the production, distribution and exhibition of films until disrupted by the outbreak of World War I.

By 1917 it was estimated that three and a half million people were going to the cinema daily. The cinema was the ultimate means of escape from anxiety and depression, and continued to be for almost half a century. This was the silent cinema although in actual fact the place was far from silent as it employed professional musicians in the orchestra of the cinemas. For many working class people cinema music was the only live music they heard. The cinema threw Music Hall into the doldrums. In the heyday of the silent film there were some 3,000 cinemas in Great Britain in action for nearly 60 hours a week.

Charlie Chaplin is a name many of us associate with early black and white silent films. He went on to become the most famous actor in early Hollywood cinema, and later as a notable director. Much of his success was due to his older brother **Sydney Chaplin**. Charlie originally signed with Mack Sennett's Keystone Pictures in California in 1913 with Sydney signing a year later. Sydney acted as Charlie's business manager and, as such, landed him such very lucrative contracts. Charlie went on to help found United Artists Films along with Mary Pickford, D.W. Griffith and Douglas Fairbanks.

The Great Dictator is regarded as Charlie's finest film and his first sound picture. As an act of defiance against Adolf Hitler and fascism, it was filmed and first released in America. It was banned in Nazi-occupied Europe but it became the biggest money spinner of 1940 breaking box office records in Great Britain as well as the United States of America.

The first sound films produced in Britain were a series of song subjects made by Walter Gibbons in 1900 under the name of Phono-Bio-Tableaux Films. They included Vesta Tilley singing *The Midnight Sun, Algy the Piccadilly Johnny* and Louisa Lou and G.H. Chirgwin giving a soulful reading of *The Blind Boy*. The earliest British talking picture was Hepworth's Vivaphone version of *Cinderella* with Gertie Potter.

In 1927 with the advent of the Talkies, it was possible for the first time to synchronise and record music onto film. The recording industry was still in its infancy. Meyer de Wolfe, a Dutchman born in 1887, came to England at the turn of the century to join the orchestra of the Duke of Devonshire as principal oboe player. He played in and conducted scores of countless silent films, including those of Charlie Chaplin, Mary Pickford and D. W. Griffith. He soon became musical director and conductor of the Provincial Cinematograph Theatres (later to become the Rank Organisation). Subsequently, he had under his control some 400 orchestras for which he was responsible for selecting music. De Wolfe set up the first library of recorded music. He first recorded music for the cinema onto 35mm Nitrate film. Gramophone recordings were cut onto wax from which a mother and master were produced from shellac and these were played at 78rpm.

Sound, as a rule, recorded separately on quarter inch magnetic tape, but carried for reproduction on a narrow track alongside the picture film, was delivered from loudspeakers placed behind the screen and sometimes also about the auditorium. The first talkie *The Jazz Singer* featured Al Jolson in 1927 and from that soundtrack the first record ever released from a film was *Mother O'Mine*. The film was quickly followed by *Gold Diggers of Broadway* and *Broadway Melody*. The first hit song from a film was *Sonny Boy*, from the film *The Singing Fool* which sold 2 million records world wide. It was only in the 1950s that magnetic tape came into use, having been developed in Germany during the Second World War. Vinyl pressings were to follow and, later still, CDs.

Although the Ealing Film Studios in Britain played an important part in establishing the British film industry it went through a difficult time in World War I (1914-1918) and they were sold to General Film Renters in 1920. Eventually new Ealing Studios were built in 1931 incorporating the talkies. One of their first signings was Gracie Fields, the Lancashire comedienne, who had been on the music hall stage since the age of thirteen and had been a popular star in the provincial theatre in the Twenties and Thirties. Her successor as Ealing's biggest box-office draw was George Formby who played the part of a gormless, well-meaning, disastrously inept character.

Pinewood Studios came into being in 1935 when Heatherden Hall, a magnificent 156-acre estate near Iver, Buckinghamshire, was purchased by General Film Distributors run by J. Arthur Rank and Charles Boot, head of a building company. They formed a new company Pinewood Studios Limited and commenced building a new studio in 1935 which was officially opened on 30 September 1936. The old manor house was retained for administrative purposes. The first film to be made there was *Talk of the Devil* in 1937. It was requisitioned by the Government during the Second World War. By then 47 films had been completed. The studio re-opened in April

1946. The *Carry On* comedy series, initiated in 1958, was one of Pinewood's successes. They became a British film institution and their audiences loved them. The last film in the series was *Carry On Columbus* made in 1992. The 1960s gave birth to the hugely successful James Bond 007 series, noted for their technical expertise and amazing sets.

Lord Rank (as he became), founder of the studios and of the organisation that bore his name, died in 1972, the year of his retirement. On 22 February 2000 it was announced that Michael Grade, the former boss of Channel 4 television and now chairman of the BBC, had purchased Pinewood Studios for £62 million. He is the nephew of Lord Lew Grade, a famous film producer in his own right and one of the founders of the ITV network. The company Pinewood Shepperton was floated on the stock market in May 2004 and in April 2005 the company purchased Teddington Studios, best known as the home of the former Thames Television, for £2.7 million. Recent TV shows produced here include *The Office* and *Harry Hill*.

Music has always played an important part of films and the cinema. In the early days it was a simple accompaniment during silent films. The resident cinema orchestra appeared as early as 1901, when Britain's first picture house, Mohawk's Hall, in Islington, appointed the 16-piece Fonobian Orchestra under their director Mr. W. Neale. Cinema organs replaced the piano and the Wurlitzer was a very popular instrument which could create many sound effects as well as most orchestral instruments. It was also cheaper than paying a full orchestra.

Quentin Maclean was a popular organist in the 1920s and 1930s. He played the mammoth 2500-pipe Christie organ which was installed at the Regal (now Odeon), Marble Arch.

In 1932 four members of Chelsea Lodge appeared in the Polygon film *The Mayor's Nest* - they were actor **Cyril Smith**, and musicians **Lew Davis, Tiny Winters** and **Max Bacon**.

Sandy Powell appeared in two films produced by Tom Arnold, made by British Lion: *It's a Grand Old World (1935)* and *I've Got a Horse (1938)*.

In the late 1930s British Lion and Pathéscope presented dance bands and variety acts on film. They were issued as "one-reelers" with a running time of eight to nine minutes. They came from three British Lion cinema musical shorts series: *Musical Film Review, Equity Musical Revue* and *British Lion Varieties*. A few were released on 9.5mm with original titles. Pathéscope released twenty-eight on 9.5mm sound under the title *Variety Number...* Musical items were generally mixed from the original British Lion releases. Amongst the artistes who appeared were **Joe Loss, Leon Cortez, Stanley Black, Stanelli** and **Roy Fox**. In addition **Syd Seymour** and His Mad Hatters appeared in an 87-minutes film, directed by Norman Lee called *Happy Days Are Here Again (1936)*. From this film a short was made which lasted nine minutes, *The Mad Hatter.*

The films provide a certain pre-war style that is of historic interest. There were vast quantities of records (78rpm) issued in those days, but little is recorded on film and, where it is, the production quality leaves a lot to be desired mainly because of the low budget assigned to such projects.

In April 2003, Daily Mail and General Trust (DMGT) signed a deal with ITN to manage and market its British Pathé News archive. The digital archive includes 3,500 hours of cinema newsreels, some more than 100 years old through to the crash of the Hindenberg air-ship and colour film of England's World Cup victory in 1966. DMGT bought the British Pathé archive, which dates from 1896 to 1970, for £10 million in 1995 and will retain ownership of the archive.

The first gold disc awarded to an individual was to bandleader Major Glenn Miller on 10 February 1942 for *Chattanooga Choo Choo*, the hit song he and his orchestra had performed in the 1941 film *Sun Valley Serenade*. *White Christmas*, composed by Irving Berling and sung by Bing Crosby in the 1942 film *Holiday Inn* has been the biggest selling record from a movie. A total of 35 million copies have been sold to date. The film soundtrack of *South Pacific* sold well in the 1950s but has been overtaken by the sales of *Star Wars* in 1977 which sold nearly four million copies. John Williams wrote the music for the film and he must be the most successful film composer of all time. Also to his credit are: *Jaws (1975), The Empire Strikes Back (1980), Raiders of the Lost Ark (1981), E.T. (1982), Return of the Jedi (1983)* and *Indiana Jones and the Last Crusade (1989).*

The cinema became the people's entertainment at an affordable price. Sound films (talkies) evolved in the 1920s and were first publicly presented in 1928. In 1932 a three-colour process known as Technicolor was developed, adding gaiety and brilliance to the production. Many of us spent long and happy hours in the cosy near-darkness of a cinema, with a constantly flickering broadening beam of light passing overhead through smoke wafting from many a cigarette to project films onto the silver screen.

By the year 1938 there were twenty-two different studios making films with sixty-five stages between them. By 1942 the number had fallen by more than half, to nine studios with thirty stages. The cinema audiences appeared to increase, however, in spite of some cinemas being bombed during the blitz. It is estimated that 19 million people went to the cinema each week by the time war broke out in September 1939 which rose to over 30 million by the end of the Second World War.

By 1950 the increasing popularity of television had seriously threatened the prosperity of the cinema industry. New techniques, such as the wide screen, were hurried forward, and costly, elaborate productions, including a number of science fiction and horror films, had some success in attracting audiences back to the cinema.

Ealing Studios were sold to the BBC in 1956. During a quarter of a century many films were made there projecting Britain and the British character. Ealing will always be remembered for its comedy films like *Passport to Pimlico, Whisky Galore* and *Kind Hearts and Coronets*, and *The Titfield Thunderbolt* which were produced in the late 1940s and early 1950s.

Hammer Films played an important part in the history of the British film industry. Located in a large country house on the banks of the River Thames at Bray, Berkshire, the company produced 152 theatrical feature films which included horror, science fiction fantasies, psychological thrillers, prehistoric extravaganzas and gritty war dramas.

The first time we heard of Hammer Films was in November 1934 when William Hinds (stage name Will Hammer) registered Hammer Productions Ltd and was based in a three-room office suite at Imperial House, Regent Street, London. Hinds was chairman, and George Gillings and Henry Fraser Passmore were joint managing directors. A member of Chelsea Lodge was a company director. He was **George Mozart** (real name David Gillings, brother of George Gillings). He shared a directorship with James Elder Wills.

Hammer's first film, in 1935, starring George Mozart was a sixty-minute comedy called *The Public Life of Henry the Ninth.* The follow-up films also starred George Mozart *The Mystery of the Mary Celeste* (1935), *The Song of Freedom* (1935), *Sporting Love* (1936) and the *Bank Messenger Mystery* (1936).

Around this time there was a massive slump in the British film industry which forced Hammer into bankruptcy and the company went into liquidation in 1937. Hammer was re-launched as an offshoot of the film company Exclusive who had Lt.Col. James Carreras as its boss. They began making films in 1947. In the early days they released an average of four films a year. However, in the year 1957 they increased the production to eleven films and features, all made at Bray. Historians say that Hammer's 'classic' period ran from *The Quatermass Xperiment* in 1954 to the *Phantom of the Opera* in 1961.

Vincent "Charles" Permane was Worshipful Master of Chelsea Lodge in 1949. He was production manager for Hammer Films and is credited with *The Crawling Eye (1957), The Trollenburg Terror* (1958)*, Circus of Horrors* (1959) and *The Witches* (1966).

By the mid-1960s a number of key personnel left the company and Hammer finally moved out of Bray on 19 November 1966. The final production to be made at Bray was *The Mummy's Shroud* filmed in 1966. The small family set-up, based in idyllic surroundings, and the independence it had afforded, had given Hammer films a style and magic that would never be repeated. To this day pop videos, advertisements

and films are still produced at Bray, but most are destined for the television market.

The USA was the first country to produce more films in colour than black and white, with 157 out of a total of 237 full-length features being shot in colour in 1954. In Britain colour became predominant in 1965, when 46 colour films were produced as against 34 monochrome. The first year in which British production was 100% colour came in 1969.

The standard cine-film is 35mm wide, but 70mm has been used. The 16mm, 9.5mm and 8mm widths are manufactured for amateurs and education films. For the amateur film maker cine film has now virtually been replaced by video.

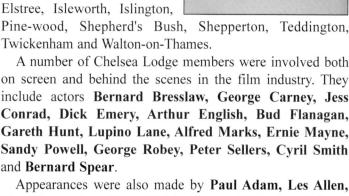

The major British film studios were located at Beaconsfield, Bray, Denham, Ealing, Elstree, Isleworth, Islington, Pine-wood, Shepherd's Bush, Shepperton, Teddington, Twickenham and Walton-on-Thames.

A number of Chelsea Lodge members were involved both on screen and behind the scenes in the film industry. They include actors **Bernard Bresslaw, George Carney, Jess Conrad, Dick Emery, Arthur English, Bud Flanagan, Gareth Hunt, Lupino Lane, Alfred Marks, Ernie Mayne, Sandy Powell, George Robey, Peter Sellers, Cyril Smith** and **Bernard Spear**.

Appearances were also made by **Paul Adam, Les Allen, Max Bacon, Issy Bonn, Teddy Brown, Billy Caryll, Leon Cortez, Jim Davidson, Freddie Davies, Reg Dixon, Ray Donn, Bunny Doyle, Marriott Edgar, Seth Egbert, Kenneth Earle, George Ganjou, Gerry George, Archie Glen, Hal Gordon, Harry Green, George Harris, Arthur Hill, Andy Ho, Davy Kaye, Jay Laurier, Edwin Lawrence, Vincent Lawson, Albert Le Fre, Reg Lever, Len Lowe, Fred McNaughton, Freddie Mills, Bob Monkhouse, George Mozart, Jimmy Nervo, Talbot O'Farrell, Paul Rich, Edmundo**

Ros, **Leslie Sarony, Harry Seltzer, Keith Skues, Charlie Smithers, Stanelli, Nat Temple, Frank Weir, Wee Georgie Wood** and **Hal Wright**.

Producers include **Stanley Goodwin, Brandon John Lee, Morton Maxwell Lewis, Laurie Mansfield, David Neale, Peter Herbert Price, Greg Smith** and **Sidney Streeter**. **Edward Frederick Harper** was a film production manager and director for Waterbury Films, based at Shepperton Studios. **George Mozart** was one of the earliest working directors for Hammer films, where **Charles Permane** was production manager. **Michael McCarthy** was a film production buyer. **Arthur Cowan** and **Frederick Fletcher** were both film renters. **Roger Wilson-Singer** was a film studio company director, **Richard William Gill** a film casting director and **Roy Graham** and **Vincent Adolph Permayne** were film managers. **Marriott Edgar** was both an actor and writer for numerous films. **Leonard Waldorf** was a film cameraman and in the very early days of black and white silent film **William Cecil Jeapes** was a cinematographer. **Robert Morgan** was a film booking manager and **Kenneth Troy** ran a film agency. **Stanley Black** began his career by accompanying silent films and later became musical director of Associated British Picture Corporation at Elstree Studios. **Phil Green** wrote music for films, as have **Ronnie Bridges, Don Percival** and **Paul Williams**

Other members of Chelsea Lodge were directors, executives, managers and proprietors of cinemas. They included **Edward Peter Beer, Roger William Gordon Bennett, Frederick Braun Box, Benjamin Brown, Herbert Lloyd Forsyth, Jack Jay, John Graham Kerr, Frank Layton, Ivan Morgan, George Mullins, Ian Norman Riches, Edwin Rudd** and **Robert Christopher Warby**.

Ivan Morgan was with Granada theatres for nearly thirty years beginning in August 1946. Training included several days in the operating box learning how to run the projectors and rewind a film as well as time spent in a poster shop to find out how publicity was designed. Granada required managers to write a weekly letter to head office describing their week. Ivan says that the local manager was better known than the town mayor, because as he was a live wire and arranged publicity stunts regularly, he was hitting the local press and his picture was in the paper more or less every week. He installed CinemaScope at the Granada, Sutton. *The Robe* was the first film there with stereophonic sound. Ambient speakers were placed all around the theatre. It was far different from anything the company had done before.

Says Ivan: "I was often asked to perform at official functions presenting prizes, opening up street parties and giving talks. I began at Granada, Rugby for £5.10.0d (£5.50) a week. My final job in the theatre was at Granada, Bedford in 1966." Ivan was so successful he was transferred to Toddington motorway service area. "But I am a theatre manager", he told his boss Lord Bernstein who replied: "You are a Granada manager. You can handle people and this is something we need - someone to handle people en masse. You have that experience and you will bring that great asset to motorways. You have had the best possible training in management."

RADIO aka The WIRELESS

Without doubt one of the most important musical events of the late 1920s was the coming of the wireless. This brought a variety of music to all kinds of people.

Entertainment had been provided by variety and music hall acts from the mid 1800s. Since the end of the Victorian era, the cinema had been the major rival to the popularity of music hall. By the end of the First World War, music hall was beginning to fade in favour of new variety acts and more sophisticated films.

By the end of the Great War technology was advancing at a rapid rate. The world of the wireless began in 1920 when Marconi made Britain's first public radio broadcast. It came from the transmitters of the Marconi Company based at Writtle, Chelmsford, Essex on 23 February

1920 when Marconi made Britain's first public radio broadcast. It came from the transmitters of the Marconi Company based at Writtle, Chelmsford, Essex on 23 February 1920. The company was subject to Parliamentary control through wireless licences being sold to the general public. The money was collected by the Post Office and paid into the Exchequer.

John Reith

The British Broadcasting Company was formed and 2LO began transmissions from London on 14 November 1922. John Reith, a former engineer, was appointed as general manager. He was a stern controller. Broadcasts were restricted mainly to talks and light classical music during the day. In the evening dance bands of the day were featured from the Savoy Hotel which was situated next door to the new company's headquarters at 2 Savoy Hill.

Meanwhile on the Continent, and also in America, experiments were being made in commercial radio. A great number of stations with the help of advertising managed to break through, but in Britain the idea of commercial radio was not liked. In 1926 the Crawford Committee said that a public monopoly of broadcasting would be successful.

The British Broadcasting Company was liquidated on 31 December 1926 and the following day Royal Charter constituted the British Broadcasting Corporation to last for ten years. The charter has been renewed on regular occasions since then. Sir John Reith was made its first Director-General. His vision was of an independent British broadcaster able to 'educate, inform and entertain' the whole nation, free from political interference and commercial pressure.

Up to and including 1924 the BBC had eight stations all transmitting different programmes. This was known as the Regional System, but it was not possible to transmit the same programme from more than one station at a time.

During the run of Julian Wylie's *Blackpool Follies* in the summer of 1928, wireless producer Victor Smythe asked **Sandy Powell** to broadcast his famous sketch *The Lost Policeman*. This posed a problem because at the time there was a good deal of controversy within the profession about the wisdom of artistes going on the air. The Variety Artistes Federation had emphatically expressed the opinion that it was detrimental to the best interests of artistes to broadcast. Sandy, however, was of the opinion that the advertising value of broadcasting could be a good thing for variety, and he became a pioneer in this medium.

This, in turn, led to Sandy broadcasting regularly from the BBC's Savoy Hill in a revue called *Sandy's Hour*, this being the very first time that a variety programme was broadcast. Variety did make in-roads into BBC broadcasts from the mid 1920s. Amongst those heard on the airwaves included Will Hay, Robb Wilton, Norman Long, Stainless Stephen, 'Wireless' Willie, Helena Millais, Vivian Foster, Leonard Henry, Tommy Handley and Mabel Constanduros.

Among the earliest variety programmes were *Songs from the Shows* and *Kentucky Minstrels* but the legendary successes of the late Thirties which created many of the first radio stars, performers and writers included *Monday Night at Eight, Bandwagon* and *ITMA* (It's That Man Again). Variety attracted the largest audiences. In many ways it was a 20th century version of the 19th century music hall. Eric Maschwitz, the founding father of BBC variety and a successful writer, produced many of the programmes from a new BBC theatre in St George's Hall, London, which opened in 1933, but was bombed during World War II.

In the 1930s there were restrictions on the type of jokes that could be broadcast on the

Radio Times   Issue 1   28 Sept 1923

airwaves. Written guidelines on what was accepted material and what was not were issued to artistes and producers. Jokes about drunkenness, religion, infidelity, effeminacy and human infirmities were unacceptable. From time to time jokes were broadcast which should have been edited (difficult on a live broadcast!).

Clapham and Dwyer, two well-known comedians, said on one broadcast: "What is the difference between a champagne cork and a baby? Answer: A champagne cork has the maker's name on its bottom." This was broadcast in January 1935. A news bulletin following the show had to apologise for "a lapse of taste in the variety programme." The newsreader said: "The BBC apologises to listeners for the inclusion in *Music Hall* of certain highly offensive remarks, violating standards, which have been firmly established by the practice of the BBC."

By 1931 radio-receiving licences in the United Kingdom exceeded four million. Radio Normandy, the first commercial station to broadcast daily sponsored programmes for British listeners, began on 11 October 1931. The BBC Empire Service began transmissions in 1932. This was the forerunner to the BBC World Service. The same year the BBC moved into Broadcasting House near Oxford Circus.

Music had been the earliest and most popular form of broadcasting, particularly dance music, although the chief pride of many in BBC management was the enlargement of serious musical taste in Britain before and during World War II. Lord Reith generally approved of dance music, unlike jazz, and it was first heard on the wireless in 1922. The Savoy Hotel Orpheans and Havana bands were popular outside broadcasts from October 1923, but later Henry Hall, with his BBC Dance Orchestra (which he took over from Jack Payne) became a major national figure. He returned during the war with *Henry Hall's Guest Night*, which had begun in 1934. His opening greeting 'Hello everyone, this is Henry Hall speaking' was an early catch phrase and his signature tune, *Here's to the Next Time,* became a hit melody of its time.

Vaudeville was represented on radio in the 1930s by Florence Desmond, **Teddy Brown, Wee Georgie Wood** and Harry Tate. The flagship programme of the time was *Music Hall*, which was broadcast on a Saturday evening throughout the decade.

The BBC began to increase its output of light entertainment programmes and by the early 1930s it was broadcasting 150 variety shows a year. Some were studio based, but the majority were live broadcasts from theatres and music halls. By the end of the 1930s 98% of the country's population could 'listen in' to the BBC's radio services. Nearly nine million ten shilling (50p) licences had been taken out.

In competition with the BBC, Radio Luxembourg began broadcasts to England from 1933. Together with Radio Normandy, they began broadcasting popular record programmes and variety shows and attracted a large audience. John Reith left the BBC in 1938. Upon his departure the Corporation mounted a major effort to rival the continental radio stations. The BBC Home Service began broadcasting in 1939, the year that the Second World War began. War correspondents included Richard Dimbleby, Frank Gillard and Wynford Vaughan-Thomas. The BBC had its secret wartime weapons waiting in the wings. Colonel ('I don't mind if I do') Chinstrap and Mrs ('Can I do yer now, sir?') Mopp were just two famous characters with which comedian Tommy Handley and his team attracted 16 million listeners each week to *It's That Man Again (ITMA)*. A Special Forces Programme was set up in 1940. This became the General Forces Programme in 1944 and the following year was renamed the Light Programme, at a similar time to Regional Broadcasting recommencing. The BBC Third Programme began in 1946.

Variety Bandbox was a very popular programme which began in 1941 and introduced new acts to radio. It was hosted by Philip Slessor. A series within a series called *Blessem Hall* was broadcast every other week from March 1950 as part of the programme. **Peter Sellers** played Major Manoeuvre the manager, Giuseppe Chipolata the waiter and Erbert Perks the night porter. Two other Chelsea members who regularly appeared were **Arthur English** who played the resident comedian and Prince of the Wide Boys and comedian **Reg Dixon** who was one of the most popular comedians in the 1940s and 1950s. He gave us the catch phrase 'I'm poorly...proper poorly."

Radio had some of the biggest stars in the 1950s, including Spike Milligan, Harry Secombe, **Peter Sellers** and Michael Bentine *(The Goon Show)*, Kenneth Horne *(Beyond Our Ken)* Ben Lyon and Bebe Daniels *(Life With the Lyons)* and Jimmy Edwards, June Whitfield and Dick Bentley in *Take It From Here*, which introduced two young comedy writers, Frank Muir and Dennis Norden.

All the domestic services were changed on 30 September 1967 with the introduction of Radio

1. The Light Programme became Radio 2, the Third Programme Radio 3 and the Home Service Radio 4. BBC Local Radio was launched with Radio Leicester. Radio 5 Live came much later, in 1990.

One of the first names from Chelsea Lodge to be featured regularly on BBC was **Stanley Black**. He was conductor of the BBC Dance Orchestra. They appeared in a number of variety shows including *Much Binding in the Marsh* (1947-1953), *The Will Hay Programme* (1944-1945), *Ray's a Laugh* (1949-1951), *Life With the Lyons* (1950-1951) and *The Goon Show* (1951). Stanley wrote the theme music for the *Goon Show* series. He was also musical director for *Happy-Go-Lucky* (1951).

Even before the BBC Dance Orchestra was established we were being entertained on the wireless by comedians **Leslie Sarony, Bud Flanagan** and **Sandy Powell. Issy Bonn** appeared in *Variety Bandbox* and *Music Hall* presenting his Finkelfeffer acts. According to the *BBC Year Book 1931* Variety artistes who broadcast that year included **Teddy Brown, Lupino Lane** and **Wee Georgie Wood.**

The dance band has its own indisputable place in the radio programmes of all countries. From earliest days music for dancing has been an important item in British broadcasting. Dance bands and orchestras were represented by **Joe Loss, 'Miff' Ferrie, Cyril Stapleton, Roy Fox, Phil Green, Edmundo Ros, Nat Temple, Frank Weir, Tito Burns, Richard Crean, Paul Adam, Harry Leader** and **Woolf Philips**. The success of a dance band or orchestra lay with the conductor, but the sidemen were an integral part of the band. Over the years a number of Chelsea Lodge musicians made a name for themselves, notably **Bert Weeden** (guitar), **Alfie Noakes** (trumpet), **Tiny Winters** (string bass and vocal), **Max Goldberg** (trumpet), xylophonist **Teddy Brown and 'Poggy' Pogson** (clarinet and alto saxophone).

Dave Carey sang with the Cyril Stapleton Orchestra in 1951 before he joined the Stargazers. Singer **Lee Lawrence** made a number of radio broadcasts in the late 1940s and early 1950s. He was in the first series of *Sing It Again* in 1949 and later joined the Cyril Stapleton Orchestra as a vocalist. In 1955 he had his own series where he sang operatic arias, show tunes and popular songs, all with the backing of the Harry Rabinowitz and the BBC Revue Orchestra.

Franklyn Boyd featured as a singer in the 1950s in *Sing It Again, Start With a Song* and *Remembered Tunes*. **Gerry Brereton** was a regular vocalist in *Come In and Sing*. **Alan Breeze** performed throughout the 1960s on Sunday lunchtimes in The Billy Cotton Show. **George Elrick** had been a popular singer with the BBC Dance Orchestra until he became a regular presenter of *Housewives Choice* from 1946.

Bob Monkhouse appeared in *Workers' Playtime* in 1948 and was soon signed as a comedy writer along with colleague Denis Goodwin. Bob had continued both in front of and behind the microphone on BBC airwaves for more than 50 years.

Comedian **Dick Emery** appeared in *Pertwee's Progress* in 1955 before becoming a popular television personality. Arthur English broadcast in comedy shows in the 1950s. His catch phrase was 'open the cage'. Actor **Alfred Marks** appeared in *Variety Bandbox, Star Bill* and *Educating Archie* in the 1950s. **Bernard Bresslaw** also appeared in *Educating Archie*. **Peter Sellers** appeared in arguably the most famous radio show of all time *The Goon Show* (1951-1960). **Bernard Spear** made over 300 broadcasts between 1945 to 1983 in a variety of shows ranging from *Henry Hall's Guest Night* to *Workers' Playtime.*

With the arrival of BBC Radio by numbers (September 1967) disc jockeys **Barry Alldis** and **Keith Skues** were heard regularly on Radios 1 and 2. **Paul Williams** became a producer to many top Radio 1 shows. Musicians **Joe Loss, Des Champ, Denny Wise** and **Zack Laurence** have been featured on the network.

TELEVISION

By the mid-1920s there were several experiments going on around the world looking at mechanically scanned television. John Logie Baird is the Scotsman who takes the credit for his work on 'true' television, by reflected light rather than back-lot silhouettes. This was shown to the general public in London in January 1926.

The BBC began broadcasting television 'test transmissions' on the Baird 30-line system in 1929 and three years later adopted this system. Technology was moving forward and the 30-line service ceased in 1935 to be replaced the following year with the world's first regular high - resolution (405 lines per picture) television service transmitted by the BBC. Though led by the need for entertainment, the development of practical television was dependent on technology.

The first performer to sing on a synchronised television and radio programme was Gracie Fields on 31 March 1930. The first musicians to make television history were Jack Payne and His Band who, at 10.50pm on 15 October 1931, played before television cameras at the Savoy Hill broadcasting studio which was described as 'the first televisation of a radio programme' put out by the BBC. It lasted thirty minutes.

The first play televised direct from a theatre, St Martin's, London, was J.B. Priestley's *When We Are Married* in November 1938. In the same year Cicely Courtneidge, **Lupino Lane**, Tommy Trinder, Basil Radford, Tommy Handley and Naunton Wayne made television comedy appearances.

Almost without exception, the early comedy stars of television were already established celebrities of music hall and radio. By the mid 1950s wall-to-wall television finished off the ailing local palais, theatre, music hall and cinema. Some artistes successfully adapted to radio and television but many more disappeared into oblivion. Sadly, some died in poverty and obscurity.

The BBC was closed down on 1 September 1939, halfway through a Mickey Mouse cartoon, and didn't transmit again until June 1946. It began with that same Mickey Mouse cartoon and it has remained ever since. Mr. Pastry (Richard Hearne) was arguably the biggest and most overworked television funny-man of that era. Joyce Grenfell became a popular television personality at this time. In the world of comedy we enjoyed *Hancock's Half Hour* and *I Love Lucy*, the latter imported from the USA. TV's biggest successes in the 1950s were light entertainment shows, comedies, game shows, US imports and *Sunday Night at the London Palladium*. Variety ruled the airwaves and ITV always scored higher rating than the BBC.

The first music hall to become a full-time television studio was also the last to be decommissioned: The Shepherd's Bush Empire which was taken over by BBC Television in 1953 and used by them as the BBC Television Theatre until the summer of 1991. The Empire had been built in 1903. The BBC made changes and added a false floor laid over the stalls at stage level, to allow the cameras to undertake tracking shots. The BBC vacated the TV Theatre in 1991, as part of the same property rationalisations that spelled the end of the former Gaumont-British studios close by at Lime Grove.

Wood Green Empire was the second theatre to switch, going 'live' in September 1955 as the first home for ATV's London operations. The Empire had been opened by impresario Oswald Stoll on 9 September 1912. As well as live entertainment, the Empire became a full-time cinema in 1929. It was closed in January 1955 after a season of the pantomime *Cinderella* starring 'Monsewer' Eddie Gray and **Arthur English**. It remained derelict for a short while before being equipped for television and taken over by ATV.

A third theatre, the Empire at Hackney, also promoted by Oswald Stoll, was opened in December 1901. It produced variety shows for 54 years, closing in February 1956 when it was taken over by ATV. The TV audiences were seated in the dress circle. One of the most famous

TV series to originate at the Empire was the rock'n'roll show *Oh Boy*. Another popular show broadcast from here was the quiz game *Take Your Pick*. Television came to an end both at Wood Green and Hackney when ATV converted the former film studios at Boreham Wood, Hertfordshire in 1962. Wood Green stood derelict for two years before much of the building was demolished to make way for a Sainsbury's supermarket. The facade, however, does remain, where the Halifax Building Society has one of its premises.

Hackney Empire was taken over by Mecca in 1963 and was converted into a bingo hall which was in constant use until November 1986. Today it is a Grade II listed building and secured Lottery funding to restore the building to its 1901 glory. This was officially opened in September 2004.

The last of the great London theatre conversions was that of Chelsea Palace in King's Road, which was converted by Granada to augment its purpose-built Manchester studio centre. Chelsea was so much part of Granada that it became 'Studio 10' in the company's hierarchy, in which Sidney Bernstein said that studios were to be given only even numbers to create a heightened impression of grandeur. The Chelsea Palace of Varieties, as it was known, upon opening, in April 1903 was later bought by Variety Theatres Consolidated in 1925. It came under Granada control in 1951. Television programmes began in the late 1950s and provided a home for *The Army Game* and the prestigious variety showcase *Chelsea at Nine*, as well as for one-off spectaculars such as the 1963 concert featuring the Duke Ellington Orchestra.

The 1950s is known as the Golden Age of Television mainly because of the variety shows which dominated the early part of the decade. Television variety shows of the period were just vaudeville on television. Most of the performers had learned their craft on vaudeville stages and many of the TV shows were structured like vaudeville revues and, as with vaudeville, these were live performances. These early variety shows spotlighted talent from many sources and they proved to be the springboard for some new faces... a place where the legends of the past gave birth to the stars of the future.

Wrestling was a popular sport on television. **Mick McManus** went on to become one of the most famous wrestlers in the United Kingdom and known as the man the wrestling fans loved to hate. He tried every trick in the book to succeed against much bigger opponents and fed off the bad reception he received from the crowd. Despite standing 5ft 6ins and weighing 13 stone, Mick used brute force to dominate wrestling in the 1950s and 1960s and he became British Welterweight Champion in 1957. He fought against all the top 'good guys' of the era including a feud with Jackie Pallo, which is still remembered to this day by the members of the wrestling fraternity.

Mick, together with Giant Haystacks, Jackie Pallo and Big Daddy were regularly seen on ITV screens each Saturday afternoon at 4.00pm.

Mick McManus

The network commenced the coverage of wrestling in 1955, hosted by Kent Walton. Between 1978 and 1988 up to six million viewers would switch on to cheer and boo the leviathans of the ring that swapped belly flops and splashdowns. It is known that members of the Royal Family were viewers, including Her Majesty The Queen, The Duke of Edinburgh, Prince Charles and the Duke of Kent. It was Greg Dyke (who later went on to become Director General at BBC until 2004) who took over *World of Sport* and dropped wrestling from ITV screens in December 1988 after a run of 33 years. He said that it was so tarnished with the old-style look of ITV it had to go.

Television pictures were in black and white. We had to wait until December 1967 for colour transmissions on BBC 2. Colour came to the BBC 1 and ITV networks in November 1969.

The BBC Television Theatre in Shepherd's Bush was opened in 1957. Amongst the shows to come from there were: *The Black and White Minstrels, The Billy Cotton Bandshow* and the *Benny Hill Show*. By the late 1950s comedy, variety, music shows and children's programmes were being scheduled. These included *The White Heather Club, Blue Peter, Juke Box Jury, 6.5 Special* and *The Good Old Days. Top of the Pops began in* 1964.

The Wakey Wakey Tavern was a very popular series featuring the Billy Cotton Band. It had begun on radio and was a 'must' to listen to on Sunday lunchtime along with *Two Way Family Favourites* as we tucked into roast beef and Yorkshire pudding. The resident vocalist was **Alan Breeze.** These rollicking broadcasts paved the way for their move into television with a colourful show, combining robust music and broad comedy, which was watched by an estimated weekly audience of 12 million. It was a happy and contented partnership and they climbed the heights together. Alan recalls the time he joined Billy Cotton:

The band singer when I joined was Cyril Grantham, who doubled on saxes and clarinet, but he was a dance-hall singer and had to use a megaphone. There were no microphones on stage in those days. Bill wanted a big voice that could be heard all over the theatre. He never bothered to take up the option after a month. It was just assumed that I would stay and I did, for 36 years. The comedy numbers used to be done on recordings by Fred Douglas, father of future bandleader Leslie Douglas. But one day Fred failed to turn up and I told Bill, "I'll do it", to which he replied 'Wotcha mean, you're a bleeding opera singer!" Anyway, in desperation, he let me have a go and it came off so well that afterwards I did all his comedy stuff.

Alan was a splendid character actor who could take off anyone from a drunken sailor to a refined country gentleman. He could perform in a variety of dialects ranging from Other Mother Riley to Maurice Chevalier. Over the years he was called upon to sing all manner of songs but without doubt he excelled on the comedy numbers, a stock trade for the Cotton band. Alan himself reckoned the most popular was *I've Got a Lovely Bunch of Coconuts*. Throughout the fifties and early sixties Billy Cotton and his Band, on radio or TV, was a weekly treat enjoyed by millions and Alan was always there to jolly the proceedings along.

That continued until the autumn of 1965 when he was dropped from *The Wakey Wakey Tavern*, the band's television series, when the show was at the peak of its popularity. It was apparently against the wishes of Billy and was a decision made by his executive son, Bill Cotton Junior, who was at that time Assistant Head of Light Entertainment for BBC TV. He decided to revamp the programme and told the press: "Alan Breeze has been in the television show for ten years and that is a very good run. But the style has changed from a band show to more of a variety show and there is really no place for him. If the show changes again, there could well be a chance for Alan to return." Friends and fans of Alan regarded this as a cruel judgment after he had devoted his entire career to old Bill.

He continued broadcasting with the *Billy Cotton Band Show* on radio until October 1968, when Bill did his final broadcast and candidly told Alan that he had nothing else in the book.

Another popular band was directed by **Nat Temple**. From 1950 they appeared in all the television shows hosted by Bernard Braden and Barbara Kelly which included *Breakfast With Braden, Bedtime With Braden, Between Time With Braden, Bedlam With Braden* and *Back With Braden*. In addition they could be seen in *Tune Times With Temple, Beauty Box* and *Dance Music Through The Ages*.

One major personality who has appeared over a period of 50 years of television is Bruce Forsyth. Some will argue and say he invented light entertainment on British television in the

1950s and went on to define it for a further five decades. It is true to say no other television personality has meant so much to so many people over so long a period. He is the link between variety and television entertainment, having mastered the old medium and graduated even more successfully to the new. He won a talent show in 1939 and later appeared on the variety circuit as Boy Bruce, the Mighty Atom. He moved into television and within a short while was attracting audiences of over 20 million in *Sunday Night at the London Palladium*. He is a walking, talking, all-singing, all-dancing, piano-playing personality who went on to entertain us in *The Generation Game, Play Your Cards Right* and more recently *Have I Got News For You* and *Strictly Come Dancing.*

ITV dominated the world of light entertainment from the 1960s to the late 1980s. The BBC was forced to make a concerted effort to be more populist, scoring a big hit with *Steptoe and Son.* Remembered as an inventive era where satire was the order of the day shows like *That Was the Week That Was, Not Only...But Also* and *The Frost Report* never caught the viewers imagination as the big-name variety shows recorded at London's premiere theatres.

Coronation Street is Britain's longest-running television soap opera set in the fictional industrial town of Weatherfield, which is based on Salford, near Manchester. Forty-five years later the show still draws in millions of viewers. Its principal rival 'soap' is the BBC's *East Enders. The Coronation Street* serial began in 1960 and was not a critical success. It was only expected to run for a few weeks but it grabbed the imagination of the viewers, not least because of its location in the North of England, which was producing some good dramas for film, and TV. The storylines in the 'Street' focused on the experiences of families, their interaction and of relationships between different ages, classes and social structures. Of the original cast on the show, only one character remains, Ken Barlow, played by William Roache, who has remained the constant link through its long run. A number of famous names have appeared in the series over the years including Davy Jones of the Monkees, Ben Kingsley who portrayed Mahatma Gandhi in Richard Attenborough's biographical film *Gandhi*, Peter Noone of Herman's Hermits, Joanna Lumley of *Absolutely Fabulous* and *New Avengers*, Arthur Lowe, who starred as Captain Mainwaring in *Dad's Army*, Roy Hudd from television and radio and Amanda Barrie who starred in many British films. Another special guest was HRH Prince Charles who appeared as himself in the 40th year anniversary show in 2000. Though no longer watched as it was in its earlier days, the decline is due to a proliferation of satellite channels, which have broken up audiences. However, it still remains ITV's most watched programme with an excess of 10 million viewers.

The 1970s were remembered fondly as the golden era of the sitcom. Popular shows during this decade included *The Two Ronnies, The Muppets, Monty Python's Flying Circus, Last of the Summer Wine, Porridge, Rising Damp*, and perhaps the greatest sitcom of all time, *Fawlty Towers.*

The 1980s produced alternative comedy featuring people like Rik Mayell, Ade Edmondson, Jennifer Saunders and Dawn French. However, some of the most popular shows of the decade were *Only Fools and Horses*, *Last of the Summer Wine* and *Bread* (one episode achieved 21 million viewers in 1988).

Chelsea member **Cecil Korer** was an important player in the world of television. Working up the ladder from being a scene shifter in 1957 he became a director and producer and later still, after a distinguished career with the BBC, Head of Programmes at Channel 4TV. He was part of the team, which brought pop music to television in *Top of the Pops*, which originated in Manchester. He was series producer on the BBC panel game *Ask the Family* (1967). He produced the long-running series *It's a Knock Out* for BBC1.

In 1981 Cecil was appointed senior commissioning editor of the fledgling Channel 4. He was an unusual choice in as much as a person who was used to conventional entertainment and enjoyed rather old-fashioned values. Channel 4 had very little money and it was to specialise in alternative, minority and innovative programming. However, Isaacs made one of the most crucial appointments of the day. Cecil's experience alone singled him out from the rest of the staff, many of whom were new to television. Unhindered and with total concentration of the project in hand, and with a hard-nosed individualism, Korer came up trumps. He scored success with the high - class import from America, *Cheers*, together with home grown shows *Mini Pops, Treasure Hunt* and *Countdown*, the latter two were consistently the highest rated shows of the 1980s. Later came *Paul Hogan, It's a Hudd, Hudd World* (Roy Hudd) and *Superfrank* (Frankie Howard). In 1990 Cecil Korer was executive producer on *Dors:The Other Diana*.

Television in the 1990s arguably was less adventurous when programme schedules changed beyond recognition. ITV gave up on sitcoms and the BBC relied heavily on repeats. Reality TV affected our tastes, but popular shows included *The Royale Family, The Day Today, The Fast Show* and *Alan Partridge. Absolutely Fabulous* was a huge success.

Chelsea members were regularly seen on the small screen. **Jim Davidson** became the host of *Generation Game* (BBC) as well as his own comedy shows from provincial theatres. He also featured in *Big Break* with snooker star **John Virgo**. **Roger Kitter** played the cowardly Italian officer Captain Alberto Bertorelli in the very successful *'Allo' Allo* series which ran for ten years. He has appeared in *Birds of a Feather, Get Back, Goodnight Sweetheart,* and *The New Statesman*. He has presented sketches in *The Frost Report, Generation Game, Jim Davidson Presents* and *It's Lulu* (all BBC) and was a regular panelist in *Punchlines* (LWT). **Bob Monkhouse** never seemed to be off our screens appearing in and also hosting comedy shows and quiz games.

As we moved into a new millennium television has seen comedy returning to the screens. *The Office, Black Books, Coupling, Little Britain* and *Look Around You,* have scored well in the ratings and some old favourites have been resurrected - *Alan Partridge* and *Absolutely Fabulous*. Impressionist shows have also been popular with *Dead Ringers, Alistair McGowan* and *2DTV*.

The ITV series *Popstars* (2001) attracted over 10 million viewers and made front-page news, following in the footsteps of *Big Brother, Castaway* and *Airport*. It has even made a star out of **Nigel Lythgoe**, a former controller of entertainment and comedy at LWT who has gained the nickname 'Nasty Nigel' for his dismissive asides like: "If they think they can sing, they're either stupid or deaf". The series' popularity appears to be that it rolls three successful programmes into one. It has the voyeurism of *Big Brother,* the putdowns of *The Weakest Link* and the talent show appeal of *Stars in Their Eyes*.

SUMMER SEASONS

At whichever branch of show business one looks there is one type of location which has endeavoured to keep entertainment 'live' and that is the seaside resort. For well over 100 years the holiday resorts have booked artistes for summer seasons. Whether it be Brighton or Blackpool, Skegness or Scarborough, Margate or Morecambe all have tried to keep the holiday makers happy.

We shall visit Great Yarmouth one typical resort to see how they have enjoyed their golden era of entertainment and if the authorities are still packing them in at the theatres and on the piers.

It would be true to say that Great Yarmouth never matched its great rival Blackpool either for the splendour of its facilities, the length of the season, or its illuminations. However, from the 1950s through to the 1970s it provided a feast of top names the like of which will not be seen again. At the turn of the 19th century Great Yarmouth had two indoor circus arenas. Today it has one which has survived.

Television has a lot to answer for. Famous names who were from the world of variety and music hall, found that doing summer seasons was a good way of putting their talents before a

An early picture postcard of Great Yarmouth Hippodrome

huge family audience. The years after World War II were the age of the family holiday. Great Yarmouth benefited from the traditional 'works holiday' weeks and fortnights, particularly from the North, Midlands and Scotland. The bracing East Coast air was a great attraction to those who

lived in industrial towns and cities. They had plenty of money and they wanted to be entertained. In its heyday Great Yarmouth had not only the permanent circus but two pier shows, plus four theatres. During the daytime some of the theatres doubled as cinemas.

Great Yarmouth had the Wellington Pier which was opened on 31 October 1853 and Britannia Pier, opened 13 July 1858. In 1898 Norwich-born George Gilbert, a famous circus equestrian built his first circus at Great Yarmouth calling it Gilbert's Modern Circus. It was opened on 25 July 1898 and the building was used until 1903 when Gilbert erected the permanent Hippodrome which to this day is still used for circus performances. The Hippodrome was opened 20 July 1903.

Following Gilbert in the ownership of the Hippodrome have been Henglers Ltd., Theophilus Edwin Read and Son, Billy Russell, Ben Dean and the Jay Family.

Chelsea members appearing at the Hippodrome have included the following: **William Permane's** Teddy Bears in a cine-variety season on 8 November 1908. He returned 6 September 1914 as Captain Permane's Five Teddy Bears in a circus season. The Five Jovers performing a horizontal bars act on 21 October 1902. **Florencio Tomas Jover** was a member of the team. Comedian and singer **Harry Marlow** on 16 March 1914 and **Charles Grantley**, comedian on 13 November 1922. Agent **Harry Zahl** presented *Hoist Yer Slacks* in December 1922 in the variety stage season. **Frank Ginnett** and partner appeared in the circus season in 1923 with lasso and whip manipulation. In the same show was the **Fossett's** equestrian act. **Tommy Fossett** would later become a featured clown at the Hippodrome. **Reg Lever** appeared in *Lucky Lads* on 19 February 1930 in the stage season. **Jack Risket** appeared in *Non-Stop Variety* performing his *Mystery Night* on 28 November 1932. **Frank Ginnett** appeared throughout the 12-week circus season in the years 1934-1938 as ringmaster. The Hippodrome remained closed from the outbreak of World War II in September 1939 to June 1951, when Frank, who had become a circus booking agent, once again acted as ringmaster and equestrian director for the whole season and again in 1952 and 1953. His place was taken by **Roberto Germains** who also performed a high school act. He, too, went on to become an agent. Frank Ginnett died 9 November 1953. It was considered that he had helped Billy Russell in re-establishing the Yarmouth Hippodrome Circus from the summer of 1951. His son Frank Ginnett Jnr. had appeared as a clown in the 1930s under the name of Lutini and in 1936 had presented a novel act of ponies, pigs and dogs.

After working as 'Count Roberto' with his riding act at the Hippodrome in 1952, Roberto Germains decided to retire as a performer and devote himself to agency work. To replace Ginnett both as ringmaster and booking agent, Billy Russell turned to Germains. He spoke a number of languages and was well-known on the continent. He was particularly adept at finding new talent in countries like Italy, Spain and Potrtugal. A number of his discoveries appeared for the first time in this country at the Hippodrome. Later he brought in acts from Korea, Hungary, Russia, China and Mongolia. The Great Yarmouth Hippodrome Circus was attracting up to a quarter of a million visitors per season.

The summer season in Great Yarmouth would run from early June to midway through September. Most theatres ran two houses a night, six nights a week. The big names were to be found in Great Yarmouth - Frankie Howerd, Morecambe and Wise, Harry Secombe, Charlie Chester, Des O'Connor, Bruce Forsyth, Mike Yarwood and Cannon and Ball. The pop music market was represented by chart toppers like Tommy Steele, Gerry and the Pacemakers, The Searchers, Billy Fury, Rolf Harris, Joe Brown, Mark Wynter and the Tornados. In 1983 Jay's World of Entertainment Company encompassed the Hippodrome, Empire, Windmill, Royalty Entertainment Centre and Rosie O'Grady's in Great Yarmouth, and the Hippodrome in Lowestoft. In the summer of 1984 Peter Jay booked Cilla Black, Jimmy Cricket and **Roger Kitter** at the Royalty Theatre on Marine Parade.

Some economic reality finally overtook the golden era and, just as television had helped promote it all, so television began to kill it off. Fewer big stars were willing to spend a summer by the seaside, as they could earn far more from a television series than from a season in Great Yarmouth.

Having said that, **Jim Davidson** remained a staunch supporter of the summer season longer than most.

Like many other coastal resorts Great Yarmouth has suffered from competition provided by the package holiday. Today it is as cheap to spend a holiday in Spain as it is in this country. Families do still come, although in decreasing numbers. Also popular now are self catering holidays and people are drawn to the holiday camps that have appeared around Great Yarmouth, where in-house entertainment is part of the package.

Sadly we are losing the old fashioned traditional British holiday when a day on the beach could be followed by an evening with some of the country's top entertainers.

One family more than any other, was responsible for putting Great Yarmouth on the entertainment map. Ben Jay arrived in the town in 1937 to begin Jay's entertainments empire. It was his son **Jack Jay** who spotted the opportunity to bring big name acts to the town and was responsible for helping many then unknown names like Norman Wisdom and Max Bygraves. The impresario died in 1995. He was also influential in re-establishing the holiday industry at critical times - after the war, and the ravaging 1953 floods. Dubbed Mr. Showbiz by his legion of friends, the importance of the Jay empire can be gauged by the fact that the family business at one time or another boasted five cinema-theatres in Great Yarmouth and Lowestoft, including the Windmill, Empire and Royal Aquarium (Royalty, previously the Three-in-One) and the Hippodrome. Jack was able to attract big names to Great Yarmouth which in turn brought thousands of visitors each summer. Block bookings from local holiday camps and hotels filled up every seat in his theatres. The list of artistes he brought to Great Yarmouth looks like a "Who's Who of Showbusiness". They include: Tommy Trinder, Sid James, John Inman, Hylda Baker, Jack Douglas, Matt Monro, Ruby Murray and George Formby. A third generation continues the name - Jack's son Peter had success with his pop group Peter Jay and the Jaywalkers in the 1960s. He has continued to build on the proud Jay entertainment legacy.

ROYAL VARIETY PERFORMANCE

Two shows took place called Royal Command Performance. The first was staged at the Palace Theatre, London on 1 July 1912 when **George Robey** performed the *Mayor of Mudcumdyke,* **Charlie Whittle** appeared in *Variety's Garden Party* finale and **Harry Claff** led the singing of the National Anthem. Also taking part was **Albert Le Fre**. The show, which was produced by Albert Toft, was held in front of Their Majesties King George V and Queen Mary. The Royal party by all accounts enjoyed the show. The only embarrassment occurred when Queen Mary saw Vesta Tilley appear on stage in trousers. Apparently she buried her face in her programme. Women were never seen in trousers until the First World War and it would have been considered most immodest in 1912.

In 1919 King George V commanded a variety performance at the Coliseum, London on 28 July to show his appreciation of the generous manner in which the artistes of the variety stage had helped the numerous funds with the First World War.

The proceeds of the two Command Performances were devoted to the Variety Artistes'

Brinsworth House located in Twickenham, home for retired members of the entertainment profession

Benevolent Fund and Institution at the request of King George V. The series of Royal Variety Performances started in 1921. They were specially arranged in aid of this fund, founded in 1907, which maintains Brinsworth House, opened in 1911, for retired performers of what was then the variety and music hall profession. Today Brinsworth House, which is located at 72 Staines Road, Twickenham TW2 5AL is the home for retired members of the entertainment profession and their dependants. President is **Laurie Mansfield**, Chairman **Peter Prichard**, OBE, Treasurer **Ray Donn** and Executive Administrator **Peter Elliott. Jim Davidson**, OBE is a vice-president.

King George V, King George VI and Queen Elizabeth II have been patrons of this fund in succession and have honoured the performances with their presence on most occasions.

The Chelsea Boys with HRH Prince Charles at Brinsworth House outside the Ganjou Brothers and Juanita dining room. Left to right Don Smoothey, Laurie Mansfield, Roger Kitter, Ray Donn, HRH Prince Charles, Paul Ganjou, Peter Elliott, Roger de Courcey and Peter Prichard OBE.

The Ganjou Brothers (Bob, Serge and George) and Juanita in full flight in a Royal Variety Performance

The Royal Variety Performance has become the longest (in length) variety show on British television and is screened annually with the television rights allotted alternatively to BBC and ITV. It was first televised in 1960 by ATV from the Victoria Palace, London on 16 May in the presence of Her Majesty the Queen and His Royal Highness, the Duke of Edinburgh. **Bud Flanagan, Alfred Marks** and **Bob Monkhouse** were among the celebrities taking part.

The Royal Variety Performance has been presented by many distinguished persons over the years. They include: Oswald Stoll, George Black, Prince Littler, Alec Shanks, Val Parnell, Jack Hylton and Bernard Delfont. In 1978 **Louis Benjamin** was asked to take over from Lord

Delfont. He continued until 1985 when BBC Television took over the presentation, alternating each year with ITV.

Amongst the members of Chelsea Lodge who have appeared in the Royal Variety Performance are: **George Robey** (1912, 1917 and 1934), **Talbot O'Farrell** (1925 and 1948), **Wee Georgie Wood** (1927), **Stanelli** (1928), **Coram** (1930), **Richard Crean** (1930), **Nervo and Knox** (1930), **Teddy Brown** (1931), **Bud Flanagan** (1932, 1933, 1935, 1947, 1950, 1951, 1954, 1955, 1956 and 1960), **Roy Fox** (1933), **George Ganjou** (1933 and 1937), **Les Allen** (1934 and 1938), **Nat Temple** (1935), **Sandy Powell** (1935, 1970 and 1980), **Leslie Sarony** (1938 and 1983), **Lupino Lane** (1938), **Nat Jackley** (1946 and 1950), **Harry Lester** (1946), **Billy Danvers** (1948), **Jack Nathan** (1949), **Reg Dixon** (1949 and 1952), **Jack Raine** (1950), **Woolf Phillips** (1949, 1950 and 1952), **Peter Sellers** (1951 and 1965), **Arthur English** (1951 and 1980), **Gerry Brereton** (1952), **Stanley Black** (1951), **Alfred Marks** (1953, 1957 and 1960), **Philip Green** (1953), **Lauri Lupino Lane** (1955), **Bernard Bresslaw** (1958), **Peter Elliott** (1958), **Dai Francis** (1958 and 1962), **Cyril Stapleton** (1955 and 1958), **Edmundo Ros** (1962), **Eric Tann** (1964-1967, 1970, 1971, 1974 and 1975), **Joe Loss** (1963 and 1980), **Billy Dainty** (1974 and 1982-1984), **Bob Monkhouse** (1957, 1960, 1986, 1988, 1996 and 2002), **Roger de Courcey** (1976), **Jim Davidson** (1979) and **Don Smoothey** (1982).

Ray Donn meets Her Majesty the Queen at the 2003 Royal Variety Performance in Edinburgh. Looking on is Laurie Mansfield.

Chapter 9

BY-LAWS of the CHELSEA LODGE

PREAMBLE

The Charter or Warrant of Constitution of this Lodge, having been granted to the Members of the Musical, Theatrical and Vaudeville professions, it is expected that none but members of these professions, or those closely allied thereto shall be proposed for election, and that such candidates shall have been at least six consecutive months in their respective professions prior to proposal.

This shall not apply to the sons of Members of the Lodge, who shall always be eligible for election.

BY-LAWS

1. Place and Dates of Meeting

The Lodge shall meet at the Freemasons' Hall, Great Queen Street, London WC2B 5AZ and shall hold regular meetings on the Third Friday in May (Installation), September, November, January and March, at such hour as the Master shall direct.

2. Election and Installation Meetings

The Master and the Treasurer shall be elected by ballot at the regular meeting in March. The Master Elect shall be installed at the regular meeting in May.

3. Election of Tyler

Subject to the provisions of Rule 113, Book of Constitutions, the Tyler shall be elected by show of hands at the regular meeting in May.

4. Lodge Committee

The Lodge Committee shall consist of the Master, Wardens, Past Masters of and in the Lodge, Treasurer, Secretary and four other members to be elected annually by the Lodge at the regular meeting in March. This Committee shall consider and report to the Lodge on all proposals for membership and on any matters specially referred to it by the Lodge. Six members of the Committee shall form a quorum.

5. Audit Committee

The Audit Committee shall consist of four members of the Lodge who shall be elected annually by the Lodge at the regular meeting in March. The accounts shall be made up to 3lst March in each year and shall be presented to the Lodge, duly audited, at the regular meeting in May. A copy of the accounts and of the Audit Committee's certificate that all balances have been checked and that the accounts have been audited shall be sent to all members with the summons convening the meeting.

6. Fee and Annual Subscription

The initiation fee shall be £50.00, the joining fee £75.00 and the rejoining fee £37.50, such fees to be exclusive of subscription. The annual subscription (except for overseas membership as provided for in By-Law No.7), due and payable in advance on 1st May shall be of such amount as the Lodge shall from time to time decide by resolution after notice on the summons. The Secretary's services shall be deemed equivalent to payment of subscription. The visitor's fee at dinners shall be such amount as the Lodge shall from time to time determine by resolution after notice on the summons. Any member whose subscription is unpaid for one year shall be liable to be excluded from the Lodge, after due notice, in accordance with Rule 181 Book of Constitutions.

7. Non-Dining or Country Membership
Any member who becomes an overseas resident and is therefore not in a position to enjoy the privileges of the Lodge regularly, may, on written application to the Secretary and by resolution of the Lodge, be considered an overseas member and shall pay a subscription annually in advance on 1st May of such less amount than that provided for in By-Law No.6 as the Lodge shall from time to time decide by resolution after notice on the summons. When attending the Lodge and dining such member shall pay the current visitor's fee.

8. Admission of Candidate
The admission of candidates for initiation and joining shall be regulated by the provisions of Rules 157 to 166, Book of Constitutions. On the ballot for a candidate for initiation or joining two black balls shall exclude.

9. Termination of Membership
Any member desirous of terminating his membership of the Lodge shall tender his resignation in writing to the Secretary, or orally in open Lodge, in accordance w1th Rule 183, Book of Constitutions, and he shall be entitled to the Certificate mentioned in Rule 175, Book of Constitutions, stating the circumstances in which he left the Lodge. Should he at any future time wish to rejoin, he shall be subject to the rules relating to joining members.

10. Payment from Lodge Funds
Payment of any sum exceeding £100.00 if for other than ordinary purposes, may be made only by resolution of the Lodge, of which notice has been given on the summons, except in a case of emergency, when such payment may be authorised by the Master and reported to the Lodge at the next regular meeting.

11. Amendment of By-Laws
Except as otherwise required by Rule 141, Book of Constitutions, amendment of these By-Laws or of any of them may be made only in the following manner:-

(a) Notice of motion in writing stating the precise amendment or amendments proposed shall be given in open Lodge at a regular meeting.

(b) The Motion shall be set out on the summons for the next regular meeting or for an Emergency meeting summoned for the purpose, and shall at such meeting be put to the Lodge.

(c) A resolution for amendment, of which notice shall have been given as aforesaid, shall be carried if a majority of the members voting shall vote in favour of it, but it shall not be effective until approved by the Grand Master.

Should there be any objection to the introduction of a Candidate for Initiation, or a Brother for Joining, it is recommended that such objection be mentioned privately to the Master or Secretary who may communicate with the proposer and give him the opportunity of withdrawing his candidate.

Approved by the M.W. The Grand Master.

M.B.S. HIGHAM, Grand Secretary
l2th August 1987

Compare the shorter By-Laws of today with the original set which were issued in 1905.

1. Acknowledgement of the Grand Lodge
This Lodge acknowledges the supremacy of the Grand Lodge of England of Free and Accepted Masons, and accepts all Laws, Rules and Regulations contained in the Book of Constitutions, or enjoined by the Resolutions of the Grand Lodge.

11. **Place and Dates of Meetings.**
The Meetings of the Lodge shall be held in the Queen's Hotel, Leicester Square, WC., on the third Friday in the months of March, April, May, June, July, August, September and October, except when Good Friday occurs on the third Friday of the month, then the meeting shall be held on the previous day; at such an hour as the WM for the time being may appoint.

111. **Officers**
The Officers of the Lodge shall consist of the Master, Senior and Junior Wardens, Treasurer, Secretary, Senior and Junior Deacons, Inner Guard, Director of Ceremonies, Organist, Stewards to any number the WM may deem necessary, and Tyler.

IV. **Reading of the Minutes**
Immediately after the opening of any Regular Lodge, the minutes and proceedings of the previous Lodge or of any intervening Lodge of Emergency shall be read, and if confirmed by the Brethren, shall be signed by the Master in the Chair.

V. **Subscription**
The Annual Subscription to this Lodge shall Two and a Half Guineas, payable in advance, on the third Friday in May in every year, which shall include the sum of Three Shillings to be paid annually to the Benevolent Fund.

VI. **Fees and Qualification**
The fee for Initiation shall be Fifteen Guineas for which each member shall be entitled to receive the three established degrees of the Order. Registration in, and Certificate from Grand Lodge. The Joining Fee shall be Seven and a Half Guineas and include Registration Fee. The Rejoining Fee shall be One Guinea. Ten Shillings and Sixpence of the Initiation Fee and Five Shillings of the Joining Fee shall be added to the Benevolent Fund, and a further Two Guineas of the Initiation Fee and One Guinea of the Joining Fee shall be placed in the name of the Lodge on the list of the WM for the time being, when going up as a Steward to represent the Lodge at one of the Charity Festivals, and failing the WM, any Brother who may so represent the Lodge, and in the event of the WM, or no Brother representing the Lodge in any particular year, the accumulated funds shall be placed on the list of the first WM or Brother so doing.
The Charter or Warrant of Constitution of this Lodge, having been granted to the Members of the Musical, Theatrical and Vaudeville professions, it is expected that none but members of these professions, or those closely allied thereto shall be proposed for election, and that such candidates shall have been at least six consecutive months in their respective professions prior to proposal.
This By-Law shall not apply to the sons of Members of the Lodge, who shall always be eligible for election.

VII. **Proposal for Initiation or Brother Joining**
Except in cases of emergency, provided for by Rule No.185, Book of Constitutions, no person shall be initiated, or Brother join without having been proposed and seconded at one regular Lodge, and balloted for at the next regular Lodge, which ballot shall not take place unless his name, age, profession, and place of abode, with the names of his proposer and seconder, shall have been put in the Summons to all the Members of the Lodge, and no ballot shall take place unless testimony be furnished by the proposer or seconder, as to the qualifications of the Candidate.

VIII. **Rules for the Same**
No Brother can be balloted for as a Joining Member, unless he has visited the Lodge at a previous Meeting, and produced a clearance certificate from his present or former Lodge, and his Grand Lodge Certificate, as provided by the Book of Constitutions, Rule No.189.

IX. **Ballot**

On a Ballot for admission of a Member, two black balls shall exclude. On a resolution passed by the Lodge, a second ballot may take place at the same Meeting, should it be considered a mistake has occurred, providing such ballot is taken at once, and that the same Members and none others shall be present, when if two black balls again appear or if no second ballot be moved for, the candidate shall not be eligible for a second nomination within twelve months.

X. **Deposit by Proposer**

The proposer of any Candidate for Initiation in this Lodge must deposit with the Treasurer at the time of such proposition, the sum of Five Guineas as part of the Initiation Fee, and this sum will be forfeited and placed in the Benevolent Fund, should the Candidate fail to appear for Initiation within one year after his election, after being notified by the Secretary to attend for Initiation, unless from circumstances which may, in the opinion of a majority of the Brethren voting in regular Lodge, be a reasonable ground for so doing, it may be deemed proper to refund it, or should the Candidate be rejected by the Lodge at the ballot.

XI. **Show of Hands**

All propositions other than those specified in the Book of Constitutions shall be by show of hands, the WM to have the casting vote on all questions to be determined by a bare majority.

XII. **Arrears**

No member shall be appointed to any Office, permitted to vote or allowed to partake of any Lodge Banquet, whose dues are not paid; should they remain unpaid for six months, the Secretary, after having given him notice in writing shall bring the case before the Lodge, when he may, by vote of two-thirds of the Brethren present, be excluded in the manner prescribed by Rule 210, Book of Constitutions.

XIII. **Privilege of WM and Regulation for Visiting Brethren at Banquet**

The WM shall have the privilege of inviting two Guests to the Annual Banquet; the Visitor's fee shall be One Guinea, payable by the Member introducing him; no visitor shall be admitted to the Installation Banquet without a Ticket of Invitation, which may be obtained from the Secretary by a Member on payment of One Guinea for each visitor invited by him at the time of making the application.

XIV. **Resignation of Members**

A Brother is discontinued as a Member, by Signifying his resignation in writing to the Secretary, or announcing it in Open Lodge, but shall remain responsible for any arrears then due by him.

XV. **Notice of Motion**

Notice of Motion shall be in writing, and handed to the Secretary, signed by the Mover and Seconder.

XVI. **Order of Discussion**

When any business shall be brought before the Lodge for discussion, any Brother desirous of speaking, shall rise and address himself to the WM, and no Brother shall be allowed to speak twice on the same subject, unless in explanation, or the Mover in reply.

XVII. **Book of Constitutions and By-Laws**

Every Brother initiated into this Lodge shall be presented with a Copy of the Book of Constitutions and the By-Laws of the Lodge.

XVIII. **Election of WM**

The Master shall be annually elected by ballot at the regular Lodge in the month of April, and at the subsequent regular Lodge in May after the Minutes of the preceding meeting are, so far at least as relates to the election of Master, confirmed, he shall be duly Installed according to the ancient custom, and afterwards appoint and invest his Wardens, and other Officers.

XIX. Election of Treasurer

The Treasurer shall be annually elected by ballot at the regular Lodge in the month of April. The Treasurer, when duly invested, shall receive from the past Treasurer the accounts of the Lodge, together with the balance of money in hand. He shall receive all monies of the Lodge, and make such payments as shall be duly vouched and sanctioned by the WM, or voted by the Lodge. He shall keep proper account books, in which his receipts and disbursements shall be regularly stated, so as to show the financial state of the funds of the Lodge, which shall be open for the inspection of any subscribing Member at every Meeting of the Lodge. These accounts shall be annually audited by the Permanent Committee, three weeks at least previous to the regular Lodge in May.

XX. Lodge Funds

The Funds of the Lodge shall be deposited in a Bank (to be selected by the Treasurer) in the joint names of the Master, the Treasurer, and Secretary, and no payments of any kind other than the Secretary's petty cash disbursements, shall be made, except by Cheque on the Bankers, signed by the Master, Treasurer, and Secretary, collectively. The Funds of the Lodge shall not be voted for any purpose (unless notice be inserted in the summons) except to be for charitable purposes.

XXI. Secretary and Duty

The Secretary shall attend all Meetings of the Lodge and its Committees and enter in a book the Minutes of all transactions, and read the same at the next regular Meeting for confirmation.

He shall issue by Post to each Member the Summons calling the Lodge Meeting at least seven clear days before the same, setting forth all notices of Motion, Elections, Initiations, Passings, Raisings and New Members proposed, and he shall also insert the amount of Subscription due from each Member. He shall keep a correct account of the Funds, and previous to the election of WM and Treasurer, shall read a statement of arrears and the finances of the Lodge.

He shall collect the fees and dues, and forthwith pay them over to the Treasurer; and make out the returns to Grand Lodge.

He shall, in the absence of the Treasurer, or during a vacancy in that office, discharge the duties of the same; he shall be free of all subscriptions, and his quarterage to the Grand Lodge of Benevolence shall be paid by the Lodge, and he shall have all the privileges of a subscribing Member.

XXII. Tyler

The Tyler shall be elected annually by a show of hands, and continue in office during the pleasure of the Lodge. He shall attend every Meeting of the Lodge punctually, and take particular care that every Member and Visitor signs his name in the book provided for that purpose, previous to entering the Lodge. He shall get out the Furniture and Regalia of the Lodge, and keep it in proper condition. For these services he shall receive the sum of Ten Shillings and Sixpence for each Meeting.

XXIII. Acceptance of Office

Every Brother elected or appointed to an office, shall, by his acceptance, be considered pledged to a strict performance of the duties attached thereto.

XXIV. Banquet

A Banquet shall be given on the day of Installation, and from time to tie, as the funds may permit; the WM, for the time being, shall have power to order light refreshments to be given after ordinary Lodge Meetings, and visitors partaking of same shall be paid for pro rata by the Member inviting them.

XXV. Honorary Members
Honorary Members shall comprehend those Brethren upon whom the Lodge may confer that distinction as a mark of respect and in consideration of services rendered to the Lodge.

XXVI. Committee on Qualification to Take Office
There shall be a Committee of Installed Masters and Past Masters, formed once in every year at a convenient date previous to the May Meeting, whose duty it shall be to examine into the capability of every Brother desirous of taking office in the Lodge, and to report to the Master upon the qualifications of the brethren so presenting themselves for the efficient discharge of their respective duties.

XXVII. Permanent Committee
A permanent Committee consisting of the WM, Wardens, Past Masters, Treasurer, Secretary and three Brethren appointed by the Lodge annually at the April Meeting, shall audit the Treasurer's account, superintend the finances and property of the Lodge, and consider any special matter regarding its interests. The Committee shall be summoned to attend previous to the Lodge Meeting in May. No business shall be transacted by the Committee unless two at least of the elected Brethren are present thereat and sign the report; the result of their proceedings shall be reported at the next regular Meeting of the Lodge for approval and a Balance Sheet shall be printed and issued with the next Lodge Summons to each Member. The expenses attending the Meeting will be paid out of the Lodge Funds.

XXVIII. Inventory
An Inventory of the Books, Furniture, Regalia and Property of the Lodge shall be entered in the Minute Book which shall be examined and compared by the Deacons or Director of Ceremonies, and by the Master Elect, previous to his Installation; and such Furniture, regalia and other Property shall be insured in the name of the Treasurer for the time being, in trust for the Lodge.

XXIX. PM Jewel
In the event of the Lodge being desirous to testify to a retiring WM the appreciation of his services to the Lodge by presenting him with a PM Jewel, the amount for the same shall be voted from the Lodge Funds at a cost of Seven Guineas.

XXX. Change of Address
Any Member changing his residence, shall forthwith send notice in writing thereof to the Secretary.

XXXI. Alteration of the By-Laws
The By-Laws shall be read once in every year in open Lodge, and notice must be given in writing, with the names of the Proposer and Seconder, to the WM, of any motion to alter, abrogate, or add to them, which the WM will appoint the Secretary to read in open Lodge, and insert the same in the Summons for the next regular Lodge Meeting, there to be discussed; and if approved by two-thirds of the members present, and confirmed by a like proportion at the next regular Lodge Meeting, shall form part of the By-Laws for the Government of the Lodge.

Confirmed by the M.W.Grand Master
E. Letchworth, G.S.
26th July 1905

Above left to right: Lord Northampton, HRH The Duke of Kent, Earl Cadogan, Charles Firth
and David Calderhead in 2001 at the London Palladium.

Below: Dick Tubb, Worshipful Master 1962-1963. Front of Ladies Festival menu.

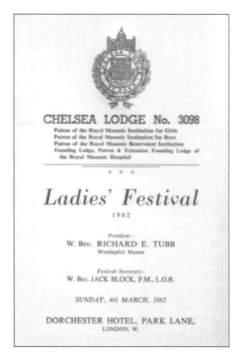

Chapter 10

PAST MASTERS OF THE LODGE

1	*JAMES W. MATHEWS, PGStB	Founder 1905
2	*ALBERT LE FRE, PAGDC	Founder 1906
3	*THEODORE SCHREIBER (Serpentello)	Founder 1907
4	*GEORGE H. COBLEY (Hy Coutts)	Founder 1908
5	*WALTER H. HITCH, PGStB	Founder 1909
6	*ALFRED W. H. BEALES, LR (Harry Bawn)	Founder 1910
7	*WALTER F.K.WALTON	Founder 1911
8	*GEORGE H. DYBALL, PAGStB	Founder 1912
9	*ERNEST R. LESTER, LR	Founder 1913
10	*WILLlAM H. ROBERTS, LGR (Atlas)	1914
11	*ALBERT BRADY (Felino)	1915
12	*HENRY W. J. CHURCH (Hal Chapter)	1916
13	*DOUGLAS WHITE	1917
14	*ERNEST J. SMITH, LGR (Erne Chester)	1918
15	*WILLIAM J. WELLS (Frank Hardie)	1919
16	*HAROLD G. HICKMOTT (Harold Findon)	1920
17	*JAMES E. YOUNG, LGR (Jimmie Athlone)	1921
18	*E. A. WARSAW, PAGStB (Erne Warsaw)	1922
19	*J. BREWSTER GREEN (Bruce Green)	1923
20	*WILLIAM H. MAY (Henry W. May)	1924
21	*W. J. MACMANUS, LGR (W. J. MacKay)	1925
22	*JOSEPH A. ELLISON, LGR (J. W. Ellison)	1926
23	*ERNEST G. GOODWIN, LR	1927
24	*JAMES PILLING (J. P. Ling)	1928
25	*W. V. MALIVOIRE (Will Collinson)	1929
26	*PHINEAS HEADWORTH, LGR	1930
27	*JOHN ENZER	1931
28	*ALFRED ARTOIS	1932
29	*J. M.T.VOST, LGR	1933
30	*W. V. PERMANE	1934
31	*GEORGE W. BATT, LGR	1935
32	*GEORGE W. BATT, LGR	1936
33	*F. BRAUND BOX, PAGDC	1937
34	*G. MARRIOTT EDGAR	1938
35	*JOE MORRISON, PAGStB	1939
36	*E. CHESTER SMITH	1940
37	*ALFRED CRUIKSHANK, LGR	1941
38	*JACK BLOCK, LGR	1942
39	*ERNEST HAMBLETON	1943
40	*A.VICTOR DREWE	1944
41	*A. J. CHESTER BISHOP, LGR (Chester Field)	1945
42	*HENRY F. THOMAS, LGR	1946
43	*PHILIP FRY, LGR (Phil Rallis)	1947
44	*REGINALD C. EAST	1948
45	*CHARLES PERMANE	1949
46	*GEORGE E. HILL	1950
47	*WALTER ARTHUR JONES (Wallie Stewart)	1951

48	*HARRY NEWMAN, PAGDC	1952
49	*CYRIL EDWARD SMITH, LGR	1953
50	*PAUL CLIFFORD	1954
51	*HARRY JAY FINK, PGStB	1955
52	*G. A. CHARLES ROSE, LGR	1956
53	*ERIC CHARLES TANN, LGR	1957
54	*CYRIL HAROLD HARLING, LGR	1958
55	*ERIC SIDNEY COOK	1959
56	*BENJAMIN WRIGHT, LGR	1960
57	*RICHARD EDWARD TUBB	1961
58	*HARRY STANLEY, LGR	1962
59	BARRY SIMONS	1963
60	GEORGE MARKS, LGR	1964
61	*ISSY BONN	1965
62	MAX LEWIN	1966
63	GEORGE F. FERRIE	1967
64	WILLIAM O. HUDSON	1968
65	RONALD RUSSELL WRIGHT	1969
66	VINCENT ADOLPH PERMANE, LGR	1970
67	JAMES EDWARD QUINN, LGR	1971
68	CHARLES DAVIS, LGR	1972
69	HUBERT WARREN, LGR	1973
70	MICHAEL R. THOMAS, PProvGDC	1974
71	PHILIP JOSEPH, LGR	1975
72	ALAN WREN	1976
73	PAUL JOSEPH, LGR	1977
74	TED ALEXANDER, PProvJGW	1978
75	*PAUL RICH, LGR	1979
76	*MICHAEL HILL, LGR	1980
77	GEORGE MULLINS, LGR	1981
78	GEORGE MULLINS, LGR	1982
79	*PHILIP WILSON	1983
80	*DOUGLAS PERRY	1984
81	PAUL GANJOU, LGR	1985
82	FREDDIE DAVIES	1986
83	LAURIE TAYLOR, LGR	1987
84	PAUL JOSEPH, LGR	1988
85	RONALD FINDON	1989
86	*BERNARD SPEAR, LGR	1990
87	DAVID CALDERHEAD, PAGDC	1991
88	Dr EDWARD CALLISTER, PPGOrg	1992
89	DAVID HILLMAN, LGR	1993
90	FRANK HOLDER, LGR	1994
91	NORMAN GRAY, SLGR	1995
92	RICHARD HILLMAN	1996
93	MICHAEL RAMSDEN	1997
94	KENNETH ANDREWS	1998
95	*PAUL RICH, LGR	1999
96	ROGER DE COURCEY, PAGDC	2000
97	JIM DAVIDSON, OBE	2001
98	PETER ELLIOTT	2002
99	PAUL WOOD	2003
100	RAY DONN	2004

* Deceased

Musical Masters of Chelsea Lodge

Chapter 11

MEETING PLACES

Freemasons' Hall, Great Queen Street, London

It seems appropriate that the first meeting place for Chelsea Lodge was in a London theatre. The Chelsea Palace of Varieties, as it became known upon opening on 13 April 1903, was located at 232-242 Kings Road, Chelsea, the site of the original Wilkinson's Sword factory, manufacturers of guns and swords. The factory had become established behind the houses in Sydney Street with an entrance onto the King's Road to the west of Manor Terrace North. Chelsea Palace was designed by the architectural practice of Wylson and Lang. The theatre, faced in terracotta, had a capacity of 2524 persons. The developer was Chelsea Palace Syndicate. **Henri Gros** was the first manager from 1903-1910. He was a Founder of Chelsea Lodge. **Edward Swanborough**, who had been manager of the London Pavilion from 1895-1898 moved in to take over as manager of Chelsea Palace from Henri Gros who took over as Director of Theatres. Gros also had control of the Metropolitan Theatre, Edgware Road from 1893-1911. In 1905 the acting manager of Chelsea Palace was **Leon Zeitlin**.

Those were days when one could be entertained in the gods for four hours - for threepence - and see about 40 turns. A penny on a programme, a penny on a packet of cigarettes and another copper for a beer afterwards. The first show in April 1903 was called Down South described as An American Show. The artistes that night were Ruth Davenport, Madge Russell and Fred Farren.

In The Referee dated 20 September 1903 the paper reported: "The sustained quality of the entertainment provided by the Chelsea Palace management has taken its place in the very front of suburban theatres".

CHELSEA PALACE

THEATRE, King,s Road, Chelsea, S.W.3

Monday, October 12th, 1925

TWICE NIGHTLY at 6.40 and 8.55

PERSONAL VISIT OF

BROMLEY CHALLENOR

IN

ARE YOU
A MASON?

A YELL IN THREE ACTS

Played by the Full London Company, including

ENID COOPER

Direct from the Successful Revival at the

KINGSWAY & FORTUNE Theatres, London

(By arrangement with Chas. Frohman, Inc.

W. SHELTON, PRINTER, HAMMERSMITH.

From 1903-1906 the manager of the Palace was **Edward Swanborough**, a Founder of Chelsea Lodge. In its heyday the Palace attracted all the famous names such as Charlie Chaplin, **George Robey**, Vesta Tilley, **Wee Georgie Wood**, Florrie Ford, Randolph Sutton, G.H.Elliott, Gracie Fields, Sir Harry Lauder and Little Tich. Also on the Palace bills has been the legendary Lily Langtree, actress Ellen Terry (who lived in Chelsea and spoke on the opening night in April 1903), Bransby Williams, Harry Tate (with his famous 'motoring' sketch), Kate Carney, Nellie Wallace, Dolly Harmer, George Gray, Syd Fields and Max Miller. The Palace staged ballet, opera, all-in wrestling as well as dramatic productions by Shaw and Shakespeare. Its Christmas pantomimes were the highlight of the year for several generations of local children. Sadly the cinema, the Second World War and television combined to put the Music Halls out of business. Even after the war, Clarkson Rose's musical shows such as *Twinkle* and Paul Raymond's mixture of circus and nude shows were still filling the stalls.

George Robey would always go for a drink after his show at "The Wellesley Arms" in Sydney Street, to the delight of the locals in the bar. The landlord at that time was William Wilmsworth.

Chelsea Palace as a cinema lasted for just a fortnight. The projection apparatus was brought for two weeks and the films shown were *One Exciting Night* and *The Prisoner of Zenda*.

Chelsea probably has more blue plaques to the square mile than anywhere else to the many

artistes, authors, actors, landed gentry, royalty, saints, eccentrics and architects that have resided or worked there.

The street names recall the history not just of Chelsea but also of nationally and internationally famous individuals who have shaped our lives, such as Viscount Cheyne, Sir Hans Sloane, Lord Cadogan of Oakley or King Charles II whose private road on which the Chelsea Palace later stood is still called the King's Road. He used the route when travelling between Whitehall and Hampton Court. As late as the reign of George III it was referred to as 'The King's Private Road' and a pass was necessary for anyone else to use it.

A circuit called Variety Theatre Consolidated bought Chelsea Palace in 1925, and it came under Granada Theatres control in 1951.

In June 1953 when HM The Queen was crowned, many theatres had closed but in Chelsea the love of music hall shone through. To celebrate the grand occasion Chelsea Palace presented an up-to-date version of the music hall, with the Beverley Sisters, Wilson, Kepple and Betty, Robin Richmond, the Crazy Gang

George Mullins the last manager of the Chelsea Palace

and a ventriloquist named Harry Benet who once lost his dummy and decided to do his act without one. On that sentimental night many stars of the early days were present and rose in their seats to acknowledge the applause of their faithful admirers.

The whole of Chelsea was shocked when they learned in March 1957 that the Palace was to close that month, the latest victim of the entertainments tax. However, the manager **George Mullins**, said; "We hope that the closure will only be a temporary measure and that the Budget may bring some entertainment tax relief which will enable us to re-open again." Apart from six months out of action due to bombing in 1940, the Chelsea Palace had never closed its doors since its audience booed and cheered its melodramatic offerings soon after the turn of the century.

The Palace closed as a live theatre in 1957. On 18 August 1957 Variety Theatre Consolidated of 123 Regent Street, London W1 wrote to the Chief Clerk of Chelsea Borough Council informing him that as from 19 August 1957 onwards Chelsea Palace would be known as Granada, Chelsea. So, Chelsea Palace, an old building, echoing with the patter of red-nosed comics and tap dancers' 'routines', came to the aid of the modern medium of entertainment - television. Granada's television operation took over and began conversion for broadcasting purposes to augment its purpose built Manchester studio centre. Chelsea was so much a part of Granada that it became "Studio 10" and operated until the mid-1960s with many top variety shows. When Granada eventually vacated Chelsea Palace, it was taken over by developers who demolished the building in 1966 and, where this once famous London landmark had stood for more than sixty years, built a branch of the furniture store Heal's on the site.

Sir John Betjeman moved to Chelsea as a child and remained there until his death. He fought valiantly to save the Chelsea Palace. "It was replaced", he said "by the cheapest and ugliest shopping and residential development in London."

A more recent mention of Chelsea Palace was in the New Year Honour List of 2004 when Roy Hudd received the OBE. He took a swipe at those who suggested the word "Empire" be deleted from future honours saying: "I don't care if it is the British Empire, Croydon Empire, Chelsea Palace or Lewisham Hippodrome, I am delighted to be thought of."

Chapter 12

SOME PERSONALITIES OF THE LODGE

Alphabetical

Mick ABRAHAMS

Musician. Born 7 April 1943. The late 1960s yielded a remarkable crop of British blues-based rock guitarists, including Eric Clapton, Jimmy Page, Rory Gallagher, Peter Green and Mick Abrahams.

The roots of Mick's musical career were typical of aspiring guitarists at that time working with various rhythm and blues groups. By 1967 he had become a founder member of Jethro Tull. The band's unique blend of blues, jazz and rock was reflected in their first album *Time Was*, which became a UK hit. Another member of Jethro Tull was flute player Ian Anderson who was noted for his wild stage persona. Having two such strong personalities of Abrahams and Anderson as a twin focus was always going to be a recipe for musical incompatibility, and at the end of 1968 Mick Abrahams jumped ship.

While Tull sailed a new course away from the blues under Captain Anderson, Mick formed his own band, dubbed Blodwyn Pig by a hippy friend just back from the Buddhist trail. The band enjoyed a hit album in 1969 *Ahead Rings Out* and the following year *Getting To This.* All was looking good for Blodwyn Pig and America, too, embraced the band in the course of two tours there. However, the old ogre of musical differences reared its ugly head, and Abrahams left his own band. The group soldiered on for a while, but Mick's presence had been too vital a factor in their success, and the Pig died.

The early seventies saw Mick on *Top of the Pops* and *In Concert* with the Mick Abrahams Band and two albums were subsequently released. The band enjoyed success throughout Europe, but record company support was less encouraging and a disillusioned Mick Abrahams effectively quit the music business.

After spending the rest of the seventies and most of the eighties in civvy street, with just the occasional appearance at charity gigs, Mick was persuaded by the enthusiastic response of the fans to these one-off concerts to resuscitate Blodwyn Pig. Far from simply trading on past glories, Mick has spent the nineties writing and recording new music, both with Blodwyn Pig and as a solo artist. In between time he has guested on a number of other artistes' albums, most notably on the Peter Green tribute album *Rattlesnake Guitar* alongside an illustrious Who's Who of the blues.

Today in the new millennium Mick continues to be as busy as he was in the sixties and seventies touring and entertaining the audiences of Europe with his powerful bluesy rock and rockin' blues.

All Mick Abraham's music has been put onto CD and these albums include: *This Was, Ahead Rings Out, Getting To This, A Musical Evening With Mick Abrahams, At Last, All Said and Done, Lies, All Tore Down, Mick's Back, One, Pig in the Middle, See My Way, the Best of Aby, Novox* and *This Is.* In addition he has recorded two videos, *25th Anniversary* and *From the Heart.*

Michael Timothy Abrahams was initiated into Chelsea Lodge on 17 September 2004.

Paul ADAM

Musical director. Real name Carl Tauber. Born 1912. He began playing violin and graduated to bandleader working at Colony Restaurant in Berkeley Square, London. By 1940 he was working at Rector's Club. At this time he was one of the 'new' bands broadcasting on the BBC, appearing in *Music While You Work* and *Late Night Uninterrupted Music.* On 10 February 1945 he took over from Harry Roy at the Milroy Club. He was the musical director on Paul Carpenter's record *There I've Said It Again* issued on Decca records in August 1945. He would play all night at the Milroy Club and go straight to the BBC studios for an early morning session. Appeared in the film *London Entertains* (1951).

Carl Tauber was initiated into Chelsea Lodge on 20 July 1945.

Bill AIREY-SMITH

Born James William Smith, Barnsley, Yorkshire, 3 June 1904. Drummer and vocalist. Father of trombonist Mike Smith. In the 1930s and 1940s worked with orchestras of Sydney Lipton, Debroy Somers, Howard Jacobs, **Harry Leader**, Reg Batten, Freddie Bretherton, Jack Payne, Jack Hylton and Mantovani. Led own bands and played in various theatre orchestras. He made two recordings for Decca Records in 1933. During World War II served in the Royal Artillery as a driver (1941-2). After being invalided out joined Ben Frankel's Orchestra (August 1942). With **John Blore**'s Orchestra, Marcel Gardner and in Alf Lewis's Trio (1947) before playing for many years for the Crazy Gang at the Victoria Palace, London. Left the music business to become a publican.

James William Smith was initiated into Chelsea Lodge on 17 February 1939. He died 12 December 1982, in Dartford, aged 78 years.

Arthur AISTON

Comedian. Born 1879, Newcastle-upon-Tyne. Educated for a commercial career, but after some three years in that line, left home and joined a travelling theatre, playing second low comedy parts. He afterwards played in many well-known companies, and fulfilled important pantomime engagements, also touring his own fresco shows. When he left the legitimate stage for variety he quickly made good and he appeared at every hall of note in London and the provinces. Arthur Aiston joined Chelsea Lodge on 17 March 1911 from Canongate and Leith Lodge No.5 in Scottish Constitution. Died 31 May 1919, Brixton, SE London, aged 40 years. He left a widow, Ruby, and a small son.

Ray ALAN

Ventriloquist. Born 18 September 1930, Greenwich, London. Educated at Morden Terrace School, Lewisham. He began his show business career as a thirteen year-old callboy at the Lewisham Hippodrome where he was taught the ukelele by George Formby. One year later he had his own act doing impersonations and magic. Moving into ventriloquism, he also played the ukelele, and created the snooty, tipsy, upper-class 'Lord Charles' who graced our television screens in the 1960s and 1970s. This was first tried out at a charity show at Wormwood Scrubs Prison.

Over the years he worked in Variety throughout the country and counts as a highlight touring with Laurel and Hardy.

On television he adapted 'Lord Charles' especially for the small screen and was responsible for a children's television series *Tich and Crackers*. He appeared in panel games and guested on many TV shows including *Good Old Days, Where in the World, Magic Circle, Check-Mates,* and *Britain By Jove.* For radio he presented a documentary on his art, *A Gottle of Gear*, which was later published as a book. He hosted *The Impressionists* on BBC Radio 2. Most of his work today comes from luxury cruise ships.

Ray Alan was initiated into Chelsea Lodge on 16 November 1962.

Frank ALBER

Acrobat. Real name Frank Jennings. Leader of the Jennings Troupe of acrobats and the Jennings Brothers. A Mr Jennings, the jester, was noted as appearing at Hengler's Circus, Dublin in 1873. He was first acknowledged as 'the great somersault thrower', at Hengler's Circus, London early 1885 and also billed as 'American rider', performing leaps and somersaults on horseback. He was seen at other Hengler's show including Manchester in 1901 and Glasgow, 1903.

Frank Jennings was initiated into Chelsea Lodge on 15 November 1907.

Ted ALEXANDER, ARCA (London), PM PProvJW

Musician. Born 1912. Son of Eddie and Ada Alexander. His father was a stage and theatre technician, his mother a teacher and pianist. At the age of eight he joined his father's *White Eyed Minstrel Show* playing the bones and singing 'Mammy' songs, solo. In his spare time he learned to play drums and by the time he was twelve he was a freelance drummer. He formed his own groups at fourteen called Teds Four and later, Teds Five. In 1935 he joined Lambert Wilson's Stage Orchestra, having done a season with Chapmans Circus. Then came a season with Monte Carlo Ballet Company, followed by sessions with George Shearing and Stefan Grapelli.

Ted married Mary Way, 4 June 1939, in

Llandudno. He was playing summer season in the resort at Payne's Ballroom with the Tommy James Band. Issue: One daughter, Christine (1956) and one son, Michael (1958).

Ted played drums and took part in broadcasts with the British Band of A.E.F. etc and many stars of the entertainment world. After demob he joined Henry Hall's Stage Orchestra being featured in a

big drum spectacular for over two years. After Henry disbanded, he played for periods with many West End orchestras - including Joe Loss, Bert Ambrose, Roberto Inglez, Al Tabor, Kenny Grahame Afro Cuban, etc etc. Much freelancing which led eventually to recordings with the group Alien Sex Fiend, led by Nik Wade who happens to be Ted's son-in-law and who is a grand nephew of Sir George Robey — yes **George Robey** - real name Ed Wade, founder member of Chelsea Lodge. It's an odd world!

He suffered three heart attacks in later life and, in February 1989, a fourth heart attack meant an end to active service in music and Masonry.

Ted Alexander was initiated into Chelsea Lodge on 19 March 1948. Climbed ladder erratically due to professional commitments. WM 1978. Other Masonic milestones include: 1969 became WM of St Canna Lodge No.6725 (Wales); 1972 WM Langley Mark Lodge No. 28; 1974 SD Provincial Mark Lodge; 1974 Elevated to Chair of Powys Rose Croix No.406; 1976 Elevated to 30th Degree; 1978 and 1988 Principal of Penarth Royal Arch Chapter; 1983 Elevated to 31st Degree.

Barry ALLDIS
He was the man who helped give The Beatles, the Rolling Stones, Buddy Holly, Paul Anka, Donovan, Petula Clark and scores of other pop stars their big break. The man who had millions of listeners tuning to his Radio Luxembourg programme under the bedclothes. The man who announced John F. Kennedy's death to much of Europe.

Barry was born in Newcastle, New South Wales, Australia in 1930. At the age of six he was playing piano at parties and during his school days he was awarded a five-year trumpet scholarship to the Sydney Conservatorium of Music. Although he was advised to continue his studies at Sydney University, Barry decided to join the staff of a country radio station, 2TM, Tamworth, where he received valuable all - round radio experience. He progressed from record packing to programme arranging, script writing, panel operating and eventually, at the age of eighteen, to announcing.

After some years, Barry was offered a job as disc jockey with 4BH, Brisbane. It was whilst at 4BH, besides presenting feature programmes and his own sponsored radio shows, he worked with visiting American and British stars on outside concerts, compèring and piano playing. In 1955 he packed his bags and headed for England. Once in London he applied for jobs in radio but a promise of work failed to materialise. After several disappointments, he went on a seven-week hitch-hiking trip through seven continental countries with an Aussie friend from Brisbane. This was followed by thirteen jobs in almost as many months ranging from van driver to fireman.

It was whilst playing the piano at a Knightsbridge Club that Barry met Dick Norton (compère of the German end of *Family Favourites* and former Radio Luxembourg disc jockey), who introduced him to an advertising man. Thanks to various old contacts Barry ended up as an announcer in the Grand Duchy.

He made his first appearance on the Radio Luxembourg airwaves on 28 December 1956 presenting the *Top Twenty Show*. On 1 October 1958 he was appointed Head of the British Department. It was whilst with the 'station of the stars' that Barry married a Luxembourg lass, Fernande Stoffels, who was working at the radio station. They had a son and a daughter. Barry was the compère for Radio Luxembourg's *Top Twenty Show* for eight years. The show was very popular throughout Europe and in Scandinavia. He can take credit for helping many pop stars become household names. One such artiste was Paul Anka. He had recorded *Diana* in 1957 and he had never been on radio before. The record was produced in America and Radio Luxembourg made it a hit before it was even released in the United States and Great Britain.

In September 1965 Barry Alldis travelled to Norway as compère and featured solo pianist in Sandefjord near Oslo and given the VIP treatment. 10,000 ecstatic fans crowded the open air auditorium, in spite of pouring rain. He was given a female judo expert as a bodyguard. Before leaving the country Barry was presented with a silver 'Billion Disc' for his unique efforts over a period of ten years for the world's recording artistes.

One of Barry's favourite hobbies was song writing. He wrote over a hundred songs, some of which were published and recorded. During 1968 a few of his compositions were heard on BBC Radio 2 performed by the BBC Radio Orchestra.

He made his debut on *Thank Your Lucky Stars* in 1961 and, at a similar time, his film debut in *Blind Corner*.

Barry Alldis moved from Luxembourg to London in 1966 in order to operate as a freelance disc jockey and compère. He was given a three - month visa by the Home Office to stay in Britain but it literally ran out whilst in the middle of a *Housewives' Choice* contract. With much help from many friends in the BBC, from his MP and also the Australian High Commissioner as well as the former Australian Prime Minister, he won his battle with the Home Office to remain in Britain...indefinitely.

Barry presented various shows for BBC radio and the British Forces Broadcasting Service. He presented a series for Scottish Television called *Bill Tennant Programme*. By 1967 he became a regular host of Radio 2's *Late Night Extra*. When this series finished he joined the *Night Ride* team.

He returned to Radio Luxembourg in 1975 where he continued to be a popular presenter.

John Barry Alldis was initiated into Chelsea Lodge on 21 November 1969. He died in Luxembourg 21 November 1982, aged 52 years.

Les ALLEN

Vocalist. Born 1902, London. Went to Canada with his parents as a child and followed in his father's footsteps and became a clarinettist as a boy.

Returned to England in 1924 as a saxophonist, clarinettist and co-leader with Hal Swain of the eight-piece band and played at the New Prince's Restaurant, Piccadilly. When Hal left in 1926 Les took control and toured with the band including a concert in Berlin. They made fifty recordings in London on the Columbia label between 1924 and 1926.

His next signing was with Alfredo's Band from 1927 to 1928. He played tenor saxophone and sang on 130 recordings with the band on the Edison Bell label.

He was vocalist with Harry Bidgood's Broadcasters on over 100 recordings on the Broadcast label in 1929, many of which were recorded in King George's Hall, London.

In 1930 he also recorded with the Blue River Band and made six recordings on the Piccadilly label. He made one recording on Decca with Sid Bright and His Orchestra and for the Dave Frost Orchestra he sang on five records on the Decca label. The following year he was recording with Howard Godfrey and His Waldorfians making seventeen recordings on the Piccadilly label. His name appears with Eddie Grossbart in the Ambassador Club Band as vocalist on six recordings on the Edison Bell label. With Harry Hudson's Band he appeared playing tenor saxophone and sang on 400 records. He must have been living in the recording studio during the years 1928-1934, because he also recorded with Pete Mandell and His Rhythm Masters (1929), New Mayfair Dance Orchestra (1929), Jay Wilbur's Band (1929-1933), Tommy Kinsman and His Orchestra (1931), Jack Leon's Band (1931) and the Hal Swain Band (1931), Arthur Lally and His Band (1932), Savoy Hotel Orpheans (1932), Nat Star's Dance Orchestra (1932), Mantovani and His Tipica Orchestra (1932-1933), Sidney Lipton's Band (1932-1934) and fellow Chelsea Lodge member **Harry Leader** and His Band (1934). He gained valuable experience on radio, not only as a musician and singer, but also as an announcer, introducing the band's programmes on the air.

Along with two other colleagues from Chelsea Lodge, **Tony Thorpe** and **Max Goldberg**, he sang with the Durium Dance Band making twenty recordings on the Durium label in 1932. At a similar time he appeared as vocalist with Fred Elizalde and His Music recording six songs on the Decca label and turned up on four recordings with Sid Firman and His Band on the Imperial label. In

1932 he was vocalist with Geraldo's Rumba Band and made two recordings on the Columbia label.

He became a huge success as singer with Henry Hall's BBC Dance Orchestra from 1932-1934. It proved a happy and successful association with broadcasts every weekday afternoon, plus Thursday and Saturday evenings from 10.30 to midnight. He took over from Val Rising who famously was the voice on *The Teddy Bear's Picnic*, which sold over a million copies. He met many celebrities of the day who appeared as guests in the show on Saturdays and the popularity of the band brought incredible displays of fan worship. When they appeared at Olympia in 1934 the mob scenes were similar to those which were later experienced by Frank Sinatra and the Beatles.

Les made hundreds of records both as a soloist and band member including, in 1934, *Little Man You've Had a Busy Day*. Assisted by his wife, Anne, and small son, Norman, and accompanied by Sidney Torch on the organ of the Regal Cinema, Edmonton, the record was so successful that it launched Les on a solo career. His good looks and pleasant style endeared him to listeners. He was replaced by Dan Donovan in the BBC Dance Orchestra, who also went on to make a big name for himself. He appeared in the film *The Rosary* (1931).

The offers began to pour in and later in 1935 he starred opposite Anna Lee in a musical film *Heatwave*. His triumphs received the final accolade with the Royal Command Performance at the London Coliseum in 1938 although it was, in fact, his second appearance in this distinguished annual event, as he was a member of the BBC Dance Orchestra when it appeared at the London Palladium in 1934.

In 1937 Les then formed his own instrumental group, the Melody Four, and a vocal group, the Canadian Bachelors, who recorded on the Columbia label. Just before the outbreak of the Second World War, Les spent a week broadcasting from the Avro radio station in Hilversum, Holland. He starred in Emile Littler's revival of the musical comedy *Miss Hook of Holland*, in 1945, touring the major cities of Britain, with **Billy Danvers** playing Mr Hook.

He enjoyed being with his family and one Christmas he played Santa even climbing down the chimney into his son's room. The child was awake and each gift was taken out of a small sack on Santa's back. He also visited hospitals to give out presents.

Les returned to Toronto in 1948 to pursue a second career in the office supply trade, which gave him an opportunity to demonstrate his business efficiency..

In 1954 he came back on a visit to Britain for a reunion with Henry Hall and the BBC Dance Orchestra. He retired in 1971, but still received offers to guest on radio and television. He lost his wife and went into a nursing home where he spent the remainder of his days.

Les Allen was initiated into Chelsea Lodge on 19 January 1945. He died in Toronto, Canada, in 1996, aged 93 years.

Ken ANDREWS, PM

Theatre executive. Born 10 June 1926. He began his professional career in cinema management at the Odeon and Gaumont cinemas in Weston-Super-Mare, Cardiff, Swindon and Bristol. He assisted in the development and operation of first cinema advance booking exercise in England and reintroduction of live shows into the Empire, Cardiff.

By 1961 he managed the fourth Tenpin Bowling Centre opened in England at Kingswood, Bristol and subsequently managed the largest Tenpin Bowl in Europe, the forty-lane Top Rank Bowl in Streatham, London. During his three-year tour he devised and operated a training school for Bowling Centre managers.

Ken Andrews (right) with Paul Ganjou (left) and George Mullins (centre)

Kenneth progressed through area management from 1964-1967 as Assistant Bowling Controller to Circuit Controller of Dancing and Bowling Division of Top Rank, administratively in charge of twenty-four bowling centres, twenty-seven ballrooms and two ice rinks.

A change of venue and company in 1967 took him to the Fortes empire where he became chief executive of Belle Vue (Manchester) Ltd which comprised a large entertainment complex of 80 acres including zoo, fun fair, eight banqueting suites, ballroom with 5,000 capacity, exhibition hall of 100,000 square feet, speedway/stock car stadium with a capacity of 20,000 and Kings Hall with a capacity of 5,800 which housed boxing, wrestling, circus and political rallies. Belle Vue had permanent staff in excess of 300, which rose by part-time employment to 1,200 in the peak season.

Kenneth was also director on joint operation of Belle Vue/Granada 32-lane Tenpin Bowl adjoining the site. During this period he renovated and operated New Brighton Pier, Merseyside. He built and operated the 1,250-seat theatre restaurant 'Golden Garter' in Wythenshawe, which presented top star billing.

In 1972 he spent two years as project executive at Fortes head office in Jermyn Street, London and project managed the building of 'Night Out' theatre restaurant in Birmingham.

Granada Theatres beckoned and in 1974 Kenneth moved across as commercial manager. The company operated thirty-six bingo clubs, twelve cinemas, two bowling centres and a night club. He was responsible for all legal licensing applications and renewals, for maintenance and development work connected with expansion (during this time fifteen new bingo clubs were opened) and for all purchasing. He was asked to stay on after official retirement in 1986 and produced a marketing report recommending expansion in tenpin bowling, which was subsequently accepted by the board.

For two years from 1989 Kenneth operated a leisure consultancy company giving advice on all aspects of leisure development and operation.

Kenneth Andrews was initiated into Chelsea Lodge on 18 March 1988 and ten years later became Worshipful Master. He was Chaplain from 2001-2002.

Stan ANDREWS

Musician, composer, arranger and conductor. Tragedy struck when Stan's mother died when he was born on 20 April 1903, Finchley, London. Son of a railway accountant and amateur bass player, he enjoyed a love for music early on in his life.

Stan was given a good education, attending the private Finchley High School. Early on he showed a great talent as a violinist. In 1914 he won the second place silver medal in one of North London music competitions. After leaving school he began taking lessons at the Royal Academy of Music. He entered the All England music competition in 1919, and won the gold medal. He began playing jazz as a semi - professional at the Brent Bridge Hotel, Hendon. He turned professional to tour with Jack Hylton.

Stan played trombone, clarinet, violin and alto saxophone and made recordings with Jack Hylton Orchestra (1930) on HMV label; Jack Jackson Orchestra (1933-1939) on HMV label; Jay Wilbur Band (1933-1935) on Rex and Eclipse labels; Hatchett's Swingtette (1940-1942) on the Decca label. He also worked with Lew Stone, Arthur Roseberry, Howard Jacobs, Carroll Gibbons and Spike Hughes. Became great friends with Stephane Grapelli with whom he worked with Hatchett's Swingtette.

In 1942 Stan joined the Jack Payne Orchestra, as first violin, deputy conductor and arranger. During the war the orchestra played all over Great Britain performing for military as well as civilian audiences. In 1944 he met Geraldine Cooper, a dancer in West End shows. They had five children, one of whom became famous as an actor, Anthony Andrews.

When Jack Payne disbanded his orchestra in 1946, Stan continued to arrange and, in 1947, began his own group in the Orchid Room in Berkeley Square. He also led his orchestra on the BBC Light programme, which he conducted weekly. The late 1940s and early 1950s gave Stan the opportunity to exercise his skills as a conductor, primarily a deputy for **Stanley Black** and the BBC Dance Orchestra.

He preferred the work of an arranger to all other musical tasks and, with his superb theoretical knowledge and perfect pitch, was a much sought after arranger for Geraldo, Carroll Gibbons, John Firman and Jack Payne. He would often stay up all night, working on arrangements which would be needed the next morning and delivering all the parts to the musicians himself by 10.00am.

Stan also deputised for **Woolf Phillips** with the Skyrockets at the London Palladium where he wielded the baton for many American acts which appeared there. He continued working around the clock, appearing at the Palladium, working through the night on arrangements, and going off to rehearsals in the morning and afternoon. He did extensive arrangements for Vera Lynn and Lizbeth Webb. Stan had been on the staff of music publishers Bradbury Wood for ten years and had written for countless leaders as a freelance. He composed many light descriptive tunes and music for shows and films.

Initiated into Chelsea Lodge 20 October 1939. Like so many of his fellow musicians, Stan was a heavy smoker, and in March 1953 he became very ill with a respiratory illness. He was diagnosed as having terminal lung cancer. He died at his Finchley home 27 October 1953, aged 50 years. His daughter Corrine was christened only three days previously, the ceremony taking place at the sick man's bedside. Stan was buried at Christ Church, Finchley, 31 October 1953.

Joe ARBITER

Musician. Born 1905. A top-flight alto-saxophonist, notably playing for Harry Roy. He later became a successful musical instrument wholesaler. He founded his own business, which became J and I Arbiter Ltd, when his son Ivor joined him, and in due course, with Ivor in control, Dallas-Arbiter and eventually CBS-Arbiter. In his younger days he lived with his cousin, the successful drummer, **Joe Daniels**.

Joseph Hyman Arbiter was initiated into Chelsea Lodge on 19 May 1944. His son, instrument maker, **Ivor David Arbiter** was initiated into Chelsea Lodge on 21 March 1952. Joe died 8 March 1962, aged 57 years.

Tom ARNOLD, OBE

Producer and theatrical manager. Thomas Charles Arnold was born in Yorkshire in 1897, son of George Henry and Louise Arnold. His ambition from an early age was to become a showman and, at eighteen, he launched boldly on the career he had deliberately chosen. He joined the office of Sir Walter de Frece, whose wife was the famous Vesta Tilley. Realising the possibilities of the touring entertainment, he formed travelling companies, whose cooperation enabled him to establish a relatively lucrative business as a promoter of many kinds of amusements. He produced over 300 revues and musical shows. In the days when revues were a novelty in London he took to the road with stage attractions bearing such titles as *The Showbox, Better and Better, Seeing Life, Love and Laughter, The Melody Box* and *The Band Box.* In September 1925 he put on a *Folies Bergère* show at the London Palladium.

As a promoter his faith in the business was justified. However, he decided to confine his amusement activities to the provincial field and continued to finance and produce musical plays for presentation at theatres throughout the country. Some were notable versions of originals staged in London by the late Sir Charles Cochran and included *Keep Dancing* and *This Year of Grace*. In 1933 he secured the right to *Waltzes from Vienna* and subsequently also toured with *Streamline, Stop Press, The Merry Widow, Anything Goes, Balalaika*, and other successful pieces featuring light music and comedy.

His first attempt at pantomime production was in 1933 at Birmingham, and he was so impressed by the result, that in the following year when, on the death of Julien Wylie, the pantomime interests of the famous manager became available, he acquired them. Tom lost no time in exploiting his new acquisition and was soon firmly established in London, where he not only set up a new high standard in Christmas pantomimes but also entered into theatrical association with Ivor Novello.

In spite of his many commitments Tom went on sending talented companies round the country in musical plays which had been a success in London, such as *Wild Oats, Me and My Girl, The Fleet's Lit Up* and *What's Going on Here?* In March 1939, he joined Ivor Novello in staging *The Dancing Years, Perchance to Dream, King's Rhapsody* and *Gay's The Word* at Drury Lane, and in March 1944, he acquired the lease of the Palace Theatre, the partnership was resumed and maintained until Novello's sudden death. Though strikingly dissimilar in some of their characteristics, the two men had much in common in theatrical matters, and were firm friends, and Tom's loss was apparent. However, the show has to go on and he continued to extend his interests, produced pantomimes in many provincial cities, presented musical comedies and big scale ice entertainment in London and Wembley Stadium, together with four seasons at the Stoll Theatre, London. He achieved fresh distinction in December 1947 by establishing a mammoth Christmas circus at Harringay Arena which added to his fame year by year. Tom Arnold's touring companies were almost as well known in South Africa and Australia as in this country. At one time his film *Waltzes from Vienna* was being shown in one New York cinema, while, as a musical, it was having record successes at another theatre.

His more ambitious projects included *Pickwick* (1963), *Maggie May* (1964), *Our Man Crichton* (1964) and *The Solid Gold Cadillac* (1965).

He presented the first operetta on ice, *Rose Marie*, 1950; promoted Noel Coward's *Ace of Clubs* (musical play), Cambridge Theatre, London, 1950; presented American-style Rodeo show at Harringay Arena, 1952; musical show starring Anna Neagle, 1952; final stage presentation of *Life With the Lyons*, 1952; he presented the annual Latin Quarter Revue at London Casino. He was joint proprietor with Emile Littler of Palace, Casino and Cambridge Theatres, London. Proprietor, Sports Stadium, Brighton. Director, Piccadilly Theatre, London; New Britannia Pier, Great Yarmouth; Brighton Palace Pier; Brighton West Pier; Ramsgate Olympia Ltd; Radio Manx etc etc.

Thomas Charles Arnold was initiated into Chelsea Lodge on 20 September 1918. For more than forty years Tom kept his finger firmly on the pulse of middle-class theatrical taste and became an impresario who was 'king of pantomime'. Appointed OBE in Queen's New Year Honours, 1969. He died in St Mary's Hospital, Paddington 2 February 1969, aged 72 years.

A.C. ASTOR

Ventriloquist/theatre director. Real name Thomas Ferguson. Born 1885. Went under the name of either Arthur Charles Astor or simply A.C. Astor. A popular personality who topped the bill at various theatres around the British Isles. He also was one of the first ventriloquists to appear on television during its experimental stages in 1936 from Alexander Palace in the series *Cabaret*. He continued to do so until 1939, when transmissions were suspended because of the outbreak of war.

Thomas Ferguson was initiated into Chelsea Lodge on 20 July 1917.

Max BACON

Comedian, drummer, raconteur. Born 1 March 1904, London. He was employed by his father as a commercial traveller, but did not come up to scratch and was sacked. He was always out drumming when he should have been getting orders. Began his career as a dance band drummer joining Ambrose in March 1927. Played with the band on radio and on tour in variety with the

Ambrose Octet. He then teamed with Sam Browne and Evelyn Dall as the variety act *Stars of Radio* and later became a bill-topping soloist with his fractured-grammar specialities, notably *Gimbel with the Cymbal, 'William To-Hell and Little Red Hooding Ride.*

He began to concentrate on comedy in 1941 and as a solo comedian he was well-known in variety and on radio, distinguishing his act with a drum

solo finale. During the latter part of his career he turned to straight acting, including a West End appearance in *The Diary of Ann Frank.*

He appeared in fourteen films: *Soft Lights and Sweet Music* (1936), *Calling all Stars* (1937), *Kicking the Moon Around* (1938), *King Arthur Was a Gentle-man* (1942), *Miss London Ltd* (1943), *Bees In Paradise* (1944), *Give us The Moon* (1944), *Gambler and the Lady* (1952), *Take a Powder* (1953), *The Entertainer* (1960), *Eyes of Annie Jones* (1963), *Privilege* (1967), *Chitty Chitty Bang Bang* (1968) and *Nine Ages of Nakedness* (1969).

He appeared in the Noel Coward musical *Present Arms* at the Prince of Wales Theatre, London in May 1940. He made an 'unofficial' appearance in the 1951 Royal Variety Performance dressed as King Farouk, and acting as a stooge for the Crazy Gang. He later played a number of straight roles in plays, including *The Diary of Anne Frank.*

He was a member of the Grand Order of Water Rats.

Max was constantly munching and carried a bag of sweets in one pocket and a packet of biscuits in the other. He loaned his drum kit to his nephew, Maurice Bacon, drummer with the 1960s pop group the Love Affair.

Max David Bacon was initiated into Chelsea Lodge on 17 December 1937. Died 3 December 1969, aged 65 years.

Dick BALL

Musician. Son of a fireman Richard Marsh Ball was born at Southwark Fire Station, London 26 December 1903. He attended Greenwich Naval

School but was discharged as unfit and chose to make a life in music, playing tuba, sousaphone and, latterly, string bass. His early career saw him in theatre and silent cinema orchestra pits, working in Cambridge and Stoke-on-Trent. He started his dance band career with 'Hutch' at the Empress Rooms, Kensington, in the late 1920s.

Dick also worked on the White Star Lines (Hamburg-New York) in addition to the land-based orchestras of Charlie Tucker, Jack Shields, Howard Jacobs and Joe Orlando where he met pianist and arranger **Stanley Black.**

He made numerous recordings in the 1930s. His first was with Marius B. Winter's Hotel Cecil Dance Band in December 1928, to be followed by the Eddie Grossbart Band who recorded on the Edison Bell record label. In 1932 he recorded with Arthur Lally and Lew Stone (1932) and Howard Jacobs (1933).

Dick moved into the big time when he joined the Ambrose Orchestra, his first recording with them being called *Memories of the Mayfair* and made 5 October 1933. He played alongside such famous names as Ted Heath, **Max Goldberg, Lew Davis** and Danny Polo. He also broadcast and recorded extensively with the Ambrose Orchestra. It is rumoured that the musicians working for Ambrose would share a £2000 per week salary and lived superstar lifestyles.

Jay Wilbur's recordings from around 1935 feature Dick on string bass. He was also two years with the Maurice Winnick Orchestra at the Dorchester and the Lyceum.

Dick performed with some of the hottest jazz groups assembled for recording sessions in Britain in the 1930s including Six Swingers (1934), Embassy Eight (1935) and the Rhythm Rascals (1935).

In 1935 Dick kept up a family tradition by buying a newsagent's shop in Upper Norwood, London SE19 that his brother Louis ran when Dick was on the road. The shop was badly damaged by enemy bombs in 1942. Sadly this affected Dick in many ways and he decided to withdraw from the world of jazz and dance bands.

In 1943 he joined the War Reserve Police and served at Bootle, Lancashire but his love for music refused to die and he joined the police band.

Dick was married and had a son (bass player Cliff Ball) and three daughters. He played string bass at their weddings and for his own golden wedding anniversary in 1974.

Richard Marsh Ball joined Chelsea Lodge on 20 December 1935. He died of cancer on 5 February 1980. *When Day is Done* was played at his funeral. There is a commemorative rose bush at West Norwood Crematorium near where his ashes were placed.

George BARCLAY

Comedian, variety agent. Born 1868. Popular comedian during the days of music hall and was one of the 'Brewers of Fun'. His songs included: *Mary Ann* (1893), *Katie McGinty* (1893) and *The Two Squires* (1894). He retired from performing and became one of Britain's top theatrical agents, so much so that from 1927 he was known as 'King of the Agents.' He operated from a large Victorian house, Boylands Oak, in Brixton which was a legend in the world of variety. Ted Ray remembers that the waiting room was a huge drawing room filled with heavy furniture and adorned by handsome silver candelabra. Round the wall were oil paintings of Derby winners. George was also a considerable figure on the turf and owned horses.

Although a big name in the world of variety George was only small in stature being just 5ft tall. He wore a cloth cap and smoked heavily, invariably Woodbines.

He married Kate Paterson (1869-1950) when she was just sixteen at St Mary's, Newington; they met at the Old Vic when it was still the Royal Victoria Palace. He was a step dancer. She was singing the coster songs that were to make her famous. George steered his wife's career and it was he who suggested she change her name of Kate Paterson to Kate Carney. She used to joke that she was the only Music Hall artiste to sleep with her agent and 'still hold her head up in public'.

Both were south Londoners born and bred. He was born at Waterloo and his wife at Trinity-Square in the Borough. For over 33 years they lived at Brixton Hill.

During the Second World War a bomb dropped near their home in Brixton and George put out a notice saying that Hitler had tried to kill him but had failed.

Kate Carney dressed in coster dress of 'pearly' and wore a large hat trimmed with enormous ostrich feathers. She played opposite the great costers of the day such as Albert Chevalier and Alec Hurley. Her songs told of street markets selling anything from cauliflowers to cock linnets. She had her own company of step-dancers and cake-walkers and, after the First World War, a mouth organ band. In 1935 she appeared in *Cavalcade of Variety*, the finale of the Royal Variety Performance at the London Palladium.

George Barclay had been a dancer, actor, theatrical agent, racehorse owner and, in the 1940s, owner of the music halls the old 'South London' which was blitzed during the Second World War, the Camberwell Palace and the Grand, Clapham.

In 1942 he reopened the Grand, which had been closed for eighteen months, with a pantomime. His wife topped the bill there shortly after her 70th birthday.

George Barclay and Kate Carney were the only couple in the theatrical business to have celebrated their golden wedding. They were just one year short of their diamond wedding anniversary when George took ill.

His last theatrical venture was at the Grand, Clapham, which he owned, where he lavished his usual generous hospitality and gave many unknown turns a chance.

George Robert Barclay was initiated into Chelsea Lodge on 15 October 1920. Died 30 January 1944, aged 75 years. He was buried at Putney Vale cemetery. On the way the cortège halted for one minute outside the Grand Theatre, Clapham, which George had owned and managed since 1941.

Kate Carney continued to perform until shortly before her death in 1950 at the age of 80.

Ken BARNES

Described as one of Britain's best pantomime dames he spanned some 30 years as a stalwart of Christmas pantomimes.

He was born 12 August 1919 at Islington, north London. His father was a Fleet Street printer who performed in his spare time in *Barnes and Elliott*, a "black and white" variety act of which he was the "white" half. After leaving school Ken followed his father on to the stage, beginning his career as a comedy conjurer.

At the outbreak of the Second World War he was seconded to ENSA (the Entertainments National Service Association). It was here he met his future wife Jeanne, a soubrette dancer specialising in acrobatics on roller-skates. She became his conjurer's assistant and he later joined her in a comedy roller-skating act, in which he performed in drag.

Towards the end of the war they were posted to

India, but told that they should fly out separately. So while Jeanne flew out first by Catalina seaplane, Ken had to wait overnight in a hotel "somewhere in southern England." That evening, in the hotel bar, he met the land and water speed record holder Malcolm Campbell who was holding forth on the dangers of flying. By far the most dangerous aircraft he had ever known was the Avro

Ken Barnes

York, said Campbell. The following morning, Ken arrived at the airfield to find an Avro York waiting to take him to India.

He and his fellow-travellers arrived in India in sweltering heat and found themselves billeted in digs above a laundry, from which the steam billowed, adding to their discomfort. When they complained that the room was too hot, they were brusquely informed: "Sorry, but Vera Lynn never complained when she was in that room last week."

Once the war had ended Ken and Jeanne took their roller-skating act to Germany to entertain the American occupation forces. The GIs had never seen a drag act before and their performances proved so popular that they were invited back for several seasons.

Back in this country they continued to perform together in variety and in pantomime, but in the 1950s Jeanne Barnes left the stage for a job as a costumier for the Black and White Minstrels.

Ken began a solo career, appearing in variety

shows during the summer season and in pantomime in the winter. He also made frequent appearances on television in the *Ken Dodd Show.*

Ken and Jeanne moved out of London in the 1960s and headed for Norfolk where they opened a rare and tropical bird farm in Dereham. Ken still carried on touring and Jeanne looked after the farm.

Ken refused to retire at 65 (show business people have not heard of the word "retirement") and appeared as an extra in Anglia Television's successful *Tales of the Unexpected* and the BBC wartime comedy series *'Allo 'Allo.*

In later years he found himself in demand as a pantomime director and he staged several shows in theatres around the country.

Ken Barnes was a joining member of Chelsea Lodge in January 1957. He died in December 2001, aged 82 years.

Harry BAWN

Real Name Alfred W.H. Beales. Theatrical Proprietor, Empire Theatre, Edmonton. Born 5 March 1872, Knightsbridge, London. Educated St Mary's College, Chelsea. Recreation: riding, motoring and golfing.

Initiated into Earl's Court Lodge 2765. Founder Chelsea Lodge. Founder Chelsea Chapter. WM Chelsea Lodge 1910-1911. Died 28 October 1928, aged 56 years.

Louis BENJAMIN

Box office manager/theatrical impresario. Born 17 November 1922, Stoke Newington, the son of a Jewish cobbler. He attended Highbury County Secondary School. Rose from office boy to become one of the most powerful figures in theatreland. In 1937 he joined Moss Empires, the variety theatre chain, as an office boy in the accounts department at the age of fourteen and returned thirty-three years later as managing director. His responsibilities included the Palladium and Victoria Palace in London and theatres in Birmingham, Bristol, Liverpool, Manchester and Nottingham.

The company later took over the Stoll group, which put Louis in charge of twelve London theatres and made him the first person to run both the Palladium and the Theatre Royal, Drury Lane. During the 1970s and 1980s he was one of the most important figures in the West End.

He described himself as "producer, entrepreneur,

investor, manager, booker and landlord". He stood for uncomplicated entertainment and tried to put on shows that would not make an audience feel embarrassed.

Louis Benjamin accompanies HM Queen Elizabeth, the Queen Mother at a Royal Variety Performance

Louis was proud of attracting big American names to the Palladium, often having to persuade them to take much lower fees than they could command at home. He engaged Shirley Maclean for her first British stage appearance and brought over Frank Sinatra, Bing Crosby, Liberace, Ginger Rogers and Liza Minnelli.

He was known in the business as Benjie. He was a small, slight man of restless energy for whom show business was a hobby as well as a job. He admitted having no interests apart from his work.

Louis Benjamin served in the Second World War in India, Burma and Singapore and, after demobilisation in 1945, became second assistant manager, the youngest on the circuit, at the London Palladium. Three years later he moved to the Victoria Palace where he was assistant manager. In 1953 he took over the Winter Gardens in Morecambe, running a theatre as well as a ballroom, fairground and wrestling.

He left theatrical management in 1959 for Pye

Records, which had been acquired by the Moss Empires parent company, ATV. Louis joined as sales controller and rose to managing director in 1963. He introduced the industry's first cheap pop label, the Golden Guinea. He built up a strong list of artistes including Kenny Ball, Petula Clark and Sandie Shaw, and once had nine out of the top ten records in the hit parade. He remained with Pye after taking charge of Moss Empires in 1970 and also became deputy chairman of ATV's successor company, Associated Communications Corporation, which was headed by Lord Lew Grade.

In 1979 Louis succeeded Grade's brother, Lord Bernard Delfont, as organiser of the Royal Variety Performance, staged to help show business charities. For his first show he engaged Yul Brynner and banned jokes about the royal family. On another occasion he banned jokes about the miners' leader, Arthur Scargill. He was prominent in other charitable work through the Variety Club of Great Britain, the Entertainment Artistes' Benevolent Fund and he was Companion of the Grand Order of Water Rats. He was one of the first members of the Westminster Synagogue and was proud of his religious tradition.

Louis brought Elizabeth Taylor to the Victoria Palace to make her first West End appearance in 1981 in *The Little Foxes.*

He retired as head of Stoll Moss in September 1989, having seen *Ziegfeld* crash at the Palladium but *Miss Saigon* successfully launched at the Theatre Royal, Drury Lane.

Louis Isaac Benjamin was initiated into Chelsea Lodge on 21 November 1952. Died 20 June 1994, aged 71 years. He is survived by Vicky, a former dancer whom he married in 1954, and by their two daughters Reica and Diana, both of whom followed him into the theatre business.

David BERGLAS

Magician. Born in Europe 30 July 1926 he was brought up and educated in six different countries and has relatives who comprise eleven nationalities. His wide-ranging early education came about because his father Alfred ran an international family textile business with factories throughout Europe. Although he spoke many languages the one he had most difficulty was with English. He arrived in England in 1938. In time he overcame the problem and later went on to join the Royal Air Force and started training to become a Spitfire pilot. All went well until the RAF

discovered he was underage. Undeterred he signed up with United States Army in 1945. Because of his knowledge of languages he went into the Intelligence Unit based in Germany and was present at the Nuremberg War Crime Trials.

On his return to the UK David studied textiles at Bradford Technical College with a view to entering the family business, but fate took a hand and his life was changed for ever. He attended a meeting of the local magical society and never looked back. David became well known through broadcasts on the BBC and he toured the country, appearing in every major variety theatre as well as performing in the top London night clubs. At a similar time he became one of the first magicians to appear on television which soon led to his first series *Meet David Berglas* in 1954. One feature of this series was his verbal predictions of events that were about to happen! He can also play thirteen different musical instruments.

His internationally acclaimed One-Man-Shows are legendary. Feats of mind-bending magic and mystery that have baffled audiences at many exclusive venues around the world. He has demonstrated the 'impossible' Indian rope trick – in India. He has caused geysers to spout on command and even made an ocean liner tilt – in still waters.

He appeared in the film *Invitation to Magic* (1956).

In 1989 David was elected President of the Magic Circle. In recent years he has devoted much of his time advising technically on films and to training business executives in personal development and memory improvement.

He is also involved in a number of charity organisations, such as the Variety Club of Great Britain and the Grand Order of Water Rats, of which he is a trustee and past King Rat.

David Berglas joined Chelsea Lodge on 17 November 1978.

Frank BIFFO

Musician. Trumpeter and leader. Born 1892. Directed Biffo and His Serenaders. Made recordings for Homochord in 1929. Was a member of Stan Greening's band and recorded for Regal records in 1924-1929; Charles 'Nat' Star in 1929 on Homochord and the Modern Dance Players, directed by Charles Renard for Regal in 1929. He was one of the bands included in the BBCs new plans for dance music in 1936 when they introduced new bands to listeners.

Frank Biffo was initiated into Chelsea Lodge on 14 June 1944.

Stanley BLACK, OBE

Pianist, arranger, composer, conductor. Born 14 June 1913, London. He was classically trained on piano and violin by Rae Robinson and went on to the Mathay School of Music. By the age of eleven he was winning prizes in most of the competitions he entered. He began accompanying silent films and then led a trio at the local Milton Cafe before gaining a scholarship at Trinity College of Music. He also led bands called The Black Hand Gang and the Modernists.

His name began to be nationally recognised after his scoring of the popular song *I Want a Little Girl*

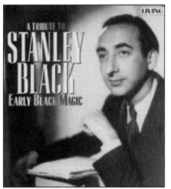

won a *Melody Maker* arranging contest.

Top leaders commissioned his arrangements and he went on to play piano in various bands, notably Harry Roy with whom he toured South America during the late 1930s. He also played professionally at the Empress Cinema, Islington, and worked with Maurice Burman's dance band.

The year 1931 was a busy one for Stanley; he won *Melody Maker* arranging contest, played with Sidney Lipton's Orchestra, and accompanied Leslie 'Hutch' Hutchinson at the London Palladium. The following year he played residency at the Empress Rooms, Kensington and worked with Howard Jacobs, Joe Orlando and Maurice Winnick before joining Lew Stone Band as an arranger and pianist.

Stanley had broadcast and recorded with some of the more distinguished American visitors to Britain, including Coleman Hawkins and Benny Carter. Hawkins had heard him on late night radio shows with Lew Stone's band. When the two eventually met in London the reviewer Edgar Jackson suggested they record together and the highlight of their work is a duet version of *Honeysuckle Rose.*

He was a member of the Harry Roy Band from 1936 to 1938, which included a trip to South

America in 1938. He played piano for Ambrose from 1938-1940 and rejoined Harry Roy from 1941-1942.

Following wartime service with the RAF Stanley became conductor of the BBC Dance Orchestra in 1945, replacing Billy Ternent. As a utility orchestra they were responsible for the music content of all kinds of programmes from light and dance music to various variety shows. He made over 3,000 broadcast during this time. He also introduced a Latin American flavour with series like *Tropical Magic.*

Stanley was also one of Decca Records contract arranger-conductors, providing many backings for solo artistes of the period plus a number of orchestral pieces. Film scoring was another string to his bow. He began writing for the cinema in 1936, with a score for the film *Rhythm Racketeers* and over the years he was associated with many others including *One Wild Oat* and *Lily Marlene.*

On Sunday 8 June 1947 Stanley married well-known vocalist Edna Kaye who sang with Carroll Gibbons and the Savoy Hotel Orpheans as well as Harry Roy, Mantovani and Lou Praeger and their Orchestras. She made many records.

Stanley took part in many vintage radio shows including *Hi Gang* and *Much Binding in the Marsh* and composed the theme music to the popular and long running series *The Goon Show.*

A very popular early fifties radio series highlighting the orchestra was *Top Score*, a peak time show that over a period of time featured the voices of Diana Coupland, Dick James, Marie Benson, Josephine Crombie, Teddy Johnson and the Stargazers. There was also *Spring Serenade* with Edmund Hockridge, Doreen Lundy and John Hanson; *Double Top* with **Alfred Marks** and Anne Shelton, Vera Lynn's *Let's Meet Again* plus many others. During those early fifties Stanley Black with the BBC Dance Orchestra was probably the most listened-to band on radio. Reflecting this they were chosen to lead *a Radio Times* feature on the 1952 Royal Variety Show at Victoria Palace during October.

Coincidentally, October 1952 was the month a rival came on the scene in the shape of the BBC Show Band under the direction of **Cyril Stapleton**. Despite denials from the BBC during November and December that its Dance Orchestra was under any threat, when Stanley's contract came up for renewal in January his eight years with the BBC came to an end.

Taking to the road, he set off on a provincial tour of one-night stands with a dance band that included vocalists Diana Coupland and Monty Norman. By the end of the year they had given way to Alma Warren and Larry Gretton. It was Alma (Lita Roza's sister) who brought Stanley's attention to a gipsy street singer, Danny Purches, and soon he too joined them on the road.

Stanley continued with his film arranging and recording work at Decca where he embarked on a series of LPs with a Latin American flavour and titles like *Sophisticat in Cuba, Tropical Moonlight* and *Stanley Black plays for Latin Lovers.* These discs featured his fine piano virtuosity. He was also to be heard on Radio Luxembourg with his series *Black Magic* (a title later also used for his television series). Not forgotten altogether by the BBC the orchestra turned up on *Star Bill* and Jack Payne's *Off the Record.*

In all he went on to compose, arrange and direct music for about 200 more movies, notably after being appointed musical director of the Associated British Picture Corporation at Elstree Studios in 1958. During the sixties he reverted to a more serious form of music and, when conducting in later years, it was more likely to be a classical orchestra. In 1965 he won a Gramophone Award for his version of Rimsky-Korsakov's *Cappricio Espangnol.*

By the 1990s Stanley had composed almost 200 film themes and signature tunes including: *It Always Rains on Sunday (1948), Laughter in Paradise (1951), The Naked Truth (1951), Too Many Crooks* (1958), *The Long and the Short and the Tall (1961), The Young Ones* (1961) and *Summer Holiday (1962).*

He recorded 40 albums for Decca, President and Hallmark Records. On 10 April 1962 he was presented with a Gold Disc from Decca Records for sales of over one million LPs.

In 1955 he was made life president of the Celebrities Guild of Great Britain. He was a member of the Grand Order of Water Rats.

He was appointed OBE in the New Year Honours, 1986. When he attended the investiture at Buckingham Palace, the military band which was playing incidental music on hearing Stanley's name called out, broke into a Latin American rhythm and played *That Old Black Magic.* The conductor winked at Stanley as he went up to meet HM the Queen.

In 1994 Stanley conducted the BBC Big Band

with Strings at the Queen Elizabeth Hall in London. **Edmundo Ros** also shared the stage. The concert was broadcast on BBC Radio 2 and was such a success that a Japanese recording company invited Stanley and Edmundo into a recording studio in London to make a CD.

In 1999 Stanley was made a Fellow of Trinity College.

Wherever he worked and with whatever orchestra he retained the effortless control of his musicians, who always held him in high regard for his consummate professionalism.

His last broadcast was a documentary on his life in the *Keith Skues Show* on BBC Eastern Counties to celebrate his 89th birthday.

Stanley Black was initiated into Chelsea Lodge in September 1947. He died in London 26 November 2002, aged 89 years.

BONN, Issy, PM

Raconteur and variety agent. Real name Benjamin Levin. Born 20 March 1903, East End of London, son of a butcher, but showed an early inclination to be an entertainer, appearing in school productions and local concert parties.

During the early years of World War I, he continued his activities and won a singing competition, which determined him to proceed with a stage career. In time he became a member of the singing and comedy act known as The Three Rascals, who became a top of the bill attraction and appeared at the Holborn Empire.

From 1923 to 1925 the act continued while Issy (then known as Benny Levin) began to appear as a solo act at the Mile End Empire and other small music halls. His line was sharp Jewish jokes and the singing of broadly sentimental songs like *My Yiddisher Mamma*.

During the 1930s comedy was very rich in Jewish humour, which generally portrayed that

race as totally concerned with the making of money. It is most frequently the other races that we laugh at, but the Jewish community always did have, and still has, a strong inclination to make jokes about themselves. One of the first comedians on British radio in its pre-war days to do so was Issy Bonn. In the early days he was known as 'The Singing Lorry Driver'.

In 1935 he was heard, singing at a cinema, by John Sharman and was given his first chance to broadcast in 1936. With his name finally modified to Issy Bonn, he now became well known on radio in such programmes as *Music Hall* and *Variety Bandbox*.

He appeared in the films *Discoveries* (1939) and *I Thank You* (1941) with Arthur Askey, Richard Murdoch and Lily Morris.

Throughout the Second World War he toured with ENSA in Italy and Germany. In 1946 he wrote and starred in a show *The Big Broadcasts* with a second edition in 1947. The following year he

toured with his own road show *And So We Go On*; in 1949 with *The Melody Lingers* In 1952 he appeared in the TV version of *Music Hall*. He also played straight parts and had been in films and pantomime, continuing throughout his career to entertain and raise money for youth clubs and children's hospitals. His hobby was collecting joke books. In August 1956 he appeared with Lita Roza at the Swansea Empire.

Issy Bonn took part in the final bill at the Metropolitan in Edgware Road on Good Friday, 12 April 1963 after a career of over 40 years on the music hall stage. He was a talented musician and played guitar, clarinet and trumpet.

He gave up appearing in shows in the 1960s and took on the management of a small theatre in Newquay, Cornwall.

During his career he recorded with the orchestras of Jay Wilbur, Harry Bidgood, **Phil Green** and **Stanley Black**. His records were originally made for the Rex record label, which was taken over by Decca Records in 1937 and phased out ten years later. Many of his old recordings were reissued as LPs on the Decca label.

In 1967 the Beatles released the album *Sgt Pepper's Lonely Hearts Club Band*. On the front cover is a montage of 68 famous people. Listed at number 48 is Issy Bonn who is seen holding a hand over the head of Paul McCartney.

He composed the Song to the Initiate *This is*

Your Finest Hour when a Candidate becomes a Freemason. This song is still sung at the Chelsea Festive Board to this day. It was registered with Performing Right Society on 21 August 1951, but never published.

Benjamin Levin was initiated into Chelsea Lodge on 17 June 1938 and became WM in 1965.

He died in a London nursing home on his birthday, 21 April 1977, aged 74 years.

Laurence BOOKIN

Musician. Born 1912, Manchester. He played clarinet, alto saxophone and violin, but made his debut by playing violin in the cinema silent film days. He joined Hal Swain when he was proficient on reeds. Made recordings with Howard Jacobs Orchestra (1933) on the Columbia label; **Phil Green** and His Orchestra (1935-1938) on Columbia label; Lew Stone Band (1938-1940) on Decca label; Jack Harris Orchestra (1939) on HMV label and George Evans Orchestra (1944) on Decca label.

During the Second World War Laurie joined the RAF and was stationed at Bridgnorth, Shropshire where he was an armourer, his only job was to set up targets for shooting practice. He played saxophone and flute in his spare time.

Laurence Bookin was initiated into Chelsea Lodge 19 January 1940.

John Edward BORELLI

Real name John Edward Blore. Musician. Born 1901. Was a violinist with the Beaufort Club Punters (1933). Recorded with Jack Hylton's Orchestra (1936) on HMV label and Billy Ternant's Orchestra (1938) on HMV. He was musical director for *Wild Oats* at the Opera House, Manchester, 1938 and *Sitting Pretty,* Opera House, Blackpool, 1939.

Under his own name appeared on both BBC Home Service and Light Programme in his own light music shows as well as *Music While You Work.*

John Edward Blore was initiated into Chelsea Lodge on 18 November 1938. Died 1948, aged 47 years.

Franklyn BOYD

Born at Luton in October 1925, Franklyn decided to take up a singing career after winning the 1941 All Britain Crooning Championship and at age l6 joined **Harry Leader's** band at Hammersmith

Palais. Following a break for wartime service in the RAF, he returned to singing, now with the Teddy Foster band staying with them until the end of the forties, when they were resident at the newly re-opened Wimbledon Palais.

During the early fifties Franklyn mostly freelanced, singing with several bands including summer seasons with Eric Winstone at Butlin camps. He did concerts and broadcast with Paul Fenoulhet and sessions with the Kathy Stobart group. There were also seasons at the Lyceum ballroom with Oscar Rabin.

Franklyn recorded with Kathy Stobart in 1951 and Eric Winstone the following year. He also made several solo recordings. Although these were popular tunes with reasonable sales (the *Melody Maker* rated his first Columbia recording, *Call Me* "an absolutely first rate performance") Franklyn never made it to chart success.

By the mid-fifties he had virtually given up stage work devoting his energies to his new position as General Manager of music publisher Aberbach Music. He continued to be heard on radio though and from July 1955 partnered Patti Lewis on an early morning series *Start with a Song*. Other radio work included another series with Patti, *Remembered Tunes and Blues, Back with Braden* with Annie Ross and Benny Lee and the long running *Sing it Again*, that also featured Benny Lee with Jean Campbell, Julie Dawn and the Coronets.

Early in 1958 by virtue of his position in Aberbach Music (they were publishers of Cliff Richard's first recording *Schoolboy Crush*) he became Cliff's guide into the world of pop music, introducing him to Jack Good producer of *Oh Boy*. Franklyn was Cliff's manager for almost a year until his father decided on professional management and the **Tito Burns** agency took over.

In 1959 Franklyn was one of the artistes providing cover versions of hits on Society Records, Top Pop Club LPs, but most of his time from here on was taken up with music publishing work.

Franklyn is currently living in Ontario, Canada.

Alan BREEZE

Vocalist. Son of concert and oratorio singer Louis Breeze who belonged to the famous D'Oyly Carte Opera Company, Alan was born in East London on 9 October 1909. His mother was a teacher with the old London County Council. Anyone who remembers Billy Cotton's Band on the BBC Light

Programme on Sunday lunchtimes or their later television shows will surely remember "Ol' Breezy", as Cotton often referred to Alan, singer with the band for 36 years.

He made his first broadcast as a boy soprano on a children's programme from 2LO at Savoy Hill. His first job was as an apprentice in a piano factory. But he could see that he would never be  any good at it, so he decided to try and make a career for himself as a vocalist and his first attempts were singing in pubs in London's East End for what he could collect in his hat, which was perched on top of the piano.

By now he was eighteen and his voice had broken, becoming a baritone, while he played the piano, having taught himself to play after a style, by ear. From a few pence every evening in pubs he graduated to working men's clubs and his earnings reached 7s 6d or even 10 shillings a night, a handsome amount in those impoverished days. "I had a hell of a hard fight to get any jobs at first, because of my stammer", he recalled. "Agents found it difficult to believe that I could sing or act with such an impediment. But I started to get a few bookings and I even sang in theatre queues in the West End so I could buy a packet of fags and afford the fourpenny bus fare back to Stratford."

Gradually his determination paid off and he was able to save enough money to study for a while with an operatic teacher who gave him favourable terms. He appeared at clubs, restaurants and theatres as a ballad singer and, when he realised that he had a flair for character acting, he did a variety tour and followed it with a revue for Archie Pitt, which he had to leave after a short time owing to adverse health. When he recovered, he started ghosting at film studios, providing the voice for artistes who couldn't sing. It was there he met Bill Cotton and they began their unbroken assocation of 36 years, unequalled by any other bandleader or vocalist. Alan was singing and Bill was appearing with his band in *The First Mrs Fraser* at Wembley Studios. Bill was impressed with Alan's voice and invited him to do an audition with the band, which took place at Hammersmith Palais in cine-variety.

Alan was booked on a month's trial at £6 a week specially to sing a concert arrangement of *Trees* at the London Palladium which at once confirmed his potential, bringing a rousing response from the audience – a great start for Alan who made his first records with Bill on 18 April 1932 *Auf Wiedersehn My Dear* and *Goodnight Vienna.* He sang almost all the vocals during his long run with the band. His songs covered a fantastic range and a few random examples will show his versatility: *There's a Lovely Lake in London, South American Joe, Your Heart and Mine, The Fleet's in Port Again, She Shall Have Music, Make It a Party, Shoe Shine Boy* and *You Can't Do That There 'Ere.* Alan was never given credit on any of his records with Bill, which were anonymously labelled 'with vocal refrain'. Everyone knew, however, it was Alan Breeze.

Alan worked with Bill on the successful television show *Wakey Wakey Tavern* until 1965 when he was 'rested', but remained with the radio series for a further three years until it ended in October 1968. At a similar time he was offered a leading role in a new musical at the Palace Theatre called *Mr and Mrs*, with John Neville, Honor Blackman and Hylda Baker, and Bill characteristically told him: "Go ahead and take it, son". Within a few months Bill was dead after collapsing at a boxing tournament at Wembley in March 1969.

Alan enjoyed his involvement with *Mr and Mrs* and it gave him a good deal of scope as a character actor, playing a retired engine driver married to Hylda Baker. However, it did not last for long and when it closed Alan decided to retire from show business. By this time he had become a licensee of a country pub called The Buck Inn, at Flixton, Suffolk, which he ran with his vivacious wife Rene (née Murdock), and their teenage daughter Melodie. The Inn (slogan on the beermats 'Don't Pass the Buck') was surrounded by a 50-acre farm, which Alan had bought for his only son Graham, who was keen on, and had studied, agriculture. Sad to say the farm proved a calamitous mistake, for it led to the tragic death of 20-year old Graham in May 1964, while Alan was appearing with the band at Torquay. A wooden stake attached to the tractor he was driving became loose and swung up, hitting him violently on the head, killing him instantly.

Alan and Rene were to suffer another heartbreak when their youngest daughter, Michelle, who had met with a serious accident whilst horse-riding as a teenager subsequently developed severe arthritis which threatened to cripple her for life. Eventually she recovered and was able to resume her acting and singing career, which included appearing in the rock musical *Evita*. Her sister Olivia is a successful actress, singer and dancer on stage and television. She appeared in the first British cast of *A Chorus Line* at Drury Lane Theatre. The third daughter Melodie, who helped Alan manage The Buck Inn, settled down as a housewife and provided Alan and Rene with two grand-daughters, Lucy and Sophie. No wonder the girls are so talented, for apart from the heritage bestowed on them by Alan, Rene was a dancer in big musical shows and that was how they first met. They married in 1938 and moved to Shepperton, Middlesex and then to a lovely Georgian house in Weybridge and finally to East Anglia.

Alan gave up the pub in 1975 when his health began to fail after a heart attack put him into hospital for about a month. They moved to a 16th century thatched cottage in the picturesque village of Hingham, Norfolk. He gradually became housebound, although he did manage to toddle the few hundred yards to the local hostelry for his favourite 'dose of poison'.

Alan Louis Breeze was initiated into Chelsea Lodge on 17 March 1944. Died West Norwich Hospital, Norfolk, 15 January 1980, aged 70 years following heart failure. He is buried in the peaceful little cemetery at Hingham. He left behind him a career of which he must have felt proud. His death was mourned by all who admired his vocal ability and his innate charm. Although he sparkled in comedy songs, he had two even greater attributes: sincerity and conviction.

Eric BREEZE

Trombonist and trumpet player. Born 27 December 1912, Newcastle-upon-Tyne. Left school to work in a house band at the Palais Royale, Manchester then completed a long stay with Phil Richardson's Band at the Oxford Galleries, Newcastle-upon-Tyne before moving to London. He worked with the Jack Hylton Band from 1932 until joining Ambrose from 1936 to 1938. He made numerous recordings for both orchestras. Moved on to play with Geraldo's Orchestra, followed by Jack Harris and **John Borelli**.

Joined RAF in 1940 where he became a member of the Squadronaires until 1948 where he joined Maurice Winnick before rejoining Ambrose in 1949.

He undertook large amounts of session work in the 1950s, including regular work with George Milacron. Later moved back to Manchester,

Eric Breeze was initiated into Chelsea Lodge on 15 November 1935.

Gerry BRERETON

Singer. Born 9 October 1921, Stockport, Cheshire, the same date as singer, and fellow Chelsea Mason, **Alan Breeze**. Educated at Stockport Grammar School. As a youngster he won an award for singing and later became head choirboy at Manchester Cathedral.

However, despite his singing prowess, Gerry had an over-riding passion to play football and he turned professional for Stockport County and later Derby County.

The clouds of war were approaching and in 1939 he was called up for the Army and joined the Durham Light Infantry. In due course he was transferred to No.9 Commando Brigade and shipped out to North Africa for the impending invasion of Sicily. His unit was one of the first to hit the beach where Gerry's life was to change dramatically. The enemy forces had booby-trapped the beach, and on 10 July 1943, sand-mines incurred tragic loss of life on the commando unit. Gerry was peppered with shrapnel, subsequently losing his eyesight through his injuries. A number of his best pals were killed on that day. He was sent back to England and admitted to the Derbyshire Royal Infirmary where he spent the following eight months. Touch replaced sight, and the touch that Gerry came to appreciate the most was that of Kay, the very first nurse to hold his hand. They were married on 16 December 1943.

Such a tragic event as happened in Sicily in a 21-year-old man's life is not easily accepted but Gerry faced the facts and decided to exploit what he considered his only asset, his voice.

There followed many years of struggle in a business where even many sighted singers didn't find work easy to come by. After his accident St Dunstan's trained him as a telephone operator but in the evenings he sang in pubs, clubs and small dance halls around his home town of Stockport, in fact anywhere he could get a booking. This led to seasons as resident vocalist with the Charles Hennessey Band at Stockport's Rex Ballroom, Tommy Smith at the Oldham Savoy and Ken Turner at the Derby Plaza, making the occasional broadcast with them. He also toured for a while with Billy Ternent. Gerry aired on the North Region *Club Night* series with comedian Dave Morris.

Encouraged by his wife Kay he decided to try his luck in London and was spotted singing in a small club by the manager of East Ham's Granada Cinema. Cine-variety, using live acts between films as an inducement to bring in the customers, was not unusual at the time and Gerry was booked for a week at the Granada. So well was he received that by the end of the week he was featured in an article in the local press and further bookings followed. Also resulting directly from this appearance he was invited to become a contestant on the *What's My Line* television panel game, and appeared on *In Town Tonight*.

George Martin, whose name within ten years was to be associated with the Beatles, was a producer at Parlophone Records. He offered Gerry a contract and his first record *Have a Good Time* coupled with *Wyoming Lullaby* was available in November 1952, quickly followed by another in December. Now a bit of a celebrity, on 3rd November 1952 Gerry was one of the honoured performers chosen to appear at the London Palladium for the Royal Variety Performance. Without assistance he walked to his correct spot on stage and sang *Here In My Heart*, receiving one of the warmest receptions of any act that included other first timers, The Beverley Sisters and

Norman Wisdom.

From here on Gerry had little trouble finding work. He seemed to be continuously touring in variety and was, for quite a while, on a bill with that Welsh funny lady with the unmistakable laugh, Gladys Morgan. For much of the time he used a blind pianist as accompanist. On radio he featured on a new series of *Come In and Sing*. A measure of his popularity is apparent from further discs appearing at the rate of almost one a month, with the April 1953 release *Windsor Waltz* obviously aimed at the forthcoming Coronation.

Always a keen sportsman, his passion became golf and he competed in the 1955 blind golfers' world tournament held in Canada, finishing second. He made several radio and TV appearances in Canada and the States.

When in 1956 trumpet star Eddie Calvert formed his own production company, Gerry became one of the performers in his *Cavalcade*, beginning with a three month summer season at Great Yarmouth. He continued to tour with Eddie for many years including overseas service camps, and after Gerry moved over to the Columbia label they made several recordings together.

It's a pity that none of Gerry's records ever made the really big time. Probably his greatest hope was the July 1954 coupling of *The Story of Tina* (a success for fellow singer Ronnie Harris) with *Smile*, two very popular tunes of the day. Other excellent offerings included *Outside of Heaven, The Book* and *From Here to Eternity.* But by the late fifties his gentle ballad style was overtaken by rock 'n' roll and the record people seemed to have forgotten him. However he did work with Norrie Paramor, Frank Chacksfield, Ronnie Hazlehurst and sang regularly with the BBC Northern Dance Orchestra and Alyn Ainsworth.

On television Gerry appeared in shows with Anne Shelton, Ken Dodd and Roy Hudd, while on radio he was a regular visitor to *Henry Hall's Guest Night*.

With the recording and big time variety days over, brushed away by a more aggressive style of music and performer, Gerry fell back on his St Dunstan's training and spent twenty-five years as a telephone operator for Barclays Bank. He didn't stop singing altogether though and still found plenty of work around the smaller clubs well into the eighties.

Although his football career had been terminated, he still enjoyed considerable success on the golf course. Blind players have caddie minders to guide them around the course. In 1955-1956 Gerry won the Blind Golf Championships in America and Canada. He has shared greens with famous names like Henry Cotton, Tony Jacklin and Seve Ballasteros.

Already in his eighties and more or less retired, Gerry, together with Kay, relaxed at their home near Hampton Court and reflected on how tragedy had been turned into happiness.

W.Bro. Gerry Brereton, LGR joined Chelsea Lodge in March 1991. Died March 2005 aged 83 years.

Bernard BRESSLAW

Actor. Born 25 February 1934 in Stepney, East London, Bernard Bresslaw was the son of a tailor's cutter and a mother who took in sewing to raise extra money for the family. He became keen on an acting career from an early age following many regular trips to the theatre in London as a child. He eventually won a scholarship to RADA, where he went on to win the Emile Littler Award for Most Promising Actor. During his time at RADA, he was picked by Laurence Olivier to play a wrestler in his production of *The MacRory Whirl*.

This early success was followed by a number of other stage appearances before Bernie landed a part in the hugely successful radio series *Educating Archie*, and later finding fame in the classic television comedy *The Army Game* in 1957 and the series' spin off *I Only Asked*. He completed two years National Service as a private in the Royal Army Service Corps. With Michael Medwin, Alfie Bass and Leslie Fyson, he enjoyed a hit record *The Army Game* in May 1958. As a solo artist he enjoyed one national hit record in September 1958, *Mad Passionate Love* which reached number 6 in the British charts. He appeared in a series for ATV in 1958-1959 called *The Bernard Bresslaw Hour.*

In 1965 Bernie was offered the role of Little Heap in *Carry On Cowboy.* He went on to star in a further thirteen 'Carry On' films and became a regular performer in the television comedies. He also appeared on stage in such productions as: *Charley's Aunt, Run For Your Wife* and *Me and My Girl.* On stage in the 1970s and 1980s Bernard appeared in *Shut Your Eyes and Think of England* at the Theatre Royal, Bath; *Lancelot and Guinevere* at the Old Vic, London 1980-1981 and *Don Juan*, Royal Exchange Theatre, Manchester

1987-1988. Few performers of recent times so ably crossed the gap between straight theatre and light entertainment. He returned to the 'Carry On' fray in 1992, alongside Barbara Windsor to star in *Wot a Carry On* for a season in Blackpool.

A complete listing of Bernard Bresslaw films in reverse order follows: *Leon, the Pig Farmer (1992), Krull (1983), Hawk the Slayer (1980), The Fifth Musketeer (1979), Jabberwocky (1977), Carry On Behind (1975), Carry On Dick (1974), Old Dracula (1974), Carry On Abroad (1974), Carry On Girls (1973), Carry On Matron (1972), Carry On At Your Convenience (1971), Up Pompeii (1971), Carry On Loving (1970), Carry On Up The Jungle (1970), Carry On Camping (1969), Moon Zero Two (1969), Carry On Up The Khyber (1968), Carry On Doctor (1967), Carry On Screaming (1966), Carry On...Follow That Camel (1966), Morgan! (1966), Carry On Cowboy (1965), It's All Happening (1963), The Ugly Duckling (1959), Blood of the Vampire (1958), Between Heaven and Hell (1956)* and *Men of Sherwood Forest(1954).*

Bernie was King Rat in the Grand Order of Water Rats in 1988, a major light entertainment honour. His wife Liz was a dancer in light entertainment productions on stage and television. They had three sons.

Bernard Bresslaw was initiated into Chelsea Lodge in March 1972. Although he never took office in the Lodge he was a regular attender, his last meeting being January 1992.

His later stage work won him great acclaim. It was just before a performance as Grumio in *The Taming of the Shrew* in Regent's Park where Bernie suffered a heart attack and died on 11 June 1993. He was 59.

Ronnie BRIDGES, PAGDC

Lyricist and musician. Honorary member. Born 15 March 1919. He began his professional career as an insurance clerk before going into the Army but was invalided out due to a foot defect. He decided to join ENSA as they were short of pianists at that time. He went to the British Liberation Army, then was promoted to stardom working with Claude Hulbert in West Africa. The show was produced by Jack Hulbert who encouraged Ronnie to write for Revue. When he returned to England he rang Vivian Van Damm of the Windmill Theatre asking if he would employ him as a lyric writer. He was put on trial for three weeks and stayed there for nineteen years until the theatre closed in 1964. He worked with colleague **Charlie Rose** who wrote the music and Ronnie, the lyrics.

Says Ronnie: I remember playing at the Windmill Theatre when **Alfred Marks** and Eric Woodburn, a famous character actor, who was also a Mason, were sharing the same roles. There were six shows a day and the two actors did three shows each. Things went terribly wrong, due to an administrative error, and both actors suddenly appeared on stage from either side to do the same show. The cast were in hysterics and the audience realised something was not quite right, but joined in the fun with their applause.

Following the closure of the Windmill, Ronnie joined Liber Southern Music as a composer and publisher. The company published songs like *Fascination* and *Under the Bridges of Paris.* For many years he was a director of the British Academy of Song Writers, Composers and Authors (BASCA). He retired from the academy when he was 70 years old, but still remains on the committee for the Gold Badge Awards.

Ronnie played the organ at Harry Secombe's wedding in 1948. He played piano for the auditions of Bruce Forsyth and **Bob Monkhouse** at the Windmill. Over the years he has been the accompanist on television for Doris Hare, Tommy Cooper, **Leslie Sarony**, Jimmy Edwards and Leslie Crowther amongst others.

For many years Ronnie appeared on the BBC Light Programme in *Roundabout* where he was specially commissioned to write original or topical songs for the programmes. With others he has written over 200 songs many of which have

been recorded including *You're Closer To Me*, Matt Monro; *The Gibraltar Anthem*, Dorothy Squires and *Where The Bullets Fly,* a song from a film, recorded by Susan Maughan. Ronnie played piano for **George Robey** from 1957-1962 for his concert acts.

Today he plays organ for thirty-seven lodges in London and Essex, and is frequently asked to perform ritual, in addition to his music.

In 2004 Ronnie and colleague Brian Willey shared a proud and historic occasion. They were invited to attend St Clement Danes, London to mark the 300 years of British rule in Gibraltar and heard a song they had written 35 years before. Due to its ongoing dispute over sovereignty on the Rock, Spain had closed the border between the two countries in 1966 – Gibraltar was under siege - so, for an entry into the 1969 Gibraltar Song Festival, Brian and Ronnie wrote *The Gibraltar Anthem (Our Rock, Our Home, Our Pride)* to help boost the morale of the population. In due course Dorothy Squires recorded the song, as did the Gibraltar Cathedral Choir. The then organiser was a local parish priest; today he is the Right Reverend Charles Caruana, Roman Catholic Bishop of Gibraltar, and he had remembered the anthem and selected it for performance in the London ceremony.

Brian noted that they were the only living composers represented during the service, but Ronnie, at 85, ruefully remarked, "Well only just!"

Ronnie Bridges was initiated into Old Brentwood's Lodge No.5342 on 15 February 1946. Grand Rank 1979; Grand Organist 1979-1981. Promoted to PAGDC in 1988.

Teddy BROWN
Musician. Virtuoso xylophone player of 1920s and 1930s, he played a six-octave instrument, two more than usual. He was born Alfred Himmelbrand, 1900 in America. He began by playing xylophone and drums with Earl Fuller's Rector Novelty Orchestra (1917-1919) and performed on Broadway, New York. They made two-dozen dance numbers from 1917-1919 on the Columbia label. Later he was a member of the legendary violinist Joseph C. Smith's Band at New York's Hotel Plaza (1919-1924) and the Mount Royal Hotel, Montreal (1924-1925). He also worked with the New York Philharmonic Orchestra. He came to England with Joseph C. Smith and His Orchestra in the autumn of 1925.

He claimed it was the Duke of Windsor who suggested he should come to Britain. He could play practically every instrument in the orchestra. His special regard for the xylophone was because he said he had raised it from obscurity and proved that it recorded better than the violin.

Teddy, who was just 5ft 2ins, but weighed in at

20-stone, made his first appearance in England at the Café de Paris, where his band made 64 recordings between 1926 and 1928 on the Imperial and Vocalion labels. He also recorded xylophone solos on the Broadcast label and guested with various orchestral or military bands. He was resident at the Kit Kat in 1927 and the following year at the Silver Slipper Club. He led a band at Ciro's Club both in Paris and in London during 1929. Also during 1929-1930 some records by Percival Mackay's Band and Harry Bidgood's Band featured Teddy on xylophone. His solo career included extensive touring of the UK and many radio appearances. He was a very popular artiste in the 1930s, although his gigantic girth staggered music hall audiences. He received big welcomes at the London Coliseum and the London Palladium and he travelled to his venues in a chauffeur-driven Rolls Royce.

Teddy was certainly a genius on the xylophone, with his sparkling performance and his wide repertoire, ranging from jazz to the classics. His nonchalant manner and dry humour added an extra appeal to his versatile act. He appeared in the following films between 1928 and 1942: *Phototone Reels No.1* (1928), *Phototone Reels No.6* (1928), *Pot Pourri* (1929). *Musical Medley* (1929), *Elstree Calling* (1930), *Indiscretions of Eve* (1932), *Clap Hands* (1935), *Radio Pirates* (1935), *Starlight Parade* (1937), *Convict 99* (1938), *Pathetone Parade of 1940* (1940) *and*

Pathetone Parade of 1941 (1941).

Teddy appeared in the Royal Variety Performance held in front of Their Majesties King George V and Queen Mary at the London Palladium on 11 May 1931. He remained in England through the Second World War and became a dedicated charity worker, a Mason and a member of the exclusive Grand Order of Water Rats, who elected him Prince Rat in 1945 and King Rat in 1946.

After the Second World War he suffered a series of heart attacks, aggravated by two serious motor accidents, and his health began to decline. He had a very bad attack during his appearance at the Liverpool Empire in 1945 and was lying prostrate on the floor of his hotel room for several hours before he was discovered. Teddy died following a further heart attack while performing on stage at the Wolverhampton Hippodrome in Lew and Leslie Grade's production *Road to Laughter* on 25 May 1946, aged 46 years. Teddy had complained to the Hippodrome manager of feeling unwell and wished to avoid climbing the stairs to the dressing room. A special room was made up for him to the side of the stage where he stayed throughout the performance. After the show he returned to the Queen's Hotel, Birmingham. At 5.00am a doctor was called who pronounced Teddy Brown dead. He was married to Sophie and they had two children, a boy and a girl. His body was taken to London and he was cremated at Golders Green Crematorium on 3 May 1946. His ashes were sent to America for interment there.

The Sussex Daily News of 1 May 1946, in a tribute, reported: "When his diary allowed him, he never failed those who called upon him in the name of any deserving cause, and his attendances at local charity concerts provided that added attraction which made them so successful financially. Teddy Brown was a big man rather than simply an unusually fat one, and an incomparable artiste." It is believed his xylophones, of which one was a magnificent Besson of his own design, went to a collection of British Music Hall instruments.

Teddy Brown became a joining member of Chelsea Lodge on 21 January 1938 and lived in an impressive house he renamed Xylophone House in Sea Road, Rustington, Sussex. This was sadly demolished in 1965 to make way for housing development. It is believed there is now a modern bungalow standing where the old house was in what is now Marama Gardens, happily once again named Xylophone!

William BUDD

Impresario and theatre manager. Born 1911. Began his career as a callboy for Ivor Novello at the Theatre Royal, Drury Lane in the 1930s. During World War II he worked with ENSA in the Middle East and gave forces' radio broadcasts. At the end of the war he became manager of the Intimate Theatre where he stayed for 18 years. This was followed by appointments at several West End theatres and he continued working until a few weeks before his death.

William Frank Budd was initiated into Chelsea Lodge on 19 September 1947. He died 30 March 1981, leaving a widow, Elvie and a son, David, a film cameraman. He was aged 70 years.

Tito BURNS

Nathan 'Tito' Burns was a tall, heavily built man with a bubbling personality and his sense of fun was such that he could probably have made it as a full time comedian had he wanted. A piano accordionist of outstanding merit, he began his professional days during the thirties with Don Marino Barreto's Band at the Embassy Club. Tito followed this with time spent in the bands of Ambrose and Lou Preager. He worked with Carl Barriteau at the Cotton Club, Dean Street, London in 1941, then led his own band at the Panama Club, London (1942) and the Nut House, London (1942).

Tito served in the RAF from 1942, and was part of the RAF Regiment Sextet (1943); then after aircrew training, was on active service in the Far East. At the end of World War II he formed the Radio SEAC Sextet. After demobilization he joined pianist Clarrie Wears' Sextet (1946) for a short while before leading his own highly successful sextet. He was invited by the BBC in December 1946 to form a small group for a new Saturday evening radio series, *Accordion Club*, which he hosted. So popular was the show with listeners that a second series quickly followed in April 1947 and the programme continued until 1949.

In August 1947 Tito took an augmented Sextet, including Bernie Fenton and Ray Ellington with singer Terry Ann Foster, into the newly opened Savoy Restaurant and Ballroom at Southsea, a venue he returned to on several occasions.

Following its popularity on radio the group was

in big demand for club work and, as Tito Burns and His Sextet, did many such engagements, plus a number of weeks in variety including London shows during February 1948 at Shepherds Bush and Hackney Empires'.

Tito was voted top British jazz accordionist, a position he held throughout the fifties.

Always a shrewd businessman, he opened his own Tito Burns Club in early 1948 in premises on Whitcombe Street in West London. This eye for business also motivated his expansion into a band-booking agency.

In June 1948 Tito announced his engagement to singer Terry Devon who at the time was a member of the newly formed Keynotes vocal group. They married on 1 November 1948 at the Grosvenor Rooms, Willesden amid a huge gathering of stars.

During the summer of 1948 the Sextet did a five week season at the Grand Hotel, Cliftonville. On radio, as Tito Burns and His Music, he was appearing on several series like *Let's Make Music* alongside Cyril Stapleton's Orchestra and playing in a more gentle manner than the Sextet who, by 1949, were available on Decca records featuring the be-bop sound imported from the States.

Terry left the Keynotes becoming full time vocalist with the Sextet and together they played a twenty-week summer season in 1949 at the Winter Gardens Ballroom, Ventnor, Isle of Wight, followed by a month at Wimbledon Palais doubling with Vic Lewis and his Orchestra. The husband and wife team of Tito and Terry were billed as "Mr and Mrs Bop".

Throughout the early fifties Tito kept busy on mainly one-night stands, including ten days in Holland during March 1950 that led to a further two months booking there during July and August at the Casino in the coastal resort Schevenengen.

In 1951 a one-off appearance on a Frankie Howerd variety bill so impressed Frankie he booked them for the whole tour, their first variety date since 1948. November and December were spent touring military service camps in Gibraltar and the Middle East. During 1951 the Sextet did several recording sessions for the Esquire label.

By the mid-fifties Tito's agency business (an

occupation his cheery personality was ideally suited to) was taking more and more of his time and finally it became necessary to give up the Sextet and touring. His wife Terry had stopped touring after the birth of a baby in early 1953.

During 1955 Tito made a one-off recording for Philips in Holland, duetting with top Continental accordion player Johnny Meyer, Although he continued to broadcast and make the odd accordion solo appearance, he never returned to touring with a full time jazz group. However, in October 1958 he was brought in by producer Russell Turner and given the task of revitalising BBC TV's *Six-Five Special* to front one of the new resident bands. During December he also led a beat group on a short lived ITV series *On The Air,* described as "a crazy show" with comedian Graham Stark and guests, but Tito left before the end of the series.

Over the years he concentrated less on band booking, giving his attention to personal management of solo artistes and for a time managed Cliff Richard and Billy Fury. During the early sixties Tito promoted a disc club, Honey Hit Records, where members received six singles a month plus specially recorded bonus discs. Later in that decade he joined the London Weekend Television Company as head of variety entertainment. Tito was still active and busy in the late 1980's.

Tito Burns, under the name Nathan Bernstein was initiated into Chelsea Lodge in November 1955. He died around 2000/2001.

David CALDERHEAD, PM PAGDC

Born 16 September 1939, Glasgow. Spent his childhood in William Quarriers Orphan Homes, Bridge of Weir, Scotland. After a four-year stint in the Army he moved south. Making the English part with their money became his hobby. In 1967 he set up what is now The Glen Cawder group of companies. A subsidiary was Corporate Productions and Entertainment Ltd. This company was formed to take over Benny Palmer's agency and thus brought him into the world of entertainment.

In 1997 David became involved with the London Gala festival now run by London Masonic Promotions, a charity of which he is chairman. He has also organised three Royal Masonic Variety shows that have raised substantial sums for Masonic and non-Masonic charities. They were held at the London

Palladium (2000) and Theatre Royal, Drury Lane (2001 and 2002).

David Glen Calderhead joined Chelsea Lodge on 21 March 1986. WM 1991. Secretary 1997-2005. Appointed to Grand Rank in 2004 (PAGDC).

Dr. Edward CALLISTER, PM M.Mus., PhD

Musician. Also known as Eddie Kaye. Born Liverpool on St George's Day, 1931 of Manx parents. His father was a professional musician and singer who played classical guitar and was a piano tuner when resting. His mother was a professional ballroom dancer. During the depression in the early 1930s his parents used to 'busk' on the streets in order to survive; his mother used to push him around in the pram whilst she went around with the hat. This is how he became interested in music.

When he was six years old Ted's father bought him a toffee hammer for his birthday and within a few days he had smashed all his father's classical record collection which were stacked in the corner of the room. One could say his music career started off with a bang.

He joined the RAF when he was 17 and was trained as a wireless operator. One of the highlights during his service was to be posted to Wilmslow in Cheshire which, at the time, was the camp for the Womens Royal Air Force. He says it was a punishment camp for him as he hardly got any sleep and was always surrounded by girls in

the NAAFI where he used to play the piano at lunch times. He was in great demand at camp concerts, but was eventually posted abroad to No.4 Flying Training School in Southern Rhodesia. This was followed by a tour in Malaya, Korea and Japan serving with distinction attached to the United Nations.

When Ted was demobbed he went to live in London and in his spare time he played piano in pubs and clubs but his first choice was the guitar. He was advised by Denny Wright a friend of his to study music professionally if he wanted to succeed and suggested he go to The Central School of Dance Music. He was taught by Ivor Mairants, sometimes by Jack Llewellan or Roy Plummer. It took him another 15 years of study at University in Bristol and Liverpool in between his professional work before he was satisfied with himself. His first audition was for the City Varieties at Leeds before going to Morecambe for a summer season working for Eddie Morrell.

He has toured all over the country with a trio and played The City Varieties at Leeds, The Floral Hall Scarborough, The Empire Circuit, Alhambra Circuit, Pigalle Restaurant and many more working with various artistes such as Alma Cogan, Don Arrol, Al Read, Eddie Hart, The Deniz Brothers, Francis Langfords Singing Scholars, Morcambe and Wise, Tony Lester and **Mike Hill.**

During this time he had learned to tap dance and do the general work required in production numbers. In 1965 he decided to work as a semi-professional as he was offered a job as a senior technician for Granada which meant travelling all over the South of England. Ted still continued with his music until he collapsed whilst playing the organ. He was diagnosed as having a rare incurable cardiac disease. Sadly this finished his career with Granada and he deteriorated to such an extent he became wheelchair bound. He was retrained in the field of watch and clock making and became a Craft Member of the British Horological Institute then started his own business but further surgery affected his eyes so he had to give that up. Undaunted he opened a recording studio, as music was the only thing left in his life apart from his family.

In 1982 he asked his doctor if anything in Freemasonry could affect his health as he had been asked if he would like to become a member. Unbeknown to Ted his doctor was a Grand Officer, who told him: "Get out of those four walls you have been looking at for the past four years. You will meet many friends and enjoy it." Ted admits that Freemasonry did save his life. After 20 years of surgery the rest is history. He is a Past Master of Proscenium Lodge No.3435; Past Provincial Grand Organist (Norfolk); Past First Principle Chelsea Chapter No.3098; Founder member of Sandringham Lodge No.9751; Norfolk Royal Air Force Chapter No.9584; and Honorary member Morning Glory Lodge No.9693. He is also a Freeman of the City of London.

Dr Edward Callister joined Chelsea Lodge on 19 September 1986. WM 1992.

David CAPRI
David was born in Nova Scotia, Canada, 2 July 1956. He has won many musical awards at song festivals, both in the UK and in Europe, as well as winning many awards for composing.

David was invited by Sir Donald Gosling to entertain the troops on HMS *Ark Royal* off the coast of Bosnia. He was subsequently asked to perform on Cunard's *Sea Goddess* along with Ned Sherrin and Terry Wogan to commemorate the 50th anniversary of the Corfu incident. He has also performed on P&O's *Canberra* and Cunard's

Seabourn Spirit.

He has shared the cabaret stage with many international artistes and has performed at major hotels in Las Vegas and Beverly Hills. He has made appearances at many private functions in London and performed before Royalty on several occasions.

DAVID CAPRI

David Capri has played lead roles in shows including *Fiddler on the Roof, Charlie Girl* and *Evita.* In concert lead roles were taken in *Les Miserables, Guys and Dolls, Evita, Buddy, Company, West Side Story, Cole Porter Story* and *Phantom of the Opera.*

He has appeared on TV many times, playing a cross section of parts ranging from comedy sketches to drama. He played the part of Johnny le Croix in *Casualty.*

David conceived the original idea for a stage musical of Paramount's *Happy Days* and was associate producer when the show toured the arenas in Australia after a very successful UK tour.

His current involvement is his own creation *Latino Nights.* It will have a number of original songs and music as well as tunes we have known and loved. It promises to be fast and energetic with stunning and exciting choreography, brilliant colourful sets and sumptuous costumes.

David Capri is a member of the Grand Order of Water Rats.

He joined Chelsea Lodge in March 1990 from Drury Lane Lodge No.2127.

Dave CAREY

Born in Warrington on 7th July 1925, Dave took piano lessons from the age of seven, later adding drums and singing. Initially playing in semi-pro

outfits, his first professional engagement was as vocalist with Lew Stone's Band when he was 16. Club work took him up to war service and after demob he returned to London's 400 Club as drummer - vocalist with Tim Clayton's Band.

In February 1951 Dave, a smooth baritone, got his big break when he joined the **Cyril Stapleton** Orchestra as vocalist, replacing Bob Dale. Appearing regularly with Cyril on stage and radio Dave quickly built up a popular following and was hailed as "the voice discovery of the year". He appeared on Cyril Stapleton's Decca recordings and soon he began making solo records for Columbia.

Almost three years on, in October 1953, Dave replaced Ronnie Milne in The Stargazers vocal group, but still continued to make solo records and appearances.

During the later fifties he took advantage of the growing commercial television industry at home and abroad, writing and recording jingles for advertisements. By the early sixties Dave had parted company with The Stargazers in favour of his business interests. In 1966 he was working for Flamingo Music Publishers.

W.Bro. Dave Carey became a Joining member of Chelsea Lodge in March 1973.

George CARNEY

Screen, stage and Vaudeville actor. Born 21 November 1887, Bristol, and educated in Ireland. Originally in the furniture trade, he made his first stage appearance in December 1906 in *Aladdin* at the Theatre Royal, Nottingham, and in London at the Holborn Empire in November 1907. He was then working a double act 'Carney and Armstrong', which toured the United Kingdom, Australia and South Africa for a number of years. With Jewish comedian Sam Harris, he later toured his own revues, in 1913 presenting *The Prize Fight*, rather strangely described on the bills as 'A New Musical Comedy Athletic Revue'.

On the music halls he attained considerable popularity as a comedian with a ripe, fruity manner, but he seemed essentially a good character actor rather than a music-hall droll. Turning solo in 1926 Carney starred in variety with his comedy studies *The Fool of the Force, The Stage Door Keeper* and, in the oldest musical hall tradition, the broken-down swell in *I Live in Leicester Square.* His last variety appearance was in 1933, but he continued to appear in revue both in London and New York in such productions as

The Good Companions and *When We Are Married.* In March 1940 he starred in *Come Out to Play* at the Phoenix.

He appeared in a number of films, notably: *Some Waiter* (1916), *The Television Follies* (1933), *The Commissionaire* (1933), *Flood Tide* (1934), *A Glimpse of Paradise* (1934), John Baxter's *Music Hall* (1934), *Lest We Forget* (1934), *Easy Money* (1934), *Say It With Flowers* (1934), *Night Club Queen* (1934), *Cock O'the North* (1935), *A Real Bloke* (1935), *The Small Man* (1935), *City of Beautiful Nonsense* (1935), *Variety* (1935), *Dreaming Lips* (1935), *It's in the Bag* (1936), *Tomorrow We Live* (1936*),* *Land Without Music* (1936), *Father Steps Out* (1937), *Lancashire Luck* (1937), *Beauty and the Barge* (1937*),* *Little Miss Somebody* (1937), *Easy Riches* (1938), *Paid in Error* (1938), *Consider Your Verdict* (1938), *Miracles Do Happen* (1938), *Weddings Are Wonderful* (1938), *Kicking the Moon Around* (1938), *Come on George* (1939), *A Widow in London* (1939), *The Stars Look Down* (1939), *Young Man's Fancy* (1939), *The Briggs Family* (1940), *The Common Touch* (1940), Henry Hardcastle in Baxter's classic *Love on the Dole* (1941), *Kipps* (1941), *Hard Steel* (1942), *Rose of Tralee* (1942), *Unpublished Story* (1942), *Thunder Rock* (1942), *Schweik's New Adventures* (1943), *Night Invader* (1943), *When We Are Married* (1943), *Tawny Pipit* (1944), *Welcome Mr Washington* (1944), *The Agitator* (1945), *Soldier, Sailor* (1945), *I Know Where I'm Going* (1945), *Waterloo Road* (1945), *Spring Song* (1946), *Woman to Woman* (1946), *Wanted For Murder* (1946), *Fortune Lane* (1947), *The Little Ballerina* (1947*),* *Brighton Rock* (1947), *The Root of All Evil* (1947) and *Good Time Girl* (1948).

George Carney joined Chelsea Lodge 17 June 1927 and later became Honorary Member. He died 9 December 1947, aged 60 years.

Billy CARYLL

Vaudeville artiste. Real name William Francis Clark. Born 1893. Worked with his wife Hilda Mundy with on-stage comic rows which had been inspired by an off-stage argument. They appeared in George Black's *Crazy Week* at the London Palladium in 1931 and 1932 which were the forerunners of the Crazy Gang shows. Billy appeared in a number of films including *Amateur Night in London* (1930), *Marry Me* (1932), *Regal Cavalcade* (1935), *Calling All Ma's* (1937), *Lassie from Lancashire* (1938) and *I Didn't Do It*

(1945), with George Formby

Billy Caryll was initiated into Chelsea Lodge 20 June 1930. Died 15 February 1953, aged 60 years at East Preston, Sussex. He had been ill for three years and in 1952 suffered the amputation of a leg.

Tony CHAPERLIN, SLGR

(A Lewis). Former night club owner. Son of **Henry Chaperlin**. Crawling on sawdust floors. Hearing the upright piano. People singing. Welcome to the world of entertainment. This was his earliest recollection at the age of three in 1948 in his grandfather's pub.

Many years later he followed his father into the nightclub business, eventually owning his own club over a period of time, under different names: 'Peacock Club', 'Chaplins' and 'Ziggys'.

Tony remembers: "In the good old days of 'proper' cabaret nightclubs, I ran what was then called 'Showcases' where we tried out our new acts, giving potential stars of tomorrow their first break. We used to have cabaret six nights a week. Many of these acts went on to become big names. I can remember paying Joe Longthorn £50 before he made it big time.

"We used to have a Star Cabaret Night once a month. One of my best memories. and one of our greatest nights was with Matt Monro. I still bump into people who remember that night some twenty-odd years ago.

"Stories about the clientele. Well this warrants a book all on its own. Could I tell some tales. The 'Famous': The infamous, gangsters and police; judges and ladies of pleasure. All such cosy bedfellows, if you will pardon the expression.

"Times changed and eventually I turned the club into a disco. It was a good investment but oh, the noise. I finally sold out in 1991. Now I just embark on whatever deals take my fancy. Perhaps I should write a book."

Anthony Douglas Chaperlin joined Chelsea Lodge on 16 September 1988. PM Annuntio Lodge No.5539.

Henry CHAPERLIN, LGR

Club owner. Born Henry John Stuart Chaperlin, 25 August 1910 in The Queen's Arms, a pub in Chapel Street, off the Edgware Road, London. He was soon nicknamed Charlie, but later refined to Charles. By the time he was going to school the cinemas were always showing Charlie Chaplin films.

At the age of seventeen he joined concert agents Ibbs and Tillett. It wasn't too long before he met many famous names at the Sir Henry Wood's concerts... Rachmaninov, Arthur Rubenstein and

Pablo Cassals to name but three.

In 1936 he joined Mecca and looked after VIPs at Sherry's in Brighton. Two years later he took over as manager of the Streatham Locarno, a purpose built ballroom and the jewel in Mecca's crown. Many of the big bands of the day appeared here including many American artistes such as Cab Calloway and Fats Waller.

During World War II Charles became Mecca's circuit manager for London and the South East and set up his headquarters at the Royal Opera House, Covent Garden. Within weeks he initiated a series of fund raising activities in support of the war effort, much boosted by the appearances of celebrities from both sides of the Atlantic. They included Jack Buchanan, Jessie Matthews, Anna Neagle, **George Robey** and Clark Gable, all of whom gave their services free.

The Stork Club established alongside the Streatham Locarno in 1948 was a Charles Chaperlin 'exclusive' and was unique as the only suburban club to match the very best the West End could offer. Membership was none too easy. As *The Stage* newspaper stated: "Charles Chaperlin ruthlessly, though charmingly denies membership to any unless he feels quite certain they are they type of people whose company will be welcomed by other members". Once a member one could

rub shoulders with the likes of Evelyn Laye, Joe Davis, Frankie Howerd and Audrey Hepburn.

Charles auditioned over 10,000 new acts for cabaret, many of whom later became household names. They include Pat Kirkwood, Mike and Bernie Winters, Barry Took, Matt Monro, Engelbert Humperdinck, Sandie Shaw, Mike Reid, Ronnie Corbett, Roy Hudd, **Ray Alan,** Cardew Robinson and Gary Wilmot. The complete list of his successes would fill a "Who's Who in Show Business".

Roy Hudd said of Charles: "What a friend he was to me and my partner when I was just beginning. He made all the acts who worked for him feel like stars."

With the arrival of the disco boom in 1964 the Stork Club closed down. Charles opened the Peacock Club which he continued to run until 1984.

Henry John Stuart Chaperlin joined Chelsea Lodge on 21 November 1988. He was a PM of Annuntio Lodge No.5539. Died 1992, aged 82 years His son **Anthony Douglas Chaperlin** joined Chelsea Lodge in 1988.

Sydney CHAPLIN
Actor/entertainer/comedian. Born 16 March 1885 to sixteen-year old seamstress Hannah Hill in London. There is a mystery as to who his father was. The story is that it was a man named Sydney Hawkes, a middle-aged Jewish bookie but there is no record of Hannah's marriage to a Mr Hawkes.

Sydney was not fatherless for long. On 22 June 1885 Hannah Hill married Charles Chaplin (senior) and he became Sydney John Chaplin. Hannah and Charles enjoyed success in the music halls. On 18 April 1889 Charles Spencer Chaplin was born. This made Charlie and Sydney half brothers. Sadly the Chaplin's marriage broke up around 1891. Hannah became pregnant by another music hall turn, Leo Dryden, who kidnapped their six-month old baby from the lodging in the spring of 1893. Four years later Hannah, Sydney and Charlie were all in a workhouse. It is an improbable rags to riches story.

In 1897, at the age of twelve, Sydney was sent on a training ship called HMS *Exmouth*, while Charlie and his mother struggled to make a living in London. On 13 May 1901 Charles Chaplin Snr died an alcoholic. Both Charlie and Sydney worked very hard to help their mother. Sydney continued his work on the ships and it was while he was gone he became ill and had to stay at a port while he was recovering. Neither Hannah nor Charlie had received word of Sydney's illness. The strain of waiting for Sydney's return was too much for his mother who was already weak from malnutrition.

In 1903 Hannah's struggles came to a sad end. Aged fourteen, Charlie had to take his mother to the infirmary where she was committed as insane and sent to Cane Hill asylum. Hannah would eventually die on 28 August 1928, aged 59 years. By the time Sydney returned, he found his brother Charlie in a terrible state. Not wanting to be sent to the workhouse again, Charlie was living on the streets by day, working odd jobs, and staying out of sight during school hours.

Sydney, of quiet manner, clever brain and steady nerve, played a major role in Charlie Chaplin's life. He was well rested from travels and had saved money from his shipping job. He told his brother that with the money saved he was going to enter the theatres and resigned his job as a steward on the SS *Kinsfairn Castle*. The two brothers wasted no time in seeking their dreams. Charlie landed the first job. Sydney knew that his brother lacked schooling and jumped in to help Charlie memorise his lines for the theatre production. Undoubtedly it was Charlie's special talents that made him a success.

Sydney finally was given his first break in 1906 with the famous London performing company of acrobatic comedians run by Fred Karno. Two years later he got Charlie a job with Karno as well. When Karno needed performers for their American tour in 1910, it was Charlie Chaplin who was sent, not Sydney. Charlie created quite a name for himself in the States and was invited back for a second tour. Whilst in America he signed with Mack Sennett's Keystone Pictures in California on 25 September 1913 and in 1914 Sydney followed, and also signed with Keystone in November 1914. It was Sydney who landed Charlie an amazing million-dollar contract in 1917, the largest salary paid to anyone at that time. Sydney acted as Charlie's business manager and helped him land the First National contract that gave Chaplin ownership of the films and allowed Charlie to build his own studio. Sydney co-starred with Charlie in a few of the First National films. He played in *The Bond, A Dog's Life, Pay Day, The Pilgrim* and most famous of these *Shoulder Arms*. In all there were a total of 33 films in which Sydney appeared.

According to Charlie, in his book *My Autobiography*, he later helped start United Artists, the famous film company founded mainly by Mary Pickford, D.W. Griffith, Douglas Fairbanks and himself.

Sydney Chaplin married twice but had no children. His first wife, Minnie, passed away in the South of France in April 1935. His second wife, Gypsy (Henriette), died later of a broken heart after Sydney died in 1965. The couple had lived for many years in France. Darryl F. Zanuck, who worked for Sydney Chaplin in the 1920s, referred to him as, "the greatest ladies' man in Hollywood history – better even than Erroll Flynn".

Before Sydney's death he visited Charlie and his family many times in Switzerland often reflecting on the struggles it took to achieve their success. Charlie had the talent, but it was Sydney who helped make that talent pay off.

In 2001 Charlie and Sydney Chaplin came back in the news. Two younger members of the Chaplin family, Christopher and Victoria, discovered a very old valise in a disregarded corner of the house. When the lock was forced, this modest piece of luggage yielded something infinitely precious – a brown leather suitcase bearing the ghosts of a dozen ancient baggage stickers and the initials 'SC' in stencilled white letters. Inside the suitcase were dozens of old colour films taken by Sydney during the filming of *The Great Dictator*.

These rare 16mm Kodachrome films, the only colour footage of Chaplin on and off the film set, show the actor in colour at a time he is most clearly remembered in black and white. Many of the film outtakes we see today of Chaplin at work resulted from Sydney carefully keeping film that Charlie had ordered to be buried. *The Great Dictator* is regarded as Charlie's finest film and his first sound picture. Chaplain played a fascist dictator clearly modelled on Hitler (also with a certain physical likeness), as well as a Jewish barber cruelly persecuted by the Nazis. The film was refused screenings in Nazi-occupied Europe, but went on to become the biggest money-spinner of 1940, breaking box-office records in Great Britain and the United States of America. Sydney Chaplin's footage records key scenes in colour, including the barber's first confrontation with the black shirts. It is believed that Adolf Hitler attended two private screenings.

The Unknown Chaplin television documentaries by Kevin Brownlow are responsible for much of the renewed interest in Charlie Chaplin. Now Brownlow's *The Tramp and the Dictator* has brought attention not only to Charlie, but Sydney as well. These old films have now been transferred onto DVD and VHS and became commercially available in the year 2003.

Brothers are important. Sydney was always there for his younger brother. This was a fact that Charlie Chaplin knew more than anyone.

A recent bequest to the British Film Institute has yielded new evidence of the brothers shared comic technique: the unedited rushes of *King, Queen, Joker* (1921), a film shot in France and made under the terms of Sydney's million-dollar contract with Famous Players-Lasky. Sydney wrote and directed this film in 1921 and was director for *Submarine Pirate* (1915).

In the latter half of the 1920s, Sydney devoted his full attention to his own film career. In 1925 he signed a six-picture deal with Warner Brothers, for whom, in the words of one trade paper, he 'turned out one smash hit after another'. He appeared in *Charley's Aunt* (1925), *The Man in the Box* (1925), *The Better 'Ole* (1926) *Oh! What a Nurse* (1926), *The Fortune Hunter* (1927) and *The Missing Link* (1927).

In 1929 Sydney was preparing a talking picture adapted from *Mumming Birds*, a sketch he and Charlie had performed with the Karno troupe. To help him write the script, he had recruited **George Carney**, an old music hall artiste who had known Charlie in his clog-dancing days. The film was never made. After what the cinema trade-press delicately described as "an incident at Elstree", Sydney Chaplin vanished, leaving only a stack of unpaid tax demands behind him. It was his final visit to the country of his birth.

Sydney Chaplin was initiated into Chelsea Lodge on 21 August 1908. He died on 16 April 1965 (his brother Charlie's birthday), aged 80 years. He is buried at Clarens-Montreaux Cemetery, France. Charlie Chaplin was the most famous actor in early Hollywood cinema, and later also a notable director. He was knighted by HM The Queen on 4 March 1975. He died on Christmas Day 1977, aged 88 years.

The author is grateful to Linda Wada, Dominque Dugros, Matthew Sweet and Lisa Stern for their help in compiling this biography.

Sydney CHASID

Musician. Began life as a classical violinist in Newcastle. He changed track and formed his own dance band called the Californians in 1930. He was under contract to ABC cinemas appearing with his musicians. In 1931 he made eight tracks with his Serenaders on the Phonycord record label; and fourteen tracks in 1934 with his orchestra on the Hudson label.

Sydney Chasid was initiated into Chelsea Lodge on 15 May 1936.

Albert CHRISTIAN

Vocalist. Made his D'Oyly Carte debut in *Patience* in February 1883. and remained with the company for two years appearing in *Trial By Jury*, *Iolanthe*, *The Mikado*, *The Sorcerer*, *The Pirates of Penzance* and *HMS Pinafore*. After leaving D'Oyly Carte he went on to appear in *Dorothy* and *La Serenata*. Following a series of provincial tours he completed a concert tour of America.

By 1890 Albert left the comic opera stage to  pursue a career in the music halls around the time of Queen Victoria's Diamond Jubilee. He specialised in military songs, achieving his greatest success as the original exponent of the famous song *The Soldiers of the Queen*, composed by Leslie Stuart. He was great, too, in Irish songs and made a great feature of *Father O'Flynn,* always an excellent lesson in humorous singing.

Albert was married to fellow D'Oyly Carte and music hall artiste Katie Cohen, daughter of Isaac Cohen, manager of the Pavilion Theatre, Mile End. When he toured America in 1893 he was billed as 'D'Oyly Carte's leading baritone'. For some years husband and wife fulfilled joint engagements on the halls. They had two sons, both of whom served in the Army in the First World War.

He was a member of the Grand Order of Water Rats.

Albert Christian was initiated into Chelsea Lodge on 4 May 1906. Died 16 June 1915.

Harry CLAFF
Baritone. Real name Hyman Clapp. Born c1880. Established a reputation in musical comedy and light opera during the 1900s and turned to the music hall stage with even greater success. He studied singing under Garcia, won a scholarship to the Royal Academy of Music, and while appearing in an RAM operetta was heard by Richard D'Oyly Carte and given a three-year contract to appear at the Savoy. Much of the time was spent in the chorus beginning in 1897 with *The Grand Duchess of Gerolstein.* His only named part was Kedas in *The Lucky Star* (January-March 1899). From parts in Gilbert and Sullivan he went to George Edwardes at the Gaiety, singing the baritone leads in *The Shop Girl, The Circus Girl, A Gaiety Girl* and *San Toy.* He made his first variety performance with Sir Alexander Mackenzie's *Knights of the Road* at the Palace Theatre, London. Soon afterwards he turned solo touring the variety theatres singing operatic arias in character. In a lighter mood he presented a double act with his wife Winnie Wager, billed as 'Harry Claff and Lady – The Demon and the Fairy'. His most famous act *The White Knight* where he appeared in shining silver fish-scale armour was followed by a series of historical musical sketches, *King Henry VIII*, etc., with which he toured America, New Zealand and South Africa. His repertoire included such popular songs *Let's All Go to the Music Hall* and *Till We Meet Again.*

Dressed in silver armour he was very proud at being chosen to lead the singing of the National Anthem at the first Royal Command Performance at the Palace Theatre on 1 July 1912 and from then on made it a feature of his publicity. A great

pantomime favourite, he appeared for twelve years in Howard and Wyndham's productions and in six pantomimes at the Theatre Royal, Drury

Lane, London. He took a prominent part in the Variety Artistes Federation, of which he was honorary chairman from 1928 to 1938. He had a son Harry Claff Junior (who at one time was married to Joan Regan) and who was box office manager of the London Palladium.

He was a member of the Grand Order of Water Rats.

Harry Claff joined Chelsea Lodge 19 July 1912. He died on 8 May 1943, aged 63 years.

Harry CONN
Musician. Born 1921, Hoxton, London. Alto and tenor saxophone player. As a teenager he suffered from asthma and he had a serious attack whilst on holiday in Brighton in 1935. A local doctor advised him to take up the trumpet. Harry was a great admirer of Benny Goodman, so took up the clarinet and alto saxophone instead. At the age of sixteen he auditioned successfully on clarinet at Mac's Academy in Great Windmill Street, London and on alto for a juvenile band, the Savoy Juniors. His first date was at Brighton Hippodrome. Also in the band were **Woolf Phillips** and **Aubrey Frank**.

Harry's big break came in 1941 when Oscar Rabin added a saxophonist and trombonist to his eleven-piece band. He took over the alto chair with **Tony Thorpe** on trombone. He recorded forty-five tunes with the Oscar Rabin Band on the Rex label in the 1940s. The band also toured extensively in England, Scotland and Wales.

By the end of 1944 Harry joined the Eric Winstone eighteen-piece band and made recordings and they were the first civilian band to cross into Germany. They played for troops in Holland and Germany. When the war ended the band moved to Paris where it played for wounded soldiers in a local hospital and also broadcast to Britain from the British Embassy.

Harry then joined the Ambrose Orchestra and still played on the continent. A short while later he was employed by Carroll Gibbons at the Savoy Hotel in London and made recordings with the famous Savoy Opheans.

In 1947 he took a job at £7 a week playing on the Queen Mary, replacing Johnny Dankworth.. The trip took him to New York . On return to the UK he continued working at the Savoy Hotel in addition to playing with Victor Silvester's Orchestra for BBC TVs *Come Dancing* and **Tiny Winters** Café Society Orchestra.

Harry Conn was initiated into Chelsea Lodge 18 November 1955.

Jess CONRAD

(A Lewis) Actor/Singer. Real name Gerald Arthur James. Born 24 February 1940, Brixton, London. Left school at the age of fifteen for a job with a steel merchant in Kingston, Surrey. When a colleague lost two fingers in an accident, Jess decided that his future lay elsewhere, and he began working in his father's flower business in Shepherd's Bush, London. His ambition at the time was to act, and he managed to find work as a film extra and in repertory with the famous Charles Danville Company.

On Valentine's Day, 1959, he played a rock and roll singer in the ATV play *Rock-A-Bye-Barney*, then had a part in the Arthur Askey film *Friends and Neighbours.* TV producer Jack Good saw him in *Rock-A-Bye-Barney* and is reported to have said to him: "Jess, you can't sing, but you have a certain teenage quality."

He made his first appearance in *Boy Meets Girl* in 1960, then moved on to *Oh Boy* and *Wham.* Was voted the most popular singer in the *New Musical Express* poll in 1961.

Standing 6ft 2ins tall and with striking looks he recorded his first single *Cherry Pie* which appeared at the lower end of the British Top 40 in June 1960. This was followed by his only Top 20 hit *Mystery Girl* in January 1961. *Pretty Jenny* reached number 50 in the British charts in October 1962. A record, which had a second lease of life, appeared on a Kenny Everett LP of his favourite worst records. The song was *This Pullover.*

Jess is one of the most versatile artistes to emerge from the 1960s. He went on to become an accomplished actor and has appeared in many films, musicals and TV shows, as well as continuing to present his individual style of cabaret act.

He has played the London Palladium, Wembley Pool and concert tours throughout the world.

In the early 1970s Jess made the transition from pop singer to musical star playing Jesus in H.M. Tennent's *Godspell.* This was followed by the Andrew Lloyd Webber musical *Joseph and His Amazing Technicolour Dreamcoat,* in which he played the part of Joseph. Other West End credits include: *The Knack, Romance* and *A Slice of Saturday Night.* In addition he has appeared in fifteen major shows touring the British Isles.

Amongst the TV shows in which Jess has appeared are: *Des O'Connor Show, Jim Davidson Special, Rock Gospel Gala, Pebble Mill, The Runnable Stag, Dixon of Dock Green, Paradise Suite, Someone Who Cares, Give Us a Clue,*

Punchliners, Through the Keyhole, Noel's House Party, Big Break, Generation Game, Paul Daniels Christmas Show, Are You Being Served, Miss Marple, Crossroads and *Ideal World TV.* He has appeared in twelve Royal Variety shows.

Theatre work includes: *Leave Him to Heaven, Seagulls Over Sorento, Sweet Charity, Boeing Boeing, A Slice of Saturday Night.* He also headlined a national tour of the Rick Wakeman musical *The Gospells* He has starred in over twenty pantomimes.

Film credits include: *The Pack, Rag Doll, Friends and Neighbours, The Ugly Duckling, Sapphire, Follow a Star, Too Young to Love, The Queen's Guards, Kill, Konga, Aliki My Love, The Boys, The Golden Head, The Amorous Adventures of Moll Flanders, Hell is Empty, The Assassination Bureau, Cool it Carol, The Flesh and Blood Show, The Great Rock and Roll Swindle, Claudia, Absolute Beginners, Tank Mullings* and *The Punk and the Princess.*

A keen sportsman, Jess is the manager of the Show Business Football Team and plays golf for the Variety Club of Great Britain. He is a member of the Grand Order of Water Rats and has been raising money for a host of worthwhile charities since the early 1960s.

He is married to former Dutch model Renée Bergman and they have two daughters.

Gerald Arthur James was initiated into Chelsea Lodge on 15 September 1995.

CORAM

Ventriloquist. Real name Thomas Mitchell Whitaker. Born 2 June 1878, Sowerby, Yorkshire. Known as **Coram.** As a teenager he entertained holidaymakers on the beach at Morecambe, Lancashire with a small knee figure given to him by his uncle. Within a few years he had perfected his act and appeared at the top of variety programmes throughout the world.

He began his professional career by touring music halls in the north of England. His London début was made in 1905, at the age of twenty - seven with his dummy Jerry Fisher in a sketch entitled *The Joys of a Motorist.* As the curtain rose, Jerry was seen sitting by himself on a stile. Coram then drove on stage in a motor car. During the dialogue which followed, Coram sat in the car the whole time, operating the figure movements by a compressed air mechanism. After a lively exchange of words, Coram eventually drove off-stage, leaving Jerry to receive the applause. We have to remember that in England at this time in history the motor car was a relatively new invention.

Coram's act made an immediate impact upon the London audiences and, together with Jerry, they found themselves in great demand. The duo began to headline at the principal theatres throughout the country and also made an extensive tour of America. However, on 18 April 1906 whilst in the USA the Jerry figure was destroyed in the San Francisco earthquake, the worst ever to hit an American city. Two-thirds of the city was destroyed, 452 died and 250,000 were made homeless. Fortunately Coram escaped with his life. Back in England a new Jerry figure was made by **Leonard Insull** who had designed and constructed the first dummy for Coram. Various refinements were made and it was not long before Jerry could wink, smoke, spit and even walk. He was very realistic and could move each eye independently. They were the first ventriloquist act to appear on radio.

To keep ahead of the game Coram was always on the lookout for new ideas. His act later changed when he adopted a military theme, appearing on stage as an Army officer with Jerry as Private Fisher. Without doubt this military act greatly enhanced the popularity of his entertainment. He even composed a song for the soldier which became known amongst his audience who often would join in:

I'm Jerry Fisher, one of the militia
I'm Jerry Fisher in the morning
One of the rank and file
No wonder the ladies smile,
But I'm every inch a soldier.

In 1919 Coram wrote a book, published in London, *How to be a Ventriloquist.*

Coram appeared with Jerry in the Royal Variety Performance at the London Palladium on 22 May 1930 and in the radio programme *The White Coons Concert Party*, the first ventriloquist to broadcast.

Many years later veteran comedian **Sandy Powell** appeared as a caricature of Coram dressed in a military uniform with a soldier dummy in an act called 'The World's Worst Ventriloquist'.

Coram was married with two sons, Billy and Ralph, and a daughter, Helen, all of whom went into showbusiness. His son Billy Whitaker was a well-known comedian.

Thomas Mitchell Whitaker was initiated into Chelsea Lodge on 17 September 1909. He died in London on 25 March 1937, aged 59 years. 'Jerry' was presented to the London Museum's Theatre Collection.

Stella Storey has traced the Whitaker family history. She says that the dummy Jerry is now in the Science Museum, South Kensington, London. The name Coram came about with his agent saying Whitaker was not a good commercial stage name. He looked out of his agents window and saw the name of the street - 'Coram'. It was as simple as that!

Leon CORTEZ

Screen, television, radio and Vaudeville actor, comedian, bandleader. Born Leon Chalkin on 27 May 1898, Greenwich. His father had been a horseback soldier in the Canadian Mounties and his mother ran a china and glass store.

Leon became manager of the Kennington Theatre, south London. This was a world-famous music hall, where all the great variety stars appeared. As manager he wore top hat and tails. It appears that he was the originator of several startling stunts on stage, including the use of live horses galloping on an endless revolving roller, creating the impression of a horse race.

In 1933 he met vocalist Doreen Harris and they were to work together as entertainers and lovers for 21 years. They had a son Derek. Leon began his career in Variety as the leader of a comedy band Leon Cortez and His Coster Pals, popular in the 1930s and 1940s. They dressed in pearly suits and played everything from jazz to the classics. He was a famous radio star for over three decades – ranging from the early days with his Coster Cockney band through to his own 'Appy 'Alf 'our series, which was broadcast before and after the war – to numerous broadcasts on *Music Hall* and variety programmes.

Leon was a saucy cockney comic with chubby features, natty moustache, horn-rimmed glasses, check suit and bowler hat. He appeared in a number of films including *Big Business* (1930) with Francis Day, Leslie 'Hutch' Hutchinson and Arthur Roseberry's Band and in the British Lion 9.5mm optical sound film *Calling All Stars* (1941) in which Leon and the Band performed the song *I'm A Bit of a Ruin That Cromwell Knocked About A Bit*. The film featured various bands and variety artistes linked by Flotsam and Jetsam.

In 1939 Leon was starring in the 'Appy 'Arf 'Our. One programme was due to be broadcast on 2 September 1939 but was replaced with gramophone records in anticipation of the declaration of war with Germany.

A popular record of World War II was *The Girl Who Loves a Soldier*. Leon Cortez and His Coster Pals recorded this song in London on 14 September 1939. It was re-released in 1999 on a double CD *Songs and Music of World War II*.

After the war Leon packed up the band and began his famous solo act in which he took the mickey out of Shakespeare and sang in Italian. It

was an ingenious act with outrageous patter in his coarse cockney voice and it brought him recognition and considerable financial reward. His dress was scholastic gown and bowler hat. His catch phrase was "Wotcha cocks"! Known primarily for his "Shakespearean" comedy monologues, he devoted many years to "H'edificating The H'iggerant", around all the variety theatres of the country. Leon was one of the fast-disappearing "great stars" from the heyday of the music halls.

When Variety ceased to be a popular entertainment Leon became a character actor of some repute on television in series such as *The Saint,*

Beggar My Neighbour, and *Dixon of Dock Green.* He also appeared in episodes of *One Step Beyond, Dad's Army* and *Out of the Unknown.* He also appeared films including: *Striptease Murder* (1961), *Gang War* (1962), *I Could Go On Singing* (1962), and *Secrets of a Windmill Girl* (1966). He was due to commence rehearsals for two other television plays in 1970, which was as a direct result of his outstanding portrayal of the elderly uncle in a play on BBC TV by Peter Nichols, but was taken ill.

Leon toured in Roy Plomley's *Devil's Highway* with which he came to the West End at the Comedy Theatre some years ago. He was one of the main stars of *Doctor at Sea* and during 1969 recreated the Gordon Harker role of the detective in *The Case of the Frightened Lady.*

A regular pantomime performer throughout his career he usually played "The Baron", "Will Atkins" or other similar roles for many leading managements. He spent twenty weeks working in Jersey in the summer of 1969 and that December he played "Abanazer" at the King's Theatre, Southsea. He had featured in Summer Season shows at many major resorts, although ill-health prevented him from accepting a resident season in 1970.

Leon Cortez was initiated into Chelsea Lodge on 18 December 1936. He died 31 December 1970, at Peacehaven, Sussex, aged 72 years.

Alfred CRUIKSHANK, PM LGR
Vaudeville artiste. Son of W.C. Cruikshank, well known circus jester in his day. Born 1875, Dublin. His earliest appearance was as a child in the pantomime *Cinderella.* One of three brothers, high wire walkers, the trio performed as the Cruikshank Family. As he was unable to match their skills he was dubbed 'the fool of the family'. When he discovered his talent as a clown he adopted this soubriquet as his own and was billed as 'Cruikshank: The Fool of the Family', working as a single turn. Although he learned his job in the circus, he also appeared in variety, on the Moss and Stoll circuit, as a musical clown. A Royal Command artiste he was noted at Ginnett's Circus, Dover in 1893, as a buffoon providing mirthful melody, and at Hengler's, Hull in 1895. He was with Transfield's Circus, Coventry, 1900.

Alfred was described as of neat appearance, with white face and tasselled hat, who sat on top of a high stool. He played both cello and banjo, and sang in a falsetto voice *The Old Brass Bottle*

and other popular songs of the day.

In 1917, aged 42, described as a music hall artiste, he was arrested and charged with avoiding military service. His daughter Doris Beatrice married Edward Sanger, 29 November 1928.

He was a member of the Grand Order of Water Rats.

Alfred Cruikshank was initiated 17 December 1920. WM 1941. Died 1956, aged 81 years. His brother George Cruikshank adopted the name Zalva.

Bob CURTISS
Comedian. Born Robert David Trayling, 22 March 1938. He has been a professional comedian for more than 35 years and worked in almost every aspect of the entertainment industry. He was a familiar face on Granada TV's *The Comedians.* Other television appearances include: *Rumpole of the Bailey, The Bill, Born and Bred* and *The Other Half*

Bob had made a number of television commercials: *Flora Margarine, Qualcast ('Lot less Bovver"), Chipsticks, Callard & Bowser, Mothers Pride, Woolwich, Unigate* and many more, too numerous to list Featured film

appearances include *The Hound of the Baskervilles* - (Peter Cooke/Dudley Moore) and *Fever Pitch -The 10th Kingdom.*

In cabaret he has appeared at Blazers, Caesars

Palace, The Circus Tavern, Lakeside and Jollies. He is much demand as an After Dinner speaker with various societies and has attended many business and corporate dinners. He regularly works on the cruise liners, mainly for the companies of Cunard, P&O, Saga and Fred Olsen.

Charity work takes up some of his time and he has appeared in Christmas shows and afternoon shows at Brinsworth House. He was twice Barker at the Brinsworth House Fête. In addition he has appeared at Golf Days for The Variety Club Golf Society.

Peter Hepple, who attended a recent Concert Artistes Association Ball at the London Marriott, writing in *The Stage* said:

" ...In Cabaret was one of our best comedians, Bob Curtiss, who has been ploughing his own furrow, concentrating on after dinner speaking and cruise work for a good few years now. This is a man who is a natural storyteller, specialising in tales from the domestic front, who has the virtues of clear, concise delivery and superb timing."

Robert David Trayling was initiated into Chelsea Lodge on 17 September 1999.

Billy DAINTY

Entertainer. William Hooper Frank John Dainty was born 1927, Dudley, Worcestershire. He was one of the last genuine music hall artistes and

always acknowledged his debt to the stage.

He first appeared as a dancer with the Betty Fox Babes in Birmingham followed by pantomime when he was twelve and gained early experience in such lowly roles as the back legs of a donkey. By this time his family moved to London. He won a scholarship to RADA, from which he played

truant to appear in the chorus of the George Black revue *Strike a New Note* at the Prince of Wales Theatre. It starred Morecambe and Wise.

In 1942 Billy appeared in the pantomime *Mother Goose* at the Coliseum Theatre in London.

Billy was called up for National Service in 1945 and toured the Far East in the *Stars in Battledress* revue called *Hello Alfsea*. On demob and a return to civvy street he turned to comedy, playing summer seasons and concert parties. His first performance after the war was in a revue called *Gaytime* at the Cosy Nook Theatre in Newquay. He later moved to the town and purchased a seaside home, which he called 'Gaytime' after the show.

In the 1950s Billy toured in many variety theatres of the day, but as the industry declined he made a sideways move into television and made a number of appearances on *Sunday Night at the London Palladium.*

He established a reputation as a singularly talented and energetic eccentric dancer with a large repertory of funny walks. His first television appearance was for a pilot *That's Showbusiness*, (ABC Television, 1967) where he was cast as Billy Cook, a comic cabaret artiste working the northern clubs, but no series developed. A much - praised appearance at the 1974 Royal Variety Show led to more television work. ITV (Thames Television) created *Billy Dainty Esq*, which elevated him from a club comic to his own prime time television show during 1975 and 1976. He appeared with **Don Smoothey** in BBC1 comedy series *Kindly Leave the Stage* in 1968 and in an edition of the BBC1 series *Comic Roots* (1983). He became a regular on children's TV in *Emu's Broadcasting Company* with Rod Hull where Billy played piano. Radio shows included *Stick a Geranium in Your Hat.*

He appeared in *Stars in Your Eyes* at the London Palladium with Russ Conway, Cliff Richard and Edmund Hockridge; and was in *Sleeping Beauty* with Diane Lee, **Arthur English** and Jack Douglas at the Pavilion Theatre, Bournemouth in 1980.

Billy's skills and his bluff seaside-postcard humour lent themselves readily to pantomime and he excelled in the role of Dame, his most successful scenes including a hilarious 'striptease' routine. He continued to appear in the part for thirty years, until ill-health forced him to drop out of *Aladdin* at Nottingham in 1985.

Outside of pantomime he was also known for his memorable partnership with Roy Hudd in which they revived many old music hall routines.

In his prime he was known for tireless feet, and when they began to slow he was able to turn even this to comic advantage, bidding his audience to "talk amongst yourselves for a minute or two", while he got his breath back. He was a member of the Grand Order of Water Rats.

William Hooper Frank John Dainty was initiated into Chelsea Lodge on 19 March 1971. He died 19 November 1986, Godalming, Surrey, aged 59 years, leaving a widow and a son.

Arthur DAKIN

Musician. Born 1938, Dulwich south London. His family moved to Blackpool when he was two years old. He began his professional career as a drummer working in local clubs and theatres. Later he moved back to London where he worked at the Palladium and it was there he met his future wife Jacqui, a singer.

Arthur became musical director for *Opportunity Knocks* star Lena Zavaroni and the Bachelors as well as drummer for comedians Roy Hudd and **Freddie 'Parrot Face' Davies**. As his career progressed he became tour manager for the Combined Services Entertainments organisation, travelling to both the Falkland Islands and Bosnia to entertain the troops. In recent years he worked as an orchestra contractor, fixing musicians for theatres, television and tours with such stars as Shirley Bassey, Jack Jones, Natalie Cole, Johnny Mathis and Howard Keel.

Initiated into Chelsea Lodge 17 September 1976. Died following an accident in his car when he drove through a ford near his home in Dorset and drowned, 22 November 2002. He was 64 and is survived by his wife Jacqui and two daughters Bethany and Lucy. Des Cluskey of the Bachelors said: "Arthur Dakin's funeral was a joy...nice, friendly and a good memory of a good friend...I visited the scene of the accident...what a tragedy."

Alfred DANIELS

Banjoist/musician. Real name Alfred David Toledano. Fifteenth and final child born to Clara Martin and Joseph Daniels (Toledano) on 20 November 1883. His father Joe Daniels was a renowned and respected banjo maker, teacher, composer, and performer who played for the Prince of Wales (later King Edward VII). He was presented by the Prince with a silver medallion

inscribed with the Fleur de Lys - and this was fixed to the peghead of the banjo that Joe Daniels always played in his public performances. Joe Daniels had a studio at 112 Leadenhall Street, London. He patented the "Defiance" banjo. He insisted that all of his children learn to play the banjo and produced a miniature instrument for each child's instruction. This colourful, musical family, actually resided in two houses that were connected - and named "Minstrel House", located at 34 Grove Road, London where Alfred Daniels was born.

As a youngster Alfred, the baby of the family, became quite a banjoist in his own right. At the age of twelve he had a command performance in front of Queen Victoria. He was very famous for having adapted the *William Tell Overture*

(Rossini) for the banjo. He performed throughout Great Britain. His granddaughter, Angela Heiss has an extant playbill from 1910 (Alfred was 26 years old). He was performing with Walter Dowling's Co., the "Fantastics". This troupe included: Mr Burt Durant, Mr Percival Mackenzie, Mr Roland Green and, of course, Mr. Walter Dowling. The summer tour of 1910 began in May at Southampton Pier and ended on 3 September at Harrogate.

In 1916 Alfred fell in love and married a young dancer, Rose Taylor and set up home in Hendon, north London. Their daughter, Claire, was born in 1917 and son Joseph Kenneth in 1920.

Alfred decided to quit performing and travelling in order to be with his family. He owned several businesses over the years: a Jowett car franchise (F.O.C.H. 'Fair Officer Car House'), two cinemas in Maidstone, Kent and later a neon sign factory on Brent Street known as 'Young's Signs'. Although he gave up professional performing, he continued to play the banjo for family and friends and was always the consummate showman.

Alfred's daughter Claire (now 86 years old and living in the USA) fondly remembers her father's connection to both the Chelsea and Vaudeville Lodges. She especially remembers her mother's excitement in London when the Lodges hosted their annual Ladies Nights. Both Alfred and his son, Kenneth, had been members of both Lodges prior to their emigration to California, USA.

In 1944, Alfred's daughter Claire, a WAAF flight officer during the Second World War met and married an American from California. After her departure to California in 1946, her parents and brother soon followed. Alfred, Rose, and Kenneth Daniels lived the rest of their lives in Los Angeles, California. Alfred's family remembers his show business tales, his stories of Pretty Benny and Sweaty Fred, of Little Tich and **Lupino Lane**. Alfred was worldly-wise, very witty (naming his dog 'Guess'), and adored by all who knew him. His banjo remains a treasured family heirloom as does sheet music for the banjo composed by his father.

Alfred David Daniels (Toledano) was initiated into Chelsea Lodge on 15 March 1912. His son **Joseph Kenneth Daniels** was initiated on 19 May 1944. Both resigned in 1947 when they went to live in America. Alfred died 8 December 1964 at his daughter's home in Hollywood, aged 81 years. Kenneth died 13 December 1985, aged 65 years.

Joe DANIELS

Musician. Joe, born in Zeerut, Transvaal, South Africa on 9 March 1909, was just two when his father died. Shortly after this his mother brought Joe and his two brothers to England. All three brothers ended up in show business, Len was a musician who later ran a music shop in Soho and Syd became **Sirdani** the stage magician with the catch phrase "Don't be fright" when coaxing members of the audience on stage to help him. His cousin was **Joe Arbiter** who became a top flight saxophonist with the Harry Roy Band.

Joe did his first gig as a schoolboy at a Jewish wedding in Stoke Newington. He was still attending school when he was offered a resident job every evening at Frascati's Restaurant, playing for a clowning bandleader aptly named Loonie, who danced, turned cartwheels and somersaults. It was while providing the "sound effects" for these antics that Joe began to develop his dynamic showy style which he called drumnastics and which made him famous. It wasn't long before he was playing professionally in variety with Harry and Burton Lester's Cowboy band in 1922 when he was fourteen. After that he spent a year sailing across the Atlantic from Southampton to New York and back as a member of the band on board the liner *SS Majestic*. Back on dry land he toured for a while in a revue called *There You Are Then* and played with West End club bands. For a six-month season he led his own group at the Ice Palace in Madrid, Spain. There were also spells at the Glasgow Palais de Dance and Belfast Plaza with Al Kaplan, a band which included his tenor saxophonist brother Len and his alto saxophonist cousin **Joe Arbiter..**

He played for Al Tabor for three years at the Hammersmith Palais and by 1930 was with Billy Mason's Band at London's Café de Paris, but the following year made probably the most significant move of his career joining Harry Roy's R.K.Olians at the Leicester Square Theatre. During his six years with Harry he formed a jazz group within the band that by the mid-thirties was recording on Parlophone as Joe Daniels and his Hot Shots, their first disc being *St Louis Blues* coupled with *Sweet Sue* in 1935. His first recordings were with Hal Swain and the New Prince's Orchestra on Regal on 20 June 1927 when he recorded *Muddy Water*, coupled with *Moonlight and You*. A further 34 tracks were recorded in 1927 and 1928 before Joe moved to banjoist Pete Mandell's Rhythm Masters on Imperial and Victory in 1929. During his career he made a number of drum tuition records which enjoyed excellent sales. He became enormously popular with his mischievous sense of humour and his driving beat, especially when backing the two pianists, Ivor Moreton and Dave Kaye.

In January 1937 he left Harry to tour with his fiery Hot Shots, but in 1939 war service intervened and he spent the next six years with the RAF, three years at Swinderby, Lincs and three years in Scotland, where he continued to lead a quintet and still managed to record the occasional disc.

Following his demob in September 1945 he reformed the Hot Shots with the accent now on the popular Dixieland style. Singers and dancers with the band were Joe's wife Mary Nolan, whom he had married in 1934, and Yvonne Cliff. The band, looking extremely smart in wine coloured jerseys and white flannels, toured extensively including several visits to service camps overseas. There were also times when Joe disbanded to do a solo-drumming act around the variety halls.

By the early fifties, experimenting with different styles, Joe dropped the Hot Shots title and for the summer of 1951 formed a new Dixieland group that appeared in the presence of Princess Elizabeth at the National Federation of Jazz Organisations concert at Royal Festival Hall on 14th July. One commentator noted, "This is a real jazz band". However, the following year Joe almost gave up jazz altogether, taking a dance band with vocalists Mike Stevens and Barbara Young to Butlin's Ayr Holiday Camp for the season. The same year he had become a partner in a business that turned Slough Theatre into Slough Palais de Dance. Often appearing there with his own boys he installed as resident group the Harry Conway All Stars, "the band with the beat for dancers".

Summer seasons for Butlin's became a regular thing for Joe from 1951 to 1974, taking him to camps at Filey, Skegness and Clacton. His billing read "not the biggest band, not the loudest band, but the danciest band". Campers enjoyed his relaxed big band jazz, his cheerful personality and his friendly approach. To all the children he was Uncle Joe! When summer was over Joe returned to his first love and toured with a jazz group around the clubs.

He also made two records for Parlophone in 1955 working under the name of Washboard Joe and His Scrubbers. Not a lot of people know that! Chelsea colleague **Max Goldberg** played trumpet on those two records *Paper Kisses* and *Big Banjo Band*.

During much of the sixties Joe virtually gave up touring having taken on a Wimpy Bar franchise. Slough Palais had been sold to the proprietor of Wembley Majestic Ballroom in 1955. Joe did continue with his Butlin seasons providing all - round entertainment with a big band, something that lasted twenty-three years, and in 1969 he gave up the burger bar and went back on the road.

He was still gigging with his own trios and quartets until he was over 80 years of age, but he suffered a stroke and developed muscular weakness in his legs, probably caused by playing drums in cramped conditions for years, and this virtually crippled him. His one big regret in life was never bothering to collect his records. Although he had been trying to buy a set of them, he was still many short. Towards the end of his days and leading a quiet life in Wembley he found an unexpected talent for painting. His pictures ranged from clowns and aeroplanes to animals and flowers.

Joseph Daniels was initiated into Chelsea Lodge on 20 March 1942. He died 1 July 1993 aged 86, never the world's greatest drummer but a true showman and certainly one of the most entertaining. He was cremated at Golders Green cemetery, a service attended by many musician friends and his widow Mary. At the funeral service the Rabbi told the story of how Joe, although bed ridden, had a pair of his favourite drum sticks by his bedside and how each morning he would practice drum rolls on a glass or plate. He was a drummer to the end.

Billy DANVERS

Comedian. Born 1886, Liverpool. Full name William Mikado Danvers, he owed his middle name to the fact that his comedian father was appearing in the Gilbert and Sullivan operetta, *The Mikado*, at the time of his birth. His father was Jimmy Danvers, a popular comedian in the North, his grandfather Edwin Danvers a burlesque actor of the 1860s, and his uncle the eccentric comedian Ramsey Danvers. His first appearance, at the age of four, was in a music hall comedy routine played by his father and Little Tich at the Tyne Theatre, Newcastle. He began his career as part of the double-act of 'Billy and Frank Bass', making his London appearance at the Bedford, Camden Town, in 1911. He appeared in *See-Saw* at the Comedy Theatre, London, December 1916. Touring solo in 1918 and billing himself as 'Cheeky, Cheery and Chubby', he was very much the red-nosed comic of the old school.

His success was not confined to variety; he worked in concert party, revue, and musical comedy, including two tours of *Miss Hook of*

Holland and *The Belle of New York*. He was a great pantomime artiste, appearing as Buttons at the Theatre Royal, Drury Lane, London in 1934. From 1948-1950 he toured with Don Ross's show *Thanks for the Memory* appearing with the company in the Royal Variety Performance in November 1948.

Billy never retired and in 1964 toured with another *Thanks for the Memory* company which included Hetty King, **Sandy Powell,** Marie Lloyd Junior, Cavan O'Connor and Trevor Moreton. For the week of 2 March 1964 the show played the Granada, Brixton, where in February 1948 the original company had commenced its successful tour.

He was described as an artiste whose warm geniality and friendliness reached to every corner of the theatre whatever its size. He lived and worked by the motto "If you make them laugh, you make them feel good."

William Mikado Danvers was a member of the Grand Order of Water Rats. He was initiated into Chelsea Lodge on 16 June 1922. He died 20 March 1964, aged 78 years

Jim DAVIDSON, OBE PM

Comedian Born 13 December 1953 Blackheath, London. Educated at St Austen's Catholic School, Charlton. Given his first show business break at the age of twelve in Ralph Reader's *Gang Show* at the Golders Green Hippodrome. He did five minutes of impressions. At the time he thought, 'This is great. Show business is marvellous.' His father commented, 'You may be in the *Gang Show* and you're a talented lad, but keep your feet on the ground, son, and think about getting a job.'

Jim had been given a drum kit by his parents and by the age of sixteen was playing drums in a pub in Woolwich. His first 'real' job was as a messenger at Millbank Travel in New Bond Street, London. As a hobby he enjoyed fishing and on one occasion caught a 21.5 pound carp.

He has been married (and divorced) four times 1) Sue Walpole, one daughter. 2) Julie Gullick, one son. 3) Alison Holloway and 4) Tracy Hilton, one son and two daughters.

Appeared in *New Faces* (ATV) in 1976. This was followed by numerous personal appearances as a comedian in pubs around London. His manager was Wally Dent and his agent, **Laurie Mansfield.**

His TV appearances include: *What's On Next* (1976); *Jim Davidson Show* comprising four

seasons and fifteen specials on Thames TV from 1979-1987 and won him the *TV Times* award as "Funniest Man of the Year"; *Big Break* (BBC) 1989 to date; *Generation Game* 1994 to 2002; *Jim*

Davidson – a Bit Further (BBC) from the Victoria Palace Theatre, London in 1999.

Appeared in the film *A Zed and Two Noughts* (1985). Jim starred in the high rating TV sitcoms *Up The Elephant And Round The Castle* and *Home James*. His one-man show for Thames TV *Stand Up Jim Davidson* was recorded on stage at London's Royalty Theatre and he has also starred in a number of his own TV specials for ITV and, most recently, for BBC TV. He hosted a brand new BBC1 TV series from the Cambridge Theatre, London titled *Jim Davidson Presents* and on Christmas Day 2000 he presented a TV special from HMS *Invincible*, *Homeward Bound for Christmas* on BBC1.

He has appeared in pantomime in Brighton and Oxford and summer seasons in Bournemouth, Blackpool, Margate, Great Yarmouth, Southampton and Torquay.

Jim formed a Charity Trust in 1995 and applied to the Lottery Commission and the Arts Council for some money to renovate Wellington Pier and Pavilion in Great Yarmouth which was falling to pieces. He paid £750,000 out of his own money to put the theatre into good order but then learned that the Lottery people would not give the Trust any money. Next door to the Pier was the Winter Gardens which he gutted, borrowed £200,000 from a brewery and built a brand new nightclub made of glass which can accommodate 1,250 people at a time. Not only did he own a pier and a theatre but a nightclub as well.

Highlights of an outstanding career have included five visits to the Falkland Islands and engagements throughout the world entertaining British Service personnel. In 1999 he travelled to Macedonia to entertain the forces and in the same year he launched and became Chairman of The British Forces Foundation charity.

Jim wrote and produced a 'blue' pantomime Sinderella which was a huge success. This was followed by Sinderella 2 and Sinderella Comes Again.

His theatre production credits include West End shows *Buddy* and *Great Balls of Fire*.

Jim's success has also embraced videos, audio cassettes, CDs and books. His current album is *Watching Over You* (Universal) produced by Greg Lake. His best-selling autobiography *Close To The Edge* (Ebury Press) and his latest adult video Jim *Davidson Uncovered and Uncensored* (Universal) were released at the end of 2001

Since 1997 he has received three coveted Showbusiness Personality of The Year Awards - from the Variety Club of Great Britain; Comic Heritage and in November 1998 from The Grand Order of Water Rats. Jim is today firmly established as one of the most popular entertainers in British show business and one of the country's funniest comedians.

In the New Year's Honours List 2001 he received an OBE for his services to charity.

In Spring 2002 he embarked on his sell-out 25th Anniversary Tour - a series of one-night live dates in his hilarious adult stand-up show. Throughout the summer he appeared every Friday in Great Yarmouth and every Sunday in Bournemouth.

Earlier in 2000 his TV appearances included a major BBC project *Jim Davidson Falklands Bound* which was screened during the 20th anniversary of the end of hostilities.

James Cameron Davidson was initiated into Chelsea Lodge in September 1991. WM from 2001-2002, although he resigned half way through his term of office. IPM Roger De Courcey took over the helm.

In his autobiography he says how important Freemasonry has been to him: "Freemasonry has taught me that we are all equal and that death is a great leveller. Freemasonry's just like that. You can go and sit in a Freemasons' Temple and find a Charlton supporter sitting next to a Millwall supporter; it's where a Hindu can sit next to a Sikh, or a Catholic can sit next to a Protestant and they promise to get on well…"

An in-depth interview with Jim Davidson conducted for *Freemasonry Today* can be found in Chapter 16 *Press Cuttings*.

Freddie DAVIES, PM

Comedian, actor. A Londoner born in Brixton, Freddie was evacuated in 1940 and after several stops along the way his family settled in Salford, Lancashire in 1941, where he stayed until National Service call up resulted in him joining the Royal Army Pay Corps. On demob in 1958, Freddie became a famous Butlin Redcoat alongside other budding comedians Dave Allen, Mike Newman and Jimmy Tarbuck. He stayed with Butlin's until 1963 after which, with just one appearance on Hughie Green's *Opportunity Knocks* on 1 August 1964, he went on to develop the character that was to become a national favourite, Parrotface. The rest is show business history and he has become one of Britain's best - loved and funniest comedians.

Freddie's fantastic career has taken him from the tough working men's clubs of the North East for thirty shillings a night (£1.50) to the Royal Shakespeare Company; seasons at the London Palladium, television shows with the legendary Judy Garland, touring the world with his stand-up comedy act and counting among his many fans, film idol, the late, Cary Grant. In a career spanning over forty years in show business he has seen the demise of the music halls, variety circuits and night clubs during the 1960s and 1970s.

His grandfather, Music Hall and Variety comedian, Jack Herbert, toured from the 1920s until the late 1950s, and much of Freddie's knowledge and experience was gained by studying many of the great performers of the day from the privileged position of the stage wings. This learning experience was invaluable in the development of his future performances. Many years later this memory and first hand background knowledge became very useful in forming the basic story line idea and premise for the critically acclaimed Disney backed film *Funnybones*, in which Freddie co-starred with Jerry Lewis, Leslie Caron, Oliver Reed and newcomer, Lee Evans.

An acting career always seemed inevitable but it was not until 1992, after a spell in the USA that Freddie was taken seriously as an actor. He has now appeared in many television drama series including *Casualty, Heartbeat, Preston Front, Hetty Wainthrop Investigates, Band of Gold, Medics, Micky Love, Last of the Summer Wine* and two series as George Blade in Nick Berry's *Harbour Lights.*

On stage Freddie starred in the nationwide theatre tour of Victoria Wood's play *Talent* and more recently in a record-breaking tour of Agatha Christie's mystery *Murder at the Vicarage.*

From September 2000 until June 2001 Freddie appeared in his first West-End musical as Ben the Gardener in the stunning RSC production of *The Secret Garden* at the Aldwych Theatre.

Frederick Shenstone Davies was initiated into Chelsea Lodge on the 16 March 1966. In the chair was W.Bro. **Issy Bonn** and he performed the ceremony of initiation. Afterwards at the festive board Issy sang the initiate song, *This is Your Finest Hour*, which he wrote and performed for the Lodge.

Freddie's proposer was **Frank Mansell** and was seconded by **Maurice Fogel**. Says Freddie "Frank became the entertainment boss for Butlin's and had been the mentor to many a show

biz starter. He had also been the first to see the potential and kick-started my budding career having given me a job as a Redcoat in 1958. I left Butlin's in 1963 after six wonderful years. Frank was a great encouragement.

"The 'Amazing Fogel' did a one man magic show mainly mental and thought-provoking illusions but sensational none the less."

Freddie proudly went through all the chairs of the lodge and became Worshipful Master in 1986-1987.

Lew DAVIS

Musician. Born 4 August 1903. One of the most highly respected trombone players in Great Britain in the 1920s and 1930s. Played in the Darnswells (directed by Syd Roy, and including Harry Roy) in 1920. With the Happy Six (with Jack Block) and in Mitchell's Syncopated Band at Rector's Club, London (1921). Worked in Dixie Five in Norway (1921, and with Laurie  Huntingdon's Dixie Five in Ostend. Returned to London and worked in Frolic Club's Five Blues (with his brother, sax-ophonist, Ben Davis) and with Harry and Syd Roy in the Original Lyrical Five. He was with Mitchell's Syncopated Number One Orchestra at Hammersmith Palais and later toured British music halls in a band led by pianist Billy Jones.

Lew has appeared on dozens of old 78s of dance band music. He joined Jack Hylton's band about 1923 and was featured on all their recordings from February 1923 through until June 1930, a total of 950 different tracks. The recordings were made in London, Glasgow and Berlin. Some were recorded at the EMI studios in Hayes, Middlesex but the majority took place in the Queen's Hall, Langham Place (opposite Broadcasting House, where the Langham Hotel stands today). There were two auditoria within the building, the main hall and the small Queen's Hall. Both were destroyed by enemy action during the Second World War together with many valuable instruments stored in the building.

After Lew left the Jack Hylton band he continued to record for the **Roy Fox** Band and Harry Hudson. In addition he worked with Jack

Harris, George Hurley, Joe Crossman and Ray Starita. In 1931-1932 he toured with Louis Armstrong. This was followed by time with Carroll Gibbons and he later rejoined Lew Stone.

He joined Ray Noble with the New Mayfair Dance Orchestra in 1932 for two years. This is where he worked with another trombone player and colleague **Tony Thorpe**. This included a tour of Holland in August 1933.

Lew moved to the Ambrose Orchestra in December 1934 and remained with them until 1937, although he did record for the Lew Stone Band during this time.

He became increasingly active in managing his own music business in Charing Cross Road, which included designing mutes and mouthpieces. He combined this with freelance music making, but then gave up playing to concentrate on a highly successful business enterprise located in the centre of the music industry, an area surrounded by music publishers and dominated by the giant Selmer instrument store. It was next to the Phoenix Theatre, controlled by Ben Davis who had long given up being an active musician when he secured the Selmer agency, and spent the remainder of his life selling instruments of all kinds to fellow musicians including Jimmy Dorsey and Louis Armstrong during their visits to the UK.

Lew is reported as saying: "If I had a million pounds, I'd take a trip around the world, something I have wanted to do ever since I was a kid. I'd travel through the East, but miss out Australia. I have never wanted to go there. Then through India, China (if things gets a bit quieter), South America and finishing up in America. I'd probably stay in New York and drink in my fill of those American bands I have enjoyed on my radio and gramophone. I'm not sure whether I'd settle in England or America. I am told there is not much tax in America, but if you have a million you don't have to worry much - or do you?"

Lewis Davis was initiated into Chelsea Lodge on 20 April 1934. He died 24 November 1986, aged 83 years.

Roger De COURCEY, PM PAGDC

Entertainer/ventriloquist. Born 10 December 1944, London, Roger has established himself as one of Britain's leading entertainers and two highly successful seasons in Las Vegas plus an engagement at the giant O'Keefe Centre in Toronto, Canada have added an international reputation to his credit.

He has appeared several times at the London Palladium, including a Royal Variety Performance and has starred in theatres and nightclubs throughout the UK including summer seasons and pantomimes.

Roger first broke into showbusiness as an opera singer. As a singer he moved into the West End stage, appearing in such musicals as *Sweet Charity* and *Company*. However, it was on an engagement in the domestic cabaret circuit that he discovered 'Nookie' and he then decided to develop an act around ventriloquism.

The irrepressible 'Nookie Bear' first delighted viewers in the series *New Faces* from which Roger went on to win the 1976 Grand Final. Since then TV appearances have been numerous including his own series *Now For Nookie* and guest spots in virtually every major light entertainment show.

He appeared in the Royal Variety Performance in front of Her Majesty Queen Elizabeth The Queen Mother at the London Palladium on 15 November 1976.

More recently Roger has appeared with 'Nookie' as the guest manager on the cult TV show *Fantasy Football League*, BBC2's *The Sunday Show*, *The Alphabet Game* for BBC1, Channel 4's *Light Lunch* and BBC1's *The Generation Game*.

Roger is a keen golfer and in 1992 was honoured with the position of Captain of the Variety Club Golfing Society. 1993 saw him inaugurated at Prince Rat and in 1994 he was delighted to have been elected the prestigious position of King Rat for the Grand Order of Water Rats, which is the highest honour in this order. This meant a full year of charity work throughout 1994.

He continues to enjoy outstanding success in all spheres of the entertainment industry travelling worldwide to various functions both as cabaret artiste and after-dinner speaker. He is a Lord's Taverner.

Roger recently joined forces with the former head of entertainment for Rank Leisure, Kyran Jesson, to form Universal Show Entertainments Agency.

W.Bro. Roger De Courcey joined Chelsea Lodge in March 1990 from Lodge of Manna No.7602 where he was initiated in 1975, and became Master in 1988. WM of Chelsea in 2001 and for part of 2002. Promoted to Grand Rank in 2003.

Joe DINDOL

Stand up comedian. Born February 1920. Began his show business career in the Royal Air Force in 1940 at St. Athan, South Wales. After the war he married and had two children and joined his family's clothing business, but was often asked to do after dinner speeches. He regularly performed at hotels, on cruise liners and at charity functions and eventually became noticed by a variety show producer who booked him for a season at the London Palladium and then the Talk of the Town; he subsequently went on to perform at every major venue in London.

W.Bro. **Cyril Packer** saw him at one of these performances, met him and became friends and eventually Joe was invited to join Chelsea Lodge. He not only loved Chelsea, but it is fair to say that he rapidly became one of the Lodges best-loved Festive Board performers. A surprisingly quiet and unassuming man, all that changed as soon as he got on his feet and hilarity would reign. His dry sense of Jewish humour, quick wit, masterful timing and delivery never failed to bring the house down and visitors to the Lodge invariably asked to be invited again after one of his sessions.

Joe has been a wonderful supporter of Chelsea Lodge and has performed at countless functions and Ladies' Nights. One of his favourite roles was as "The Great Dindole" a "stand-up comedic magician", whose tricks always managed to go hilariously wrong and for ever had the audience rolling in the aisles. Sadly, failing health now prevents Joe attending Lodge but he is very proud of his long association with Chelsea.

Joseph Dindol joined Chelsea Lodge 28 September 1984 from King David Lodge No.5719.

Reg DIXON

Comedian. Born 24 February 1915. Began his show business career as a child actor in his hometown of Coventry and as a teenager toured with Lord George Sanger's Circus. Quite a competent musician and songwriter he later played in Variety as half of a piano double act Scott and Dixon, while developing his droll humour and songs.

He became one of the most popular radio comedians of the 1940s and 1950s and is well remembered for his catch phrase "I'm poorly... proper poorly" and for the song *Confidentially* that he wrote himself.

After wartime service in the Royal Air Force,

where he appeared in the *RAF Gang Show*, and toured with **Peter Sellers**, Tony Hancock, **Dick Emery**, Graham Stark and Cardew Robinson, Reg returned to the boards playing summer seasons and pantomime. However, it was on radio that most people heard him. During the early fifties he was one of the regular comedians on, and often compered, radio's *Variety Bandbox* and promoted his own stage show under the title *To Look at Me* (another catch phrase) which played variety theatres around the country. He appeared in a feature of music hall songs in the 1952 Royal Variety Performance and in *Happy Holiday* at the Palace Theatre, London in December 1954.

Reg had parts in two films *Love in Paris* (1953) and *No Smoking* (1955) and made his first television appearance in a live telecast from Blackpool Tower Ballroom during July, 1953. He was on ITV's opening night variety show *Channel Nine* on 22 September 1955. Reg continued to tour in variety through the sixties and seventies, while his broadcasts included a straight role playing a stable lad in the series *Confidentially, They're Off*.

Reg was a member of the Grand Order of Water Rats.

Used to playing Buttons in pantomime, in later years he became an excellent 'dame' and was still professionally active in the early eighties. Reg died 26 June 1984 at his home in Bournemouth, where his wife Gladys was still living a decade later. He was 69. As well as his signature tune Reg recorded several songs, most displaying his humourous North Country style.

Ray DONN

For someone who began life in the licensed trade Ray has met and worked with a galaxy of stars and Royalty. He entered the licensed trade in 1961. In all he spent 36 years running pubs, clubs and hotels. He also ran Ray Donn (Leisure) Ltd., a licensed entertainment and management agency-booking artistes for clubs, theatre and TV (1970-1984).

From 1966-1980 he produced and directed the annual Publand *Variety Show* featuring the top performers from pub and club entertainment. This was presented at major London Theatres concluding at the London Palladium.

Ray was secretary of the Comedians Golfing Society from 1978-1984.

Perhaps his most treasured charity is the Entertainment Artistes' Benevolent Fund with which he has been involved since 1974. He is currently Treasurer.

Ray took early retirement from the licensed trade in 1997, sold up and headed for a new career as a film extra or supporting artiste (SA) as they are now known. His first appearance was in the film *Notting Hill*. Since then he has appeared in over 50 films and 30 television commercials. He says that being a professional extra has enabled him to dress in period or unusual costume, working at locations including stately homes and famous buildings.

He has worked with dozens of major names including: Robert Hardy, Bob Hoskins, Julia Roberts, Martin Clunes, Neil Morrissey, Edward Fox, Hugh Grant, John Voigt, Derek Jacobi, Edward Woodward, Christopher Plummer ... and the list goes on.

Asked what has been his most interesting assignment to date Ray says: "I was sent by my agent for a casting to play the character Hercule Poirot the David Suchet version (someone said I resemble him). When I got there the room was full of Poirot's, all shapes and sizes some in full costume.... very professional! It came to my turn to go in front of the casting director. I slipped off my raincoat, took out my little "Poirot" moustache from my pocket and stuck it under my nose. Profile left and right in front of camera, muttered some French type gibberish, thanked them for seeing me and I was gone!

"Four days later my agent rang and informed me that I had been successful at the casting and I have got the job. "Great", I said..."Where?"... "Denmark" she said. "The street?", I asked... "No Copenhagen!"... "Fine fax me the details"... as if it happened every day.

"The job was a commercial for "Tele Danmark" (similar company to our BT) I was flown out to Copenhagen on a Friday night, met at the airport, and taken to a nice hotel. The next morning costume and make-up came to the hotel got me ready and took me to the set, a tourist tour boat on the canal, with 20 extra's.

"I performed as Hercule Poirot all day as a tour guide, with a microphone at the front of the boat pointing out the places of interest to a bunch of my fellow SAs.

"The plot of the commercial was 'You do not have to be a well-known detective to understand the new Denmark telephone directory'...go ask!

"I was shipped back to the UK on the Saturday night...job done.

"The commercial was shown all over Denmark,

nice fee and a star for a day!"

Since 1997 Ray has been Honorary Treasurer of the Vaudeville Golfing Society.

He designed and also maintains the websites for the Entertainment Artistes' Benevolent Fund, The Actors Charitable Trust, Grand Order of Lady Ratlings, Grand Order of Water Rats, Vaudeville Golfing Society and The Bud Flanagan Leukemia Fund.

Ray has been presented to Her Majesty the Queen, HM The Queen Mother and HRH Prince of Wales on numerous occasions in the capacity of Hon.Treasurer to the Entertainment Artistes Benevolent Fund at the annual Royal Variety Performance.

Ray Donn was initiated into Chelsea Lodge on 19 September 1997. Proposed by Bro. **Peter Elliott** and Seconded by Bro. **Peter Prichard** OBE.

Bunny DOYLE

Comedian. Real name Bernard Doyle. Born Hull, 1898. Described as 'The Minister for Idiotic Affairs.' He was a Pierrot at the age of twelve and appeared in various seaside concert party shows. He was particularly popular in the north of England. Bunny later moved into revue, Variety and pantomime.

He was activated into the First World War and he won the Croix de Guerre for 'Conspicuous Gallantry'. In the Second World War he performed for ENSA, appeared in the film *Facing the Music* (1941) and by the age of fifty he was a well-known character actor.

Bernard Doyle was a member of the Grand Order of Water Rats. He was initiated into Chelsea Lodge on 15 September 1944. Died 27 August 1955, aged 57 years.

Jimmie DUNEDIN

Variety artiste and later variety agent. Born 1853, Australia. Real name James Edward Donegan. Manager and trainer of Dunedin Troupe of bicyclists who were formed in 1883. Previously he was a well-known Australian sportsman.

In the space of thirty weeks in 1906 the troupe completed a successful tour of America playing in 171 towns with the Ringling Brothers' Circus. In New York they appeared at all the leading establishments, including the Hippodrome. The reception given to the clever band of trick cyclists was of a most enthusiastic nature. Press notices were abundant, one of them in a New York newspaper being as follows:

"A review of the Dunedin Troupe of bicyclists could begin and end by the statement that it is the best bicycle act in show business. That it is. The team riding commences where all the others leave off, and the troupe continues with a boy who stands far above all other riders for straight fancy work. This young man does two complete whirls around the handle-bars while in motion before alighting upon the seat. It has been done by others, but with one whirl only. He also rides a ''quad' upon one wheel, and there is not the least bit of riding throughout done on two wheels, either by the boys or the girls. There are two of each. The young women are riders, dancers, singers and are doing something all the time to keep the stage alive. Both are excellent acrobats in addition. Besides the bicycle riding on the stage, there is balancing on a tight wire by one boy and one girl seated on machines. Even the music is good".

After leaving the American capital, there were appearances in Chicago, Los Angeles, Salt Lake City, Cincinnati, Boston, Philadelphia and many other towns and cities. The Dunedin Troupe then moved on to Canada appearing in Ottawa, Montreal and Toronto before returning to England on the *SS Cedric*, which left New York on 18 June 1907.

Talking to *The Era* newspaper on 11 July 1908, Jimmie said: "We were treated very well in the States, and our tour was a big success. Fortunately there were no accidents but, of course, several very narrow squeaks. The Americans are first-rate judges of good acts, and they like anything that is really clever. Their enthusiasm is most encouraging. I have travelled all over the world, and I find that America is one of the best countries I was ever in. There are so many opportunities for everybody with ability, especially young ones."

Jimmie proudly boasted that he took around with him a couple of his grandchildren, who were keen bicyclists. And how old was grandad at the time? Just fifty-four years of age.

He was the fourth initiate into Chelsea Lodge on 16 June 1905.

Jimmy DURRANT

Musician and arranger. Born 1911. Played clarinet, soprano saxophone, alto saxophone, tenor saxophone and baritone saxophone. Made recordings with Brian Lawrence and the Lansdowne House Orchestra (1936-1940) on the

Rex and Decca labels. He attended 114 recording sessions between 1935-1950 playing soprano, alto and baritone saxophones, clarinet and viola as well as arranging musical scores.

Was a member of the Royal Air Force Dance Orchestra and also the Squadronaires during Second World War. *Melody Maker*, January 1941 described a radio concert of the Squadronaires as: "The greatest dance band ever broadcast this side of the Atlantic". Playing everything from Dixieland to Jive, the Squadronaires was the first British service band to make its mark. They created adventurous swing, which, thanks to quality records on the Decca label, can still be savoured to this day. They also appeared in a 1943 film *The Life and Death of Colonel Blimp*. The Squadronaires played on into the post-war era under Ronnie Aldrich, disbanding a civilian group in the early 1960s.

James Durrant was initiated into Chelsea Lodge on 17 February 1939.

Robert EARL

Vocalist. Real name Montague Leigh. Born 17 November 1926 just off the Whitechapel Road in London's East End. From a schoolboy he always wanted to sing. He learned his singing at dances, small clubs and weddings close to where he lived. Those days he would earn in the region of fifteen shillings per show, he was singing for people, that was the important thing. However, he had to earn a living and he worked in a gown shop. There he made tea, swept floors, kept the books and travelled around selling gowns by day and singing at night. Slowly but surely he became more established with his singing and worked with the orchestras of Sidney Lipton, **Nat Temple** and **Van Straten.**

Robert auditioned for Norman Newell at Philips Records and was given a four-year contract which meant he could give up his day job and turn professional. This he did in 1950 and appeared regularly on television and radio in *The Jack Jackson Show* and *Off The Record*. He didn't have to wait too long before his name appeared in the best selling records of the day. His first record was *If You Love Me* backed with *Crying in the Chapel* in September 1953 beating Perry Como to the British charts. *I May Never Pass This Way Again* entered the British charts at number fourteen in April 1958 where it remained for nearly three months and sold in excess of a quarter of a million copies. *Come Prima* followed in the same year

and in 1959 he enjoyed his third and final top thirty hit, *Wonderful Secret of Love*. In all he recorded fourteen singles, two LPs and four EPs.

Robert's first radio broadcast was *In Town Tonight*, followed very quickly by *Workers' Playtime* where he appeared with **Peter Sellers.** Robert, who sang a couple of songs, earned the fee of seven guineas whereas Sellers, as top of the bill comedian, collected nine guineas.

He has worked with many artistes over the years including Bruce Forsyth, Tommy Cooper, Harry Worth, Ken Dodd, **Dick Emery, Bud Flanagan, Issy Bonn,** Josef Locke and Morecambe and Wise and has fond memories of summer seasons in Blackpool and Great Yarmouth when thousands of holidaymakers would flock to see the shows.

Robert, who has a rich and resonant voice, is always in demand. He toured the variety theatres until their day finally waned. Since then he has been a richly paid performer in clubs, in pantomime and summer seasons. He has also travelled the world performing in luxury liners. He is married to Daphne and they have a son Robert who lives in Orlando, Florida and has kept the Earl name alive as President of Planet Hollywood restaurants. He has a son Robert Earl III who is already showing signs of entering the world of show business.

Robert retired as a singer in 1970 and then joined London Management as an agent for five years until he retired permanently.

For many years the Earl family lived in Hendon,

but now they split their affection between America and Britain, spending six months in each country.

He is a member of the Grand Order of Water Rats, The Entertainment Artistes' Benevolent Fund and the Bud Flanagan Leukemia Fund and an energetic worker for various charities. He is a golfing fanatic and belongs to the Vaudeville Golfing Society.

Robert Earl was initiated into Chelsea Lodge on 15 September 1967.

Kenneth EARLE

(A Lewis). Actor, comedian, theatrical management and consultancy. Born 1930, Liverpool, into a theatrical family, his parents were jugglers (Percy Rich and Eva) and he toured with them until he was nine years old. Became a boarder at Dulwich College. Completed National Service in the RAF.

Kenneth began his show business career as an actor in films before becoming the comedy half of Kenneth Earle and Malcolm Vaughan. Both met during the Old Mother Riley road show. The

double act achieved a high profile in the entertainment world during the eighteen years they were together. They played all the major theatres, appeared in numerous television programmes and many pantomimes. Malcolm enjoyed ten hit records in the British charts between 1955 and 1959. Both were honoured to become "Members of the Grand Order of Water Rats" on 15 October 1961. When the act folded Kenneth returned to acting and appeared in a few films.

In 1972 he chose the path to management and became an agent looking after personalities appearing in Las Vegas, the London Palladium, films, television and West End plays. Additionally he has written, produced and directed a number of pantomimes and summer seasons in England and Jersey, in theatres, hotels and nightclubs.

The famous London Management asked him to join them, where he stayed for ten years, booking most of the American artistes for the *Des O'Connor Show*, looking after artistes such as Des, Patrick McNee, Hugh Lloyd, Linda Lusadi, Kit and the Widow, Jon Pertwee and many more,

including directors and writers.

When the time came to move on Kenneth was offered the position of account holder for the whole of the Butlin's circuit of worlds and hotels under the Rank banner. During his four years with the company he booked thousands of artistes and many major stars, both English and American. He devised and produced comedy / rock / adult / festivals, also writing and producing shows for the circuit.

In June 1995 he opened his own agency Kenneth Earle Personal Management with a high profile client list incorporating actors, actresses, authors and directors. He has directed pantomimes and conceived, directed and co - produced the successful touring show *Spirit of the Dance* in 1996. He is also busy as a theatrical consultant.

Kenneth was honoured to become President of the Agents Association (GB) in 1993. He is now Joint Trustee of the Agents Benevolent Fund, Joint Secretary of the Variety and Light Entertainment Council, and sits on the Theatres Advisory Council Committee. He is a member of the Grand Order of Water Rats.

Kenneth Earle was initiated into Chelsea Lodge on 18 March 1988. He says: "**Freddie Davis** and **Bernard Bresslaw** proposed and seconded me. My father was about 90 at the time and I thought I would not mention it to him, as he was rather frail. Subsequently he died at the age of 92. Going through his effects I came across his apron. I never knew for positive that he was a Freemason. Imagine my astonishment when I saw he was initiated in 1930 under his given name Percy Richards (known as **Beaucaire**) into Chelsea Lodge. Out of all the lodges in the UK we were both initiated into the same one, without either knowing…imagine the odds on that!"

Jim EASTON

Musician. Born 1908. Played clarinet, baritone, tenor and alto saxophones who worked with Brian Lawrence and Sydney Lipton Bands in the 1930s. Recorded with **Roy Fox** Band from 1930 to 1932 on Decca records. Recorded with Lew Stone and his Band from 1932-1940 on Decca records. He replaced Freddy Gardner for radio broadcasts in August 1933. After Freddy died Jim was given Freddy's tenor saxophone. Recorded with the Jack Hylton Orchestra from 1935 to 1937 on HMV.

He was a keen golfer and played with Lew

Stone and Noel Webb.

William James Easton was initiated into Chelsea Lodge on 19 July 1940.

Marriott EDGAR

Born George Marriott Edgar, 5 October 1880, Kirkudbright, Scotland. Began his career in 1896 by being apprenticed to the scene-painter, H.P. Hall of the St James Theatre. He stayed there for two years, afterwards painting under Walter Hann and Pritchard Barrett. He went on tour with Percy Hutchison, became tired of scene-painting and began to play small parts. Later he went on tour with Charles Frohman's *Adventure of Lady Ursula Company*, and later still with W.W. Kelly's *New East Lynne* doubling the parts of Richard Hare and Lord Mountsevern.

Marriott was at the Prince's, Bristol for four years, as assistant stage-manager and general understudy. Leaving Bristol he went to the Prince's, Manchester to appear in pantomime.

During the Boer War he toured South Africa with George Edwardes' company. Returning to England, he toured as stage-manager for *The Torreador* and *Messenger Boy* companies. In 1903 he conceived the idea of going on the halls. He wrote for himself a couple of songs and started at the Palace, Camberwell. Subsequently he went out on tour with Eugene Stafford in the musical comedy *His Fatal Beauty*. Whilst on this tour George Scott saw Marriott, advised him to return to variety, and gave him a letter of introduction to Richard Warren, who immediately employed him.

By 1908 he had written some 25 songs. *The Reason Why I Dress in Red* proved to be one of his most popular. Two years later he made his fourth tour of South Africa.

Marriott was a very successful writer of monologues, made famous by Stanley Holloway, scriptwriter and actor for films.

In monologues he wrote: *Albert and the Lion, Albert and His Savings, Albert and the 'Eadsman, Albert's Return, Asparagus, Battle of Hastings, Balbus, Burghers of Calais, Canute the Great, Channel Swimmer, Fair Rosamund, George and the Dragon, Goalkeeper Joe, Gunner Joe, Henry the Seventh, Joe Ramsbottom, Jonah and the Grampus, Jubilee Sovereign, Little Aggie, Magna Carter, Marksman Sam, 'Ole in the Ark, Queen Matilda, Recumbent Posture, Richard Coeur de Lion, Runcorn Ferry, Sam Goes to It, Sam's Christmas Pudding, Sam's Racehorse, Three Ha' pence a Foot, Up'ards* and *William Rufus*.

Combined Filmography: *Top of the Form* (1953) [Writer], *Bees in Paradise* (1944) [Writer], *Miss London Ltd* (1943) [Writer], *Back-Room Boy* (1942) [Writer], *King Arthur Was a Gentleman* (1942) [Writer], *Ghost Train* (1941) [Writer], *Hi Gang!* (1941) [Writer], *I Thank You* (1941) [Writer], *Charlie's Big-Hearted Aunt* (1940) [Writer], *Gasbags* (1940) [Writer], *Ask a Policeman* (1939) [Writer], *Band Waggon* (1939) [Writer], *Convict 99* (1939) [Writer], *Frozen Limits* (1939) [Writer], *Where's That Fire?* (1939) [Writer], *Alf's Button Afloat* (1938) [Writer], *Hey! Hey! USA* (1938) [Writer], *Old Bones of the River* (1938) [Writer], *Good Morning, Boy's* (1937) [Writer], also known as *Where There's a Will* (1937) (USA), *Oh, Mr Porter!* (1937) [Writer], *Okay for Sound* (1937) [Writer], *Said O'Reilly to McNab* (1937) [Writer], *Windbag the Sailor* (1936) [Writer], *Hello, Sweetheart* (1935) [Actor], *Here's George* (1932) [Actor and Writer] and *Spare Room* (1932) [Writer].

Between the years 1920 and 1950 on stage Marriott appeared in *Tom, Tom, The Piper's Son; King of the Golden Mountain; The Forty Thieves; Co-Optimists; Robinson Crusoe and Jack and Jill* all at the Prince's Theatre, Bristol. He appeared in *Jack and the Beanstalk* at Drury Lane, London and *Cinderella* at the Coliseum, London and Hippodrome, Bristol.

Marriott was King Rat (1935) in the Grand Order of Water Rats.

Many of his famous monologues were read by Stanley Holloway in a television programme *The Barnstormers* broadcast on BBC2 in September 1969.

George Marriott Edgar was initiated into Chelsea Lodge 15 March 1912. WM 1938. Died 14 May 1951, Battle, Sussex, aged 70 years.

Tom EDWARDS

Born 1879. A popular personality who topped the bill at various theatres around the British Isles, Tom was known as 'The Huntsman Ventriloquist'.

Thomas Joseph Edwards was initiated into Chelsea Lodge on 19 June 1908. Died 1933. Buried in West Norwood Cemetery.

Albert and Seth EGBERT

Screen actors and music hall performers. One of the earliest knockabout acts of great prestige. Albert and Seth (real name Jee) were brothers in more senses than one. Albert, who was born in

1881 and his brother Seth (born 1879), appeared in a number of W.P. Kelline black and white silent comedy films in 1902. In addition *Temperance Lecture* (1913), *Inkey and Co* (1913), *Potty's Wedding Day* (1915), *Dustman's Outgoing* (1916), *Hushabye Baby* (1919) *Bill's Monickee* (1915) and *Further Adventures of the Flag Lieutenant* (1927).

Albert and Seth wrote the scripts for direction for *The Temperance Lecture* and *Inkey and Co.*

Seth appeared in some additional films: *Hot Heir* (1931, *Bull Rushes* (1931), *My Old China* (1931), and *The Temperance Fete* (1932) which starred **George Robey** and *Old Timers* (1936).

Albert and Seth, who were members of the Grand Order of Water Rats, were both initiated into Chelsea Lodge on 16 September 1921. They were cleft together in a bond of affection seldom known among genuine brothers. Albert died 18 March 1942.

Chas H. ELLIOTT, PAGDC

Theatrical producer. Born 8 May 1949. In 1968 he began his career in show business by donning the famous Butlin's Redcoat. He teamed up with his now, life-long friend Jimmy Cricket as one half of the comedy duo Cohen and Kelly. This partnership inspired Chas to embark on a six-year spell on the U.K. club circuit as a solo performer. Equally suited for a behind the scenes production role, when aged 21, he produced and presented his first show for Chandris Lines on-board their voyages between U.K. and Australia and Far East passenger services.

Chas later developed a concept of *Theatre in Business* and headed up his own company producing on behalf of multi-national companies such as Coca-Cola, Whitbread and Halifax, corporate one-night spectaculars, product launches and conferences worldwide. Throughout the 1990s Chas's association with Paul Elliott's (no relation) West End Production Company E & B Productions, resulted in numerous successful Theatre projects including *Rebecca, The Goodbye Girl* and *Buddy - The Musical* in London and on Broadway.

In 1995 Chas co-produced *Jolson - The Musical* with E & B Productions. The show opened at the Victoria Palace, London where it ran for 18 months prior to touring Canada and the USA, before the curtain finally came down in Sydney, Australia in 1999. Warmly received and recognised as Best Musical by the *Laurence*

Olivier Awards in 1996, the show marked a genuine career highlight for Chas, but sharing in Al Jolson's sentiment, he will be the first to tell you "You ain't seen nothing yet."

Other production credits include Cleo Laine & John Dankworth at the Royal Albert Hall, U.K.Provincial tours with The Royal Philharmonic Orchestra Beatles *Classical Anthology* and Louis Clark's *Hooked on Classics, Freddie Starr Unwrapped* and several '60s music' concerts and tours with The Searchers, The Swinging Blue Jeans, The Merseybeats, Marmalade, The Tremeloes, P.J. Proby, Billie Davis and Peter Sarstedt.

Running parallel to Chas's professional life has been his Masonic career. Initiated into Tabula Rotunda Lodge No.8607 (Province of Essex) in 1979, Chas progressed through all of the offices before becoming the youngest Worshipful Master of the Lodge in 1991. After being appointed as an Active Provincial Grand Steward in 1992 he became Past Senior Grand Deacon in 1997 before being promoted again in 1998 to Past Provincial Deputy Grand Sword Bearer. In 1999 Chas became a joining member of Chelsea Lodge when Bro. **Roger Kitter** proposed him seconded by W.Bro. **Jim Davidson**. He attained Grand Rank in 2004.

Chas was exalted into Tabula Rotunda Chapter in 1990 and rapidly rose to First Principal in 1995. He was appointed as an Active Provincial Grand Chapter Steward in 1998 and promoted to Past Provincial Grand Sojourner in 2002. He is currently also a member of Essex Masters Lodge, Essex Provincial Grand Stewards Lodge and Essex Provincial Grand Stewards Chapter.

Freemasonry has provided an important influence on Chas's life, and in 1992 he was happy to marry both Masonic and professional careers in aid of R.M.B.I. He organised a Gala Charity performance of *Buddy* at the Cliffs Pavilion, Southend. His work on behalf of the R.M.B.I continued when he produced several more classical music concerts for the Freemasons of Essex including *Last Night of the Provincial Proms.* In 2000 and 2003 on behalf of the Province he produced two outdoor concerts in the grounds of The Lord Lieutenant of Essex, Lord Petre's ancestral home Ingatestone Hall featuring the Band of The Royal Artillery.

Peter ELLIOTT, PM

A Lewis. Son of Horace and Jesse Elliott. Born 12 May 1935, Chatham, Kent. His father had been

Past Master of St Peter's Lodge, Rochester, Kent and holder of Provincial Grand Rank. Peter was educated at Kings School, Rochester. He moved on to the Buddy Bradley Stage School, Piccadilly, London. Trained as a dancer and subsequently worked in many shows firstly as a chorus dancer and finishing as a principal dancer in the Howard and Wyndham production of *5 Past 8* in Glasgow. He began his show business career as one half of The Elliotts (his wife Billy was the other half). They toured the British Isles and, in 1952, did a long summer season in Leven, Scotland.

He was called up for National Service and served two years with the Royal Air Force (1953-1955).

On leaving the service Peter toured Italy as a single dancing act and was invited to appear in the 1958 Royal Variety Performance held in the presence of Her Majesty The Queen and The Duke of Edinburgh at the London Coliseum. Peter had earlier worked at the Windmill Theatre where he met Jimmy Edmundson and they formed the very successful double act of Edmundson and Elliott. They worked in Variety, summer season, and pantomime and as resident comedians on television with Billy Cotton and Rolf Harris. They completed spells at London's Prince of Wales Theatre, Victoria Palace and The Palladium until the late 1960s. Jimmy decided to call it a day in 1967 and Peter joined **Dick Emery**, as his straight man on stage, in cabaret and on television and for many years received the slap after Dick said 'Ooooh you are awful, but I like you'. In 1973, after a career of thirty years, he quit personal appearances and went into management via the Grade Organisation. He managed Dick Emery for fifteen years as well as the careers of Norman Wisdom, Kathy Kirby, American singer Dick Haymes and many others.

Peter Elliott was one of Britain's top pantomime producers undertaking production of sixteen major pantomimes per year in Great Britain, plus The London Palladium. In 1986 he was invited by Lord Delfont, President of the Entertainment Artistes' Benevolent Fund to run the charity as its chief executive and administrator which he has been doing ever since, transforming the Fund's home, Brinsworth House in Twickenham, Middlesex. In addition Peter is partly responsible for the annual Royal Variety Performance which is staged in the presence of either Her Majesty The Queen or His Royal Highness The Prince of Wales.

Peter Elliott with HM Queen Mother attending 'Beauty and the Beast', at the Dominion, Tottenham Court Road in 2000.

His other charitable interests apart from the EABF are his work in seven Masonic Lodges and the Grand Order of Water Rats. His sporting interests are golf and cricket as a spectator.

Initiated into St. Peter's Lodge, Rochester, Kent, 1968. He joined Chelsea Lodge on 19 November 1977. WM 2002. His son **Daniel ELLIOTT** was initiated into Chelsea Lodge on 17 November 1995. Peter initiated his son **Simon Peter ELLIOT** on 17 November 2004.

George ELRICK, FRSA

Vocalist, comedian, song-writer, bandleader, disc jockey. Active well into his nineties, Mrs. Elrick's wee son George enjoyed over seventy years in show-business, twenty-one of them as business manager to bandleader Mantovani.

Only five feet tall, he was born in Aberdeen on 29th December 1903. As a lad George was a drummer in the Boy's Brigade and before the age of twenty was leading his own 10-piece Embassy Band, that won a *Melody Maker* dance-band contest.

Having widened his talents, adding vibraphone and xylophone to his drum-kit, George formed a professional band resident at Aberdeen's Beach Dance Hall. Soon, taking the plunge, he went to London and after some time gigging around landed the plum job of second percussionist in the famous Ambrose Orchestra (**Max Bacon** was the drummer at the time but often went up front to take a vocal). Listening to the applause Max got when he finished a song led George to decide giving it a try and he began taking singing lessons.

In 1935 Henry Hall invited him to join the BBC Dance Orchestra where he stayed for two years making probably hundreds of broadcasts. George made several records with the band and added vocal on many jolly songs like *The Music Goes Round and Around, 'Got a Brand New Suit, There's a Song They Sing in Sing Sing, I Like*

Bananas Because They Have No Bones and *I Laughed So Hard I Nearly Died* (the latter being so popular George told journalist Chris Hayes he had to sing it on radio almost every day). It's pretty obvious that with his cheery manner he was the ideal person to sing a comedy song. These weren't his first recordings though, for he had already played drums on a couple of sessions with pianist Billy Mason's orchestra.

From 1937 until the early 1940s George toured music halls with his own band show and made a number of recordings with his Swing Music Makers. He appeared in some Jack Hylton stage shows and had his own *George Elrick Band Party* on radio. When the BBC began their long running series *Housewives Choice* in 1946 George was one of the first presenters, famous for humming along with the shows signature tune *In Party Mood*, and known as "the smiling voice of radio" became one of the most popular, often on air a month at a time while other presenters only got a week.

Housewives Choice continued into the late seventies, but long before then George had become right-hand man and manager to top orchestra leader Mantovani, accompanying him on numerous tours across America and to other corners of the globe. They remained a first class team until Mantovani died in 1974.

George was King Rat in the Grand Order of Water Rats in 1954 and again in 1973.

He joined Chelsea Lodge from St Clements Lodge No 688, Aberdeen, Scottish Constitution, in November 1936.

In later years George continued his role in show-business management and wrote his biography, aptly titled *When You're Smiling*. Ill health dogged him in old age; he had a life saving stomach operation in 1990 and blood circulation problems in 1996. George's wife of sixty years died in 199I and he passed away on 15 December 1999, aged 95.

Dick EMERY

Actor. BBC televisions longest running sketch - show, from 1963 until 1981, was one that introduced some of the mediums most memorable and enduring comedic characters, skilfully brought to life by an undisputed master of his craft.

Richard Gilbert Emery was born on 19 February 1917 at the University College Hospital in St Pancras, London, and was probably destined for a life in show business. His parents were a double-act known as Callan and Emery that performed around the country at various music hall venues throughout much of Dick's childhood, a fact that deprived the youngster of a formal education. However, his parents divorced in 1926 and Dick went to live with his mother who, realising her son had inherited a talent for enter-taining, insisted that he perform whenever possible. This led Emery to admit later in life that although he adored his mother he was also frightened of her.

During the Second World War he joined Ralph Reader's *Gang Show* entertaining the troops. However, like many others with an ambition to go into show business by the end of the war, he found work hard to come by and struggled through many auditions only to be (more often than not) turned down. He ap-peared in *Sun-day Starlight*, a band show with guests recently out of the forces. In 1948 he man-aged to secure an engagement at London's famous Windmill Theatre, and appeared

there around the same time as another new and generally unknown comedian, Tony Hancock. In 1948 Dick appeared in pantomime playing an Ugly Sister with George Formby, in Tom Arnold's *Cinderella* at Leeds Grand Theatre. In the 1950s Emery began getting regular work on BBC radio and in 1955 established himself on Jon Pertwee's show, *Pertwee's Progress*. It was at this time that he began developing one or two regular characters including a doddery old man by the name of Lampwick. He had already made a number of TV appearances (the earliest being in *Kaleidoscope* on 13 June 1952) when he, Pertwee and his cousin Bill Pertwee joined forces with **Lupino Lane** for five 60-minute entertainment specials broadcast once a month between October 1955 and March 1956. He appeared in *Educating Archie* on BBC radio from 1956 to 1959 which gave him a wider following and he began to build up his repertoire of outrageous characters which would get a bigger showcase when he landed his own show. Emery turned up on a variety of shows with great regularity and his face soon became well known to the viewing public. In the 1960-61 season he turned up as Private 'Chubby' Catchpole, a regular character in the popular comedy series *The Army Game*.

Dick Emery continued to divide his time between TV and radio (in fact he continued to do so throughout his career), but in 1963 the BBC offered him his own TV series. Drawing on many of the characters he'd developed over the years and benefiting from scripts written by US comedy writers such as Mel Brooks and Mel Tolkin, Emery quickly established himself as a class act. His characters were some of the best remembered on British television and included the breath-catching First World War veteran, Lampwick, the old codger who would connive to get his own way and cause trouble between his daughter and son-in-law, Hettie, the frustrated spinster, the toothy Vicar; the 'bovver boy' Gaylord, and his dad (played by

Roy Kinnear), the effeminate swinger who referred to everyone as 'Honky Tonk' the upper-class tramp, College and most famously Mandy, the brassy blonde who always misunderstood the street interviewer (a feature that opened every show), and interpreted his question to have a suggestive meaning so that it would lead her to slap him on the shoulder as she announced, "Oooh you *are* awful - but I like you!" It became a national catchphrase and was so popular that it also became the title of Emery's full-length feature film in 1972. The television series, the longest running sketch-show, ran from 1953 to 1979.

Dick appeared in the Royal Variety Performance held at the London Palladium on 26 November 1972 in front of Her Majesty Queen Elizabeth II and The Duke of Edinburgh, the same year he was voted 'Entertainer of the Year'.

In 1979, following 166 shows and fifteen successful years in the BBC Television series, Emery decided to switch channels to Thames for *The Dick Emery Comedy Hour*. There were two more comedy specials for ITV before he returned to the BBC in 1982 for two series of comedy thrillers *Emery Presents* in which he played Bernie Weinstock, the boss of a private detective agency. However, in the latter years of his life Emery was plagued with ill health as well as bouts of depression and periods of insecurity, and before the second series of *Emery Presents* could be shown he passed away, in January 1983. The second series, which was due to air on 13 January, was held over until later in the year. His manager for fifteen years was **Peter Elliott.**

Dick Emery entertained the British public for the best part of thirty years, and in the process left behind a legacy of comedic characters that will be enjoyed for years to come. In his lifetime he won countless awards, national fame and, more importantly, the hearts of an adoring audience. In terms of quantity his creations were unrivalled by any of his contemporaries. In terms of quality they were, like the man himself, in a class of their own.

He appeared in a number of films. They included: *Super Secret Service* (1953), *Case of the Mukkinese Battle Horn* (1956), *A Taste of Money* (1960), *Light Up the Sky* (1960), *The Fast Lady* (1972), *Mrs Gibbons' Boys* (1962), *Crooks Anonymous* (1962), *Just For Fun* (1963), *The Big Job* (1965), *River Rivals* (1967), *Yellow Submarine* (1968), *Baby Love* (1968), *Loot* (1970), *Get Charlie*

Tully (1972), *You Are Awful* (1972) and *Find the Lady* (1976).

Dick enjoyed two minor hit records in the British charts *If You Love Her* (1969) and *You Are Awful* (1973). Both were released by Pye Records.

He owned and flew his own aircraft; he also enjoyed fast cars and motorcycles and had a portable gym. Dick was a member of the Grand Order of Water Rats.

He married five times – all his wives were show girls – and left the last one to set up home with yet another showgirl thirty years younger than him.

Richard Gilbert Emery was initiated into Chelsea Lodge in September 1971. He died 2 January 1983, aged 65 years.

Arthur ENGLISH

Comedian/Actor. Born 9 May 1919, Aldershot. After working as an errand boy, waiter and shop assistant, he spent six years in the Army during the Second World War reaching the rank of sergeant. He was demobilised in 1946 and started work as a painter and decorator. His brother Walter put his name forward for an audition at the Windmill Theatre in London. Arthur's spiv act made an immediate impact on Windmill impresario, Vivian Van Damm. Striding the stage, he delivered his gags at a reputed 300 words a minute. Even a journalist using shorthand would have found it difficult to quote him verbatim. He moved into Variety where, playing the part of Tosh the Spiv, Prince of the Wide-Boys with a four-foot-long, spectacularly colourful kipper-tie, draped-jacket with wide lapels and accentuated shoulder-pads, a trilby 'titfer' at a jaunty angle, elongated sideburns and pencil lined moustache, he delivered a stream of Cockney patter at machine-gun rate.

Having established what would have seemed to be a peculiarly visual image in the variety theatres of the day, he transposed it to the non-visual medium of radio, becoming one of the most popular stars of programmes like *Variety Bandbox, Star Show* and *Workers' Playtime.* He made his first broadcast in 1950. One year later he became resident comedian on *Variety Bandbox.* He had catch phrases including "They're laughing at me, Mum". "Sharpen up there, the quick stuff's coming" and "Play the music, open the cage."

He also spent four years working a double act with 'Monsewer' Eddie Gray (of Crazy Gang fame). However, as the Fifties progressed, the appeal of the Spiv went out of fashion and Arthur

Sporting his Kipper tie, Arthur English and Teddy with Lew Lane

found himself at the crossroads. Changing direction, he took a chance and made his straight acting debut in 1959 in a short tour of *Meet Mr Tombs.* He then moved into repertory at the Palace Theatre, Watford. A series of Whitehall farces followed, along with roles in pantomime and old time music hall, before he started to pick up character parts in a succession of films and television programmes, gaining particular acclaim for his portrayal of a burnt out variety comic in *Clap Hands for the Walking Dead.*

Following his casting as Slugger in the children's show *Follyfoot,* Arthur became a household name again and he was constantly in demand. Alongside his top-ranking roles in situation comedies like *Are You Being Served?* and *Ghosts of Motley Hall,* he constantly popped up doing cameo parts and commercials. In 1974 he appeared in the thriller *A Coffin for the Bride* (ATV) which was also shown in the USA. He also succeeded in moving into distinguished roles, such as in the English National Opera's production of *Die Fledermaus,* in which he registered as the police sergeant, as well as playing Twiggy's father in the 1981 television version of *Pygmalion.*

Other television credits include: *In Sickness and In Health, Follyfoot; Cooper's End; How's Your Father; Dixon of Dock Green; Crown Court; Not In Front of the Children; Doctor in the House; Jack Squalor's Time* and *Funny Man.* He appeared in pantomime, revues, Royal Variety Performances (1951 and 1980) and summer seasons. He made a number of films including *The Hi-Jackers* (1963), *Echo of Diana* (1963),

For the Love of Ada (1972), *Love Thy Neighbour* (1973), *Malachi's Cove* (1974), *Are You Being Served* (1977) and *The Boys in Blue* (1983).

In 1987 he joined fellow veterans Charlie Chester and Irene Handl in *Never Say Die*, a comedy series set in an old people's home.

From Prince of the Wide Boys in variety to straight roles in plays by Shaw, Arthur was certainly a performer who successfully crossed the boundaries of his profession. His career plunged into the doldrums on one or more occasion, but each time he was able to pick himself up and return to celebrity status wearing a new persona.

A sociable man, he was an active Water Rat and Rotarian, supporting numerous local activities in his beloved hometown of Aldershot.

He had a son and a daughter with his wife Ivy, and when she died in 1975, he fell into a deep depression which threatened his thriving career. Forcing himself back to work, he found new happiness with a young dancer he met in pantomime. Regardless of the raised eyebrows (she was 35 years his junior) they married and had several happy years together, Arthur finding a new lease of life with the birth of their daughter whom he idolised.

Although the work offers were still pouring in he was forced into early retirement – much to his dismay – by ill health, and he spent his last years indulging in his hobbies, such as painting and reflecting on a lifetime which had included such accolades as appearing in the Royal Variety Performance and being made a Freeman of the City of London.

Arthur Leslie Norman English was initiated into Chelsea Lodge on 21 November 1952. He died in hospital in Camberley, Surrey, 18 April 1995, aged 75 years. It seemed that the whole of Aldershot, as well as many celebrity friends, turned out to honour him, giving the funeral a feeling of a state occasion. The following year a bar in the local Princes Hall was named after him and filled with memorabilia devoted to his career.

Will EVANS

Comedian. Born 29 May 1875, London. One of the finest slapstick comedians who made his first stage appearance in the traditional theatrical family manner, being carried on stage as a baby during a pantomime at Drury Lane, in which his parents, Fred Evans and Amy Rosaling, were appearing. At the age of six Will appeared in the *Harlequinade of Robinson Crusoe*, the Drury Lane pantomime for 1881-1882, with Fanny Leslie as principal boy and Arthur Roberts as dame. He received good early training as a knockabout comedian and instru-mentalist with his father's pantomime troupe, touring the UK and Europe with the *Cats on the Tiles* acrobatic comedy act. Later he and his older brother Fred Evans Junior, with another partner, turned to the music halls as a musical trio. When Fred Evans married Minnie Jee and joined her and her two brothers to appear in variety as 'The Florador Quartette'. Will Evans married Ada Luxmore and the couple worked a comedy musical act as 'Evans and Luxmore'. In 1894 his wife became fatally ill (she died on 11 May 1897) and he turned solo, becoming famous for his eccentric clown-like make-up and series of slapstick sketches and monologues, *The Derby Winner, Building a Chicken House, Harnessing a Horse, Whitewashing a Ceiling, Papering the Parlour,* etc. At his funniest in pantomime, he is considered to have originated the now traditional slapstick kitchen scenes and knockabout routines.

He was a popular Christmas attraction in London and the provinces for nearly 30 years. He appeared in every pantomime at Drury Lane between 1911 and 1919, playing Potterini in *Hop O'My Thumb* (1911-1912), Pompos for three consecutive years in the Arthur Collins *Sleeping Beauty* (1912-1914), the Grand Duke in *Puss in Boots* (1915-1916), the Grand Duchess in *Puss in Boots* (1916-1917). the Slave of the Ring in *Aladdin* (1917-1918), Little Flossie. one of the *Babes In The Wood* (1918-1919), and the Baroness in *Cinderella* (1919-20).

He recorded a number of his comedy songs on Regal Records including: *The Missing Actress, I'm a Soldier, The Beauty Doctor, Who Am I, The Butcher, The Alpine Guide, Polly, The Novelette, The Knight in Armour, Keeping Bees, Food Versus Love* and *Spontaneosities.*

Will Evans was co-author of the very successful farce *Tons of Money,* first produced at the old Shaftesbury Theatre in 1922 with Tom Walls and Ralph Lynn. Transferring to the AIdwych in 1923, it was the first of an era of famous farces associated with that theatre and ran for nearly 800 performances. He retired on his share of the proceeds.

Together with F.L. Lyndhurst, a scenic artist, Will founded the Sunny South and Sealight Film Company based at Shoreham, Sussex in 1913.

Will Evans was a Founder of Chelsea Lodge. He died 11 April 1931, aged 56 years.

Grisha FARFEL

Musician. Born 27 April 1921 in Russia where his parents died. His brother, Aleksey, had been in the Red Army, but later moved to America where he settled in Orlando, Florida. Best remembered as featured trumpet player in Billy Cotton's Band, he also spent several years fronting his own groups.

 During the war years Grisha toured for ENSA in a swing band led by saxophonist Sasha Borstein. In l947 he joined Billy Cotton, but after about a year left and formed his own quartet. Vocalist with the group was Grisha's wife, ex-Windmill notability and film starlet, Phyllis French. Over the next year or so they played residencies at Richmond's Palm Court Hotel, Southend's Palace Hotel and The Twenty One Room. At the latter, in September 1949, he was leading a five piece using the name Grisha Romaine. The band made their first broadcast on the BBC Home Service early morning on 22 December 1948.

By the early fifties he was directing both a dance band and a rumba band at the Empress Club in London's Dover Street and from February 1951 took a six piece out to Nairobi for a twelve month contract at the exclusive Avenue Hotel.

Back in Britain, Grisha rejoined Billy Cotton in March 1952 and so re-established what was to become a long association with the band on stage, radio and television.

During the sixties he went back to club work, while continuing his broadcast duties with Cotton.

Jenny Adams-Barbero, a professional singer, was thirteen when she discovered her father was a musician and someone she had seen many times on television. She had never known her father, who had left her mother when she became pregnant, telling her only then that he was already married. Her mother told her the one who came out to play solo trumpet each week on the Billy Cotton Show on BBC TV was her father. Jenny tried to find him.

She put an advert in the *Jewish Chronicle* and her searches took her to America. Grisha had married again and his widow took the phone call in Los Angeles. Alas, Grisha had died six months previous, so Jenny never did meet her father. It was Phyllis Farfel who informed Chelsea Lodge of Grisha's death.

He doesn't appear to have recorded under his own name but did make three sides for Oriole, using the name Gay Brill and His Music.

Grisha Farfel was initiated into Chelsea Lodge in January 1961. He died 5 May 1988, Los Angeles, aged 66 years.

George Frederick 'Miff' FERRIE, PM

Musician and agent. Born 1911, Edinburgh. He was a choir boy at seven, then started on the violin but soon played cornet, euphonium, clarinet and trombone. During his career 'Miff' Ferrie was the creator of several vocal groups. He began his musical career with **Stanelli**'s Orchestra (1932) , **Roy Fox** (1933) and Ambrose (1935).

In the late 1930s he formed The Jackdauz, a group that broadcast with Jack Jackson's Band from London's Dorchester Hotel. With a slight change of spelling, as The Jakdauz they also had a regular spot on radio's *Bandwagon*, the series that starred Richard Murdoch and Arthur Askey. The group also aired with Miff's band, which included musicians George Crow and Harry Parry in another comedy series *Airs and Disgraces*.

Miff was called up for military service in 1941 but was invalided out of the Army after a year due to injuries sustained through enemy action. After the Second World War, Miff reformed The Jakdauz for Arthur Askey's *Forever Arthur* series. The same year he introduced his new group The Vocaltones, three boys and three girls, who made their first appearance on *Navy Mixture* on 20 July and went on to broadcast over many years, including their own *Songbag* series. The Vocaltones were led by Beatrice Findlay who also led the all-girl Merry Maids, another Ferrie vocal group. Born on 24 January 1915 she was married to 'Miff' and died 2 December 2000 in Folkestone.

Miff's band The Ferrymen, following the war, had spells at the Panama and Nut House clubs and spent two years at the exclusive Windermere Club in London's Regent Street, where The Jakdauz also featured. In April 1949 they replaced Ambrose when he unexpectedly pulled out of the Nightingale Club. He was also involved musically in The Ovaltinies with **Phil Green** on Radio Luxembourg and featured in the BBC radio variety series *Bandwagon* with Arthur Askey and Richard Murdoch.

During 1950 his band was appearing regularly on Radio Luxembourg in *Radio Roundabout* with comedian Max Wall. Shortly afterwards Miff gave up performing to concentrate on music publishing and his band agency. Miff recorded two records with his Ferrymen on Decca. March 1945, *In a little Spanish Town / Jungle Jive* and November 1945, *Sweetheart of all my Dreams / Palais Jive.*

He later became an artistes' manager. Among his clients were Tommy Cooper, Bruce Forsyth and Terry Thomas.

His brother Joe Ferrie became a well known trombone player from 1920s to 1950s.

George Frederick 'Miff' Ferrie was initiated into Chelsea Lodge in January 1952 and was WM in 1967. Died 9 July 1994, aged 84 years.

Charles FIRTH, SLGR MetGStwrd

Executive director. Born 29 May 1943, Bucks. Director of Corporate Productions & Entertainment Ltd and of London Masonic Promotions Ltd, producers of the Royal Masonic Variety Shows and other entertainment events for London Freemasons.

Initiated into Chelsea Lodge on 20 September 1991. Assistant Secretary of the Lodge since 1997.

Bud FLANAGAN, OBE

A comedian so popular that he became an English institution. Born 14 October 1896, in Hanbury Street, opposite Spitalfields Market, Whitechapel, London where a blue plaque has been put up to mark his birth. His parents were Polish Jewish, originating in a small town called Radon in Poland, and he was named Chaim Reeven. The family name was changed and he became known as Reuben Weintrop (Robert Winthrop).

His father who was named Wolf was nineteen when he married Kitty Price (aka Yetta). She was seventeen. They were advised to emigrate to America where they had relatives.

They had just enough money for the passage to New York but they would have to sail from Hamburg, nearly six hundred miles away, and so their adventure of life began.

In Hamburg the shipping agent took their two guineas and gave them, unknowingly, a 7/6d ticket to London. With tears in their eyes they crossed the channel hoping their luck would change.

They settled in Spitalfields, London and the two of them were welcomed by local tongues. These turned out to be sweet shop owners looking for cheap labour. Wolf was offered a job with a boot and shoe maker. Work started at 6.30 a.m. through to 8.30 at night.

His father worked hard and soon found a part time job as a Cantor in a small synagogue, this brought in a welcomed extra 5/- a week, he also found singing in local pubs at weekends paid 3/6d a week. After a couple of years they had enough saved to buy a small grocery shop from a neighbour who was moving to the States. Yetta worked in the shop while Wolf continued with his boot and shoe job.

This carried on until Yetta was expecting their first child. They had to sell the shop so she could have the baby. A girl was born, they named her Esther, but she died, aged 9, whilst at school, following a caning by a teacher.

Bud's young days were much like any other child in and around the East End during the turn of the century…school, boys clubs and street fights. Also, being Jewish, three nights a week were spent at Chedar for Hebrew lessons. These were run by the local Rabbi who ruled the lessons with a rod of iron.

He also joined the Boy Scouts, camping in Epping Forest and smelling real fresh air after the filthy streets of London's East End.

By now his father ran a local fish and chip shop, where even the salt cans were chained to the tables and counter to avoid them being stolen.

In his early days he became interested in conjuring and used to walk to Gamages in High Holborn and look longingly at the tricks they sold but without the coppers to buy them. To raise the money he took a job as a call boy at the Cambridge Music Hall, at the age of ten. The job was very handy for earning a small wage but the extra money that could be earned from running errands for the Pros. was even more welcomed. When they wanted fish and chips, as they did most nights, off he went to his father's shop. There were no wages from this but the tips were good. Soon he had enough to buy some tricks and those he couldn't afford he made himself.

Bud would run shows after his father's shop was closed on Sunday nights, charging the kids a farthing and the older ones a halfpenny. He was making a local name for himself until one evening out shot a big rat and cast its evil eye over the audience, there were screams and before he could say abracadabra the place was empty. This wasn't surprising as the shop was next door to a horse repository and the traps laid would yield at least two or three large rats each morning. The news however spread like wild fire, and was neither good for Bud nor his father's business.

It was from these humble beginnings that Bud was to make his debut on stage. The year was 1908 and the Music Hall performers were on strike. The Cambridge, where he worked as a call boy, also ran the London in Shoreditch and Collins in Islington, collectively known as LCC, London, Collins and Cambridge.

It was at the London that he made his first stage appearance. Every Saturday afternoon at 2.30 they had an extra time matinee when the acts worked for nothing. The place was packed with a good sprinkling of agents looking for acts. The audience were hard to please and the first prize was fifty shillings and a week's work at the theatre. He was by this time quite good with manipulating the cards and doing a few other tricks besides. He gave his name as Fargo, the Boy Wonder. His turn finally arrived and the audience at first were sympathetic being a kid. He messed up the first trick. He had to pour water from a tumbler, turning milk into beer, but he hadn't smeared enough chemicals on the glass. For his second trick he first asked the audience for a bowler hat. A bowler in Shoreditch? Big mistake! That was it, and down came the curtain.

Bud collected his props and sneaked out of the stage door, only to be met by his father who planted a stinging right hand across his face and twisted his ear saying, "I'll give you working on the Sabbath." He was pushed and shoved all the way home. His props lay somewhere in the Shoreditch High Street, never to be seen again.

He ran away to sea at the age of 14 ending up in the USA where he did a Jewish comedy act in vaudeville and was later in a blackface duo with Dale Burgess.

After returning to England to serve in the Army from 1915-1918, he toured in variety with various partners until he met Chesney Allen in 1924 and adopted his guise of moth-eaten fur coat, enormous shabby clothes and tattered straw hat.

Flanagan and Allen began working for the Florrie Forde company in the early 1920s. They were given their break in 1924 and the famous partnership was born. Bud was an eccentric hobo,

whereas Chesney was always well dressed but their voices blended perfectly in songs like *Down Forget-Me-Not Lane* and *We're Just Ordinary People.*

In 1931 they quit the Florrie Forde company and went to the Argyle Theatre, Birkenhead to run their *Underneath the Arches* act. A few weeks later they were appearing at the Holborn Empire and eventually the London Palladium.

Curly and Bud Flanagan at Buckingham Palace, 1959 on Bud's appointment to OBE

During World War II Flanagan and Allen worked with ENSA boosting the morale of the British troops with songs like *Run Rabbit Run, The Umbrella Man*, and *We're Going to Hang out the Washing on the Siegfried Line.* They appeared in wartime revues *Top of the World* (1940), *Black Vanities* (1941) and *Hi De Hi* (1943).

The post-War Crazy Gang were formed in April 1947 with the comedians **Nervo** and Knox, 'Monsewer' Eddie Gray, **Caryll** and Munday and Naughton and Gold, making their debut at the Victoria Palace. In Jack Hylton's *Together Again.* They went on to appear in shows like *Life Begins at Oxford Circus, Give Me a Ring, Happy Returns* and *Swing is in the Air.*

Due to ill health Chesney Allen was forced to retire in 1946. Bud did a few solo performances but was soon reunited with his colleagues from the Crazy Gang. Their successes included *Together Again* (1947) which ran for 1566 performances, *Knights of Madness* (1950), *Ring Out the Bells* (1952), *Jokers Wild* (1954), *These Foolish Kings* (1956) *Clown Jewels* (1959) and *Young in Heart* (1960).

Flanagan and Allen recorded many songs on HMV Records including: *Down Forget-Me-Not-*

Lane, Sierra Sue, I Don't Want to Walk Without You, Let's Be Buddies, On the Outside Looking In, We'll Smile Again, There's a Boy Coming Home on Leave, Down Every Street, Rose O'Day, If a Grey-Haired Lady Says "How's Your Father?", Underneath The Arches, Round the Back of the Arches, Franklin D. Roosevelt Jones, Run Rabbit Run, Yesterday's Dreams, What More Can I Say?, Music Maestro Please, Home Town, Maybe It's Because I'm a Londoner, Umbrella Man, Home Is Where Your Heart Is, Strollin', Nice People, Galloping Major, Can't We Meet Again?, Dreaming, Hey Neighbour and *On the Other Side of Town*.

Flanagan and Allen appeared in the Royal Variety Performance on no less than ten occasions in 1932, 1933, 1935, 1947, 1950, 1951, 1954, 1955, 1956 and 1960.

Bud was King Rat in the Grand Order of Water Rats on no less than three occasions in the years 1945, 1946 and 1951.

In 1958 Bud Flanagan was appointed OBE.

After the Crazy Gang broke up in 1962 Bud continued to appear in pantomime, for the idea of retirement did not appeal to him.

He adopted the name Flanagan which was in part a compliment to Florrie Forde whose maiden name was Flanagan and in part a good humoured revenge upon his Irish Sgt Major Flanagan who 'didn't like Jews'. Robert Winthrop has promised the Irishman that he would make his name famous as a joke, and he spent the rest of his life doing so.

Just as he began to relax and take life more easy he was asked, in 1968, to sing the song *Who Do You Think You're Kidding Mr Hitler* which was to be used over the credits of the TV series *Dad's Army*. The series ran well into the 1980s with numerous repeats.

Flanagan and Allen appeared in a number of films between 1930 and 1958 including: *The Bailiff* (1932), *The Dreamers* (1932), *They're Off* (1933), *Wild Boy* (1934), *A Fire Has Been Arranged* (1935), *Okay For Sound* (1937), *Underneath the Arches* (1937), *Alf's Button Afloat* (1938), *The Frozen Limit (1939), Gasbags* (1940), *We'll Smile Again* (1942), *Theatre Royal* (1943), *Dreaming* (1944), *Here Comes the Sun* (1945) *Judgement Deferred* (1952), *Life is a Circus* (1958) *and The Wild Affair* (1963).

Chesney Allen died 13 November 1982 in Midhurst, Sussex.

Bud Flanagan was initiated into Chelsea Lodge on 20 October 1939. Died 20 October 1968 aged 72 years. There is a memorial for him at Golders Green Crematorium.

Maurice FOGEL

Magician and mind-reading act known as 'The Amazing Fogel'. Born 7 July 1911, London. Made his first variety appearance at the age of eighteen, doing a straight magic act at Collins Music Hall, Islington. He developed his thought transmission routine while serving in the army and used it as an intriguing form of entertainment with George Black's famous service show *Stars in Battledress*. In 1946 he toured the act in variety, topping bills for Moss and Stoll, and led the field in this kind of speciality act. He toured the world with his own show and presented a top spot in variety and cabaret.

At the headquarters of the Magic Circle in London are a set of X-rays, which show bullets lodged in Maurice's chest and hip, the result of his attempt to catch a bullet in his teeth.

Maurice Fogel was initiated into Chelsea Lodge on 15 July 1938. Died 1981, aged 70 years.

Don FOX

Described as looking a lot like film star Jeff Chandler, with a pleasing personality and good singing voice, Don Fox had all the ingredients needed to succeed in show-business, but never got any higher than the lower steps on the stairway to stardom. Nevertheless he never seemed to be out of work either, in constant demand as a variety support artiste. From Stamford Hill, North London he was always well turned out too, not so surprising considering he began work as a tailor.

Don made his professional debut as a 22-year-old at Collins Music Hall early in 1956 and on 23 April opened in cabaret at the Astor Club. The next couple of years was an uphill struggle constantly on tour, often with Tony Crombie and his Rockets.

His debut record came on the Decca label in August 1957, a cover of Jim Dale's hit *Be My Girl* and he could be seen miming to it on his first television date, ITV's *Jack Jackson Show* on 27 October. The following month his second disc *Party Time* hit the shops. Plugging it on BBCTV's *Off The Record* on 16 January 1958, Don had postponed his honeymoon to do so. He had married Evelyn Gold at Edgware Road synagogue on 9 January.

Further TV and variety, including tours of Middle East and Cyprus service camps, kept him busy over the remaining 1950s and into the 1960s. There were two more singles from Decca and a few more on various labels, but none made the British charts.

Bro. Donald Fox became a joining member of Chelsea Lodge in May 1980.

Roy FOX

Cornet player and musical director. Born 25 October 1901, Denver, Colorado, USA, Roy Fox became one of the worlds top society bands in the 1930s. The family, who were members of the Salvation Army, moved to Hollywood when Roy was just a few months old. At the age of eleven, he started studying the cornet. He had his first job with a small band in Santa Monica when he was just sixteen years of age. Later, he joined the Abe Lyman orchestra. In time, he achieved a reputation as "The Whispering Cornetist", confirming it by adopting the 1920 hit song *Whispering* as his signature tune from then on.

His first band, in 1920, was booked into the Club Royale, in Culver City, California. They toured coast to coast, and then Roy was offered a position as musical director for the Fox Film Studios (no relation), which later became the 20th Century Fox Studios. While working for Fox Studios, London's Café de Paris contacted him and made an offer which he accepted and opened at the Café de Paris on 29 September 1930. He travelled by sea from New York to Southampton and brought with him six other musicians from California. The opening night was one of only mild enthusiasm. However one exception made up for all the rest. A gentleman asked Roy Fox to play the popular tune *Without a Song*. The band obliged. It turned out that the gentleman in question was none other than the Prince Of Wales and from then on whenever the future King arrived in the ballroom they would strike up the music for that song.

Roy was able to obtain a British Work Permit when Decca Records asked him to form a recording band. He was offered £50 a week. Recording started in January 1931 and Roy made over 400 titles for the company. The band opened at the new Monseigneur Restaurant, London on 27 May 1931 and each Wednesday evening the show was broadcast live on BBC radio from 10.30pm to midnight. That band included Nat Gonella, Billy and Mickey Amstell, Syd Buckman, Joe Ferrie, Harry Berly, Lew Stone, and Bill Harty. Roy helped a young guitarist who

had been heard busking on the streets of London in 1930 to a new career as singer - Al Bowlly.

In October 1931, Roy was taken ill with pleurisy caused by overwork and had to enter a sanatorium. He spent six months recuperating in Switzerland and in his absence Lew Stone fronted the band. Fox returned in April 1932 and again assumed leadership. In addition he was given a prestige booking of twice nightly at the London Palladium. However, in October 1932, the Monseigneur management objected to this doubling of stage work and Roy parted company. All of the musicians, except Syd Buckman, stayed at the restaurant with Lew Stone as leader.

Roy formed a second band built around just 5 musicians who had been working in a club called the Spider's Web. Just a few days later, 14 August 1932, they were booked into London's Café Anglais where they enjoyed an instantaneous success. Part of this was due to the pianist **Jack Nathan**, whose arrangements formed the style of the new Fox band for the next six years. The band appeared in the Royal Variety Performance on 8 May 1933 at the London Palladium in the presence of King George V and Queen Mary.

Early in January 1933, Roy received an offer from the Kit-Kat Club and once again the band were on the move. The Café Anglais released him from his contract and he opened on 16 January 1933(using the name of Roy Fox and his Kit-Kat Orchestra). He stayed until 5 March when he returned to the Café de Paris, and remained there until 16 January 1934. Seven months later Roy and the band appeared in Deauville Casino in Normandy much to the delight of the French audiences.

Roy's mid-1930s orchestra had such sidemen as: George Rowe and Freddie Welsh (trombones); **Jack Nathan** (piano); Syd Buckman and Les Lambert (trumpets); Maurice Burman (drums); Denny Dennis (Vocalist); George Gibbs (bass); Ivor Mairants (guitar); Reg Owen, Art Christmas, Hughie Tripp and Harry Gold (saxes) and Peggy Dell on piano. In the years following, Roy toured the theatre circuit until disbanding in August 1938. They had also appeared in three films in the 1930s: *A Night Like This, On the Air* and *Radio Pirates.*

Roy and his band appeared in most of the London's top night spots. They made numerous records on the Decca and HMV labels from 1930-1938.

In 1938, Roy went to Australia, possibly due to health problems, where he rather unsuccessfully fronted Jay Whidden's Orchestra at the St Kilda Palais in Melbourne. Unable to return to Britain during the war years, he travelled to the USA where he led small combos in New York City. In 1946, he was again granted permission to work in Britain and returned to form a new band with only Syd Buckman and Bobby Joy from the pre-war days.

This band worked one summer on the Isle of Man and then was booked into London's Potomac Club. However, the big band era was effectively over, due to the war, economics and many other factors, and Roy decided to call it a day in England although he became a British citizen. In 1949 he was appointed musical director of Dublin's Theatre Royal where he discovered Rose Brennan who went on to bigger things with the **Joe Loss** Orchestra. Sadly the Inland Revenue made him bankrupt in 1951 with tax debts of £10,000. He won his discharge in 1964. His final job was as a theatre agent in Birmingham in 1952. He was married three times.

Roy Fox was initiated into Chelsea Lodge on 16 January 1937. Towards the end of his life he moved to Brinsworth House, the Benevolent Home for retired entertainers. where he died on 20 March 1982, aged 80 years.

Teddy FOX

Actor. Real name Edward James Dixon. Born 1890. Appeared in *Dear Billie* (1925) at the Lyceum, Sheffield. The production toured the country eventually coming to the Shaftsbury Theatre, London.

Edward James Dixon was initiated into Chelsea Lodge on 18 September 1931.

Dai FRANCIS

Vocalist, best known as one of the Black and White Minstrels. Born 1930, Swansea, son of a music hall performer who at one time knew more than 200 Dixieland songs. His knowledge and singing ability rubbed off on young Dai, and before the age of ten the boy was "blacking up" his face with burnt cork to sing at jazz band processions for local village carnivals. He left school at the age of 14 and began work as a wages clerk at the Neath Valley colliery.

Dai was called up for National Service in 1946 and stationed at the RAF's Record Office at Insworth, Gloucester. It was whilst there he took part in a Carroll Levis talent competition at Cheltenham. He won first prize with his impression of Al Jolson, which he had learned from his father.

On return to 'civvy street' he toured for four years in the *Zuyder Zee* show, singing, doing impressions and playing the trumpet. The show's organist was Elsie Monks, whom he married in 1952. They had a daughter Cheryl Maria.

Dai teamed up with fellow Chelsea Lodge musician **Woolf Phillips** when they worked at the Pigalle nightclub in London, as well as the Embassy Club. Dai was employed as a singer and trumpeter. In 1954 he joined the George Mitchell Singers in the chorus but within three years had risen to soloist when the first *Black and White Minstrel Show* was staged by George Mitchell and George Inns for BBC Television

At the 1957 National Radio Show held during September at London's Earl's Court, George Inns presented for the BBC 'The 1957 Television Minstrels'. This was a visual format of an earlier radio series 'The Kentucky Minstrels', the male singers having blackened faces. That would be sneered upon these days of political correctness - and it was at that time. The show provoked a review by Tony Brown in *Melody Maker* criticising its bad taste and insult to coloured people. A number of follow up comments, for and against, appeared in the letter's column of this and other papers.

Undaunted, on 14 June 1958 the *Black and White Minstrel Show* began its long run on BBC Television. Featured on that first show were Dennis Lots and Jackie Lee, the George Mitchell

Minstrels, Big Ben Banjo Band and the Television Toppers.

This successful television series ran for 21-years and Dai appeared in every edition, as well as 6,500 performances over ten years at the Victoria Palace Theatre, where it is estimated that seven million tickets were sold over this period of

time. The Black and White Minstrels were the only artistes to hold first, second and fourth places simultaneously in the Top Ten LP ratings.

Dai Francis was a major star of the Black and White Minstrel Show which beat Fred Astaire and the Kirov Ballet to win the Golden Rose (for Best Television Show in the World) at the first Montreux Festival in 1961 and dominated television variety for more than two decades, regularly attracting audiences of 15 million. With his fellow bass-baritone Tony Mercer and tenor John Boulter, Dai was one of the Minstrels' trio of lead vocalists.

During the summer season of 1960 a stage version was tried out at Scarborough followed by a short tour. Encouraged by the favourable reaction a more ambitious production opened in May 1962 at London's Victoria Palace Theatre. Over the years touring versions played many theatres around the country, until a changing public attitude towards colour and race made such a concept unacceptable to many people and on stage and screen the final curtain fell on the Black and White Minstrels.

Several long playing records made in the format of the show, many by the George Mitchell Singers themselves, were available during its lifetime.

The television show was eventually axed in 1978 on the grounds that the blacking up, a long tradition in the theatre, was racially offensive. A subsequent series of the shows in which the performers did not black up failed to pull in the viewers.

Dai spent the remainder of his working life appearing in summer shows, pantomimes and Variety in most of the major theatres in the United Kingdom. His tribute to Al Jolson established him as Britain's foremost Jolson impressionist. He also appeared in two Royal Variety Performances (1958 and 1962) and became a member of the Grand Order of Water Rats in April 1967.

Each year the surviving Minstrels and Television Toppers would gather at a country club near Wolverhampton to share memories over lunch. Although Dai will be best remembered for his renditions of Al Jolson, his enthusiasm for his trade was such that he gave an instant lift to any scene in which he appeared.

Dai Francis was initiated into Chelsea Lodge in January 1968. He died on 27 November 2003, aged 73 years. He was separated from his wife and is survived by his daughter.

Jack FRANCOIS
Variety artiste. Born 1911, Scotland, son of a Belgian acrobat who had been in the circus since childhood. Followed in his father's footsteps, making his debut in Berlin, as a child acrobat at the age of ten. Returning to Britain after four years on the continent he went into variety and concert party work, perfecting his eccentric dancing act and incorporating singing with verbal comedy.

In the 1930s Jack moved into musical comedy, appearing in the original London production of *Anything Goes* at the Palace and also in *Sunny Side Up* at His Majesty's. He also appeared in cabaret production shows at leading West End hotels and restaurants.

Called up in 1940, he joined the Rifle Brigade, serving for six years, during which time he produced Army shows and measured his career, largely in variety, making several appearances at the London Palladium, a theatre where he was a great favourite, personally and professionally and touring in *Piccadilly Hayride* with **Nat Jackley.**

He also worked as a double act with his brother Manny who, with his wife Joy, continued in the business. When he retired from performing, Jack worked as a company manager for Bernard Delfont and, for fourteen years, looked after his summer shows and pantomimes.

After the death of his wife, Dorothy whom he met when she was one of the Betty Hobbs Dancers, he moved into Brinsworth House, a home for retired show business people, where he stayed for five years and became one of the most popular residents.

Jack Francois was initiated into Chelsea Lodge on 17 November 1950. He died at Brinsworth House, 11 January 1997, aged 86 years.

Aubrey FRANK

Musician. Brilliant tenor saxophone and clarinet player. Born East End of London 3 June 1921 and educated at Mile End Central School. He was interested in music whilst still at school, and, at the age of 15, he made his first broadcast playing with the Savoy Junior Band. His first professional work was playing with Stan Atkins and with Reg Arnold at the Nest Club, London (late 1939). After a brief time with Hetty Booth's Band he joined Jack Harris (1940). For the next two years he freelanced with Eddie Carroll, Jack Simpson, Josephine Bradley, George Evans, The Skyrockets and Geraldo. Aubrey played jazz whenever the opportunity arose.

He joined the RAF in 1941 and succeeded in combining service duties with musical commitments including the orchestras of Ted Heath, Lew Stone and Ambrose. He was also a regular member of RAF Fighter Command Band, based at Uxbridge. Demobilised from the RAF in 1945 he joined Ambrose the following year. In 1947 he teamed up with **Frank Weir** for several months.

He worked with **Jack Nathan** from 1949 to 1954. From the mid-1950s he specialised in studio and session work with BBC Review Orchestra, BBC Concert Orchestra, BBC Big Band, Muir Matheson, Ben Frankel and also the London Symphony Orchestra. He played on many television programmes, primarily with Eric Robinson and Steve Race, and worked with American singers such as the Andrews Sisters, Dinah Shore, Betty Hutton and Judy Garland.

Towards the end of his musical career Aubrey concentrated on teaching and would stress the timeless qualities of the pioneers who laid the foundation of jazz saxophone. One of his pupils was Tommy Whittle who went on to become an accomplished tenor saxophonist.

He was single and had a flat in the prestigious White House in Regent's Park, London.

Aubrey Frank was initiated into Chelsea Lodge on 20 January 1956. Died on his 72nd birthday at University College Hospital, London. Lifelong friend and saxophonist, **Harry Conn**, who was born on exactly the same day said: "Aubrey was a perfect gentleman, too nice to have been a professional. He was a wonderful jazz player and an enormously popular man."

Morton FRASER

Harmonica player. Born Leeds, 1906. Real name Mannie Fish, the younger brother of impresario Dan Fish. It was in America that he was first discovered when he won a National All-America harmonica contest in Philadelphia. From then he has played his way all around the world appearing in variety theatres and concert halls. This came to a halt in 1939 when war broke out. He joined the Royal Artillery and within a short time was a member of the entertainment troupe *Stars in Battledress*. It was whilst in the Army he met other harmonica enthusiasts and the idea was born of forming a 'harmonica group'. This came to fruition in 1946 and was based on the American act Borrah Minevitch's Harmonica Rascals. They set up business as Morton Fraser's Harmonica Gang. They were an immediate hit in this country and were booked into the London Palladium on many occasions including a 17-week season. They appeared on television and were firmly established as one of the funniest and most popular comedy acts in Great Britain.

They made records for EMI including one called *Chelsea.*. They backed Don Cameron on his minor hit of 1954 *I See the Moon*. All members of the Gang were multi-instrumentalists and fine vocalists as well.

Writing in *Harmonica News* in 1951, Morton Fraser says: "During the time I spent in the Forces I did a lot of entertaining in the various theatres of war, and met several harmonica players in battledress and I kept in touch with them until the war ended. On 3 June 1946 the Morton Fraser Harmonica gang made their first public appearance. By 1950 I decided to use my efforts to far better advantage attending the production of the act and to looking after the business full time."

The Gang remained successful throughout the 1950s and into the 1960s until they finally disbanded.

The harmonica began to be manufactured from the 1850s. Morton Fraser and his Gang certainly helped to popularise the instrument, as did virtuoso Larry Adler. In the 1960s the mouth organ became popular again with folk singers Bob Dylan and Donovan. To keep their hands free to play the guitar, they held the mouth organ in a frame worn around the neck.

Morton Fraser was initiated into Chelsea Lodge on 18 January 1946. He died 10 June 1982, leaving a widow, daughter and grandchildren.

Clinton 'Froggy' FFRENCH

Born about 1908 and learned trumpet while serving in the RAF. Later became part of the Cavendish Dance Band when they won three All-England contests organised by *Rhythm* magazine in 1931, 1932 and 1933. He turned professional to join Percival Mackey's Band in 1933. Was briefly with Lew Stone in 1934, then joined Howard Jacobs. Teamed up with Eddie Carroll in late 1934 for a year, but also freelanced with Sydney Kyte at a similar time. He was with the Ambrose Orchestra from late 1935 until September 1936. His first record was *A Little White Gardinia* backed with *I Knew You When*, released on the Parlophone label on 19 February 1935, playing trombone with Eddie Carroll and his Music. The same day they recorded *Whistling Lovers Waltz* and '*I'm Popeye the Sailor Man*'. He then worked mainly with Geraldo (1936-1940) regularly appearing in the BBC radio programme *Romance in Rhythm* before rejoining the RAF during Second World War. He became a member of the Squadronaires along with **Eric Breeze**. Worked with George Melachrino's Orchestra in the late 1940s. He made numerous recordings with dance bands over a ten-year period. Was also active in many studio and theatre orchestras including a long stay with the *Black and White Minstrel Show* in the 1960s.

George GANJOU

Variety artiste, impressario. Born 1 January 1901, Poland. George was a member of one of the world's greatest variety acts, The Ganjou Brothers and Juanita. A peerless family act, they appeared in three Royal Variety Performances, toured the world many times and often topped the bill, the only adagio dancing act ever to do so. The three Ganjous, George, Bob and Serge, were half Russian and half Polish and escaped from Russia as teenagers after the Russian Revolution. Their story is an involved one, but if anyone wanted a romantic adventure story from the world of Variety, this is it!

When the Great War started in 1914 they left Poland for Russia first to Moscow and then the Ukraine. George, the eldest, fought in the Polish army and had many adventures including a miracle escape from the wrong end of a firing squad - after the rifles had been cocked! He learned music and played the flute and piccolo for a symphony orchestra in Warsaw before journeying through Europe learning five languages along the way, eventually crossing the Atlantic to New York where he joined a symphony orchestra. He had lost contact with Bob but met him again through a million to one chance. He was late for a concert one night, hailed a taxi to get to the theatre - and brother Bob was driving it!

Bob had dramatically escaped from a Russian war prison years earlier, riding on horseback for many days through the Russian winter to Odessa where he jumped onto the side of a ship and hauled himself up on its ropes while it was setting sail! He ended up in America where he contacted friends in the Russian Ballet and as he was very strong he worked with them as an adagio dancer before starting his own act with another Russian boy and Natasha Natova, the ballerina. They were a sensation in New York and starred in one of the earliest sound films, MGM's Spectacular *Hollywood Revue of 1929* billed as Natasha Natova and Company.

Bob soon talked George in to joining him and they changed the name to "The Ganjou Brothers and Juanita". They quickly reached star-status in America and were invited to tour England in 1933 when they also recruited Serge, who had had many adventures of his own and had to be persuaded to give up a highly successful career as a singer/guitarist in Warsaw, specialising in Russian gypsy songs. They were in great demand on the Variety circuit and were the first speciality act to command fees of over £100 per week, a huge sum at the time. When Natova got married, English ballerina Joy Marlowe joined the team as "Juanita" and they starred in the Royal Variety Performance the following year.

The act soon developed into a family affair with Serge marrying Joy; and George's wife, Adela, conducting the orchestra during their performances as the music timing required intimate knowledge of the act's tempo and routines. An excerpt from the act appears in the 1943 film *Variety Jubilee* which also featured the great comedian **George Robey** and that other wonderful speciality act, Wilson, Kepple and Betty with their unique sand dance routine. A giant porcelain clock is the backdrop with Juanita gently swinging on the pendulum and the three boys as porcelain figures, dressed in magnificent blue and red costumes and white wigs. The clock strikes 12, the figures come to life and the action begins to the beautiful strains of Strauss's *Blue Danube* - a series of elegant acrobatic dance routines, spins and throws, most of which had never been seen before and all of which were quite breathtaking - but also dangerous. The climax of the act was a spectacular routine where George and Serge end up throwing Joy 10 feet up and 22 feet across the stage to be caught by Bob, above his head and with Joy in an arabesque position. (Do not try this at home!) Joy was dropped many times during her career but always had a smile on her face as she flew through the air, well-knowing that she might end up in the orchestra pit at any moment - and indeed she did on more than one occasion. Joy was a wonderfully brave little lady.

Their last show was at London's Prince of Wales Theatre in 1956, when the boys were well into their fifties and Joy her forties, an amazing age considering the physical demands of their act, which they often performed two or three times a day. Two little-known comedians were on that same bill - Tommy Cooper and Benny Hill - both of whom became good friends of the Ganjous and they hosted Benny's thirtieth birthday party that year.

George became an impresario, concentrating on speciality acts, though his most notable discovery was Cliff Richard, whom he passed on to another management when he realised that the pop scene was not his forte. A new act he handled at the time was Jimmy Tarbuck and for many years was associated with Billy Butlin's organisation. With Serge and Bob he also owned and ran the famous showbiz retreat, the Empire Billiards Club in Frith Street, frequented by agents like Lew and Leslie Grade as well as countless well-known artistes. Bob directed and managed a new adagio act called The Dior Dancers, based on the Ganjous and married the beautiful Merian Morris, the new "Juanita". The family also owned the Daquise Restaurant in South Kensington, specialising in traditional Polish and Russian dishes which is still a popular haunt for Polish ex-pats to this day. They were active in many Charities, Joy becoming Queen Ratling of the Grand Order of

Lady Ratlings in 1960 and Serge, Treasurer of the Entertainment Artists Benevolent Fund and the Grand Order of Water Rats "Rat of the Year" in 1988.

One of George's last visits to Chelsea Lodge was in 1978 where he saw the Initiation of his son Paul, who became WM in 1985 and Director of Ceremonies in 1997. When asked at that meeting why he never went through the Chair himself, he said that he would have been more nervous than facing another firing squad!

George Ganjou was initiated into Chelsea Lodge on 18 March 1936. He died 1 November 1988. Cliff Richard acknowledged the debt he owed to George and sent a large floral tribute to his funeral which was held at the Russian Orthodox Cathedral in Kensington, followed by cremation at the South London Crematorium, where the ashes of his brother Bob rest.

Paul GANJOU, PM LGR

(A Lewis). Born 16 July 1947, London, and the only son of George, the eldest of the three brothers in The Ganjou Bros and Juanita adagio act. Paul readily admits he had no talents as a performer but recalls an amusing role he fulfilled in the 1965 production of the Lerner and Loewe musical, *Camelot,* at the Theatre Royal Drury Lane. He remembers his time there with great affection, mixing with stars like Richard Harris and Paul Daneman. As assistant stage manager (stagehand in the vernacular) his main duty was clearing the stage after Sir Lancelot's horse had been on for a few minutes and then chased off by the evil Mordred: but it was a real horse that often forgot where it was and the stage is one of the steepest in London, so fleetness of foot was often essential in order to prevent the orchestra suffering an embarrassing bombardment of what

Richard Harris used to mischievously describe as "equine rolling stock". Paul was once asked why he put up with such an unpleasant job every night and why he didn't do something more edifying: he said, "What! - and leave show business?"

But he eventually did – and spent three years as a management trainee with an international oil company, although being an enthusiastic sportsman, he spent more time representing them at Golf, Snooker and Table Tennis than he did learning about the oil business: so he decided he would be better off in another career and entered the Insurance industry. Starting as an Adviser he gained rapid promotion and by 1985 he had become the Sales and Marketing Director of a major national Financial Services group. He was fortunate enough to visit many parts of the world during his career and has addressed meetings and conventions in places as far apart as Paris, Hong Kong and San Francisco.

Paul married Chrissie, in 1978, and has two sons, Anthony and Alastair. He took early retirement from his main career in 1997 and as well as Masonic and Charity work, he now acts as a consultant and helps Chrissie run her Central London Apartments business, mainly providing accommodation for the Royal Opera House and theatrical people in the West End shows.

Paul was initiated into Chelsea on 21 January in 1977, became Worshipful Master in 1985 and Ceremonies and Lodge of Instruction Preceptor in 1997. He was promoted to London Grand Rank in 1999 and was Almoner of the Lodge from 1997 – 2000. He is a Past First Principal of the Chelsea Chapter and a member of the Old Pauline Lodge No.3969. He was also made a Freeman of the City of London in 1980.

Following **Benny Wright** and **George Mullins** as Director of Ceremonies and Preceptor was very much the definitive "hard act to follow" as they were both outstanding in their own ways: but Paul quickly gained the confidence of the Lodge through his knowledge and presentation of the ritual and particularly his enthusiasm at the Lodge of Instruction, which he runs every Wednesday at Freemasons Hall in London.

Paul believes a successful Lodge of Instruction is an essential foundation stone for any Lodge and encourages as many Officers, Past Masters and Members as possible to attend. He feels that as well as the important and serious side of the Ceremonies and the learning and presentation of the ritual, attending Lodge and the LOI must also

be fun: and he does all that he can to ensure that it is.

Harold GELLER
Musical Director. Worked every aspect of the music business from session musician, through to arranger, manager, leader of his own orchestra and a major executive in music publishing.

Harold Geller was initiated into Chelsea Lodge on 18 March 1949.

His son **Laurence Stephen Geller** was initiated on 21 March 1969.

Gerry GEORGE
Actor. Real name Gerald Victor Francis de Weld Nicholas. Born 12 April 1939. As far as Gerry is concerned, there is no secret about his being a Freemason: indeed he is proud to own that he is part of a worldwide family, where a sense of belonging, fellowship and goodwill - without prejudice or bigotry – are the rigid mainstays of the Masonic superstructure.

Former Variety kid Gerry started in show business when barrage balloons loomed over the provincial theatres, in Blitz-weary England. His love of stars like George Formby and Frank Randle, lead him into child extra work in films, and later into Variety and Pantomime, and afterwards Repertory Theatre.

A Christmas Island veteran – and armed forces amateur entertainer - after RAF national service he served a journalistic apprenticeship, working on a litany of provincial newspapers, before joining Mirror Group Newspapers, and later news-editing the Somerset Branch of their provincial Sunday tabloid, in the West Country.

He simultaneously served three decades in the elite Territorial Army Pool of Public Information Officers, retiring with the rank of Major, in 1990, having seen service in military hot-spots all over the world, and for which he received a Queen's Decoration.

Throughout this time, he still retained a foothold as a professional entertainer – and actor – so it was not surprising when, in 1981, he gave up everything else, to return to acting, and entertaining, full time.

Since then he has appeared as a character actor in a string of feature films and television plays, and has done numerous personal appearances, either in the guises of the many celebrity characters he portrays – including Churchill, Captain Mainwaring, Bud Flanagan, Frank

as Winston Churchill   Gerry as himself

Randle, Robb Wilton or George Formby – or as a lecturer or basic role player in corporate seminars.

Gerry has also appeared as a comedy foil on television with such stars as Lenny Henry, Paul Whitehouse, Frank Skinner and latterly, Harry Enfield.

One of two semi-biographical books he has written, concentrates on his story of Frank Randle, and this has been turned into a screenplay, and is due to go into production in the next year.

Gerry feels privileged to belong to Chelsea Lodge, because he sees it as the epitome of Show business, itself, in addition to being the realisation of his life's ambition…and, not least, the fulfilment of a once inexplicable and mysterious recurring childhood dream in which he always found himself in Masonic carpeted surroundings… always knocking at a door, and asking for admission.

Gerald Victor Francis de Weld Nicholas was initiated into Chelsea Lodge on 21 November 1997.

Roberto GERMAINS
Theatre agent. Born 1918, Illmau, Austria, son of the Latvian proprietor of the Circus Carlo Germains, his mother being an Italian circus rider. He made his debut as a clown at the age of six, and two years later was a member of his family's bareback act. As he grew up, he added the skills of acrobatics, trapeze work, tumbling and musical clowning as he travelled with the circus throughout Europe and Asia, learning several languages as he did so. He first came to England in 1931 to appear with Bertram Mills Circus at Olympia, London, returning later to work with his sister, Valeska, in Chapman's Circus.

The Second World War, during which he worked as a translator, interrupted his career, but immediately afterwards he joined Don Ross' Stage Circus, where he met his wife, the trapezist

Dandy Mery, though they later parted. In 1949 he went to Ireland with the Albert Jeserich Circus, learning the managerial ropes in addition to appearing as ringmaster and presenting a trained pig act. Two years later he began as booker for the Coliseo Dos Recreios, Lisbon, run by the Corvoes family.

In 1952 he presented a high school act at the Hippodrome, Great Yarmouth, where he eventually became ringmaster and booking agent. He played a vital, if not largely back-stage role in introducing many Continental circus artistes to Great Britain. He was named as the Equestrian Director and was a man of many languages and many parts who dealt with all the performers and their problems.

He became ringmaster at Belle Vue, Manchester in the late 1960s, later taking over as booking agent, by which time he had achieved a reputation in this field, having started his own agency in the Fifties, which was run for many years, until 1993, in association with Noel Gay Artistes.

Roberto presented a number of circuses outside London, booked artistes for Blackpool Tower Circus and provided acts for ten years to the mid-1980s. He also assisted Prince Rainier with the international circus festivals in Monte Carlo. He booked many of the overseas acts which were featured on such television productions as the *Paul Daniels Magic Show*. He had two daughters both of whom were musicians. Undoubtedly he became the most celebrated circus booking agent in this country. He appeared in the James Bond film *Octopussy* (1983) as the circus ringmaster.

Roberto Germains became a British citizen and joined Chelsea Lodge on 16 September 1966. He died 9 July 1994, aged 76 years.

Max GOLDBERG
Musician. Born 19 March 1905, London's East End. Real name Max Gorginski. His family originally came from Lithuania. One of five children, he emigrated with his parents to Toronto, Canada when he was just nine months old. Played mellophone and at the age of nine took up the cornet. Played in Jewish Boys' Band and toured Canada and USA as part of the Russian Juvenile Band. The first professional work was with the Novelty Sextet at Moshers Arcade in Toronto in 1919.

He was one of the greatest jazz trumpeters of the 1920s-1940s rising to fame with the Ambrose

Orchestra and becoming one of the most sought after musicians in Canada and England. Max returned to England in 1923 as part of Bill Shenkman's Buffalo Orchestra and played long residency at Birmingham Palais (1924). Led his own band at Moody's Club, London (late 1925). Worked with Kal Leech and his Band (1926) and the Criterion Dance Band (1926). Was also at the Kit-Kat Club with Al Payne.

He worked with Savoy Havana Band for a year from 1926, transferred to the Savoy Hotel Orpheans in October 1927. He went on tour to Germany with the Orpheans (1927-1928).

Max, who enjoyed cinematography as a hobby, as well as golf, undertook extensive freelance work from 1928 onwards making 10,000 records during his lifetime. As a session man he backed most of the soloists then recording – George Formby, Gracie Fields, Jessie Matthews and Richard Tauber, and played in bands led by Marek Weber, Ambrose, Ray Noble and many more. His session work from 10am to 5.00pm on most days of the week was followed by his usual job with Ambrose from 9.00pm to 2.00am. Musicians were paid £5.00 a session. He worked regularly with Al Collins (1928), Blue Lyres (1929), Arthur Lally (1930), Billy Mason (1931) and Melville Gideon (1931). He was with the Ambrose Orchestra from 1931-1935 and again in 1937 and shared the stand with such names as Joe Crossman, Ted Heath, Billy Amstell, Joe Jeanette, Bert Read, plus all other top musicians that made the Ambrose Orchestra amongst the finest in the world. He became a stalwart in the Ambrose organisation, performing at various venues across London's West End, and the nationwide stage shows, plus the now legendary Saturday night broadcasts in the 1930s, listened to throughout Europe; he recorded *Brighter Than the Sun* with the Ray Noble Orchestra in 1933; he played with Sidney Lipton (1936); Jack Harris (1938) and Geraldo (1939) at the Savoy Hotel and made 50 records while with him. Was activated for duty during Second World War and joined RAF where he played in various service bands until he was demoblised in 1944. His postings had included RAF stations Uxbridge, Wittering, Wisbech, Leicester, Peterborough, Stamford and finally Shetland, before returning to Uxbridge. Worked with **Frank Weir** (1944) and Ted Heath (1945) and played five weeks in Monte Carlo in 1946. He also featured with Bert Firman's Rhythmic Eight and Louis Levy's Orchestra until emigrating to

Australia in 1957. Worked with the Royal Theatre Orchestra in Brisbane then moved to Melbourne where he joined Channel Nine's Television Orchestra until his retirement in the 1970s.

During the 1960s and 1970s he also taught music for the Australian Department of Education until 1981 when he suffered a stroke which followed the death of his wife.

Max Goldberg was initiated into Chelsea Lodge on 16 November 1934. He died in Melbourne, Australia 11 February 1990, aged 84 years. At his funeral service, the Ronnie Munro arrangement of *When Day is Done* by the Ambrose Orchestra, made in January 1935 at the Decca studios in Chelsea, was played. It was one of Max's favourite recordings on which he appeared.

Joe GOODMAN

Comedian/entertainer. Born 12 January 1939, Essex. Real name Joey Cotterill. His life-story is fascinating and very moving, which he will reveal in detail as and when he writes his autobiography. Suffice it to say that at just six weeks old his mother left him in downpour of rain in a shop doorway as she could not afford to look after him, and her other children did not know they had a brother. As luck would have it, an older woman saw her walking away, comforted her and offered to help - and took Joey in along with her other children. A tough start in life inevitably followed, but it bred self-confidence and an ability to literally sing for his supper when necessary.

He was introduced to variety and pantomime at

a young age as friends of the family were script writers for amateur shows and pantomimes and asked the eight year-old Joey if he would like to play the part of the cat in *Dick Whittington*. He was very nervous until he took the head off the cat's costume in the finale and heard the applause - and that was that. As for Joey Cotterill and show business there was no looking back.

In 1949 he won the then huge sum of seven shillings and sixpence singing *Goodnight Irene* at a Labour social club. He appeared in four pantomimes between the ages of nine and fourteen and by eighteen was earning £5 a night acting as an MC and a singer at dances and weddings and sang with several dance bands in and around Essex. At age of twenty-five he started to enter talent contests and won most of them, including a national Butlin's competition and a Sunday Newspaper Star Trail competition and he also appeared on ITV's *Opportunity Knocks* and *New Faces*.

As Joe Goodman, he became renowned and extremely popular as a stand-up comedian and after dinner speaker and soon earned the enviable label as "The King of the One Liners". He later won 'Club Entertainer of the Year' and 'Southern Entertainer of the Year' and Joe starred in TV's *The New Comedians* in 1986 and became one of Britain's best-loved comics on the charity and fund raising circuit enhancing his career to the versatile entertainer he is today.

In 2003 Joe decided to find out more about his four blood brothers and sisters and after an extraordinary story and some intricate windings, he finally did! Sadly one had passed away, but he found the other three in wonderful and touching circumstances.

Joe has appeared in *The Not Forgotten Variety Show* at Buckingham Palace as well as four Royal shows at the London Palladium and Theatre Royal, Windsor, The City Varieties, Leeds, British Music Hall Society Annual Ball and *The Comedians* television series produced by Granada Television.

He was made Captain of the Vaudeville Golfing Society, 1998 and is a proud member of the Grand Order of Water Rats.

Joe does find time to pursue his hobbies, the love of golf, and his inventions, designing 'Clive the Cone' and many more of his own 'props'

Happily married to Maureen for 25 years, Joe has four children of his own and nine grandchildren and stays as close as he can to his family. His maxim is: 'If laughter is the milestone of your journey then depend on it and you'll never get lost'.

Joe Goodman was initiated into Chelsea Lodge on 17 January 1997.

Phil GOODY

Musician. Born 1897. Played alto saxophone, tenor saxophone and flute. He was a military musician in the Royal Artillery and was co-opted into Geraldo's Swing Septet. Appeared on over 100 tracks with the Geraldo Orchestra on Parlophone Records between 1943 and 1945. Phil appeared In a performance of Ravel's *Bolero* at the Coliseum in St Martin's Lane in a programme called *Music for the Millions* with the Geraldo Orchestra. The piece commences with a solo drum, then the flute. He was late so not there for the entry. Geraldo appeared not to notice, so Phil slipped into his place, but nothing had happened until the entry of the oboe. There were suppressed giggles throughout the orchestra, Geraldo never let on he knew what had happened.

Phil recorded ten records with George Evans Orchestra on Decca in 1944. Made numerous broadcasts from the BBC with Geraldo Orchestra in 1950s.

Fellow musician Billy Amstel described Phil as "the gentleman of the Geraldo Orchestra and an extremely good flautist."

Philip Goody was initiated into Chelsea Lodge on 15 September 1944. Died 8 November 1968, aged 71 years.

Norman GRAY, PM SLGR

Showman. Born 22 February 1935, Norwich into a fairground family. Norman's paternal grandmother was Jane Elliot and many of her descendants still travel the Essex fairgrounds to this day. Jane's family had a large travelling 'Boxing Booth' and she used to spar on the front of the show with a boxer called Joe Leggat. When Norman's grandmother was a very young girl, they were at a fairground in Halstead, Essex. Their caravan was near a tree when, during a storm, lightning struck the tree and it fell across the caravan killing the mother and father, but the children were asleep at the other end and were rescued safely.

Today Norman operates a successful amusements business at Vickers Point, Ingoldmells, Lincolnshire.

Norman Gray was initiated into Proscenium Lodge No.3435, 18 November 1980. He joined

Chelsea Lodge 19 January 1990. WM 1995. Also a member of Lumley Lodge No.1893, Skegness; Chelsea Chapter. MEZ 1993 and 1997. Exalted in Tableau Chapter Noo.4875, London10 December 1987. MEZ 1992; joined Skegness Earl of Scarborough Mark Masons No.1932 on 10 December 1999; joined Skegness Royal Ark Mariners No.1032 on 24 November 1999.

His son **Richard Gray** was initiated into Chelsea Lodge 15 November 1996.

Bruce GREEN

Comedian. Born 1876. Real name Joseph Brewster Hamilton Green. Enjoyed a long and successful career as a pantomime and music hall dame. The inspiration to tread the boards came when, ten years old, he toured England as a choir boy with St Paul's Choir. His father was not best pleased and Bruce became a clerk in the Science and Art Department of the Public Service. According to an interview in *Era,* 6 June 1917 he started at thirteen and stayed until he was twenty-six. He practiced singing and inventing songs. He was heard singing in Littlehampton by a theatre company man who put him in a show, playing a 'bibulous old cockney woman'. He was then offered the Cannibal King and Demon King in the north of England, for the same manager. After a week he was made the dame.

Bruce had three years touring with the pantomime company acting also as the baggage man when the company could not afford porters. Acton Philips engaged him to play in stock dramas at the Lyric Theatre, London. He made his career impersonating old cockney women, playing seventeen consecutive years on the Moss Circuits, never missing a performance; arguably the longest run ever.

He appeared as a male in *Copper Nob* at the Derby Hippodrome, 7 April 1924, a musical comedy revue. He played professional visits to South Africa and Australia, where he received rave notices. His popular opening numbers were *Washing Day* and *Spanish Burlesque.*

By 1930 he had taken a partner into his act, Edith James. In March 1937 he was elected the Honorary Chairman of the Variety Artistes Federation. He was still performing in the 1940s.

Joseph Brewster Hamilton Green was initiated into Chelsea Lodge on 15 March 1912. WM 1923. Died at Waterloo Station, London on 18 December 1944 on his way to Southsea to play the dame. He was 68.

Harry GREEN

Actor. Real name Henry Blitzer. Born 1893, New York. Studied law as a young man and became a barrister. Later he turned to acting and appeared in about 60 films in Hollywood.

When talking pictures came in Harry found himself at Paramount, playing mildly stereotypical Jewish characters in such films as *The Kibitzer* (1929) and *Close Harmony* (1931).

Highlights of his Hollywood output include his plaintive rendition of *Isadore the Toreador* in *Paramount on Parade* (1930) and his portrayal of one Jose Pedro Alesandro Lopez Rubinstein in Fox's *She Learned About Sailors* (1934).

Harry Green spent the last ten years of his life in England playing character roles in films like *Joe Macbeth.* (1956) and Chaplin's *A King in New York* (1957). One of Harry's favourite parts was that of Perlmutter in the play *Potash and Perlmutter*, in which he appeared on radio and television in the United Kingdom.

Some of the other films he appeared in include: *The Man I Love* (1929), *Why Bring That Up* (1929), *The Light of Western Stars* (1930), *Honey* (1939), *Be Yourself* (1930), *The Spoilers* (1930), *True to the Navy* (1930), *Sea Legs* (1930), *No Limit* (1931), *Marry Me* (1932), *Mr Skitch* (1933), *Too Much Harmony* (1933), *This Day and Age* (1933), *Love Time* (1934), *Wild Gold* (1934), *Bottoms Up* (1934), *Born to Be Bad* (1934),

Coming Out Party (1934), *The Cisco Kid and The Lady* (1939), *Stardust* (1940), *Glad Tidings* (1951) and *Next to No Time* (1958). He was the screenwriter for the film *Last of the Mohicans,* which was produced in 1971.

Harry was an accomplished card manipulator and conjurer and showed many of his tricks to members of the Royal Family.

He joined Chelsea Lodge on 21 January 1949 from Bohemian Lodge (South Africa) No.4755. He died in hospital after collapsing at a television studio in Wembley on 30 May 1958, aged 65 years.

Phil GREEN

Musical Director. Born 19 July 1911, London. After entering Trinity College of Music at the age of 14, within two years he was appointed musical director of the Prince of Wales Theatre in London's West End. He also played piano, piano accordian and harpsichord. In 1935 he began a long recording career with Decca and EMI Records, during which time he was involved with every type of band from small ensemble to full concert orchestra. His many records appear on a variety of labels ranging from Decca to Parlophone, from Columbia to MGM and HMV. As a composer, arranger and conductor, he regularly encompassed radio, television, films and advertising jingles. From the mid-1930s to early 1940s he recorded under the names: Phil Green and His Rhythm, Bravour Dance Orchestra, Phil Green Orchestra, Seven Kings of Rhythm, Phil Green and His Musketeers, Don Miguel and His Cuban Music, Phil Green and Swing on Strings, The Victory Band, Phil Green

and His Basin Street Band, The Studio Orchestra, Phil Green and His Rhythm on Reeds, Don Felipe and His Cuban Caballeros, The Dixieland Band, The Darktown Strutters, and The Ballyhooligans. He also directed the New Mayfair Dance Orchestra from 1940-1942. He was a musical adviser to Rank Studios and scored more than 200 films including *The Dambusters, League of Gentlemen, Escape in the Sun, Innocent Strangers, Saints and Sinners, Murder Without Crime, Rooney, The Square Peg, The Franchise Affair* and *Masquerade*.

During World War II, Phil conducted many shows for the BBC that were designed for the armed forces. His many programmes included *Salute to Rhythm, Band Call, Cuban Caballeros* and *Music Society of Lower Basin Street.*

He conducted the Ovaltinies Orchestra which was heard regularly on Radio Luxembourg. He played for *Guys and Dolls* at the London Coliseum for seventeen months appearing in 777 performances and the Royal Command Performance of 1953. In 1956 he was presented with an Ivor Novello Award for Outstanding Contribution to the Score of a Stage Play, Film, TV Programme or Radio Programme for *The March Hare.* He also received nominations in other years.

Phil spent the last years of his life in Dublin where he figured prominently in the Irish music scene, running two studios and publishing companies. He had a number one hit record in Ireland with *Suffer Little Children To Come Unto Me.* He was a devoted family man and married to the former singer Dorothé Morrow. He wrote *St Patrick's Mass* which was performed regularly in Ireland. The sleeve notes on the album were written by Cardinal Heenan.

Harry Philip Green was initiated into Chelsea Lodge on 17 February 1937. He died 6 October 1982, Dublin, aged 71 years.

Henri GROS

Director of Variety. Born c1850. French-Jew who came to England originally as the representative of a commercial house, and subsequently became an agent in London for French wines. His business brought him into contact with the old fashioned music hall enterprises and his first venture in music hall enterprise was in 1892 by acquiring an interest in the variety theatre, the Metropolitan, Edgware Road, London where he became managing director.

He was also managing director of Variety Theatres Consolidated, which owned the Metropolitan, Chelsea, Euston, South London and Walthamstow Palaces of Variety, and managing director of the United Varieties Syndicate, which ran the East Ham and Tottenham Palaces.

Henri acquired the Metropolitan in 1892. Six years later he formed a company under whose auspices he transformed the hall into a handsome palace of varieties, some £30,000 being spent on the work. He also took an enthusiastic interest in the Chelsea Palace, which he opened in April 1903, and of which he had chief control.

He was an uncompromising opponent of anything in the shape of vulgarity on his stage and more than once came into conflict with his artistes on the subject. The secret of his success in business lay principally in the fact that he recognised the worth of every man in his employ and placed him in a position most suited to his capacity. He was a strict disciplinarian.

His influence on the contemporary music hall was immeasurable and he threw himself whole heartedly into its development.

In 1900 Henri Gros was appointed president of the London Entertainments Protection Association (an association of music hall managers), a position to which he was elected for many years in succession. He was known as a speaker who 'went on a bit'. On one occasion, presiding at an annual dinner of the Licensed Victuallers' Protection Association, he astonished his colleagues by making a speech lasting an hour and a quarter. He wrote many letters to *The Times* and other newspapers. In the arbitration proceedings arising out of the music hall strike in 1907, Henri was the leading spokesman of the managers, and his popularity in all grades of his profession undoubtedly promoted the restoration of peace. He was president of the Music Hall Benevolent Fund and remained a member of the executive up to the termination of that society in 1908.

Henri Gros was a Founder member of Chelsea Lodge. He died 25 July 1910 and was buried in the Jewish Cemetery, Willesdon. His wife predeceased him in 1900 and he left two sons and two daughters.

Brian HALLARD

Theatrical Producer. Born 10 June 1947, Dalston, East London. Educated at Sir John Cass Foundation School in the City of London where

his after school activities included playing tag with the Beefeaters' sons in the Tower of London moats. He left school at fifteen, at a time when jobs could be changed as often as underwear, and teenagers were affluent. During the swinging sixties when he was a brash young kid of sixteen, Brian deejayed in the trendy Chez Don Club in Dalston, popular because of its gimmicky table telephones used for chatting up purposes without the effort of crossing the room!

He also worked at Leyton Baths and Coronation Gardens – both local venues where the best music was played, alongside top sixties groups The Searchers, The Dave Clark Five and the late Screaming Lord Sutch.

From working locally, Brian went on to deejay at some of the top clubs in London's West End. Free time was spent listening to the latest sounds at The Last Chance Saloon and the notorious Discotheque in Wardour Street, where, before he was famous, David Bowie, (then Davey Jones), often performed with his band, The Lower Third.

Gaining experience along the way, Brian's entrepreneurial skills rapidly developed. He soon progressed to managing a slick team of Go-Go dancers who worked on the East End pub circuit, including the outrageous Deuragon Pub, where infamous drag queens of the day strutted their stuff on the same bill as 'blue' comedians. In the early seventies, Brian was invited to manage Zambuc, a brilliant up and coming five piece band. With Brian's ebullient personality and drive behind them they were soon playing all the 'in' venues on the London scene.

Eventually, there came a time when, albeit reluctantly, Brian had to grow up and shoulder the responsibilities that came with a young family. Being both resilient, ambitious and a quick learner, he reinvented himself and eventually became quite a successful property developer.

In spite of his various achievements, Brian still hankered after the buzzing world of rock music. Then fate took a hand; after hearing the incomparable Johnny Curtiss sing Orbison, the idea behind *Rockin' On Heaven's Door* took shape and took over his life.

Seven years on, *Rockin' On Heaven's Door* has played every major venue from Lands End to The Shetland Isles, including The London Palladium. The year 2005 sees the show go into Europe for a seventy-date tour, as well as an open air performance in Moscow's Red Square.

In May 2004, Brian launched *Elvis in Concert – The Vegas Years*. This show proved so popular over a fifteen-night run that it will be going out again during 2005.

Brian has recently been informed that he is to receive the *Encore* magazine, Producer of the Year award for 2004.

Brian and his wife, Diana, moved to Hunstanton in 2002 where they have settled happily and enjoy the sea views from their office window.

Brian Vincent Hallard joined Chelsea Lodge on 31 May 2002 from Good Samaritan Lodge No.4991 where he was WM in 1996.

Cyril HARLING, PM LGR

Musician. Born 1907. Played tenor and baritone saxophones and violin. Worked with the Edgar Jackson Band in 1932 and made eighteen records on the Decca label. Took part in seventy recordings with Henry Hall and the BBC Dance Orchestra on Columbia between 1935 and 1937.

Cyril Harling was initiated into Chelsea Lodge on 17 March 1939. WM 1958. From 1963 to 1979 he held the office of Secretary to the Lodge. Died 7 June 1986, aged 79 years.

Albert HARRIS

Musician. Born 13 February 1916, London. A top guitarist, but was also a talented pianist who went straight from school to Edgar Jackson's Band at the Grand Hotel, Brighton. In 1933 he recorded with Stanley Barnett in the Madame Tussaud's

Dance Orchestra (London label). In 1934 he joined **Lew Stone** as guitarist and later, Ambrose, making recordings with both bands. In 1939 he appeared at the Pakefield Holiday Camp, Lowestoft with Stan Atkins. He appeared on recordings with Maurice Winnick, Benny Carter, Howard Jacobs, and Seven Kings of Rhythm, directed by **Phil Green**.

Albert Montague Harris was initiated into Chelsea Lodge on 19 September 1975. Died September 1978, aged 62 years.

Tony HARRISON

Band booker agent. Born 4 June 1920. Through his company Harrison and Willis Ltd, he was agent for the Harry Roy, **Woolf Phillips** and **Harry Leader** bands and with Harry Roy ran the Directors' Club in New Bond Street, London from 1961 to 1966.

Tony was Vice President of the Variety Club of Great Britain from 1975 to 1982. He is a London Liveryman of the Worshipful Company of Painter-Stainers, and was one of the ADC's to the Lord Mayor of London in 1981.

He founded the Coda Club in 1987, the rendezvous for all musicians that meet monthly at the Phoenix, 37 Cavendish Square, London W1 at 3.00pm. There is a membership over 300.

Anthony Augustus Harrison joined Chelsea Lodge from Vaudeville Lodge No.5592 on 18 November 1994.

Ralph HEARSUM, PJGD

Cabaret Agent. Son of Frederick and Lillian Hearsum. Born 14 December 1925, Clapham, London. Served in RAOC from 1944-1947. On leaving the Army he became a director of family business in market gardening.

A colleague, W.Bro. **Clive Stock**, who ran the theatrical agency Derwent Entertainments from the 1950s moved from London to Llandudno, North Wales in 1979. Ralph took over the London side of the business and ran the office. He has worked with many well-known names in show business particularly comedian Ken Goodwin. He continues to be involved in the entertainment scene.

Ralph Henry Charles Hearsum was initiated into Streatham Vale Lodge No.5623 in 1952. WM in 1971. Member of Surrey Grand Stewards Lodge No.8297. Member of Elizabethan Jubilee Lodge No.8814 and WM in 1978. Member of Surrey Provincial Grand Stewards Lodge No.8207. Joined Chelsea Lodge 16 September 1994. Currently Chaplain of the Lodge. PAGStB 1988, PAGDC 1994, PJGD 2000.

Dick HENDERSON

Comedian and vaudeville artiste. Born Hull, East Yorkshire 1891. He was described as a 'fat bowler-hatted cigar-chewing comic' and, according to his famous son Dickie Henderson, was the first comic to finish with a straight song. He was also the father of Winnie and Theresa, the Henderson Twins.

Dick Henderson was initiated into Chelsea Lodge on 15 February 1918. Died 1958.

Mike HILL, PM LGR

Musician. Mike Hill who was organist for Chelsea Lodge for 21 years passed away on 1 May 2002 and left behind a legacy that will never be surpassed. He was the finest exponent of the ad-lib song which always came at the appropriate time during a ceremony or when brethren arrived late.

His great friend, **Dr Ted Callister**, who took over the organ whilst Mike was being invested with his collar at Installation always played *The Hills are Alive with The Sound of Music*. The song *There'll Never be Another You* summed him up.

What of the real Mike Hill? Very few people could get close to him as he was a very private person, but from his personal papers and comments from his friends and acquaintances a fascinating story emerges.

Mike Hill, born in Hartlepool on the 11 November 1935, came from a musical family. His mother was a piano teacher, his father a violinist and his brother Paul a drummer so he had a good grounding in music. Mike was a natural and gifted musician (in fact a child prodigy) and at the age of

13 was introduced by telephone live on radio to Hughie Green for *Opportunity Knocks*. He played four instruments: piano, vibes, harpsichord and orchestra bells going from one instrument to the next until he had completed the song he was asked to do. Hughie Green invited him to the show and he won. He then became a regular on the show and travelled the country, playing for Jack Taylor's Juveniles, Ralph Reader's *Gang Shows* and many more.

He became resident with the Merry Magpies doing stage and radio work with Tommy Thompson, Ted Alex, Edna Dean, Michael Hibbert and Terry Moore. He had offers from Scotland, Ireland, Jersey and abroad.

He went to Birmingham to audition for ITV's *Bid For Fame*, a contest that he won. He worked quite a lot on TV and played the American Bases. Mike continued working until 1960 when he took a break for a month, then it was back to the grindstone. According to his diary (written by his mother) the list of engagements, far too numerous to detail, reads like a Who's Who in Showbusiness. They include working with Derek Foulds, Connie Francis, Graham Hill, Jon Pertwee, Wally Whyton and Jack Wild. Mike appeared on the BBC Light Programme in *Tuesday Rendezvous*.

During this time he worked for Dick James Music and released his first record *Jukes Jingle* backed with *Joey's Song.* His second record was released on 14 October 1960 called *Beatnik Boogie* backed with *Mike's Song.* In all he composed about eighteen songs.

Mike then went on tour again with **Tito Burns** and The Allisons and he later became resident on TV with the *Five o'clock Club* and *Stubby Kaye's Silver Star Show.* Overseas engagements in 1967 took him to Germany and Sweden as musical director to Jayne Mansfield. He returned to Dick James and was invited to be musical advisor to The Beatles. A signed photo of the group was a proud possession but when funds were drying up in 1997 he sold the photo at an auction at Sotherby's. No asking price is listed in his diary, nor is what the photo realised in hard cash.

Throughout the 1970s Mike played in almost every pub and club in London and continued recording changing labels to the Edmat label. His final recording was *From Us To You* together with Kenny Williams and Guy Saville. On the record sleeve DJ Adrian Love said: "You have in your hands the product of three of the best entertainers in London."

Around this time Mike's health began to deteriorate but he continued to be the unofficial ambassador to the widows of the Lodge and was always in touch with them.

Mike Hill was a very artistic person and renovated numerous Lodge banners during his time as a Freemason. He left behind another legacy in the form of a Yorkshire terrier called Bobo who became known as "The Chelsea Mascot".

He had so many facets to his life and will be remembered by someone, for something, for the good he has done.

Michael Hill was initiated into Proscenium Lodge No.3435 on 1 September 1968 and was Master in 1978. Joined Chelsea Lodge, 18 January 1974 and became Master in 1980. LGR, 1991. He died 1 May 2002, aged 66 years. A Memorial Service was held at St Paul's (the Actors Church), Bedford Street, London WC2 on 16 September 2002.

HILLMAN Family

Three generations of the family have been members of Chelsea Lodge.

Cyril (known as Michael) Hillman (right) senior electrician at Finsbury Park Empire with film star and actor Terry Thomas in 1953.

Merson James HILLMAN

Born 1896. Electrician and later stage manager at Finsbury Park Empire from 1930-1950s. Initiated

into Chelsea Lodge 17 November 1944. His son **Cyril Merson HILLMAN** (known as Michael), senior electrician at the Finsbury Park Empire during the 1950s was initiated into Chelsea Lodge on 17 July 1953. Died 22 October 1986. He had two sons both of whom became members of Chelsea Lodge. **David Russell HILLMAN** was born 28 October 1964, London and initiated on 19 September 1986, becoming WM in 1993. He attained LGR in 2002. **Richard Michael HILLMAN** was born 22 March 1968 and initiated on 15 September 1989, becoming WM in 1996.

Frank HOLDER. PM LGR

This singer-bongo player from Guyana arrived in Britain with the RAF in 1944 and on demob decided to stay. Frank, a superbly fit body builder, came from a musical family and had been a professional entertainer in Guyana, singing with various dance bands. During his service career he sang with a number of RAF groups. He was also an accomplished athlete, boxing and running for the RAF. He ran the 100 yards in 9.9 seconds. He played cricket for his station.

In 1948 Frank joined Leslie 'Jiver' Hutchinson's band as vocalist, playing mainly one night stands around England, Scotland and Wales. During a year spent with 'Jiver' he began developing as a notable bongo player and it was this expertise that led Kenny Baker to enlist him for his band at London's Churchill Club. He also played at the Mecca dance hall, The Paramount, with Andre Messeder's Band, with whom he took the first Latin American band to the Ritz Ballroom in Manchester. Frank then had a spell in the London Casino *Latin Quarter* show, before joining Johnny Kerrison's Rumba Band at the Café de Paris. During this period he would visit various jazz clubs and sing with the jazz groups.

In May 1950 Johnny Dankworth was looking for a singer to replace Marion Williams in the band and a mutual friend recommended Frank. So began an association that lasted through until 1956. His first recording was with the John Dankworth Seven, adding the vocal on *Don't Blame Me*, released in January 1951. Other recordings with the band followed including *I Get a Kick Out of You* and *I've Got You Under My Skin*. Frank was voted 4th Most Popular Singer in the *Melody Maker* Poll of 1953. In late 1954 came his own solo debut, *Mambo in the Moonlight* on the Parlophone label.

Frank's reason for leaving Dankworth was to pursue a solo variety career, making his debut at the Glasgow Empire on 15 October 1956. A nationwide tour supporting artistes like Anne Shelton, Tommy Cooper, Arthur Haynes and others was followed by another in a beat package *Music Music* with Johnny Duncan's Blue Grass Boys and the Alex Welsh Band. Television appearances included the *Benny Hill Show* and *Six Five Special*. He acted in *Cry the Beloved Country* on ITV and appeared in Noel Coward's *Nude with Violin* at the Bromley Theatre.

With calypso at the time quite popular Frank was a natural, a fact he soon began to regret when record producers considered him for little else. He even invested his own cash into some demo ballads, with little success. As well as Parlophone he recorded on Pye and Decca, making LPs *Calypso Time, Mambo in the Moonlight* and *Stop! Proceed with Caution*. He sang the title song on the sound-track of the 1958 film *Nor the Moon by Night* that was set in Africa.

As variety bookings at home became scarce he often worked abroad and in 1958 was appearing on some Bill Haley concerts in Europe. Frank has continued to be a popular cabaret artist, at home and abroad.

Frank Holder was initiated into Chelsea Lodge in January 1967. He was WM in 1994. Now holds LGR.

John HOLLINGSWORTH

Toastmaster. Born 26 March 1938, York. He was on the first boatload of families to the British Zone of Germany after WWII. He attended the British Forces Education Service boarding school, Prince Rupert School, Wilhelmshaven, returning to the UK at the age of sixteen.

After various part time jobs he joined the Metropolitan Police, spending the entire time in Special Branch at Scotland Yard. This involved periods of protection with various Kings, Presidents, Chancellors and government ministers both foreign and domestic.

Following retirement John became a toastmaster at leading West End Hotels and Beadle to various Livery Companies in the City of London. He is a Past President of the Society of London Toastmasters.

Joined Chelsea Lodge 21 March 1997. PM of Jubilee Lodge No.6936. Currently Almoner of Chelsea Lodge.

Sydney HOWARD

Vaudeville Artiste. Born Yeadon, Leeds, West Yorkshire 1883. Known as the 'slow-witted droll from Yeadon'. Known for his unusual humour and eccentric walk, he was a cartoon character in the children's comic *Radio Fun.*

Robert Sydney Howard was initiated into Chelsea Lodge 21 March 1924. Died 1946.

Gareth HUNT

Actor. Real name Alan Leonard Hunt. Born 7 February 1943, London. Nephew of actress Martita Hunt. Served in the Merchant Navy for six years after which he had a variety of jobs before training at Webber Douglas Academy of Dramatic Art. Appeared in repertory at Ipswich, Bristol Old Vic, Coventry, Royal Court in London, and Watford before the Royal Shakespeare Company and the National Theatre.

His first taste of real exposure came in the Doctor Who series *Planet of the Spiders* (1974) on BBC television. Next came *Upstairs Downstairs* (1971) where he played Frederick Norton the footman. After this came his first lead role: *The New Avengers – The Eagles Nest* (1976) - a show that he remembers with much fondness.

Stage productions include *Conduct Unbecoming, Alpha Beta* and *Deathtrap.* He is famed for the television Nescafé advertisements in the 1980s where he shook coffee beans in his hands.

Films include: *The World is Full of Married Men* (1979), *Licenced to Love and Kill* (1979), *The House on Garibaldi Street* (1979), *Funny Money* (1982), *Gabrielle and the Doodlemen* (1984), *And the Wall Came Tumbling Down*

(1984), *Bloodbath at the House of Death* (1983), *Hazard of Hearts* (1987), *It Couldn't Happen Here* (1988), *A Chorus of Disapproval* (1988), *The Lady and the Highwayman* (1988), *The Castle of Adventure* (1990), *The Ghost of Monte Carlo* (1990), *The Forgotten Wells* (1992), *Fierce Creatures* (1997), *The Incredible Adventures of Marco Polo* (1998), and *Parting Shots* (1998).

Guest starring roles on television include: *The Hanged Man* episode *Bless This House* (1971), *For the Love of Ada* (1972), The *Bridge Maker* (1975), *The Brotherhood* (1975), *Space: 1999* in episode *The Guardian of Piri* (1975), *The Old Curiosity Shop* (1981), *Minder* (1982), *And the Walls Came Tumbling Down*, (1984), *A Hazard of Hearts* (1987), *Chorus of Disapproval* (1998), *The Lady and The High-wayman* (1989) A *Ghost in Monte Carlo* (1990), *Grottmorden* (1990), *Side by Side* (1992), *Upstairs Downstairs Remembered* (1996). *The New Adventures of Robin Hood* (1997), and *The Best Show in the World... Probably* (1997) *Harry and the Wrinklies* (1999) *BBC Hall of Fame* (2000) and *Night and Day* (2001). He also made a cameo appearance on *EastEnders* in 2001.

Gareth decided to pursue business interests through his ideas for a CD-ROM containing details of hundreds of British actors and clips from their performances. This has now been turned into a website e-Media-c.

Twice married, he has two sons. He collapsed from a suspected heart attack whilst appearing on stage in *Absurd Person Singular* at the Pier Theatre, Bournemouth in July 2002. He suddenly cried out "Oh, please God," slumped across a table and then fell to the floor. Members of the audience did not realise it wasn't part of the script and began applauding until co-star Robert Beck rushed on stage and shouted: "Is there a doctor in the house? I'm being serious." Sadly there were no doctors on hand, but people who were qualified to practise first aid responded immediately before he was taken to hospital. Previously Gareth had had a heart attack in the year 2000 and needed a bypass operation.

Alan Leonard Hunt was initiated into Chelsea Lodge on 19 March 1993.

Len HUNT
Musician. Played drums with The John Birmingham Band, also known as the Big Twelve. Recorded a number of records in 1925 and 1926 on the Edison Bell Winner label. Guested with the Percival Mackay Band at the Shaftsbury Theatre, London(1928) and with Harry Perritt and His Orchestra (1932). Was drummer with the Original Havana Band (1928-1929) and made records on Broadcast label; he was with Nat Star and His Dance Orchestra (1928-1932) and recorded on the Sterno label. Recorded with **Phil Green** (1942) in the Victory Band and recorded on the Decca label. Also guested on recording sessions in 1941 with Hatchett's Swingtette on the Decca label. He also worked with Geraldo and was the drum doyen of Archer Street where musicians used to congregate seeking work from the 1920s to the 1960s. His little shop, through a small alley off Archer Street, was packed to the ceiling with drums and effects. Arguably every drummer in the world knew Len and his drummers headquarters, as he proudly described it, and his weekly advertisements in the music papers with jolly slogans which always contained a caricature of his jovial face. Len was the friend of everyone in the business; he was kind, fatherly, helpful, patient and obliging, always ready with advice and guidance. That's why he became known as 'Doc' Hunt.

Leonard W. Hunt was initiated into Chelsea Lodge on 19 March 1937. Died July 1981, aged 77 years.

Leonard John INSULL
Born 1893. Began his career as a comedy illusionist appearing under the name of **Hinsle**. For twenty years he performed in theatres around the world assisted by his wife, who appeared under the name of Miss Gertie Ross.

Shortly after the end of World War I, Len began a stage property business in Wolverhampton. It was there that ventriloquist **Thomas Mitchell Whittaker**, known on stage as **Corum** challenged him: "I bet you couldn't make me a dummy." Len produced 'Jerry' and from thereon he never looked back. Len became the most sought after British maker of ventriloquist properties.

After successfully making the first figure for

Corum, he began to experiment and made a series of 'cheeky boy' heads to which he fitted complicated movements that enabled their faces to become fully animated. His work, which is often distinguishable by the fine leather mouth movement and delicately painted face, was supplied to artistes around the world. Among his famous creations were Archie Andrews made for Peter Brough and Lord Charles for **Ray Alan**.

Leonard John Insull was a joining member of Chelsea Lodge on 16 April 1920. He continued to produce ventriloquial properties until his death in 1974, aged 81 years.

Ian IRVING

Comedian. Born 25 January 1958. Began his show business career in 1986 in talent shows at various venues around southern England. His first television appearance was on *Surprise, Surprise* in 1987, then *New Faces* also in the same year. He has appeared at many of the top venues in the country supporting numerous leading performers including Lionel Richie, Elkie Brooks, **Jim Davidson**, Russ Abbott, Bonnie Tyler, Smokey Robinson, The Four Tops, and The Drifters.

When Ian performed at the London Palladium he supported Dame Vera Lynn, Mike Yarwood, David Copperfield plus a host of other top showbiz stars, which led to him supporting Richard Digance for a third time, culminating with an appearance at Her Majesty's Theatre in London. In addition, he has worked at home and abroad for all the armed services, as well as performing internationally for companies in Barbados, South Africa, Cyprus, Portugal, Germany, Spain and the USA.

Ian's extensive cabaret performances have incorporated many summer seasons on the holiday circuit for companies including Butlins, Pontins, Warners, Havens and other holiday venues in the UK. He has also performed on Mediterranean cruises run by the major tour companies.

As a regular on the after-dinner speaking circuit, Ian has travelled around the world with luminaries from varied sports, including Sir Bobby Charlton, Sir Geoff Hurst, Sir Henry Cooper, Nick Faldo, Kevin Keegan, Lennox Lewis, Frank Bruno, Barry McGuigan, Graham Gooch, Allan Lamb, Willie John McBride, Gareth Edwards, and Bill Beaumont.

Sport plays a major part in Ian's life – his hobbies include golf, skiing, football, karate and cricket. He says: "One of my many sporting achievements was winning the Jimmy Tarbuck Golf Classic in Portugal – a major trophy among entertainers. Golf is my speciality subject, and I play in a number of corporate events during the year. I incorporate sports-related material into an entertaining and amusing routine. The functions vary in size and range from large occasions to smaller gatherings and I am equally at home in either setting."

Ian has experience from both sides of the camera having been a warm-up artiste for the BBC on *Blankety Blank, Fast Friends, Bread, Brush Strokes,* and *In Sickness and in Health,* with walk-on parts in *The Chief, Kilroy,* and *Pebble Mill.* He has also appeared on *Celebrity Squares* with **Bob Monkhouse,** which led to his own half -hour TV show called *Stand And Deliver.*

He supports various charity organisations including The Variety Club, SPARKS, Lord's Taverners, The Wooden Spoon Society and is a proud member of the Grand Order of Water Rats.

Ian lives in rural Essex with his wife Joanne and two sons Dale and Ryan.

Ian Irving was initiated into Chelsea Lodge on 20 January 2000.

Jimmy JACK

Musician. Born 1904. Played drums with The Masterkeys (1934), Scott Wood's Six Swingers (1935), Billy Thorburn and His Music (1936-1937) and the Henry Hall Orchestra (1939). He appeared in variety shows with Jack Jackson and his Pavilion Serenaders at the Pavilion Hotel, Scarborough.

James Jack was initiated into Chelsea Lodge on 18 January 1957. Died 25 July 1957, aged 53 years.

Nat JACKLEY

Variety Artiste and rubberneck comedian. Born 16 July 1909, Sunderland. Son of Chelsea member **George Jackley,** famous comedian and panto-mime dame. Began his career as a dancer with the Eight Lancashire Lads at the Hippodrome, Chesterfield in 1920. He left the group in 1927 and travelled around the variety theatres with his sister Joy.

In 1942 he appeared at the London Palladium in George Black's *Best Bib and Tucker* and in 1946 in *High Time* at the same theatre. He took part in the Royal Variety Performance on 4 November 1946at the London Palladium in front of Their Majesties

King George VI and Queen Elizabeth.

In the book *Kindly Leave The Stage* Nat is quoted as saying: "Joy was a very good pianist; we did concerted numbers and a pal of mine used to come on and do spoken gags with me and then I would do my clog-dance on a steel table. Then we had an eight-step staircase which was formed into a xylophone, and we used to do our tap dancing and play tunes on the xylophone."

After his sister became ill Nat moved into verbal comedy and became known as a sketch artiste. He worked in an almost unintelligible voice. Tall and thin, with an unusual length of neck, he was known as "rubber neck". This came about by Nat wearing a coat which was forever slipping off his shoulders. He was forced to jerk it back on, in the process producing a curious twitch of the neck which the audience loved. He worked on this feature during his performance, evolving the 'rubber neck' which became his hallmark.

He appeared in a number of films including: *Demobbed* (1944), *Under New Management* (1946), *Stars in Your Eyes* (1956), *Magical Mystery Tour* (1967), *Mrs Brown You've Got a Lovely Daughter* (1968) and *The Ploughman's Lunch* (1982).

In 1980 he played the grandad, Harry Haward, in ITV's *Spoils of War.* He was a member of the Grand Order of Water Rats.

Nathan T. Jackley Hirsch was initiated into Chelsea Lodge on 19 June 1942. He died 17 September 1988, aged 79 years. He left a widow, Pam, and four children.

Jack JAY

Entrepreneur. Born 20 May 1915. Son of Ben Jay, a London impresario who built up a chain of over thirty cinemas in London, Oxford and Hastings in the 1930s.

At the age of sixteen Jack became Britain's youngest cinema manager for one of his father's cinema chain. He first went to Great Yarmouth with his father, Ben, in 1937.

During the war, with the bombing of inner city areas, many of the cinemas were destroyed but some coastal ones, two in Hastings, two in Lowestoft and one, the Windmill, in Great Yarmouth remained intact. Jack turned the Windmill back into a live theatre and brought in big name attractions in the 1950's which included Tommy Trinder, who became a life long friend, George Formby, Max Bygraves, Norman Wisdom and later Tommy Steele, Frankie Howerd, Bernie Clifton, Fiona Richmond and Billy Fury. These trail blazing shows firmly established Great Yarmouth on the showbusiness summer circuit.

Jack headed 'Jay's World of Entertainment', which by the early 1960s encompassed theatres, cinemas, social clubs, discotheques, a pub and a restaurant. He pioneered the start of the Cash Bingo clubs in the country, first at the Windmill and later at the Empire on Great Yarmouth's seafront and the Hippodrome in Lowestoft.

The Lowestoft Hippodrome had been built by George Gilbert as one of his circus arenas and in 1903 Gilbert opened another circus building, the Hippodrome in Great Yarmouth, a few yards away from Jays' Windmill Theatre. After the Second World War, it was mooted that two Great Yarmouth showmen, Jack Jay and Billy Russell, would take over the running of the Hippodrome and its amusement forecourt, Jack to run the circus and Russell the arcade. As it turned out Russell ended up running both the circus and the 6,000 square feet forecourt, building up a very successful circus business, carried on by executors after his death in 1957. However, at the end of the 1978 summer season the Hippodrome was sold, and Jack and his son Peter Jay found themselves as the owners of a form of entertainment in which they had no experience whatsoever. They were determined, however, that the circus traditions would continue unbroken.

After booking in complete circuses for a couple

of years, Jack allowed his son to take over the running of the circus and Peter Jay went on to become one of the leading circus impresarios of the postwar years in Britain also presenting circuses in Blackpool Tower and at Blackpool Pleasure Beach since the early 1980s.

Jack Jay was a charter founder member and past president of the Great Yarmouth Lions Club and founder and past chairman of the Great Yarmouth Publicity Association which he started in the 50s after the East Coast disastrous floods to specifically help Great Yarmouth recover its position in the Holiday Trade.

Together with the late Lord Delfont and Sir Harry Secombe, Jack Jay was a trustee of the Entertainment Artists Benevolent Fund, a charity which raises thousands of pounds for Artistes welfare, and a Companion Water Rat the highest honour in Showbiz, which he shared with Prince Charles and Prince Philip.

A keen footballer and cricketer he started the legendary Stars Showbiz Charity Football and Cricket matches which pulled in large crowds in the 60s and raised thousands of pounds for showbiz and local charities.

He also started and produced for many years the annual showbiz *Midnight Matinee* for the Publicity Association and the Entertainment Artistes Benevolent Fund Charities.

In 1982 Jack expanded his East Coast empire buying Trusthouse Fortes three-in-one cinema and disco complex which had originally been the Royal Aquarium, renaming it the Royalty and bringing back live entertainment there after a gap of over ten years. Peter Jay had worked there himself in the 1960s on a bill headed by Helen Shapiro and Jimmy Savile, while at the bottom of the bill had been a then-unknown comic, Ronnie Corbett. Subsequently the Jays have featured summer variety bills at the Royalty with such artistes as Brian Conley, the Grumbleweeds, Michael Barrymore, the Bluebell Girls, Bobby Davro, Duncan Norvelle, Gary Wilmot, Freddie Starr, Cilla Black and **Jim Davidson.** They also presented all-star wrestling at the Hippodrome with bill-toppers Big Daddy and Giant Haystacks.

Jack Jay retired from his showbusiness empire in 1985, handing over to son Peter and daughter-in-law Christine (the daughter of another well-known Great Yarmouth showman, Gordon Edwards) and grandsons Ben, Joe and Jack Junior, who represent the fourth generation of Jays in Great Yarmouth's showbusiness traditions.

Although originally from London, Jack Jay made Great Yarmouth his home for fifty years. He was happily married to Freda for 55 years.

Jack Jay was initiated into Chelsea Lodge on 19 November 1948. Died in the James Paget Hospital, Great Yarmouth, 26 June 1995, aged 80 years. His passing marked the end of an era in the history of the Great Yarmouth Entertainment Industry, a time that had seen the resort become established as one of the country's major holiday destinations. Jack Jay will be remembered for all his pioneering work for the town and his major contributions to charities along the way.

Many showbiz stars, local friends and hundreds of mourners were present at his funeral on 13 July 1995 held at the St Nicholas Parish Church, Great Yarmouth; they included sixties star Marty Wilde who sang an acoustic rendition of *Tears in Heaven,* **Johnnie Riscoe**, who helped Jack Jay create his vast entertainment empire, singer **Robert Earl** who sang the celebrity anthem *My Way* and local artist Len Lowe.

Mike JEROME

Comedian. Born 18 May 1947. Describes himself as 'The International Toy Boy', introducing the  character in 1986. He began his show business career when he joined his first band The Kentucky Kids as a youngster. The band featured Brian Connelly who later went on to form the pop group The Sweet. In 1979 Mike became a redcoat and it was during his years with Billy Butlin and Pontins, winning Pontins' Entertainer of the Year, that he decided to embark on his now well-acclaimed solo career.

He has worked various summer seasons across the UK, Jersey's Caesar's Palace, Lakeside and seasons for Butlins, Pontins and Warner Holidays.

Mike's act is well suited for pantomime. He has appeared in *Peter Pan, Goldilocks* and the *Three Bears* in addition to being a member of the Crazy Gang in *Dick Whittington.*

His role in theatre has taken him to The London Palladium, the Royal Albert Hall and St David's Hall, Cardiff.

Mike was the outright winner of *Opportunity*

Knocks in 1987, featured on many TV shows including *Pebble Mill* and LWT's *Six O'Clock Show*. He is a well-known warm-up comedian for many television productions including *Last of the Summer Wine, Bread* and *Ready, Steady, Cook*.

In 1987 and 2000 he was voted Captain of the Comedians Golf Society. His career has enabled him to work, tour and become friends with some of his comedy and music colleagues including Michael Barrymore, Brian Conley, **Jim Davidson**, Shane Richie, Mike Reid, Jimmy Jones, The Drifters, Three Degrees, Neil Sedaka and Frankie Valli of the Four Seasons.

Since 1994 Mike's love of music and singing has allowed him to write, record and release six songs including *Toyboy, Gone and Lost my Little Yo-Yo* and *Not Another Christmas*. He is the manager of the tribute band Blues Brothers Inc. Says Mike: "If you are doing a tribute show to one of the most successful movies of all times, it has to be not only in keeping with the original attitude and atmosphere of the film, but also to the highest musical performances possible. It takes time and a lot of effort but at the end of the day you see and hear classic tunes, professional choreography, commitment and a performance of rare quality."

Michael James Jerome was initiated into Chelsea Lodge on 11 May 2001. He relates: "It was my proudest moment and the actual day (not year) that Chelsea Lodge was Consecrated (11 May 1905). The ceremony took place in the Grand Temple. **Roger De Courcey** was Worshipful Master, **Jim Davidson** was Senior Warden, **Peter Elliott**, Junior Warden, **Paul Wood**, Senior Deacon and **Ray Donn**, Junior Deacon. Inner Guard was **Ron Smiley**. There were over 700 brethren present."

David George JOHNSTON

Musician. Born Upper Norwood, London 29 September 1932. Learned piano from the age of eight and then the organ from twelve. He played organ at his local church and always wanted to be a theatre organist. The opportunity came in the mid-Fifties starting at the Granada, North Cheam when he filled in with various appearances when required. He graduated to playing at all the Granada organs in and around the London area.

After the demise of the theatre organs David turned to teaching music and has continued in this field for over thirty years, combined with cabaret work, mainly in the London area.

David George Johnston joined Chelsea 18 September 1998. PM of St Mary Abbots Lodge No.1974. Took over as organist of the lodge following the death of **Michael Hill** in May 2002.

Tommy JOVER

Vaudeville Artiste. Born 1895. Real name Florencio Tomas Jover. Member of the Five Jovers and a third generation circus artiste. He had two children Nena and Raf. Allegedly Tommy did some bull-fighting when his family hit hard times.

Florencio Tomas Jover was initiated into Chelsea Lodge on 15 December 1922. Died 1983.

Ken JOY

Variety Artiste. Born 9 December 1945. Spanning a period of some 200 years, Ken Joy's theatrical history dates back to the early Victorian era. His family can be traced back to George Edwardes' Gaiety Theatre in the Strand, where Ken's great grandmother first appeared as one of the original Gaiety Girls. Since that time, the Joy family have always been associated with the theatre in one way or another.

His Father was a 'pit' and orchestral violinist and musician, playing and appearing at most of the well-known variety theatre's during the 'hey day' of variety.

Ken's son, Richard, an established and well known drummer/performer, carries on the theatrical tradition.

Ken first 'trod the boards', at a very early age when he appeared with his sister on Blackpool's Central Pier Theatre, and from that time has appeared in most of this country's major, and not so major, theatres...from the Palace Theatre,

Attercliffe to the Palladium Theatre, London!

As well as having his own unique comedy and instrumental speciality act, he has also acted as comedy 'feed' to some of our greatest comedians...the last one being the great 'Rubber Neck' comedian, **Nat Jackley**.

Ken's past experience takes in all aspects of the theatre, from Variety to 'straight' acting. After the decline of the Variety Theatre, Ken decided to go into the 'legitimate' side of the theatre. He studied at the Webber Douglas Drama School and then went into the Repertory Theatre, both as an actor and as a director. The lure of variety was too strong and when the cabaret and club scene took hold, Ken returned and he still remains one of the country's leading comedy and instrumental speciality acts, entertaining audiences either on the Cruise Ships or in London's West End.

A proud member of the famous theatrical Order, The Grand Order of Water Rats, Ken had the 'Joy' of bringing 'in' his son Richard, who is now the youngest member of this grand old Order.

Ken Joy was initiated into Chelsea Lodge on 15 September 2000.

Harry KARR

Musician. Canadian. Real name Harry Kurnasky. Played alto saxophone, clarinet, flute, piccolo and oboe. He spent time with the bands of Jack Jackson, Jack Harris and Jack Hylton. He could play *Flight of the Bumble Bee* on the alto saxophone with great ease! His hobbies included transcribing saxophone solos and making wine.

When once asked what he would do if he had a million pounds he said: "First and foremost I would start a fund to build free hospitals (like you have here in England) for the people of Canada. One of the saddest memories of my life is of a young girl cousin of mine in Vancouver. When still only a child she was suddenly stricken with a serious disease. Immediate attention was essential, but in Canada hospitals will not admit patients until they are paid for. My cousin never had a chance because her folks hadn't enough money to meet the bills. She died. After I had started the fund rolling with a good few thousand dollars, I would settle in London in a big house on Hampstead Heath. Under the house I would have a large wine cellar, for one of my pet hobbies is making wine. Musicians would be welcome any time at my house or in my wine cellar. Then I would get the biggest car I could find and in it do a tour of the Continent with my wife. When I got tired of pleasure, I would start a saxophone school, but only real enthusiasts would be taught. I'd make them pay according to their means, because if you don't pay for a thing, you don't appreciate it."

Harry Karr joined Chelsea Lodge on 21 September 1934 from Meridian Lodge No.108, Vancouver, British Columbia, Canada.

Nat KARSON

Theatrical and television producer. Born 1908, Zurich, Switzerland, son of a refugee Russian architect, who took him to Chicago as an infant. He attended public schools. He won a scholarship to the Chicago Art Institute, painted office murals in Chicago for a while and, after the 1929 stock market crash, went to New York where the Ainslie Galleries put on a one-man show of some of his caricatures.

Finally he edged his way into the theatre world through the Federal Theatre Project. In 1936 he collaborated with Orson Welles and John Houseman on a highly successful all-Negro production of *Hamlet.*

From that he jumped to the Radio City Music Hall, where for seven years from 1936 he designed the sets for the large-scale theatre productions. He became producer and director of the *Fashions of the Times* in 1948 and 1949. After leaving the music hall Nat plunged into the hectic world of theatrical production. He and Eddie Cantor made their debuts as producers together in the musical *Nellie Bly* which, sadly, was a disaster and lost $300,000.

In 1948, he wrote for the *New York Times* a highly critical article on the artistic side of television and shortly after was engaged as a consultant producer for the Columbia Broadcasting Company. He moved to London to set up operations and he produced a series of revues for the New Empire Theatre. He returned to America in 1954 and became producer of the National Broadcasting Company's television *Comedy Hour.*

Nat Karson was initiated into Chelsea Lodge on 18 January 1952. He collapsed and died of a heart attack on 27 September 1954 in New York City. He was 46 years old.

Davy KAYE, MBE

Born on 25 March 1916 in London's East End, Davy made a name for himself in theatre, film and television. Moving easily from one to the other with a natural skill and professionalism that earned him respect from everyone who knew him. One of this countries most experienced and versatile entertainers, his international career has also been wide ranging, covering revue, cabaret as well as film and television.

As a schoolboy, Davy was already doing amateur and school shows, but his first professional engagement came in 1935 at the Mile End Empire. This was followed by appearances at many other venues. With a partner in the 1930s he worked as Kaye and Vale as 'The Only Two Jewish Cowboys in Captivity'. At the outbreak of war 4ft 11ins, Davy volunteered, but was told by the medical officer, "When we declare war on the pygmies we'll send for you!!" He spent the war years working in shows all over England at RAF bases, army camps, munitions factories and on radio.

After the war, he started touring his own revues in partnership with his agent Joe Collins (father of Joan and Jackie), an association which lasted over 30 years. During this period, Davy played `Benny Southstreet' in the original London production of *Guys and Dolls* at the London Coliseum. He will also be remembered by many for his outstanding performance playing five different characters in the Wolf Mankowitz musical *Belle – the Story of Doctor Crippen* at the Strand Theatre, London. He was the principal comedian in the revue *Fanny Get Your Fun*. Then came work in film, television, theatre and cabaret. From 1954 to 1968 Davy presented and starred in a new show each month at London's smartest nightspot The Embassy Club in Bond Street.

He starred in *Androcles and the Lion* and *The Bishop's Bonfire* at the Mermaid Theatre, London and featured in films such as *Wrong Arm of The Law, The Biggest Bundle of Them All, The Pot Carriers, Crooks in Cloisters, Satan's Harvest, Those Magnificent Men in Their Flying Machines, Chitty Chitty Bang Bang, Alice in Wonderland, Carry on Cowboy, Carry on Regardless, Carry On at Your Convenience, The Millionairess, Fun at St Fanny's, A Nightingale Sang in Berkeley Square* and many more.

TV appearances include*: It Takes a Thief* (1968), *Adventure Five* of the cult TV series *Sapphire and Steel* (1981*). I Love Christmas* (archive footage), (2001) and *Drake's Progress* (archive footage), (2001).

His final television appearance was with Michael Barrymore on the *Barrymore* show

where he performed his world famous one-man band routine to the tune of *Macnamara's Band*.

Since 1985, when The Variety Club of Great Britain honoured him with a luncheon at the Hilton Hotel to celebrate his Fifty Years in Show Business, Davy personally raised more than £1 million for various charities including: Duke of Edinburgh Award Scheme and Prince Philip Trust Fund (Windsor and Maidenhead). He was a Past King Rat - Preceptor Grand Order of Water Rats. Awarded Badge of Merit and Bar; Bud Flanagan Leukemia Fund Celebrity Committee Chairman and Executive Committee Member; and Nightingale House Home for the Aged - Life Governor.

Davy was one of the very few people to have been awarded a 'Silver Heart' by the Variety Club of Great Britain on two occasions, once in 1975 and again in 1985 for his work on behalf of underprivileged children. He has organised five *Royal Gala Shows* for HRH The Duke of Edinburgh and in 1990 Davy organised and produced a Variety Show at The London Palladium for International Spinal Research which raised £120,000.

Awarded the MBE in Her Majesty The Queen's 1995 New Years' Honours List, Davy was a little man in physical stature, but as a talent - he was a GIANT!

Davy Kaye was initiated into Chelsea Lodge on 21 August 1956. He died 4 February 1998, aged 81 years. Following his death Prince Philip wrote from Windsor Castle: "Davy Kaye died suddenly while on holiday in the Caribbean earlier this year. That very sad event seemed to spell the end of the series of highly entertaining and successful fundraising concerts, but I was mistaken. Davy's son, **Kaplan Kaye**, very generously offered to organise a special concert as a tribute to his father." This was held at the Theatre Royal, Windsor on 14 June 1998.

Prince Philip went on: "I have no doubt at all that Davy would have been delighted to know that this tribute will bring great pleasure to all of us attending it and very welcome funds for his two favourite charities."

Kaplan KAYE

A Lewis. Son of **Davy Kaye**. Born 7 August 1948 After originally training as an actor, soon found himself appearing on television and in films and West End theatre productions such as *Oliver, Blitz* and *Bye Bye Birdie*, as well as playing the coveted role of 'Puck' at Covent Garden in Benjamin Britten's opera *A Midsummer Night's Dream*. He also appeared as 'Henry' in the original BBC television series *Just William*. Whilst appearing at Covent Garden and playing 'Billy' the grandson in the radio series *Mrs Dales Diary*, Kaplan wrote and recorded *Do You Believe in Magic?* his first single that graced the lower end of the hit parade. By now Kaplan had decided that the thing he most wanted to do was enter the music business. This he did by securing a job working for Dick James Music, publishers of the Beatles and Elton John. He worked at Dick James Music for eight years starting as a dub-cutter in DJM's studio, before soon becoming an in-house sound engineer and then Artistes and Repertoire manager for DJM Records working with such recording stars as Elton John and Joe Cocker.

After leaving DJM, Kaplan concentrated on record production, music publishing, writing and management, and was responsible for launching the successful career of Judie Tzuke with the release of her major world hit *Stay With Me Till Dawn*.

Kaplan's other hits include *Chalk Dust* by the Brat, a send-up of tennis star John McEnroe and *Listen to the Budda* by reggae group Ozo. As writer/producer Kaplan has had his songs recorded by Lulu, Geno Washington, Lance Ellington and Karan Knowles. In 1994 he won the British Academy of Songwriters and Authors (BASCA) Award for Best British Song at the Cavan International Song Festival with his song *You Will Find Me There*. He has composed the musical *Circumstances.*

Kaplan now runs his own theatrical agency

KAL Management, incorporating Kaplan Kaye Music. He has produced *Royal Gala Shows* for HRH The Duke of Edinburgh in aid of The Prince Philip Trust Fund (Windsor and Maidenhead) and The Bud Flanagan Leukemia Appeal since 1989.

He is a member of the show business charity The Grand Order of Water Rats.

Kaplan Kaye was initiated into Chelsea Lodge on 21 March 1997.

Roger KITTER

Entertainer. Born 20 October 1949. Educated at

Clifton College Bristol . He has enjoyed a career in show business which has spanned thirty-six years. It is very rare for any performer to be able to pursue a career which combines stand up comedy and acting, but he has managed to do this very successfully, in addition to performing as a radio presenter, game show host and voice-over man.

Roger has appeared many times at the famous London Palladium "opening" for international stars including Diana Ross, Dionne Warwick, Frankie Valli and The Four Seasons, Vic Damone, Josephine Baker, Petula Clark, and the legendary Perry Como. He has also starred in West End farces such as *Run For Your Wife, Pyjama Tops* and *What No Pyjamas?* and toured nationally in the farce *Women Of A Certain Age* and appeared as "Oberon" in William Shakespeare's *A Midsummer Night's Dream.* Roger received rave reviews when he starred as Howard Cunningham in the musical version of the it TV series *Happy Days.*

As a presenter, auctioneer, and after dinner

speaker Roger appears at numerous corporate events and golf days (he plays to a 15 handicap) and is regularly to be seen at most of the top West End hotels for clients such as Top Shop, Coca Cola, The Insolvency Practitioners Association and The Ford Motor Company, to name but a few.

Television and Radio have played a major part in Roger's career, constantly appearing in shows such as *Birds of a Feather, Get Back, Goodnight Sweetheart*, and *The New Statesman.* He has presented sketches in *The Frost Report, Generation Game, Jim Davidson Presents* and *It's Lulu* and was a regular panellist in *Punchlines.* He is probably best known for playing the cowardly Italian officer Captain Alberto Bertorelli in the hugely successful BBC series '*Allo 'Allo*, which ran for ten years. He also starred in the West End version of the show which also toured nationally and culminated in a record breaking run in Australia. In 1997 the team got together for the last time to perform the show for the season in Bournemouth.

Roger has recorded numerous television commercials including: Lego (Tommy Cooper voice), The Sun Newspaper (different characters), Smiths Potato Tubes (as John McEnroe), Thomson Local (different character voices) and Millennium Dome (the voice of the brain). He has appeared at numerous Corporate Dinners, Golf Days, Auctions, and Presentations.

A regular BBC Radio 2 broadcaster Roger starred for eight years in the series *The Impressionists* before developing his career by devising his own BBC Radio 2 quiz *The Names the Game*, which ran for nine years.

He made quite an impact on the music scene in July 1982 with his top twenty hit record, a send up of tennis ace John McEnroe called *Chalk Dust - The Umpire Strikes Back* was released under the name of 'The Brat'. Not only was it successful in the UK, it reached No.2 in Holland, No.4 in Belgium, and No.8 in South Africa.

In 2002 Roger undertook the first half of a mammoth 49-night tour with **Jim Davidson** celebrating Jim's 25 years in show business. He continued throughout the summer and the remainder of the year doing concert dates and corporate entertaining until pantomime , in which he starred as Sarah the Cook in *Dick Whittington* at the Bristol Hippodrome. He is constantly in demand for pantomime and is acknowledged to be one of the country's top panto "Dames"!

During the summer 2003 Roger spread the time evenly, five days a week, between Bournemouth, Weymouth, and Great Yarmouth, doing concerts, once again with Jim Davidson, and then toured during the autumn months until appearing in the pantomime *Aladdin* at the Mayflower Theatre Southampton.

In the spring of 2004 The BBC repeated *Spywatch,* a ten part children's series in which Roger plays "Professor CD Rom", alongside Keith Barron. The year 2004 also saw him star in his first feature film role with Summer Phoenix, sister of the late River Phoenix. The comedy, called *Susie Gold,* in which Roger played Tony, the promiscuous father-in-law of Susie's sister, was a major release in March.

Currently, Roger is co-writing a six part, one hour comedy/drama series about the life of his father, known as 'Sir' Leonard, who was a colourful character known throughout the racing and casino world. This is a project in which he will also take the role of executive producer, and may even take a supporting role. At a similar time he has been asked to do the narration on a one hour documentary, for the UK and American markets, about the life of a larger than life property millionairess with whom Roger went to school, and who is a close friend.

The 2004-5 pantomime season saw Roger co-starring in *Aladdin* alongside Brian Blessed at The Derngate Theatre, Northampton.

He has been happily married to former actress Karan David for 29 years and they have a 15-year-old daughter, Chloe, and a Yorkshire terrier called Bertie Buttons.

Roger Daniel Kitter was initiated into Chelsea Lodge on 17 March 1995.

Cecil KORER

TV producer. Born 17 October 1924, Stockport, Cheshire. Educated Chapel Allerton School, Leeds and Leeds College of Technology.

With Britain at war with Germany, Cecil, aged nineteen, was called up for military service in 1944 and served in the RAF as a pilot/flight engineer. He returned to civilian life and took on various jobs including repertory actor, stage manager and stage director (1946-1956).

His BBC career began as a scene shifter in 1957 progressing up the ladder the following year to call boy and assistant floor manager, Drama, then Light Entertainment. In 1959 Cecil moved to BBC TV in Manchester first as an outside broadcast stage manager, becoming an assistant producer/director in 1964. He was a member of the team that brought to television the first three years of *Top of the Pops,* a show which went on to enjoy audiences of 15 million viewers. The programme was launched on New Year's Day 1964, by Jimmy Savile, from a converted church in Manchester.

He took up the post of producer, general features at BBC TV, London in 1967 and three years later was promoted to executive producer. For five years from 1975 Cecil was based in Europe as executive producer of *It's a Knockout* and *Jeux Sans Frontieres.*

By 1980 he was back working at BBCTV at the White City, London where he became senior editor to Head of Programme Purchasing/Acquis-itions.

After thirty-four years with the BBC he opted for a change of scenery and in 1981 he was appointed senior commissioning editor, entertainment for Channel 4 Television by Jeremy Isaacs. One of his first successes was the commissioning of *Countdown*, which is still attracting huge audiences to this day. The programme calculator on the programme named CECIL (Countdown's Electronic Calculator In Leeds) we believe is really a tribute to CECIL Korer. Other credits include: *Treasure Hunt, Paul Hogan* and the British Film Institute award for the high powered import from America, *Cheers.* In 1983 the programme won the Best Imported Programme in the annual Broadcasting Press Guild Television Awards.

Cecil moved away from national television studios and he became managing director and producer of Gambit Productions in 1984. After six years it was time to move on when he became a production consultant. He has been running Korermedia since 1996.

For over forty years Cecil has been a major player in both BBC and Independent Television as a producer of variety and entertainment shows.

He is author of *Ask the Family*, Book 1, 1972; *Ask the Family*, Book 2, 1973; and *Ask the Family*, Book 3, 1974.

Cecil Harry Korer was initiated into Chelsea Lodge on 20 September 1970.

Harry LANDAU
Musician. Drummer. Born 10 July 1909, Mile End, London. He learned his trade whilst in the Boys' Brigade and at eighteen obtained his first professional job when the entertainers, Scott and Whaley, headed a variety show in the Channel Isles for a summer season.

In the early 1930s he became associated with Sid Roy, and through him, brother Harry, for whose wedding reception he led a band at the Mayfair Hotel in 1935. Following a year with Al Leaver he joined **Bram Martin** at the Holborn Restaurant in 1937, broadcasting weekly and recording thirty tunes for Regal Zonophone.

In 1939 he played firstly for Al Saxon at Madame Tussauds and then at Landsdowne House and the Coconut Grove for Barney Gilbraith, until both he and Barny were called up for military service at the outbreak of the Second World War. Both joined the RAF in March 1940. Harry played in a station dance band for two years until he was invalided out of the service. Fully fit again in 1943 he led Syd Roy's Lyricals for a while at the Café de Paris before being taken ill again.

In 1944 Harry made some broadcasts with Lou Praeger followed by a summer season leading a seven-piece band at the Pier Ballroom, Eastbourne. He was with Syd Roy again in 1951, leading the Lyricals in the Empress Club, playing for Frank Sinatra on the occasion of a Duke of Edinburgh Anglo-American charity.

Harry also led a band for a farewell party to George Raft at the Zuyda Zee Roadhouse. Over the years Harry worked with a number of different bands including Jack Jackson, **Alf van Straten**, Teddy Foster, **George Elrick** and Sidney Lipton, whilst in the late 1960s he became part of 'Geraldo's Navy', leading an eight-piece band on the *Empress of Canada.*

Harry Landau was initiated into Chelsea Lodge on 18 September 1960. Died 28 November 1992, aged 83 years.

Lew LANE
Stage director. At the age of twelve he learned to be a ventriloquist and took part in shows at senior citizens' clubs after school. He tried straight acting with a couple of roles in films for children's Saturday morning pictures. He attended

Theatre School with **Billy Dainty** and believes he hit the big time when he had to play opposite Sir Alec Guinness in *Kind Hearts and Coronets*. He recalls: "My big part consisted of playing a dinner companion to Sir Alec for a scene in which he had an accident with the mustard pot and pie. I was the one who got the mustard-pie in my face."

He completed national service in the Royal Air Force from 1949-1951 and undertook the production of many Combined Services Entertainment shows. On return to civilian life he worked for **Johnnie Riscoe** in various reviews around the British Isles. He also appeared in live trailers for RKO films and spent eighteen months working at the Pavilion, Glasgow with Tommy Morgan.

Lew worked for many years from 1960 onwards as producer and director of the cabaret for London's Churchill Club. He was very much a one-man band…booking acts, stage directing, playing props man, artiste's dresser and arranging the lighting.

Looking back to those days Lew says that crises was what his job was all about. Once, a Wild West act misfired and some customers lost their drinks as glasses were shattered by the shooting. Another time, a tight-rope walker disappeared into 'heaven' as clouds of smoke billowed from the stage and engulfed the audience. There was also the occasion when fifteen minutes before the lights splashed on to a stage filled with pretty girls in lavish costumes that the costumes did not arrive. Lew tried to sooth thirteen panicky dancers in a tiny dressing-room and at the same time rack his brain for a solution. He peeped out front and saw a show business friend and signalled to her that he was in trouble. The lady came to the rescue. She loaned her lace dress to the principal girl and the rest of the dancers improvised with pretty bras and bikinis.

Churchill's was a breeding ground for talent. Many of the speciality acts went on to appear in *Sunday Night at the Palladium*. Magicians Johnny Hart, Vic Burnett and Michael Allport were groomed at Churchill's. Other artistes made the London debut at Churchill's – George Shearing, Tommy Cooper, Ron Moody, Dusty Springfield, Tony Hancock, Terry Thomas and Shirley Bassey.

Lew has worked with nearly every name in show business. Asked to summarise his years directing stage shows he says:

"Swapping gags with Bob Hope, talking magic to Sir Carol Reed, sparring with Peter Finch, arranging parties for the Marquis of Milford Haven and splitting a magnum of champagne with Dick Van Dyke. Also at 4a.m.saying goodnight to Frank Carson, still trying to make the doorman laugh and vowing not to move until he did. On another occasion I remember Marlene Dietrich buttonholed me to enquire how I handled my back projection and cordless microphones."

Collecting old show business photographs is a hobby of Lew. Many of these have appeared in books he has been involved with including *Roy Hudd's Cavalcade of Variety Acts*, Lord Delfont's *Curtain Up*, *Golden Age of Radio* by Andy Foster, *Kindly Leave the Stage* by Alan Wilmott and this book *That's Entertainment*.

Lew Lane was President of the British Music Hall Society from 1980-1983.

He is an active member of the Grand Order of Water Rats and has staged and directed many galas and cabaret nights for them from 1958 right up to the centenary in 2000. He has arranged many continental acts to take part in the annual Royal Variety Performance for over forty years. He was initiated into Chelsea Lodge on 21 March 1975.

Lupino LANE

Actor, singer, dancer, choreographer, author, director and producer. Real name Henry William George Lupino. Son of Harry Lupino and born 16 June 1892, London. Best remembered as a brilliant stage comedian and an accomplished acrobat rather than for his years as a silent film comedian.

Lane was born into a theatrical family which could trace its connection with the stage back to 1632. One of his famous ancestors was the clown Grimaldi. His cousin was actor Stanley Lupino.

At the age of four Lupino made his first appearance at the Prince of Wales's Theatre, Birmingham, at a benefit performance for Vesta Tilley. In his early days he was known as 'Nipper' Lane. He appeared under that name at the London Pavilion in 1903. He developed his own individual style of extremely skilful (and sometimes dangerous) comic acrobatic dancing and appeared in many English and American two-reelers. However, his greatest impact was made in stage musicals where his trademark bowler hat and Cockney persona endeared him to audiences, especially those in London.

From 1915 through to 1934 he appeared in the West End musical productions of: *Watch Your Step (1915), Follow the Crowd (1916), Afgar (1919), League of Notions (1921), Puss-Puss (1920), Brighter London (1923), Turned Up (1926), Silver Wings (1930)* and *The One Girl (1933)*. During this time he travelled to and from America and appeared in a number of films including *Maid in Morocco (1925)* and *The Love Parade (1929)*, as well as starring in the Broadway show *Afgar* from 1920-1922. The *New York Times*, reviewing the production on 9 November 1920 said: "Stunning Alice Delysia was obliged to share the honours of the evening with Lupino Lane, one of the Lupinos whose comedy and knockabout talents have so long provided the most amusing interludes of the London pantomimes. He is not of a style familiar on this side of the water; he is perhaps best comparable to Fred Stone. He has all of Stone's comedy knack and a good deal of his acrobatic talent, if not his versatility. Last night his acrobatics definitely halted the show in the first act."

He acted in shorts and features for Fox Films. In 1924 he acted in D. W .Griffiths *Isn't Life Wonderful*. From 1925-1929 he acted and directed shorts for Educational Films.

Writing in the American magazine *Photoplay*, January 1927, James R. Quirk gave a short portrait of Lupino:

"Chaplin's forte is pathos, Langdon's metier is infantile appeal. Lloyd's trick is the conquest of an inferiority complex. Lupino Lane is broad, clean burlesque.

"Most men are born clowns and don't know it. Lupino Lane can outboast the ginger ale that advertises six month's preparation for its perfection. It took 227 years to make him a comedian. His pantomime ancestry is as long as a transcontinental railroad ticket. His Lupino grandfathers were Pierroting on the London stage in 1700. His Lane grandmothers were the Desdimonas of their day - he himself is one of the original theatrical mergers. He was supposed to get a fortune from his grandmother for twisting the names so that the first should be last and the last should be first. The old lady broke his heart by leaving him nothing but a good recipe for tumbling without breaking his neck.

"As British as bad cooking, the Lane-Lupinos survived when the newest chip from the family numskull announced his departure for America. They never understood the lack of concentration that kept him from being the hit of the 'Follies' but then they had never seen a glorified American Chorus Girl. All even went well when the boy entered the movies. When he returned and told them his movie salary, his grandfather did a back flip in his grave.

"His comedies are released by Educational, but don't let that fool you. He gags and he spins and Solomon in all his wisdom never thought up such stomach-laughs as his."

He quit Hollywood in 1930 returning to London to direct and act in British stage productions.

Lupino Lane tried his hand as director and producer for the first time in 1935 in the stage musical *Twenty To One*. He also acted in the production, which was a musical with a plot about horse racing.

In 1937 he enjoyed the biggest hit of his career with *Me and My Girl* at the Victoria Palace which set the town singing and dancing the enormously popular *Lambeth Walk*. He appeared in 1550 consecutive performances.

J.D. White wrote *Born To Star: The Lupino Lane Story* in 1937. The following year Lupino Lane appeared in the Royal Variety Performance at the London Coliseum.

In the 1940s Lane continued with more London stage productions including: *La-Di-Da-Di-Da (1943), Meet Me Victoria(1944)* and *Sweetheart Mine* (1946). Although he had enjoyed success in silent films during the 1920s, he was unable to recreate his later stage appeal in talkies. However he and Lillian Roth were acclaimed for their performances as second leads in *The Love Parade* (1929) which starred Maurice Chevalier and Jeanette MacDonald.

A list of the films in which Lupino Lane appeared were: *The Man in Possession* (1915), *A Friendly Husband* (1923), *Isn't Life Wonderful* (1924), *Hectic Days* (1928), *The Love Parade* (1929), *His Private Life* (1929), *Only Me* (1929), *Bride of the Regiment* (1930), *The Yellow Mask* (1930), *Golden Dawn* (1930), *Love Lies* (1931), *No Lady* (1931), *Never Trouble Trouble* (1931), *The Love Race* (1931), *Why Saps Leave Home* (1932), *Old Spanish Customers* (1932), *The Maid of the Mountains* (1932), *A Southern Maid* (1933), *My Old Duchess* (1933), *Letting in the Sunshine* (1933), *Who's Your Father* (1935), *Trust the Navy* (1935), *The Deputy Drummer* (1935), *Hot News* (1936) and *The Lambeth Walk* (1940).

In 1946 Lane published *How to Be a Comedian*. An announcement was made in 1946 that he had bought the Gaiety Theatre, London for £200,000, but he disposed of the property four years later without having managed to reopen it. The name of Lupino had been associated with the Gaiety for more than 100 years.

Lupino Lane married Violet Blyth and they had one son, **Lauri Lupino Lane**, who appeared with his father in *Me And My Girl,* and was a regular performer in British variety theatres until television closed them down in the 1960s. He made an appearance in the Royal Variety Performance in 1955. Lauri was initiated into Chelsea Lodge on 21 September 1945 and died in 1986, aged 64 years. He was the last in the line of celebrated family of entertainers, which had spanned 350 years.

Lupino Lane, who was a member of the Grand Order of Water Rats, was initiated into Chelsea Lodge on 18 September 1914. Died London 10 November 1959, aged 67 years.

The Times obituary of 11 November 1959 described him: "A small, lithe man with remarkably mobile features, he was an engaging comedian whose perfect timing always disguised the unflagging energy he put into his work. He had, too, a touch of the clown's endearing pathos and, a relic of his early clowning days, he could hold an audience without speaking a word while he mimed his way through some elaborate and usually quite improbable fantasy."

Another well-known member of the family was Stanley Lupino (born 15 May 1894, London and died 10 June 1942 London). He was an athletic dancer and a talented all-round performer. He appeared in a number of London musical productions from 1917 until 1941, and introduced several amusing songs including *I Lift Up My Finger and say Tweet Tweet* by **Leslie Sarony**. Among his shows were: *Love Lies, Suzette, Arklette, Hullo America, Cinderella, Jigsaw, The Peep Show, Phi-Phi, Dover Street to Dixie, Puppets, Better Days, So This Is Love, The Love Race, Hold My Hand, Sporting Love, Over She Goes, Crazy Days, The Fleet's Lit Up, Funny Side Up* and *Lady Behave*.

Stanley Lupino, who was the father of actress Ida Lupino, made 20 films himself. Ida went to Hollywood and was the star in many 1930s films and was very successful right through to the 1980s. In all she appeared in 79 films between 1932 and 1992. She also directed many television series including *The Untouchables* and *The Fugitive.* Ida Lupino was born on 4 February 1916 in London and died 3 August 1995, Burbank, California, aged 79 years.

The Lupinos were one of England's most

celebrated theatrical families. The earliest traceable Lupino, who spelled his name 'Luppino' is believed to have lived in Italy in 1612 and billed himself as Signor Luppino. His descendant, George William (1632-1693), a singer, reciter and puppet master, came to England as a political refugee. The family tree shows nearly all descendants to have been connected with the stage. George Hook Lupino (1820-1902) had 16 children, at least 10 of whom became professional dancers, two marrying into the family of the well-known actress Sara Lane. Lupino Lane took the stage name from his auntie, Sara (Lane).

Fred LATHAM

Vocalist, saxophonist and racing cyclist. Born 9 September 1905, New Mills Derbyshire, son of an engraver. He was given his first break at the age of nineteen with the Charleston Dance Band. He applied to the Jack Jackson Band for an audition and cycled from Manchester to the Dorchester Hotel, London and got the job. He made his first broadcast with them on his 28th birthday on the BBC Empire Service and later made numerous records with the Jackson band on the HMV label, but also freelanced with Jay Wilbur and Billy Reid on Rex and Eclipse records making over 200 recordings. In addition he sang for a Pathétone Weekly film. Fred formed a trio with Jack Jackson at the Dorchester Hotel which was called the 'Jacdors' made up from the first three letters of 'Jackson' and 'Dorchester', but is soon became the 'Jackdaws'. This in turn led to Fred appearing with bandleader Jack Harris, a patron of the Dorchester, on Radio Luxembourg for a programme sponsored by Beecham's Pills.

By the mid-1930s Fred joined the Jack Harris Band as regular singer first at the Café de Paris and then at Ciro's. He made recordings on HMV and also appeared in broadcasts with Jack.

Later in the 1930s **'Miff' Ferrie** approached Fred suggesting reforming The Jackdaws, which he did with George Crowe joining Miff and Fred. They changed their spelling to Jackdauz and appeared in numerous broadcasts – on Radio Luxembourg they sang in the Palmolive Programme with Carroll Gibbons and in the Ovaltine Programme with **Phil Green**. On the BBC they were with Arthur Askey and Richard Murdoch in *Bandwagon* and with Jack Jackson's Band from the Dorchester. The Jackdauz also broadcast and recorded with Lew Stone,

providing accompaniment to singer Al Bowlly.

Fred later left the Jackdauz and formed the 'Harristocrats' with Chick Smith and Freddy Williams. The new trio sang at Ciro's and made recordings for Radio Luxembourg with Carroll Gibbons. He was the featured singer in a commercial radio programme series on Luxembourg, *Cycling Magazine of the Air,* sponsored by Dunlop, after winning the Dunlop Jubilee Meeting in 1938.

Prior to the outbreak of the Second World War, Fred quit the Jack Harris Band to turn freelance. He broadcast with Percival Mackey, **Bram Martin**, Carroll Gibbons, Billy Gerhardi and Al Collins and made stage appearances with **Harry Leader**, Maurice Frolic and Al Berlin. He made a second appearance in *Pathé Pictorial* in 1939. He led his own band 'Fred Latham and his Cuba Swing Band' at the Cuba Club in London's Gerrard Street and was approached by Henry Hall to become a full member of his band.

He married nurse Anne Turner in 1940 and they had one daughter, Susan.

Fred was called up for military service with the Royal Navy in 1941. He sang and played drums for the Navy Dance Band, The Blue Mariners. They appeared in the radio shows *Navy Mixture* and *Merry-go-Round.*

After demobilisation in 1945 Fred worked with various bands including Wally Chapman, Tommy Regan and Tim Clayton.

He decided to quit the music business at the age of 45 and went into the licensing trade. During the 1950s he managed the 'Adam and Eve' in Hackney, 'The Lord Stanley' in Camden Square and later moved to Essex to become landlord of the 'Yachtsman's Arms' in Brightlingsea. He was a keen amateur racing cyclist and throughout his life won many medals. Even into his 70s he regularly cycled fifty miles a day.

Fred Latham was initiated into Chelsea Lodge on 18 March 1938. He died 12 September 1985, just three days after his 80th birthday.

Zack LAURENCE

Musician. Born 1945, East London, a stone's throw from singer Helen Shapiro. Zack Laurence started his career as a child prodigy pianist. He gave his first classical concert at the age of 9, and his exceptional talent for writing and playing just about everything from Jazz to Rock 'n' Roll very soon led him into the world of commercial music. He made his first solo recording at the age of 14;

the piece of music was his own composition *Magic Fingers.* The company was EMI, the producer George Martin of Beatles fame and, at the same time, his manager was Dick James, the publisher of the Beatles' many song successes. So young Zack started out in good company. As a teenager he appeared on TV's *Discs A Gogo* and in *Thank Your Lucky Stars.* In 1961 he joined the Performing Right Society and was one of the youngest ever members to be accepted by that organisation.

He is known to millions not only for his EMI recordings but also for his many radio broadcasts playing piano with his Quartet as well as conducting and performing with The BBC Radio Orchestra. His talents as an orchestral composer, arranger and conductor are highlighted on several successful albums by The Zack Laurence Orchestra.

Zack has built a reputation as a versatile writer, performer and producer of many different styles of music, resulting in a succession of hit records for which he has used a variety of enigmatic pseudonyms. Of these, probably the most famous ones are: *Groovin' With Mr. Bloe* under the eponymous pseudonym Mr. Bloe, - a million selling Disco record - which reached No. 2 in the UK and No. 1 in many other countries in June 1970; *The Spirit Is Willing* under the compelling pseudonym The Hands Of Dr. Teleny, - a work for synthesiser and orchestra which reached the Top 40 in the UK in 1972; and the orchestral theme from the highly-acclaimed TV mini-series *The Flame Trees Of Thika* under the pseudonym Video Symphonic - a huge romantic orchestral piece - which also reached the UK Top 40 in October 1981.

His arrangements have graced the recordings of many world-famous artistes from Eartha Kitt to Roger Whittaker and, as a songwriter, he has notched up hits with major artistes all over the world, also achieving several first prize International Song Contest winners - in the Spanish Costa Del Sol Contest, the Japanese Yamaha Song Contest and the Irish Castlebar Song Contest. He currently writes for film and TV and has composed music for all kinds of media productions for which he has built up a comprehensive collection of recorded compositions covering every aspect of descriptive music. He is also the composer of the popular themes for two of TV's longest-running award winning series, *Treasure Hunt* and *The Crystal Maze.*

Zack has never allowed his writing commitments to get in the way of the entertainer in him. He continues to perform as 'Zack + A Piano', playing and singing his way through an astonishingly vast and varied amount of material to the delight of his audiences. Current albums are *The Singalong Piano, The Sound of Musicals,* and classical ballet favourites transcribed for solo piano in *Piano Music For Young Dancers.*

Zack Laurence was initiated into Chelsea Lodge on 21 March 1980.

Jay LAURIER

Comedian and Shakespearian actor. Born in Birmingham on 31 May 1879, he first appeared on stage at Abertillery in 1896 in *The Arabian Nights.* For many years he was a 'top-liner' on the halls where he sang songs which combined great innocence and complete fatuity. The included *'I'm Always Doing Something Silly', 'Ring o'Roses',* and *'S'what's S'nicer than a S'nice S'ice S'ice?'.* He was also a successful pantomime performer. He recorded a number of comedy songs for Regal Records including: *Silly Billy Brown, Sneezing, I Can't Keep the Flies Off My Lunch* and *Get Away You're Kidding.* He played in several musical productions like *The Merry Widow, Phi-Phi* and *Les Cloches de Corneville,* but he always hoped to play in more serious works and in 1937 he achieved his ambition. That year he joined the Old Vic company playing first Alfred Doolittle in Shaw's *Pygmalion* and then Pompey in *Measure for Measure.* In 1938 he acted through the Stratford season as the Porter in *Macbeth,* Sir Toby in *Twelfth Night,* Launce in *Two Gentlemen of Verona,* Bottom in *A Midsummer Night's Dream',* and as Stephano in *The Tempest.* He made the most of these parts and was engaged again at Stratford in 1939 playing Christopher Sly in *The Taming of the Shrew.* He was seen in 1947 as Sir Toby Belch at the Savoy. He also appeared in numerous films including *Hobson's Choice* (1931), *Pyjamas Preferred* (1932), *I'm Stuck To You* (1933), *Waltz Time* (1933), *The Black Tulip* (1937) and *Oh Boy* (1938).

Jay Laurier was initiated into Chelsea Lodge on 19 April 1919. Died in Durban, South Africa, April 1969, aged 89 years

Lee LAWRENCE

Vocalist. Born Leon Siroto, 1921, Salford, Lancashire. Following in the footsteps of his parents, who both sang with the Carl Rosa Opera Company, Lee set out to become a classical singer and in 1938 he won a scholarship to study operatic singing in Italy. Unfortunately this came to an abrupt end with the outbreak of World War Two.

Lee came home and joined the Royal Tank Regiment, spending much of the following six years in the Middle East. On demob, and determined to join the music profession, he secured his first job touring service camps for ENSA. After this he did the odd club date and broadcast on *Beginners Please*, but generally found work hard to come by and was considering giving up and returning to a regular job in Manchester until, in 1948, BBC producer Roy Spear gave him a spot on *Showtime*, another radio series featuring new talent. On this live show, broadcast from The People's Palace in London's East End, Lee sang *Everybody Loves Somebody* and *Falling in Love With Love*.

Further radio bookings followed and soon Lee was regularly broadcasting with several top bands including Ronnie Pleydell, Geraldo, **Stanley Black**, George Melachrino and Louis Levy's Music From the Movies Orchestra. Often on air three or more times a week, for a couple of years, except for the occasional concert he did little else. Lee had regular spots on *Dancing With Strings* with the Ray Martin Orchestra, *Starlight Hour* with Peter Yorke and The Radio Revellers, the late night *Rhythm Reverie* series with Oscar Grasso and his Intimate Music, Geraldo's *Melody Time* and Norman Evans *Over the Garden Wall* shows where he even joined in the comedy sketches. He was in the first series of radio's *Sing It Again* that began 19 January 1949, alongside Sam Browne, Johnny Eager, Carole Carr, Pearl Carr and Stella Nichol.

Decca Records took notice and in February 1949 issued his first disc *How Can You Buy Killarney* backed with *Helene* (that resurfaced several years later as *The Story of Tina*). With his fan mail building up to what was to become over a thousand letters a week, Lee set off on a variety tour beginning 27 February 1950 at Portsmouth's Theatre Royal, followed by a week in March at London's Finsbury Park Empire with Max Wall and Wilson, Kepple and Betty. In December he played in his first and only pantomime, *Jack and the Beanstalk* at Bolton's Theatre Royal with The Radio Revellers.

When **Cyril Stapleton** formed the BBC Show

Band in October 1952, Lee was one of the original vocalists on the show alongside Jean Campbell and The Johnston Singers. In early 1953 Dick James took over, but Lee was soon back on air in another series, *Pleasure Boat*, that also featured Anne Shelton and Julie Andrews.

Continuing on his almost non-stop variety tour gave Lee the chance to let the public hear *Crying in the Chapel*, one of his biggest hits. The BBC had banned its broadcast on religious grounds, but despite this the record reached No.7 in the British hit parade charts in December 1953.

During 1955 Lee had his own BBC Light Programme series where he indulged himself singing a mix of operatic arias, show tunes and popular songs, all with the backing of Harry Rabinowitz and the BBC Revue Orchestra. While over on Radio Luxembourg there was his *Scrapbook of Song*. With both shows scheduled at the same time on the same day, the BBC observed that their better sound reproduction drew the biggest audience.

Overlooked by BBC Television, the new ITV service had him on *Music Shop* in November 1955, singing his second chart entry *Suddenly There's a Valley*. He sang it again in December on ATV's *On the Town*.

With the record scene becoming more and more under pressure from the rock and roll brigade, Lee obviously decided 'if you can't beat them join them' and consequently raised a few eyebrows with his November 1956 offering. On the disc classical tenor Lee gave them an up-market beat number with his rendition of *Rock and Roll Opera*. Record Mirror reviewer Dick Tatham compared it to "using a Derby winner as a dray horse".

On radio Lee rejoined the Show Band crew on their Friday night *Music For Always* broadcasts for three months from January 1957 and made one of his rare BBC TV appearances on *Monday Melody* on 4th March with the Northern Dance Orchestra, Cleo Laine and Joe 'Mr. Piano' Henderson.

On the road Lee had put together his own touring stage show *Music For Everyone* on which he was supported by the Johnny Lenniz Jazz Group whose drummer was a real aristocrat, the rocking Earl of Wharncliffe, with a family estate in Yorkshire. Not a success, the road show came to a halt after only four weeks, and Lee admitted he had lost more than £2,000 on the venture.

Aware that Variety as he knew it was on the wane and finding bookings harder to come by, in October 1957 Lee with his wife Pearl and young daughter Suzanne, left Britain in search of a better deal in America. He was already booked for a season at Hollywood's Coconut Grove and also had some TV work. He made a record for Apollo in the States and this was released here by Top Rank.

Lee believed that the beat craze would soon die out and his kind of singing would be back in demand, but things didn't turn out that way. He found it hard going, but was beginning to build up a reputation as a quality performer around the U.S. clubs when he died.

A keen sportsman with a strong interest in Yoga, he was a fine vocalist with a rich, powerful voice, excellent diction and an extensive range. Lee deserved better recognition during his lifetime and has been sadly overlooked on the re-issue market ever since.

During his time in this country he made 40 singles for Decca, twelve for Columbia and just one for Top Rank.

Lee Lawrence, a member of the Grand Order of Water Rats, was initiated into Chelsea Lodge on 20 September 1957. He died from a heart attack in the West Indies on 25 February 1961, aged 40 years.

Harry LEADER

Bandleader. Real name George Henry Lebys that was legally changed by Deed Poll in the 1930s to Harry Leader. Born 18 January 1906, Poplar, London. Son of Wolf Lebys, a professor of music from the St Petersburg Conservatoire who settled in London's East End to run a grocery store. His father taught him the violin and made a living by working for him during the day and accompanying silent movies.

With the coming of jazz in the 1920s he switched allegiance to the alto saxophone, which was becoming all the rage at that time. He was soon playing dates in the many clubs, which mushroomed around Piccadilly Circus and toured all over Europe. An accomplished musician, he later played clarinet, tenor, also, baritone and soprano saxophones, as well as flute.

From 1931 to 1933 he conducted an American style band in Italy, and when he returned to Britain he decided to set up his own dance orchestra. From 1933 onwards he made many recordings on the Panachord, Eclipse and Broadcast labels. One record '*Little Man You've Had a Busy Day*', recorded in London on 28 June 1934, sold nearly half a million copies, a huge number in those pre-war years. He made numerous broadcasts with the BBC in the 1930s. His first show was in 1933 in an Overseas programme for Cecil Madden, followed by the discovery show *First Time Here*, in 1934. His first theme tune was *Memories of You*, but later changed it to *I'm Just Wild About Harry*, and later still to his catch-phrase *Music, Maestro, Please*. Harry was on the air regularly after that for over 30 years in all sorts of programmes.

Harry also worked under the pseudonym of Wally Bishop and His Band, Max Murray and His Orchestra, The International Novelty Orchestra, Joe Taub and his Melodians, and dozens of others. He directed the New Mayfair Dance Orchestra from 1936 to 1937.

Though well-known in the recording industry, (he completed his 3,000th recording in three years) the Harry Leader Band did not have a regular engagement until 1940, when it became resident at the Hammersmith Palais de Danse for four years. Harry was called up for military service, but rejected on medical grounds, so he took his band out to entertain the troops whenever he could do so, including a most rewarding radio series for the Canadian Forces Network and also for the Canadian Forces Sunday Concerts.

Harry specialised in modern dance music. He moved on to the Astoria Danse Salon in the Charing Cross Road, London, through to 1957 where he enjoyed a record-breaking run of nearly fifteen years. He shared with Oscar Rabin the honour of being the first bandleader to broadcast on VE day, 8 May 1945. In 1946 he broadcast on the BBC in *Music While You Work* and continued with the series until it was taken out of the schedules in 1983. He was a top purveyor of music, the chief feature of which was his ability to remain in harmony with popular demand. In 1947 he presented his own *Harry Leader Show* on BBC Television. After a very long tour in 1959 he went to the Brighton Regent Ballroom where he stayed until 1963 when it became a bingo hall.

He discovered many latent musical talents whom he encouraged. A friend suggested that Harry take a trip to Hornsey Town Hall to listen to a young singer named Terry Parsons, whose regular job was driving a No.27 bus. He engaged him and launched him on a career as the crooner, Matt Monro. Others included Freddy Gardner, Steve Race, Chick Henderson and others.

When Harry was playing at the Charing Cross Astoria, a fourteen-to-fifteen-year-old pianist was brought by his father to see Harry. Harry saw the potential talent in this young man, but at the time he was heavily involved in a project with the BBC, so could not take the risk with an inexperienced pianist he was always very sad at having to reject this young man, and in other circumstances he would not have hesitated to take him on. In later years the young pianist became a multi-millionaire composer, arranger and musical director Les Reed, OBE, FCL!

Harry's first marriage was dissolved and in 1967 he married vocalist Rona Nye. He and Rona were prolific songwriters and wrote over 300 songs.

Harry Leader joined Chelsea Lodge on 15 March 1968 from Proscenium Lodge No.3435. He died 19 January 1987, aged 80 years. Chris Hayes writing in *Melody Maker* described Harry as "a brisk, bustling little man, with a round rosy face, a giant smile, sparkling eyes behind his horn rimmed spectacles, and a perpetual carnation in his buttonhole. He was unquestionably a bandleader of great charm and personality. He talked rapidly, with warmth and conviction, his words spouting at you like bullets from a machine gun! He could talk your head off, but he always managed to make his conversation interesting."

Harry was a supporter of several charitable ventures and had the honour of being a member of the Royal Variety Club.

Gus LE CLERQ

Vauderville artiste/comedian. Born 29 July 1884, London. Real name Augustus Howard. Also known as Gus McNaughton and appeared with The McNaughtons (Fred and Tom). He was a successful pantomime dame. Under the name Gus McNaughton he appeared in sixty-six films, his first *The Comets* (1930) and his last *The Turners of Prospect Road* (1947).

Gus Le Clerq, a member of the Grand Order of Water Rats, joined Chelsea Lodge on 21 October 1910 from Kilwinning Lodge No.2, Edinburgh, Scottish Constitution. Died 18 November 1969, aged 85 years.

Albert LE FRE, PM PAGDC

Music Hall Artiste. Founder. Born 3 March 1870, London. Son of James Albert De Voy and his wife Sarah (née Lefevre). Made his first appearance on the stage as a child, at the Criterion, Sheerness, 1876, in pantomime, appearing as a dancer and skater. For many years he appeared with the Le Fre Trio. He made his first appearance in London, at the Surrey Theatre, at Christmas, 1879, under William Holland, playing in the pantomime *Aladdin*. Toured in the United States with the Hanlon-Lees Troupe. He later worked as a solo act, an original comedian with some excellent songs.

Among the sketches for which he achieved popularity included *The Gentleman Scamp, The Professor*, and *The Dancing Family*, where he appeared with his brothers. As a solo artiste he has introduced *That's What You See in the Halls* and *The Tip-top Topper*. He performed on the theatrical stage in musical comedy and appeared in the 1936 film *She Knows What She Wanted.*

His standing in the profession was recognised by his appearance in the First Royal Command Performance at the Palace Theatre, London on 1 July 1912.

Albert Le Fre was initiated in the Lodge of St Asaph, No.1319, during the last year of Queen Victoria's reign, and was installed as the second Master of the Lodge in 1906. He was Preceptor of the Vaudeville Lodge of Instruction. He at one time or another occupied all the offices in the Lodge and was well remembered by the more senior members of Chelsea Lodge as a great Director of Ceremonies. He also fulfilled the role as Treasurer to the satisfaction of all members. He was greatly respected for his serenity, depth of Masonic knowledge and willingness to advise and assist the younger brethren.

'Our Albert', as he was affectionately known, was made an Honorary member of Chelsea Lodge in 1955.

Arrangements were well in hand for him to occupy the chair in his centenary year. Sadly he passed away on 14 December 1969, just three months short of his 100th birthday. His son **Eric Le Fre** was later made an Honorary member of Chelsea Lodge.

Reginald LEOPOLD

Violinist/Musical Director. Born 1907 into a musical family in Tufnell Park, North London. At an early age won a scholarship to Trinity College of Music, where he led the Symphony Orchestra and formed a chamber group which numbered the future bandleaders Mantovani and George Melachrino among its members.

Reg worked with the Savoy Orpheans under Carroll Gibbons in the late 1920s who introduced him to broadcasting. He also recorded with the band. He went on to do similar work with Lew Stone and Eddie Carroll in the 1930s and during the war his music was broadcast as background to British propaganda messages to continental Europe.

By the early 1950s, Reg had become a wel-known name in his own right, helped by the success of his novelty records *The Laughing Violin* (made in 1949 with the Charles Williams Orchestra) and Prokofiev's *Peter and the Wolf*, narrated by Bob Danvers-Walker. In the 1960s he was active in the recording studios, providing string backing for some of the biggest hits of the period, including Cilla Black's *Anyone Who had a Heart* and Petula Clark's *Downtown*. He also led the strings on the Beatles' film and album *A Hard Day's Night* and provided the backing for singers as varied as Matt Monro and Gracie Fields.

Perhaps his biggest claim to fame was at 7.00 p.m. on Sundays throughout the 1960s on the BBC Light Programme. Reginald Leopold's weekly broadcasts 'from the Palm Court of the Grand Hotel' epitomised British light music. With its mixture of light classics and popular dance tunes, he provided the musical background for a generation of wireless listeners. However, for almost all its fifteen-year run, the programme emanated not from the dance floors of the Waldorf or the Ritz, but from the concert hall at Broadcasting House in London. His other long-running radio series was *In a Sentimental Mood*, featuring romantic music more suited to the late evening.

Reginald Leopold was initiated into Chelsea Lodge on 17.03.1950. He died in Sussex, 26 February 2003, aged 95 years.

Harry LESTER

Variety Artiste. Born 9 July 1895, Forth Worth, Texas, son of John and Clara Lester who were touring the Western States, was christened after the hotel (Harrold), and given the middle name of Worth, after the town.

In 1898, the family (stranded and broke) were living with an Indian family in Oklahoma during the great land rush. By 1900 Harry's brother Burton had arrived and the family moved to Chicago. In winter quarters with a circus in Waco, Texas in 1907, the brothers learned acrobatics and high wire work, which their father included in the act, previously consisting of drama and comedy. The early jazz music the boys heard in the South has a big influence on them and they learned to play almost every instrument. In 1908 Harry and Burton were a featured aerial act at the San Antonio State Fair and spent a lot of time mixing with the cowboys.

When Harry was fifteen the family worked the

riverboats with the aerial act, travelling the length of the Mississippi, returning to circus and working their way up to the Ringling, Barnum and Bailey outfit. The next year, 1914, they were booked by Hugh D. McIntosh for a tour of Australia and South Africa, after which they arrived in England, in December 1915, opening in the following April as the Four Aerial Lesters at the Grand, Birmingham in *A Band Upside Down*. They then became John Lester and his Family, next they were called the Frisco Five, being the first act to introduce jazz into England. By 1920 they were working as a trio, John, Harry and Burton Lester, until Harry and Burton formed the Ten Cowboy Syncopators, which were very successful featuring in *The Roundup, Hollywood Follies* and *A Jazz Roundup,* all big-cast shows in the West End.

After the band broke up in 1928 Harry returned to the States but was soon back, this time forming the Midget Circus at Blackpool Tower, where he stayed for four years. Always the showman, he brought an embalmed whale to England and exhibited it throughout the country, also starting the miniature golf craze over here. In 1937 he and Burton were together again with the famous Cowboy band, both on tour and in a resident season in Birmingham. By the end of the decade the brothers had parted company again, Harry forming his best-remembered act the Hayseeds, which was on radio and television before the war, toured throughout the war years and continued until he retired in 1957. The band was in the first post-war Royal Command Performance and recorded for Decca.

At the age of 96 he visited Birmingham with his son Bob. He was still a big man with a strong voice and very humorous, looking nowhere near his great age. In 1993 his wife Babs, whom he had married in 1925, died and he was not the same afterwards.

Harry Worth Lester joined Chelsea Lodge 16 June 1939 from Dramatic Lodge No.571, Scottish Constitution. He died on 4 July 1993, just a few days short of his 98th birthday. He had always retained his American citizenship and he told a friend John M. Hall that it was his wish he would die in America. Sadly this was not fulfilled, though leaving the world on American Independence Day would doubtless have appealed to his sense of humour.

Reg LEVER

Vaudeville Artiste. Real name Stanley Edward Russell. Born 1904. He was one of the country's foremost revue entertainers, occasionally to be seen in London's West End. He also worked extensively during World War II organising and playing in numerous musical entertainments abroad and on the home front. In the autumn of 1939 Reg Lever's *Hello Happiness* Company was in France before the country was occupied and the Allied forces were evacuated from Dunkirk. It was described as 'A great laughter show. Girls galore'.

By the 1950s Reg had become one of a dwindling band of such regular entertainers, but continued to be the life and soul of the party in which he figured. He was a popular member of the Savage Club where, for many years, he had helped to organise the regular entertainment which was such a feature with his originality, wit and very good humour. He appeared on Children's TV as 'Mr Happy' and in pantomime in different parts of the country in addition to starring in *Carnival* at the Lyric Theatre, London in February 1963.

Reg appeared in a number of films including *The Celestial Toymaker* (1966) where he played the joker and *Twinky* (1969), portraying the old gentleman. Hammer films used him in their 1969 film *Wolfshead,* also known as *The Legend of Robin Hood.* He played the Punch and Judy man in *Scrooge* (1970) and appeared in the BBC 1 television series *Pennies From Heaven* (1978).

He was a member of the Concert Artistes' Association and the Grand Order of Water Rats.

Stanley Edward Russell was initiated into Chelsea Lodge on 20 July 1928. He died 18 August 1985, aged 81 years. A Memorial Service was held at St Paul's Church, Covent Garden, 2 October 1985. The Rev. Michael Hurst-Bannister, senior Chaplain to the Actor's Church Union, officiated. Rowena Vincent, Concert Artistes' Association, read Noel Coward's poem *I Can Remember*, and Geoffrey Wheeler gave an address. Marietta and Vernon Midgley sang *Panis Angelicus* and members of the Savage Club sang *The Long Day Closes.*

Ernie LEWIS

Musician. Real name Ernie Kapinsky. Born London, but was discovered in South Africa playing violin and leading a classical trio. Changed his name to Ernie Lewis when he was cabled to tour India and then East Africa with Al Bowlly. Joined the Ambrose Orchestra in 1928 and made hundreds of recordings with them on Decca in studios in Chelsea and later on HMV from the Mayfair Hotel, London. Ernie remained with the Ambrose orchestra until the end of 1939.

Ernie Lewis joined Chelsea Lodge on 15 May 1936.

Ted 'Kid' LEWIS

cabled to tour India and then East Africa with Al
Boxer. Born Solomon Mendeloff, 24 October 1893, he was one of eight children born in London's East End to Russian Jewish immigrant parents. His father was a cabinet-maker. Ted was classed as one of the greatest English fighters of the early 1900s who had the nickname 'The Crashing, Bashing, Dashing Kid'. To this day he is still the only British-born boxer to win the undisputed weltereight championship of the world twice – *and* in the USA. He was a non-stop, all-action, relentless attacker who fought often and had a long career. Lewis had his first fight at the age of fourteen and was a champion by eighteen. He and Jack Britton comprised one of the greatest ring rivalries in boxing history. They fought twenty times for a total of 224 rounds and traded titles several times. There was hardly a

tactic or a manoeuvre employed by either man that the other hadn't seen before and knew how to counter.

Lewis held thirteen championships including European Featherweight Champion (1913-1914); British Feather, Welter and Middleweight Champion (1914-1924); and World Welterweight Championship (1915-1919). He was the first Briton to make an impact in America where almost 100 of his 299 fights took place. He also won many more British, European, Empire and World titles. No British boxer ever had more success against American opposition, for no one ever adapted himself so completely to the two handed American style which dominated professional boxing from the 1930s.

Ted Lewis fought 2625 recorded rounds in his career. He was the first boxer to wear a gumshield, and was its co-inventor. He was the first British boxer to be featured in Hollywood films, and the first boxer to run for Parliament, and the first fighter to command world record £26.25 ringside seats, until TV money and inflation took over. He was the youngest World, British and European champion ever, the first boxer to be in both the UK and American armed forces, and he featured in the first big fight ever held at the Royal Albert Hall, against Matt Wells on Boxing Day, 1919. He was also the first British boxer to have a fight broadcast on the radio in the UK, on station 2LO, in 1922, and was the youngest boxer to top the bill in the music halls.

Ted made his farewell appearance in London on 13 December 1929. He made a winning exit, knocking out Johnny Basham in the third round.

He retired from the boxing ring after twenty years as a fighter. He had no savings from his long and gruelling career, but he made ends meet for his family by appearing in a revue called *Hello Sweetie* and from refereeing, film work and personal appearances. He was an 'easy touch' for every confidence man he met, however, and he invested money in ventures that hadn't the remotest chance of success. The most extraordinary episode of his colourful life was when, in 1931, he met Sir Oswald Mosely, thought by some destined to be British prime minister. He was one of the brightest young politicians of his day and sat successfully as a Conservative, Independent, and Labour MP before founding the British Union of Fascists in 1932. Lewis was hired for £60 a week to be the physical youth training instructor for the 'New

Party'. Within a short time Lewis headed Mosley's bodyguards, a group of East End toughs.

Within a year Mosley's party was lagging in popularity. After visiting the Italian dictator Benito Mussolini, Moseley returned to England and disbanded the 'New Party' and formed the 'National Union of Fascists,' a political party which failed to find the mass support enjoyed by its European cousins. Rumours spread that Mosley hated Jews. Ted 'Kid' Lewis and his son Morton paid one final visit to Mosley's headquarters. In his book *Ted Kid Lewis. His Life and Times* (Robson Books, 1990) Morton Lewis vividly remembers "...when we arrived there were two big men, clad not in the black shirts of Mosley's New Party, but in the brown shirts of the Nazi Party. TK momentarily froze...he mounted the stairs to Mosley's office and, without knocking, opened the door...Mosley was seated...with two of his henchmen in brown shirts standing at his elbows...The two men gave TK the traditional raised arm salute. "Is it true you're anti-Semitic? And I want the truth this time. Are you anti-Jewish?"

Mosley confirmed he was. Lewis "struck with an open hand across Mosley's face, sending him and his chair crashing against the wall. The two brown-shirted men came round the desk and grappled with TK." Both men were flattened. On his way out of the building Lewis knocked out the two guards standing at the door. Sir Edward Mosley was imprisoned for most of the Second World War and made an unsuccessful attempt to form a new right-wing party in Britain after its end.

In 1970 Mike Tyson paid tribute to Lewis in a BBC TV interview. He said: "You rate a fighter by his longevity and for years Ted 'Kid' Lewis beat the greatest American fighters...why, he won the title twice and it's unbelievable, the guys he had to fight! Benny Leonard, Jack Britton, Mike Gibbons, Willie Richie – the *Who's Who* of boxing, the greatest of the great, and yet he still prevailed as number one."

Lewis was elected to the Boxing Hall of Fame in 1992.

Ted 'Kid' Lewis joined Chelsea Lodge on 19 May 1961. He died 20 October 1970, London, just four days short of his 76th birthday. *The Times* obituary of 21 October 1970 said of Lewis: "In the ring he was a hard man, but outside the ropes he was generous to a fault. He will be remembered not only for his fiery attack and incredible determination, but also for his dignity and modesty in old age whenever lesser men, all of us, toasted him for his deeds of long ago."

Maurice and Benny LOBAN

Maurice and Benny arrived from Canada in 1929.

Maurice, a violinist, joined the Jack Hylton Band in 1930 and took part in many recordings. He remained with them until 1936. He also played with the Debroy Somers Band from 1930 to 1931 and with Sidney Lipton's Orchestra from 1937-1940.

Benny (born 16 April 1902) joined the New Savoy Orpheans, becoming leader in 1930. When he took the band away with him on tour, however, the Savoy made him rename it. As the Music Weavers they remained together for a further twelve months.

Benny then joined Debroy Somers but reformed his own band in 1937, playing for another five years. He gave up music as a livelihood and turned to the property market, or real estate as it is known in America and Canada. This proved to be highly successful and he only completely retired aged 88. He lived in Winnipeg, Canada and enjoyed good health to the end.

Maurice was initiated into Chelsea on 21 November 1930. Benny was initiated on 15 March 1935. He died 7 March 1993, aged 90 years in Winnipeg following a stroke.

Peter LOCKE, SLGR

Television producer. Born 14 May 1943, Edgware. Educated locally and then at Kneesworth Hall school near Royston. Attended Regent Street Polytechnic, School of Photography and began his professional career in 1965 as a studio TV cameraman with Rediffusion and worked on programmes such as *Take Your Pick, Double Your Money* and *Ready Steady Go.* He continued with LWT after the takeover in 1968 and turned freelance from 1972. Peter has worked with all the major UK TV companies and many facility houses.

He relates: "During my career I have been involved in shooting medical operations, pop concerts, all kinds of sports, including Wimbledon and the F.A. cup final, covered the Iraq/Iran war from Baghdad, where I was lucky enough, on a day off, to visit Babylon, a city few Westerners ever see, met lots of interesting people and had a great time."

He started his own production company in the late 80s with exciting corporate videos such as *Choosing a Parrot,* EMAP annual awards, training video for the London Institute, and many more. Masonic videos include: *The Treasurer* and *Grand Lodge the Ultimate Tour.*

Peter Alan Locke joined Chelsea Lodge on 20 November 1998 from Seven Stars Lodge No.5892 where he was WM in 1984 and 1991. He is also a PM of Gallery Lodge No.1928; MEZ Quintinian Chapter 1986 and 1995 and MEZ Chelsea Chapter 2002. LGR 1994, SLGR 1996 and LGCR in 1995. In the year 2004 he was in the Chair of four different Orders.

His son **Robert Peter Locke** joined Chelsea Lodge on 20 November 1998 from Seven Stars Lodge No.5892 where he was a PM.

John LOGAN

(A Lewis). General Secretary of PRS Members Fund. Born 6 September 1955, London. Attended John Betts Primary and Christopher Wren Comprehensive schools in West London. Joined full-time staff of Performing Right Society in 1973 as a junior clerk. In 1975 he was appointed Assistant to the Registrar where his role in the organisation's 'front-line' membership department included promoting PRS membership services to potential and existing writer and publisher members and advising pop and classical writers and music publishers about the music business in general and copyright matters. Other aspects of the job were to give guidance to widows and other relatives of recently deceased writer members regarding future royalty payments; maintaining correct membership and accounting records for prompt and accurate royalty payments and assisting with the arrangements for the Society's AGM. He was appointed Deputy Registrar of the Society in 1978 (aged 23) when he became part of the Society's management team. Promotion to Registrar followed in 1985.

In 1977 John was successful in his application to become involved with the Society's Benevolent Fund for members and their widows and other dependants. He was appointed Assistant Secretary, a part-time post that involved combining this task with his normal duties in the Registrars department. He was appointed Secretary in 1985. He managed the two roles successfully until 1999 when corporate restructuring made the job of Registrar redundant.

John accepted an invitation to become the Fund's first ever full-time General Secretary, a position he holds to this day.

He was made a Freeman of the City of London in 1999. John Jeffrey Logan was initiated into Chelsea Lodge on 16 November 2001.

Joe LOSS, LVO OBE

Dance band leader. Born Joshua Alexander Loss 22 June 1909. He was a student at Trinity College of Music. His father did not approve of jazz but by 1934 Joe was topping the bill at the Holborn Empire. Married Mildred Blanch Rose, 1939. One son, Kevin and one daughter, Jennifer. Began his show business career by playing as silent film accompanist at the Coliseum Cinema, Ilford and Tower Ballroom, Blackpool, 1926. He formed his own orchestra at the Astoria Ballroom, Charing Cross Road, 1930 and, at 21, was the youngest West End bandleader. First broadcast, 1934, followed by regular appearances on BBC radio. He was one of the first West End bands to play in ballrooms in the provinces and to top the bill in variety theatres.

During the Second World War Joe toured variety theatres and concert halls across the country. He also worked for ENSA playing for servicemen at home and abroad, his band being one of the first to visit Europe after liberation in 1944.

After the war he continued to tour the country and during the 1950s did an annual summer season at the Villa Marina on the Isle of Man.

Joe joined Mecca in 1959 and became resident at the Hammersmith Palais. Recorded for the Regal Zonophone record company. He earned a gold disc for *Begin the Beguine*, recorded in 1936 which, over a period of 25 years, sold a million copies. Later joined EMI Records. His record for them was *I Only Have Eyes For You*. He enjoyed many hits over the years including: *Wheels Cha Cha, The Maigret Theme, The Steptoe Theme, Must Be Madison* and *March of the Mods*; gold discs for long-playing albums *Joe Loss Plays Glenn Miller* and *All Time Party Hits*.

His television programmes included: *Come Dancing, Bid For Fame, Home Town Saturday Night,* and *Holiday Parade.* He was featured in *This Is Your Life,* 1963 and 1980, panel member *New Faces Awards, 15 Carl Alan Awards, New Musical Express Top Big Band Award, Weekend Magazine Top Musical Personality Award* and *Music Publishers Association Award.*

Films included*: British Lion Varieties Nos 1-9* (all 1936)and *The Mood Man* (1965).

The Joe Loss Orchestra was the first dance orchestra from the western world to appear in China in 1979. The orchestra played for dancing on many QE2 world cruises, at Buckingham Palace and Windsor Castle, and at pre-wedding balls for Princess Margaret, Princess Alexandra and Princess Anne. He also played at the Queen's 50th birthday celebrations and for the Queen Mother's 80th birthday.

He appeared in the Royal Variety Performance in 1980. Was awarded Queen's Silver Jubilee Medal, 1979. Freeman, City of London, 1979; Liveryman, Musicians Company, 1983. He was a Life Member of the MCC.

Bro. Joe Loss joined Chelsea Lodge in March 1936. He died of kidney failure 6 June 1990, aged 80 years.

Len LOWE

Actor/writer. Real name Leonard Alfred Smoothey. Born 17 September 1916, London. At the age of six he could sing all the comic songs of the day and by the time he was nine he was performing at British Legion Clubs and such like in his neighbourhood. At the age of thirteen he trained in drama, ballet and tapdance at the Italia Conti Stage School and was on the boards from childhood. He appeared in the original West End productions of *White Horse Inn, Cavalcade* and *All God's Children* (with Paul Robeson and Flora Robson).

Len's first appearance at a 'proper' theatre was in 1929 at the Holborn Empire. After six weeks there he went on tour in *Peter Pan*.

He sang, played guitar and danced with the Jack Hylton Orchestra. They played the London Palladium for six months in 1934, after which they made a film *They Shall Have Music*. A tour of the continent followed where the band played thirty-six towns and cities in thirty-four days. Len toured with Jack Hylton in America in 1935.

He left the Jack Hylton Orchestra in 1938 and teamed up with Bill Redman, an old chum from schooldays. They formed the act Len and Bill Lowe. They worked in revue and later moved to the Coconut Grove night-club in London.

They received their call-up papers and both joined the Royal Air Force. They soon became involved with the *RAF Gang Show* and toured military bases throughout England. They were demobbed in 1945 and went straight into a Tom Arnold production in London, which ran for a year. The next stop was at the London Palladium working with Laurel and Hardy in 1947. Len and Bill dressed smartly in Saville Row suits and their style (straight man and comedian) was adopted later by Morecambe and Wise. The act was dissolved in 1950.

Len produced another double act with his brother Don and they became known as Lowe and Ladd. They played the London Palladium and all the number one dates, summer shows and pantomimes. Abroad they were hugely popular in Australia and New Zealand and toured both countries. They remained together until 1956.

Len moved into television as a straight man and feed. One of his first shows was with Charlie Chester in his TV show *Pot Luck*. In 1959 he returned to Australia for more Variety and revue. He had his own weekly television show out there for which he wrote the script, appeared in and produced. Back in this country he made appearances in *Colditz* and *The Benny Hill Show.*

He has appeared in a number of films including: *A Date with a Dream,* (1948), *Melody Club* (1949), *Countess from Hong Kong,* (1967), *Carry on Loving* (1970). He appeared in the Thames Television programme *Will the Real Mike Yarwood Stand Up?* (1968).

Len is a Past King Rat in the Grand Order of Water Rats (1983) and organised charitable events for the Entertainment Artistes Benevolent Fund. Joined Chelsea Lodge on his 77th birthday, 19 September 1993, from Prospect Lodge No 7618.

Greg LUNNON LR

Born 6 October 1957. When the Lunnon family were looking through an alphabetical listing of careers for their children they got no further than the letter 'A', it was either Acting or Accountancy. Greg's father Denis was an actor, his brother and sister accountants. It seemed inevitable that the young Lunnon's career would go one way or the other. In fact Greg was earning a good living at the age of seven from various roles in commercials and films. However coming up to senior school Greg's mother, who was in business, decided that if he was ever going to make it in accountancy a line would need to be drawn under his acting career which was taking him out of school for long periods of time, she was also in need of a trainee bookkeeper. So at age 12 Greg's acting career was ended and finance took centre stage where it has remained to this day.

Progressing on as a teenager from juggling his school studies with a bookkeeping role Greg trained at several firms eventually establishing a Wealth Management business in his early 20's and now providing financial services to a range of clients including some of the world's foremost names in the Music business. Greg has played most popular sports competitively and competed in various extreme sports achieving national titles and international level in highboard diving. He continues to be a keen marathon runner covering over 1500 road miles per year many of which raise money for charity.

Greg was initiated into Proscenium Lodge No.3435 in 1990 becoming treasurer shortly afterwards. He was passed in Chelsea Manor Lodge and raised on 16 January 1991 by the late W.Bro. **Bernard Spear**, also in Chelsea Manor where neither of them were members. He joined Chelsea Lodge on 19 September 1997 when he became the treasurer and his responsibilities now include the finances of Chelsea Lodge and Chelsea Chapter, Proscenium Lodge and various Masonic Charity initiatives including the Royal Masonic Variety Show. Member of Chelsea Chapter. He attained London Rank in the craft in 2002.

Nigel LYTHGOE

TV producer/director/actor. Born 1949, Wallasey. Son of George, a Birkenhead docker and Gertrude Lythgoe. He auditioned for a talent competition at the age of eleven at the Tower Ballroom, New Brighton, but his father was totally against him entering the world of show business. However, at the age of twenty-one he eventually got his own way. His professional career began as a dancer and choreographer before he became a television executive, producing and directing many light entertainment shows. In 1968 he was a dancer in the thirty-strong team of BBC's Young Generation dance troupe. In 1976 he was the choreographer for *The Muppets TV Show* and the *Morecambe and Wise Show*. He worked on 500 shows in the 1970s, including Lulu, Two Ronnies, Vera Lynn and five Royal Variety Performances, As producer they are: *Mates and Music* (1984), *TV Weekly* (1988), *You Bet* (1989), *Brian Conley Show* (1992), *Gladiators* (1992), *An Audience with Alf Garnett* (1997), *An Audience with Elton John* (1997), *An Audience with Ronnie Corbett* (1997), *Dame Edna Kisses It Better* (1997), *Thoughts of Chairman Alf (1998)*, *Animals Do the Funniest Things* (1998), *Popstars (2000)*, *The Way They Were-Coronation Street Special (2000)*, *An Audience With Des O'Connor* (2001), *Pop Idol* (2001-2002), *American Idol* (2002), *All American Girl* (2003), *American Juniors* (2003), *An American Idol Christmas* (2003).

As director: *TV Weekly* (1988), *An Audience with Shirley Bassey* (1995), *Happy Birthday Shirley* (1996), *Survivor* (2001) and *American Idol* (2002-2003).

For twenty-seven years he remained behind the camera until the arrival of *Popstars* where he found fame and was given the nickname 'Nasty Nigel' for his cruel jibes and acid wit reducing hundreds of wannabe singers to tears; he later presented the BBC show *The Enemy Within* (2001). He has appeared in *American Idol - The Phenomenon* (2004) as well as *The Hear'Say Story* and *Top Ten Bastards* (2000).

In January 2000 Nigel suffered a heart attack in the United States of America.

He left his job with LWT to work for the production company 19, run by ex-Spice Girls manager Simon Fuller. He joined the company in June 2001. He is married to Bonnie and they have two grown up sons Simon and Kristopher and their home is in Hertfordshire.

Nigel Lythgoe joined Chelsea Lodge on 18 September 1992 from Broxbourne Lodge No.2253.

Laurie MANSFIELD

Born 27 March 1943, Birmingham. Left school in 1959. First job was in the accounts office at Cadbury's, Bourneville. A colleague who knew of his interest in music (Laurie knew the record numbers, together with titles of the A and B sides of every chart record) and was offered a job as a salesman in the Birmingham firm of A.A. Woods where he sold new singles to local record shops. Following his success here Laurie joined the newly formed CBS Records, London, in the mid 1960s as a salesman. He remembers: "It was a very exciting time. We had the Tremeloes, Marmalade, Chicory Tip and Love Affair in this country and Bob Dylan, Scott Mackenzie, Simon and Garfunkel and The Byrds in the States. There was a lot of very good material around in the mid to late 1960s."

Following his time as a salesman with CBS Laurie decided he would try his luck as an independent producer working with Morgan Records in London. They were very successful as a recording studio working with artistes on the Island record label, but wanted to set up their own record label. Laurie helped them achieve this. Another step up the ladder led him into the agency business in November 1969 and since then he has been responsible for building International Artistes Limited into one of the most successful all purpose management and agency companies in the United Kingdom, where he is now Chairman.

He has helped guide the careers of such artistes as Rolf Harris, Cannon and Ball, Cleo Laine, Johnny Dankworth, Peters and Lee, **Jim Davidson**, Sacha Distel, Ronnie Corbett, Hale and Pace, Richard Digance, Brian Conley and Max Boyce.

International Artistes has co-produced on a number of occasions with Paul Elliot, notably their production of *Babes in the Wood* at the Palace Theatre, Birmingham which, as it did at the London Palladium, broke all box office records.

In the 1980s he was responsible for the company's move into production of London's West End shows including the musical *Buddy* (The Buddy Holly Story), which was staged for fifteen years and *Jolson* (Olivier Award Best Musical, 1997), *Defending the Caveman* (Olivier Award Best Entertainment, 1999) and most recently *Great Balls of Fire* (The Jerry Lee Lewis Story). In 2000 Laurie was executive producer of the film *Agnes Brown* starring and directed by Anjelica Houston. In 2002 he was executive producer for the BBC1 TV series *Jim Davidson – On the Edge,* from Southampton's Mayflower Theatre.

Laurie is Vice-chairman of the British Forces Foundation which works in conjunction with Services Sound and Vision Corporation (SSVC) in helping to finance artistes and back-up crew who

travel overseas to entertain the troops. Patron is HRH Prince Charles and Lady Thatcher is their President.

Each year Laurie is involved with the organisation of the Royal Variety Performance and is President of the Entertainment Artistes' Benevolent Fund, which maintains Brinsworth House, Twickenham, the home for retired members of the entertainment profession.

Laurie Mansfield was initiated into Chelsea Lodge in September 1987.

Alfred MARKS
Actor. Born Alfred Edward Touchinsky, 28 January 1921, Holborn, London. His first stage appearance was at the age of nine in a Boys' Brigade concert party. His first professional appearance was at The Kilburn Empire in variety, in 1946. He studied singing in Italy and was a trained operatic baritone for three years before being called up at the outbreak of the Second World War. In the RAF he spent four years organising ENSA concerts in the Middle East.

Back in civilian life he became an apprentice comedian working at the Windmill Theatre in London where he stayed for 20 months.

He began broadcasting in the late 1940s. Appeared on BBC Radio Shows: *Variety Bandbox* (early 1950s), *Star Bill* (1953) and *Educating Archie* with Peter Brough and Archie Andrews.

Alfred appeared in the Royal Variety Performance of 1960 held at the Victoria Palace, London. He was married to comedienne /

impressionist Paddie O'Neil.

By the 1960s he had moved into straight theatre taking on musical roles as well as works by Shakespeare. He appeared on radio and television as well as in films.

The films in which he appeared were: *Penny Points to Paradise* (1951), *Johnny You're Wanted* (1956), *Desert Mice* (1959), *There Was a Crooked Man* (1960), *Weekend with Lulu* (1961), *Frightened City* (1961), *Status Symbol* (1962), *She'll Have to Go* (1962), *Fire Crackers* (1964) TV series, *Paris 1900* (1964), *Scream and Scream Again* (1969), *Scramble* (1969), *Jokers Wild* (1969) TV Series, *Albert and Victoria* (1970) TV Series, *Our Miss Fred* (1972), *Mission Monte Carlo* (1974), *Valentine* (1977), *Yeoman of the Guard* (1982), *Fanny Hill* (1983), *Lost Empires* (1986) TV Series and *Antonia and Jane* (1991).

Alfred Marks also guested in a number of television programmes including: *Lovejoy. Virtual Murder, Kenny Everett Television Show, Minder, Target, Raffles, The Sweeney, Joker's Wild, Jason King, The Adventurer* and *The Persuaders.*

He inaugurated the Seagull Theatre at the Lowestoft Theatre Centre, Suffolk in 1981.

Alfred Edward Marks was initiated into Chelsea Lodge on 16 September 1955. He died 1 July 1996, aged 75 years. A plaque by the Heritage Foundation was unveiled to him on 11 October 1996 at Broadcasting House, London.

Manny MARRON

Musician. Played alto saxophone, baritone saxophone and clarinet. This diminutive Londoner was born in 1906. He bought a clarinet to take to a party and it went well so he decided to make music his profession. He went to the Cottage at Bow and was employed there. He toured the provinces as well as the continent. After two years service at the Regent Palace Hotel he joined Maurice Winnick. His hobbies included motoring, swimming and golf.

Emmanuel Marron joined Chelsea Lodge on 16 January 1970 from Assiduity Lodge No.4844. He died September 1980, aged 74 years.

Bram MARTIN

Musical director. Real name Bramwell Martinez. Born 22 June 1901, London. His ancestors were Spanish/Portuguese. Began his career as a cellist in classical and light music working in pit orchestras in cinemas for silent films and playing with symphony orchestras in Covent Garden Opera House. By the age of sixteen he was playing in George Byng's Queens Hall Light Orchestra, recording at HMV, backing such renowned performers as Sir Harry Lauder.

He was in the orchestra at Covent Garden Opera House for two seasons between 1921 and 1923, playing under Bruno Walter. Thereafter he played in more cinema orchestras, including the legendary Regal Cinema Orchestra directed by Emmanuel Starkey. He also took up the banjo and guitar while playing in dance combinations and claimed to have been the first guitarist in a British dance band.

Bram made his bandleading debut quite by chance when he was asked by a friend to provide a dance band for a charity concert at the London Hippodrome in 1934. He recruited sixteen musicians and the concert was a big success. From there they were offered a residency at the Holborn Restaurant which began in August 1935. The band broadcast regularly on the BBC and also for Horlicks on Radios Luxembourg and Normandy and they were given a recording contract by Regal Zonophone. Their first record *I Dream of San Marino* was published on 4 November 1936. They made over 70 records for the company between 1936 and 1938. His singers included Gene Crowley, Sam Costa and Al Bowlly. His theme song was *Out of a Clear Blue Sky.*

There must be very few bandleaders whose instrument was the violincello, but that was the case of Bram whose years as a dance band leader were only a small part of a long and varied career. He was not a showman, but a first class musician whose success was born of musical talent, leading a fine professional band with the emphasis on melody and lightness of touch.

Bram was offered a summer season at Blackpool's North Pier with Lawrence Wright's *On With the Show.* He took on the engagement and never returned to the Holborn Restaurant. He was booked for another four seasons in Blackpool and liked the area so much he bought a bungalow in Cleveleys, near Blackpool where he moved his family away from London. He alternated theatre work with the summer seasons at Blackpool. In 1943, he took his band to the Plaza Ballroom, Derby for a two-year residency and this is believed to be his last engagement as a dance band leader. In 1945 he decided to retire from the music business and bought the Palladium Restaurant, between the two piers at Brighton, where he enjoyed entertaining his artist friends who were playing the resort. He bought an imposing Regency House in peaceful Norfolk Square and thought he had finished with music for good, but like many other performers before him he was tempted back into show business. He returned to playing the cello and recorded for Geoff Love, George Melachrino, Mantovani, Michel le Grand, Gordon Jenkins and Nelson Riddle. Bram appears as a cellist on the Beatles 1967 recording of *I Am a Walrus.*

He launched an orchestral agency which supplied ensembles of every size and style, for any sort of programme. He acted as musician, musical director, arranger, producer, administrator and 'fixer', working phenomenal hours until he reached the age of 79. He was married to Jane (Jenny) Blank and they had one son and four daughters.

Bram Martin was initiated into Chelsea Lodge on 16 July 1936. Died 18 July 1984, aged 83 years.

Mike MARTIN

(A Lewis) Entertainer/musician. Born 23 March 1954, son of George Martin (The Casual Comedian), a household name in 1950s/60s variety theatre, television and radio who later became a prolific scriptwriter for many British stars of the day.

Studied film and television production at West Surrey College of Art, Guildford, 1971-74. Worked as a Butlin's Redcoat for several seasons. Joined *The Stage* newspaper full time, 1976-79, in the advertisement department, occasionally reviewing shows. Also semi-pro in bands and duos. In May 1979, he turned fully professional in showbusiness. Since then has worked in virtually every branch of the entertainment business as a performer, actor, singer, musician and presenter.

On television Mike has appeared in: *Arrivals* 1 and 2 (ATV), *The Bill* (Thames), *EastEnders* (BBC) and as Kenny Everett's double in his hugely successful BBC series. In 1986 he was a founder member of the cult American country roots band 'Peace on the Panhandle' which found considerable success on the circuit of the time. 1988 he teamed up with versatile singer/musician Martyn Oram, a partnership which has lasted over the years in a variety of guises, specialising in themed events which include medieval minstrels, pirates, Irish buskers, Mexican Mariachi and cowboys.

He has worked solo and in a variety of bands, duos and trios, appearing at every conceivable venue, including clubs, pubs, theatres, festivals, military bases, theme parks, hotels, ferries and even, on one occasion, a funeral!

Mike plays a variety of instruments including guitar, banjo, harmonica and ukulele. In 2001 he and Martyn were the founder members of The London Philharmonic Skiffle Orchestra, a comedy/musical band which performs eclectic world music and original compositions with the energy of old time skiffle and the spirit of true variety.

He is also a writer who has had two vastly contrasting books published, reflecting his interests in many fields. *Noddies* (The Film Extras Guide) by Arlon House Publishing and *From Crockett to Custer,* Trafford Publishing.

Mike is a keen historian specializing in the old American West, but he also occasionally works as a London tour guide, noted for his Jack the Ripper walks!

Also, he is a regular contributor to *The Stage* newspaper as a feature writer and reviewer, as well as supplying material for a wealth of other publications on a variety of topics.

He is a member of Equity, The Grand Order of Water Rats and several historical organisations.

Michael George Martin was initiated into Chelsea Lodge 20 September 2003.

James W. MATHEWS, PM PGStB

Actor and business manager. Born Dunedin, New Zealand, son of the famous comic opera prima donna, Julia Mathews. Brought to England by Charles D. Dillingham. Educated St Mary's College, Derbyshire. Travelled throughout Africa and Australia. Made his first appearance on the stage at the Princess Theatre, London, under the management of the late Wilson Barrett, on 6th December, 1883, when he played the part of the Captain of the Scythians in *Claudian*. He acted in various companies for ten years, and then he became business manager for William Lestocq and Harry Nicholl's 'Jane' company; subsequently toured with his own companies playing *The Real Little Lord Fauntleroy, Gloriana* etc.

From the year 1895 to 1915 J.W. Mathews officiated as business manager at the Duke of York's Theatre for Charles Frohman; after the death of Mr. Frohman, was engaged by Charles B. Dillingham for the Hippodrome, New York and in July 1915, left England to take up his position full time there. Whilst in England he had also been manager of the Globe Theatre as well as The Hippodrome.

James W. Mathews was initiated into Asaph Lodge No 1319 in 1888. Founder of Chelsea Lodge. Founder and PZ Chelsea Chapter. Appointed PGStB in the Grand Lodge of England in 1909. Representative of the Grand Lodge of New Zealand in the Grand Lodge of England. He was a member of the Savage, Sketch, Genesius and Logic Clubs of London.

Was the first Master of Chelsea Lodge 1905-1906. Appointed Honorary Member, 1911. Died Charing Cross Hospital 14 December 1920.

Eugene MATTHIAS

Magician and agent. Born 15 July 1956, Bombay, India. Three weeks after his birth his family moved to England and settled in Maidenhead, Berkshire. The family had business interests around the world and therefore by the age of six he found himself placed into a private boarding school called Presentation College in Reading.

Life seemed very hard for him at the time as bullying and caning was an everyday affair not only from the teachers but also from prefects. That was until one day when he saw Tommy Cooper performing magic on TV and this changed his life for good, because from that day onwards he decided he was going to be a magician.

He would go to the library every day during study periods and read books on magic, and joined the library in Reading where he would go on Saturdays to read more about the famous magicians and learn how to perform magic.

Eugene recalls: "One day the bullies came up to me and said: 'we understand you do magic'. 'Yes', I said. They went on: 'show us a trick then', which I did with my stomach turning over not knowing what was going to happen. They loved it and over a period of about a month I became accepted and they even called me by my name. There was no looking back."

By the age of fourteen Eugene had put on his first magic show before the school of 600 pupils and even got a write up in the local newspaper. But life goes on and suddenly he found out about the opposite sex and when the testosterone starts pumping ones whole life changes; magic becomes a thing of the past. For Eugene marriage and family life settled in together with children and a career in sales with a large multi-national company. All of a sudden he realised that magic would play a major part in his success in sales as his prospective customers loved it and it broke down barriers and made him the number one salesman. On the back of magic he made it to the top of his career.

By now he was in his mid-twenties and realised that people really did like magic. His local pub was holding a show evening and asked if he would like to take part - they even paid him to perform. He was amazed at the response from those present. It was his first ever paid gig and he decided this was the way forward.

Says Eugene: "Over the next five years I made the switch and set up a magic dealership selling magic around the country at outdoor shows. A club was formed and we would send the members a newsletter and arrange meetings around the country. From those beginnings the club has grown over the years into The Magic Club of Great Britain with over 400 active members. I am now the President of The Magic Club of Great Britain which holds an annual magic convention, puts on magic shows around the country and is there for anyone who wishes to learn about magic. We have lectures from many of the top magicians in this country including Paul Daniels and Wayne Dobson.

"I made numerous friendships and became aware that many of my friends were Freemasons, and they had Ladies Festivals and asked if I would like to come to one. I said 'yes', it sounded great. As we were going away for a weekend with friends what could be nicer. Little did I know that within two years I would become a Freemason, and I was initiated into Cymbeline Lodge No.9004. Magic introduced me to other performers and I was asked if I would like to come down to visit their Lodge, which was called Chelsea Lodge, which I did. When I became Master of Cymbeline Lodge I was asked what I was going to do about my cabaret. I said I did not know, but was told not to worry about it. Chelsea Lodge members W.Bro. **Frank Holder**, W. Bro. **Ivan Morgan**, Bro. **John Star**, Bro. **Ron Smiley**, Bro. **Jess Conrad** and the Wilde Cats turned up and put on a two-hour variety show for my Lodge, truly an evening never to be forgotten. So when I was asked would I like to become a member of Chelsea Lodge (it's amazing the lengths some Lodges go to for members) what else could I say but yes!

"It's funny how things go full circle because I am now back working with multi national companies, only this time performing my magic in cabaret."

Eugene Patrick Reynold Matthias joined Chelsea Lodge on 16 November 2001.

Ernie MAYNE

Comedian. Real name Percy Ernest Barrett. Born 17 March 1871, Topsham, Devon. He was described as a hilariously funny personality with

well rounded face and figure, accentuated by eccentric costume and make-up. Many of his songs revolved around eating and its consequences. They included: *A N'Egg and some N'Ham and a N'Onion, I Like a C'Hip of C-Hocoa, You Can't Get Many Pimples on a Pound of Pickled Pork* and *I Can't Do My Bally Bottom Button Up.*

By 1897 he was appearing in shows at the Empire, Portsmouth as well as touring in pantomime in Scotland and the North of England. The provincial tours continued for the next five years. After years of successful music hall work, Ernie moved to London appearing at Greenwich, Woolwich and the Hammersmith Palais. He sang a tune composed by Wallis and Terry, *Cupid*, which became very popular. The song was later incorporated into an act with **George Robey**.

Ernie wrote to *The Era* newspaper on 25 April 1903:

"In your issue of Saturday last I notice that you give a report on Mr George Robey's new song called *Cupid*. May I point out that I am the absolute originator of this character on the halls as a comedy patter song, and have worked it for the past two years. As I have now arrived in London, and am meeting with success in the song, I don't want to be considered a 'copy' of Mr Robey, but the originator."

Ernie Mayne recorded over seventy songs on the Winner label between 1905 and 1926.

He also appeared in films. In 1906 he appeared in *Excelsior* and the following year *Cupid,* both released by Gaumont Chronophone and featured in the Variety programme at the London Hippodrome. He is also believed to have appeared in the 1920 film *Pimple's Topical Gazette,* a burlesque newsreel

In 1924 Ernie appeared in a touring musical production *A Working Girl* which finished its seven-month run in London. He told *Era,* 3 February 1926: "I am an actor before anything else. I have even gone so far as to play in my early days, Henry Irving parts. When I went into revue last summer, some people were astonished that I should play such a part. They thought I was simply a comic singer in vaudeville."

For the remainder of the 1920s he returned to pantomime and variety.

Ernie had two sons Percy and Alec who appeared in variety acts and another son Jack who worked in the musical department of a Sussex firm.

Although in semi-retirement Ernie made his radio debut singing three of his original favourite songs in December 1933. His last appearance in pantomime, *Robinson Crusoe,* was at the Connaught Theatre in Worthing not too far from his residence at Shoreham-by-Sea. This was staged at Christmas 1936.

In April 1937, Ernie went into the Royal Sussex Hospital, Brighton to undergo an operation for appendicitis. Complications set in, the operation could not be performed, and Ernie's condition was reported as 'seriously ill'.

Percy Ernest Barrett was initiated into Chelsea Lodge on 17 April 1914. He died on 14 May 1937, aged 66 years.

Harry MAYVILLE

Vaudeville Artiste. Born July 1874. With his wife, Elsie, he had been working as a popular Lilliputian marionette act. They fulfilled most successful engagements at the chief London and provincial halls. When at the London Hippodrome in April 1903, the following paragraph describes their clever entertainment:

'By a clever contrivance Harry and Elsie

Mayville, the actors and inventors of this Lilliputian comedy, manage to completely deceive the eye, and so dainty is the entire production – so artistic from start to finish, that not only is it worthy of the first vaudeville establishment in the land where it is being presented, but the drawing-room of a duchess would not feel ashamed to welcome the sparkling little company from the Theatre Mayville.'

Henry Richmond Mayville joined Chelsea Lodge on 27 July 1905 from Glasgow Dramatic Lodge No.571, Scottish Constitution. On 12 February 1912 while travelling in the 9.20am train from London Euston to Birmingham to fulfill an engagement at the Grand Theatre, Birmingham, he suddenly took ill and died. The train was stopped at Berkhampstead and his body removed to a waiting-room. An inquest was held at Berkhampstead, the verdict returned being death from heart failure, due to chronic dyspepsia. The funeral took place at Tooting Cemetery 16 February 1912. He was 37 and left a widow and four children.

Billy McCOMB

Inventor, comedian, doctor of medicine, actor, author and magician. Born 1924 in Northern Ireland, son of Sir Charles Henry McComb, who was knighted by King George V for his valuable research in the field of X-rays. Billy graduated as a doctor of medicine to please his family but soon learned that he had to please himself so he gave up medicine and moved to London to pursue his dream as an entertainer. He began with voice-overs and soon moved into films and radio, becoming well known in the nightclub scene. He even opened for Bob Hope at the Prince of Wales Theatre. Within a few years Billy was headlining shows with an original blend of comedy and magic. He was asked to appear in a Royal Variety Performance at the London Palladium in front of HM the Queen.

He has made over 300 television appearances and appeared in films. He has worked the best theatres, cruise ships, and clubs around the world and is now recognised in the world of magic for his innovative effects. Billy has published books on magic and has enough magic awards to fill a warehouse.

During the summer months of 1969 he appeared in an ITV (Tyne Tees) black and white sitcom series *On the Rocks* in which he plays a mad producer at Seaview Television, the smallest station in Britain where the company transmits its signals from a lighthouse, aiming its ramshackle programming at a handful of residents in Kipper Cove and Mumbling Bay. Also in the show are Arthur Mullard and Pip Hinton.

Today he lives in Hollywood and is still actively performing. He is vice-president of the prestigious Magic Castle and an honorary lifetime member. His self-deprecating remarks about his age now play an integral part in his show, helping to enhance it even more. The worlds largest leprechaun has spent over six decades presenting magic and his work performed in front of an audience is now available on a 2 hour DVD which takes us through every nuance and subtlety that he has worked out over the last 60 years, including the vanishing bird cage which we learn is not a self-working illusion, but artistry in sleight of hand.

Billy McComb, a member of the Grand Order of Water Rats, was initiated into Chelsea Lodge on 18 September 1964.

Mick McMANUS

Wrestler. Born William George Michael McManus, 11 January 1927, London.. One of professional wrestling's best known figures with over 300 televised bouts plus guest appearances on many major TV shows with Tommy Cooper. Terry Wogan, Bruce Forsyth. Jimmy Tarbuck, **Bob Monkhouse,** Morecambe and Wise, Cannon and Ball and Little and Large.

Held the British Welterweight and European Middleweight titles during his career. Wrestled extensively on the continent, the Middle East and African states. His non-stop all action style of wrestling, at times bending the rules, earned him the title of 'The Man They Love To Hate'. Wrestling dominated televised sport on Saturday afternoons for 33 years with viewing figures of 6 million, which was staggering at that time.

Mick twice appeared in wrestling tournaments at the Royal Albert Hall in 1963 and 1968 before HRH the Duke of Edinburgh and again in 1973 in the presence of HRH the Duke of Kent. He was invited to Buckingham Palace to meet HRH Prince Charles and to 10 Downing Street at the invitation of Margaret Thatcher, the Prime Minister at that time.

A keen follower of all sports with special interest in rugby and cricket and has been a member of the MCC since the 1970s. Has always been involved with a great number of charities including the Lords Taverners, Sparks, National Playing Fields Association, The Variety Club and the Bud Flanagan Leukemia Fund. He plays in many Pro/AM/Celebrity golf tournaments for various charities and benefits.

Edited *The Mick McManus Wrestling Book*, published in 1970 which gives insights into the lives of Britain's best-known professional wrestlers of the 1960s.

Mick retired in 1982 and is now a Public Relations Consultant with a large global distributor of wire, cable and network systems organising golf days, lunches, dinners and sporting functions.

William George Michael McManus was initiated into Chelsea Lodge on 15 November 1991.

Fred McNAUGHTON

Comedian. James Frederick Norton was born 27 May 1869. With his brother Tom worked as sketch artistes: The McNaughtons. When Tom married Alice Lloyd in 1909 and left for the United States, he was replaced by Augustus Le Clerq, also known as Gus McNaughton who later married Lottie Poluskis.

Fred McNaughton was a Founder member of Chelsea Lodge in 1905. Died 24 February 1920, aged 51 years.

Freddie MILLS

Boxer. Born 26 June 1919, Parkstone, Dorset. His courage and dogged determination was legendary. He learned his craft in the West Country by joining Sam McKeowen's boxing booth. A challenger was invited to take on a travelling boxer at £5 to win and £100 knock-out. He turned professional at sixteen. His brawling style and heavy punching made him a crowd puller. He seemed impervious to pain. By 1942 he was a contender from middle - weight to heavyweight, but his big chance came at

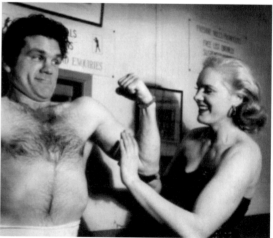

Strong man meets strong woman. Freddie Mills flexing his muscles for Joan Rhodes the lady who tore telephone books as if they were bus tickets

light heavyweight when he knocked out Len Harvey to win the British and Empire titles and the domestic version of the world title.

He completed war service in the RAF stationed at Netheravon with No. 1FTS as a sergeant physical training instructor.

Freddie was British and Empire Light Heavyweight champion 1942-1950, European champion 1947-1950 and World champion 1948-1950. He retired after losing his world title to Joey Maxim in 1950.

In 97 contests throughout his life he won 74, drew 6 and lost 17.

In 1947 he opened a Chinese restaurant at 143 Charing Cross Road, London WC2, together with businessman and actor Andy Ho. Freddie Mills Chinese Restaurant was one of the first in London and was a most popular venue for show business personalities and ran until 1963 when Chinatown set up in the same area.. Freddie and Andy then decided to turn the restaurant into a night club after extensive and expensive refurbishment. Freddie Mills Nite Spot opened on 9 May 1963.

Freddie married Christine Marie Broadribb, daughter of his boxing manager, Edward Broadribb, 30 September 1948 at The Methodist Church, Half Moon Street, London SE5. She had a son (Donald, 1939) by a previous marriage to the boxer Don McCorkindale. Freddie and Christine had two daughters Susan (1950) and Amanda (1956).

He was the author of *Battling For a Title* (1955), *Learn Boxing With Me* (1955) and *Forward the Light Heavies* (1956).

BBC Television introduced a new pop music show on 16 February 1957called *Six-Five Special* introduced by Peter Murray and Josephine Douglas. Later in the series Freddie Mills was recruited to present a sports item featuring lesser-known activities.

He appeared in the 1961 black and white film *Carry on Regardless*, which starred Sid James, Kenneth Williams, Charles Hawtrey, Kenneth Connor, Fenella Fielding, Joan Sims, Liz Fraser and Terence Alexander. Other film appearances included: *Emergency Call* (1952), *One Jump Ahead* (1955), *Breakaway* (1956), *Fun at St Fanny's* (1956), *Kill Me Tomorrow* (1957), *6.5 Special* (1958), *Chain of Events* (1958), *Carry On Constable* (1960), *The Comedy Man* (1963) and *Saturday Night Out* (1964).

Freddie Mills was initiated into Chelsea Lodge on 20 November 1964, the same day that **Reg** *'Confidentially Yours'* **Dixon** was initiated and **Bob Monkhouse** who was raised to the degree of a Master Mason..

He was found slumped in the back of his car in a Soho alleyway outside his London night club on 26 July 1965. He had been shot in the head and a small calibre rifle was resting between his knees. Many of his colleagues were convinced he had been murdered by the Kray Twins but police said it was suicide.

The funeral service took place at the Parish Church of St Giles, Camberwell, 30 July 1965. Pall bearers were Bruce Forsyth and Henry Cooper with members of the Boxing Board of Control. Boxing promoter Jack Solomons led the procession from the church to the New Cemetery, south London. One thousand people were in attendance in the church with a further thousand spectators outside.

Paul MILLS

Theatre director. Born 30 June 1948. He has directed many pantomimes with some of the biggest names in light entertainment from Aberdeen to Torquay, from Belfast to Richmond and as far a field as Tel Aviv.

He previously worked as an actor and stage manager in tours and repertory throughout the country. Paul's West End credits include: *Jesus Christ Superstar, Anything Goes, Cafe Puccini, The Normal Heart, Run For Your Wife, Orphans* with Albert Finney, *Rick's Bar, Casablanca, The Goodbye Girl* and *Cats*, where he met his wife,

choreographer, Rosita Yarboy.

Paul's other directing credits include *Commitment* and *The Dumb Waiter* at the Kenneth More Theatre. Ilford. *Oh! Calcutta!* in New Zealand and *Run For Your Wife* in both Chelmsford and Eastbourne. Rock 'n' Roll shows in Spain.

In 2002 he directed *Over The Rainbow* for the Edinburgh Festival and produced and directed *Dinomime* - three children's musicals for Butlins' resorts.

In 2003 Paul directed a new U.K. and Denmark tour of *Buddy — The Buddy Holly Story,* having directed previous productions in Germany, Japan, Minneapolis and two tours of the U.S.A., as well as being Associate Director of the London production and first U.K. tour. His work in the U.S.A. led to him being asked to become a consultant for the American Theatre Network. He has been the consultant to a National tour of *Summer Holiday* and has directed the stage musical *Sweet Home Chicago.* He continues to oversee his productions of *Buddy* and *Dinomime.*

Paul Edward Valasco Mills was initiated into Chelsea Lodge 18 January 2001.

Bob MONKHOUSE, OBE

An entertainer who was born on 1 June 1928 in Beckenham, Kent. Freelance cartoonist from the age of twelve, drawing comic strips and writing short stories. Sold his first jokes to Max Miller in 1944. Trained as a cartoon film animator with Gaumont-British at the age of 17. Conscripted into RAF in 1946 and posted as a clerk to Central Medical School in London.

Bob's first radio show *Works Wonders* took place in 1948 at a similar time to his first television appearance in *New To You*, where he received a fee of two guineas (£2.20p). At this time he was still in the RAF and demobbed in 1949. He made his name via radio in the post-war years, followed by television in 1953. He became BBC's first contract comedian. With Denis Goodwin he formed a script-writing team and together they scripted thousands of radio and television comedy shows for Arthur Askey, Bob Hope, Jack Benny, Jack Buchanan, Frank Sinatra, Rosemary Clooney, Bing Crosby, Billy Eckstine, Johnnie Ray and Jimmy Durante. For a year they wrote up to seven weekly shows simultaneously.

Bob made his London West End debut as compere of *Sauce Piquante* in 1950 with Norman

Wisdom and Tommy Cooper at the Cambridge Theatre. Five years later he appeared on stage in a summer show at Blackpool and subsequently

toured the British Isles in variety, pantomime, summer seasons and musical comedy, as well as appearing in hundreds of television programmes.

Credits include: *Beat Up the Town, Bury the Hatchet, For Love or Money, Candid Camera, What's My Line, The Golden Shot, Celebrity Squares, Bob's Full House, The Bob Monkhouse Show, Fast and Loose, My Pal Bob, Bob Monkhouse On The Spot, Bob Says Opportunity Knocks, Bob Monkhouse Comedy Hour, The Bob Monkhouse Disturbance, The Bob Monkhouse Offensive, The Big Noise, Mad Movies, Looks Familiar, The Bob Monkhouse Breakdown, London Palladium Show, Family Fortunes, $64,000 Dollar Question, This Is Your Life, Wipeout* and *An Audience With Bob Monkhouse*. He made a 26-week comedy series, *Bonkers*, for the CBS network filmed at Borehamwood, Hertfordshire.

Bob appeared in his first film, *The Secret People*, directed by Thorold Dickinson in 1952. This was followed by *All in Good Fun* (1956), *Carry on Sergeant* (1958), *Dentist in the Chair* (1960), *Dentist on the Job* (1961), *A Weekend With Lulu* (1961), *She'll Have to Go* (1962), *Bliss of Miss Blossom* (1968) and *Simon, Simon* (1970).

Songwriter Alan Jay Lerner used the title *How To Handle a Woman* suggested by Bob when they met, together with Frank Loesser, in a New York restaurant in 1958. The song was recorded by Richard Burton and featured in the stage production and film *Camelot*.

Bob was the host of the 75th anniversary of the Royal Variety Performance (1996) and has appeared in four other Royal Variety Performances in 1957, 1960, 1986 and 1988. Awards: Top Comedian in Cabaret (1981 and 1987), Best After Dinner Speaker (1988), British Comedy Award - Lifetime Achievement (1995). Publications: *Just Say a Few Words, The Complete Speaker's Handbook* and *Crying With Laughter.*

Robert Alan Monkhouse was initiated into Chelsea Lodge in November 1956. His grandfather John Monkhouse, who had died in 1938, was a Grand Officer in Craft and Chapter. Bob died 29 December 2003, aged 75 years.

Louis MORDISH

Musician. Born 1 July 1908. Described as the first gentleman of the music profession. Taught himself music until age of fourteen when he started his professional career as a pianist in a cinema in the days of silent films. He was a versatile musician, cinema organist, pianist, conductor, arranger and composer. His radio broadcasts were as organist and conductor. Both as an organist and a composer he was entirely self-taught. His first composition was a suite for full orchestra, which had its first performance by the BBC Concert Orchestra under Stanford Robinson. Apart from a number of songs, his compositions were primarily orchestral: the suites *New York, Legend of the Words* and *This Happy Health* and individual genre movements such as the *Can Can Polka, Toy Shop Polka, Madrilena, Calling All Notes, Spectre on the Spree, Pattern in Rhythm, Mexican Devil Dance, Mexican Promenade, A Cuban Romance, A-Spook Goes a Swinging,* described as a "rhythmic absurdity" and featuring a solo for piano or xylophone *Phantom Phingers.* A popular composition of his was *Turkish Delight.*

During the 1930s Louis was a regular organist at the Regal Cinema, Norwood. In those days the cinemas showed two films. All cinemas had a theatre organ which, during the interval, rose on a hydraulic ramp, so that the audience could see the organist. Sometimes the words of the song he was playing would be projected onto the screen so that the audience could join in the singsong. When their musical performance was completed the organist would slowly disappear into the bowels of the cinema, their hands waving goodbye to the audience. Louis also played regularly at the Regal cinema, Edmonton.

Amongst the recordings he made was as pianist with the Commodore Grand Orchestra on the Regal Zonophone label. He recorded *Knave of Hearts* at the Commodore Theatre, Hammersmith in 1933. Following war service in the RAF he became organist of the New Victoria Cinema, London and a regular broadcaster.

Author of the book *So I Think I'll Become a Musician.*

Louis Mordish was initiated into Chelsea Lodge 19 March 1954. Died 5 March 1996, aged 87 years.

Ivan MORGAN, LGR

Theatre manager. Born 23 March 1922, Rugby, Warks. As a teenager he was articled to Truslove and Harris, agricultural auctioneers. He volunteered for military service in World War II and served as a wireless operator/air gunner in the RAF from April 1940 to June 1946. He flew on missions in the Middle East on Blenheims and Wellingtons and in Europe on Dakotas, eventually ending up as signal's officer on Ramree Island, off the Burma coast.

On demobilisation from the RAF he joined Granada having seen an advertisement for assistant managers, the first to be taken on after the war. He joined Granada, Rugby on August Bank Holiday Monday 1946. This was followed by the Regent, Rugby later renamed the Century. Ivan wanted to take over a London theatre but had to gain ex-perience first so he became house manager at Granada, Woolwich where he stayed for nine months.

West Ham Kinema was Ivan's first London theatre and it was a tough house to run. On one occasion a customer pulled a knife on him - on another, a loaded pistol was aimed at him. Fortunately, in both cases, the trouble makers were arrested and given custodial sentences. Further moves were on the cards for Ivan who took over Granada, Sydenham and had to stop the film and go on stage when it was announced that King George VI had died. All cinemas and theatres were shut immediately. Sydenham was followed by Dartford, Sutton, Welling, Woolwich and finally, in 1960, to Granada, Bedford.

Ivan started something completely different when he went to the Granada, Welling. He presented a spring parade of farm animals and had baby chicks hatching out in the foyer in an incubator, and lambs, calves, piglets and little ponies on stage. At the Granada, Bedford, for the first time at any theatre anywhere in the world he ran a sheep-shearing competition on stage, advertising *Hot Enough for June*. He also started disc jockey shows on stage on Sunday nights which progressed to band shows and competitions, which proved a huge success.

During his years with Granada he has worked with hundreds of top names in the music business. He particularly remembers Tommy Steele, The Beatles, Mollie and Robinson Cleaver, Del

The Proscenium from the Circle, Granada, Woolwich

Shannon, Roy Orbison, Gene Vincent, Joe Brown, Matt Monro, The Rolling Stones, Little Richard, Vera Lynn, Russ Conway, Sam Cooke and Eden Kane. He discovered Marty Wilde and put him on the road to stardom. In the world of opera and ballet he has worked with Alicia Markova, Nadia Nerina, Anton Dolin, Moira Shearer and Beryl Gray.

Says Ivan: "I had a most enjoyable week playing the *Student Price* with John Hanson. I also remember Joe Collins who produced some of the Granada pantomimes and often he was accompanied by a young Joan Collins and her sister Jackie. Memories which will stay with me for the rest of my life are time spent with Ingrid Bergman and Charlie Chaplin. What wonderful people they were!"

In 1959 Ivan was the first manager to promote wrestling in a Granada theatre at Woolwich. The ring was on stage and Paul Lincoln, who ran the Two I's Coffee Bar in Soho, was the promoter who wrestled under the name Doctor Death with a mask on. From then on, wrestling was adopted throughout Granada.

He enjoyed his twenty years working in the various Granada theatres but was surprised to receive a call from Lord Bernstein in 1966 asking him to take over the Toddington motorway service area as general manager. Once the service area was up and running Ivan controlled some 1,200 staff, 84 managers, 1,200 seats with an extra 400 for party catering, plus 64 petrol pumps and eight breakdown vehicles.

He was made a Freeman of the City of London in the year 2000. Ivan remained an active member of the National Equine Welfare Committee and was one of the four organisers of the British Horse Society Rescue Centre. He was regional welfare officer for 18 years for the six counties in the East of England, retiring in December 2002. He is the only Englishman in 105 years to have driven a pair or team of four horses from the seat of a wagon in the Frontier Days parades at Cheyenne, Wyoming, USA.

He first took an interest in Freemasonry whilst in the RAF when he met a colleague Billy Hughes. It was Billy who, in 1955, initiated Ivan into Lakedale Lodge No.4044. WM of St Mary Abbotts Lodge No.1974 in 1999. Thomas Ivan James Morgan joined Chelsea Lodge 20 March 1987.

Gil MORRIS

Comedian/Actor. Born 8 December 1942. Began his career at the Birmingham Theatre School. He first stood on stage as a comedian in Newcastle 1965, turned professional in 1973, and worked for four seasons in holiday camps to gain further experience then continued on the Club circuit with his very funny routines.

Gil was featured in *Taming of the Shrew* for BBC2 plus various character parts in the successful series *Last of the Summer Wine* and many popular television commercials.

He relaxes with a game of golf with his many fellow comedians of the Comedians Golfing Society which he founded in 1977.

Gilbert Joseph Morris was initiated into Chelsea Lodge on 16 January 2004.

George MOZART

Comedian. Born David Gillings, 15 February 1864, Great Yarmouth, Norfolk. From the age of fourteen he received musical training as a volunteer bandsman with the Prince of Wales Own Artillery and later played with local music hall and theatre orchestras. His first professional appearance was as a clown with John Henry Cooke's circus in Edinburgh.

He married at twenty-two and his father bought him a public house, and he might have remained a publican but for a serious illness. On the variety stage he joined the Livermore Brothers Court Minstrels, first as a musical director and violinist, and then as corner man. His London debut was as a black-faced minstrel at the Marylebone Music Hall in 1886. For the next twelve years he worked with a partner as 'Engist and Orsa - Musical Clowns', and then teamed with Charles Warrington as the comedy and musical act 'Warrington and

Gillings'. Changing their name to 'the Mozarts' they made their first London appearance at the Queen's Music Hall, Poplar, in 1893. Other London bookings followed including a season in 1893 with Charles Morritt's magic and variety company at the Prince's Hall, Piccadilly, London and a 12-month engagement for Charles Morton. at the Palace.

While playing in *Aladdin* at the Grand Theatre, Islington, in 1895, George Mozart was seen by Sir Augustus Harris who offered him a part as solo comedian in his next pantomime at Drury Lane. Harris died two weeks later, but the offer helped to make up George's mind to turn solo and he appeared soon after at the Westminster Aquarium and the Canterbury.

He became one of the finest character comedians and pantomime artistes, topping bills at all the major halls for nearly 30 years notably with the one-man sketches *A Soldier and a Maid* and *The Family Album*. With his own variety company he toured the USA in 1907, appearing in New York at the Colonial, Hammerstein's and the Orpheum theatre. (On the same tour Marie Dressler was appearing in vaudeville with her burlesque of David Belasco's *Girl of the Golden West*). He first appeared in revue in 1915, playing Queen Elizabeth in Andre Charlot's *Now is the Time* at the Alhambra. From the earliest days he had an interest in film-making and was one of the first directors of Hammer Productions. He appeared in *Indiscretions of Eve* (1932), *Public Life of Henry the Nineth* (1935), *The Mystery of the Mary Celeste* (1935), *The Bank Messenger Mystery* (1936), *Polly Two Father's* (1936), *Strange Cargo* (1936), *Café Mascot* (1936), *Song of Freedom* (1936), *Full Speed Ahead* (1936), *Two on a Doorstep* (1936), *Overcoat Sam* (1937) and *Dr Sin Fang* (1937).

Throughout his interesting life he topped the bill at all the major British theatres and music halls and was a great success in America and Australia.

During the 1920s he was the landlord of the Green Man, Woodford and French Horn in St Martin's Lane, London, the latter with disastrous financial results, but also continued to play London variety engagements, including a season in 1928 with Maskelyne's *Mysteries at the St George's Hall*.

During the Second World War he took part in more than 3,000 shows put on especially for the troops.

In 1947 *The Times* described George as 'a short,

sturdy, dapper, monkey-faced little man, bouncing with energy, and his chief success was in imitating – without much, if any, change of costume – a whole series of persons, the people at a wedding, at a race meeting, or merely crossing the street at a busy corner. In these he showed a good deal of genuine humorous observation. He used also to conduct a band composed of a few grotesque-looking players – but in this act he relied on methods too primitive to seem funny except to very simple-minded audiences.'

He was the author of novels *July* and *Mary Ann* and an autobiography *Limelight*.

George Mozart, a member of the Grand Order of Water Rats, was a Founder of Chelsea Lodge. He died on 9 December 1947, aged 83 years.

George MULLINS, PM LGR

Born 4 July 1914, Ireland. Came to England at the age of fourteen. He put his age up so he could join the Irish Guards. He signed on for ten years, but was subsequently recalled at the outbreak of World War II in 1939 when he rejoined the Irish Guards. He was promoted in the field to major.

George was a great friend of the late Queen Mother. She always talked to him at the annual Trooping the Colour. They got on well together. Privately he was a proud man. He is the last link between Chelsea Lodge and the Chelsea Palace being the final manager before it was taken over by Granada TV. He went on to manage the Metropolitan Theatre, Edgware Road for two years.

George and **Ivan Morgan,** have remained pals since 1949. Says Ivan: "George was an outstanding Director of Ceremonies for seven or eight years following on from **Benny Wright**. He was a

George Mullins with Ivan Morgan in 1996, friends since 1946

fantastic ritualist, probably one of the best the Lodge has ever had. In addition he was a good coach and taught the officers everything they ever wanted to know. When he retired as DC in 1998 the Past Masters organised a dinner to show their appreciation for his exemplary work. Quite simply he was a great pillar of strength to Chelsea Lodge.

"As an ex-military man his floor work was immaculate. I remember on one occasion at a rehearsal, the Deacons were looking at the ground and he shouted, 'What are you looking for, money? Get your eyes up. You're on parade now.' He commanded huge respect. Nobody argued with him as he was 6ft 3ins and bore himself like a Guards officer the whole of the time."

Francis George Mullins was initiated into Chelsea Lodge on 20 March 1970. WM 1981. Made an Honorary Member, 20 March 2001. Died 22 January 2005, aged 89 years.

Jack NATHAN

Musician. Born 23 August 1910, London, A brilliant pianist, he soon added arranging, becoming an asset to any bandleader, and it didn't take **Roy Fox** long to realise this after Jack joined his band in October 1932. He composed *Here's Looking at You* which was the signature tune of the first TV programme transmitted on 26 August 1936.

Originally planning on a career in accounting, he had played in semi-professional bands around London before opting for a full time musical career as a member of Jack Padbury's Band at the Prince's Restaurant in Piccadilly, moving over to **Roy Fox** just three months later. Jack stayed with Fox six years, then had a year in Billy Bissett's band at the Café de Paris, before forming his own band in September 1939 for a new night-spot in the West End called Le Suivi.

A year later Jack was in uniform serving his country in the RAF, during which time he led his station dance band. Demobbed in 1946 he worked with Harry Hayes at Churchill's Club and his old boss Roy Fox at The Milroy. He then went into the orchestra for the show *Annie Get Your Gun* at London Coliseum while at the same time arranging for several top bandleaders, including Geraldo, Lew Stone and Jack Payne.

In July 1947 he formed his own band again, an eight-piece that replaced Jack Jackson at Churchill's, the plush society night club in Bond Street. Vocalist with the band was Charles Judah.

He was there until the club experienced a little licensing trouble and was closed by the police in January 1949. It soon re-opened and Jack, who had moved to the Nightingale, went back in April. He appeared in the Royal Variety Performance in November 1949, as pianist to *Annie Get Your Gun* star Dolores Gray.

By 1950 his outfit (that could boast the impressive line-up of **Aubrey Frank** and Ronnie Scott tenor-saxes, Wally Stott and Harry Klein alto-sax, Kenny Baker trumpet, Joe Muddell bass and Basil Kirchin drums) had taken up residency at the New Coconut Grove alongside the **Edmundo Ros** Band.

During his six-year stint at the Coconut Grove, Jack and his band made several broadcasts (his first had been some private recordings made at Churchill's that were played by Ralph Moffatt over the American Forces Network from Munich in 1947 - something the BBC quickly followed up with a Home Service broadcast on New Year's Eve 1947) and on 11 May 1951 their first television appearance came on *It's Fun To Dance,* a show that included the Butlins' Square Dance Team. Jack married dancer and cabaret artiste Patricia Worth on 3 June 1954 at the West London Synagogue.

In June 1956 Jack moved back into Churchill's Club for a further five years until January 1961 when he took over from **Woolf Phillips** as leader at the famous Pigalle Restaurant. For Jack this was a full circle, because the Pigalle had previously been the Prince's Restaurant where he began his professional career. The Pigalle was a show-case for many visiting American stars and during his time there Jack provided the backing for several of these, including Patti Page, Tony Bennett, Betty Hutton and Peggy Lee plus numerous home grown artistes.

In 1966 Jack left the Pigalle and had about a year freelancing. This included a role as musical director for *Who's Pinkus? Where's Chelm*, a musical play in two parts in which **Bernard Bresslaw** played Pinkus. It opened at the Jeanette Cochrane Theatre, London 3 January 1967 and ran for just ten performances. In December 1967 he was tempted back to Churchill's for another seven-year stay, then went straight from there into another night club residency, his longest yet, almost eight years at the Stork Club.

During his final years at the Stork Club, Jack suffered long spells of ill health and when it closed in 1981 he gave up full time work, concentrating more on his arranging. He worked on film scores and did some special arrangements of Jewish folk songs that were broadcast by Radio Two. Jack's first recordings were as part of the Roy Fox Band in 1932 and he recorded with his own band but, other than a few LP's for Philips in the late 1960's that featured current songs played in the Glenn Miller style, it is not known if there were any other records issued.

Jack Nathan was initiated into Chelsea Lodge in January 1972. An aristocrat of the music profession, he died 20 March 1990, London, aged 79 years. He left a wife, Patricia, who was a dancer with the Television Toppers, and three children.

David NEALE

Film and video producer. David Allan Neale was born 25 June 1944, Mottingham, London, fifth son of George and Katie Neale. Educated at Edgebury Secondary Modern School London SE9.

His first job was as a post boy with Pearl & Dean the screen advertising company in the heart of London's Mayfair. David remembers: "My father was a London Dock Worker. My four elder brothers, my uncles and the other male members of my family were London Dockers. So my future was mapped out for me, I was destined to become  a docker as well. When the time came to leave school the intake of Port of London messenger boys had already taken place and I was advised to get a job for six months until they "opened the books" again. A friend asked me to join him at George Munro, Fruit Importer, Covent Garden. I duly undertook an interview one Monday and was offered a job to start the following Monday as a post boy at £3 per week – I gladly accepted. On the way home I bought a copy of the *Evening Standard* and saw an advertisement for a company called Pearl & Dean, they also required a post boy.

"I knew something of Pearl and Dean. They were "Hollywood". Every time you went to the cinema you saw their Grecian ornamental gates on the screen opening onto a technicolour blue sky and those wonderful Chinese restaurant commercials followed. So I rang them and booked an interview for the following day. They, too, offered me a job as a post boy to start the following Monday but at £3.50 per week. So, naturally I went for the money and joined Pearl & Dean as a post boy. I left them twenty years later having risen to the board as their Director of Production to form my own commercial production company. To this day I've never had another employer. I never did inform George Munro of my change of mind – I guess they're still waiting for me to arrive!"

In his role as director David has shot for virtually most well known products both for this country and international markets. Products like British Airways, English Tourist Board, Pepsi, the Government (Video for Norman Tebbit when he was secretary of state for industry) Capital Radio, Cadbury's products, Proctor & Gamble, many of the major beer companies and a couple of cigarette companies when they were allowed to advertise.

He has worked with many well known 'faces' from Terry Wogan, Kenny Everett, Noel Edmonds, Roy Kinnear, Clement Freud, Loraine Chase, Annika Rice, Abba, Shakin' Stevens, Lennie Henry, Chris Tarrant, Sir Bob Geldorf, Paul Edington, Joanna Lumley, John Culshaw, even a very young **Freddie Davies** would you believe and many more. David says: "The trouble with the commercial business you do so much work it all pales into insignificance."

More recently David has branched out into TV and Feature production. In so far as children's television is concerned he produced the current BBC2 series, *Snailsbury Tales* and previous to that a Central TV series, *Windfalls.* His company is currently developing three feature projects one targeting French and Saunders, another Michael Caine and a third that Joan Collins has agreed to do.

David Allan Neale joined Chelsea Lodge on 21 January 2000 from Durobrivae Lodge No.6956 where he was initiated in March 1994 and became WM in 2000. Exalted into St Peter's Holy Royal Arch Chapter No.4193 in December 1995. The following year he was appointed Treasure of the Howard Masonic Hall (Kent) and later became a Trustee. In 1998 Advanced into St Peter's Mark Master Masons Lodge No. 842. In 1999 he was Elevated into St Peter's Royal Ark Mariners Lodge

No.842.

In addition in 1998 he was elected chairman of the Durobrivae Lodge Golden Anniversary organisation committee. He wrote the Lodge's 50th Anniversary booklet. In 2001 appointed Principal Sojourner, St Peter's Holy Royal Arch Chapter No.4193. In 2001 he became a joining member Mid Kent Masters Lodge No.3173 as well as a joining member of Chelsea Chapter No.3098. In 2002 was appointed information officer for Medway by the Province of East Kent. He also became an associate member East Kent First Principals Chapter No.3931.

Fred NEIMAN

Ventriloquist Real name Jacob Neiman. Born 16 October 1860, Brighton. A very popular personality in the late 1800s and early 1900s. At the age of seventeen he toured for nine months with a company presenting a panorama of the Russian-Turkish War, using at that time two knee figures with great success. Subsequently he was secured by 'The Wizard of the North', Professor Anderson, and then fulfilled a two years' engagement with Leonard Bosco. Billed as 'Neiman-The Youngest Ventriloquist in the World', he made his first music hall appearance at the Star, Liverpool, in 1878 and developed ventriloquism to a standard previously unsurpassed in scale and originality.

The ventriloquial figure known as the dummy or doll did not become the fashionable accompaniment of the ventriloquist until the latter part of the nineteenth century. Fred Neiman used a wooden knee figure in the 1870s. A simple spring mechanism animated the jaw which was controlled through the back of the head.

Not content with just one dummy, Fred went on to develop the Ventriloquial Minstrels. Eight figures filled the stage, dressed in the traditional minstrels' attire and through the voice of them all he gave a complex minstrel show. The movements of the figures were operated by a complicated system of bulbs, wires and tubes. Fred also produced a 'Ventriloquial Parliament', which included all the leading politicians of the day including Rt. Hon.W.E.Gladstone, Disraeli, Beaconsfield and Lord Randolph Churchill.

Fred left England in 1887 for a two-year tour of the USA, appearing at the White House, Washington, before President George Cleveland in 1888. On his return to England he toured with the Livermore Brothers Court Minstrels and on 24 May 1890 presented his 'Ventriloquist Minstrels' at the opening of the Tivoli Music Hall, London where he remained some considerable time and went on to play all the leading tours in England. He later teamed up with **Willie Benn** to help run a variety agency at 108 The Strand, London WC.

Fred had always been a hard worker in many charitable causes, being a Royal Arch Freemason of the Chelsea Lodge and a member of the Benevolent and Protective Order of Ellis of America, his lodge being Newark No.21, New Jersey. He was also a member of the committee of the Music Hall Artistes' Railway Association, of which he was one of the founders; a founder and vice-president of the Music Hall Home Fund, in which he took a keen interest; and a founder of the Terriers Association, of whose executive he was likewise a member. He belonged to the Antidiluvian Order of Buffaloes, his name being enrolled in one of the oldest lodges, The Pride of Sheppey.

Jacob Neiman was initiated into Chelsea Lodge on 17 August 1906. He died on 25 December, 1910, aged 50 years. He was interred in the Jewish Cemetery at Willesdon.

Jimmy NERVO

Juggler, acrobat, comedian. Real name James Henry Holloway. Born 1890, son of George Holloway of the Brothers Holloway, circus acrobatic act. He began his career as a juggler and acrobat at the Bedford, Camden Town, London in 1912. Later worked for two years with Fred Karno (who discovered Charlie Chaplin) in the show *Nosey Nose.* It was here where he met Teddy Knox (born 1896) who had been part of the double act 'Chink and Kaufman'.

Nervo and Knox teamed up in 1919, appearing as gymnasts and knock-about comedians in variety and touring in revue for Albert de Courville. In 1923 they presented their *Fantastic Frolics* on an all-British variety bill at the Palace Theatre, New York, followed by a season in the *Ziegfeld Follies.*

While appearing in their own touring revue *Young Bloods of Variety* at the Empire, Nottingham, they were seen by Val Parnell, then booking manager for George Black. Nervo and Knox were booked to appear at the London Palladium on 30 November 1931and then were signed to George Blacks *Crazy Shows.* With time off for revue and pantomime, Nervo and Knox appeared in the 'Crazy Gang' shows at the Palladium between 1932 and 1940 and from 1947 to 1962 at the Victoria Palace. The Crazy Gang comprised **Flanagan** and Allen, Naughton and Gold, Nervo and Knox and 'Monsewer' Eddie Gray. Nervo appeared in a number of films including *It's In the Bag* (1936), *Skylarks* (1936), *Okay For Sound* (1937), *Cavalcade of the Stars* (1938), *Alf's Button Afloat* (1938), *The Frozen Limits* (1939), *Gasbags* (1940) and *Life Is a Circus* (1958).

In his book *Cavalcade of Variety Acts* Roy Hudd says of Nervo and Knox: "Jimmy Nervo was the man who dealt with the management and came up with, and developed, most of the best ideas. Nervo and Knox had a spot called *Making a Talkie*, very topical at the time. In this sketch one played a returning husband who, after discovering his wife's lover in the house, has a terrific punch-up with him. After this the stage lights were dimmed. When they came up again the whole piece was replayed in slow motion. Eye witnesses say it was a masterpiece of timing and acrobatic prowess. Totally unique."

Nervo and Knox lived in Sussex and they were friends of 15th Reconnaissance Regiment who were stationed at Angmering-on-Sea, set between the sparkle of the Channel and the dapple of the Downs. In October 1944 the duo entertained members of the regiment and 8th Armoured Brigade in Nijmegan, Holland some 2,500 yards from the German front line and in a building frequently hit by enemy shell fire.

Teddy Knox died at his home in Salcombe. Devon, December 1974.

James Henry Holloway, a member of the Grand Order of Water Rats, was initiated into Chelsea Lodge on 21 September 1921. He was married to Minna in 1939. He died 5 December 1975, aged 85 years and is buried in St Marylebone (now East Finchley) cemetery.

Harry NEWMAN, PJGD

Accountant. Has been described as a 'life saver' during the 1930s and 1940s. He was proposed into Chelsea Lodge, as a joining member by Bro. **Teddy Brown**, famed bandleader and Music Hall star. Harry occupied every office in Chelsea Lodge and held every office with great distinction. His appointment as Director of Ceremonies in 1955, marked not only a milestone in his career, but also that of Chelsea Lodge, and during the ensuing

years his sterling work brought him Grand Honours.

Harry Newman joined Chelsea Lodge on 15 July 1938. WM 1952. Died 27 July 1983.

Alfie NOAKES

Popular session musician in the 1930s and 1940s. Born Toronto, Canada about 1902. Probably best known as a trumpeter in the Lew Stone Band in the 1930s. Appearing on records and in daily radio broadcasts he became a household name.

He began working in Canada with Gilbert Watson's Band before moving to Britain with Hal Swain's Toronto Band in 1924, as did trombonist **Tony Thorpe.**

With Alfredo's New Prince's Orchestra he recorded 150 tracks on the Electron label between 1925 and 1930. With the Ambrose Orchestra he recorded 110 different tracks between 1936-1940 on the Decca label. With Dave Frost and His Orchestra he recorded 12 tracks on the Decca label in 1930. With the Geraldo Orchestra he recorded 210 tracks on the Parlophone label between 1941-1945. He appeared on one of Nat Gonella's recordings for Decca in 1932. He played trumpet with the Jack Harris Orchestra in 1936 and recorded 80 tracks for the HMV label. With Sydney Kyte and His Piccadilly Hotel Band he recorded 46 tracks on the Regal Zonophone label. With the New Mayfair Dance Orchestra directed by Ray Noble he recorded 150 tracks between 1932-1934 on the HMV label. With the Harry Roy Band he recorded 12 tracks for Regal Zonophone in 1940. With Lew Stone and the Monsigneur Band and, later, the Lew Stone Band he recorded 360 different tracks between 1932-1941 on Regal Zonophone and Decca labels. He appeared on one recording session with **Frank Weir** and His Orchestra in August 1944. With the Jay Wilbur Band he recorded 100 different tracks. With the Maurice Winnick Orchestra he appeared in 40 recordings in 1937 and 1938.

He remained with the Geraldo Orchestra from 1941-1951, then joined George Melachrino and played for various West End shows before again working with Lew Stone (1953). He quit full time playing and moved to Bournemouth to run his own shop.

Alfie Noakes was initiated into Chelsea Lodge on 19 November 1937. He died 1982, Liss, Hampshire.

Gerald Vincent O'CONNOLLY

Publicity manager of Moss and Stoll Administrative Offices. Born 1881. Initiated into Chelsea Lodge 12 September 1907. Died at the Cooperative offices, Moss and Stoll, Cranborne Street, Leicester Square, London WC on 8 May 1909, aged 28 years. He was interred at Kensal Green Cemetery 11 May 1909.

Talbot O'FARRELL

Variety artiste. Born 1879. Real name Will Parrott. Started his professional life as a policeman in Hull. Began his show business career on the halls as Jock McIver, Scottish comedian and vocalist. As a Scot he enjoyed only mediocre fame, but then he changed to an Irish character and became a star of his time.

A burly, smiling man, with a broad face and projecting chin, Talbot O'Farrell wore a grey top hat, a somewhat extravagantly cut frock-coat and grey trousers, his monacle secured by a broad black ribbon. He would stand easily before the footlights, singing mildly risky patter songs, telling stories in a manner which depended for its effect almost entirely upon clever timing and sudden variations of speed, usually ending with some songs of extreme sentimentality such as *That Old Fashioned Mother of Mine* or *When Irish Eyes Are Smiling*. He had a pleasing light tenor voice and this, combined with his rich brogue and general air of knowing geniality, made an effective vehicle for his art.

He appeared in *Hanky Panky* at the Empire, London in March 1917. He recorded the song *Come Back to Ireland* with George W. Byng and His Orchestra taken from this musical show. He also recorded for Regal Records and his releases include: *Sweet Mary O'Neill. Search for a Four-leafed Shamrock, A Little Bunch of Shamrocks, Ballyhooly, Take Me Back to the Home of Childhood, The Whistling Thief, At the End of the Road, I Will Love You More Than Ever, Finnegan's Wedding, Ballyhooly Races, The Wedding of Maggie Malone, Fat Men Are Wonderful, Donnybrook Fair, Gilligan's Jaunting Car* and *Dear Little Irish Mother.*

Talbot made an appearance in the Royal Variety Performance of 1925 at the Alhambra, London.

Having fulfilled engagements as a music hall artiste since 1912 he fell on hard times financially. By 1929 his weekly earnings ranged from £60 to £200. Owing to the despression in the theatrical

world his earnings had further decreased and he appeared before the Bankrupty Court in December 1933. when accounts were lodged showing total liabilities £4,648 and assets £154. Talbot O'Farrell, who was then living at Greystones, Sheldon Avenue, Hampstead, stated that in January 1930, he paid £100 for shares in a company formed in 1928 to carry on a theatrical agency. He acted as director and advanced £250 to the company, which proved a failure, and was dissolved in 1931. In October 1930, he formed a company which produced *Fancy Free*, a music hall entertainment, in which he played the principal part. That production was unsuccessful and caused a loss of between £1,500 and £2,000, which was partly paid with money provided by his wife. When he entered on that venture he was perfectly solvent and, in fact, he was worth £10,000 in 1928, the failure being due to depression in the theatrical profession and lack of engagement in the latter years.

He refused to be beaten and made a successful return to the stage with another appearance in the Royal Variety Performance given at the Palladium in 1948 when, with six other performers, he was part of the *Thanks for the Memory* company.

He appeared in a number of films including: *Born Lucky* (1933), *Music Hall Cavalcade; Stars of Yesterday and Today* (1937); *Kathleen Mavourneen* (1937); *Rose of Tralee* (1938); *Little Dolly Daydream* (1938); *Lily of Laguna* (1938) and a new version of *Rose of Tralee* (1942). He wrote a column called 'And More Again' in *The Performer*. He had been a pierrot and wrote about music hall matters.

Talbot O'Farrell, a member of the Grand Order of Water Rats, was married to Minnie Talbot and they had one son and two daughters. He joined Chelsea Lodge from Thailia Lodge No.5177 on 18 July 1947. Died 2 September 1952, aged 72 years.

Minnie O'Farrell was three times Queen Rat of the Grand Order of Lady Ratlings, and had connections with the society of music hall performers and, in 1931, was president of the 'Cup of Kindness', which Ratlings organised to help performers in difficulty, and whose history she wrote in 1948.

Thomas O'FARRELL, LGR PProDepGReg (Surrey), PPADC (Middlesex)

Company director. Born 31 March 1933. He has enjoyed a professional career in land and property development progressing to appointment at board level of a publicly quoted company with subsequent profit and loss responsibility as managing director within the leisure, retails and public service industries.

He has served with numerous professional and voluntary bodies in the pubic and private sectors including Fellow, Council and Founder Member of the Incorporated Guild of Surveyors; Fellow of the Architects and Surveyors Institute; Fellow of the Institute of Chartered Builders; Member of the Royal Institute of Chartered Surveyors; Lay Member Independent Tribunals Social Services Appeals Tribunal; Member Police Consultative Committee; Vice Chairman Independent Monitoring Board, HM Wormwood Scrubs Prison (Home Office appointment); and National Interviewer Independent Monitoring Board in addition to Trustee of a charity managing homes for mental health in Camden and Brent and Care in the Community and Fund Raiser for MENCAP, Windsor.

Tom is Grand Commander of the Order of Saint John of Jerusalem, Freeman of the City of London, member of the Guild of Freeman, Liveryman Guild of Plumbers and Companion of the Grand Order of Water Rats.

His is a member of many Craft Lodges including Upper Thames No.6138 - WM 1982-1984; Columbia No.2397 – WM 1989-1990 and 1992-1993; Lodge of Brotherly Union No.8649 –WM 1998-1999 – resigned 2002; Founder Member New Morning Lodge No.9207 – WM 1987-1988 – resigned 1998; Justice and Peace Lodge No.8668 – WM 1997-1998; Barbican Lodge No.8494 – WM 1999-2000; Founder Member Steadfast Lodge No.9654; Motspur Lodge No.6106 – WM 2004-2005; and Westminster City Lodge No.2882.

Tom holds Senior London Grand Chapter Rank and is a member of various Royal Arch Chapters. These include Redwood No.3411; Faith No.141; Columbia No.2397; New Morning No.9207 and Chelsea No.3098.

Thomas O'Farrell joined Chelsea Lodge 15 May

1992. Currently Junior Warden.

Cyril PACKER

Hairdresser to the stars and wig maker, Cyril was born 31 October 1919 to Benjamin and Minnie Packer, London's East End. Educated at Central School, St George's in the East, his first job was a lather boy working in his father's barber shop and in the evenings he attended a hairdressing school. Studied in the Dempsey Street School to learn wig making and trichology. At the age of seventeen he rented his first salon in Cliftonville, Margate and from there after three summer seasons was called up in the Army. Joined Royal Artillery and in 1940 was sent to France, Norway, Dunkirk, Singapore, Burma, India and Germany. He married Sadie Cunningham on 4 August 1941.

Cyril returned to Civvy Street in August 1945 and joined Associated British Film Distributors but the company closed down two years later. In 1947 he returned to hairdressing and was asked to manage a salon in Streatham which he ran for 18 months. It was here he met famous stars. Regular clients were **Peter Sellers**, who had a difficult head of hair, and Morecambe and Wise. He then opened his own shop in Tottenham Court Road and also taught hairdressing at the Academy of Haircraft, which he owned. He opened his own salon in Curzon Street in London's Mayfair in 1961. He has groomed numerous personalities over the years

A young Cyril Packer with an equally young Cliff Richard

and on occasions travelled to where they are appearing. Celebrities include Harry Secombe, Peter Sellers, Norman Vaughan, Cliff Richard, Frank Ifield, Norman Wisdom, Jimmy Young, Danny Kaye, Bernard Delfont, Lonnie Donegan, Ronnie Carroll, Anthony Newley, Roy Castle and many others.

Cutting was only part of his job for the stars. A

big slice of Cyril's business with them was tinting and perming. He remembers: "I didn't set out to give a curly head of hair or row of waves. All I did was to make a man's hair sit properly and permanently in the way that he wanted it."

Cyril had unusual requests as well. "Peter Sellers gave me a problem. How to cut his hair longer! First he wanted, and got, a special convict haircut for a film. Easy – and short. Two days later he was calling me on the phone. 'It's all changed. I need a Teddy Boy haircut instead. You've got to cut my hair longer!' Somehow I managed it even though it was not more than an inch long. When Peter was working with the Goons on radio I was the regular hairdresser for the whole team. When Peter and Spike Milligan were appearing on a TV programme in the 1960s I was the hairdresser in the sketch.

"Cliff Richard rang me and said 'I've been swimming and my hair won't stay put.' So out came the little black bag, full of the tools of my trade. And then it suddenly dawned on me that Cliff was in Blackpool and I was in London. Cliff had a show to do that night. Fortunately he had called me early in the day, so I set off on the 476-mile round journey. It's all in a day's work."

Many of the stars were touring around the country and so Cyril had to go with them. He has given haircuts in hotels, dressing rooms, shops, television studios, even in the back of a car. There have been unusual requests as well. Cyril had to teach a lady how to cut a man's hair. In this case her husband. Channing Pollock made the request himself. He was going on tour and was determined not to let just anyone cut his hair – so Cyril had to train Mrs Pollock to cut his hair. It took three lessons to get the rudiments across to her. She picked up enough to cope with the situation for the duration of the tour.

He was the regular hairdresser for the stars of *Sunday Night at the London Palladium* for twenty years.

Cyril Packer was initiated into Astral Seven Lodge No.6489 on 23 November 1962, becoming WM in 1981. He joined Chelsea Lodge on 16 May 1980 and remembers the time he was Senior Deacon and had to decline the offer to become JW as he was moving to the USA for a couple of years. He recommended **Bernard Spear** take his place who went on to become WM in 1990. Cyril has attended more LOIs that any other member of Chelsea Lodge.

His son **Barry Packer,** a musician, was initiated on 18 September 1981 and his grandson **Simon Robert Packer** was initiated by Cyril on 15 March 2002.

Norman PAYNE

Musician. Born July 1911, London. Played trumpet and mellophone. Was younger brother of saxophonist Laurie Payne. He took up cornet, studied briefly in Germany, then returned to London. Turned professional and played at Florida Club, London in trio with Lionel Clapper and Ginger Conn (1927).

He played residency at Southport Palais with Sidney Lipton's Orchestra before returning to London to join Fred Elizalde (December 1927). He worked with Arthur Lally (1930) and Howard Jacobs (1930). He appears on hundreds of recording with Spike Hughes, Carroll Gibbons, Ray Noble, Bert and John Firman, Jay Whidden and Van Phillips.

During Second World War served in RAF. On demob joined Savoy Hotel Orpheans, followed by the Ted Heath Orchestra.

Norman retired from playing in 1944 to run a booking agency (J.P. Productions) with drummer Jock Jacobsen. The business was later sold to MGM and he was employed by the company for a number of years as a booker.

Norman Payne was initiated into Chelsea Lodge on 20 December 1935. He died 11 February 1992, London, aged 80 years.

Don PERCIVAL

(A Lewis). Musician. Born 2 October 1930, Swansea, son of singers/performers on the Moss Empire circuit, professionally known as Elsie Bowen and Percy Wilton. Educated to grammar school level at a variety of schools due to parent's touring, but most of the time lived with his maternal grandmother in Swansea, as did his two brothers, Norman and Alan. Don began learning the double bass in 1944 and three years later took it to London to make his fortune. At a similar time his brother Norman was studying composition, orchestration and conducting at the Guildhall School of Music and became a useful contact.

Don was called up for National Service in 1948 and on demob returned to London where he joined a trio and played at a club in Sussex Gardens. He was renting a furnished room in Kilburn. His landlord was an agent who made him an offer to work in Calcutta. It turned out to be one of the best tours of his life.

It was in Calcutta where Don was introduced into Freemasonry when his father wrote to a Scottish Lodge, Calcutta Kilwinning, asking the secretary to contact him with a view to becoming a member of the craft. He was initiated in 1951.

Returning from India, he took a job on the P & O ship *Strathmore* for a three-months return journey to Australia in the ship's orchestra, a loosely applied term as there were only four members on board. This was followed by several cruises on *Himalaya*.

Eventually Don returned to England and joined the Basil Kirchin band and spent the best part of 1953 in Edinburgh. He recalls it was a tremendous learning period with a phenomenal band. He left Edinburgh for London and freelanced with various bands and later joined the Barry Morgan Trio at the Blue Angel Club in Berkeley Street where the cabaret performers included David Frost, Lance Percival, The Clarke Brothers, Donna Hightower, Noel Harrison, Kathy Kirby and Hutch. He still freelances doing radio, television and recording sessions.

However, things were to change. Don had married in 1963 and had two young sons whom he seldom saw. He became a fourth partner in a company called Morgan Records and learned about the record business. Sadly the job did not work out the way he wanted, although he did gain a great deal of experience. He didn't have to wait long before he was offered the job as head of promotion at Phonogram Records. He worked with David Bowie, Harry Secombe, Esther Ofarim, Dusty Springfield and David Essex, amongst many others. He instituted a film department (the first promotional films) and produced videos from 16mm film of 10cc, Thin Lizzy and Peters and Lee, but his most successful campaign was with Demis Roussos.

In 1980 Don left Phonogram to look after various artistes' promotion and public relations on an independent basis and worked with many names who have since become good friends like Jose Carreras, Jessye Norman, Des O'Connor, Charles Aznavour and Julie Andrews. He had done the initial promotion work for Diana Krall and Natalie Cole.

As a composer Don has written the title and incidental music for several BBC TV series and productions. These include: *Fighter Pilot, Airline,*

Star Memorie and *Year of the Balloon.* He also sings a song in the movie *Bladerunner* for Vangelis who wrote the music for that film.

At the turn of the century Don was all set to retire when a friend approached him regarding an idea to form a company manufacturing and selling fine bone china. He hopes it will become a successful venture.

Bro. Donald John Percival became a joining member of Chelsea Lodge 15 May 1959.

Vincent 'Charles' PERMANE

Film production manager. Born 20 April 1899, Stockholm, Sweden. Began his career in the film business as an assistant production manager on *Henry V* with Laurence Olivier. Freelance Production Manager and worked on a number of Hammer Films including: *The Crawling Eye* (1957), *The Trollenberg Terror* (1958), *Circus of Horrors* (1959) and *The Witches* (1966).

Married Doreen Katie Fuller Neary. Issue: two sons and one daughter. Joining member of Chelsea Lodge. WM in 1949.

William PERMANE

Vaudeville artiste. Son of William Permane, the gymnast. Born 28 March 1864 at Bell Barn Road, Birmingham. At age six he was apprenticed to Charles Adams, the circus proprietor, and became a rider. He was noted at Hengler's from about 1880. He travelled widely with Ciniselli's Circus, and while in Russia met Johnny Watson who had a riding bear. Being ill, Watson allowed Permane to deputise for him. In time William decided to train his own bears and on 1 August 1888 'Permane's Bears' made their debut at the Djurgarden, Stockholm, Sweden. In May 1899 he introduced his bears at Circo Place, Madrid. In August 1889 they were at the Grand Eden Cirque, Nova. Their fame spread and the bears came to England, first appearing at Covent Garden Circus for the 1889-1890 season, when people were astounded to see bears standing on their heads, walking a narrow pole, barrel rolling, riding a tricycle and even seated at a table enjoying a meal. Two of the bears were named Wodki and Sacuski. They appeared at the Canterbury Theatre of Varieties, and in August 1890 they appeared at the Royal Aquarium, Westminster. Permane appeared with many circuses, including Tudor's and Ohmy's, visiting the Continent several times. For Christmas 1893 he was in William Holland's *Noah's Ark* at Covent

Garden having earlier presented a boxing kangaroo in France. In 1938 he exhibited a trained monkey, having lost a finger the previous year.

In an old edition of *The Strand Magazine* (date obliterated, but it would be around 1900) Albert H, Broadwell interviewed William Permane who had many narrow escapes with his bears: "It was a hot summer in Madrid," said Permane, "and the weather seemed to affect my pets rather more than usual. After feeding time I went to caress one of the bears, who was chained up. Not seeming in a mood to accept my overtures, however, the brute seized me by the arm just above the shoulder, and shook me as a terrier would a rat, and then threw me in a heap into the furthermost corner of the stable. This being the second time she had attacked me in a determined manner that week, I thought it high time that the good people of Madrid were enjoying some bear's meat for supper – and so they did!

"After a certain age, which after all depends much upon the temperament of the animal, a bear will become unmanageable. There is no coaxing it into good behaviour, either by threats or kindness. The bear will have his own way, and then the best thing to do is to get rid of him at an early stage."

William Vincenti Permane was initiated into Chelsea Lodge on 15 September 1905. WM 1934. Died 5 June 1939, aged 75 years.

Woolf PHILLIPS

Musician. Born 5 January 1919, London, the youngest of a large musical family, and watched his older brothers, Sid, Ralph and Harry succeed in musical careers. He studied the piano when he was just five years old. As a child, he attended the Mile End Central Foundation School and became their best cricketer. His older brother, Sid, would take

him to lessons at Aubrey Faulkner's Cricket School. Both remained life-long cricket enthusiasts.

When he was only 13, Woolf had his first professional job when he and his brothers, Ralph and Harry, played in a band for a one-night engagement in the ballroom at Lord Rothchild's mansion. (Woolf played tenor saxophone).

One year later he began to study the trombone under **Tony Thorpe**, one of the Ambrose Orchestra's trombone trio (the others were **Lew Davis** and Ted Heath).

His career really started when he worked as a writer/arranger in both the Lawrence Wright and Campbell Connelly Music Publishing companies. After that, at age 16, he got his first orchestral job, as trombonist, with the Teddy Joyce Juvenile Band, touring theatres and cinemas throughout England. Woolf left Joyce and joined the Ambrose Orchestra, then called the "Ambrose Orchestra conducted by Evelyn Dall". Evelyn, a blond bombshell, was "fronting" the band. Ambrose stayed in the wings and didn't appear on stage. After that particular tour of Moss Empires he again worked with Ambrose at the Café de Paris just before war broke out, again near the end of the war, and at Ciro's after the war ended.

It should be noted that as a writer/arranger, Woolf invariably conducted at rehearsals with such people as **Joe Loss** (1935) and Harry Roy (1941-1943), leading the band through more than one complete broadcast while Harry did the vocals, Ted Heath (1942-1945), Ambrose (1945), and Geraldo (1945-1946). He joined Geraldo as an arranger. Wally Stott, Bob Farnon and Woolf were the band's arrangers.

Woolf has written that there was a programme called *Romance and Rhythm*, with a choir and a big orchestra (Geraldo's). One night their guest was to be Irving Berlin. He relates: "I did a big thing for that, and this particular night they had Irving Berlin as the guest, which was marvellous. I started writing on the Monday and by Thursday I couldn't see straight! I had done about 268 pages of score with the choir, singers and so on and, at the end of it, Irving Berlin came over to me and he said, 'I must congratulate you Sir.' He called me Sir - thank you - I was 25!"

In 1936, Woolf joined Joe Loss at the Astoria, on Charing Cross Road. Also in the band were **Harry Latham** and Joe Cordell (trombone). Woolf later recalled that he 'liked Joe Loss immensely - a very nice man'. It was a seven-day-a-week job at the Astoria, and the band played all the time for dancing.

In 1937, Woolf left the Joe Loss Band and was playing with the Jack Hylton Band, many of whom were also avid cricketers. The band was touring all the big theatres, working on the *Rinso Radio Revue* and other broadcasts as well as recording for HMV.

While Woolf was with Hylton, the band was seen on the very first television show from Alexandra Palace.

With the start of the Second World War he was called up on 1 November 1939and remained in the Army for six years. When the Royal Army Medical Corps saw Jack Hylton's name on his papers, they sent him to the band quarters at Church Crookham, where he was musically tested on Tommy Dorsey's *Song of India*. (The band was under the baton of Bandmaster Harry Johnson, another trombonist). In 1945, after serving in Africa and the Middle East, he became Musical Director of the Concert Orchestra of the RAMC (he was listed simply as Bandsman Private Phillips, W.) for its tour of Holland, Belgium and Germany. In private correspondence Woolf has recalled that the band excelled as a Concert Orchestra. They built up an excellent show, which gave much joy to the troops in the United Kingdom, Middle East, Iran and Iraq Commands, and later in Holland, Belgium and Germany. At one time, they recorded background music for the famous Pathé News and several times played under the baton of the famous bandleader George Melachrino who was then the conductor of the Allied Expeditionary Forces British Band.

On leave from the RAMC Band, he played with his brother Sid's Quintet at 'Le Suivi', recorded with Sid for Decca, *Darktown Strutter's Ball*, and later was in Sid's band for a concert at the Alma Theatre in Luton. In 1942-1943, Harry Roy asked Woolf to do an arrangement of *Brazil* and subsequently he did most of Harry Roy's arrangements (sent on to him from various military establishments). He maintained a close social and musical relationship with American bandleader Glenn Miller.

Whenever Woolf was home on leave he would either play with Harry Roy's Band at the Milroy night-club or Le Suivi with his brother Sid's band. Sid was a Corporal before he received his commission as an intelligence officer. In private correspondence, Woolf recalled that on one particular night, he played with Sid Phillips at Le Suivi, with Leslie "Jiver" Hutchinson on trumpet, Yorkie de Sousa on piano, Woolf on trombone, and Max Abrahams on the drums. Actor Robert Newton was lying drunk on the stand. They were all in civilian clothes when Air Chief Marshal Sir William Sholto danced by with his escort. The Air Chief asked, "Hello Sid, is everything fine?" Sid

replied, "Yes sir, thank you very much." So, they now knew that the air marshal was yet another Sid Phillips fan.

After the war ended, Woolf played with the Ambrose Orchestra at Ciro's and wrote many of their arrangements. Ambrose was instrumental (if you'll pardon the pun!) in getting Woolf some extended leave from the Army so that he could score for the Ambrose and Anne Shelton radio programme.

From November 1947 to September 1949, Woolf led the famous Skyrockets orchestra on broadcasts and on HMV recordings. In addition, he led his own orchestra at London's Palladium from November 1947 to September 1953. In July 1949, the bill at the Palladium comprised the Benny Goodman Sextet, and the Skyrockets Orchestra, directed by Woolf Phillips. The band included alto-saxophonist Johnny Dankworth and guest trumpeter Kenny Baker. During the months of August and September 1949, the original Ink Spots appeared at the London Palladium along with the Woolf Phillips Orchestra. Also on the Bill were Borah Minevitch's Harmonica Rascals, and others. Woolf was a peerless variety conductor, which was why he was so successful at the Palladium, and he played for the last performances of Max Miller and George Formby.

From 1952 to 1960, Woolf's own orchestra was part of the glitzy night life of London's West End. From 1953 - 1960 he replaced the Lew Stone Orchestra at the Pigalle Theatre Restaurant.

Woolf became quite involved with both ITV and the BBC, working with such stars as Terry Thomas, Joan Regan, Kay Starr, Vera Lynn, Jack Buchanan, Al Read, Betty Hutton, Michael Miles and others. Woolf's own orchestra was featured in the *Paris in Piccadilly* production, supported Cecily Courtneidge in her show and also substituted, on many shows, for all BBC Staff Orchestras during their holidays. He led a 27-piece orchestra on the BBC *Morning Music* and was Musical Director for both Vera Lynn and Donald Peers Radio Luxembourg shows.

During all this time Woolf was also scoring music for various Palladium shows and worked with Judy Garland, The Marx Brothers, Jack Benny, Ella Fitzgerald, Noel Coward, Nat 'King' Cole, Duke Ellington, Johnnie Ray and Donald O'Connor, amongst others. Woolf even hosted the radio show, *Housewives Choice* for a week. He composed the theme music for the English version of the popular TV show *What's My Line*. He was the Musical Director for the London production of Cole Porter's *The Decline and Fall of the Entire World*.

He was regular band at the Pigalle in London from 1953-1960 and worked with Frank Sinatra, Bob Hope, Danny Kaye and Sammy Davis Jnr. He conducted six Royal Variety Performances before The Queen and The Duke of Edinburgh. In addition to performing on radio and television, he conducted orchestras in all genres of music from symphonies to jazz and even wrote advertising jingles for radio and television. He recorded the million-selling *Tenement Symphony* with Tony Martin and appeared in the film *Vote for Huggett* (1948), for which he wrote three songs. He made recordings for Coral Records in America where he settled in 1966. He became conductor for Donald O'Connor, then Shari Lewis, June Allyson, Pat Boone, Frankie Avalon, Anthony Newley and Milton Berle.

Woolf was a vice-president of ASMAAC (American Society of Musicians, Arrangers, and Composers) and captain of the California Cricket Association. He remained active until shortly before his death and resided in Camarillo, California, USA, where he led the Camarillo Symphony Orchestra.

Woolf Phillips, a member of the Grand Order of Water Rats, was a Joining member of Chelsea Lodge on 21 November 1952 from Anglo Colonial Lodge No.3175. He married Sylvia Brower at the West London Synagogue on 12 December 1948. She survives him, as do their son, daughter and five grandchildren. He died in Reseda, California, 11 July 2003, aged 84 years.

Edward Owen "Poggy" POGSON

Musician. Born 20 October 1904, Acton, London. Talented all rounder in music playing saxophones, all reeds including bassoon, violin and he also sang. He first started playing violin on gigs as a schoolboy in short trousers for 3/6d (17½pence) per week. Whilst a pupil at Middlesex Grammar School in Isleworth, he bought a saxophone from a pawnbroker's shop which cost him £6.00. His first professional job was with a quartet at the Wimbledon Palais in 1920 when he was sixteen, then spent nine months with Herman Darewski's Stage Band. Also worked with Bert Firman and Al Starita's Kit-Kat Band before joining the Jack Hylton Orchestra in the 1920s. He joined Jack Jackson's Orchestra for six years, but also did freelance work with Ray Noble, including a tour of Holland in 1933. Was with Hugo Rignold, George Melachrino and Debroy Somers (1939); Billy Ternent, Geraldo and Jack Jackson (1940); Chappie D'Amato (1941), Jack Payne (1931-1933 and 1942-1943). He worked with the Victor Silvester Orchestra for 26 years.

Throughout the 1940s, 1950s and 1960s he did much freelance work, regularly in Kenny Baker's Dozen. He is also credited with being in many editions of the *Goon Show* on BBC radio. He was employed by symphony orchestras as a specialist 'extra' and has played soprano saxophone in Ravel's *Bolero,* bass sax in *Don Quixote,* alto sax in *Façade* and hecklephone in *Salome.*

Poggy was taken ill in 1967 and decided to move away from London to Somerset where he taught music until shortly before his death. He was married to Kay, a former secretary to EMI record producer Norman Newell.

He was an authority on tropical fish, antique clocks and antique musical instruments. He was a founder member of the Horological Society and a member of the Galpin Society. In sport he particularly enjoyed golf and yachting. He loved vintage cars and at different times owned seven old Rolls Royce's.

Colleagues described Poggy as 'friendly, loyal, modest and serene'. He was in every way a perfect gentleman and loved by everyone around him.

Edward Owen Pogson was initiated into Chelsea Lodge on 16 November 1934. He died 31 January 1980, Crewkerne Hospital, aged 75 years.

Felix POWELL

Song writer/musician. Born 1879, St Asaph, North Wales, son of a master painter and decorator. His younger brother, George Henry, was born a year later. The two boys were educated at the local Cathedral School. Felix had shown an early interest in music and was something of a piano prodigy, giving public performances when he was twelve. Eight years later he and George had taken an interest in music hall and moved to London. It was during this time that they met the Brook Sisters, Mabel and Leila. In time Felix married Mabel and George married Leila. With another couple of male supports, they toured on stage together as the Harlequinaders. Later Felix and Mabel called their only son Harley!

Felix wrote the music to one of the most popular

songs of World War I *Pack Up Your Troubles in Your Old Kit Bag and Smile, Smile, Smile.* The words were written by George who worked under the pseudonym 'Asaf.'

Neither had great faith in the song about 'a funny little codger, Private Perks', and it lay on a shelf for a while. It was dusted down a few years later and submitted in a competition for a marching song, which it won. It was then incorporated into the brothers' music hall act and became an instant hit.

Music during any war helps to boost morale amongst servicemen and women. Often the positive, optimistic words of many of the songs belied the actual savagery of the fighting when, during World War I, tens of thousands of our troops were killed in battle. Some of these patriotic songs survived well into World War II. The song composed by the Powell brothers falls into this category and we still sing the song today. At the time of World War I it was described as 'a philosophy song being sung and whistled by our troops as they march along'. The song became a hit all around the world. It was published in London and later in America.

Pack up your troubles in your old kit bag
And smile, smile, smile.
While you've a lucifer to light your fag
Smile, boys, that's the style.
What's the use of worrying?
It never was worthwhile,
So pack up your troubles in your old kit bag
And smile, smile, smile.

A 'lucifer' is a match and a 'fag', a cigarette.

The song was later featured in the 1942 black and white film *For Me and My Gal* which starred Judy Garland, George Murphy and Gene Kelly.

Felix also wrote the music for: *Have You Seen the Ducks Go By? There's a Friend in Every Milestone, Queen of Summer, When the Sun Sinks to Rest, Music of the Harlequinaders,* version of Gay's *Beggar's Opera* and *Rubicund Castle* (operetta).

Felix Powell lived for a time in Peacehaven where he was involved in the Tatler Cinema and theatre, the Peacehaven Philharmonic and orchestral society. During the year 1936 he was an estate agent in Peacehaven. He was married with one son. He was collecting a minimum of £400 a year in royalties and by 1936 had earned £12.000

for *Pack Up Your Troubles.*

Many people try to cover the harsh realities of life with a smile. They try to hide their anger and anxiety behind their smile. That was the philosophy behind *Pack Up Your Troubles in Your Old Kit Bag,* but remarkably in 1942 Felix Powell sat down at his piano at home with a few friends to play his hit tune. He began singing the words to the song. When he finished he stood up, walked to his bedroom, took out a revolver from a bedside drawer, put it to his head and shot himself. He could write a song about not worrying, but he was unable to overcome personal worries himself.

Felix Lloyd Powell was initiated into Chelsea Lodge 20 October 1922. He died 1942, aged 64 years. His brother George (born 1880) died in 1951.

Sandy POWELL, MBE

Music Hall Artiste. 'Can your hear me mother'? This was Sandy Powell's catch phrase. Albert Arthur Powell was born in a small house in Russum's Yard, Bridgegate, Rotherham on 30 January 1900. His father called him 'Sandy' because of his ginger hair. Sadly, his father left home when Sandy was four years old and never came back. His mother, Lillie La Maine, who had been a variety artiste, quickly returned to work first as a waitress/singer in a pub and then contracted as a feature artiste. Young Sandy used to go along with her and hide under the piano out of the way.

Lillie obtained a number of dates and Sandy was taken on tour with her. At the age of five he got his first part - sitting in the audience belting out the choruses to encourage the audience to sing along.

In 1907 he first appeared on the stage as a boy soprano, but when his voice broke he gave up singing and concentrated on comedy and impressions. He was taught to read and write by his mother but had little formal education, the law requiring him to attend school in whatever town his mother was appearing, being largely unobserved.

He made his London debut at the Palace, Bow, in 1915, and later that year appeared at the London Hippodrome in Harry Day's *Business as Usual* playing one of the boys in Harry Tate's sketch, *Fortifying the Garden*. He and his mother worked a double variety act in 1916 billed as 'Lillie and Sandy', and while playing the Dewsbury Empire were seen by a Stoll talent scout and booked for the Shepherd's Bush, Empire. Lillie La Main eventually dropped out of the act as Sandy developed as a solo comedian, but she was not to be forgotten. Sandy's 'Can you hear me, Mother'? became the first radio catch phrase and one of the most famous of variety.

At the age of sixteen he played his principal comedian role in pantomime at the Rotunda, Liverpool and two years later repeated this success at the Princess Theatre, Glasgow. From 1921 he appeared on the halls with a series of comedy sketches, over 40 of which he recorded.

By the time the First World War broke out he was in regular work and topped the bill when he was just eighteen. He was called up on 30 April 1918 but was rejected as unfit for service. Due to shortage of manpower he was called up again on 11 November 1918- Armistice Day as it happened.

Sandy Powell had a long career on the stage and in pantomime. In addition to this he made his first broadcast on the radio in 1928 which was the start of many years of radio comedy. He also recorded many of his music hall and radio sketches, the first of these *The Lost Policeman* in 1929 which sold half a million copies. These were very popular and earned him a very comfortable sum in royalties over the years. His total output of gramophone

records has been estimated at seven million. He made two short films of his most popular sketches in 1930 *The Lost Policeman* and *Sandy the Fireman* and later starred in eight feature films: *The Third String* (1932), *Can You Hear Me, Mother?* (1934), *Leave It To Me* (1935), *It's a Grand Old World* (1935), *I've Got a Horse* (1938) *All at Sea* (1939), *Home From Home* (1939) and *Cup Tie Honeymoon* (1948). During the Second World War Sandy was an entertainer to the troops.

In 1933 he produced his own summer concert party at Onchan Head Pavilion, Douglas, Isle of Man. He also produced the first complete variety show on television in 1933. He was a huge success in South Africa.

He made his first Royal Variety Performance at the London Palladium in 1935, assisted by Jimmy Fletcher and Roy Jeffries in *The Test Match*. His second was in 1970, assisted by his wife Kay White, when he presented his hilariously funny ventriloquist burlesque. His philosophy in life 'To blazes with subtlety, make 'em laugh and feel good'.

Sandy Powell was married three times: 1) Peggy Whitty with whom he had a daughter Peggy and a son Peter. This marriage ended in divorce. 2) Katie Hughes in 1942 but she died in 1947. 3) Kay White whom he married in 1951. He was appointed MBE in 1975.

Harry Stanley wrote his biography *Can You Hear Me. Mother* (1975).

Sandy was initiated into Chelsea Lodge on 20 January 1933. He died on 26 June 1982 in Eastbourne, still the old trouper preparing for his next show. He was aged 82 years.

Twenty years after his death his Master Mason's apron came into the hands of Bro. Rev. Howard John of Eastbourne via a friend of his widow. This was presented to the WM of Chelsea Lodge by Bro. Rev. John on 31 May 2002.

Peter PRICHARD, OBE
Agent. Born 30 November 1932, Shepherd's Bush, London. Left school at fourteen. Took an interest in show business which had been handed down from his grandmother who had been an entertainer. He began by moving scenery at the Shepherd's Bush Empire and generally helping out. Whilst at school he met an agent called **Hymie Zahl** who gave him a job as office boy. The only way to become an agent, Zahl had said, was to sit at an agent's desk. Peter sat on a chair between him and another great

agent who was a mason, Cyril Berlin. Within three years the company had taken over the Harry Foster agency who were highly respected in the world of light entertainment. Peter stayed with the company until he was called up for national service with the King's Royal Rifle Corps.

On return to civilian life he rejoined Foster's and within three years was working for Lew and Leslie Grade where he stayed for fifteen years. Peter remembers: "I joined Fosters at the beginning of Variety at the London Palladium so I was sent backstage to look after artistes like Danny Kaye and Jack Benny. With the Grades I looked after Bob Hope and Dorothy Lamour when they appeared at the Palladium."

Peter was then sent to America where he worked in the Grades New York office and he took over as road manager to Johnnie Ray who travelled all over the world. He then returned to England in the early 1960s and brought over Hugh O'Brien who was television's Wyatt Earp to do a Christmas

Western show at London's Dominion Theatre in Tottenham Court Road. His next assignment was with Mario Lanza. Again his job took him all over the world which included the making of two films. Sadly Mario died at the early age of 38.

Still working for Lew and Leslie Grade Peter then represented them at two casinos – The Dunes and The Sands – in Las Vegas. All the European talent which went to these two casinos was booked by him. Whilst in the USA he joined the Ed Sullivan show working as European representative for sixteen years.

In 1967 Peter split from the Grades and he took

over Kavanagh's agency in Hertford Street, London. The company had been set up by Ted Kavanagh one of Britain's funniest scriptwriters and the creator of the ITMA radio series. Here he represented **Bob Monkhouse**, Pete Murray, Jack Douglas, Windsor Davies, Anita Harris and Jimmy Tarbuck. Three years later he set up Peter Prichard Ltd where he remained until he was 65 when he decided not to run a large company anymore and went into partnership with his colleague **Laurie Mansfield** at International Artistes where he remains to this day.

Peter has devoted much of his life to charity work. He is a Commander of the Order of St John of Jerusalem where he has spent twenty years as a fund raiser as well a serving officer. He has spent a similar amount of time with the Entertainment's Artistes Benevolent Fund where he holds the position of chairman. He was recently made a life-governor of the Fund. The main responsibilities are the Royal Variety Performance and administering Brinsworth House in Twickenham which costs £1.4 million a year to run. Peter has seen almost every Royal Variety Performance since 1947. He remembers the day when Britain invaded Suez and the show was cancelled at 3 o'clock in the afternoon, the only show since the Second World War which did not take place. He says: "The Royal Variety Performance is the only show on television which still has that tradition of variety which produced artistes from ballet, opera classics, drama and light entertainment and pulling them all together for an enjoyable evening. Her Majesty the Queen is the Patron and each performance is attended by a member of the royal family. It is my job to escort Her Majesty during the interval when she meets and chats to members of the cast and has a glass of champagne with them. She is well informed about the charity and the home and always takes an interest in knowing how much will be made on that evening."

Peter Prichard was appointed OBE in 1992. A letter arrived at his home from the Prime Minister's office asking if he would accept an award should he be granted it. Peter remembers: "I showed my wife the letter saying it doesn't name which artiste it is for, because I thought it was for one of my clients. I rang the Prime Minister's office and said you have forgotten to put the name of the artiste on the letter. They said. 'No. The award we are considering is for you!' I was truly amazed." Peter's top two artistes were also appointed OBE – Jimmy Tarbuck and **Bob Monkhouse.**

Peter Prichard was initiated into Chelsea Lodge on 18 January 1990.

Jack RAINE

Trumpet player and violinist. Born 1891, Rotherham, South Yorkshire. Served in Army during World War One. Returned to civvy street and joined the Rag Pickers at Hammersmith Palais, London and later the Albany Five at Birmingham Palais (1921). He appeared in the musical show *The Blue Train* at the Prince of Wales Theatre, London in May 1927. Worked with the Jack Hylton Band from 1922-1936, followed by freelance work with Debroy Somers and **John Borelli**. During World War Two he served in ENSA.

His main work following the war was playing violin in various theatre orchestras. In 1950 he was invited to play trumpet for the 1950 Royal Command Performance reunion of the Jack Hylton Band.

John Alfred Raine was initiated into Chelsea Lodge on 19 July 1935. He died, 1952, in Sussex.

Mike RAMSDEN

Born 18 February 1939. He comes from a theatrical family on his mother's side. His mother and aunts were all dancers and his uncle was the well-known comedian George Betton. His wife, Elizabeth, was the dancing half of The Max Sisters a popular sister act in the 50s. Mike met Elizabeth when they were both Ballroom Dancing Instructors at a local academy in Surrey.

In 1960 he joined Granada Theatres and remained with them for fifteen years before moving into Local Authority Theatre Management. After a spell at Surrey Heath he moved to Derby to open the prestigious Assembly Rooms. The opening concert was in the presence of the late Queen Mother and his last event there before moving to Eastbourne was in the presence of HRH The Prince of Wales.

In Eastbourne he was responsible for all the shows at the towns four theatres. One of his Highlights in Eastbourne was producing and directing a Royal Variety Performance for the Fire Brigade Benevolent Fund in the presence of the late Princess Margaret.

Having retired he is now a very busy Toastmaster and Master of Ceremonies in East Sussex and Kent.

Michael Richard Ramsden was initiated into Chelsea Lodge 17 January 1986. WM 1997.

His son **David Richard Ramsden** was born 3 March 1976. He started a theatrical career at stage school in Brighton and subsequently won funding from the local authority to continue his studies at the Doreen Bird Academy of Performing Arts were he gained his diploma.

With a flourishing dancing career ahead of him David unfortunately had a serious injury to his ankle whilst dancing on board a cruise liner in Alaska. The injury would not heal and an operation was needed which resulted in him being unable to dance again. He is now a self-employed painter and decorator in Eastbourne.

David Richard Ramsden was initiated into Chelsea Lodge by his father 19 January 2001 who also performed the Second Degree ceremony in September 2001 and Third Degree ceremony, March 2002.

Ivor RAYMONDE

Musical Director/composer/arranger/record producer. Born 22 October 1926. He studied at Trinity College of Music and initially entered professional music as a jazz and classical pianist. For five years he had his own Sextet at The Norfolk Hotel, Bournemouth. He played in a variety of bands, including one led by Ronnie Scott, before he took a position as a musical director at the BBC, where he supervised recording sessions and occasionally played or sang (bass) on various artistes' broadcast recordings. He worked  on the *Billy Cotton Band Show*, *Hancock's Half Hour* and *Great Scott, It's Maynard*. He also worked as a session musician on occasions, playing on and arranging skiffle star Johnny Duncan's hit *Last Train From San Fernando*.

From the BBC, he moved on to become a producer at Philips Records, where he worked with artistes such as British rock 'n roller Marty Wilde, Roy Orbison, Paul Anka, Los Bravos, Helen Shapiro, Kathy Kirby, Alan Price and the folk-pop trio The Springfields. He was one of the few arrangers who worked with the legendary Joe Meek of *Telstar* fame, Britain's first independent record producer. Raymonde was among the very few British record producers of his day who became an influence on his American counterparts - he told author Lucy O'Brien that he found his arrangement of the Marty Wilde song *Donna* getting copied by American producers and arrangers. Raymonde also produced hits for Frankie Vaughan and Anne Shelton, but it was his work with the Springfields that was ultimately to prove fateful to his career when the girl in the trio, Dusty Springfield, decided to go solo with a new, soulful sound, late in 1963. He had written a tune while on holiday that he played for her, which the singer enjoyed, and then got lyricist Mike Hawker to add words. That song became *I Only Want To Be With You*, one of eight cut at Dusty's first solo session and the one chosen as her debut single. Its over-the-top arrangement, the orchestra playing too loud and over-recorded as well, with Dusty Springfield singing at the top of her lungs to compete, became something of a trademark for the singer and her arranger over the next four years. It was as distinctive as any records ever made at Philips or, for that matter, in England. Raymonde's relationship with Springfield lasted until the late 1960s, when she moved toward a more distinctly American-style soul sound in Memphis and Philadelphia. He regarded the writing of *I Only Want To Be With You* as a lucky accident and never concentrated on composing to any great length.

Ivor gained recognition in many fields of music, but was ultimately and especially known for his powerful vocal and string arrangements. Most memorable, apart from Dusty's own hits were the backings created on the records of Billy Fury *Halfway To Paradise*, The Walker Brothers *The Sun Ain't Gonna Shine Anymore*, Marty Wilde *Jezebel*, Frankie Vaughan *Tower of Strength* and The Bachelors *I Believe* to mention a few at random. Ivor produced dozens of other artistes during the 1960s, including the Hawaiians and the Honeybus, both on Deram Records.

From the middle Fifties to the late Seventies, he worked with recording artistes in England and abroad: Roy Orbison, Julio Iglesias, Richard Anthony, Paul Anka, Los Bravos, Helen Shapiro, Kathy Kirby, Anne Shelton, Alan Price, Ian Dury and many more.

During the 1970s, Raymonde also worked as an arranger and producer at DJM Records on albums by the actor Edward Woodward *The Equaliser, The Wicker Man* etc. However, it was his work with Dusty Springfield as an arranger and songwriter that dominated his reputation. *I Only Want to Be With You* was the first song Ivor Raymonde ever wrote, yet to date it has been recorded by numerous artistes and on five occasions – when sung by Dusty Springfield, Annie Lennox (with the Tourists), Samantha Fox, the Bay City Rollers and Nicolette Larson – became a chart topper. No matter how much time had elapsed, when the Bay City Rollers covered *I Only Want To Be With You* in 1976, they adapted his arrangement to their instruments, scarcely changing anything. When the Continental Miniatures covered the Raymonde/Hawker song *Stay Awhile* they, too, used the same arrangement that Raymond had used with Springfield.

What is not generally known is that Ivor was responsible for the release of a number of records on the Deram label by Whistling Jack Smith. *I Was Kaiser Bill's Batman* was a Top Ten hit in March 1967.

He married Nita Archer in 1956 (two sons and two daughters). The sons followed their father into the music business. The eldest, Nicholas, who was formerly director of A & R at BMG Records, now owns a successful production company. Simon Raymonde, formerly a bassist with Drowning Craze, carries on the family's musical tradition as a member of the Cocteau Twins where he served as bassist starting in 1983 and, increasingly, as a songwriter and arranger.

Ivor Raymonde was initiated into Chelsea Lodge on 18 January 1963. He died 4 June 1990, aged 63 years.

David REDFEARN

Magician. Born 19 August 1958. He was waiting to join the London Fire Brigade and filling in with part time jobs. In one of those jobs a fellow worker at the company showed him a very clever coin trick. David begged him to teach him the trick, which he did, and that was his start in magic.

Says David: "I can remember rushing home from school to watch Kreskin predict serial numbers and thinking how does he do that? As a youngster I have fond memories of Johnny Hart and his budgerigar act at the Seven Dials in London. I guess I have always had an interest in magic. I later met a magician named John Kenton. That night he bent my Yale door key, and performed a chop cup routine which ended with the chop cup being sold. I was totally hooked and fascinated by magic. I could not read enough books and there didn't seem enough hours in the day. I went through the stage of attending conventions and buying all the props but eventually realised I was best suited to sleight of hand study."

David joined the London Fire Brigade in 1983 and passed out as top recruit. He still enjoyed his hobby and joined the Magic Circle as an associate. He had an enthusiastic group of onlookers at the fire station, but they were not slow in coming forward with their criticism if they were not happy with a particular trick. Bookings began to come in on a regular basis. Eventually he decided to take the plunge and leave the London Fire Brigade. It was at a similar time to the King's Cross fire.

David Redfearn became a full time professional magician and his work took him from London to Hong Kong, from Europe to Las Vegas and from Cyprus to South America.

He has also performed for some of the most bizarre audiences - not least a branch of the Russian mafia: "I wasn't allowed any prior information about what the party was actually for", he recalls. "I turned up and everyone there was huge with big black coats and automatic weapons. I asked no questions!"

David believes that magic is as popular today as it ever was thanks to magicians that have changed the presentation of it on a television medium.

He has performed before HRH The Duke of Edinburgh at a private party in London. He has appeared on the same bill as Russ Abbott and Bobby Davro and has been resident magician for socials at Chelsea Football Club for over five years.

His TV credits include: *Absolutely Celebrities*, ITV 1; *Trick Saturday*, BBC1; *Shattered*, Channel 4; and numerous live performances in *This Morning*, Granada TV. In 2004 he was awarded 'Member of the Inner Magic Circle with Gold Star'.

David concludes: "Magic has given me the opportunity to perform at some incredible parties and meet the most wonderful people. Sometimes I have to pinch myself to make sure it is not a dream"

David George Redfearn was initiated into Chelsea Lodge on 16 March 2001.

Charlie RICH

Comedian. Born 1871. Real name Henry Charles Levy. He and his brother Harry, looking not dissimilar to today's Little and Large, were a popular duo on the Edwardian music hall and pantomime scene. They started their partnership as Rich and Rich on Jubilee Day, 22 June 1897, having previously played in minstrel troupes, drama and burlesque. In common with other acts, for example **Brothers Egbert,** they became great pantomime favourites playing Mother Goose and Jack and in similar roles in provincial theatres. In May 1912 they appeared in Australia and in December 1913, in South Africa. They were not prolific recorders, only four sides by them being issued on Regal and Pathe labels between 1910 and 1911: *We Don't Want a Girl, Jenny, My Own True Love, The King of Karactacus* (many years later recorded by Rolf Harris) and *Wishing.*

Other songs Rich and Rich performed on stage included: - *Charley Take Hold of my Arm, The Best of Everything, Walk Out With Nothing in Your Pocket, They Still Stand Saying Good Night* and a parody on *Loch Lomond.*

The act broke up in 1914 when Harry became active in the War. Charlie appeared after the War with his wife Elsie Roby, under the advertising slogan 'Get Rich Quick'. They toured the provinces with revue productions such as *Bubble and Squeak (*Christmas 1922) and *Babes in the Wood* (Christmas 1927). Charlie retired in 1927 and became landlord of 'The Royal Oak' in Halifax. His son Roy Rich was manager of the London Hippodrome and with the production department of Moss Empires.

Henry Charles Levy was initiated into Chelsea Lodge 16 August 1918.

Paul RICH, PM LGR

Singer, musician and music publisher. Born 20 August 1921, London the son of Russian immigrants. Although the family were poor his mother had a great passion for music and, despite the family's limited means, Paul's elder brothers Boris and Joe were given classical music lessons and became professional classical musicians. Paul was originally earmarked to follow in his father's footsteps as a tailor, but possessed a fine singing voice and a yearning to be an entertainer. He studied guitar under Ivor Mairants and went on to play in the bands of **Harry Leader**, Eddie Carroll, Ronnie Munro and Oscar Rabin before finally joining Lou Preager. By now he was just as likely to be singing as playing guitar and provided the vocal on over fifty of the band's recordings on Regal Zonophone, Parlophone and Columbia Records.

In 1942 he began his long association with the Lou Preager Band at London's Hammersmith Palais. He became Lou's longest serving singer staying with the band over thirteen years.

On many occasions, after all the dancers at the Palais had gone home, Paul would head back into town to perform his guitar-vocal solo act in West End nightspots. He also appeared in two films: 1) In the 1950 thriller *Pool of London*, for which the

Preager band supplied the music and Paul was in a pub scene and 2) in *Counter Spy* a few years later where he sang a specially written song (by Eric Spear) *Slightly Mad in Mexico* in a music hall scene, accompanying himself on guitar.

One of the records he made was *Cruising Down the River*, recorded in 1946. The fast waltz was written by two elderly ladies, Nellie Tollerton and Eileen Biddell as part of a 'Write a Song and Win £100' competition sponsored by the BBC. Paul was contracted to sing the winning entry and it became the country's second biggest sheet music seller ever (second only to *Doing the Lambeth Walk*).

Paul married Marion White at Bayswater Synagogue on 24 June 1952. Issue: one son, Clive.

He left the Preager band in 1955 because he needed more time to run his private business venture. He had built up a small chain of sweet and tobacco shops and he felt the time had come to give them his full attention.

However, within a year he was back performing

his solo act around London's clubs and coffee bars and even formed a group, The Fortune Airs. Back on record too, in May 1957 he began a long list of 63 singles on Woolworth's Embassy label, becoming one of their most popular artistes staying with them until the label folded in 1965. His last record was called *Keep Searchin'* backed with *Marie* in June 1965.

By the 1960s Paul had moved into music publishing, joining **Franklyn Boyd**, Al Leslie and Cyril Baker in running a string of companies from an office in Saville Row. At Carlin, where he became vice-president, Paul forged his reputation as publisher with a rare gift for nurturing young song writing talent, spotting hits and placing the right songs with the right singer. During the years 1966 to 1976 Carlin received the UK's Top Publisher Award from *Music Week* for ten years out of eleven. The success of the company was based on song writing deals with the likes of Bacharach and David and Lieber and Stoller, together with publishing deals with the best of UK talent, such as Cliff Richard, The Shadows, Eric Burdon and The Animals, The Kinks, Roy Wood, ELO, The Sweet, Genesis, Van der Graef Generator and Nazareth. The company also had an enviable reputation as a successful sub-publisher of US artistes and catalogues. It represented Elvis Presley, Michael Jackson and the Jackson 5, Dolly Parton and the Osmonds and the entire Tamla Motown catalogue during Motown's most successful years in which it produced hits by Four Tops, Diana Ross and The Supremes, Marvin Gaye, Smokey Robinson and many more.

After several decades in the music publishing business Paul ended up running the Music Publishers Association. He retired in 1996 after 54 years in the business.

Paul Rich was initiated into Chelsea Lodge in January, 1960. He was WM on two occasions - 1979 and 1999. He attained LGR. He died 23 February 2000, aged 78 years. The BRIT school's 'Paul Rich Award for Musical Composition' is dedicated to his memory.

Dickie RICHARDS

Comedy singer. Real name Brian Richard James Pearce. Born 31 December 1935. Began entertaining at the age of seven, doing puppet shows and magic for his fellow school pupils and later, at college, he wrote, produced and appeared in shows, this time as a comedian. From here he joined a revue company, appearing in sketches, production numbers (many of which he wrote or adapted) as well as doing his 'spot'.

Whilst serving in the Royal Air Force he continued producing shows and also established the base radio station, which involved him at all levels from programming to presenting. On leaving the RAF he was seen by Jack Good and was invited to compère shows which launched the careers of many of the rock stars of the 1950s and 60s, including Marty Wilde, Adam Faith, Craig Douglas, John Barry Seven, Cliff Richard, Gene Vincent, Freddie and the Dreamers and many more.

By now the cabaret scene was gaining momentum and this was Dickie's next step – appearing at many leading UK venues, Cesar's Palace, Heart of the Midlands, Talk of the Midlands, Lakeside Country Club to mention but a few with artistes like Buddy Greco, Lovelace Watkins and Des O'Connor, as well as appearances for Butlins, Warners and Pontins, which prompted a record deal with Phoenix Records. He was to become a firm favourite with holidaymakers at home and abroad with his *Do it with Dickie* feature having worked for many tour and cruise operators.

A change of direction took Dickie into television productions as an actor, appearing in promotional films for BBC's *EastEnders* as well as commercials in the United Kingdom and Europe. He can also be seen in corporate videos for such organisations as British Telecom, Trust House Forte, British Rail, G.E. Life, Everest Double Glazing and many others.

Dickie appears in newspapers and magazines advertising a wide range of products including insurance, pharmaceuticals, holidays, consumer products, cars and service industries. He is also seen in TV productions, one of the most recent being a reconstruction of the assassination attempt on Hitler towards the end of the Second World War and, with the help of computers, he is transformed into President Roosevelt. The production for the Discovery channel was shown in July 2004.

He is still very active on the cabaret and theatre scene and continues as children's entertainer and toastmaster/MC at prestige functions, corporate and charity events.

Brian Richard James Pearce joined Chelsea Lodge on 18 November 1988 from Loyalty Lodge No.7154.

J.W. RICKABY

Vaudeville Artiste. Born circa 1869. Real name James Emanuel Platt, son of an Army sergeant-major. He grew up in the Manchester area, where he trained to be an engineer, but he was to find a more profitable career in front of the footlights. He spent a short time appearing as a straight baritone vocalist at concerts in Manchester before achieving some success as a comedian at 'free-and-easies'.

He joined music hall proper at the Hull City Empire Theatre of Variety on 15 August 1898 and was described as 'an eccentric vocal comedian'. He specialised in burlesque soldier songs and made a number of provincial engagements before appearing in London at Sadlers Wells. In September 1908 he embarked on a seventeen-week engagement in Australia, his first professional visit abroad. He also appeared in America at a similar time and continued his success at the British halls. In 1921 he paid his first visit to South Africa and the following year revisited Australia and America. It was in South Africa where he became a major success and to keep his fans happy he once again returned to perform in 1924. The *South Africa Pictorial*, 2 February 1924 painted a very positive picture:

"J.W. Rickaby, the Burlesque character comedian, played two seasons of three weeks at the Johannesburg Empire. He became a tremendous – almost unprecedented – favourite. His work contains some peculiar quality, elusive possibly to the few, which is exactly what Empire audiences love. It rips them out of their phlegmatic stolidity into transports of shouting, singing, cheering ecstasy. Attribute his phenomenal success to whatever you will, the fact remains that Mr Rickaby can return to England and tell them the time-honoured story of how in Johannesburg he packed the Empire to the doors and then, in the expressive cant of the halls, proceeded to 'tear them to pieces'; the only difference in this case being that it will happen to be perfectly and completely true. A huge audience filled even the 'top-shelf' boxes (and the Empire has to be very full indeed for that to happen). He held the stage for fifty minutes and sang seven numbers. Between numbers, the audience sang or whistled the preceding air and at the end of each song yelled vociferously for its favourites. The songs were: *Then London Will Belong to Me, The Rajah of Nincompoo Islands, The Italian Ice-Cream Vendor's Song, The Shreik of Palestine,* a burlesque of *The Sheik of Araby, I'm the Biggest Guy on Broadway, Piccadilly* and *PC49,* still one of the funniest songs ever written."

Other songs performed by J.W. Rickaby included: *What ho! She Bumps, Oh, It's Lovely, Why Can't It Always Be Saturday, Napoleon's White Horse, I Hope I'm Not Keeping You Up, The Gentleman Jockey, The Farmer's Boy; Burlesque on Nero, They Built Piccadilly For Me* and *I Maka-de-Hokey de Pokey So Nice.*

Songs J.W. Rickaby recorded on the Bulldog and Winner labels between 1916 and 1928 were: *Major General Worthington, There's a Good Time Coming, First I Went and Won the DCM, I'm Always Thinking of Her, Okey de Poke, I'm An Airman, The Mountaineer, Three Meals a Day, Don Alfonso, Oh, Pola Nicoli* and *I'm a Bad Man from Buffalo.*

Comedians Tommy Trinder and Max Wall both said they had high regard of J.W. Rickaby who was one of the best in his profession. He was a member of the Vaudeville Golfing and Snooker Societies, and an early member of the Variety Artistes Federation. His brother, also a comic singer on the Halls, was Ted Waite, The Spasmodic Comedian.

Around July 1929 J.W. Rickaby was confined at his home in Brixton. During this illness, a VAF outing detoured to pass his house and he struggled to the window to wave to them.

J.W. Rickaby was initiated into Chelsea Lodge on 16 April 1908. He died peacefully on 1 October 1929, after an illness lasting three months. He was buried at Putney Vale Cemetery. He was aged 60 years. He left a widow, Margaret Alston Platt, who was not present at the funeral as she had collapsed in Charing Cross Road two days after his death and had been taken to hospital.

Johnny RISCOE

Variety artiste and theatrical agent. Born 21 June 1910, Leeds. He came from a theatrical background, his parents being a song and dance act, and by the age of twelve was earning a living by playing in pantomime at the city's Theatre Royal as a stilt walker.

Throughout his teens he was engaged in touring revues both as an acrobat and eccentric dancer. He signed with George Black who was influential in getting him to try his hand at the then experimental television production that was being aired at Alexander Palace.

Whilst appearing on a bill with Tessie O'Shea

and DeHaven and Page in 1929 Johnnie was spotted by an agent who offered him four weeks in Holland. Whilst he learned some Dutch and stayed, with much success, becoming a headline comic. This led to him touring Europe.

He was activated for military service in the Second World War and served in the Intelligence Corps, rather than Army entertainments, perhaps because of his knowledge of the Dutch life and language. On demobilisation he formed a double act with Violet Terry, a soubrette in variety, who had been on the stage almost as long as himself.

Riscoe and Terry were very successful on the post-war variety stage, working the Moss Empires circuit, appearing annually in Christmas pantomimes, and frequently broadcasting on shows like *Midday Music Hall* and *Worker's Playtime*

In 1950 Johnnie retired from performing and opened up his own variety agency. He worked in conjunction with BBC television, supplying suitable acts for the variety series *The Good Old Days.* Among his finds in their early careers were Norman Wisdom, Harry Secombe, Hope and Keen, Frank Carson, Mike and Bernie Winters and many others.

He was a member of the Grand Order of Water Rats and in 1949 was elected King Rat, and in addition help to found the Variety Club of Great Britain. Both he and his wife were tireless workers for show business charities, she in turn being elected Queen Ratling of the female half, the Grand Order of Lady Ratlings.

Johnnie Riscoe joined Chelsea Lodge on 16 July 1943 from Lodge Solomon.

He died 9 April 2000, aged 89 years having enjoyed one of the longest and most distinguished careers in variety. He is survived by his wife Vi and daughter Patsy.

Jack RISKIT

Gymnast and wire-walker. Real name John Richard Evans. Born 8 August 1879, Manchester. Made his first stage appearance at Barnard's Music Hall, Chatham, in 1898. Soon afterwards he went to South Africa as a wire-walker and comic singer. In 1902 he opened for Harry Rickards at the Opera House, Melbourne, Australia presenting a drag wire act billed as 'The Girl on the Slack Wire'. This was followed by a tour of Australia, playing the Rickard's Tivoli theatres and Fulbar's variety circuit.

On his return to London in 1909 Jack appeared at the Oxford Music Hall in July where he presented a novel speciality act known as 'Dental Riskit'. He toured in variety with a partner and in 1914 went back to Australia. Later he toured South America, North Africa and Spain with his own variety company.

While appearing at a charity show in West Bromwich during the Second World War, he fell from the slack wire and spent several months recovering. Forced to give up active stage work he went into theatre management.

John Richard Evans was initiated into Chelsea Lodge on 15 June 1923.

Harry ROBBINS

Musician. Xylophone player, vibraphone and drummer. In 1922 he was the drummer with Jack Hylton Orchestra and the Queen's Dance Orchestra making 60 records. He recorded with Bert and John Firman's Band in 1924 and 1925 making 40 records for Zonophone records. In 1926 was working at Jade's Club in Golden Square and he appeared as a member of the Romaine Five doubling drums and xylophone on a recording session for Columbia records. The following year The Daventry Experimental radio programmes began transmissions on the old BBC Birmingham wavelength. The London Radio Dance Band performed every Saturday night for two hours from 8.00pm in *Dancing Time* with Harry playing xylophone. The same year he recorded with Jay Whidden and his New Midnight Follies Band.

In 1928 Harry went on tour to Germany with the Jack Hylton Orchestra and whilst in Berlin made a recording for HMV Records returning later in the year to do more records with Jack Hylton at the Small Queen's Hall, London as well as freelancing with Arthur Lalley and Percival Mackey and his Kit-Kat Band

Harry remained with Jack Hylton until 1932 when he joined the BBC Dance Orchestra under Henry Hall and recorded 60 tracks on the Columbia label.

He continued to freelance and recorded with the Debroy Somers Band in 1935 and 1936 and the Jack Jackson Orchestra in 1937.

Harry Robbins was initiated into Chelsea Lodge on 18 September 1936. Died 8 March 1983.

Bobby ROBERTS Snr

Circus Director. Born 1912, Kingsthorpe,

Northampton. Second son of Paul Otto, a continental clown and tumbler, who married Mary Fossett, a sister of Sir Robert Fossett, one of England's best known circus owners. Their first son, Paul, died in infancy and their third, Tommy, was born two years after Bobby. The two brothers, virtually inseparable for most of their lives, became one of the most successful and enduring family and business partnerships of the circus world.

Christened Robert Fossett, Bobby later changed his name to that of Roberts. Their father had travelled England with the famous Bostock Wombwell and Bailey's Circus and, when the show closed in 1896, his father-in-law set up Sir Robert Fossett's Circus and Bobby and Tommy spent their early days at Tiffield, where the Fossetts had their winter farm. Paul and Mary Otto were with the Fossett show after the First World War and it was with the Fossett Circus that Bobby grew up. He made his circus debut as a very young clown and, at the age of eleven, was a featured solo rider in Sir Robert Fossett's Circus. The brothers subsequently became part of the Fossett family riding troupe, with Bobby, Bailey and Mary Fossett. They also appeared in an aerial rings act and on the horizontal bars.

The brothers also took part in a number of other circuses including Rosaire's and Chapman's No.1.

Bobby Roberts married Kitty Mednick in June 1941. She was part of the musical act known as the Norman Sisters and Michael, which also comprised her brother and his wife. Their children were Bobby Jnr (1942), Maureen (1951) and Tommy (1961). In turn all three have married and their children have all gone into the circus profession.

Over the years Bobby and Tommy acquired more and more animals and their acts were seen at prestigious British venues like Blackpool Tower, Harringay Arena and Brighton Centre as well as most of the leading European circuses. At one time they had seventeen elephants in their stables and Bobby was proud to see his elder son, Bobby Jnr., take over as elephant trainer, appearing on several occasions before members of the Royal family, including the Queen and the late Princess Margaret and at the Royal Tournament at Earl's Court, London in 1980.

In 1966 their animals were featured in the film *Doctor Dolittle.*

The Robert's Circus hit the big time when they

took over the BBC Television contract, which had been held by Billy Smart's Circus for 25 years.

By 1980 the two Robert's families had grown so steadily, that in 1982, they decided to divide the ample resources of Roberts Brothers' Circus, with each brother and his family going their separate ways with their own show, but came together for the BBC Television shows and Circus World Championships. Bobby Roberts Snr and his wife Kitty, along with sons Bobby Jnr and Tommy formed Roberts Brothers' Super Circus, which travelled until 1982.

Bobby Roberts Snr was the elder statesman of the circus world. For a number of years he was Honorary President of the Association of Circus Proprietors of Great Britain.

Robert Fossett Otto Roberts joined Chelsea Lodge on 18 September 1970. He died 5 April 1999, aged 87 years.

Bobby ROBERTS

(A Lewis). Circus Artiste. Born December 1942. Son of **Robert Fossett Otto Roberts**. He was aged four when he first fell into the sawdust ring as a clown with his uncle, the famous Jacko Fossett. His early years were spent watching and learning the basic circus skills from his father. He then developed his own personality into the routines. He perfected his solo-juggling act but later teamed up with Ringmaster Norman Barrett as the Barro Boys. Later still as a ground acrobat he was a member of the Teenage Tumblers act. He learned to walk the low wire, then graduated to high wire, walking above the big cage with a group of lions roaming below.

Bobby had a passion for the Wild West. Following on from his skills as a horse rider, he developed a cowboy act which incorporated sharp shooting, gun juggling, rope spinning and whip cracking. In 1980, for the showmanship, quality and skill in his act he won the Western category at the Circus World Championships.

His partner in the act was his wife Moira, who is now the overall administrator of the circus. They met in Kelvin Hall, Glasgow where her family operated a shooting and archery stall in the Carnival, which was always held beside the circus. They married in 1965 and Moira was soon in the ring as 'Princess Moira' demonstrating her prowess with the bow and arrow in the Western act.

Bobby took over from his father in 1961 in presenting the elephants and trained many through the years and is now recognised as one of the world's greatest elephant trainers.

In 1990 Bobby, along with his brother Tommy, were honoured by the Circus Friends Association who presented them with the award for the Best Equestrian Act in Britain for their highly original presentation of Arabian and Palomino horses in the Superdrome Circus, Blackpool. He has won numerous other awards including Best Circus for 1997 and 2000.

Bobby is a member of the Grand Order of Water Rats.

He was initiated into Chelsea Lodge on 12 March 1973.

Sir George ROBEY, CBE

Comedian and entertainer. Called 'The Prime Minister of Mirth' he was one of the most phenomenally successful of music hall comedians. Unlike most music hall artistes he had a middle-class upbringing.

He was born George Edward Wade on 20 September 1869, Herne Hill, London. His father, also George, was a civil engineer whose profession involved much overseas travel. At the age of eleven he went to live in Germany and, as a result having left school in Dresden, where he learned to speak fluent German, he studied science at the University of Leipzig. On his father's return to England, it was his intention to send George to Cambridge. What must have seemed like a catastrophe at the time eventually led him to the halls. As he tells his life story in *Looking Back on Life*, "I was sent to Cambridge until some of my father's speculations went wrong, and I had to face the facts of life and carve out a career for myself."

George began training as an engineer on Birmingham's first cable tramway but found that had little interest for him. He enjoyed legitimate drama but it was a chance visit to the Westminster Aquarium that led to his becoming a music hall performer.

His first London appearance as a comic singer was on 28 April 1891, at the Horns Assembly Rooms, Kennington singing *He Was Never Used to Luxuries* and *Where Did You Get That Hat*. His West End debut followed at the Oxford Music Hall on 6 June 1891 and he was signed on for a year's contract as 'George Robey – The Coming Man'. He was just twenty-one years old.

He was soon promoted from 'an extra' to star

George Robey

billing and adopted his own stage persona. In common with his contemporaries the red-nose was *de reguer*, but George added strongly blackened eyebrows, top hat (later discarded for a squashed bowler) and clergyman's coat that were to become his trademark throughout his career. He was equally as successful in pantomime, revue and on the musical stage, and his character studies, including *The Prehistoric Man, The Mayor of Mudcumdyke, The German Musician* and others are still remembered.

He played his first pantomime at the Alhambra, Brighton, in 1892. For years his Widow Twanky and Dame Trot so delighted the audiences of the main provincial cities that he only found time to appear in one London pantomime, *Jack and the Beanstalk* at the Hippodrome in 1921.

During World War I George served with the Motor Transport Service from 1914-1918,

He married Ethel Haydon of Melbourne, Australia. Issue: One daughter, Eileen, and one son who, as Sir Edward Robey, was a Metropolitan magistrate 1954-1972. He married for a second time, to Blanche Littler, theatrical proprietor and producer.

Robey realised that to survive as the 'Prime Minister of Mirth' he had to change with the times and move into all the entertainment media he could – revue, music hall, pantomime and musical comedy, Shakespearian drama and cinema..

George was the star of ten silent films between 1914 and 1924, but really came into his own with sound. These included: *The Barrister* (1928), *Safety First* (1928), *The Bride* (1929), *Mrs Mephistopheles* (1929), *The Temperance Fete* (1931), *Don Quixote* (1932), *Marry Me* (1932), *Chu Chin Chow* (1934), *Birds of a Feather* (1935), *Royal Cavalcade* (1935), *Southern Roses* (1936), *Men of Yesterday* (1936), *Calling the Tune* (1936), *A Girl Must Live* (1939), *Salute John Citizen* (1942), *Variety Jubilee* (1943), *They Met in the Dark* (1943), *Waltzing Time* (1945), *Henry V* (1945), *The Trojan Brothers* (1946) and *The Pickwick Papers* (1952).

Although he began as a singer, George was more noted on the halls for his acting rather than his songs. The most closely associated with him *If You Were The Only Girl in the World* is not a music hall song at all. The song became enormously popular in the First World War, following his singing it with Violet Lorraine, not in the music halls but, significantly, in revue.

George Robey enjoyed playing with language in the tradition of hyperbolic chairmen of the old halls. "Kindly temper you hilarity with a modicum of reserve," he would urge his audiences, to be followed by the blunt, deflationary, "Desist".

His particular brand of audacious songs included: *Fancy That, Bang Went the Chance of a Lifetime, The Simple Pimple, Archibald, Certainly Not!* and *Oh How Rude.*

He made recordings for the Columbia and Broadcast labels.

George Robey enjoyed a very successful stage career. In the early 1930s he had made his first musical comedy appearance as Menglaus in *Helen.* The hero of the *Bing Boys,* the much loved Prime Minister of Mirth with his whitened face and huge, beetling eyebrows, was a star of the first magnitude and an enormous asset to *Jolly Roger* which was staged in 1933.

It was also through him that *Jolly Roger*, a new musical comic opera in three acts, gained publicity on which it had not counted. After a promising enough opening in Manchester and a week in Birmingham, the *Jolly Roger* company headed for the Savoy in London where they received surprising news. The fledgling actors' union, Equity, was about to ask them not to work with their star. Robey had refused to become a member of Equity, which was attempting to force a closed shop agreement in the West End Theatres. He was not the only actor, nor even the only prominent one, to do so, but it was he and his position which hit the headlines. Robey and *Jolly Roger* were ready to open at the Savoy and Equity was threatening the production.

Things came to a head at a meeting on 26 February 1933 at Drury Lane Theatre. Godfrey Tearle, Equity's president, made conciliatory noises in his speech but the unionists had packed the theatre with the faithful and to achieve a closed shop was their mission. Percy Heming got up to say that Rita John, who was financing the production from her own personal funds, had more than met all the conditions which Equity wished to demand of employers and another confirmed that the whole cast was behind her. The entire cast that was except Cecil Musk who declared that Robey has 'promised' he would join Equity, which was an outright lie.

By the time the meeting was finished the extreme unionists, led by Llewellyn Rees and Reginald Bach, had won the day through pure force of oratory; but they counted without Robey. The comedian reiterated that he could not join a union. To save Miss John, the show and the rest of the cast he sent Equity a ten-guinea cheque - the equivalent of a life membership – as a donation.

Once again Tearle was forced by his more militant colleagues to demur. The cheque was returned. They did not want his money but his submission to their 'law' and his membership. That Robey refused.

The test was to come. If Equity issued an order to the cast of *Jolly Roger* not to work, would anyone except Musk 'come out'? It was doubtful. Then George Robey let Equity off the hook. He joined Miss John as co-producer of *Jolly Roger*. Actor-managers were dispensed from becoming members owing to a possible conflict of interest. The union grabbed gratefully at the excuse to avoid a memorable climb-down (although many newspapers reported it as such) and *Jolly Roger* was able to open on 1 March 1933 without any further problem.

The opening night reception was quite tremendous, although Robey recorded: "The first

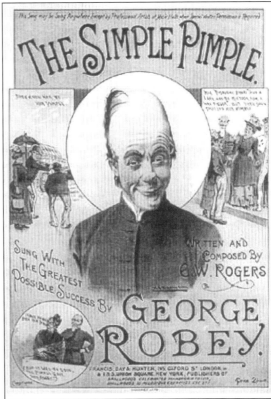

night audience on my first entry gave me the most prolonged ovation I have ever received. On that occasion, however, there was a principle involved and, no doubt, at least half that applause was for the principle."

Robey's characterful performances as Ben won laurels everywhere. The press enjoyed his performance as is evident in this write-up from the *Daily Telegraph*:

"From first to last he is pure joy, whether being made to walk the plank or rescuing beauty in distress, or giving a castanet solo on a couple of pairs of bones or sewing his little sampler. This is a really great performance."

Jolly Roger settled into the Savoy Theatre and, with Robey as one of its principle attractions, ran there profitably for three months.

George Robey had unintentionally polarized the closed shop ideal in such a way that Equity had succeeded in getting it accepted by West End managers.

Equity could now crush the rival Stage Guild in the same way that Equity itself might well have been crushed had Robey not adjusted his case to allow it to retain credibility.

On 5 June 1933 *Jolly Roger* transferred to the Lyceum Theatre. It had undergone a few alterations during its run. Robey had a new song *Thingamebob*. It retained its essentials and its grossly burlesque character and, above all, retained Robey and his performance: his eyebrows, his comicalities, his bits of business from tatting to turning (at 63) a pretty good cartwheel, his gravelly singing and his radiant star quality. The show ran for 199 performances, closing on 19 August 1933.

He made his first broadcast in 1936 in *The Spice of Life* programme and in 1937 was appointed a member of the BBC General Advisory Council. He made his television debut in 1938. His last appearance in pantomime was in 1942, as Mrs Crusoe at the Bristol Hippodrome.

During his life George organized many shows and concerts to entertain the troops in the First World War and raised over £500,000 for war charities, for which he was honoured with a CBE. His charity work continued throughout his life.

Publications included: *My Life Up To Now* (1908), *Pause* (1910), *Mental Fireworks* (1925), *Don't* (1926) and *Looking Back on Life* (1933).

George, a Founder of Chelsea Lodge, lived and worked to a distinguished old age, receiving a knighthood in the New Year Honours List for 1954, the year in which he died on 29 November in Saltdean, Sussex. He was eighty-five.

Rex ROPER

Variety Artiste. Born Charles Victor Knight, 17 October 1919, Bristol. As a youngster he was inspired to perform rope-spinning and whip cracking by seeing Will Rogers in the *Ziegfeld Follies* in the USA. His father was a Texas Ranger and champion sharpshooter Two Gun Rix, who started a Wild West show in England.

Charles Victor Knight became Rex Roper at the age of fourteen, having previously been billed as 'Young Rex' in variety. Worked in all the major variety halls and venues in Britain, appearing with the comedian Max Miller and singing duo Flanagan and Allen. He met Stan Laurel at the age of fourteen who had come to see the show *The Young and the Old*. Rex was top of the bill for the young and Harry Champion top of the bill for the old.

At seventeen Rex toured America with his sister Enid as Rex Roper and Maisie. Whilst over there he met 'Schnozzle' Durante and had the pleasure of cutting a cigar in half out of his mouth with his whip. Schnozzle kept the half cigar as a souvenir!

He volunteered and joined the RAF in 1939 and during World War II he served in Ralph Reader's *Gang Show* where he spent six years entertaining the troops in the Middle East. He also performed for King Farouk in Cairo. It was whilst in Cairo he met up with Tommy Cooper, who he later helped to join the Variety Artistes Federation when he became a professional entertainer. Once on a night

out with Tommy Cooper and some friends the comedian unknowingly caught the back of his trousers on a nail and his rear end was exposed. Rex and his friends decided not to tell Tommy about this. Tommy was wearing his new white jacket that was his pride and joy. On passing a mirror in a club they were at, Tommy decided to admire himself and noticed the rip in his trousers with his rear end protruding. Realising that Rex and his friends knew about it but had said nothing about it, Tommy proceeded to chase Rex and company out of the club.

Once the war had ended it appeared the RAF wanted Rex to stay another year as they conveniently lost his records. In charge of these was a certain **Peter Sellers**. Rex remembers: "I confronted Peter years later at an RAF Gang Show Reunion and reminded him about the lost records and not being able to leave immediately after the war. Peter said: 'You were doing too well entertaining the remaining troops for us to let you go.'

On completing the extra year and having done shows for the army, as well as the RAF, Rex was offered a post to take out another Combined Services Entertainment Show which he politely declined to enable him to get back home and continue where he left off before the war and back to civilian entertainment.

His wife joined the act, and they became known

as Rex Roper and Billie the Kid. They spent much time in Germany and France in cabaret and circus and eventually returned to England. They appeared on a number of television programmes as well as doing the Bailey Club circuit, supporting many top line acts. They completed two tours with Edith Piaf plus many TV shows and top clubs around the world.

From 1986 to 1992 Rex played host, and performed his routines as Sheriff of Silver City American Adventure Theme Park, South Derbyshire, where this real-life character brought the flavour of the Wild West, to thousands of visitors each year. His speciality act was roping, spinning a lariat in ever decreasing circles, while jumping through the loops he made. He dressed in a black suit and stetson. He had always wanted to visit the Will Rogers Ranch in Hollywood and his dream came true in 1992. There he won the Gold Award for roping and showmanship, Senior Division.

The name Rex Roper was used in the 1990 television film *Opposites Attract* where Rex Roper was an ageing cowboy played by movie star John Forsythe.

Rex tutored Justin Bohan the new star of the Trevor Nunn/Susan Stroman production of *Oklahoma* in 1999.

He recalls: "I really have enjoyed my time in variety. I have never made a great deal of money as a performer, but my life has been enriched by all the wonderful people I have worked with over the years. I am also a Past Chief Trap Guard in the Grand Order of Water Rats."

Rex Roper joined Chelsea Lodge on 20 January 1995 from Prospect Lodge No.7618.

Edmundo ROS, OBE

Bandleader. Born 7 December 1910, Trinidad, but brought up in Venezuela. Edmundo, did more than anyone to popularise Latin American music in Britain. His Scottish-Canadian father and Venezuelan mother hoped he would become a lawyer, but young Edmundo had other ideas and as a lad was quite rebellious. To instil some discipline they sent him off to a military college. It was here he developed his interest in music when he joined the college band. Initially expected to play a baritone euphonium, he was allowed to transfer to bass drum when it became apparent he was too small to handle the large euphonium - although he did grow up to become a 6ft. 2in. adult. He also learned to play the saxophone.

Leaving military college after four years Edmundo went straight into the Orquesta Sinfonica De Venezuela as a percussionist under the direction of Vincente Emilo Sojos. At the same time he ran his own dance band that was so popular it eventually became his full time job when he secured a contract to play in all the Venezuelan government's seaside hotels.

Ambitious and eager to further his musical knowledge he used his savings to travel, first to the United States and then to Britain, where he arrived in 1937. Wishing to study arranging at the Royal Academy of Music he needed a source of income. His first job was with Ciro Rimac's Rumba Band in the Cochrane revue *Follow the Sun*. After the show's run he toured the Continent with the same band.

In 1938 he was playing drums and tenor-sax in a small group at The Nest Club, where he was spotted during a visit there by Fats Waller. Fats asked Edmundo to play drums on a recording session that he made in London on 21 August 1938, when they recorded *Ain't Misbehavin', The Flat Foot Floogie, Pent up in a Penthouse, Music, Maestro, Please* and *A-tisket, A-tasket.*

Edmundo formed his own Cuban Trio and worked at several London night-spots including the Bermuda Club. By now he had discovered the public were favourably responsive when he added his own unmistakable reedy tenor vocals to the Latin-American rhythms he played and this now became an important part of his performance.

In March 1939 Don Marino Barretto was asked to assemble a band for the Embassy Club and Edmundo agreed to help and become deputy leader. This was the first Latin-American style orchestra to be formed in this country. After about a year, following a policy disagreement, Edmundo left and for a while became a full time emergency ambulance driver.

In August 1940 he reformed his own band, working at the Cosmo Club in Wardour Street, Soho as Edmundo Ros and his Rumba Band. The job was short lived when under wartime emergency regulations the basement club premises were requisitioned for use as an air-raid shelter. A booking at the St Regis Hotel off Piccadilly suffered a similar fate when the building was bombed during a performance, just two weeks after they opened there. Out of work and in desperation he took his band into the almost deserted Coconut Grove.

With Latin American rhythm now catching on with the British public, it wasn't long before fans of the music, and of Edmundo Ros, were flocking to the club and he was playing to packed houses.

In 1941 he began recording with his band on Parlophone where he released fourteen singles between 1943, switching to Decca about a year later. His 1949 Decca recording of *Wedding Samba* is reported to have sold three million copies over the years. It reached No.16 on the American Hit Parade. The Ros band appeared on one of the first Decca long play records to be issued in this country, *L.A. Rhythms*, a 10-inch album in June 1950.

Becoming something of a household name, late in 1942 he left the Coconut Grove to join George Black's London Palladium revue *Best Bib and Tucker, that* also featured Tommy Trinder and **Nat Jackley** and ran well in to the following year. At a similar time Ros was doubling at the Bagatelle (publicised as Mayfair's smartest restaurant). The band appeared in the 1945 musical film *Flight From Folly* and the spy thriller *Night Boat To Dublin* the following year. They also appeared in a night club sequence in the 1948 Huggetts' film *Wedding Bells*.

While continuing to appear at the Bagatelle, a venue he worked for twelve years, Ros doubled at other clubs. On 4 August 1947 his band returned to the Astor, a club Edmundo had been associated with since 1943. He had left in a bit of a frenzy in February after a disagreement with the management over the fact that the other band at the club (Harry Roy) was playing Latin American numbers. Ros made such a fuss over this, he was virtually sacked. He took up residency at Churchill's in Bond Street but after a few months the Astor asked him back with a new contract that forbade any other band there from playing Latin American. Harry Roy had left at the end of July.

In 1950 the band undertook one of its rare variety tours, but confined itself to just London theatres. Beginning at Finsbury Park Empire on 6th March they progressed a week at a time to Shepherds Bush, Chiswick and Hackney Empires and Lewisham Hippodrome, and after every second house it was back to the Bagatelle for the late-shift.

With seemingly little time for anything other than music, Edmundo sneaked in a lightning courtship and on 19th October 1950 married 24-year old Swedish model Britt Kolming at Paddington Register Office. They had two children. Some time later Britt left Edmundo and went to live with someone else in Columbia.

On 5 February 1951 the band made its first appearance in a public ballroom (other than a club or restaurant), playing a one-night-stand at Hammersmith Palais. This led to a two month season at the Strand Lyceum from May 1951, followed by one of their few out-of-London appearances, a Sunday concert at the Blackpool Opera House on 29 July.

By 1951 Edmundo was in a position to take a controlling interest in the Coconut Grove and he let it be known he intended to return to his old haunt, renaming it the Edmundo Ros Dinner and Supper Club. Only those mentioned in *Who's Who* were allowed into the club. The management of the Bagatelle Restaurant were loathe to lose such an excellent band who had been resident for nine years and persuaded him to stay. So came about the unique situation in which Edmundo recruited a new band for the Dinner and Supper Club the New Coconut Grove and fronted them both!

Not content with this, on 29 October 1951 he added another season at the London Palladium to his busy schedule which gave him seven weeks in the fast moving, colourful revue *Peep Show* with Vera Lynn, Jack Jackson and Bryan Johnson. Despite his hectic lifestyle and late nights, from New Year's Eve Edmundo was up early in the morning when he began a spell introducing *Housewives Choice* on the BBC Light Programme. With his easy manner he was an ideal compere and over the months presented various programmes. The band could currently be heard on air in the series *Golden Slipper Club*, a series that had featured the Ros band since it began in 1948. They played before a studio audience at the BBC's studio in the old Paris Cinema, Regent Street and broadcast Saturday evenings.

Each summer Edmundo took the band out of London's clubland on a three week 'holiday' break. During the summer of 1952 they played their first season at Blackpool's Empress Ballroom. The following year they toured several holiday resorts with a variety package and in 1954 really lived it up with five weeks at Monte Carlo Sporting Club. Obviously hooked on the Mediterranean air (and no doubt the agreeable fee) Edmundo and the band returned to the Sporting Club most summers throughout the remaining 1950s.

On radio they joined forces with the Ray Ellington Quartet for a Sunday lunchtime mix of musical styles in the series *Mr. Ros and Mr. Ray*. Edmundo was a mainstay of *Latin American Ballroom* that turned up on radio and television. On Radio Luxembourg the band appeared on *Topps With Ros* sponsored by Topps furniture polish while Edmundo presented a record show called the *Samuel Driver Record Club*.

Over the years he has recorded 123 singles with Decca Records, although during 1955 he did defect for a short while to Columbia to record four singles. Popular songs, show tunes and South American standards (some of them with unpronounceable names) were all presented in his inimitable style. He even had a go at the classics with the LP *Ros at the Opera*, just one of the dozens of albums he made.

Edmundo was also booked for private functions at parties arranged by King George VI at Windsor Castle. He claims to have taught the then Princess Elizabeth (now Queen Elizabeth II) and her sister the late Princess Margaret, to dance.

During April 1960 Edmundo's band was in Nigeria to play at that country's independence celebrations, attended by Princess Margaret who was reported to be a big fan of Ros. Edmundo was also a big favourite in Japan, playing numerous concerts there. He recorded an album of Japanese marches arranged in Western style.

The Edmundo Ros Orchestra appeared on the 1962 Royal Variety Performance at the London Palladium during October in a *Broadway Goes Latin* feature.

Reaching the mid-1970s and retirement age, Edmundo decided to give up while he was still on top and went to live in Javea, Alicante, Spain with his second wife Susan (née Smith), where they bought a house overlooking the sea. Few sightings have been made outside of Spain since, although he did present a series of record shows for the BBC in the early nineties.

In 1994 Edmundo conducted and sang with the BBC Big Band with Strings at the Queen Elizabeth Hall in London. **Stanley Black**, as guest conductor, also shared the stage. The concert was broadcast on BBC Radio 2 and was such a success that a Japanese recording company invited Edmundo into a recording studio in London to make yet another CD.

Not totally forgotten, he was awarded an OBE in the Millennium New Year Honours list and BBC TV screened a documentary about him during October 2000, in which Edmundo, fast approaching his 90th birthday, seemed to have lost none of his energy and wry humour.

There are currently more than 20 CDs of the Edmundo Ros Orchestra on the market.

Bro. Edmundo Ros, a member of the Grand Order of Water Rats, joined Chelsea Lodge in May 1952.

Charlie ROSE, PM LGR

Musician. Born 1906. Worked at the Windmill Theatre as a composer/musician. Honorary member **Ronnie Bridges** remembers him well as the two worked together in their professional careers:

"At the Windmill Theatre, Charlie composed the music and I wrote the lyrics. I knew he was a Freemason, but was very secretive about it. Shortly after the Second World War one tended to keep those things close to one's chest. However, he came to my initiation in Old Brentwoods Lodge, as well as passing and raising, exaltation into Royal Arch, and my installation as Master. We were very good friends. He was always very keen on Masonry and became secretary of the Chelsea Lodge after having been organist.

"When Charlie became secretary I was invited to play organ for his lodge – for free. I think organists were paid about two guineas those days. In my opinion he should have been as successful as Andrew Lloyd Webber. He was that brilliant. However, he was successful in Masonry and this is all he wanted. It made up for the lack of being successful elsewhere other than the Windmill. He should have been up amongst the Franz Lehar's of this world."

Ronnie and Charlie wrote some 200 songs between them and some of them were later published. In the year 2003 one was used in a film in New York called *Cha Cha on the Moon*, fifty years after they wrote it.

George Alfred Charles Rose was initiated into Chelsea Lodge on 17 May 1945. WM 1956. Died 12 March 1976, aged 82 years.

Austin RUDD

Vaudeville artiste/songwriter. Real name Arthur Rudd. Born 1869, Holborn, London. Choirboy in St Alban's Church, Holborn. Away from church he sang comic songs, took part in Gilbert and Sullivan operas and sang comic songs at temperance meetings in Holborn.

His first job was in the civil service and, having developed his talents as a comic vocalist at the temperance meetings, he wrote two or three songs and one evening presented himself at Deacon's Music Hall in Clerkenwell. He had a long wait until he was allowed to show his ability by singing

three songs for 'nothing per song'. After four of these 'extra turns', all without payment, he was given a whole week's engagement for which he received one pound. The first paid appearance at Deacon's was on August Bank Holiday 5 August 1889. He was billed as Arthur Rudd, which was his real name. *The Entr'acte* of 10 August reported on the entertainment at Deacon's: "included in the programme which has been framed for us this week have been the comic contributions of Mr Arthur Rudd, who is well-known and much liked here…" It appears he wasted little time making a favourable impression with the patrons of the hall.

Austin later wrote that on the programme with him in his first full week was Marie Lloyd with whom he struck up a lifelong friendship. Researchers have since found that information is not quite accurate as Marie Lloyd appeared at Deacon's between 24 June and 6 July. Austin wrote: 'I remember with sincere gratitude her praise of my initial efforts'. It would seem that her

engagement at Deacon's coincided with his 'trial runs'.

Austin continued at Deacon's, and on 2 September 1889also appeared at the Royal Cambridge Hall of Varieties, Bishopsgate, London. Continuing at these two establishments he added the Oxford to his nightly round of halls. Around this time he announced a change of stage name: 'Arthur Rudd begs to inform Proprietors and Managers that, acting under the advice of his agent (George Ware), he will in future be known as Austen Rudd'.

Whether by mistake or design, Austen often appeared in the bills as Austin, and by the end of the year the 'e' had been permanently replaced. Austin Rudd made his bow at a West End hall, the Oxford, just six weeks after his first appearance on any music hall bill. He stayed at the Oxford until December 1889, during which time Dan Leno, Little Tich, Harriet Vernon and **Harry Randall** starred at the hall. Other engagements followed in the next six months: the Metropolitan, the Bedford, the Middlesex, Hammersmith, and Marylebone. Carados writing in the *Referee* in their 20 April 1890 edition was impressed with Austin: 'One of the special successes at the Oxford has been Mr Rudd, a comic vocalist new to me, but evidently already in high favour with music hall audiences'.

His engagements at the Oxford were followed by the Pavilion, Trocadero and other London halls. On 27 October 1890 he started a provincial tour, taking in Southampton, Brighton, Chatham, Liverpool and Dublin.

His first pantomime appearance was at the Coliseum, Oldham at Christmas 1893, playing 'Sinbad' in *Sinbad the Sailor*. The following Christmas he returned to play the wicked uncle in *Babes in the Wood*. In 1896 he was booked for South Africa and in 1898 completed his first appearance in Australia for Harry Rickards, He revisited Australia in 1901.

Austin Rudd introduced several popular songs, many of which he wrote himself, but the song for which he is probably best remembered was *Bobbing Up and Down Like This*. Written by Worton Dand and Norman Reeve, this song was introduced by Austin in February 1899 and was a huge success. He enjoyed another big hit during the First World War with *Sailors Don't Care*.

Two cylinder recordings by Austin Rudd were made in August 1905: *They Found Me* and *Parody on Fancy Faces*. They were released on Sat Gold-

Moulded cylinders 611 and 612.

He composed a number of songs between 1889 and 1920 including: *Oh My, Is That the Eiffel Tower?, Love's Golden Dream Was O'er, Oh What A Relief, I Was Off; Oh, the Difference, I Put It Somewhere Else, That Was Dutch To Me, We Had To Part, How Pleasant, I'm The Lodger, I Saw Him Home, We Shall All Have To Wear 'em, The Pro's Supper, Suppose You Haven't Got It, I Must Have Been Drunk, Raid On The Club, She Was In My Class, I've Been And Got A Separation, Come And Help Your Daddy Shoot The Moon, After He's Taken His Wages, Red Light – Danger, It Never Could Happen Here, I Hope They Never Do It To Me Again, I Can't Get It Out, And She Did, I Supplied A Long Felt Want, Now We're Getting On, He's Making Ladies Laugh* and *The Body's Upstairs.*

Arthur Rudd joined Chelsea Lodge on 18 September 1926. As Austin Rudd he continued performing into the 1920s and in March 1929 he went to stay with his only son, Edwin, licensee of the King's Arms, Edgware Road, London, having just lost his wife. The idea was to help him run the pub. However Austin was taken ill shortly after his arrival and died from pernicious anaemia at the Lancaster Nursing Home, Swiss Cottage, London on 24 March 1929, aged 60 years. He was buried in the family grave at Morden Parish Church.

His son **Edwin Austin James Rudd** (a Lewis), a retired cinema proprietor, later a licensee, joined Chelsea Lodge 21 June 1929 from Lodge No 2743.

Leslie SARONY

Singer, comedian, dancer and composer. Born Leslie Legge-Sarony-Frye on 22 January 1897 in Surbiton, Surrey. His first stage appearance was in the music hall in 1911, when he joined the Arthur Gallimore Trio and earned five bob a week! Then he became a dancer with the Park Eton Boys. Only 5ft 2ins tall he was lively, dapper and very energetic and appeared in the revue *Hello Tango* at the Hippodrome in 1913 and in various concert party groups up to the war years, when he served in the London Scottish Regiment in France and was one of the few to survive the campaigns on the Somme. After the war he played in pantomime and in various revues such as *The Peep Show* (1921), *His Girl* (1922), the musical *Phi-Phi* (1922), *Dover Street to Dixie* (1923), *Brighter London* (1923), *The Whirl of the World* (1924), *Rat-a-Tat* (1925), in cabaret at the Cafe de Paris, and in music hall, *Up*

With the Lark (1927), *Show Boat* (1928), *Rio Rita* (1930), *Silver Wings* (1930) and many more. In the 1930s he moved into the variety world and became well-known on radio.

In 1935 he teamed up with Leslie Holmes (1901-1958), former dance band drummer and music publishing manager, to form the popular variety and radio duo the Two Leslies, appearing in a Royal Variety Performance in 1938 and touring North Africa, Italy and Germany to entertain the troops in the Second World War in a regimental concert party known as The Barnstormers. With Holmes at the piano, Leslie did his song and dance act and they enjoyed an immense vogue from 1935. The act itself was unusual in that both men were comedians as opposed to the more usual comedian and straight man set-up. Their records show how they overcame this. They took it turns to sing the verses of their songs, and sang the choruses together. Holmes sat at the piano while the more agile Sarony tap-danced. Sarony was known as 'Snodgrass' and Holmes was 'Birkentwitt'. Sarony had first broadcast in Savoy Hill days and was a pioneer of fast revue, introducing various characters in the programme *Radio Pie*. Holmes left the act in 1946 and, after working with another partner, Michael Cole, for three years, Sarony decided to become a solo entertainer, singing, dancing, and presenting a number of eccentric acts like *Jake the Peg* and, with animal noises, *There Was an Old Farmer Who Had An Old Sow*. He appeared in the film *Chitty Chitty Bang Bang* (1968) and *Yanks* (1979), in straight plays and on TV, remaining very active into his eighties. He was successful in a television series *I Didn't Know You Cared* in which he played a senile delinquent.

Roy Hudd describes Leslie Sarony as 'a tiny, old-fashioned, dynamic, forthright and hard-working dyed-in-the-wool professional'.

He composed about 300 successful songs which he and others performed, although he always considered song writing a hobby; these included: *Don't Do That to the Poor Pussy Cat* (1928), *Forty-Seven Ginger-Headed Sailors* (1928), *I Lift Up my Finger and I say "Tweet-Tweet"*, (1929), *Mucking About in the Garden* (1929), *Over The Garden Wall* (1930), *The Empire Party* (1930), *Jollity Farm* (1930), *Rhymes* (1931), *Three Little Times* (1931), *When the Guards Are on Parade* (1931, *Ain't It Grand to be Bloomin' Well Dead* (1932), *Wheezy Anna* (1933), *Come Pretty One*

(1934) and *When a Soldier's On Parade.* (1934). In addition he recorded under various pseudonyms. One song he wrote *Mucking About in the Garden* was under the name Q. Kumber. Leslie won the Golden Badge of Honour of the Songwriters' Guild.

Limericks have been around since Edward Lear, and Leslie reworked one called *Rhymes* recorded on 5 November 1931. The last line of each limerick was omitted to give the audience food for thought. The recording sold over a quarter of a million copies and was Decca's biggest selling record until Vera Lynn's *Auf Wiedersehn.*

On radio Leslie broadcast on the BBC frequently and was in the second *Henry Hall's Guest Night* on 24 March 1934.

Leslie appeared in a number of films including: *Soldiers of the King* (1933), *Rolling in Money* (1934), *Where's George* (1935), *Wedding Eve* (1935), *When You Come Home* (1947), *Noddy in Toyland* (1958), *Game for Three Lovers* (1965), *It Shouldn't Happen to a Vet* (1976) and *The Taming of the Shrew* (1980).

He went on to appear in seaside shows on the south coast. He was involved in the Arthur Lane production *The Golden Years of Music Hall* at Eastbourne alongside **Sandy Powell, Nat Jackley** and Elsie and Doris Waters. The show also toured South Africa for three seasons in the 1970s. Leslie appeared in a similar show at the Palace Pier Theatre, Brighton. This had the dubious distinction of being the last summer season at the old Victorian Theatre because a barge rammed the pier in autumn 1973 and caused considerable damage.

A greatly loved member of most of the professional organisations and fraternities, his contributions to the dinners of such bodies as the Grand Order of Water Rats and the Vaudeville Golfing Society were eagerly awaited.

Leslie Sarony was initiated into Chelsea Lodge on 20 July 1923. He was President of the Concert Artistes' Association from 1983-85. He died 12 February 1985, aged 87 years.

George SAUNDERS

Comedian. Born 11 August 1944. After 10 years service on minesweepers with the Royal Navy, George began his show business career as a Butlin Redcoat in Bognor Regis in 1971, working alongside such legendary greats as Jimmy Wheeler, Tommy Trinder and Sandy Powell. He is a keen golfer and in 1997 was voted Captain Jester

of the Comedians Golfing Society, who raise thousands of pounds for children's charities.

As a Comedian, George was the top compère on the Bailey Circuit for ten years, appearing with famous names from both sides of the Atlantic including Elton John, Roy Orbison, Tommy  Cooper, Les Dawson and Brian Conley. His comedy work has taken him to clubs, theatres and holiday venues the length and breadth of the United Kingdom, in fact from the Shetlands to the Channel Islands. More recently George performed at Jongleurs where his demonstration of the art of mainstream comedy received rapturous applause from a discerning audience.

As an actor he has appeared in *Lovejoy, Hercule Poirot, Middlemarch, The Chief* and various TV plays.

As an after dinner speaker George has entertained at hundreds of top venues ranging from The Institute of Directors, University College, Oxford and The Belfrey to Round Table, Rotary, Masonic and Sporting Dinners. He regularly performs at military, naval and police functions as well as corporate golfing days and charity events.

George is at his best working to an all male audience who demand their humour a little stronger. However, in mixed company he is well experienced in 'reading the room' and will tailor his act to the level required. He is a master at the risqué and innuendo; he can be bold and bawdy without being blue. Above all, very funny.

The Stage recently described him as: 'An endless reservoir of funny stories, smiling, smooth and unflappable'.

George William Saunders was initiated into Chelsea Lodge on 20 September 2001.

Arthur SCOTT

Secretary of the Variety Artists' Benevolent Fund. Born 1902. He lived near Brinsworth House, Twickenham, the retirement home where twenty-five ex-artistes are looked after. The fund helped organise the Royal Variety Performance and raised an average of £32,000 in the 1960s.

He met his wife, the former Miss Betty Foster, when they were playing in a concert party. They had two sons.

Arthur Scott joined Chelsea Lodge on 20 September 1957 from Aarheus Lodge No.6854. Died 11 April 1968, aged 66 years.

Peter SELLERS, CBE

(A Lewis). Actor and Variety Artiste. Came from a music hall family. His mother and father worked in an acting company run by his grandmother. His father, Bill, was a pianist and his mother, Peg, was a singer and dancer. Peter was a drummer in his early show business career and toured with several bands prior to his enlistment in the RAF as part of the service's Entertainment Division. During this time he developed his talents as an impressionist. Whilst in the services he met Michael Bentine and both appeared in the RAF Gangshow.

Born Richard Henry Seller on 8 September 1925 at Southsea, Hampshire, Peter said that Ted Ray was a major influence on his career. He was just 23 year-old when he rang Roy Speer the producer of *Ray's a Laugh*. He pretended to be Kenneth Horne, insisting that Sellers was a wonderful new performer and then 'Richard Murdock' came on the line to put in a few good words. Sellers did admit it was a wind-up but nevertheless Speer agreed to audition him. He was successful and became a regular member of the cast. The characters he played included Soppy, a small boy with a catchphrase 'Just like your big red konk'! *Ray's a Laugh* ran for 65 weeks, beginning on the BBC Home Service on 4 April 1949. Music was provided by The BBC Dance Orchestra conducted by **Stanley Black**.

The Goon Show is often referred to as the most famous radio show of all time; it made Peter Sellers, Spike Milligan, Harry Secombe and Michael Bentine household names. Peter's ability to mimic was legendary and by the early 1950s he was a well-respected impressionist. Each of his Goon characters had a unique vocal tone and his ability to switch from one to the other seamlessly is mind-boggling. Whilst Sellers and Bentine were in the RAF during the war, Milligan and Secombe were in the Army, serving in the Western Desert; all four enjoyed a unique brand of humour that continued throughout their lives. The *Goon Show* ran to a series of 10 from 1951 to 1960 broadcast on BBC Home Service. Michael Bentine quit after the second series. In the *Goon Show* Peter Sellers

played the part of Major Dennis Bloodnok, Bluebottle, Henry Crun and Hercules Grytpype-Thynne.

Whilst Peter was appearing regularly on radio he was also establishing himself as a movie star and he made his debut in the film *Penny Points to Paradise* in 1951, which was followed one year later by *Down Among The Z Men*. His first major success was in 1959 playing the union man, Fred Kite, in *I'm Alright Jack*. From then on he never looked back. It was also in 1959 that he appeared in the film *The Mouse That Roared* in which he played three of the major roles. Not content with that he also took on the role of several extras. In all he appeared in over 70 films between 1951 and 1980. *The Fiendish Plot of Dr. Fu Manchu* was completed just before his death. He will be best remembered as the indefatigably inept French detective Inspector Jacques Clouseau in the Pink Panther series, directed by Blake Edwards. Peter Sellers had become one of the greatest comedy actors of all time.

He was married four times. 1) To Anne Howe, 1951-1961, divorced; 2) Britt Eckland, 1964-1968, divorced; 3) Miranda Quarry, 1969-1971, divorced; and 4) Lynn Frederick, 1977 to his death in 1980.

Peter Sellers enjoyed success in the British Music charts with the Goons *I'm Walking Backwards for Christmas/Bluebottle Blues*, 1956. The record reached No.4. *Bloodnok's Rock and Roll/Ying Tong Song* reached No.3 in 1956 and No.9 in 1973. His solo records were: *Any Old Iron*, No.17 in 1957; *Goodness Gracious Me* (with Sophia Loren), No.4 in 1960; *Bangers and Mash* (with Sophia Loren), No.22 in 1961; and *A Hard Day's Night*, No 14 in 1965 and No.52 in 1993.

He also released some very successful LPs including: *The Best of Sellers* (1958), *Songs For Swinging Sellers* (1959), *Peter and Sophia* (1960), *Sellers Market* (1979), and *A Celebration of Sellers* (1993). He also appeared with other artistes in LPs: *Bridge on the River Wye* 1961 with Peter Cook, Jonathan Miller and Spike Milligan, *Fool Britannia* 1963 with Anthony Newley and Joan Collins.

The complete list of films starring Peter Sellers was: *The Trial of the Pink Panther* (1982), *Fiendish Plot of Dr. Fu Manchu* (1980), *Being There* (1979), *Prisoner of Zenda* (1979), *Revenge of the Pink Panther* (1978), *To See Such Fun* (1977), *Pink Panther Strikes Again* (1976), *Murder by Death* (1976), *Great McGonagall* (1974), *Return of the Pink Panther* (1974), *Soft Beds, Hard Battles* (1974), *Blockhouse* (1973), *Ghost in the Noonday Sun* (1973), *Optimists* (1973), *Alice's Adventures in Wonderland* (1972), *Where Does It Hurt?* (1972), *Last Goon Show of All* (1972) (TV), A *Day at the Beach* (1970), *Hoffman* (1970), *Simple Simon* (1970), *Wiltons - The Handsomest Hall in Town* (1970) (TV), *There's a Girl in My Soup* (1970), *Magic Christian* (1969), *Goon Show* (1968) (TV), *I Love You, Alice B. Toklas!* (1968), *The Party* (1968), *Alice in Wonderland* (1967) (TV), *With Love, Sophia* (1967) (TV), *The Bobo* (1967), *Woman Times Seven* (1967), *Casino Royale* (1967), *Wrong Box* (1966), *Caccia Alla Volpe* (1966), *Music of Lennon and McCartney* (1965) (TV), *What's New, Pussycat* (1965), *Carol for Another Christmas* (1964), (TV), *World of Henry Orient* (1964), *A Shot in the Dark* (1964), *Dr. Strangelove or How I Learned to Stop Worrying and Love the Bomb* (1964), *Telegoons* (1963) TV Series, *Pink Panther* (1963), *Heavens Above!* (1963), *Dock Brief* (1962), *Wrong Arm of the Law* (1962), *Waltz of the Toreadors* (1962), *Lolita* (1962), *Road to Hong Kong* (1962), *Only Two Can Play* (1962), *Mr. Topaze* (1961), *The Millionairess* (1960), *Two Way Stretch* (1960), *Never Let Go* (1960), *Battle of the Sexes* (1959), *Carlton-Browne of the F.O.* (1959), *I'm Alright! Jack* (1959), *The Mouse That Roared* (1959), *The Running Jumping and Standing Still Film* (1959), *Up the Creek* (1958), *Tom Thumb* (1958), *The April 8th Show (Seven Days Early)* (1958) (TV), *Yes, It's the Cathode Ray Tube Show* (1957) TV series, *Insomnia Is Good for You* (1957), *The Naked Truth* (1957), *The Smallest Show on Earth* (1957), *Idiot Weekly, Price 2d* (1956) TV series, A *Show Called Fred* (1956) TV Series, *Son of Fred* (1956), TV Series, *Case of the Mukkinese Battle Horn* (1956), *Man Who Never Was* (1956) *John and Julie* (1955), *The Ladykillers* 1955, *Our Girl Friday* (1954), *Down Among the Z Men* (1952), *Let's Go Crazy* (1951), and *Penny Points to Paradise* (1951).

Awards: Best Actor for 1959 British Film Academy Award; Golden Gate Award, 1959; San Sebastian Film Award for Best British Actor, 1962; Best Actor Award, Tehran Film Festival, 1973 and *Evening News* Best Actor Award, 1975.

Peter Sellers, a member of the Grand Order of Water Rats, was initiated into Chelsea Lodge on 16 July 1948.

He died of a heart attack on 24 July 1980, aged 54 years, ironically the day before a Goon Reunion.

SIRDANI

Variety artiste. Real name Solomon Sydney Daniels. Born 1899, Transvaal, South Africa, he was just ten when his father died. Shortly after this his mother brought Sydney and his two brothers to England. All three brothers ended up in show business. Len was a musician who later ran a music shop in Soho and Joe became a well-known drummer.

Sydney adopted the name Sirdani and affected an Italian accent for a radio broadcast – magic on radio. All the tricks had to be explained to a studio audience but he became very popular.

Solomon Sydney Daniels, a member of the Grand Order of Water Rats, was initiated into Chelsea Lodge on 16 June 1939. He died in 1982.

Keith SKUES, MBE AE LGR

Radio presenter and producer. Son of Richard and Doris Eileen (née Hughes) Skues. Born 4 March 1939, Timperley, Cheshire. Editor *Youth Fellowship Times* (1956-1958).

National Service, Royal Air Force - British Forces Network, Cologne, Germany (1958-1960). Civilian commission as an announcer BFBS. Service in Kuwait (1961) and Nairobi, Kenya (1961-1964). Whilst in East Africa he and an RAF team from Eastleigh successfully climbed to the summit of Mount Kilimanjaro (19,340 feet) on 2 October 1962. The following year he reached the summit of Mount Kenya (17,058 ft). Wrote articles for *East African Standard*; edited a weekly features page for *Sunday Post* and compiled a pop page each week for *Daily Nation*. His radio shows *Skues Me* and *Skueball Speshall* collected awards in 1962 and 1963. When Kenya gained independence in 1963 Forces radio closed down and Keith was posted to Aden early in 1964.

He returned to England after three months, resigned from BFBS and joined Radio Caroline as a disc jockey (1964-1965), Radio Luxembourg (1965) and Radio London (1966-1967).

Was chosen as a member of the original team of disc jockeys on BBC Radio One in 1967 and remained with BBC until 1974 during which time he broadcast regularly on Radios 1 and 2 as well as appearing on television. Radio shows included: *Saturday Club, What's New, Album Time, Radio*

One Club and *Night Ride*. Television shows included *Juke Box Jury, Top of the Pops, Wembley Festival of Stars, Pop the Question, Rough With the Smooth, Kenneth Williams Show, Ronnie Corbett Show, Thank Your Lucky Stars, Late Night Line Up, Pop Quest, About Anglia, The Weakest Link, Calendar* and *Look East*. His last series with the BBC was the award winning *Story of Pop*, which ran for 26 weeks on Radio One.

In 1972 Keith was appointed a vice-president of National Association of Youth Clubs (now Youth Clubs UK) whose patron was HM The Queen Mother. He is still actively involved in charity work up and down the country.

Pilot member of Aircraft Owners and Pilots Association, committee member for Scope (formerly Stars Organisation for Spastics), Lord's Taverner, Member of Society of Genealogists, Fellow of International Biographical Association, Squadron Leader (Rtd), RAFVR and Liveryman of the Worshipful Company of Clockmakers. He was made a Freeman of the City of London in July 1997.

In his spare time enjoys writing and to his credit are *A Short History of Heanton Punchardon, North Devon (1958), Radio Onederland (1968), This is Hallamland (1975), Cornish Heritage (1983), 21 Years of the Red Arrows (1985), Pop Went the Pirates (1994)* and *Centenary Book of Harringay Lodge No.2763* (1999). In addition he has written many articles for newspapers and magazines.

He has written sleeve notes for LP records, appeared in the film *Sunday Bloody Sunday,* been the voice behind many television and radio commercials and film documentaries and has represented Great Britain as a disc jockey in South Africa (1971).

Keith Skues was appointed programme director of Radio Hallam (South Yorkshire) in May 1974 and became a full board member. In 1977 he won the National Hit Pickers award and in the following two years compèred the National Radio Awards in London. By 1980 he was the longest serving programme director in Independent Radio.

Keith was granted his own armorial bearings from the College of Arms on 4 March 1981.

He was activated for military service in the Royal Air Force at the outbreak of hostilities in the Gulf where he served in Dhahran, Saudi Arabia as a public relations officer. Whilst on active duty his radio station made him redundant. On return to civilian life in March, 1991 he was offered a daily show for BBC Radio Sheffield which he presented throughout the year. In November 1991 Keith presented the afternoon show on BBC Radio 2.

As a squadron leader he attended a staff course at the NATO Defence College in Rome, June 1991 and in January 1992 he was presented with Gulf Campaign Medal. He returned to Saudi Arabia in 1992 as Public Relations Officer for the RAF Detachment in Dhahran for two months. He was a member of the public relations team at RAF Marham for the 75th anniversary of the Royal Air Force which was attended by five members of the Royal Family on 1 April 1993.

During 1993 he guested on Radio 2, BBC East, Radio Norfolk and British Forces Broadcasting Service.

A documentary television programme *Rockin' the Boat*, based on his book *Pop Went the Pirates,* was produced by ITV and transmitted in October 1994.

Keith was presented with the Air Efficiency decoration in January 1995 for services to the Royal Air Force.

In April 1995 he joined BBC East to present the regional share programme across East Anglia (10.00 p.m.-1.00 a.m.) each weekday evening. His programmes are broadcast nightly on BBC Radios Norfolk, Suffolk, Essex, Bedfordshire, Bucking-hamshire, Hertfordshire (3CR), Northampton, Peterborough and Cambridge. They have proved to be the most popular late-night listening in the whole of the country, his share of audience topping any other station in Great Britain, national or local, BBC or commercial radio. (RAJAR, Autumn, 2004)

Keith was appointed MBE in the New Year Honours List 2004. He joined Chelsea Lodge on 19 November 1999. PM of Harringay Lodge No.2763 (1984) and Sandringham Lodge No.9751 (2004).

Ron SMILEY
Entertainer. Real name Ronald Charles Rigby-Saunders. Born 9 August 1944, Manor Park, London. Took an interest in music from an early age. Whilst in primary education he was playing the banjo! Aged five he was an entrant in the *Carroll Levis Discoveries Show*. One year later he was attending the Betty May School of Dance. After four years at the Stally School of Art he attended Water Lane College of Music in Stratford, East London.

In 1959 Ron transferred to guitar and started the skiffle group 'The Tellafrets' doing the rounds on the London circuit and in working men's clubs. The same year he commenced an apprenticeship as a diamond mounter in Hatton Gardens, London.

His music was near and dear to him and in 1963 Ron joined Steve Marriott and 'Marriott's Moments', also played for sessions with various groups of the 1960s. He joined the Roy Royston

Sextet in 1965 playing on the dance band circuit as well as appearing in BBC broadcasts. This led to various sessions for Cyril Ornadel and the 'World Wide Record Club', in addition to working in London studios like the Marquee Club, BBC Maida Vale and Olympic Sound.

The next five years was to see Ron move to East Anglia, start the Nightriders country and western group. He toured the UK, Germany and Turkey and at the age of twenty-seven decided to retire from the business, marry and start a family.

Retirement did not last long. In 1975 he was back performing as a cabaret artiste on the London and Midlands club circuit working under the stage name Ron Smiley. He became an extra, walk on, also bit part actor for BBCTV, Anglia TV and Central TV. In 1981 he did a tour of Germany with Wayne Dobson as Ron Smiley 'The Musical Memory Man'. He married again in 1990 and returned to the club circuit as a cabaret artiste.

Ron Smiley was initiated into Chelsea Lodge on 20 November 1998 and two years later became a member of the International Masonic Poetry Society. The same year he discovered and

produced a synopsis of a concept of Masonic allegory applied to the ancient puzzle of Solitaire. With his wife Janet he started the Charity of the Mystic Tye organisation and its subsequent products in 2001 and the following year he received publication and distribution to concept of 'Solitaire' unto Masonic allegory by ARS Quatuor Coronatorum Transactions Correspondence Circle.

Cyril SMITH, PM LGR

Screen and stage actor. Son of Cyril E. and Elsa (née Goddard) Bruce-Smith. Born 4 April 1892, Peterhead, Scotland. His first London part was that of the Fairy Peasblossom in *A Midsummer Nights' Dream* for Beerbohm Tree on 10 January 1900 at Her Majesty's Theatre. Subsequently he toured with Sir Henry Irving as Geoffrey in *Becket*, continuing until 1905. Appeared in New York at the Criterion Theatre with John and Ethel Barrymore in *Alice Sit-by-the-Fire* and was seen in numerous films. He played the hen-pecked husband, Henry Hornet, in the successful comedy *Sailor Beware.* He was married to actress Anne Rendall.

Subsequently toured in *Dr Jekyll and Mr Hyde* and *Princess Clementina, Ever Been Had, Full Inside* and *Love Birds.* From 1917 to 1923 Cyril was engaged as assistant director by the Gaumont Film Company and was for a time editor of the *Gaumont Graphic.* He returned to the stage in September 1923 when he toured as Rodney Martin in *It Pays to Advertise.* Other productions he appeared in between 1899 and 1958 included: *A Midsummer Night's Dream,* Her Majesty's Theatre, London; *The Queen's Husband,* Prince's Theatre, Bristol; *Espionage,* Apollo Theatre, London; *Heaven and Charing Cross,* St Martin's Theatre, London; *Black Velvet,* London Hippodrome; *Black Vanities,* Victorian Palace, London, *Arsenic and Old Lace,* Strand Theatre, London; *Wild Horses,* Hippodrome, Bristol and *Sailor Beware,* Bristol Hippodrome.

To his credit are over 600 films some of which include: *His First Car* (1930), *The Mayor's Nest* (1932), *Innocents of Chicago* (1932), *Waltzes from Vienna* (1933), *The Roof* (1933), *It's a Cop* (1934), *The Black Abbot* (1934), *Wild Boy* (1934), *Lend Me Your Wife* (1935), *Hello Sweetheart* (1935), *Bulldog Jack* (1935), *Key to Harmony* (1935), *Brown on Resolution* (1935), *The Frog* (1937), *OHMS* (1937), *No Parking* (1938), *Return of the Frog* (1938), *The Challenge* (1938), *Traitor Spy*

(1939), *Sword of Honour* (1939), *The Flying Squad* (1940), *Law and Disorder* (1940), *One Exciting Night* (1944), *Meet Sexton Blake* (1944), *The Echo Murders* (1945), *Don Chicago* (1945), *Appointment with Crime* (1946), *It's Hard to be Good* (1948), *The Rocking Horse Winner* (1949), *The Interrupted Journey* (1949), *Conspirator* (1949), *Old Mother Riley, Headmistress* (1950), *Body Said No!* (1950), *The Dark Man* (1951), *Green Grow the Rushes* (1951), *The Night was our Friend* (1961), *The Third Visitor* (1951), *Mystery Junction* (1951), *Stolen Face* (1952), *The Lost Hours* (1952), *Women of Twilight* (1952), *Wheel of Fate* (1953), *The Strange Case of Blondie* (1954), *Burnt Evidence* (1954), *Sailor Beware!* (1956), *Light Up the Sky* (1960), *Over the Odds* (1961), *Watch it Sailor!* (1961) and *She Knows Y'Know* (1962).

Cyril Edward Smith was initiated into Chelsea Lodge on 17 May 1940. He became WM in 1953. Died 5 March 1963, London, aged 70 years.

Greg SMITH

One of the most successful independent film and television producers in Europe. On leaving drama school in London at the age of 15, Greg joined the Argyle Theatre Touring Company and then took a job as a runner to impresario Bernard Delfont. Subsequently he became an agent with MCA until its enforced closure in 1964. Shortly afterwards he established his own talent agency and assembled a respectable client list of producers, directors and writers.

With Norman Cohen he made two documentary films *Brendan Behan's Dublin* and *The London Nobody Knows.*

Their success enabled Greg and Norman to acquire the film rights to the BBC TV series *Dad's Army* for Columbia Pictures. This was quickly followed by the film of Spike Millgan's novel *Adolf Hitler - My Part in His Downfall.*

His return to Columbia Pictures led to the hugely successful *Confessions of ....* series, the first in 1974 - *Confessions of a Window Cleaner* grossed a higher sum per dollar spent than any other Columbia film in the non-US markets and gained entry into the Guinness Film Book of Records. At the same time he also produced *Never Too Young to Rock* for GTO and the award-winning documentary *The Importance of Being Dublin* in 1975, and for Warner Brothers, arising from his association with Leslie Thomas, the successful

Stand Up Virgin Soldiers in 1976/77.

Greg then persuaded the Rank Organisation to allow him to recreate *The Thirty Nine Steps,* starring Robert Powell, John Mills and David Warner, from Buchan's original book rather than as a remake of the famous Hitchcock version. In 1979 he turned his attention to television, both film and series. This led to the making of the series *Tropic of Ruislip,* for ATV's 1979-80 season. In 1980 came the TV movie *The Shillingbury Blowers* starring Trevor Howard and leading to the popular series *Shillingbury Tales* in 1981-82; then another Leslie Thomas creation *Dangerous Davies - The Last Detective,* both for ITC.

The early 1980s saw Greg making the independently financed movie *Funny Money,* as well as *The Boys in Blue* for the Rank Organisation and the TV series *Cuffy* for the 1982-83 season. He has been mainly involved in TV production since then, with a 12 x 1 hour series for Euston Films *Prospects* (1984-85) and two series of the Channel 4 sitcom *Rude Health. Great Expectations* followed in 1988-89, a 3 x 2 hour mini-series for The Disney Channel/Primetime/HTV, (starring Anthony Hopkins, Jean Simmons, Ray McAnally and John Rhys Davies) which received two *ACE* awards and four *EMMY* nominations.

Greg co-produced *Buddy (The Buddy Holly Story)* in association with **Laurie Mansfield** and Paul Elliott, opening at the Victoria Palace Theatre, London in 1989. The stage production proved a major hit worldwide and, having moved to the Strand Theatre, is now in its 13th year. *Buddy* has been nominated for many international awards including two English *Laurence Olivier Awards,* one US *Tony Award* and six *Canadian Dora Mavor Moore Awards*.

During 1987-8. Greg chaired the British Cannes Action Committee and the British Pavilion at the Cannes Film Festival.

In 1989-90, he produced Trevor Nunn's highly acclaimed production of *Othello* for BBC and *Primetime* (starring Sir Ian McKellan and Willard White), which received two BAFTA nominations and in 1992 Trevor and Greg joined forces again to make the world television production of Gershwin's operatic masterpiece *Porgy and Bess* for BBC, American Playhouse and Primetime based on Nunn's renowned Glynbourne and Royal Opera House production.

Following the production of *The Old Curiosity Shop* as a mini-series for Disney and Hallmark, starring Sir Peter Ustinov and Tom Courtney, and filmed in Ireland, Greg and Trevor Nunn jointly formed Circus Films Limited which in 1995-96 produced *Twelfth Night* for New Line. Also in 1995, and continuing his association with Laurie Mansfield and Paul Elliott, they brought *Jolson* to the Victoria Palace, London with Brian Conley playing the title role. The show collected the *Laurence Olivier Award* for 'Best Musical 1996'. In the spring of 1996, Greg produced Neil Simon's *London Suite* for RHI/Hallmark Entertainment Inc., to appear initially on NBC and which was filmed at the Grosvenor House Hotel and Shepperton Studios.

In 1998 Greg, as producer, set up a production studio site in Luggala Valley in the Wicklow Mountains of Ireland to film George Orwell's *Animal Farm* for TNT/Hallmark, using both live animals and animatronic doubles. Postproduction took place in London. Within weeks of the completion of this shoot, *David Copperfield*, again for TNT/Hallmark, commenced shooting in Dublin, with Greg as co-producer. This was accomplished in March 1999

During this period he and Laurie Mansfield also co-produced *Agnes Brown* with Jim Sheridan and Morgan O'Sullivan for October Films/Hells Kitchen.

In the London theatre, Greg and Laurie Mansfield, with Chris Davis, Chris Marino and Effective Productions, brought *Animal Crackers* - a Marx Brothers comedy classic - to the West End. In July 1999 Greg, Laurie, **Jim Davidson** and Robin Clark launched *Great Balls of Fire*, the Jerry Lee Lewis story, in Plymouth, Birmingham and at the Cambridge Theatre, London.

Greg Smith was initiated in Chelsea Lodge in November 1991.

Charlie SMITHERS

He is the Cockney comedian known for his highly individual and cheeky humour. Born 1927, Shoreditch, London. He served a hard showbiz apprenticeship in working men's clubs, pubs and private parties but gradually emerged to top the bill in the glittering night clubs and well-known cabaret spots and is the only comedian to have signed a three-year contract at the London Palladium. He achieved this at the age of 50 in 1978. On no less than nine occasions he has had the honour of performing for the Royal Family. Although a television break always eluded him, he has guested on numerous shows including *The Golden Shot, Meet'n'Greet, The Comedians, Des O'Connor Show, Celebrity Squares, Frankie Vaughan Show, Double Trouble* and *Look Who's Talking.* He has appeared in various radio programmes and has been a popular guest speaker at all of London's West End Hotels, including the Dorchester, Savoy, Grosvenor and Café Royal. The Variety Club of Great Britain presented him with the Top Award for Comedy in 1973. He has many comedy LPs to his credit, appeared in the film *Showcase* (1972) and has toured the world.

Charlie was the resident after - dinner speaker for five years at the World Sporting Club's monthly meetings and had a regular slot at boxing evenings staged at London's Grosvenor House Hotel by promoter Jack Solomons.

He made regular appearances at the Lakeside Club, Camberley and Cesar's Palace, Luton. He remains true to the traditions of his Cockney humour showing the funny side of life around him, digging at officialdom and captivating audiences wherever he appears.

"God gave you a mouth to do something with, so use it to smile! I served in the Fleet Air Arm during World War Two and often used to tell jokes to the lads when they were feeling a little depressed but I never really thought about being a comedian until I entered a talent contest at a dance hall in London after the war," he says. "The funny thing was, I entered as a singer. To be honest I am not a Frank Sinatra but I was willing to have a go. When I got on stage the people started laughing. I stopped the music, grinned and asked them to give me a chance. I started singing again and they laughed even louder! I made the most of it and although I flopped as a singer, it was a wonderful feeling to see all those smiling faces out there. I started getting bookings as a comedian at ten shillings (50p) a night and I had to work hard to earn it. But it was a great experience. I learned a lot about people and I learned my trade. Basically you have to get to know your audience. Once they like you, there is no problem. People will laugh at a friend, but not at a stranger."

He has entertained on the cruise liners working on the *Oriana* and *Canberra.* Charlie was on board the P & O liner *SS Canberra,* the second largest in the British Merchant Navy in the Mediterranean when the ship was requisitioned for war service in the Falklands on 3 April 1982. The crew, entertainers and customers were all taken off and returned to England and troops from 40 Commando Royal Marines, 42 Commando RM and 3 Parachute Brigade put on board. They sailed on 9 April on their voyage south.

Charlie, known as the comedian's comedian and who lived in a council house in Islington for much of his life, was Rat of the Year (1977) and King Rat of the Grand Order of Water Rats (1982), the oldest and most prestigious show business charity. He has helped raise small fortunes for needy causes. Charlie appeared in the Royal Gala Show at the Theatre Royal, Windsor in 1998.

He has worked with a veritable list of personalities that read like a Who's Who. They include: Baroness Thatcher, Des O'Connor, Ken Dodd, Mohammed Ali, Henry Cooper, Les Dawson, Steve Davis, Michael Caine, Sacha Distel, **Bert Weedon**, Lonnie Donegan, Bernard Delfont, Ginger Rogers, Donald O'Connor, Morecambe and Wise, Danny la Rue, Vera Lynn, Sean Connery, **Peter Sellers**, Harry Secombe, Anne Shelton, Tommy Cooper, **Joe Pasquale** and Lennox Lewis.

Charlie is still in demand and gives a hand whenever he is asked to make a personal appearance. He now lives with his wife Julie in Suffolk.

Charles Smithers was initiated into Chelsea Lodge on 17 November 1978.

Don SMOOTHEY PPAGDC

Theatrical Entertainer. Born 11 April 1919, Fulham, London. At the age of twelve he attended the famous Italia Conti School where his brother Len Lowe was a star pupil. Began his show business career as a child in 1932 appearing at the Holborn Empire in the production of *Where the Rainbow Ends.* This was followed by a time in *Cavalcade* at Drury Lane. His big break came at the outbreak of World War II when he joined the army and started entertaining as half of a double act with Len Marten and in 1942 became a member of the official army organisation *Stars in Battledress.*

Don was demobbed in 1946 and returned to civilian life and Variety by appearing at the Grand, Clapham Junction. He went through one or two name changes. For a time he was known as Don Maxwell and later, Chester Ladd.

He completed a long tour in *The Old Town Hall,* which was followed by Ralph Reader's *The Gangs All Here.* In 1950 he joined his brother Len, as half of a new act Lowe and Ladd. They enjoyed great success in this country as well as in Australia and

New Zealand but nothing lasts forever. The brothers broke up as Len wanted to do more television appearances. From now on Don would use his real name appearing as a solo comic until singer Dickie Valentine persuaded him that Tommy Layton wanted to work with Don and so Smoothey and Layton were born. They stayed together until 1960. Since then Don has continued his career working in Variety, numerous summer shows and pantomimes.

Asked what he has enjoyed most about his long time in show business Don adds: "I have to say appearing in the Royal Variety Performance in the presence of Her Majesty Queen Elizabeth The Queen Mother in 1982 in the feature *Underneath the Arches* was very special. This took place at the Theatre Royal, Drury Lane. In our particular sketch there was Roy Hudd, Joe Black, Tommy Godfrey, Billy Gray, Peter Glaze, Christopher Timothy and myself.

A highlight of the Royal Command Performance was the appearance of Ethel Merman who flew in especially from America to sing *There's No Business Like Show Business.* Sitting with her hairdresser before going on stage, she asked if she could have her hair all up front. The stylist remarked that there would be nothing to cover the back of her head.

'Honey, my name is Ethel Merman', replied the great singer, 'and I've never turned my back on an audience in all my life. So put it all up at the front and to hell with what anyone behind sees!'

"Backstage, dressed in a terrible old dressing gown, Ethel stumbled by mistake into our dressing room. She apologised, 'Oh boys I'm sorry, I've got the wrong dressing room.'

"'You'll be alright,' said my colleague Tommy Godfrey. 'You stay with us, darling,' and sat on her knee.

"'That's it boys' she exclaimed. 'I'm dressing in here from now on!' – and she stayed there for ages talking about American Vaudeville."

Don has been a member of the Grand Order of Water Rats since 1967. Past King Rat, 2001. His brother Len Lowe was also King Rat in 1983 the first brothers of the order to be made King Rats.

Donald Ralph Smoothey was initiated into Hamilton Lodge No.3309 on 21 April 1971. WM 1983. He was presented with Provincial Honours in 1995 by Companion of the Grand Order of Water Rats, HRH Prince Michael of Kent, KCVO. He joined Chelsea Lodge 19 May 1995.

Judd SOLO

Musician. Born 3 November 1916, Brick Lane, East London, son of a musical family. His father was a tenor and he was responsible for getting Judd to sing at the Dukes Palace Synagogue. When he was nine he sang at the old Pavilion Theatre in Whitechapel. In those days there were no house microphones!

On 3 September 1939 Judd immediately volunteered to join the army, and with only three weeks' training was sent to the BEF in France. He was later in the Dunkirk evacuation and was wounded resulting in his being discharged from the army.

As a violinist/guitarist he spent the later years of the war gigging around. His first big break came in 1945 when he was installed as the leader of the band at the exclusive Albany Club in Saville Row, a post he held for over ten years.

Bearing in mind his vocal talents, he then formed the Quartetto Italiano, which was to tour all over Europe and two trips to the USA. This group included the Grand Lodge officer Benny Wright, who was Master of Chelsea Lodge in 1960.

In 1963 he was established as the leader in the Roof Restaurant of the newly-opened Hilton Hotel in Park Lane. An unbroken stretch of fifteen years ensued, leaving in 1978 when the hotel decided to use pop groups.

Judd Solo was initiated into Chelsea Lodge on 18 March 1960. He now lives in a retirement home in Potters Bar, Hertfordshire.

Bernard SPEAR, PM LGR

Actor. Born 11 September 1919, Croydon, son of a Polish-Jewish father and Russian mother, he was educated at the Central Federation School, London. His first job after leaving school was for R & J Hills of Shoreditch, tobacco and cigarette manufacturers, as an invoice clerk when they found he could speak German and French. He was duly promoted to exports manager and earned an extra ten shillings a week, bringing his weekly wage to thirty-five shillings.

At the outbreak of World War II Bernard was conscripted and he served three years in the

Gunners (Royal Artillery) much of the time in Gibraltar. He met up with a few 'pros.' and they organised a concert party called the *Gunflashes,* which Bernard re-established at Woolwich Barracks in 1942. In Gibraltar the boys worked out of the Theatre Royal, which they kept going with plays, shows and pantomimes. It was in Gibraltar that Bernard Spear learned the trade of being a disc jockey. He remembers: "We were heard in Franco's Spain from where we used to receive fan mail and requests. They particularly liked our swing records." Whilst in Gibraltar he got into an argument with a bomb crater on Upper Rock whilst riding his motorcycle.

Back in Britain, after discharge from the Army, he began his career at the Windmill Theatre as resident comedian in 1943. This was followed by twelve years of touring in Variety and Music Hall shows until 1955 when he started in the West End in *Wonderful Town* with Pat Kirkwood, Shani Wallis and Sid James, followed by *Plain and Fancy* at Drury Lane. Worked with Van Johnson in *The Music Man* (1960-1961), *How To Succeed in Business* (1962-1963) and *Little Me* with Bruce Forsyth (1964-1965).He enjoyed a season of Moliere plays at the 'Mermaid' for Bernard Miles (1965-1966), then Vandergelder in *Hello Dolly* (1966-1967) at Drury Lane. The following year he played Sancho Panza in *Man of La Mancha*, which ran through into 1969. From 1970-1971 he appeared at the Prince of Wales Theatre in the Neil Simon musical play *Promises Promises.* In 1978 he was invited by the author David Mamet to appear in his one-act comedy *Duck Variations* at the Regent Poly Theatre. He then worked for Jonathan Lynn in Thornton Wilder's *The Matchmaker,* this for the Cambridge Theatre tour, which proved so successful that it transferred to Her Majesty's in the Haymarket.

In the world of radio from 1945 until 1983 Bernard made over three hundred broadcasts from *Henry Hall's Guest Night* to *Workers' Playtime.* He was in 300 airings as Loopy Lou, the Mexican chef who introduced chilli sauce to the Great British listener. He also had his own *Mid-Day Floor Show*.

Bernard worked for some of the most prestigious studios, both here and on the continent, giving credible voice characterisations, including, for one engagement, such differing creatures as an elephant, two flies, a bumblebee, a rabbit, a hare, a wolf, a bear, a stork and two mice for a Thames TV programme. His television commercials include a

two-year stint as the White Tide Man (1962-1963) and the Breville Toaster Man in 1970.

He appeared in many films including *Daleks' Invasion Earth 2150AD,* (1966) with Bernard Cribbins, *Chitty Chitty Bang Bang* (1968) where he played one of the comedy spies and when Barbra Streisand came to this country to film *Yentl* (1983) she booked Bernard to play the tailor who shared all her scenes. He worked with Tony Curtis in *Drop Dead Darling*, Peter Cooke and Dudley Moore in *Bedazzled*, Barry Humphries in *Adventures of Barry McKenzie*, Frances de la Tour in *Wombling Free* and *Not Quite Jerusalem* for Lewis Gilbert.

Bernard was the first British actor to appear live on London ITV in 1955 *Xavier Cugat Show*. He made his television debut at 'Ally Pally' (Alexander Palace) in 1950 in *Rooftop Rendezvous*. He played straight roles on TV in *Quatermass, Mother Courage* with Dame Flora Robson, The *Maigret* series, *The White Guard*, Harold Pinter's *Night School* and the Somerset Maugham series. He was also present when the new Rediffusion Studios opened in 1960 and he and Stanley Holloway played the two main comedy characters in the lavish *Arabian Nights* special.

He took the role of Mike and Bernie Winter's agent, Lionel Ross, "The Lew Grade of Lewisham", in Vince Powell and Harry Driver's *Mike and Bernie* (1971-72), the stand up comedians' first venture into sitcom. He played numerous character parts since then including a seven-year stint of *Never Mind the Quality* and his own series for Thames TV, *My Son Reuben,* especially written by Vince Powell. He celebrated the BAFTA prize awarded for the best play on television in 1977 for the BBC's *Barmitzvah Boy* by Jack Rosenthal, where he played the part of the father, Victor Green. He took the role of Morris Ransome, the chairman of the Market Traders' Association, in the short-lived Granada soap *Albion Market* from 1985-1986. His final appearance on television was in the sitcom *My Family* (2003).

He mastered most known dialects and accents and featured in such diverse parts as a French sculptor with Charlie Drake and Irene Handl, an Irish surgeon in the *Lister Story* for BBC TV. He played a Hampshire businessman with Milo O'Shea in the *Dobson Doughnut,* an American impresario in the *Lenny Henry Show*, an Austrian artist in Pinter's *The Schoolmistress,* a Brummie removal man in the *Kelly Montecito Show,* many stand-up comedy appearances in *The Good Old Days.* All these apart from guest appearances in such shows as *Celebrity Squares*, *Love Thy Neighbour* and *The Jim Davidson Show*.

Altogether Bernard made over 300 feature and guest appearances on television spanning fifty years.

For services to Charity he was made a Freeman of the City of London in 1982.

He returned to cabaret and after-dinner speaking and even hosted a night at the Royal Albert Hall for the Burma Star Reunion to celebrate the new Century.

Said Bernard: "I've been a lucky lad and I know it. A wonderful marriage to ex-dancer Mary Logan, (great-niece of the famous Marie Lloyd), who has written a great book, *Bring on the Dancing Girls*, about her 'war' as a dancer entertaining the troops. We met in a Summer Show at Hunstanton, Norfolk in 1948, run by Carroll Gibbons, who tried his luck as an impresario, as a change from only the Savoy. We developed a double-act 'Bernard Spear and Mary, To Say Nothing of the Dog', a reference to the pet who shared the stage with us. We married in 1949 and have never looked back. We have a smashing son, Julian Spear, who works in the music business running his own independent promotion company, Red Shadow. There is one grandson, Taran who is a drummer in the punk band Anonymous Tip, a grand-daughter Talitha, who is still at school, and a daughter-in-law, the actress Carol Royle."

Bernard Spear was initiated into Vaudeville Lodge No.5592 in January 1955 and became Master in 1963. At the time he was appearing in *How To Succeed in Business,* so he never presided at one festive board in his year of office. Joined Chelsea Lodge 17 May 1968. WM Chelsea, 1980. LGR, 1973. Died 9 May 2003, aged 83 years.

STANELLI

Comedian and musician. Real name Edward Stanley De Groot. Born Dublin, 1895. Began his career as a classical musician. He was a scholarship student at the Royal Academy of Music and the Royal College of Music studying violin. He guested as conductor of the Bournemouth Symphony Orchestra, later conducting the London Symphony Orchestra and the Hallé Orchestra. He composed several tunes.

Made his first music hall appearance at the Metropolitan in 1914. He worked a musical double act with a partner as 'Stanelli and Douglas', appearing at the Royal Variety Performance at the London Coliseum on 1 March 1928 as *Fiddle Fanatics*. Later Stanelli worked as a solo comedian in variety and on radio and then teamed up with another partner as 'Stanelli and Edgar'. The act comprised two violinists who played both popular and classical compositions. They also danced, tap/soft shoe, while they played in unison. Eventually the act broke up and Stanelli went solo in his own touring show *Stanelli's Stag Parties, Stanelli's Bachelor Parties and Stanelli's Crazy Cruise.*

He had a good ear for sound and this gift was exploited on the stage in his ingenious variation of the one-man band, this took the form of a collection of car horns – some bulb, some electric – mounted on a frame and 'played' as an instrument by their dextrous owner.

In August 1935 Stanelli appeared at the Radio Olympia broadcast on the BBC together with **Leslie Sarony**, Tommy Handley and Geraldo and His Gaucho Tango Orchestra. In January 1946 he appeared on the BBC Home Service when he conducted the Queen's Hall Light Orchestra for a performance of his own composition *Atlantis.*

Appeared in the films: *Greek Street* (1930), *Fiddle Fanatics* (1931), *British Lion Varieties No.1* (1936), *Pathetone Parade of 1938* and *The Adventures of Jane* (1949).

On 2 April 1937 Stanelli made his television debut, introducing viewers to the 'Hornchestra', another device of his own creation – and already well-known to radio listeners – which comprised a weird collection of electric and bulb motor-horns on which he played jazz music.

Edward Stanley De Groot was initiated into Chelsea Lodge on 19 December 1941. He died 12 February 1961, aged 65 years.

Harry STANLEY, PM LGR

Magician. Born 29 November 1905, London, son of Barnet and Rose Ruderman who ran a tobacconist and sweet shop in Stoke Newington. He first took an interest in magic whilst at school and once a week gave a magic concert in his parents garden shed and charged a penny a show. As a schoolboy he used to go along to Hoxton Music Hall to see the various acts.

He became a musician playing guitar and

singing. He played with various North London groups before joining the Jan Ralfini Band. In turn he joined Sid Seymour's Band and it was whilst in Blackpool he was recommended to Jack Hylton's Band. He made various recordings with Hylton's Band and on one occasion radio disc jockey Christopher Stone described his voice as: 'not a crooner, but he is a true singer'.

Harry toured with the Hylton Band and in the 1930s went to Germany but by then had changed his name by deed poll from Ruderman to Stanley. The German authorities under Adolf Hitler said to Hylton that they did not want any Jewish musicians playing in the concert which also featured Peggy O'Dell. The German secret police found out that Harry was Jewish and asked Hylton to keep him at the back of the band for disobeying their instructions. The band returned to England and played regularly at the London Palladium and other well-known venues.

In 1934 Harry decided to give up the work with the Jack Hylton Band and concentrate on his hobby – magic. He first bought a shop in Wardour Street and a factory in Peckham. He went into partnership with Jack Hughes (maker of magic tricks) and comedian Arthur Dowler, who also performed magic tricks and later bought them out. In 1945 he became founder, manager and owner of the Unique Magic Studio for 30 years, following his demobilisation from the Army where he served in the Royal Artillery.

Harry issued conjuring's first regular fully comprehensive instruction sheets and helped to pioneer the sturdy purpose-built children's apparatus magic which is all taken for granted today. With his wife, Rita, published the first magic magazine *The Gen*. He became the most important publisher of magical books in the last seventy years, revolutionising in the process techniques in card, close-up, and manipulative conjuring which described that at last magic had arrived in the modern age.

He acted as a pioneer in the areas of secret two-way communication apparatus and was at the vanguard in the discrete use of remote control mechanisms in tables and rising cards, and that of magnets in coins, both individual growth industries at the time in Europe and the USA. In a pre-video age Harry produced a series of magicians' educational films, in addition to acting as associate producer of *Focus on Hocus*, the first magic show on ITV. In addition he gave concerts and entertained at top social functions, including a private party at the home of Lord and Lady Mountbatten where he brought across magicians from America complimenting them with top British names, including **David Berglas**. On another occasion in 1950 he hired the Scala Theatre in London for one week when he promoted the top magicians from Norway, Denmark and Holland. Representing Great Britain were **Maurice Fogel** and David Berglas.

He went on to manage the career of the first 'Young Magician of the Year', Johnny Hart, who made six appearances on the *Ed Sullivan Show* in America as well as performing in Las Vegas.

BBC TV Producer John Fisher remembers Harry Stanley : "While his achievements were important, he never became self-important. It is a fact of life that in any sphere of activity the pioneers and innovators are often the ones soonest forgotten. Harry Stanley pioneered a magical venture the like of which had never been seen before and which

may not be seen again. The world of magic has an obligation never to forget him."

He was the author of a number of books on magic and he wrote the bio-graphy of **Sandy Powell** *Can Your Hear Me Mother* (1975).

Harry Stanley with Sandy Powell

Harry married Violet (known as Rita) Parks in May 1929 and they had one son Bill (1946). He decided to retire in the mid-1970s and sold his magic studio to a group of people who asked to pay back the money over a period of years. Harry reluctantly agreed. The men never honoured the contract and Harry was left destitute. In fact he was so upset that he threw away all his souvenirs of the world of magic, including books he had written over years and magazines to which he had contributed articles and moved with his wife to Pevensey Bay, Sussex. In 1987 they moved to Shropshire to be near their son.

Harry Stanley was initiated into Chelsea Lodge on 21 January 1949. He became WM 1962-1963 and was later honoured with LGR. He initiated his son **William Stanley** on 12 September 1968. Harry compiled *The First Seventy-Five Years of Chelsea Lodge* published in 1980. Died 20 September 1991, aged 86 years.

Cyril STAPLETON

Orchestra leader. Son of a Nottingham building worker, Cyril was born on 31 December 1914 at Mapperley, Notts. Given an old fiddle as a lad, by the age of twelve he had made his first broadcast on solo violin from Nottingham's 5NG local radio station. Like so many of his contemporaries, Cyril's early career found him playing in cinema 'pit orchestras' accompanying silent films. Musical scholarships took him to Trinity College of Music in London and to Czechoslovakia, where he studied under Sevcik, the famous teacher of the violin.

In 1932 Cyril joined Henry Hall's BBC Dance Orchestra, appearing on radio and on 78s made by Columbia Records. By 1937, after a spell with Jack Payne and a few café orchestras, he was leading his own eight piece at Fischer's Restaurant in London's New Bond Street. In 1939 a larger outfit he assembled for Jack Hylton at the London Casino was short lived when war intervened and the venue closed.

Cyril married comedienne and impersonator Beryl Orde in December 1939.

After a few months with Billy Ternent's BBC Orchestra Cyril enlisted for war service with the RAF, initially as an air gunner, where he played in a number of service bands and toured America as a violinist with the RAF Symphony Orchestra.

Following his demob in December 1945 he worked with the bands of Fred Hartley, Geraldo, The London Studio Players and just about every large classical orchestra, including the London Symphony, National Symphony and the Philharmonia, until in July 1946 he went back, leading an eleven piece, to Fischer's Restaurant, broadcasting from there every Tuesday night.

Decca Records signed him up and so began a long association with the label. He recorded 80 singles, sometimes backing David Whitfield, Jimmy Young, Reggie Goff, The Stargazers, Dick James, Sally Douglas, Pearl Carr and Bob Dale.

In June 1947 Cyril moved down the road to The Embassy Club, with Dick James and a newcomer Pam Deeming as vocalists. Radio work continued on the likes of *Band Parade, On The Sweeter Side* and *Morning Music* and from 2 February 1948 his own series *Cyril Stapleton Entertains* with songs from Sally Douglas and Denny Dennis.

During the summer of 1948 Cyril took the band on a tour of holiday resorts including Weston-Super-Mare, Ramsgate and Great Yarmouth. They also played a three-week season at Green's Playhouse Glasgow.

More radio work followed: from January 1949, a new Saturday evening BBC series *Golden Slipper Club* where he shared the bandstand with **Edmundo Ros**. On Radio Luxembourg there was the regular Sunday *Treasure Hunt*. On Tuesdays he was back on the BBC with *Hit Parade* that featured his 35-piece string orchestra and on Thursdays joined Reggie Goff and the **Tito Burns** Sextet on *Let's Make Music*.

His wife Beryl collapsed shortly after appearing on a *Music Hall* show and later died. On Monday 8th January 1951 he married 22-year old Sheila Shardlow the daughter of a Lieutenant Colonel who had served in India, where she had been born. He rushed back 400 miles from Edinburgh, where the band was appearing, to make the Paddington Register Office ceremony.

The early fifties usually found the Stapleton Band on tour, while regularly hopping back to London for their many broadcasts; these included *Let's Make Music* and *Variety Bandbox* where they replaced the Billy Ternent Band (who'd been on the show seven years) in September 1951.

For two months from March 1951 the orchestra followed Ted Heath into a resident season at London's Savoy Hotel. **Dave Carey,** Jean Campbell and The Staplejacks were handling vocals.

Now leading what was being billed as 'Britain's biggest dance band' the 20- piece outfit played an early summer season at the Palace Ballroom on the Isle of Man, followed by two weeks at Blackpool's Winter Gardens. Each Sunday they had to travel back to London for their *Variety Bandbox* duties.

He recorded a few LPs on the Decca label including *Paris After Dark, Italy After Dark, New York After Dark* and *Music for a Starry Night*.

Cyril's first entry into the Top 40 charts in England occurred in the summer of 1955 with *Elephant Tango*. He enjoyed four more hits: *Blue Star (The Medic Theme), The Italian Theme, The Happy Whistler* and *Forgotten Dreams*. Although it was never a chart success the *Children's Marching Song, Nick Nack Paddy Wack,* from the film *Inn of the Sixth Happiness* was a 'turntable' hit.

Cyril's was now regarded as one of the most popular broadcasting bands and from January 1952 began a new monthly radio series *Hit Parade*, which featured Eve Boswell, Carole Carr, Dick James, **Lee Lawrence** and The Stargazers. However, there were rumours of something going on at the BBC and that Cyril was involved. There were tales of 'secret' auditions being held in Studio One at Aeolian Hall (in New Bond Street, London). The truth is that Cyril had been approached by the BBC to form a new radio big band to rival anything that was available anywhere. The 'secret' auditions were being held by him to recruit the 18-plus top class musicians who would make up this all star 'show' band.

Despite numerous denials, the BBC finally made an official announcement at the end of July heralding the forthcoming arrival of the BBC Show Band. Cyril announced that he would be disbanding his touring orchestra on 7th September 1952 to take up leadership of the Show Band. The band's first broadcast was on 2 October, the beginning of a commitment that saw them on air three times every week. Vocalists on the early shows were **Lee Lawrence**, Jean Campbell, Louise Trail and Johnny Johnston with his Johnston Brothers and Johnston Singers. The BBC Show Band programmers soon became a national favourite. Stars from America appeared on the show including Nat 'King' Cole and Frank Sinatra.

1955 saw the Show Band on television every other week on a Sunday evening with Janie Marden, Ronnie Hilton and The Stargazers. The band featured on November's Royal Variety Show at London's Victoria Palace. Cyril and his Show Band also appeared in a CinemaScope film *Just For You* which was released to the Odeon Cinema circuits late in 1955.

Cyril, with his growing family (a daughter in 1952 and twin boys in 1954), was voted by readers of The Daily Mail as Britain's most popular musical entertainer in their 1955 national Radio and TV Awards poll.

As so often happens when a radio or television series becomes very popular it is taken off the air. Such was the case with the BBC Show Band after a very successful run of almost five years. The final show was broadcast on the BBC Light Programme on 28 June 1957. However, when one door closes another one opens and the new Cyril Stapleton Show Band began a countrywide tour with a TV show celebrating 21 years of BBC Television on 7 September 1957.

In 1958 the band began a series of BBC TV shows and in April were on the opening show from the Corporation's new Birmingham studios.

On 3 November 1958 Cyril and the band were at the London Coliseum on another Royal Variety Performance. They appeared on BBC Radio in a series called *Swingalong* and Cyril had a spell as presenter of *Housewives Choice.*

The touring came to an end in 1961 when Cyril took on his first London ballroom residency at the Hammersmith Palais. This was followed, in 1962, with a residency at the Strand Lyceum Theatre.

In 1966 he became artistes and repertoire manager at Pye Records and recorded nine singles of his own, as well as overseeing numerous recording sessions with bands and singers.

Cyril Stapleton was initiated into Chelsea Lodge on 20 November 1953. He died from a heart attack on 25 February 1974, aged 59 years.

John STAR, AIMC

Comedy Magician. Born Reading, Berkshire 1941. Took up magic whilst at school at the age of fourteen after being beaten up! Was a DJ at the Playboy Club from 1966-1968.

In the 1960s met up with David Bailey and Lord Litchfield who helped him 'develop' his interest in photography. He is still a keen photographer and is asked to produce work for magazines, calendars and private functions.

John has been a professional magician for over 30 years and has performed both with his comedy magic in cabaret, TV, theatre and also in the more intimate settings of close-up magic at tables in

some of Europe's finest restaurants.

He is an Associate of the Inner Magic Circle, the Society of American Magicians and a member of the Magic Circle, Hollywood, USA. His humour has been compared to 'a British Woody Allen', with his magic second to none. His business card tells us he is guaranteed to amuse and amaze! Given the Freedom of the City of London, April 2003.

John Star was initiated into Chelsea Lodge on 20 September 1996.

Maurice STERNDALE

Musician. Violinist and arranger. Born 1897, Durban, South Africa. He was a scholar of the Cape of Good Hope University and after his solo violin act he teamed up with Harry Revel. Came to England in the 1930s with a touring group, husband and wife comics **Billy Caryll** and Hilda Mundy. He then went solo and toured England with his act *Cat and the Fiddle,* and in the late Thirties joined drummer **Joe Daniels** when they appeared on early television. Subsequently they both joined Harry Roy. Maurice went on to become the longest serving member of the Harry Roy Band from 1932 to 1945 appearing on hundreds of records on the Parlophone label.

During the Second World War Maurice drove ambulances in London and when war ceased, he toured with Tony Britton in various musical comedies. He then did summer seasons in Brighton and bought a sea front property at Westgate-on-Sea, Kent. He was married to Sonia, dancer and vocalist who, in 1986, told *Memory Lane*: "Maurice was always up to some little trick. We never knew what he would do next. A good example was when we were playing *The Navarro Trail* and we suddenly saw Maurice wearing a headband of feathers and stirring a pot on a fake camp fire!"

Described as a much-loved musician, an admirable little man, kind and gentle full of fun, with a twinkling smile and a mildly teasing sense of humour, Maurice Sterndale was initiated into Chelsea Lodge on 20 September 1951. Died 27 March 1986, aged 89 years.

Eric TANN, PM LGR

Musician. Trombone/arranger. Born 15 November 1911, East Ham, son of an East Anglian military bandmaster and brother of tenor saxophonist Ernie Tann. At the age of eleven he broadcast on the BBC's *Children's Hour.* Did first professional work at Birmingham Palais, then moved back to London and joined Hal Swain in the late 1920s. Worked with Savoy Hotel Orpheans, **Bennie Loban**, Sydney Kyte and Arthur Roseberry. With **Roy Fox** (1932-4). Briefly with Alfred Myerscough's Band before joining Henry Hall in November 1934. Played regularly in Louis Levy's Orchestra for film work from the mid-1930s. With Jack Jackson (1934-5), Ambrose (1935) and with Jack Harris and Eddie Carroll's Band (1938), before working with Lew Stone (1939-40). Joined Royal Army Ordnance Corps (1940) and played in regimental band before becoming leader of its dance band, the Blue Rockets, in 1941. Injured in 1942 and discharged from Army in spring 1943. Worked with Geraldo (autumn 1943 to January 1945), followed by Mantovani and then formed own band (March 1945). Played trombone with Harry Roy (spring 1946), then worked as musical director for an Australian radio station and led own band before returning to Britain in summer 1949. Freelanced on sessions and worked with George Melachrino and Cyril Ornadel in the 1950s becoming a member of the augmented Skyrockets Orchestra, playing in the pit and on stage at the London Palladium. He gave up regular playing in 1960 to work as a conductor and arranger. Became musical director for the Moss Empires theatre chain which entailed choosing the musicians for all their theatres, including the Palladium.

Eric was Musical Director for the 1964-1967, 1970, 1971, 1974 and 1975 Royal Variety Performances all held at the London Palladium.

Eric and his wife, Doris, emigrated to Australia in 1976, to join their two sons and daughter, who had settled out there. Eric taught brass players until failing health caused retirement following a stroke.

Eric Charles Tann was initiated into Chelsea Lodge on 21 July 1939. WM in 1957. Later appointed LGR. Died Adelaide, Australia, 28 July 1988, aged 76 years.

Laurie TAYLOR, PM LGR

Band Leader. Born 2 November 1946, Hammersmith, London 'to be near his mother'. Interested in music from an early age and is reported as holding a clarinet when he was eleven. He knew even then he was destined to enjoy a career in music. In his early teens he would buy *Melody Maker* and read with interest the various jobs on offer to musicians. In one particular edition he noticed 'Musicians wanted to register for ships. Sydney Lipton Orchestra'. In 1970 he turned professional, worked on *Oriana*, and became the youngest bandleader (aged 24) to work for P & O.

Laurie worked at sea for three years and, coming ashore, joined Sydney Lipton's function band playing clarinet and saxophone and working extensively in London's Five Star hotels. In 1975 he took over as 'fixer' of musicians for Lipton and three years later through strange circumstances was offered the chance to learn the agency side of the music business. He recalls: "It seemed a natural progression, and one with which I was very happy, so I grabbed it with both hands."

When Sydney Lipton's wife became ill in the late 1970s he decided to semi retire and was looking to sell the business. In 1982 Laurie visited his bank manager the result being he took over the Lipton empire some twenty years after seeing the advert in *Melody Maker* when he was a sixteen year-old.

Since 1982 Laurie has continued to lead his own band for some of the largest corporates in the world, as well as Royalty. He provided the band for Prince Andrew's engagement to Sarah 'Fergie' Ferguson, and also for her father, Major Ronald Ferguson, at the Guards Polo Club, where the Jazz Band was a favourite of Prince Charles.

"I have recently found out that poignantly, I am mentioned in **Bob Monkhouse's** latest book. I had the pleasure of playing for him twice – firstly at his 65th birthday party at his home, and then at his 70th birthday party at Woburn. It was this second occasion that he has mentioned me in his book, something of which I am very proud. Thanks Bob."

Through his agency Laurie has worked with some of the biggest names in show business and found them all wonderful people with whom to work.

Initiated into Chelsea Lodge 18 January 1980. WM 1987. Currently Almoner. Laurie has organised the annual Chelsea Lodge Ladies Festival since 1999.

Nat TEMPLE

Musician. Alto saxophone and clarinet player. Son of a tailor, he was born in Stepney, East London on 18 July 1913, one of four musical brothers. By the age of 15 Nat was gigging around town, before spreading his wings working at ballrooms as far apart as the Plaza in Dublin and Dreamland in Margate.

In 1931 he joined the new band being assembled by Syd Roy for cine-variety at the Leicester Square Theatre. Known as the RKOlians the outfit was fronted by Syd's brother Harry and Nat stayed with the band until 1940. During that time they moved around London's clubland with seasons at the London Pavilion, the Cafe Anglais and the Mayfair Hotel. The band appeared on the 1935 Royal Variety Performance and featured in two films *Everything in Rhythm* and *Rhythm Racketeer.*

In May 1940 Nat went off to war, joining the Band of the Grenadier Guards, where he played clarinet and saw service in Italy and North Africa. But for most of the time he was stationed at Wellington Barracks, in London, and like all the top musicians, was able to do sessions when off duty. He played for dozens of bandleaders and was the first musician in Britain to play the demanding clarinet introduction to George Gershwin's *Rhapsody in Blue*, at a concert in the Royal Albert Hall conducted by Sir Malcolm Sargent.

In 1944 Nat formed his own band for broadcasting work and began recording as Nat Temple and his Club Royal Orchestra. He appeared on the BBC Home Service in the series *It's a Pleasure* in January 1946.

He had a short spell with Ambrose at Ciro's Club before being discharged on medical grounds from the army in November 1946.

Nat took several months' convalescence before forming a new band that in 1947 was booked by Billy Butlin for the summer season at his Skegness Holiday Camp. Among the 14-piece line up were such fine musicians as pianist Roland Shaw, drummer Joe Watson and Syd Lawrence on trumpet. Vocalists were Helen Mack and Dave Kidd. The band made its first broadcast during September 1947 and it wasn't long before Nat and his boys were regulars on the airwaves. He formed his smaller Octet for much of this work.

After the Butlin season Nat took the band out on the road, beginning with a week at the Redcar Pier Pavilion Ballroom from 29 September. By May 1948 he was resident at Brighton's Martinique Club with a six piece, plus Benny Lee on vocals, spending the summer there. After this he went back on tour playing mainly one-night-stands up and down the country. In addition he did ninety per cent of all university engagements at both Oxford and Cambridge, including the annual May Balls. He played on many occasions for Queen Elizabeth, the Queen Mother, the late Princess Margaret and at Windsor Castle for other members of the Royal Family.

Between 1945 and 1953 Decca Records used his band as backing on 28 singles by a number of artistes including Joy Nichols, Benny Lee, Denis Lotis, David Whitfield and The Keynotes. Frankie Vaughan owed much of his early encouragement in the business to Nat, who used him as vocalist and introduced him to Decca Records.

Finding touring and club work a bit of a strain Nat decided to concentrate more on radio work, including a regular series with Joyce Grenfell called *A Note With Music*, on which Nat played some music and Joyce read a letter to an imaginary friend. During 1949 his 21-piece woodwind and string orchestra could be heard on *Bright and Early* and he had a 13-week Monday evening series *Enchanted Rhythm*. On Fridays his ragtime band was resident on *The Bowery Bar*. Then there was *Twelve Men and a Girl* with Benny Lee and Beryl Davis.

1950 saw the beginning of Nat's long running association with Bernard Braden and his wife Barbara Kelly, also the series of radio and television sagas written by Frank Muir and Dennis Norden. Starting off with *Breakfast With Braden*, they continued through *Bedtime With Braden*, *Between Time With Braden, Bedlam With Braden, Barbara With Braden* and *Back With Braden*. Nat became an integral part of these shows not only supplying the music but also becoming involved in the humour as the somewhat bumbling bandleader. Singers on most shows were Pearl Carr and Benny Lee, except for the latter series that featured Annie Ross and **Franklyn Boyd.**

Almost fully committed to the media, other radio series to feature his band were *The Peter Ustinov Show*, Michael Bentine's *Round The Bend, Good Evening Each* starring Beryl Reid and Ken Platt that was set in an imaginary dance hall where Nat was the manager and *Emery At Large* with **Dick Emery**. He also took his turn as presenter on *Housewives Choice.*

On television he worked on the children's series *Jack in the Box* supplying not only the music but the script as well. Other TV included Richard Afton's *Beauty Box, Frankie Howerd's *Nuts In May, Tune Times With Temple, A Jolly Good Time, Dance Music Through The Ages* and *Starstruck.*

Nat did find time to play the occasional ballroom season and during the 1960s returned to summer

seasons at Butlins. Nat, still active in the business well into the 1980s, had by the 1990s decided to take things a bit slower spending more time with his wife Freda at their beautiful neo-Georgian house in a quiet tree-lined avenue on the outskirts of Woking, Surrey. They celebrated their Sixtieth Wedding Anniversary on 6 December 2002: they have four daughters.

Nat Temple was initiated into Chelsea Lodge in July 1950.

Emlyn THOMAS
Musician. Born 1889. Violinist who later led his own orchestra and directed also the London Band with musicians Nat Star, Debroy Somers, Jay Wilbur and Ronnie Munro all of whom went on to direct their own bands. Emyln recorded 38 tracks for HMV and Vocalion Records between 1923 and 1925.

He was initiated into Chelsea Lodge on 19 July 1925. Died August 1940, aged 51 years.

Michael THOMAS, JP PProvGDC
(A Lewis). Born 14 January 1936, Quorn, Leicestershire, a Fifth generation Travelling Showman. Educated at Uppingham School, Rutland. On leaving school at eighteen he travelled the length and breadth of England and Wales with Thomas's Fun Fair.

At the age of twenty-one he settled in Hunstanton, Norfolk and established two large Family Leisure Centres, which he still operates with his wife Gloria and daughter Michelle.

Michael has enjoyed a very distinguished career outside as well as inside Freemasonry. He has served 35 years on the local council and has been elected Mayor for unprecedented four times, the most recent being in 2003. He has spent over 20 years as one of Her Majesty's Justices of the Peace for the Commission of Norfolk, and is a Past President of the local Chamber of Commerce, Past Chairman of Round Table, Founder and President of Hunstanton Rotary Club, President of Hunstanton Festival of Arts and President of Local Branch of Save the Children Fund and has served on three sets of School Governors and trustee of numerous Charities.

Michael Richard Thomas was initiated into Chelsea Lodge on 20 November 1959. Proposed by his father Bro. **John Freeman Thomas,** seconded by his eldest brother **John Keeble Thomas** and followed his elder brother **James David Thomas.**

Installed as the 70th Master in 1974 and later initiated his two nephews **John Chaplain Thomas** and **Simon James Thomas** and his son **Thomas Christian Thomas.** Father, three sons and three grandsons all members of Chelsea Lodge - "From generation to generation!"?

Although, he seldom misses a Chelsea meeting, he has been particularly active masonically in Norfolk, where he has been recently promoted to PPJGW. He has been a founder of two Lodges and member of five Norfolk Craft Lodges and has been WM five times having been elected as WM of Old Uppinghamian Lodge (his old school lodge) in 2003.

He was 1st Principal in Le Strange Chapter and later served as Provincial Treasurer in the Royal Arch. He was MWS in the Albert Edward Chapter and later promoted to 30th Degree.

In is early days as a Steward and Junior Officer he regularly made the round trip of 260 miles every Wednesday, to attend Lodge of Instruction at the Horseshoe Hotel, Tottenham Court Road and learnt most of his ritual on the train!

Michael has a special claim to fame regarding the Chelsea Lodge Ladies' Festival. He has attended every Chelsea Lodge Ladies Festival for the last 50 years! (which is believed to be a record!).

Although an outstanding ritualist, his favourite Masonic toast is to the initiate, which he has made his own and proposed over 40 times. He says, "It is always very special to be present and be part of *When a Man becomes a Mason.*

Anthony THORPE

Tony Thorpe was a trombone player well-known amongst the dance bands in the 1930s and early 1940s. Born about 1898 in Nottingham he served in the Royal Flying Corps during World War I, then emigrated to Canada and became a Canadian citizen. Worked in Toronto with Gilbert Watson's Band. Returned to England in 1926 as part of Bill Shenkman's Buffaloes, as did trumpeter **Alfie Noakes.** Played with numerous bands over the years and appeared on countless recordings. He worked with: Ambrose and His Orchestra (1931-1936), Blue Mountaineers (1932), Durium Dance Band (1932-1933), George Glover Band (1933), Henry Hall and the BBC Dance Orchestra (1936-1938), Jack Jackson Orchestra (1933-1935), Howard Jacobs Orchestra (1930), Arthur Lally (1930-1932), Percival Mackey's Band (1940),

Mantovani (1941), New Mayfair Dance Orchestra (1928-1935), Savoy Havana Band (1926-1927), Savoy Orpheans (1928) including a trip to Germany, George Scott Wood Orchestra (1934-1940), Van Phillips Orchestra for the show *Good News* (1928), Jay Widden Band (1928-1929), Jay Wilbur Orchestra (1929-1933) and Eric Winstone Band (1943).

As a member of the Savoy Havana Band, Tony took part in the bands initial broadcast for the BBC in April 1923 and five months later it became the first dance band to have regular weekly broadcasts relayed from the Savoy Hotel. Tony, together with **Max Goldberg**, trumpet, would become future stalwarts of the Ambrose Band. Another member of the Savoy Havana Band who went on to bigger things was Rudy Valee, an American saxophone player. He would become one of America's first singing idols. Pianist Billy Mayerl would also make a name for himself in Britain as a pianist and composer.

When the dance band days were over Tony moved to the London Symphony Orchestra where he played bass trombone. He was known for his eccentricity and telling yarns which kept members of the orchestra amused for hours on end. He was best when playing fast, loud and high and had adapted from his days with the dance bands. However Tony left the LSO about 1957 by which time the orchestra was into high quality recording work and what would pass for casual concerts would not be acceptable for the microscopic ear of the recording studio. During the 1960s was a member of the Royal Opera House Orchestra.

Anthony Thorpe was initiated into Chelsea Lodge on 16 June 1933. He died in June 1973, aged 72 years.

Alfred VAN DAM

Musical conductor. Born 1 March 1902, London. Educated at Guildhall School of Music. Joined the Carl Rosa Opera Company at the age of seventeen. Married Dorothy Gascoyne. Two daughters. Musical Director, Gaumont-British circuit 1921-1930, Trocadero, Elephant and Castle 1930-1937, Gaumont State, Kilburn 1937-1940 and Golders Green Hippodrome from 1940. Began broadcasting in 1931. Enjoyed golf and bridge and was a member of the Musicians Golfing Society.

Alfred Van Dam was initiated into Chelsea Lodge 17 October 1930.

Alfred VAN STRATEN, SLGR

Musical Director. Tenor saxophonist/leader. Born 1904. He was of Dutch descent and trained and practised as an accountant, playing the violin in his spare time, later taking up the saxophone. He led a five-piece band at 'The Mudies', which was followed by the Astoria Club, Brighton. From there he moved to the Casino, Finchley. Later he secured a job at the Grand Hotel in Margate without playing a note of music, because the manager liked his face! After a time in Rochester, Alfred moved back to Holland where he concerted his five-piece into a modern dance band. He was billed as 'The Singing Saxophonist from England' and was not allowed to speak Dutch, but eventually the story got out. Back in England he joined Harry Saville in Regent Street, London. He later joined his brother, Joe, in Jack Hylton's Ketner's Five. Another brother, Leon, came from Australia and opened the Ambassador's Club, with **Max Bacon** on drums. Alf took over the band at the Café Anglais and finally became the musical director of Quaglino's Club, staying there ten years, with short visits to the USA in 1935 and 1938.

Alf was in the band which did the pioneer broadcast from the old 2LO station in Savoy Hill, which was relayed over the Empire Service. He was later given a series called *We're Calling You From Home Across the Sea,* and his theme tune was *Struttin' with Straten*. His recordings include: *Just a Bird's Eye View, Indian Butterfly, Mary Lou* and *Pining For You,* the last two having vocals. They were recorded on Duophone unbreakable records (allegedly!). He also recorded a couple of titles for Parlophone with his band at Quaglino's in 1939. He gave up bandleading to form a band-booking agency in Soho with rival bandleader Sid Simone.

Alfred Van Straten was initiated into the Golden Rule Lodge No.1261 in 1936. Joined Chelsea Lodge 19 June 1942. He played at the Silver Wedding anniversary for Winston Churchill. Colleagues referred to him as a gentleman and a very considerate employer. He was a member of Chelsea Lodge for 47 years. Died 4 December 1988, aged 84 years.

John VIRGO

Snooker player. Born 4 March 1946, Salford, Manchester. Learned his snooker skills in Potter's Club, Salford. He made his mark as one of the country's leading amateurs in the 1960s and 1970s when he captured both the British under 16s and under 19s title and represented England. National Paris Champion, 1975. In 1976 he turned professional and three years later became the UK Champion. He reached the World Professional Snooker Championship semi-finals, 1979, and was the Professional Snooker League Winner, 1984.

John became a household name when he brought his skills to the job as a co-presenter of the phenomenally successful BBC quiz show *Big Break* with comedian **Jim Davidson.** Versatility is his byword and laughter is never far away. His ability to amuse and entertain was first exposed to a major audience when his side-splitting impersonations of fellow stars were broadcast on BBC TV during the coverage of the Embassy World Championship in Sheffield. His version of Ray Reardon, Terry Griffiths, Cliff Thornton, Steve Davis and others were uncannily accurate and extremely funny. He is a former chairman of the World Professional Billiards and Snooker Association and a popular after dinner speaker. He appears each year at the Crucible as a commentator on the Embassy World Championship.

John Trevor Virgo was initiated into Chelsea Lodge on 12 March 1998.

Bob VOICE

Born 1948, Hackney, London. Took an interest in music whilst at school and played percussion and drums with the Boys Brigade. Worked with various pop groups including Paul Brett's Sage and sessions with Mungo Jerry on tour throughout Europe, Portugal and Italy in the 1960s and, with the group Fire, were the second artistes to sign with the Beatles Apple label.

At the age of 24 he realised he wasn't going to be a rockstar anymore so joined the family business in Bournemouth. Met Mike Yarwood at the Pavilion Theatre, became his tour manager and later agent. Bob joined International Artistes in 1982 taking Mike with him. His brief with the company was to find new talent which he did in the form of Brian Connolly who was with a group Tom Follery. Bob sent him on his way as a solo artiste. Hale and Pace were with a group called Foundation. They seemed a natural double act who went on to enjoy fourteen years on television. Other new signings included Alan Davis, (Jonathan Creek), Bill Bailey, Joe Pasquale and Sean Lock. Bob says that his main brief is to find his artistes work on television and radio and the rest follows on. "If they like watching an artiste on television or hearing him on radio, the chances are they will buy a theatre ticket."

With Mandy Ward, is now joint managing director of International Artistes.

Bob Voice was initiated into Chelsea Lodge on 15 March 1985.

Danny WALTERS

Musical Director. Born 1908. Began his career as a cinema violinist and was rapidly promoted to Musical Director for Gaumont British and Stoll. At 25 he was the youngest MD in the West End of London at the Alhambra in 1933. He gave up conducting in 1937 to join Jack Hylton as lead violinist for two years and spent the Second World War fronting a quintet in the RAF. He was described as placid and gentle, a bit like a favourite uncle, with a jolly, round face, slight moustache, flickering smile and natty spectacles.

Over the years Danny worked in cine-variety, music hall, operetta, ballet, musical comedy, popular concerts, summer seasons and pantomimes. He accompanied a galaxy of stars including Richard Tauber, Billy Eckstine, Sophie Tucker, Al Read, Billy Fury, Shirley Bassey, Tommy Steele, Hutch, Max Bygraves, Max Miller, Joan Regan, Bobby Howes, Anton Dolan and Alicia Markova. He was employed by a long series of respected names – Gaumont British, Sir Oswald Stoll, Jack Hylton, Gerard Heath, Bernard Delfont, Geraldo, Moss Empires, Howard and Wyndham, Henry Hall, Larry Parnes, Tom Arnold and Harold Fielding.

He was married to Edith, a theatre catering manageress, who predeceased him in 1978, after 30 years of marriage.

Daniel Rhys Walters was initiated into Chelsea Lodge 16 May 1969. Died 23 December 1985, aged 78 years.

Hubert WARREN, PM LGR

Musical director. Born 1911. Known for many years as one of the principal providers of orchestras and musicians for cruise ships.

Hubert Edward Warren was initiated into Chelsea Lodge 21 September 1962. WM 1973.

Died 6 February 1992, aged 81 years.

Erne WARSAW, PM PAGStB

Musician. Born 1877. When he was Director of Ceremonies at Chelsea colleagues who remembered him said he was the strictest disciplinarian they had ever known. On one occasion a candidate did not answer the questions leading from second to the third degree in a satisfactory manner and Erne refused to let him advance.

Erne Warsaw was initiated into Chelsea Lodge 21 August 1908. WM 1922. Died 26 December 1948, aged 71 years

Jeff WAYNE

Singer/entertainer. Born 6 November 1940, Yougal, County Cork, Ireland. He comes from a large family of seventeen children, all of whom were gifted with excellent singing voices. At the age of sixteen Jeff came to England to take singing lessons with a view to joining an opera company but he became influenced by various ballad singers of the time and decided on a career in variety.

He auditioned for the Howard and Wyndham company and was given a six months engagement in *The Five Past Eight Show* in Glasgow. Following this he worked for the same company in long running seasons throughout the country. These included a tour in *The Bachelors Show*, Bournemouth, *The Josef Locke Show,* Blackpool and the *Ken Dodd Show* in Blackpool and Liverpool. It was in fact Ken Dodd who suggested to Jeff that he should expand his act with comedy and impressions which he took on board with successful results.

Over the years Jeff has appeared in most of the country's leading night clubs and restaurants. He was given repeated engagements by Mecca International at The Lyceum, London, Café de Paris, London and The International Cabaret in Birmingham.

He has varied his career with musicals and pantomimes. He was given a ten-month engagement in *On The Twentieth Century* at H.M. Theatre, London, and he also played Little John in *Babes in the Wood* at the Churchill Theatre, Bromley.

In recent years Jeff has become interested in acting and is often seen on television. Appearances have included *Murphy's Stroke, The Gentle Touch, Secret Army, Open University, Dr. Who, Just Good*

Friends, EastEnders, The Two Ronnie's, Cause Celebre, Death on the Rock, The Bill and *Crime Monthly.*

Jeff has also recorded a number of television commercials for: Woolworths, American Express, Sainsbury's, Caledonian Airways, Hoffmeister, Myer's Beds, Carlsberg Lager and Toshiba.

On the big screen Jeff has appeared in a number of films including: *Top Secret, Morons From Outer Space, John and Yoko, Strong Medicine, White Knight, The Two Mrs Grenvilles, Secret Weapon, Indiana Jones and the Last Crusade* and *Not a Penny More, Not a Penny Less.*

In addition he is a variety artiste singer, comedy performer, carpenter and decorator and at one time was a boxer.

Jeff Wayne joined Chelsea Lodge on 11 November 2002 from Drury Lane Lodge No.2127.

Ray WEBB

Guitarist, double bass, vocalist and arranger. Worked on guitar with Benny Parker in Scheveningen, Holland during the summer of 1937. Returned to London and played double bass in Don Barrigo's Bandits in 1938. On guitar with Dan Donovan's Music (1938). With drummer Phil Watts (1939). Doubled with Jack Jackson (1939-40). Served in the RAF from 1941. On demobilisation joined '**Miff**' **Ferrie** (1946), then went overseas to Canada (1947). Returned to Britain in 1948 and settled in Thornton Heath, Surrey where he freelanced as a musician and writer.

Ray Webb was initiated into Chelsea Lodge on 15 March 1963.

Bert WEEDON, OBE

Hubert Maurice William Weedon, a Londoner, was born at East Ham on 10 May 1920. His father was a train driver and was also one half of a semi-pro comedy duo. He gave young Bert his first guitar when he was twelve. It was a rather battered guitar off a stall in London's famous Petticoat Lane Street Market which had cost fifteen shillings in old money (75 pence). And so began the career of one of Britain's most accomplished instrumental stars. Learning to play in the classical style, he was taught by James Newall.

After leaving school Bert had several jobs before taking up music full time in 1937. Working with small bands, he began to be noticed when he became a *Carroll Levis Discoveries* winner in 1939.

He played in John Shakespeare's Band in Romford (1939); Laurie Payne's Band (1940) and then led his own Scatterbrains in a *Melody Maker* contest in 1940.

He played Number One Rhythm Club in 1942 and the following year he was in the West End at Hatchetts' Restaurant, a member of the famous Swingtette with Stephane Grappelli.

In 1944 he was in Frank Weir's Quartet and also worked in the Ambulance Service during World war II. After the war Bert mainly freelanced with many radio and record producers using his skilful electric guitar playing to great effect. He also worked with several bands including Ambrose, Ted Heath, Mantovani, **Harry Leader**, Howard Baker, **Nat Temple**, Teddy Foster, Harry Gold, **Cyril Stapleton** and The Squadronaires.

In 1947 while playing as a session musician during the day, at night he was a member of the Arnold Bailey Quartet at Quaglino's Restaurant in Bury Street.

For four years during the fifties Bert was a regular member of the instrumental group backing the acts on radio's travelling *Workers Playtime* shows. A mainstay of the BBC Show Band, joining them on various radio and television shows, he was also a regular on many others including *Slater's Bazaar* an early advertising feature hosted by John Slater on ITV, *Emney Enterprises, The A to Z of Show Business* and AR-TV's *Lucky Dip* on which he featured over many years.

Year after year he was voted Britain's top guitar player by record buyers, listeners and viewers.

Bert wrote a guitar tutor book *Play in a Day* in 1957 that sold over two million copies and he had a late 1950s children's television series on ITV, *Bert Weedon's Guitar Corner*, on which he showed them how to play. He followed up the success of his first book with another *Bert Weedon's Rock, Skiffle and Blues Album*.

On record, after many years backing artistes like Winifred Atwell, Tommy Steele, Terry Dean and lots more, plus duets with violinist Max Jaffa, Bert began making his own solo discs with his 1959 offering *Guitar Boogie Shuffle* reaching No.10 on the charts. He became the first British guitarist to get a solo record in the Hit Parade. About a half-dozen of his other recordings reached the lower regions of Britain's Top Fifty. One that didn't was his theme for the 1956 ITV quiz series *The 64,000 Question* (based on the American '$64,000 Question' its UK version only offered multiples of sixpence with a maximum of £1,600), although with the alternative title of *The Old Haunted Castle* the theme was top of the pops in Finland. Surprisingly Top Rank chose Bert to lead a small strict tempo band issued as Bert Weedon and his Music for Dancing.

In 1959 Bert, aged almost forty and with years of professional playing behind him, joined a bunch of young 'beat' singers that included Craig Douglas and Billy Fury on the road in a teenage pop package tour making his variety debut at the Newcastle Empire on 28 September.

Nowadays no record will sell without a video to back it up - but nothing's new. For his February 1960 single *Big Beat Boogie*, Bert made a two-minute film 'short' featuring him playing the tune backed by the visual attraction of TV's *Cool For Cats* dance team. This was shown in over 600 Rank cinemas (he was recording at the time for Top Rank), but it only managed four weeks on the charts and the highest position it made was No.37.

During the early 1960s Bert was regularly on radio shows (sometimes solo, sometimes with either his trio, quartet or sextet) - shows like *Guitar Club, Easy Beat, Saturday Club, Workers' Playtime* and *Midday Music Hall*. His Sextet was the resident band on *Music With A Beat* that also featured singers Loris Mann and **Franklyn Boyd.** On television he often guested on Russ Conway's show and in October 1960 Russ presented him with a miniature cricket bat inscribed '5001 - NOT OUT' to commemorate Bert's achievement of over 5000 radio and TV appearances. He compered AR-TV's *Tuesday Rendezvous* for over three years.

In 1961 he appeared in his first summer season,

on Blackpool North Pier with Matt Monro, Lyn Cornell and the Paul Burnett Orchestra and he was back there again the following year with Edmund Hockridge, Sheila Buxton, **Billy Dainty** and Harry Worth. Bert played regular summer seasons after that.

His virtuosity in all fields of music has enabled Bert to accompany such artistes as Frank Sinatra, Tony Bennett, Rosemary Clooney, Nat King Cole, Judy Garland and many top British names.

Come the 1990s Bert was as busy as ever, playing in cabaret and the recording studio, and his *Play in a Day* tutor is now out on video. He was the victim for an ITV *This Is Your Life* programme shown in December 1992.

Over the years Bert has recorded singles for Columbia, Parlophone, Beltona, Top Rank, HMV, Fontana, Polydor and Celebrity Records.

Three Chelsea members Bert Weedon (centre) with Bob Monkhouse and David Berglas at a meeting of the Grand Order of Water Rats

In live shows Bert has played concert tours throughout the country and appeared at the Royal Albert Hall, London Palladium, Victoria Palace, London and Manchester Opera House and every top summer season in Britain. He has also been featured as the cabaret star on many top Cruise Liners including the *QE2, The Canberra* and the *Sagafjord.*

Although Bert's first love has always been the guitar, a very close second is his work for Charities. Over the years he has helped to raise endless amounts of money for worthy causes, both by appearing and contributing. His main charity is The Grand Order of Water Rats where he was honoured to be King Rat in 1992. He has been Barker of The Variety Club of Great Britain since the late 1950s and a member or an active supporter of many major charities too numerous to mention.

He was honoured with the *British Music Hall Society Lifetime Achievement Award* in December 2000. Was appointed OBE in the Queen's Birthday Honours in June 2001.

Herbert M. Weedon was initiated into Chelsea Lodge in November 1989.

Frank WEIR

Frank, born on 30 January 1911, came from a show-business family. His mother was a singer and his father a comedian. He was himself not only a fine saxophone and clarinet player but also an accomplished singer and dancer and over the years made several film and television appearances in straight acting roles.

He learned to play the clarinet during his three years in the Army, serving with the Argyll and Sutherland Highlanders and then the Dorset Regiment, between 1925 and 1928. Returning to civilian life he worked hard at honing his military band style to suit a dance band public and spent a year at the Spa Ballroom, Torquay. He then freelanced around London's clubland, during which time he took up the saxophone as an alternative instrument.

Expanding his musical range still further he played in the Queen's Hall Light Orchestra and Boyd Neel's String Orchestra. During the mid-thirties he had a spell in Jack Hylton's Band and made his first recordings with them. For a year he played in Fred Hartley's Novelty Quintet. Frank also broadcast and recorded pre-war with the bands of Teddy Foster, Jack Payne, Van Phillips, Peter Yorke, Ambrose, Arthur Young, Lew Stone, Howard Jacobs and Sydney Lipton.

At the outbreak of World War Two he was leading his own group at Fischer's Restaurant off London's Bond Street, where his pianist was George Shearing. He began making broadcasts under his own name. Anne Shelton was vocalist on some of those broadcasts.

In 1941 Frank was playing at the Bagatelle Restaurant while training as a ferry pilot. It was in this capacity that he saw war-time service with the Air Transport Auxiliary. Invalided out in 1943 he led a band at Hatchetts for a time and then was at the Astor Club for almost a year before returning to Fischers, from where he made several broadcasts.

It was in December 1943 that Decca made the first recordings with Frank's own Sextet, following up six months later with several sides from his twenty-two piece orchestra that included a string section. At a time when Frank was still not widely known, his version of *Clarinet a la King* with the orchestra received much acclaim from critics who compared it very favourably with Benny Goodman's original. While he was at the Astor, Decca issued a number of recordings by his Astor Club Seven with vocals from Anne Lenner and Lynne Shaw. Frank had an acting role in the mild ghost story film *Dead o' the Night* made in 1945.

Replaced at Fischer's Restaurant by **Cyril Stapleton** in June 1946, Frank went on the road with seasons at Southampton's Royal Court Hotel and Green's Playhouse, Glasgow. The band was on radio's *Saturday Night at the Palais* from Green's in December 1946.

He then had a spell with a small group working at the Studio and La Melanite Clubs, both in Knightsbridge, until May 1947 when he opened with a 10 piece at the Lansdowne Hotel. The orchestra included Ken Mackintosh on the lead alto sax and George Shearing on accordian (an instrument on which he also excelled.), with singers Vivien Paget and Alan Dean.

In June 1947 Frank was guest soloist with the London Symphony Orchestra at a concert in Harringay Stadium, held before an audience of over 11,000 people. He also freelanced with the London Philharmonic Orchestra.

As well as their late night broadcasts from the Lansdowne Hotel, the band provided music for the new radio comedy series *Hello Anybody* that featured Dandy Nichols, Charlie Clapham and Gene Crowley. During 1948 Frank was host of the television series *New to You*.

In April 1949 he moved with a new orchestra into the exclusive Churchill Club in Bond Street.

Having kept up his flying skills, in June 1949 Frank took part in the Kings Cup Air Race at Elmden Airfield near Birmingham. He piloted *Windmill Girl*, a Proctor light aircraft belonging to Windmill Theatre owner Vivian Van Damm, coming fifth in his heat.

During September 1949 American film star Jane Russell was appearing in variety at London's Princes' Theatre and Frank left Churchill's to take another change in direction, leading the 16-piece orchestra supporting her. He then took a band on the road again and in March 1950 was the first

British 'name' band to play for US servicemen in Germany.

An extensive tour of dance halls included ten weeks at the Samson and Hercules Ballroom in Norwich during the summer of 1950. The band broadcast regularly on programmes as diverse as *BBC Ballroom, Music While You Work, On the Sweeter Side,* and *Jazz Club.* In July 1951 he had a solo acting role playing a bandleader named Gil Martin in a radio detective play *The Inch Man.*

Following redecoration of the Churchill Club Frank was back there with a new resident band opening on 4 December 1950, the fifth anniversary of its original opening. Six weeks later Johnny Gray took over the band at Churchill's while Frank formed a new outfit to return to the Astor Club, where he first established himself almost ten years previously. His Astor Club Nine broadcast live on 8 March on *Tonight We Dance.* Frank had a solo clarinet spot on Tommy Cooper's *Its Magic!* TV show the following week.

To say that Frank was living out of a suitcase would be an understatement. At the end of April 1950 he moved from the Astor to the Milroy Club and this became the pattern for the fifties. Working mainly clubs and dance halls the orchestra went through many changes of size and personnel throughout the decade. His band played seasons at the Empress Club Crystal Room, the Don Juan Club and the Copacabana.

Frank made many radio and TV appearances and from 1954 his orchestra recorded several more singles for Decca often featuring the brilliant soprano saxophone playing of its leader. A popular combination was his 1954 disc *The Little Shoemaker* coupled with *The Never Never Land.*

In June 1954 his version of *The Happy Wanderer,* a German tune that did much for the Obenkirchen Children's Choir, reached No. 4 position on the US hit parade. American *Billboard* magazine placed him No. 3 in their 'Most promising newcomer' poll. Over here it was the children's choir and the Stargazers that took chart honours.

Frank provided the backing music for a number of solo artistes on disc, including Vera Lynn. In 1956 he moved to the Parlophone label.

During January 1954 he had another straight acting role in a Midland's radio thriller serial *Suspicion in the Air,* written by Edward J. Mason (one of the creators of *Dick Barton* and *The Archers).* Frank played a sinister musician and he

also wrote the theme music. He played solo soprano sax on *Variety Playhouse, Midday Music Hall* and *The Show Band Show,* while his Quintet made a number of broadcasts on *Music While You Work.*

In 1955 he went on tour with a new orchestra whilst still making guest appearances on radio and television.

During the winter months of 1956 Frank presented a series of *Hit Parade* concerts in Battersea Town Hall, playing 24 numbers from the current hit parade.

More radio and television broadcasts continued throughout 1957. After a handful of discs for Parlophone, Frank made a few on the Oriole label including an LP *20th Century Folk Mass,* with the Peter Knight Singers. His one and only UK chart entry was the September 1960 Oriole offering *Caribbean Honeymoon,* but only low down at No. 42. By 1961 he moved to the Phillips label that issued three singles.

In 1958 the orchestra played a 13-week summer season in the Isle of Man and the following December were backing the Frankie Vaughan holiday show in Southampton.

By 1961 Frank was back in London's clubland at the Colony Restaurant. A year later he was leading a quintet at Paul Raymond's new club the Bal Tabarin that opened on New Year's Day 1962. The same year he played the summer season leading an orchestra for the variety show *Stars at Night* at Jersey's Opera House. Frank continued to play for summer season shows during the 1960s and 1970s and also worked as a musical director in the theatre.

Frank Weir was initiated into Chelsea Lodge on 16 September 1938. He died on 12 May 1981 aged 70 years.

Charles WHITTLE

Comedian. Born 24 August 1874, Manningham, Yorkshire, son of Peter and Betsy Whittle. At the age of ten he was working as a half-timer in a Bradford silk mill for half-a-crown a week. He later became a clog iron maker and served an apprenticeship as a shoesmith. By this time he was adding to his income by appearing at public-house concerts in Bradford, for which he was earning six shillings a night with a pie for his supper. He also appeared at the Mechanics Institute in Bradford where singing contests were often held. The next step up the ladder was the City Varieties, Leeds in

December 1900 followed by appearances in various minor theatres in London.

He gave up the forge for the footlights. His first on-stage song was called *Why Hasn't Daddy Come Home,* a ballad about a daughter missing her father, lost in the Boer War. The *Chatham Observer* said on 30 September 1902: "Charles Whittle, versatile comedian, has some capital songs of a somewhat fresh order." Charles went on to enjoy huge success with songs like *Put me Amongst the Girls, Let's all Go Down the Strand* and *Kelly From the Isle of Man.*

His recording career ran from 1911-1916. They were issued on the Regal and Corena labels: *Play us Another Before You Go, We All Go the Same Way Home, We're All Going to the Seaside, Tommy Trouble, Toddling Home, We All Go Home in Ragtime, Let's All have the Lights Up* and *Dance With Your Uncle Joseph.*

He performed many of his chorus songs in top hat, suit and spats. In the first Royal Command Performance held at the Palace Theatre on 1 July 1912, Charles was one of the artistes selected to appear in *Variety's Garden Party* finale.

The string of successful songs continued, alongside his ever-popular old favourites, as he went on performing into the 1920s. He retired in 1930, aged 56, still living in Yorkshire but appeared at local concerts, socials, and charity performances.

On 20 February 1939 George Black opened at the Adelphi Theatre in the Strand with a new revue-cum-variety policy. The first show was a revue *Let's All Go Down the Strand,* named after one of Charlie's successful songs. Appropriately Charlie appeared in the production, which ran for seven nights, the house then converting to variety. Charlie's appearance at the Adelphi led to offers to appear in other London variety theatres, where he was credited with showing all his old vigour in putting across his chorus songs.

He appeared in a 1946 Forces Broadcasting Service programme and in a BBC TV show in 1947 after which Lew Lake invited him to go to America to make a film about the old days. Sadly this never came to fruition as he died before the contract was signed.

Charles Richard Whittle was initiated into Chelsea Lodge on 17 July 1908. Died St Luke's Hospital, Bradford 27 November 1947, aged 73 years, and was buried at Undercliffe Cemetery. Charlie's wife Margaret had predeceased him (September 1941) as did two of their daughters and a son. Another daughter survived.

Des WILLIAMS
Musician. Winner of a talent show in 1949. He replaced Dick James in the Paul Fenhoulet Orchestra. Later joined **Paul Adam** before going solo. He also led the Brighton Aquarium Orchestra in the mid-1950s.

Desmond Williams was initiated into Chelsea Lodge on 16 March 1962.

Paul WILLIAMS
Composer and musician. Paul Williams, aka Terry Day, was born 3 September 1940, Kingston, Surrey. Educated at Tiffin School, Kingston. As a teenager he played in various combos in the 1950s alongside John Barry and Craig Douglas. He studied piano and music composition at the Royal College of Music before going on to read Music at Jesus College, Cambridge, where he gained a Master of Arts degree in 1964. He has been composing since the age of eight and plays a variety of keyboard instruments. Paul has also worked as a session musician with numerous bands and orchestras, and for a while was a pianist on the cruise liners. More recently he has worked with Phil Manzanera of Roxy Music fame.

For a time he was a music teacher at St Paul's School, Hammersmith, but moved back into the music business on the advice of the late Joe Meek, producing independent records and becoming a music arranger.

Today Paul is a versatile, talented and experienced writer of media music. He has been composing for radio, television, films and the recording industry for several years. Major credits include television commercials such as: Flash Cascade, Heineken, Hewlett-Packard, ICI, National Panasonic, Sony, Suchard, Tetley Tea, Uncle Ben's Rice, Brittany Ferries, Lunn Poly, Ericsson and the music for Neptune's Kingdom - Thorpe Park.

Paul also composes for major international publishing companies, including Carlin Music and Zomba Publishing with over 1500 titles published. He has also composed music for films and television including the Love Theme for *Crocodile Dundee,* incidental music for Stephen Speilberg's film *Deep Impact* and TV series *Oprah Winfrey Show* and *Neighbours.* He composed the theme and incidental music to BBC1 TV series *House of*

Gristle and BBC1 TV documentary *Out of This World,* amongst many others.

In June 1964 Paul joined the BBC as a general trainee later becoming a radio producer working on programmes such as: *Morning Music, Those Were The Days, Bandbeat, Music Through Midnight, Scene and Heard* and *The Joe Loss Bandshow.* Since then he has been directing and making programmes for BBC Radio One and Radio Two innovating BBC pop music radio on the national networks with great success, involving record programming and participation with top international artistes.

Many of these programmes have been heard and appreciated by a wide international audience and have had a strong musical bias, featuring people at the very peak of the music business such as Phil Collins, Elton John and Bruce Springsteen. In 1980 Paul captured on tape John Lennon's final interview in New York – an historical interview which was broadcast worldwide. Other BBC productions have included *The Morning Show*, Saturday and Sunday sequences and Radio One arts features.

He has won three prestigious Sony Awards for *The Paul McCartney Story* (1988), BBC Radio and international syndication, *Backchat* (1990), BBC Radio One magazine programme and *The Nicky Campbell Show* (1992), BBC Radio One which ran on air nationwide for over four years, featuring live studio interviews with guests such as Princess Michael of Kent, Prime Minister John Major, plus many famous guests from the worlds of art, politics and music from Andrew Lloyd Webber to Jackie Collins. Paul also won the STEMRA Composer Award winner, Netherlands, 1994. He has also written classical pieces for the annual Cathcart Spring Proms at the Royal Albert Hall, London.

Married to Rosalind Anne (née Burns) with one son and two daughters Paul is living in Surrey, and spends the majority of his time composing and recording to commission in his state of the art recording studio.

David Paul Gifford Williams was initiated into Chelsea Lodge on 11 November 1965.

Fred WINN

Actor. Real name Frederick Thompson. Born 1866. Appeared in *Who's Hooper* at the Adelphi, 1919. He recorded a collection of songs including: *It's Nice to be Home Once More, Wonderful Love,* *What Are the Wild Waves Saying, and It Must Be Very Trying to be Mad,* all featuring the Mayfair Dance Orchestra conducted by George W. Byng on Columbia Records.

Frederick Thompson was initiated into Chelsea Lodge on 15 June 1905.

Tiny WINTERS

Musician. Born Frederick Gittens, 24 January 1909. Dalston, London, but later worked under the name Frederick William Winters, better known as 'Tiny' as he was by build and by voice. He first appeared in a touring concert party and married the leading lady, his first wife, Bebe. His first job was as a boot and shoe salesman, then stocktaking, but he preferred music, playing clarinet and fiddle as well as string bass. He entered the dance band business with Lew Stone's Orchestra at the Monseigneur Restaurant in the 1930s and became a renowned exponent of the slapped-bass technique which he picked up by listening to American recordings. This is where he plucked the strings so hard they rebounded and slapped against the backboard. During his career in the dance band world Tiny played double bass with most of the top

London professional bands. He was also immensely popular for his girlish comedy vocals. He was a radio favourite with his unique voice on such numbers as *Sing Me a Swing Song* and *Little Nell*.

He was with the Ambrose Orchestra and **Roy Fox** (both in 1932). The following year he was with the Ray Noble Orchestra which included a summer season in Holland. He then joined a jazz outfit called The Heralds of Swing before rejoining the Lew Stone Band. He also freelanced with Spike Hughes and Coleman Hawkins.

With the Roy Fox Band Tiny recorded 54 different tracks in 1932, some made in Chelsea Town Hall. With the New Mayfair Dance Orchestra, directed by Ray Noble, he recorded nearly 200 tracks between 1932-1934 on the HMV label. With Lew Stone and the Monsigneur Band and, later, the Lew Stone Band he recorded nearly 300 different tracks between 1932-1937 on Regal Zonophone and Decca labels. Whilst with the band one of his singles *Sing Me a Swing Song* was issued on Decca in 1937 shortly before he left Lew Stone. With Nat Gonella and His Georgians he recorded 50 different tracks between 1932-1935 on the Parlophone label. He made one record on Decca for Edgar Jackson's Gargoyle Five in 1932. With the Ambrose Orchestra he recorded 270 different tracks between 1937-1941 on the Decca label. With the Teddy Foster Orchestra he recorded two singles in April 1937 on the HMV label.

In 1939 he was with Ambrose at the Mayfair Hotel. He gave extra bounce to the rhythm section of a band and was in big demand for post-war performances. During the mid-1930s he led an offshoot of the Ambrose Band which recorded jazz tracks under the name of 'Tiny Winters and his Bogey Seven'. He was activated for military service during World War Two in 1940 and played in various service bands including a station band at RAF Wittering 1940-1941 and regularly with Billy Amstell's Quintet (The RAF Rhythm Five) from 1941. Demobilised in September 1945, he again teamed up with Lew Stone in the summer of 1947. From the 1950s onwards he did night club and theatre work as well as many freelance sessions.

In 1953 Tiny moved to Canada. Later went to India for a while before returning to England. In the 1980s he formed a band to recreate the classic 1930s dancing at the Park Lane Hotel, London. Called the Café Society Orchestra they recorded one LP on the Zodiac label. Tiny also led a trio

which played nightly in front of the National Theatre and was a member of George Chisholm's famous Jazzers, an integral and popular part of the televised *Black and White Minstrel Show,* where he played sousaphone from 1962-1972. Continued to freelance into the 1980s playing on many sessions, leading his Trio and Café Society Orchestra, touring with Digby Fairweather in a *Nat Gonella Tribute* (1982) and subsequently worked with Fairweather in the Kettners Five. Led his trio into the 1990s until ill-health caused his retirement in 1994. He compiled his life story, appropriately titled *It Took a Lot of Pluck,* which still awaits publication.

Frederick William Winters was initiated into Chelsea Lodge 15 March 1935. He died 7 February 1996, aged 87 years. Having married again he left a widow, Lillian.

Bob WISE
Musician. Joined the Arthur Roseberry and His Kit-Kat Dance Band and made many recordings on the Parlophone label between 1928 and 1931. Worked with the Savoy Orpheans and, later, Carroll Gibbons and the Savoy Hotel Orpheans between 1930 and 1939. Recorded with Jay Wilbur's Band between 1933 and 1935.

Was a member of the Ray Noble Band and the New Mayfair Dance Orchestra. A talented musician, he played clarinet, alto saxophone and baritone saxophone. Appeared on many recordings on the HMV label with the band between 1931 and 1935.

Robert Wise was initiated into Chelsea Lodge 17 May 1935.

Denny WISE
Bandleader/vocalist/musician/ Born 12 September 1947, Bedford. Began singing at the age of ten, making his first appearance at the Weavers Club in Bedford with his father playing piano and Denny singing the Nat King Cole Standard, *When I Fall In Love.* During the performance the audience started throwing money at him. He turned to his father and said, "Why are they throwing these coins Dad"? His father replied "Don't worry about it just keep ****** singing."

At the age of eleven, due to family situations, Denny moved to Leicester to live with his grandmother. Later he was put into a children's home and also spent time with foster parents. The family break up did not deter him and he kept singing and tinkling on the piano. Four years later he joined a semi-professional band called The Colorado's. They won a local talent competition in Leicester as 'Best Local Band'. At seventeen Denny joined a Manchester band and he went touring with them in Germany and performed at the famous Star Club in Hamburg alongside Cliff Bennett and the Rebel Rousers, Wayne Fontana and the Mindbenders, Small Faces and many more.

Denny decided on a change of direction at the age of twenty and wanted to become involved in the big band scene. He auditioned with Ken Mackintosh, was successful and appeared on numerous BBC broadcasts. He gained invaluable experience with the Mackintosh Orchestra and this enabled him to go on and form his own band for Mecca at the age of 25. His first band was called Rainbow Bridge and performed at the Stevenage Locarno in the Nocturne Club. Mecca then asked Denny to move to Wimbledon Tiffany's. He later teamed up with the Johnny Howard Band on the road and after a spell with Johnny decided to venture into the private and corporate music scene. The Denny Wise Band went on to perform at parties for **Bert Weedon** who was King Rat in 1992. His special guests included the Prince and Princess Michael of Kent. The band played for Sir Elton John's *Birthday Party Special*. Guests were the Duke and Duchess of Kent and a host of famous show business names. They have also played at Gleneagles where the special guest was the Princess Royal, the Miss World Ball, special guest Prince Andrew, and performed with the Supremes in 1999 and 2000, appeared at the Savoy, Hilton, Claridges, Grosvenor House and all the top hotels in London, plus many other venues and hotels all over the country and abroad, where Denny had the honour of performing in front of dignitaries and celebrities who have included The Duke of Edinburgh and Prince Charles.

Denny and his band have performed for several charity events including the Variety Club and the Helen Rollason Cancer Care Ball. He has appeared on numerous LPs on the Hallmark and EMI labels many of which have reached the best selling album charts, particularly in the 1970s with various volumes of *Hot Hits*. In addition he recorded a duet for EMI called *Time* with Marian Davies of the Ladybirds. The Denny Wise Band have appeared on the BBC in the *Jimmy Young Show, Terry Wogan Show* and *Music Through Midnight*, in addition to shows on Capital Radio and broadcasts in Germany.

Denny is a Vice Patron of the Heal Cancer Charity, Prostate Cancer Research Appeal; he sits on the committees of The Royal Star and Garter Home (Richmond) who recently presented him with a medal for his services; Life Line 4 Kids (Handicapped Children's Aid Committee) and Robert Burns Club (London) incorporated with the Robert Burns Worldwide Federation.

Denny Wise joined Chelsea Lodge 15 March 1996 from Holy Well Lodge No.6178 where he was WM in the year 2001.

Paul WOOD, PM

Vocalist. Born Paul Woodcock, 16 November 1964, Romford, Essex. He began singing at the age of six, and ten years later was working regularly as a semi-profess-ional in cabaret in Taunton and Great Yarmouth. During this time he became more involved in the jazz music scene and worked with a number of local bands.

Paul has been billed in various London venues with many familiar names from the world of stage and screen including Barbara Windsor, The Bachelors, The Barron Knights, Richard Briers and **Jim Davidson**. He has also worked with some of Britain's leading musicians including Don Lusher, the late George Chisholm, Kenny Ball and Terry Lightfoot.

The Royal Festival Hall, Royal Ascot, Café Loire and the Pizza Express are amongst the venues where Paul has performed and he took part in the 50th anniversary Celebrations at the Goodwood Motor Circuit organised by the Earl and Countess of March.

He has sung on radio programmes in this country and in Europe and has been interviewed on television talk shows. He performed a two-hour live radio broadcast at the Film Festival Hall in Cannes, France, and successfully completed a sell-out tour throughout France called *Salute to Frank Sinatra* including the Palais des Congress where he played to an audience of 5,000.

Paul has completed twelve European Tours with a 20-piece orchestra which has taken him all over Europe and North Africa. A highlight was singing in front of the late Prince Ranier and Princess Caroline of Monaco at the Sporting Club in Monte Carlo. He works with a number of orchestras including the Glenn Miller Memorial Orchestra, the BBC Big Band, The Tommy Dorsey Orchestra, the Syd Lawrence Orchestra and Lex Vanwel and his Swing Orchestra. He has appeared on the same bill as the Royal Philharmonic Orchestra.

Classed as a ballad singer, his expertise lies mainly with standards and jazz songs, although Paul performs a wide repertoire of musical styles and techniques including popular songs and chart music. This, combined with a pleasant and engaging approach to his profession makes him a good, warm and friendly, all-round entertainer. His polished performance has resulted from much hard work and effort and his wide experience over recent years.

He has his own band of top class musicians which accompanies him on tour when he does concert dates, cabaret and other functions.

Paul Woodcock was initiated into Chelsea Lodge on 18 November 1994. WM 2003.

Wee Georgie WOOD, OBE

Comedian. Real name George Bamlett. Born 17 December 1895, Sunderland, he made his first appearance in Will Elliott's concert party in the castle grounds at Barnard Castle in July 1904. Of diminutive stature at four feet, nine inches and because of his height he specialised in little boy characters. His complexion seemed to remain youthful until almost the last years of his life. He was very knowledgeable about music hall and Variety. Not only popular in this country but also in America and South Africa doing impersonations of Marie Lloyd and Vesta Tilley. He began touring at the age of eleven and continued on the road until he was into his 50s.

In 1904 he worked a single turn as a mimic at the Empire Music Hall, South Shields, and the following year appeared with Levy and Caldwell's Juveniles.

He made his first London appearance in variety at the Shepherd's Bush Empire on 9 April 1909 in a sketch *Nursery at Bedtime*. He toured South Africa later that year and was so popular that he returned two years later. In January 1915 he starred

GEORGIE WOOD

in *High Class Vaudeville* at B.F. Keith's Colonial Theatre, New York.

In 1917 Mr Julian Wylie presented him with Dolly Harmer in a play *Some Detective*. It was not particularly successful but from it sprang a stage partnership between the two players which lasted for nearly forty years. During that time they appeared in a long series of comedy sketches all based on one central theme. Dolly was the stage mother of a precocious son, Wee Georgie Wood, who was always getting into scrapes. The sketches normally consisted of little more than the attempts of the mother to make her son behave properly with Wood pouring out plenty of comedy and a certain amount of sentiment in a battle of wits.

With Dolly he toured the USA, South Africa, Canada, Australia and New Zealand. During the Second World War they worked for ENSA in North Africa and the Middle and Far East and travelled some 70,000 miles to entertain the troops. For nearly forty years Wee Georgie appeared in pantomime as well as comedy shows and straight plays in addition to making an appearance in the film *The Black Hand Gang*. With Dolly and colleague Tom Blacklock they appeared in the Royal Variety Performance at the Victoria Palace on 24 February 1927. Dolly died in 1956. He married Ewing Eaton, an American vaudeville performer, in the States in 1933 although the marriage only lasted two years. He retired in 1953. He wrote his own personal jottings *Stage Man's Diary* for *The Stage* and a regular column for *The Performer*, in addition to writing a play called *Music Hall* which traced the rise to fame of a young couple in radio and music hall. He was a member of the British Music Hall Society, Savage Club and of the Grand Order of Water Rats becoming King Rat in 1936.

George Bamlett joined Chelsea Lodge on 20 April 1923 from Wythenshawe Lodge No.2688. To the end of his days he retained the voice, face and figure of a boy of tender years. He died 19 February 1979, London, aged 84 years.

Benny WRIGHT, PM PAGStB

Musician. Born 1917. Well-known double bass player in the 1940s and 1950s and played with many of the top bands of the day, including Jack Hylton and Syd Lawrence. Highly thought of by his peers. Bachelor. Legend has it that he was so impressed by the Ancient Charge at his initiation, he learned the whole thing the following week! He delivered it at the first Lodge of Instruction he attended.

Following on from becoming WM he devoted 25 years to the offices of Treasurer and Director of Ceremonies. In addition he was Preceptor of Chelsea Lodge of Instruction for many years from 1968 and chief organiser of the annual Ladies Festival. He is remembered as a very strict, but nevertheless, outstanding ritualist who ran a tight ship.

Benjamin Wright was initiated into Chelsea Lodge on 17 September 1954. He attained Grand Rank 1982. In November 1985 he decided to settle in the USA and very much regretted having to resign as DC but requested to stay an overseas member of the Lodge. In November 1986 he was made an Honorary Member of Chelsea Lodge. Died 23 November 2003, aged 86 years.

Chapter 13

LIST OF MEMBERS 1905-2005

in ALPHABETICAL ORDER

Lists full name, profession and area where they were living at the time of becoming a member, together with their age, date of initiation (I), passing (P) , raising (R) or joining and any other information of interest. In many instances members were known by pseudonyms in which case their real name will be given and readers will be directed to the pseudonym. If the member was the son of a Freemason he will be listed as '(A Lewis)'.

A

ABERY, MICHAEL, LGR
New Southgate N11 2NT. Joined from Mount Zion Lodge No.7664 on 17.11.1978.

ABRAHAMS, ABY EMANUAL
Company Director. Forest Gate, E15. Aged 37. Joined 17.05.1940. Died 1979.

ABRAHAMS, DAVID
(A Lewis). London W1. I.16.01.1976 P.19.03.1976 R.17.09.1976. Excluded May 1985.

ABRAHAMS, MICHAEL TIMOTHY
Musician. Milton Keynes. Born 07.04.1943. I.17.09.2004.

ABRAHAMS, NATHANIEL See HARRY BANCROFT

ADAKER, WILLIAM SCOTT
Vaudeville Artiste. Brixton. Rejoined 20.07.1923.

ADAM, PAUL
Musical Director, Real name Carl Tauber. London SW2. Age 33. I.20.07.1945 P.17.05.1946 R.18.03.1949. Excluded 30.04.1994.

ADRIAN, JULES
Music Hall Artiste. Real name Henry Godowski. Age 48. Joined 21.01.1944 from Greenock Lodge 175, Scottish Constitution.

AIREY-SMITH, BILL
Musician. Real name James William Smith. Brondesbury Park, London,NW6. Age 36. I17.02.1939 P.21.07.1939 R.20.10.1939. Died 12 December 1982, aged 78 years.

AISTON, ARTHUR
Comedian. West Kensington. Joined 17.03.1911 from Canongate & Leith No 5. Died 31.05.1919, aged 40 years.

AITKIN, JOHN GEORGE See JACK

ALBERT ALAN, RAY
Variety Artiste. Real name Raymond Alan Whybird. Hornsey, London N8. Age 33. I.16.11.1962 P.15.03.1963 R.24.04.1964.

ALBER, FRANK
Acrobat. Real name Frank Jennnings. Age 27. I.15.11.1907 P.16.04.1908 R.13.08.1909.

Excluded 15.05.1914.

ALBERT, JACK
Vaudeville Artiste. Real name John George Aitken. London WC2. Age 37. I.21.10.1921 P.06.12.1921 R.07.02.1922.

ALEXANDER, FRANK
Scenic Artiste. East Finchley. Age 32. I.16.07.1948 P.18.03.1949. Excluded 16.09.1955.

ALEXANDER, MICHAEL ANTHONY HOWELL
Scientific Officer. Chelworth, Cricklade. I.16.03.1979 P.16.11.1979 R.18.01.1980. Resigned May 1986.

ALEXANDER, TED Prov.AGDC
Musician. Lewisham, SE18. Age 36. I.19.03.1948 P.19.11.1948 R.18.11.1949. WM 1978. Was made Hon. Member 20.01.1992.

ALEXANDRA, WALTER LEOPOLD See J. REGAN

ALLDER, ROBERT ERNEST EDWARD
Organist. Romford, Essex. Born 30.07.1949. Joined 21.05.2004 from Loughton Lodge No.8455 of which he was WM in 1993.

ALLDIS, JOHN BARRY
(A Lewis). Disc jockey. Ealing, London W5. Age 38. I.21.11.1969 P.16.01.1970 R.20.03.1970. Died 21 November 1982, aged 52 years.

ALLEN, CHARLES HERBERT
Theatrical Manager. Fulham, London SW6. Age 40. I.19.06.1925 P.18.09.1925 R.18.09.1926. Excluded.

ALLEN, ERNEST
Variety Artiste. London WC. Age 39. I.19.03.1926 P.18.06.1926 R.16.07.1926. Excluded.

ALLEN, JACKSON
Comedian. Real name Jackson Allen Rand. Brighton, Sussex. Age 43. I.21.09.1928 P.19.07.1929 R.18.10.1929. Excluded.

ALLEN. LES
Vocalist. Maida Vale, London. Age 42. I.19.01.1945 P.18.06.1946 R.15.06.1946. Died 1996, Toronto, Canada, aged 93 years.

ALVAREZ, EDWARD DAVID

Musician. Joined 21.11.1975. Died 20.06.1993.

ALVAREZ, ROBIN JULIAN
(A Lewis). London W1. I.16.09.1977 P.18.11.1977
R.20.01.1978.

AMANDUS
Vaudeville Artiste. Real name Amandus Carl
Linden. Stamford Hill, London N. Age 44.
I.19.08.1910 P.21.10.1910 R.17.03.1911.
Excluded 20.05.1920.

ANDERSON, VICTOR
Circus Artiste. London SE. I.21.11.1975
P.16.01.1976 R.17.09.1976. Died 11.03.1989.

ANDREWS, KENNETH, PM
Theatre Executive. Leighton Buzzard, Beds. Age
62. Born 10.06.1926.I.18.03.1988 P.18.11.1988
R.17.11.1989. WM 1998.

ANDREWS, STANLEY THOMAS
Musician. Finchley, London N3. Age 36.
I.20.10.1939 P.18.01.1946 .Died October 1953.

ANDREWS, WILLIAM BOWKER
Author and Composer. Age 32. I.17.07.1908
P.21.08.1908 R.16.10.1908.

APPLE, MAURICE
Sound expert. London WC1. J.19.05.1972. PM of
Probity Lodge No 4911. Died 09.07.1979.

**APPLEBOOM, JOEL See PAUL JOHN
CLIFFORD**

ARBITER, IVOR DAVID
Instrument Maker. London WC1. Age 22.
I.21.03.1952 P.16.01.1953 R.17.07.1953.

ARBITER, JOSEPH HYMAN
Musician. London WC1. Age 39. I.19.05.1944
P.17.11.1944 R.21.09.1945. Died 08.03.1962.

ARCHER, JOSEPH WILLIAM
Vaudeville Artiste. London SW4. Age 45.
I.15.07.1921 P.18.08.1921 R.15.09.1921.

ARDLEY, ALBERT CHRISTOPHER
Creative Director. Streatham, London SW16. Age
38. J.15.11.1991 from Geomatic Lodge No.6214.

ARMSTRONG, FRANK
Vocalist. Real name Frank Percy Strong. London
N. Age 36. I.16.01.1916 P.21.07.1916
R.18.08.1916.

ARNOLD, HENRY CLARK Junior
Theatrical Manager. Age 28. New Brighton,
Cheshire. J.20.08.1920 from Liverpool Dramatic
Lodge No.1609. Excluded 1924.

ARNOLD, THOMAS CHARLES
Publicity Manager. Stockwell, London SW. Age
24. I.20.09.1918 P.18.10.1918 R.21.03.1919.

**ARRENDELL, HORACE EDWARD See
HORACE O'MALLEY**

ARTHUR, HARRY
Vaudeville Artiste. Real name Arthur Harry
Charles King. Brixton, London SW2. Age 37.
I.18.07.1924 P.17.10.1924 R.20.03.1925.
Excluded.

ARTHUR, LOUIS
Musical Director. Real name Arthur Hawkins.
Brixton, London SW2. Age 59. I.18.03.1949

P.18.11.1949 R.15.09.1950. Excluded 1957.

ARTOIS, ALFRED
Vaudeville Artiste. Real name Alfred Eugene
Lilley. Margate, Kent. Age 43. I.19.07.1918
P.16.08.1918 R.20.09.1918. WM 1932.

ASCOT, RONNIE
Manager. Real name Walter Alexis Groves.
London SE24. Age 49. I.18.07.1948 P.19.07.1947
R.19.03.1948. Died 07.03.1967.

ASHER, ANGELO ANDREW
Musical Conductor. Founder. Organist. Resigned
17.04.1913.

ASHFULL, FREDERICK JAMES
Manager. London SW1. Age 36. I.18.09.1926
P.18.03.1927 R.22.06.1927. Excluded.

ASTOR, ARTHUR CHARLES
Ventriloquist and later theatre director. Real name
Thomas Ferguson. Worthing, Sussex. Age 32.
I.20.07.1917 P.17.08.1917 R.21.09.1917.
Resigned but later rejoined on 15.01.1960. Died
17.02.1966.

ATHLONE, JIMMIE,PM LGR
Gymnast. Real name James E. Young. Brixton,
London SW. Age 37. I.18.07.1913 P.15.08.1913
R.19.09.1913. WM 1921. Died 07.09.1955.

ATLAS, PM LGR
Vaudeville Artiste. Real name William Hedley
Roberts. Age 41. Joined from Liverpool Dramatic
Lodge No.1609. 16.03.1913. WM 1914. Died
1946.

ATLAS, GUS
Vaudeville Artiste. Real name Ernest Augustus
Roberts. London SW6. Joined 19.06.1920 from
Proscenium Lodge No.3435.

AUSTEN, BRIAN HENRY
Circus Proprietor. I.21.03.1979 . Excluded 1985.

AUSTIN, HERBERT
Theatrical Manager. Real name Charles John
Joseph Fitzowen. Age 40. I.12.07.1905
P.18.18.1905 R.15.09.1905. Died December
1927

**AYRES, RICHARD See RICH HAYES AZA,
BERT**
Theatrical Manager. Real name Bert Selinger.
Balham, London SW12. Age 35. I.21.04.1922
P.16.06.1922 R.21.07.1922.

B

BACON, MAX DAVID
Musician/Raconteur. London W1, I.17.12.1937
P.17.03.1939 R.15.03.1940. Died 03.12.1969,
aged 65 years.

BAIN, JAMES WILLIAM See JAMES STEWART

BAKER, AUGUSTUS GEORGE
Comedian. London WC. Age 37. I.18.06.1926
P.16.07.1926 R.20.08.1926. Excluded.

BALL, RICHARD MARSH
Musician. London SE19. I.20.12.1935
P.17.01.1936 R.16.10.1936. Excluded May 1948.

BAMLETT, GEORGE WOOD See WEE

GEORGIE WOOD

BANCROFT, HARRY
Actor/Vocalist. Real name Nathaniel Abrahams.
Age 31. I.21.02.1908 P.14.05.1908 R.18.09.1908.
Died. Date not known

BAND, THOMAS EVANS
Musician. Wembley, Middlesex. Age 45.
I.17.07.1942 P.20.11.1942 R.15.01.1943.

BANNERMAN, HARRY
Manager. Real name Harry Allen Phillips.
Clapham Park, London SW4. Age 39.
I.18.06.1926 P.20.08.1926. Excluded.

BARCLAY, GEORGE ROBERT
Variety Agent. Brixton Hill, London SW2. Age 33.
I.15.10.1920 P.17.12.1920 R.21.01.1921.

BARGATE, GEOFFREY NORMAN
HM Forces. RAF. I17.01.1937 P.15.07.1938
R.21.07.1939. Departed for South Africa 1947.
Resigned May 1949.

BARKER, MARTIN See M.MARTINI

BARKER, REGINALD WALTER
Musician. Leyton, London E10. Age 24.
I.21.08.1931. P.18.09.1931 R.18.03.1932.

BARLOW, JOHN
Vocalist. Restalrig, Edinburgh. Age 30.
I.31.12.1915 P.04.04.1916 R.02.05.1916.
Excluded.

BARNES, KENNETH VERNON
Variety Artiste. Edmonton, London N18. Age 37.
Joined 18.01.1957. Resigned May 1982. Died
December 2001, aged 82 years.

BARONI
Vaudeville Artiste.Real name George Henry
Cobley. Also known as Henry Coutts. Founder.
WM 1908. Died 21.11,1910

BARRATT, PERCY FRED THOMAS
Vaudeville Artiste. Clapham, London SW. Age 22.
I.11.04.1919 P.13.06.1919 R.18.07.1919.

**BARRETT, PERCY ERNEST See ERNIE
MAYNE**

BARRY, LEOPOLD
Comedian. Real name Louis Bonhomme.
London,SE. Age 44. I.17.04.1914 P.19.06.1914
R.17.07.1914. Excluded 20.05.11920

BARTLETT, WILLIAM HUBERT
Sketch Artiste. Age 41. I.20.09.1907 P.15.11.1907
R.21.02.1908. Resigned 25.11.1912.

BARTON, GEORGE EDWARD
Musician. London SW17. Age 43. I.17.01.1969
P.21.03.1969 R.19.09.1969.

BATES, HOWARD JOHN
Musician. Isleworth, Middlesex. Age 44.
I.15.11.1968 P.17.01.1969 R.19.09.1969.

BATT, GEORGE WALKER LGR
Vaudeville Artiste. Poplar, London E14. Age 27.
I.18.07.1919 P.15.08.1919 R.19.09.1919. WM
1935 and 1936. Died 29.04.1957.

BATTLE, LEONARD
Vaudeville Artiste. Gorton, Manchester. Age 27.
I.17.08.1928 P.21.09.1928 R.15.03.1929.

Excluded March 1933.

BAWELL-BRADER, JOHN TREHARNE
Retired Manager. Streatham Hill, London SW2.
Age 24. I.20.09.1929 P.03.12.1929 R.21.03.1930.
Resigned 15.04.1932.

BAWN, HARRY, PM
Music Hall Manager. Real name Alfred William
Henry Beales. Founder. Born 05.03.1872. WM
1910. Died 28.10.1921, aged 49 years.

BAYLEY, MONTY
Sketch Artiste. Real name Alfred Bernard Bayley.
Age 28. I.19.07.1907 P.16.08.1907 R.20.09.1907.
Excluded 19.05.1916.

**BEADLE, RONALD WALTER ALEXANDER
LESLIE**
(A Lewis). Para - Legal. Barons Court, London
W14. Age 22. I.18.11.1988 P.18.01.1991
R.15.03.1991.

**BEADLE, RONALD WALTER WILLIAM
GEORGE See RON ROWLANDS**

**BEALES, ALFRED WILLIAM HENRY See
HARRY BAWN**

BEASLEY, THOMAS ALFRED
Actor. Brixton, London SW2. Age 48.
I.21.07.1922 P.20.10.1922 R.19.01.1923.
Excluded.

BEAUCAIRE
Vaudeville Artiste. Real name Percy Richards.
East Tuebrook, Liverpool Age 30. I.25.04.1929
P.20.01.1933 R.20.10.1933. Excluded September
1941.

BEER EDWARD PETER
Cinema Manager. Thornton Heath, Surrey. Age
36. I.21.01.1955 P.18.03.1955 R.16.09.1955.
Excluded 16.05.1980.

BELINFANTE SEM
Musician. London SW9. I.20.11.1925
P.19.02.1926 R.16.04.1926. Excluded.

BELL, H. LESLIE
Vaudeville Artiste. Real name James Richardson
Bell. Age 33. I.16.04.1908 P.19.06.1908
R.17.07.1908. Excluded May 1914.

BENJAMIN ISAAC LOUIS
Box Office Manager. Stoke Newington, London
N16. Age 30. I.21.11.1952 P.17.07.1953
R.01.10.1953. Excluded 1959.

BENN, WILLIE
Vaudeville Artiste. Real name William Joseph
Garrett. Age 38. I.20.09.1907 P.20.03.1908
R,16.04.1908. Died 13 May 1919.

BENNETT, ROGER WILLIAM GORDON
Administrative Executive Odeon Cinemas. High
Wycombe, Bucks. Age 62. I.15.01.1993
P.19.03.1993 R.19.11.1993.

BENTLEY, FREDERICK
Musician. Stockwell, London SW9. Age 39.
I.18.09.1931 P.19.03.1933 R.21.04.1933. Died
22.03.1953.

BENTON, THOMAS OWEN
Musician. Victoria Park, London E9. Age 45.

I.18.07.1952 P.21.11.1952 R.15.07.1953.

BERGLAS, DAVID
Magician. Wiltshire. Joined 17.11.1978. Resigned May 1986.

BERMON, LEN
Comedian. London W4. I.15.05.1936 P.20.11.1936 R.19.02.1937. Excluded September 1941.

BERNSTEIN, NATHAN See TITO BURNS

BERZIN LOUIS
Nottingham. Age 43. I.18.01.1946 P.15.03.1946 R.19.07.1946. Resigned May 1981.

BEST, LEONARD THOMAS
Amusement Caterer. Woodford Green, Essex. Age 56. Joined 15.01.1965 from Alhambra Lodge 2657. Died 11.09.1973.

BEWSEY, ERNEST WALTER See ERNIE MOSS

BIFFO, FRANK
Musician. Age 52. I.14.06.1944 P.17.11.1944 R.21.09.1945. Excluded May 1953.

BIGNEY, BERT ALEXANDER
Clerk (Empire). Founder. Excluded 18 May 1911.

BINGHAM HENRY
Refreshment Caterer. St James, London SW. Age 32. I.16.06.1905 P.21.07.1905 R.18.08.1905. Excluded 19.03.1911.

BINNICK, SONNY
Professional Dancer. Real name Norman Binnick. East Sheen, London SW4. Age 56. I.17.11.1972 P.21.09.1973 . Excluded May 1987.

BINNIE, HARRY
Retired Dancer. London NW8. Age 54. Joined 15.05.1959. Died June 1980.

BIRKBY, ARTHUR
Actor. Age 36. I.18.02.1944 P.14.06.1944 R.15.09.1944. Excluded May 1953. Rejoined 17.1.64.

BLACK, MICHAEL
Variety Agent. London NW1. Age 38. Joined 18.01.1963 from Joppa Lodge No.188.

BLACK, STANLEY, OBE
Musical Director. Edgware, Middlesex. Age 34. I.18.07.1947 P.19.03.1948 R.19.11.1948. Died 26 November 2002, aged 89 years.

BLAKE, JACK, PM LGR
Vaudeville Artiste. Real name Jack Block. Stamford Hill, N16. Aged 30. I.19.10.1928 P.19.04.1929 R.19.07.1929. WM 1942. LGR. Died 21.07.1966.

BLAKE, WALTER THOMAS See TOM PAYNE

BLAND, ALAN VICTOR
Entertainment Agent. Hemel Hempstead, Herts. Age 58. Born 13.12.1943. Joined 16.03.2001. PM from Christopher Lodge No.2309.

BLATCHLY, JOHN JOSEPH See JACK WYNNE

BLECH, NEVILLE FRANKLIN, LGR
Broadcaster on Food and Wine. London SW7. Age 64. Born 07.07.1937. Joined 16.11.2001. PM from Mozart Lodge No.6997.

BLEWITT, JOSEPH

Musician. London W1. Age 38. I.21.09.1951 P.20.03.1953 R.19.11.1954. Resigned August 1973.

BLINDT, NATHAN DAVID
Musician. London SE5. Age 32. I.21.10.1932 P.20.01.1933 R.21.04.1933. Excluded September 1941.

BLITZER, HENRY See HARRY GREEN

BLOCK, DAVID
Script Writer. London SW1. Joined 16.05.1980.

BLOCK, IVAN MARTIN
Diamond Cutter. London W1. Age 40. I.21.03.1947 P.18.07.1947 R.21.11.1947.

BLOCK, JACK See JACK BLAKE

BLOCK, JOSEPH CLAUDE See ZOLA

BLOCK, ROBERT
Merchant. Coventry, Warwickshire. Age 39. I.21.01.1944 P.18.02.1944 R.21.06.1944. Resigned 1959.

BLOOMFIELD, JACK
Retired Artiste. London WC2. Aged 29. I.20.04.1928 P.15.06.1928 R.20.07.1928. Excluded. Rejoined 17.03.1950. Was then a licensed victualler in London W1.

BLORE, JOHN EDWARD See JOHN BORELLI

BOATWRIGHT, ALBERT EDWARD
Musician. Kingsbury, London NW9. Age 42. I.15.10.1943 P.14.06.1944 R.19.01.1945. Excluded March 1952.

BODLEY LESLIE CYRIL
Stage Manager. Finsbury Park, London N4. Age 29. I.19.09.1930 P.17.10.1930 R.21.11.1930. Resigned.

BODNER, MONTY See MONTY BOND

BOND, GEORGE FRANK
Theatre Executive. Thornton Heath, Surrey. Age 58. I.15.01.1965 P.17.09.1965 R.21.01.1966. Resigned May 1986. Rejoined 20.01.1989.

BOND, MONTY
Entertainments Manager. Real name Monty Bodner. Potters Bar, Herts. I.16.01.1981 P.18.09.1981 R.20.11.1981.

BONHOMME, LOUIS See LEOPOLD BARRY.

BONN, ISSY, PM
Raconteur and Variety Agent. Real name Benjamin Levin. London NW8. Age 35. I.17.06.1938 P.20.01.1939 R.21.07.1939. Rejoined 19.11.1948. Died 21.04.1977, aged 74 years.

BOOCOCK, GEORGE See GEORGE BRADLEY

BOOKIN, LAURENCE
Musician. Age 28. I.19.01.1940 P.16.02.1940 R.21.11.1941. Resigned June 1947.

BORELLI, JOHN
Real name John Edward Blore. Musical Director. London SW2. Aged 37. I.18.11.1938 . Excluded. Died 1948, aged 47 years.

BOWEN, WILLIAM HILL See BILLY HILL

BOWMAN, ALFRED
Company Director. Camberley, Surrey. Age 42.

Joined 17.03.1967 from Albert Edward Lodge No. 1714.

BOWMAN, JERRY
Musician. Edmonton, London N9. Age 48. I.21.09.1962 P.18.01.1963 R.15.11.1963. Died 01.06.1966.

BOWN, BENJAMIN
Cinema Manager. London SW9. Age 38. I.16.12.1921 P.20.01.1922 R.17.03.1922.

BOX, EDMUND CHARLES See TED. E. BOX

BOX, FREDERICK BRAUND, PM PAGDC
Theatre Proprietor. Holborn Circus, London EC1. Age 56. I.18.01.1918 P.15.02.1918 R.15.03.1918. Resigned 24.05.1920. Rejoined 16.09 1921. WM 1937.

BOX, TED. E.
Comedian. Real name Charles Edmund Box. Age 32. I.19.07.1907 P.16.08.1907 R.18.10.1907. Excluded 16.05.1912.

BOYD, FRANKLYN
Music Publisher. New Malden, Surrey. Age 27. Joined 21.05.1965.

BOYD, SYD
Variety Artiste. Real name John Ernest Stewart Henderson. Streatham Hill, London SW2. Age 46. I.20.04.1945 P.21.09.1945 R.16.11.1945.

BRADLEY, GEORGE
Musician. Real name George Boocock. Changed his name by Deed Poll to Bradley. London SW2. Age 35. I.20.09.1963 P.20.03.1964 R.18.09.1964.

BRADSHAW COLIN
Musician. North Finchley, N12. Age 31. I.19.07.1929 P.16.08.1929 R.20.09.1929.

BRADY, ALBERT See ALBERT FELINO

BRANSBY, PHIL
Vaudeville Artiste. Real name Alexander Edward Phillips. East Ham, London E. Joined 19.07.1918. Joined from Proscenium Lodge No.3435.

BRAY, SYDNEY
Vaudeville Artiste. Real name William Zaccheaus Putner. Greenwich London SE10. Age 25. I.20.07.1917 P.19.04.1918 R.21.06.1918.

BREEZE, ALAN LOUIS
Vocalist. Weybridge, Surrey. Age 34. I.17.03.1944 P.20.03.1945 R.16.03.1945. Died 15.01.1980, aged 70 years.

BREEZE, ERIC
Musician. London NW1. I.15.11.1935 P.21.02.1936 R.19.11.1937.

BRERETON, GERALD, LGR
Singer. East Moseley, Surrey. Age 69. Joined 15.03.1991 from Blackheath Lodge No.1320.

BRESSLAW, BERNARD
Actor. Totteridge, N20. Age 37. I.17.03.1972 P.16.11.1973 R.18.01.1974. Died 11.06.1993, aged 59 years.

BRETT, EDWIN WILSON
Vaudeville Artiste. Age 36. Joined 20.04.1906 from Earl's Court Lodge No.2765. Resigned 24.10.1920.

BREWER, MARK ANTONY
Vaudeville Artiste. Battersea, SW11. Age 52. I.21.11.1919 P.16.04.1919 R.16.07.1920. Excluded 1923.

BRICKWELL, PINERO JEROME
Theatrical Manager. Streatham, SW16. Age 40. I.17.04.1931 P.16.10.1931 R.15.09.1933.

BRIDGES, RONALD V. PAGDC
Musician. Shenfield, Essex. Hon. Member. Elected 19 May 1995.

BRITTON, ERNEST CHARLES, LGR
Merchant. Age 56. Joined 16.03.1945. Died 19.11.1957.

BRITTON, NORMAN ERNEST
Food Company Director. Buckhurst Hill, Essex. Age 35. I.21.03.1947 P.16.01.1948 R.21.01.1949. Resigned 04.07.1959.

BROCKDORFF, JOHN DILLENG
Revue Proprietor. London W1. Aged 40. I.18.01.1918. P.15.02.1918 R.15.03.1918.

BROOK, ERNEST EDWARD See LEO TELL

BROWN, ALAN WILLIAM
Comedian. St Leonard's-on-Sea, East Sussex. Born 18 June 1942. I.21.01.2005.

BROWN, JACK SAMUEL See JACK ROYAL

BROWN, LORD NEVILLE KENNARD
Variety Artiste. Kenton, Middlesex. Age 44. I.16.11.1945 P.15.02.1946 R.08.04.1949.

BROWN, TEDDY
Musical Conductor. London WC1. Joined 21.01.1938. Died 25.05.1946, aged 46 years.

BROWN, WILLIAM ERNEST
Actor. Chelsea Manor, London SW3. Age 64. Joined 15.09.1989. Resigned.

BRUCE, JOHN CHARLES See JACK IDENTO

BRUCE-SMITH, CYRIL EDWARD See CYRIL SMITH

BRUSKE, CHARLES
Musician. London E1. Age 33. I.20.06.1924 P.18.07.1924 R.15.08.1924. Excluded.

BRYAN, CARSON
Vaudeville Artiste. Real name Lawrence Dunn. Brixton, London SW2. Age 34. I.20.04.1917 P.15.06.1917 R.20.07.1917. Excluded 1924.

BRYANT, ROBERT
Motor Engineer. London SW14. Age 42. I.20.09.1940.

BUDD, ARTHUR
Vaudeville Artiste. Kennington, London SE11. Age 31. I.18.01.1924. P.20.06.1924 R.18.07.1924. Died 22.02.1963.

BUDD, WILLIAM FRANK
Stage Director/Producer. London SE14. I.19.09.1947 P.21.11.1947 R.17.09.1948. Died 30.03.1981.

BUNGEY, EDWARD HARRY
Music Hall Clerk. Founder. Resigned 12.03.1907.

BUNTING, GEORGE HUGH ALLEN
Stage Manager. Folkestone, Kent. Age 50.

I.15.06.1923 P.21.09.1923 R.19.09.1923.
Excluded.

BURDEN, JOHN HAROLD
Musician. Great Missendon, Bucks. Age 38.
I.18.03.1960 P.16.09.1960 R.21.09.1962.
Resigned 16.05.1980.

BURNETT, THOMAS S.
Vaudeville Artiste. Founder. Died, date not
known.

BURNOFF, JACK
Variety Artiste. Real name John Thomas Burns.
South West Lake, Los Angeles, USA. I.7.07.1936
P.18.09.1936 R.16.10.1936. Resigned May 1946.

BURNS, JACK, LGR
Toastmaster. Benfleet, Essex. Aged 62. Born
30.11.1939. Joined 16.03.2001. PM from City
Wall Lodge No.6793.

BURNS, JOHN THOMAS See JACK BURNOFF

BURNS, TITO
Variety Artiste. Real name Nathan Bernstein.
Maida Vale, London W9. Age 34. I.8.11.1955
P.20.01.1956 R.16.03.1956.

BURTON, CHARLES HAROLD
Violinist. Age 31. I.21.06.1907 P.19.07.1907 R.16.
08.1907. Excluded 19.05.1916.

BYFIELD, PETER PHILIP
Club Proprietor. Chelsea, London SW10. Aged
34. I.20.01.1984 P.21.09.1984 R.18.01.1985.

**BYRON-BARHYDT, ROMAN VICTOR JOSE
See MORAN**

C
CADWALL, EDWIN HORACE
Variety Agent. Balham, London SW. Age 39.
I.17.10.1919 P.21.11.1919 R.19.03.1920.

CALDERHEAD, DAVID GLEN, PM PAGDC
Hotel Director. Lee, London SE12. Aged 46.
Joined 21.03.1986 from Mithraic Lodge No.6396.
WM 1991.

CALLISTER, EDWARD Dr. PM PPGorg
Musician. London SW2. Age 56. Joined
19.09.1986 from Proscenium Lodge No.3435.
WM 1992.

CAMP, FREDERICK THOMAS
Musical Conductor. Holloway, London N. Age 33.
I.15.10.1909 P.18.03.1910 R.15.04.1910.
Resigned January 1917.

**CAMPKIN, GEORGE See GEORGE
D'ORMONDE**

CAPRI, DAVID
Singer/Actor. Rochester Row, London SW1. Age
39. Joined 16.03.1990 from Drury Lane Lodge
No.2127.

CAREY, DAVID CHARLES
Music Publisher/Vocalist. Norbury, London SW16.
Joined 16.03.1973. PM from Royal Naval Lodge
No 59. Resigned.14.07.1993.

CARLILE, CHARLES ALFRED
Actor. Upper Tulse Hill, London SW. Joined
21.04.1911 from St John's Lodge No. 1306.

Excluded May 1917.

CARLILE, CHARLES DOUGLAS
Actor. Clapham Common, London SW. Joined
21.04.1911 from St John's 1306. Excluded May
1915.

CARNEY, GEORGE
Comedian. London NW2. Joined 17.06.1927.
Rejoined and later became Honorary Member.
Died 9 December 1947, aged 60 years.

CARNEY, GEORGE ARTHUR
Vaudeville Artiste and Comedian. Wandsworth
Common, SW. Aged 30. Born 21 November
1877, Bristol. I.21.07.1911 . Excluded March
1917. Died 9 December 1947, London. Aged 70
years.

CARPENTER, EDWARD JAMES
Motor Dealer. Brixton Hill, London SW2. Age 37.
I.16.02.1940 P.21.11.1958 R.18.03.1960.
Rejoined 17.01.1958.Died 1971.

CARPENTER, JOHN RAYMOND
Musician. Rainham, Essex. Age 55. Born
23.09.1941. Joined 17.05.1996 from St Helens &
St Giles Lodge No.9133.

CARR, CHARLIE
Vaudeville Artiste. Real name Charles Albert
Leslie Carter. London, SE5. Age 33. I.20.08.1926
P.15.10.1926 R.14.04.1927. Excluded

**CARTER, CHARLES ALBERT LESLIE See
CHARLIE CARR**

CARTWRIGHT, EDWARD HENRY
Vaudeville Artiste. Leicester. Age 35. I.17.10.1924
P.21.11.1924 R.20.11.1925.

CARYL, CHARLES RONALD RAMSDEN
Musical Director. Hanworth, Middlesex. Age 60.
I.16.03.1984 P.18.01.1985 R.17.11.1985. Died
15.02.1996.

CARYLL, BILLY
Vaudeville Artiste. Real name William Francis
Clark. Streatham, London SW1. Age 35.
I.20.06.1930 P15.08.1930 R.17.04.1931. Died
February 1953.

CASHTIEN, ISAAC See LEN JACKSON

CASSIDY, MICHAEL DAVID
Comedian/Magician. Tunbridge Wells, Kent. Age
46. Born 14.01.1948. I.16.09.1994 P.19.11.1994
R.15.03.1996.

CATLIN, WILLIAM HENRY
Comedian. Real name William Henry Fox. Age
36. I.17.07.1908 P.16.10.1908 R.15.04.1910.
Resigned 18.05.1915.

CHAMP, DESMOND HERBERT
Musical Director. Winchmore Hill, London N21.
Age 40. I.21.11.1969 P.20.11.1970 R.15.01.1971.
Resigned May 1987.

CHAPERLIN, ANTHONY DOUGLAS, SLGR
Night Club Owner. Streatham, London SW16.
Age 43. Joined 16.09.1988. PM from Annuntio
Lodge No.5539.

CHAPERLIN, HENRY
Club Owner. Streatham, London SW16. Age 76.

Joined 21.11.1986. WM Annuntio Lodge No. 5539 in 1971. Died 25.03.1993, aged 82 years.

CHAPLIN, SYDNEY
Comedian. Age 23. Born 17.03.1885, London. I..21.08.1908 P.18.09.1908 R.16.10.1908. Excluded 17.05.1918. Died 15.04.1965, Nice, aged 80 years.

CHAPMAN, CHARLES ERNEST
Music Hall Agent. Founder. Excluded 20.05.1909.

CHAPMAN, HARRY See HARRY MARASO

CHAPMAN, HENRY
Vaudeville Manager. Cleethorpes, Lincs. Age 38. I.18.01.1935 P.15.03.1935 R.20.09.1935. Resigned 21.11.1941.

CHAPMAN, WILLIAM THOMAS
Musical Director. London W1. Age 45. I.17.11.1950 P.16.03.1951 R.16.01.1953.

CHAPTER, HAL
Comedian. Real name Henry William John Church. Age 34. Joined.20.10.1905 from Metropolitan Lodge No. 1507. WM 1916.Died 11.06.1953.

CHARLTON, CHRIS
Illusionist. Clapham Common SW11. I.16.10.1936 P.19.02.1937 R.18.02.1938. Excluded September 1941.

CHASID, SIDNEY
Musician. Stamford Hill, London N16. I.15.05.1936 P15.05.1936 R18.11.1955. Excluded 1940. Rejoined 21.05.1954.

CHEEK, CLIFFORD HAMILTON See KRANTON

CHESTER-BISHOP, ALFRED JOHN, PM **See CHESTER FIELD**

CHESTER, ERNE, PM LGR
Vaudeville Artiste. Real name Ernest James Smith. Age 35. Joined 20.04.1906 from Duke of Fife Lodge Nio.2345. WM 1918. Died 07.04.1950.

CHILD, WILLIAM NELSON
Comedian. London W1. Age 31. I.16.08.1929 P.25.04.1930 Excluded March 1933.

CHILLINGWORTH, STANLEY THOMAS
Musician. Leyton, London E10. Age 24. I.18.10.1929 P.21.03.1930 R.25.04.1930.

CHISHOLM, ARTHUR
Vaudeville Artiste. Real name Arthur Alexander Clarke. Age 50. London W1. Age 45. I.19.09.1930. P.30.03.1931 R.17.07.1931. Died May 1960.

CHRISTIAN, ALBERT
Vocalist. Age 46. I.04.05.1906 P.15.06.1906 R.20.07.1906. Resigned 18.05.1911. Died 16 June 1915.

CHRISTO, SID
Vaudeville Artiste. Real name Sidney Ralph Owens. Spark Brook, Birmingham. Age 36. I.16.09.1927 P.21.10.1927 R.19.03.1929. Excluded.

CHURCH, HENRY WILLIAM JOHN See HAL CHAPTER

CLAFF, GEORGE
Make Up Artiste. London NW1. Age 61. I.17.01.1964 P.20.11.1964 R.15.01.1965. Died 26.02.1982.

CLAFF, HARRY
Vaudeville Artiste. Real name Hyman Claff. Balham, London SW. Born c1880. Joined 19.07.1912 from Liverpool Dramatic Lodge No.1609. Died 08.05.1943

CLARK, DAN H.
Vaudeville Artiste. Real name Frederick Henderson. London EC. Age 29. I.19.03.1915 P.16.07.1915 R.20.08.1915.

CLARK, WILLIAM FRANCIS See BILLY CARYLL

CLARKE, ALEXANDER HUGHES See CON STUART

CLARKE, ARTHUR ALEXANDER See ARTHUR CHISHOLM

CLARKE, ERNEST LEATHLEY
Variety Agent. Age 36. I.20.09.1907 P.18.10.1907 R.15.11.1907. Excluded 18 May 1911.

CLARKE, LAURIE
Musician, London W4. Age 35. I.21.01.1949 P.16.09.1949 . Excluded May 1954. Rejoined 17.05.1957. Excluded May 1959.

CLARKE, ROBERT GEORGE See HARRY FIELDS

CLAY, FREDERICK THOMAS
Theatre Proprietor. Founder. Excluded 16.05.1912.

CLAYTON, HENRY
Variety Producer. Real name Larry Gordon. London N1. Age 30. I.16.11.1951 P.21.03.1952 R.21.03.1952.

CLIFFORD, HARRY
Vaudeville Artiste. Real name Henry Francis Glen. Stockwell, London SW. Age 39. I.15.10.1909 P.15.04.1910 R.21.10.1910. Excluded.15.05.1914.

CLIFFORD, LEN
Variety Artiste. Real name Charles Smith.Hyams Park, London,E. Age 44. I.19.06.1942. Excluded April 1947.

CLIFFORD, PAUL JOHN , PM
Real name John Appleboom. Musical Director. Brixton Hill, SW2. Age 27. I.18.07.1919 P. 15.08.1919 R.19.09.1919. Excluded 24.02.1920 Changed name by Deed Poll. Rejoined 18.11.1938. WM 1954.

CLIFTON, JOSHUA
Vaudeville Artiste. Balsall Heath, Birmingham. Age 38. I.16.04.1909 P.18.06.1909 R.13.08.1909. Excluded 20 May 1920.

CLINTON, WAL
Comedian. Real name Walter Crooks. East Ham, London E. Age 21. I.19.06.1914 P.17.07.1914 R.21.08.1914.

CLOETINS, ANTOINE
Musical Conductor. Founder. Resigned

15.01.1907.

COBLEY, GEORGE HENRY See BARONI

COHEN, ABRAHAM See ARTHUR COWAN

COHEN, GERALD
Maida Vale. I.17.03.1944. P.20.03.1945.
R.16.11.1945.

COLE, MERVYN DAVID
(A Lewis) Law student. North Harrow, Middlesex.
Age 21. I.15.09.1967 P.17.11.1967 R.15.03.1968.
Resigned May 1983.

COLE, MICHAEL DAVID
Musician. Borehamwood, Herts. Aged 59. Born
09.06.1943. Joined 31.05.2002. PM from Oliver
Goldsmith Lodge No.5924.

COLE, NAT
Musician. Rayners Lane, Harrow, Middlesex. Age
40. I.16.03.1951 P.21.09.1951 R.21.03.1952.
Resigned 14 July 1993.

COLLINSON, WILLIAM, PM
Comedian. Real name William Valentine
Malivoire. Age 29. I.21.09.1906 P.19.04.1907
R.18.10.1907. WM 1929. Died. Date not known.

COLQUHOUN, IAN
Vocalist. Real name John Colquhoun Manifold.
Age 37. I.22.01.1907 P.19.07.1907 R.16.08.1907.
Excluded 21.05.1915

CONDON, CHRISTOPHER THOMAS
Musician. South Croydon, Surrey. Age 46.
I.18.11.1966 P.17.03.1967 R.19.01.1968.
Resigned 10.03.1996.

CONN, HARRY
Musician. Southampton Row, London WC1. Age
34. I.18.11.1955 P.16.03.1956 R.21.09.1956.

CONN, WILLIAM See BILLY MAHER

CONNOLLY, WILFRED JAMES
Manager. New Malden, Surrey. I.15.01.1926
P.19.02.1926 R.18.06.1926. Resigned May 1942.

CONWAY, TOM
Comedian. Real name Thomas William Cowlam.
Age 48. Tulse Hill, Brixton, London SW. Age 52.
I.17.02.1914 P.20.03.1914 R.17.04.1914. Died
27.06.1917.

CONRAD, JESS
Actor/Singer. Real name Gerald Arthur James.
Denham, Bucks. Age 59. Born 24.02.1936.
I.15.09.1995 P.20.09.1996 R.21.03.1997.

COOK, ERIC SYDNEY
Musician. London, W1. I.19.09.1947
P.19.03.1948 R.16.07.1949. WM 1959. Died
01.10.1985.

COOPER, FRED
Vaudeville Artiste. Real name Leopold Arthur
Goldschede. Age 36, London SE5. Age 35.
I.19.06.1925 P.19.07.1925 R.21.08.1925. Died
09.12.1968.

CORAM
Ventriloquist. Real name Thomas Mitchell
Whitaker. Telford Park, London SW. Age 31.
I.17.09.1909 P.21.10.1910 R.13.12.1912.
Excluded 19.05.1916.

**CORBETT, ROWLAND JOHN See JOHN
ROWLAND**

CORFIELD, ALFRED See ALFRED DEAN

CORTEZ, LEON
Musician. London SW9. I.18.12.1936
P.19.02.1937 R.19.03.1937. Excluded April 1946.
Died 31 December 1970, aged 70 years.

COTTERILL, JOEY See JOE GOODMAN

COUSINS, BERTIE PHILLIP
Musician. Plumstead, SE18. Age 36.
I.21.08.1931 P.16.10.1931 R.14.04.1932

COUTTS, HENRY, See BARONI

COWAN, ARTHUR
Film renter. Real name Abraham Cohen.
Birmingham. Age 43. I.15.02.1918 P.15.03.1918
R.19.04.1918.

COWBRICK, CHARLES ERNEST
Musician. London NW1. Age 47. I.14.04.1927
P.15.07.1927 R.20.04.1928. Excluded.

**COWLAM, THOMAS WILLIAM See TOM
CONWAY**

COX, ALAN VICTOR
Organist. Guildford, Surrey. Age 46. Joined
15.01.1988 from Benefaction Lodge No.5318.
Died September 1928.

COX, JAMES ALFRED
Stage Manager. Poplar, London E14. Age 42.
I.16.10.1925 P.20.11.1925 R.19.03.1926. Died
September 1928.

**CRAMER, ARTHUR JOEL See ARTHUR C.
KINGSLEY**

CRAMP, WILLIAM ALFRED
Musician. Ealing, London W. Age 26.
I.21.04.1911 P.16.06.1911 R.18.08.1911.
Resigned 08.04.1913.

CRANBY, WALTER
Vaudeville Artiste. Real name Harry Styck Tullett.
Eastbourne, Sussex. Age 30. I.16.12.1921
P.21.04.1922 R.20.04.1923. Died 21.12.1928.

CREAN, RICHARD
Musical Director. Fulham, London SW. Age 42.
I.17.10.1919 P.19.03.1920 R.16.04.1920. Died
14.11.1955.

CREASEY, FREDERICK JOSEPH
Theatre Manager. Maida Vale, London W9. Age
47. I.15.01.1954 P.18.03.1955. Disappeared...and
he wasn't a magician!

CREGAN, JOSEPH See DION WADE

CROCKER, HENRY
Stage Manager. Age 33. Born c.1875.
I.20.03.1908 P.16.04.1908 R.21.08.1908.
Excluded 16.05.1913. Died 12 10.1937, Thorpe
Bay, Essex.

CROKE, LEO THOMAS
Musical Director. Fulham, SW6. Age 39.
I.19.08.1927.P.16.03.1928 R.20.04.1928.
Excluded May 1934.

CROMWELL, WILL
Juggler. Real name William Cromwell Knox.
Herne Hill, London,SE. Age 21. I.18.03.1910

P.16.09.1910 R.18.08.1911 Resigned
17.09.1917.

CROMWELL-KNOX, ALBERT EDWARD
Vaudeville Artiste. Brixton Hill, London SW2. Age
27. I.21.09.1923 P.19.10.1923 R.21.03.1924.
Excluded March 1932.

CROOKS, WALTER See WAL CLINTON

CROSSLAND, EDWARD
Musical Sketch Proprietor. London SW. Age 34.
I.16.07.1909 P.15.07.1910 R.04.10.1910.

CROSSLEY, LIONEL DOYLE
Vaudeville Artiste. Highgate, London NW5. Age
27. I.19.11.1920 P.17.06.1921 R.18.11.1921.
Excluded.

CROWTHER, GEORGE FRANCIS MORGAN
Vaudeville Artiste. Cardiff. Age 29. I.19.09.1919
P.21.11.1919 R.19.03.1920. Excluded.

CRUIKSHANK, ALFRED LGR
Vaudeville Artiste. Clapham, London SW. Age 44.
I.17.12.1920 P.17.06.1921
R.18.11.1921.Rejoined 1940. WM 1941.
Resigned March 1952.

CUMBERBIRCH, HENRY
Music Hall Artiste. Founder. Resigned
04.05.1907.

CUMMINGS, RAYMOND FREDERICK
Consultant & Musician. Sanderstead, Surrey. Age
45. I.17.03.1989 P.19.01.1990 R.16.03.1990.
Resigned 30.03.1994.

CURTISS, BOB
Comedian. Real name Robert David Trayling.
Cheam, Surrey. Age 61. Born 22.03.1938.
I.17.09.1999 P.19.01.2001 R.15.03.2002.

CUTTS, WILFRED, MBE
Sidcup, Kent. Joined 20.03.1969. PM of Cheyne
Lodge No.4443.

D

DAINTY, BILLY
Variety Artiste. Real name William Hooper Frank
John Dainty. Ruislip, Middlesex. Aged 41.
I.19.03.1971. P.17.03.1972 R.17.11.1972. Died
19.11.1986.

DAINTY, HENRY JAMES
Entertainment Caterer. London WC1. Aged 48.
I.20.09.1946 P.21.03.1947 R.18.07.1947. Died
18.12.1968.

DAKIN, ARTHUR H.A.
Musician. Mappowder, Dorset. I.17.09.1976
P.21.01.1977 R.18.03.1977. Died 22 November
2002, aged 64 years.

DALE, PHILIP CHANDELER
Theatrical agent London WC2E. Born
23.04.1957. I.15.11.2002. P.19.09.2003.
R.21.01.2005.

DALLAS, STAN
Entertainment Agent. Real name Stanley Jones.
Bushby, Leics. Age 46. Born 04.04.1935.
I.20.10.1981 P.21.05.1982 R.17.09.1982.

DALTON, THOMAS See ARCHIE GLEN

DALY, PAUL
Vaudeville Artiste. London SE11. Age 32.
I.19.08.1921 P.18.11.1921 R.21.04.1922.

DANIEL, HERBERT BERNARD
Entertainment Promoter. London SW1. Age 36.
Joined 19.01.1962 from Assembly Lodge
No.4357.

DANIELS, ALFRED
Banjoist. Real name Alfred David Toledano.
London EC. Age 27. I.15.03.1912 P.19.04.1912
R.21.06.1912. Resigned May 1947, USA.
Rejoined 21.11.1958. Died 08.12.1964.

DANIELS, JACK
Musician. Streatham, London SW2. Age 43.
I.18.09.1953 P.15.01.1954 R.19.03.1954.

DANIELS, JOSEPH
Variety Artiste. Standlake, near Witney, Oxford.
Age 36. I.20.03.1942 P.17.07.1942 R.20.11.1942.
Died 01.07.1993, aged 85 years.

DANIELS, JOSEPH
Electrician. Real name Joseph Kenneth
Toledano. Golders Green, London NW11. Age
24. I.19.05.1944 P.20.03.1945 R.15.02.1946.
Went to America. Resigned March 1947.

DANIELS, SOLOMON SYDNEY See SIRDANI

DANTE, TROY
Snooker Manager. Real name Noel Frederickson.
Blackpool, Lancashire. Age 62. Born 25
December 1936. I. 20.03.1998. P.21.05.1999.

DANVERS, WILLIAM
Vaudeville Artiste. Offerton, Stockport. Born 1884.
Age 36. I.16.06.1922 P.20.04.1923 R.21.09.1923.
Died 20.03.1964, aged 80 years.

DARBY, ERIC GEORGE
Musician. London SE16. Aged 37. I.17.01.1958
P.16.01.1959 R.19.01.1962. Resigned May 1965.

DAROS, ED
Vaudeville Artiste. Real name Harold Rhymer.
Spennymoor, County Durham. Age 31.
I.15.08.1924 P.16.07.1926 R.20.11.1927.

DAVEY, CYRIL JAMES
Self-employed film extra. Born 7 July 1932.
Master Mason. Joined 19.11.2004 from
Petersham Lodge No.4514.

DAVEY, ROY HERBERT
(A Lewis). Musician. Maida Vale London W9. Age
47. I.16.01.1970 P.20.03.1970 R.18.09.1970.
Excluded 18.05.1999.

DAVIDSON, HOWARD
Musician. Herts. I.19.11.1976 P.21.01.1977
R.16.09.1977.

DAVIDSON, JAMES CAMERON, OBE PM
Entertainer. Ewhurst, Surrey. Aged 37.
I.20.09.1991 P.15.11.1991 R.17.01.1992. WM
2001. Resigned whilst in office as Master.

DAVIES, DENNIS
Catering Manager. Tynemouth, Tyne and Wear.
Joined 16.05.1980 from Hadrian Lodge No. 6772.

DAVIES, EDWIN BARNARD BERTRAM
Theatrical Manager. Earl's Court, London SW5.

Age 26. I.15.03.1918 P.19.04.1918 R.21.06.1918.
Died 1927.

DAVIES, FREDERICK SHENSTONE, PM
Variety Artiste. Blackpool, Lancs. Age 29.
I.18.03.1966 P.18.11.1966 R.17.11.1967. WM
1986.

DAVIS, CHARLES, PM
Vocalist. London W7. Age 35, I.19.01.1951
P.21.09.1951 R.18.01.1952. Resigned 1974.
Rejoined 19.09.1975.WM 1972. LGR. Died
27.05.1987.

DAVIS, FREDERICK FAY
Manager. Stratford, London E15. I.20.08.1937
P.17.12.1937 R.16.09.1938. Excluded April 1947.

DAVIS, LEWIS
Musician. Maida Vale, London W9. Age 30.
I.20.04.1934 P.15.06.1934 R.20.07.1934.
Resigned.

DAVIS, MARCUS
Musician. Shepherd's Bush, W12. Age 34.
I.17.07.1931 P.21.08.1931 R.16.10.1931.

DAVIS, THOMAS GUNNING See SPOT

DAWSON, CYRIL
Manager. London NW6. Age 60. I.15.03.1957
P.15.11.1957 R.21.03.1958. Died 1969.

**DAY, ARTHUR HERBERT WILLIAM See
ARTHUR LEWIS**

DE COURCEY-COOKE, ROGER, PM PAGDC
Ventriloquist and entertainer. Bushey, Herts. Age
45. Born 10 December 1944. Joined March 1990
from Lodge of Manna No.7602 where he was
initiated in 1975. WM 2001 and part of 2002.
PAGDC 2003.

**DE GROOT, EDWARD STANLEY See
STANELLI**

DE MOUNTFALCON, DAVID MAURICE
Magician. London W1. I.20.03.1987 P.15.01.1988
R.16.09.1987.

DE VOY, JAMES ALBERT PM PAGDC, **See
ALBERT LE FRE**

**DE VOY, PERCIVAL FREDERICK See PERCY
LE FRE**

DE YOUNG, JOSEPH See JOE YOUNG

DEAN, ALFRED
Vaudeville Artiste. Real name Alfred Corfield.
Brixton, London SW2. Age 2.5 I.19.08.1927
P.18.11.1927 R.16.03.1928. Resigned May 1934.

DEKKER, CORNELIUS
Vaudeville Artiste. Merton, London SW19. Age
32. Joined 17.03.1922 from Proscenium Lodge
No.3435. Resigned 21.01.1929

DELMAR, NEVILLE JACK
Vaudeville Artiste. Westcliffe-on-Sea, Essex. Age
39. I.17.09.1920 P.19.11.1920 R.15.07.1921.
Rejoined 20.09.1935. Died March 1952.

DENNIS, HARRY
Theatre Agent. Real name Harry Gilbert.
Holloway, London N7. Age 54. I.16.09.1949
P.21.07.1950 R.20.07.1951. Died 1971.

DENNY, FRANK

Stage Director. Empire, Finsbury Park.
I.17.03.1944 P.21.07.1944 R.15.09.1944.

DESWARTE, ALFRED
TV Theatrical Agent. Stanmore, Middlesex.
Joined 19.05.1972 from Proscenium Lodge
No.3435. Died 2 February 1991.

DICKSON, GEORGE See G. DIXON KENWIN

DIGBY, JAMES
Variety Agent. London NW10. Age 49.
I.16.01.1948 P.16.07.1948 R.15.09.1949.
Resigned May 1986.

DILLON, ERNEST
Vaudeville Artiste. Merton, Surrey. Age 36.
I.19.02.1909 P.18.06.1909 R.16.07.1909.
Excluded 1924.

DINDOL, JOSEPH
Comedian. Southgate, London N14. Aged 64.
Joined 21.09.1984 from King David Lodge
No.5719.

DITTRICH, ALBERT BERNARD
Musician. Frockenham. Age 38. I.15.01.1943
P.16.07.1943 R.16.10.1943. Excluded 1958.

DIX, FRANK JOHN WINGATE
Dramatic Author. Aged 34. I.15.03.1907
P.19.04.1907 . Excluded 19.05.1911.

DIX, MARK JOHN
Events Manager. Walton-on-the-Hill, Surrey. Born
15.03.1944. Joined 19.03.2004 from Claremont
Lodge No.1861 of which he was WM in 1994.

**DIXON, FRANK EDWARD JAMES See TEDDY
FOX**

DIXON, REG
Comedian. Coventry. Age 49. I.20.11.1964
P.19.03.1965 R.19.11.1965. Died 26.06.1984.

DOLINOFF, DANIEL TEPPER
Dancer. London W1. Age 44. I.19.09.1941
P.19.12.1941 R.19.06.1942. Excluded
16.09.1955.

DOLTON, EDGAR
Musician. Walthamstow, London E. Age 22.
I.18.04.1913 P.20.06.1913 R.18.07.1913. Died
04.10.1955.

DOMKE, LEO See LEE DONN

DONEGAL, JOHN
Actor/vocalist. London SW9. Age 49.
I.20.01.1950 P.15.09.1950 R.19.01.1951.
Resigned November 1965.

**DONEGAN, JAMES EDWARD See JIMMIE
DUNEDIN**

DONN, LEE
Musician. Real name Leo Domke. London WC.
Aged 39. I.16.09.1932 P.17.03.1933
R.21.07.1933.

DONN, RAPHAEL
Theatrical Manager. Wouldham, Kent. Age 60.
Born 07.08.1937. I.19.09.1997 P.16.01.1998
R.20.03.1998.

DOONAN, GEORGE VINCENT
Comedian. Claygate, Surrey. Age 44.
I.17.11.1939 P.17.01.1941 R.16.05.1941.

Excluded May 1950.

D'ORMONDE, GEORGE
Variety Artiste. Real name George Camkin. Great Richmond. Aged 43. I.16.03.1945. Excluded May 1949

DOUGHTY, CHARLES JOHN
Independent. Founder. Secretary. Died. Date not known.

DOUST, WILLIAM
Vaudeville Artiste. Age 32. I.20.04.1906 P.15.06.1906 R.21.09.1906. Died. Date not known,

DOVE, JOHN
Musician. Known as Jack Dove. Hatfield, Herts. Age 45. I.16.09.1960 P.17.11.1961 R.17.05.1963.

DOYLE, BUNNY
Comedian, Real name Bernard Doyle. Wimbledon, London. Age 49. I.15.09.1944 P.19.03.1954. Died 27.08.1955

DOYLE, JOHN
Variety Artiste. Brixton, London SW9. Age 41. I.21.09.1951 P.21.11.1952 R.21.11.1958.

DRAKE, WILLIAM
Musician. London NW4. Age 55. I.18.09.1964 P.15.01.1965 R.15.03.1965.

DRAPER, THOMAS ALFRED
Toastmaster. Chiswick, London. Age 83. Joined 20.03.1992 from Proscenium Lodge No.3435. Died 13.10.92.

DREWE, ALFRED VICTOR, PM
Secretary, VAF. Maida Hill, London W9. Age 34. I.19.06.1931 P.17.07.1931 R.18.09.1931. WM 1943. Died 1946.

DUCE, ROBERT WILLIAM
Music Hall Manager. Joined 19.10.1906 from Henry Muggeridge Lodge No.1679. Died 13.04.1926.

DUDLEY, ERIC
Vaudeville Artiste. Real name Charles Henry Eric Hunter. Balham, London SW. Age 28. I.18.02.1921 P.15.04.1921 R.16.09.1921. Excluded 1924.

DUGGAN, TERENCE RUSSELL
Actor/Comedian. Ilford, Essex IG1 1HE. Age 58. I.21.09.1990 P.18.01.1991. R.20.09.1991.

DUNEDIN, JIMMIE
Vaudeville Artist and later Variety Agent. Real name James Edward Donegan. I.16.06.1905 P.21.07.1905 R.20.10.1905. Rejoined 18.02.1921 from New York. Excluded.

DUNN, LAWRENCE See CARSON BRYAN

DURHAM, GEORGE
Catering Manager. London WC2, Age 34. I.21.07.1939. Excluded April 1947. Rejoined 19.11.1948.

DURHAM, GEORGE HENRY
Bookkeeper. London NW1. Age 43. I.21.07.1939 P.19.11.1948 R.18.11.1949. Rejoined. Excluded 1979.

DURRANT, JAMES

Musician. London SW11. Age 28. I.17.02.1939 P.21.07.1939 R.17.11.1939.

DYBALL, GEORGE H., PM PAGStB
Stage Manager. Founder. WM 1912 Died. Date not known.

DYER, FREDERICK
Vaudeville Artiste. Oxford Street, London W. Age 38. I.18.10.1926 P.19.11.1926 R.18.03.1927. Excluded.

E

EARL, ROBERT
Vocal Entertainer. Real name Montague Leigh. Hendon, London NW4. Age 47. I.15.09.1967 P.17.11.1967 R.15.03.1968. Resigned May 1991. Rejoined 20.11.1992.

EARLE, EDDIE
Dancer. Real name Alfred Thomas Preedy. Kingston-on-Thames, Surrey. Age 49. I.17.11.1944. Excluded May 1948.

EARLE, KENNETH
(A Lewis)Theatrical Agent. Real name Charles Kenneth Earle Richards. London SW9. I.18.03.1988 P.16.09.1988 R.20.01.1989.

EAST, REGINALD CHARLES, PM
Licensed Victualler. London SW11. Age 37. I.16.09.1938 P.17.02.1939 R.18.08.1939. WM 1948. Resigned May 1981.

EASTON, EDWARD VERNON See TED RAYMOND

EASTON, FREDERICK LESLIE See FRED RAYMOND .

EASTON, WILLIAM JAMES
Musician. Croydon. Age 32. I.19.07.1940 P.19.01.1945 R.18.06.1946. Excluded 1952.

EATON, FREDERICK WILLIAM
Vaudeville Artiste. Finsbury Park, London N4. Age 32. I.15.07.1932 P.19.08.1932.

EATON, JACK ALEXANDER
Sales Director. Streatham Common, London SW16. Joined 16.11.1945 from City of London Lodge No.901. Died 23.02.63.

EBERHARDT, ADOLPH CHARLES
Manager. Muswell Hill, London N10. I.20.11.1936 P.18.12.1936 R.19.11.1937. Excluded May 1943.

EDERMANIGER, ROBERT LUSBY See BOB MEZZETTI

EDGAR, MARRIOTT, PM
Vaudeville Artiste. Real name George Marriott Edgar. Kingston by Sea, Brighton. Age 31. Born 05.10.1880, Kirkcudbright, Scotland. I.15.03.1912 P.19.04.1912 R.19.07.1912. WM 1938. Died 5 May 1951, aged 70 years.

EDLIN, JACK
Comedian. Real name Ernest Harold Green. Wandsworth, London SW18. Joined 15.11.1935. Resigned July 1941. Rejoined 17.07.1942.

EDMONDS, COLIN JOHN
Comedy Writer. Chalfont St Peter, Bucks. Joined 19.03.1993.

EDWARDS, THOMAS JOSEPH
Ventriloquist. Age 28. I.19.06.1908 P.04.12.1908
R.21.07.1911.

EGBERT, ALBERT
Vaudeville Artiste. Real name Albert Edward Jee.
Brixton, London SW2. Age 40. I.16.09.1921
P.17.03.1922 R.16.06.1922.

EGBERT, SETH
Vaudeville Artiste. Real name Seth Jee. Brixton,
London SW2. Age 42. I.16.09.1921 P.17.03.1921
R.16.06.1922.

EISNER, COLLIE
Musician. Hyde Park, London W2. I.21.01.1938
P.18.11.1938 R.17.03.1939. Died 20.02.1970.

ELLIOT, CHARLES HOWARD, PPDepGStdB
Theatrical Producer. Emerson Park, Essex. 50.
Born 08.05.1949. Joined 19.03.1999 from Tabula
Rotunda Lodge No.8607.

ELLIOTT, DANIEL
(A Lewis). Student. West Runton, Norfolk. Age
21. Born 18.09.1974. I.17.11.1995 P.19.01.1996
R.15.11.1996.

ELLIOTT, PETER
Agent. Longhope, Gloucestershire. Joined
19.11.1976 from St Peter's Lodge No.4193.

ELLIOTT, SIMON PETER
(A Lewis). Business consultant. Sheringham,
Norfolk. Born 11.02.1972. I.19.11.2004.

ELLIS, JOHN GARDINER
Music Hall Clerk. Founder. Excluded 20.05.1909.

ELLISON, JOSEPH ALFRED, PM LGR
Comedian. Known as J.W.Ellison. Age 28.
I.15.11.1907 P.21.02.1908 R.20.03.1908. WM
1926, Died 1946.

ELLWANGER, WILLIAM THEODORE
Sketch Artiste. Age 39. I.20.11.1908 P.19.02.1908
R.18.06.1909. Excluded 1924.

ELRICK, GEORGE, FRSA
Vocalist and later Impressario. Kensington,
London W8. Joined 20.11.1936 from St Clements
Lodge No 688, Aberdeen, Scottish Constitution.
Resigned May 1977. Rejoined 19.11.1982. Died
15 December 1999, aged 95 years.

**ELTON, WALTER LEONARD See SYDNEY L.
HAMPTON**

ELVIO
Comedian. Real name James Ross. London,SW.
Age 30 I.17.09.1909 P.18.03.1910 R.19.08.1910.
Excluded 19.05.1921. Died May 1949

EMERIC, HENRY CHARLES
Vaudeville Artiste. Bexhill-on-Sea, Sussex. Age
37. I.16.07.1920 P.17.09.1920 R.15.10.1920.
Excluded.

EMERY, RICHARD GILBERT
Actor. Known as Dick Emery. St George's Hill,
Weybridge, Surrey. Age 55. I.17.09.1971
P.15.03.1974 R.19.03.1976. Died 02.01.1983,
aged 65 years.

ENGLISH, ARTHUR LESLIE NORMAN
Variety Artiste. Aldershot, Hants. Age 33.

I.21.11.1952 P.18.09.1953 R.18.01.1957. Died
18.04.1995, aged 75 years.

ENZER, JOHN, PM
Vaudeville Artiste. Sheffield, South Yorkshire.
Joined 21.06.1918 from Proscenium 3435. WM
1931. Died 28.04.1932

EVANS, JOHN RICHARD See JACK RISKIT

EVANS, WILLIAM E.
Comedian. Founder. Resigned 28.04.1911.

EYDMANN, EDWIN ALBERT
Musician. Plumstead, London SE18. Age 43.
I.19.03.1943 P.17.09.1943 R.16.10.1943.
Excluded 1953.

F

FARFEL, GRISHA
Musician. Real name Frank Peters. Boreham
Wood, Herts. Age 39. I.20.01.1961 P.17.11.1961
R.18.01.1963. Died 5 May 1988, aged 65 years.

FARR, STEPHEN FRANCIS
Musician/Tourman. Boxmoor, Herts. Aged 51.
Born 18.11.1947. I.15.03.1996 P.17.01.1997
R.21.11.1997.

FARR, WILLIAM EDWARD
Vaudeville Artiste. Known as Eric Farr. Age 37.
I.20.04.1906 P.15.06.1906 R.21.09.1906.
Resigned 20.03.1914.

FARRAR, JABEZ SMITH
Variety Artiste. London WC1. Age 56. Joined
19.05.1961. Excluded.

FARRAR, JABEZ SMITH
Musician. Hammersmith, London W6. Age 60.
I.19.07.1935 P.15.11.1935 R.21.02.1936.
Excluded September 1941.

FARREN, FRED
Comedian. Real name Michael Rouhan. Age 32.
I.15.06.1906 P.17.08.1906 R.19.10.1906.
Excluded 17.05.1918

FAULKES, JOHN SEBASTIAN
Musician. Greenford, Middlesex. Age 28.
I.20.10.1933 P.16.03.1934 R.15.06.1934. Died
29.10.1973.

FAWCETT, DAVID EDWARD
Singer/Producer. Flimwell, East Sussex. Born
09.02.1954. Joined 19.03.2004 from Holmesdale
Lodge No.874 of which he was WM in 2002.

FAWCETT, HECTOR ARTHUR
Musician. London E12. Age 29. I.21.04.1933
P.16.06.1933 R.21.07.1933.

FEATHER, LESLIE
Clothing Manufacturer. Marylebone, London W1.
Age 49. I.15.03.1946 P.17.05.1946 R.21.03.1947.
Died March 1952.

FELD, ALFRED, PPAGDC
Innkeeper. Brighton, Sussex. Joined 21.03.1969.
PM from Lodge of Light No.7218. Died
07.10.1990.

FELD, ROBERT P., PM
Joined November 1981

FELINO, ALBERT

Real name Albert Brady. Vaudeville Artiste.
Hampstead London NW. Age 28. Joined
16.06.1905 from St Clement's Lodge, Aberdeen
No.688, Scotland. WM 1915.

**FERGUSON, THOMAS See ARTHUR
CHARLES ASTOR**

FERRIE, GEORGE FREDERICK, PM
Musician. London W1. Age 40. I.18.01.1952
P.18.07.1952 R.18.09.1952. WM 1967. Died
09.07.1994.

FIELD, CHESTER, PM LGR
Vaudeville Artiste. Real name Alfred John
Chester-Bishop. Harringay, London N4. Age 32.
I.15.07.1927 P.18.11.1927 R.16.03.1928. WM
1945 Died 18.02.1964.

FIELDS, HARRY
Vaudeville Artiste. Real name Robert George
Clarke. Dalston, London NE. Age 30.
I.18.06.1915 P.20.08.1915 R.17.09.1915.

FFRENCH, CECIL CLINTON
Musician. Chiswick, London W4. I.17.01.1936
P.15.05.1936 R.18.12.1936. Resigned May 1984.

FINCH, ERNEST SIDNEY
Theatrical Manager. Known as Teddy Finch.
Stockwell, SW5. Age 44. I.17.07.1942
P.18.09.1942 R.15.01.1943. Died 03.10.1985.

FINDEN, HAROLD, PM
Sketch Artiste/Actor. Real name Harold George
Hickmott. Age 52. Chiswick, London W4.
Joined.18.03.1910 from New Concord Lodge
No.813. WM 1919. Rejoined June 1926. Died
02.07.1950.

FINDON, RONALD, PM
Musician. Edgware, Middlesex. Age 55. Born
08.11.1927. I.21.01.1983 P.18.03.1983
R.03.09.1983.

FINGLASS, THOMAS See TONE.E

FINK, HARRY JAY, PGStB
Musician. London SW5. I.17.05.1935
P.19.07.1935 R.15.11.1935. WM 1955. Died
21.12.1961

FIRMAN, ALEC
Musician. Harrow, Middlesex. Joined 21.07.1950
from Portman Lodge No.4747.

FIRTH, CHARLES MICHAEL, SLGR MetGStwrd
Executive Director. London SE14. Age 48. Born
29.05.1943. I.20.09.1991 P.15.11.1991
R.17.01.1992.

FISH, MANNIE See MORTON FRASER

FISHER, LEON
Musician. Real name Louis Fishburg. London
EC1. Age 30. I.21.06.1929 P.19.11.1929 in
Bohemian Lodge No.4475, Johannesburg, South
Africa. R.19.11.1930. Resigned.

**FITZGERALD, MAURICE CHARLES See
M.GERALDO**

**FITZOWEN, CHARLES JOHN JOSEPH See
HERBERT AUSTIN**

FLANAGAN, BUD, OBE
Variety Artiste. Real name Reuben Weintrop.

Portman Square, London W1. Age 43.
I.20.10.1939 P.19.01.1940 R.16.05.1941. Died 20
October 1968, aged 72 years.

FLETCHER, FREDERICK
Musician. Crouch End, London N8. Age 39.
I.20.11.1925 P.15.01.1926 R.16.04.1926.

FLETCHER, FREDERICK ALBERT
Film Renter and later, accountant. Kingston Hill.
Age 36. I.15.02.1924 P.15.08.1924 R.21.11.1924.
Excluded Sept 1941. Rejoined 16.05.1958.

FOGEL, MAURICE
Age 28. I.15.07.1938 P.17.02.1939 R.15.03.1940.

FORD, EDWARD McMULLEN
Vaudeville Artiste. Known as Ed. E. Ford. London
SW. Age 38. I.20.11.1908 P.19.02.1909
R.19.03.1909.

FORESTER, FREDERICK See FREDDIE FOSS

FORRESTER, JOHN See JACK LESTER

FORSYTH, HERBERT LLOYD
Cinema Manager. Folkestone, Kent. Age 46.
I.19.07.1918 P.13.06.1919 R.21.11.1919.
Excluded 1924.

FORSYTH, WILLIAM ROBERT JOHN
Theatrical Proprietor. Victoria Pier, Folkestone.
Age 47. I.16.01.1916 P.21.07.1916 R.18.08.1916.

FORT, FRANK
Comedian. Real name Frank Gude. Age 32.
I.18.10.1907 P.15.11.1907 R.21.02.1908. Died.
Date not known.

FOSS, FREDDIE
Music Hall Artiste. Real name Frederick Forester.
Colwyn Bay, North Wales. Age 45. I.16.01.1942
P.18.03.1942 R.16.03.1945. Died 15.02.1966.

FOSSETT, JAMES HAROLD
Acrobat. London SW4. Age 42. I.19.03.1943
P.16.10.1943 R.19.11.1943. Excluded 1952.

FOSSETT, THOMAS
Circus Artiste. Lowsonford, near Henley-in-Arden,
Warks. Age 37. I.20.10.1933. P. 20.04.1934
R.15.03.1935. Excluded September 1941. Grand
Lodge Certificate returned to GL. November
1960.

FOSSETT, THOMAS JOHN
Circus Artiste. Chilbolton, Hants. I.21.11.1980
P.16.01.1981 R.20.03.1981. Died 23.01.1996.

FOSTER, ALBERT
Vaudeville Artiste. Real name Albert Wilkinson.
Chiswick, London W4. Age 35. I.15.08.1919
P.19.03.1920 R.16.04.1920.

FOSTER, ERNEST
Theatrical Manager. Real name Ernest George
Goodwin. Age 38. I.16.04.1908 P.17.07.1908
R.21.08.1908. WM 1927. Secretary of the Lodge
until his death May 1939.

FOX, CHARLES
Theatrical Producer. London WC1. Age 30.
I.18.09.1942 P.19.03.1943 R.16.07.1945. Died
05.09.1984.

FOX, DONALD
Script writer. Kingsbury, London NW9. Joined

16.05.1980 from United Hearts Lodge No.6590.

FOX, ROY

Musical Director. Piccadilly, London W1.
I.13.01.1937. Died 20 March 1982, aged 80
years.

FOX, TEDDY

Actor. Real name Frank Edward James Dixon.
Maida Hill, London W9. Age 41. I.18.09.1931
P.18.03.1932 R.16.09.1932.

FOX, WILLIAM H. See CATLIN, WILLIAM H.

FRANCIS, BARRY MICHAEL EDWARD

Musical Director. Enfield, Middlesex. Age 45.
Joined 18.05.1984 from Asaph Lodge No.1317.

FRANCIS, DAI

Variety Artiste. Wembley Park, Middlesex. Age
39. I.19.01.1968 P.15.03.1968 R.15.11.1968.
Excluded 30.04.1995.

FRANCOIS, JACK

Variety Artiste. Clapham, London SW4. Age 38.
I.17.11.1950 P.16.03.1951 R.20.03.1953. Died 11
January 1997.

FRANK, AUBREY

Musician. London NW1. Age 34. I. 20.01.1956
P.21.09.1956 R.16.11.1956. Died 03.06.1993, on
his 72nd birthday.

FRANKEL, ALEXANDER

Musician. London E1. Age 27. I.19.06.1931
P.18.09.1931 R.18.03.1932.

FRAZER, MORTON

Variety Artiste. Real name Mannie Fish. Bognor
Regis, Sussex. Age 40. I.18.01.1946
P.15.03.1946 R.19.07.1946. Died 10 June 1982.

FREDERICKSON, NOEL See TROY DANTE

FRIDKIN, BORIS

Vaudeville Artiste. Age 31. I.20.11.1908
P.23.02.1909 R.16.07.1909.

FRIESNER, ABRAHAM See FRED KEETON

FRY, PHILIP, PM, **See PHIL RALLIS,**

**FRYE, LESLIE-LEGGE-SARONY See LESLIE
SARONY**

FULLER, LESLIE

Vaudeville Manager. Margate, Kent. Age 39.
I.20.04.1928 P.20.07.1928 R.17.08.1928. Died
1948.

G

GANJOU GEORGE

Dancer. London SW1. I.18.03.1938 P.18.11.1938
R.17.02.1939. Died 1 November 1988.

GANJOU, PAUL ANTHONY, PM LGR

(A Lewis) London W1. I.21.01.1977 P.18.03.1977
R.17.03.1978. WM 1985.

GARFIELD, JOHN FRANK

Singer/entertainer. Brookmans Park, Herts. Born
21.05.1929. I.17.01.2003.

GARNER, STUART REAY

General Manager. Café de Paris, London. Age
27. I.16.09.1966 P.20.01.1967 R.17.03.1967.
Excluded.

GARRETT, WILLIAM JOSEPH See WILLIE

BENN

GELLER, HAROLD

Musical Director. Edgware, Middlesex. Age 32.
I.18.03.1949 P.18.11.1949 R.21.07.1950.

GELLER, LAURENCE STEPHEN

(A Lewis). Management Consultant. Edgware,
Middlesex. Age 22. I.21.03.1969 P.17.09.1971
R.21.01.1972. Expellled!

GEORGE, GERRY

Actor. Real name Gerald Victor Francis de Weld
Nicholas. Acton, London W3. Age 58. Born
12.04.1939. I.21.11.1997 P.18.09.1998
R.19.03.1999.

GERALDO, M.

Vaudeville Artist. Real name Maurice Fitzgerald.
Age 33. I.16.07.1909. Excluded 16.05.1913.

GERMAINS, ROBERTO

Theatre Agent. London WC2. Age 49. Joined
16.09.1966. Died 09.07.1994.

GIGGS, EDWARD

Stage Manager. London SE 30. I.17.04.1924
P.18.07.1924 R.15.08.1924. Excluded.

GILBERT, HARRY See HARRY DENNIS

GILBEY, GEORGE

Comedian. Real name John Kildear. Age 34.
I.20.10.1905 P.16.03.1906 R.20.04.1906.
Excluded May 1915.

GILDER, ISRAEL

Musician. Limehouse, London E. Age 27.
I.19.04.1912 P.21.06.1912 R.19.07.1912.

GILL, RICHARD WILLIAM

Film Casting Director. Forest Gate, London E7.
Age 34. I.16.09.1960 P.20.01.1961 R.17.03.1961.
Died 22.10.1992.

**GILLANDERS, WILLIAM ROBB See WILLIAM
WARD**

**GILLINGS, DAVID GEORGE See GEORGE
MOZART**

GINNETT, FRANK JACK

(A Lewis) Circus Artiste. Streatham, SW16. Age
52. I.21.09.1973 P.16.11.1973 R.20.09.1974.

GINNETT, LOUIS ALBERT

Circus Proprietor. London SW9. Age 34.
I.19.03.1926 P.16.04.1926 R.18.09.1926.
Excluded.

GLEN, ARCHIE

Vaudeville Artiste. Real name Thomas Dalton.
Ravescroft Park. London W6. Age 36,
I.21.10.1927 P.19.10.1928 R.20.09.1929.

**GLEN, HENRY FRANCIS See HARRY
CLIFFORD**

GLOVER, GEORGE ERIC CALLAND

Musician. London NW2. Age 34. I.19.07.1940
P.17.01.1941 R.18.07.1941. Resigned May 1948.
Went to live in Australia.

GODOWSKI, HENRY See JULES ADRIAN

GOLD, HENRY

Vocalist. Real name Henry James Ricks. Age 40.
I.15.11.1907 P.21.02.1908 R.20.03.1908. Died.
Date not known.

GOLD, JACK
Musician. Real name Jack Goldblatt. Forest
Gate, London E7. Age 31. I.21.08.1925
P.18.09.1925 R.19.03.1926. Excluded.

GOLDBERG, MAX
Musician. London NW6. Age 29. I.16.11.1934
P.18.01.1935 R.15.11.1935. Died 11 February
1990, aged 84 years.

GOLDBLATT, JACK See JACK GOLD

GOLDMAN, HAROLD LEWIS, PGStB
Managing Director. London NW8. Age 49. Joined
21.07.1944.

**GOLDSCHEDE, LEOPOLD ARTHUR See FRED
COOPER**

GOLDSTEIN, ALFRED, See ALFRED GRAHAM

GOLDSTEIN, MARTIN
Conductor. I.15.03.1974 P.20.09.1974
R.15.11.1974. Resigned May 1984.

GOODMAN, JOSEPH
Comedian/Entertainer. Real name Joey Cotterill.
Southend-on-Sea, Essex. Age 58. Born
12.01.1939. I.17.01.1997 P.18.09,1998
R.19.03.1999.

GOODMAN, SOLOMON
Theatrical Proprietor. Age 28. I.19.10.1906
P.22.01.1907 R.15.03.1907. Resigned
15.03.1917.

**GOODWIN, ERNEST GEORGE See ERNEST
FOSTER**

GOODWIN ERNEST SIDNEY
Manager. London E1. Age 29. I.17.06.1927
P.16.09.1927 R.18.11.1927. Resigned
15.04.1932.

GOODWIN, STANLEY
Film Producer. Edgware, Middlesex. Age 67.
Born 20.09.1933. Joined 21.01.2000 from
Endeavour Lodge No. 5506.

GOODY, PHILIP
Musician. Mottingham, London SE9. Age 47.
I.15.09.1944 P.16.01.1948 R.15.05.1953. Died
08.11.1967.

GORDON, HAL
Comedian. Real name Harold Rushen.
Wraysbury, Middlesex. I.29.03.1936 P.15.05.1936
R.17.07.1936. Died February 1952.

GORDON, LARRY See HENRY CLAYTON

GRAHAM, ALFRED
Commission Agent. Real name Alfred Goldstein..
London WC1. Age 41. I.16.07.1943 P.17.09.1943
R.19.11.1943. Changed name by Deed Poll,
1958. Died 1968.

GRAHAM, GEORGE
Actor. Real name George Gloyne Papps. Age 35.
I.20.04.1906 P.15.06.1906 R.20.07.1908.
Resigned 04.04.1915.

GRAHAM, JOHN DIXON See GANTY LITTLE

GRAHAM, ROY JEFFREY
Films Manager. Hatch End. Age 58. Born
02.04.1928. I.16.01.1987 P.18.09.1987
R.20.11.1987.

GRANT, JOHN THOMAS WILLIAM
Stage Manager. Age 34. I.16.04.1908
P.19.06.1908 R.17.07.1908. Resigned
01.04.1914.

GRANTLEY, CHARLES
Comedian. Real name Ambrose Charles Grantley
Thorn. Birmingham. Age 34. I.16.10.1914
P.19.03.1915 R.16.04.1915. Died 1931.

GRAY, NORMAN JAMES, PM SLGR
Amusement Caterer. Age 55. Joined 19.01.1990.
WM 1995.

GRAY, RICHARD JAMES ALFRED
Amusement Caterer. Farnborough, Hants. Age
23. I.15.11.1996 P.19.09.1997 R.20.03.1998.
Born 29.09.1973.

GRAYDON, JAMES LAURENCE
Music Hall Agent. Age 24. I.19.04.1907
P.19.07.1907 R.20.09.1907. Excluded
18.05.1911.

GRECO, BERNARD
Musical Director. Manor Park, London E. Age 3. I.
18.01.1924 P.20.06.1924 R.19.09.1924. Excluded
1936. Died 1940.

GREEN, BRUCE
Comedian. Real name Joseph Brewster Hamilton
Green, PM Chiswick, London,W. Age 33.
I.15.03.1912 P.19.04.1912 R.21.06.1923. Died
1946.

GREEN, ERNEST HAROLD See JACK EDLIN

GREEN, HARRY
Actor. Savoy Hotel, London. Real name Henry
Blitzer. Joined 21.01.1949 from Bohemia Lodge
No.4475, (South Africa). Died 30 May 1958,
aged 65 years.

GREEN, HARRY PHILIP
Musician. Stamford Hill, London N16.
I.19.02.1937 P.16.07.1937 R.18.03.1938.
Excluded 30.04.1943. Died 06.10.1982, aged 71
years.

GREEN, JOSEPH BREWSTER HAMILTON, PM

GREY, FREDERICK
Joined 20.03.1936. Resigned.

GRIFFITHS, HENRY HADDON
Music Hall Artiste. Known as Griff. Founder. Born
05.04.1864, Liverpool. Excluded May 1915. Died
14.04.1945, aged 81 years.

GRIFFITHS, JOHN
Comedian. Tylorstown, Rhondda, South Wales.
Age 25. I.16.08.1929 P.25.04.1930 R.17.10.1929.

GROS, HENRI
Director of Variety. Founder. Born c1850.
Resigned 05.04.1907. Died 24.07.1910, London.

**GROVES, WALTER ALEXIS See RONNIE
ASCOT**

**GRUHLER, KARL FREDERICK See KARL F.
HOOPER**

GUDE, FRANK See FRANK FORT

GULBENKIAN, KRIKOR PARSEGH
Stamp Dealer. London W11. Age 38. I.18.11.1938
P.16.06.1939 R.18.08.1939.

H

HADLEY, WALTER CHARLES
Theatre Manager. London WC2. Aged 31. Joined 21.01.1938. Excluded 1943.

HAGGERTY, JAMES HENRY See JIMMY KIDD

HALES, FREDERICK JOHN
Recording Engineer. Hampton, Middlesex. Age 42. I.15.01.1965 P.17.09.1965 R.20.01.1967. Died 21.08.1996.

HALL, ARTHUR ROBERT See A. HALL MENZIES

HALL, HARRY THOMAS CHAMBERLAIN
Night Club Owner. Folkestone, Kent. Aged 47. Born 07.05. 1950. Joined 19.09.1997. PM Proscenium Lodge No. 3435.

HALLARD, BRIAN VINCENT
Theatrical Producer. London E17. Age 55. Born 10.06.1947. Joined 31.05.2002. PM from Good Samaritan Lodge No.4991.

HAMBLETON, ERNEST, PM
Stage Manager. Brixton, London SW. Age 35. I.21.01.1921 P.18.02.1921 R.18.03.1921. WM 1943. Died June 1943.

HAMPTON, SYDNEY L.
Musical Director. Real name Walter Leonard Elton. Palace Theatre, East Ham, London E. Age 35. I.16.07.1920 P.20.08.1920 R.17.09.1920.

HANCOCK, WILLIAM HENRY
Musician. London NW6. Joined 17.04.1925. Died March 1947, South Africa.

HANDKO Junior
Vaudeville Agent. Real name James Shaw. Sheffield 3. I.17.01.1937 P.18.03.1938 R.16.09.1938. Died February 1951.

HANDS, JAMES EDWARD
Musician. Wembley, Middlesex. Age 25. I.14.04.1932 P.17.06.1932 R.19.08.1932. Died 04.09.1964.

HANDS, MICHAEL JAMES
Purser. Steeple Claydon, Bucks. Age 21. I.15.01.1954 P.17.09.1954 R.16.09.1955.

HARDIE, FRANK, PM
Sketch Proprietor. Real name William James Wells. Age 35. I.20.04.1906 P.15.06.1906 R.20.07.1906. WM 1919. Died 1947.

HARDING, CHARLES
Musician. Real name Charles Katz. Edgware, Middlesex. I.20.11.1936 P.18.12.1936 R.16.07.1937. Excluded 16.05.1980.

HARDING, WILLIAM See BILLY KLOOF

HARDLE, FREDERICK ROBERT JESSE
Vaudeville Artiste. Leytonstone, London E . Age 24. I.17.04.1914 P.02.06.1914 R.04.03.1916. Resigned May 1915. Passed and Raised in Lodge No.3435.

HARLEY, ALFRED WILLIAM
Licensed Victualler. Parson Hotel, Sheesley, Warwickshire. Age 48. Joined 17.05.1940. Rejoined. Excluded May 1953.

HARLEY, ALFRED WILLIAMS

Vaudeville Artiste. Handsworth, Birmingham. Age 26. I.19.01.1923 P.21.12.1923 R.18.01.1924.

HARLING, CYRIL H.PM LGR
Musician. Balham, London SW17. Age 32. I.17.03.1939 P.18.08.1939 R.16.02.1940. WM 1958. Died 7 June 1986.

HARMAN, ARTHUR GORDON
Music Hall Manager. Palace Theatre, Bow, London E. Age 29. I.15.04.1910 P.17.06.1910 R.15.07.1910. Excluded 15.05.1914.

HARPER EDGAR CHARLES
Music Hall Manager and, later, Variety Artiste. Stanmore, Middlesex. Age 36. I.19.06.1914 P.16.07.1915 R.20.08.1915. Rejoined 18.07.1947. Died 1948.

HARPER, EDWARD FREDERICK
Film Director. Shepperton, Middlesex. Age 31. I.20.11.1970 P,19.03.1971 R.17.09.1971.

HARPER, PERCY
Musician. London W14. Age 33. I.21.11.1930 P.19.06.1931 R.21.08.1931.

HARRINGTON, TOM
Artiste. Crouch Hill, London N4. I.20.03.1936 P.17.07.1936 R.20.11.1936. Died 04.05.1989.

HARRIS, ALBERT MONTAGUE
Musician. Wembley. I.19.09.1975 P.16.01.1976 R.19.03.1976. Died September 1978.

HARRIS, GEORGE
Company Director. Brompton Road, London SW3. Age 59. Joined 17.05.1957. Rejoined 17.05.1957.

HARRIS, Wee GEORGIE
Vaudeville Artiste. Real name Isaac Silverman. Dalston, E8. Age 21. I.18.06.1920. P.17.12.1920 R.21.01.1921. Excluded. Rejoined 15.03.1935. Excluded September 1941.

HARRIS, JACK
Assistant Manager. Greenwich, London SE10. Age 28. I.21.04.1933 P.21.07.1933 R.20.10.1933. Excluded September 1941.

HARRISON, ANTHONY AUGUSTUS
Band Booker Agent. Teddington, Middlesex. Age 74. Born 04.06.1920. Joined 18.11.1994 from Vaudeville No, 5592.

HART, JOHN BERNARD
Magician. Preston, Lancashire. Age 25. I.15.03.1968 P.15.11.1968 R.21.03.1969. Died 19.01.1987.

HART, LOUIS LESLIE
Musician. Highbury London N5. Age 46. I.18.09.1953 P.20.11.1953 R.15.01.1954. Excluded May 1987.

HARTMAN, ALPHONSI CHARLES
Vaudeville Artiste. Brussels, Belgium. Age 39. I.20.08.1926 P.15.10.1926 R.17.06.1927. Excluded.

HARVARD, CHAS
Vaudeville Artiste. Real name Charles Paulson. Nottingham. Aged 39. I.20.07.1925 P.17.04.1925 R.20.11.1925.

HARVEY, ALBERT WILLIAM
Vaudeville Artiste. London SW2. I.19.11.1937
P.18.02.1938 R.18.11.1938.

HARVEY, ROBERT E.
Vaudeville Artiste. London SW2. Age 34. Joined
19.11.1937.

HAWKINS, ARTHUR See LOUIS ARTHUR

HAWKINS, FREDERICK WILLIAM
Theatrical Proprietor. The Hippodrome,
Peterborough. Age 41. I.17.11.1916 P.07.08.1917
R.21.09.1917. Excluded 19.05.1921.

HAYDN, WALLACE
Vaudeville Artiste. Real name Hayden Wallace
Vanderstay. Mornington Crescent, London NW1.
Age 30. I.16.10.1931 P.14.04.1932 R.21.10.1932.
Died January 1961.

HAYES RICH
Real name Richard Ayres. Vaudeville Artiste.
Born c.1890,York. Age 36. I.18.03.1921
P.18.11.1921 R.17.03.1922. Died 01.10.1933.

HAYWARD, PATRICK THOMAS
Entertainer. Cumnor, Oxon. Age 46. I.15.01.1988.
Resigned.

HEADWORTH, ERNEST JOHN
Musician. Dalston, London NE. Age 29.
I.18.08.1916 P.15.09.1916 R.20.10.1916.

**HEADWORTH, PHINEAS, PM See FRED
LYSTER,**

HEARSUM, RALPH HENRY CHARLES, PJGD
Cabaret Agent. Kenley, Surrey. Age 69. Born
04.12.1925. Joined 16.09.1994. Member of four
other lodges. PAGStB 1988, PAGDC 1994, PJGD
2000,

HEDDON, LEONARD CHARLES
Theatre Manager. Hackney, London E9. Age 47.
I.15.01.1943 P.16.07.1943 R.17.09. WM 1943.
Died July 1949.

HEDGES, DENNIS AUGUSTUS
Musician. Leytonstone, London E11. Age 30.
I.19.01.1940 P.16.02.1940 R.20.09.1940.
Resigned May 1988.

HELM, JOHN BLACKWWELL
Theatrical Manager. Age 47. I.04.05.1906
P.20.07.1906 R.19.10.1906. Excluded
19.05.1911.

HEMME, HENRY See HARRY LAMORE

HEMMINGS, WILLIAM ROBERT
Musician. Southgate, London N14. Age 43.
I.18.03.1955 P.16.09.1955 R.18.11.1955.
Resigned March 1965.

**HENDERSON, FREDERICK See DAN H.
CLARK**

**HENDERSON, JOHN ERNEST STEWART See
SYD BOYD**

HENDERSON, MARTIN
Blind Musician. Whitely Bay, Northumberland.
Age 29. I.17.06.1910 P.04.04.1911 R.02.05.1911.
Resigned 27.02.1927.

HENDERSON, RICHARD
Vaudeville Artiste. Hull, East Yorkshire. Age 27.

I.15.02.1918 P.15.03.1918 R.19.04.1918.
Excluded 1924.

HENRY, CHARLES
Musician. London W4. Age 58. I.15.11.1957
P.03.01.1958 R.21.03.1958. Died 21.04.1978.

HENSLEY, CLIFFORD THEODORE
Entertainer. Richmond, Surrey. Age 64.
I.17.11.1972 P.19.01.1973 R.16.03.1973.
Member of CAA. Died 29.09.1973.

**HENSMAN, REGINALD MOORE See ARTHUR
REYNOLDS**

**HICKMOTT, HAROLD GEORGE PM See
HAROLD FINDEN, PM**

HILL, BILLY
Real name William Hill Bowen. Musician. Queens
Gate, London SW7. Aged 35. I.15.09.1950.
P.20.07.1951 R. 21.09.1951. Excluded May 1962.

HILL, EDWIN ARTHUR
Actor/Singer. Friern Barnet, London N11. Age 35.
I.20.11.1953 P.19.03.1954 R.19.11.1954.
Resigned August 1967.

HILL, GEORGE EDMUND, PM
Camera expert. New Barnet, Herts. Age 40.Born
13.09.1896 I.16.07.1937 P.17.09.1937
R.7.12.1937. WM 1950. Died 02.08.1977

HILL, GEORGE HENRY
Music Hall Clerk. Founder. Excluded 15.05.1914.

HILL, HERBERT HERIOT, Rev.
Clerk, Holy Orders. Age 40. I.20.07.1906
P.17.08.1906 R.21.09.1906. Excluded
19.05.1911.

HILL, JOHN GEORGE
Manager, Cafe de Paris, Stanmore, Middlesex.
Age 47. Joined 20.09.1963 from St James,
Edinburgh. Died 10.09.1964.

HILL, JOHN WILLIAM
Vaudeville Manager. Grimsby, Lincs. Age 36.
I.18.01.1935 P.15.03.1935 Resigned May 1940.

HILL, MICHAEL, LGR
Musician. Joined 18.01.1974 from Proscenium
Lodge No.3435. Master Proscenium Lodge 1978.
WM 1980. Died 01.05.2002, aged 66 years.

HILL, STANLEY JAMES
Musician. West Kensington, London W14. Age
45. I.19.04.1929 P.21.06.1929 R.16.08.1929.
Resigned 03.12.1934.

HILLMAN, CYRIL MERSON
Theatre Electrician. Finsbury Park, London N4.
Age 26. I.16.01.1953 P.17.07.1953 R.18.09.1953.
Died 22.10.1986.

HILLMAN, DAVID RUSSELL, PM LGR
(A Lewis). Food Merchandiser. Lee, London
SE12. Age 21. I19.09.1986 P.16.01.1987
R.20.03.1987. WM 1993.

HILLMAN, MERSON JAMES
Electrician. Finsbury Park Empire. Age 48.
I.17.11.1944 P.20.04.1945 R.20.07.1945.

HILLMAN, RICHARD MICHAEL, PM
(A Lewis). Financial Consultant. Lee, SE12. Age
21. I.15.09.1989 P.19.01.1990 R.16.03.1990. WM

1996.

HINSLE
Illusionist. Real name Leonard John Insull. Wolverhampton. Joined 16.04.1920 from Cinque Ports Lodge No. 1206. Excluded. Died 1974, aged 81 years.

HIRSCH, DAVID JACKLEY
Hotelier. Drift Bridge Hotel, Epsom, Surrey. Age 40. I.19.11.1954 P.16.11.1956 R.15.01.1960.

HIRSCH, GEORGE PHILLIP See GEORGE JACKLEY

HIRSCH, LOUIS See LOUIS LE SINE

HIRSCH, NATHAN T. JACKLEY See NAT JACKLEY

HITCH, WALTER HENRY, PGStB
Auctioneer. WM 1909. Founder. Died 1946.

HO, ANDREW C.G.
Actor. Stanmore, Middlesex. Age 46. I.16.01.1959 P.20.03.1959 R.18.11.1960.

HODGSON, WALLACE PROUSE See VALAZZI

HOLDER, FRANK,PM LGR
Musician. Carshalton, Surrey. Age 41. I.20.01.1967 P.15.09.1967 R.20.09.1968. WM 1994.

HOLDER, JAMES PAUL
Director of Entertainment. London E1. Age 53. Born 11.04.1939. I.20.03.1992 P.18.09.1992 R.20.11.1992. Resigned. Rejoined 18.01.2002.

HOLGATE, RAYMOND CHRISTOPHER
Vaudeville Artiste. Bloomsbury, London WC1. Age 25. I.17.09.1920 P.19.11.1920 R.31.01.1921. Resigned April 1928.

HOLLINGSWORTH, JOHN
Toastmaster. Erith, Kent. Age 59. Born 26.03.1938. Joined 21.03.1997. PM Jubilee Lodge No.6936.

HOLLOWAY, GEORGE HUGH
Vaudeville Artiste. London SW2. Joined 18.02.1921 from Glasgow Dramatic 571, Scottish Constitution.

HOLLOWAY, GEORGE SEBASTIAN
Vaudeville Artiste. Brixton, London SW2. Age 26. I.15.09.1922 P.20.10.1922 R.19.01.1923.

HOLLOWAY, JAMES HENRY See JIMMY NERVO

HOOPER, KARL F.
Vaudeville Artiste. Real name Karl Frederick Gruhler. Age 25. I.20.10.1905 P.16.03.1906 R.20.04.1906. Resigned 11.05.1921.

HOPWOOD, CHARLES HENRY
Clerk (Tivoli). Founder. Excluded 26.05.1910/

HOWARD, AUGUSTUS See GUS LE CLERQ

HOWARD, ROBERT SYDNEY
Vaudeville Artiste. Yeadon, Leeds, West Yorkshire. Age 42. I.21.03.1924 P.19.09.1924 R.16.01.1925.

HOWARD, THOMAS See CLIVE WATTS

HOWE, HENRY EDWARD
Vaudeville Artiste. Balham, London SW. Age 30. I.21.07.1911 P.15.09.1911 R.20.10.1911.

Excluded May 1915.

HOWE, LEONARD RODNEY
Comedy Actor. London SW2. Age 69. Joined 18.11.1988 from Proscenium Lodge No.3435.

HUDSON, WILLIAM OSWALD, PM
Musician. Epsom, Surrey . Joined 21.11.1958. WM 1968. Died 8 February 1983.

HUGHES, HERBERT GROSVENOR
Variety Artiste. London SE1. Age 33. I.16.04.1926 P.18.06.1926 R.15.10.1926. Resigned March 1952.

HUGHES, HERBERT JAMES
Vaudeville Artiste. Brixton Hill, SW2. Age 38. I.19.07.1925 P.21.08.1925 R.15.01.1926.

HUGHES, JAMES, SLGR LGCR
Tyler of Chelsea Lodge since May 1984. Initiated in Wantage Lodge No.3178, June 1970. Has been Tyler for 20 Lodges and 5 Chapters, the oldest of which is Antiquity No.2.

HUGHES, PETER HESKETH
Musician. Boston Manor, London W7. Age 33. I.15.09.1961 P.19.01.1962 R.16.01.1962. Resigned 1990.

HUGHES, THOMAS HENRY
Comedian. Known as Tom Hughes. London WC. Age 33. I.18.03.1910 P.17.03.1911 R.21.06.1912. Excluded 20 May 1920.

HUNT, ALAN LEONARD
Actor. Known as Gareth Hunt. Coulsdon, Surrey. Age 51. Born 07.02.1942. I.19.03.1993 P.18.11.1994 R.17.11.1995.

HUNT, LEN W.
Musician. London WC1. Age 33. I.19.03.1937 P.20.08.1937 R.21.01.1938. Resigned January 1972.

HUNTER, CHARLES HENRY ERIC See ERIC DUDLEY

HUNTERMAN, ABRAHAM
Musician. Age 34. I.17.01.1941 P.19.12.1941 R.20.03.1942. Died 07.11.1941.

HUNTERMAN, MAURICE
Musician. Whitton, Middlesex. Age 27. I.15.07.1949 P.20.01.1950 R.20.03.1953.

HURLEY, JOHN WILLIAM DAVID
Comedian. Known as Johnnie Hurley. East Ham, London E. Age 41. I.16.08.1918 P.20.09.1918 R.21.03.1919.

HUXTER, SYDNEY DOUGLAS See SYD MAKIN
Music Hall Artiste. Real name Sydney Douglas Huxter. London SW9. Age 56. I.19.03.1954 P.19.11.1954 R.18.03.1955.

HYAMS, SIDNEY
Musician. London, N17. Age 54. I.16.03.1962 P.16.11.1962 R.15.11.1963.

I

IDENTO, JACK
Real name John Charles Bruce. Vaudeville Artiste. London W1. Aged 40. I.15.06.1928 P.20.07.1928 R.21.09.1928. Died 24.06.1956. If

not 24th then 29th.

INSULL, LEONARD JOHN See HINSLE

IRVING, IAN
Comedian. Thundersley, Essex. Age 42. Born
25.01.1958. I.21.01.2000 P.17.11.2000
R.16.03.2001.

ISAACS, MYER CHARLES
Music Hall Proprietor. Llanelly, Carmarthen. Age
45. I.19.01.1923. P.20.04.1923 R.15.06.1923.
Died February 1953.

ISLES, WILLIAM BUTLER
Vaudeville Manager. Hackney, London E8. Age
45. I.20.03.1925 P.17.04.1925 R.19.06.1925.
Resigned.

ISON, FREDERICK
Vaudeville Artiste. Upper Holloway, London N19.
Age 41. I.15.07.1927 P.19.08.1927 R.18.11.1927.
Died 29.04.1957.

J

JACK, JAMES
Musician. Known as Jimmy Jack. Herne Hill,
London SE24. Age 53. Initiated 18.01.1957. Died
25.07.1957.

JACKLEY, GEORGE
Vaudeville Artiste. Real name George Philip
Hirsch. Clapham, London SW. Age 35.
I.20.09.1918 P.18.10.1918 R.13.06.1919.
Resigned. 15.01.1934.

JACKLEY, NAT
Variety Artiste. Real name Nathan T. Jackley
Hirsch. St John, Woking, Surrey. Age 33.
I.19.06.1942 P.17.07.1942 R.20.11.1942. Died
17.09.1988, aged 72 years.

JACKSON, BERTRAND GASCOIGNE
Musician. Holland Park, London W11. Age 57.
I.15.11.1963 P.24.04.1964 Resigned May 1978.

**JACKSON, HERBERT VALENTINE See VAL
SAINT**

JACKSON, JAMES
Musician. Rochdale, Lancs. Age 34. I.19.02.1909
P.27.04.1909 R.13.08.1909. Resigned May 1915.

JACKSON, JOHN
Music Hall Artiste. London W11. Age 45.
I.21.01.1955 P.18.11.1955 R.18.01.1957.
Excluded May 1961.

JACKSON, JOHN
Musician. Rochdale, Lancs. Age 31. I.19.02.1909
P.27.04.1909 R.13.08.1909. Resigned May 1915.

JACKSON, JOHN WILLIAM
Manager. London SW4. Age 43. I.18.09.1926
P.19.11.1926 R.21.10.1927.

JACKSON, LEN
Vaudeville Artiste. Real name Isaac Cashtien.
Bow, London,E3. Age 29. I.18.03.1927
P.19.10.1928 R.19.07.1929. Excluded.

**JACKSON, LEONARD STONEWALL See
PROBUS**

JACOBS, BERNARD
Vaudeville Agent. Known as Barney Jacobs.

London W1. Joined 17.07.1942. Died January
1949.

JACOBS, JIMMY
Cabaret Artiste. Stanmore, Middlesex. Age 41.
Joined 15.03.1964 from Royal George Lodge
No.3535. Died 12.12.1980.

JAMES, ALBERT
Musician. Real name Roger Smith. London N19.
Joined 19.11.1967.

**JAMES, GERALD ARTHUR See JESS
CONRAD**

JAMES, GORDON
Vaudeville Artiste. Holloway, London N7. Age 33.
I.18.11.1927 P.15.06.1928 R.20.07.1928

JAMESON. HOWARD LESLIE
Theatre Proprietor. London WC2H. Age 45. Born
16.06.1955. Joined 17.03.2000 from South West
Polytechnic Lodge No.3680.

JAY, JACK
Cinema Director. Southgate, London N14. Age
33. I.19.11.1948 P.20.01.1950 R.17.11.1950.
Died 27 June 1995.

JEAPES, WILLIAM CECIL
Cinematographer. Founder. Excluded
16.05.1912.

JEE, ALBERT EDWARD See ALBERT EGBERT

JEE, BURNELL FRED
Vaudeville Artiste. London WC. Joined
20.11.1925 from Glasgow Dramatic No.571,
Scottish Constitution.

JEE, SETH See SETH EGBERT

JENNINGS, FRANK See FRANK ALBER

JEPSON, FREDERICK
Musician and Music Hall Artiste. London NW2.
Age 26. I.17.09.1937 P.19.11.1937 R.18.02.1938.
Resigned 1943. Rejoined 21.01.1944.

JEROME, MICHAEL JAMES
Comedian. Portsmouth, Hants. Age 54. Born
18.05.1947. I.11.05.2001 P.18.01.2002
R.21.03.2003.

JESSON, KYRAN MARTIN
Entertainments Director, Rank Organisation.
Alcombe, Minehead, Somerset. Age 40. Born
23.08.1957. Joined 21.11.1997 from Cudlow
Lodge No.8738.

JOHNSON, GEORGE
Musician. London N11. Age 60. I.18.11.1966
P.17.03.1967 R.15.09.1967. Excluded
31.03.1978.

JOHNSON, JOHN
Musical Director. London N4. Age 41.
I.17.12.1943 P.17.03.1944 R.20.07.1945.
Excluded April 1947.

JOHNSON, THOMAS CHARLES
Musician. London N6. Age 49. I.19.07.1946
P.16.08.1946. Excluded May 1954.

JOHNSON, WILLIAM HENRY
Comedian. Known as Will Johnson. Tooting,
London SW. Age 35. I.17.06.1910 P.15.07.1910
R.19.08.1910. Died July 1940.

JOHNSON, WILLIAM HENRY Jnr
(A Lewis) Manager. London SW. Age 21.
I.18.03.1927 P.17.06.1927 R.15.07.1927.
JOHNSTON, DAVID GEORGE
Theatre Organist. Scole, Norfolk. Age 66. Born
29.09.1932. Joined 18.09.1998. PM of St Mary
Abbotts Lodge No.1974.
**JONES, CHARLES FREDERICK STIRLING See
CHARLES F. STIRLING**
JONES, KENNETH PAUL See PAUL KAYE
JONES, STANLEY See STAN DALLAS
**JONES, WALTER ARTHUR PM See WALLY
STEWART, PM**
JONES-VALENTINE, LOUIS CHARLES
(A Lewis). South Wales. I.19.01.1979
P.16.11.1979 R.18.01.1980. Died 20.11.1983.
JOSEPH, PAUL DAVID, PM
(A Lewis) Accountant. Streatham, London SW16.
Age 22. Born 18.11.1945. I.17.03.1967
P.15.09.1967 R.19.01.1968.
JOSEPH, PHILIP, PM
Co-Director. London SW16. Age 53. Joined
17.09.1965. WM 1975.
JOSEPHS, LOUIS See HARRY WEBBER
JOVER, FLORENCIO TOMAS
Vaudeville Artiste. Walworth, London SE17.
Known as Tommy Jover. Age 26. I.15.12.1922
P.15.06.1923 R.20.07.1923. Member of the Five
Jovers. Resigned May 1949.
JOY, KENNETH
Variety Artiste. Westbrook, Margate, Kent. Age
55. Born 09.12.1945. I.15.09.2000. P.20.09.2003.
R.19.11.2004

K
KACHARIA, PAUL
Agent. Lunsford Cross, Sussex. I.18.11.1977
P.17.03.1978 R.17.11.1978.
KAGAN, ADOLPHE
Musical Director. London NW6. Age 32.
I.21.04.1922 P.16.06.1922 R.21.07.1922.
Excluded.
KAPLAN, HYMAN See HAL STONE
KARR, HARRY
Musician. Real name Harry Kurnasky. London
SW10. Joined 21.09.1934 from Meridian Lodge
No.108, Vancouver, British Columbia, Canada.
Excluded.
KARSON, NAT
Producer. London WC1. Age 41. Born Zurich,
Switzerland. I.18.01.1952. Went to live in New
York. Died 27.09.1954.
KASRAC. CHARLES
Vaudeville Artiste. Real name Charles Moore
Warner. Brixton Hill, London SW. Age 31.
I.18.04.1913 P.18.07.1913 R.15.08.1913. Died
March 1948.
KATCHKEY, SYDNEY
Band Leader. London WC2. Joined 20.05.1938.
Excluded 1947.

KATO, HARRY
Vaudeville Artiste. Real name William Henry
Phillips. Age 38. I.19.07.1907 P.16.08.1907
R.21.02.1908. Excluded 16.05.1912.
KATZ, CHARLES See CHARLES HARDING
KAYE, DAVY, MBE
Variety Artiste. London W4. Age 40. I.21.08.1956
P.15.03.1957 R.20.03.1959. Died 04.02.1998,
aged 81 years.
KAYE, KAPLAN
(A Lewis). Theatrical Agent/Producer. Hampton,
Middlesex. Age 48. Born 07.08.1949.
I.21.03.1997 P.16.01.1998 R.20.11.1998.
KAYE, PAUL
Singer/songwriter. Real name Kenneth Paul
Jones. Petersfield, Hants. Born 13 March 1947.
I.21.03.2003. P.16.01.2004. R.21.01.2005.
KAZANZI, GEORGE,SLGR
Operatic Singer. London W1. Age 60. Joined
16.05.1986. PM Savage Club Lodge No.2190.
Initiated Orpheus Lodge No.1706.
KEATS, ALBERT WILLIAM
Musical Director. Leyton, London E. Age 31.
I.17.08.1923 P.15.02.1924 R.19.09.1924.
Excluded September 1941.
KEETON, FRED
Comedian. Real name Abraham Freisner. Age
27. I.15.03.1907 P.19.04.1907 R.21.06.1907.
Died 28.05.1934.
**KELLEY, STANLEY THOMAS See JACKSON
OWEN**
KELLEY, THOMAS
Actor. London SW14. Age 45. I.21.11.1941
P.16.01.1942 R.17.07.1942. Left for Vancouver,
Canada 1948. Resigned1948.
KELLY, VICTOR
Vaudeville Artiste. Real name George Victor
Leglere. Age 28. I.16.08.1907 P.20.03.1908
R.19.06.1908. Excluded 16.05.1912.
KEMP, ARTHUR FREDERICK
Joined 17.11.1978.
KENDALL, ALEC
Comedian. Real name Alexander Thomson.
Brixton, London SW. Age 36. I.19.04.1912
P.18.10.1912 R.01.07.1913. Excluded 21.05.1919
KENT, ERNEST ARTHUR
Vaudeville Manager. East Dulwich, London SE15.
Age 44. I.17.04.1925 P.19.06.1925 R- - -.
Excluded 1928.
KENWIN, G. DIXON
Actor. Real name George Dickson. London N7.
Age 36. I.15.10.1920 P.21.01.1921 R.21.12.1923.
Excluded.
KERR, JOHN
Musician. Ruislip, Middlesex. Age 40.
I.17.09.1948 P.08.04.1949 R.20.01.1950. Died
14.06.1956.
KERR, JOHN GRAHAM
Director. Wokingham, Berks. Age 40.
I.21.11.1986. Excluded 30.04.1994.

KIDBY, ALBERT ROBERT
Stage Director. Shepherd's Bush, London W12.
Age 47. I.21.11.1947 P.16.07.1948 R.19.11.1948.
Died 01.08.1970.

KIDD, JIMMY
Variety Artiste. Real name James Henry
Haggerty. Sydenham, London,SE. Age 59.
I.19.03.1965 P.17.09.1965 R.21.01.1966

KILDEAR, JOHN See GEORGE GILBEY

**KIMM, VICTOR LEOPOLD See VICTOR
LEOPOLD**

**KING, ARTHUR HARRY CHARLES See HARRY
ARTHUR**

KING, BASIL
Vaudeville Artiste. Real name Basil Henry
Richardson. West Norwood ,London SE. Joined
21.03.1924 from Army and Navy Lodge No.1971.

KING, CHARLES LEDIARD
Vaudeville Artiste. Age 26. I.15.09.1905
P.20.10.1905 R.20.04.1906. Died. Date not
known.

KINGSLEY, ARTHUR C.
Vaudeville Artiste. Real name Arthur Joel Cramer.
London WC1. Joined 19.06.1920 from Glasgow
Dramatic 571, Scottish Constitution.

KISBY, HERBERT JOSEPH
Manager. Brixton, London SW2. Joined
21.07.1944. Resigned April 1951.

KITTER, ROGER DANIEL
Entertainer. London NW3. Age 49. Born
20.10.1949. I.17.03.1995 P.15.09.1995
R.17.11.1995.

KLOOF, BILLY
Vaudeville Artiste. Real name William Harding.
London,SE. Age 35. I.21.08.1914 P.16.07.1920
R.115.04.1921

KNIGHT, CHARLES VICTOR See REX ROPER

KNIGHT, GEORGE
Musician. Shepherd's Bush, London W12. Age
39. I.16.09.1949 P.17.03.1950 R.15.09.1950.
Died 29.03.1967.

KNIGHT, GEORGE VICTOR
Comedian. Known as Victor Knight. Upper
Tooting, London SW17. Age 38. I.21.01.1921
P.15.04.1921 R.15.07.1921.

KNIGHT, WILLIAM JOHN WINGROVE
Musician, Edgware, Middlesex. Age 45.
I.17.07.1953 P.18.09.1953 R.20.11.1953.
Resigned 18.05.1963.

**KNOX, WILLIAM CROMWELL, See WILL
CROMWELL**

KORER, CECIL HARRY
BBC TV Producer. Whitton, Middlesex. Age 45.
Initiated 18.09.1970.

KRANTON
Vaudeville Artiste. Real name Clifford Hamilton
Cheek. Taunton, Somerset. Age 36. I.18.11.1921
P.21.04.1922 R.15.12.1922.

KRIEGER, LAURENCE, LGR
Managing Director Harlequin Records. Edgware,

Middlesex. Joined 18.09.1970. from St James
Lodge No.765. Died 11.05.1996.

KURNASKY, HARRY See HARRY KARR

L

LAIKIN, BUNNY
Musical Director. Real name Herzl Laiken.
London NW9. I.21.05.1954. Joined from
Orchestral Lodge No. 3028.

LA MARLINE, HERBERT
Vaudeville Artiste. Real name Thomas Herbert
Sherry. Age 23. I.20.11.1908 P.19.02.1908
R.19.03.1909. Excluded 1923.

LAMORE, HARRY
Vaudeville Artiste. Real name Henry Hemme.
Thames Ditton. Age 39. I.19.07.1912
P.14.03.1913 R.20.03.1913. Excluded
21.05.1919.

LAMPE, CARL RICHARD
Musician. Dalston, London E8. I.30.03.1931
P.17.04.1931 R.19.06.1931.

LAND, DAVID
Company Director. London W1. Age 40. Joined
16.05.1958. Died 23.12.1995, aged 77 years.

LANDAU, BARNET
Theatrical Manager. Southampton. Joined
20.03.1925. Excluded.

LANDAU, HARRY
Musician. Edgware, Middlesex. Age 50.
I.18.11.1960 P.20.01.1961 R.15.09.1961 Died 4
December 1992..

LANE, ARTHUR HORACE GREELY
Comedian. Brixton Hill, SW2. Age 32.
I.16.08.1912 P.20.09.1912 R.18.10.1912.
Excluded 17.05.1918. Rejoined 14.04.1932.
Resigned.

LANE, LEW
Comedian. Stoke Newington N16. Age 50.
I.16.10.1925 P.15.01.1926 R.18.03.1927.
Excluded.

LANE, LEW
Stage Director. Age 47. I.21.03.1975
P.19.09.1975 R.21.11.1975.

LANE, LUPINO
Vaudeville Artiste. Real name Henry William
George Lupino. Clapham, London. Age 22.
I.18.09.1914 P.16.10.1914 R.16.04.1915.
Rejoined 15.03.1946. Excluded 16.09.1953. Died
10.11.1959, aged 67 years.

LANE, LAURIE LUPINO
Actor. Real name Lauri Henri Lupino. Ham
Island, Old Windsor.Age 24. I.21.09.1945
P.15.02.1946 R.16.08.1946. Excluded
16.09.1953. Died 04.06.1986, London.

LANE, WILLIAM CHARLES
Cabaret Artiste. Ilford, Essex. Age 59. Joined
15.09.1967 from Aarheus Lodge No.6854.

LARTER, CYRIL LOUIS
Musician/Stage Manager. East Finchley, London
N2. Age 40. I.15.11.1946 P.21.11.1947

R.19.03.1948. Died 1953.

LATHAM, FRED
Vocalist. London SW2. I.18.03.1938 P.16.09.1938 R.18.11.1938. Resigned March 1953.

LAUGHTON, RALPH MARK HUDSON
Colindale, London NW. Age 35. I.17.06.1932 P.15.07.1932 R.19.08.1932. Resigned.

LAURENCE, ZACK
Musician. Stanmore, Middlesex. I. 21.03.1980 P.19.09.1980 R.21.11.1980.

LAURIER, JAMES
Comedian. Known as Jay Laurier. Hampstead, London NW4. Age 39. I.11.04.1919 P.19.09.1919 R.17.10.1919.

LAW, RONALD JOHN
Variety Artiste. Ilford, Essex. Age 25. I.16.01.1953 P.20.11.1953 R.18.09.1953.

LAWRENCE, EDWIN CHARLES
Vaudeville Artiste. Harrogate, Yorkshire. Age 44. I.21.11.1924 P.16.01.1925 R.18.09.1925. Resigned.

LAWRENCE, JOSEPH
Music Hall Manager. The Pavilion Theatre, Leicester. Age 48. I.19.10.1917 P.16.11.1917 R.18.01.1918. Died October 1941.

LAWRENCE, LEE
Variety Artiste. Real name Leon Sirota. Stanmore, Middlesex. Age 37. I.20.09.1957. Died in West Indies 26.02.1961, aged 40 years.

LAWSON, VINCENT WADE
Actor. Cirencester, Gloucester. Age 34. I.19.11.1920 P.18.03.1921 R.21.10.1921.

LAYTON, FRANK
Cinema Manager. Real name James McDonald. Ranelagh Cinema, Barnes. Age 45. I.16.10.1931 P.14.04.1932 R.17.06.1932. Died 12.01.1945.

LE CLERQ, GUS
Vaudeville Artiste/Comedian. Real name Augustus Howard. Also known as Gus McNaughton. Brixton, London SW. Age 28. Born 29 July 1884. Joined 21.10.1910 from Kilwinning No.2 Edinburgh, Scottish Constitution. Excluded 19.05.16. Rejoined 17.08.1917. Died November 1969.

LE FRE, ALBERT, PM PAGDC
Vaudeville Artiste. Real name James Albert de Voy. Upper Tulse Hill, Brixton, London SW2. Founder. Born 03.03.1870, London. WM 1906. Died 14 Dec 1969, aged 99 years.

LE FRE, ERIC
(A Lewis). Honorary member.

LE FRE, PERCY
Vaudeville Artiste. Real name Percival Frederick de Voy. Upper Tulse Hill, London SW2. Joined 19.06.1920 from Proscenium Lodge No.3435.

LE SINE, LOUIS
Comedian. Real name Louis Hirsch. London SW4. Age 37. I.16.04.1920 P.16.07.1920 R.20.08.1920. Resigned 15.04.1921.

LEADER, HARRY

Band Leader. London SW17. Real name George Henry Lebys. Joined 15.03.1968 from Proscenium Lodge No.3435. Died 19.01.1987, aged 81 years.

LEE, BRANDON JOHN
Film Producer. London SW11. Age 32. I.20.03.1964 P.18.09.1964 R.20.11.1964. Died March 1982.

LEE, BRINLEY ARNOLD
Film Producer. London W14. Age 29. I.20.03.1964 P.18.09.1964 R.15.03.1965.

LEE, DAVE
Entertainer. Real name David Legge. Herne Bay, Kent. Age 46. Born 02.03.1947 I.19.11.1993 P.16.03.1994 R.20.01.1995.

LEE, HERBERT
Comedian. London SW9. Age 26. I.18.06.1920 P.15.10.1920 R.19.11.1920. Excluded 1924.

LEGGE, DAVID See DAVE LEE

LEGLERE, GEORGE VICTOR See VICTOR KELLY

LEIGH, MONTAGUE See ROBERT EARL

LEOPOLD, REGINALD
Musical Director. Radlett, Herts. Age 42. I.17.03.1950 P.16.11.1951 R.21.09.1956. Died 26 February 2003, aged 95 years.

LEOPOLD, VICTOR
Vaudeville Artiste. Real name Victor Leopold Kimm. Eltham, London SE9. Age 25. I.20.02.1925 P.17.04.1925 R.20.11.1925. Excluded.

LESLIE, LEWIS ALFRED
Pantomime Producer. Shepherd's Bush, W. Age 37. Joined 21.07.1911 from Star Glasgow Lodge No. 219, Scottish Constitution.

LESTER, ERNEST THOMAS ROBBINS, LR
Comedian. Founder. WM 1913. Died March 1939.

LESTER, HARRY WORTH
Variety Artiste. Age 44. Real name Harrold Worth. Joined 16.06.1939 from Dramatic Lodge No.571, Scottish Constitution. Died 4 July 1993, aged 97 years.

LESTER, JACK
Manager. Real name John Forrester. London NW10. Age 33. I.17.06.1927 P.19.08.1927 R.16.09.1927

LESTER, JOHN BURTON
Musician. London NW2. Age 22. I.21.03.1952 P.20.01.1956 R.16.01.1959.

LEVENE, SIMON
Musician. Lower Clapton, London E5. Age 31. I.16.06.1933 P.18.08.1933 R.16.03.1934. Died July 1949.

LEVER, REG
Vaudeville Artiste. Real name Stanley Edward Russell. Rock Ferry, Cheshire. Age 24. I.20.07.1928 P.21.09.1928 R.31.07.1931. Excluded. Rejoined 1946. Died 18.08.1985

LEVEY, CHARLES FELICE

Sketch Artiste. Merton Park. Age 32. I.17.09.1909
P.15.10.1909 R.05.04.1910. Excluded
16.05.1913.

LEVIN, BENJAMIN See ISSY BONN

LEVINGER, JOSEPH, LGR
Millinery Manufacturer. Age 45. London WC1.
Age 39. I.18.09.1942 P.19.03.1943 R.17.12.1943.
Died 06.07.1981.

LEVY, HENRY CHARLES See CHARLIE RICH

LEWIN, DAVID JOHN
(A Lewis). Salesman. St Alban's, Herts. Age 26.
I.16.01.1970 P.20.03.1970 R.18.09.1970.
Resigned May 1986.

LEWIN, MAX, PM
Musician. London W12. I.16.10.1936
P.20.11.1936 R.16.07.1937. WM 1966. Died
24.09.1995.

LEWIS, ARTHUR
Vaudeville Artiste. Real name Arthur Herbert
William Day. Stockwell, London SW9. Age 32.
I.17.11.1922 P.19.01.1923 R.15.06.1923.

LEWIS, BERTRAM
Musician. London N3. Age 44. I.19.11.1954
P.21.01.1955 R.18.03.1955. Died 19.01.1995.

LEWIS, DAVID JOHN
Manager. Rhondda, Glamorgan. Age 35.
I.21.10.1927 P.16.03.1928 R.17.08.1928.

LEWIS, TED 'KID'
Boxer/Film Artiste. Real name Solomon
Mendeloff. London NW8. Age 66. Joined
19.05.1961 from Mount Moriah Lodge No.29,
New York. Died 20.10.1970, aged 75 years.

LEWIS, ERNEST
Musician. West Norwood, London SE27. Joined
15.05.1936.

LEWIS, LEON
Musician. London SW2. Age 47. I.16.11.1956
P.18.01.1957 R.15.03.1957. Died June 1988.

LEWIS, MORTON MAXWELL
Film Producer. Streatham Hill, London SW2. Age
42. I.18.09.1959 P.20.11.1959 R.18.11.1960.

LEWIS, PERCIVAL
Musical Director. London SW8. Age 32.
I.19.03.1920 P.16.04.1920 R.18.06.1920.
Excluded. Rejoined 21.06.1929. Excluded.

LIDIARD, FREDERICK ARTHUR
Musician. Catford, London SE6. Age 54.
I.20.08.1920 P.15.10.1920 R.19.11.1920.

**LILLEY, ALFRED EUGENE See ALFRED
ARTOIS**

LILLEY, GEORGE ROBERT See G.R. RANGER

LINDEN, AMANDUS CARL See AMANDUS

LING, J.P.
Entertainer. Real name James Pilling. Rochdale,
Lancs. Age 32. I.15.07.1910 P.17.03.1911
R.04.07.1911. WM 1928. Died 26.03.1938.

LINSEED, CHARLES See CHAS MILDARE

LIPTON, DAN
Author. Real name William James Mundy. Age
33. I.19.04.1907 P.21.06.1907 R.19.07.1907.

Died. Date not known.

LIQUORISH, CHARLES
Musician. South Ealing, London W. Age 30.
I.20.10.1911 P.15.03.1912 R.19.04.1912.
Excluded 19.05.1916. Rejoined 15.07.1927. Died
12.04.1962.

LITTLE, GANTY
Comedian. Real name John Dixon Graham.
London SE. Age 38. I.17.10.1913 P.17.02.1914
R.16.10.1914. Excluded 17.05.1915.

LOBAN, BENNIE
Musician. St John's Wood, London NW. Age 26.
I.15.03.1935 P.20.09.1935 R.20.12.1935.
Resigned May 1953. Went to Canada. Died
07.03.1993, aged 90 years.

LOBAN, MAURICE
Musician. London NW6. Age 21. P.21.11.1930
P.16.06.1933 R.16.03.1934 . Excluded
September 1941.

LOCKE, PETER ALAN, SLGR
TV Producer. Kenton, Middlesex. Joined
20.11.1998 from Seven Stars Lodge No.5892.

LOCKE, ROBERT PETER
TV Presenter. Southgate, London N14. Joined
20.11.1998. PM Seven Stars Lodge No.5892.

LOGAN, JOHN JEFFREY
General Secretary, Performing Right Society
Members Fund. Pinner, Middlesex. Age 46. Born
06.09.1955. I.16.11.2001 P.20.09.2002.
R15.11.2002.

LOGAN, JOHNNY T.
Singer/Musician. Real name John McMonagle.
London N1. Born 29 October 1944. Joined
19.03.2004 from Clydesdale Lodge No.556.

LORD, BERT
Vaudeville Artiste. Real name Herbert Myers.
Brixton Hill, London SW2. Age 35. I. 21.12.1923
P.21.03.1924 R.20.06.1924. Excluded.

LORIMER, GEORGE HENRY
Musician. Brondesbury, London NW. Age 42.
I.19.04.1918 P.21.06.1918 R.19.07.1918.
Excluded 1924.

LOSS, JOSHUA ALEXANDER, LVO OBE
Musical Director. Known as Joe Loss.
Hampstead, London NW2. Joined 20.03.1936.
Died 06.06.1990, aged 80 years.

LOVELL, HERBERT AUGUSTUS THOMPSON
Sketch Artiste. Known as Harry Cuthbert Lovell.
Age 28. I.17.07.1908 P.04.12.1908 R.18.03.1910.
Excluded 17.04.1919.

LOVICK, JOSEPH HENRY
Variety Artiste. Blackpool, Lancashire. Age 47.
Joined 19.03.1926 from Forfar Lodge No.309,
Scottish Constitution.

LOWE, LEN
Actor/Writer. Real name Leonard Alfred
Smoothey. Stanmore, Middlesex HA7. Age 77.
Born 17.09.1916. Joined 17.09.1993.

LUBELLE, BARNEY
Musician. London NW3. Age 41. I.15.10.1943

P.21.03.1947 R.18.03.1949. Rejoined
19.03.1975. Died 10.07.1983.

LUNNON, GREGORY STEPHEN
Financial Advisor. Walton-on-Thames, Surrey.
Age 40. Born 06.10.1957. Joined 19.09.1997
from Proscenium Lodge No.3435.

LUPINO, HENRY WILLIAM GEORGE See LUPINO LANE

LUPINO, LAURIE HENRI See LAURIE LUPINO LANE

LUTON, JOHN WALTER
Writer/director. Brookmans Park. Herts. Age 57.
Born 05.01.1945. I.20.09.2003. P.12.09.2004.

LYNCH, WILLIAM FRANK See BILLY REJANE

LYON, ALFRED EMANUEL
House furnisher. Montreal, Canada. Age 23.
I.04.12.1908 P.09.04.1909 R.14.05.1909.
Resigned 16.05.1913. Rejoined 15.08.1919.

LYON, JAMES SIMON
Solicitor. Age 23. I.16.08.1907 P.20.09.1907
R.18.10.1907. Resigned 19.05.1912.

LYON, JOHN REUBEN
5th Canadian Rifles. Canadian Pay Office,
Millbank, London SW1. Age 30. I.16.11.1917
P.18.01.1918 R.15.02.1918. Resigned
15.04.1921.

LYON, MICHAEL LEWIS
Vaudeville Agent. London WC2. Age 39.
I.15.07.1921 P.21.10.1921 R.20.01.1922.
Rejoined 16.06.1933. Died 19.08.1952.

LYON, WOLFE SIMON
Theatrical Upholsterer. Founder. Treasurer. Died
date not known.

LYSTER, FRED, PM
Musician. Real name Phineas Headworth.
Dalston, London NE. Joined 17.11.1916 from
Proscenium Lodge No.3435. WM 1930.

LYTHGOE, NIGEL BRUCE
TV Producer. Cuffley, Herts. Age 43. Joined
18.09.1992 from Broxbourne Lodge No.2253

LYTON, BILLY
Comedian. Real name William George Shinn.
Chiswick, London W4. Age 43. I.13.06.1919
P.18.07.1919 R.15.08.1919.

M

MACKAY, W.J.
Sketch Artiste. Real name William John
McManus. Hammersmith, London,W. Age 42.
I.15.04.1910 P.17.06.1910 R.19.08.1910. WM
1925. Took over Secretary of the Lodge in 1939.
Died 1947.

MACLEOD, HAMISH WILLIAM
Actor. London NW3. Age 32. I.21.11.1958
P.20.03.1959 R.18.03.1960.

McCARTHY, IAN
Vaudeville Artiste. Real name Edward Noble.
London WC2. Age 39. I.18.08.1922 P.15.09.1922
R.17.11,1922. Excluded.

McCARTHY, MIKE

Film Production Buyer. Hatch End, Middlesex.
Age 50. I.17.03.1961 P.15.09.1961 R.19.01.1962.
Died 22.08.1982.

McCOMB, BILLY
Magician. Edgware, Middlesex. Age 40.
I.18.09.1964 P.15.01.1965 R.19.11.1965.

McDONALD, JAMES See FRANK LAYTON

McIVER, JOCK: See TALBOT O'FARRELL

McKAY, PAUL See PAUL MURRAY

McLEOD, ALEXANDER
Variety Artiste. Known as Tex McLeod. Banstead,
Surrey. Age 59. I.18.11.1949 17.P.11.1950
R.16.03.1951. Excluded 1957.

McLEOD, JAMES CAMPBELL
Variety Artiste. Known as Jimmy Mac. London
N8. Age 63. I.19.11.1965 P.18.03.1966
R.20.01.1967. Excluded May 1979.

McMANUS, WILLIAM GEORGE MICHAEL
Entertainer. Denmark Hill SE5. Age 64. Born
11.01.1927. I.15.11.1991 P.20.03.1992
R.18.09.1992.

McMANUS, WILLIAM JOHN, PM LGR See W.J. MACKAY

McMONAGLE, JOHN See LOGAN, JOHNNY

McNAUGHTON, FRED
Comedian. Real name James Frederick Norton.
Founder. Born 27 May 1869. Excluded
26.05.1910. Died 26 February 1920, London,
aged 50 years.

McNAUGHTON, Gus See LE CLERQ, Gus

MAGNUS, JOSEPH
Retired. Aveley, Essex. Age 62. Joined
17.09.1965. Died 1979.

MAHER, BILLY
Vaudeville Artiste. Real name William Conn.
London SW9. Age 36. I.18.08.1922 P.15.09.1922
R.17.11.1922.

MAINWARING, JOHN PETER RODERICK See PETER WARING

MAITLAND, PHILIP
Theatrical Producer. Woolpit, Bury St Edmonds,
Suffolk. Joined 18.09.1970. Died May 1995.

MAKIN, SYD
Music Hall Artiste. Real name Sydney Douglas
Huxter. London SW9. Age 56. I.19.03.1954
P.19.11.1954 R.18.03.1955.

MALIVOIRE, WILLIAM VALENTINE See WILLIAM COLLINSON

MANIFOLD, JOHN COLQUHOUN See IAN COLQUHOUN

MANLEY, THOMAS HENRY
Variety Artiste. Burnley, Lancashire. Age 36.
I.15.03.1946 P.17.01.1947 R.21.11.1947.
Excluded May 1953.

MANSELL, FRANK ROBERT
Entertainments Manager. Finchley, London N12.
Age 46. I.19.01.1962 P.16.03.1962. Died
18.09.1983.

MANSFIELD, LAURENCE
Theatrical Agent. Walton-on-Thames, Surrey. Age

Four members who have exchanged time for eternity

Reg East

Dick Ball

Stanelli and his Hornchestra

Wallie Stewart

45. I.18.09.1987 P.18.11.1987 R.20.01.1989.

MARASO, HARRY
Variety Agent. Real name Harry Chapman. North Wembley, Middlesex. Joined 20.04.1923 from Asaph Lodge No. 1319. Died March 1947.

MARCHMISKE, ALBERT See RAMESES

MARKS, ALFRED EDWARD
Actor. East Finchley, London N2. Real name Alfred Edward Touchinsky. Age 34. I.16.09.1955 P.16.11.1956 R.15.01.1960. Excluded May 1985. Died 01.07.1996, aged 75 years.

MARKS, GEORGE, PM LGR
Musician. London NW2. Age 52. I.16.03.1956 P.21.09.1956 R.16.11.1956. Died 10.01.1997.

MARKS, HERBERT See BERT RAY

MARKS, LEWIS FREDERICK See LEWIS RAY

MARLOW, HARRY
Vaudeville Artiste. London NW1. Age 40. I.20.10.1922 P.17.11.1922 R.16.03.1923. Resigned 23.04.1929.

MARRON, EMANUEL
Musician. Known as Manny Marron. London NW4. Age 59. Joined 16.01.1970 from Assiduity Lodge No. 4844. Died September 1980.

MARSDEN, BERT
Comedian. Real name Albert Edward Williams. Clapton, London NE. Age 34. I.15.07.1910 P.19.08.1910 R.16.09.1910. Excluded 19.05.1916.

MARSHALL, JAMES CHARLES
Chairman. Aspley Guise,Bucks. Age 69. Joined 20.03.1992 from Luculas Lodge No.5258.

MARTI, JOSEPH
Variety Artiste. Half of the Chevalier Brothers. Wimbledon, SW19. Joined 19.03.1948 from Liverpool Dramatic 1609. Resigned January 1965.

MARTI, MARTIN PABLO
Variety Artiste. Half of the Chevalier Brothers. Wimbledon, SW19. Joined 19.03.1948. Died 10.08.1958.

MARTI, MARTIN PAUL
Vaudeville Artiste. Ilford, Essex. Joined 17.06.1921 from Liverpool Dramatic No.1609. Rejoined 20.09.1935. Died 17.08.1958.

MARTIN, BRAM
Musical Director. Real name Bramwell Martinez. Northwick Park, Middlesex. I.17.07.1936 P.18.09.1936 R.16.01.1937. Resigned August 1939.

MARTIN, MICHAEL GEORGE
Entertainer/musician. Waltham Abbey. Born 23.03.1954. Son of comedian George Martin. I.20.09.2002. P.23.11.2003.

MARTINI, M.
Real name Martin Barker. Vaudeville Artiste. Hampstead, NW3. Age 40. I.17.11.1922 P.16.03.1923 R.20.04.1923. Excluded.

MASON, GARY
Boxing Promoter. Sutton, Surrey. Age 37. Born 15.12.1962. I.19.11.1999 P.17.03.2000 R.15.09.2000.

MASON, HENRY
Gymnast. Real name Henry Tinkler. Age 26. I.20.04.1906 P.15.06.1906 R.20.07.1908. Resigned 20.07.1922

MATHER, CECIL CARTER
Musician. Brixton, London SW2. I.16.07.1943 P.15.10.1943 R.17.12.1943. Resigned Nov 1947. Went to live in New York. Rejoined 18.05.1962.

MATHEWS, JAMES WILLIAM, PGStB
Theatrical Manager. Bedford Park, London W. Age 42. Born in Dunedin, New Zealand. Founder. WM 1905. Elected Honorary member 1911. Died 14.12.1920, London.

MATHEWS, RONALD GEORGE KENNETH
Musician. Clapham Park, London SW4. Age 30. I.19.01.1951 P.20.07.1951 R.21.09.1951.

MATTHIAS, EUGENE PATRICK REYNOLD
Magician and Agent. Woburn, Beds. Age 45. Born 15.07.1956. Joined 16.11.2001. PM from Cymbaline Lodge No.9004.

MAURICE, AL
Vaudeville Artiste. Real name Alfred David Morris. Birmingham. Age 36. I.15.08.1930 P.19.09.1930 R.17.04.1931.

MAURICE, NEWMAN
Manager. Clapham Common, SW12. Age 37.I.18.03.1932 P.19.08.1932 R.16.09.1932. Excluded.

MAXIM, JOHNNY
Musical Entertainer. Real name Johnny Pluck. Islington London N1. Age 54. Joined 21.05.1982 from Citizen Lodge No.2911.

MAXIM, JOHNNY Junior
Musician. Real name John Reginald Pluck. Lee, London SE12. Age 41. Born 29.07.1953. Joined 20.05.1994.

MAY, JACK HYMAN
Theatrical light supplier, Leicester. Age 49. I.19.11.1971 P.17.03.1972 R.17.11.1972.

MAY, WILLIAM HENRY, PM
Musician. Known as Henry W. May. Hammersmith, London W. Age 46. I.17.04.1914 P.19.06.1914 R.17.07.1914. WM 1924.

MAYNE, ERNIE
Real name Percy Ernest Barrett. Comedian. Age 37. I.17.07.1908. P.18.09.1908 R.20.11.1908.

MAYVILLE, HENRY RICHMOND
Vaudeville Artiste. Age 32. Joined 21.07.1905 from Glasgow Dramatic Lodge No. 571, Scottish Constitution. Died 12.02.1912, aged 37 years.

MEAD, CHARLES SYDNEY
Musician. Upper Tooting, London SW17. Age 57. I.19.09.1952 P.20.03.1953 . Excluded May 1960.

MEERS, ALFRED GEORGE CHARLES
Vaudeville Artiste. Leicester Square, London WC. Age 41. Joined 15.10.1909 from Glasgow Dramatic 571, Scottish Constitution. Resigned 10.05.1913.

MELLOR, THOMAS WILLIAM
Entertainer and composer. Age 27. I.19.07.1907
P.20.09.1907 R.15.11.1907, Excluded
18.05.1911.

MENDELOFF, SOLOMON See TED 'Kid' LEWIS

MENZIES, A. HALL
Vaudeville Artiste. Real name Arthur Robert Hall.
Sydenham, London,SE. Age 39. I.16.06.1911
P.21.07.1911 R.19.04.1912. Resigned
20.03.1918

MERCADO, LIONEL DAVID
(A Lewis). Managing Director. London NW1. Age
21. I.17.11.1967 P.19.01.1968 R.20.09.1968

MERCADO, NATHAN
Commission Agent. London NW8. Age 63. Joined
17.09.1965. Died 10.06.1973.

**MEREDITH, HENRY JAMES See PETE
MURRAY**

MERRELL, CHARLES
Vaudeville Artiste. Real name Charles Newhouse.
London SW. Age 31. I.15.08.1913 P.19.09.1913
R.17.10.1913. Excluded.

MEZZETTI, BOB
Gymnast.Real name Robert Lusby Edermaniger.
Walthamstow, London E. Age 40. I.17.04.1914
P.19.06.1914 R.17.07.1914. Excluded 1924.

MILDARE, CHAS
Vaudeville Artiste. Real name Charles Linseed.
Westcliffe-on-Sea, Essex. Age 53. I.19.09.1919
P.17.10.1919 R.21.11.1919. Excluded.

MILLER, LESLIE
Musician. Kenton, Middlesex. Age 41.
I.15.11.1957 P.21.03.1958 R.19.09.1958. Died
13.01.1980.

MILLS, FREDERICK PERCIVAL
Boxer and Entertainer. Denmark Hill, London
SE5. Age 45. I.20.11.1964 P.19.03.1965 Died 26
July 1965, aged 46 years.

MILLS, MURRAY
Vaudeville Manager. Real name Abraham Morris
Somerfield. London, W1. Age 30. I.21.11.1924
P.16.01.1925 R.18.09.1925. Resigned.

MILLS, PAUL EDWARD VALASCO
Theatre Director. Whitstable, Kent. Age 54. Born
30.06.1948. I.18.01.2002 P.17.01.2003.

MILLWARD, ALBERT See AUSTIN WEBB

MINDEL, DAVID RICHARD
(A Lewis). Furniture Buyer. London W1. Age 21.
I.15.03.1968 P.15.11.1968 R.17.01.1969.

MINDEL, MONTY
Co-Director. London N3. Age 52. Joined
17.09.1965. Died Sept 1976.

MITCHELL, CECIL C.
Musical Director. St John's Wood,London NW2.
Age 41. I.20.01.1939. Died 28.07.1984.

MITELLE, LEONARD
Theatrical producer and variety agent. London
NW6. Age 47 18.09.1942 19.01.1945 17.11.1961.
Excluded April 1947. Rejoined 19.01.1951.

MOIR, JAMES JOHN

Music Hall Manager. London SW9. Age 43.
I.17.06.1921 P.15.07.1921 R.16.09.1921.

MONKHOUSE, ROBERT ALAN, OBE
Entertainer. London NW11. Age 28. I.16.11.1956
P.21.09.1962 R.20.11.1964.

MOON, BARRY
Comedian/Musician. Real name Barry Weir.
Staines, Middlesex. Age 51. Born 11.10.1949.
I.19.05.2000 P.19.01.2001 R.16.11.2002

MOORE, WILLIAM BERNARD
Cabaret Artiste. Known as Billy Moore. Forest
Gate, London E7. Age 50. Born 27.04.1926.
I.21.09.1984 P.16.11.1984 R.15.03.1985.

MORAN
Real name Toman Victor Jose Byron-Barhydt.
Vaudeville Artiste. Aged 30. I.16.03.1906
P.15.06.1906 R.22.01.1907. Excluded May 1910.

MORDISH, LOUIS
Musical Director. London W10. Age 46.
I.19.03.1954 P.17.09.1954 R.21.01.1955.
Resigned 30.04.1996. Died 1996.

MORGAN, FRED
Vaudeville Artiste. Real name Jim O'Callaghan.
Sefton Park, Liverpool. Age 44. I.20.03.1925
P.17.06.1927. Excluded.

MORGAN, ROBERT MYRDDIN
Film Booking Manager. Bromley, Kent. Age 56.
Born 15.11.1927. I.18.11.1983 P.20.01.1984
R.16.03.1984. Treasurer, 1990-1994.

MORGAN, THOMAS IVAN JAMES LGR
Theatre Manager. Bedford. Age 55. Joined
20.03.1987 from Lakedale Lodge No.4044.

MORRICE, LAWRENCE STEWART
Musician. Putney, London SW15. Age 48. Born
20.05.1947. I.20.01.1995 P.15.09.1995
R.15.03.1996.

MORRIS, ALFRED DAVID See AL MAURICE

MORRIS, GILBERT JOSEPH
Comedian. Reading, Berks. Known as Gil Morris.
Born 08.12.1942. I.16.01.2004. P..12.09.2004.

MORRIS, JOSEPH
Musical Conductor. Kennington, SE11. Age 38.
I.17.06.1921 P.15.07.1921 R.19.08.1921. Later
changed his name to Joseph Salcot.

MORRIS, MIKE
Vaudeville Artiste. Real name Thomas Newsham.
Age 30. Joined 16.06.1905 from Earl's Court
Lodge No.2765.

MORRIS, WALTER
Musician. London W12. Age 32. Joined
15.03.1935 from Atlantic Phoenix Lodge No.224,
Hamilton, Bermuda.

MORRISON, JOSEPH TURNER, PM PAGstB
Revue Proprietor. Middlesborough. Age 44.
I.21.08.1925 P.16.10.1925 R.19.02.1926. WM
1939.

MOSELEY, WILLIAM GRAY
Vocalist. Joined 19.04.1907. Joined from Earl's
Court Lodge No.2765. Excluded 16.05.1912.

MOSLEY, TONY

Joined 15.05.1964.

MOSS, ERNIE
Comedian. Real name Ernest Walter Bewsey. Hayes, Kent. I.23.02.1936 P.20.03.1936 R.20.11.1936. Died January 1949.

MOSS, PHILIP
Merchant. Blackpool. Age 39. I.19.01.1945 P.16.11.1945 R.15.02.1946. Died 13.05.1964.

MOTIMURA
Illusionist. Real name Albert James Powell. Age 31. I.18.10.1907 P.15.11.1907 R.18.03.1910. Excluded 19 May 1916.

MOYNIHAN, Lord ANTONY PATRICK
Theatrical Manager. Chelsea, London SW3. Age 31. I.19.01.1968 P.15.03.1968 R.15.11.1968. He was The Lord Moynihan of Leeds. Excluded May 1972..

MOZART, GEORGE
Comedian. Real name David John Gillings. Founder. Born 15.02.1864, Great Yarmouth, Norfolk. Resigned 02.02.1910. Died 09.12.1947, aged 83 years.

MOZR, GEORGE ANTON
Musician. London SW2. Age 35. I.17.01.1947 P.21.03.1947 R.16.01.1948. Died 22.08.1983.

MULLER, JOHN CHARLES ERNEST
Dancer. Southport, Lancashire. Age 20. I.21.06.1912 P.19.07.1912 R.20.09.1912. Excluded 19.05.1921.

MULLINS, FRANCIS GEORGE PM LGR
General Manager, Granada. Clapham Common, London SW4. Age 55. Born 04.07.1914. I.20.03.1970 P.20.11.1970 R.15.01.1971. WM 1981. Honorary Member. Died 22 January 2005, aged 89 years.

MUNDY, WILLIAM JAMES See DAN LIPTON

MURANYI, GEORGE JASON
Musician. London NW8. Age 31. Born 07.01.1969. Joined 21.01.2000 from Lodge of Fidelity No.7974.

MURRAY, CHRISTOPHER See FRED ROMA

MURRAY, PAUL
Vaudeville Agent. Real name Paul McKay. Age 23. I.17.07.1908 P.21.08.1908 R.18.09.1908. Resigned May 1912.

MURRAY, PETE
Music Hall Manager. Real name Henry James Meredith. Brixton, London SW. Age 40. I.18.06.1909 P.16.07.1909 R.13.08.1909. Resigned 21.04.1912.

MURRAY, SID
Entertainer. Real name Sydney Percy Orford. London E. Age 32. I.15.09.1916 P.20.10.1916 R.17.11.1917.

MUSIKANT, DAVID
Confectioner. London NW6. Joined 17.11.1967 from Covent Garden Lodge No.1614.

MUSIKANT, HARRY
Musician. London N17. Age 64. Joined 15.11.1968 from Amicus Lodge No 3772.

Resigned 16.05.1980.

MUSIKANT, LEON
Musician. North Wembley, Middlesex. Age 53. Joined 15.11.1968 from Morton Lodge No 89, Scottish Constitution. His father was David Musikant, his uncle Harry Musikant.

MYERS, ERNEST MOSS
Comedian. Age 35. I. 16.04.1908 P.19.03.1909 R.13.08.1909. Died 07.04.1914.

MYERS, GEORGE
Musician. Middleton, Leeds. Age 28. I.30.03.1931 P.17.04.1931 R.16.10.1931. Excluded 1950.

MYERS, HERBERT See BERT LORD

N

NASH, JOHN E.
Manager. London W1. Joined 16.06.1911 from Liverpool Dramatic No.1609. Excluded May 1915.

NATHAN, JACK
Bandleader. London NW4. Age 60. I.21.01.1972 P.15.09.1972 R.16.03.1973. Resigned due to ill health May 1985. Died 20.03.1990, aged 79 years.

NEALE, DAVID ALLAN
Film Producer. Gillingham, Kent. Age 58. Born 25.06.1944. Joined 21.01.2000 from Durobrivae Lodge No.6956.

NEIMAN, JACOB
Ventriloquist. Known as Fred Neiman. Age 46. Born 16.10.1860, Brighton. I.17.08.1906 P.21.09.1906 R.19.0.1906. Died 25.12.1910, aged 50 years.

NELSON, THOMAS YOUNG
Comedian. Camberwell, London SE. Age 34. I.16.08.1912. Died 16.06.1918.

NERVO, JIMMY
Vaudeville Artiste. Real name James Henry Holloway. Brixton Hill, SW2. Age 26. I.21.09.1923 P.19.10.1923 R.21.03.1924. Excluded March 1932. Died 05.12.1975, aged 85 years.

NEWHOUSE, CHARLES See CHARLES MERRELL

NEWMAN, ARTHUR CECIL See PRIMOVESI

NEWMAN, BERNARD
Manufacturer. Baker Street, London NW1. Age 42. Joined 16.05.1943.

NEWMAN, HARRY, PM PAGDC
Accountant. London W1. Joined 15.07.1938. WM 1952. Died 27.07.1983.

NEWSHAM, THOMAS See MIKE MORRIS

NICHOLAS, GERALD VICTOR FRANCIS de WELD See GERRY GEORGE

NICHOLSON, GEORGE
Maitre de Hotel. Age 30. I.20.01.1939 P.17.03.1939 R.16.06.1939. Excluded May 1962.

NICKLIN, ALBERT EDWARD
Fancy Goods Manager. Founder. Resigned 19.03.1913.

NIGHTINGALE, RICHARD HENRY

Theatrical Manager. Llanfairfechan, North Wales. Age 48. I.16.03.1928 P.17.08.1928 R.21.09.1928. Excluded.

NIXON, JOHN
Master Baker. Camberwell, London SE5. I.17.05.1935 P.19.07.1935 R.15.11.1935. Excluded September 1941.

NOAKES, ALFRED SAMUEL
Musician. London SE27. I.19.11.1937 P.18.03.1938 R.20.01.1939. Resigned 20.11.1953. Died 1982.

NOBLE, EDWARD See IAN McCARTHY

NOLAN, H.S.
Music Hall Agent. Real name Herbert Edward Scott. London SE. Age 23. I.16.04.1909 P.16.07.1909 R.13.08.1909. Excluded 1924.

NOONAN, PATRICK JOSEPH
Stage and Screen Artist. London SW1. Age 46. Joined 17.03.1933 from Knight Lodge No.3918.

NORTON, JAMES FREDERICK See FRED McNAUGHTON

NORTON, RONALD GEORGE
Joined 17.11;1978. Died 28.01.1980

NURTHEN, ERNEST HENRY
Musician. Hendon, London NW4. Age 46. I.19.11.1948 P.15.07.1949 R.17.03.1950.

O

O'CALLAGHAN, JIM See FRED MORGAN

O'CONNOLLY, GERALD VINCENT
Publicity Manager of Moss and Stoll Administrative Offices. Age 26. I.20.09.1907. P.18.10.1907. R.15.11.1907. Died 8 May 1909.

O'DONNELL, DEREK THOMAS
Musician. London SW15. Age 44. I.18.03.1966 P.18.11.1966 R.17.11.1967. Resigned May 1981.

O'FARRELL, TALBOT
Variety Artiste. Real name Will Parrot. Also known as Will McIver. London WC1. Age 69. Joined 18.07.1947 from Thailia Lodge No.5177. Died 02.09.1952.

O'FARRELL, THOMAS MICHAEL, LGR PPAGSuptW
Company Director/Producer. London W1. Age 59. Born 31.03.1933. Joined 15.05.1992. Joined from Upper Thames Lodge No.6138.

OGDEN, ERIK
Musical Director. London N7. I.21.01.1938 P.18.02.1938 R.15.07.1938.

O'HARA, SAMUEL FREDERICK
Vaudeville Artiste. Streatham Hill, London SW2. Age 42. I.21.09.1928 P.01.01.1929 R.15.03.1929.

OLIVELLI, ENRICO
Restauranteur. London WC1. Age 46. I.19.03.1937 P.16.07.1937 R.20.08.1937. Died 08.04.1961.

O'MALLEY, HORACE
Real name Horace Edward Arrendell. Comedian. Hampstead, London NW. Age 32. I.04.12.1908 P.15.04.1910 R.19.08.1910. Excluded May 1915.

ORFORD, SYDNEY PERCY See SID MURRAY

OVERS, ALBERT
Stage Manager. Camden Town, London NW. Age 26. I.13.12.1912 P.14.03.1913 R.18.04.1913. Resigned 14.04.1915.

OWEN, JACKSON
Comedian. Real name Stanley Thomas Kelley. Brixton, London SW2. Age 33. I.21.11.1919. Excluded 1924.

OWENS, SIDNEY RALPH See SID CHRISTO

P

PACKER, BARRY
Musician. Conniburrow, Bucks. Age 35. I.18.09.1981 P.15.01.1982. R.19.03.1982.

PACKER, CYRIL
Wig maker. Stanmore,Middlesex. Joined 16.05.1980 from Astral Seven Lodge No.6489.

PACKER, HENRY FRANK
Theatre Agent. London SE13. Age 46. Joined 17.03.1961.

PACKER, SIMON ROBERT
(A Lewis) Student. Milton Keynes, Bucks. Age 20. Born 10.05.1982. I.15.03.2002.

PAGE, DANDY
Vaudeville Artiste. Real name Joseph Pessis. Holloway, London,N. Age 27. I.20.07.1923 P.21.09.1923 R.16.11.1923.

PALMER, GEORGE
(A Lewis) Musician. Streatham, London SW16. Age 35. I.19.03.1948 P.17.09.1948 R.16.09.1948. Excluded 18.05.1979.

PALMER, JEREMY DAVID
Theatrical Agent. South Woodham Ferrers, Essex. Age 32. I.20.11.1992 P.15.01.1993 R.17.09.1993.

PAPPS, GEORGE GLOYNE See GEORGE GRAHAM

PARKER, HENRY THOMAS
Comedian. Age 28. I.19.04.1907 P.21.06.1907 R.19.07.1907. Excluded May 1913.

PARNELL, ARTHUR RUSSELL
Theatrical Manager. London, WC1. Age 50. I.17.01.1947 P.19.09.1947 R.21.06.1949.

PARROTT, WILL See TALBOT O'FARRELL

PARSONS, ROBERT JOHN SHORE
Entertainments Manager. Rochdale, Lancashire. Age 56. I.20.03.1981 P.20.09.1981 R.20.11.1981. Resigned May 1987.

PARTLETON, WILLIAM THOMAS
Makeup Artiste. London E18. Age 30. I.18.07.1941 P.20.03.1942 R.19.03.1943.

PASQUALE, JOSEPH ELLIS
Comedian/Entertainer. Higham, Kent. I.18.03.2005.

PAULSON, CHARLES See CHAS HARVARD

PAYNE, NORMAN
Musician and Variety Agent. London W9. Aged 25. I.20.12.1935 P.17.01.1936 R.16.01.1937. Died 11.02.1992, aged 80 years.

PAYNE, TOM
Real name Walter Thomas Blake. Vaudeville and Variety Artiste. London W12. Joined 21.04.1911 from Coppin Lodge No.94, Victoria, Australia. Excluded Rejoined 19.03.1926. Excluded 1956.

PEARCE, CHARLES
Vaudeville Artiste. Aged 31. Joined 20.04.1906 from Earl's Court Lodge No.2765. Resigned 13.05.1907.

PEARCE, BRIAN RICHARD JAMES See DICKIE RICHARDS

PEARCE, GAVIN RICHARD
Children's Entertainer. Yately, Camberley, Surrey. Age 29. Joined 21.09.1990 from Benefaction Lodge No.5318. Resigned 1995.

PEARSON, WILLIAM JOHN See W.H. WALLIS

PEDGRIFT, FREDERICK HENCHMAN
Professor of Singing. Age 49. I.04.05.1906 P.15.06.1906 R.20.07.1906. Excluded 19.05.1916.

PEPPER, PHILLIP
Musician. Lewisham. Age 49. I.21.06.1918 P.19.07.1918 R.16.08.1918. Resigned March 1939.

PERCIVAL, DONALD JOHN
Musician and PR Consultant. London W14. 70. Born 02.10.1930. Joined 15.05.1959. Resigned. Rejoined 19.05.2000.

PERMANE, CHARLES HENRY
Vaudeville Artiste. Brixton, London SW9. Age 39. I.19.11.1937 P.17.12.1937 R.19.07.1940. WM 1949. Resigned January 1964.

PERMANE, VINCENT ADOLF, PM LGR
Film Manager. London W14. Age 58. I.21.03.1958 P.19.09.1958 R.18.09.1959. WM 1970. Died 08.11.1991, aged 91 years.

PERMANE, WILLIAM VINCENTI
Vaudeville Artiste. Age 41. I.15.09.1905 P.20.10.1905 R.11.01.1906. WM 1934. Died 05.06.1939, aged 75 years.

PERRY, DOUGLAS ROBERT, PM
Musician. Herts. Age 32. I.15.09.1978 P.19.01.1979 R.21.09.1979. WM 1984. Died 16.09.1996.

PESSIS, JOSEPH See DANDY PAGE

PETERS, FRANK See GRISHA FARFEL

PETERS, JOHN
Sports Promoter. Brighton, Sussex. Age 48. Joined 17.01.1969 from Lodge of Light No.7218. Resigned 05.1979.

PETERS, JOHN PETER Jnr
(A Lewis) Site Manager. London SW17. Age 23. I.15.01.1971 P.19.03.1971 R.17.09.1971.

PHILLIPS, ALEXANDER EDWARD See PHIL BRANSBY

PHILLIPS, HARRY ALLEN See HARRY BANNERMAN

PHILLIPS, WILLIAM HENRY See HARRY KATO

PHILLIPS, WOOLF
Musical Director. Woodside Park, London N12.

Born 05.01.1919. Joined 21.11.1952 from Anglo Colonial No.1561. Excluded May 1969 Died 11 July 2003, USA, aged 84 years..

PIKE, BRIAN H.M.J.
Dentist. Luton, Beds. Age 21. I.21.11.1958 P.16.01.1959 R.18.09.1959.

PIKE, HENRY CHARLES WALTER
Age 34. I.20.09.1940 P.21.07.1944 R.16.03.1945.

PILLING, JAMES See J.P. LING

PITMAN, FRANCIS
Circuit Supervisor. Kingsbury, London NW9. Age 52. I.16.01.1948 P.17.09.1948 R.16.09.1949. Died March 1961.

PLANT, JOSEPH
Builder. Neathfield, Birmingham. Age 56. Joined 20.09.1946 from Lodges 4472, 5224, 5546, 5747. Excluded 1947.

PLATT, JAMES EMANUEL See J.W. RICKABY

PLUCK, JOHN REGINALD See JOHNNY MAXIM Junior

PLUCK, JOHNNY See JOHNNY MAXIM

PLUMMER, THOMAS WALLACE See TOMMY WALLIS

POGSON, EDWARD OWEN
Musician. London SW18. Age 31. I.16.11.1934 P.18.01.1935 R.15.03.1935. Excluded Died 31.01.1980, aged 75 years.

PORTER, TREVOR, PPSGD
Theatrical Legal Representative. Blackpool, Lancashire. Joined 20.11.1998 from Peace and Unity Lodge No.3966.

POTTER, EDWARD
Musician. East Molesey, Surrey. Age 27. I.16.09.1955. Excluded 1959.

POTTER, ERNEST GEORGE
Musical Director. Chelsea Embankment, London SW3. Age 47. I.17.03.1950 P.19.01.1951 R.16.11.1951. Excluded 1958.

POULTEN-ROGERS, ALAN JOHN
Musician/Conductor. Chipperfield, Herts. Age 45. Born 09.12.1948. I.21.01.1994 P.16.09.1994 R.20.01.1995.

POWELL, ALBERT ARTHUR
Music Hall Artiste. Known as Sandy Powell. Neasden, London NW10. Age 33. I.20.01.1933 P.17.12.1943 R.21.01.1944. Excluded. Died 20.06.1982, aged 82 years.

POWELL, ALBERT JAMES See MOTIMURA

POWELL, ARTHUR HEDLEY
Musician. Upper Tooting, London SW17. Age 40. I.16.03.1951 P.16.11.1951 R.21.03.1952. Resigned May 1986.

POWELL, FELIX LLOYD
Musician. Harrow, Middlesex. Age 44. I.20.10.1922 P.17.11.1922 R.15.12.1922. Died 1942, aged 64 years.

PRAEGER, ALFRED PHILLIP BERNARD
Theatrical Agent. London, W1. Age 44. Joined 17.03.1961 from Silver Jubilee Lodge No.5535. Excluded.

PREEDY, ALFRED THOMAS See EDDIE EARLE

PRICE, PETER HERBERT
Assistant Film Producer. Laleham, Middlesex. Age 35. I.21.01.1966 P.18.03.1966 R.16.09.1966. Excluded May 1991. Rejoined 15.01.1993.

PRICHARD, PETER JOHN, OBE
Theatrical Agent. Chelsea, London SW10. Age 57. Born 30.11.1932. I.19.01.1990 P.21.09.1990 R.16.11.1990.

PRIDDY, THOMAS
Musician. Holloway, London N. Age 33. I.16.07.1926 P.20.08.1926 R.15.10.1926. Excluded 1959.

PRIMOVESI
Real name Arthur Cecil Newman. Joined 16.06.1905 from Scottish Constitution. Resigned 18.03.1910

PRIOR, HERBERT LESLIE
Electrician. Brockham, Surrey. Age 23. I.12.1943 P.18.02.1944 R.17.03.1944.

PRIOR, JAMES GEORGE
Radio Engineer. Brockham, Surrey. Age 36. I.18.09.1942 P.20.11.1942 R.19.03.1943. Excluded 1951.

PRIOR, JIMMIE
Comedian. Real name James Pryer. Age 37. I.04.05.1906 P.17.08.1906 R.21.09.1906. Excluded 19.05.1911.

PROBERT, ALBERT EWART
Musical Director. Colindale, London NW9. Age 39. I.17.09.1943 P.19.11.1943 R.18.02.1944. Excluded 1959. Grand Lodge Certificate returned To GL November 1960.

PROBST, ROBERT EDWARD
Musical Director. London SW15. Age 59. I.20.09.1963 P.20.03.1964 R.15.05.1964. Died 15.02.1979.

PROBUS
Theatrical Manager. Real name Leonard Stonewall Jackson. Porchester, Nottingham. Age 30. I.20.11.1942 P.19.03.1943 R.17.09.1943.

PRYER, JAMES See JIMMIE PRIOR

PUNCHARD, HERBERT
Vaudeville Artiste. London W12. Age 29. I.20.06.1924 P.19.09.1924 R.21.11.1924.

PURI, Dr VIKRAM
Medical Doctor. London SE15. Age 43. Born 24.02.1948. Joined 18.01.1991 from St George's Lodge No.1098.

PURNELL, EDWARD CALSTON See EDDIE REINHART

PURSLOE, THOMAS See HAL WRIGHT

PUTNER, WILLIAM ZACCHEAUS See SYDNEY BRAY

Q

QUINN, JAMES EDWARD PM, LGR
Theatrical Agent. Dolphin Square, London SW1. Age 52. I.17.11.1961 P.19.01.1962 R.16.03.1962.

Died 16.07.1982.

R

RADFORD, HENRI C.
Comedy Juggler. Age 27. I.20.10.1905 P.15.06.1906 R.21.09.1906. Excluded 16.03.1913.

RAINE, GEORGE GLADNEY
Musician. London W4. Age 41. I.16.02.1940 P.19.07.1940 R.20.09.1940. Resigned. Went to Australia in 1951. Rejoined 21.03.1954. Resigned 11.04.1961.

RAINE, JOHN ALFRED
Musician. Chiswick, London W4. I.19.07.1935 P.21.02.1936 R.20.03.1936. Excluded July 1942. Died 1952.

RALFINI, IAN
Recording Executive. London SE12. Age 26. I.15.03.1963 P.20.09.1963 R.24.04.1964. Excluded.

RALLAND, BERTIE
Music Hall Manager. Real name William Herbert Randall. Age 24. I.16.10.1908 P.20.11.1908 R.19.02.1909. Excluded 1923. Died 01.02.1942, Melbourne, Australia.

RALLIS, PHIL, PM
Vaudeville Artiste. Real name Philip Fry. Stockwell, London SW9. Age 26. I.20.08.1920 P.17.09.1920 R.15.10.1920. WM 1947. Died 05.07.1966.

RAMESES
Magician. Real name Albert Marchmiske. Bethnal Green, London E. Age 33. I.15.04.1910 P.07.06.1910 R.05.07.1910. Excluded 21.05.1915.

RAMSDEN, DAVID RICHARD
(A Lewis). Dancer. Lewes, East Sussex. Age 25. Born 03.03.1976. I.19.01.2001 P.21.09.2001 R.15.03.2002.

RAMSDEN, HENRY KAY
Musical Director. Joined 19.10.1906 from Lancastrian Lodge No.2528. Died 01.06.1909.

RAMSDEN, MICHAEL RICHARD, PM
Theatres Director. Eastbourne, Sussex. Age 46. Born 18.02.1939. I.17.01.1986 P.21.03.1986 R.21.11.1986.

RAND, JACKSON ALLEN See JACKSON ALLEN

RANDALL, HENRY THOMAS WILLIAM
Comedian. Known as Harry Randall. Founder. Excluded 16.05.1913.

RANDALL, WILLIAM HERBERT See BERTIE RALLAND

RANGER, G.R.
Vaudeville Artiste. Real name George Robert Lilley. Longsight, Manchester. Age 22. I.16.04.1909 P.13.01.1910 R.17.06.1910. Excluded 15 May 1914.

RAWLINS, DENNIS
Magician. London W3. Age 34. Joined

20.09.1957 from Fairfax Lodge No.3014.

RAY, BERT
Review Manager. Real name Herbert Marks.
Southsea, Hants. Age 31. I.17.04.1924
P.15.08.1924 R.17.10.1924. Excluded. Rejoined
21.07.1944. Excluded May 1952.

RAY, LEWIS
Vaudeville Artiste. Real name Lewis Frederick
Marks. East Finchley, London N. Age 34.
I.21.03.1924 P.20.02.1925 R.14.04.1927.
Excluded 1928. Rejoined 16.05.1945.

RAYE, PAUL
Musician. Real name Christopher Williams.
London W11. Age 37. I.21.11.1947 P.18.03.1949
R.21.07.1950. Excluded 1958

RAYMOND, FRED
Vaudeville Artiste. Real name Frederick Leslie
Easton. Clapham Park, London SW. Age 29.
I.31.12.1915 P.17.03.1916 R.14.04.1916.
Resigned.

RAYMOND, TED
Vaudeville Artiste. Real name Edward Vernon
Easton. Clapham Park, London SW. Age 29.
I.31.12.1915 P.17.03.1916 R.14.04.1916.
Resigned 11.11.1919.

RAYMONDE, IVOR
Musical Director. Croydon, Surrey. Age 36.
I.18.01.1963 P.17.01.1964 R.20.03.1964.
Resigned May 1987. Died 1990.

RECO
Circus Artiste. Real name Herbert Wroe.
Darlington. Age 36. I.16.03.1945 P.16.11.1945
R..... Excluded 18.05.1979

READ, IAN SHAW
Public Relations. Harrow, Middlesex. Age 27.
I.19.09.1958. Excluded May 1962.

READ, SIDNEY JOHN
Caterer. Kenton, Middlesex. Age 34. I.15.03.1940
P.19.07.1940 R.14.02.1946. Excluded 1951.
Rejoined 16.11.1956. Excluded May 1962.

REDFEARN, DAVID GEORGE
Magician. West Wickham, Kent. Age 43. Born
19.08.1958. I.16.03.2001 P.18.01.2002.

REED, WILLIAM NEWMAN
Theatrical. Brixton Hill, London SW2. Age 47.
I.18.11.1949 P.21.07.1950 R.16.03.1951. Died
10.08.1964.

REES, ERNEST THOMAS
Actor. Age 32. I.17.08.1906 P.19.10.1906
R.22.01.1907. Excluded 19.05.1911.

REGAN, J.
Real name Walter Leopold Alexandra. Vaudeville
Artiste. London SW6. Age 31. I.16.03.1923
P.16.11.1923 R.21.12.1923. Excluded.

REID, CLIFFORD
Proprietor and Manager. Folkestone, Kent. Age
33. I.18.06.1915 P.16.07.1915 R.20.08.1915.
Resigned 16.05.1919.

REID, JAMES
Theatrical Manager. Ripley, Derbyshire. Age 49.

I.18.03.1921 P.19.08.1921 R.18.11.1921.

REINHART, EDDIE
Comedian. Real name Edward Calston Purnell.
Also known as Eddie Reindeer. Age 35.
Westcliffe-on-Sea, Essex. Age 33. I.15.03.1940
P.18.07.1941 R.14.09.1941. Died 17.10.1983.

REJANE, BILLY
Vaudeville Artiste. Real name William Frank
Lynch. London N1. Age 35. I.16.01.1925
P.19.07.1925 R.15.01.1926. Excluded.

REYNOLDS, ARTHUR
Vaudeville Artiste. Real name Reginald Moore
Hensam. Clapham, London SW. Age 41.
I.16.03.1917 P.20.04.1917 R.20.07.1917.

REYNOLDS, EARLE
Vaudeville Artiste. Broadway, New York, USA.
Age 38. I.18.06.1909 P.16.07.1909 R.13.08.1909.
Excluded 16 May 1913.

RHYMER, HAROLD See ED DAROS

RIAT, FREDERICK EBOR
Vaudeville Artiste. Regent Street, London SW.
Age 33. I.17.07.1914 P.21.08.1914 R.16.10.1914.

RICH, CHARLES CONGERE
Vaudeville Artiste. London SW. Age 28.
I.18.07.1930 P.21.11.1930 R.19.06.1931. Died
November 1933.

RICH, CHARLIE
Comedian. Real name Henry Charles Levy.
London SW9. Age 47. I.16.08.1918 P.20.09.1918
R.18.10.1918.

RICH, PAUL
Guitarist/Vocalist. London NW6. Age 38.
I.15.01.1960 P.16.09.1960 R.20.01.1961. WM
1979 and 1999. Died 23.02.2000, aged 78 years.

**RICHARDS, CHARLES KENNETH EARLE See
KENNETH EARLE**

RICHARDS, DICKIE
Comedy Singer. Real name Brian Richard James
Pearce. Farnborough, Hants. Age 53. Born
31.12.1935. Joined 18.11.1988 from Loyalty
Lodge No.7154.

RICHARDS, PERCY See BEAUCAIRE

**RICHARDSON, BASIL HENRY See BASIL
KING**

RICHES, IAN NORMAN
Cinema Executive. London W2. Age 41.
I.21.03.1986 P.16.01.1987 R.20.03.1987.

RICKABY, J.W.
Vaudeville Artiste. Real name James Emanuel
Platt. Age 38. Born 1870, Manchester.
I.16.04.1908 P.16.08.1909 R.16.07.1909.
Excluded 16.05.1919. Died 01.10.1929, London.

RICKS, HENRY JAMES See HENRY GOLD

**RIGBY-SAUNDERS, RONALD CHARLES See
RON SMILEY**

RISCOE, JOHNNIE
Comedian. Age 33. Joined 16.07.1943 from
Solomon Lodge. Resigned March 1955.

RISKIT, JACK
Vaudeville Artiste. Real name John Richard

Evans. Lower Broughton, Manchester. Age 43.
I.15.06.1923 P.17.08.1923 R.18.09.1925.

ROBBERDS, JOHN HENRY
Electrician. Hither Green, London SE. Age 34.
I.19.10.1923 P.21.12.1923 R.15.02.1924.
Excluded March 1932.

ROBBINS, HARRY
Musician. London W1. I.18.09.1936 P.16.06.1937
R.17.06.1938. Excluded May 1949. Died
08.03.1983.

**ROBERTS, ERNEST AUGUSTUS See GUS
ATLAS**

ROBERTS, ROBERT FOSSETT OTTO
Circus Director. Polebrook, Peterborough. Joined
18.09.1970. Excluded 30.04.1994. Died Easter
Monday, 5 April 1999, aged 87 years.

ROBERTS, ROBERT MAURICE PAUL
(A Lewis). Circus Artiste. Known as Bobby
Roberts. Polebrook, Peterborough. Age 30.
I.16.03.1973 P.15.03.1974 R.20.09.1974.

ROBERTS, VICTOR CHARLES
Musical Director. Clapton, London E5. Age 38.
I.15.06.1928 P.17.08.1928 R.19.10.1928.
Excluded March 1933.

**ROBERTS, WILLIAM HEDLEY, PM LGR See
ATLAS**

ROBEY, GEORGE, Sir CBE
Comedian. Real name George Edward Wade.
Founder. Resigned May 1909. Died 29.11.1954,
aged 85 years.

ROBINS, JOE
Vaudeville Artiste. Real name Joseph William
Robinson. Age 30. I.16.08.1907 P.20.09.1907
R.21.08.1908. Excluded May 1913.

**ROBINSON, JOSEPH WILLIAM See JOE
ROBINS**

**ROBINSON, LESLIE HOLLINGS See JACK
STRAND**

ROGERS, ALBERT
Showman. Smethwick. I.18.08.1939 P.19.01.1940
R.21.03.1941.

ROGERS, NOEL FREDERICK
Music Publisher. Blackheath, London SW3. Age
38. I.20.11.1959 P.18.03.1960 R.15.03.1963.
Excluded.

ROGERS, SAMUEL
Musical Director. Upton Park, London E13. Age
30. I.16.03.1923 P.17.08.1923 R.19.10.1923.
Excluded March 1928.

ROLFE, LEONARD
(A Lewis). Concert Artiste. Edgware, Middlesex.
Age 44. I.15.09.1972 P.21.09.1973 R.18.01.1974.

ROMA, FRED
Vaudeville Artiste. Real name Christopher
Murray. Bedford Park, London W. Age 37.
I.13.12.1912 P.14.03.1913 R.18.07.1913.
Excluded 1919. Died 1947.

ROPER, REX
Variety Artiste. Real name Charles Victor Knight.
London SW18. Age 42. Born 17.10.1919. London

SW18. Joined 20.01.1995 from Prospect Lodge
No.7618.

ROS, EDMUNDO, OBE
Musical Director, London W2. Joined 16.05.1952
from Cheyne Lodge No.4443.

ROSE, GEORGE ALFRED CHARLES, PM LGR
Musician. London SW20. Age 40. I.17.05.1946
P.16.08.1946 R.20.09.1946. WM 1956. Died
12.03.1976, aged 82 years.

ROSS, JAMES See ELVIO

ROSS, WILLIAM LESLIE
Vaudeville Artiste. Stamford Hill, London N16.
Age 31. I.19.10.1928 P.16.08.1929. Excluded
March 1933.

ROUHAN, MICHAEL See FRED FARREN

ROWLAND, JOHN
Concert Artiste. Real name John Rowland
Corbett. London, W7. Joined 20.07.1951 from
Winnington Lodge No. 4559. Died 08.01.1972

ROWLANDS, RON
Real name Ronald Walter William George
Beadle. Theatrical Artiste. London W12. Age 35.
I.16.11.1962 P.15.03.1963 R.17.01.1964.

ROYAL, JACK
Stage manager. Real name Jack Samuel Brown.
Fulham, London SW6. Joined 19.10.1917 from
Glasgow Dramatic Lodge No.571, Scotland. Died
15.06.1952.

RUDD, ARTHUR
Vaudeville Artiste. Holland Park, London W. Age
59. Joined 18.09.1926. Died 24.03.1929.

RUDD, EDWIN AUSTIN JAMES
(A Lewis). Retired Cinema Proprietor. London
W2. Age 34. Joined 21.06.1929 from Lodge
No.2743.

RUDERMAN, HARRY See HARRY STANLEY
RUSHEN, HAROLD See HAL GORDON
**RUSSELL, STANLEY EDWARD See REG
LEVER**

S
SAINT, VAL
Vaudeville Artiste. Real name Herbert Valentine
Jackson. Nottingham. Age 37. I.20.04.1917
P.20.07.1917 R.17.08.1917.

SALIH, NEJ
Actor and Writer. Southgate, London N14. Age
44. Born 23.12.1956. I.17.11.2000 P.21.09.2001
R.16.11.2002.

SALMONS, MICHAEL
Musician. London NW2. Age 51. I.16.01.1959
P.18.09.1959 R.20.11.1959. Died 01.10.1987.

SARONY, LESLIE
Vaudeville Artiste. Real name Leslie Legge
Sarony-Frye. East Sheen. Age 25. I.20.07.1923
P.18.01.1924 R.17.04.1924. Excluded. Rejoined
20.09.1857. Died 12.02.1985, aged 87 years

SAUNDERS, GEORGE WILLIAM
Comedian. Leavesden, Herts. Age 57. Born
11.08.1944. I.21.09.2001 P.20.09.2002.

SAW, ARCHIBALD THOMAS
Provision Merchant. London W12. Age 45.
I.19.09.1943 P.19.11.1943 R.21.07.1944.

SCENIS, JOHANNES THORVALD MARIUS
Conjurer. Copenhagen. Age 27. I.15.07.1910
P.21.10.1910 R.18.07.1913. Excluded
19.05.1916.

SCHEEL, DAVID
Entertainer. Kensington, London W8. Age 32.
Joined 17.05.1985. MM from Thespian Lodge
No.195, Australia. Emigrated.

SCHNEIDERMAN, WALTER
Make Up Artiste. Edgware, Middlesex. Age 35.
I.17.01.1958 P.21.11.1958 R.16.09.1960.

SCHREIBER, THEODORE, PM **See
SERPENTELLO**

SCHUBERT, EGON
Music Publisher. Known as Elias Schubert. Maida
Vale, London W9. Age 61. I.18.01.1957
P.20.08.1957 R.15.11.1957. Died 26.07.1976.

SCOTT, ARTHUR
Secretary Variety Artistes Benevolent Fund.
London SW6. Age 56. Joined 20.09.1957 from
Aarheus Lodge No.6854.

SCOTT, HERBERT EDWARD See H.S.NOLAN

SCOTT, KEN E.
Vaudeville Artiste. Real name Thomas William
Skeer. Gorton, Manchester. Age 29. I.21.06.1918
P.11.04.1919 R.17.10.1919.

SCOTT, TONY
Comedian. Apse Heath,Isle of Wight. Age 63.
Joined 17.05.1985. MM from Phaeton Lodge
No.7820. Died April 2004, aged 81 years.

SCOTT-DODD, RONALD DAVID
Theatre Manager. London SW19. I.20.01.1978
P.15.09.1978 R.16.03.1979.

SEENER, ELIAS BORIS
Vaudeville Artiste. Age 31. I.20.11.1908
P.23.02.1909 R.16.07.1909. Excluded
20.05.1920.

SELINGER, BERT See BERT AZA

SELLER, WILLIAM
Vaudeville Artiste. Known as William Sellers.
Bradford, Yorkshire. Age 26. I.18.07.1924
P.17.10.1924 R.20.03.1925. Excluded 1928.
Rejoined 25.03.1946. Resigned March 1956.
Died 1960

SELLERS, PETER, CBE
(A. Lewis) Variety Artiste. East Finchley, London
N2. Age 22. I.16.07.1948 P.21.01.1949
R.16.11.1951. Died July 1980, aged 54 years.

SELTZER, HARRY
Variety Artiste. London WC1. Age 30.
I.18.08.1939 P.20.10.1939 R.19.01.1940.
Excluded May 1954.

SERPENTELLO, PM
Vaudeville Artiste. Real name Theodore
Schreiber. WM 1907. Founder. Resigned
24.04.1911.

SEYMOUR, SYD
Theatrical Artiste. Real name Seymour Solomon.
Edgware, Middlesex. Age 35. I.17.05.1940
P.19.12.1941 R.17.09.1943.
Died 13.12.1958.

SEYMOUR, TOM
Vaudeville Artiste. Real name Thomas Robert
Woolford. Camden, London NW. Age 42.
I.15.10.1915 P.31.12.1915 R.17.03.1916.
Resigned 17.05.1918.

SHAINBERG, MARK
Musician. St Pancras, London NW1. Age 23.
I.18.03.1932 P.15.07.1932.

SHARE, MAURICE
Manager. Bermondsey, London SE16. Age 31.
I.16.07.1937 P.20.08.1937 R.21.01.1938. Killed in
Second World War, September 1940.

SHARPE, LAUCHLAN GEORGE
Concert Agent. Founder. Resigned.

SHATTER, JACK
Musician. Stoke Newington, London N16.
I.15.11.1935 P.20.12.1935 R.21.02.1936.

SHAW, CHARLES
Vaudeville Agent. Sheffield 3. I.19.02.1937
P.19.03.1937 R.20.08.1937. The house in which
he was living in Sheffield was bombed in
September 1940.No trace of any of his personal
belongings, including Masonic regalia and
papers, including Grand Lodge Certificate. Died
12.07.1956.

SHAW, CHARLES
Theatre Manager. Streatham, London SW16. Age
32. I.18.07.1952 P.19.09.1952 R.21.11.1952.
Died 16.04.1993.

SHAW, JAMES See HANDKO JUNIOR

SHEPHERD, ALEXANDER
Age 38. Joined 15.07.1938.

**SHERRY, THOMAS HERBERT See HERBERT
LA MARLINE**

SHINN, WILLIAM GEORGE See BILLY LYTON

**SILVERMAN, ISAAC See WEE GEORGIE
HARRIS**

SIMMONDS, ANTHONY IAN
(A Lewis). Solicitor. London W1. Age 26.
I.18.01.1963 P.20.09.1963 R.17.01.1964.

SIMMONDS, DAVID HOWARD
(A Lewis). Estate Agent. London W1. Age 22.
I.15.11.1963 P.24.04.1964 R.18.09.1964.

SIMMONDS, GEOFFREY AUBREY
(A Lewis). Executive Salesman. London W3. Age
35. I.19.03.1965
P.17.09.1965 R.18.11.1966.

SIMMONDS, LOUIS
Musical Director. London W1. Age 55. Joined
19.01.1962 from Solomon Lodge No.1209
(Scottish Constitution) Died1968

SIMMONDS, PHILIP MICHAEL
Music Publisher. Hampstead, London NW3. Age
66. Born 25.11.1932. I.18.09.1998 P.19.11.1999.

SIMMONS, KEITH PAUL
Entertainer/scriptwriter. Dartford, Kent. Age 52.

More Personalities of Chelsea Lodge

Harry Marlow

Barry Simons

Harry Stanley

Cyril Stapleton

Born 22.03.1947. I.19.03.1999 P.17.11.2000 R.16.03.2001.

SIMONS, BARRY, PM
Theatrical Profession. Hendon, London NW4. Age 21. I.17.09.1948 P.21.01.1949 R.17.03.1950. WM 1963.

SIMONS, CECIL DAVID
Theatrical Representative. Putney Heath, London SW15. Age 48. I.21.03.1958 P.19.09.1958 R.20.03.1959.

SIMONS, ELKAN
Variety Agent and Theatre Producer. Westcliffe-on-Sea, Essex. Age 28. I.21.12.1923 P.17.04.1924 R.20.06.1924. Excluded. Rejoined 17.11.1944. Secretary 1955. Died 03.01.1969.

SIMPSON, WILLIAM JOHN
Secretary. Kilburn, London NW6. Age 38. I.14.04.1927 P.15.07.1927 R.16.09.1927.

SINCLAIR, EPHRAIM
Musician. London W. Age 35. I.20.04.1934 P.15.06.1934 R.20.07.1934.

SIRDANI
Variety Artiste. Real name Solomon Sydney Daniels. Tufnell Park, London N7. Age 40. I.16.06.1939 P.20.10.1939 R.19.01.1940.

SIROTA, LEON See LEE LAWRENCE
SKEER, THOMAS WILLIAM See KEN E. SCOTT
SKUES, RICHARD KEITH, MBE AE LGR
Radio Broadcaster. Horning, Norfolk. Age 60. Born 04.03.1939. Joined 19.11.1999. PM Harringay Lodge No.2763 and Sandringham Lodge No.9751.

SLATER, PERCY RANDOLPH
Vaudeville Artiste. London SW9. Age 34. I.18.02.1921 P.16.09.1921 R.16.12.1921.

SMILEY, RON
Entertainer. Real name Ronald Charles Rigby-Saunders. Heston, Middlesex. Age 54. Born 09.08.1944. I.20.11.1998 P. 15.01.1999 R.17.09.1999.

SMITH, CHARLES See LEN CLIFFORD
SMITH, CYRIL EDWARD, PM LGR
Actor. London W1. Born 04.04.1892, Peterhead, Scotland. Aged 48. I.17.05.1940 P.20.09.1940 R.21.03.1941. WM 1953. Died 05.03.1963, aged 70 years.

SMITH, ERNE CHESTER, PM
Musician. London SW4. Age 20. I.16.07.1926 P.18.09.1926 R.18.03.1927. WM 1940.

SMITH, ERNEST JAMES, PM LGR **See ERNE CHESTER,**
SMITH, GEORGE ALEXANDER
Agent. London E11. Age 39. I.21.09.1945 P.15.02.1946 R.17.05.1946. Died 17.02.1976.

SMITH, GREGORY IVOR
Film/TV Producer. London NW6. Age 52 Born 04.11.1939. I.15.11.1991 P.20.03.1992 R.20.11.1992.

SMITH, HARRY

Musician. Neasden, London NW2. Age 53. Joined 21.05.1965. Died 16.06.1995.

SMITH, JAMES WILLIAM, See BILL AIREY-SMITH
SMITH, MICHAEL JOHN
(A Lewis) Musician. Sidcup, Kent. Age 36. I.19.09.69 P.21.11.69 R.16.01.70. Son of Bill Airey – Smith.

SMITH, ROGER See ALBERT JAMES
SMITH, WILLIAM LESLIE
Musician. London..Age 42. I.21.09.1956 P.20.09.1957 R.15.11.1957.

SMITHERS, CHARLES
Comedian. London N1. Age 51. I.17.11.1978 P.19.09.1980 R.20.03.1981.

SMOOTHEY, LEONARD ALFRED See LEN LOWE
SMOOTHEY, DONALD RALPH, PPAGDC
Theatrical Entertainer. Richmond, Surrey. Age 75. Born 04.11.1919. Joined 19.05.1995. P M Hamilton Lodge No.3309.

SNIDERMAN, WILLIAM
Musician. London NW8. Age 30. I.18.02.1938 P.15.07.1938 R.17.02.1939. Moved to New York.

SNOWDEN, ALBERT HENRY
Vauderville Artiste. Known as Bert Snowden. Upper Norwood, SE. Age 37. I.17.12.1920 P.18.03.1921 R.17.06.1921. Excluded May 1952.

SOAR, THOMAS HAROLD
Musical Director. London E13. Age 32. I.17.04.1931 P.17.07.1931 R.18.09.1931.

SOLO, JUDD
Musician. Maida Vale, London W9. Age 42. I.18.03.1960 P.18.11.1960 R.20.01.1961.

SOLOMON, MICHAEL
Theatrical Manager. Known as Marcus Solomon. Empire Theatre, Ebbw Vale, Monmouth. Age 44. I.15.04.1921 P.19.08.1921 R.21.10.1921. Excluded.

SOLOMON, SEYMOUR See SYD SEYMOUR
SOMERFIELD, ABRAHAM MORRIS See MURRAY MILLS
SOMERS, ROBERT GEORGE
Musician. Kingsbury, London NW9. Age 38. I.21.11.1930 P.19.06.1931 R.21.08.1931.

SPEAR, BERNARD,PM SLGR
Actor. Streatham, London SW16, Joined 17.05.1968. WM 1990. PM of Vaudeville Lodge No. 5592. Died 9 May 2003, aged 83 years.

SPOT
Vaudeville Artiste. Real name Thomas Gunning Davis. Age 35. I.16.06.1905 P.21.07.1905 R.15.09.1905. Excluded 20.05.1909.

STACEY. CHARLES WILLIAM
Musician. Dalston, London E8. Age 33. I.20.06.1930 P.18.07.1930 R.15.08.1930.

STAIG, ERNEST HAROLD
Variety Artiste. Kingsbury, London NW9. Age 43. I.08.04.1949 P.15.09.1950 R.19.01.1951. Died June 1968.

STANELLI
Music Hall Artiste. Real name Edward Stanley De Groot. London NW1. Age 47. I.19.12.1941 P.19.06.1942 R.18.02.1944. Rejoined 1948. Resigned May 1949. Died 12.02.1961.
STANILAND, DENNIS GORDON
Insurance Agency. Sheffield. Age 41. I.16.11.1951 P.21.03.1952 R.20.03.1952. Excluded May 1961.
STANILAND, JOHN
Publicity Manager. Sheffield 8. 54. I.16.01.1942 P.19.06.1942 R.17.07.1942. Died January 1956.
STANILAND, LEONARD
Representative. Sheffield. Age 34. I.15.07.1949 P.17.03.1950 R.17.11.1950. Resigned May 1974.
STANLEY, CHARLES WARREN
Music Hall Artiste. London WC. Age 32. I.20.01.1933 P.20.10.1933 R.20.04.1934. Excluded May 1962.
STANLEY, EDWARD ROBERT
Gymnast. Mottingham, London SE8. I.20.08.1937 P.17.09.1937 R.17.12.1937.
STANLEY, HARRY, PM, LGR
Magician. Real name Harry Ruderman. East Barnet, Herts. Age 42. I.21.01.1949 P.15.07.1949 R.20.01.1950. WM 1962. Died 20.09.1991, aged 86 years.
STANLEY, JOSEPH ELMER
Gymnast. Mottingham, London SE9. I.18.09.1936 P.16.10.1936 R.18.12.1936. Died March 1947, Los Angeles.
STANLEY, WILLIAM
(A Lewis). Shop Proprietor. New Barnet, Herts. Age 21. I.20.09.1968 P.19.01.1969 R.21.03.1969.
STAPLETON, CYRIL
Musical Director. London W2. Age 39. I.20.11.1953 P.16.03.1956 R.18.10.1960. Died 25.02.1974, aged 59 years.
STAR, JOHN, AIMC
Comedy Magician. London W14. Age 55. Born 12.09.1941. I.20.09.1996 P.19.09.1997 R.20.11.1998.
STERN, ALFRED See BOBBY WRIGHT
STERNDALE, MAURICE
Theatrical. Hampstead, London NW3. Age 52. I.20.07.1951 P.18.01.1952 R.20.03.1953. Excluded 18.05.1979.
STERZELLY, JACK
Vaudeville Artiste. Stockwell London SW9. Joined 19.04.1918 from Proscenium Lodge No.3435. Excluded 1924.
STEVENS, JEFFREY BRIAN see JEFF STEVENSON
STEVENSON, JEFF
Comedian. Real name Jeffrey Brain Stevens. Ruislip, Middlesex. Age 33. Born 03.03.1961. I.17.03.1995 P.20.09.1996 R.21.11.1997.
STEWART, FRANK
Musician. Barnes, Middlesex. Joined 20.05.1938. Excluded May 1948.

STEWART, JAMES
Musician. Real name James William Bain. Hornsey, London N. Age 35. I.17.04.1910 P.15.07.1910 R.15.08.1913. Excluded 19.05.1921.
STEWART, RODNEY
Musician. London SW13. Age 26. I.19.09.1958 P.15.11.1963 R.15.05.1964.
STEWART, WALLY, PM
Stage Manager. Real name Walter Arthur Jones. Orpington, Kent. Age 36. I.16.06.1939 P.18.08.1939 R.17.11.1939. WM 1951.
STIRLING, CHARLES F.
Musician. Real name Charles Frederick Stirling Jones. Shepherd's Bush, London W12. Age 41 I.15.07.1910 P.19.08.1910 R.04.10.1910. Resigned 15.04.1913.
STOLBERG, JOHN
Musician. Folkestone, Kent. Age 43. I.16.11.1923 P.21.03.1924 R.17.04.1924. Excluded 1928.
STONE, HAL
Variety Artiste. Real name Hyman Kaplan. London WC1. Age 44. I.17.03.1939 P.19.07.1946 R.16.08.1946. Died June 1947.
STONE, SOLOMON SIDNEY
Company Director. Harringay, London N8. Age 39. I.21.01.1944 P.17.03.1944 R.21.07.1944. Resigned November 1946. Went to live in Denver, Colorado, USA. Rejoined 10.11.1959.
STONE, WILLIAM ALBERT
Theatrical Proprietor. Roath Park, Cardiff. Joined 19.03.1948. Died 27.03.1951.
STRAND, JACK
Vaudeville Artiste. Real name Leslie Hollings Robinson. Wisbech, Cambridge. Age 30. I. 16.09.1927. P.21.10.1927 R.19.03.1929. Excluded.
STRAUSS, ARTHUR
Musician. Age 45. I.20.09.1946 P.21.03.1947 R.18.07.1947. Excluded 1952. Died 07.09.1993.
STREETER, SIDNEY STANLEY STEPHEN
Film producer. Stanmore, Middlesex. Age 28. I.17.01.1941 P.21.03.1941 R.18.07.1941. Resigned May 1948.
STRICKLAND, ALEXANDER
Recording Executive. Edgware, Middlesex. Age 39. Joined 15.03.1964 from Aspiration Lodge No.6086.
STRICKLAND, NORMAN MARTIN
Company Director. Finchley, London N3. Age 46. Joined 20.01.1967 from Old Quintinian's No. 3307. Resigned May 1979.
STRONG, FRANK PERCY See FRANK ARMSTRONG
STUART, CON
Musical Act. Real name Alexander Hughes Clarke. London W14. Age 40. I.21.07.1944 P.20.07.1945 R.18.01.1946.
STUBBS, JAMES WILFRED
Grand Secretary. Freemasons Hall, London

WC2. Elected Honorary Member 18.03.1960.

SULLY, WILLIAM
Joined 21.09.1973

SWANBOROUGH, EDWARD
Manager, Chelsea Palace. London W. Founder.
Honorary Member May 1908. Died 21.12.1908,
aged 67 years.

SWINNY, JOSEPH HENRY
Vaudeville Artiste. Cricklewood, London NW2.
Age 51. I.19.08.1921 P.16.09.1921 R- - -.
Resigned.

SYMONS, ROBERT EDWARD
Accountant/Musician. Age 25. Edgware,
Middlesex. Age 41. Born 01.04.1947. Joined
18.11.1988 from Tolerance Lodge No.7998.

T

TANN, ERIC,PM LGR
Musician. Harrow, Middlesex. Age 28.
I.21.07.1939 P.17.11.1939 R.16.02.1940.
Resigned. Died 28.07. Australia, aged 76 years.

TAPLIN, FRANCIS GEORGE
Theatre Manager. Mitcham, Surrey. Age 55.
Joined 19.01.1962 from Dobie Lodge No.889.
Died 13.03.1984.

TAUBER, CARL See PAUL ADAM

TAYLOR, ERNEST
Comedian. Age 39. I.15.03.1907 P.19.04.1907
R.16.08.1907. Resigned May 1918.

TAYLOR, ERNEST CHARLES
Musician. Harlesdon, London N10. Age 33.
I.17.05.1946 P.19.07.1946 R.20.09.1946.
Resigned March 1952.

TAYLOR, ERNEST CHARLES
Make Up Artiste. California, USA. Age 44. Joined
20.09.1957.

TAYLOR, HENRY IRVING
Manager. London W6. I.18.12.1936 P.16.01.1937
R.19.03.1937. Excluded September 1941.

TAYLOR, JOHN ALEXANDER
Variety Agent. Golders Green, London NW11.
Age 30. I.15.06.1917 P.17.08.1917 R.19.10.1917.
Excluded May 1921.

TAYLOR, KENNETH DOUGLAS
Vaudeville Artiste. London SW15. Age 32.
I.17.10.1924 P.20.03.1925 R.16.10.1925.
Excluded.

TAYLOR, LAURIE
Band Leader. Hainault, Essex. Age 34. Born
02.11.1946. I.18.01.1980 P.21.03.1980
R.10.09.1980.

TEAPE, DANIEL REGINALD
Musician. Childshill, London NW2. Joined
20.11.1998 from Almondale Lodge No. 1658.

TELL, LEO
Real name Ernest Edward Brook. Mimic. Age 36.
I.20.07.1906 P.17.08.1906 R.21.06.1907.
Excluded 16.05.1913.

TEMPLE, NAT
Musical Director. Dolphin Square, London SW1.

Age 38. I.21.07.1950 P.19.01.1951 R.18.01.1952.
Resigned 30.04.1994.

THOMAS, EMLYN
Musician. Clapham, London SW4. Age 36.
I.19.07.1925 P.21.08.1925 R.19.02.1926. Died
August 1940, aged 51 years.

THOMAS, HENRY FRANCIS
Stage Director. Kenton, Middlesex. I.17.01.1936
P.20.03.1936 R.17.07.1936. WM 1946. Died
14.07.1967.

THOMAS, JAMES DAVID
Amusement Caterer. Quorn, Leicester. Age 21.
I.20.01.1956 P.15.03.1957 R.16.01.1959.

THOMAS, JOHN CHAPLAIN
Entertainments Director. Leicester. I.16.11.1979
P.21.03.1980 R.21.11.1980.

THOMAS, JOHN FREEMAN
Amusement Caterer. Edgware Road, London
W2. Age 39. I.20.10.1939 P.15.01.1943
R.16.07.1943. Died 11.08.1982.

THOMAS, JOHN KEEBLE
Amusement Caterer. Leicester. Age 22.
I.17.07.1953 P.15.01.1954 R.19.03.1954.

THOMAS, MICHAEL RICHARD, PM PPGDC
(A Lewis). Amusement Caterer. Tibidaba, Quorn.
Age 23. Born 14.01.1936. I.20.11.1959
P.18.03.1960 R.17.11.1961. WM 1974.

THOMAS, SIMON JAMES
(A Lewis) Entertainment. Chelsea Harbour,
SW10. Age 22. Born 20.06.1965. I.20.01.1989
P.15.09.1989 R.17.11.1989.

THOMAS, THOMAS CHRISTIAN
(A Lewis). Student. Hunstanton, Norfolk. Age 21.
Born 30.09.1974. I.19.01.1996 P.17.01.1997
R.21.03.1997.

THOMPSON, FREDERICK See FRED WINN

THOMSON, ALEXANDER See ALEC KENDAL

THORN, AMBROSE CHARLES GRANTLEY
See CHARLES GRANTLEY

THORNTON, FRANK CHARLES WILLIAM
Musician. Cockfosters, Herts. Age 33.
I.18.03.1955 P.16.09.1955 R.18.11.1955.

THORPE, ANTHONY
Musician. London N16. Age 32. I.16.06.1933
P.18.08.1933 R.16.03.1934. Died June 1973.

TINKLER, HENRY See HENRY MASON

TIPPER, FREDERICK THOMAS
Musician. Balham, London, SW12. Age 50.
I.15.06.1917 P.20.07.1917 R.17.08.1917.

TODD, ERIC ROLAND
Musician. Manor Park, London E12. Age 22.
I.25.04.1930 P.17.10.1930 R.21.11.1930.

TOLEDANO, ALFRED DAVID See ALFRED
DANIELS

TOLEDANO, JOSEPH KENNETH See JOSEPH
DANIELS

TONE.E
Vaudeville Artiste. Real name Thomas Finglass.
London WC. Age 29. I.19.08.1910 P.21.10.1910
R.17.03.1911. Resigned 20.03.1915.

TOUCHINSKY, ALFRED EDWARD See ALFRED MARKS

TRACEY, SID
Variety Artiste. London WC1. Age 42.
I.20.11.1942 P.15.01.1943 R.19.01.1945.
Excluded May 1948.

TRAYLING, ROBERT DAVID See BOB CURTISS

TRESADERN, ALBERT ARTHUR HENRY
Victoria Park, London E2. Age 30. I.21.10.1932
P.21.04.1933 R.20.04.1934. Excluded 1943.

TROY, S. KENNETH
Film Agency. Grove Park, London SE12. Age 72.
Born 30.06.1921. Joined 17.09.1993.

TUBB, RICHARD EDWARD, PM
Comedian. High Seycom, Peacehaven, Sussex.
Age 29. I.19.11.1943 P.21.01.1944 R.14.06.1944.
Resigned May 1978.

TUBB, RICHARD JOHN CORNELIUS
Vaudeville Artiste. Wembley Park, Middlesex. Age
34. I.18.11.1921 P.16.03.1923 R.16.11.1923.

TUCKER, ALFRED
Musician. Edgware, Middlesex. Age 49.
I.20.03.1959 P.16.03.1962 R.20.09.1963. Died
02.11.1972.

TULLETT, HARRY STYCK See WALTER CRANBY

TURNBULL, ARTHUR ELLIOT
Vaudeville Artiste. Pompalett, Plymouth. Age 35.
I.18.11.1927 P.18.03.1932 . Excluded.

TURNER, FRANK
Theatrical Manager. Ferndale, Glamorgan. Age
36. I.15.04.1921 P.21.10.1921 R.16.12.1921.
Excluded.

TURNER, PERCY MELVILLE
Theatrical Manager. Brockley, London SE4. Age
38. I.21.07.1922 P.19.01.1923 R.16.03.1923.

TYLER, DONALD LESLIE
Leisure Centre Director. Bedford. Age 49.
I.19.03.1982 P.21.05.1982 R.09.11.1982.
Resigned May 1985.

U

UNDERWOOD, JOHN
Musician. London SW6. Age 53. I.14.06.1944
P.20.07.1945 R.17.05.1946. Grand Lodge
Certificate returned to GL November 1960.

UNSTEAD, STANLEY ALBERT
Bedding manufacturer. London SE1. Age 55.
Joined 20.01.1967 from Tudor Lodge No.6681.
Died 09.08.1983. Left a legacy to Chelsea Lodge.

V

VALAZZI
Juggler. Real name Wallace Prouse Hodgson.
Age 25. I.18.08.1905 P.15.09.1905 R.20.10.1905.
Resigned 07.07.1915.

VAN DAMM, ALFRED
Musical Director. London SE17. Age 28.
I.17.10.1930 P.21.11.1930 R.30.03.1931.

Excluded.

VAN STRATEN, ALFRED, SLGR
Musical Director. Joined 19.06.1942. Died
04.12.1988.

VANDERSTAY, HAYDN WALLACE See WALLACE HAYDN

VARNEY, FRANK
Vaudeville Artiste. Real name Frank Wooll.
Highgate, London N6. Age 39. I.17.08.1928
P.15.03.1929 R.21.06.1929. Resigned May 1950.

VEGODA, ROBERT SAMUEL
Video cameraman/director. Born 07.05.1951.
Joined 20.09.2002. MM Goliath Lodge No.5955.

VIRGO, JOHN TREVOR
Snooker Player. Weybridge, Surrey. Age 52. Born
04.03.1946. I.20.03.1998 P.21.05.1999
R.17.03.2000.

VOCKINS, HERBERT JOHN
Amusement Caterer. Folkestone, Kent. Age 39.
I.16.11.1917 P.18.01.1918 R.02.04.1918.
Excluded 1924.

VOGELBEIN, HANS BORGE
Theatrical Artiste. London SW16. Age 41.
I.17.01.1964 P.20.11.1964 R.15.01.1965.
Excluded 18.05.1979.

VOICE, ROBERT CHARLES
Theatrical Agent. Sandhurst, Berkshire. Age 37.
Born 18.04.1948. I.15.03.1985 P.20.09.1985
R.19.01.1986.

VOST, JOHN MILNER TELFORD, PM LGR
Theatre Manager. Longsight, Manchester. Age
35. I.19.10.1917 P.16.11.1917 R.18.01.1918. WM
1933. Died 02.08.1970.

W

WADE, DION
Vaudeville Artiste. Real name Joseph Cregan.
London SE. Age 27. I.21.04.1911 P.21.07.1911
R.20.10.1911. Died 14.02.1919.

WADE, GEORGE EDWARD See GEORGE ROBEY

WALDORF, JOE
Theatrical Artiste. London NW4. Age 31.
I.17.05.1957 P.15.11.1957 R.21.11.1958.
Excluded 16.05.1980.

WALDORF, LEONARD
Film Cameraman. North Finchley, London N12.
Age 34. I.17.05.1957 P.15.11.1957 R.17.01.1958.

WALKER, DAVID
Theatre Agent. Crayford, Kent. Joined
15.01.1993 from St Barnabos Lodge No.6315.

WALKER-DREDGE, WILLIAM
Circus Manager. Ashford, Kent. Age 41.
I.18.09.1959 P.20.11.1959 R.16.09.1960. Died
03.10.1987.

WALLEN, ARCHIBALD STANLEY
Concert Party Proprietor. Cotham, Bristol. Age
34. I.19.10.1923 P.15.02.1924 R.17.10.1924.

WALLIS, TOMMY
(A Lewis) Entertainer. Real name Thomas

Wallace Plummer. New Malden, Surrey. Age 46.
I.16.11.1943 P.18.01.1974 R.21.03.1975

WALLIS, W.H.
Comedian. Real name William John Pearson.
Age 40. I.17.07.1908 P.18.03.1910 R.06.09.1910.
Excluded 15.04.1914.

WALTERS, DANIEL RHYS
Musical Director. London WC1. Age 61.
I.16.05.1969 P.19.09.1969 R.21.11.1969. Died
23.12.1985.

WALTERS, OWEN
Musical Director. Green Lanes, London N8.
I.17.06.1938 P.16.09.1938 R.17.03.1939.
Excluded April 1947.

WALTON, IAN ANTHONY
Actor. Norwich, Norfolk. Age 55. Born
28.03.1944. Joined 17.09.1999. PM Burlington
Lodge No.96.

WALTON, WALTER FOGARTY KELLY
Comedian. 1911 Founder. Died. Date not known.

WARBEY, ROBERT CHRISTOPHER
Cinema Executive. Kingston Vale, London SW15.
Age 45. I.20.11.1987 P.18.03.1988 R.16.09.1988.

WARD, WILLIAM
Press Manager. Real name William Robb
Gillanders. Age 38. I.20.11.1908 P.19.02.1908
R.19.03.1909. Resigned 15.06.1911.

WARING, PETER
Variety Artiste. Real name John Peter Roderick
Mainwaring. London,W1. Age 26. I.16.11.1945
P.15.02.1946 R.17.01.1947. Died July 1949

**WARNER, CHARLES MOORE See CHARLES
KASRAC**

WARREN, DALE
Theatrical Entertainer. Forest Gate, London E7.
Age 59. Joined 18.01.1991 from Proscenium
Lodge No.3435.

WARREN, HUBERT EDWARD, PM LGR
Musical Director. Bushey, Herts. Age 51.
I.21.09.1962 P.18.01.1963 R.20.09.1963. WM
1973. Died 08.02.1992.

WARSAW, DAVID
Clerk. London SW2. Age 25. I.19.07.1946
P.16.08.1946 R.15.11.1946.

WARSAW, ERNEST ALEXANDER PM PAGStB
Musician. Known as Erne Warsaw. Age 31.
I.21.08.1908 P.18.09.1908 R.19.02.1909. WM
1922. Died 26.12.1948, aged 71 years.

WATTS, CLIVE
Comedian. Real name Thomas Howard. Age 32.
I.15.11.1907 P.21.02.1908 R.16.04.1908.
Excluded 16 May 1912.

WAYNE, JEFF
Singer/entertainer. Hildenborough, Kent. Born
06.11.1940. Joined 15.11.2002. MM of Drury
Lane Lodge No.2127.

WEBB, AUSTIN
Vaudeville Artiste. Real name Albert Millward.
Islington, London N. Age 35. I.17.08.1923
P.16.11.1923 R.18.01.1924. Excluded.

WEBB, RAY
Musician. Thornton Heath, Surrey. Age 42.
I.15.03.1963 P.17.01.1964 R.20.03.1964.

WEBBER, HARRY
Comedian. Real name Louis Josephs. Age 25.
I.21.08.1908 P.20.11.1908 Excluded 16.05.1912.

WEBSTER, DEREK JOHN
Theatrical Agent. Datchet, Berks. Age 55. Born
16.11.1944. I.15.01.1999 P.17.11.1999
R.21.01.2000.

WEEDON, HERBERT MAURICE WILLIAM,
OBE
Musician. Beaconsfield, Bucks. Age 69.
I.17.11.1989 P.16.11.1989 R.18.01.1991.

WEIR, BARRY HENRY See BARRY MOON

WEIR, FRANK
Musician. I.16.09.1938 .ied 12.05.1981, aged 70
years..

**WELLS, WILLIAM JAMES PM See FRANK
HARDIE PM**

WESTON, IVAN
Chairman, General Entertainment Company.
Hendon, London NW4. Age 37. I.17.11.1967
P.20.09.1968 R.17.01.1969.

WHIDDEN, JAMES MICHAEL
Vaudeville Artiste. London SW. Age 37.
I.16.11.1923 P.18.01.1924 R.15.02.1924.
Excluded.

WHITAKER, THOMAS MITCHELL See CORAM

WHITE, DOUGLAS, PM
Licensed Victualler. Age 57. Joined 21.07.1905
from Dalhousie 860 Scottish Constitution. WM
1917. Died. Date not known.

WHITELEY, BENJAMIN JAMES
Acrobat. Age 27. I.17.08.1906 P.22.01.1907
R.10.04.1907. Died October 1920.

WHITESON, LEWIS SOLLY
Conductor/violinist. Wembley Park, Middlesex.
Age 47. I.15.01.1960 P.18.11.1960 R.17.03.1961.
Resigned May 1992.

WHITE-REWSE, DONALD
Manager. Warwick Avenue, London W2.
I.13.01.1937 P.19.03.1937 R.17.06.1937.
Excluded September 1941.

WHITTLE, CHARLES RICHARD
Comedian. Age 33. I.17.07.1908 P.20.11.1908
R.19.02.1909. Died December 1947.

WHITTLE, JAMES A.
Dental Surgeon. Clapham, London SW9. Age 28.
I.16.07.1926 P.18.09.1926 R.18.03.1927.
Resigned May 1931.

WHYBIRD, RAYMOND ALAN See RAY ALAN

WICKS, BARRY STANTON
Theatre Agent. London NW3. Age 37.
I.20.01.1950 P.17.11.1950. Excluded May 1953.

WILD, VICTOR AUGUSTUS
Comedian. Age 31. I.20.11.1908 P.18.11.1910
R.15.04.1910. Excluded May 1915.

WILDING, ROBERT EDGAR
Musical Director. Age 23. I.19.04.1907

P.21.06.1907 R.19.07.1907. Resigned May 1910.
WILKINSON, ALBERT See ALBERT FOSTER
WILKINSON, CHARLES JOHN
Musician. Catford, London SE. Age 23.
I.19.06.1914 P.17.07.1914 R.21.08.1914.
Excluded 1923.
WILLIAMS, ALBERT EDWARD See BERT MARSDEN
WILLIAMS, CHRISTOPHER See PAUL RAYE
WILLIAMS, CHRISTOPHER MICHAEL
Musician. Worcester Park, Surrey. Age 23.
I.16.09.1966 P.20.01.1967 R.17.03.1967.
WILLIAMS, DAVID PAUL GIFFORD
BBC Producer. Surbiton, Surrey. Age 25.
I.19.11.1965 P.21.01.1966 R.18.03.1966.
WILLIAMS, DESMOND
Musician. Southall, Middlesex. Age 35.
I.16.03.1962 P.16.11.1962 R.15.03.1963.
Excluded.
WILLIAMS, EVAN
Variety Artiste. Sutton, Surrey. Age 49.
I.20.07.1951 P.20.03.1953. Excluded 1959.
WILLIAMS, SYDNEY
Leader/Musical Conductor. Hanworth, Middlesex.
Age 43. I.19.09.1952 P.20.03.1953 R.20.11.1953.
WILLIAMS, WILLIAM ARTHUR
Amusement Caterer. Casino, Rhyl, North Wales.
Age 23. I.21.01.1966 P.16.09.1966 R.18.11.1966.
Died 15.09.2002.
WILLIS, BEN
Music Publisher. Born 30.04.1974. London NW1.
I.19.03.2004. P.18.03.2005
WILLIS, ROBERT JOHN
Show Business Manager. Sandy, Beds. Born
26.07.1970. I.19.03.2004. P.18.03.2005
WILLOUGHBY, FRANK HENRY
Musician. London SE24. Age 48. I.17.01.1969
P.21.03.1969 R.21.11.1969. Resigned May 1991.
WILSON, PERCIVAL THOMAS
Musician. Acton W3. Age 34. I.21.06.1929
P.18.10.1929 R.21.03.1930. Excluded.
WILSON, PHILIP ERIC, PM
Company Director. St John's Wood Park, London
NW8. Age 52. Joined 17.01.1969 from Nucleus
Lodge No.5893. WM 1983.
WILSON-SINGER, ROGER
Films Studio Company Director. London W6. Age
40. I.19.01.1962 P.21.09.1962 R.17.05.1963.
Died 29.09.1994.
WINN, FRED
Actor. Real name Frederick Thompson. Brixton,
London SW. Age 39. I.16.06.1905 P.21.07.1905
R.18.08.1905. Excluded 21.03.1915.
WINSTON, ROY GEORGE
Film Executive/Musician. Hampstead, NW2. Age
43. Born 08.08.1946. I.16.03.1990 P.21.09.1990
R.16.11.1990.
WINTER, ERIC HENRY, SLGR PJGW
Theatrical Costumier. Clapham, London SW12.
Age 66. Joined 20.03.1987 from Baron Renfrew

Lodge No. 5120. Died 09.06.1994.
WINTERS, FREDERICK WILLIAM
Musician. Known as Tiny Winters. Chiswick,
London W4. Age 26. I.15.03,1935 P.15.11.1935
R.20.03.1936. Resigned May 1953. Died
07.02.1996, aged 87 years.
WEINTROP, REUBEN See BUD FLANAGAN
WISE, DENNY
Bandleader. Epsom Downs, Surrey. Age 51. Born
12.09.1947. Joined 15.03.1996 from Holy Well
LodgeNo.6178.
WISE, LLOYD GEORGE ROBERT
Musician. London SW6. I.17.05.1935
P.20.09.1935 R.15.11.1935. Resigned May 1940.
WOLLHEIM, ERIC
Variety Agent. Walton-on-Thames. Age 59.
Joined 17.05.1940. Died April 1948.
WOOD, ALEXANDER NATHAN
Film Artiste and Athlete. Known as Micky Wood.
London NW2. Age 63. Joined 18.11.1960. Died
20.11.1963.
WOOD, WEE GEORGIE, OBE
Real name George Wood Bamlett. Vaudeville
Artiste and Actor. London NW3. Age 26.
J.20.04.1923 from Wythenshaw Lodge 2688.
Excluded 1928. Rejoined 17.11.1944. Resigned
May 1949. Died 19.02.1979, aged 84 years.
WOOD, JOSEPH ROBERT
Comedian. Stroud, Gloucester. Age 35.
I.19.11.1926 P.18.03.1927 R.15.07.1927.
WOOD, PAUL
Vocalist. Real name Paul Richard Woodcock.
Ilford, Essex. Age 30. Born 16.11.1964.
I.18.11.1994 P.19.01.1996 R.15.11.1996.
WOOD, PHILIPLGR
Retired. Edgware, Middlesex. Age 73. Joined
17.09.1965. Died 19.09.1973.
WOODCOCK, PAUL RICHARD See PAUL WOOD
WOODRUFF, RONALD, PM PPGJD
Retired Military Bandsman. Liss, Hants. Age 70.
Born 16.06.1919. Joined 19.05.1989 from St
Vincent Lodge No.5295.
WOODWARD, BRIAN PHILIP
Wrestler/Actor/Singer. Streatham, London SW16.
Joined 18.09.1987 from Prospect Lodge
No.7618.
WOODWARD, JOHN WILLOUGH WILSON
Scenic Artist. Founder. Resigned 15.03.1908.
WOOLFORD, THOMAS ROBERT See TOM SEYMOUR
WOOLL, FRANK See FRANK VARNEY
WORTH, HARROLD See HARRY WORTH LESTER
WREN, ALAN CHARLES
Variety Artiste. London W3. Age 29. I.20.09.1957
P.21.03.1958 R.19.09.1958. WM 1976.
WRIGHT, BENJAMIN, LGR
Musician. London NW6. Age 37. I.17.09.1954
P.19.11.1954 R.21.01.1955. WM 1960. Honorary

Member. Died 23 November 2003, aged 86 years.

WRIGHT, BOBBY

Actor. Real name Alfred Stern. Kensington, W11. Age 38. I.18.07.1930 P.15.08.1930 R.17.10.1930. Emigrated to Australia. Resigned 1949.

WRIGHT, HAL

Vaudeville Artiste. Real name Thomas Pursloe. Brixton Hill, London SW2. Age 46. I.17.04.1925 P.19.06.1925 R.16.10.1925. Excluded.

WRIGHT, RONALD RUSSELL, PM

Musician. London SW9. Age 44. I.20.03.1959 P.18.09.1959 R.20.11.1959. Died 19.01.1981.

WROE, HERBERT See RECO

WULFF, RAFAEL

Vaudeville Artiste. A member of The Five Jovers. Walworth, SE17. Age 36. I.15.12.1922 P.15.06.1923 R.20.07.1923.

WYNN, CHARLES VICTOR

Vaudeville Artiste. Age 30. Joined 21.07.1905 from St Clement's Lodge No.688, Scottish Constitution. Resigned 12.12.1905.

WYNN, CLARENCE EATON

Vaudeville Artiste. Known as Sam Wynn. Stockwell, London SW. Age 43. I.20.04.1923 P.20.07.1923 R.17.08.1923. Excluded.

WYNN, HAL

Variety Artiste. Age 41. I.20.04.1945 P.16.08.1946 R.17.01.1947. Went to Australia. Excluded May 1950.

WYNNE, JACK

Real name John Joseph Blatchly. Vaudeville Artiste. Peckham, London. Age 37. I.15.02. 1924 P.17.04.1924 R.18.07.1924.

WYNN, MICHAEL JAMES

Master Carpenter. St Alban's, Herts. I.17.09.1937 P.19.11.1937 R.15.07.1938. Excluded September 1941.

Y

YARDLEY, MAURICE ABRAHAM

Accountant. London E8. Age 29. I.19.11.1943 P.17.12.1943 R.17.03.1944. Died 09.07.1976.

YOUNG, JAMES EDWARD, See JIMMIE ATHLONE PM LGR

YOUNG, JOE

Vaudeville Artiste. Real name Joe De Young. London SE11. Age 41. I.19.04.1929 P.18.09.1929 R.20.09.1935.

YOUNG, JOSEPH

Musician. Upper Clapton, London E5. I.18.02.1938 P.17.06.1938 R.20.01.1939.

Z

ZAHARIA, ALEXANDER

Dental Surgeon. London N5. Age 45. Joined 18.03.1938.

ZAHL, HARVEY

Variety Agent. Cardiff. Age 31. I.20.08.1915 P.15.10.1915 R.31.12.1915.

ZAHL, HYMAN

Vaudeville Agent. London W1. Joined 16.09.1938. Resigned 1956

ZEITLIN, LEON

Vaudeville Agent. Age 27. I.21.08.1908 P.04.12.1908 R.17.09.1909. Resigned May 1910.

ZIDERMAN, BARRY LEON

Gaming Inspector. London N12. Age 39. I.20.09.1985 P.17.11.1985 R.19.09.1986. Born 13.05.1946.

ZOLA

Real name Joseph Claude Block. I.15.07.1938 P.20.01.1939 R.20.10.1939.

Chapter 14

COMPLETE LIST OF MEMBERS

In CHRONOLOGICAL ORDER

1905-2005

Excluding Founders

Bro. THOMAS NEWSHAM	Joined	Jun. 1905		Bro. ABRAHAM FRIESNER	Initiated	Mar. 1907
Bro. ALBERT BRADY	Joined	Jun. 1905		Bro. ERNEST TAYLOR	Initiated	Mar. 1907
Bro. ARTHUR CECIL NEWMAN	Joined	Jun. 1905		Bro. WILLIAM GRAY MOSELEY	Joined	Apr. 1907
Bro. HENRY BINGHAM	Initiated	Jun. 1905		Bro. ROBERT EDGAR WILDING	Initiated	Apr. 1907
Bro. FREDERICK THOMPSON	Initiated	Jun. 1905		Bro. JAMES LAURENCE GRAYDON	Initiated	Apr. 1907
Bro. THOMAS GUNNING DAVIS	Initiated	Jun. 1905		Bro. WILLIAM JAMES MUNDY	Initiated	Apr. 1907
Bro. JAMES EDWARD DONEGAN	Initiated	Jun. 1905		Bro. HENRY THOMAS PARKER	Initiated	Apr. 1907
Bro. CHARLES JOHN J. FITZOWEN	Initiated	Jul. 1905		Bro. CHARLES HAROLD BURTON	Initiated	Jun. 1907
Bro. CHARLES VICTOR WYNN	Joined	Jul. 1905		Bro. WILLIAM HENRY PHILLIPS	Initiated	Jul. 1907
Bro. DOUGLAS WHITE	Joined	Jul. 1905		Bro. EDMUND CHARLES BOX	Initiated	Jul. 1907
Bro. HENRY RICHMOND MAYVILLE	Joined	Jul. 1905		Bro. THOMAS WILLIAM MELLOR	Initiated	Jul. 1907
Bro. WALLACE PROUSE HODGSON	Initiated	Aug. 1905		Bro. ALFRED BERNARD BAYLEY	Initiated	Jul. 1907
Bro. CHARLES LEDIARD KING	Initiated	Sep. 1905		Bro. JOSEPH WILLIAM ROBINSON	Initiated	Aug. 1907
Bro. WILLIAM VINCENTI PERMANE	Initiated	Sep. 1905		Bro. HERBERT JOSEPH KISBEY	Initiated	Aug. 1907
Bro. HENRY WILLIAM J. CHURCH	Joined	Oct. 1905		Bro. JAMES SIMON LYON	Initiated	Aug. 1907
Bro. HENRI C. RADFORD	Initiated	Oct. 1905		Bro. GEORGE VICTOR LEGLERE	Initiated	Aug. 1907
Bro. JOHN KILDEAR	Initiated	Oct. 1905		Bro. WILLIAM HUBERT BARTLETT	Initiated	Sep. 1907
Bro. KARL FREDERICK GRUHLER	Initiated	Oct. 1905		Bro. ERNEST LEATHLEY CLARKE	Initiated	Sep. 1907
W. Bro. WILLIAM HEDLEY ROBERTS	Joined	Mar. 1906		Bro. WILLIAM JOSEPH GARRETT	Initiated	Sep. 1907
Bro. ROMAN V.J. BYRON-BARHYD	Initiated	Mar. 1906		Bro. GERALD V. O'CONNOLLY	Initiated	Sep. 1907
Bro. WILLIAM SCOTT ADAKER	Initiated	Mar. 1906		Bro. ARTHUR RUDD	Initiated	Sep. 1907
W. Bro. ERNEST JAMES SMITH	Joined	Apr. 1906		Bro. FRANK GUDE	Initiated	Oct. 1907
Bro. EDWIN WILSON BRETT	Joined	Apr. 1906		Bro. ALBERT JAMES POWELL	Initiated	Oct. 1907
Bro. CHARLES PEARCE	Joined	Apr. 1906		Bro. JOSEPH ALFRED ELLISON	Initiated	Nov. 1907
Bro. WILLIAM DOUST	Initiated	Apr. 1906		Bro. HENRY JAMES RICKS	Initiated	Nov. 1907
Bro. WILLIAM EDWARD FARR	Initiated	Apr. 1906		Bro. FRANK JENNINGS	Initiated	Nov. 1907
W. Bro. WILLIAM JAMES WELLS	Initiated	Apr. 1906		Bro. THOMAS HOWARD	Initiated	Nov. 1907
Bro. GEORGE GLOYNE PAPPS	Initiated	Apr. 1906		Bro. NATHANIEL ABRAHAMS	Initiated	Feb. 1908
Bro. HENRY TINKLER	Initiated	Apr. 1906		Bro. HENRY CROCKER	Initiated	Mar. 1908
Bro. FREDERICK H. PEDGRIFT	Initiated	May. 1906		Bro. ERNEST MOSS MYERS	Initiated	Apr. 1908
Bro. ALBERT CHRISTIAN	Initiated	May. 1906		Bro. ERNEST GEORGE GOODWIN	Initiated	Apr. 1908
Bro. JAMES PRYER	Initiated	May. 1906		Bro. JAMES EMANUEL PLATT	Initiated	Apr. 1908
Bro. JOHN BLACKWELL HELM	Initiated	May. 1906		Bro. JAMES RICHARDSON BELL	Initiated	Apr. 1908
Bro. MICHAEL ROUHAN	Initiated	Jun. 1906		Bro. JOHN THOMAS W. GRANT	Initiated	Apr. 1908
Bro. ERNEST EDWARD BROOK	Initiated	Jul. 1906		Bro. THOMAS JOSEPH EDWARDS	Initiated	Jun. 1908
Bro. HERBERT HERIOT HILL, Rev.	Initiated	Jul. 1906		Bro. WILLIAM ALBERT STONE	Initiated	Jun. 1908
Bro. ERNEST THOMAS REES	Initiated	Aug. 1906		Bro. CHARLES RICHARD WHITTLE	Initiated	Jul. 1908
Bro. JACOB NEIMAN	Initiated	Aug. 1906		Bro. HERBERT A.T. LOVELL	Initiated	Jul. 1908
Bro. BENJAMIN JAMES WHITELEY	Initiated	Aug. 1906		Bro. WILLIAM JOHN PEARSON	Initiated	Jul. 1908
Bro. WILLIAM V. MALIVOIRE	Initiated	Sep. 1906		Bro. WILLIAM BOWKER ANDREWS	Initiated	Jul. 1908
Bro. ROBERT WILLIAM DUCE	Joined	Oct. 1906		Bro. PAUL McKAY	Initiated	Jul. 1908
Bro. HENRY KAY RAMSDEN	Joined	Oct. 1906		Bro. WILLIAM HENRY FOX	Initiated	Jul. 1908
Bro. SOLOMON GOODMAN	Initiated	Oct. 1906		Bro. PERCY ERNEST BARRETT	Initiated	Jul. 1908
Bro. JOHN COLQUHOUN MANIFOLD	Initiated	Jan. 1907		Bro. LOUIS JOSEPHS	Initiated	Aug. 1908
Bro. FRANK JOHN WINGATE DIX	Initiated	Mar. 1907		Bro. LEON ZEITLIN	Initiated	Aug. 1908

W. Bro. ERNEST A. WARSAW	Initiated	Aug. 1908
Bro. SYDNEY CHAPLIN	Initiated	Aug. 1908
Bro. WILLIAM HEBBERT RANDALL	Initiated	Oct. 1908
Bro. THOMAS HERBERT SHERRY	Initiated	Nov. 1908
Bro. WILLIAM T. ELLWANGER	Initiated	Nov. 1908
Bro. WILLIAM ROBB GILLANDERS	Initiated	Nov. 1908
Bro. BORIS FRIDKIN	Initiated	Nov. 1908
Bro. ELIAS BORIS SEENER	Initiated	Nov. 1908
Bro. VICTOR AUGUSTUS WILD	Initiated	Nov. 1908
Bro. EDWARD McMULLEN FORD	Initiated	Nov. 1908
Bro. HORACE E. ARRENDELL	Initiated	Dec. 1908
Bro. ALFRED EMANUEL LYON	Initiated	Dec. 1908
Bro. ERNEST DILLON	Initiated	Feb. 1909
Bro. JOHN JACKSON	Initiated	Feb. 1909
Bro. JAMES JACKSON	Initiated	Feb. 1909
Bro. GEORGE ROBERT LILLEY	Initiated	Apr. 1909
Bro. JOSHUA CLIFTON	Initiated	Apr. 1909
Bro. HERBERT EDWARD SCOTT	Initiated	Apr. 1909
Bro. HENRY JAMES MEREDITH	Initiated	Jun. 1909
Bro. EARLE REYNOLDS	Initiated	Jun. 1909
Bro. EDWARD CROSSLAND	Initiated	Jul. 1909
Bro. MAURICE C. FITZGERALD	Initiated	Jul. 1909
Bro. THOMAS MITCHELL WHITAKER	Initiated	Sep. 1909
Bro. CHARLES FELICE LEVEY	Initiated	Sep. 1909
Bro. JAMES ROSS	Initiated	Sep. 1909
Bro. HENRY FRANCIS GLEN	Initiated	Oct. 1909
Bro. FREDERICK THOMAS CAMP	Initiated	Oct. 1909
Bro. ALFRED GEORGE C MEERS	Joined	Oct. 1909
Bro. HAROLD GEORGE HICKMOTT	Joined	Mar. 1910
Bro. THOMAS HENRY HUGHES	Initiated	Mar. 1910
Bro. WILLIAM CROMWELL KNOX	Initiated	Mar. 1910
Bro. ALBERT MARCHMISKE	Initiated	Apr. 1910
Bro. ARTHUR GORDON HARMAN	Initiated	Apr. 1910
Bro. WILLIAM JOHN McMANUS	Initiated	Apr. 1910
Bro. JAMES WILLIAM BAIN	Initiated	Apr. 1910
Bro. WILLIAM HENRY JOHNSON	Initiated	Jun. 1910
Bro. MARTIN HENDERSON	Initiated	Jun. 1910
Bro. ALBERT EDWARD WILLIAMS	Initiated	Jul. 1910
Bro. JAMES PILLING	Initiated	Jul. 1910
Bro. CHARLES F. S. JONES	Initiated	Jul. 1910
Bro. JOHANNES T. M. SCENIS	Initiated	Jul. 1910
Bro. THOMAS FINGLASS	Initiated	Aug. 1910
Bro. AMANDUS CARL LINDEN	Initiated	Aug. 1910
Bro. AUGUSTUS HOWARD	Joined	Oct. 1910
Bro. ARTHUR AISTON	Joined	Mar. 1911
Bro. CHARLES ALFRED CARLILE	Joined	Apr. 1911
Bro. CHARLES DOUGLAS CARLILE	Joined	Apr. 1911
Bro. WALTER THOMAS BLAKE	Joined	Apr. 1911
Bro. WILLIAM ALFRED CRAMP	Initiated	Apr. 1911
Bro. JOSEPH CREGAN	Initiated	Apr. 1911
Bro. JOHN E. NASH	Joined	Jun. 1911
Bro. ARTHUR ROBERT HALL	Initiated	Jun. 1911
Bro. GEORGE ARTHUR CARNEY	Initiated	Jul. 1911
Bro. HENRY EDWARD HOWE	Initiated	Jul. 1911
Bro. LEWIS ALFRED LESLIE	Joined	Jul. 1911
Bro. CHARLES LIQUORISH	Initiated	Oct. 1911
Bro. ALFRED DAVID TOLEDANO	Initiated	Mar. 1912
Bro. JOSEPH BREWSTER H. GREEN	Initiated	Mar. 1912
Bro. GEORGE MARRIOTT EDGAR	Initiated	Mar. 1912
Bro. ISRAEL GILDER	Initiated	Apr. 1912
Bro. ALEXANDER THOMSON	Initiated	Apr. 1912
Bro. JOHN CHARLES E. MILLER	Initiated	Jun. 1912
Bro. HENRY HEMME	Initiated	Jul. 1912
Bro. HYMAN CLAFF	Joined	Jul. 1912
Bro. THOMAS YOUNG NELSON	Initiated	Aug. 1912
Bro. ARTHUR HORACE G LANE	Initiated	Aug. 1912
Bro. CHRISTOPHER MURRAY	Initiated	Dec. 1912
Bro. ALBERT OVERS	Initiated	Dec. 1912
Bro. EDGAR DOLTON	Initiated	Apr. 1913
Bro. CHARLES MOORE WARNER	Initiated	Apr. 1913
W. Bro. JAMES EDWARD YOUNG	Initiated	Jul. 1913
Bro. CHARLES NEWHOUSE	Initiated	Aug. 1913
Bro. JOHN DIXON GRAHAM	Initiated	Oct. 1913
Bro. THOMAS WILLIAM COWLAM	Initiated	Feb. 1914
Bro. WILLIAM HENRY MAY	Initiated	Apr. 1914
Bro. LOUIS BONHOMME	Initiated	Apr. 1914
Bro. ROBERT L. EDERMANIGER	Initiated	Apr. 1914
Bro. FREDERICK R. J. HARDLE	Initiated	Apr. 1914
Bro. EDGAR CHARLES HARPER	Initiated	Jun. 1914
Bro. CHARLES JOHN WILKINSON	Initiated	Jun. 1914
Bro. WALTER CROOKS	Initiated	Jun. 1914
Bro. FREDERICK EBOR RIAT	Initiated	Jul. 1914
Bro. WILLIAM HARDING	Initiated	Aug. 1914
Bro. HENRY WILLIAM G LUPINO	Initiated	Sep. 1914
Bro. AMBROSE C. G. THORN	Initiated	Oct. 1914
Bro. FREDERICK HENDERSON	Initiated	Mar. 1915
Bro. ROBERT GEORGE CLARKE	Initiated	Jun. 1915
Bro. CLIFFORD REID	Initiated	Jun. 1915
Bro. HARVEY ZAHL	Initiated	Aug. 1915
Bro. THOMAS ROBERT WOOLFORD	Initiated	Oct. 1915
Bro. JOHN BARLOW	Initiated	Dec. 1915
Bro. EDWARD VERNON EASTON	Initiated	Dec. 1915
Bro. PREDERICK LESLIE EASTON	Initiated	Dec. 1915
Bro. FRANK PERCY STRONG	Initiated	Jan. 1916
Bro. WILLIAM ROBERT J. FORSYTH	Initiated	Jan. 1916
Bro. ERNEST JOHN HEADWORTH	Initiated	Aug. 1916
Bro. SYDNEY PERCY ORFORD	Initiated	Sep. 1916
W. Bro. PHINEAS HEADWORTH	Joined	Nov. 1916
Bro. FREDERICK WILLIAM HAWKINS	Initiated	Nov. 1916
Bro. REGINALD MOORE HENSMAN	Initiated	Mar. 1917
Bro. LAWRENCE DUNN	Initiated	Apr. 1917
Bro. HERBERT V. JACKSON	Initiated	Apr. 1917
Bro. FREDERICK THOMAS TIPPER	Initiated	Jun. 1917
Bro. JOHN ALEXANDER TAYLOR	Initiated	Jun. 1917
Bro. THOMAS FERGUSON	Initiated	Jul. 1917
Bro. WILLIAM ZACCHEAUS PUTNER	Initiated	Jul. 1917
Bro. AUGUSTUS HOWARD	Rejoined	Aug. 1917
Bro. JACK SAMUEL BROWN	Joined	Oct. 1917
Bro. JOSEPH LAWRENCE	Initiated	Oct. 1917
Bro. JOHN MILNER TELFORD VOST	Initiated	Oct. 1917
Bro. JOHN REUBEN LYON	Initiated	Nov. 1917
Bro. HERBERT JOHN VOCKINS	Initiated	Nov. 1917
Bro. FREDERICK BRAUND BOX	Initiated	Jan. 1918
Bro. JOHN DILLENG BROCKDORFF	Initiated	Jan. 1918
Bro. ABRAHAM COHEN	Initiated	Feb. 1918
Bro. RICHARD HENDERSON	Initiated	Feb. 1918
Bro. EDWIN BARNARD B. DAVIES	Initiated	Mar. 1918
Bro. JACK STERZELLY	Joined	Apr. 1918
Bro. GEORGE HENRY LORIMER	Initiated	Apr. 1918
W. Bro. JOHN ENZER	Joined	Jun. 1918

Bro. THOMAS WILLIAM SKEER	Initiated	Jun. 1918
Bro. PHILLIP PEPPER	Initiated	Jun. 1918
Bro. ALFRED EUGENE LILLEY	Initiated	Jul. 1918
Bro. HERBERT LLOYD FORSYTH	Initiated	Jul. 1918
Bro. ALEXANDER E PHILLIPS	Joined	Jul. 1918
Bro. JOHN WILLIAM DAVID HURLEY	Initiated	Aug. 1918
Bro. HENRY CHARLES LEVY	Initiated	Aug. 1918
Bro. GEORGE PHILLIP HIRSCH	Initiated	Sep. 1918
Bro. THOMAS CHARLES ARNOLD	Initiated	Sep. 1918
Bro. PERCY FRED T. BARRATT	Initiated	Apr. 1919
Bro. JAMES LAURIER	Initiated	Apr. 1919
Bro. WILLIAM GEORGE SHINN	Initiated	Jun. 1919
Bro. GEORGE WALKER BATT	Initiated	Jul. 1919
Bro. PAUL JOHN APPLEBOOM	Initiated	Jul. 1919
W. Bro. ALFRED EMMANUAL LYON	Rejoined	Aug. 1919
Bro. ALBERT WILKINSON	Initiated	Aug. 1919
Bro. CHARLES LINSEED	Initiated	Sep. 1919
Bro. GEORGE F. M. CROWTHER	Initiated	Sep. 1919
Bro. EDWIN HORACE CADWALL	Initiated	Oct. 1919
Bro. RICHARD CREAN	Initiated	Oct. 1919
Bro. MARK ANTONY BREWER	Initiated	Nov. 1919
Bro. STANLEY THOMAS KELLEY	Initiated	Nov. 1919
Bro. PERCIVAL LEWIS	Initiated	Mar. 1920
Bro. LOUIS HIRSCH	Initiated	Apr. 1920
Bro. LEONARD JOHN INSULL	Joined	Apr. 1920
Bro. HERBERT LEE	Initiated	Jun. 1920
Bro. ISAAC SILVERMAN	Initiated	Jun. 1920
Bro. PERCIVAL FREDERICK DE VOY	Joined	Jun. 1920
Bro. ERNEST AUGUSTUS ROBERTS	Joined	Jun. 1920
Bro. ARTHUR JOEL CRAMER	Joined	Jun. 1920
Bro. WALTER LEONARD ELTON	Initiated	Jul. 1920
Bro. HENRY CHARLES EMERIC	Initiated	Jul. 1920
Bro. FREDERICK ARTHUR LIDIARD	Initiated	Aug. 1920
Bro. PHILIP FRY	Initiated	Aug. 1920
Bro. HENRY CLARK ARNOLD Jnr.	Joined	Aug. 1920
Bro. RAYMOND C. HOLGATE	Initiated	Sep. 1920
Bro. NEVILLE JACK DELMAR	Initiated	Sep. 1920
Bro. GEORGE ROBERT BARCLAY	Initiated	Oct. 1920
Bro. GEORGE DICKSON	Initiated	Oct. 1920
Bro. LIONEL DOYLE CROSSLEY	Initiated	Nov. 1920
Bro. VINCENT WADE LAWSON	Initiated	Nov. 1920
Bro. ALFRED CRUIKSHANK	Initiated	Dec. 1920
Bro. ALBERT HENRY SNOWDEN	Initiated	Dec. 1920
Bro. ERNEST HAMBLETON	Initiated	Jan. 1921
Bro. GEORGE VICTOR KNIGHT	Initiated	Jan. 1921
Bro. PERCY RANDOLPH SLATER	Initiated	Feb. 1921
Bro. CHARLES HENRY E. HUNTER	Initiated	Feb. 1921
Bro. JAMES EDWARD DONEGAN	Rejoined	Feb. 1921
Bro. GEORGE HUGH HOLLOWAY	Joined	Feb. 1921
Bro. RICHARD AYRES	Initiated	Mar. 1921
Bro. JAMES REID	Initiated	Mar. 1921
Bro. FRANK TURNER	Initiated	Apr. 1921
Bro. MICHAEL SOLOMON	Initiated	Apr. 1921
Bro. JAMES JOHN MOIR	Initiated	Jun. 1921
Bro. JOSEPH MORRIS	Initiated	Jun. 1921
Bro. MARTIN PAUL MARTI	Joined	Jun. 1921
Bro. MICHAEL LEWIS LYON	Initiated	Jul. 1921
Bro. JOSEPH WILLIAM ARCHER	Initiated	Jul. 1921
Bro. PAUL DALY	Initiated	Aug. 1921
Bro. JOSEPH HENRY SWINNY	Initiated	Aug. 1921
Bro. SETH JEE	Initiated	Sep. 1921
Bro. ALBERT EDWARD JEE	Initiated	Sep. 1921
W. Bro. FREDERICK BRAUND BOX	Rejoined	Sep. 1921
Bro. JOHN GEORGE AITKIN	Initiated	Oct. 1921
Bro. RICHARD JOHN C. TUBB	Initiated	Nov. 1921
Bro. CLIFFORD HAMILTON CHEEK	Initiated	Nov. 1921
Bro. BENJAMIN BOWN	Initiated	Dec. 1921
Bro. WALTER CRANBY	Initiated	Dec. 1921
Bro. HARRY STYCH TULLETT	Initiated	Dec. 1921
Bro. CORNELIUS DEKKER	Joined	Mar. 1922
Bro. ADOLPHE KAGAN	Initiated	Apr. 1922
Bro. BERT SELINGER	Initiated	Apr. 1922
Bro. WILLIAM DANVERS	Initiated	Jun. 1922
Bro. PERCY MELVILLE TURNER	Initiated	Jul. 1922
Bro. THOMAS ALFRED BEASLEY	Initiated	Jul. 1922
Bro. EDWARD NOBLE	Initiated	Aug. 1922
Bro. WILLIAM CONN	Initiated	Aug. 1922
Bro. GEORGE S. HOLLOWAY	Initiated	Sep. 1922
Bro. FELIX LLOYD POWELL	Initiated	Oct. 1922
Bro. HARRY MARLOW	Initiated	Oct. 1922
Bro. MARTIN BARKER	Initiated	Nov. 1922
Bro. ARTHUR HERBERT W. DAY	Initiated	Nov. 1922
Bro. FLORENCIO TOMAS JOVER	Initiated	Dec. 1922
Bro. RAFAEL WULFF	Initiated	Dec. 1922
Bro. ALFRED WILLIAMS HARLEY	Initiated	Jan. 1923
Bro. MYER CHARLES ISAACS	Initiated	Jan. 1923
Bro. WALTER L. ALEXANDRA	Initiated	Mar. 1923
Bro. SAMUEL ROGERS	Initiated	Mar. 1923
Bro. CLARENCE EATON WYNN	Initiated	Apr. 1923
Bro. GEORGE WOOD BAMLETT	Joined	Apr. 1923
Bro. HARRY CHAPMAN	Joined	Apr. 1923
Bro. JOHN RICHARD EVANS	Initiated	Jun. 1923
Bro. GEORGE HUGH A. BUNTING	Initiated	Jun. 1923
Bro. LESLIE LEGGE SARONY FRYE	Initiated	Jul. 1923
Bro. JOSEPH PESSIS	Initiated	Jul. 1923
Bro. WILLIAM SCOTT ADACKER	Rejoined	Jul. 1923
Bro. ALBERT MILLWARD	Initiated	Aug. 1923
Bro. ALBERT WILLIAM KEATS	Initiated	Aug. 1923
Bro. ALBERT E. CROMWELL-KNOX	Initiated	Sep. 1923
Bro. JAMES HENRY HOLLOWAY	Initiated	Sep. 1923
Bro. JOHN HENRY ROBBERDS	Initiated	Oct. 1923
Bro. ARCHIBALD STANLEY WALLEN	Initiated	Oct. 1923
Bro. JAMES MICHAEL WHIDDEN	Initiated	Nov. 1923
Bro. JOHN STOLBERG	Initiated	Nov. 1923
Bro. HERBERT MYERS	Initiated	Dec. 1923
Bro. ELKAN SIMONS	Initiated	Dec. 1923
Bro. ARTHUR BUDD	Initiated	Jan. 1924
Bro. BERNARD GRECO	Initiated	Jan. 1924
Bro. FREDERICK A. FLETCHER	Initiated	Feb. 1924
Bro. JOHN JOSEPH BLATCHLY	Initiated	Feb. 1924
Bro. LEWIS FREDERICK MARKS	Initiated	Mar. 1924
Bro. ROBERT SYDNEY HOWARD	Initiated	Mar. 1924
Bro. BASIL HENRY RICHARDSON	Joined	Mar. 1924
Bro. EDWARD GIGGS	Initiated	Apr. 1924
Bro. HERBERT MARKS	Initiated	Apr. 1924
Bro. CHARLES BRUSKE	Initiated	Jun. 1924
Bro. HERBERT PUNCHARD	Initiated	Jun. 1924
Bro. ARTHUR HARRY C. KING	Initiated	Jul. 1924
Bro. WILLIAM SELLER	Initiated	Jul. 1924
Bro. HAROLD RHYMER	Initiated	Aug. 1924

Bro. EDWARD H. CARTWRIGHT	Initiated	Oct.1924
Bro. KENNETH DOUGLAS TAYLOR	Initiated	Oct.1924
Bro. ABRAHAM M. SOMERFIELD	Initiated	Nov.1924
Bro. EDWIN CHARLES LAWRENCE	Initiated	Nov.1924
Bro. WILLIAM FRANK LYNCH	Initiated	Jan.1925
Bro. CHARLES PAULSON	Initiated	Jul.1925
Bro. VICTOR LEOPOLD KIMM	Initiated	Feb.1925
Bro. JIM O'CALLAGHAN	Initiated	Mar.1925
Bro. WILLIAM BUTLER ISLES	Initiated	Mar.1925
Bro. BARNET LANDAU	Joined	Mar.1925
Bro. THOMAS PURSLOE	Initiated	Apr.1925
Bro. ERNEST ARTHUR KENT	Initiated	Apr.1925
Bro. WILLIAM HENRY HANCOCK	Joined	Apr.1925
Bro. LEOPOLD A. GOLDSCHEDE	Initiated	Jun.1925
Bro. CHARLES HERBERT ALLEN	Initiated	Jun.1925
Bro. CHARLES PAULSON	Initiated	Jul.1925
Bro. HERBERT JAMES HUGHES	Initiated	Jul.1925
Bro. EMLYN THOMAS	Initiated	Jul.1925
Bro. JACK GOLDBLATT	Initiated	Aug.1925
Bro. JOSEPH TURNER MORRISON	Initiated	Aug.1925
Bro. LEW LANE	Initiated	Oct.1925
Bro. JAMES ALFRED COX	Initiated	Oct.1925
Bro. BURNELL FRED JEE	Joined	Nov.1925
Bro. FREDERICK FLETCHER	Initiated	Nov.1925
Bro. SEM BELINFANTE	Initiated	Nov.1925
Bro. WILFRED JAMES CONNOLLY	Initiated	Jan.1926
Bro. LOUIS ALBERT GINNETT	Initiated	Mar.1926
Bro. ERNEST ALLEN	Initiated	Mar.1926
Bro. WALTER BLAKE	Rejoined	Mar.1926
Bro. JOSEPH HENRY LOVICK	Joined	Mar.1926
Bro. HERBERT G. HUGHES	Initiated	Apr.1926
Bro. HARRY ALLEN PHILLIPS	Initiated	Jun.1926
W. Bro. HAROLD GEORGE HICKMOTT	Rejoined	Jun.1926
Bro. AUGUSTUS GEORGE BAKER	Initiated	Jun.1926
Bro. THOMAS PRIDDY	Initiated	Jul.1926
Bro. ERNE CHESTER SMITH	Initiated	Jul.1926
Bro. JAMES A. WHITTLE	Initiated	Jul.1926
Bro. ALPHONSI C. HARTMAN	Initiated	Aug.1926
Bro. CHARLES ALBERT L. CARTER	Initiated	Aug.1926
Bro. ARTHUR RUDD	Rejoined	Sep.1926
Bro. JOHN WILLIAM JACKSON	Initiated	Sep.1926
Bro. FREDERICK JAMES ASHFULL	Initiated	Sep.1926
Bro. FREDERICK DYER	Initiated	Oct.1926
Bro. JOSEPH ROBERT WOOD	Initiated	Nov.1926
Bro. ISAAC CASHTIEN	Initiated	Mar.1927
Bro. WILLIAM HENRY JOHNSON Jnr	Initiated	Mar.1927
Bro. WILLIAM JOHN SIMPSON	Initiated	Apr.1927
Bro. CHARLES ERNEST COWBRICK	Initiated	Apr.1927
Bro. ERNEST SIDNEY GOODWIN	Initiated	Jun.1927
Bro. JOHN FORRESTER	Initiated	Jun.1927
Bro. GEORGE CARNEY	Joined	Jun.1927
Bro. CHARLES LIQUORISH	Rejoined	Jul.1927
Bro. ALFRED J. CHESTER-BISHOP	Initiated	Jul.1927
Bro. FREDERICK ISON	Initiated	Jul.1927
Bro. ALFRED CORFIELD	Initiated	Aug.1927
Bro. LEO THOMAS CROKE	Initiated	Aug.1927
Bro. LESLIE HOLLINGS ROBINSON	Initiated	Sep.1927
Bro. SIDNEY RALPH OWENS	Initiated	Sep.1927
Bro. THOMAS DALTON	Initiated	Oct.1927
Bro. DAVID JOHN LEWIS	Initiated	Oct.1927
Bro. ARTHUR ELLIOT TURNBULL	Initiated	Nov.1927
Bro. GORDON JAMES	Initiated	Nov.1927
Bro. RICHARD H. NIGHTINGALE	Initiated	Mar.1928
Bro. JACK BLOOMFIELD	Initiated	Apr.1928
Bro. LESLIE FULLER	Initiated	Apr.1928
Bro. JOHN CHARLES BRUCE	Initiated	Jun.1928
Bro. VICTOR CHARLES ROBERTS	Initiated	Jun.1928
Bro. STANLEY EDWARD RUSSELL	Initiated	Jul.1928
Bro. LEONARD BATTLE	Initiated	Aug.1928
Bro. FRANK WOOLL	Initiated	Aug.1928
Bro. JACKSON ALLEN RAND	Initiated	Sep.1928
Bro. SAMUEL FREDERICK O'HARA	Initiated	Sep.1928
Bro. WILLIAM LESLIE ROSS	Initiated	Oct.1928
Bro. JACK BLOCK	Initiated	Oct.1928
Bro. JOSEPH DE YOUNG	Initiated	Apr.1929
Bro. STANLEY JAMES HILL	Initiated	Apr.1929
Bro. PERCIVAL THOMAS WILSON	Initiated	Jun.1929
Bro. LOUIS FISHBURG	Initiated	Jun.1929
Bro. EDWIN AUSTIN JAMES RUDD	Joined	Jun.1929
Bro. PERCIVAL LEWIS	Rejoined	Jun.1929
Bro. COLIN BRADSHAW	Initiated	Jul.1929
Bro. WILLIAM NELSON CHILD	Initiated	Aug.1929
Bro. JOHN GRIFFITHS	Initiated	Aug.1929
Bro. JOHN T. BAWELL-BRADER	Initiated	Sep.1929
Bro. STANLEY T. CHILLINGWORTH	Initiated	Oct.1929
Bro. PERCY RICHARDS	Initiated	Apr.1929
Bro. ERIC ROLAND TODD	Initiated	Apr.1930
Bro. CHARLES WILLIAM STACEY	Initiated	Jun.1930
Bro. WILLIAM FRANCIS CLARK	Initiated	Jun.1930
Bro. CHARLES CONGERE RICH	Initiated	Jul.1930
Bro. ALFRED STERN	Initiated	Jul.1930
Bro. ALFRED DAVID MORRIS	Initiated	Aug.1930
Bro. LESLEY CYRIL BODLEY	Initiated	Sep.1930
Bro. ARTHUR ALEXANDER CLARKE	Initiated	Sep.1930
Bro. ALFRED VAN DAMM	Initiated	Oct.1930
Bro. ROBERT GEORGE SOMERS	Initiated	Nov.1930
Bro. PERCY HARPER	Initiated	Nov.1930
Bro. MAURICE LOBAN	Initiated	Nov.1930
Bro. GEORGE MYERS	Initiated	Mar.1931
Bro. CARL RICHARD LAMPE	Initiated	Mar.1931
Bro. PINERO JEROME BRICKWELL	Initiated	Apr.1931
Bro. THOMAS HAROLD SOAR	Initiated	Apr.1931
Bro. ALFRED VICTOR DREWE	Initiated	Jun.1931
Bro. ALEXANDER FRANKEL	Initiated	Jun.1931
Bro. MARCUS DAVIS	Initiated	Jul.1931
Bro. REGINALD WALTER BARKER	Initiated	Aug.1931
Bro. BERTIE PHILLIP COUSINS	Initiated	Aug.1931
Bro. EDWARD JAMES DIXON	Initiated	Sep.1931
Bro. FREDERICK BENTLEY	Initiated	Sep.1931
Bro. HAYDN W. VANDERSTAY	Initiated	Oct.1931
Bro. JAMES McDONALD	Initiated	Oct.1931
Bro. MARK SHAINBERG	Initiated	Mar.1932
Bro. NEWMAN MAURICE	Initiated	Mar.1932
Bro. ARTHUR HORACE G. LANE	Rejoined	Apr.1932
Bro. JAMES EDWARD HANDS	Initiated	Apr.1932
Bro. RALPH MARK H. LAUGHTON	Initiated	Jun.1932
Bro. FREDERICK WILLIAM EATON	Initiated	Jul.1932
Bro. LEO DOMKE	Initiated	Sep.1932
Bro. NATHAN DAVID BLINDT	Initiated	Oct.1932
Bro. ALBERT A. H. TRESADERN	Initiated	Oct.1932

Bro. PATRICK JOSEPH NOONAN	Joined	Mar.1933
Bro. ALBERT ARTHUR POWELL	Initiated	Jan.1933
Bro. CHARLES WARREN STANLEY	Initiated	Jan.1933
Bro. HECTOR ARTHUR FAWCETT	Initiated	Apr.1933
Bro. JACK HARRIS	Initiated	Apr.1933
Bro. ANTHONY THORPE	Initiated	Jun.1933
Bro. SIMON LEVENE	Initiated	Jun.1933
Bro. MICHAEL LEWIS LYON	Rejoined	Jun.1933
Bro. JOHN SEBASTIAN FAULKES	Initiated	Oct.1933
Bro. THOMAS FOSSETT	Initiated	Oct.1933
Bro. LEWIS DAVIS	Initiated	Apr.1934
Bro. EPHRAIM SINCLAIR	Initiated	Apr.1934
Bro. HARRY KURNASKY	Initiated	Sep.1934
Bro. EDWARD OWEN POGSON	Initiated	Nov.1934
Bro. MAX GORDINSKI	Initiated	Nov.1934
Bro. HENRY CHAPMAN	Initiated	Jan.1935
Bro. JOHN WILLIAM HILL	Initiated	Jan.1935
Bro. HYMAN CLAFF	Initiated	Mar.1934
Bro. ISAAC SILVERMAN	Rejoined	Mar.1935
Bro. WALTER MORRIS	Initiated	Mar.1935
Bro. BENNIE LOBAN	Initiated	Mar.1935
Bro. FREDERICK WILLIAM WINTERS	Initiated	Mar.1935
Bro. JOHN NIXON	Initiated	May.1935
Bro. LLOYD GEORGE ROBERT WISE	Initiated	May.1935
Bro. HARRY JAY FINK	Initiated	May.1935
Bro. JABEZ SMITH FARRAR	Initiated	Jul.1935
Bro. JOHN ALFRED RAINE	Initiated	Jul.1935
Bro. NEVILLE JACK DELMAR	Rejoined	Sep.1935
Bro. MARTIN PAUL MARTI	Rejoined	Sep.1935
Bro. ERIC BREEZE	Initiated	Nov.1935
Bro. JACK SHATTER	Initiated	Nov.1935
Bro. ERNEST HAROLD GREEN	Joined	Nov.1935
Bro. RICHARD MARSH BALL	Joined	Dec.1935
Bro. NORMAN PAYNE	Initiated	Dec.1935
Bro. HENRY FRANCIS THOMAS	Initiated	Jan.1936
Bro. CECIL CLINTON FFRENCH	Initiated	Jan.1936
Bro. ERNEST WALTER BEWSEY	Initiated	Feb.1936
Bro. TOM HARRINGTON	Initiated	Mar.1936
Bro. HAROLD RUSHEN	Initiated	Mar.1936
Bro. JOSHUA ALEXANDER LOSS	Joined	Mar.1936
Bro. FREDERICK GREY	Joined	Mar.1936
Bro. LEN BERMON	Initiated	May.1936
Bro. SIDNEY CHASID	Initiated	May.1936
Bro. ERNEST LEWIS	Joined	May.1936
Bro. JOHN THOMAS BURNS	Initiated	Jul.1936
Bro. BRAMWELL MARTINEZ	Initiated	Jul.1936
Bro. HARRY ROBBINS	Initiated	Sep.1936
Bro. JOSEPH ELMER STANLEY	Initiated	Sep.1936
Bro. CHRIS CHARLTON	Initiated	Oct.1936
Bro. MAX LEWIN	Initiated	Oct.1936
Bro. ADOLPH C. EBERHARDT	Initiated	Nov.1936
Bro. CHARLES KATZ	Initiated	Nov.1936
Bro. GEORGE ELRICK	Joined	Nov.1936
Bro. HENRY IRVING TAYLOR	Initiated	Dec.1936
Bro. LEON CORTEZ	Initiated	Dec.1936
Bro. DONALD WHITE-REWSE	Initiated	Jan.1937
Bro. ROY FOX	Initiated	Jan.1937
Bro. JAMES SHAW	Initiated	Jan.1937
Bro. CHARLES SHAW	Initiated	Feb.1937
Bro. HARRY PHILIP GREEN	Initiated	Feb.1937
Bro. ENRICO OLIVELLI	Initiated	Mar.1937
Bro. LEN W. HUNT	Initiated	Mar.1937
Bro. MAURICE SHARE	Initiated	Jul.1937
Bro. GEORGE EDMUND HILL	Initiated	Jul.1937
Bro. FREDERICK FAY DAVIS	Initiated	Aug.1937
Bro. EDWARD ROBERT STANLEY	Initiated	Aug.1937
Bro. FREDERICK JEPSON	Initiated	Sep.1937
Bro. MICHAEL JAMES WYNN	Initiated	Sep.1937
Bro. ALBERT WILLIAM HARVEY	Initiated	Nov.1937
Bro. ROBERT E. HARVEY	Joined	Nov.1937
Bro. CHARLES HENRY PERMANE	Initiated	Nov.1937
Bro. ALFRED SAMUEL NOAKES	Initiated	Nov.1937
Bro. MAX DAVID BACON	Initiated	Dec.1937
Bro. GEOFFREY N. BARGATE	Initiated	Jan.1937
Bro. JAMES SHAW	Initiated	Jan.1937
Bro. ERIK OGDEN	Initiated	Jan.1938
Bro. COLLIE EISNER	Initiated	Jan.1938
Bro. TEDDY BROWN	Joined	Jan.1938
Bro. WALTER CHARLES HADLEY	Joined	Jan.1938
Bro. JOSEPH YOUNG	Initiated	Feb.1938
Bro. WILLIAM SNIDERMAN	Initiated	Feb.1938
Bro. FRED LATHAM	Initiated	Mar.1938
Bro. ALEXANDER ZAHARIA	Joined	Mar.1938
Bro. GEORGE GANJOU	Initiated	Mar.1938
Bro. FRANK STEWART	Joined	May.1938
Bro. SYDNEY KATCHKEY	Joined	May.1938
Bro. BENJAMIN LEVIN	Initiated	Jun.1938
Bro. OWEN WALTERS	Initiated	Jun.1938
Bro. JOSEPH CLAUDE BLOCK	Joined	Jul.1938
Bro. MAURICE FOGEL	Initiated	Jul.1938
Bro. ALEXANDER SHEPHERD	Joined	Jul.1938
Bro. HARRY NEWMAN	Joined	Jul.1938
Bro. FRANK WEIR	Initiated	Sep.1938
Bro. REGINALD CHARLES EAST	Initiated	Sep.1938
Bro. JOHN EDWARD BLORE	Initiated	Nov.1938
Bro. KRIKOR P. GULBENKIAN	Initiated	Nov.1938
Bro. HYMAN ZAHL	Joined	Sep.1938
Bro. PAUL JOHN CLIFFORD	Rejoined	Nov.1938
Bro. GEORGE NICHOLSON	Initiated	Jan.1939
Bro. CECIL C. MITCHELL	Initiated	Jan.1939
Bro. JAMES WILLIAM SMITH	Initiated	Feb.1939
Bro. JAMES DURRANT	Initiated	Feb.1939
Bro. HYMAN KAPLAN	Initiated	Mar.1939
Bro. CYRIL HARLING	Initiated	Mar.1939
Bro. SOLOMON SYDNEY DANIELS	Initiated	Jun.1939
Bro. WALTER ARTHUR JONES	Initiated	Jun.1939
Bro. HARRY WORTH LESTER	Joined	Jun.1939
Bro. ERIC TANN	Initiated	Jul.1939
Bro. GEORGE DURHAM	Initiated	Jul.1939
Bro. HARRY SELTZER	Initiated	Aug.1939
Bro. ALBERT ROGERS	Initiated	Aug.1939
Bro. ROBERT WINTHROP	Initiated	Oct.1939
Bro. JOHN FREEMAN THOMAS	Initiated	Oct.1939
Bro. STANLEY THOMAS ANDREWS	Initiated	Oct.1939
Bro. GEORGE VINCENT DOONAN	Initiated	Nov.1939
Bro. DENNIS AUGUSTUS HEDGES	Initiated	Jan.1940
Bro. LAURENCE BOOKIN	Initiated	Jan.1940
Bro. EDWARD JAMES CARPENTER	Initiated	Feb.1940
Bro. GEORGE GLADNEY RAINE	Initiated	Feb.1940
Bro. SIDNEY JOHN READ	Initiated	Mar.1940

Bro. EDWARD CALSTON PURNELL	Initiated Mar. 1940	Bro. JOHN UNDERWOOD	Initiated Jun. 1944
W. Bro. ALFRED CRUIKSHANK	Rejoined May. 1940	Bro. ALEXANDER HUGHES CLARKE	Initiated Jul. 1944
Bro. ALFRED WILLIAM HARLEY	Joined May. 1940	Bro. HERBERT JOSEPH KISBY	Rejoined Jul. 1944
Bro. ERIC WOLLHEIM	Joined May. 1940	Bro. HERBERT MARKS	Rejoined Jul. 1944
Bro. ABY EMANUAL ABRAHAMS	Joined May. 1940	W. Bro. HAROLD L. GOLDMAN	Joined Jul. 1944
Bro. CYRIL EDWARD BRUCE-SMITH	Initiated May. 1940	Bro. BERNARD DOYLE	Initiated Sep. 1944
Bro. SEYMOUR SOLOMON	Initiated May. 1940	Bro. PHILIP GOODY	Initiated Sep. 1944
Bro. WILLIAM JAMES EASTON	Initiated Jul. 1940	Bro. ELKAN SIMONS	Rejoined Nov. 1944
Bro. GEORGE ERIC C. GLOVER	Initiated Jul. 1940	Bro. GEORGE WOOD BAMLETT	Rejoined Nov. 1944
Bro. HENRY CHARLES W. PIKE	Initiated Sep. 1940	Bro. ALFRED THOMAS PREEDY	Initiated Nov. 1944
Bro. ROBERT BRYANT	Initiated Sep. 1940	Bro. MERSON JAMES HILLMAN	Initiated Nov. 1944
Bro. SIDNEY STANLEY S STREETER	Initiated Jan. 1941	Bro. LES ALLEN	Initiated Jan. 1945
Bro. ABRAHAM HUNTERMAN	Initiated Jan. 1941	Bro. PHILIP MOSS	Initiated Jan. 1945
Bro. WILLIAM THOMAS PARTLETON	Initiated Jul. 1941	Bro. EDWARD RUSSELL	Rejoined May. 1945
Bro. DANIEL TEPPER DOLINOFF	Initiated Sep. 1941	W. Bro. ERNEST C. BRITTON	Joined Mar. 1945
Bro. THOMAS KELLEY	Initiated Nov. 1941	Bro. HERBERT WROE	Initiated Mar. 1945
Bro. EDWARD STANLEY DE GROOT	Initiated Dec. 1941	Bro. GEORGE CAMPKIN	Initiated Mar. 1945
Bro. JOHN STANLAND	Initiated Jan. 1942	Bro. JOHN STEWART HENDERSON	Initiated Apr. 1945
Bro. FREDERICK FORESTER	Initiated Jan. 1942	Bro. HAL WYNN	Initiated Apr. 1945
Bro. JOSEPH DANIELS	Initiated Mar. 1942	Bro. LEWIS FREDERICK MARKS	Rejoined May 1945
Bro. CHARLES SMITH	Initiated Jun. 1942	W. Bro. STANLEY EDWARD RUSSELL	Rejoined May 1945
Bro. NATHAN T. JACKLEY HIRSCH	Initiated Jun. 1942	Bro. CARL TAUBER	Initiated Jul. 1945
W. Bro. ALFRED VAN STRATEN,	Joined Jun. 1942	Bro. GEORGE ALEXANDER SMITH	Initiated Sep. 1945
Bro. ERNEST HAROLD GREEN	Rejoined Jul. 1942	Bro. LAURIE HENRI LUPINO	Initiated Sep. 1945
Bro. BERNARD JACOBS	Joined Jul. 1942	Bro. JACK ALEXANDER EATON	Joined Nov. 1945
Bro. THOMAS EVANS BAND	Initiated Jul. 1942	Bro. LORD NEVILLE K. BROWN	Initiated Nov. 1945
Bro. ERNEST SIDNEY FINCH	Initiated Jul. 1942	Bro. JOHN PETER R. MAINWARING	Initiated Nov. 1945
Bro. LEONARD MITELLE	Initiated Sep. 1942	Bro. LOUIS BERZIN	Initiated Jan. 1946
Bro. JAMES GEORGE PRIOR	Initiated Sep. 1942	Bro. MORTON FRAZER	Initiated Jan. 1946
Bro. JOSEPH LEVINGER	Initiated Sep. 1942	Bro. THOMAS HENRY MANLEY	Initiated Mar. 1946
Bro. CHARLES FOX	Initiated Sep. 1942	Bro. LESLIE FEATHER	Initiated Mar. 1946
Bro. LEONARD S. JACKSON	Initiated Nov. 1942	Bro. HENRY WILLIAM G. LUPINO	Rejoined Mar. 1946
Bro. SID TRACEY	Initiated Nov. 1942	Bro. WILLIAM SELLAR	Rejoined Mar. 1946
Bro. LEONARD CHARLES HEDDON	Initiated Jan. 1943	Bro. JACK ALEXANDER EATON	Joined Nov. 1945
Bro. ALBERT BERNARD DITTRICH	Initiated Jan. 1943	Bro. ERNEST CHARLES TAYLOR	Initiated May. 1946
Bro. JAMES HAROLD FOSSETT	Initiated Mar. 1943	Bro. GEORGE ALFRED C. ROSE	Initiated May. 1946
Bro. EDWIN ALBERT EYDMANN	Initiated Mar. 1943	Bro. DAVID WARSAW	Initiated Jul. 1946
Bro. BERNARD NEWMAN	Joined May. 1943	Bro. THOMAS CHARLES JOHNSON	Initiated Jul. 1946
Bro. JOHNNIE RISCOE	Joined Jul. 1943	Bro. LEOPOLD A. GOLDSHEDE	Rejoined Jul. 1946
Bro. ALFRED GOLDSTEIN	Initiated Jul. 1943	Bro. ARTHUR STRAUSS	Initiated Sep. 1946
Bro. CECIL CARTER MATHER	Initiated Jul. 1943	Bro. HENRY JAMES DAINTY	Initiated Sep. 1946
Bro. ARCHIBALD THOMAS SAW	Initiated Sep. 1943	Bro. NORMAN PAYNE	Rejoined Sep. 1946
Bro. ALBERT EWART PROBERT	Initiated Sep. 1943	W. Bro. JOSEPH PLANT	Joined Sep. 1946
Bro. BARNEY LUBELLE	Initiated Oct. 1943	Bro. CYRIL LOUIS LARTER	Initiated Nov. 1946
Bro. ALBERT E BOATWRIGHT	Initiated Oct. 1943	Bro. GEORGE ANTON MOZR	Initiated Jan. 1947
Bro. RICHARD EDWARD TUBB	Initiated Nov. 1943	Bro. ARTHUR RUSSELL PARNELL	Initiated Jan. 1947
Bro. MAURICE ABRAHAM YARDLEY	Initiated Nov. 1943	Bro. IVAN MARTIN BLOCK	Initiated Mar. 1947
Bro. HERBERT LESLIE PRIOR	Initiated Dec. 1943	Bro. NORMAN ERNEST BRITTON	Initiated Mar. 1947
Bro. JOHN JOHNSON	Initiated Dec. 1943	Bro. TALBOT O'FARRELL	Joined Jul. 1947
Bro. ROBERT BLOCK	Initiated Jan. 1944	Bro. EDGAR CHARLES HARPER	Rejoined Jul. 1947
Bro. SOLOMON SIDNEY STONE	Initiated Jan. 1944	Bro. WALTER ALEXIS GROVES	Initiated Jul. 1948
Bro. FREDERICK JEPSON	Rejoined Jan. 1944	Bro. STANLEY BLACK	Initiated Jul. 1947
Bro. HENRY GODOWSKI	Initiated Jan. 1944	Bro. WILLIAM FRANK BUDD	Initiated Sep. 1947
Bro. ARTHUR BIRKBY	Initiated Feb. 1944	Bro. ERIC SYDNEY COOK	Initiated Sep. 1947
Bro. GERALD COHEN	Initiated Mar. 1944	Bro. CHRISTOPHER WILLIAMS	Initiated Nov. 1947
Bro. ALAN LOUIS BREEZE	Initiated Mar. 1944	Bro. ALBERT ROBERT KIDBY	Initiated Nov. 1947
Bro. FRANK DENNY	Initiated Mar. 1944	Bro. FRANCIS PITMAN	Initiated Jan. 1948
Bro. JOSEPH HYMAN ARBITER	Initiated May. 1944	Bro. JAMES DIGBY	Initiated Jan. 1948
Bro. JOSEPH KENNETH TOLEDANO	Initiated May. 1944	Bro. WILLIAM ALBERT STONE	Rejoined Mar. 1948
Bro. FRANK BIFFO	Initiated Jun. 1944	Bro. MARTIN PABLO MARTI	Rejoined Mar. 1948

Bro. ALFRED TUCKER	Initiated	Mar.1959
W. Bro. RONALD RUSSELL WRIGHT	Initiated	Mar.1959
Bro. HARRY BINNIE	Joined	May.1959
Bro. DONALD JOHN. PERCIVAL	Joined	May.1959
Bro. MORTON MAXWELL LEWIS	Initiated	Sep.1959
Bro. WILLIAM WALKER-DREDGE	Initiated	Sep.1959
Bro. NOEL FREDERICK ROGERS	Initiated	Nov.1959
Bro. MICHAEL THOMAS	Initiated	Nov.1959
Bro. THOMAS FERGUSON	Rejoined	Jan.1960
Bro. PAUL RICH	Initiated	Jan.1960
Bro. LEWIS SOLLY WHITESON	Initiated	Jan.1960
Bro. JAMES WILFRED STUBBS	Elected	Mar.1960
Bro. JOHN HAROLD BURDEN	Initiated	Mar.1960
Bro. JUDD SOLO	Initiated	Mar.1960
Bro. JOHN DOVE	Initiated	Sep.1960
Bro. RICHARD WILLIAM GILL	Initiated	Sep.1960
Bro. ALEXANDER NATHEN WOOD	Joined	Nov.1960
Bro. HARRY LANDAU	Initiated	Nov.1960
Bro. FRANK PETERS	Initiated	Jan.1961
Bro. HENRY FRANK PACKER	Joined	Mar.1961
Bro. ALFRED PHILIP B. PRAEGER	Joined	Mar.1961
Bro. MIKE McCARTHY	Initiated	Mar.1961
Bro. JABEZ SMITH FARRAR	Joined	May1961
Bro. SOLOMON MENDELOFF	Joined	May1961
Bro. PETER HESKETH HUGHES	Initiated	Sep.1961
Bro. JAMES EDWARD QUINN	Initiated	Nov.1961
Bro. FRANK ROBERT MANSELL	Initiated	Jan.1962
Bro. ROGER WILSON-SINGER	Initiated	Jan.1962
W. Bro. FRANCIS GEORGE TAPLIN	Joined	Jan.1962
W. Bro. HERBERT BERNARD DANIEL	Joined	Jan.1962
Bro. LOUIS SIMMONDS	Joined	Jan.1962
Bro. DESMOND WILLIAMS	Initiated	Mar.1962
Bro. SIDNEY HYAMS	Initiated	Mar.1962
Bro. CECIL CARTER MATHER	Rejoined	May.1962
Bro. JERRY BOWMAN	Initiated	Sep.1962
W. Bro. HUBERT EDWARD WARREN	Initiated	Sep.1962
Bro. RAYMONND ALAN WHYBIRD	Initiated	Nov.1962
Bro. RONALD W. W. G. BEADLE	Initiated	Nov.1962
Bro. ANTHONY IAN SIMMONDS	Initiated	Jan.1963
Bro. IVOR RAYMONDE	Initiated	Jan.1963
Bro. MICHAEL BLACK	Joined	Mar.1963
Bro. RAY WEBB	Initiated	Mar.1963
Bro. IAN RALFINI	Initiated	Mar.1963
Bro. JIMMY JACOBS	Joined	Sep.1963
Bro. ROBERT EDWARD PROBST	Initiated	Sep.1963
Bro. JOHN GEORGE HILL	Joined	Sep.1963
Bro. GEORGE BRADLEY	Initiated	Nov.1963
Bro. DAVID HOWARD SIMMONDS	Initiated	Nov.1963
Bro. BERTRAND G. JACKSON	Initiated	Nov.1963
Bro. GEORGE CLAFF	Initiated	Jan.1964
Bro. HANS VOGELBEIN	Initiated	Jan.1964
Bro. BRANDON JOHN LEE	Initiated	Mar.1964
Bro. ALEXANDER STRICKLAND	Joined	Mar.1964
Bro. BRINLEY ARNOLD LEE	Initiated	Mar.1964
Bro. TONY MOSLEY	Joined	May.1964
Bro. ARTHUR BIRKBY	Rejoined	May.1964
Bro. WILLIAM DRAKE	Initiated	Sep.1964
Bro. BILLY McCOMB	Initiated	Sep.1964
Bro. FREDERICK PERCIVAL MILLS	Initiated	Nov.1964
Bro. REGINALD DIXON	Initiated	Nov.1964

Bro. FREDERICK JOHN HALES	Initiated	Jan.1965
Bro. GEORGE FRANK BOND	Initiated	Jan.1965
W. Bro. LEONARD THOMAS BEST	Joined	Jan.1965
Bro. JAMES HENRY HAGGERTY	Initiated	Mar.1965
Bro. GEOFFREY A. SIMMONDS	Initiated	Mar.1965
Bro. HARRY SMITH	Joined	May1965
W. Bro. PHILIP WOOD,	Joined	Sep.1965
Bro. NATHAN MERCADO	Joined	Sep.1965
Bro. MONTY MINDEL	Joined	Sep.1965
Bro. JOSEPH MAGNUS	Joined	Nov.1965
Bro. FRANKLYN BOYD	Initiated	Nov.1965
Bro. DAVID PAUL G. WILLIAMS	Initiated	Nov.1965
Bro. JAMES CAMPBELL McLEOD	Initiated	Nov.1965
W. Bro. PHILIP JOSEPH	Joined	Nov.1965
Bro. PETER HERBERT PRICE	Initiated	Jan.1966
Bro. WILLIAM ARTHUR WILLIAMS	Initiated	Jan.1966
Bro. FREDERICK S DAVIES	Initiated	Mar.1966
Bro. DEREK O'DONNELL	Initiated	Mar.1966
Bro. CHRISTOPHER M. WILLIAMS	Initiated	Sep.1966
Bro. ROBERTO GERMANS	Joined	Sep.1966
Bro. STUART REAY GARNER	Initiated	Sep.1966
Bro. GEORGE JOHNSON	Initiated	Nov.1966
Bro. CHRISTOPHER T. CONDON	Initiated	Nov.1966
Bro. STANLEY ALBERT UNSTEAD	Joined	Jan.1967
W. Bro. NORMAN MARTIN STRICKLAND	Joined	Jan.1967
Bro. FRANK HOLDER	Initiated	Jan.1967
Bro. PAUL DAVID JOSEPH	Initiated	Mar.1967
Bro. ALFRED BOWMAN	Joined	Mar.1967
Bro. WILLIAM CHARLES LANE	Joined	Sep.1967
Bro. MERVYN COLE	Initiated	Sep.1967
Bro. MONTAGUE LEIGH	Initiated	Sep.1967
Bro. DAVID MUSIKANT	Joined	Nov.1967
Bro. IVAN WESTON	Initiated	Nov.1967
Bro. LIONEL DAVID MERCADO	Initiated	Nov.1967
Bro. ANTHONY P. MOYNIHAN Lord	Initiated	Jan.1968
W. Bro. ROGER SMITH	Joined	Jan.1968
Bro. DAI FRANCIS	Initiated	Jan.1968
Bro. DAVID RICHARD MINDEL	Initiated	Mar.1968
Bro. HARRY LEADER	Joined	Mar.1968
Bro. JOHN BERNARD HART	Initiated	Mar.1968
W. Bro. BERNARD SPEAR,	Joined	May.1968
Bro. WILLIAM STANLEY	Initiated	Sep.1968
Bro. HOWARD JOHN BATES	Initiated	Nov.1968
Bro. HARRY MUSIKANT	Joined	Nov.1968
Bro. LEON MUSIKANT	Joined	Nov.1968
Bro. FRANK HENRY WILLOUGHBY	Initiated	Jan.1969
Bro. GEORGE EDWARD BARTON	Initiated	Jan.1969
Bro. WILFRED CUTTS	Joined	Mar.1969
Bro. LAURENCE STEPHEN GELLER	Initiated	Mar.1969
Bro. PHILIP ERIC WILSON	Joined	May.1969
W. Bro. JOHN PETERS	Joined	May.1969
Bro. DANIEL RHYS WALTERS	Initiated	May.1969
W. Bro. WILFRED CUTTS, MBE,	Joined	May.1969
W. Bro. ALFRED FELD	Joined	May.1969
Bro. MICHAEL JOHN SMITH	Initiated	Sep.1969
Bro. JOHN BARRY ALLDIS	Initiated	Nov.1969
Bro. DESMOND HERBERT CHAMP	Initiated	Nov.1969
Bro. EMANUEL MARRON	Joined	Jan.1970
Bro. DAVID JOHN LEWIN	Initiated	Jan.1970
Bro. ROY HERBERT DAVEY	Initiated	Jan.1970

Bro. FRANCIS GEORGE MULLINS	Initiated	Mar. 1970
W. Bro. LAURENCE KRIEGER	Joined	Sep. 1970
Bro. CECIL HARRY KORER	Joined	Sep. 1970
Bro. PHILIP MAITLAND	Joined	Sep. 1970
Bro. ROBERT FOSSETT O ROBERTS	Joined	Sep. 1970
Bro. EDWARD FREDERICK HARPER	Initiated	Nov. 1970
Bro. JOHN PETER PETERS Jnr.	Initiated	Jan. 1971
Bro. WILLIAM HOOPER F..J. DAINTY	Initiated	Mar. 1971
Bro. RICHARD GILBERT EMERY	Initiated	Sep. 1971
Bro. JACK HYMAN MAY	Initiated	Nov. 1971
Bro. JACK NATHAN	Initiated	Jan. 1972
Bro. BERNARD BRESSLAW	Initiated	Mar. 1972
W. Bro. MAURICE APPLE	Joined	May 1972
Bro. ALFRED DESWARTE	Joined	May 1972
Bro. LEONARD ROLFE	Initiated	Sep. 1972
Bro. CLIFFORD T. HENSLEY	Initiated	Nov. 1972
Bro. NORMAN BINNICK	Initiated	Nov. 1972
Bro. ROBERT M. P. ROBERTS	Initiated	Mar. 1973
W. Bro. DAVID CHARLES CAREY	Joined	Mar. 1973
Bro. FRANK JACK GINNETT	Initiated	Sep. 1973
Bro. WILLIAM SULLY	Joined	Sep. 1973
Bro. THOMAS WALLACE PLUMMER	Initiated	Nov. 1973
W. Bro. MICHAEL HILL	Joined	Jan. 1974
Bro. MARTIN GOLDSTEIN	Initiated	Mar. 1974
Bro. LEW LANE	Initiated	Mar. 1975
Bro. BARNEY LUBELLE	Rejoined	Mar. 1975
W. Bro. CHARLES DAVIS	Rejoined	May. 1975
Bro. ALBERT MONTAGUE HARRIS	Initiated	Sep. 1975
Bro. EDWARD DAVID ALVAREZ	Joined	Nov. 1975
Bro. VICTOR ANDERSON	Initiated	Nov. 1975
Bro. DAVID ABRAHAMS	Initiated	Jan. 1976
Bro. ARTHUR DAKIN	Initiated	Sep. 1976
Bro. HOWARD DAVIDSON	Initiated	Nov. 1976
Bro. PETER ELLIOTT	Joined	Nov. 1976
Bro. PAUL ANTHONY GANJOU	Initiated	Jan. 1977
Bro. ROBIN ALVAREZ	Initiated	Sep. 1977
Bro. PAUL KACHARIA	Initiated	Nov. 1977
Bro. RONALD DAVID SCOTT-DODD	Initiated	Jan. 1978
Bro. DOUGLAS ROBERT PERRY	Initiated	Sep. 1978
Bro. CHARLES SMITHERS	Initiated	Nov. 1978
Bro. ARTHUR FREDERICK KEMP	Joined	Nov. 1978
Bro. MICHAEL ABERY	Joined	Nov. 1978
W. Bro. DAVID BERGLAS	Joined	Nov. 1978
Bro. LOUIS C. JONES-VALENTINE	Initiated	Jan. 1979
Bro. MICHAEL A. H ALEXANDER	Initiated	Mar. 1979
Bro. BRIAN HENRY AUSTIN	Initiated	Sep. 1979
Bro. JOHN CHAPLAIN THOMAS	Initiated	Nov. 1979
Bro. LAURIE TAYLOR	Initiated	Jan. 1980
Bro. ZACK LAURENCE	Initiated	Mar. 1980
Bro. DAVID BLOCK	Joined	May 1980
Bro. DENNIS DAVIES	Joined	May. 1980
Bro. DONALD FOX	Joined	May. 1980
W. Bro. CYRIL PACKER	Joined	Jun. 1980
Bro. THOMAS.JOHN. FOSSETT	Initiated	Nov. 1980
Bro. MONTY BODNER	Initiated	Jan. 1981
Bro. ROBERT JOHN S. PACKER	Initiated	Mar. 1981
Bro. BARRY PACKER	Initiated	Sep. 1981
Bro. STANLEY JONES	Initiated	Nov. 1981
W. Bro. ROBERT P. FELD	Joined	Nov. 1981
Bro. DONALD LESLIE TYLER	Initiated	Mar. 1982
Bro. GEORGE ELRICK	Rejoined	Nov. 1982
Bro. RONALD FINDON	Initiated	Jan. 1983
Bro. ROBERT MYRDDIN MORGAN	Initiated	Nov. 1983
Bro. PETER BYFIELD	Initiated	Jan. 1984
Bro. CHARLES RONALD R. CARYL	Initiated	Mar. 1984
Bro. BARRY MICHAEL E. FRANCIS	Joined	May. 1984
Bro. WILLIAM BERNARD MOORE	Initiated	Sep. 1984
Bro. JOSEPH DINDOL	Joined	Sep. 1984
Bro. ROBERT VOICE	Initiated	Mar. 1985
Bro. DAVID SCHEEL	Joined	May. 1985
Bro. TONY SCOTT	Joined	May. 1985
Bro. BARRY LEON ZIDERMAN	Initiated	Sep. 1985
Bro. MICHAEL RICHARD RAMSDEN	Initiated	Jan. 1986
Bro. IAN NORMAN RICHES	Initiated	Mar. 1986
W. Bro. DAVID G. CALDERHEAD,	Joined	Mar. 1986
W. Bro. GEORGE KAZANZI,	Joined	May. 1986
Bro. DAVID RUSSELL HILLMAN	Initiated	Sep. 1986
W. Bro. EDWARD CALLISTER	Joined	Sep. 1986
Bro. HENRY CHAPERLIN	Joined	Nov. 1986
Bro. JOHN GRAHAM KERR	Initiated	Nov. 1986
Bro. ROY JEFFREY GRAHAM	Initiated	Jan. 1987
Bro. DAVID M. de MOUNTFALCON	Initiated	Mar. 1987
W. Bro. ERIC HENRY WINTER	Joined	Mar. 1987
Bro. THOMAS IVAN J. MORGAN	Joined	Mar. 1987
Bro. BRIAN PHILIP WOODWARD	Joined	Sep. 1987
Bro. LAURENCE MANSFIELD	Initiated	Sep. 1987
Bro. JOHNNY PLUCK	Joined	Sep. 1987
Bro. ROBERT C. WARBY	Initiated	Nov. 1987
W. Bro. ALAN VICTOR COX,	Joined	Jan. 1988
Bro. PATRICK THOMAS HAYWARD	Initiated	Jan. 1988
Bro. KENNETH ANDREWS	Initiated	Mar. 1988
Bro. CHARLES K. E. RICHARDS	Initiated	Mar. 1988
W. Bro. ANTHONY D. CHAPERLIN	Joined	Sep. 1988
Bro. RONALD WALTER A.L. BEADLE	Initiated	Nov. 1988
W. Bro. BRIAN R. J. PEARCE	Joined	Nov. 1988
W. Bro. ROBERT EDWARD SYMONS	Joined	Nov. 1988
Bro. LEONARD RODNEY HOWE	Joined	Nov. 1988
Bro. GEORGE FRANK BOND	Rejoined	Jan. 1989
Bro. SIMON JAMES THOMAS	Initiated	Jan. 1989
Bro. RAYMOND F. CUMMINGS	Initiated	Mar. 1989
W. Bro. RONALD WOODRUFF	Joined	May. 1989
Bro. WILLIAM ERNEST BROWN	Joined	Sep. 1989
Bro. RICHARD MICHAEL HILLMAN	Initiated	Sep. 1989
Bro. HERBERT M. W. WEEDON	Initiated	Nov. 1989
Bro. PETER JOHN PRICHARD	Initiated	Jan. 1990
W. Bro. NORMAN GRAY	Joined	Jan. 1990
Bro. ROY GEORGE WINSTON	Initiated	Mar. 1990
Bro. DAVID CAPRI	Joined	Mar. 1990
W. Bro. ROGER de COURCEY-COOKE	Joined	Mar. 1990
Bro. TERENCE RUSSELL DUGGAN	Initiated	Sep. 1990
W. Bro. GAVIN RICHARD PEARCE	Joined	Sep. 1990
Bro. VIKRAM PURI Dr.	Joined	Jan. 1991
Bro. DALE WARREN	Joined	Jan. 1991
W. Bro. GERRY BRERETON	Joined	Mar. 1991
Bro. JAMES CAMERON DAVIDSON	Initiated	Sep. 1991
Bro. CHARLES MICHAEL FIRTH	Initiated	Sep. 1991
Bro. GREGORY IVOR SMITH	Initiated	Nov. 1991
Bro. ALBERT CARDLEY	Joined	Nov. 1991
Bro. WILLIAM GEORGE M.McMANUS	Initiated	Nov. 1991
Bro. THOMAS ALFRED DRAPER	Joined	Mar. 1992

Bro. JAMES PAUL HOLDER	Initiated	Mar.1992
Bro. JAMES CHARLES MARSHALL	Joined	Mar.1992
W. Bro. THOMAS M. O'FARRELL	Joined	May.1992
Bro. NIGEL BRUCE LYTHGOE	Joined	Sep.1992
Bro. MONTAGUE LEIGH	Rejoined	Nov.1992
Bro. JEREMY DAVID PALMER	Initiated	Nov.1992
Bro. ROGER WILLIAM G. BENNETT	Initiated	Jan.1993
W. Bro DAVID WILLIAM WALKER	Joined	Jan.1993
Bro. ALAN LEONARD HUNT	Initiated	Mar.1993
Bro. COLIN JOHN EDMONDS	Joined	Mar.1993
W. Bro. KENNETH TROY	Joined	Sep.1993
Bro. LEONARD ALFRED SMOOTHEY	Joined	Sep.1993
Bro. DAVID LEGGE	Initiated	Nov.1993
Bro. ALLAN J. POULTON-ROGERS	Initiated	Jan.1994
Bro. JOHN REGINALD PLUCK	Joined	May 1994
Bro. MICHAEL DAVID CASSIDY	Initiated	Sep.1994
W. Bro. RALPH HENRY C. HEARSUM	Joined	Sep.1994
Bro. ANTHONY A. HARRISON	Joined	Nov.1994
Bro. PAUL RICHARD WOODCOCK	Initiated	Nov.1994
Bro. CHARLES VICTOR KNIGHT	Joined	Jan.1995
Bro. LAWRENCE S. MORRICE	Initiated	Jan.1995
Bro. JEFFREY BRIAN STEVENS	Initiated	Mar.1995
Bro. ROGER DANIEL KITTER	Initiated	Mar.1995
W. Bro. RONALD BRIDGES	Elected	May 1995
W. Bro. DONALD RALPH SMOOTHEY	Joined	May 1995
Bro. GERALD JAMES CONRAD	Initiated	Sep.1995
Bro. DANIEL ELLIOTT	Initiated	Nov.1995
Bro. THOMAS CHRISTIAN THOMAS	Initiated	Jan.1996
Bro. STEPHEN FRANCIS FARR	Initiated	Mar.1996
Bro. DENNY WISE	Joined	Mar.1996
Bro. JOHN RAYMOND CARPENTER	Joined	May.1996
Bro. JOHN STAR	Initiated	Sep.1996
Bro. RICHARD JAMES A. GRAY	Initiated	Nov.1996
Bro. JOSEPH GOODMAN	Initiated	Jan.1997
W. Bro. JOHN HOLLINGSWORTH	Joined	Mar.1997
Bro. KAPLIN KAYE	Initiated	Mar.1997
Bro. RAPHAEL DONN	Initiated	Sep.1997
W. Bro. HARRY THOMAS C. HALL	Joined	Sep.1997
Bro. GREGORY STEPHEN LUNNON	Joined	Sep.1997
Bro. GERALD V.F. de W. NICHOLAS	Initiated	Nov.1997
Bro. KYRAN MARTIN JESSON	Joined	Nov.1997
Bro. NOEL FREDRICKSON	Initiated	Mar.1998
Bro. JOHN TREVOR VIRGO	Initiated	Mar.1998
Bro. PHILIP MICHAEL SIMMONDS	Initiated	Sep.1998
W. Bro. DAVID GEORGE JOHNSTON	Joined	Sep.1998
Bro. RONALD C. RIGBY-SAUNDERS	Initiated	Nov.1998
W. Bro. TREVOR PORTER,	Joined	Nov.1998
W. Bro. ROBERT PETER LOCKE	Joined	Nov.1998
W. Bro. PETER ALAN LOCKE	Joined	Nov.1998
Bro. DANIEL REGINALD TEAPE	Joined	Nov.1998
Bro. DEREK JOHN WEBSTER	Initiated	Jan.1999
Bro. KEITH PAUL SIMMONS	Initiated	Mar.1999
W. Bro. CHARLES HOWARD ELLIOT	Joined	Mar.1999
Bro. ROBERT DAVID TRAYLING	Initiated	Sep.1999
W. Bro. IAN ANTHONY WALTON	Joined	Sep.1999
Bro. GARY MASON	Initiated	Nov.1999
W. Bro. RICHARD KEITH SKUES	Joined	Nov.1999
Bro. IAN IRVING	Initiated	Jan.2000
Bro. GEORGE JASON MURANYI	Joined	Jan.2000
W. Bro. DAVID ALLAN NEALE	Joined	Jan.2000

Bro. STANLEY GOODWIN	Joined	Jan.2000
Bro. HOWARD LESLIE JAMESON	Joined	Mar.2000
Bro. BARRY HENRY WEIR	Initiated	May.2000
Bro. DONALD JOHN PERCIVAL	Rejoined	May.2000
Bro. KENNETH JOY	Initiated	Sep.2000
Bro. NEJ SALIH	Initiated	Nov.2000
Bro. DAVID RICHARD RAMSDEN	Initiated	Jan.2001
Bro. DAVID GEORGE REDFEARN	Initiated	Mar.2001
W. Bro. JACK BURNS	Joined	Mar.2001
W. Bro. ALAN VICTOR BLAND	Joined	Mar.2001
Bro. MICHAEL JAMES JEROME	Initiated	May.2001
Bro. GEORGE WILLIAM SAUNDERS	Initiated	Sep.2001
Bro. JOHN JEFFREY LOGAN	Initiated	Nov.2001
W. Bro. NEVILLE FRANKLIN BLECH	Joined	Nov.2001
W. Bro. EUGENE PATRICK R MATTHIAS	Joined	Nov.2001
Bro. JAMES PAUL HOLDER	Rejoined	Jan.2002
Bro. PAUL EDWARD V. MILLS	Initiated	Jan.2002
Bro. SIMON ROBERT PACKER	Initiated	Mar.2002
Bro. MICHAEL DAVID COLE	Joined	May.2002
Bro. BRIAN VINCENT HALLARD	Joined	May.2002
Bro. KENNETH JOY	Initiated	Sep.2002
Bro. ROBERT SAMUEL VEGODA	Joined	Sep.2002
Bro. MICHAEL GEORGE MARTIN	Initiated	Sep.2002
Bro. JEFF WAYNE	Joined	Nov.2002
Bro. PHILIP CHANDELER DALE	Initiated	Nov.2002
Bro. JOHN FRANK GARFIELD	Initiated	Jan.2003
Bro. KENNETH PAUL JONES	Initiated	Mar.2003
Bro. JOHN WALTER LUTON	Initiated	Sep.2003
Bro. GILBERT JOSEPH MORRIS	Initiated	Jan.2004
Bro. ROBERT JOHN WILLIS	Initiated	Mar.2004
Bro. BEN WILLIS	Initiated	Mar.2004
Bro. DAVID EDWARD FAWCETT	Joined	Mar.2004
W. Bro. JOHN McMONAGLE	Joined	Mar.2004
Bro. MARK JOHN DIX	Joined	Mar.2004
W. Bro. ROBERT ERNEST E. ALLDER	Joined	May.2004
Bro. MICHAEL TIMOTHY ABRAHAMS	Initiated	Sep.2004
Bro. CYRIL JAMES DAVEY	Joined	Nov.2004
Bro. SIMON PETER ELLIOT	Initiated	Nov.2004
Bro. ALAN WILLIAM BROWN	Initiated	Jan.2005
Bro. JOSEPH ELLIS PASQUALE	Initiated	Mar.2005

Chapter 15

ANECDOTES ABOUT THE WORLD OF

SHOW BUSINESS

Tell Us Another One!

From **Kenneth EARLE**

Years ago in variety Malcolm Vaughan and I were in digs in Chester, and in the digs was the Amazing Paul. His act, as he had no arms, consisted of using his feet for all jobs that would require arms and hands…and had a special chair to accommodate this social difficulty. At the breakfast table one morning he stretched over with his foot to borrow the sauce bottle and knocked it over. One of the pros there commented: "Dear me…Buttertoes!"

From **Bernard SPEAR**

On my Installation as Master of Chelsea Lodge Joe Dindol approached me with an idea. He said would I mind if he pulled a gag on me with my connivance. He suggested that in the third rising he would stand and ask if we could donate our whole collection to this widow and four children who were being evicted for non-payment of rent.

I said: *"But that would be out of order."* He said he knew that but I was to object and he would take it from there. He then explained what he wanted me to do. So sure enough in the third rising, he proposed that we donate our entire collection (over £500) to this young widow. *"W.Bro. Joe,"* I replied, *"You are out of order. You* must *bring it up to the attention of the Almoner, besides what is your interest in the lady. Are you related?"*

"No," said Joe, "I'm her landlord!"

As you can well imagine there was one almighty roar. We had nearly three-hundred men in there that day and I think it was the biggest laugh I've ever heard, on stage or off. It took us a long time to get back to "Any Other Business".

From **Dennis DAVIES**

In March 1983 I was attending lodge having travelled down from Newcastle. The DC, W.Bro. **Benny Wright,** approached me and asked if I could help out. The candidate for initiation hadn't turned up because his mother had died suddenly. They had rehearsed the ceremony and that afternoon it was going to be held in front of the Deputy Grand Master, Major-General Sir Allan Adair. Would I stand in as the candidate? I said I would be delighted. I reported to the Tyler's Room and explained to the DGM what was happening. Sir Allan said: "That's a good story to tell your grandchildren…that you were initiated twice, and once in front of the Deputy Grand Master." I was first initiated in Hadrian Lodge No.6672 in Wallsend-on-Tyne on 9 November 1959.

From **Harry LEADER**

I was told by musical director **Phil Green** at the BBC in 1939 that my band was not good enough to broadcast. Just for the record I had been broadcasting since 1934 and making gramophone records since 1933.

From **Ivan MORGAN**

I used to organise a lot of charity shows, raising money for local hospitals, On this occasion we were raising money for Bexley Hospital, Kent. In the interval there was a skiffle group playing and I was very impressed with this tall guy playing guitar. I went up to him and said I wanted to put him on stage. I worked on him for about three Sunday afternoons. His name was Reg Smith, leader of the Hound Dogs Skiffle Group. We subsequently put him on stage at Granada, Welling. I had him booked onto the Granada circuit and later managed to get him onto the Empire Circuit which had eight theatres. Later still I got him a booking at the Two I's Coffee Bar in Soho with Paul Lincoln. Then he changed his name to Marty Wilde and the rest is musical history. He lived next door to the Granada, Greenwich at the time. I knew his parents very well. His father was a bus driver from Camberwell, the same depot which produced Matt Monro.

From **Michael THOMAS**

Many years ago **Bob Monkhouse** and **Alfred Marks** used to compère the cabaret at Ladies' Night and were a wonderful double act! Alfred Marks you may recall had the kind of haircut, "short back and sides and polish the top!" Bob said, "That Alfred Marks hasn't always been a comedian; he started out as a Ladies' Shoe Salesman. He didn't last long - one day he was knelt down trying a lady's shoe on. She looked down, saw his head, thought it was her knee, covered it over with her dress, and he got the sack!"

From **George ROBEY**

A successful comedian has a reputation to keep up, and his greatest difficulty is to procure good songs and new ideas. The British public is very fickle, and apt to bring your old and brilliant successes to compare with your fresh efforts. I hope I shall be spared the anxiety of ever having a song that becomes 'the rage', because the probability is I should never find another to equal it in the eyes of the public. I do not trust to catchy melodies, which are quickly appropriated by the crowd. It isn't what you sing that brings the house down, it is the funny way you sing it. A comical look will gain as much applause as the smartest repartee ever written. Singing is very much like drawing – the few the strokes the better the result.

From **Laurie MANSFIELD**

I was with **Roger de Courcey** at a stag evening at Woking Football Club. Roger was there with Nookie the Bear and doing a great ventriloquist act. However, in the audience was a heckler, so Roger decided to give this chap some of his own medicine back, through the bear. The heckler did not see the funny side and began to turn nasty. So Roger said to the bear: "You had better be careful because he could come up here on stage and cause you some grief." And the bear replied, "It's not me he's going to hit!"

Roger De Courcey with Nookie Bear.
Looking on, a young Laurie Mansfield

From **Mick McMANUS**

Wrestling in this country really got the seal of approval when members of the royal family used to come... Prince Philip and the Duke of Kent to name but two. I was attending a charity concert on one occasion when I was introduced to Princess Anne. The man acting as host said: "This is Mick McManus, the wrestler." She replied: "Oh yes, but I am not used to seeing you with your clothes on."

From **Sandy POWELL** talking about his children

I don't want my daughter, Peggy, to go into the business. Not unless she turns out to be a great artiste. It's a pretty tough business for a woman. But my son, Peter, he's only ten, has made up his mind to be the same as his father. He came to me the other day. "Dad", he said, "I want to have a quiet talk with you." "What's the matter?" I said and wondered what on earth was coming next. "Dad," he said, "I don't want you to spend any more money on my education. What's the good of education to me? I'm just like you, and I always shall be, and you never went to school. Why should I?"

From **Ivan MORGAN**

Ritual at Chelsea Lodge has always been superb. There was a certain amount of ad-libbing going on, but the ceremony flowed and was always entertaining. You could always have fun in the lodge without showing any disrespect to the ceremonies. W.Bro. **Mike Hill** was a brilliant organist and he would always give a lot of humour in his music without any detriment to the lodge workings.

From Ted RAY

Charlie Austin was a very popular sketch comedian and was famous for his invention of 'Parker-P.C'. He and Charles Coburn (he recorded the popular song *The Man Who Broke the Bank at Monte Carlo*) attended the funeral of music hall star Harry Tate. As they stood beside the grave, Austin to said to Coburn: "You're getting on a bit now aren't you Charles?"
"Yes, I am," replied Charles, "I'm over ninety."
"Blimey," said Austin, "It's hardly worth you going home!"

From **Harry LEADER**

If it hadn't been for a terrible humiliation in earlier life I might never have been a bandleader at all. I'd been studying the saxophone in my spare time and one night I was given my first 'gig'. Well, the leader packed me off home after the very first dance. And that was what spurred me on to make good.

From **Kenneth EARLE**

Who was the agent that received a call for two strippers and informed the party concerned that was not his line of business? The caller said: "That's a pity, I've got £50,000 to spend."
Agent: "Oh well, I think I can help." He duly booked two ladies at a very reasonable fee. Thinking about it he felt that perhaps because of the 'mark up' he better go along. Putting on his best suit and looking extremely smart he arrived. Standing in the wings watching the stripper perform, a man stood next to him…the following dialogue ensued:

Man: "Pick those costumes up which she has left on stage."
Agent: "I beg your pardon! … do you know who I am?"
Man: "No I don't…do you know who I am?"
Agent: "No!"
Man: "I'm the man paying the wages here…who are you?"
Agent: (after a short pause) "I'm the man that cleans up after the strippers."
No prizes for guessing the agent.

From **Max GOLDBERG**

Poggie Pogson had a little run in with the tax man. He applied to the Inland Revenue for an allowance for carting his instruments around. He listed his repertoire and was not believed, so he hired a pantechnicon and delivered the instruments to his local tax office to back up his claim.

Leon CORTEZ

Leon was appearing in the revue '*Appy 'Arf 'Our* in 1938. His script had to be submitted to the Lord Chamberlain's Office who had the power to censor scripts. On this occasion they must have been on a tea break.

Met a nice girl this morning, she'd been out shopping with her arms all full of parcels. What struck me most was the way she was dressed all in the latest fashion – tightly cut jacket, striped skirt, with hip pocket just like us men. Crossing the road she dropped her handkerchief. I picked it up and said: "Excuse me, madam, you've dropped your handkerchief."

She said; "It's very nice of you to pick it up – would you mind putting it in my pocket?" I put it in her pocket, and I've never felt such an ass in all of my life.

From **Kenneth EARLE**

Wilfred Hyde White was appearing in Leeds in *The Jockey Club Stakes*, a most amusing farce. From opening Monday, Tuesday, Wednesday (including matinee), not a sound, not a titter. On the evening performance during the piece there was a very slight half laugh from one member of the audience. Wilfred stopped the whole action, went to the front of the stage and shouted in a most exasperated voice, "Oh what's wrong now!"

From **Ray DONN**

I was raised in Chelsea Lodge with Bro. **Kaplan Kaye** on 20 March 1998. On leaving the Lodge after the raising ceremony W.Bro. **Mike Hill** (the lodge organist) played us out with *Donnkaye Serenade.* Very appropriate!

From Billy AMSTELL

Max Goldberg was a keen 'keep fit' guy and was fond of good wholesome food, especially fresh fruit. We took a stroll through Soho one day and a particular fruit stall attracted his attention. Picking up a lovely large pear and admiring it seemed to give the Italian stallholder cause to frantically shout in his native tongue to stop ruining his fruit. After snatching the pear from Max's hand he observed that dear old Max only had half a thumb. The stallholder was under the impression that Max was testing the pear…you know the way one does by pressing the top with one's thumb. The Italian was most apologetic! Max had lost half his thumb whilst fiddling with his bicycle a few years earlier.

From **Michael THOMAS**

At a Chelsea Ladies' Festival singer Yana topped the bill at the cabaret. When she finished her act, (singing *In A Persian Market*), she received a standing ovation and when the applause eventually died down. Bob Monkhouse said, "Ladies and Gentlemen, if *manana* means tomorrow, I hope *Yana* means tonight!"

From **Ivan MORGAN**

I am led to believe Chelsea Lodge had special dispensation from Grand Lodge regarding what the brethren wear at its meetings. I used to come once or twice a year as a visitor and saw a number of guys in stage clothing rather than the standard dark suit. Some would go off after or during the meeting to appear on stage in different theatres in the West End and come back later on for the festive board in strange costume. I can remember one particular act was a tap dancer and he was in the lodge in white tap shoes. Some of these personalities didn't even take off their make up, wearing a black jacket on top of their stage costume!

From **Peter LOCKE**

In the mid seventies I was shooting a commercial at ITN's studios with a producer named **David Neale.** It wasn't until years later, when we met again, that we realised we had shared the same experience. Halfway through the commercial ITN's production manager came into the studio control room and asked David and his team to leave. We were then inundated with 'Deaf Sheriffs' my term for CIA bodyguards. Easily recognised because they all wear mohair suits, sported earpieces, have small stars in their lapels and have large bulges under their armpits. Top brass from ITN took over the control room, in walked Richard Nixon, and we were to shoot an interview with him. The previous day Jimmy Carter had launched a failed attempt to rescue the American hostages from Iran. Alistair Burnett asked him, "As one of the most devious men in the world, what did Carter do wrong, and what would you have done in his place?" The question did not upset Nixon, in fact he seemed to enjoy that reputation. After all the commotion was over, David returned and we continued selling bedroom furniture, or some such mundane item.

From **Peter PRICHARD**

In 1950 I was working with Johnnie Ray at the Latin Quarter Night Club in New York where we did two shows a night – one at 9 O'clock and the other at midnight. On one occasion Johnnie had gone out with a few celebrities after the 9 O'clock show and by the time he returned for the midnight show he was a little the worse for wear. The gangland- related owners were not too amused and threatened all sorts of nasty things if he didn't perform. So I got Johnnie to sit at the piano all the time rather than stand at the microphone. By the end of each number as he was slowly drifting off I would fade the stage lighting into blackout, walk on stage slap him across the face and wake him up for the next number. Fortunately we didn't have any problems from 'the boys'.

From **Leslie SARONY**

I was waiting to go on stage in Showboat in 1928. There were a couple of these gorgeous six-foot showgirls having a devil of a row at the side of the stage, calling each other anything but a lady! I went up to them and said, "Now, if anybody said a thing like that to me, I'd lift up my finger and I'd say tweet tweet, shoosh shoosh, now now, come come," and with that I went to my dressing room, got my uke out it just flowed like that!

So a theme song was born. The finished song *I Lift My Finger and I Say Tweet Tweet* found its way into the show *Love Lies* at the Gaiety Theatre where it was sung by Stanley Lupino. Leslie recorded the song on HMV B 5629 on 7 April 1929 with Jack Hylton's Orchestra

From **Lew LANE**

Roy Hudd and myself attended the preview of the musical *Aspects of Love* in London which didn't do a lot for either of us. After the show I asked a stage hand what was the huge lorry for outside the stage door. "It's full of new scenery for tomorrow night," he replied. Said I, "Scenery you don't need – tunes you do!"

From **Laurie MANSFIELD**

Jim Davidson has an act which can sometimes upset people. He received a letter of complaint from a viewer who saw one of his television shows complaining that as far as he was concerned Jim Davidson talked out of his a***". Jim replied to the letter by saying "Thank you for your comments about my manner of speech. If we ever meet in the street I hope you don't mind if I clear my throat in your general direction."

From Charlie WINTER

My wife worked in a tailoring establishment supplying Masonic clothing and equipment. **Teddy Brown,** the giant xylophonist arrived to try on his regalia. When he placed the traditional blue and white apron around his 72inch girth, the girls fell about laughing because the apron looked like a G-string!

From **Ivan MORGAN**

Sidney Bernstein had a flat in Grosvenor Square and film star Ingrid Bergman, a great friend of his, was appearing at the Kingsway Theatre in *Joan of Arc* and he asked me as Granada group office manager to collect her from the theatre at the end of the show and take her to his flat. I went with the chauffeur to the stage door where she was signing photographs. I persuaded her to get into the car in the back and I went to sit next to the chauffeur in the front. Ingrid said: "You come and sit with me." I said Miss Bergman may I be very personal…and she replied "Please call me Ingrid." I said I fell in love with you in the early Forties when I saw you in the film *For Whom the Bell Tolls* with Gary Cooper. She leant over and gave me a kiss. I was thrilled. She was a lovely, lovely person.

From **Cyril PACKER**

I was a hairdresser by profession working with many top names in show business. On one occasion I was asked to appear in a TV recording session. "There I was peacefully cutting Lonnie Donegan's hair prior to the show when it was announced, on a note of panic, that the bass player needed for a sketch was missing and there wasn't time to find him before the musical number. Lonnie said to me, 'Cy look like a bass player and take over.' It says something for the residual capacity of all hairdressers that I did, and so became the only non-playing bass-player barber to appear on television."

From **Peter LOCKE**

I was the first freelance called to work for Channel 4, just before its launch date. They wanted shots of their facilities, using what they called their studio hand held camera. This turned out to be what the manufacturers described as a portable camera, very much heavier than a proper hand held one. After the shoot the booking clerk asked if I would come back next day and shoot a fairly long interview in the office area. I said I didn't mind doing it, but I would need a set of legs and a head. Looking at me as if I was mad, and wondering what I was standing on, and what was keeping my ears apart, I had to explain these meant a tripod and a pan and tilt head. She then asked who supplied such things and could I bring them with me. Having overheard my conversation, the lighting director thought he might join in the fun, and told her he would need a couple of red heads and a blonde. All went well in the end, and I spent several months working for the company after their launch.

Bud FLANAGAN

Told in the Roy Hudd Book of *Music Hall, Variety and Showbusiness Anecdotes* following a Royal Variety Performance when the Royal family chatted to the artistes who had taken part. Prince Philip asked Bud and other members of the Crazy Gang: "What are you doing next?" Said Bud: "I've got a crate of brown ale in the dressing-room. I thought we might all go back to your place."

From **Albert LE FRE**

Giving a toast to the visitors and well into his 90s. 'On my journey into Freemasons Hall today I travelled by train. At my local railway station I saw three very pretty girls and thought to myself I wish I were ten years younger!'

From **Peter PRICHARD**

One of the saddest nights I experienced was Tommy Cooper's last appearance on stage when he died following a fatal heart attack. He literally died in my arms. We were working at Her Majesty's Theatre on a live television show with Jimmy Tarbuck, whom I managed. Tommy, who was a Mason and well-known at Chelsea Lodge, was a guest on the show. He began sliding down the tabs to the floor which was not in the act. I went round to the side of the stage and pulled him half-way through the curtains. I couldn't pull his whole body as he was too heavy. I began to give him the kiss of life, but got no response. The ambulance people came very quickly but Tommy was declared dead on arrival at the hospital.

From actress and singer Olivia COFFEE

I remember on one occasion when my father, **Alan Breeze,** had to appear in court as a witness to a road traffic accident. Because of his bad stammer, he passed a note to the judge, asking if he could sing his evidence. Permission was granted!

From **John VIRGO**

Working with snooker players is both interesting and, on occasions, amusing. Alex Higgins, is my favourite player. He was great for the game and created tremendous excitement. He was returning to London from New York with an ink pad and stamp, and on the stamp in capital letters it said A.HIGGINS. Instead of signing autographs, he just stamped the fans autograph books. Only Alex could get away with that.

From **Ronnie BRIDGES**

I remember one of our founder members quite distinctly. **Albert Le Fre** lived to a great age and was a brilliant ritualist. He was not very tall, but excelled at giving the address to the Brethren on every occasion that he did so, at times of Installation. Sadly he passed away a few weeks short of his 100th birthday.

From **Billy CARYLL**

In 1938 I had to make an entrance through a trap door in a pantomime. When the time came for me to shoot up through the stage there was only one man there to pull the trap. Instead of taking ten seconds to get me up, it took more than five minutes. My head and shoulders had just appeared when the stage hand got exhausted and let me back down again. "Be up in a minute," I yelled as I disappeared.

From **Cyril PACKER**

On one occasion when I was in my London hairdressing salon there was a bang on the door and in came a dirty, old tramp. He lurched towards a chair, wiping his grimy hands on a greasy sweater that was, if anything, slightly dirtier than he was himself.

"Ere you," he said aggressively, "you'll do. 'aircut!"

I whispered to my assistant "Get him out of here." I'm no snob, but when your salon is a tidy, pleasant sort of place, you try to keep it so. In two shakes we had him outside. Bang went the door again. He was back. Big-built fellow, too. Looked as though he could cause quite a bit of trouble.

"When I says 'aircut", he began again, "I means 'aircut. Now come on Cy, give your old mate an 'aircut."

It was Harry Secombe all made up for a film part, and having his little joke. Well, he fooled me. But I wasn't half as surprised as the people who saw the 'tramp' walk out of the salon and whistle for his Rolls Royce."

From **Eric BREEZE**

I was playing saxophone with the RAF Dance Orchestra in 1940. **Tiny Winters** was the vocalist. We had a chorus of girls dancing a type of Astaire number with top hats and walking canes. I made a book offering odds on which girl would be the next to drop her cane! I had to pack it in though when I was threatened with the sack!

From **Keith SKUES**

After a particularly convivial festive board a visitor stood up to reply on behalf of the guests. After the usual compliments paid to the Master and members of the Lodge for a most enjoyable meeting he told us that he was an undertaker by profession. 'As Masons we have nothing to fear …death is a great leveller. We came into this world with nothing and we shall leave with nothing. In my professional life as well as dealing with the funeral itself I have to comfort the relatives of the deceased. When it comes to paying for the funeral most people are appreciative of what we do and write and tell us. There are, however, one or two argumentative people who would haggle over the price of the funeral. I always personally reply to them in writing and sign the letter 'Yours eventually!'

From **Lew LANE**

When I was working at Churchill's in the West End I have fond memories of Eartha Kitt and Danny La Rue. Eartha made her professional debut as a singer at Churchill's while appearing with the Katherine Dunham troupe at the Prince of Wales Theatre. She was also the first international star to appear at the Talk of the Town but for a lot more money than the £15 per week we were paying her at Churchill's.

Danny La Rue was a star from the moment he set foot on our stage. He had complete control over the audience with his ready wit and the rare capacity to silence or get a laugh out of any heckler. As for people changing when they become stars, if they were nice at the beginning stardom simply magnifies their niceness. Danny has never changed. He has always been generous with his time and unfailingly kind and considerate towards those who know him or work with him.

From Mickey LEWIS

Max Goldberg was the most wanted session man and lead trumpeter in dance bands in England in the 1920s. There is a set of footprints in the pavement leading to HMVs recording studios which just fit Max Goldberg's shoes – he has been there so often, he has worn his own track!

From **Michael THOMAS**

'Miff' Ferrie was Tommy Coopers agent and when 'Miff' was Master, he called on Tommy to propose the toast to the Ladies. It was with out doubt the funniest speech I have ever heard. He started off by producing several small bottles out of his pocket and said, "Aspirins, aspirins, aspirins, every bloody chemist shop I went into this afternoon had a lady serving!"

From Ted RAY

I remember sharing digs with the **Egbert Brothers** in Swansea. One night, (in a particularly mischievous mood), they had a brainwave. One of them took off his shoes, removed his socks and rubbed the soles of his feet liberally with soot from the grate.

The other got into position and the bare footed 'brother' jumped on to his shoulders and went into a handstand and proceeded to walk over the ceiling.

It really was an extraordinary sight – a pattern of black footprints stood out against the slightly off-white background. The boys waited until the landlady came into the room. She took one look at the ceiling and broke into a piercing scream and then she fled. Forever after the poor creature swore the house was haunted!

You have to be pretty fly to get the better of the Egberts. Even those who ought to have known better – and I count myself among these – were sometimes caught. I was on the same bill as the Egbert Brothers one on occasion when Seth came up to me and whispered very confidentially: "I've got a great stunt for tonight, Ted."

I remember thinking to myself that this meant trouble for somebody and I lent an appreciative ear to what he went on to say. Seth pressed a parcel in my hand and said: "Look, Ted, here are half a dozen mouth organs. Sometime during your act I want you to call for six volunteers from the audience." I must have looked as mystified as I felt, for he went on even more confidentially: "I've dipped these in bitter aloes. You just ask your volunteers to play and watch their faces. Now this is your mouth organ. This one's all right."

I did as Seth asked me, took the mouth organs, which were all wrapped in cellophane, and at the appointed time duly handed them out to half a dozen willing victims. I told them to unwrap the instruments and asked them to do exactly as I did. Of course, you've guessed the result of this particular bit of Egbert fooling – my mouth organ was the only one with bitter aloes on it!

From **Cecil KORER**

On New Year's Day 1964 the now familiar words, 'Yes! It's Number One – It's Top of the Pops''', rang out for the first time from a converted church in Manchester. That historic occasion was introduced by Jimmy Savile and the featured artistes were the Rolling Stones, Dusty Springfield, the Dave Clark Five, the Hollies and the Swinging Blue Jeans. It was important we maintained a youthful image on the show. I was assistant producer in 1964 and on one occasion was horrified to see a bald head bobbing about on screen, and was even more appalled to discover the dome belonged to me. I had accidentally appeared in front of the cameras. To ensure there was no repetition I asked the BBC wardrobe department to fit me with a teenage wig. Basking in my new growth I said 'Now, I'll look like one of the dancers.' The Daily Mirror picked up the story and the headline read 'Toupee the Pops'.

From **Ivan MORGAN**

The Chelsea festive boards were always great fun. There was always such a lot of excitement going on. It was and is such a vibrant lodge. We had many visitors. On one occasion I remember Channing Pollock sat opposite me. He was the number one illusionist at the time. Out of his brief case he brought a piece of glass measuring 20 inches by 12 inches and about a quarter of an inch thick and passed it around the table. We had to tap the glass with our knives. Then he put his finger straight through the middle. It was remarkable. He took a handkerchief out of his top pocket and out came a dove!

From **Harry STANLEY**

I remember **Albert Le Fre** 'Father of Chelsea Lodge' at a Chelsea Ladies Festival night at the Dorchester Hotel, London, when he gave an impromptu turn in the cabaret. He sang *Give Me the Moonlight, Give Me the Girl,* complete with straw hat, cane, and a series of high kicks, that Frankie Vaughan would envy. How old was he at the time? Ninety-six!

From **Bob VOICE**

I was with Mike Yarwood on a gruelling tour with twelve musicians. We had reached King's Theatre, Edinburgh, and it was the last night. Coming towards the end of the show Mike was on stage doing an impersonation of Ken Dodd. I was at prompt corner and reached up to give the guys on the fly floor the standby for dropping the house tabs for the end of the show. The orchestra was playing and Mike was on the stage and accidentally I pressed the 'go' button instead of 'standby'. The house tabs, which were on a counterweight, were thrown. Once they start moving there is no way you can stop them. Mike was mid flight saying, "How tickled I am…what a wonderful night for…" when the curtain landed right on top of his head. Without even hesitating he continued, "How tickled I am. What a wonderful night for having the house tabs drop on you." Mike stormed off stage with a large cloud over his head. I thought to myself what a thing to do. I let him return to his dressing room to calm down. After about fifteen minutes I plucked up enough courage to go round to his dressing room. I knocked on the door and he said, "Come in!" As I walked in the musical director and supporting comic, Brian Marshall, and Mike were standing on chairs with their hands above the door. They had somehow managed to get a pair of curtains into the dressing room and just threw the whole lot all over me. I thought I was going to be fired, but fortunately Mike saw the funny side of it.

From **Harry LEADER**

As a teenager I fought in a six-round contest at Premierland (an East End boxing hall). I won the fight and thirty shillings, and decided to make it my living. But in my second fight I got such a good hiding I changed my mind and stuck to my music lessons.

From **Peter LOCKE**

When Princess Anne opened the Harrod's food hall, I was booked as one of the two cameramen to cover the event. My first shot was on the street, as the Royal car arrived. Then I was to go to the top floor, as quickly as possible, where the Princess would be presented to all the Harrod's dignitaries. Running inside I found that the lift I had used in rehearsals was now guarded, ready for the exclusive use of Her Royal Highness. I rushed up the emergency stairs and, on reaching the top, found that every door was now sealed by a steel shutter. Eventually I found someone who directed me through the staff kitchens, just in time to line up my shot as Princess Anne arrived. Anxious to get the best possible shot, I closed in on the presentation, whereupon Princess Anne exclaimed, "Who is that man? Ask him to move aside!" Ah well, that's showbiz.

From **Kenneth EARLE**

Malcolm Vaughan and I were approached by the late, sadly missed, Billy Forrest who did not enjoy the best of health. In fact a comic once sent him for Christmas a tube of penicillin tablets, for the man who has everything. However, he asked us to appear at a venue to show his client the act for a long summer season. I have to say we went exceedingly well and Billy laughed so much, his wife Maureen helped him out of the room. When we came off stage, obviously with the summer in our pocket, we went to find Billy who was in another room lying down. It turned out he wasn't laughing at all during the act…he was passing a stone. No, we didn't get the summer season!

Joe LOSS

On the subject of society dances. 'The smarter the crowd, the worse they dance'!

From **Greg LUNNON**

One lasting memory is of **Bernard Spear** who raised me in the craft and exalted me into Chelsea Chapter. He substantially increased the membership during his year as Scribe E. This concerns Chapter. Roger Kitter and Dave Lee were candidates of Jim Davidson. Following their exaltation we assembled at the festive board and Jim Davidson stood up to propose a toast to the candidates and began by introducing the officers. When he reached Bernard's name he said something to the effect, "You must both know Bernard Spear. Not only is he the Scribe E, but also the owner of Chelsea Chapter." This was most amusing at the time because Bernard was going through one of his prompting periods. Jim went on to give the most incredible toast I have ever heard at a festive board. We also had an incident at the dinner where a member found a large piece of wire in his lamb chop which, after some negotiations with the Drury Lane hotel, resulted in them cancelling our entire bill for the festive board. Being the treasurer of the Lodge most of my memories centre around the logistics of counting large wads of cash at the meetings that on occasions reached over 500 visitors. In the year 2003 there was an episode with the Connaught Rooms where several members noticed some unwelcomed furry, four legged visitors with long tails, running around under sprig one at the festive board. It took some persuading to encourage the Connaught to realise that this was not really acceptable. We were eventually assured that the unwelcomed visitors moved on.

From **Peter ELLIOTT**

My show business partner, Jimmy Edmundson, and I were doing a summer season at the Opera House, Jersey and Jimmy Wheeler was appearing at the Watersplash. Every evening when he finished he used to come to our dressing room with a crate of light ales and two bottles of whiskey which we used to consume until the early hours of the morning. We were given the stage door keys so that we could lock up. One morning on leaving the theatre Jimmy Wheeler walked toward a grey Jaguar car. I advised Jimmy not to drive as he could kill somebody. He then enquired what time it was. I answered that it was 4.15am. Jimmy replied, "Anybody out at 4.15 in the morning deserves to be killed." He then said I wasn't to worry as he usually got the car up to 40 miles per hour and jumped in the back!

From **Jim DAVIDSON**
Having learned from the Treasurer's report that he had inadvertently paid his subs twice at the City of Westminster Lodge No.2882 replied:
Our Treasurer is a remarkable man. He is the only person in the world who has ever caused me to pay for something twice over without having been married to me.

From **Norman GRAY**
One evening at a Festive Board in the Connaught Rooms, Great Queen Street, I and some other brethren were laughing and talking to **Bernard Bresslaw**. He was telling us about an experience he had. It seems the police entered his theatre dressing room, telling him they were searching the theatre for a suspected pervert who had been seen entering the theatre, and was suspected of molesting one of the young boys. Bernard sat in his dressing room and said to the police how awful it was, and that he could never understand anyone being a pervert. Then he realised he was sitting there dressed in stockings, suspenders, large petticoat and corset, large false eyelashes, heavy make-up and a very large ladies wig. He was playing the dame in a pantomime at the time. We have no comment whatsoever from the police.

From Ted RAY
In conversation with **Reg Dixon** one day he told me that Emile Littler telephoned and asked him to take over George Formby's part in *Zip Goes a Million*. Reg couldn't think of anything to say but: "Oh, but I couldn't do that. I've fixed to go on my holiday." It was several seconds later before the penny dropped and the comedian from the Midlands realised he was being offered the chance of a lifetime!

From **Mike JEROME**
At my initiation I knelt in front of the WM I suddenly realised my left trouser leg was split from my knee to my crutch. At this point I was in a state of *panic*, but nobody said a word. I thought *oh good, nobody can see the split*. At the festive board I related the incident in my short speech that I was surprised that nobody had noticed.
I was shocked when all I could hear was the words, "Oh yes we did!!!!" I quickly finished and sat down with a very red face.

From **Ivan MORGAN**
I won a national publicity competition for promoting the film *The King in New York* and my prize was an antique chair which appeared in the film and which I still have at home, plus supper with Oonagh and Charlie Chaplin at the Dorchester Hotel. He was a very quiet little man but ever so charming. Much later Sidney Bernstein asked me to buy Charlie a present for his 80th birthday. What can you buy a multi millionaire who has everything and lives in Switzerland? I arranged for Lord Bernstein to see six telescopes on stands. We bought the best one for him and had it delivered by courier to his mountain hideout in Switzerland.

Sandy POWELL
Story appeared in the book *Kindly Leave the Stage* by Roger Wilmut
I was working in a club near Sheffield. I did the ventriloquist act in the first half, and didn't get one laugh. I was working away…dropping the doll and it's agony to be on there, knowing you've got to be on for twenty minutes and they don't think you're funny. During the interval I went in the bar and the barman said: "I've just had three fellows in here, and one of them said Sandy Powell's not in the same street as Ray Alan"…they thought I meant it, you see…Anyway, in the second half I did my conjuring routine – mucking up the tricks – and I went in the bar again and said, "Have your friends been in?" The barman replied: "Yes –

they say you're a bloody sight worse as a conjurer." So I didn't work any more clubs!

Variety magazine discussing **Wee Georgie Wood**

He can do things on the stage that no one else can do. He can utilise a hackneyed melodramatic situation, plaster it with pathos, kid the life out of it, and make you like it.

And finally Tommy COOPER

He was initiated into St Margaret's Westminster Lodge No.4518, London on 16 December 1952. Tommy was a visitor to Chelsea and had given replies for the visitors and also entertained at Ladies' Festivals. This collection of amusing 'ramblings' have been collected over a period of time and remembered by various members of Chelsea Lodge. A certain amount of poetic licence has been allowed in the telling of the stories.

"Worshipful Master I apologise for being late. I had to go to the doctor and there was this chap there who had a strawberry growing out of his head. The doctor said, 'I'll give you some cream to put on it'."

The WM says to Tommy that he is very welcome and to sit where he likes. "I'll begin by sitting in your seat," said Bro. Cooper. The WM replied: "Before you sit anywhere, I suggest you have a look at your dress. You have put your apron on inside out!"

At the festive board Tommy replied on behalf of the visitors: "I was driving home the other night when this policeman stopped me. He tapped on the window and said 'Would you blow into this bag, Sir?' I said: 'What for officer?' He said: 'My chips are too hot.' The following night I got stopped again by a different policeman. He said: 'I'd like to follow you to the nearest police station.' I said 'What for?' he said: 'I've forgotten the way.' The next night I decided not to drive and got a taxi. I said to the driver, 'King Arthur's Close.' He said: 'Don't worry, we'll lose him at the next set of traffic lights.' So I arrived home and paid the taxi fare. The cabby was just sitting there waiting for a tip. So I gave him a teabag and said, 'Have a drink on me!' When I got inside the phone was ringing. I picked it up, and said 'Who's speaking please?' And a voice said: 'You are'!"

Commenting at another festive board about the meal Tommy said: 'Waiter, this chicken I've got is cold.' He replied: 'I should think so. It's been dead for two weeks.' 'Not only that,' I said: 'It's got one leg shorter than the other.' He said: 'What do you want to do, eat it or dance with it?'

The next day Tommy went into an ice cream parlour and said to the assistant, 'I'd like a vanilla cone.' She said: 'Hundreds and thousands?'. I replied: 'No – I'll just have the one.' She said: 'Knickerbocker glory?' I said: 'I do get a certain amount of freedom in these trousers, yes.' I then went along to the dentist. He said: 'Say Aaah.' I said: 'Why?' He said: 'My dog's died.' Now most dentist's chairs go up and down, don't they? The one I was in went back and forward. I thought - this is unusual. And the dentist said to me: 'Mr Cooper, get out of the filing cabinet.' When I came out from the dentist somebody complimented me on my driving. They left a little note on the windscreen. It said: 'Parking Fine'. So that was nice.

Chapter 16

PRESS CUTTINGS

The Era, 26 May 1906
MASONS AT FRASCATI'S

The Chelsea Lodge of Freemasons, which was established twelve months ago in the interest of members of the theatrical and music hall professions, held its installation meeting at Frascati's Restaurant, Oxford Street, London W., on Friday 18 May.

A special dispensation from the Grand Lodge was read permitting the Lodge to be held at this restaurant instead of their regular meeting-place The Chelsea Palace. On the completion of the usual formal business the W.M. Bro. James W. Mathews installed as his successor in the chair Bro. Albert Le Fre, the ceremony being impressively performed. The new W.M. then appointed Bro. Mathews, IPM. The other officers were invested as follows:- Mr T. Serpentello, SW; Mr H. Baroni, JW; Mr W.S. Lyon, treasurer; Mr C.W. Doughty, secretary; Mr Walter H. Hitch, SD; Mr Harry Bawn, JD; Mr Fred Clay, DC; Mr W.F.K. Walton, IG; Mr Angelo A. Asher, organist; Mr George H. Dyball, first steward; Mr Bert A. Bigny, second steward; Mr L.G. Sharpe, third steward; Mr E.T. R. Lester, fourth steward and Mr J. H. McNaughton, tyler. The WM afterwards referred to the unavoidable absence, through illness, of the acting Past Master for the past year, Bro. Edward Swanborough, and on behalf of the Lodge sent, by special messenger, a Past Master's jewel, together with a letter expressing hopes for his speedy recovery.

Dinner was afterwards served, the brethren present numbering seventy-eight. The loyal and Masonic toasts having been duly honoured, the WM proposed the toast of "The Grand Officers", and said he was delighted to be honoured by the presence of three Grand Officers on the night of his installation. Bro. Harry Nicholls was an honorary member, whilst Bro. Times had always taken a great interest in the Lodge. He had received nothing but kindness from all the Grand Officers he had ever met. All seem willing and anxious to further the interests of the craft in every way in their power.

Bro. Nicholls said that he felt hardly equal to the occasion, and he felt the responsibility of his position very much. He gave way to none of the Grand Officers in his respect of the Craft, but he must say he thought he could sing a comic song better than make a dignified speech. Mr Nicholls concluded by saying that the variety profession - the sister of the dramatic profession - was become more strong every year, and he was glad to see it was reaching its proper place in the world of amusements.

Bro. Henry James also replied, and said that it was the first time he had visited the lodge and he assured the members that he was not paying empty compliments when he said the installation ceremony could not have been more perfectly rendered.

The toast of the WM was proposed by Bro. Mathews, IPM, who said: "Our WM has this evening proposed several toasts; he has had the quantity, but I feel that I have had the quality, for I have the pleasant duty to propose that of the Worshipful Master. I am sure he must feel delighted that he has taken up the reins of office. Bro. Le Fre is a member of my mother lodge - 1319 - and was initiated only six years ago, which is a short period for him to have reached the high office which he now adorns. He should be greatly flattered to occupy the chair of this lodge, formed as it is to bring vocal artistes and actors together. We all know that he is as well known as an actor as he is a singer. I prophesy a very good year of office for him, and I am sure the officers will assist him as they assisted me in my year of office."

The Worshipful Master, in his reply, said he thanked the IPM and Lodge heartily for the kind manner in which they had drunk his health. he hardly thought he deserved all the kind words which were said by the IPM, but he hoped he would be able to follow the footsteps of the IPM and at the expiration of his year of office, when he had done the work of the year, that the members would be satisfied that he had worked to the best of his ability.

The toast of the IPM was then felicitously proposed by the WM, and responded to by Bro. Mathews, who thanked them most heartily for the handsome cup which had been presented to him. If there was a regret in saying farewell it was sweetened by the thought that Bro. Le Fre would be the next Master. In announcing that the lodge would in future meet in the Chelsea Town Hall, Mr Mathews thanked the directors of the Chelsea Palace, especially Mr Henri Gros, for the accommodation and kindness which had been offered to the lodge.

The toast of The Visitors was acknowledged by Colonel Landon and Mr W. Lestocq, the former referring gracefully to the service actors as soldiers had rendered during the South African War.

Mr Lestocq spoke eloquently on the subject of Masonry, his words making a deep impression. The atmosphere of the Chelsea Lodge, he said, was one of attention and earnestness. "If we don't bring heart to it," said Mr Lestocq, "if we don't think about it, if we don't gather some good from it, then Masonry is of no good to any of us. As artistes we know there is only one way to attain perfection, and that is rehearse! rehearse! rehearse!"

While the dinner was in progress a reply was received, and this was read out. Mr Henri Gros made sympathetic reference to Mr Swanborough's state of health and announced that he and his co-directors were arranging a benefit matinee for Mr Swanborough which would shortly take place at the London Pavilion.

Among members present at the installation were Bros. Albert Le Fre (WM), James W. Mathews (IPM), T. Serpentello (SW), H. Baroni (JW), Wolfe S. Lyon (treasurer), C.J. Doughty (secretary), Walter H. Hitch (SD), Harry Bawn (DC), Angelo A. Asher (organist), W.T.K. Walton, L.G. Sharpe, Geo H. Dyball, and B.A. Bigny (stewards), J.H. McNaughton (Tyler), Henry G. Neville (PAGDC), J. Percy Fitzgerald (PGStB), Harry Nicholls (PGStB), Henri Gros, F. Clay, Hal Chapter, Valazzi, Primavesi, F. H. Pedgrift, W. Scott Adaker, Geo. Gilby, Fred Winn, Mike Morris, H.R. Mayville, G.H. Hill, J.B. Helm, E.T.R. Lester, E.W. Brett, A. Nicklin, Herbert Austin, Douglas White, Jimmie Prior, K.T. Hooper, Chas. King, H.F. Bingham, W. H. Atlas, Albert Christian, A. Cloetins, Frank Hardie, George Grahame, J.G. Ellis, A. Felino, W.C. Jeapes, Spot, C.E. Chapman, and C.H. Hopwood.

Included amongst the visitors were Bros. Henry Times (PAGDC), Chas Cruickshanks (AGStDBr), Mr W. Lestocq, Colonel W.F.B. Landon, Colonel H. Walker, G.E. Seabright, R.F. Campbell, V.H. Lanyi, R. Cobley, Chas Macdona, Herbert Chenery, G.H. Radford, J. Venner, Henri de Neut, A.C. Girard, W.H. Stephens, S.A. Weedon, T.W. Rumble, N.S. Lyon, L. Carson, G. Burgess, S. Grogan, J.W.P. Mark, E.T. Steyne, J.E. Borelli, D.M. Trytel and Max Rose.

The Era, 7 July 1916

Mr CHARLES WHITTLE

Appearing at the Ealing Hippodrome, Charles Whittle is one of those amusing vocalists whose mere appearance at the footlights is the signal for an outburst of merriment. He is funny without effort, every line of his patter is really droll. In *I'm Muggins the Juggins* the artist is at his best, and some of his facial contortions are irresistibly comic.

The Era, 25 May 1907

MASONS AT WORK

Chelsea Lodge No.3098 held its annual meeting on Friday afternoon, 17 May 1907, at Frascati's, Oxford Street, London, when Mr Theodore Schreiber (Serpentello) was installed Master for the ensuing year by Mr Albert Le Fre, who retired from the governorship of the Lodge. The ceremony, which was witnessed by a large gathering of the members and visitors was most impressively performed by the retiring Master. The Master then appointed and invested his officers, to

support him during the forthcoming year, as follows: Mr G.H. Cobley (Baroni), SW; Mr Walter H. Hitch, JW; Rev. H. Heriot Hill, chaplain; Mr W.S. Lyon, PM, treasurer; Mr C.J. Doughty, secretary; Mr Harry Bawn, SD; Mr W.F.K. Walton, JD; Mr J.W. Mathews, PM, DC; Mr Angelo Asher, organist; Mr G.H. Dyball, IG; and Messrs Clay, Bigny, Sharp and Lester, stewards; and Mr J.H. McNaughton, tyler.

At the subsequent banquet, after the usual loyal and Masonic toasts had been duly honoured, Mr Albert le Fre, IPM, proposed the health of the Worshipful Master, a toast which was rapturously received by all present. Serpentello was received with great cheering. In the course of his reply, he stated that, although, like Othello, he was rude in speech, his heart was in his work, and assured those present that nothing should be wanted on his part to maintain the reputation and usefulness of the Lodge. He then retired from the board for a short period, during which time Mr J.W. Mathews occupied the chair, and in proposing the health of the Immediate Past Master, took the opportunity of enlightening those assembled on the remarkable growth of the Lodge during the short time it had been in existence, showing that it must have been needed by the members of the profession, who had taken advantage of the existence by becoming members, and mentioned that it must be a very proud day for Mr Lyon, from whose idea the Lodge emanated. Amongst statistics, he stated that the Lodge had paid away in two years no less a sum than fifty guineas to the Masonic charities. Forty-odd guineas to its own benevolent fund, and still had a balance, after paying all expenses of every description, of sixty odd pounds. He concluded his remarks by calling upon those present to drink to the health of the IPM, wishing him long life and a successful career, and took the opportunity of presenting him with a very massive and handsome silver-gilt cup, emblazoned with the arms of the Lodge and suitably inscribed.

Mr Albert Le Fre expressed his gratitude to the brethren for the handsome cup and jewel which had been presented to him, and assured them that he had only one regret connected with his year of office, and that was that distance had prevented him attending his duties once or twice during the time.

The toast of the Visitors was proposed by the WM, and responded to by the Rev. C.E.I. Wright, PGD; Mr Harry Nicholls, PGStB; and Mr W. Lestocq, PM of the Asaph Lodge. The artists who appeared under the direction of Messrs F. Neiman and G.H. Dyball, were Miss Julia Leslie, Miss Linda Dale, Miss Agnes Hansom, Miss Alma Murray; Messrs Albert Christian, Jimmy Prior, Leo Tell, Tom Mellor, Charles Penrose, E. Leathley and Miss Viola Russell at the piano.

The following members were present: Mr Albert Le Fre, Mr T. Schreiber (Serpentello), Mr G.H. Cobley (Baroni), Rev. H. Herriot Hill, Mr W.S. Lyon, Mr

C.J.Doughty, Mr Walter H. Hitch, Mr Harry Bawn, Mr A.A. Asher, Mr G.H. Dyball, Mr B.A. Bigny, Mr L.G. Sharpe, Mr Fred Clay, Mr James W. Mathews, Mr J.H. McNaughton, Mr G.H. Hill, Mr W. Permayne, Mr T.H. Parker, Mr Leo Tell, Mr Fred Neiman, Mr R.W. Duce, Mr W. Atlas, Mr Edwin Brett, Mr R.E.Wilding, Mr Frank Hardie, Mr W. Collinson, Mr Dan Lipton, Mr T.S. Burnett, Mr A.E. Necklin, Mr Douglas White, Mr James Prior, Mr H.T. Bingham, Mr Albert Christian, Mr Hal Chapter, Mr Fred Farren, Mr H.K. Ramsden and Mr Herbert Austin.

The visitors were: Rev. C.E.L. Wright, PGD; Mr Harry Nicholls, PGStB: Bro. Chas Cruikshank, APGStd; Mr W. Lestocq, Asaph 1319; J.J. Kern, Mozart, 198; J.J. Orr, Earl's Court 2765; H. Chenery, Knightsbridge, 2978; H. Lindsay, St Andrew 110; W.H. Wolsey, Kennington 1381; T. Davis, London Welsh 2867; Mr L. Carson, Savage Club 2190; J.M. Fortune, Sir Walter Raleigh 2432, T.W. Rumble, Caledonian, 134; W.H. Gay, Bollingbrook 2417; J.H. Smith, Earl's Court 2765; N.S. Lyon, Joppa 188; C.W. Peachey, Fulham 2512 and M.H. McDowell, Skelmersdale 1658.

The Era, 26 December 1908
EDWARD SWANBOROUGH DEAD

After a long illness over a period of two years, Mr Edward Swanborough passed away on Monday at the residence of his sister, Mrs William Lyon, of 1 Hill Street, Berkeley Square, London where he had been nursed with loving care and tenderness. He was 67. He finished his active work in connection with the management of Chelsea Palace in the spring of 1906.

Mr Henri Gros, managing director of the Metropolitan and Chelsea, recognising the seriousness of his case, put himself at the head of a movement which resulted in a testimonial matinee that was held at the London Pavilion on 20 June 1906 when, among others, Mr Charles Hawtrey appeared.

Before his appointment as manager of Chelsea Palace in 1903, the deceased manager had been out of employment for a considerable period, and for a long time he was hampered with financial responsibilities not of his own creation, which he honourably and secretly discharged.

A son of Mrs Swanborough, the highly esteemed lady who for so long directed the fortunes of the old Strand Theatre, the deceased gentleman filled the position of treasurer at that house for many years. He was the brother of Ada Swanborough, who played principal parts at the Strand in the palmy days of burlesque and Byronic comedy; and his brother Arthur Swanborough, was one time manager of the Royal Music Hall.

Mr Swanborough had many happy and humorous recollections of the old Strand Theatre. On two occasions as a youngster he decorated the house with cheap gold and red French paper bought in Cannon Street, being assisted in this undertaking by the printer's labourer, Tom Christian – who, by the way, had a pension from the proprietress until the day of his death – and Mr Swanborough used to recall, with a laugh, that the newspapers at the time highly complimented him upon his artistic and decorative abilities. Another little anecdote he used to relate did not appear to flatter the old playhouse in the Strand. A piece called *The Woman in the Dusthole,* written by John Oxenford, was produced there, and Oxenford wrote his own criticism upon it in *The Times,* stating in the course of his remarks that a more appropriate title could not have been chosen, as the place in which the play was produced was, indeed, a dusthole. Later on, however, when Mr Swanborough's sister took possession, very great alterations and improvements were effected in the old house.

The Prince of Wales (now the King), accompanied by the Princess and their children, as a rule paid three or four visits a month to the Strand, and the Prince's first request was always, "I want to be received by my boys," meaning Mr Swanborough and his brother Arthur.

Mr Swanborough was the first theatrical manager who went over to the music halls. At the time of his becoming connected with the London Pavilion – which, by the way, had been rebuilt since he managed it – there were no stalls, the space where these are now then occupied by lounges and tables.

The deceased gentleman stood on a high rung of the ladder of Masonry. In December 1864 he was passed into the Lodge of Joppa, No.188, some years later becoming a member of the Asaph Lodge with which he was associated for thirty-six years. In 1879 he was Master of this Lodge and journeyed to Truro with the Grand Lodge of England to witness the Prince of Wales lay the foundation-stone of Truro Cathedral. He was also, together with Mr James Willing, one of the founders of the Strand Lodge, and its first Senior Warden.

Mr Swanborough's sister, Mrs Lyon, is the original Miss Swanborough who played at the Olympic with Robson and Emden, and, prior to that, she was at the Haymarket Theatre, under J.B. Buckstone's management, playing Juliet to Miss Cushman's Romeo. It was William Swanborough, a brother, who built the Prince of Wales's Theatre in Birmingham, the other brother, Arthur, being the acting-manager of the Strand for many years.

The deceased gentleman was buried at Brompton Cemetery.

The Era, 21 June 1916
MARRIOTT EDGAR

He wrote the book and most of the lyrics in the revue *Frolics* and Marriott Edgar plays the parts of *Tipps* the waiter, and Timekeeper. *Frolics* played to packed houses at Chelsea last week, and after two weeks in the provinces opens at the Middlesex on

July 3rd. The tent-scene in the revue is one of the funniest to be seen on the halls today.

The Era, 21 June 1916
WEE GEORGIE WOOD
He paid £4 recently for a pedigree fox terrier puppy at an auction in aid of our blinded heroes at the Hippodrome, Birkenhead. He is arranging a draw for it on July 13 at the Argyle, Birkenhead. The proceeds will be given to St Dunstan's Hostel, less 10 per cent to the Music Hall Ladies Guild. Tickets 2s 6d each.

The Era, 21 May 1919
FREEMASON KILLED IN MOTOR ACCIDENT
The deepest sympathy will be extended to Mr and Mrs Albert Le Fre in the terrible bereavement they have sustained by the death of their son Sydney (Sydney Harold De Voy), who expired on Thursday as a result of injuries sustained in a motor accident the previous Sunday.

The young man, who was only 23, was on his way to Shoreham on a motor-cycle to meet the members of his family, when a motor car coming in the opposite direction collided with him, and he was heavily thrown. He was taken to the cottage hospital at Horsham, where he lingered till the following Thursday without recovering consciousness, and died in his mother's arms.

A curious feature of the sad tragedy is that Mr **Albert Le Fre** was himself motoring in the neighbourhood, and was held up by a puncture. His son **Percy Le Fre** went back to the garage to get another tyre, and there heard about the accident to a motor cyclist, but was unaware until the following morning that the victim was his brother. Mr Le Fre sent to London at once for a specialist, but he could give no hope of his son's recovery.

Young Sydney was the chief comedian of *The Latest Craze,* a revue successfully produced at the Hippodrome, Derby, on 28 April. He had several other successes to his credit. He was a member of Proscenium Lodge of Freemasons, which his father founded, and of the Chelsea Royal Arch Chapter.

The Times, 22 May 1922
A VAUDEVILLE MASONIC LODGE
The annual installation meeting of the Chelsea Lodge No 3098, membership of which is limited to vaudeville performers, was held last week at Frascati's when Mr **Ernest A. Warsaw** (Erne Warsaw) was installed as Master in succession to Mr **James E. Young** (Jimmie Athlone), who was presented with a Past Master's jewel.

The officers appointed included: Mr J.B.H. Green (Bruce Green) and Mr Henry W. May, Wardens; Mr G.H. Dyball, LR, Chaplain, Mr Wolfe S. Lyon, PAGP, Treasurer; Mr C.J. Doughty, LR, Secretary; and Mr Albert Le Fre, LR, DC.

The Performer, 21 May 1924
WITH THE MASONS
The Twentieth Installation Meeting of the Chelsea Lodge of Freemasons, No.3098, was held on Friday at the Restaurant Frascati, Oxford Street, close upon one hundred members of the Lodge and visitors being present.

The retiring Master, W.Bro. Bruce Green performed the ceremony of installing his successor, Bro. Henry W. May, as Worshipful Master for the ensuing year, and performed his duties in an impressive and dignified manner.

The next 'business' was of a very interesting character, W.Bro. Wolfe S. Lyon, PAGP, and Treasurer of the Lodge, investing W.Bro. Ernest T.R. Lester, LR, with the regalia of London Rank, which honour has recently been conferred upon him.

The newly installed Master then appointed and invested those of his officers who were present as follows: W.Bro. Ernest Warsaw, PM, being the Acting Director of Ceremonies; Bro. W.J. MacKay, SW; Bro. J.W. Ellison, JW; W.Bro. George.H. Dyball, PM, LR, Chaplain; W.Bro. Wolfe S. Lyon, PAGP, Treasurer; Bro. Ernest G. Goodwin, Secretary; W.Bro. Albert Le Fre, PM, LR, DC; Bro. Israel Gilder, SD; Bro. J.P. Ling, JD; W.Bro. Walter H. Hitch, PM, LR, Almoner; Bro. Ernest J. Headworth, Organist; Bro. Will Collinson, IG; W.Bro. Fred Lyster, W.Bro John Enzer, Bros Alfred Artois, J.M.T. Vost, E.J. Headworth, and Percy Le Fre, Stewards; and W.Bro. J.F. MacNaughton, Tyler.

After other business had been transacted the brethren and visitors dined together in the York Room.

In addition to those mentioned above, the following members were present: W.Bro. Herbert Chenery, PAGStB, W.Bro. W.H. Atlas, Erne Chester. Albert Felino and Bros. Jack Wynne, Edward Giggs, J. Stolberg, Fred Keeton, P.M. Turner, A.H. Snowden, Billy Danvers, C. Isaacs, W. Scott Adacker, Dick Crean, J.M. Whidden, E.B. Daniels, Jas. W. Laurence, F. Tipper, Alf Daniels, Will Johnson, E. Hambledon, Lewis Leslie, Harry Gold, Bert Lord, Dan Lipton, S.L. Hapton, S. Murray, Tom Arnold, Walter Cranby, Edgar Hooper, Will Stone, C.R. Whittle, Tom Edwards, Geo. Jackley, A. Bown, Jack Royal, George Harris, James Robberds, J.J. Moir, P. Pepper, Herbert Jackson, Harry Marlow, Leslie Sarony, Dan MacCarthy, A.E. Lyon and E.H. Cadwell.

The visitors included the following: A. Briscoe, T. Pullen, Norman White, C.J. Cawood, Thomas Vosper, Leonard Neville, G.F. Messer, John Warren, James Brown, P. Morgan, Victor Andre, John Haxon, Edward Bawn, Chas. A. Cohen, Fred Scott, J.W. Winn, Geo.

Bolton, Geo. de Grande, J. Millehir, T.E. Crofts, Fred Alexander, T.S. Burnetti, S.P. Briginshaw, W. Davidson, Arthur E. Were, J.C. MacMahon, Ben Hill, H.J. Scott, Walter P. Valls, Evered Digby, C. Douglas Stewart, E.A. Westoby and W. Collins.

Following the banquet the usual loyal and Masonic toasts were duly given and replied to, the W.Master giving an example of brevity and conciseness.

A specially entertaining and attractive musical programme had been arranged by W.Bro. Henry W. May, the direction of which was in the excellent hands of Bro. Harry Marlow. The following well-known artistes appeared: George Doonan, Sammy Shields, Violet King, Olga Charna, Naughton and Gold, S.W. Wyndham, Sydney Hott, Mr and Miss Treet, in a thought transmission act (their first appearance in this country from Australia), Thornley Dodge, Doris Ashton and George Bolton. Mr Percy Langdon was an efficient accompanist.

Performer, 23 May 1929

CHELSEA LODGE

The twenty-fifth Installation meeting of the Chelsea Masonic Lodge No.3098 was held at Frascati's Restaurant, Oxford Street, on Friday, 17 May. There was a large attendance of members and friends of over 120. W.Bro. J.P. Ling was the Installing Master and performed the ceremony of installing W.Bro. Will Collinson as W. Master in a most impressive and dignified manner. The newly elected W. Master then appointed and invested his officers as follows:

Phinneas Headworth, SW; W.Bro. John Enzer, JW; W.Bro. George.H. Dyball, PM, LR, Chaplain; W.Bro. Albert Le Fre, PAGStB, Treasurer; Bro. Ernest G. Goodwin, Secretary; W.Bro. Erne Warsaw, PM, DC; Bro. Alfred Artois, SD; Bro. J.M.T. Vost, JD; W.Bro. Walter H. Hitch, PM, LR, Almoner; W.Bro. Erne Chester, PM, LR, Assistant Secretary; W. Bro. Fred B. Box, ADC; Bro. Frederick A. Lidiard, Organist; Bro. William V. Permane, IG; and Bros. George Jackley, George Batt, Chas Kasrac, Alf Cruikshank, Johnny Hurley and Bert Snowden as Stewards; and W.Bro. J.H. MacNaughton, Tyler.

The WM presented the IPM, W.Bro. Ling with a Past Masters jewel from the Lodge.

The annual balance sheet was submitted and adopted, and other business transacted, after which the Brethren and their visitors adjourned to the Alexandra Room for dinner. The usual Masonic toasts then followed, which, at the request of the WM were commendably brief and to the point, owing to the length of the concert. W.Bro. Storr, PGADC, replied for Grand Lodge, and W.Bro. Geo. Messer for the visitors.

During the evening an interesting presentation was made by W.Bro. Erne Warsaw to the popular new master, W.Bro. William Collinson, of a smoker's companion, subscribed to by those brethren he had introduced into Freemasonry.

An excellent programme of well-known artistes was given during the evening, under the direction of Bro. Bob Lloyd, when the following appeared: Troy Sisters and Helen, Australian Boys, Harry Moore, Jones and Thomas, Carr Lynn, Winifred Hammond, Jim Nolan, Doris Ashton and Billy Rawson, Connie Bonnick, Marie and Nora, Rudarni Sisters and Billy Carlton, Millie Love, Will Dellar, and Chas Whittle. Mr Chas. Lucas was the accompanist. Space prevents the names of all present, but in addition to those already referred to, were the following members of the Lodge: W.Bro. W.H. Atlas, PM, LR, W.Bro. W.J. Mackay, PM, W.Bro. J.W. Ellison, PM, W. Bro. Henry May, PM, W.Bro. Harold Finden, PM, and Bros. Fred Ison, Chas. Carr, E.S. Goodwin, Alfred Dean, L.Lester, Chas. Bruske, Phil Rallis, Frank Varney, F.A. Fletcher, B. Green, Dan Lipton, Syd Howard, F. O'Hara, W.J. Conelly, Victor C. Roberts, Chas Allen, A.Kingsley, S. Belinfante, H. Maraso, F. Forrester, Will Johnson (Sen), Will Johnson (Jun), L. Croke, J.W. Jackson, A. Daniels, Richard Crean, Elkan Simons, Harry Claff, Fred Maple, Fred Cooper, E.C. Harper, William Stone, J.W. Robberrds, E. Hambledon, E. Cadwell, Joe Lawrence, Geo. Holloway, Fred Murray, Jack Gold; and W. Bro. F.W.G. Golby, PAGDC.

Among the visitors we noticed were: W. Bro. John E. Pinder, PPGIG, W.Bro. C. Douglas Stuart, LR, W.Bro. Horace Sheldon, and Bros. Henry Supper, L. Morris, J.S. Charters, M. Mordecai, G. Field, G. Fenton, Percival Lewis, J. Williams, William Arthur, George Le Mox, and W.Bro Arthur E. Were.

Stage, 21 May 1931

THE CHELSEA LODGE

The usual efficiency and enthusiasm marked the proceedings at Chelsea Lodge on Friday, at Frascati's Restaurant, when John Enzer was installed as WM by the outgoing Master, Phineas Headworth, LR. The addresses after the installation were delivered by Phineas Headworth, W.J. Mackay and Albert Le Fre. A jewel and pastmasters's collar were presented to the retiring master, and £10. 10s was voted to the Variety Artistes' Benevolent Fund. Later at the dinner Mr Headworth was presented with a loving cup, a gift which has been made to every retiring master since the Lodge was started.

Mr Enzer appointed and invested those who were present, the following as his officers for the year: Alfred Artois, SW; J.M.T. Vost, JW; George H. Dyball, Chaplain; Albert Le Fre, PAGStB, Treasurer; Ernest G. Goodwin, PM, Secretary; Erne Warsaw, LR, DC; W.V. Permane, SD; George Jackley, JD; Walter H. Hitch, PM, Almoner; Erne Chester, PM, Assistant Secretary; Fred B. Box, Assistant DC; Frederick A. Lidiard, Organist;

George Batt, IG; Charles Kasrac, Alf. Cruikshank, Bert Snowden, Arthur C, Kingsley, George Marriott Edgar and Jack Wynne as Stewards and J.H. MacNaughton as Tyler.

The Lodge is celebrated for its musical entertainments, and this year's programme was quite up to the usual high standard. The following artistes kindly gave their services: Vin Kaley, Kathleen Destourel, Bert Erroll and his daughter Betty, Chic Farr and Wells Farmer, Rosie Lloyd, Bud Flanagan and Chesney Allen, A.C. Astor, Ruby Shepherd and Guiseppe Ceci, De Vas and Charlie Whittle.

W.Bro. T.W. Bambridge, PAGStB, responded for the Grand Officers toast. W. Bros. Eric Le Fre and A.W. Ward replied to that of the visitors, proposed by W.Bro. T.B. Box. W.Bro. W.H. Hitch responded for the Past Masters, and W.Bro. Erne Warsaw, LR, replied to the toast of London Rank given by W.Bro. W.J. MacKay.

News of the World, 10 December 1933

In a larger article the newspaper reported that all **Lew Davis'** saxophonists were bachelors, all the brass section were married with a daughter each, and all the rhythm section were married and childless except **Tiny Winters** whose wife had recently given birth to a daughter. The paper jokingly suggested that Tiny, who played string bass, should be transferred to the brass section.

Radio Pictorial, 1 November 1935
WORST MOMENT OF MY LIFE

The Two Leslies
LESLIE SARONY & LESLIE HOLMES
The *Famous Composers,* B.B.C. and Recording Stars

Leslie Sarony of the Two Leslie's fame, is inclined to think his worst moment came when he was playing in *Showboat* at Drury Lane. At the beginning of the play he and a fellow actor had a scene which explained the plot of the whole show. This was most important, and without it all that followed was practically meaningless. "On the first night," remarked Leslie, "you can imagine the state of nerves I was in! Opening scene. Opening night. Drury Lane Theatre and the meaning of the show, to a great extent, depending on the way we put our scene over. I was shaking like a leaf. The curtain went up, but my partner never appeared! I had to say his words and mine, too, with as much sense and presence of mind as I could muster. Not so good!" said Leslie.

Radio Pictorial, 23 October 1936
HARRY LEADER and his BAND IN HOLLAND

Harry Leader's recent trip to Holland provided him and the boys with plenty of fun, excitement and kudos. There was the time when, for a gag, the boys decided to rehearse on a barge on one of the canals. When the brass section got really enthusiastic, the barge tipped over and many of the boys got a ducking!

Radio Pictorial, 20 November 1936
TWO LESLIE'S PARTY

The two Leslie's threw a 'swell' party to celebrate their brilliant *Radio Pie Show.* It started at 10.00pm and went on until about 5.30am. Quite a night! The Two Leslie's are two of the most popular fellows in show business, as was evident by the 80 to 100 top stars and music publishers who arrived to do them honour. A high spot was **Leslie Sarony**'s solo 'drunk' dance with Tessie O'Shea.

Radio Pictorial, 20 November 1936
ALAN BREEZE AND HIS CARS
by Buddy Bramwell

Vocalist **Alan Breeze** has got himself a new car – built to his own design. I am wondering how long this one will last, for Alan has a flair for getting mixed up in car smashes. Returning from the North, his car (the one before the present one!) hit a saloon car head-on. Alan was unscathed, his only worry being whether he could get to the show in London in time. Prior to that he was peacefully driving his car (the one before the one that came before the present one!) when it suddenly burst into flames. Alan escaped with nothing more serious than singed eyebrows and hair! And once before when he was driving his car (the one before the one that preceded the one before the present one!) he hit a lorry (only Alan says that the lorry hit him!) The folks around eventually found Alan sitting among the wreckage unhurt and busy learning the words of a new song! A Breezy sort of life…

Radio Pictorial, 4 December 1936
ROY FOX RESCUED BY HIS TRUMPET
If it hadn't been for **Roy Fox**'s trumpet they might have found a body in the strong-room of a certain bank. Roy's body! Roy used to work in a bank, and, around lunch-time he'd slither off to a tiny strong-room in the depths of the building, to practice on his beloved trumpet out of everybody's earshot! The door of the strong-room was self-locking, and one day it was slammed shut by accident. Roy was inside… the room (a very small one) was airproof! Frenziedly Fox shouted for help, but his voice didn't carry through the massive steel door. So he took off his jacket and sat down to blow that trumpet in earnest. For hours he kept blowing using up the all-precious oxygen. Hours later a passing clerk heard the trumpet and rescued the perspiring player. Roy was almost literally at his last gasp.

Radio Pictorial, 18 June 1937
JOE DANIELS SETS UP SHOP
by Edgar Jackson

A journalist popped into a shop in Soho Street, London to buy a pack of cigarettes, He was surprised when a fat, grinning face appeared from behind the counter and proved to be none other than Harry Roy's former drummer, **Joe Daniels**, who had recently been making a big success on the Halls with his own musical act. The cigarette shop, it transpired, was owned by Joe's brother, Len, and Joe had taken the next door premises and set up as a musical instrument dealer. The place was most imposing and the astonishingly large stock seemed to embrace everything from trombones to gramophone records and needles.

"I'm another," said Joe, "who doesn't propose to be left high and dry should the day arrive when the theatre public gets tired of my ugly mug. Already, I'm doing good business here." Joe was nothing if not a good showman. One of his stunts was to play his drums with two large silk handkerchiefs and very effective it was with various coloured lights thrown on them. While he was on tour, Joe's wife, Amy, looked after the shop. On leaving the shop a neat arrangement of fairy bells over the door tinkled 'Get Your Hair Cut'.

Radio Pictorial, 16 July 1937
RIGHT BAND, WRONG HALL
The first time **Joe Loss** wore evening 'tails' at a hotel engagement, he forgot to pack a white tie –

and had to make one out of a white table napkin.

He took his band to St George's Hall, Langham Place, to make his first gramophone records. Amazed officials stared goggle-eyed and then Joe discovered he should have gone to St George's Hall, Tottenham Court Road.

Radio Pictorial, 16 July 1937
ROY FOX IN HOLLYWOOD
Roy Fox used to play 'sob-music' in Hollywood studios to help film stars to cry. He was once too successful. It was a scene between Janet Gaynor and Charles Farrell. Fox struck up a sentimental tune and Janet switched on the tears. Then "Cut" yelled the director, for lo and behold Charles Farrell (playing a 'tough guy') had likewise started to weep!

Radio Pictorial , 10 January 1938
BILLY and HYLDA with 'MIKE' FRIGHT
A man and a woman sat in St George's Hall watching a rehearsal. They were artistes. At any moment they would be called upon by Eric Maschwitz to go on stage and do their stuff. The woman was so nervous that when she lit her cigarette her hands trembled and we all noticed. The man was just as bad. They both confessed they felt physically sick out of pure funk. "If we feel like this at rehearsal," said the man, "what on earth is going to happen tonight, when we do the show?"

Now Hilda Mundy and **Billy Caryll** have worked together on the Halls for fourteen years. There is nothing they do not know about their job. In comedy cross-talk they are brilliant. But the other night in the Gala Variety programme with Nelson Keys, they went on the air for the first time. In the words of Hilda Mundy: "We don't know what to do! We don't know how to time our laughs unless we have an audience to give us applause."

Hilda Munday and Billy Caryll have grown famous in a husband - and - wife act. They always quarrel. Sometimes Billy gets romantic and sings a passionate love song in a voice throbbing with emotion. And then, in the middle of it, Hilda gives a violent sneeze, which leads to another quarrel.

In real life they seem to adore each other and have been married for fourteen years. They met in a variety show in 1921. Billy says: "I didn't like Hylda and she hated me. But everyone said we ought to work together. Well, when we did work together Hylda changed all her lines and I had a terrible time trying to give the right answers.

Anyway, the idea to quarrel on stage came to both of us." Said Hylda: "It was the natural thing to do." Said Billy: "At one time I used to do an acrobatic act. I used to walk on my hands and stand on my head." Said Hylda: "The blood never went back to his feet. Isn't it a pity?"

Radio Pictorial, March 1938

THE BIGGEST MOMENT OF MY CAREER

Barry Wells

When **Bram Martin** first heard he was going to broadcast he was so bewildered that it hardly occurred to him that this was his 'big moment'. But, in retrospect, he realises that it stands out in bold relief from any other date in his professional calendar.

"All I ever hoped and planned for came true when I heard that my band was to go on the air," said Bram, "I had done many solo broadcasts, but it seemed hopeless trying to break into the select circle of broadcasting bands. But Eric Maschwitz and Max Kestner dined at the Holbom Restaurant and seemed to like the band. Months passed and then came my official notification that the band was to broadcast. Hectic rehearsals followed and during the actual broadcast I felt emotionally battered. It had simply got to be a success, part of my brain insisted... and another part seemed to stand aloof as if it took no responsibility for the outcome, based as it was on capricious whims of fate. When it was all over and I knew that the band was on its upward way I felt sick. But it was a grand moment!" grinned Bram.

Radio Pictorial, 6 May 1938

ALL FALL DOWN

Maurice Sterndale – always up to tricks – was very impressed with a couple of amazing acrobats. One night an appalling crash was heard, which sounded as if the theatre had fallen in. In his dressing room, Maurice was found sitting on the floor ruefully rubbing his head.

Fired by the acrobats he had carefully stood a piano stool on a table, balanced two phone books on that, and a milk bottle on the books. Then he had contrived to stand on the milk bottle! But only for an instant. The appalling crash was the result of Maurice discovering that he might be a darned fine instrumentalist but, as an acrobat, he wasn't in the first three!

Radio Pictorial, 2 December 1938

'I WANT A ROCKING HORSE

Leslie Sarony was caught one Christmas to do his stuff at a Church Bazaar. "I was getting along fine, except that the whiskers tickled so much I wanted to sneeze," Les said, "and then suddenly there emerged one of those awful little pests who are their mother's darlings but a pain in the neck to everybody else. The little blighter stood and goggled at me until I gave him the present. He looked at it – it was a snappy line in jig-saw puzzles - and then suddenly he yelled: 'I want a rocking horse!'

"There, there little man", I said, "we haven't got any rocking horses. Run along and work out your puzzle!" But the little brute was inconsolable. He kept clutching at my leg and I was beginning to despair. In the end I looked round for help, and a man came over to me and said: "Now it's no use losing your temper. Children can only be won over by kindness and a knowledge of psychology." He turned to the child and said: "I want to talk to you little man," and drew him aside.

"Three minutes later the kid disappeared, and I didn't see him again. So I said to my benefactor; "Gosh, that was psychology. What on earth did you say to him to get rid of him so quickly?" He looked at me and winked wisely: "I just whispered in his ear that if he didn't go pretty darned quick I'd put him over my knee and tan his little behind!" Kindness, psychology! Well, well..."

Radio Pictorial, January 6 1939

ALL FOR A PENNY!

If the late - goers in Birmingham the other week wondered who was the extremely robust bald - headed gentleman with the smile who was seen shortly after midnight strolling along the lamp - lit streets near the Hippodrome Theatre sucking an enormous stick of barley sugar which protruded several inches from his mouth, here is his identity.

Max Bacon, Ambrose's famous drummer - comedian, who, of course, is noted for his Yiddish -interpreted monologues among which have been '*Red Hooding Ride', 'William To-Hell', 'Noah's Ark'* and, his latest and greatest, which he is now performing with Ambrose on tour, '*Nero',* who fiddled about at the most critical moment!

Max is an inveterate joker from the time he wakes in the morning until he falls asleep at night. Some nights he even tells funny stories in his sleep - and did he get the poor trying-to-be-obliging chemist in the all night Boots' in Birmingham tied in a knot when he went in with brilliant sax-player, accompanist, orchestrator and stylish cricketer Sid Phillips, who wanted to get some toilet necessities.

After exercising his absurd wit on nearly every article on view in the shop he bought that stick of barley-sugar for a penny! He then trundled out, leaving the assistant behind the counter scratching his head and wondering.

Radio Pictorial 21 July 1939
VAN STRATEN at the SAVOY HOTEL
Looking positively immaculate in his suit of tails in front of his excellent band at Quaglino's, **Van Straten** (he has definitely abandoned the Alf now!) sometimes finds his mind darting back to the first time that he ever entered the precincts of a lavish restaurant such as he makes almost a home-from-home now.

The picture conjured up is of a youth in scout's uniform blowing for all that he was worth at a well-polished bugle as he sat on top of a motor-bus on Armistice Night in 1918.

Young Alf had been doing his stuff with some street-corner batch of lads addicted to doing their daily good deed, when a decidedly riotous party of revellers literally dumped him on the bus they had commandeered because he added such a lot of noise to their lustiness. They had the bus driven clear into the courtyard of the Savoy Hotel and there carried their little trumpeter into the soft-carpeted interior and treated him to the biggest feed he had ever had before or since.

Daily Sketch 14 September 1959
MUSICIAN JOE CALLED TO THE BAR
Thirty pounds a week - and more. That's what you can easily earn in your Wimpy Bar. How much more? Well, look at bandleader **Joe Daniels**. His Wimpy Bar is just a sideline. A £100-a-week sideline.

Joe's Wimpy bar is near the ITV studios at Wembley, a Wimpy where the stars pop in for a cuppa or a quick snack. It all started when Joe's band was in the middle of a spate of one-night stands. One quick appearance and off to the next town.

Joe hated these jobs although they seemed essential. But one foul night in Inverness the band's coach driver misjudged a turn on a mountain road and nearly ended the entire band's career. Says Joe: "That finished it. I made up my mind on the spot to break with one-night stands

and find something else."

So Joe decided to go into business. But what business? That was a problem, until he walked into a South Coast Wimpy Bar with its air of obvious prosperity. "I had intended just to buy a Wimpy hamburger but I ended up buying a Wimpy Bar. Altogether it cost me about £6000 to open this place, but I look like getting most of my money back in a year. What I like most about these Wimpy Bars is that they're easy to run. You can learn all you need to know in a day. I guarantee that almost anyone with absolutely no experience could walk in here and start making £100 a week."

Joe has his one-night stand days far behind him. He still has a pretty full musical bill with his orchestra. He picks and chooses his jobs and while he is away his wife, Mary, who was a professional singer, runs the business.

Melody Maker 30 December 1961
YOUTHFUL SUCCESS
Sixteen-year-old composer **Zack Laurence** is signed up to Dick James Music and plays his latest composition *Snowman's Land* on a Parlophone disc. He has already broadcast the tune in *Discs A Gogo* and in *Thank Your Lucky Stars.*

Zack has just joined the Performing Right Society and is one of the youngest ever members to be accepted by that organisation. He was born, and lives a stone's throw away from Helen Shapiro in East London and composed his first two songs when he was twelve, *Magic Fingers* and *Zsa Zsa,* and then recorded them four years later as his debut disc for Parlophone.

The Times 18 September 1975
Review by Leonard Buckley of *Billy Dainty Esq,* Thames Television Show, September 1975.

Billy Dainty has long been a visiting fireman on the box. Time and again when we have been watching some television spectacular which has proved so dreadful as to leave us too stricken to switch it off the situation has been saved by his timely arrival with his twinkling eyes and his tireless feet. Oozing with good nature like Roy Hudd, whom he much resembles, and not taking himself too seriously, he is the sort of performer who can turn his hand to anything. It comes of years on the boards.

It is, of course, his eccentric dancing that has chiefly won our hearts. Perhaps the feet do grow a little tired these days. But like the good trouper he is he can even turn exhaustion to comic advantage. "Could you just talk among yourselves for a minute or two?" he gasps to the audience after some frenzied caper, as he struggles, or appears to struggle, to catch his breath.

Last night he had a show of his own. He could display his versatility in humorous sketches as well as in song and dance.

Much of the material supplied to him by Vince Powell and Brian Cooke was end-of-the-pier stuff. We had the barber-shop quartet that goes awry. There were jests about the wife. There was even the concert pianist with the stool that falls apart. As in the joke about the curate's egg, which we might

easily have had as well, some parts were excellent but others were not so good. It scarcely mattered. As each item, good or bad, was finished Mr Dainty had something different ready for the next.

It was pleasant, however, to see a television show for once in which the star did not entirely hog the limelight. Victor Spinetti had full scope for the inarticulate verbals with which he takes off the Thespian, the drill sergeant and so on. Kate Williams, lovely comic actress, was there. There were others. Moreover, Mr Dainty seemed to have invested them all with his own good humour. It would indeed have been churlish not to enjoy a show in which such a happy time was being had by one and all.

Freemasonry Today, August 1999

FREEMASONRY SAVED MY LIFE

Doug Pickford talks to Jim Davidson, the public Jack the Lad who is champion of the Craft

THE PUBLIC FACE of Jim Davidson is that of a Jack the Lad comedian whose sometimes saucy stage shows blend with his much-publicised fight against alcoholism and his reputation for the number of marriages he has notched up. Yet divest him of this façade and the real Jim Davidson will stand up and be counted as a champion of Freemasonry who regards the Craft as the crux of his life and is happy to acknowledge that becoming a mason not only changed his life but saved it.

Indeed, he holds the Craft in such high esteem that he is looking forward to studying for a degree in Freemasonry at the recently-opened Canonbury Masonic Research Centre, sponsored by the Marquess of Northampton.

The Blackheath born entertainer had his first taste of treading the boards at the age of twelve when he was chosen to appear in Ralph Reader's Gang Show at the Golders Green Hippodrome when he was given his own spot, telling gags and doing impressions. He then got totally disillusioned with show-business after failing the audition for the part of the Artful Dodger in the movie "Oliver!". He was thirteen.

It was by chance that he found his way back into show-business. One Sunday evening he went along to a pub in Woolwich where the

regular stand-up comic had not turned up. Pushed into it by his friends, he ended up on stage telling gags... and the audience laughed. From then on he would appear as often as possible in pubs and clubs across London and soon turned professional. Appearing on television's "New Faces" in 1976 proved to be the turning point for his career and he was quickly starring in his own shows and won the *TV Times* accolade as "The Funniest Man on Television". Now he is undoubtedly one of the top comedians in the United Kingdom.

There have not been any Masonic connections in his life, and he only joined Chelsea Lodge eleven years ago because a couple of his friends were in the lodge and he "felt left out". It was Laurie Mansfield, his manager, who told him he would only get out of it as

much as he put in; he liked this and so joined. In his own words, he has never looked back.

What perceptions did he have of Freemasonry before he joined?

"I thought Freemasons were people like JPs. They were the Establishment if you like; they were the ones who were not getting into trouble! They were the leaders, if you like."

What were his first impressions?

"My first reaction was that we don't seem to be doing much, just getting people to join."

Before the interview had concluded I realised that that was the way he was: forthright, no-holds barred, and if another cliché was required, he pulls no punches. I asked him how his Freemasonry developed.

"I read all the standard works on Freemasonry, the histories and usual publications, the obvious books concerning Freemasonry, and then about five years ago I started to read other books, *The Hiram Key*, for instance, which I thought was splendid but they were a bit naughty giving away too many secrets. There's nothing wrong with having secrets like the rituals but I don't think we should be so secretive about everything else we do. I re-read the Bible about this time, too, and now I have built up a library of the esoteric. I eventually hope to take a degree in Freemasonry at the Canonbury Masonic Research Centre founded by the Assistant Grand Master, who I feel is doing a first-rate job for the Craft."

After a while he added: "I think clamping down does not help; we should be even more open."

So just what does Jim Davidson, the man behind the mask, get from Freemasonry?

"I think that Freemasonry is the chisel to smooth down the rough edges of society; when people talk about it being a secret society well, yes, we do have secrets, but they are there to allow people to fit into society, and we will only give them to people to try to fit into society. I believe Freemasonry finds order from chaos."

He is "taking the chair" at the City of Westminster Lodge next year and has undertaken many degrees including Mark Masonry, Knights Templar, Knights of Malta and the Royal Order of Scotland, about which he said proudly:

"I love this very much. I have a bit of Scottish blood."

He began to reflect on his fascination for the historical and esoteric aspects of the Craft and said he believed its origins started almost at the time of the pyramids and does not think it is much at all to do with freestone-masons and the like.

"Eventually it came through the Knights Templar to what we have today," he entrusted.

So what has Freemasonry done for him?

"I need a set of rules," he told me. "As a person I suffered from drinking a lot and Freemasonry helped me to stop. I try to live my life today as the Freemasonry Book of Rules. I practise Freemasonry's concepts and indeed, every morning I practise and endeavour to live my life as a true Freemason. It was the ideals of Freemasonry that made me see sense and stopped me from drinking. I was killing myself and I now feel we should all help other people to overcome their problems."

He elaborated by mentioning that at Chelsea Lodge he sat on a committee where a prospective candidate was being interviewed. "This guy had a lot of mis-behaviour up until 18 (he is a famous boxer)," he explained. "And I said if we could not get this man in, who had promised to be good, we were nothing more than a golf club. We should help him to help himself and give him the opportunity to let Freemasonry help him."

He returned to his views on lodges merely getting candidates through degrees, saying, "I think that all it needs for a lot of lodges to get a candidate through their first and second degrees is an empty date in the diary. To my mind they should serve their apprenticeship for as long as possible. They should learn all the aspects of the Craft; if it takes three years then so be it. Freemasonry is a learning process and it should not be a race to see how quickly an Apprentice can be passed."

He was modest when I asked him to tell me about some of the work he had undertaken for Freemasonry. He mentioned visiting a Freemasonry-funded home for the elderly in Essex and speaking to the residents there. "That's the sort of thing we should all do," he said. He also mentioned `doing a show' for the Marquess of Northampton to raise money. He

did not mention the many thousands of pounds this raised through his talents. However, he did cite that he endeavoured to turn up to support any Freemasons he knew whenever he could, such as a Third Degree ceremony for a 53 year- old friend at another lodge in the near future. "I'll be there to support him. That's how it should be."

There was a pause for obvious reflection, before he pronounced: "I am very proud to be a Freemason. It is the light from the dark; for me it is the resurrection. I get told off for saying it sometimes, but it is a religion. It is for me anyway."

We discussed some of the people who knock Freemasonry and he spoke of Chris Mullin MP. "I wrote to him and invited him to lunch so I could explain what Freemasonry means to me, and said if he wanted to know what it is all about he should come and find out and he would see we were fellow human beings."

And what happened?

"He did not reply."

So is Freemasonry going the right way?

"We need to take on the role of a probation service in a way within the ranks of Freemasonry. We need to help people more. For example, a friend of mine has just found himself in Ford Open Prison for fraud and we should be helping people like him to go back into society. We should work a little harder on it:"

I asked him to elaborate on his religious views and he told me, "I went to a Catholic school (St. Austen's in Charlton). I was a lapsed C of E until I became a Gnostic Christian. I found Christianity through knowledge, not through faith. It is not difficult to find if the Kingdom of God is within.'

What then of the future?

On the professional side, he can only go from strength to strength. He opened a brand new musical based on the life of Jerry Lee Lewis called "Great Balls of Fire" in the West End in October and his hugely successful *Jim Davidson's Generation Game* and *Big Break* keep pulling in viewers by the many millions. Of the Freemasonry side, he said: "Once I am in the chair at my lodge and I have attained my degree in Free-masonry, then Freemasonry had better watch out - we'll really be coming out of the closet!"

Finally, I asked him if he knew a joke about Freemasonry. He thought for a while, then laughed. "Er, no, I can't recall one. Mind you, I have a terrible memory sometimes. I was carrying out Senior Warden duties recently and had my words hidden everywhere around me!"

After an intriguing discussion it was obvious that the public and private sides of the man are as different as chalk and cheese. He is as committed a show-biz pro-fessional as he is a committed Freemason. He is the kind of person who puts everything, plus a further ten per cent, into anything he undertakes and his contagious enthusiasm for the Craft certainly gets that.

The Square June 2003

Peter Sellers - Mason for the wrong reason?

By Yasha Beresiner

To label any subject unsuitable for comedy is to admit defeat. Peter Sellers

Peter Sellers epitomised the unhappy clown. He was a brilliant comedian and a sad man. His brief involvement and attitude to freemasonry reflected his discontented life.

Peter was very nearly born on stage. His mother began her labour contractions in the middle of an act and performed to the finish before being rushed to hospital in Southsea, Hampshire to deliver her baby. It was the 8th of September 1925 and an ominous start to a difficult childhood. He was the second son of the vaudeville artists, Peggy and William Seller and was named Richard Henry. He was called Peter in memory of the couple's first child who had sadly died at birth two years earlier. His mother, a singer and dancer, was back on stage two weeks later, Peter in her arms crying to the audience's applause! Just a year earlier on 18 July 1924 his father was initiated into Freemasonry in the Chelsea Lodge number 3098 in London. This was to influence Peter's limited Masonic career.

He could have been named Daniel after his illustrious great-great-grandfather, Daniel Mendoza (1764-1836), famed Portuguese-Jewish bare-fisted pugilist, who styled himself *Mendoza the Jew* and was known as the *father of scientific boxing*. In 1792 he defeated William Ward becoming the heavy weight-boxing champion of England, a title he retained for three years. Peter Sellers once said . . . '*Both my mother (who is Jewish) and I bear a most remarkable resemblance to him – it is almost uncanny.*' Was it a hereditary tendency then, that may explain Peter Sellers recorded aggressive streak, which did not serve him well through his life? His earliest professional performances as a teenager were as a drummer and he became almost obsessed with his addiction to the drums. This has been interpreted as an outlet for his bad tempered predisposition. It manifested itself in his early youth. He was defiant as a toddler and naughty and disobedient.

Whilst his mother doted on him, an imposition of her emotions that was to influence him throughout his life, she also, by the nature of her work, often neglected him for days on end. His father, a pianist, was an intelligent but uneducated and weak man, frequently absent from home. They were a poor family. Peter recalled his early youth always in the back of his parent's car moving from venue to venue and, almost as often, moving homes to avoid paying rent. It was a sad childhood made no happier by his parents sending him to the Catholic *St Marks and St Aloysius School*, run by the *Brothers of Our Lady of Mercy*. He was the only Jewish boy in the school, and quipped later than he recited Christian prayers far better than any other boy in the school.

The War Years

In 1940, as England declared war on Germany, Peter was 14 years old and typically refused to move out of London to Cambridge, with the rest of the youngsters and women being evacuated. It interrupted his education. His natural talents, however, were already beginning to surface. He impressed young girlfriends with his almost eerie talent for mimicking. On his 17th birthday in September 1943 Peter was obligated to enlist. He chose the Air Force in the hope of becoming a pilot but ended up in the Entertainment Division of the RAF known as the Gang Shows. Here he first met Michael Bentine with whom he was later to found the *Goons*. Within a year Peter was posted to India and after the war served in both occupied Germany and France before his demobilisation in December 1946.

It is not clear what may have induced Peter to become a Freemason on 16 July 1948. As already mentioned, his father William had been initiated in 1924, thus allowing Peter the special privilege of being known as *a Lewis*, a term applied to initiates into Freemasonry who were born after their father had joined the Craft. William Sellers, who originally spelt his name *Seller* without the last 's', was passed on 17th October 1924 and raised March 1925 aged 27 in Chelsea Lodge. At the time he gave his address as 85 Sydenham Place, Bradford, York but was excluded for non-payment of fees in 1928; a reflection of the financial state of affairs of the Sellers family when Peter was just 3 years old. In November 1945, no doubt aware of his son's possibility to become a Mason, Bill rejoined the Lodge now giving the familiar address, also used by Peter, in East Finchley, North London. He was present at Peter's initiation, as well as his passing on 21 January 1949 and raising on 19 November 1951. The Chelsea Lodge number 3098 founded in 1905 was an almost obvious if not a natural choice for both father and son. It was and remains the mother Lodge of the variety profession, founded by 34 brethren consisting entirely of theatrical managers, music hall artistes, comedians, stage managers and musical directors. It is still today the best-known Lodge for the entertainment industry and has had, and still has, a myriad of famous and lesser-known artist as members.

Although Peter Sellers remained a member of the Chelsea Lodge to his dying day in July 1980, he never once appears to have attended Lodge except for the three meetings in which he took part. This period in his life was both a busy and important one. He was an ambitious man and was building his career. In 1949 he used his talent for

impersonation in a most mischievous way to obtain his first audition at the age of 23. He rang Roy Speer, the producer of the popular radio program *Ray's a Laugh* and using Kenneth Horne's voice, insisted that Speer should really consider auditioning *this youngster called Peter Sellers, a wonderful new performer.* He admitted on the telephone line who he really was and his cheeky approach paid off. He was soon to become a regular member of the cast.

The First Step

It is not inconceivable that Peter's purpose in joining Freemasonry was to attain his commercial ambitions through the contacts that he was able to make. There were a host of variety artists, entrepreneurs and musical directors present at Peter's initiation.

Peter Sellers

Although the minute books for the period from 1925 to 1956 are missing, the attendance register shows 76 brethren present, a considerably smaller number than the 200 or more usually in attendance as recorded for most meetings. Rather unusually Peter Sellers' signature appears among those of the members of the Lodge. (A candidate would normally sign a '*declaration book*' and only sign in as a member on his second attendance.) Among the guests at his initiation on 16 July 1948, I was pleasantly surprised to find the name of Bro.

Ronnie Bridges who signed in as a Master Mason of the Old Brentwood Lodge No 5342 and a guest of Charles Rose. (Ronnie was later to become a joining member of Lodge). Many Brethren in England will know Bro Ronnie. At 82 he is still very active as an organist to many lodges and lectures as often as he is invited to do so, especially in the London Area. Ronnie knew Peter Sellers personally very well. When in March 1948, three months before his initiation into freemasonry, Peter Sellers applied to the well known impresario Vivian Van Damm for a job at the famous Windmill Theatre. Van Damm had already employed Ronnie some years earlier and Ronnie was asked to accompany Peter on the piano for his audition. Peter was singing a song written for him by his father William. This was a small community of artistes. It was here that Peter Sellers met Harry Secombe. His army pal, Michael Bentine was also soon to join the Windmill and it is from here they recruited Spike Milligan and launched the legendary *Goons.*

Ronnie and Peter began a friendship and visited each other's homes until Peter began to make a name for himself. *I was dumped* are the words Ronnie uses *as were many other of his friends.*

There were at least eight freemasons amongst the staff at the Windmill and many were members of Chelsea Lodge. None of them had much good to say about Peter Sellers joining the fraternity. It became apparent that it was his ambition driving him. There were soon rumours, repeated and substantiated, that Peter, having set his sights on a radio and television career, was attempting to make suitable contacts in the BBC hierarchy by using Masonic signs and words to gain introductions. One report has him ridiculing the Craft, although no doubt, his very special brand of humour may have been misinterpreted. None the less, the Brethren of the Lodge were disenchanted with him. He attended the dinner after his initiation but did not do so after his passing and raising.

Peter Sellers joined the Craft for the wrong reasons. He may have followed in his father's footsteps and complied with the fashion, following the war period, when many demobilised soldiers joined the Craft to find companionship. This does not, however, appear to have been the reasoning behind Peter's intentions. He brought little into freemasonry and derived even less benefit from it because Peter Sellers never embraced the true and basic spirit of Freemasonry.

Chapter 17

ANY OTHER BUSINESS
Incorporating
NEWS IN BRIEF

The arms of Chelsea Lodge are very much based on the arms of the Borough of Chelsea, namely red, within a double cross of gold, a crozier; in the first quarter a winged bull, in the second a lion rampant with its head turned to the rear, in the third a sword, point downwards, between two bears' heads cut off at the neck and in the fourth a stag's head; the motto beneath is 'Nisi Dominus frustra' (It is vain without the Lord). The winged bull represents St. Luke, patron saint of Chelsea; the lion comes from the arms of Lord Cadogan, Lord of the Manor. The bears' heads and sword and stag's head are taken respectively from the arms of the Sloanes and Stanleys. The lodge was named to honour Chelsea Palace of Varieties. The motto of Chelsea Lodge is derived from the second verse of Psalm 127, the first two verses of which are:

Nisi Dominus aedificaverit domum, in vanum laboraverunt qui aedificant eam.
Nisi Dominus custodierit civitatem, frustra vigilat qui custodit eam. This is translated in the Book of Common Prayer as:
Except the Lord build the house; their labour is but lost that build it.
Except the Lord keep the city; the watchman waketh but in vain.

The Prayer Book version forms the basis of the final anthem currently used in London in the ceremony for Consecration of a new lodge (or chapter). A setting of the same anthem was specially composed by the then Grand Organist, Dr Henry Goss Custard, for the dedication of Freemasons' Hall, London, in 1933.

THE ROYAL BOROUGH OF KENSINGTON & CHELSEA

COAT OF ARMS

The Kensington and Chelsea Council received its Charter of Incorporation as a London borough on 10 March 1964, following the reorganisation of London government. Prior to this the separate boroughs of Kensington and Chelsea had been metropolitan boroughs since 1 January 1900. The title 'Royal Borough' was originally granted to the Kensington Council by Royal Charter dated 20 November 1901 to fulfil a wish expressed by Queen Victoria to confer a distinction on her birth place. The use of this Royal Title was graciously conferred by Letters Patent dated 7 April 1964, on the new borough.

The Council's Coat of Arms was granted by the College of Arms on 10 December 1965, and is of an entirely new design incorporating none of the features of the arms of the old boroughs.

The Shield comprises three Crowns on ermine symbolising the Royal status of the borough, and an Abbot's Mitre signifying the centuries old connection of Kensington with the Abbey of Abingdon and of Chelsea with the Abbey of Westminster.

The Crest consists of a Bush of Broom. This indicates the connecting link between the two former boroughs of the 'Brompton' Ward of Kensington which, for Parliamentary purposes, forms part of the constituency of Chelsea. Brompton, in mediaeval times, was an area famous for its fields of gorse and the name itself is a corruption of "Broom tun", a gorse farm.

The Supporters are a Blue Boar and a Silver Winged Bull. The Boar is taken from the Arms of the De Vere family who were Lords of the Manor of Kensington for 500 years. The Winged Bull is associated with St Luke, the Patron Saint of the ancient Parish of Chelsea.

The motto 'Quam Bonum In Unum Habitare' is the Latin version of the opening words of the 133rd Psalm – 'What a good thing it is to dwell together in unity'.

The Arms were designed by Sir Anthony Wagner, KCVO, D.Litt., Principal Garter King of Arms.

The Rev. Herbert Heriot-Hill was at one time Chaplain of Chelsea Lodge. His son Captain E.W.M. Heriot-Hill of 43rd (Wessex) Division, and of Grays Inn, a barrister-at-law wrote to the

Lodge on 6 July 1929 to say his father had died on 29 June 1929. He wanted to return to the Secretary of Chelsea Lodge the books and documents he found among his father's papers. He asked for financial assistance for his mother who was left destitute with four children.

The 11th Regular Meeting of Chelsea Lodge was held at Chelsea Town Hall, King's Road, Chelseain September 1906. Albert Le Fre was in the Chair. The May 1907 Installation Meeting was held at Frascati's Restaurant. Albert Le Fre installed Theodore Schreiber (Serpentello) who, in his response at the Festive Board, said that, "He would like to see Chelsea as one of the biggest and most successful lodges in London" – and so it became. W.S. Lyon, Treasurer, was identified as the originator of the idea to found Chelsea Lodge. During its first two years of existence, Chelsea had bought all their own furniture and organ and given 25 guineas to Charity. The Festive Board was attended by 23 visitors and 13 members. In August 1907 Wolfe S. Lyon initiated his son J.S. Lyon, a solicitor, after a new Bye Law was passed permitting sons of members not in the theatrical profession to join.

According to *The Freemason*, 10 June 1911Chelsea Lodge sprung from the Earl's Court Lodge, No. 2765. Two of those initiated into Earl's Court Lodge at a similar time became Masters of Chelsea Lodge namely Alfred W.H. Beales (Harry Bawn)in 1909 and Walter F.K. Walton (1910).

A letter from Lupino Lane is retained at Grand Lodge. It was written on 3 January 1924 from Alladin pantomime, Theatre Royal, Birmingham. It was addressed to **Ernest G. Goodwin**, Secretary, Chelsea Lodge. It reads:

Dear Bro. Goodwin,
I have seen copies of two letters, one dated 17 December 1923from the United Grand Lodge of England to yourself regarding my Certificate and one from you to Worshipful Brother Arthur Burr, Secretary of Old Concord Lodge, No.172. I wish to thank you for the trouble you have taken in the matter and I am enclosing herewith 6/6d in payment of the expense for issuing a duplicate of my Certificate, and shall be glad if you will be good enough to ask Grand Lodge to urge forward the matter as I am leaving in the course of a couple of weeks or so for America and am most anxious to have the Certificate before my departure.
Again my thanks in anticipation.
Yours faithfully and fraternally,
LUPINO LANE (Signed)

Grand Secretary's office endorsed and posted the Certificate to Lupino Lane on 18 January 1924.

Former Secretary of Chelsea Lodge dies
A letter from **Frederick B. Box**, PM PAGDC, of 8 Bartlett's Building, Holborn Circus, London EC4, dated 5 July 1939 writing to the Grand Secretary Sydney A. White (later Sir Sydney A. White) said he had learned that the Chelsea Lodge Secretary, W.Bro.**E.G. Goodwin** had died, believed to be in April 1938.

He understood it was then found that the books had been very badly kept, and there was a serious deficiency. Non accounts could be submitted at the Installation Meeting in May. W.Bro. **George Batt** had very kindly consented to try and put the books straight. W.Bro. Box went on: "I was WM in 1937/1938. We found that a Return had been sent in with my signature on it, but this had been forged. No return had ever been submitted to or signed by me."
Note: Sadly the Secretarial Returns covering this period in time have been destroyed by Grand Lodge.

Honoured with London Rank in 1908

Bro. **Wolfe S. Lyon**, Treasurer of Chelsea Lodge in the early 1900s was appointed London Rank in 1908. He said he felt very proud of the honour, and the pleasure was so much more keen that it was presented in the presence of his son, whom he was allowed to initiate into Chelsea Lodge which, in the space of three and a half years, had a membership of 114 men who were daily making the influence of Freemasonry in its fullest sense, felt not only in Great Britain, but also in all parts of the civilised globe, as from the nature of their profession they were veritable birds of passage – here today and gone tomorrow; and a further proof of the interest taken, if further proof were required, was emphasised by the fact that there were present at that meeting, members who had come from Brighton, Reading, Southampton, Nottingham, and elsewhere to attend their Masonic duties, and who would have to rush off to catch trains which would enable them to return in time to attend to their business in the evening.

Presentations and gifts to Chelsea Lodge

Sword presented to the Lodge by Bro. **W.H. Roberts**, LR on 20 December 1936.

Candle Snuffer presented by Bro. **Ivan Morgan**, November 1995.

Framed picture of **Issy Bonn** presented by Bro. Mike Digby of Rectitude Secundus Lodge No.6778 as a thank you to Chelsea Lodge for the welcome and entertainment given to all visitors past and present.

Framed line drawing of **George Mullins** with a backdrop of Chelsea Palace presented by W.Bro. **Ivan Morgan**, LGR, May 2005.

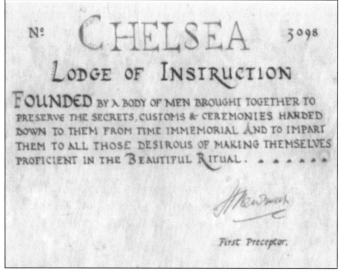

Chelsea Lodge of Instruction

In September 1912, permission was given to Chelsea Lodge and Proscenium Lodge, to operate a Lodge of Instruction. The joint venture carried on for many years, sometimes having to work in rooms of various sizes and with modest facilities. Then in 1956, W.Bro. **Harry Jay Fink** was able to 'manoeuvre' Chelsea Lodge of Instruction into the Horse Shoe Hotel, Tottenham Court Road, W1, adjoining Dominion Cinema. It was a well equipped Temple, used by many London Lodges for their regular meetings.

The first meeting of the Lodge of Instruction at the Horse Shoe Hotel took place at 12 noon on Wednesday 4 January 1956. Officers elected on the day were: Preceptor W.Bro. **Harry Newman**, Assistant Preceptor W.Bro. **Henry Thomas**, Treasurer W.Bro. **Charles Rose**, Secretary W.Bro. **Cyril Harling** and Assistant Secretary Bro. **Dick Tubb.**

For those who studied Latin at school you may remember that the motto – Cras florebit res hodierna – literally means 'tomorrow will flourish the things of today', but in vernacular it means:

'It will be Alright on the Night'.

Paul Ganjou writes:
Anyone who has ever attended a rehearsal will know that people often say this little phrase tongue in cheek, but with fingers tightly crossed behind their back! As Preceptor at Chelsea Lodge's weekly LOI (Lodge of Instruction), I have to confess that I have said it more often than most - but thankfully, with never any need for crossed fingers.

Every Lodge has a LOI, where the Officers regularly meet and rehearse their ritual and ceremonies. Most meet in the evenings but being a show business Lodge it is easier for us to attend in the day-time, which we do, at noon on Wednesdays. Past Masters and Officers attend along with members interested in becoming Stewards of the Lodge and possibly eventually being invited to take Office. Chelsea has a tradition of always being "alright on the night" and no Preceptor or Director of Ceremonies could have more enthusiastic Officers and Past Masters.

I was lucky that my immediate predecessor, W.Bro **George Mullins**, was an exceptional role model. Not only an outstanding Freemason, W.Bro George was also an excellent ritualist and coach as well as a true Gentleman. He set and maintained high standards but was always the first to appreciate the funny side of life and, mercifully, the funny side of life is oft to be found in Chelsea Lodge.

In order for anyone to do something on a voluntary basis, as we do in Freemasonry, above all else it has to be fun. If we did not enjoy it, we would stop attending the LOI, Lodges would slowly disband and eventually there would be no Freemasonry: so I am very conscious that the LOI is a vital foundation stone in our continuing development and of not just setting and maintaining high standards, but also ensuring that we never lose the capacity to laugh at ourselves and have fun along the way.

We take pride in our performances in Lodge but we never take ourselves too seriously and despite the countless slips we make along the way and doubtless will continue to make, we are supremely confident that it will always be alright on the night!

I would particularly like to thank these Past Masters and Members (and even two visitors) whose regular attendance and support in recent years has added so much value and fun to our meetings and Wednesday rehearsals:

W.Bro. Ralph Hearsum, W.Bro. Roger de Courcey, W.Bro. George Mullins, W.Bro. Frank Holder, W.Bro. Norman Gray, W.Bro. Kenneth Andrews, W.Bro. Peter Elliott, W.Bro. Cyril Packer, W.Bro.Ivan Morgan, W.Bro. Denny Wise, W.Bro. Peter Locke, Bro. Roy Graham and Bro. John McGonigle.
Also visitors: Bro Bob Carrigan and W.Bro Philip Calickman.'

BIBLIOGRAPHY

The undermentioned includes all the printed sources consulted, sorted in alphabetical order by the title, author, publisher, locations and publication dates are also given. In addition some information has been obtained from the internet. The author is grateful to the following authors and publishers for allowing him to quote extracts from their works.

Ballad Years, The, Don Wickes, Privately published, Weston Super Mare, 1990

Big Bands Go to War, Chris Way, Mainstream Publishing, Edinburgh, 1991

British Dance Bands, This England Books, Cheltenham, 1999

British Dance Bands on Record 1911-1945, Brian Rust and Sandy Forbes, Gramophone, Harrow, 1987

British Music Hall, Raymond Mander and Joe Mitchenson, Gentry Books, London (1975)

British Music Hall, Roy Busby, Paul Elek Ltd, London, 1976.

British Musical Theatre, Kurt Ganzl, MacMillan Press, 1986

Can You Hear Me Mother, Harry Stanley, Jupiter Books, London 1975

Century of Boxing Greats, A, Patrick Myler, Robson Books, London, 1999

Chelsea, Patrick Loobey, Tempus, Stroud, Glos, 1999

Complete Index to Sound Films since 1928. Alan Goble. Bowker-Saur, East Grinstead, Sussex, 1999

Crying With Laughter, Bob Monkhouse, Century/Randem House, 1993

Curtain Up, Lord Bernard Delfont, Robson Books, London, 1989

Dance Band Years, The, Albert McCarthy, Spring Books, London, 1974

Database of Big Bands, Murray L. Pfeffer, 1994, Internet

Encyclopedia of Pantomime, Gale Research International Ltd, Andover, Hants, 1993

Encyclopedia of Popular Music, Colin Larkin, MacMillan, 1998

First 75 years of Chelsea Lodge, Harry Stanley, London, 1980

Forever Ealing, George Perry. Pavilion Books, London, 1994

Limelight, George Mozart, Hurst and Blackett, London, 1938

Golden Age of the Circus, Howard Loxton, Grange Books, London, 1997

Golden Age of Radio, Denis Gifford, Batsford, London, 1985

Grace, Beauty and Banjos, Michael Kilgarriff, Oberon Books, London, 1998

Guinness Book of Movie Facts and Feats. Patrick Robertson. Guiness Publishing Ltd., London, 1994

Guinness Book of TV Facts and Feats, Kenneth Passingham, Guinness Superlatives Ltd, Enfield, Middlesex, 1984

Hammer Films – the Bray Studio Years, Wayne Kinsey, Reynolds and Hearn, London, 2002

Hard Act To Follow, A,, Peter Leslie, Paddington Press, London and New York (1978)

Hippodrome, Great Yarmouth, Don Stacey, Jays UK Limited, Great Yarmouth, 2003

History of the Circus, George Speaight, Tantivy Press,1980, London

I Can See Your Lips Moving, Valentine Vox, Kaye and Ward Ltd, Windmill Press, Tadworth, Surrey, 1981

Jim Davidson Close to the Edge, Alec Lom, Ebury Press, London 2001

Kindly Leave The Stage, Roger Wilmut. Methuen, London, 1985

Oxford Companion to Popular Music, Peter Gammond, OUP, London, 1993

Peter Sellers The Man Behind the Mask, Peter Evans, Leslie Frewin, London, 1969

Popular Music of 20s, Ronald Pearsall, David and Charles, Newton Abbot, 1976

Raising a Laugh, Ted Ray, Werner Laurie, London, 1952

Roy Hudd, Music Hall, Variety and Showbiz Anecdotes, Robson Books, London, 1993

Roy Hudd, Cavalcade of Variety Acts, Robson Books, London, 1997

Radio Comedy 1938-1968, Andy Foster and Steve Furst, Virgin Publishing, London, 1996

Radio Companion, The, Paul Donovan, Harper Collins, London, 1991

Radio Times Guide to Television Comedy, Mark Lewisohn, BBC Books, London, 2003

Seventy Years of Broadcasting, John Cain, BBC Books, London, 1992

Stage and Film Musicals, Colin Larkin, Virgin, London, 1999

Stage Deaths 1850-1990, George B. Bryan, Greenwood Press, Westport, USA, 1991

Stars Who Made the Halls, S.Theodore Felstead. T Werner Laurie Ltd. London. 1946

Talking Swing, Sheila Tracy, Mainstream Publishing, Edinburgh, 1997

There Goes That Song Again, Colin Walsh, Elm Tree Books, London (1977)

Those Variety Days, Donald Auty, Internet, 2003

Ultimate Encyclopedia of Boxing, Harry Mullan, Hodder and Stoughton, London, 1996

Who's Who in British Jazz, John Chilton, Cassel, London 1977.

Who's Who on Screen, Evelyn Mack Truitt. R.R. Bowker, New York, 1983.

Wrestling, The, Simon Garfield, Faber And Faber, London, 1996

Also consulted were copies of the following newspapers: *The Era, Stage, The Times, The Freemason, Freemasonry Today, Daily Telegraph, Guardian, Radio Times, Radio Pictorial, TV Times* and *Memory Lane.* as were numerous websites on the Internet including *BBC News Online, British Big Bands Database* and *All Music Guide*